Phaidon Press Inc.
180 Varick Street
New York, NY 10014

www.phaidon.com

First published in English 2005
Reprinted 2005, 2006 (four times)
© 2005 Phaidon Press Limited

US edition:
ISBN-13: 978 0 7148 4531 9
ISBN-10: 0 7148 4531 0

First published in Italian by Editoriale
Domus as *Il cucchiaio d'argento* 1950.
Eighth edition (revised, expanded and
redesigned) 1997.
© Editoriale Domus

A CIP catalogue record for this book is
available from the British Library.

The Publishers would like to thank
Lagostina, Paderno and Wedgwood for
having kindly provided some of the
china, pots, pans and tools illustrated
in this book.

Designed by Italo Lupi with Marina del
Cinque and Alessandra Beluffi

Photography by Jason Lowe

Drawings by Francesca Bazzurro

The Publishers would also like to thank
Hilary Bird, Tessa Clark, Linda Doeser,
Clelia d'Onofrio, Carmen Figini, Trish
Hilferty and Tom Norrington-Davies for
their contributions to the book.

Printed in Italy

THE

SILVER

SPOON

CONTENTS

EATING IS A SERIOUS MATTER

Eating is a serious matter in Italy. Cooking and food are among the finest expressions of Italian culture, vividly portraying the country's history and traditions. Like all other arts, cooking is based on measures and proportions, on the balance and fusion of different elements. It blends ancient traditions with contemporary innovation and evolves constantly, even in the twenty-first century, as a result of its position at the center of Italian family life. At home with family or friends, for a special occasion, in a fancy restaurant or in a humble trattoria, or even when preparing a simple everyday meal, for Italians, cooking is synonymous with good food, good wine and good company. Whether rustic or sophisticated, Italian cooking is traditionally based on excellent, fresh, seasonal ingredients. This is one of the main reasons why Italian food varies so much from region to region and even from village to village. In the north, where cattle and dairy farming are prevalent, we find a cuisine based on butter, meat and Parmigiano, while travelling towards the south we encounter olive oil (extra vergine, of course), ripe tomatoes, gorgeous eggplants and fresh fish. Italian cooking is based on Italy's rural traditions and depends very much on the vast variety of the country's agricultural produce. Yet even if nowadays you can find almost any kind of food at any time of the year, Italians still follow the rhythm of the seasons and will wait until spring to enjoy asparagus, or the summer for a fresh Insalata caprese. But as soon as the temperature falls in the autumn, everyone is ready for a warming plate of Braised Beef with Barolo. In Italian families, special occasions are still celebrated at home with a five-course meal (antipasto, first course, main course with vegetables, cheese and dessert). But, when eating everyday, a one-meal dish such as lasagne, pizza or ribollita will satisfy even the most demanding of appetites. The country's infinite variety of dishes allows Italians to create an excellent and healthy meal whether they choose to spend their entire day cooking, putting together a stunning Brodetto Marchigiano (a fish soup made using several varieties of fish and shellfish), or if, instead, they go home and make a simple but authentic dish of Spaghetti aglio olio e peperoncino, with its four ingredients never missing from any Italian kitchen. Authentic Italian dishes are very often based on just a few, humble ingredients. What makes them so tasty and delicious is that, over the centuries, Italians have discovered exactly how to achieve the perfect mix of flavors. It sometimes seems that

Italians learn to cook before they learn to talk and their skills are handed down from one generation to the next. The perfection of Italian cooking has been achieved through centuries of testing in family kitchens, with millions of dishes served to the most discerning of critics. *The Silver Spoon* is the result of a labor of love, with only the very best recipes from Italian families and cooks within its covers. This is the one cookbook every Italian passes on to their children, teaching them the skills of their parents and grandparents, and allowing them to understand what Italian cooking is really about. It shows them how to prepare a healthy and delicious meal by, firstly, choosing the right ingredients and then by following a variety of recipes that may be either simple or complicated, but always explained in the clearest and simplest of ways. For these reasons *The Silver Spoon* is the most successful cookbook in Italy, the book that has its place in every family kitchen, the one that many brides have received as a wedding gift. Conceived by Editoriale Domus, publisher of *Domus*, the Italian design and architectural magazine famously directed by Gio Ponti, the first edition came out in 1950 with the title *Il cucchiaio d'argento* (the silver spoon). This name stems from an English phrase that symbolizes plenty, wealth and good fortune: to be born with a silver spoon in your mouth describes how someone has been born with a fortunate heritage… just like the culinary heritage *The Silver Spoon* gives to its readers. From its very first appearance, the book immediately made its mark on the world of gastronomy, and from that point onwards it has never been out of print, quickly becoming the classic volume of Italian cooking and the leading authority in Italy. To compile *Il cucchiaio d'argento*, experts were commissioned by Editoriale Domus to collect hundreds of traditional recipes from throughout the Italian regions, showing every regional specialty. During the more than 50 years in which the book has been in print, it has been constantly updated, with various successive editions, each one adapting the recipes and techniques to our modern lifestyle without losing the principles of authentic Italian cuisine. The result is an extraordinary cookbook containing over 2,000 recipes. Now translated for the first time into English, *The Silver Spoon* can transform every English-speaking reader into an experienced Italian cook, teaching them the thousands of secrets of how to cook a truly authentic Italian meal.

OUR
SPOON

As we started working on the English-language edition of *Il cucchiaio d'argento*, it quickly became obvious that it was not enough to simply translate the recipes without any adaptation as there is a fundamental difference between the Italian approach to cooking and that of the English-speaking countries. English-language cookbooks tend to contain far more detailed explanations than their Italian counterparts. We have moved the original Italian recipes much nearer to what is expected by English-speaking readers but we have also been careful to retain the Italian character of the book. Also, when a recipe indicates ingredients that are not readily available outside Italy, we have tried to suggest alternative and more commonly found ingredients alongside the originals. In this way, we have made as many of the recipes as possible available to everyone. To preserve the authenticity of the Italian edition, we have included all of the recipes that feature in *Il cucchiaio d'argento*, even if some of them seem unfamiliar to an English-speaking audience. In this way, the book remains an authentic Italian cookbook and includes all of the dishes that Italians like to prepare and eat. *The Silver Spoon* is organized in chapters by course, with each course using a different color in the design of its pages. The recipes are listed according to the alphabetical order of their original Italian titles, though each recipe also has an English

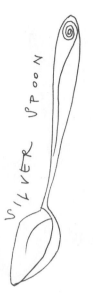

translation of its name alongside. In the final section of the book there is a collection of menus comprising signature dishes by 14 celebrated Italian cooks, together with a further 9 menus from some of the very best Italian restaurants and chefs throughout the world. There is a comprehensive index that allows the reader to look up specific ingredients, to find the recipes in which that ingredient is used and, of course, it also includes the names of the recipes both in English and Italian. For this English edition we have commissioned 200 new images from the distinguished food photographer, Jason Lowe. An expert cook prepared each dish using only natural, authentic ingredients and, as soon as the food was ready, it was photographed on pure white crockery or in the pan in which it was cooked. In this way, we have ensured that the food looks both as delicious and natural as possible, with all the little imperfections that make home cooked recipes so appealing. Illuminated only using natural daylight, the photography in *The Silver Spoon* conjures up the flavors and aromas of the authentic cuisine of Italy.

GUIDE TO USING
THE SILVER SPOON

This book contains over 2,000 recipes; some are traditional and regional Italian dishes, while others are more contemporary additions. For this latest edition, the ingredients and cooking times of some recipes have been updated in the light of changing tastes and lifestyles. Others have been left virtually untouched to retain their unique characteristics. The majority can be easily adapted to suit your personal requirements. Most of the recipes are designed for four servings. (The number of servings for each recipe is usually specified.) This is a convenient quantity and can be usually be halved or doubled to accommodate smaller groups or for entertaining guests. Some recipes, such as roasts, work better in slightly larger quantities and may serve six or eight. Other recipes - antipasti, salads and sauces, for example - do not list the number of servings, as quantities may be varied without compromising the results. Where no quantity is specified these ingredients should be used according to personal taste.

NOTES ABOUT COOKING

Like most specialist fields, cooking has its own vocabulary. Many foreign terms, often French and, in the case of *The Silver Spoon*, Italian, are frequently used – blanquette and al dente, for example. We have included a glossary of common terms, particularly those used in this book. This chapter also includes a guide to tools and equipment.

WHERE TO FIND WHAT YOU WANT

SAUCES, MARINADES AND FLAVORED BUTTERS

Recipes for both hot and cold classics, such as béchamel and mayonnaise, are included here.

→ Marinades may be used to flavor and tenderize a wide range of ingredients before cooking. Let ingredients marinate in a cool place rather than the refrigerator for up to 2 hours. If marinating for longer, place the mixture in the refrigerator. In both cases, it is sensible to cover the dish.

→ Flavored butters may be used for cooking, but are more often added when the dish is served. Note that quantities can sometimes seem excessive, but there is always a reason for the amount specified.

ANTIPASTI, APPETIZERS AND PIZZAS

Antipasti and appetizers are designed to stimulate the taste buds and are served in small quantities to leave plenty of room for the dishes that will follow. This chapter also includes recipes for pizzas, although nowadays these tend to be served as a main dish.

FIRST COURSES

This chapter is divided into the traditional Italian classifications of 'in broth' and 'dry'. 'In broth' includes recipes for a wide range of soups; 'dry' includes fresh and dried pasta, rice, risottos, polenta and gnocchi.

EGGS AND FRITTATA

The recipes are arranged according to the different ways of cooking eggs.

VEGETABLES

Vegetables have always played an important role in the Mediterranean diet. Over 30 sub-sections describe the basic preparation and cooking techniques of individual vegetables, followed by a collection of mouth-watering recipes.

FISH, CRUSTACEANS AND SHELLFISH

Italy is rightfully famous for its fish and shellfish dishes and this chapter is packed with recipes for more than 40 different kinds. It is divided into sub-sections, covering sea fish, freshwater fish, crustaceans, and shellfish, and also includes general advice on preparation and cooking techniques. Where particular types of fish may be difficult to obtain, more readily available varieties have been suggested. This chapter also includes a collection of recipes for fish soups and for cooking frogs and snails.

MEAT AND VARIETY MEATS

This chapter is sub-divided into sections covering all the different types of meat eaten in Italy. The introductions to the main sub-sections offer a helpful guide to the different cuts of meat and the techniques most suitable for cooking them.

→ The chapter concludes with a wide range of variety meat recipes. Both familiar and less familiar types are included. This chapter also includes a selection of recipes for Italian sausages.

POULTRY

Chicken is very popular in Italy. This chapter also includes recipes and information on all other farmed birds and is one of the few places where the English-language edition differs from the Italian. Even though rabbit is now widely farmed it is classified as furred game and the recipes appear within Game. Quail recipes are also included within Game.

GAME

This chapter includes both furred and feathered game and, given Italian enthusiasm for hunting, it is not surprising that the recipes are simply fabulous. Much of what is classified as game is now widely available farmed.

CHEESE

Italy is rightly proud of the more than 400 different types of cheese it produces, many of them protected by DOC controls. The introduction to this chapter provides advice on choosing, using and storing cheese, plus a guide to tasty combinations with cheese.

DESSERTS AND BAKING

Home-made desserts are not widespread in Italy as people tend to buy them at the local pasticceria. But don't let this put you off. The many fabulous recipes included here are joined by basic recipes for a range of pastry doughs for those who really love baking.

MENUS BY CELEBRATED CHEFS

This chapter features menus by some of the most famous chefs in Italy from the past five decades. This edition has the additional bonus of including menus by a galaxy of international chefs, from countries as far apart as the United Kingdom, the United States, Australia and New Zealand.

LIST OF RECIPES AND INDEX

The book concludes with a complete list of recipes arranged by chapter and a comprehensive index.

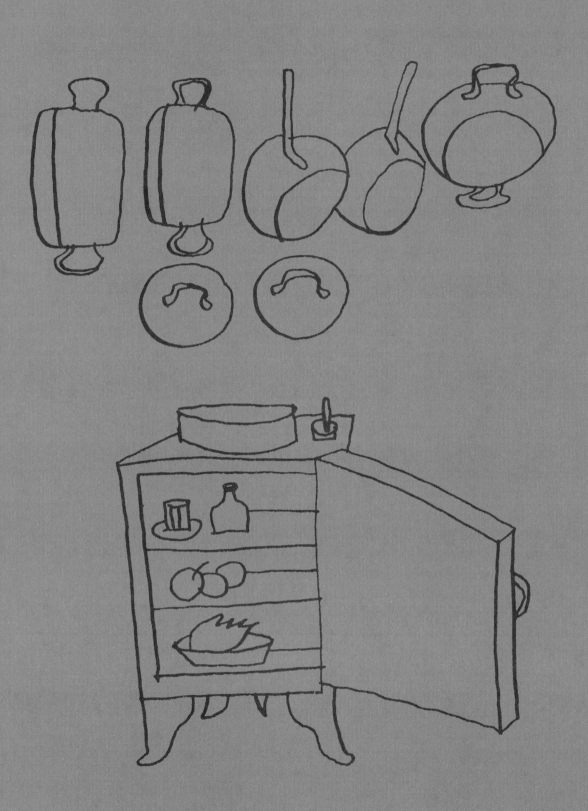

COOKING TERMS →

COOKING TERMS

To poach, to soften, and to deglaze – these verbs describe a way of cooking an egg, a method of making a mixture more delicate, and how to dilute cooking juices. Busecca, carpione and fricassée are the words for tripe in Milan, spiced water and vinegar for marinating fried meat and vegetables, and a sauce made of eggs and lemon juice for cooking meat and vegetables. Pie, blini, and soubise mean a pastry shell with a savory or sweet filling, a small pancake, and an onion sauce. These are some of the more than 200 entries that make up this short dictionary of cooking terms and idioms which you frequently read in cookbooks and magazines and which we all use, often without knowing precisely what they mean.

VINEGAR

ACETO BALSAMICO

Vinegar made from cooked and concentrated wine must from Trebbiano grapes. It is matured for at least 10 years and sometimes much longer, and can be made only in a designated area surrounding the city of Modena. It is quite expensive but has a unique mellow flavor.

ACIDULATE

To add vinegar or lemon juice to water (or another liquid) for immersing some vegetables, such as globe artichokes, to prevent them from turning black before cooking.

ADD WHILE COLD

To add an ingredient to a liquid or sauce before heating. For example, meat is put in cold water when the flavor of the stock is more important than that of the meat.

ADD WHILE HOT

To add an ingredient to a hot or boiling liquid or sauce. For example, meat is put in hot water when the flavor of the meat is more important than that of the stock.

AGRODOLCE

This dressing made with herbs, wine vinegar, sugar, onion, and garlic is served with fish, game, and vegetables, particularly onions and eggplant.

AÏOLI

This garlic-flavored mayonnaise was originally called ailloli, and is a specialty of the south of France, where it is usually served with fish.

À LA MAÎTRE D'HÔTEL

A dish served with butter flavored with chopped parsley and a little lemon juice. It is usually chilled in a roll, then sliced and served on meat or fish.

À LA TARTARE

Lean ground steak served raw, mixed with egg yolk, lemon juice, pickles, olive oil, herbs, and spices. For instructions on how to prepare this dish, see page 802.

AL DENTE

The point during cooking at which pasta and rice become tender but are still firm to the bite and should, therefore, be removed from the heat and drained. Vegetables cooked al dente are tastier and retain more nutrients.

ALL'INGLESE

Meaning 'in the English style' this, perhaps rather unflatteringly, describes food cooked and seasoned in a very simple way, such as vegetables boiled and served with melted butter or plain boiled rice seasoned with just a drop of oil.

AMARETTI

Sweet cookies flavored with almond or apricot kernels, these are served with creamy desserts such as mousse.

APFELSTRUDEL

Among the various Austrian strudels — filled, wafer-thin pastry rolls — this is perhaps the most popular. It consists of a thin sheet of pastry filled, with apples, sugar, golden raisins, cinnamon, dried fruit, and nuts, then rolled up and baked.

ARRABBIATA

Literally 'angry', meaning hot, this is a method of cooking chops, rabbit, and chicken in a skillet with plenty of spices. It is also used to describe penne or other pasta covered with a tomato and hot chile sauce.

ARROWROOT

A powdered root used for thickening sauces. It is similar to cornstarch but has the advantage of producing a transparent sauce.

A'SCAPECE

This is a typically Neapolitan mixture of eggplant, zucchini, and other vegetables, which are fried, and then left to marinate in vinegar and chopped garlic. It keeps for a long time in the refrigerator.

ASPIC

This is a French term meaning meat, fish, or vegetables that have been set in gelatin and prepared in a steel or copper mold with, and turned out and served with characteristic decoration.

ASSIETTE

A French term for a dish of mixed cold meats.

AU GRATIN

When a dish is sprinkled with grated cheese or topped with béchamel sauce, dotted with butter and sprinkled with bread crumbs, then cooked in the oven until golden, it is said to be au gratin.

BAKE IN A PACKET

To wrap food in foil, baking parchment, or waxed paper and bake in the oven. This method requires very little oil or fat and is excellent for meat, fish and vegetables as it retains the cooking juices and aroma.

BARD

To wrap a roast or a breast of poultry or game with slices of pancetta or bacon, pancetta fat or bacon fat, or ham partly to flavor the meat and partly to protect it from fierce heat which might otherwise dry it

out. Three-fourth of the way through the cooking time the barding is removed so that the covered area may brown like the rest.

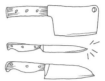

BATTUTO

Onion, carrot, celery, and garlic chopped with a sharp heavy knife form the basis of many Italian dishes. It is sometimes sautéed with pancetta, pancetta fat, or pork-back fat as a base for minestrones and meat dishes.

BED

A base of vegetables, salad greens, or other ingredients on which a dish is served.

BEURRE MANIÉ

A paste made from equal quantities of all-purpose flour and butter used to thicken sauces. It is added in small pieces at a time and the sauce is stirred until the beurre manié is completely incorporated before another piece is added.

BLANCH

To partially cook fruit or vegetables briefly in boiling water to make them softer or easier to peel.

BLANQUETTE

Veal, chicken, or lamb is cooked without browning. It is typical of French cuisine.

BLEND

To combine ingredients, by hand or with an electric mixer, until creamy and fully incorporated.

BLINI

Pancakes made of flour, milk, butter, eggs, and a little salt, cooked in the oven and served hot. In traditional Russian cuisine, they are often served with caviar, smoked salmon, and sour cream.

BOIL

To cook meat, vegetables, or other ingredients for a specified time in water or stock.

BOLOGNESE

Meaning from the city of Bologna, this term describes a series of typical Emilian dishes that are part of classic Italian cuisine, such ragù (meat sauce), tagliatelle, tortellini, and lasagne.

BONE

To remove the bones from fish or meat.

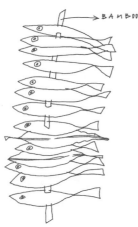

BORTSCH

Also sometimes spelt borsch, this thick meat and vegetable soup, served with sour cream, is made with beet which gives it its characteristic red color. It is an eastern European specialty and is very popular in Russia.

BOTTARGA

Salted, pressed stripe mullet (or tuna) roe is prepared like a salami. Slices, drizzled with olive oil and lemon juice or spread on toast, make a tasty antipasto. Crumbled and lightly heated in oil, it makes a pleasant sauce for spaghetti. It is a Sardinian speciality.

BOUILLABAISSE

A French fish soup or stew which always includes spiny lobster and scorpion fish and never contains mussels. Among its many ingredients are saffron, garlic, tomatoes, and dried orange rind. It is a typical Provençal dish and is a recipe that is particularly associated with the port of Marseille.

BOUILLON CUBES AND POWDER

Seasoning made of meat extract and monosodium glutamate which brings out the flavor and aroma of foods. It is used for stocks and soups and to flavor sauces, gravies, meat and vegetables.

BOUQUET GARNI

Fresh herbs tied together so that they may be easily removed from stock or other dishes after cooking. The Italian bouquet garni consists of flat-leaf parsley, basil, thyme, and bay leaves. However it may vary and include celery, sage, and other herbs.

BRAISE

To cook slowly in a covered pan or casserole on low heat with a small quantity of liquid, usually specified in the recipe. Braising is mainly used for red meats, poultry, and game.

BREAD CRUMB

To coat meat, fish, or vegetables in bread crumbs – after dipping them in beaten egg – before frying.

BRESAOLA

Slices of raw beef tenderloin are salted and air-dried, rather like prosciutto. It is a specialty from Valtellina.

BRODETTO

Adriatic fish soup. There are many regional variations, but the most classic is from Romagna.

BROIL

To cook meat, fish, or vegetables under a broil or in a griddle pan. You can also cook over glowing charcoal on a barbecue.

BROWN IN A PAN

To cook vegetables over low heat in butter or oil until they go a light golden color. This is particularly common with thinly sliced onion or garlic cloves. Meat or vegetables may also be cooked in oil or butter in a skillet over high heat until a rich, even brown in color during the first or final stage of cooking.

BROWN IN THE OVEN

To make the top of a dish cooked in the oven, such as lasagne, become golden brown in color. To brown meat and fish, just add oil, butter, or a mixture of the two. Pastry is brushed with beaten egg yolk so that it turns golden brown.

BRUNCH

More substantial than breakfast and less filling than lunch, this meal is eaten in Britain and the United States, mainly on holidays and at weekends, between eleven o'clock and midday. Nowadays, it has been adopted in Europe too.

BRUSCHETTA

Meaning lightly toasted, this consists of a slice of home-made bread, lightly toasted, rubbed with garlic, seasoned with salt, and drizzled with olive oil. Chopped tomato, oregano, and wild fennel may be added.

BUSECCA

Milanese tripe with kidney beans.

BUTTERFLY

A preparation method used particularly for chickens and Cornish hens, in which they are cut along the back, opened out, pounded, marinated in oil, lemon and pepper, and cooked on the broiler or barbecue.

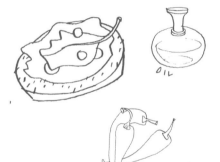

CACCIATORE

Meaning 'in the style of a hunter', this is a method of cooking chicken, and rabbit, combined with mushrooms, onions, white wine, herbs, and spices. There are many regional variations.

CACCIUCCO

This Tyrrhenian fish soup, almost a stew, exists in many local versions, but the most classic is cacciucco from Livorno.

CAGNONE

Boiled rice, seasoned with chopped garlic and sage, fried in butter, and served with plenty of grated Parmesan cheese.

CANAPÉS

Slices of bread, often toasted or fried in butter, topped with a variety of ingredients, such as flavored butter, cheese, caviar, smoked salmon, anchovies, hard-cooked eggs, cured ham, tapenade, and so on. They are served as an antipasto or with pre-dinner drinks.

CANDY

To immerse fruit in a sugar syrup several times until the sugar is absorbed. The fruit loses most of its water content, becomes thicker, and can be stored for a long time. Candying is, however, a long and laborious process.

CAPONATA

This famous Sicilian dish is, according to some, Catalan in origin. Diced vegetables, mainly eggplant, cooked in sweet and sour sauce, are served warm, cold, or as an antipasto.

CARAMELIZE

To melt sugar by heating it with a little water and using it to cover fresh fruit, to prepare a brittle or praline, or to decorate molds.

CARPIONE

This pan-fried mixture of olive oil, chopped onion, sage, celery, and carrot combined with water and vinegar, is poured piping hot onto vegetables and freshwater fish.

CHANTILLY

Both a savory and sweet ver-sion of this sauce exist. The savory sauce is based on mayonnaise and whipped cream, while the sweet version is based on whipped cream and sugar. It takes its name from a château in France.

CHATEAUBRIAND

This describes steaks of about 11–14 ounces in weight and about 1 inch thick, cut from the heart of the tenderloin and broiled, roasted, or pan-fried. They may be served with various sauces, including sweet and sour sauce and flavored butters. According to some, the name derives from the beef-rearing farms of Chateaubriand but others think it derives from the writer René de Chateaubriand.

CHITARRA

A utensil, traditionally from Abruzzo, used to make macaroni alla chitarra, which resembles square spaghetti. It is a wooden frame with stretched metal wires on which fresh pasta is placed and cut and its name derives from its similarity to a guitar.

CHOP

To cut vegetables, herbs, bacon, and other ingredients into small pieces using a heavy knife.

CLARIFY

This is a procedure for making meat stock clearer by adding beaten egg white about 30 minutes before cooking is complete, simmering the stock, then straining it. Butter may also be clarified (see page 88).

CLEAN

To immerse brains, sweetbreads, kidneys, or game in water with a little lemon juice or vinegar, to reduce their odor and strong flavor; to immerse shellfish in water to remove sand and impurities; and also to gut fish or draw feathered game.

COCOTTE

A thick, round porcelain, terracotta, or metal vessel. It absorbs heat well, transmitting it evenly to the food.

COMPOSTA

Various fruits – both fresh and dried – are cooked over low heat in syrup, with vanilla, cinnamon, lemon rind, and other flavorings. It is served cold.

COOK OVER LOW HEAT

Dishes, such as stews, which require long cooking times to tenderize ingredients, are cooked over low heat, that is, with the heat turned down to its lowest setting.

COOK UNTIL SOFTENED

To cook vegetables gently over low heat. Typically, onion is cooked in butter or oil until soft – that is, until it has lost its moisture content and becomes translucent.

COVER

To seal a pan or dish with a lid or foil, either to shorten the cooking time or to slow down evaporation and, therefore, prevent the ingredients from drying up.

COVER WITH A THIN LAYER

To pour on, or brush a dish with, a thin layer of cream, gelatin, or sauce.

CROISSANT

A sweet or savory crescent-shaped, flaky pastry. It is ideal for breakfast and may be filled with cream, jelly, cheese, cured ham, etc.

CRUSH

To grind ingredients, such as peppercorns, whole spices, and garlic, to help release their aroma. This is traditionally done in a mortar with a pestle. A spice grinder may also be used and if you don't have a pestle and mortar, you can use the end of a rolling pin or two spoons.

CURDLE

When the egg in a sauce coagulates rather than mixes in smoothly, it is said to curdle. This may happen with mayonnaise and egg custards.

CURRIED

A dish cooked with curry powder or curry spices, an Indian or South-east Asian mixture of such spices as turmeric, pepper, cumin and ginger. Curry sauce goes very well with rice, chicken, mutton, lamb, eggs, and many different types and combinations of vegetables.

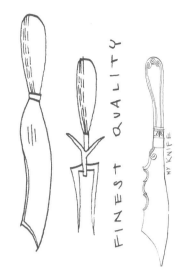

FINEST QUALITY

MY KNIFE

CUT INTO PORTIONS

To cut poultry or game birds into serving pieces using poultry shears or a very sharp knife.

DECORATE

To decorate single plates or serving dishes of sweet ingredients with fruit, sifted sugar and/or unsweetened cocoa powder, swirls of cream, or other finishes to make them look attractive and to achieve a balance between the various shapes and colors.

DEEP-FRY

To cook in plenty of hot oil or fat over high heat. Olive or vegetable oils may be used for deep-frying, although olive oil has a lower smoke point than oils such as peanut. Margarine and butter are not suitable for deep-frying as they tend to burn when cooked at very high temperatures. Lard may not be advisable for dietary reasons.

DEGLAZE

To loosen sediment and dissolve the cooking juices produced in roasting pans and skillet with water, wine, or stock to make a gravy or sauce.

DICE

To cut vegetables, meat, or other ingredients into small, even cubes.

DILUTE

To make a thick sauce or season-ing thinner by adding relevant quantities of a liquid.

DISSOLVE

To mix a dry ingredient, such as sugar, in a liquid until it forms a solution.

DOUBLE BOILER

This is for a cooking method whereby delicate ingredients are cooked in a container over a pan of barely simmering water. This method of cooking is used to make delicate sauces, to melt chocolate without its becoming 'grainy' and to heat or reheat dishes without changing their flavor and consis-tency.

DRIPPINGS

The cooking juices which collect on the base of a roasting pan. When diluted with water, stock, or wine and heated, the resulting liquid may be used as a sauce and poured directly on meat or served separately in a sauce boat.

DUST WITH FLOUR

Meat, vegetables, and fish are often dusted – lightly coated – with flour before frying. Baking pans, counters, and pastry dough are also dusted with flour to stop the dough sticking to the rolling pin.

EMULSIFY

To mix two liquids of different densities, such as oil and vinegar or lemon juice, by whisking them together. You should be aware that the resulting mixture is unstable and the ingredients will separate again after a while.

EVAPORATE

To dry off an added liquid, such as stock, wine, or liqueur, to give dishes extra flavor.

FILL

Layers of a cake are alternated with, and puffs are filled with, custard, chocolate, cream or jelly. Patty shells are also filled with various mixtures.

FILLET

To remove fillets of raw or cooked fish from the bones. A very sharp, flexible knife is required to fillet raw fish.

FLAMBÉ

From the French flamber, this means to pour an alcoholic liquid, such as brandy, on a dish after cooking and then ignite it to burn off the alcohol and keep the aroma.

FLAVOR

To give additional flavor and aroma to food by adding herbs, such as parsley, rosemary, sage, or thyme, and/or vegetables, such as carrots, onions and celery.

FRATTAU BREAD

This Sardinian bread, also known as music paper, is a thin round of dough made with water, durum wheat flour, and salt, cooked for a few minutes over low heat. It is called frattau bread when it is boiled in water and served with a poached egg, tomato sauce, and cheese on top.

FRICASSÉE

A sauce consisting of eggs and lemon poured onto veal, lamb, rabbit, or chicken. When heated, it thickens and takes on a creamy consistency. The dish must be removed from the heat as soon as it is ready, otherwise the sauce thickens excessively and develops an unpleasant flavor.

FROST

Cakes and cookies are frosted by covering the surface with a shiny sugar layer, which may be colored to taste with chocolate or food dyes. There are a number of different types of frosting.

FRUIT SALAD

Mixed, thinly sliced or diced fresh or cooked fruit, sprinkled with lemon juice, orange juice, sugar, and, sometimes, liqueur. Fruit salads vary according to the season. In the winter there is a limited choice and they may be enriched with dried fruit and nuts – raisins, walnuts, figs, etc. In the summer, they may be served with ice cream.

FRY LIGHTLY

To cook a mixture, such as chopped vegetables, in oil or butter over low heat without browning.

GALANTINE

A boned boiling fowl or chicken filled with a mixture of diced meat, hard-cooked eggs, cured ham, truffle, and other ingredients. It is

sewn up and poached. Galantine is served cold, thinly sliced, and is often set in aspic.

GARNISH

To decorate single plates or serving dishes of savory ingredients with cut vegetables, herb sprigs, lemon slices, or other garnishes to make them look attractive and to achieve a balance between the various shapes and colors.

GAZPACHO

A famous, chilled Spanish soup made from chopped raw tomatoes, onion, cucumbers, bell peppers, and bread crumb. It is partly puréed, drizzled with olive oil and vinegar and served ice-cold.

GIARDINIERA

A mixture of vegetables, mainly pearl onions, carrots, cauliflower, bell peppers, and cucumbers, preserved in vinegar. It is similar to the French 'a la jardinière', meaning garden vegetables.

GIUDIA

A method of frying globe artichokes popular among the Jewish community in Rome, from which the name derives. Whole artichokes are deep-fried in a pan of hot oil. They open like flowers and go a beautiful copper color.

GLAZE

To glaze a roast means to spread shiny, clear cooking juices over the meat. To glaze vegetables means to cook them in lightly sugared liquid which makes them shiny.

GRANOLA

A mixture of oat and barley flakes, dried fruit, nuts, wheat germ, honey, etc. served with milk or yogurt. It is the most popular breakfast in Switzerland and today is widespread in many other countries.

GREASE

To brush a baking pan, roasting pan, mold, or baking parchment with oil or melted butter or to smear it with butter to prevent the mixture from sticking during cooking. Sweet butter is better as it is less likely to burn than salted butter.

GRIND

To grind ingredients, such as beef for hamburgers, very finely using a grinder or food processor.

HANG

To leave meat for a length of time after butchering so that it becomes tender and succulent. The process still continues when the meat is frozen, although very much more slowly. As a rule, fish should not be hung.

HEAP

This is the classic way of arranging flour on a counter before mixing.

Sift the flour into a small pyramid, make a hollow in the center, and break the eggs into it or add other ingredients.

JULIENNE

Vegetables cut into very thin sticks, which absorb oil, lemon juice, or mayonnaise well.

KNEAD

To mix solid and liquid ingredients by 'working them' for varying lengths of time by hand, with a spatula, or with an electric mixer fitted with dough hooks. Pasta and yeast doughs are kneaded vigorously, whereas pastry dough is kneaded lightly.

KNÖDEL

A large dumpling, 3–4 inches in diameter, made from bread crumbs soaked in milk and kneaded with herbs, spices, and various other ingredients, such as eggs and bulk sausage. They are served in clear soup or alone as a first course.

LARD

To make small incisions in a piece of meat and insert pieces of pancetta or bacon fat, pancetta, bacon, or cured ham. The fat melts during cooking and tenderizes and seasons the dish.

LINE

To cover the inside of a tin or mold with pastry, or slices of pancetta, or bacon, or vegetables to prepare it for a filling.

MARINATE

To place meat, game, or fish in an aromatic mixture, usually based on olive oil, lemon juice, vinegar, wine, spices and herbs, in order to flavor and tenderize it.

MEAT OR VEGETABLE EXTRACT

This is similar to a bouillon cube. It is a meat or vegetable concentrate in the form of a thick liquid or granules. It is used to flavor stocks, gravies, and sauces.

MILANESE

Meaning 'from the city of Milan', this is a cooking method in which meat or vegetables are dipped in beaten egg and then coated with bread crumbs before frying. Milanese chops fried in butter are particularly famous.

MOCETTA

A specialty from Valle d'Aosta, this is a type of raw cured 'ham' made from the thigh of an ibex, chamois, or goat. It is preserved in brine with herbs and air-dried. It is served as an antipasto.

MOUSSAKA

A famous Greek dish, similar to Italian Parmesan eggplant, with alternate layers of eggplant, ground beef or lamb sauce, local cheeses, tomato sauce, etc.

MOUSSE

A soft, frothy preparation which sets in the refrigerator. It may be

savory, flavored with cured ham, tuna, goose liver, salmon, etc., or sweet, flavored with chocolate, vanilla, etc.

MUGNAIA

The Italian translation of the French 'a la meunière', literally meaning 'in the style of the miller's wife'. Fillets of fish are dusted with flour and browned in butter. This method is particularly recommended for sole, but also works well with other white fish.

MUSTARD

This condiment is made from mustard seeds mixed with vinegar, pepper, and other spices. Cremona mustard is an Italian specialty of candied fruit immersed in a syrup of honey, mustard, and wine. It may be mild or strong, and is eaten with roast and boiled meat and sharp cheeses. Venetian mustard is similar to Cremona mustard, and Mantuan mostarda is made from sliced apple. For salad dressings and flavoring stews, Dijon mustard is usually the preferred type.

OLLA PODRIDA

This very popular Spanish hotch-potch consists of mixed boiled meats, including chorizo, as well as garbanzo beans.

PAELLA

This is the national dish of Spain. There are a huge number of regional variations and it even varies from town to town. The classic version, the Valencian paella, is made with rice, chicken, shellfish, vegetables, spices, and saffron, and cooked in a big iron skillet also called a paella.

PANCETTA

Cured pork taken from the belly of the pig, like streaky bacon, but cured differently. It may be smoked or unsmoked, natural or rolled, and flavored with spices. It is used in pasta sauces, kabobs and to add flavor to many other dishes. If pancetta is not available, use bacon.

PANSOTTI

Genoese ravioli, with a rich filling of mixed herbs and vegetables, such as borage and Swiss chard. Pansotti are served with walnut sauce.

PARFAIT

A French word meaning 'perfect', this describes a soft, frothy chilled dessert made from cream and eggs and flavored with vanilla or other flavorings.

PARMENTIER

A number of potato-based dishes take their name from the man who popularized the potato in France.

PARMIGIANA, ALLA

Eggplant in Parmesan are famous. They are first fried, then baked au gratin in the oven. This method is also suitable for other vegetables.

PARMIGIANO, AL

This describes cooked pasta, rice, or

vegetables seasoned with melted butter and grated Parmesan cheese.

PASSATA

Bottled strained tomatoes which are less concentrated than tomato paste.

PÂTÉ

A mixture of finely chopped cooked meat or fish, usually smoked, mixed with butter and left to set for a few hours in the refrigerator. It is served as an antipasto to be spread on toast. Probably the most famous is goose liver pâté, but chicken liver pâté is also immensely popular.

PIE

A farmhouse pie made with beef, game, chicken, or fruit, arranged in layers in a pastry shell, topped with another sheet of pastry, and baked in the oven. It is a traditional British and American dish.

PILAF

Long-grain rice is boiled in a small quantity of water or stock, dried in the oven and seasoned in various ways. It can be used in a variety of recipes.

PILLOTTO

A cooking method involving a broiler or a spit. When the meat is half-cooked, a piece of bacon fat is wrapped in a sheet of thick paper, slipped on to a toasting fork, and passed over the flame. The paper catches fire and the heat causes the fat to drip and spread out over the meat.

PINZIMONIO

A dressing consisting of olive oil, salt, lemon juice or vinegar and pepper. It is used as a dip for raw vegetables cut into strips.

POACH

To cook eggs by breaking them into boiling water and cooking them for a few minutes. Fish, meat and poultry may also be poached in gently simmering water or stock.

POTACCHIO

Chicken, rabbit, or lamb stewed in tomato sauce.

POT–AU–FEU

French mixed boiled meat of various kinds with legumes, cooked in the same pan and served together.

POUND

To soften the texture of ingredients using various utensils, such as a meat bat. For example, dried cod, octopus, and some cuts of meat are softened by pounding in order to break up their fibers.

PRE–SALÉ

The meat from flocks of sheep allowed to graze on salt marshes. It has a very pleasant flavor.

PROSCIUTTO

This is the Italian word for any kind of cured ham, including cooked

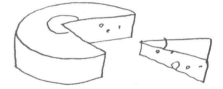

RED WINE

ham. However, in the United States it is used to refer exclusively to raw, dry-cured ham, usually from Parma. Other fine versions of prosciutto are produced in Veneto and San Daniele.

PUNTARELLE

A type of thinly sliced catalogna – Italian dandelion – dressed with oil, vinegar, salt, garlic, and anchovies. It is typical of Roman cuisine.

PURÉE

To reduce a solid or semi solid substance or mixture to a semi-liquid or smooth cream using a food processor or blender.

QUENELLE

A French dish consisting of small meat or fish dumplings poached in simmering water and served with sauce or au gratin.

QUICHE

A tart originally made in Alsace-Lorraine. The quiche Lorraine is the most famous – a pastry shell filled with bacon and beaten eggs.

RACLETTE

A cheese from Valais in Switzerland, the word raclette also describes the way it is served. A half wheel is heated with an open flame and half melted flakes are scraped from the middle and served immediately with boiled potatoes and dill pickes.

RAGÙ

Interestingly, the name derives from the French ragoût, but this is the quintessential Italian pasta sauce. It is either made with ground meat (Bolognese) or by prolonged stewing of a piece of meat with tomatoes, oil, and spices, as is the custom in southern Italy.

REDUCE

To make a liquid, such as a stock or sauce, thicker and more concentrated by heating it for longer.

RIBOLLITA

This Tuscan peasant soup has today now become a delicacy of classic Italian cuisine. It is based on Tuscan cabbage (cavolo nero) and beans. It is cooked, then left to stand until the next day, when it is put back on the heat – the name, which literally means 'reboiled', derives from this method of preparation.

ROAST

To cook meat, fish, or vegetables in the oven, on a spit, or in a pan (pot roast), after initially browning over high heat.

ROLL OUT

To roll out pastry or other dough on a flat surface to an even thickness. You should always roll in only one direction, occasionally turning the dough a quarter turn to ensure an even result.

SALMÌ

This is a way of preparing game, that is similar to the French civet and English jugged. The meat is cut into pieces, marinated for a couple of days in wine with plenty of spices, and, finally, stewed.

SALMORIGLIO

This sauce made of olive oil, lemon juice, parsley, oregano and salted water is prepared in Calabria and Sicily to season slices of grilled swordfish.

SALT

To sprinkle sliced eggplant, cucumbers, and, sometimes zucchini with salt to draw out their juices. This was once essential with eggplant which used to have very bitter juices, but contemporary varieties are much milder.

SANDWICH

Two slices of buttered bread filled with cured ham, salami, cheese, salad, etc. It takes its name from John Montagu, 4th Earl of Sandwich, an inveterate card player who had sandwiches brought to the gaming table in order to avoid interrupting play. The club sandwich is a multi-layered sandwich with three slices of bread, sometimes toasted. Open or Danish sandwiches consist of a single slice of bread, often rye bread, with a topping. Filled rolls or baguettes are known as submarines, poor boys or torpedoes.

SASHIMI

A typical Japanese dish in which fillets of raw fish are sliced according to strict rules, and served with wasabi, Japanese horseradish.

SAUTÉ

To cook meat, fish, or vegetables in a skillet or sauté pan with oil or butter until browned and cooked through. Pasta and risotto may also be sautéed.

SCHIDIONATA

Birds and small chickens cooked on a spit.

SEASON

To enrich the taste of a dish by adding salt, pepper and other condiments, such as paprika.

SHRED

To cut ingredients, such as cabbage and lettuce, into very thin strips.

SIFT

Flour, superfine sugar, unsweetened cocoa powder, and other dry ingredients may be shaken through a fine strainer before mixing with oil, melted butter, or milk to prevent lumps from forming.

SIMMER

To bring a liquid to just below boiling point or to turn down the heat under a liquid that has reached boiling point so that the surface of the liquid barely ripples. For example, the court-bouillon in which fish is poached and the water in a double boiler should barely simmer.

SINGE

To pass chickens, squab, and game quickly over a flame to remove any feathers or quills remaining on the skin.

SKIM

To remove the scum or froth that forms on the surface of some liquids, such as stock, during boiling. A skimmer or a slotted spoon is the most suitable tool.

SKIM THE FAT

To remove the excess fat which sometimes forms on the surface of stock. The easiest way is to chill the stock in the refrigerator and then remove the solid layer of fat that will set on the surface.

SLASH

When whole fish is to be broiled or baked, two or three diagonal slashes may be made on both sides to make it easier for the heat – and flavorings – to penetrate. The surface of risen yeast dough, particularly for breads, is slashed, so that it rises well during baking.

SMETANA

A yogurt-like product made with sour cream which Eastern Europeans use copiously even in their beet soup (bortsch).

SNIP

To make small cuts in ingredients for a variety of purposes. For example, the edges of steaks are often snipped so that they do not pucker. Chives are often snipped with kitchen scissors rather than chopped with a knife, as this is quicker, easier, and doesn't bruise them.

SOAK

To soften and rehydrate some foods, such as sheets of gelatin, dried fruit, and dried mushrooms, in water or other liquid so that they regain volume and freshness.

SOFT BUTTER

SOFTEN

To make a food softer, for example, by taking the butter out of the refrigerator and leaving it at room temperature for 30 minutes so that it can be spread more easily, or beaten.

SOUBISE

A sauce based on mashed or puréed onions, invented by the Prince de Soubise, an amateur gourmet.

SPECK

A smoked pork ham that is a typical, very tasty specialty from Alto Adige in Italy, Germany and Scandinavia.

SPRINKLE

Sprinkling ingredients with a small quantity of wine, liqueur or

juice during cooking is better than drowning them by pouring all the liquid in at once. This also refers to sprinkling small quantities of sauce or cooking juices on the surface of various dishes.

STEEP

To leave ingredients to soak in a liquid or spice mix, such as wine, liqueur, or seasoning, for a specified period.

STEW

To cook meat or fish on low heat with a little liquid in a covered pan.

STIR IN

To mix a liquid or semi-liquid ingredient with a dry ingredient. This is usually carried out in several stages to obtain an even mixture – liquid is added to dry ingredients or vice versa, a little at a time, and the rest is added only when the mixture is smooth and even.

STIR IN BUTTER OR CREAM

To give an even and velvety texture to a dish by stirring in butter or cream when it has finished cooking. A classical example is risotto.

STUFATO

A large piece of beef cooked, without browning, in a covered pan over low heat with wine, herbs, and spices.

STUFF

To put a savory mixture inside the main roast or baked ingredient, such as turkey, or fish, or vegetable 'shells' such as hollowed-out tomatoes.

STUFFING

Any filling for chicken, turkey, squab, pheasant, or fish. It consists of many finely chopped ingredients, which vary according to the recipe, mixed with bread crumb, moistened with milk, and bound with egg.

SUPPLÌ

Rice croquettes stuffed with a little ground meat or, more commonly, a piece of mozzarella cheese. The melted mozzarella stretches into thin threads resembling telephone wires when you bite into it, hence its name supplì al telefono. Supplì are extremely tasty and are very popular in Rome and central Italy.

SUSHI

Morsels of rice garnished with wasabi, Japanese horseradish, and a fillet of raw fish.

TABASCO SAUCE

Made from vinegar, herbs, hot chile, salt, and sugar, this sauce takes its name from a Mexican state where chile cultivation predominates. It should be used sparingly. The most famous brand of Tabasco is made in Louisiana.

TAHINI

A mixture of sesame seeds, lemon juice, and water, this is one of the most typical hors d'oeuvres of Arabian cuisine and is widely used in Middle Eastern cooking.

TARAMASALATA

A type of pâté or dip made with smoked striped mullet roe, olive oil, bread, milk, egg yolk, olives, and other ingredients. Nowadays, smoked cod's roe is more often used than smoked striped mullet roe. It is spread on bread, particularly pitta bread, and is one of the most popular hors d'oeuvres in Turkey and Greece.

TATIN, TARTE

A French apple pie in which slices of apple are arranged like the rays of the sun, sprinkled with plenty of sugar and covered with puff pastry dough. When the pie dish is turned out, the apples look as if they are covered with a caramel 'mirror'.

TEMPURA

A typical Japanese dish in which fish or vegetables are dipped in a light batter and fried in soya or other seed oils.

THICKEN

To make a sauce thicker by adding flour, cornstarch, beurre manié (see page 88), egg yolk or heavy cream, and heating for a few minutes.

TOFU

A cake with a cheese-like texture made from a milky substance derived from soybeans. It has very little flavor, but is rich in protein and quickly absorbs the flavors of other ingredients. It is popular in China and Japan and is now widely available. It is also known as beancurd.

TRIFOLATO

Various types of ingredients cooked in a skillet with olive oil or butter and garlic and/or onion. Parsley is added at the end.

UMIDO

This is usually meat stewed or braised in tomato sauce and flavored with olive oil, parsley, other herbs, and spices. This method of cooking may be used with meat, fish, chicken and rabbit.

UNLEAVENED BREAD

Bread made without yeast or other raising agents.

VICHYSSOISE

A leek and potato soup that is served chilled. The name is French, as was its inventor, but the dish comes from North America.

VINAIGRETTE

The classic salad dressing — olive oil, wine vinegar and salt — whisked together to an even mixture.

WHISK/BEAT

Cream, egg whites, butter, and sauces are whisked or beaten with a hand-held or electric whisk to increase their volume and make them frothy. Flavorings may be beaten into softened butter.

WORCESTERSHIRE SAUCE

A sweet and sour condiment for seasoning meat, fish, and vegetables. An English specialty that is essential for the cocktail Bloody Mary.

TOOLS
AND EQUIPMENT

Large kitchens are making a comeback in suburban homes around large cities. The once revolutionary kitchenette, which solved several space problems, is today considered a bit cramped even for the increasing population of singles, who are very often amateur gourmets anyway. In any case, whatever the size of your kitchen, it is advisable to purchase equipment in stages and buy accessories and electrical appliances according to real needs and changing habits. It is also important for all utensils to be ready for use and always at hand. Otherwise, you might just as well not have them.

POTS AND PANS

COPPER

This is ideal for pans, as copper is an excellent conductor of heat and ensures even heat distribution. However, copper pans are heavy, they dent easily, require a high level of maintenance, and are expensive.

STAINLESS STEEL

Hygienic and robust, but mediocre conductors of heat, stainless steel pans are not recommended for dry dishes which tend to stick to the base. On the other hand, they are excellent for boiling meat and cooking pasta. Some of the best manufacturers make steel pans with a copper base, which improves heat distribution. Enamelled steel pans have rather fallen into disuse, partly because they chip rather easily and also because they are not dishwasher safe.

ALUMINUM

Light and good heat conductors, aluminum pans are, however, porous and not very hygienic. Decades ago aluminum was considered a cheap material, but today it is more appreciated thanks to modern manufacturing techniques which make it smoother, more resistant to chipping, and easier to clean. Thick aluminum pans are often found in professional kitchens. It is best to use uncoated metal for boiling. For other cooking methods, aluminum with a non-stick coating is recommended because it allows cooking without fat. This coating is delicate and it is advisable to use wooden or plastic utensils to avoid scratching it. The secret of any pan, whether it is made of steel or aluminum, is its thickness. The thicker the metal on the base, the better it is at transmitting heat, and therefore cooking ingredients quickly and evenly.

SPECIAL PANS AND DISHES

The starting point for correctly preparing a dish is a sound knowledge of cooking methods and an understanding that each foodstuff often requires its own method and a pan or dish made of the appropriate material. The best way to meet these requirements – as learned from the experience of cooking professionals – is to have a range of pots, pans, casseroles, and dishes made from a variety of materials. As well as metal ones, pans and dishes made from earthenware, porcelain and ovenproof glass are suitable for some cooking techniques. Without excluding the ever-versatile steel pans, other equipment is also of great help in the kitchen. For example, the classic nonstick cast-iron skillet is an incomparable natural controller of the temperature of oil. Oil, in fact, should never reach smoke point, which is bad for your health and also when it could catch fire. A fish kettle is a long oval pan with a removable rack and lid, designed for cooking whole fish. Rhomboid fish kettles are also available for cooking large flat fish, such as halibut, but are rarely found in domestic kitchens. The choice of specialist equipment is vast, since fish kettles and other pans are available in a variety of materials, from copper to steel and aluminum. The price varies considerably too. A tall, narrow pan for cooking asparagus is also useful, as well as oval pans of various sizes for pot-roasts and poultry. A cast-iron griddle pan can be used to cook vegetables and small slices of meat without additional fat, an important consideration in these health-conscious days.

A double boiler with a set of nested copper or ceramic bowls is also invaluable. No less useful are stainless steel baskets used for steaming. Alternatively, to give an exotic touch to the kitchen, why not buy a classic set of Chinese stackable bamboo steaming baskets? Lastly comes the pressure cooker. It is purely a matter of choice – some people cannot live without one, while others rule it out right from the start. It certainly can be useful for people with limited time.

The shapes of cooking vessels are important and are not simply dictated by the whim of their designers. They are linked with various cooking techniques and designed for correct heat diffusion. One example is the sauté pan, made with high, flared sides and a strong long handle that is easy to grip. It is ideal for cooking dishes, such as creams and zabaglione, which have to be stirred frequently. Another example is the flat shape of some skillets designed for cooking meat and vegetables or omelets and crêpes, which must be turned over and cooked on both sides.

A WORKING KITCHEN

SMALL APPLIANCES

Knives, cutting boards, ladles, and can openers are utensils that everyone is familiar with. However, when choosing small electrical appliances it is easy to make mistakes, attracted by promises of convenience. Be wary of appliances that promise lots of functions – kneading, grating, puréeing, grinding, etc. Bear in mind that it is necessary to take them apart, and wash, dry, and replace the components each time you use them. When possible, choose appliances with specific purposes that match your needs and place them on the counter or hook them onto the wall under the wall units so that they are readily available.

POWER SOCKETS

Have a suitable number of power sockets installed, away from the sink for safety reasons. It is best to connect appliances used every day, such as a coffee machine, citrus juicer, toaster, microwave oven, etc., to specific sockets. Others, such as an electric grill, bread machine, electric carving knife, or a deep-fryer, may be connected only when needed. Electrical appliances do not always save time. For example, if you use a deep-fryer only occasionally, remember that it has to be emptied each time and thoroughly cleaned. A traditional iron skillet may well be more practical. A food processor takes up a lot of room and unless you use it frequently, you may be better off with hand-held food mill.

GOOD ORGANIZATION

The practicality of a kitchen depends to a great extent on the space available. For example, a sink unit under the window may be pleasant, but often means having no space for a draining board. The most useful unit is one with two sinks. An extractor fan or cooker hood that recirculates the air is not very effective against odors. It is better to have one connected to the outside. Storage located under the counter is especially practical if it can be pulled out, like drawers, so that you can see the contents at a glance. The most frequently used objects should be placed in the wall units, arranged in lines on shelves, or hung on hooks to avoid opening and closing drawers and cupboard doors.

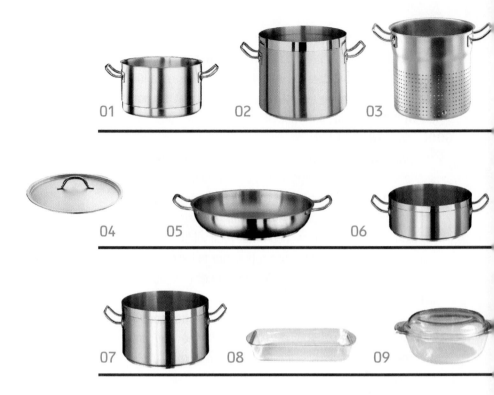

POTS
AND PANS

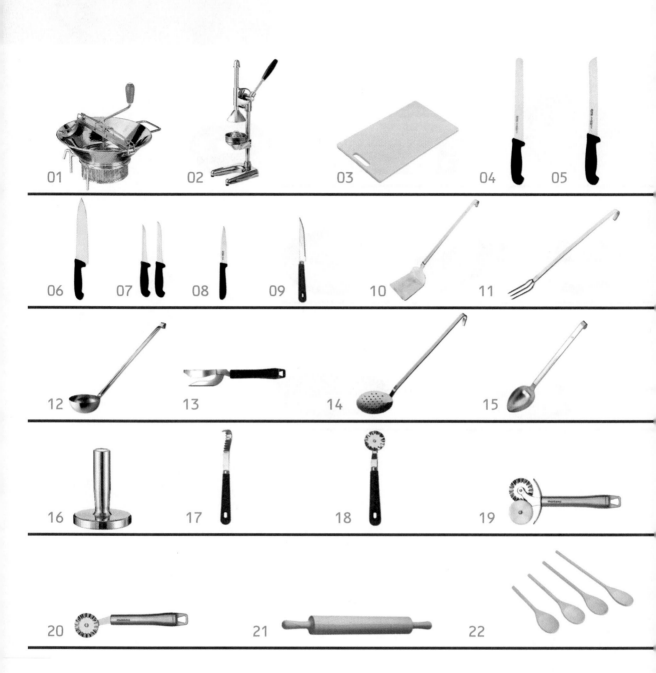

UTENSILS

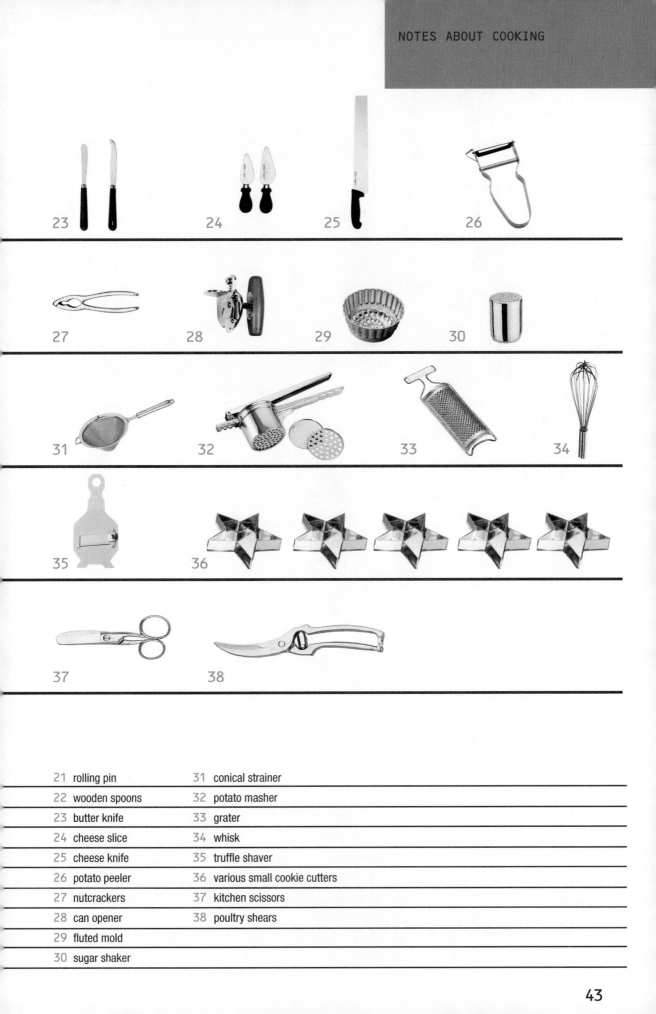

INSIDE

?

PICKLE JARS

LITTLE SPOON

SOUP & SAUCE

POT

ELEGANTLY DECORATED DISH

BUTTER!

SAUCES →

MARINADES →

FLAVORED BUTTERS →

SAUCES

This subject is without doubt a delicate one. Hot, cold, sweet or spicy…with sauces there are no half-measures: they can enhance the flavor of a dish or completely smother it with disastrous consequences. Nevertheless, it is almost impossible to do without them. Almost since the dawn of time, people have striven to add flavor to food. Indeed, there are foods which, without an appropriate sauce, would be inedible or, at least, would not be eaten with any enthusiasm. Just think about pasta. Try to imagine spaghetti without a fragrant fresh tomato sauce, trenette without the subtle aroma of pesto or baked lasagne without the delicate texture of a béchamel. All sauces need careful preparation: the various ingredients react chemically with each other and even the best cook cannot break the laws of nature. It is worth pointing out that almost all sauces are derived from a few basic recipes. These recipes were subsequently developed and transformed by professional chefs or amateur enthusiasts. Anyone who wants to develop their culinary skills must start by getting to know the basic sauces and learning how to make them perfectly. Only later can you move onto more complicated sauces and, perhaps, even invent your own. Before tackling the various traditional, new, revised, lightened recipes, here are a few tips and suggestions: as the quality of a sauce lies in its fragrance, lightness and aroma, all the ingredients must be extremely fresh as well as top quality. Butter, for example, where required, should be the finest available and, in Italy, is always sweet unless otherwise stated. Pans should be heavy-based to insure even cooking. To keep a sauce hot until you are ready to serve, it is best to sit the pan in another pan full of hot water. To prevent a skin from forming on the surface, sprinkle a little diced butter or a few tablespoonfuls of liquid on the surface and don't stir in until serving. Finally, remember not to overdo sauces: they need to be used with discretion. This means their flavor must complement the food with which they are served not smother it.

MARINADES

When you want to spice up a meat or game dish and tenderize it, a marinade will produce the best results. One of the most common ingredients is red or white wine, depending on the desired result: one gives a strong flavor to the mixture and the other brings out the taste of the meat.

FLAVORED BUTTERS

Also known as compound butters or by their French name, beurres composés, these are made by mixing another ingredient with butter to give it a strong flavor: herbs, mustard, anchovies, tuna, etc. Flavored butters may be used to add extra zest to steaks, fish and omelets and may also be spread on canapés.

HOT
SAUCES

BAGNA CAUDA

Bring a pan of water to a boil, then lower the heat and simmer. Heat the olive oil with the butter in a smaller pan without letting them brown. Add the garlic and place the pan in the simmering water. Chop the anchovies, add them to the oil mixture and mash with a wooden spoon until they have disintegrated and the sauce is smooth. Just before serving, add the truffle. Pour the bagna cauda into a fondue pot or dish and serve.
For poached cardoons or raw vegetables.

BAGNA CAUDA

Serves 4

5 tablespoons olive oil

6 tablespoons butter

2 garlic cloves, finely chopped

3¹/₂ ounces salted anchovies, heads removed, cleaned and filleted (see page 596), soaked in cold water for 10 minutes and drained

1 small white truffle, very thinly sliced

BÉCHAMEL SAUCE (BASIC RECIPE)

BESCIAMELLA

Serves 4

1/4 cup butter

1/4 cup all-purpose flour

2 1/4 cup milk

pinch of freshly grated nutmeg (optional)

salt and pepper

Melt the butter in a pan over medium heat. Whisk in the flour. Pour in all the milk, whisking constantly until it starts to boil. Season with salt, lower the heat, cover and simmer gently, stirring occasionally, for at least 20 minutes. Béchamel sauce should not taste floury. Remove the pan from the heat. Taste and add more salt if necessary and season with pepper and/or nutmeg. If the sauce is too thick, add a little more milk. If too runny, return to the heat and add a pat of butter mixed with an equal quantity of all-purpose flour. Making this delicious sauce, considered a basic sauce because of the numerous variations to which it has given rise, is an essential skill for anyone keen to cook. For a richer béchamel sauce, replace half the milk with the same amount of heavy cream; for a lighter béchamel sauce, add half milk and half water. For gratins, soufflés or stuffings.

MUSHROOM BÉCHAMEL

BESCIAMELLA AI FUNGHI

Serves 4

2 tablespoons butter

2 cups cultivated mushrooms, thinly sliced

1 quantity Béchamel Sauce (see above)

3 tablespoons heavy cream

salt and pepper

Melt the butter in a pan. Add the mushrooms, cover and cook over low heat for about 10 minutes until they release all their liquid. Remove the lid, increase the heat and boil off the liquid. Season with salt. Heat the béchamel sauce and stir in the mushrooms. Season with pepper to taste and gently fold in the cream. For short pasta, veal scallops or poached eggs.

MAÎTRE D'HÔTEL BÉCHAMEL

BESCIAMELLA MAÎTRE D'HÔTEL

Serves 4

1/2 quantity Béchamel Sauce (see above)

1 tablespoon chopped fresh parsley

juice of 1 lemon, strained

3 tablespoons butter

Add 4–5 tablespoons warm water to the béchamel sauce and stir well. Bring just to a boil and stir in the parsley and lemon juice. Remove the pan from the heat and stir in the butter. For poached eggs, fish or sautéed vegetables.

BÉCHAMEL WITH CREAM

BESCIAMELLA ALLA PANNA

Serves 4

1 quantity Béchamel Sauce (see above)

1 cup light cream

As soon as the béchamel has finished cooking, remove the pan from the heat and stir in the cream, mixing well. Made like this, the sauce is more delicate. For gratins.

PAPRIKA BÉCHAMEL

Melt the butter in a pan. Add the onion and cook over low heat, stirring occasionally, until softened and translucent but not browned. Whisk in the flour. Pour in all the milk, whisking constantly until it starts to boil. Season with salt, lower the heat, cover and simmer gently, stirring occasionally, for at least 20 minutes. A few minutes before removing the pan from the heat, stir in the paprika.
For meat, fish or boiled vegetables.

BESCIAMELLA ALLA PAPRICA

Serves 4

¼ cup butter

1 pearl onion, chopped

½ cup all-purpose flour

2¼ cups milk

1 tablespoon hot paprika

salt

MUSTARD BÉCHAMEL

Mix the mustard powder with a little warm water to a paste. Add to the béchamel sauce and stir in the butter.
For fish, poultry or broiled meat.

BESCIAMELLA ALLA SENAPE

Serves 4

1 teaspoon mustard powder

½ quantity Béchamel Sauce (see opposite)

1½ tablespoons butter

YOGURT BÉCHAMEL

When the béchamel sauce is ready, add the cream and simmer, stirring the mixture constantly, for approximately 15 minutes. Remove the pan from the heat and let cool slightly. Stir in the yogurt and lemon juice, then stir in the mustard. Season with salt if necessary.
For broiled fish or poached chicken.

BESCIAMELLA ALLO YOGURT

Serves 4

1 quantity Béchamel Sauce (see opposite)

scant ½ cup heavy cream

⅔ cup low-fat plain yogurt

juice of 1 lemon, strained

2 teaspoons mild mustard

salt

MORNAY SAUCE

Beat the egg yolk with the cream in a small bowl. When the béchamel sauce is ready, remove the pan from the heat and stir in the Swiss cheese and Parmesan, then stir in the egg yolk mixture. Season to taste with salt and pepper. Pour into a sauce boat.
For poached eggs, fish, vegetables or gratins.

BESCIAMELLA MORNAY

Serves 4

1 egg yolk

scant ½ cup heavy cream

1 quantity Béchamel Sauce (see opposite)

1 cup Swiss cheese, freshly grated

1 cup Parmesan cheese, freshly grated

salt and pepper

SOUBISE SAUCE

BESCIAMELLA SOUBISE

Serves 4

1 pound 2 ounces white onions, thinly sliced

¹/₄ cup butter

1 quantity Béchamel Sauce (see page 50)

1 cup heavy cream

salt

Parboil the onions for 5 minutes, then drain well and let cool. Melt the butter in a pan and add the onions, a pinch of salt and a few tablespoons of warm water. Cover and cook over low heat for about 1 hour until mushy, but not brown. Stir the onion purée into the béchamel sauce. Add the cream and heat through, stirring, over medium heat.

For poached eggs or boiled vegetables.

BOLOGNESE MEAT SAUCE

RAGÙ ALLA BOLOGNESE

Serves 4

3 tablespoons butter

2 tablespoons olive oil

1 onion, chopped

1 celery stalk, chopped

1 carrot, chopped

9 ounces ground steak

1 tablespoon concentrated tomato paste

salt and pepper

Heat the butter and olive oil in a small pan and add the onion, celery, carrot and ground steak. Season with salt and pepper to taste. Mix well and cook over low heat for a few minutes until the vegetables have softened and the meat starts to brown. Mix the tomato paste with a little water to dilute it and add to the pan. Cover and cook over a very low heat for 1¹/₂ hours, adding a little hot water if the sauce seems to be drying out. This ragù (meat sauce) may be made with mixed meats and flavored with mushrooms.

For timbales or tagliatelle.

WHITE MEAT SAUCE

RAGÙ BIANCO

Serves 4–6

2 tablespoons olive oil

¹/₄ cup butter

1 onion, finely chopped

1 celery stalk, finely chopped

1 carrot, finely chopped

2 ounces pancetta or bacon, diced

14 ounces mixed ground beef and pork

scant ¹/₂ cup white wine

scant 1 cup Chicken Stock (see page 209)

2–3 tablespoons heavy cream (optional)

salt

Heat the olive oil and butter in a shallow pan. Add the onion, celery, carrot and pancetta or bacon and cook over low heat for 5 minutes until softened. Increase the heat to high, add the meat and mix well. Cook, stirring frequently, until browned. Add the wine and cook until it has evaporated. Season to taste with salt and add a ladleful of the stock. Lower the heat and cook for 1¹/₂ hours, adding more stock as the sauce dries out. Finally, stir in the cream to give a more mellow flavor.

For all types of pasta.

CHICKEN LIVER SAUCE

Melt the butter in a skillet. Add the chicken livers and cook, stirring frequently, for 4 minutes. Be careful not to overcook the livers or they will become tough. Add the wine and cook over low heat until evaporated. Season with salt and stir in the cream. Remove the pan from the heat and season with pepper.

For timbales, pasta, as an omelet filling, on scallops or with a vegetable soufflé.

RAGÙ CON FEGATINI

Serves 4

5 tablespoons butter

9 ounces chicken livers, trimmed and chopped

2–3 tablespoons dry white wine

3 tablespoons heavy cream

salt and pepper

SPINACH SAUCE

Put the spinach in a large pan with just the water clinging to its leaves after washing and cook for 5 minutes. Drain, squeeze out as much liquid as possible, then purée in a food processor. Melt the butter in another pan and pour in the milk and spinach purée. Season with salt. Cook over medium heat, stirring the mixture occasionally, until thickened. If the sauce remains runny, stir in the flour and cook for 10 minutes. Remove the pan from the heat and add more salt, if necessary, and white pepper to taste. If this sauce is served with pasta, such as farfalle or pennette lisce, hand around plenty of grated Parmesan cheese.

For short pasta or poached eggs.

SALSA AGLI SPINACI

Serves 4

1³/₄ pounds spinach

3 tablespoons butter

1 cup milk

1 tablespoon all-purpose flour (optional)

salt and white pepper

LEEK SAUCE

Melt the butter in a pan. Add the leeks and cook over low heat, stirring occasionally, for about 5 minutes until softened but not browned. Sprinkle in the flour and gradually stir in the boiling stock. Cook for a further 10 minutes. Remove the pan from the heat and push the leek mixture through a strainer into a clean pan. Re-heat the sauce gently, then stir in the lemon juice, cream and chopped parsley. Season with salt and white pepper to taste.

For chops.

SALSA AI PORRI

Serves 4

2 tablespoons butter

2 leeks, trimmed and thinly sliced

¹/₄ cup all-purpose flour

2¹/₄ cups boiling Chicken or Vegetable Stock (see page 209)

juice of ¹/₂ lemon, strained

scant ¹/₂ cup heavy cream

1 tablespoon chopped fresh parsley

salt and white pepper

BUTTER SAUCE

SALSA AL BURRO

Serves 4

¹/₂ white onion, finely chopped

scant ¹/₂ cup white wine vinegar

¹/₄ cup, softened and cut into small pieces

1–2 tablespoons chopped fresh parsley

salt and pepper

Put the onion and vinegar in a small pan. Set over medium heat and cook until the liquid has reduced by one-third. Process the mixture in a food processor, then pour back into the pan. Place the pan only partially over the heat so that the sauce is heated very slowly. Add the softened butter, a piece at a time, stirring constantly. The sauce will increase in volume and become white and creamy. Stir in the parsley and season with salt and pepper to taste.
For poached fish.

CURRY SAUCE

SALSA AL CURRY

Serves 4

¹/₄ cup butter

¹/₄ onion, chopped

2 tablespoons curry powder

1 tablespoon all-purpose flour

salt and pepper

Melt the butter in a pan. Add the onion and cook over low heat, stirring occasionally, for about 5 minutes until softened. Mix the curry powder with a little hot water to make a paste. Sprinkle the flour into the pan and stir well, then stir in the curry paste. Cook over low heat for 30 minutes, gradually adding more water as it is absorbed. Season with salt and pepper.
For vegetables, eggs or poultry.

ONION SAUCE

SALSA ALLE CIPOLLINE

Serves 4

6 tablespoons butter

4 pearl onions, finely chopped

2 egg yolks

6 fresh basil leaves, chopped

salt and pepper

Melt the butter in a pan over low heat. Add the onions and cook, stirring occasionally, for 15 minutes. Remove the pan from the heat and process the mixture in a food processor to a purée. Scrape the purée into a bowl and stir in the egg yolks, mixing gently. Stir in the basil and season to taste with salt and pepper.
For broiled fish or würstel (northern Italian sausage rather like a frankfurter).

APPLE SAUCE

SALSA ALLE MELE

Serves 4

2 russet apples, peeled, cored and thinly sliced

2 tablespoons butter

juice of 1 lemon, strained

3 tablespoons heavy cream

1 tablespoon grated horseradish

salt and pepper

Pour water into a pan to a depth of ³/₄ inch. Add the apples, cover and cook over medium heat, stirring occasionally with a wooden spoon, for about 15 minutes until very soft. Gently stir in the butter, lemon juice and cream and season with salt and pepper. Finally, stir in the grated horseradish, then serve.
For pork, goose or duck.

SAFFRON SAUCE

Pour the fish stock into a pan and heat gently. Place the saffron in a bowl and add about 5 tablespoons of the hot stock. Set aside. Melt the butter in another pan. Add the flour, a pinch of salt and the saffron mixture. Stir carefully, then gradually stir in the remaining hot stock. Cover and simmer for 15 minutes. Remove the pan from the heat, taste and add more salt if necessary. Garnish with extra saffron threads.

For poached or roasted fish.

SALSA ALLO ZAFFERANO

Serves 4

1 1/4 cups Fish Stock (see page 208)

1 teaspoon saffron threads, plus extra to garnish

6 tablespoons butter

3 tablespoons all-purpose flour

salt

MARSALA SAUCE

Melt the butter in a pan and stir in the flour. Cook, stirring constantly, until lightly browned. Stir in the stock, a little at a time, and bring to a boil, stirring constantly. Lower the heat and continue cooking until reduced by half. Season to taste with salt and pepper. Pour in the Marsala, bring to a boil and turn off the heat so that the wine's aroma is not lost. If using, stir in the black truffle.

For smoked ham, kidneys or sautéed chicken fillets.

SALSA AL MARSALA

Serves 4

6 tablespoons butter

1/4 cup all-purpose flour

1 1/4 cups Chicken Stock (see page 209)

3 tablespoons Marsala

1 black truffle (optional), thinly sliced

salt and pepper

BÉARNAISE SAUCE (BASIC RECIPE)

Pour the vinegar into a stainless steel pan. Add the shallots, tarragon and a pinch of salt. Set over medium heat until the liquid has reduced by more than half. Strain and let cool slightly. Lightly beat the eggs yolks with 1 teaspoon water. Stir the egg yolk mixture into the cooled vinegar, then add the lemon juice. Pour the mixture into the top of a double boiler or a heatproof bowl. Set over a pan of barely simmering water and whisk constantly until increased in volume. Add the melted butter and whisk until thickened. Season with the cayenne pepper.

For all kinds of broiled or spit-roasted meat and steamed vegetables, such as asparagus spears, green beans or zucchini.

SALSA BEARNESE (RICETTA BASE)

Serves 4

scant 1/2 cup white wine vinegar

4 shallots, chopped

2 tablespoons fresh tarragon leaves

3 egg yolks

1 tablespoon lemon juice, strained

1 cup butter, melted

pinch of cayenne pepper

salt

EASY BÉARNAISE SAUCE

SALSA BEARNESE SEMPLIFICATA

Serves 4

2 egg yolks

2 tablespoons heavy cream

1 tablespoon white wine vinegar

pinch of cayenne pepper

6 tablespoons butter, cut into pieces

1 tablespoon chopped fresh tarragon

1 tablespoon chopped fresh flat-leaf parsley

salt

Combine the egg yolks, cream, vinegar, cayenne pepper and a pinch of salt in the top of a double boiler or a heatproof bowl. Set over barely simmering water and heat gently, whisking constantly. When the sauce starts to thicken, add the butter, a few pieces at a time, whisking constantly. Stir in the tarragon and parsley and remove the pan from the heat.

For all broiled or spit-roasted meat.

CHINESE SAUCE

SALSA CINESE

Serves 4

scant 1 cup white wine vinegar

2 tablespoons sugar

pepper

Pour the vinegar into a pan and add the sugar and a pinch of pepper. Bring to a boil and simmer for 15 minutes. Serve while still very hot.

For rice or poached chicken.

ANCHOVY SAUCE

SALSA D'ACCIUGHE

Serves 4

9 ounces salted anchovies

scant 1 cup olive oil

1 garlic clove

Place the anchovies flat on a board, skin side up. Press along the backbones with your thumb, then turn them over and remove the bones. Rinse the fish and then chop. Heat the oil in a pan. Add the garlic and cook until it has turned brown, then remove and discard. Add the anchovies and cook, mashing with a wooden spoon until they have completely disintegrated.

For poached eggs, hot boiled vegetables or pasta.

MARCHAND DE VIN SAUCE

SALSA DEL VINAIO

Serves 4

2 shallots, finely chopped

1 cup red wine

pinch of chopped fresh thyme

1/2 bay leaf, crumbled

5 tablespoons butter, softened and cut into pieces

juice of 1/2 lemon, strained

salt and pepper

Put the shallots in a pan and add the wine, thyme and bay leaf and season with salt and pepper. Cook over low heat until the liquid has reduced by about half. Remove the pan from the heat, strain and whisk in the butter, one piece at a time. When the mixture is thick and frothy, whisk in the lemon juice. Pour into a sauce boat and serve.

For red meat or broils.

BRAIN SAUCE

Fill a large pan two-thirds full with water, add the bay leaf and bring to a boil. Drain the brain, add to the pan and cook for about 10 minutes. Drain the brain, place in a bowl and crush carefully with a wooden spoon. Shell and halve the eggs and scoop out the yolks into the bowl. Stir the mixture, drizzling in sufficient olive oil to obtain a pouring consistency. Stir in the onion, parsley and capers and season with salt and lemon juice to taste.
For boiled meat.

SALSA DI CERVELLA

Serves 4

1 bay leaf

1 small lamb brain, membranes
and blood vessels removed
and soaked in cold water for 1 hour

2 eggs, hard-cooked

olive oil, for drizzling

1 pearl onion, chopped

1 fresh parsley sprig, chopped

1 tablespoon capers, drained, rinsed and chopped

juice of 1 lemon, strained

salt

WALNUT SAUCE

Place the walnuts in a bowl and pour in boiling water to cover. let stand for 3 minutes, then drain. When the nuts are cool enough to handle, rub off the skins. Chop the nuts and put in a bowl with the olive oil and cream. Season with salt and white pepper. Mix to an even sauce.
For fresh fettuccine or boiled turnips.

SALSA DI NOCI

Serves 4

2¹/₄ cups shelled walnuts

4 tablespoons olive oil

2 tablespoons heavy cream

salt and white pepper

RED BELL PEPPER SAUCE

Blanch the bell peppers in salted, boiling water for a few minutes, then drain. Peel off the skins, halve and remove the seeds and membranes. Chop coarsely, then process in a food processor to a purée. Pour the vinegar into a pan, add the garlic and heat for a few minutes. Strain the vinegar into the food processor and add the oil. Process until smooth.
For steamed fish or bollito misto (mixed boiled meats).

SALSA DI PEPERONI

Serves 4

2 large red bell peppers

2 tablespoons white wine vinegar

2 garlic cloves, chopped

3 tablespoons olive oil

salt

TOMATO SAUCE

Put the tomatoes with their can juice, if using canned tomatoes, into a pan and add the sugar, garlic and a pinch of salt. Cover and cook over a very low heat for about 30 minutes without stirring. Mash the tomatoes with a wooden spoon and, if using canned tomatoes, cook for a further 15 minutes. Remove the pan from the heat and let cool. Stir in the olive oil and basil.
For spaghetti or scallops.

SALSA DI POMODORO

Serves 4

9 ounces canned tomatoes or
fresh tomatoes, peeled

pinch of sugar

2 garlic cloves

2 tablespoons olive oil

10 fresh basil leaves, torn • salt

QUICK TOMATO SAUCE

Blanch the tomatoes in boiling water for a few seconds, then peel, seed and dice. Place in a small pan and add the olive oil, garlic, parsley and a pinch of salt. Cook, uncovered, over medium heat for 10 minutes. Remove and discard the garlic and parsley. Taste and add more salt if necessary. Pour the sauce directly onto drained pasta while still hot. Do not sprinkle with grated Parmesan cheese. If you like a stronger flavor, thicken the sauce over high heat for the last 5 minutes of the cooking time, making sure it does not stick to the pan. For short or long pasta.

SALSA DI POMODORO VELOCE

Serves 4

6 plum tomatoes

4 tablespoons olive oil

2 garlic cloves

1 fresh parsley sprig

salt

HORSERADISH SAUCE

Melt the butter in a small pan. Stir in the flour and cook, stirring constantly, until the flour turns brown. Stir in the stock. Add the grated horseradish and sugar and cook, stirring frequently, for 10 minutes.
For poached meat.

SALSA DI RAFANO O CREN

Serves 4

2 tablespoons butter

$1/4$ cup all-purpose flour

$2/3$ cup Meat Stock (see page 208)

1 tablespoon grated horseradish

pinch of sugar

NORMANDY SAUCE

Melt the butter in a pan and stir in the flour, nutmeg and a pinch each of salt and pepper. Mix well, then pour in the wine, cream and lemon juice. Cook over low heat, stirring constantly, until fairly thick.
For lamb chops.

SALSA NORMANNA

Serves 4

2 tablespoons butter

$1/4$ cup all-purpose flour

pinch of freshly grated nutmeg

3 tablespoons white wine

scant $1/2$ cup heavy cream

1 tablespoon lemon juice, strained

salt and pepper

HOLLANDAISE SAUCE

Beat the egg yolks with 3 tablespoons water in a heatproof bowl. Set the bowl over a pan of barely simmering water and whisk well. Whisk in the butter, one piece at a time, and continue whisking for about 15 minutes until the sauce is thick and frothy. Remove from the heat and stir in the lemon juice.
For broiled or poached turbot or salmon.

SALSA OLANDESE

Serves 4

3 egg yolks

scant 1 cup butter, softened and cut into pieces

juice of $1/2$ lemon, strained

PIQUANT SAUCE

SALSA PICCANTE

Serves 4

3 hard-cooked egg yolks

1 tablespoon white wine vinegar

1 tablespoon mild or hot mustard

pinch of sugar

11 ounces tomatoes, peeled and diced

2 raw egg yolks

2 tablespoons butter

salt and pepper

Mash the hard-cooked egg yolks in a pan, then stir in the vinegar, mustard, sugar and tomatoes and season the mixture with salt and pepper. Set the pan over low heat to warm through, then move it slightly off the heat and add the raw egg yolks, stirring the mixture thouroughly until combined. Remove the pan from the heat and beat in the butter.
For boiled rice.

ROYAL SAUCE

SALSA REALE

Serves 4

2 white bread slices, crusts removed

hot milk, for soaking

2 tablespoons butter

1 pearl onion, finely chopped

1 carrot, finely chopped

2 tablespoons finely chopped fresh flat-leaf parsley

2 tablespoons all-purpose flour

scant 1 cup Chicken or Vegetable Stock (see page 209)

scant 1 cup white wine

Tear the bread into pieces, place in a bowl and pour in enough hot milk to cover. Set aside to soak. Melt the butter in a pan. Add the onion, carrot and parsley and cook over low heat, stirring occasionally, for about 5 minutes until the onion has softened. Sprinkle in the flour and stir in the stock and wine. Cook for about 30 minutes. Remove the pan from the heat and pour the mixture into a food processor. Process, then squeeze out the bread and add to the sauce. Process the mixture again and re-heat the sauce before serving.
For short pasta or boiled rice.

ESPAGNOLE SAUCE

SALSA SPAGNOLA

Serves 4

2 tablespoons butter

3 ounces prosciutto, diced

1 carrot, chopped

1 onion, chopped

fresh flat-leaf parsley sprig

6 black peppercorns

1 clove

1 quantity Vegetable Stock (see page 209)

salt

Melt the butter in a pan. Add the prosciutto, carrot, onion, parsley, peppercorns and clove and cook over medium heat, stirring occasionally, for about 5 minutes. Add the stock and season with salt to taste. Cook for about 45 minutes, then push through a strainer into a bowl or sauce boat. This sauce should be served hot, so re-heat it in a double boiler if necessary.
For pasticcio (baked pasta pie) or fresh pasta.

SPECIAL SAUCE

Pre-heat the oven to 350°F. Tie the beef into a neat round with kitchen string if this has not already been done. Sprinkle the butter over the base of an oval roasting pan. Place the meat on top, cover with the onion slices and roast for about 1 hour until the cooking juices are thick and dark. Season with salt and white pepper halfway through the cooking time. Remove the pan from the oven and place the meat on a plate. Place the roasting pan on the stovetop over low heat, add the brandy and cook until evaporated. Stir in the cream, a tablespoonful at a time, making sure the sauce does not become too runny. Mix well to combine the flavors and serve with tagliatelle. The meat can be served cold with Mayonnaise (see page 65).
For fresh tagliatelle.

SALSA SPECIALE
Serves 4
1 pound 10 ounces top round of beef
7 tablespoons butter, diced
1 large white onion, very thinly sliced
$^1/_4$ cup brandy
scant $^1/_2$ cup heavy cream
salt and white pepper

SPICY SAUCE

Melt the butter in a pan. Add the onion and cook over low heat, stirring occasionally, for about 10 minutes until lightly browned. Add the brandy and cook until the liquid is reduced by half. Add the tomatoes and simmer for 5 minutes. Add the chervil, cayenne pepper and Worcestershire sauce. Mix well and pour into a sauce boat.
For broiled steak.

SALSA SUPERPICCANTE
Serves 4
$^1/_4$ cup butter
1 pearl onion, finely chopped
scant 1 cup brandy
2 tomatoes, peeled, seeded and finely chopped
1 tablespoon chopped fresh chervil
pinch of cayenne pepper
generous dash of Worcestershire sauce

VELOUTÉ SAUCE (BASIC RECIPE)

Melt the butter in a pan over low heat. Sprinkle in the flour and stir until the mixture becomes golden brown and smooth. Gradually stir in the stock, a little at a time. Bring to a boil and cook, stirring frequently, for about 15 minutes. Season with salt and pepper to taste.
For lasagne or meatballs.

SALSA VELLUTATA (RICETTA BASE)
Serves 4
3 tablespoons butter
$^1/_3$ cup all-purpose flour
2$^1/_4$ cups Meat, Fish or Vegetable Stock
(see pages 208–209)
salt and pepper

SAUCE AURORE

Place the tomatoes in a food processor and process to a purée. Add the purée to the velouté sauce and cook until thickened. Season to taste with salt and pepper.
For broiled fish, poached chicken or poached eggs.

SALSA VELLUTATA AURORA
Serves 4
14 ounces tomatoes, peeled, seeded
and coarsely chopped
1 quantity Velouté Sauce (see above)
salt and pepper

SEAFOOD SAUCE

SUGO AGLI SCAMPI E CAPPESANTE

Serves 4

5 tablespoons olive oil

4 shallots, chopped

2 salted anchovies, heads removed, cleaned and filleted (see page 596), soaked in cold water for 10 minutes, drained and chopped

4 sea scallops, shelled and chopped

1 tablespoon brandy

1 cup bottled strained tomatoes

7 ounces langoustines or jumbo shrimp, peeled

scant ½ cup white wine

2 tablespoons chopped fresh flat-leaf parsley

salt and pepper

Heat 2 tablespoons of the olive oil in a pan. Add the shallots and cook over low heat, stirring occasionally, for 3–5 minutes until softened and translucent. Add the anchovies and cook, mashing with a wooden spoon until they have completely disintegrated. Add the sea scallops and cook for 1 minute, then sprinkle with brandy and cook until evaporated. Pour in the strained tomatoes and cook over medium heat for about 10 minutes, then season with salt and pepper to taste. Meanwhile, heat the remaining olive oil in a skillet. Add the langoustines or shrimp and cook for 2–3 minutes. Sprinkle with the white wine and cook until evaporated, then add the parsley and season with salt. Cook over low heat for 5 minutes. Tip the langoustine or shrimp mixture into the tomato mixture and stir to mix.

For fresh taglierini, ricotta and spinach ravioli or tagliatelle.

TUNA SAUCE

SUGO AL TONNO

Serves 4

9 ounces canned tomatoes

1 garlic clove

4 ounces canned tuna in oil, drained

2 tablespoons olive oil

1 salted anchovy, head removed, cleaned and filleted (see page 596), soaked in cold water for 10 minutes, drained and finely chopped

salt

Tip the tomatoes and their can juice into a pan, add the garlic and a pinch of salt and bring to a boil over medium heat. Cook for 15 minutes, then lower the heat, mash the tomatoes with a wooden spoon and cook until the liquid has reduced slightly. Remove the pan from the heat. Remove and discard the garlic. Flake the tuna with a fork and stir into the tomato sauce. Add the olive oil and anchovy and spoon over very hot spaghetti.

For spaghetti.

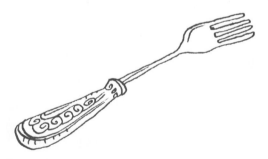

COLD SAUCES

AÏOLI

Serves 4

2 egg yolks

3 garlic cloves, finely chopped

scant 1/2 cup olive oil

lemon juice, strained, to taste

salt and pepper

AÏOLI

Beat the egg yolks with the garlic in a bowl. Gradually add the olive oil, as if making mayonnaise. Season with salt, pepper and a few drops of lemon juice to taste. This sauce can also be made in a food processor (see basic recipe for Mayonnaise, opposite).

For fish.

CHUTNEY AL RIBES E MELE

Serves 4

generous 1/3 cup golden raisins

14 ounces green apples, peeled, cored and diced

9 ounces red currants

3 1/2 ounces chopped walnuts

scant 1/2 cup white wine vinegar

scant 1/2 cup orange juice

3 1/2 ounces sugar

2 cloves

2-inch cinnamon stick

RED CURRANT AND APPLE CHUTNEY

Place the golden raisins in a bowl, add hot water to cover and set aside to soak for 15 minutes, then drain. Place all the ingredients in a large pan and bring to a boil over low heat, stirring occasionally. Simmer, uncovered, for at least 30 minutes until the mixture has the consistency of jam. Pour into a bowl and let cool. Discard the cloves and cinnamon stick. This sauce is widely eaten in India. It can be stored in a screw-top jar in the refrigerator for a few days.

For broiled meat.

ONION CHUTNEY

Put the raisins, onions, sugar, tomato paste, bay leaf, green peppercorns and cayenne pepper in a large pan. Pour in 1 cup water and the vinegar. Cover and cook for 2 hours. Remove the lid and cook for 1 hour more to reduce.
For game or curries.

CHUTNEY DI CIPOLLINE
Serves 4

generous $1/3$ cup, soaked in warm water

for 15 minutes and drained

1 pound 2 ounces pearl onions

$1/3$ cup sugar

3 tablespoons concentrated tomato paste

1 bay leaf

10 green peppercorns

pinch of cayenne pepper

1 cup wine vinegar

MAYONNAISE (BASIC RECIPE)

Mayonnaise is probably the best loved and most frequently eaten sauce in the world. It is almost always bought ready made and there are several good brands available. However, it is useful to know how to make it by hand or in a food processor and it is worth savoring the delicacy of homemade mayonnaise every now and again. Both techniques are described here. Always make sure that the oil and eggs are at room temperature; if they are too cold, the mayonnaise may not bind. Add the oil a drop at a time and do the same with the lemon juice or vinegar. If the mayonnaise separates, whisk a fresh egg yolk in another bowl and gradually whisk in the separated mixture a drop at a time. To make mayonnaise by hand, put the egg yolks in a bowl and season with a pinch each of salt and pepper. Add the oil, a drop at a time, beating constantly with a small whisk or wooden spoon. As soon as the mixture thickens, whisk in a drop of lemon juice or vinegar. Continue adding the oil and lemon juice or vinegar alternately, beating constantly, until all the ingredients are used. To make mayonnaise in a food processor, place an egg yolk and a whole egg in the food processor, season with salt and pepper and add 2 tablespoons of the oil and a drop of the lemon juice or vinegar. Process for a few seconds at maximum speed. When the ingredients are thoroughly mixed, add the remaining oil and lemon juice or vinegar and process for 1 minute. For both methods, taste and adjust the seasoning if necessary. Pour the mayonnaise into a sauce boat and store in the refrigerator.
For boiled or roasted meat, raw or cooked vegetables or as a garnish.

MAIONESE (RICETTA BASE)
Serves 4

2 egg yolks or 1 egg yolk and 1 egg (see method)

scant 1 cup sunflower oil

2 tablespoons lemon juice or white wine vinegar

salt and pepper

CURRY AND CREAM MAYONNAISE

Gently stir the cream into the mayonnaise and season with the curry powder. Mix well. Pour into a sauce boat and serve.
For seafood and chicken salads or hard-cooked eggs.

MAIONESE AL CURRY E PANNA

Serves 4

3 tablespoons light cream

1 quantity Mayonnaise (see page 65)

1 teaspoon curry powder

GORGONZOLA MAYONNAISE

Make the mayonnaise with vinegar instead of lemon juice and beat the mustard into the egg yolks before adding the oil. Cream the Gorgonzola in a bowl and beat into the mayonnaise, a little at a time. Season to taste with salt if necessary. Pour into a sauce boat.
For cold meat.

MAIONESE AL GORGONZOLA

Serves 4

1 quantity Mayonnaise (see page 65)

1 teaspoon Dijon mustard

3¹/₂ ounces Gorgonzola cheese, crumbled

salt (optional)

WHIPPED CREAM MAYONNAISE

Stir the mustard into the mayonnaise, then fold in the whipped cream. Serve in a sauce boat.
For fish or shellfish.

MAIONESE ALLA PANNA MONTATA

Serves 4

1 teaspoon Dijon mustard

1 quantity Mayonnaise (see page 65)

3 tablespoons heavy cream, whipped

AVOCADO MAYONNAISE

Stir the cream, ketchup, lime juice, Worcestershire sauce and a dash of Tabasco into the mayonnaise and season with salt to taste. Peel and halve the avocado and remove the pit. Cut into wedges, then slice thinly. Add to the mayonnaise and mix gently. Spoon into a sauce boat and garnish with slices of lime.
For shrimp, chicken and rice or poached eggs.

MAIONESE ALL'AVOCADO

Serves 4

3 tablespoons heavy cream

2 tablespoons tomato ketchup

2 tablespoons lime juice, strained

2 tablespoons Worcestershire sauce

dash of Tabasco sauce

1 quantity Mayonnaise (see page 65)

1 avocado

salt

lime slices, to garnish

HERB MAYONNAISE

Cook the spinach in a little salted, boiling water for 5 minutes, then drain and let cool. When cool, place the spinach, tarragon and watercress or arugula in a food processor and process to a purée. Stir the purée into the mayonnaise until the mixture is an even green color. Season with salt to taste.
For poached fish or hard-cooked eggs.

MAIONESE ALLE ERBE

Serves 4

7 ounces spinach

1 fresh tarragon sprig

¹/₂ bunch of watercress or arugula

1 quantity Mayonnaise (see page 65)

salt

HORSERADISH MAYONNAISE

MAIONESE AL RAFANO

Serves 4

1 tablespoon grated horseradish

1 quantity Mayonnaise (see page 65)

Stir the horseradish into the mayonnaise, mixing well.
For cold meat.

ANDALUSIAN MAYONNAISE

MAIONESE ANDALUSA

Serves 4

4 tablespoons tomato paste

1 quantity Mayonnaise (see page 65)

1 green bell pepper, halved,
seeded and finely chopped

$^1/_4$ dried red chile, crumbled

Stir the tomato paste into the mayonnaise, 1 tablespoon at a time.
Stir in the green bell pepper and chile.
For raw vegetables.

MALTESE MAYONNAISE

MAIONESE MALTESE

Serves 4

1 blood orange

1 quantity Mayonnaise (see page 65 and method)

salt

Using a small, sharp knife, peel the orange, avoiding the bitter white pith. Blanch the orange rind in a small pan of boiling water for 1 minute, then drain and refresh under cold running water. Chop finely. Squeeze the orange and strain the juice. Prepare the mayonnaise, but do not add lemon juice or vinegar. Stir in the orange rind, then beat in the juice. Season with salt if necessary.
For asparagus, artichokes or poached chicken.

PESTO

PESTO

Serves 4

25 fresh basil leaves

scant $^1/_2$ cup extra virgin olive oil

$^1/_3$ cup pine nuts

1 cup Parmesan cheese, freshly grated

$^1/_3$ cup romano cheese, freshly grated

salt

Put the basil leaves in a food processor with the olive oil, pine nuts and a pinch of salt. Process briefly at medium speed. Add the grated cheeses and process again.
For asparagus, egg dishes, spaghetti or gnocchi.

RÉMOULADE SAUCE

RÉMOULADE

Serves 4

1 garlic clove

1 egg yolk

about $^2/_3$ cup olive oil

1 teaspoon white wine vinegar

1 fresh flat-leaf parsley sprig, very finely chopped

salt

Rub the garlic around the inside of the bowl you are going to use to make the sauce. Put the egg yolk in the bowl, season with a pinch of salt and gradually beat in the olive oil, a drop at a time. The exact amount of oil depends on how much the egg absorbs. When the sauce has reached the desired consistency, beat in the vinegar and parsley. Season with salt to taste.
For poached fish.

PINE NUT SAUCE

Drain the anchovy and pat dry with paper towels. Shell and halve the egg, then scoop out the yolk. Finely chop together the anchovy, egg yolk, pine nuts, capers, olives, bread, parsley and garlic. Put the mixture in a bowl and drizzle with olive oil, stirring constantly, as if making mayonnaise. Season to taste with salt and pepper. Serve in a sauce boat.
For poached fish.

SALSA AI PINOLI

Serves 4

1 salted anchovy, head removed, cleaned and filleted (see page 596), soaked in cold water for 10 minutes and drained
1 egg, hard-cooked
1/2 cup pine nuts
1 1/2 tablespoons capers, drained and rinsed
4 stoned green olives
1 white bread slice, crusts removed
1 fresh flat-leaf parsley sprig • 1/2 garlic clove
olive oil, for drizzling
salt and pepper

GORGONZOLA SAUCE

Cream the Gorgonzola in a bowl, then gradually beat in the cream or milk. When the mixture has a creamy consistency, season with salt and pepper and add the grated horseradish. Mix well and serve.
For canapés or raw vegetables.

SALSA AL GORGONZOLA

Serves 4

11 ounces mild Gorgonzola cheese, crumbled
2 tablespoons light cream or scant 1/2 cup milk
1 tablespoon grated horseradish
salt and pepper

BALSAMIC VINEGAR SAUCE

Put the capers, parsley, boiled potato and a pinch of salt in a food processor and process to a purée. Scrape into a bowl and gradually beat in the olive oil to make a thick sauce. Stir in the balsamic vinegar.
For short pasta or spaghetti.

SALSA ALL'ACETO BALSAMICO

Serves 4

3 tablespoons capers, drained and rinsed
1/2 bunch of fresh flat-leaf parsley, coarsely chopped
1 potato, boiled and coarsely chopped
about 2/3 cup olive oil
1 tablespoon balsamic vinegar
salt

PAPRIKA SAUCE

Shell and halve the eggs, then scoop out the yolks into a bowl. Mash well with a fork and stir in the mustard. Add a pinch each of salt and pepper and stir in the paprika. Stir in the cream and lemon juice. Mix well and serve.
For celery root or rice salad.

SALSA ALLA PAPRICA

Serves 4

2 eggs, hard-cooked
1 tablespoon Dijon mustard
1/2 teaspoon paprika
scant 1/2 cup light cream
1 tablespoon lemon juice
salt and pepper

RICOTTA SAUCE

SALSA ALLA RICOTTA

Serves 4

generous 1 cup ricotta cheese

4 tablespoons mascarpone cheese • 2 tablespoons milk

1 egg yolk • 4 walnuts, peeled and chopped

1–2 tablespoons chopped fresh chives

salt and pepper

Place the ricotta in a bowl and stir in the mascarpone and milk. Season to taste with salt and pepper. Stir in the egg yolk and add the walnuts and chives. Mix well, then taste and adjust the seasoning if necessary.

For short pasta or canapés.

YOGURT SAUCE

SALSA ALLO YOGURT

Serves 4

4 dill pickles, drained and very finely chopped

4 fresh mint leaves, very finely chopped

2/3 cup plain yogurt

dash of olive oil (optional) • salt

Stir the dill pickles and mint into the yogurt and season to taste with salt and a dash of olive oil if you like.

For griddled and grilled meat or baked potatoes.

GRAPEFRUIT SAUCE

SALSA AL POMPELMO

Serves 4

scant 1 cup mascarpone cheese

juice of 1 grapefruit, strained

1 tablespoon chopped fresh chervil

salt and pepper

Beat the mascarpone in a bowl with a small whisk until light and smooth. Gradually whisk in the grapefruit juice. Season with salt and pepper and stir in the chervil. Mix gently and pour into a sauce boat.

For roast pork.

BLACK TRUFFLE SAUCE

SALSA AL TARTUFO NERO

Serves 4

2 fresh black truffles • 3 salted anchovies, heads removed, cleaned and filleted (see page 596), soaked in cold water for 10 minutes, drained and finely chopped • about 2/3 cup light olive oil

dash of lemon juice

Clean the truffles with a small damp brush. Grate into a bowl and add the anchovies. Stir in the olive oil to make a fairly runny sauce. (Use a light, delicately flavored oil so that the truffle flavor dominates.) Just before serving, sprinkle with a dash of lemon juice.

For tagliolini or poached chicken.

BARBECUE SAUCE

SALSA BARBECUE

Serves 4

2 tablespoons mustard

3 tablespoons milk • 3/4 cup olive oil

5 tablespoons mixed pickles, such as capers, dill pickles, onions and carrots, chopped

2 tablespoons chopped fresh flat-leaf parsley

juice of 1/2 lemon, strained • salt and pepper

Combine the mustard and milk in a bowl. Gradually whisk in the olive oil a drop at a time. When the sauce has thickened, season to taste with salt and pepper, then stir in the pickles, parsley and lemon juice. Mix well and pour into a sauce boat.

For broiled meat or fish.

COCKTAIL SAUCE

SALSA COCKTAIL

Serves 4

3 tablespoons tomato ketchup

1 tablespoon Worcestershire sauce

1 teaspoon brandy

1 teaspoon sherry

1 cup heavy cream

salt and white pepper

Combine the tomato ketchup, Worcestershire sauce, brandy and sherry in a bowl. Lightly whisk the cream, then gently fold into the other ingredients. Season with a little salt and white pepper. Stir shellfish into this sauce and place in a dish lined with lettuce leaves.

For lobster, langoustines or shrimp.

CAPER SAUCE

SALSA DI CAPPERI

Serves 4

3 tablespoons capers, drained

²/₃ cup olive oil or to taste

juice of ¹/₂ lemon, strained

Place the capers in a bowl, add cold water to cover and let aside to soak for 15 minutes. Drain well and chop finely. Transfer the capers to a sauce boat and stir in the olive oil and lemon juice. Taste and, if necessary, add more olive oil or lemon juice.

For breaded veal chops.

MINT SAUCE

SALSA DI MENTA

Serves 4

10–15 fresh mint leaves, chopped

1 tablespoon sugar

4 tablespoons white wine vinegar

Put the mint in a bowl and pour on 3 tablespoons boiling water. Let steep and cool slightly. Stir in the sugar and vinegar and mix well. Let the sauce stand for at least 30 minutes before serving.

For boiled zucchini.

WHIPPED CREAM AND RADISH SAUCE

SALSA DI PANNA MONTATA E RAVANELLI

Serves 4

3 bunches of radishes, trimmed

1 teaspoon Bordeaux mustard

lemon juice, to taste

1 cup heavy cream, stiffly whipped

salt

Place the radishes in a bowl, add cold water to cover and let soak for about 30 minutes. Drain, then process briefly in a food processor to chop finely. Do not over-process into a purée. Transfer to a bowl and add a little salt. Stir in the mustard and a few drops of lemon juice. Gently fold in the whipped cream, 1 tablespoon at a time, taking care not to knock out the air.

For fish or cold meat.

GRIBICHE SAUCE

Shell and halve the eggs, then scoop out the yolks into a bowl and mash well with a wooden spoon. Finely chop the egg whites and set aside. Add the mustard and vinegar to the egg yolks and season with salt and pepper. Gradually beat in the olive oil a drop at a time. Stir in the tarragon, parsley and capers. Stir gently. Just before serving, stir in the reserved egg whites.

For deep-fried langoustines or jumbo shrimp or poached eggs.

SALSA GRIBICHE

Serves 4

3 eggs, hard-cooked

1 teaspoon Dijon mustard

2 tablespoons white wine vinegar

1 cup olive oil

1 tablespoon chopped fresh tarragon

1 tablespoon chopped fresh flat-leaf parsley

6 tablespoons capers, drained,

rinsed and finely chopped

salt and pepper

MEDITERRANEAN SAUCE

Combine the mustard and milk in a bowl. Gradually whisk in the olive oil a drop at a time. When the mixture has the desired consistency, season with salt and pepper to taste. Add a drop of lemon juice, then stir in the tomato paste until the mixture takes on an even, slightly pink color. Taste and adjust the seasoning if necessary. Serve in sauce boat.

For fish, poultry or cold meat.

SALSA MEDITERRANEA

Serves 4

1 tablespoon Dijon mustard

2 tablespoons milk

scant 1 cup olive oil

lemon juice, to taste

1 tablespoon concentrated tomato paste

salt and pepper

RUSSIAN GARLIC SAUCE

Crush the garlic with a little salt in a bowl using a large spoon. (A garlic press may also be used.) Stir in the warm stock, let cool and then pour into a sauce boat.

For broiled meat.

SALSA RUSSA ALL'AGLIO

Serves 4

4-5 garlic cloves, halved

scant $\frac{1}{2}$ cup warm Chicken Stock (see page 209)

salt

TARTAR SAUCE

Nowadays, in order to save time, this sauce is usually made by adding pickled onions, parsley and vinegar to mayonnaise. However, the genuine recipe is somewhat different. Shell and halve the hard-cooked eggs, then scoop the yolks into a bowl. Add the raw yolk and mash together until smooth and even. Season with a little salt and pepper, and stir in the onions and parsley. Gradually whisk in the olive oil, a drop at a time. When the sauce has begun to thicken, whisk in a little of the vinegar. Continue adding the olive oil and vinegar alternately, whisking constantly. If a stronger flavor is required, add some tarragon.

For cold meat or poached fish.

SALSA TARTARA

Serves 4

3 eggs, hard-cooked

1 egg yolk

2 baby onions, finely chopped

2–3 tablespoons chopped fresh flat-leaf parsley

scant 1 cup olive oil

4 tablespoons white wine vinegar

1 tablespoon chopped fresh tarragon (optional)

salt and pepper

SALSA TONNATA

Serves 4

3¹/₂ ounces canned tuna in oil, drained

5 tablespoons capers, drained and rinsed

2 salted anchovies, heads removed, cleaned and

filleted (see page 596)

1 hard-cooked egg yolk

scant 1 cup olive oil

juice of ¹/₂ lemon, strained

salt and pepper

TUNA SAUCE

Finely chop the tuna, capers and anchovies and place in a food processor. Crumble in the egg yolk and season with salt and pepper. Add a few tablespoons of the olive oil and process for a few seconds. Add the remaining oil and process briefly again. If the sauce is too thick, add a little more oil. Pour into a sauce boat, add the lemon juice, mix well and let stand for 10 minutes before serving.

For poached meat or fish.

SALSA VERDE

Serves 4

1 small potato

2 eggs, hard-cooked

2 salted anchovies, heads removed, cleaned and

filleted (see page 596), soaked in cold water for

10 minutes and drained

1 fresh flat-leaf parsley sprig, leaves only

¹/₂ garlic clove

1 dill pickle, drained

scant 1 cup olive oil

2 tablespoons white wine vinegar

salt and pepper

GREEN SAUCE

Cook the potato in lightly salted, boiling water for 15 minutes or until tender. Drain and peel. While still hot, put in a bowl and mash well with a fork. Shell and halve the eggs, then scoop the yolks into the bowl and mix with the mashed potato. Drain the anchovies, pat dry and chop finely with the parsley, garlic and dill pickle. Add to the potato and mix well. Gradually beat in the olive oil, a drop at a time. Season with salt and pepper and stir in the vinegar.

For boiled meat or cold, poached fish.

TAPÉNADE

Serves 4

3¹/₂ ounces salted anchovies, heads removed,

cleaned and filleted (see page 596), soaked in

cold water for 10 minutes and drained

1³/₄ cups pitted black olives

¹/₂ cup capers, drained and rinsed

3¹/₂ ounces canned tuna in oil, drained

1 teaspoon Dijon mustard

olive oil, for drizzling

¹/₄ cup brandy

2 tablespoons lemon juice, strained

pinch of fresh thyme

¹/₂ garlic clove, finely chopped

pepper

TAPÉNADE

Drain the anchovies, pat dry and chop with the olives, capers and tuna. Place in a bowl and stir in the mustard. Drizzle in olive oil to taste, stirring constantly. Add the brandy, lemon juice, thyme and garlic. Season lightly with pepper. (The fairly strong taste of this Provençal sauce may be made less intense by omitting the pepper.) Some people prefer to mix all the ingredients with Mayonnaise (see page 65). The result is equally pleasant. Store in the refrigerator.

For boiled meat, hard-cooked eggs or fish.

VINAIGRETTE

VINAIGRETTE

Serves 4

2 tablespoons white wine vinegar

6 tablespoons olive oil

salt

Whisk a generous pinch of salt into the vinegar in a bowl. Add the olive oil and whisk well. To make the dressing even tastier, you can add a little anchovy paste, 1 tablespoon natural yogurt or 1 teaspoon Dijon mustard.
For all salads.

FONDI DI COTTURA | BASES FOR SAUCES

ROUX

I ROUX

$^1/_4$ cup butter

$^1/_2$ cup all-purpose flour

2$^1/_4$ cups meat or vegetable stock (see page 209)

salt and pepper

The word roux is French and means reddish. In cooking, it refers to a mixture of butter and flour cooked for a varying length of time according to what is required. Roux are divided into white (briefly cooked), blond (cooked a little longer) and brown (cooked thoroughly). It is not possible to give precise cooking times as you can only check the progress of the roux by looking at it. Roux are used to thicken soups and sauces, and in both cases the dish becomes tastier. Melt the butter in a pan and, as soon as it turns golden brown, sprinkle in the flour, stirring constantly to prevent lumps from forming. Gradually stir in the stock. Cook, stirring occasionally, for about 20 minutes. Season with salt and pepper to taste. If a runnier roux is needed, use only $^1/_4$ cup of the flour and 2 tablespoons of the butter but the same amount of stock.

STOCKS

I FONDI

These are generally meat, fish and vegetable stocks which are added to roux to make various sauces. To make a classic meat stock, cook a few beef and veal bones in olive oil and butter, add water and continue cooking for several hours until the liquid thickens. A quicker method is to use the dripping from any roasted meat mixed with a little stock or water. To ensure a smooth sauce without lumps use cold stock if the roux is hot and add hot stock if the roux is cold.

For more stock recipes see pages 208–209.

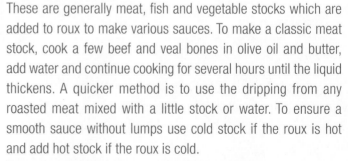

MARINADES

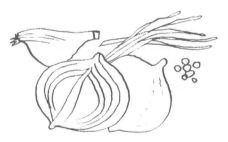

BRANDY MARINADE

Combine the brandy, olive oil, thyme and bay leaf and season with salt and pepper. Marinate meat for a few hours.
For white meat.

MARINATA AL BRANDY

3 tablespoons brandy

4 tablespoons olive oil

1 fresh thyme sprig

1 bay leaf

salt and pepper

JUNIPER MARINADE

Pour the wine into a large bowl, add the onion and juniper berries and season with salt and pepper. Marinate meat for 5–12 hours, stirring frequently.
For white meat.

MARINATA AL GINEPRO

4 cups red wine

1 onion, sliced

8–10 juniper berries, crushed

salt and pepper

VINEGAR MARINADE

MARINATA ALL'ACETO

scant 1 cup white wine vinegar

scant 1 cup olive oil

juice of 1 lemon, strained

2 teaspoons finely chopped fresh rosemary

1 tablespoon finely chopped fresh flat-leaf parsley

pinch of dried oregano

salt and pepper

Combine the vinegar, olive oil and lemon juice in a large bowl. Add the rosemary, parsley and oregano and season with salt and pepper. Marinate fish for a couple of hours before cooking.
For fish.

YOGURT MARINADE

MARINATA ALLO YOGURT

1 onion, coarsely chopped

2¼ cups low-fat plain yogurt

salt and pepper

Place the onion in a food processor and process to a purée, then push through a strainer into a bowl. Add the yogurt and season with salt and pepper. Marinate meat for 3–4 hours.
For lamb or kid.

WHITE WINE MARINADE

MARINATA AL VINO BIANCO

1 onion, sliced

4 cups dry white wine

1 cup olive oil

juice of 1 lemon, strained

salt and pepper

Place the onion in a bowl, add the wine, olive oil and lemon juice and season with salt and pepper. Marinate fish for 2 hours.
For fish.

RED WINE MARINADE

MARINATA AL VINO ROSSO

2 carrots, thinly sliced

2 red onions, thinly sliced

2 garlic cloves, thinly sliced

4 fresh thyme sprigs

6 bay leaves

6 black peppercorns

4 cups red wine

1¾ cups olive oil

2½ cups red wine vinegar

salt

Combine the carrots, onions and garlic and arrange half the mixture in a layer on the base of a large bowl. Add half the thyme and half the bay leaves, then place meat on top. Cover with the remaining sliced vegetables, thyme and bay leaves and sprinkle with the peppercorns and salt. Combine the wine, olive oil and vinegar in a pitcher, then pour into the bowl. Marinate for at least 12 hours.
For red meat or game.

HERB MARINADE

MARINATA AROMATICA

1 onion, sliced
3 tablespoons chopped fresh flat-leaf parsley
1 tablespoon chopped fresh thyme
2 bay leaves, torn into pieces
2 garlic cloves, thinly sliced
5 tablespoons olive oil
2 teaspoons lemon juice, strained
salt and pepper

Season meat with salt and pepper and cover with the onion, parsley, thyme, bay leaves and garlic. Combine the olive oil and lemon juice and pour over the meat. Marinate in a cool place for about 2 hours.
For sliced meat or chicken breasts.

COOKED MARINADE

MARINATA COTTA

5 tablespoons olive oil
2 carrots, chopped
2 onions, chopped
1 celery stalk, chopped
1³/₄ cups red wine
4 cups red wine vinegar
2 teaspoons chopped fresh thyme
6 black peppercorns
salt

Heat the olive oil in a large pan. Add the carrots, onions and celery and cook over low heat, stirring occasionally, for about 10 minutes until lightly browned. Add the wine, vinegar, thyme and peppercorns and season with salt. Simmer over low heat for 30 minutes. Let cool before using to marinate meat for about 24 hours.
For red meat or game.

SPICY MARINADE

MARINATA PICCANTE

1³/₄ cups olive oil
3 tablespoons Worcestershire sauce
juice of 1 lemon, strained
dash of Tabasco sauce
salt

Pour the olive oil into a large bowl, add the Worcestershire sauce, lemon juice and a dash of Tabasco and season with salt. Whisk well to mix. Marinate meat for 2 hours.
For red or white meat.

QUICK LEMON MARINADE

MARINATA VELOCE AL LIMONE

1³/₄ cups olive oil
juice of 1 lemon, strained
2 fresh flat-leaf parsley sprigs, leaves only
1 small shallot, chopped
1 fresh thyme sprig, leaves only
1 bay leaf
salt and pepper

Combine the olive oil, lemon juice, parsley, shallot, thyme and bay leaf in a bowl and season with salt and pepper. Marinate meat or fish for 30 minutes.
For fish or steak.

Chicken breasts in herb marinade

FLAVORED BUTTERS

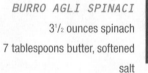

BURRO AGLI SPINACI 3 1/2 ounces spinach 7 tablespoons butter, softened salt	**SPINACH BUTTER** Cook the spinach in just the water clinging to its leaves after washing for 5 minutes until tender. Drain well, squeezing out as much liquid as possible, and chop finely. Cream the butter in a bowl, then beat in the spinach and season with salt. For roast meat.

BURRO AI FUNGHI 7 tablespoons butter, softened, plus extra for frying scant 1 1/2 cups mushrooms, sliced 1 tablespoon chopped fresh flat-leaf parsley salt and pepper	**MUSHROOM BUTTER** Melt 2 tablespoons of the butter in a pan. Add the mushrooms, season with salt and pepper and cook over medium heat, stirring occasionally, for about 5 minutes until tender. Transfer to a food processor and process to a purée, then let cool. Cream the remaining butter in a bowl, then beat in the mushrooms and parsley. For canapés, crostini or broiled meat.

SHRIMP BUTTER

Cream the butter in a bowl, then beat in the shrimp and season with salt and pepper.
For canapés or crostini.

BURRO AI GAMBERETTI

7 tablespoons butter, softened
scant 1 cup peeled, cooked shrimp, finely chopped
salt and white pepper

BASIL BUTTER

Place the butter in the top of a double boiler or in a heatproof bowl and melt over barely simmering water. Remove the pan from the heat, whisk in the basil and lemon juice and season with salt and pepper.
For fish or shellfish.

BURRO AL BASILICO

7 tablespoons butter, diced
1 large bunch of fresh basil, leaves torn into pieces
2–3 tablespoons lemon juice, strained
salt and pepper

CAVIAR BUTTER

Gently stir the caviar to a cream in a bowl, then mix with the butter. Stir the mixture until soft.
For canapés.

BURRO AL CAVIALE

2 tablespoons caviar
7 tablespoons butter, softened

CURRY BUTTER

Cream the butter in a bowl and beat in the curry powder, mixing well.
For crostini or hamburgers.

BURRO AL CURRY

7 tablespoons butter, softened
pinch of curry powder

FENNEL BUTTER

Blanch the garlic in a small pan of boiling water for about 1 minute, then drain, peel and mash well with a fork. Cream the butter in a bowl and beat in the garlic. Grind the fennel seeds in a mortar with a pestle or in a spice grinder and beat into the butter. Beat in the lemon juice and a pinch of white pepper.
For meat or broiled fish.

BURRO AL FINOCCHIO

1 garlic clove
7 tablespoons butter, softened
2 teaspoons fennel seeds
juice of $1/2$ lemon, strained
white pepper

BUTTER WITH CHEESE AND ALMONDS

Cream the cheese in a bowl and beat in the almonds. Add the butter and mix well.
For crostini.

BURRO AL FORMAGGIO E MANDORLE

$3^{1}/_{2}$ ounces strong soft cheese
10 blanched almonds, chopped
7 tablespoons butter, softened

GORGONZOLA BUTTER

BURRO AL GORGONZOLA

Beat together the butter and Gorgonzola in a bowl until smooth and even. Beat in the parsley.
For broiled meat.

7 tablespoons butter, softened
scant 3/4 cup Gorgonzola cheese, crumbled
1 fresh flat-leaf parsley sprig, chopped

BUTTER WITH DRIED SALTED ROE

BURRO ALLA BOTTARGA

Pour the wine into a pan, add the roe and cook until tender. Remove from the heat and let cool, then drain. Cream the butter in a bowl, then crumble in the roe and beat well. Beat in the mustard.
For crostini.

scant 1 cup dry white wine
3 ounces pressed dried gray mullet or tuna roe, sliced
7 tablespoons butter, softened
1/2 teaspoon Dijon mustard

BURGUNDY BUTTER

BURRO ALLA BOURGUIGNONNE

Cream the butter in a bowl, then beat in the shallot, garlic and parsley. Season with salt and pepper and mix gently.
For snails or steak.

7 tablespoons butter, softened
1 shallot, finely chopped
1/2 garlic clove, finely chopped
1 fresh flat-leaf parsley sprig, finely chopped
salt and pepper

ANCHOVY BUTTER

BURRO ALL'ACCIUGA

Cream the butter in a bowl. Beat in the anchovies, then beat in the anchovy paste.
For broiled meat.

7 tablespoons butter, softened
2 ounces salted anchovies, heads removed, cleaned and filleted (see page 596) and finely chopped • 1 teaspoon anchovy paste

GARLIC BUTTER

BURRO ALL'AGLIO

Blanch the garlic in boiling water for about 1 minute, then drain, peel and mash. Cream the butter in a bowl, then beat in the mashed garlic. Mix carefully.
For warm garlic bread or steaks.

3 1/2 ounces garlic cloves
7 tablespoons butter, softened

MAÎTRE D'HÔTEL BUTTER

BURRO ALLA MAÎTRE D'HÔTEL

Cream the butter in a bowl, then beat in the parsley, some salt, very little pepper and a few drops of lemon juice. Make into a roll and wrap in foil. Chill in the refrigerator until set. Cut into slices to serve.
For steaks, scallops or poached fish.

7 tablespoons butter, softened
1 tablespoon chopped fresh flat-leaf parsley
lemon juice, strained, to taste
salt and pepper

↑ Broiled steak with anchovy butter

BUTTER SAUCE

Put the butter in a small pan and melt over low heat. As soon as it begins to color, add the lemon juice, a pinch of salt and a pinch of pepper.
For poached fish or boiled vegetables.

BURRO ALLA MUGNAIA

7 tablespoons butter

2 tablespoons lemon juice, strained

salt and pepper

LOBSTER BUTTER

Break off the lobster's head, then twist off and reserve the claws. Remove and discard the stomach sac. Cut open the shell along the belly and push apart to remove the meat in one piece. Remove the dark vein along the back with the point of a knife. Finely chop the meat, coral and liver. Crack open the claws, pick out the meat and chop finely. Cream the butter in a bowl, then stir in the lobster meat, coral and liver. Lightly season with salt.
For canapés.

BURRO ALLA POLPA D'ARAGOSTA

1 small boiled lobster

7 tablespoons butter, softened

salt

SAGE BUTTER

Melt the butter in a small pan over low heat. As soon as it starts to color, add the sage leaves and season with salt. When the leaves are crisp, remove the pan from the heat and serve the butter immediately.
For boiled rice, broiled meat or ravioli.

BURRO ALLA SALVIA

7 tablespoons butter

15 fresh sage leaves

salt

MUSTARD BUTTER

Cream the butter in a bowl, then beat in the mustard and a pinch of salt. Mix until the color is even.
For canapés.

BURRO ALLA SENAPE

7 tablespoons butter

1 teaspoon Dijon mustard

salt

SARDINE BUTTER

Skin the sardines and remove the bones. Mash or work through a food mill. Cream the butter in a bowl, then beat in the sardines. Season with a pinch of white pepper.
For canapés or toast.

BURRO ALLE SARDINE

4 canned sardines in oil, drained

7 tablespoons butter, softened

white pepper

← Ravioli with sage butter

BURRO AL RAFANO 7 tablespoons butter, softened 2 ounces horseradish, grated salt	## HORSERADISH BUTTER Cream the butter in a bowl, then beat in the horseradish. Season with salt. For canapés or roast meat.
BURRO AL SALMONE AFFUMICATO 7 tablespoons butter, softened 2 ounces smoked salmon, finely chopped	## SMOKED SALMON BUTTER Cream the butter in a bowl, then gently stir in the salmon. For canapés or crostini.
BURRO AL TONNO 7 tablespoons butter, softened 2 ounces canned tuna in oil, drained and flaked	## TUNA BUTTER Cream the butter in a bowl, then gently stir in the tuna. For white bread canapés or milk rolls.
BURRO CHIARIFICATO 4 1/2 cups butter	## CLARIFIED BUTTER Put the butter in the top of a double boiler or a heatproof bowl and set over barely simmering water. Heat for 1 hour. At this point, the water content of the butter will have evaporated and the casein will be deposited on the base in a hazelnut-color layer. Line a strainer with cheesecloth and pour the liquid through. Pour the clarified butter into a screw-top jar, close the lid and store in the refrigerator. If used instead of normal butter, halve the quantity.
BURRO FUSO 7 tablespoons butter salt and pepper dash of lemon juice, strained (optional)	## MELTED BUTTER Put the butter in the top of a double boiler or in a heatproof bowl and set over a pan of barely simmering water to melt. When slightly frothy, add salt and pepper, stir and pour into a sauce boat. To accentuate the taste of the butter, add a dash of lemon juice if you like.
BURRO 'INFARINATO' butter all-purpose flour	## BEURRE MANIÉ This butter is used to thicken sauces, so exact quantities cannot be specified as they will vary according to the amount of sauce. As a general guide, blend together 1 1/2–2 tablespoons butter with 3–4 tablespoons flour and add to the cooking juices in small pieces, stirring well. The butter should melt without the liquid boiling.

SOFT BUTTER

Smoked salmon butter on canapés →

ANTIPASTI →

APPETIZERS →

PIZZAS →

ANTIPASTI

Classic Italian antipasti are based on cold meats, such as cured ham, salami, bresaola (dried salted beef), coppa (rolled and cured pork rump shoulder in a sausage casing in northern Italy or brawn made from pig's head in central Italy) and culatello (cured pork rump), served with pickles or vegetables preserved in oil, such as baby artichokes, mushrooms, dill pickles and pickled onions. A more international selection consists of bowls of shrimp, shells full of fish, and shellfish (lobsters, crabs and oysters), salmon and smoked sturgeon. Another alternative – by far the most expensive – is caviar served on a bed of ice. Finally, something lighter is required for the summer, such as the traditional combination of prosciutto and melon, or prosciutto and figs. Antipasti served with pre-dinner drinks before sitting at the table are completely different. Practicality and good sense indicate a choice of small assorted hot and cold morsels that can be picked up with the fingers and finished off in one or two bites – canapés, various kinds of puffs and pizzette (mini pizzas). In any case, antipasti must be served and enjoyed in sensibly limited quantities, so that your guests will be able to do justice to the courses which follow. Antipasti based on vegetables, even if they also contain eggs, tuna, anchovies or cheese, should comply with the following rules for serving wine. In general serve light white wines, suitable for the beginning of a meal. When eggs are a major component, a soft white wine like Soave, dry Albana, Castel del Monte Bianco or Cirò Bianco should be served. If the flavor of tuna or anchovies dominates, choose a structured wine such as Gavi, Sylvaner, Pinot Bianco or Chardonnay. When vegetables are combined with grated cheese, choose light wines but if the dish contains a lot of cheese, some red wines are also fine, so long as they are not full-bodied and not aged. It's not usually recommended to serve any wine with artichokes because of their tannin content but partnering them with highly aromatic white wines, such as dry Malvasia, aromatic Traminer or dry Moscato, is something of a taste sensation. Cold meats are the most classic Italian antipasto, and if you want the right wine to go with them, it is best to choose a traditional one from among those typical of their origin. The ideal partner for smoked cold meats is a rosé or a light red wine. Sparkling wine is normally served with appetizers like barquettes, tartlets, patty shells, etc.

APPETIZERS

Puffs, crêpes, tartlets, assorted small patty shells, game terrines, crusty pies, mousses and anything else which is served at the beginning of a meal are considered appetizers and are normally served only on formal occasions. Their deliberate abundance is intended to give an idea of the richness of the menu to follow.

PIZZAS

If there is a dish that is simultaneously a food, a symbol and a ritual, that dish is the pizza. As a food it could hardly be more complete, as a symbol it could hardly be clearer, and as a ritual it could hardly be more enjoyable. When Italians say pizza, it is taken for granted that they are referring to the Neapolitan pizza, topped with mozzarella cheese and tomato. Pizzas are included in this section of the book because, although they are generally thought of as a dish in themselves, they make great antipasti too when cut into small pieces or baked as miniatures, known in Italian as pizzette. Not quite so famous, but deeply rooted in its region of origin, is the Ligurian version of pizza, better known as focaccia. The surface of the different types is sprinkled with oil, onions, vegetables and anchovies.

ITALIAN ANTIPASTI

ANTIPASTI

Prosciutto, cooked, cured and smoked hams; regional salamis, small cacciatore sausages, coppa (cured pork shoulder) and soppressata (smoky pork salami); bresaola (dried salted tender loins of beef); and mortadella (Bologna sausage). Any of these served with fruit, including exotic fruit, make delicious antipasti.

PROSCIUTTO AND FIGS

Whether they are green or black, the figs must be ripe; they are served peeled and cut into star shapes for a decorative effect. A mild type of prosciutto is best for this dish.

PROSCIUTTO AND PINEAPPLE

A pleasant combination as a result of the sweet-savory contrast. The pineapple must be fresh, peeled and cut into slices.

PROSCIUTTO AND MELON

This is truly the best-loved antipasto among Italians. It has also been very successfully exported abroad. The melon is served cut into wedges which are left attached to the rind at one end or, more simply, completely rindless. Melon may be combined either with mild or strongly flavored prosciutto.

COOKED, CURED HAM AND KIWI FRUIT

A delicate, pleasant combination in terms of both flavor and color. The peeled kiwi fruits are thinly sliced.

BRESAOLA WITH OIL AND LEMON

An hour before serving, the bresaola is cut into wafer-thin slices and dressed with a drizzle of olive oil, lemon juice to taste, salt and pepper.

BRESAOLA AND GRAPEFRUIT

Wrap single segments of completely peeled grapefruit in small slices of bresaola and fasten with a toothpick. Together they have a pleasant fresh taste.

TOMATO BRUSCHETTA

Toast the slices of bread on both sides under the broiler or on a spit. Rub them with garlic while they still hot and put back under the broiler for a moment. Arrange the tomatoes on the bread. Season with salt and pepper and drizzle with olive oil.

BRUSCHETTA AL POMODORO

Serves 4

8 country-style bread slices

4 garlic cloves

6–8 ripe plum tomatoes, diced

extra virgin olive oil, for drizzling

salt and pepper

PIEDMONTESE TARTAR

Place the veal in a bowl and drizzle with olive oil and lemon juice. Add the mustard, season with salt and pepper and mix well. Set aside for about 2 hours to allow the flavors to mingle. When serving, arrange the meat in a dome in the middle of a platter and garnish with the mushrooms and shavings of truffle.

CARNE CRUDA ALLA PIEMONTESE

Serves 4

$3/4$ cup veal, ground

olive oil, for drizzling

lemon juice, strained, to taste

$1/4$–$1/2$ teaspoon Dijon mustard

$2^3/4$ cups mushrooms, thinly sliced

1 white truffle, thinly shaved

salt and pepper

SEMOLINA BASKETS

Bring the milk to a boil in a pan over low heat and sprinkle in the semolina, whisking constantly to prevent lumps from forming. Simmer for 10 minutes, stirring constantly. Season with salt and remove the pan from the heat. Stir in 4 tablespoons of the butter, the eggs and lemon rind. Dampen a counter with a little water and pour the semolina onto it in a layer about $3/4$ inch thick. Let cool. When the semolina has set, stamp out rounds using a damp cookie cutter or the rim of a glass. Use a smaller cutter or glass to stamp out the center of half of the rounds to make rings. Discard the centers. Place the rings on top of the complete rounds to form 'baskets'. Place on a cookie sheet and brush with a little milk. Preheat the oven to 350°F. Heat the remaining butter in a skillet. Add the onion and sage leaves and cook over low heat, stirring occasionally, for about 5 minutes until the onion has softened. Add the chicken livers and cook, stirring constantly, for 3–5 minutes until lightly browned and tender. Pour in the Marsala and cook until it has evaporated. Sprinkle in the flour, stir in the tomato paste and the hot stock and season with salt and pepper. Cook until reduced and thickened, then remove from the heat and use the mixture to fill the baskets. Heat through for a few minutes in the oven.

CESTINI DI SEMOLINO

Serves 6

4 cups milk, plus extra for brushing

$1^1/2$ cups semolina

$5^1/2$ tablespoons butter

2 eggs, lightly beaten

grated rind of 1 lemon

$1/2$ onion, chopped

4 fresh sage leaves

7 ounces chicken livers, trimmed and chopped

4 tablespoons dry Marsala

1 teaspoon all-purpose flour

1 tablespoon tomato paste

2 tablespoons hot Chicken Stock (see page 209)

salt and pepper

HAM MOLDS

Slice the carrot into eight rounds and then cut each one into a decorative flower shape. Cut the dill pickles into thin slices, then cut into 16 small leaf shapes. Melt the butter in a small pan. Stir in the flour, then gradually stir in the stock. Bring to a boil, stirring constantly, then simmer for 10 minutes, stirring. Season to taste with salt, pepper and nutmeg. Remove the pan from the heat and let cool. Process the ham in a food processor, then stir into the sauce. Chill in the refrigerator for 30 minutes. Prepare the gelatin according to the instructions on the packet. Add the Marsala and heat for longer than the packet instructions state in order to reduce the mixture. Rinse eight individual molds in cold water, dry and pour 1 tablespoon of the gelatin mixture into each. Put a carrot 'flower' on the base of each mold with two dill pickle 'leaves' alongside. Return to the refrigerator and chill until set. Once set, add another tablespoon of the gelatin mixture to each mold and return to the refrigerator. Meanwhile, stir the ham mixture until light and frothy. Whisk the cream until soft peaks form, then fold into the ham mixture. Divide this mousse among the molds and return to the refrigerator to set. To serve, turn each mold out onto a separate lettuce leaf and arrange on a platter.

CUPOLETTE DI PROSCIUTTO

Serves 6–8

1 carrot

2–3 dill pickles, drained

2 tablespoons butter

1 tablespoon all-purpose flour

scant 1 cup Chicken Stock (see page 209)

pinch of freshly grated nutmeg

1 pound 2 ounces lean cooked cured ham, chopped

1 envelope gelatin

1 tablespoon Marsala

scant 1/2 cup heavy cream

salt and pepper

8 lettuce leaves, to serve

GRAPE LEAF PARCELS

Blanch the grape leaves in boiling water for 3 minutes. Drain and spread out on a dish towel. Tear the bread into pieces and place in a bowl with the milk. Let soak. Melt 2 tablespoons of the butter in a pan. Add the onions and cook over low heat, stirring occasionally, for about 10 minutes until golden. Stir in the prosciutto. Melt half the remaining butter in a small skillet. Add the veal and cook, stirring occasionally, until golden brown all over. Put the onion and prosciutto mixture and the veal in a food processor. Squeeze out the bread and add to the food processor with the egg and nutmeg. Season with salt and pepper and process to a purée. Place 1 tablespoon of the purée in the middle of each grape leaf and wrap into a parcel. Melt the remaining butter in a pan and add the parcels. When hot, sprinkle with the wine and cook until it has evaporated. Pour in 2 1/2 cups water and cook for 40 minutes until the liquid has almost completely evaporated. Drizzle with the lemon juice and serve.

FAGOTTINI DI FOGLIE DI VITE

Serves 6

24 grape leaves

2 thick bread slices, crusts removed

scant 1/2 cup milk

6 tablespoons butter

2 onions, chopped

2 ounces prosciutto, chopped

7 ounces veal, chopped

1 egg

pinch of freshly grated nutmeg

scant 1/2 cup dry white wine

juice of 1 lemon, strained

salt and pepper

MORTADELLA PARCELS

FAGOTTINI DI MORTADELLA

Serves 4

scant 1/2 cup ricotta cheese

1 yellow bell pepper, halved, seeded and finely chopped

4 shelled walnuts, chopped

4 thick slices mortadella, cut into fourths

salt

Place the ricotta in a bowl and stir until smooth. Add the yellow bell pepper and walnuts and season with salt. Spoon a little of the ricotta mixture onto the point of each mortadella triangle and roll up. Place the parcels in the refrigerator until ready to serve.

RUSSIAN SALAD ROULADES

INVOLTINI DI INSALATA RUSSA

Serves 4

4 fairly thick slices of cooked cured ham

1 quantity Russian Salad (see page 116)

8 pickled pearl onions, drained

lettuce leaves, to serve

Place the slices of ham flat on a counter. Spread a heaping tablespoon of Russian salad on each one. Roll up and insert a pickled pearl onion at each end of the rolls. Place the roulades on a bed of lettuce leaves arranged in the shape of a fan on a serving platter.

SOUSED BOILED BEEF

LESSO DI MANZO IN CARPIONE

Serves 4

1 pound 2 ounces boiled beef, chopped

3 tablespoons olive oil

1 onion, sliced

4 fresh sage leaves

1 fresh rosemary sprig

2/3 cup white wine vinegar

3/4 cup white wine

salt

Place the beef in a heatproof dish and set aside. Heat the olive oil in a pan. Add the onion and cook over low heat, stirring occasionally, for about 10 minutes until golden brown. Add the sage leaves, rosemary, vinegar and a pinch salt. Simmer over low heat until the vinegar has evaporated. Pour in the wine diluted with a little water and cook for a few minutes. Pour the hot mixture over the beef and let steep in a cool place for several hours.

BOILED BEEF TORTINO

LESSO DI MANZO IN TORTINO

Serves 4

olive oil, for brushing

1 pound 2 ounces boiled beef, chopped

3 eggs

juice of 1 lemon, strained

salt and pepper

Brush a flameproof glass or earthenware dish with olive oil and add the beef. Beat the eggs with the lemon juice and salt and pepper to taste. Place the dish over low heat, pour in the egg mixture and mix quickly so that the beef is coated. Cook for 2 minutes, then remove from the heat and serve hot.

SWEET–AND–SOUR TONGUE

Cook the tongue in boiling water for 1 hour or until tender. Peel off the skin while it is still hot and cut into the tongue slices. Dust lightly with flour. Heat the olive oil and butter in a skillet. Add the tongue slices and cook for 5 minutes on each side. Drain the raisins and add them to the skillet with the pine nuts. Cook over low heat for 15 minutes. Combine the chocolate, vinegar, sugar, flour and a pinch of salt in a bowl. Add 5 tablespoons hot water and stir until the chocolate has melted and the sugar has dissolved. Pour the mixture into the skillet and bring to a boil. If there doesn't seem to be enough sauce, add a little more hot water. Season with salt to taste and serve.

LINGUA IN DOLCEFORTE

Serves 6

1 veal tongue, trimmed,
soaked in cold water overnight and drained
1 tablespoon all-purpose flour, plus extra for dusting
2 tablespoons olive oil
2 tablespoons butter
scant $1/2$ cup golden raisins, soaked in warm water
for 10 minutes
$1/4$ cup pine nuts
1 ounce bittersweet chocolate, grated or finely chopped
6 tablespoons white wine vinegar
3 tablespoons sugar
salt

NERVETTI WITH ONIONS

Place the calf's feet in a large pan with one onion, the celery and carrot. Pour in water to cover and add a pinch of salt. Bring to a boil, then lower the heat and simmer for about 2 hours. Drain well, cut the meat off the bones while it is still hot, then cut it into strips (nervetti). Place in a dish. Thinly slice the remaining onion and mix with the meat. Drizzle with olive oil and season with salt and pepper. Set aside for at least 30 minutes to steep.

NERVETTI E CIPOLLE

Serves 4

2 calf's feet, blanched and central bones removed
2 onions
1 celery stalk
1 carrot
olive oil, for drizzling
salt and pepper

SPICY QUAIL EGGS

Bring a pan of water to a boil, add the eggs and cook for 8 minutes. Drain, refresh under cold water, then shell. Cut them in half. Stack several lettuce leaves on top of each other, roll up and cut into slices to make thin strips. Repeat with the remaining lettuce. Make a bed of lettuce strips on a serving platter. Place half the quail eggs on top, in groups of four arranged like flower petals. Gently stir the cream into the mayonnaise, then stir in the orange juice. Season with salt and white pepper to taste. Pour into a sauce boat and serve with the salad.

OVETTI DI QUAGLIA PICCANTI

Serves 4

16 quail eggs
7 ounces round lettuce
2 tablespoons heavy cream, whipped
1 cup Mayonnaise (see page 65)
4 tablespoons orange juice, strained
salt and white pepper

ROSEMARY AND CHEESE ROLLS

PANINI AL ROSMARINO E FORMAGGIO

Serves 6

scant ¹/₂ cup milk

3 tablespoons butter

¹/₂ ounce dried yeast

2³/₄ cups all-purpose flour, plus extra for dusting

vegetable oil, for greasing

2¹/₂ tablespoons finely chopped fresh rosemary

scant ³/₄ cup mild provolone cheese, grated

3 tablespoons heavy cream

1 ounce smoked pancetta, cut into strips

salt

Pour the milk into a small pan, add the butter and set over low heat. When the butter has melted, remove the pan from the heat, stir well and let cool to lukewarm. Sprinkle the yeast over the milk mixture and set aside for about 10 minutes until frothy. Sift the flour and pinch of salt into a bowl and make a well in the center. Stir the yeast mixture, pour into the well and, using your fingers, gradually incorporate the dry ingredients. Knead thoroughly, then shape into a ball. Oil a clean bowl, place the dough in it and cover with oiled plastic wrap. Set aside in a warm place until doubled in volume. Turn out onto a lightly floured surface and knead again, gradually kneading in the rosemary. Divide the mixture into six pieces and shape into balls. Place on a cookie sheet and let rise for about 1 hour. Preheat the oven to 350°F. Flatten the rolls slightly with your hand and bake for 15 minutes. Meanwhile, prepare the filling. Heat the provolone, cream and pancetta in a small pan over low heat. When the rolls are cooked, remove them from the oven and increase the oven temperature to 400°F. Cut off the tops of the rolls and hollow out the soft crumb without breaking the crust. Fill the hollows with the cheese mixture and replace the tops. Reheat in the oven for a few minutes.

PINEAPPLE KABOBS

SPIEDINI ALL'ANANAS

Serves 4

7 ounces red bell peppers, halved and seeded

4 onions

7 ounces prosciutto in a single piece, cut into ³/₄-inch cubes

7 ounces fresh pineapple, cut into ³/₄-inch cubes

7 ounces fontina cheese, cut into ³/₄-inch cubes

16 fresh basil leaves

olive oil, for frying

1–1¹/₂ cups bread crumbs

1 egg • all-purpose flour, for dusting

salt and pepper

arugula, to serve

Parboil the red bell peppers and onions in boiling water for a few minutes. Drain and let cool. Cut the bell peppers and onions into ³/₄-inch cubes and thread the pieces of bell pepper, onion, prosciutto, pineapple and fontina and the basil leaves alternately onto skewers. Heat the olive oil in a large skillet. Spread out the bread crumbs on a shallow plate. Beat the egg with salt and pepper in a bowl. Lightly dust the kabobs with flour, shaking off any excess. Dip them into the egg and drain off any excess, then quickly roll in the bread crumbs several times to coat. Fry in hot olive oil and drain on paper towels. Serve on a bed of arugula.

SAGE APPETIZER

STUZZICHINI DI SALVIA

Serves 4

1 egg

30 fresh sage leaves

1 ounce fine white bread crumbs

olive oil, for frying

salt

mild provolone cheese, diced

Beat the egg with a pinch of salt in a bowl. Add the sage leaves, making sure that they are immersed, and let stand for 2 minutes. Drain the leaves well and dip in the bread crumbs to coat. Heat plenty of olive oil in a skillet, add the sage leaves and cook until golden brown. Drain on paper towels and serve with the provolone.

SCHERRER'S TARTARE

TARTARA ALLA SCHERRER

Serves 4

4 herring fillets, diced

1 green apple, diced

1 dill pickle, drained and diced

1 shallot, finely chopped

6 fresh chives, finely chopped

2 tablespoons olive oil

6 tablespoons butter

8 whole-wheat bread slices

pepper

Combine the herring fillets, apple, dill pickle, shallot and chives in a bowl, stir in the olive oil and season with pepper. Melt a pat of the butter in a skillet. Add one or two slices of bread and fry on both sides until golden. Remove from the pan and drain on paper towels. Fry the remaining slices of bread, adding more butter as necessary. Arrange the fried bread on a serving dish, top with the herring mixture and serve. Scherrer, the owner of a restaurant with the same name, created the original recipe.

TRUFFLE, CHICKEN AND CORN SALAD

TARTUFO, POLLO E SONGINO

Serves 4

4 tablespoons olive oil, plus extra for drizzling

14 ounces skinless chicken breast fillets

7 ounces corn salad

1 small black truffle, thinly shaved

salt and pepper

For the dressing

1 tablespoon anchovy paste

olive oil, for drizzling

juice of 1 lemon, strained

Heat the olive oil in a skillet. Add the chicken and cook over medium heat, turning occasionally, for 15 minutes until golden brown all over. Remove from the skillet and cut into thin strips. Make a bed of corn salad on a serving platter. Drizzle with olive oil, season with salt and pepper and toss gently. Place the chicken strips on the lettuce and sprinkle with the truffle shavings. For the dressing, place the anchovy paste in a bowl, mash with a fork and gradually drizzle olive oil in to make a smooth paste. Stir in the lemon juice. Drizzle the dressing over the chicken and truffles and serve without tossing.

FISH
ANTIPASTI

FISH FILLET

FRESH ANCHOVIES WITH LEMON

Rinse the anchovies and pat dry with paper towels. Arrange the fillets in a nonmetallic dish or soup plate, sprinkle with salt and pour in the lemon juice or vinegar. Marinate in a cool place for 24 hours. Drain the anchovies, arrange on a serving dish and sprinkle with the parsley and onion slices. Drizzle with olive oil and serve immediately.

ACCIUGHE AL LIMONE
Serves 4

16 fresh anchovies, heads removed, cleaned and filleted (see page 596)
$^1/_2$ cup lemon juice, strained, or white wine vinegar
3 tablespoons chopped fresh flat-leaf parsley
2 pearl onions, thinly sliced
olive oil, for drizzling
salt

SHRIMP BITES

BOCCONCINI DI GAMBERETTI

Serves 4

1 onion, coarsely chopped

9 ounces raw shrimp, peeled and deveined

5 fresh flat-leaf parsley sprigs, coarsely chopped

2¹/₄ cups all-purpose flour • scant ¹/₂ cup milk

1 egg • olive oil, for frying

salt and pepper

Put the onion, shrimp and parsley in a food processor, season with salt and process for 1 minute. Add the flour, milk, egg and scant ¹/₂ cup water. Process again until combined. Season with salt and pepper to taste. Heat plenty of olive oil in a skillet. Add the shrimp mixture, a tablespoonful at a time, and cook until golden brown. Remove with a slotted spoon, drain on paper towels and serve hot or cold.

CHERRY TOMATO AND CRAB BITES

BOCCONCINI DI POMODORI E GRANCHIO

Serves 4

12 red cherry tomatoes

9 ounces white crabmeat, drained if canned

3 tablespoons Mayonnaise (see page 65)

salt and pepper

12 black olives, to garnish

Cut the tops off the tomatoes and scoop out some of the pulp. Sprinkle the insides with salt and place them upside down on paper towels to drain. Combine the crabmeat with the mayonnaise in a bowl and season with salt and pepper. Fill the tomatoes with the crab mixture and garnish with the olives.

TUNA BITES

BOCCONCINI DI TONNO

Serves 4

2 eggs, hard-cooked

7 ounces canned tuna in oil, drained and flaked

scant ¹/₂ cup ricotta cheese

2 tablespoons capers, drained

2 tablespoons finely chopped fresh basil

rind of 1 lemon, grated

2 tablespoons lemon juice, strained

2 tablespoons butter, softened • salt and pepper

arugula, to serve

Shell and chop the eggs. Push the eggs, tuna and ricotta through a strainer into a bowl. Stir in the capers, basil, lemon rind, lemon juice and butter and season to taste with salt and pepper. Shape the mixture into balls and chill in the refrigerator until ready to serve. Just before serving, arrange a bed of arugula on a platter and place the tuna bites on top.

STUFFED SQUID

CALAMARI RIPIENI

Serves 4

2¹/₄ cups dry white wine

2 bay leaves • 8 squid, cleaned

11 ounces cooked, peeled shrimp

1 garlic clove, chopped

2 tablespoons chopped fresh flat-leaf parsley

juice of 2 lemons, strained

scant ¹/₂ cup olive oil, plus extra for drizzling

salt and pepper

Pour 4 cups water into a large pan and add the white wine, bay leaves and a pinch of salt. Bring to a boil, add the squid and simmer for 20 minutes. Drain and let cool. Place the shrimp, garlic, 1 tablespoon of the parsley and 2 tablespoons of the lemon juice in a bowl, drizzle generously with olive oil and season with pepper. Mix well. Stuff the squid sacs with the shrimp mixture and arrange on a serving dish. Whisk together the olive oil, the remaining lemon juice and the remaining parsley. Season with salt and pepper and pour the dressing over the squid.

FISH CARPACCIO

Place the fish in the freezer or refrigerator for 1–2 hours to firm up. Using a very sharp knife, cut the swordfish and salmon into thin slices. Arrange on a serving dish and keep in the refrigerator until ready to serve. Put the olive oil, garlic, brandy, parsley and thyme in a food processor and season with salt and pepper. Process to mix well. Just before serving, sprinkle the carpaccio with the dressing.

CARPACCIO DI PESCE

Serves 4

9-ounce swordfish fillet

9-ounce salmon fillet • scant 1/2 cup olive oil

1 garlic clove, finely chopped

1 tablespoon brandy

1/2 bunch of fresh flat-leaf parsley, coarsely chopped

1 teaspoon fresh thyme leaves • salt and pepper

BABY SQUID IN BASKETS

Discard any mussels that do not close immediately when sharply tapped. Put the mussels in a skillet with 2 tablespoons of the olive oil, the wine, parsley, garlic and a pinch of pepper. Set over high heat for 3–5 minutes until the shells open. Remove the skillet from the heat and discard any mussels that have not opened. Strain the mussels, reserving the cooking liquid, and remove them from their shells. Strain the cooking liquid through a cheesecloth-lined strainer. Preheat the oven to 425°F. Grease eight individual ramekins with butter. Roll out the dough on a lightly floured surface and line the ramekins. Place in the refrigerator until required. Heat the remaining olive oil in another skillet. Add the shrimp and cook, stirring frequently, for 3–5 minutes. Add the squid and mussels and simmer gently. Whisk together the egg yolks, reserved mussel cooking liquid, grated Parmesan and shallot in a bowl and season with salt and pepper. Add the seafood mixture, stir well and divide among the ramekins. Place on a cookie sheet and bake for 15–20 minutes until set and golden. Serve warm.

CESTINI DI CALAMARETTI

Serves 6–8

5 ounces live mussels, scrubbed and beards removed

4 tablespoons olive oil

3 tablespoons dry white wine

2 tablespoons chopped fresh flat-leaf parsley

1 garlic clove, finely chopped

butter, for greasing

9 ounces ready-made puff pastry dough,

thawed if frozen

all-purpose flour, for dusting

3 1/2 ounces raw shrimp, peeled and deveined

7 ounces baby squid, cleaned, blanched and chopped

2 egg yolks

generous 1/2 cup Parmesan cheese, freshly grated

1 shallot, chopped

salt and pepper

LANGOUSTINE COCKTAIL

Bring a pan of lightly salted water to a boil. Add the langoustines or shrimp, onion and carrot and cook for 2–5 minutes until tender. Drain well and peel the langoustines or shrimp. Combine the mayonnaise, cream, Worcestershire sauce and ketchup in a bowl. Sprinkle with gin and whisky, season with salt to taste and stir. Line four serving dishes with the most tender lettuce leaves. Divide the langoustines or shrimp among them and spoon the sauce over them. Chill in the refrigerator until ready to serve.

COCKTAIL DI SCAMPI

Serves 4

1 3/4 pounds langoustines or jumbo shrimp

1 onion, chopped • 1 carrot, chopped

1 1/4 cups Mayonnaise (see page 65)

scant 1 cup light cream

1 teaspoon Worcestershire sauce

1 teaspoon tomato ketchup

1 teaspoon gin, or to taste

1 teaspoon whisky, or to taste

1 lettuce • salt

DELIZIE DI TROTA IN CREMA ROSA

Serves 4

6 tablespoons butter

14 ounces smoked trout fillets,
skinned and coarsely chopped

1 tablespoon brandy, or to taste

2 tablespoons olive oil

1/2 onion, chopped

1 red bell pepper, halved, seeded and chopped

scant 1/2 cup tomato paste

scant 1/2 cup heavy cream

salt and pepper

SMOKED TROUT
IN PINK CREAM

Melt the butter in a double boiler or a heatproof bowl set over a pan of barely simmering water, then remove from the heat. Meanwhile, place the trout in a food processor and process to purée. Scrape into a bowl, stir in the melted butter and brandy and season with salt and pepper. Divide the mixture among four individual molds and put in the refrigerator for a few hours to set. Heat the olive oil in a skillet. Add the onion and red bell pepper and cook over low heat, stirring occasionally, for 5 minutes until softened. Add the tomato paste, season with salt and pepper and cook for 15 minutes. Remove the skillet from the heat and let cool slightly. Spoon the vegetable mixture into a food processor and process to a purée. Scrape into a bowl and stir in the cream. To serve, pour 2 tablespoons of the pink cream into the middle of each of four plates and turn out the molds on top.

GRANCEOLA GRATINATA

Serves 4

4 live or freshly cooked blue crabs

3 tablespoons butter, plus extra for greasing

3 tablespoons brandy

2 egg yolks

1/2 quantity Béchamel Sauce (see page 50)

1/2 cup Swiss cheese, grated

salt

CRAB AU GRATIN

If using live crabs, plunge them into a large pan of salted, boiling water, cover and cook for about 15 minutes. Drain and let cool. When the crabs are cold, remove the claws and legs. Using a small strong knife, force the shells apart, inserting it under the tail flaps. Remove and discard the gills and stomach sacs. Extract the white meat and pinkish-red corals, if present, from the bodies, then crack the claws and legs and pick out the meat. Wash and dry the crab shells to use as serving dishes, then grease with butter. (You can also use individual gratin dishes.) Preheat the oven to 350°F. Stir the corals and brandy together in a bowl. Stir the crabmeat, egg yolks and brandy mixture into the béchamel sauce and spoon into the crab shells or dishes. Sprinkle with the grated cheese and dot with the butter. Place on a cookie sheet and bake for 15–20 minutes until golden and bubbling.

CRAB AND LANGOUSTINE CUPS

Wash the grapefruit well and cut in half. Cut around the flesh and scoop it out without damaging the 'shells'. Chop the flesh and reserve the shells to use as serving dishes. Grate the carrots into a bowl and immediately stir in the lemon juice. Cook the langoustines or shrimp in a pan of lightly salted, boiling water for 2–5 minutes until tender. Drain, peel and chop. Stir the langoustines or shrimp, crabmeat, olives and 4 tablespoons of the grapefruit flesh into the carrot mixture. Season to taste with salt and pepper. Divide the mixture among the grapefruit shells and chill in the refrigerator until ready to serve.

GRANCHI E SCAMPI IN COPPETTE

Serves 4

2 grapefruit

3 small carrots

juice of 1 lemon, strained

12 langoustines or jumbo shrimp

4 ounces canned crabmeat, drained

4 tablespoons black olives, pitted

salt and pepper

BABY OCTOPUS AND GREEN BEAN SALAD

Cook the beans in lightly salted, boiling water until just tender, then drain and put in a salad bowl. Bring a pan of water to a boil and add the octopuses. Cook for 1 minute, then drain and halve the larger ones, leaving the smaller ones whole. Pour the vinegar into a small pan and add the basil, marjoram, parsley, garlic and chile. Bring to a boil and cook for a few minutes until reduced. Remove from the heat and strain into a bowl. Flake the tuna and sprinkle it over the beans, then add the octopuses. Drizzle olive oil over the salad, then spoon over the spiced vinegar and season with salt and pepper. Chill in the refrigerator for 2 hours before serving.

INSALATA DI MOSCARDINI E FAGIOLINI

Serves 6

$2^{1}/_{4}$ pounds green beans, trimmed

14 ounces baby octopuses, cleaned and skinned

$^{3}/_{4}$ cup red wine vinegar

2 tablespoons chopped fresh basil

2 tablespoons chopped fresh marjoram

1 tablespoon chopped fresh flat-leaf parsley

1 garlic clove, chopped

1 fresh chile

5 ounces canned tuna in oil, drained

olive oil, for drizzling

salt and pepper

WHITEBAIT SALAD

Wash the fish carefully and thoroughly. Parboil for a few minutes in salted water. Drain carefully and let cool. Combine the olive oil and lemon juice in a bowl and season with salt and white pepper. Pour the dressing over the whitebait and toss. Let stand for 10 minutes before serving.

INSALATA DI BIANCHETTI

Serves 4

1 pound 2 ounces whitebait

4 tablespoons olive oil

juice of $^{1}/_{2}$ lemon, strained

salt and white pepper

OCTOPUS AND ARUGULA SALAD

Put a little water in a pan and add the wine and peppercorns. Bring to a boil, add the sea salt and immerse the octopus. Cook for 1 hour or until the thickest tentacles can be pricked with a fork. Remove the pan from the heat and let the octopus cool in the water for at least 20 minutes. Meanwhile, combine the arugula, pine nuts and apple. Drain the octopus, pull off and discard the skin and chop the flesh. Add to the arugula mixture. Whisk together the olive oil and lemon juice in a pitcher, season with salt and pepper and pour over the salad.

INSALATA DI POLPO E RUCOLA

Serves 6

scant $^1/_2$ cup dry white wine

6 black peppercorns

1 teaspoon coarse sea salt

$1^3/_4$-pound octopus, cleaned and tenderized

2 bunches of arugula, chopped

4 tablespoons pine nuts

$^1/_2$ apple, peeled, cored and diced

$^1/_2$ cup olive oil

juice of 1 lemon, strained

salt and pepper

LANGOUSTINE AND FIG SALAD

Bring a pan of lightly salted water to a boil. Add the langoustines or shrimp and cook for 2–5 minutes until tender. Drain and peel, then set aside. Place the tomatoes in a food processor with the lemon juice, grapefruit juice and Tabasco, season with salt and pepper and process to a purée. Pour the sauce into a bowl and gradually whisk in the olive oil. Using a melon baller or teaspoon, scoop out about 40 small balls of melon flesh. Using a dampened knife cut each fig into four wedges. To serve, divide the arugula among four serving plates, placing it in the center, and arrange the figs, langoustines or shrimp and melon balls around like sun rays. Spoon over the sauce and serve.

INSALATA DI SCAMPI E FICHI

Serves 4

1 pound 2 ounces langoustines or jumbo shrimp

4 plum tomatoes, peeled, seeded and coarsely chopped

juice of $^1/_2$ lemon, strained

juice of $^1/_2$ grapefruit, strained

dash of Tabasco sauce

4 tablespoons olive oil

1 melon, halved and seeded

4 fresh figs, peeled

1 bunch of arugula

salt and pepper

SHRIMP WITH ARUGULA

Arrange the arugula on a serving dish. Peel and devein the shrimp, reserving any roe for the garnish. Put the shrimp in the top of a steamer and cook over medium heat for 4 minutes. Meanwhile, whisk together the lemon juice and olive oil and season with salt. Arrange the shrimp on the bed of arugula, garnish with the reserved roe and drizzle with the lemon dressing. Serve immediately while the shrimp are still warm.

MANZZANCOLLE ALLA RUCOLA

Serves 4

7 ounces arugula

$1^3/_4$ pounds large raw shrimp

juice of 1 lemon, strained

scant $^1/_2$ cup olive oil

salt

OYSTERS

Just before serving open the oysters. Protect the hand holding the oyster with a dish towel and insert an oyster knife or small strong knife into the hinged edge, then twist to prize the shells apart. Slide the blade along the inside of the upper shell to sever the muscle and lift off the shell. Taking care not to spill the juices, slide the blade under the oyster to sever the lower muscle. Arrange the oysters on the halfshells on a bed of crushed ice. They may be eaten as they are, with a dash of lemon juice or with thin slices of lightly buttered toast.

OSTRICHE

Serves 4

24 oysters

crushed ice, to serve

lemon (optional)

buttered toast (optional)

RAW SOLE WITH CHILE

Place the sole fillets in a serving dish. Combine the tomatoes, onion, lemon juice, orange juice, Worcestershire sauce, chili powder and a pinch of salt in a bowl. Pour this mixture over the fish and set aside in the refrigerator to marinate for at least 4 hours. Remove the dish from the refrigerator 10 minutes before serving.

SOGLIOLETTE CRUDE AL PEPERONCINO

Serves 4

2¼ pounds sole fillets, skinned

2 tablespoons bottled strained tomatoes

2 tablespoons chopped onion

2 tablespoons lemon juice, strained

1 tablespoon orange juice, strained

dash of Worcestershire sauce

pinch of chili powder

salt

VEGETABLE ANTIPASTI

Serves 4

1³/₄ pounds eggplants, diced

¹/₂ cup olive oil

1 celery stalk, chopped

1 onion, thinly sliced

11 ounces ripe tomatoes, peeled and diced

1¹/₂ teaspoons sugar

scant ¹/₂ cup white wine vinegar

1 tablespoon pine nuts

scant 1 cup pitted green olives

3 tablespoons capers

1 tablespoon golden raisins, soaked in hot water

for 10 minutes and drained

salt and pepper

fresh basil leaves, to garnish

SWEET–AND–SOUR CAPONATA

Put the eggplants in a colander, sprinkle with salt and let stand for 30 minutes. Rinse and pat dry with paper towels. Heat 5 tablespoons of the oil in a large skillet. Add the eggplants and cook over medium heat, stirring frequently, until golden brown all over. Meanwhile, heat the remaining olive oil in another skillet. Add the celery, onion and tomatoes and cook over low heat for 10–15 minutes until thickened and pulpy. Season with salt and pepper to taste. Stir in the sugar, vinegar, pine nuts, olives, capers and raisins and bring to a boil over low heat. Add the eggplants and simmer for 10 minutes. Serve the caponata hot or warm, sprinkled with small basil leaves.

ARTICHOKES JARDINIÈRE

Half-fill a bowl with cold water and add the lemon juice. Working on one artichoke at a time, break off the stems and cut off the coarse outer leaves. Trim off the top ³/₄ inch. Scoop out and discard the chokes, then cut the artichokes into wedges. Drop them in the acidulated water to prevent discoloration. Pour 2¹/₂ cups water into a pan and add the olive oil, clove, bay leaf, onion, peppercorns and sea salt. Drain the artichokes, add them to the pan and bring to a boil. Cook over medium heat until most of the liquid has evaporated and the artichokes are tender. Drain, reserving 2–3 tablespoons of the cooking liquid. Discard the clove, bay leaf and peppercorns. Line a wide, shallow salad bowl with lettuce leaves. Arrange the artichoke wedges on top. Whisk together the reserved cooking liquid and the anchovy paste in a pitcher, then pour the sauce over the artichokes. Add the olives to the bowl and sprinkle the salad with the chopped eggs.

CARCIOFI ALLA GIARDINIERA

Serves 4

juice of 1 lemon, strained
8 globe artichokes
4 tablespoons olive oil
1 clove
1 bay leaf
¹/₂ onion, thinly sliced
6 black peppercorns
1 teaspoon coarse sea salt
1 lettuce
¹/₂ teaspoon anchovy paste
3¹/₂ ounces pitted black olives
2 eggs, hard-cooked and finely chopped

STUFFED ARTICHOKES JARDINIÈRE

Beat the egg with the grapefruit juice in a bowl and season with salt and pepper. Add the Parmesan, bread crumbs, capers and anchovies and mix well. Set aside. Half-fill a bowl with cold water and add the lemon juice. Working on one artichoke at a time, break off the stems and cut off the coarse outer leaves. Trim off the top ³/₄ inch. Scoop out and discard the chokes. Drop the artichokes in the acidulated water to prevent discoloration. Half-fill a large pan with water, stir in the flour and a pinch of salt. Drain the artichokes, add them to the pan and bring to a boil. Lower the heat and simmer for about 15 minutes until tender. Preheat the oven to 400°F. Drain the artichokes and stuff with the Parmesan and anchovy mixture. Arrange the artichokes in an ovenproof dish and drizzle with olive oil. Bake for 20 minutes and serve warm.

CARCIOFI GIARDINIERA SAPORITI

Serves 4

1 egg
juice of ¹/₂ grapefruit, strained
²/₃ cup Parmesan cheese, freshly grated
2 tablespoons bread crumbs
1 tablespoon capers
2 salted anchovies, heads removed,
cleaned and filleted (see page 596),
soaked in cold water for 10 minutes,
drained and finely chopped
juice of 1 lemon, strained
8 globe artichokes
1 tablespoon all-purpose flour
olive oil, for drizzling
salt and pepper

CIPOLLE GRATINATE

Serves 4

4 large onions, peeled

butter, for greasing

5 ounces cooked cured ham, chopped

4 tablespoons bottled strained tomatoes

4 tablespoons Parmesan cheese, freshly grated

$^1/_2$ quantity Béchamel Sauce (see page 50)

salt and pepper

STUFFED ONION GRATIN

Bring a large pan of salted water to a boil. Add the whole onions and parboil for a few minutes. Drain well, cut in half horizontally and gently scoop out the middles to leave eight 'shells'. Preheat the oven to 350°F and grease an ovenproof dish with butter. Chop the scooped-out onion and mix with the ham and tomatoes in a bowl. Season with salt and pepper. Stuff the onion shells with this mixture. Arrange them in the prepared dish. Stir the Parmesan into the béchamel sauce and season with salt and pepper to taste. Pour the sauce over the stuffed onions and bake until golden brown and bubbling. Serve immediately.

CIPOLLINE ALLA SENAPE ARANCIONE

Serves 4

16 pearl onions

2 teaspoons olive oil, plus extra for drizzling

2$^1/_2$ cups dry white wine

2 tablespoons butter

2 carrots, chopped

2 tablespoons all-purpose flour

2 tablespoons mustard

generous 1 cup bacon, diced

$^1/_4$ cup heavy cream

salt and pepper

ONIONS IN ORANGE MUSTARD

Preheat the oven to 350°F. Place the onions in a high-sided roasting pan and drizzle with a little olive oil. Pour in 1$^3/_4$ cups of the white wine and season with salt and pepper. Bake for about 30 minutes until the liquid has almost completely evaporated. Melt the butter in a skillet. Add the carrots and cook over low heat, stirring occasionally, for 5 minutes. Sprinkle with the flour and stir in, then add the mustard and season with salt and pepper. Cook, stirring frequently, until thickened. Heat the olive oil in another skillet. Add the bacon and cook, stirring occasionally, for 4–5 minutes. Sprinkle with the remaining wine and cook until it has evaporated. Stir in the cream, then pour the mixture into the pan of carrots and stir well. Transfer the onions to a serving dish and pour the sauce on top.

CUORICINI DI SPINACI

Serves 6

1 pound 2 ounces spinach

1 quantity Béchamel Sauce (see page 50)

pinch of freshly grated nutmeg

2 egg yolks

$^1/_2$ cup all-purpose flour

1 cup bread crumbs

2 eggs

6 tablespoons olive oil

salt and pepper

SPINACH HEARTS

Cook the spinach in lightly salted, boiling water for about 5 minutes until tender. Drain, squeezing out as much liquid as possible, then chop and let cool slightly. Season the béchamel sauce with the nutmeg and salt and pepper to taste, then stir in the spinach and beat in the egg yolks. Spread out the mixture on a counter and let cool completely. Spread out the flour on a plate, spread out the bread crumbs on another plate and beat the whole eggs in a shallow dish. Heat the olive oil in a large skillet. When the spinach mixture is cold, stamp out shapes using a heart-shaped cookie cutter. Dip them first in the flour, then in the beaten eggs and, finally, in the bread crumbs. Cook in the hot oil, in batches if necessary, until golden brown all over. Drain on paper towels and serve warm.

MUSHROOM SALAD

Thinly slice the mushrooms and sprinkle with the lemon juice. Combine the mushrooms with the shrimp in a serving bowl. Season with salt and pepper, drizzle with oil and garnish with parsley.

FUNGHI IN INSALATA

Serves 4

11 ounces Caesar's mushrooms
or other exotic mushrooms
juice of 1 lemon, strained
14 ounces cooked shrimp, peeled and deveined
olive oil, for drizzling • salt and pepper
fresh flat-leaf parsley, chopped, to garnish

BELGIAN ENDIVE WITH HAM

Put the diced fontina and mozzarella in a bowl, add the milk and let soften for 1 hour. Bring a large pan of salted water to a boil. Add the endive heads and simmer for 15 minutes, then drain well. Preheat the oven to 400°F. Grease an ovenproof dish with butter. Wrap each head of endive in a slice of prosciutto and arrange in the prepared dish. Tip the cheese and milk mixture into a skillet and heat gently, stirring, to make a thick, smooth cream. Season with salt and pepper. Remove the pan from the heat, stir in the egg yolks and pour the mixture over the prosciutto-wrapped endive. Sprinkle with the Parmesan, dot with the butter and bake for 10 minutes.

INDIVIA AL PROSCIUTTO

Serves 4

5 ounces fontina cheese, diced
1 mozzarella cheese, diced
1 cup milk
4 Belgian endive heads
2 tablespoons butter, plus extra for greasing
4 prosciutto slices
2 egg yolks, lightly beaten
2 ounces Parmesan cheese, freshly grated
salt and pepper

CAULIFLOWER SALAD (1)

Cook the cauliflower flowerets in boiling water until al dente. Drain, let cool, then place in a salad bowl. Mash the anchovy fillets in the lemon juice in a bowl and add the olive oil, garlic and tuna. Season with salt, mix and use to dress the cauliflower.

INSALATA DI CAVOLFIORE (1)

Serves 4

1 cauliflower, cut into flowerets
6 canned anchovy fillets, drained
juice of 1 lemon, strained
6 tablespoons olive oil • 1/2 garlic clove, chopped
5 ounces canned tuna in oil, drained and flaked
salt

CAULIFLOWER SALAD (2)

Cook the cauliflower flowerets in salted, boiling water until al dente. Drain, let cool, then place in a salad bowl. Combine the olive oil and vinegar in a bowl, add the parsley and tarragon and season with salt and pepper. Use to dress the cauliflower and let stand for 1 hour. Serve separately with mayonnaise with a little mustard.

INSALATA DI CAVOLFIORE (2)

Serves 4

1 cauliflower, cut into flowerets
6 tablespoons olive oil
3 tablespoons white wine vinegar
1 tablespoon chopped fresh flat-leaf parsley
2 teaspoons chopped fresh tarragon
salt and pepper • mustard mayonnaise, to serve

INSALATA DI CETRIOLI E GAMBERI

Serves 4

4 cucumbers, peeled and cut into thin batons

14 ounces cooked shrimp, peeled and deveined

scant $^1/_2$ cup heavy cream

juice of 1 lemon, strained

1 teaspoon paprika

2 tablespoons chopped fresh flat-leaf parsley

salt

CUCUMBER AND SHRIMP SALAD

Place the cucumbers and shrimp in a salad bowl. Combine the cream and lemon juice in a bowl, stir in the paprika and season with salt. Pour the dressing over the salad, sprinkle with parsley and toss well. If you do not like the flavor of cucumber, substitute boiled zucchini.

INSALATA RUSSA

Serves 4

scant 1 cup shelled peas

$^2/_3$ cup green beans

6 cauliflower flowerets

2 potatoes • 2 carrots

3 cornichons or small dill pickles, drained and diced

1 cooked beet, diced

1 egg, hard-cooked, shelled and diced

1 quantity Mayonnaise (see page 65)

RUSSIAN SALAD

Cook the peas, beans, cauliflower, potatoes and carrots in separate pans of boiling water until al dente. Drain well and chop them, apart from the peas. Put all the vegetables in a salad bowl with the cornichons or dill pickles, beet and egg. Stir in enough mayonnaise to form a soft mixture. Chill in the refrigerator for 2–3 hours. Shortly before serving, arrange the Russian salad in a dome in the middle of a dish and garnish to taste.

MELANZANE RIPIENE

Serves 4

4 eggplants

3 tablespoons olive oil, plus extra for brushing

1 onion, chopped

1 celery stalk, chopped

3 red or green bell peppers, halved, seeded and chopped

4 ripe tomatoes, diced

2 eggs, lightly beaten

3 tablespoons Parmesan cheese, freshly grated

salt and pepper

STUFFED EGGPLANTS

Halve the eggplants lengthwise and scoop out the flesh without piercing the 'shells'. Chop the flesh and reserve the shells. Heat the oil in a large skillet. Add the onion and cook over low heat, stirring occasionally, for 5 minutes until soft. Add the chopped eggplant flesh, celery, bell peppers and tomatoes, season with salt and pepper and cook over low heat for 15 minutes. Meanwhile, preheat the oven to 350°F. Brush an ovenproof dish with olive oil. Remove the pan from the heat and stir in the eggs. Fill the eggplant shells with the mixture and place in the prepared dish. Sprinkle with the Parmesan and bake until golden and bubbling. Remove from the oven and let cool. Serve cold.

ROLLED BELL PEPPERS

Place the bell peppers on a cookie sheet under a preheated broiler. Broil, turning frequently, until charred and blackened. Transfer to a plastic bag, tie the top and let cool. Peel off the bell pepper skins, rinse gently under cold running water and pat dry. Halve and seed the bell peppers, then cut the flesh into two or three large slices. Place the tuna, olives, tomato, chile and basil in a food processor and process to a purée. Add enough lemon juice to make a soft mixture and add the olive oil. Spread each slice of bell pepper with the tuna sauce and roll up. Keep in a cool place before serving.

PEPERONI ARROTOLATI

Serves 4

4 large red or green bell peppers

11 ounces canned tuna in oil, drained

10 pitted black olives, coarsely chopped

1 tomato, peeled, seeded and coarsely chopped

1 fresh red chile, seeded and coarsely chopped

12 fresh basil leaves

3–4 tablespoons lemon juice, strained

1 tablespoon olive oil

TOMATO FLOWERS

Cut off the tops of the tomatoes and scoop out the seeds. Sprinkle with salt and place upside down on paper towels to drain. Meanwhile, shell the eggs and halve lengthwise. Scoop out the yolks without breaking the whites. Place the tuna, olives, egg yolks, mayonnaise and mustard in a food processor and process to a purée. Season with salt to taste. Spoon the mixture into eight of the egg-white halves, doming it on top. Arrange arugula leaves in the tomatoes so that they look like a whorl of petals, and place the filled egg halves in the middle. Garnish with mayonnaise and arrange on a serving dish. Chop the remaining egg whites and sprinkle them around the tomato flowers. Serve cold.

POMODORI FIORITI

Serves 4

4 large tomatoes, about the same size

6 eggs, hard-cooked

3½ ounces canned tuna, drained and flaked

1 tablespoon pitted green olives, coarsely chopped

1 tablespoon Mayonnaise (see page 65), plus extra to garnish

1 teaspoon Dijon mustard

1 bunch of arugula

salt

STUFFED PORCINI MUSHROOMS

Preheat the oven to 325°F. Line a roasting pan with baking parchment. Remove the mushroom caps, reserving the stalks. Place the caps in the roasting pan and bake for 5 minutes. Remove from the oven and increase the temperature to 350°F. Transfer the mushroom caps to a plate, discard the baking parchment and brush the roasting pan with oil. Slice the stalks. Chop the anchovy fillets. Heat 1 tablespoon of the olive oil in a skillet. Add the onion, parsley, garlic and anchovies and cook over low heat, stirring occasionally, for 5 minutes. Add the mushroom stalks, cook for 3–4 minutes more, then season with salt and pepper. Remove the skillet from the heat. Squeeze out the bread and stir it into the pan with the egg and remaining olive oil. Place the mushroom caps in the roasting pan gill sides uppermost and fill with the mixture. Sprinkle with the bread crumbs and bake for 20 minutes.

PORCINI RIPIENI

Serves 4

8 porcini mushrooms

2 tablespoons olive oil, plus extra for brushing

2 salted anchovies, heads removed, cleaned and filleted (see page 596), soaked in cold water for 10 minutes and drained

1 onion, thinly sliced

1 tablespoon fresh flat-leaf parsley

1 garlic clove, chopped

2 bread slices, crusts removed, soaked in cold water for 10 minutes

1 egg, lightly beaten

4 tablespoons bread crumbs

salt and pepper

SACCHETTI DELL'ORTOLANO

Serves 4

4 yellow bell peppers

2 tablespoons olive oil, plus extra for brushing

4 eggplants, diced

1 garlic clove

1 tablespoon concentrated tomato paste

1 tablespoon capers

6 fresh basil leaves, chopped

6 black olives

1 mozzarella cheese, diced

salt and pepper

4 fresh basil leaves, to garnish

GARDENER'S BAG

Place the bell peppers on a cookie sheet under a preheated broiler. Broil, turning frequently, until charred and blackened. Transfer to a plastic bag, tie the top and let cool. Peel off the bell pepper skins, cut off the tops and remove the seeds and membranes without piercing the 'shells'. Preheat the oven to 350°F. Brush an ovenproof dish with oil. Heat the olive oil in a skillet. Add the eggplants and garlic and cook over low heat for 5 minutes until golden brown. Mix the tomato paste with 1 teaspoon hot water and add to the skillet with the capers, chopped basil leaves and olives. Cook for a few more minutes. Remove and discard the garlic and season with salt and pepper. Remove the skillet from the heat and add the mozzarella. Fill the bell peppers with the mixture and place in the prepared dish. Bake for 10 minutes. Garnish each bell pepper with a basil leaf and serve warm.

STRUDEL DELL'ORTO

Serves 8

2³/₄ cups baby peas, shelled

2 cups green beans, halved

11 ounces asparagus spears

11 ounces artichoke hearts, cut into fourth

1 cup carrots, chopped

³/₄ cup potatoes, chopped

²/₃ cup butter

1 garlic clove

4 tablespoons light cream

1 pack ready-made puff pastry dough, thawed if frozen

all-purpose flour, for dusting

1 egg yolk, lightly beaten

salt and pepper

VEGETABLE–GARDEN STRUDEL

Preheat the oven to 350°F. Cook the baby peas, beans, asparagus, artichoke hearts, carrots and potatoes in separate pans of boiling water until al dente. Drain well. Heat 7 tablespoons of the butter with the garlic in a large skillet. Remove and discard the garlic, add all the vegetables and cook, stirring frequently, for 5 minutes. Season with salt and pepper to taste. Remove the pan from the heat and stir in the cream. Roll out the pastry into a fairly thin rectangle on a lightly floured surface. Melt the remaining butter and brush it over the surface of the pastry. Sprinkle the vegetables over the pastry and roll up gently, crimping the edges to seal. Brush the strudel with the egg yolk, place on a cookie sheet and bake for about 30 minutes until golden. Let stand for 10 minutes before serving.

BELL PEPPER PIE

TORTINO DI PEPERONI

Serves 4

Heat the butter and olive oil in a skillet. Add the onion and cook over low heat, stirring occasionally, for 10 minutes until golden brown. Add the bell peppers and potatoes. Cook over low heat for 15 minutes. Preheat the oven to 400°F. Grease an ovenproof dish with butter. Chop the anchovies and put them with the eggs, basil and marjoram in a food processor and process to a purée. Transfer to a bowl, season with salt and add the onion and bell pepper mixture. Mix well, then spoon into the prepared dish and bake for 20 minutes. Turn out onto a warm platter and serve warm.

2 tablespoons butter, plus extra for greasing

2 tablespoons olive oil

1 onion, chopped

1 each red, yellow and green bell peppers, halved, seeded and sliced

3 potatoes, diced

2 salted anchovies, heads removed, cleaned and filleted (see page 596), soaked in cold water for 10 minutes and drained

2 eggs

1 tablespoon chopped fresh basil

1 tablespoon chopped fresh marjoram

salt

ZUCCHINI PIE

TORTINO DI ZUCCHINE

Serves 4

Preheat the oven to 400°F. Grease a roasting pan with butter. Spread out 3 tablespoons of the flour and the Parmesan in separate shallow plates. Beat 1 egg in a bowl. Dip the zucchini slices first in the flour, then in the egg and finally in the Parmesan. Heat the olive oil in a skillet. Add the zucchini slices and cook over medium heat until golden brown and crisp. Drain on paper towels and arrange on the base of the prepared roasting pan. Separate the remaining eggs. Place the butter, fontina, Swiss cheese, the remaining flour and the milk in a skillet over low heat. Melt, stirring constantly. Season with the nutmeg, salt and pepper. Remove the skillet from the heat and add the salami and egg yolks, one at a time. Whisk the egg whites until stiff, then fold into the sauce. Pour the sauce over the zucchini and bake until the top of the pie is golden brown. Serve hot.

1/4 cup butter, plus extra for greasing

5 tablespoons all-purpose flour, for dusting

3 tablespoons Parmesan cheese, freshly grated

4 eggs

4 zucchini, trimmed and sliced into rounds

4 tablespoons olive oil

5 ounces fontina cheese, diced

5 ounces Swiss cheese, diced

scant 1 cup milk

pinch of freshly grated nutmeg

scant 1 cup salami, diced

salt and pepper

121

NEST EGGS

UOVA NEL NIDO

Serves 4

2 salted anchovies, heads removed, cleaned and filleted (see page 596), soaked in water for 10 minutes and drained

6 tablespoons pine nuts

7 tablespoons olive oil

2 tablespoons butter

8 artichoke hearts

dash of tomato ketchup

dash of Worcestershire sauce

4 eggs, hard-cooked

salt and pepper

fresh flat-leaf parsley, chopped, to garnish

Place the chopped anchovy fillets in a food processor with the pine nuts, 6 tablespoons of the olive oil and the butter and process to a purée. Heat the remaining olive oil in a skillet, add the purée and artichoke hearts and cook, stirring gently, for a few minutes. Season with ketchup, Worcestershire sauce, salt and pepper and cook for 10 minutes. Meanwhile, shell the eggs and cut in half. Arrange the artichoke hearts on a serving dish, put an egg half in the middle of each heart and sprinkle with cooking juices. Garnish with the parsley.

STUFFED ZUCCHINI

ZUCCHINE RIPIENE

Serves 4

olive oil, for brushing and drizzling

4 zucchini, halved lengthwise

3½ ounces canned tuna in oil, drained and flaked

2 eggs

2 tablespoons Parmesan cheese, freshly grated

2 tablespoons bread crumbs

1 sprig fresh flat-leaf parsley, chopped

1 tablespoon white wine

salt and pepper

Preheat the oven to 350°F. Brush a roasting pan with oil. Scoop out most of the zucchini flesh with a teaspoon without piercing the 'shells'. Reserve the shells. Place the flesh in a bowl with the tuna, eggs, half the Parmesan, 1 tablespoon of the bread crumbs and the parsley and season with salt and pepper to taste. Drizzle with olive oil, mix well and spoon into the zucchini shells. Arrange the zucchini in the prepared pan and sprinkle with the remaining Parmesan, remaining bread crumbs and the wine. Bake for about 30 minutes. Serve hot or warm.

CANAPÉS

Canapés consist of square slices of bread, crusts removed, that are cut into halves or fourth or into small triangles. They may be left as they are, lightly toasted or quickly fried in butter to give extra flavor. Ingredients such as hard-cooked eggs, anchovies, cured ham and cheese are arranged on top according to taste and with careful consideration of how flavors and colors combine.

CHICKEN LIVER CANAPÉS

Melt the butter in a skillet. Add the chicken livers and cook over medium heat, stirring frequently, until browned. Sprinkle with the brandy and cook until it has evaporated. Chop the anchovy fillets, add to the skillet and season with salt, if necessary, and pepper. Stir for 1 minute, then remove the skillet from the heat. Lightly toast the bread slices on both sides, cut in half and spread with the liver mixture. Serve cold or warm.

CANAPÉ AI FEGATINI

Serves 4

¹/₄ cup butter

11 ounces chicken livers, trimmed and
coarsely chopped

¹/₂ cup brandy

3 salted anchovies, heads removed, cleaned and
filleted (see page 596)

4 white bread slices, crusts removed

salt and pepper

CHEESE CANAPÉS

CANAPÉ AL FORMAGGIO

Serves 4

3 small fresh goats' cheeses, at room temperature

3¹/₂ ounces sharp Gorgonzola cheese

4 whole-wheat bread slices

fresh chives, chopped, to garnish

Put the cheeses into a bowl and mash well with a fork. Cut the bread slices in half and spread with the cheese mixture. Sprinkle with chives to garnish and store in a cool place until ready to serve.

NIÇOISE CANAPÉS

CANAPÉ ALLA NIZZARDA

Serves 4

2 eggs, hard-cooked

4 ripe tomatoes, sliced, outer slices discarded

olive oil, for drizzling

4 white bread slices, crusts removed

butter, for spreading

salt

scant ¹/₂ cup pitted black olives, sliced

Shell the eggs, slice thinly, preferably with an egg slicer, and sprinkle with salt. Place the tomatoes in a shallow dish and drizzle with olive oil. Spread the bread with butter and cut in half. Place two slices of tomato, slightly overlapping, on each half-slice of bread and put a slice of egg between them. Garnish with the olives.

LOBSTER CANAPÉS

CANAPÉ ALL'ARAGOSTA

Serves 4

¹/₂ quantity Mayonnaise (see page 65)

1 tablespoon brandy

1–2 teaspoons tomato ketchup

4 whole-wheat bread slices, crusts removed

1 small cooked lobster tail, shelled and sliced into 8 pieces

8 small fresh thyme sprigs, to garnish

Combine the mayonnaise, brandy and ketchup in a bowl. Cut the slices of bread in half and spread with the mayonnaise mixture. Place a slice of lobster in the middle of each and garnish with a sprig of thyme.

HOT CANAPÉS WITH MOZZARELLA

CANAPÉ CALDI CON LE OVOLINE

Serves 4

4 salted anchovies, heads removed, cleaned and filleted (see page 596)

4 white bread slices, crusts removed

8 small buffalo milk mozzarella cheeses, halved

2 tomatoes, sliced

fresh flat-leaf parsley, chopped, to garnish

Preheat the oven to 425°F. Cut the slices of bread in half. Place half a mozzarella cheese and an anchovy fillet on each. Arrange tomato slices all round. Place the canapés on a cookie sheet and bake for a few minutes until the cheese has melted. Sprinkle with parsley and serve.

CANAPÉ DI AVOCADO E POMODORI

Serves 4

¹/₂ quantity Mayonnaise (see page 65)

1 tablespoon chopped fresh flat-leaf parsley

dash of Worcestershire sauce

4 white bread slices, crusts removed

¹/₂ avocado

juice of 1 lemon, strained

8 cherry tomatoes

AVOCADO AND TOMATO CANAPÉS

Combine 2 tablespoons of the mayonnaise with the parsley and Worcestershire sauce. Cut the bread in half and spread with the remaining mayonnaise. Peel, halve and pit the avocado, then cut into slices crosswise. Sprinkle with the lemon juice to prevent discoloration. Cut a cross in each tomato without cutting all the way through and open it out like a star. Put a tomato in the middle of each piece of bread and garnish with the parsley, mayonnaise and avocado.

CANAPÉ DI CAROTE

Serves 4

1 carrot

¹/₂ green apple, cored

juice of ¹/₂ lemon, strained

4 white bread slices, crusts removed

2 tablespoons chopped fresh flat-leaf parsley

2 ounces pickles, chopped

¹/₂ quantity Mayonnaise (see page 65)

CARROT CANAPÉS

Cut the carrot and apple into thin batons, combine and sprinkle with the lemon juice to prevent the apple from going brown. Cut the bread in half. Combine the parsley, pickles and mayonnaise, then spread the mixture on the bread. Place a little carrot and apple in the middle of each half-slice.

CANAPÉ DI PROSCIUTTO

Serves 4

¹/₄ cup butter

generous ¹/₂ cup lean cooked cured ham, very finely chopped

4 white bread slices, crusts removed

8 baby artichokes in oil, drained, to garnish

HAM CANAPÉS

Cream the butter, then beat in the ham. Cut the bread in half and spread with the ham mixture. Garnish by placing a baby artichoke, opened out like a small rose, in the middle of each half-slice.

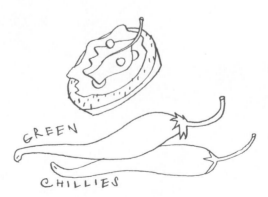

GREEN CHILLIES

CROSTINI

Crostini are synonymous with tastiness. There is an extensive choice of bases: homemade breads of all types are ideal, but you can also use baguettes, focaccia – plain and flavored – soda bread, sourdough loaves, breads made with polenta, rice, millet or buckwheat and rye bread. Chicken and game livers are the classic toppings, but you can also spread crostini with chopped meat flavored with herbs, mature cheeses and game mousses.

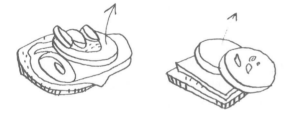

TUSCAN ANCHOVY CROSTINI

Place the anchovy fillets in the base of a dish. Squeeze out the white bread and combine with the parsley, onion, garlic, capers and chile, then beat in the olive oil and vinegar. Pour this sauce over the anchovies and let stand for a day. Just before serving, toast the rye bread, spread with butter and top with the anchovy mixture.

CROSTINI ALLA TOSCANA

Serves 4–6

7 ounces salted anchovies, heads removed, cleaned and filleted (see page 596), soaked in cold water for 10 minutes and drained

1 white bread slice, crusts removed, soaked in cold water for 10 minutes

2 tablespoons chopped fresh flat-leaf parsley

1/2 small onion, chopped

1 garlic clove, chopped

2 ounces capers, chopped

1 fresh red chile, seeded and chopped

6 tablespoons olive oil

3 tablespoons white wine vinegar

4–6 rye bread slices

butter, for spreading

CHICKEN LIVER CROSTINI

CROSTINI CON FEGATINI DI POLLO

Serves 4–6

2 tablespoons olive oil

1 carrot, chopped

$^1/_2$ onion, chopped

1 celery stalk, chopped

6 chicken livers, trimmed

3 tablespoons red wine vinegar

scant $^1/_2$ cup dry white wine

2 egg yolks

juice of 1 lemon, strained

4–6 whole-wheat bread slices, lightly toasted

salt and pepper

1 tablespoon capers, to garnish

Heat the olive oil in a skillet. Add the carrot, onion and celery and cook over low heat, stirring occasionally, for 5 minutes. Dip the chicken livers into the vinegar, pat dry with paper towels and add to skillet. Pour in the wine and season with salt and pepper. Cook, stirring frequently, until browned. Remove the chicken livers from the skillet and chop finely, then return them to the skillet and cook for 2 minutes more. Beat together the egg yolks and lemon juice in a bowl. Remove the skillet from the heat and stir in the egg yolk mixture. Spread on slices of lightly toasted bread and garnish with the capers. Serve immediately.

CHICKEN LIVER AND PROSCIUTTO CROSTINI

CROSTINI CON FEGATINI DI POLLO E PROSCIUTTO

Serves 4–6

3 tablespoons olive oil

3 tablespoons butter

$4^1/_2$ ounces prosciutto

1 onion, chopped

about 6 tablespoons warm milk or Meat Stock (see page 208)

5 ounces chicken livers, trimmed and chopped

2 fresh sage leaves

4–6 country-style bread slices, lightly toasted

8 fresh rosemary sprigs

Heat the olive oil and half the butter in a pan. Add the prosciutto and onion and cook over very low heat, stirring occasionally, for 30 minutes, gradually adding the milk or stock to keep the mixture moist. Add the chicken livers and sage leaves and bring to a boil. Boil for 3 minutes, stirring constantly. Remove the pan from the heat, grind the mixture with a meat grinder or in a food processor and return to the pan. Bring to a boil, adding a little more milk or stock if necessary. Stir in the remaining butter and cook for 3 minutes more. Cut the toasted bread in half and spread with the liver mixture. Arrange crisscross sprigs of rosemary on the base of a serving dish and lay the crostini on top.

MUSHROOM AND CAPER CROSTINI

CROSTINI CON FUNGHI E CAPPERI

Serves 4–6

3 tablespoons olive oil

scant $4^1/_2$ cups porcini mushrooms, chopped

$1^1/_2$ teaspoons chopped fresh marjoram

1 garlic clove, chopped

about 6 tablespoons Meat Stock (see page 208)

1 tablespoon capers

1 tablespoon chopped fresh flat-leaf parsley

1 loaf of country-style bread, sliced and lightly toasted • salt and pepper

Heat the oil in a skillet. Add the mushrooms, marjoram and garlic and cook, stirring frequently, over medium heat for 20 minutes, gradually adding the stock. Add the capers and parsley and season with salt and pepper. Increase the heat and boil off the liquid. Spread the mixture on slices of lightly toasted bread and serve.

CROSTINI WITH MUSHROOMS IN A LIGHT SAUCE

CROSTINI CON FUNGHI IN GUAZZETTO

Serves 4–6

2 garlic cloves

2 tablespoons olive oil

2 Italian sausages, chopped

1 tablespoon chopped fresh flat-leaf parsley

scant 1 cup dry white wine

scant 4$\frac{1}{2}$ cups mixed wild and cultivated mushrooms, coarsely chopped

5 ounces tomatoes, peeled and chopped

about 6 tablespoons Meat Stock (see page 208)

4–6 Tuscan or whole-wheat bread slices, toasted

salt and pepper

fresh mint leaves, to garnish

Chop one garlic clove. Heat the oil in a skillet. Add the sausages, chopped garlic and parsley and cook over low heat, stirring occasionally, for 5 minutes. Pour in the wine and cook until evaporated. Add the mush-rooms and cook for a few minutes, then add the tomatoes. Cook, gradually adding the stock, until cooked through and tender. Season with salt and pepper to taste. Lightly toast the bread on both sides. Rub with the remaining garlic and spread the mushroom mixture on top. Garnish with the mint leaves and serve immediately.

GRAPEFRUIT CROSTINI

CROSTINI CON POMPELMO

Serves 4–6

1 tablespoon butter, plus extra for greasing

juice of 2 grapefruit, strained

1 tablespoon Swiss cheese, grated

5 ounces mild Gouda cheese, grated

2 tablespoons heavy cream

1 egg yolk, lightly beaten

4–6 white bread slices, crusts removed

salt and pepper

Preheat the oven to 350°F. Grease a cookie sheet with butter. Pour the grapefruit juice into a small pan and add the butter, and cheeses. Sprinkle with salt and pepper. Stir in the cream and cook over low heat, stirring constantly, for 10 minutes. Remove the pan from the heat and stir in the egg yolk. Return to the heat and cook, stirring until smooth; do not let the mixture boil. Spread the slices of bread with the mixture and place on the prepared cookie sheet. Bake for a few minutes until lightly browned. Serve hot.

SAUSAGE CROSTINI

CROSTINI CON SALSICCIA

Serves 4–6

3 Italian sausages, skinned

5 ounces stracchino cheese, such as taleggio or robiola, crumbled

1 tablespoon fennel seeds

4–6 country-style bread slices

salt

Preheat the oven to 350°F. Crumble the sausages into a bowl and mix in the cheese and fennel seeds. Season with salt to taste and stir well. Spread the mixture on the slices of bread, place on a cookie sheet and bake for 15 minutes. Arrange on a platter and serve immediately while still very hot.

CROSTINI IN AGRODOLCE

Serves 4–6

generous 1/3 cup golden raisins, soaked in
hot water for 10 minutes and drained

1/2 cup capers, coarsely chopped

1/4 cup pine nuts, coarsely chopped

1/3 cup prosciutto, finely chopped

2 tablespoons butter

1 teaspoon sugar

1 1/2 teaspoons all-purpose flour

juice of 1 small orange, strained

3 tablespoons white wine vinegar

1 baguette, sliced diagonally

salt and pepper

SWEET–AND–SOUR CROSTINI

Coarsely chop the raisins. Combine the raisins, capers, pine nuts and prosciutto in a bowl. Put the butter, sugar and flour in a small pan and stir over low heat. When the mixture starts to froth, pour in the orange juice and vinegar and cook for a few minutes more. Pour the sauce over the prosciutto mixture, season with salt and pepper to taste and mix gently. Lightly toast the bread on both sides and spread with plenty of the prosciutto mixture. Arrange on a serving dish and serve warm. These crostini are also good served cold. They have an unusual flavor, but are really worth tasting.

CROSTINI MARINARI

Serves 6

9 ounces small squid, cleaned

9 ounces cooked shrimp, peeled and deveined

1 egg, lightly beaten

1 garlic clove, chopped

1 sprig fresh flat-leaf parsley, chopped

2 tablespoons fresh bread crumbs

olive oil, for drizzling

1 baguette, sliced diagonally

salt and pepper

SEAFOOD CROSTINI

Preheat the oven to 350°F. Coarsely chop the squid and shrimp and place in a bowl. Mix in the egg, garlic, parsley and bread crumbs. Drizzle with olive oil and season with salt and pepper. Thickly spread the mixture on the slices of bread, place on a cookie sheet and bake for 15 minutes. Serve immediately.

CROSTINI MONTANARI CON SPECK E CREMA DI MELE

Serves 6

2-inch piece of horseradish, grated

1 green apple, peeled, cored and chopped

juice of 1/2 lemon, strained

scant 1/2 cup low-fat plain yogurt

scant 1/2 cup heavy cream

1 baguette, sliced diagonally

7 ounces speck or smoked ham, sliced

salt and pepper

MOUNTAIN CROSTINI WITH SPECK AND APPLE CREAM

Combine the horseradish and apple in a bowl and sprinkle with the lemon juice. Stir in the yogurt, then add the cream and season with salt and pepper to taste. Spread the mixture on the slices of bread, top with a slice of speck or ham and serve.

TARTINES

Tartines are always served cold and must have a distinctive flavor. They are closely related to ordinary canapés and crostini (which are also served hot), so it's worth following a few rules to distinguish them. First, tartines must be small and not overloaded. As far as shape is concerned, you can let your imagination run riot: stars, hearts, ovals, diamonds, squares or small triangles. You can use almost any kind of bread, apart from rye bread, which would crumble. For all kinds of bread, the crusts must be removed. The surface of the bread should almost always be lightly buttered to prevent the tartines from becoming soggy. Remove the butter from the refrigerator at least 1 hour before using so that it is easy to spread. Tartines prepared in advance may be stored, covered with foil.

SHRIMP BUTTER TARTINES

Reserve eight shrimp and chop the remainder. Cream the butter in a bowl, then beat in the chopped shrimp, parsley, marjoram and basil and season with salt and pepper. Spread the mixture on the squares of bread and place on a serving dish. Garnish each one with a whole shrimp, a small leaf of arugula and a few capers.

TARTINE AL BURRO DI GAMBERETTI

Serves 4

14 ounces cooked shrimp, peeled and deveined

scant 1 cup butter, at room temperature

1 tablespoon chopped fresh flat-leaf parsley

2 teaspoons chopped fresh marjoram

4 fresh basil leaves, chopped

2 white bread slices, crusts removed,

cut into small squares

salt and pepper

small arugula leaves, to garnish

capers

CAVIAR TARTINES

TARTINE AL CAVIALE

Serves 4

2 lemons, sliced

5 teaspoons vodka

3–4 tablespoons butter, at room temperature

pinch of paprika

4–6 white bread slices

scant 1 cup caviar

salt

Place the lemon slices in a soup plate and sprinkle with the vodka. Beat the butter with the paprika and a pinch of salt in a bowl. Stamp out rounds from the slices of bread using a cookie cutter or glass and spread with the paprika butter. Place a slice of drained lemon on each with a teaspoonful of caviar on top.

CUCUMBER TARTINES

TARTINE AL CETRIOLO

Serves 4

2 cucumbers, peeled

¹/₄ cup cream cheese

dash of lemon juice, strained

1 teaspoon chopped fresh flat-leaf parsley

¹/₂ whole-wheat loaf, cut diagonally and crusts removed

salt and pepper

Halve one cucumber lengthwise, then cut into very thin semicircular slices. Place in a colander, sprinkle with salt and let drain. Chop the other cucumber and stir it into the cream cheese. Add a dash of lemon juice and the parsley and season with salt and pepper. Cut the slices of bread into squares and spread with the mixture. Arrange the cucumber slices on top as if they were fish scales. Serve cold.

WATERCRESS TARTINES

TARTINE AL CRESCIONE

Serves 4

4 eggs, hard-cooked

4 tablespoons Mayonnaise (see page 65)

juice of 1 lemon, strained

1 bunch of watercress or arugula, coarsely chopped

4–8 white bread slices, crusts removed

salt and pepper

Shell and chop the eggs, then combine with the mayonnaise and lemon juice. Season with salt and pepper and stir in the watercress or arugula. Cut the slices of bread in half and spread with the mixture. Chill in the refrigerator until ready to serve.

CHEESE AND BRANDY TARTINES

TARTINE AL FORMAGGIO E BRANDY

Serves 4

7 ounces robiola cheese, crumbled

scant ¹/₂ cup brandy

5 walnuts, chopped

1 tablespoon pine nuts, finely chopped

4–8 white bread slices

pepper

walnut halves, to garnish

Cream the cheese in a bowl, then beat in the brandy, walnuts and pine nuts and season with pepper. Stamp out rounds from the bread using a cookie cutter or glass and spread with the cheese mixture. Garnish each round with a walnut half. The robiola may be replaced with Gorgonzola or Roquefort.

RUSTIC TARTINES

Cream the cheeses in a bowl, then beat in the olives, chiles and tuna. Season with salt to taste. Stamp out rounds from the slices of bread using a cookie cutter or glass and spread with the mixture. Garnish with the pickled pearl onions.

TARTINE ALLA CAMPAGNOLA

Serves 4

5 small fresh goat cheeses

12 green olives, pitted and sliced

4 pickled chiles, seeded and chopped

about 2 ounces canned tuna in oil,

drained and flaked

4–8 white bread slices

salt

pickled pearl onions, to garnish

GRAPPA AND PEAR TARTINES

Beat the mascarpone with the farmer's cheese in a bowl, then beat in the grappa. Peel, halve, core and cut the pear into wedges. Cut each quarter in half and sprinkle with the lemon juice. Cut each slice of fontina into four triangles. Spread the bread with the mascarpone mixture and top each with a wedge of pear and a triangle of fontina.

TARTINE ALLA GRAPPA CON LE PERE

Serves 4

scant 1 cup mascarpone cheese

scant 1 cup farmer's cheese

1 tablespoon grappa

1 pear

juice of $1/2$ lemon, strained

2 slices fontina cheese

2–4 white bread slices,

crusts removed, cut into squares

PIZZAIOLA TARTINES

Sprinkle the insides of the tomatoes with salt and place upside down on paper towels to drain for 5 minutes, then chop. Combine the tomatoes, scallions, olives and parsley in a bowl, season with salt and pepper and drizzle with olive oil. Stir well to mix. Stamp out rounds from the bread with a cookie cutter or glass and toast lightly on both sides. Spread the toast with butter and then with the tomato mixture. Top with a slice of mozzarella and sprinkle with oregano.

TARTINE ALLA PIZZAIOLA

Serves 4

2 firm ripe tomatoes, halved and seeded

2 scallions, chopped

6 green olives, pitted and chopped

1 tablespoon very finely chopped

fresh flat-leaf parsley

olive oil, for drizzling

4–6 white bread slices

3–4 tablespoons butter, at room temperature

1 buffalo milk mozzarella, thinly sliced

salt and pepper

fresh oregano, chopped, to garnish

AVOCADO TARTINES

Peel, halve and pit the avocados, then chop the flesh. Place in a food processor with the cream cheese, lemon flesh and juice, Worcestershire sauce and chives and season with salt and pepper. Process until smooth. Spread the bread with the avocado mixture and top each piece with a tomato half. Garnish with the basil leaves.

TARTINE ALL'AVOCADO

Serves 4

2 avocados

$^2/_3$ cup cream cheese

$^1/_2$ lemon, peeled and chopped

juice of $^1/_2$ lemon, strained

dash of Worcestershire sauce

1 tablespoon chopped fresh chives

4–6 white bread slices,

crusts removed, cut into squares

10 cherry tomatoes, halved

salt and pepper

fresh basil leaves, to garnish

ROQUEFORT TARTINES

Beat the cheeses together in a bowl with a fork. Beat in the cream, season with salt and pepper and beat with a small whisk until soft and creamy. Cut the slices of the bread in half and spread with the cream cheese mixture. Garnish each piece with one white grape and one black grape.

TARTINE AL ROQUEFORT

Serves 4

3$^1/_2$ ounces Roquefort cheese, crumbled

scant $^1/_2$ cup cream cheese

2 tablespoons heavy cream

4–6 whole-wheat bread slices, crusts removed

salt and pepper

white and black grapes, to garnish

TUNA TARTINES

Shell and coarsely chop the egg. Place the tuna, capers and onions in a food processor and process to a purée. Cream the butter in a bowl. Push the hard-cooked egg through a strainer into the bowl and beat in with the tuna purée. Beat in lemon juice to taste, season with salt and drizzle with olive oil. Beat well until combined. Cut the slices of bread in half and spread with the mixture using a damp knife or metal spatula. Garnish each tartine with olive rings and a few strips of pickled bell pepper.

TARTINE AL TONNO

Serves 4

1 egg, hard-cooked

3 ounces canned tuna in oil, drained and flaked

1$^1/_2$ teaspoons capers

$^1/_4$ cup pickled pearl onions, drained

2 tablespoons butter, at room temperature

juice of 1 lemon, strained

olive oil, for drizzling

4–6 white bread slices, crusts removed

salt

To garnish

3 ounces green olives, pitted and sliced

1 pickled bell pepper, cut into strips

TWO—COLOR OMELET TARTINES

TARTINE BICOLORE DI FRITTATINE

Serves 4

2 eggs

3 fresh chives, finely chopped

1 sprig fresh flat-leaf parsley, finely chopped

1 tablespoon olive oil

4–8 white bread slices, crusts removed

black olive paste, for spreading

salt and pepper

Beat the eggs with the chives and parsley in a bowl and season with salt and pepper. Heat a little of the olive oil in a small omelet pan. Pour in one-third of the egg mixture, tilt the pan to coat and cook over medium heat until the underside is set and the omelet is crisp. Slide out onto a plate and make two more omelets in the same way. Cut into ¼-inch wide strips. Lightly spread the bread with olive paste and place strips of omelet diagonally on top.

ANCHOVY AND EGG SAUCE TARTINES

TARTINE CON ACCIUGHE IN SALSA

Serves 4

1 egg, hard-cooked

1 tablespoon white wine vinegar

2 tablespoons olive oil

2 tablespoons chopped fresh flat-leaf parsley

2–4 white bread slices, crusts removed

2 ounces canned anchovy fillets, drained

salt and pepper

pickled pearl onions, halved, to garnish

Shell and halve the egg, then scoop the yolk out into a bowl. Stir in the vinegar, olive oil and parsley and season with salt and pepper. Cut the slices of bread into triangles and toast lightly on both sides. Spread with a little of the egg mixture, arrange two anchovy fillets on top and garnish with the pickled pearl onion halves.

CRAB AND APPLE TARTINES

TARTINE DI GRANCHIO ALLE MELE

Serves 4

4 ounces canned crabmeat, drained

2 tablespoons Mayonnaise (see page 65)

1 green apple

juice of 1 lemon, strained

4–6 white bread slices, crusts removed

1 tablespoon chopped fresh flat-leaf parsley

salt and pepper

Flake the crabmeat in a bowl with a fork, then stir in the mayonnaise and season with salt and pepper. Peel, core and finely dice the apple and sprinkle with a little of the lemon juice. Add the apple to the crabmeat and stir in the remaining lemon juice. Cut the slices of bread in half and spread with the crab mixture. Sprinkle with the parsley. Store in the refrigerator until ready to serve.

JELLIED TONGUE TARTINES

TARTINE GELATINATE ALLA LINGUA

Serves 4

1 envelope (about ⅓ ounce) powdered gelatin

or ⅛ ounce leaf gelatin

4 dill pickles, drained

1 small round loaf, thinly sliced and crusts removed

7 ounces foie gras pâté

16 slices cooked pickled tongue

Prepare the gelatin according to the instructions on the packet and let cool. Slice each dill pickle lengthwise into four. Spread the bread with plenty of foie gras pâté, place a small slice of tongue on top of each piece and garnish with a dill pickle slice. Dip a pastry brush in the gelatin and gently brush the tartines with several layers until evenly coated. Chill in the refrigerator for 2 hours until set.

JELLIED MUSTARD TARTINES

Prepare the gelatin according to the instructions on the packet and let cool. Shell and slice the eggs, preferably with an egg slicer. Cut the slices of bread in half. Cream the butter in a bowl, then beat in the mustard. Spread each half-slice with the mustard cream, place a slice of egg on top and arrange two anchovy fillets on opposite sides. Dip a pastry brush in the gelatin and gently brush the tartines with several layers. Chill in the refrigerator for 2 hours until set.

TARTINE GELATINATE ALLA SENAPE

Serves 4

1 envelope (about $1/3$ ounce) powdered gelatin
or $1/8$ ounce leaf gelatin

3 eggs, hard-cooked

8 whole-wheat bread slices, crusts removed

6 tablespoons butter, at room temperature

2 tablespoons Dijon mustard

32 canned anchovy fillets, drained

JELLIED RUSSIAN SALAD TARTINES

Prepare the gelatin according to the instructions on the packet and let cool. Shell and slice the eggs, preferably with an egg slicer. Lightly butter the slices of bread and spread with a layer of Russian salad. Place a slice of egg on top and put a shrimp in the middle. Dip a pastry brush in the gelatin and gently brush several layers over the tartines. Chill in the refrigerator for 2 hours until set.

TARTINE GELATINATE
ALL'INSALATA RUSSA

Serves 4

1 envelope (about $1/3$ ounce) powdered gelatin
or $1/8$ ounce leaf gelatin

3 eggs, hard-cooked

6 tablespoons butter, at room temperature

16 slices whole-wheat bread

11 ounces Russian Salad (see page 116)

16 cooked shrimp, peeled and deveined

BARQUETTES AND TARTLETS

APPETIZERS

When you are serving aperitifs or cocktails, these delightful, little morsels – mostly served hot – are the perfect accompaniment. Their delicious, mellow flavor comes from their pastry shells, which contain varying amounts of butter and hold the filling. They are made from pâte brisée, which is used to line boat-shaped pans for barquettes, and round pans in the case of tartlets. They are baked, left to cool, then filled in a variety ways just before serving so that the pastry does not become soggy. Unfilled barquettes and tartlets may be stored in bags in the freezer. Thaw at room temperature before use.

PÂTE BRISÉE

PASTA BRISÉE

Makes 35–50 barquettes or tartlets

2¼ cups all-purpose flour, plus extra for dusting

¾ cup butter, softened and diced

1 egg, lightly beaten

salt

Sift the flour and a pinch of salt into a mound on the counter and add the diced butter. Rub in the butter with your fingertips until the mixture resembles bread crumbs. Shape into a mound, make a well in the center and pour in the beaten egg and 2 tablespoons water. Knead lightly by hand (your hands should be cold – if necessary hold them under cold running water) or using a metal spatula. Wrap the pastry in plastic wrap, flatten gently with a rolling pin and chill in the refrigerator for 1 hour. Preheat the oven to 350°F. Divide the pastry into several pieces, roll out on a lightly floured surface and use to line boat-shaped, oval or round tartlet tins. Line with baking parchment or wax paper and fill with baking beans. Bake for 15–20 minutes. Remove the pans from the oven, remove the beans and parchment or paper and let cool before filling. The quantity of pastry given here is also enough for two 9-inch round pies. Halve or double the quantity according to your requirements.

SHRIMP BARQUETTES

Put the onion, celery, carrot and parsley in a pan, pour in water to cover, bring to a boil and add a pinch of salt. Add the shrimp and cook for 3–4 minutes, then drain, reserving the cooking liquid. Return the cooking liquid to the pan, add the potatoes and cook for 10–15 minutes until tender. Drain and mash with 2 tablespoons of the butter and as much hot milk as required. Heat the remaining butter in a small pan, add the tomatoes and cook over low heat for 3–4 minutes until tender. Remove the pan from the heat and season to taste with salt. Peel and devein the shrimp. To serve, divide the mashed potato among the pastry shells and arrange the shrimp and tomatoes on top. Heat in a preheated oven, 400°F, for a few minutes before serving.

BARCHETTE AI GAMBERETTI

Makes 35–50 barquettes

^{1}/$_4$ onion

1 celery stalk

1 carrot

1 fresh flat-leaf parsley sprig

35–50 raw small shrimp

3 potatoes, diced

3 tablespoons butter

about ^{2}/$_3$ cup hot milk

2 tomatoes, diced

35–50 Pâte Brisée barquette shells (see opposite)

salt

FOUR–CHEESE BARQUETTES

Cook the pasta in salted, boiling water for 8–10 minutes until al dente. Drain and stir in the butter and all the cheeses. To serve, fill the pastry shells with a little of the pasta mixture and cover with 1–2 tablespoons of the béchamel sauce. Place on a cookie sheet and bake in a preheated oven, 400°F, until golden and bubbling.

BARCHETTE AI QUATTRO FORMAGGI

Makes 35–50 barquettes

1^1/$_4$ cups ditalini pasta

^{1}/$_4$ cup butter

^{1}/$_2$ cup fontina cheese, grated

^{1}/$_2$ cup Emmenthal cheese, grated

^{1}/$_2$ cup caciotta cheese, grated

^{1}/$_2$ cup mozzarella cheese, finely chopped

35–50 Pâte Brisée barquette shells (see opposite)

1 quantity Béchamel Sauce (see page 50)

salt

ANCHOVY BARQUETTES

Heat the oil in a small pan. Add the garlic and onion and cook over low heat, stirring occasionally, for 5 minutes until softened. Stir in the tomato paste, cook for a few minutes more and then remove from the heat. Stir in the capers and anchovies. To serve, fill the pastry shells with the mixture and garnish with the olives.

BARCHETTE DI ACCIUGHE

Makes 35–50 barquettes

1 tablespoon olive oil

1 garlic clove, finely chopped

1 onion, finely chopped

2 tablespoons concentrated tomato paste

2 tablespoons capers

6 canned anchovy fillets, drained and chopped

35–50 Pâte Brisée barquette shells (see opposite)

pitted black olives, cut into fourths, to garnish

CRAB BARQUETTES

Melt the butter in a skillet. Add the pancetta and onion and cook over low heat, stirring occasionally, until the onion is soft. Remove the pan from the heat. Beat the eggs with the Parmesan and cream in a bowl and season with salt and pepper. Stir the crabmeat, pancetta, and onion, into the egg mixture. To serve, spoon the mixture into the pastry shells. Place on a cookie sheet and bake in a preheated oven, 400°F, for about 10 minutes or until the filling has set.

BARCHETTE DI POLPA DI GRANCHIO

Makes 35–50 barquettes

2 tablespoons butter

1 ounce pancetta, diced

1/2 onion, finely chopped

2 eggs

1 ounce Parmesan cheese, freshly grated

2 tablespoons heavy cream

3 1/2 ounces white crabmeat, drained if canned

35–50 Pâte Brisée barquette shells (see page 140)

salt and pepper

CHEESE TARTLETS

Melt the butter in a pan. Add the leek and cook over low heat, stirring occasionally, for about 5 minutes until softened. Add the baby peas, season with salt and pepper and cook, stirring occasionally, for about 20 minutes. Beat the eggs with the milk, nutmeg and a pinch of salt in a bowl. To serve, spoon the leek and baby peas mixture into the pastry shells, cover with 1 tablespoon of the egg mixture and top with a few cubes of Roquefort. Place on a cookie sheet and bake in a preheated oven, 400°F, for about 10 minutes.

TARTELETTE AL FORMAGGIO

Makes 35–50 tartlets

2 tablespoons butter

1 leek, trimmed and thinly sliced

1 1/4 cups shelled baby peas

2 eggs

scant 1/2 cup milk

pinch of freshly grated nutmeg

7 ounces Roquefort cheese, diced

35–50 Pâte Brisée tartlet shells (see page 140)

salt and pepper

GORGONZOLA TARTLETS

Beat together the mascarpone and Gorgonzola in a bowl, then stir in the parsley and season with salt and pepper. To serve, spoon the cheese mixture into a pastry bag fitted with a star tip and fill the pastry shells with the mixture. Garnish each tartlet with a walnut half and a pistachio.

TARTELETTE AL GORGONZOLA

Makes 35–50 tartlets

scant 1 cup mascarpone cheese

3 1/2 ounces Gorgonzola cheese

1 tablespoon chopped fresh flat-leaf parsley

35–50 Pâte Brisée tartlet shells (see page 140)

salt and pepper

To garnish

walnut halves

pistachios

Makes 35–50 tartlets

25 cherry tomatoes, halved and seeded

2 ripe avocados

1 teaspoon lemon juice, strained

1 1/4 cups farmer's cheese

2 tablespoons heavy cream

35–50 Pâte Brisée tartlet shells (see page 140)

salt and pepper

35–50 fresh basil leaves

AVOCADO TARTLETS

Sprinkle the insides of the tomatoes with salt and place upside down on paper towels to drain. Peel, halve and pit the avocados. Chop the flesh, place in a food processor with the lemon juice and process to a purée. Beat together the farmer's cheese and cream in a bowl, then stir in the avocado purée and season with salt and pepper to taste. To serve, fill the pastry shells with the avocado mixture. Top each with a tomato half and garnish with a basil leaf.

Makes 35–50 tartlets

11 ounces skinless, boneless chicken breasts

2 eggs, hard-cooked

2 tablespoons Mayonnaise (see page 65)

1 tablespoon heavy cream, whipped

35–50 Pâte Brisée tartlet shells (see page 140)

salt

cornichons or small dill pickles, drained and thinly sliced, to garnish

CHICKEN TARTLETS

Place the chicken breasts in a pan, add water to cover and bring to a boil. Lower the heat, cover and simmer gently for about 20 minutes until cooked through. Drain and let cool, then chop coarsely and grind with a meat grinder or in a food processor. Shell and halve the eggs, then scoop out the yolks and mix with the chicken. Stir in the mayonnaise and cream and season with salt to taste. To serve, fill the pastry shells with the chicken mixture and garnish with the cornichons or dill pickles.

SAVORY PUFFS

The puffs made according to the recipe for Savory Puff Batter on page 1011 may also be filled with cream cheese, fish, vegetables, etc. If more flavor is required, you can also add a pinch of salt or pepper or even 2 tablespoons grated cheese.
It is best to keep the puffs small so that they are easier to eat at cocktail parties or stand-up buffets. Puffs are always served warm or hot and arranged on serving dishes in concentric circles or piled up in pyramids. If they are to accompany aperitifs, allow four per person. If they are large, two is sufficient.

BIGNÉ AI FUNGHI

Serves 4

2 tablespoons butter

1 tablespoon olive oil

scant 4$^1/_2$ cups mushrooms, coarsely chopped

$^3/_4$ cup heavy cream

$^1/_2$ cup Emmenthal cheese, grated

8 large puffs (see page 1011)

salt and pepper

MUSHROOM PUFFS

Heat the butter and oil in a skillet. Add the mushrooms and cook for about 7 minutes until tender. Stir in the cream and grated cheese, season with salt and pepper and remove the skillet from the heat. Make a slit in the top of each puff and stuff with plenty of the mushroom mixture. Place on a cookie sheet and bake in a preheated oven, 400°F, for a few minutes to warm through, then serve.

BIGNÉ ALLA CREMA DI FORMAGGIO

Serves 4

$^2/_3$ cup heavy cream

3$^1/_2$ ounces Gorgonzola cheese, diced

3$^1/_2$ ounces fontina cheese, diced

3$^1/_2$ ounces provolone cheese, diced

1 tablespoon chopped celery leaves

pinch of freshly grated nutmeg

16 small puffs (see page 1011)

salt and white pepper

CREAMY CHEESE PUFFS

Divide the cream equally among three pans. Add the Gorgonzola to one pan, the fontina to another and the provolone to the third. In turn, melt the cheeses into the cream over low heat, stirring constantly. Season with salt before removing each pan from the heat. Stir the celery leaves into the Gorgonzola mixture, a pinch of white pepper into the fontina and the nutmeg into the provolone mixture. Make a slit in the puffs and fill with the three cheese mixtures. Serve piled into a pyramid.

SALMON PUFFS

BIGNÉ AL SALMONE

Serves 4

1 quantity Béchamel Sauce (see page 50)

pinch of freshly grated nutmeg

3 tablespoons heavy cream

1$\frac{1}{3}$ cups ricotta cheese

3 ounces smoked salmon, chopped

1 tablespoon chopped fresh flat-leaf parsley

8 large puffs (see page 1011)

4 tablespoons Parmesan cheese, freshly grated

salt and pepper

Preheat the oven to 400°F. Season the béchamel sauce with a little nutmeg. Beat together the cream and ricotta in a bowl, stir in the salmon and parsley and season with salt and pepper. Spoon the mixture into a piping bag. Make a slit in the puffs and fill with the salmon mixture. Place the filled puffs in an ovenproof dish, sprinkle with the Parmesan and spoon the béchamel sauce over them. Bake for 10 minutes and serve.

BACON FRITTERS

FRITTELLE AL BACON

Serves 4

2 tablespoons butter

3 bacon slices

1$\frac{1}{2}$ teaspoons chopped fresh flat-leaf parsley

$\frac{1}{2}$–1 teaspoon Dijon mustard

1 quantity Savory Puff Batter (see page 1011)

vegetable oil, for deep-frying

pepper

Melt the butter in a skillet. Add the bacon slices and cook until crisp. Remove from the pan and chop. Mix the bacon with the parsley, a pinch of pepper and mustard to taste in a bowl. Stir the bacon mixture into the batter, then shape into small balls. Heat the vegetable oil to 350–375°F or until a cube of day-old bread browns in 30 seconds. Add the paste balls and deep-fry for a few minutes until puffed up and golden brown. Drain on paper towels and serve hot.

TOMATO FRITTERS

SGONFIOTTI DI POMODORI

Serves 4

20 cherry tomatoes

1 mozzarella cheese, diced

8 fresh basil leaves, chopped

2 anchovy fillets in oil, drained and chopped

vegetable oil, for deep-frying

1 quantity Savory Puff Batter (see page 1011)

salt

Slice off the tops (stalk end) of the tomatoes with a small sharp knife and remove the seeds. Sprinkle the insides with salt and place upside down on paper towels to drain. Meanwhile, combine the mozzarella, basil and anchovies in a bowl. Heat the vegetable oil to 350–375° or until a cube of day-old bread browns in 30 seconds. Fill the tomatoes with the cheese mixture, then dip them, one at a time, in the batter. Deep-fry in the hot oil until puffed up and golden brown. Drain on paper towels and serve hot.

BOUCHÉES
AND PUFF PASTRY

These small puff or rough puff pastry shells containing a variety of fillings are among the most delectable antipasti. (They make great desserts too.) They can be shaped like tartlets, bowls or simple rectangles, but the classic shape is the patty shell, which the French make very small and call bouchées since they may be eaten in a single bite. The extremely light pastry is a little difficult and time consuming to make and ready-made pastry is almost always used. There are some excellent brands of frozen pastry and they are all sufficiently light. Bouchées and puffs are almost always served hot so that the pastry, which is based on butter, and the filling melt in the mouth. Therefore, keep them warm in a low oven until ready to serve.

RICOTTA MORSELS

Mix the ham with 1 tablespoon of the ricotta in a bowl and set aside. Make a soft Pâte Brisée (see page 140) with the remaining ricotta, the butter, flour and a pinch of salt, and let stand for 1 hour. Preheat the oven to 350°F. Line a cookie sheet with baking parchment. Roll out the dough on a lightly floured counter into a fairly thin sheet. Stamp out rounds using a cookie cutter or a glass. Spoon a little of the ham mixture in the middle of each round, fold in half and crimp the edges to seal. Brush with the egg yolk and place on the prepared cookie sheet. Bake for 20 minutes. Serve warm or cold. These morsels have a subtle flavor and are ideal as elegant appetizers.

BOCCONCINI DI RICOTTA

Serves 6

3 1/2 ounces cooked cured ham, chopped

scant 1 cup ricotta cheese

7 tablespoons butter

generous 3/4 cup all-purpose flour,

plus extra for dusting

1 egg yolk, lightly beaten

salt

COUNTRY BOUCHÉES

BOCCONCINI RUSTICI

Serves 6

1 tablespoons butter

12 ounces chicken livers, trimmed and coarsely chopped • 3 fresh sage leaves

1 fresh marjoram sprig, leaves only

2 tablespoons all-purpose flour, plus extra for dusting

2 tablespoons Marsala • scant ¹/₂ cup heavy cream

9 ounces ready-made puff pastry dough, thawed if frozen

18 ready-to-eat prunes • 1 egg yolk, lightly beaten

salt and pepper

Melt the butter in a skillet. Add the chicken livers, sage and marjoram and cook over medium heat, stirring frequently, for a few minutes until lightly browned. Sprinkle in the flour and stir well. Pour in the Marsala and cook until it has evaporated. Lower the heat, stir in the cream, season with salt and pepper and cook, stirring occasionally, for about 10 minutes. Preheat the oven to 400°F. Meanwhile, roll out the pastry on a lightly floured surface and cut into 18 squares. Place a little of the chicken liver mixture in the middle of each square and top with a prune. Brush the sides of the squares with egg yolk, fold over and press to seal. Place on a cookie sheet and bake for about 20 minutes until golden brown, then serve.

PARISIAN BRIOCHES

BRIOCHES ALLA PARIGINA

Serves 6

¹/₂ cup butter • 5 ounces smoked pancetta, diced

5 ounces cooked cured ham, diced

5 ounces Swiss cheese, diced

4 würstel or frankfurters, chopped

1¹/₄ cups heavy cream

¹/₄ cup brandy • 18 small brioches

salt and pepper

Preheat the oven to 350°F. Melt the butter in a pan, add the pancetta, ham, Swiss cheese and sausages and mix well. Add the cream and brandy and cook, stirring frequently, until the mixture has thickened. Remove the pan from the heat and season to taste. Slice the brioches horizontally just over halfway up and set the tops aside. Carefully pull out some of the soft crumb and fill the hollows with the pancetta mixture. Replace the tops. Arrange the brioches on a cookie sheet and bake for about 10 minutes. Serve warm.

COUNTRY BONBONS

CARAMELLE RUSTICHE

Serves 6–8

¹/₂ cup bread crumbs

4 tablespoons milk

2 tablespoons butter

11 ounces ground meat, such as beef or veal

5 ounces mortadella, finely chopped

1 tablespoon chopped fresh flat-leaf parsley

¹/₂ cup Parmesan cheese, freshly grated

2 eggs, lightly beaten

9 ounces ready-made puff pastry dough, thawed if frozen

all-purpose flour, for dusting

1 egg yolk

salt and pepper

Preheat the oven to 400°F. Line a cookie sheet with baking parchment. Put the bread crumbs in a bowl, add 3 tablespoons of the milk and let soak. Melt the butter in a skillet. Add the meat and cook over medium heat, stirring frequently, for about 5 minutes until lightly browned. Remove from the heat and tip into a bowl. Squeeze out the bread crumbs and add to the bowl with the mortadella, parsley and Parmesan. Stir in the beaten eggs and season with salt and pepper. When everything is thoroughly combined, shape the mixture into 30 small balls. Roll out the pastry on a lightly floured surface to a fairly thin sheet and cut out 30 squares with a fluted pastry wheel. Place a ball of the meat mixture in the middle of each square, then roll up and twist the ends like a candy wrapper. Lightly beat the egg yolk with the remaining milk, then brush over the bonbons. Place on the prepared cookie sheet and bake for about 20 minutes.

RADICCHIO BUNDLES

Preheat the oven to 400°F. Grease a cookie sheet with butter. Melt the butter in a pan. Add the radicchio and cook over low heat, stirring occasionally, for a few minutes until soft. Season with salt and pepper and remove from the heat. Roll out the pastry on a lightly floured surface into a thin sheet and stamp out rounds with a cookie cutter or a glass. Put a little radicchio in the middle of each round and place two slices of cheese and one slice of truffle on top. Brush the edges of the pastry with egg yolk and gather into bundles. Brush with egg yolk, place on the prepared cookie sheet and bake for about 10 minutes until golden brown.

FAGOTTINI DI RADICCHIO

Serves 6

2 tablespoons butter, plus extra for greasing

2 heads of radicchio, coarsely chopped

9 ounces ready-made puff

pastry dough, thawed if frozen

all-purpose flour, for dusting

3 ounces quartirolo or taleggio cheese, thinly sliced

1 small white truffle, thinly sliced

1 egg yolk, lightly beaten

salt and pepper

SMALL CHEESE CRACKERS

Preheat the oven to 350°F. Cook the potatoes in lightly salted, boiling water for 15–20 minutes or until tender. Drain, peel and mash with a potato masher, then stir in the flour and half the butter. Knead the mixture well and roll out on a lightly floured surface to $1/4$ inch thick. Combine the Gorgonzola, the remaining butter and the walnuts in a bowl. Cut the potato dough into small triangles and cover half of them with slices of cheese cut to shape. Spread with the Gorgonzola mixture, cover with another potato dough triangle and seal the edges well. Place on a cookie sheet and brush the tops with egg yolk. Bake for 15 minutes, then remove from the oven, brush with more egg yolk and sprinkle with finely chopped walnuts to garnish. Return to the oven for 2 minutes, then serve.

GALLETTINE AL FORMAGGIO

Serves 6–8

$2^{1}/_{4}$ pounds potatoes

$1^{1}/_{4}$ cups all-purpose flour, plus extra for dusting

7 tablespoons butter, softened

3 ounces Gorgonzola cheese, crumbled

$1/_{2}$ cup shelled walnuts, chopped

5 Italian sottilette or thin Swiss cheese slices

1 egg yolk, lightly beaten

salt

walnuts, finely chopped, to garnish

ROMAN CRESCENTS

Sift the flour with a pinch of salt into a mound on a counter. Make a well in the center and add the butter, egg yolks and 1 teaspoon water. Using your fingers, gradually incorporate the flour, adding more water if necessary. Knead lightly, then form into a ball and let rest for 1 hour. Roll out the dough on a lightly floured surface to a thin sheet, then stamp out rounds with a cookie cutter or a glass. Heat the vegetable oil to 350–375°F or until a cube of day-old bread browns in 30 seconds. Meanwhile, combine the ham, sage, provolone, Parmesan and whole egg in a bowl and season with salt and pepper. Spoon a little of the mixture into the middle of each round, fold over and crimp the edges to seal. Brush the crescents with the egg white and deep-fry in the oil until golden brown. Drain on paper towels and serve hot.

MEZZELUNE ALLA ROMANA

Serves 6

$2^{3}/_{4}$ cups all-purpose flour, plus extra for dusting

$1/_{4}$ cup butter, softened

2 egg yolks

vegetable oil, for deep-frying

$3^{1}/_{2}$ ounces cooked cured ham, chopped

10 fresh sage leaves, chopped

$3^{1}/_{2}$ ounces sharp provolone cheese, diced

$2^{1}/_{2}$ tablespoons Parmesan cheese, freshly grated

1 egg, lightly beaten

1 egg white, lightly beaten

salt and pepper

PICONCINI FROM MARCHE

Sift the flour with a pinch of salt into a mound on a counter. Make a well in the center and add the egg, butter and 2 tablespoons of the milk. Using your fingers, gradually incorporate the flour, adding more milk if necessary. Knead lightly, form into a ball and let rest in the refrigerator for 20 minutes. Preheat the oven to 350°F. Line a cookie sheet with baking parchment. Roll out the dough on a lightly floured surface to a fairly thin sheet and stamp out 2-inch rounds with a cookie cutter or a glass. To make the filling, beat the eggs with a pinch salt in a soup plate, then stir in the Parmesan. If the mixture is too runny, add more grated Parmesan. Put a teaspoonful of filling on each round, fold over and crimp the edges. Gently pinch the middle of each piconcino with a pair of scissors and brush with milk. Place on the prepared cookie sheet and bake for about 20 minutes. Serve warm with aperitifs.

PICONCINI MARCHIGIANI

Serves 6–8

2³/₄ cups all-purpose flour, plus extra for dusting

1 egg

7 tablespoons butter, softened and diced

2–3 tablespoons milk, plus extra for brushing

salt

For the filling

2 eggs

1²/₃ cups Parmesan cheese, freshly grated

salt

CURRIED CHICKEN PUFFS

Preheat the oven to 400°F. Roll out the dough on a lightly floured surface and stamp out 12 rounds with a cookie cutter or a glass. Place on a cookie sheet and bake for 15–20 minutes until puffed up and golden. Transfer to a wire rack to cool. Place the chicken meat in a processor and process until very finely chopped. Transfer to a bowl and season to taste with curry powder. Stir in the béchamel sauce and egg yolks and season with salt and pepper to taste. When ready to serve, sandwich the chicken mixture between pairs of pastry rounds. Place on a cookie sheet and heat through in a preheated oven, 350°F, for 10 minutes.

SFOGLIATINE AL POLLO E CURRY

Serves 6

9 ounces puff pastry dough, thawed if frozen

all-purpose flour, for dusting

7 ounces cooked chicken meat, coarsely chopped

curry powder, to taste

1 cup Béchamel Sauce (see page 50)

2 egg yolks, lightly beaten

salt and pepper

SFOGLIATINE CON FUNGHI

Serves 6

2 tablespoons butter, plus extra for greasing

11 ounces mushrooms

juice of 1 lemon, strained

9 ounces puff pastry dough, thawed if frozen

all-purpose flour, for dusting

6 cooked cured ham slices, halved

1/2 envelope pine nuts

5 ounces fontina cheese, sliced

1 egg yolk, lightly beaten

salt and pepper

MUSHROOM PUFFS

Preheat the oven to 400°F. Lightly grease a cookie sheet with butter. Slice the mushrooms and sprinkle with the lemon juice. Melt the butter in a skillet. Add the mushrooms and cook over medium heat, stirring frequently, for about 7 minutes until tender. (If all the liquid evaporates, add 1 tablespoon warm water.) Roll out the dough on a lightly floured surface to 1/8 inch thick. Stamp out 4-inch rounds with a cookie cutter or a glass. Spread out the half-slices of ham and put a few slices of mushroom, a few pine nuts, a strip of fontina and a pinch of salt and pepper on each. Fold in the sides to enclose the other ingredients, and lay a ham bundle in the middle of each pastry round. Fold the pastry over and crimp the edges to seal. Arrange the puffs on the prepared cookie sheet, brush with the egg yolk and bake for about 15 minutes or until golden brown.

SFOGLIATINE CON RAFANO E WÜRSTEL

Serves 6

6 würstel or frankfurters

1 quantity Horseradish Butter (see page 88)

12 puff pastry rounds

(see Curried Chicken Puffs, page 153)

HORSERADISH AND SAUSAGE PUFFS

Cook the sausages in gently simmering water for about 8 minutes. Drain, let cool, then skin and chop very finely. Combine the sausage meat and horseradish butter. When ready to serve, sandwich the sausage mixture between pairs of pastry rounds. Arrange on a dish and serve cold. Highly recommended with aperitifs.

SFOGLIATINE CON SCAMPI AL CURRY

Serves 6

7 ounces langoustines or jumbo shrimp

1/2 onion, sliced

1 1/2 tablespoons butter

1 teaspoon all-purpose flour

1/4 teaspoon curry powder

1 egg yolk

12 puff pastry rounds

(see Curried Chicken Puffs, page 153)

salt

CURRIED LANGOUSTINE PUFFS

Bring a large pan of lightly salted water to a boil. Add the langoustines or shrimp and onion and cook for 2–5 minutes. Drain, reserving the cooking liquid, and peel the langoustines or shrimp. Combine the butter and flour in a pan over low heat and gradually stir in the reserved cooking liquid. Simmer, stirring constantly, for 15 minutes. Season with salt and stir in the langoustines or shrimp, curry powder and egg yolk. Remove the pan from the heat. When ready to serve, sandwich the mixture between pairs of pastry rounds. Place on a cookie sheet and heat through in a preheated oven, 350°F, for 5 minutes.

CRÊPES

There are dozens of different types of crêpes, both sweet and savory. They offer lots of scope and are equally suitable for solving the problem of how to start an elegant dinner party or what to serve as a fun snack. Crêpes are easy, but quite time-consuming, to make. Therefore it is a good idea to make a few more than you think you will need and keep them in the refrigerator to fill when required. A small, heavy-based non-stick crêpe pan is generally the most successful and popular utensil for cooking crêpes. Electric hotplates with a non-stick coating have been on the market for several years. A ladleful of batter is poured onto the hotplate and, once the underside is cooked, the crêpe is flipped over with a spatula to cook the other side. Whichever way you cook them, crêpes should always be fairly thin.

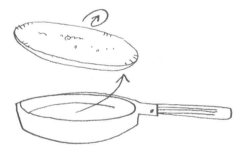

CRÊPE BATTER (BASIC RECIPE)

Sift the flour into a bowl, add the eggs and 3 – 4 tablespoons of the milk and mix well. Gradually stir in the remaining milk to make a fairly runny batter. Melt the butter in a double boiler in a heatproof bowl over a pan of simmering water, let cool almost completely, then add to the batter. Season with salt, beat again for a few minutes with a small whisk, then let stand for at least 1 hour. Brush the base of a crêpe pan with oil and heat, then pour in 2 tablespoons of the batter. Turn and tilt the pan so that the batter covers the base evenly. Cook for 3 – 4 minutes until the underside is set and golden brown, then flip over with a spatula and cook the other side for about 2 minutes until golden. Slide the crêpe out of the pan onto a plate. Make more crêpes in the same way until all the batter is used. If sweet crêpes are required, replace the salt with sugar.

PASTELLA PER CRÊPES (RICETTA BASE)

Makes 12

scant 1 cup all-purpose flour

2 eggs

1 cup milk

2 tablespoons butter

vegetable oil, for brushing

salt

ASPARAGUS CRÊPES

CRÊPES AGLI ASPARAGI

Makes 12

1³/₄ pounds asparagus, trimmed

¹/₄ cup butter, plus extra for greasing

12 crêpes (see page 155)

²/₃ cup heavy cream

²/₃ cup Parmesan cheese, freshly grated

salt

Cook the asparagus in lightly salted, boiling water for 15 minutes. Drain and chop coarsely. Melt half the butter in a large skillet, add the asparagus and cook over low heat, stirring occasionally, for 5 minutes. Preheat the oven to 400°F and grease an ovenproof dish with butter. Brush the crêpes with some of the cream, sprinkle half with the Parmesan, place the asparagus on top and roll up. Arrange in a single layer in the prepared dish, pour in the remaining cream, dot with the remaining butter and sprinkle with the remaining Parmesan. Bake for about 10 minutes until golden and bubbling. Remove from the oven and cut each roll into three or four sections before serving.

MUSHROOM CRÊPES

CRÊPES AI FUNGHI

Makes 12

¹/₄ cup butter, plus extra for greasing

¹/₂ cup mushrooms, thinly sliced

1 tablespoon chopped fresh flat-leaf parsley

¹/₄ cup brandy

1 quantity Béchamel Sauce (see page 50)

12 crêpes (see page 155)

3 tablespoons Parmesan cheese, freshly grated

salt and pepper

Preheat the oven to 400°F. Grease an ovenproof dish with butter. Melt half the butter in a skillet. Add the mushrooms and cook over low heat, stirring occasionally, for 5 minutes. Add the parsley, season with salt and pepper, sprinkle with the brandy and cook for a further 3–4 minutes until the liquid has evaporated. Spread 1 tablespoon of the béchamel sauce on each crêpe, top with 1 tablespoon of the mushrooms and roll up. Arrange in a single layer in the prepared dish, pour the remaining béchamel sauce over them, sprinkle with the Parmesan and dot with the remaining butter. Bake for 10–15 minutes.

ANCHOVY CRÊPES

CRÊPES ALLE ACCIUGHE

Makes 12

12 crêpes (see page 155)

16 canned anchovy fillets, drained

7 tablespoons butter, softened

Keep the crêpes warm or reheat stored crêpes. Finely chop four of the anchovy fillets. Cream the butter in a bowl, then beat in the chopped anchovies. Gently spread the mixture over the crêpes and put a whole anchovy fillet in the middle of each. Roll up and serve.

HAM AND FONTINA CRÊPES

CRÊPES AL PROSCIUTTO E FONTINA

Makes 12

2 tablespoons butter, plus extra for greasing

12 crêpes (see page 155)

generous 1 cup cooked cured ham, chopped

3¹/₂ ounces fontina cheese, diced

1 quantity Béchamel Sauce (see page 50)

3 tablespoons Parmesan cheese, freshly grated

pinch of freshly grated nutmeg

Preheat the oven to 400°F. Grease an ovenproof dish with butter. Sprinkle the crêpes with the ham and fontina. Roll up and arrange in a single layer in the prepared dish. Pour the béchamel sauce over them, sprinkle with the Parmesan and nutmeg and dot with the butter. Bake for about 10 minutes until golden and bubbling. Serve the crêpes whole or halved diagonally.

PÂTÉS

AND TERRINES

When the assistant at the delicatessen cuts a chunk off that soft block covered in gelatin and lays the slices of 'pâté' that we requested on a tray, assuring us that it is the very best quality, we are all using the term wrongly, even though this misuse has now become standard: we should, in fact, say mousse. The French word pâté really means something quite different. First, it is always covered in pastry which is cooked together with the filling, which may consist of a mashed or chopped mixture of meat, vegetables, fish or pulses. It is also usually served hot as an hors d'oeuvre or as the main course of a formal dinner. Terrines are part of the pâté family. Here, the filling, which is partly ground and partly cut into strips or slices, is arranged in an earthenware container lined with strips of bacon so that when it is sliced it reveals a decorative mosaic pattern. To cook, the terrine is covered and placed in a water bath or bain-marie before being baked in the oven. It is then left to cool, chilled in the refrigerator, turned out and thinly sliced.

PINEAPPLE BAVAROIS

Serves 4

4 sheets leaf gelatin

9 ounces fresh pineapple, coarsely chopped

juice of ¹/₂ lemon, strained

4 tablespoons milk

¹/₂ cup heavy cream, whipped

prosciutto slices, to serve

Soak the sheets of gelatin in cold water for 5 minutes to soften. Place the pineapple in a food processor and process at maximum speed to a purée. Scrape into a bowl and stir in the lemon juice. Squeeze out the gelatin and place in a small pan with the milk and heat gently until the gelatin dissolves. Remove from the heat and let cool slightly, then add the pineapple. Let cool completely, then fold in the cream. Rinse out a mold with cold water and drain. Spoon the mixture into the mold and chill in the refrigerator for 6–7 hours. To serve, turn out onto a serving dish. Serve with slices of prosciutto.

FLORENTINE MOLD

Heat the oil in a skillet. Add the onion and cook over low heat, stirring occasionally, for 5 minutes until soft. Add the steak, increase the heat to high and cook, stirring frequently, until browned. Sprinkle with the brandy and cook until it has evaporated, then season with salt and pepper and remove the pan from the heat. Let cool, then grind very finely with a meat grinder or in a food processor. Scrape into a bowl and beat in scant 1 cup of the butter, then chill in the refrigerator. Cook the carrots and peas in salted, boiling water until tender, then remove with a slotted spoon and add the chicken portion to the pan. Poach for 15 minutes or until cooked through and tender. Drain the chicken, chop and mix with the remaining butter, the truffle pâté, if using, and the Marsala. Stir until thoroughly combined, then season with salt and pepper to taste. Gently stir in the peas, carrots and ham. Grease a 8³/₄-cup mold with butter. (In Florence, a dome-shaped zuccotto mold is used.) Spoon in the steak pâté and smooth the surface with the back of a damp tablespoon. Spoon the chicken mixture on top. Tap the mold on the counter several times to release any air pockets. Cover with plastic wrap and chill in the refrigerator for 4–5 hours. Remove from the refrigerator about 10 minutes before serving to bring back to room temperature. Turn out onto a dish and garnish with parsley sprigs and rose-cut radishes.

GRAN ZUCCOTTO DI PÂTÉ

Serves 10–12

2 tablespoons olive oil

1 onion, thinly sliced

1 pounds 5 ounces lean steak, finely chopped

5 tablespoons brandy

scant 1 cup butter, softened, plus extra for greasing

¹/₂ cup carrots, diced

scant 1 cup shelled peas

1 skinless, boneless chicken portion

1 ounce truffle pâté (optional)

scant ¹/₂ cup Marsala

5 ounces cooked cured ham, finely chopped

salt and pepper

To garnish

fresh flat-leaf parsley sprigs

rose-cut radishes

GORGONZOLA MOUSSE

Put the three cheeses and the butter in a food processor and process to a soft, even cream. Line a pie pan with plastic wrap. Spoon in the mixture, smooth the surface and cover with more plastic wrap. Chill in the refrigerator for about 3 hours. Turn out onto a serving dish and garnish with the walnut halves arranged in a circle. Serve with raw carrots.

MOUSSE DI GORGONZOLA

Serves 6–8

7 ounces Gorgonzola cheese, crumbled

11 ounces stracchino cheese,

such as taleggio, diced

3¹/₂ ounces robiola cheese, diced

7 tablespoons butter, softened

walnut halves, to garnish

raw carrots, to serve

MOUSSE DI PICCIONE
CON VINAIGRETTE AL TARTUFO

Serves 10–12

³/₄ cup Armagnac brandy

1 teaspoon sugar

2 squab, boned and livers reserved

3¹/₂ ounces goose liver, sliced

3¹/₂ ounces chicken livers, trimmed

generous ¹/₂ cup olive oil

scant 1 cup heavy cream, whipped

3 shallots, finely chopped

1 sprig fresh flat-leaf parsley, finely chopped

scant ¹/₂ cup white wine vinegar

¹/₂ tube truffle pâté

1 tablespoon Dijon mustard

salt and pepper

crackers, to serve

SQUAB MOUSSE WITH TRUFFLE VINAIGRETTE

Pour the Armagnac into a bowl and stir in the sugar and salt and pepper to taste. Chop the squab meat and add to the bowl with the squab livers, goose liver and chicken livers. Marinate for 12 hours. Heat 3 tablespoons of the oil in a large skillet. Drain all the meat, reserving the marinade, and add to the skillet. Cook over medium heat, stirring frequently and gradually adding the reserved marinade. Season with salt and pepper to taste, remove the pan from the heat and let cool. Grind all the meat with a meat grinder or in a food processor and place in a bowl. Gently fold in the whipped cream, cover and chill in the refrigerator for 12 hours. Meanwhile, combine the shallots, parsley, the remaining olive oil, the vinegar, truffle pâté and mustard. Store in the refrigerator until required. To serve, scoop almond-shaped balls from the squab mousse, using two dessert spoons, and put two on each individual plate. Sprinkle with the vinaigrette and serve with crackers.

MOUSSE DI PRATOLINE

Serves 6

30 edible flowers, such as violas, marjoram, heartsease or tansy

scant ¹/₂ cup mascarpone cheese

1 tablespoon milk

dash of lemon juice, strained

salt and white pepper

toasted bread, to serve

MEADOW FLOWER MOUSSE

Wash the flowers, pat dry, set eight aside for the garnish and chop the remainder. Beat the mascarpone with the milk and lemon juice in a bowl, then stir in the chopped flowers and season with salt and pepper to taste. Shape into a dome on a serving dish and garnish with the whole flowers. Serve with toasted bread.

MOUSSE DI PROSCIUTTO E KIWI

Serves 6–8

2¹/₃ cups cooked cured ham, diced

4 ounces robiola cheese, diced

¹/₄ cup butter, softened

salt and pepper

3 kiwi fruits, peeled and sliced, to garnish

HAM AND KIWI FRUIT MOUSSE

Put the ham, cheese and butter in a food processor and season with salt and pepper. Process until smooth. Line a mold with plastic wrap, spoon in the ham mousse and smooth the surface. Cover with more plastic wrap and chill in the refrigerator for 3 hours. Turn out and garnish with kiwi fruit.

SALMON MOUSSE WITH SHRIMP CREAM

Preheat the oven to 325°F. Grease a ring mold with butter. Skin and chop the salmon fillets and place in a bowl. Put the skin, any trimmings, the bones and head in a large pan. Add water to cover, bring to a boil, then lower the heat and simmer for 30 minutes. Whisk the egg whites in a grease-free bowl until stiff. Stiffly whip the cream in another bowl. Fold the egg whites, then the cream into the chopped salmon and season with salt and pepper. Pour the mixture into the ring mold and place in a roasting pan. Pour in boiling water to come about halfway up the side of the mold and bake for 45–50 minutes. Meanwhile, strain the salmon stock into a bowl. Make the shrimp cream. Peel and devein the shrimp and finely chop the shells. Heat half the butter in a skillet, add the shells and cook, stirring frequently, for a few minutes. Sprinkle with the brandy and cook until it has evaporated, then season with salt and pepper. Combine the remaining butter and the flour to a paste and add to the skillet, stirring. Stir in as much of the hot salmon stock as required to make a slightly runny sauce. Strain into a bowl and add the shrimp. Turn out the mousse and pour the shrimp cream in the middle. Serve immediately.

MOUSSE DI SALMONE CON CREMA

Serves 6–8

butter, for greasing

1 pound 5 ounces salmon, cleaned and filleted, bones and head reserved

2 egg whites

1 cup heavy cream

salt and white pepper

For the shrimp cream

18 cooked shrimp

$1/4$ cup butter

$1/4$ cup brandy

1 tablespoon all-purpose flour

salt and pepper

COLD TOMATO MOUSSE

Sprinkle the insides of the tomatoes with salt and place upside down on paper towels to drain for 10 minutes. Place the tomatoes in a food processor and process to a purée. Scrape into a large bowl, add the chives and garlic and mix well. Gently stir in the mayonnaise, then the yogurt, then the cream and season with salt and pepper to taste. Spoon into individual dishes and chill in the refrigerator. Serve garnished with the basil leaves.

MOUSSE FREDDA DI POMODORI

Serves 6

8 ripe tomatoes, peeled and seeded

1 tablespoon chopped fresh chives

1 garlic clove, chopped

1 quantity Mayonnaise (see page 65)

$2/3$ cup low-fat plain yogurt

scant 1 cup heavy cream

salt and pepper

fresh basil leaves, to garnish

CHICKEN LIVER PÂTÉ

PÂTÉ AI FEGATINI

Serves 6

²/₃ cup butter

14 ounces chicken livers, trimmed

¹/₂ onion, chopped

5 fresh thyme leaves

2 tablespoons Marsala

1 tablespoon brandy

2 tablespoons heavy cream, whipped

salt and pepper

Melt scant ¹/₂ cup of the butter in a heatproof bowl over a pan of barely simmering water. Remove from the heat and let cool. Melt the remaining butter in a skillet. Add the chicken livers, onion and thyme and cook over medium heat, stirring frequently, for 2 minutes. Sprinkle with the Marsala, season with salt and pepper and cook for 3 minutes. Remove the skillet from the heat, chop the chicken livers and place in a bowl. Stir in the cooled melted butter, then add the brandy and fold in the cream. Chill in the refrigerator for 6 hours.

DELICATE CHICKEN PÂTÉ

PÂTÉ DELICATO DI POLLO

Serves 8

¹/₂ cup butter, softened

7 ounces skinless, boneless chicken breast, sliced

11 ounces cooked cured ham

1 small potato

scant 1 cup heavy cream

scant 1 cup Béchamel Sauce (see page 50)

5 tablespoons brandy

1 envelope powdered gelatin

1 egg, hard-cooked

1 fresh flat-leaf parsley sprig, leaves only

salt and pepper

Chill a rectangular mold in the freezer. Melt 2 tablespoons of the butter in a skillet. Add the chicken and cook over medium heat, stirring occasionally, for 8–10 minutes until cooked. Remove from the skillet and chop together with 7 ounces of the ham, then place in a bowl. Cook the potato in a pan of lightly salted, boiling water for 10 minutes until tender, then drain, peel and mash. Add the potato to the chicken and ham mixture, then gently stir in the remaining butter, the cream and béchamel sauce and season with salt and pepper. Sprinkle with 1 tablespoon of the brandy and mix, then set aside. Meanwhile, prepare the gelatin according to the packet instructions and add the remaining brandy. Spoon a little gelatin into the chilled mold and turn so that it coats the sides and base. Put in the refrigerator to set. Using a heart-shaped cutter, stamp out small hearts from the remaining ham. Shell and slice the egg, preferably with an egg slicer. Arrange the ham hearts on the base of the mold alternating with slices of egg and the parsley leaves. Spoon in another layer of gelatin and brush some over the sides. Return to the refrigerator for at least 30 minutes. When the gelatin has set, spoon in the chicken mixture, pressing it down gently with the palm of your hand. Spoon the remaining gelatin on top. Chill in the refrigerator for at least 5 hours until set. Turn out onto a serving dish and serve immediately.

DELICATE CALF'S LIVER PÂTÉ

PÂTÉ DELICATO DI VITELLO

Serves 6–8

12 ounces calf's liver, sliced

all-purpose flour, for dusting

1/2 cup butter

scant 1/2 cup Marsala

generous 1/2 cup prosciutto, chopped

1 egg yolk

salt and pepper

fresh sage leaves, to garnish

toast triangles, to serve

Lightly dust the liver with flour. Melt 2 tablespoons of the butter in a skillet, add the liver and cook over high heat, stirring frequently, for 5 minutes. Pour in the Marsala and cook for about 7 minutes until it has evaporated. Season with salt and pepper to taste and remove from the heat. Chop the liver and dice the remaining butter. Place them in a food processor with the pan juices, prosciutto and egg yolk and process until smooth. Line a rectangular mold with plastic wrap, spoon in the pâté and chill in the refrigerator for at least 5 hours until set. Turn out, slice thinly and garnish with the sage. Serve with toast triangles.

SMOKED SALMON PÂTÉ

PÂTÉ DI SALMONE

Serves 6–8

2 tablespoons butter, melted, plus extra for greasing

3 potatoes

7 ounces smoked salmon, chopped

3 tablespoons pitted black olives, coarsely chopped

2 canned anchovy fillets in oil, drained and chopped

salt and pepper

cornichons or small dill pickles, drained, to garnish

Grease a mold with butter. Cook the potatoes in lightly salted, boiling water for 15 minutes or until tender. Drain, peel and mash with a potato masher. Put the salmon, olives, melted butter and anchovies in a food processor, season with salt and pepper and process to a purée. Stir the purée into the mashed potatoes. Spoon the mixture into the prepared mold, smooth the surface and chill in the refrigerator for 6 hours. Turn out and garnish with cornichons or dill pickles.

TUNA PÂTÉ

PÂTÉ DI TONNO

Serves 6

3 1/2 ounces canned anchovy fillets in oil, drained

11 ounces canned tuna in oil, drained

juice of 1 lemon, strained

2/3 cup butter, softened

olive oil, for brushing

salt and pepper

To garnish

2 smoked salmon slices, cut into strips

Italian mixed pickled vegetables (sottaceti)

Put the anchovies and tuna in a food processor and process to a purée. Scrape into a bowl, stir in the lemon juice, then the butter. Season with salt and pepper and mix well. Brush a mold with olive oil, spoon in the mixture and smooth the surface. Chill in the refrigerator for at least 3 hours. Just before serving, turn out onto a serving dish and garnish with strips of smoked salmon and Italian pickles.

TERRINA D'ANATRA

Serves 8–10

butter, for greasing

1 duck, boned, liver reserved

9 ounces lardons

3¹/₂ ounces prosciutto, cut into strips

scant ¹/₂ cup brandy

1¹/₄ cups ground veal

1¹/₄ cups ground pork loin

2 eggs, lightly beaten

salt and pepper

DUCK TERRINE

Grease a terrine or loaf pan with butter. Chop the duck meat and put into a large bowl. Cut 3¹/₂ ounces of the lardons into strips and add to the bowl with the prosciutto. Sprinkle with the brandy, season with salt and pepper and mix well. Cover and set aside for 2 hours. Preheat the oven to 325°F. Chop 3¹/₂ ounces of the remaining lardons with the duck liver and mix with the veal and pork. Season with salt and pepper and stir in the eggs. Combine with the duck meat mixture and spoon into the prepared dish, pressing down well. Lay the remaining lardons on top. Cover with a lid or foil, place in a roasting pan and add boiling water to come about halfway up the sides. Bake for 2 hours. Remove from the oven and uncover. Place a sheet of foil on the surface, put a weight on top and chill in the refrigerator for 24 hours. Before turning the terrine out, remove any fat that has formed on the surface.

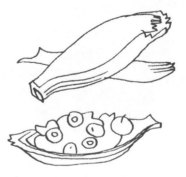

MOLDS
AND SOUFFLÉS

Both molds and soufflés are important antipasti, make elegant second courses and can be served as unusual and delicious accompaniments. For example, serving a succulent veal roast with a soufflé is a sure sign of a certain culinary sophistication. It is not at all true that molds and soufflés are difficult to make. All you have to do is carefully follow the method in each recipe and, above all, allow yourself enough time to do so. The difference between the two dishes lies in their consistency: a mold is firmer and a soufflé is lighter and airier. In practice, a soufflé is a mixture that puffs up during cooking until it is higher than the rim of the dish. The basic element for the success of both is eggs. For example, in vegetable molds the eggs help to keep the mixture together. However, you should never add an extra egg to be 'on the safe side', as the mixture may become too tough during cooking and acquire an unpleasant flavor. A mold is cooked when you can push a wooden toothpick into it and it comes out dry. After cooking, in general let stand for 5 minutes, then turn out onto a dish and serve. In soufflés, on the other hand, whisked egg whites carry out the main task. The incorporated air bubbles increase the volume of the mixture and make it softer, and at the same time almost 'elastic'. Soufflés are made by mixing the chopped or mashed main ingredient (cheese, ham or fish) with a firm béchamel sauce, egg yolks and stiffly whisked egg whites. Two important warnings: fill the dish only two-thirds full so that the soufflé puffs up and rises over the rim; and do not open the oven door during cooking. Serve the soufflé in the dish it is cooked in.

TUNA MOLD WITH LEEK SAUCE

FLAN DI TONNO CON SALSA AI PORRI

Serves 4

butter, for greasing

7 ounces canned tuna in spring water, drained

4 eggs, separated • salt and pepper

fresh flat-leaf parsley, chopped, to garnish

For the sauce

2 tablespoons butter

2 tablespoons heavy cream

4 leeks, trimmed and sliced

salt and pepper

Preheat the oven to 350°F and grease a quiche pan with butter. Place half the tuna and the egg yolks in a food processor, process to a purée and scrape into a bowl. Stiffly whisk the egg whites, then fold them into the tuna mixture. Finely chop the remaining tuna, season with salt and pepper and fold in. Pour the mixture into the prepared pan, place in a roasting pan and pour in boiling water to come about halfway up the side. Bake for about 45 minutes. For the sauce, heat the butter and cream in a pan, add the leeks and cook over low heat for 20 minutes. Season with salt and pepper. Turn out the mold and top with the leek sauce. Garnish with parsley and serve immediately.

LEEK MOLDS

SFORMATINI DI PORRI

Serves 6

butter, for greasing

2¼ pounds leeks, trimmed • ½ cup pine nuts

⅔ cup Parmesan cheese, freshly grated

2 eggs, separated

salt

For the béchamel sauce

2 tablespoons butter • ¼ cup all-purpose flour

scant 1 cup milk • ¼ cup heavy cream

pinch of freshly grated nutmeg

First make the béchamel sauce (see page 50) with the ingredients listed, then let cool. Preheat the oven to 350°F and grease six individual quiche pans with butter. Meanwhile, cook the leeks in salted, boiling water for 10 minutes until tender. Drain, pass through a food mill into a bowl and add the pine nuts. Stir the mixture into the cold béchamel sauce, then stir in the Parmesan and egg yolks and season with salt. Stiffly whisk the egg whites and fold in. Pour the mixture into the prepared pans and bake for 30 minutes. Remove the pans from the oven and let stand for a few minutes, then turn out onto a serving dish.

ZUCCHINI MOLDS

SFORMATINI DI ZUCCHINE

Serves 4

2 tablespoons butter, plus extra for greasing

9 ounces zucchini, sliced

1 tablespoon olive oil • 1 shallot, finely chopped

2 eggs, lightly beaten

2 tablespoons Parmesan cheese, freshly grated

salt and pepper

For the béchamel sauce

2 tablespoons butter

3 tablespoons all-purpose flour • scant 1 cup milk

pinch of freshly grated nutmeg

Preheat the oven to 350°F and grease four dariole molds with butter. Cook the zucchini in salted, boiling water for 10 minutes until tender. Drain and mash with a fork. Heat the oil and butter in a skillet, add the shallot and cook over low heat, stirring occasionally, for 4–5 minutes until softened. Stir in the zucchini and season with salt and pepper. Cook for a few minutes more until all the liquid has evaporated, then remove from the heat. Make the béchamel sauce (see page 50) with the ingredients listed, then stir in the zucchini mixture, eggs and Parmesan. Divide the mixture among the molds, then place in a roasting pan and add boiling water to come about halfway up the sides. Bake for 30–35 minutes. Let stand for 5 minutes, then turn out the molds and serve.

TWO—COLOR MOLD

Cook the spinach, in just the water clinging to the leaves after washing, for 5 minutes until tender. Drain, squeezing out as much liquid as possible, and chop. Melt half the butter in a small pan, stir in half the flour, then gradually stir in half the milk. Bring to a boil, stirring constantly. Cook, stirring, until thickened, then remove from the heat, stir in the thyme and season with salt and pepper. Beat in two egg yolks, one at a time, then add the spinach, Emmenthal and potato flour. Let cool, then stiffly whisk one egg white and fold in. Preheat the oven to 350°F and grease a quiche pan with butter. Cook the carrots in salted, boiling water for 10 minutes until tender. Drain and pass through a food mill into a pan. Stir in the remaining butter, flour and milk and cook over low heat, stirring constantly, until thickened. Remove from the heat, stir in the Parmesan and nutmeg and season with salt and pepper. Let cool slightly, then beat in the remaining egg yolks. Stiffly whisk the remaining egg whites and fold in. Spread 3 tablespoons of the spinach mixture on the base of the prepared pan, pour the carrot mixture on top and cover with the remaining spinach. Place in a roasting pan, add boiling water to come about halfway up the side and bake for about 1 hour. Remove the pan from the oven, let stand for 5 minutes, then turn out onto a serving dish. This dish may also be served as a first course.

SFORMATO BICOLORE

Serves 4

1³/₄ pounds spinach

¹/₄ cup butter, plus extra for greasing

¹/₂ cup all-purpose flour

2¹/₄ cups milk

¹/₂ teaspoon chopped fresh thyme

4 eggs, separated

¹/₃ cup Emmenthal cheese, grated

1 teaspoon potato flour

12 ounces baby carrots

¹/₂ cup Parmesan cheese, freshly grated

pinch of freshly grated nutmeg

salt and pepper

ARTICHOKE HEART MOLD

Preheat the oven to 350°F. Grease a quiche pan with butter, then sprinkle in the bread crumbs, turning the pan to coat. Tip out any excess. Bring a pan of salted water to a boil and add the lemon juice. Break off the artichoke stalks, strip off all the leaves, remove the chokes and add the hearts to the pan. Cook for 15 minutes, then drain, chop and let cool slightly. Lightly beat the eggs and Parmesan in a bowl and stir in the artichoke hearts. Stir the mixture into the béchamel sauce and season with salt and pepper. Pour into the prepared pan and bake for about 45 minutes. Remove from the oven, let stand for 5 minutes, then turn out onto a dish and serve.

SFORMATO DI CARCIOFI

Serves 4

butter, for greasing

1³/₄ cups fresh bread crumbs

juice of ¹/₂ lemon, strained

6 globe artichokes

2 eggs, lightly beaten

¹/₂ cup Parmesan cheese, freshly grated

1 quantity Béchamel Sauce (see page 50)

salt and pepper

CARROT MOLD

SFORMATO DI CAROTE

Serves 4

butter, for greasing

2¹/₂ pounds baby carrots

1¹/₄ cups Béchamel Sauce (see page 50)

scant 1 cup Emmenthal cheese, grated

¹/₂ cup Parmesan cheese, freshly grated

3 eggs, lightly beaten

pinch of freshly grated nutmeg

salt and pepper

Preheat the oven to 350°F. Grease a quiche pan with butter. Steam the carrots for 8–10 minutes until tender. Set four or five carrots aside and pass the remainder through a food mill. Slice some of the reserved carrots lengthwise into strips and arrange in a star shape on the base of the pan. Slice the remaining reserved carrots into rounds and arrange in rows around the sides of the pan. Pour the carrot purée into a pan and set over low heat to dry out. Remove from the heat, stir in the béchamel sauce, Emmenthal, Parmesan, eggs and nutmeg and season with salt and pepper. Pour the mixture into the quiche pan without disturbing the garnish. Place in a roasting pan and add boiling water to come about halfway up the side. Bake for 45–50 minutes. Let stand for 5 minutes, then turn out onto a serving dish.

CARROT AND FENNEL MOLD

SFORMATO DI CAROTE E FINOCCHI

Serves 6

3 tablespoons butter, plus extra for greasing

1 pound 2 ounces carrots

6 small fennel bulbs, quartered

scant 1 cup milk

4 tablespoons Parmesan cheese, freshly grated

¹/₂ quantity Béchamel Sauce (see page 50)

2 eggs, separated

Preheat the oven to 350°F. Grease a quiche pan with butter. Cook the carrots in salted, boiling water for 10 minutes until tender, then drain. Meanwhile, cook the fennel in salted, boiling water for 10–15 minutes until tender, then drain. Melt half the butter in a skillet, add the carrots and cook over low heat, stirring occasionally, for 5 minutes. Add half the milk and cook until it has been absorbed. Process the carrot mixture in a food processor to a purée. Melt the remaining butter in a skillet, add the fennel and cook over low heat, stirring occasionally, for 5 minutes. Add the remaining milk and cook until it has been absorbed. Process the fennel mixture in a food processor to a purée. Stir the Parmesan into the béchamel sauce and divide the mixture in half. Stir the carrot purée into one bowl of sauce and the fennel purée into the other. Beat one egg yolk into each bowl. Stiffly whisk the egg whites and fold half into each mixture. Pour the mixtures in alternate layers into the prepared pan. Place the pan in a roasting pan and add boiling water to come about halfway up the side. Bake for 40–50 minutes. Let stand for 10 minutes, then turn out onto a serving dish. This dish may also be served as an original first course instead of risotto or pasta.

CAULIFLOWER MOLD

Preheat the oven to 350°F. Grease a quiche pan with butter. Cook the cauliflower in salted, boiling water for 8–10 minutes until tender, then drain well. Melt the butter in a skillet, add the cauliflower and cook over low heat, stirring occasionally, for 5 minutes until lightly browned. Season with salt and pepper, pour in the milk and cook until it has been absorbed. Remove the pan from the heat and push the mixture through a strainer. Beat the eggs into the béchamel sauce, one at a time, then stir in the Swiss cheese and puréed cauliflower. Pour into the prepared pan, place in a roasting pan and add boiling water to come about halfway up the side. Bake for 1 hour. Let stand for a few minutes, then turn out onto a serving dish.

SFORMATO DI CAVOLFIORE

Serves 6

2 tablespoons butter, plus extra for greasing

2¹/₂ pounds cauliflower, cut into flowerets

scant 1 cup milk

3 eggs

1 quantity Béchamel Sauce (see page 50)

³/₄ cup Swiss cheese, grated

salt and pepper

BELGIAN ENDIVE MOLD

Preheat the oven to 350°F. Grease a quiche pan with butter. Cook the Belgian endive in salted, boiling water for 10 minutes until tender. Drain, squeezing out as much liquid as possible, and chop coarsely. Melt the butter in a skillet, add the Belgian endive and cook over low heat, stirring occasionally, for 5 minutes, then remove from the heat. Lightly beat the eggs with a pinch of salt, then stir into the Belgian endive. Stir the Belgian endive mixture into the béchamel sauce and pour into the prepared pan. Place in a roasting pan, add boiling water to come about halfway up the side and bake for 45–50 minutes. Let stand for 5 minutes, then turn out onto a serving dish.

SFORMATO DI CICORIA

Serves 4

2 tablespoons butter, plus extra for greasing

2¹/₄ pounds Belgian endive

2 eggs

1¹/₄ cups Béchamel Sauce (see page 50)

salt

FENNEL MOLD

Preheat the oven to 350°F. Grease a quiche pan with butter. Melt the butter in a skillet, add the fennel and cook over low heat, stirring occasionally, for 5 minutes. Season with salt and pepper, pour in the milk and cook until it has been absorbed. Transfer the fennel to a bowl, let cool, then mash with a fork. Beat the eggs with the Parmesan and stir into the fennel. Stir the fennel mixture into the béchamel sauce and pour into the prepared pan. Place in a roasting pan, add boiling water to come about halfway up the side and bake for 45 minutes. Let stand for 5 minutes, then turn out and serve hot.

SFORMATO DI FINOCCHI

Serves 6

2 tablespoons butter, plus extra for greasing

3¹/₄ pounds fennel bulbs, cut into wedges

scant 1 cup milk

3 eggs

²/₃ cup Parmesan cheese, freshly grated

1¹/₄ cups Béchamel Sauce (see page 50)

salt and pepper

PEA AND AMARETTI MOLD

SFORMATO DI PISELLI DOLCI

Serves 6

¹/₄ cup butter, plus extra for greasing

³/₄ cup bread crumbs

6¹/₂ cups shelled peas

²/₃ cup Chicken Stock (see page 209)

pinch of ground cinnamon

1 tablespoon all-purpose flour

2 amaretti, crumbled

2 tablespoons heavy cream

3 eggs, separated

salt

Preheat the oven to 350°F. Grease a quiche pan with butter, sprinkle with the bread crumbs and turn the pan to coat. Tip out any excess. Melt half the butter in a pan, add the peas and cook over low heat, stirring occasionally, for 5 minutes. Add the stock and cinnamon and simmer for 5 minutes or until the peas are tender. Drain and pass through a food mill. Melt the remaining butter in a pan. Pour in the pea purée, sprinkle with the flour and cook over low heat, stirring constantly. Add the amaretti, cream and egg yolks and season to taste with salt. Remove from the heat and let cool. Stiffly whisk the egg whites and fold in. Pour into the prepared pan and bake for about 45 minutes then serve.

CELERY AND HAM MOLD

SFORMATO DI SEDANO AL PROSCIUTTO

Serves 6

2 tablespoons butter, plus extra for greasing

2 bunches of celery, chopped

1 quantity Béchamel Sauce (see page 50)

²/₃ cup Parmesan cheese, freshly grated

scant 1 cup cooked cured ham, chopped

3 eggs, separated

salt

Preheat the oven to 350°F. Grease a quiche pan with butter. Cook the celery in salted, boiling water for 15 minutes, then drain. Melt the butter in a pan, add the celery and cook over low heat, stirring frequently and breaking up the pieces with a spoon, for 5 minutes. Stir into the béchamel sauce with the Parmesan and ham. Beat in the egg yolks, one at a time. Stiffly whisk the egg whites and fold in. Pour into the prepared pan and bake for 45–50 minutes. Let stand for 5 minutes, then turn out onto a serving dish.

SPINACH MOLD

SFORMATO DI SPINACI

Serves 6

2 tablespoons butter, plus extra for greasing

³/₄ cup bread crumbs

2¹/₄ pounds spinach

¹/₂ cup Italian salami, diced

2 ounces fontina cheese, diced

1 quantity Béchamel Sauce (see page 50)

3 eggs, separated

salt and pepper

Preheat the oven to 350°F. Grease a ring mold with butter, sprinkle with the bread crumbs and turn the mold to coat. Tip out any excess. Cook the spinach, in just the water clinging to the leaves after washing, for 5 minutes. Drain, squeezing out as much liquid as possible, and chop. Melt the butter in a pan, add the spinach and cook over low heat, stirring occasionally, for 4–5 minutes. Stir the spinach, salami and fontina into the béchamel sauce and season with salt and pepper to taste. Beat in the egg yolks, one at a time. Stiffly whisk the egg whites and fold in. Pour the mixture into the mold, place in a roasting pan and add boiling water to reach about halfway up the side. Bake for 45–50 minutes. Let stand for 5 minutes, then turn out onto a serving dish and serve. Mushroom Trifolati (see page 486) or small meatballs may be served in the middle of the ring.

SEA TROUT MOLD

Preheat the oven to 350°F. Grease six small molds or ramekins with butter. For the stock, put the fish heads, onion, carrot, leek and a pinch of salt in a pan, pour in 4 cups water, bring to a boil and simmer for 5 minutes. Strain into a clean pan, set over high heat and cook until reduced by half. Remove from the heat and let cool. Coarsely chop the fish fillets, place in a food processor, season with salt and pepper and process to a purée. Add the egg yolks, potato flour and all but 1 tablespoon of the cream. Pour the mixture into the prepared molds, place in a roasting pan and add boiling water to come about halfway up the sides. Bake for about 25 minutes. Let stand for 5 minutes before turning out. For the vegetables, melt the butter in a pan, add the carrots, celery, leeks and zucchini and cook over low heat, stirring occasionally, for 5 minutes. Remove from the heat and keep warm. For the sauce, stir the potato flour into the cooled fish stock. Bring to a boil over low heat, stirring constantly. Add the saffron and reserved cream, bring back to a boil and season with salt and pepper to taste. Add the wine and simmer gently for a few minutes. Remove from the heat, stir in the butter and spoon a thin layer of the sauce onto a warm serving dish. Arrange a layer of vegetables on the dish and turn out the sea trout molds on top. Sprinkle with the parsley and garnish with the tomato. Serve immediately with the remaining sauce handed separately.

SFORMATO DI TROTA SALMONATA

Serves 6

butter, for greasing
2¼-pound sea trout, filleted and skinned
2 egg yolks
1 tablespoon potato flour
1 cup heavy cream
2 tablespoons chopped fresh flat-leaf parsley
salt and pepper
1 tomato, peeled and diced, to garnish

For the stock
a few white fish heads, gills removed
1 onion • 1 carrot • 1 leek
salt

For the vegetables
2 tablespoons butter
2 carrots, cut into thin strips
2 celery stalks, cut into thin strips
2 leeks, cut into thin strips
2 zucchini, cut into thin strips

For the sauce
1 tablespoon potato flour
pinch of saffron threads
scant ½ cup dry white wine
2 tablespoons butter

CLAM AND MUSSEL MOLD

Preheat the oven to 350°F. Grease a quiche pan with butter. Place the shellfish in a pan, add 1 cup water and cook over high heat until the shells open. Remove the shellfish, discarding any that remain closed, and strain the cooking liquid through a cheesecloth-lined strainer. Make the velouté sauce with the shellfish cooking liquid, season with salt and pepper and let cool slightly. Remove the mussels and clams from the shells and chop. Stir the egg yolks, poached fish and shellfish into the sauce. Stiffly whisk the egg whites and fold in. Pour the mixture into the prepared pan and bake for 40 minutes. Let stand for 5 minutes, then turn out onto a dish and serve.

SFORMATO DI VONGOLE E COZZE

Serves 6

butter, for greasing
1 pound 2 ounces clams, scrubbed
1 pound 2 ounces mussels, scrubbed and beards removed
1 quantity Velouté Sauce (see page 61 and method)
4 eggs, separated
3½ ounces poached white fish fillet, flaked
salt and pepper

PUMPKIN MOLD

SFORMATO DI ZUCCA

Serves 4

2 tablespoons butter, plus extra for greasing

1 onion, sliced

7³/₄ cups pumpkin, peeled, seeded and diced

1 quantity Béchamel Sauce (see page 50)

²/₃ cup Parmesan cheese, grated

2 egg yolks

¹/₃ cup pine nuts

salt and pepper

Preheat the oven to 325°F. Grease a quiche pan with butter. Melt the butter in a pan. Add the onion and cook over low heat, stirring occasionally, for 5 minutes until softened. Add the pumpkin and ²/₃ cup water and cook, stirring and mashing occasionally, until the pumpkin is very soft. Remove from the heat, stir in the béchamel sauce, Parmesan, egg yolks and pine nuts and season with salt and pepper. Pour the mixture into the prepared pan and bake for 1 hour. Increase the oven temperature to 350°F and bake for 10 minutes more. Let cool in the pan, then turn out. This mold is excellent served with spinach sautéed in butter.

CHESTNUT SOUFFLÉ

SOUFFLÉ DI CASTAGNE

Serves 4

¹/₄ cup butter, plus extra for greasing

1 pound 5 ounces chestnuts, shelled

²/₃ cup Meat Stock (see page 208)

2 egg whites

salt

Preheat the oven to 400°F. Grease a soufflé dish with butter. Parboil the chestnuts in a pan of salted water, then drain and rub off the skins. Pass the nuts through a food mill into a pan. Pour in the stock, add the butter and season with salt. Place on low heat and stir until the purée is fairly dry, then remove from the heat and let cool. Stiffly whisk the egg whites and fold into the mixture. Spoon into the prepared dish and bake for about 20 minutes, then lower the temperature to 350°F and bake for 5 minutes more. Serve immediately.

ONION SOUFFLÉ

SOUFFLÉ DI CIPOLLE

Serves 6

2 tablespoons butter, plus extra for greasing

11 ounces small onions, finely chopped

1 cup hot Meat Stock (see page 208)

¹/₄ cup brandy

pinch of sugar (optional)

1 cup Emmenthal cheese, grated

4 eggs, separated

1 cup Béchamel Sauce (see page 50)

pinch of grated nutmeg

salt and pepper

Melt the butter in a pan, add the onions and cook over low heat, stirring occasionally, for 10 minutes until lightly browned. Pour in the stock and simmer for 1 hour. Preheat the oven to 400°F. Grease a soufflé dish with butter. Season the onions with salt and pepper and add the brandy with a pinch of sugar if the mixture tastes a little sour. Cook until the liquid has evaporated, then stir in the Emmenthal and remove from the heat. Stir the egg yolks into the béchamel sauce, one at a time, then stir in the onions and nutmeg and season with salt. Stiffly whisk the egg whites and fold in. Spoon the mixture into the prepared dish and bake for 20 minutes. Lower the oven temperature to 350°F and bake for 5 minutes more. Serve immediately.

GREEN BEAN SOUFFLÉ

SOUFFLÉ DI FAGIOLINI

Serves 4

butter, for greasing
1³/₄ pounds green beans, trimmed
2 tablespoons Parmesan cheese, freshly grated
4 eggs, separated

For the béchamel sauce
6 tablespoons butter
²/₃ cup all-purpose flour • 2¹/₄ cups milk
salt and pepper

Preheat the oven to 400°F. Grease a soufflé dish with butter. Cook the beans in boiling water for 5 minutes until al dente. Drain and pass through a food mill. Make the béchamel sauce (see page 50) with the ingredients listed and season with salt and pepper. Stir in the beans, remove from the heat and stir in the grated cheese. Let cool slightly, then beat in the egg yolks, one at a time. Stiffly whisk the egg whites and fold in. Spoon into the prepared dish and bake for about 20 minutes. Lower the oven temperature to 350°F and bake for 5 minutes more. Serve immediately.

CHEESE SOUFFLÉ

SOUFFLÉ DI FORMAGGIO

Serves 4

butter, for greasing
³/₄ cup bread crumbs
1 quantity Béchamel Sauce (see page 50)
5 ounces Emmenthal cheese, thinly sliced into strips
3 eggs, separated
salt

Preheat the oven to 400°F. Grease a soufflé dish with butter, sprinkle with the bread crumbs and turn to coat. Tip out any excess. Pour the béchamel sauce into the top of a double boiler or into a heatproof bowl set over a pan of barely simmering water, add the Emmenthal and stir until melted. Season with salt and let cool. Beat in the egg yolks, one at a time. Stiffly whisk the egg whites and fold in. Spoon into the prepared dish and bake for 20 minutes. Lower the oven temperature to 350°F and bake for 5 minutes more. Serve immediately.

MUSHROOM SOUFFLÉ

SOUFFLÉ DI FUNGHI

Serves 4

2 tablespoons butter, plus extra for greasing
³/₄ cup bread crumbs
3 tablespoons olive oil
1 onion, chopped • 1 garlic clove, chopped
1 salted anchovy, head removed, cleaned and filleted (see page 596)
1 pound 10 ounces mushrooms, preferably porcini, thinly sliced
3–4 tablespoons Meat Stock (see page 208)
2 tablespoons chopped fresh flat-leaf parsley
5 ounces fontina cheese
1 quantity Béchamel Sauce (see page 50)
3 eggs, separated
salt and pepper

Preheat the oven to 400°F. Grease a soufflé dish with butter, sprinkle with the bread crumbs and turn to coat. Tip out any excess. Heat the olive oil and butter in a small pan, add the onion, garlic and anchovy and cook over low heat, stirring occasionally, for 5 minutes. Add the mushrooms, season with salt and pepper and cook, stirring occasionally, for 30 minutes. Add a little stock if the mixture seems to be drying out. Towards the end of the cooking time increase the heat and add the parsley. Dice about three-quarters of the fontina and slice the remainder. Stir the diced cheese into the béchamel sauce, then beat in the egg yolks, one at a time. Stiffly whisk the egg whites and fold in. Spoon half the mixture into the prepared dish, add the mushrooms with their cooking juices and cover with the remaining soufflé mixture and the sliced fontina. Bake for 20 minutes, then lower the oven temperature to 350°F and bake for 5 minutes more. Serve immediately.

CRAB SOUFFLÉ

Preheat the oven to 400°F. Grease a soufflé dish with butter. Melt the butter in a pan, add the pepper and cook over low heat, stirring occasionally, until softened. Transfer to a food processor and process to a purée. Sprinkle the crabmeat with the vermouth and set aside. Beat the egg yolks into the velouté sauce, one at a time, then stir in the crabmeat and red bell pepper purée. Season with salt and pepper. Stiffly whisk the egg whites and fold in. Spoon into the prepared dish and bake for about 20 minutes, then lower the oven temperature to 350°F and bake for 5 minutes more. Serve immediately.

SOUFFLÉ DI GRANCHIO

Serves 4

2 tablespoons butter, plus extra for greasing

1 red bell pepper, halved, seeded and diced

7 ounces crabmeat, drained and flaked

1 tablespoon vermouth

4 eggs, separated

1 quantity Velouté Sauce (see page 61)

salt and pepper

SPICY CORN SOUFFLÉ

Preheat the oven to 400°F. Grease a soufflé dish with butter. Melt the butter in a small pan over low heat, stir in the flour and gradually stir in the milk. Cook, stirring constantly, until the mixture is thickened and smooth, then remove from the heat, stir in the Emmenthal and let cool slightly. Beat in the egg yolks, one at a time, then stir in the corn, bell pepper, chile and paprika and season with salt and pepper. Stiffly whisk the egg whites and fold in. Spoon into the prepared dish and bake for 20 minutes, then lower the oven temperature to 350°F and bake for 5 minutes more. Serve immediately.

SOUFFLÉ DI MAIS PICCANTE

Serves 4

2 tablespoons butter, plus extra for greasing

2 tablespoons all-purpose flour

scant 1 cup milk

$2^3/_4$ cups Emmenthal cheese, grated

3 eggs, separated

2 cups canned sweetcorn, drained

$^1/_2$ red bell pepper, seeded and chopped

$^1/_2$ fresh chile, seeded and chopped

pinch of paprika

salt and pepper

POTATO SOUFFLÉ

Cook the potatoes in salted, boiling water for 20 minutes until tender, then drain and mash with a potato masher. Place in a pan and stir in the butter and cream over low heat. Cook, stirring constantly, for 15 minutes, then remove from the heat, stir in the nutmeg and season with salt and pepper. Let cool slightly. Preheat the oven to 400°F. Grease a soufflé dish with butter, sprinkle with the bread crumbs and turn to coat. Tip out any excess. Beat the egg yolks into the potato mixture, one at a time, then stir in the ham and Parmesan. Stiffly whisk the egg whites and fold in. Spoon into the prepared dish and bake for 20 minutes, then lower the oven temperature to 350°F and bake for 5 minutes more. Serve immediately.

SOUFFLÉ DI PATATE

Serves 6

$1^3/_4$ pounds potatoes

6 tablespoons butter, plus extra for greasing

scant 1 cup heavy cream

pinch of freshly grated nutmeg

$^3/_4$ cup bread crumbs

4 eggs, separated

scant 1 cup cooked cured ham, diced

4 tablespoons Parmesan cheese, freshly grated

salt and pepper

TOMATO SOUFFLÉ

SOUFFLÉ DI POMODORI

Serves 6

1¹/₂ tablespoons butter, plus extra for greasing

¹/₂ onion, thinly sliced

11 ounces tomatoes, peeled and chopped

4 fresh basil leaves, chopped

¹/₃ cup Parmesan cheese, freshly grated

¹/₄ cup Swiss cheese, freshly grated

1 quantity Béchamel Sauce (see page 50)

4 eggs, separated

salt and pepper

Melt the butter in a pan, add the onion and cook over low heat, stirring occasionally, for 10 minutes until golden brown. Add the tomatoes and basil and season with salt and pepper. Increase the heat and cook for 10–15 minutes until thickened and pulpy. Preheat the oven to 400°F. Grease a soufflé dish with butter. Stir the tomato sauce, Parmesan and Swiss cheese into the béchamel sauce and season with salt and pepper. Beat in the egg yolks, one at a time. Stiffly whisk the egg whites and fold in. Spoon into the prepared dish and bake for 20 minutes. Lower the oven temperature to 350°F and bake for 5 minutes more. Serve immediately.

HAM SOUFFLÉ

SOUFFLÉ DI PROSCIUTTO

Serves 4

6 tablespoons butter, plus extra for greasing

9 tablespoons all-purpose flour

1 cup milk

³/₄ cup bread crumbs

2 eggs, separated

generous 1 cup Parmesan cheese, freshly grated

generous ¹/₂ cup cooked cured ham, coarsely chopped

salt

Melt the butter in a pan, stir in the flour and cook, stirring constantly, for 3–4 minutes until lightly browned. Gradually stir in the milk, add a pinch of salt and cook, stirring, until the mixture comes away from the sides of the pan. Remove from the heat and let cool. Preheat the oven to 400°F. Grease a soufflé dish with butter, sprinkle with the bread crumbs and turn to coat. Tip out any excess. Beat the egg yolks into the cooled sauce, one at a time, then stir in the Parmesan and ham. Stiffly whisk the egg whites and fold in. Spoon the mixture into the prepared dish and bake for 20 minutes, then lower the oven temperature to 350°F and bake for 5 minutes more. Serve immediately.

SAVORY PIES, AND
QUICHES

At one time, savory tarts and pies were eaten only as snacks, at picnics or stand-up buffets. Today they increasingly replace the appetizer at elegant luncheons. They almost always have a pastry casing or base, which may be made of puff pastry, rough puff pastry or Pâte Brisée (see page 140). In most cases, savory Italian quiches are filled with vegetables mixed with béchamel sauce, ricotta, eggs and soft and hard cheeses. Although mostly round, quiches may also be baked in square or rectangular pans so that they can be cut more easily into squares and served with aperitifs. At the table they are served warm and whole, on wooden, wickerwork or rough pottery plates. Some are also good served cold.

ASPARAGUS QUICHE

Cook the asparagus in salted, boiling water for about 20 minutes until tender. Drain well and chop the spears, leaving the tips whole. Preheat the oven to 325°F. Dust a quiche pan with flour. Roll out the dough on a lightly floured surface to a round and line the prepared pan. Prick the base all over with a fork, line with baking parchment, fill with baking beans and bake blind for 15 minutes. Remove the beans and parchment, then spoon the asparagus over the base and sprinkle with the Swiss cheese. Increase the oven temperature to 400°F. Beat together the eggs, cream, milk and nutmeg in a bowl, season with salt and pepper and carefully pour into the pie shell. Bake for about 20 minutes and serve hot.

QUICHE AGLI ASPARAGI

Serves 6

9 ounces asparagus spears, trimmed

all-purpose flour, for dusting

7 ounces puff pastry dough, thawed if frozen

scant 1 cup Swiss cheese, freshly grated

3 eggs

$^2/_3$ cup heavy cream

$^2/_3$ cup milk

pinch of freshly grated nutmeg

salt and pepper

SMOKED SALMON QUICHE

QUICHE AL SALMONE AFFUMICATO

Serves 6

all-purpose flour, for dusting

7 ounces Pâte Brisée

(see page 140), thawed if frozen

3 smoked salmon slices, chopped

1¼ cups Swiss cheese, grated

4 eggs

1 cup heavy cream

salt and pepper

Preheat the oven to 325°F. Dust a quiche pan with flour. Roll out the pâte brisée on a lightly floured surface to a round and line the prepared pan. Prick the base all over with a fork, line with baking parchment, fill with baking beans and bake blind for 15 minutes. Remove the beans and parchment, scatter the salmon over the base of the pie shell and sprinkle with the Swiss cheese. Increase the oven temperature to 350°F. Beat together the eggs and cream in a bowl, season with salt and pepper and pour over the salmon. Bake for 45 minutes.

QUICHE LORRAINE

QUICHE LORRAINE

Serves 6

all-purpose flour, for dusting

11 ounces puff pastry dough, thawed if frozen

scant 1 cup bacon, diced

3 eggs

1–1¼ cups heavy cream

pinch of freshly grated nutmeg

salt and pepper

Preheat the oven to 325°F. Dust a quiche pan with flour. Roll out the dough on a lightly floured surface to a round and line the prepared pan. Prick the base all over with a fork, line with baking parchment, fill with baking beans and bake blind for 15 minutes. Meanwhile, cook the bacon in a small nonstick skillet, stirring frequently, for 5–8 minutes until golden brown but not crisp. Drain on paper towels. Beat together the eggs, cream and nutmeg in a bowl and season with salt and pepper. Remove the beans and parchment from the pie shell. Increase the oven temperature to 350°F. Sprinkle the bacon over the base of the pie shell, pour the cream mixture over it and bake for about 30 minutes. Serve hot or warm in slices.

MUSHROOM PIE WITH WALNUT CREAM

For the walnut cream, tear the bread into pieces, place in a bowl, add the milk and let soak. Melt the butter in a small skillet, add the shallot and cook over low heat, stirring occasionally, for about 5 minutes until softened. Squeeze out the bread, put it in a food processor with the egg, ham, walnuts and shallot and process until smooth. Scrape into a bowl, season with salt and pepper and chill in the refrigerator for 45 minutes. Meanwhile, parboil the mushrooms in salted water for 5 minutes. Drain, pat dry and slice thickly. Preheat the oven to 325°F. Sprinkle a quiche pan with flour. Roll out the dough on a lightly floured surface, and line the prepared pan. Line with baking parchment, fill with baking beans and bake blind for 10 minutes. Melt the butter in a small skillet, add the garlic and cook for 2–3 minutes. Remove the garlic. Remove the walnut mixture from the refrigerator and stir in the cream. Remove the beans and parchment from the pie shell and increase the oven temperature to 400°F. Pour the walnut cream into the pie shell, arrange the mushrooms on top like sunrays, brush the rim with the garlic-flavored butter and bake for 30 minutes.

SFOGLIA DI FUNGHI ALLA CREMA DI NOCI
Serves 6–8

2¹/₂ pounds mixed mushrooms, such as porcini, honey fungus and white mushrooms
all-purpose flour, for dusting
11 ounces puff pastry dough, thawed if frozen
1 tablespoon butter
1 garlic clove, halved

For the walnut cream
1 ounce bread (1 thick slice), crusts removed
3 tablespoons milk
2 tablespoons butter
1 shallot, thinly sliced
1 egg
¹/₃ cup cooked cured ham, chopped
scant 1 cup shelled walnuts, chopped
¹/₂ cup heavy cream
salt and pepper

BROCCOLI PIE

Preheat the oven to 350°F. Line a quiche pan with baking parchment. Parboil the broccoli in salted water for about 5 minutes. Drain and chop, leaving the flowerets whole. Melt the butter in a pan, add the broccoli and a little salt and cook over low heat, stirring occasionally, for 5 minutes. Remove from the heat. Roll out the dough on a lightly floured surface and line the prepared pan, trimming the edges. Prick the base all over with a fork. Mix half the fontina with the nutmeg and sprinkle evenly over the dough base. Arrange the broccoli on top. Mix the remaining fontina with the béchamel sauce and pour over the broccoli. Roll the dough edges over and brush with the egg yolk. Bake for about 40 minutes.

TORTA AI BROCCOLETTI
Serves 4–6

1 pound 2 ounces sprouting broccoli, cut into flowerets
2 tablespoons butter
11 ounces puff pastry dough, thawed if frozen
all-purpose flour, for dusting
9 ounces mild fontina cheese, grated
pinch of freshly grated nutmeg
1 quantity Béchamel Sauce (see page 50)
1 egg yolk, lightly beaten
salt

TORTA ALLA MARINARA

Serves 6

butter, for greasing

all-purpose flour, for dusting

7 ounces Pâte Brisée (see page 140), thawed if frozen

4 tablespoons chopped fresh flat-leaf parsley

2 tablespoons olive oil

1 garlic clove

7 ounces shelled clams

scant 1 cup ricotta cheese

2 eggs, lightly beaten

3 tablespoons heavy cream

7 ounces small cooked shrimp, peeled

salt and pepper

SEAFOOD PIE

Preheat the oven to 325°F. Grease a quiche pan with butter and dust with flour. Sprinkle the pâte brisée with 2 tablespoons of the parsley and roll out on a lightly floured surface, then line the prepared pan. Trim the edges and reserve the trimmings. Prick the base all over with a fork, then line with baking parchment and fill with baking beans. Bake blind for 15 minutes, then let cool. Remove the parchment and beans. Heat the olive oil in a pan, add the garlic and clams, plus a drop of water if necessary, and cook for 3−4 minutes. Remove and discard the garlic, add the remaining parsley and remove from the heat. Combine the ricotta and eggs in a bowl, season with salt and pepper, then stir in the cream, clams and shrimp. Spoon the filling into the pie shell, spreading it out evenly. Roll out the trimmings, cut into thin strips, brush the ends with water and arrange in a lattice over the top of the pie. Bake for 40 minutes.

TORTA ALLA RUCOLA E TALEGGIO

Serves 6

1³/₄ cups all-purpose flour, plus extra for dusting

1 tablespoon poppy seeds

1 tablespoon chopped fresh marjoram

scant 1 cup butter, chilled and diced, plus extra for greasing

For the filling

7 ounces arugula

1¹/₃ cups cream cheese

7 ounces Taleggio cheese, diced

2 tablespoons bread crumbs

2 eggs

salt and pepper

ARUGULA AND TALEGGIO PIE

Sift the flour with a pinch of salt into a mound on the counter, sprinkle with the poppy seeds and marjoram and rub in the butter with your fingertips. Add enough cold water to make a soft pastry, then shape into a ball, cover with plastic wrap and let rest for 1 hour. Preheat the oven to 350°F. Grease a quiche pan with butter. Parboil the arugula for a few minutes in salted water, then drain, squeezing out as much liquid as possible. Put the arugula in a food processor with both cheeses, the bread crumbs and eggs. Process at low speed, then season with salt and pepper. Roll out the dough on a lightly floured surface, and line the prepared pan, trim the edges and reserve the trimmings. Fill with the arugula and cheese mixture and roll the dough edges over slightly. Roll out the trimmings, cut into thin strips, brush the ends with water and arrange in a lattice over the top of the pie. Bake for about 40 minutes.

COD AND MUSHROOM PIE

Pour 2¼ cups water and the wine into a pan. Stud the onion with the cloves, add to the pan and bring to a boil. Add the fish and cook over low heat for about 20 minutes. Remove the cod with a metal spatula and boil the stock to reduce slightly, then set aside. Sprinkle the cod with the marjoram, thyme and parsley, and season with pepper. Melt the butter in a skillet, add the mushrooms and cook over low heat, stirring occasionally, for about 10 minutes. Remove from the heat and set aside. Preheat the oven to 325°F. Grease a quiche pan with butter. Make the béchamel sauce using half milk and half fish stock, then stir in the mushrooms, Swiss cheese, cream and eggs and season with salt and pepper. Roll out the pâte brisée on a lightly floured surface and line the prepared pan. Prick the base all over with a fork, line with baking parchment and fill with baking beans. Bake blind for 15 minutes, then remove from the oven and increase the temperature to 350°F. Remove the parchment and beans. Chop the fish and sprinkle evenly over the pie shell. Cover with the béchamel sauce mixture and return to the oven for 40 minutes. Serve warm.

TORTA DELICATA DI MERLUZZO
AGLI CHAMPIGNON

Serves 6

2¼ cups dry white wine

1 large onion, halved

2 cloves

6 cod fillets, skinned

1 tablespoon chopped fresh marjoram

2 teaspoons chopped fresh thyme

1 fresh flat-leaf parsley sprig, leaves only

2 tablespoons butter, plus extra for greasing

2¼ pounds mushrooms, thinly sliced

1 quantity Béchamel Sauce

(see page 50 and method)

scant 1 cup Swiss cheese, grated

2 tablespoons heavy cream

2 eggs, lightly beaten

9 ounces Pâte Brisée

(see page 140), thawed if frozen

salt and pepper

SAVORY CABBAGE PIE

Sift the flour into a bowl, add ⅔ cup of the butter and rub in with your fingertips. Stir in 3–4 tablespoons water to make a firm pastry. Set aside for 1 hour. Cook the carrots and cauliflower in separate pans of lightly salted, boiling water for 10 minutes until tender, then drain. Cut the cauliflower into flowerets. Melt 3 tablespoons of the remaining butter in a pan, add the cauliflower and cook, stirring frequently, for 5 minutes, then season and remove from the pan. Melt the remaining butter in the pan, add the cabbage and cook, stirring frequently, for 5 minutes until softened, season and remove from the heat. Preheat the oven to 400°F. Grease a large pie dish with butter. Divide the dough into two pieces, one larger than the other. Roll out the large piece on a lightly floured surface and line the prepared dish. Shell the eggs and slice, preferably with an egg slicer. Make a layer of egg slices in the base of the dish, cover with a layer of cauliflower flowerets, then a layer of fontina, then a layer of cabbage and carrots. Continue making layers until all the ingredients are used. Roll out the remaining dough, cover the pie, trim and crimp the edges to seal. Cut a hole in the center of the lid and prick the surface with a fork. Bake for 30 minutes and serve hot.

TORTA DI CAVOLI

Serves 6–8

2¼ cups whole-wheat flour, plus extra for dusting

generous 1 cup butter, plus extra for greasing

3 carrots, sliced

1 medium cauliflower

½ white cabbage, shredded

4 eggs, hard-cooked

5 ounces fontina cheese, sliced

salt

TORTA DI CIPOLLE ALL'ANTICA

Serves 6

4 tablespoons butter, plus extra for greasing

all-purpose flour, for dusting

1 cup golden raisins

1 cup dry white wine

7 ounces Pâte Brisée

(see page 140), thawed if frozen

2^1/$_4$ pounds onions, thinly sliced

marrow from 2 beef bones, diced

pinch of sugar

salt and pepper

OLD—FASHIONED ONION PIE

Preheat the oven to 325°F. Grease a quiche pan with butter and sprinkle with flour, tipping the pan to coat. Put the golden raisins in a bowl, pour in the wine and let soak. Roll out the pâte brisée on a lightly floured surface and line the prepared pan, trimming the edges. Reserve the trimmings. Prick the base all over with a fork. Line with baking parchment, fill with baking beans and bake blind for 15 minutes. Remove the pie shell and increase the oven temperature to 350°F. Meanwhile, melt the butter in a skillet, add the onions and cook over low heat, stirring occasionally, for 10 minutes until golden brown. Stir in the beef marrow, the golden raisins with the wine and a pinch of sugar, season with salt and pepper and cook until the wine has evaporated. Remove the parchment and beans from the pie shell, pour in the onion mixture and spread evenly. Roll out the trimmings, cut into thin strips, brush the ends with water and arrange in a lattice over the top of the pie. Bake for 30 minutes. Serve warm, cut into slices.

TORTA DI ERBETTE E CARCIOFI

Serves 6

4^1/$_2$ cups all-purpose flour, plus extra for dusting

6 tablespoons olive oil

2 white bread slices, crusts removed

^{1}/$_2$ cup pint milk

1 pound 2 ounces leafy green vegetables,

such as Swiss chard, spinach and turnip greens

juice of 1 lemon, strained

12 globe artichokes

butter, for greasing

1 onion, thinly sliced

generous 1 cup romano cheese, freshly grated

^{2}/$_3$ cup Parmesan cheese, freshly grated

1 tablespoon chopped fresh marjoram

salt and pepper

WILD GREENS AND ARTICHOKE PIE

Sift the flour with a pinch of salt into a mound on the counter, then add 4 tablespoons of the olive oil and just enough water to knead to a soft pastry. Let rest in the refrigerator for 30 minutes. Tear the bread into pieces, place in a bowl and pour in the milk. Let soak. Cook the greens in salted, boiling water for 5—10 minutes until tender, then drain, squeezing out as much liquid as possible, and chop. Half-fill a bowl with water and add the lemon juice. Remove and discard the outer leaves from the artichokes, cut off the top 2 inches of the remaining leaves and remove the chokes. Drop into the acidulated water and set aside for about 10 minutes. Preheat the oven to 400°F and grease a quiche pan with butter. Drain the artichokes, chop and put in a pan with the onion and the remaining oil. Cook over low heat for 10 minutes until softened. Squeeze out the bread and add to the pan with the greens and cheeses. Mix well, season with salt and pepper and sprinkle with the marjoram. Roll out the dough on a lightly floured surface into two rounds, one larger than the other. Place the larger one in the prepared pan, spoon in the vegetable mixture, cover with the second pastry round and crimp the edges to seal. Prick with a fork in a spiral pattern and bake for about 40 minutes. This pie may be served hot, warm or cold.

CHICKEN AND CHERVIL PIE

Preheat the oven to 325°F. Grease a quiche pan with butter. Melt half the butter in a pan, add the onion and cook over low heat, stirring occasionally, for 5 minutes until softened. Pour in 2¹/₄ cups water and the wine, bring to a boil and add the chicken. Bring back to a boil, then remove the chicken and onion with a slotted spoon and boil the liquid until reduced. Heat the remaining butter in another pan, add the chervil and cook, stirring frequently, for a few minutes. Stir in the flour, the reduced cooking liquid and the milk, season with salt and pepper and bring to a boil, stirring constantly. Turn out the heat and stir in the chicken, onion, Swiss cheese and cream. Roll out the pâte brisée on a lightly floured surface to a round and line the prepared pan. Prick the base all over with a fork, line with baking parchment and fill with baking beans. Bake blind for 15 minutes. Remove the beans and parchment, spoon in the filling, roll the pastry edges inwards slightly and prick with a fork. Increase the oven temperature to 350°F and bake for about 40 minutes. Serve warm.

TORTA DI POLLO AL CERFOGLIO

Serves 6

¹/₄ cup butter, plus extra for greasing

2 ounces onion, thinly sliced

2¹/₄ cups white wine

1 pound 2 ounces skinless,

boneless chicken portions, diced

2 bunches of fresh chervil, chopped

¹/₂ cup all-purpose flour, plus extra for dusting

3 cups milk

scant 1 cup Swiss cheese, grated

scant ¹/₂ cup heavy cream

7 ounces Pâte Brisée

(see page 140), thawed if frozen

salt and pepper

LEEK PIE

Preheat the oven to 325°F. Grease a quiche pan with butter. Melt the butter in a pan, add the leeks and cook over a low heat, stirring occasionally, for 5 minutes until softened. Sprinkle with the Parmesan and season with salt and pepper, then remove from the heat. Beat together the milk, cream, eggs, flour, Emmenthal and nutmeg in a bowl. Stir in the leeks and set aside. Roll out the pâte brisée on a lightly floured surface to a round and line the prepared pan. Prick the base all over with a fork, line with baking parchment and fill with baking beans. Bake blind for 15 minutes. Remove the beans and parchment, spoon in the filling and bake for about 40 minutes. Serve warm.

TORTA DI PORRI

Serves 6

2 tablespoons butter, plus extra for greasing

1³/₄ pounds leeks, trimmed and thinly sliced

1 tablespoon Parmesan cheese, freshly grated

1 cup milk

²/₃ cup heavy cream

3 eggs, lightly beaten

1 teaspoon all-purpose flour, plus extra for dusting

generous ¹/₂ cup Emmenthal cheese, grated

pinch of freshly grated nutmeg

7 ounces Pâte Brisée

(see page 140), thawed if frozen

salt and pepper

HAM AND TARRAGON PIE

TORTA DI PROSCIUTTO AL DRAGONCELLO

Serves 6

¼ cup butter, plus extra for greasing

2 bunches of fresh tarragon, finely chopped

½ cup all-purpose flour, plus extra for dusting

3 cups milk

generous 1 cup cooked cured ham, diced

scant 1 cup Swiss cheese, grated

scant ½ cup heavy cream

7 ounces Pâte Brisée

(see page 140), thawed if frozen

salt and pepper

Preheat the oven to 325°F. Grease a quiche pan with butter. Melt the butter in a pan, add the tarragon and cook over low heat, stirring frequently, for a few minutes. Stir in the flour, then gradually stir in the milk and season with salt and pepper. Bring to a boil, stirring constantly, then remove from the heat. Add the ham, Swiss cheese and cream and set aside. Roll out the pâte brisée into a round on a lightly floured surface and line the prepared pan. Prick the base all over with a fork, line with baking parchment and fill with baking beans. Bake blind for 15 minutes. Remove the beans and parchment, spoon in the ham and tarragon mixture, roll the pastry edge inwards slightly and prick with a fork. Increase the oven temperature to 350°F and bake for 30 minutes. Let cool slightly, then serve.

SPINACH AND SALMON PIE

TORTA DI SPINACI AL SALMONE

Serves 6

3 tablespoons butter, plus extra for greasing

4 salmon fillets

2¼ pounds spinach

½ cup all-purpose flour, plus extra for dusting

2¼ cups milk

pinch of freshly grated nutmeg

2 teaspoons chopped fresh thyme

scant 1 cup Swiss cheese, grated

scant ½ cup heavy cream

7 ounces Pâte Brisée

(see page 140), thawed if frozen

salt and pepper

Preheat the oven to 325°F. Grease a quiche pan with butter. Place the salmon in a pan, add water to cover and a pinch of salt and bring just to a boil. Lower the heat and poach for 10 minutes. Meanwhile, cook the spinach, in just the water clinging to the leaves after washing, for 5 minutes, then drain well, squeezing out as much liquid as possible, and chop. Drain the salmon, reserving 1¼ cups of the cooking liquid, and flake. Melt the butter in a pan, stir in the flour, milk, reserved cooking liquid, nutmeg and thyme and season with salt and pepper. Remove from the heat and stir in the Swiss cheese, cream, spinach and salmon. Roll out the pâte brisée into a round on a lightly floured surface and line the prepared pan. Prick the base all over with a fork, line with baking parchment and fill with baking beans. Bake blind for 15 minutes. Remove the beans and parchment, spoon in the spinach and salmon mixture, roll over the pastry edges slightly and prick with a fork. Increase the oven temperature to 350°F and bake for 30 minutes. Serve warm.

RUSTIC VEGETABLE PIE

Cook the spinach, chard, salad greens, zucchini and leeks in salted, boiling water for 5–10 minutes until tender. Drain, squeeze out as much liquid as possible and chop coarsely. Beat the eggs with the romano, add the vegetables and 6 tablespoons of the oil and season with salt and pepper. Mix well and let stand. Preheat the oven to 400°F and line a rectangular pie dish with baking parchment. Sift the flour with a pinch of salt into a mound on a counter. Make a well in the center, add the remaining oil and generous 1 cup warm water and gradually incorporate the flour using your fingers. Knead well, then roll out on a lightly floured surface into two rectangles, one larger than the other. Line the pie dish with the larger sheet and spoon in the vegetable mixture. Cover with the smaller sheet of pastry, trim and crimp the edges to seal. Make a hole in the center. Bake for 30 minutes. This pie, called 'scarpazza' in Tuscany, may be served warm or cold.

TORTA DI VERDURE DELLA LUNIGIANA

Serves 6–8

1 pound 2 ounces spinach

1 pound 2 ounces Swiss chard

1 pound 2 ounces wild salad greens,
such as borage, arugula and dandelion

2 zucchini, sliced

2 leeks, trimmed and sliced

2 eggs

$2/3$ cup romano cheese, grated

$2/3$ cup olive oil

$2^{3}/4$ cups all-purpose flour, plus extra for dusting

salt and pepper

PUMPKIN PIE

Preheat the oven to 350°F. Grease a pie dish with butter. Place the mushrooms in a bowl, add warm water to cover and let soak for 20 minutes. Place the pumpkin in an ovenproof dish, drizzle with the oil and bake for 20 minutes, then push through a strainer. Increase the oven temperature to 400°F. Drain and chop the mushrooms. Melt the butter in a small pan, add the onion and mushrooms and cook over low heat, stirring occasionally, for 5 minutes. Add the pumpkin purée and cook, stirring constantly, for 10 minutes. Remove the pan from the heat and stir in the Parmesan, egg and egg yolk and season with salt and pepper. Divide the dough in half and roll out one piece to a round on a lightly floured surface. Line the prepared dish, cover the base with the Swiss cheese and spoon in the pumpkin mixture. Roll out the remaining dough into a round and cover the pie. Trim and crimp the edges together to seal, prick all over with a fork and bake for 1 hour.

TORTA DI ZUCCA

Serves 6–8

$1/4$ cup butter, plus extra for greasing

$1/3$ cup dried mushrooms

$2^{1}/4$ pounds pumpkin, peeled, seeded and sliced

2 tablespoons olive oil

1 onion, thinly sliced into rings

4 tablespoons Parmesan cheese, freshly grated

1 egg

1 egg yolk

11 ounces puff pastry dough, thawed if frozen

all-purpose flour, for dusting

2 ounces Swiss cheese, sliced

salt and pepper

TORTA PASQUALINA

Serves 12

butter, for greasing

1 pound 5 ounces Swiss chard

10 eggs

1¹/₃ cups ricotta cheese

2 tablespoons Parmesan cheese, freshly grated

2 tablespoons bread crumbs

scant 1 cup heavy cream

1 tablespoon chopped fresh marjoram

14 ounces puff pastry dough, thawed if frozen

all-purpose flour, for dusting

olive oil, for brushing

salt and pepper

EASTER PIE

Preheat the oven to 400°F. Grease a large pie dish with butter. Cook the chard in salted, boiling water for 10 minutes until tender, then drain and chop. Beat together four of the eggs. Push the ricotta through a strainer into a bowl, add the beaten eggs, Parmesan, bread crumbs and cream and season. Stir in the chard and marjoram. Roll out half the dough on a lightly floured surface into two thin sheets. Line the prepared dish with a sheet of dough, letting the edges overhang, and brush with oil. Place the second sheet on top and pour in half the chard mixture. Make six small hollows in the chard mixture and break an egg into each. Season, cover with the remaining chard mixture and smooth the surface with a damp knife. Roll out the remaining dough into two thin sheets. Place one on the filling and brush with oil, then top with the second and crimp carefully around the sides to seal. Prick the surface with a fork. Bake for about 1 hour. Easter pie may be served hot or cold.

TORTA RUSTICA ARCOBALENO

Serves 8–10

2³/₄ cups all-purpose flour, plus extra for dusting

scant 1 cup dry white wine

1 tablespoon olive oil

1 pound 2 ounces spinach

2 tablespoons butter, plus extra for greasing

scant ¹/₂ cup heavy cream

4 tablespoons Parmesan cheese, freshly grated

1 tablespoon chopped fresh thyme

2 red bell peppers

2 yellow bell peppers

7 ounces cooked cured ham, thinly sliced

7 ounces fontina cheese, thinly sliced

1 egg yolk, lightly beaten

salt and pepper

FARMHOUSE RAINBOW PIE

Sift the flour with a pinch of salt into a mound on a counter. Make a well in the center and pour in the wine and oil, then gradually incorporate the flour with your fingers, adding enough water to make a smooth pastry. Knead lightly, form into a ball and place in the refrigerator to rest for 30 minutes. Cook the spinach, in just the water clinging to the leaves after washing, for 5 minutes, then drain, squeezing out as much liquid as possible, and chop. Melt the butter in a skillet, add the spinach and cook, stirring frequently, for 5 minutes, then season with salt and pepper and stir in the cream, Parmesan and thyme. Place the bell peppers on a cookie sheet and set under a preheated broiler, turning frequently, until the skins are charred and blistered. Transfer to a plastic bag and tie the top. When cool enough to handle, peel off the skins, halve and seed the bell peppers and cut into large slices. Preheat the oven to 350°F. Grease a large pie dish with butter. Divide the dough in half. Roll out one piece on a lightly floured surface and line the prepared dish. Arrange a layer of ham on the base, cover with a layer of the spinach mixture, then a layer of red bell pepper and a layer of fontina. Repeat the layers, using yellow bell pepper instead of the red. Continue making layers until all the ingredients are used, gently pressing each one down. Roll out the remaining dough, cover the pie, trim and crimp the edges to seal. Prick with a fork and brush with the egg yolk. Bake for 1 hour, then serve hot or cold.

TORTA RUSTICA ZIA MARIA

Serves 6–8

2³/₄ cups all-purpose flour

3 eggs

1 tablespoon sugar

scant 1 cup butter, softened

3–4 tablespoons milk

2 tablespoons Parmesan cheese, freshly grated

7 ounces mozzarella cheese, diced

5 ounces cooked cured ham, cut into strips

3¹/₂ ounces mortadella, cut into strips

¹/₂ quantity Béchamel Sauce (see page 50)

AUNT MARIA'S FARMHOUSE PIE

Preheat the oven to 350°F. Sift the flour into a mound on a counter, make a well in the center and add one of the eggs, the sugar, butter and half the milk. Gradually incorporate the flour with your fingertips, adding more milk if necessary to make a soft dough. Knead lightly. Beat the remaining eggs in a bowl, then add the Parmesan, mozzarella, ham and mortadella and mix well. Set a small piece of dough aside, roll out the remainder on a lightly floured surface and line a pie dish. Spoon in the filling, level the surface and cover with a thin layer of béchamel sauce. Roll out the remaining dough, cut into thin strips, brush the ends with water and arrange in a lattice over the top of the pie. Brush with milk and bake for 45 minutes. Serve warm.

PATTY SHELLS

The famous French chef and pastry cook Antonin Carême (1784–1833) not only invented pièces montées, table center-pieces, but also created the fragile and delicious patty shell known as vol-au vent. An extremely fine puff pastry he put in the oven one day started to rise with the heat and puffed up so wonderfully that one of his assistants drew his attention to it by calling out, 'It is flying in the wind' hence 'vol-au-vent'. The experts say that a classic patty shell should be 6 inches in diameter, but both bigger and smaller ones are now made. Nowadays, most people buy patty shells ready made or order them from bakeries, so it's probably sensible to consider how different-sized ones are used. The small or extremely small ones, just over $1^1/_4$ inches in diameter, that can be eaten in one bite, are suitable for filling with ragù (meat sauce), creamed mushrooms or peas and for serving at stand-up buffets with aperitifs. Medium-size ones, $2^1/_2$ inches, filled with chicken giblets, brains with butter or asparagus and mushrooms, are an alternative first course instead of pasta or risotto. The biggest ones, 6–8 inches, filled with tortellini, raviolini or maccheroncini, are suitable for formal dinners because of their impressive appearance.

VALLE D'AOSTA PATTY SHELLS

Place the fontina in a bowl, pour in half the milk and let soak for 4–5 hours. Preheat the oven to 300°F. Drain the cheese, place in the top of a double boiler or a heatproof bowl set over a pan of barely simmering water, pour in the remaining milk and melt the cheese, stirring constantly. Stir in the egg yolks, one at a time, and season with salt and pepper to taste. Pour the cheese sauce into the patty shells, place them on a cookie sheet, and warm through in the oven for a few minutes before serving.

VOL–AU–VENT ALLA VALDOSTANA

Serves 4

11 ounces fontina cheese, thinly sliced

$1^3/_4$ cups milk

2 egg yolks

8 medium patty shells

salt and pepper

CHICKEN IN PATTY SHELLS

VOL-AU-VENT AL POLLO

Serves 4

2 tablespoons olive oil

1 onion, thinly sliced

$3^{1}/_{2}$ ounces leeks, white part only, thinly sliced

7 ounces skinless, boneless chicken portion, diced

$^{1}/_{3}$ cup blanched almonds, chopped

$1^{1}/_{2}$ teaspoons all-purpose flour

scant $^{1}/_{2}$ cup dry white wine

1 cup Chicken Stock (see page 209)

1 tablespoon chopped fresh flat-leaf parsley

8 medium patty shells

salt and pepper

Preheat the oven to 300°F. Heat the oil in a skillet and cook the onion and leeks over low heat, stirring occasionally, for 5 minutes until softened. Add the chicken and almonds, sprinkle with the flour, pour in the wine and cook until the liquid has evaporated. Stir in the stock, season with salt and pepper and cook until the sauce is fairly thick. Remove the pan from the heat and stir in the parsley. Fill the patty shells with the mixture, place on a cookie sheet and warm through in the oven for a few minutes.

HAM IN PATTY SHELLS

VOL-AU-VENT AL PROSCIUTTO

Serves 4

2 tablespoons butter

1 onion, chopped

generous $^{1}/_{2}$ cup prosciutto, diced

scant 1 cup shelled baby peas

$^{2}/_{3}$ cup Meat Stock (see page 208)

generous $^{1}/_{2}$ cup cooked cured ham, diced

3 tablespoons heavy cream

1 egg yolk, lightly beaten

8 medium patty shells

salt and pepper

Preheat the oven to 300°F. Line a cookie sheet with foil. Melt the butter in a small pan, add the onion and cook over low heat, stirring occasionally, for 5 minutes until softened. Add the prosciutto, baby peas and stock and cook for about 10 minutes until the liquid has evaporated. Season with salt and pepper, remove from the heat and stir in the cooked, cured ham, cream and egg yolk. Mix well, then return to the heat for a few minutes. Fill the patty shells with the mixture, place on a cookie sheet and warm through in the oven for 5 minutes.

SHRIMP IN PATTY SHELLS

VOL-AU-VENT CON GLI SCAMPI

Serves 4

2 tablespoons butter

$^{1}/_{2}$ onion, thinly sliced

pinch of curry powder

1 teaspoon all-purpose flour

scant 1 cup milk

1 teaspoon tomato paste

1 egg, lightly beaten

juice of 1 lemon, strained

7 ounces cooked shrimp, peeled and deveined

12 small patty shells

salt and pepper

Preheat the oven to 300°F. Heat the butter in a pan, add the onion and cook over low heat, stirring occasionally, for 5 minutes until softened and translucent. Stir in the curry powder and flour, then gradually stir in the milk. Stir the tomato paste with $^{1}/_{2}$ teaspoon lukewarm water and stir into the pan. Season with salt and pepper and cook until thickened. Quickly stir in the egg, lemon juice and shrimp and immediately remove the pan from the heat. Fill the patty shells with the mixture, place on a cookie sheet and heat through in the oven for 5 minutes.

PIZZAS

Yes – pizza really was a completely Italian idea which the whole world has copied. Truly the word pizza is used in every corner of the globe. All Italians take it for granted that the term refers to the Neapolitan pizza. The ingredients for the base are flour, fresh yeast, water and salt. (If fresh yeast is not available, use half the quantity of dried yeast and follow the packet instructions for dissolving it.) The topping in the case of a classic pizza is oil, tomato and mozzarella cheese. However, infinite variations are possible, using, for example, fish, a variety of cheeses, eggs and vegetables. Pizzas may be served as a first course, a snack, for dinner and as a dessert. They may vary in size from pizzette (mini pizzas), served with aperitifs, to normal and gigantic pizzas. Pizzas need fizzy drinks to stimulate the digestion. Beer is fine, but those who prefer wine may choose a sparkling white, preferably light, young and fruity.

PIZZA DOUGH (BASIC RECIPE)

Sift the flour and salt into a mound on a counter and make a well in the center. Mash the yeast in the water with a fork until very smooth and pour into the well. Incorporate the flour with your fingers to make a soft dough. Knead well, pulling and stretching until it becomes smooth and elastic. Shape into a ball, cut a cross in the top, place in a bowl and cover. Let rise in a warm place for about 3 hours until almost doubled in size. Flatten the dough with the palm of your hand and roll out on a lightly floured surface to a round about ¼ inch thick. Brush a cookie sheet with oil or line it with baking parchment. Put the dough round on it and press out until it covers the area. Make sure the rim is thicker than the center. Sprinkle with the topping ingredients, leaving a ¾-inch margin around the edge.

IMPASTO PER LA PIZZA
(RICETTA BASE)

Serves 4

1¼ cups all-purpose flour,
preferably Italian type 00, plus extra for dusting
¾ teaspoon salt
½ ounces fresh yeast
½ cup lukewarm water
olive oil, for brushing (optional)

CALZONE

CALZONE

Serves 2

olive oil, for brushing

1 quantity Pizza Dough (see page 193)

all-purpose flour, for dusting

2 ounces mozzarella cheese, diced

$^1/_4$ cup Italian salami, diced

3 tablespoons cooked cured ham, diced

1 egg, lightly beaten

2 tablespoons ricotta cheese, crumbled

salt and pepper

Preheat the oven to 425°F. Brush a cookie sheet with oil or line with baking parchment. Knead the dough for 1 minute. Roll out on a lightly floured surface into two rounds. Combine the mozzarella, salami, ham and egg, then season with salt and pepper and add the ricotta. Sprinkle the mixture on one side of each dough round and fold the rounds in half. Crimp the edges to seal. Place on the cookie sheet and bake for about 15 minutes.

MUSHROOM PIZZA

PIZZA AI FUNGHI

Serves 4

3 tablespoons olive oil, plus extra for brushing

1 garlic clove, chopped

$4^3/_4$ cups mushrooms, sliced

2 tablespoons chopped fresh flat-leaf parsley

1 quantity Pizza Dough (see page 193)

all-purpose flour, for dusting

salt and pepper

Heat the oil in a skillet, add the garlic and mushrooms and cook over low heat, stirring frequently, for 5 minutes. Season with salt and pepper, sprinkle with the parsley and simmer over very low heat for about 30 minutes. Preheat the oven to 425°F and brush a cookie sheet with oil or line it with baking parchment. Roll out the dough on a lightly floured surface, then press it out on the cookie sheet. Sprinkle the mushrooms on top and bake for 20 minutes.

PIZZA NAPOLETANA

PIZZA ALLA NAPOLETANA

Serves 4

olive oil, for brushing and drizzling

1 quantity Pizza Dough (see page 193)

all-purpose flour, for dusting

5–6 tomatoes, peeled and chopped

1 mozzarella cheese, sliced

pinch of dried oregano

8 canned anchovy fillets, drained

salt

Preheat the oven to 425°F. Brush a cookie sheet with oil or line with baking parchment. Roll out the dough on a lightly floured surface, then press it out on the cookie sheet. Sprinkle the tomato flesh evenly on top and drizzle with oil poured around, once, in a circle. Bake for about 18 minutes. Add the mozzarella, oregano and anchovies, season with salt and drizzle with oil if necessary. Bake for a further 7–8 minutes until crisp.

PIZZA ALLA PESCATORA

Serves 4

11 ounces baby octopuses, cleaned and skinned

2 tablespoons olive oil,

plus extra for brushing and drizzling

11 ounces raw shrimp

11 ounces live clams, scrubbed

11 ounces live mussels,

scrubbed and beards removed

1 onion, thinly sliced

4 garlic cloves, thinly sliced

1 fresh chile, seeded and chopped

1 tablespoon chopped fresh flat-leaf parsley

1 quantity Pizza Dough (see page 193)

all-purpose flour, for dusting

11 ounces cherry tomatoes,

peeled and cut into fourths

salt

FISHERMAN'S PIZZA

Cook the octopuses in salted, boiling water until tender, then drain well. Preheat the oven to 425°F. Brush a cookie sheet with oil and line with baking parchment. Parboil the shrimp for 2–3 minutes, then drain, peel and devein them. Discard any clams or mussels with broken shells or that do not shut immediately when sharply tapped. Place them in a dry skillet and set over high heat for 5 minutes until they open. Discard any that remain closed. Remove the clams and mussels from their shells. Heat the oil in a skillet, add the onion, garlic and chile and cook over low heat, stirring occasionally, for 5 minutes, then add the octopuses, mussels, clams and shrimp. Season with salt and cook, stirring frequently, for 5 minutes. Remove from the heat and add the parsley. Roll out the dough on a lightly floured surface, then press it out on the cookie sheet. Sprinkle the tomatoes on top, drizzle with oil and bake for about 15 minutes. Arrange the seafood on top and return the pizza to the oven for 7–8 minutes more (no longer or the seafood will become tough).

PIZZA ALLE PATATE

Serves 4

3 large potatoes

olive oil, for brushing and drizzling

1 quantity Pizza Dough (see page 193)

all-purpose flour, for dusting

generous 1 cup pancetta, diced

3¹/₂ ounces Taleggio cheese, diced

2 ounces Parmesan cheese, shaved

2 teaspoons chopped fresh rosemary

salt and pepper

POTATO PIZZA

Cook the potatoes in salted, boiling water for 20 minutes until tender. Drain, peel and thinly slice. Preheat the oven to 425°F. Brush a cookie sheet with oil or line with baking parchment. Roll out the dough on a lightly floured surface, then press out on the cookie sheet. Arrange the slices of potatoes on top and drizzle with oil. Bake for about 15 minutes, then sprinkle with the pancetta, cheeses and rosemary and season with salt and pepper. Drizzle with oil and bake for 7–8 minutes more. Serve hot.

PIZZA BIANCA

Serves 4

olive oil for brushing and drizzling

1 quantity Pizza Dough (see page 193)

all-purpose flour, for dusting

5 ounces mozzarella cheese, sliced

5 ounces Taleggio cheese, diced

pinch of dried oregano • salt and pepper

'WHITE' PIZZA

Preheat the oven to 425°F. Brush a cookie sheet with oil or line with baking parchment. Roll out the dough on a lightly floured surface, then press out on the cookie sheet. Arrange the mozzarella and Taleggio on top, sprinkle with oregano, season with salt and pepper and drizzle with oil. Bake for about 20 minutes.

SAUSAGE PIZZA

PIZZA CON LE SALSICCE

Serves 4

olive oil, for brushing and drizzling

7 ounces Italian sausages, skinned and crumbled

²/₃ cup romano cheese, freshly grated

1 quantity Pizza Dough (see page 193)

all-purpose flour, for dusting

4 tomatoes, peeled and chopped

3¹/₂ ounces smoked pancetta, sliced

1 teaspoon chopped fresh rosemary

6 fresh basil leaves, torn

salt and pepper

Preheat the oven to 425°F. Brush a cookie sheet with oil or line with baking parchment. Combine the sausages and romano in a bowl and season with salt and pepper. Roll out the dough on a lightly floured surface, then press it out on the cookie sheet. Sprinkle the tomatoes on top and drizzle with oil. Bake for 20 minutes. Sprinkle with the sausage mixture and top with the pancetta. Sprinkle with the rosemary and basil, drizzle with oil and bake for 7–8 minutes more.

BELGIAN ENDIVE PIZZA

PIZZA D'INDIVIA

Serves

2 tablespoons oil, plus extra for brushing

1 onion, chopped

1 garlic clove, chopped

3¹/₂ ounces tomatoes, peeled and chopped

4 Belgian endive heads, trimmed and separated into leaves

2 tablespoons heavy cream

1 quantity Pizza Dough (see page 193)

all-purpose flour, for dusting

3¹/₂ ounces prosciutto, sliced

salt

Heat the oil in a pan, add the onion and garlic and cook over low heat, stirring occasionally, for 5 minutes until soft. Add the tomatoes and Belgian endive, cover and cook for 10 minutes. Sprinkle with salt and continue cooking for 20 minutes more, adding a little hot water if the mixture seems to be drying out. Meanwhile, preheat the oven to 425°F. Brush a cookie sheet with oil or line with baking parchment. When the Belgian endive is very soft, stir in the cream and cook until thickened, then remove from the heat. Roll out the dough on a lightly floured surface, then press it out on the cookie sheet. Spread the Belgian endive mixture on top and bake for 20 minutes. Remove the pizza from the oven, lay the slices of prosciutto on top and serve immediately.

MARGHERITA PIZZA

PIZZA MARGHERITA

Serves 4

olive oil, for brushing and drizzling

1 quantity Pizza Dough (see page 193)

all-purpose flour, for dusting

5–6 tomatoes, peeled and chopped

1 mozzarella cheese, sliced

6 fresh basil leaves, torn

salt and pepper

Preheat the oven to 425°F. Brush a cookie sheet with oil or line with baking parchment. Roll out the dough on a lightly floured surface, then press it out on the cookie sheet. Sprinkle the tomatoes on top and drizzle with oil. Bake for 15–20 minutes. Add the mozzarella slices and basil, season with salt and pepper and drizzle with oil. Bake for 7–8 minutes more.

FOUR SEASONS PIZZA

Preheat the oven to 425°F. Brush a cookie sheet with oil or line with baking parchment. Cut the anchovy fillets in half lengthwise. Discard any mussels with broken shells or that do not shut immediately when sharply tapped. Place in a dry skillet and set over high heat for 5 minutes until they open. Remove the mussels from their shells. Roll out the dough on a lightly floured surface, then press it out on the cookie sheet. Sprinkle the tomatoes on top and mark out a cross using the back of a knife. Arrange the anchovy fillets and green olives in one fourth, the mussels in another, the ham and mozzarella in the third, and the artichokes and black olives in the fourth. Season with salt and pepper, drizzle with oil and bake for 15–20 minutes.

PIZZA QUATTRO STAGIONI

Serves 4

olive oil, for brushing and drizzling

4 salted anchovies, heads removed, cleaned and filleted (see page 596), soaked in cold water for 10 minutes and drained

3¹/₂ ounces live mussels, scrubbed and beards removed

1 quantity Pizza Dough (see page 193)

all-purpose flour, for dusting

4 tomatoes, peeled and chopped

¹/₂ cup green olives

¹/₃ cup cooked cured ham, diced

2 ounces mozzarella cheese, diced

4 baby artichokes in oil, drained and halved

¹/₂ cup black olives

salt and pepper

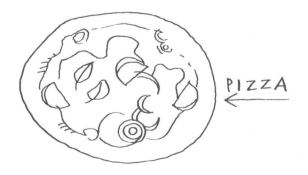

PIZZA

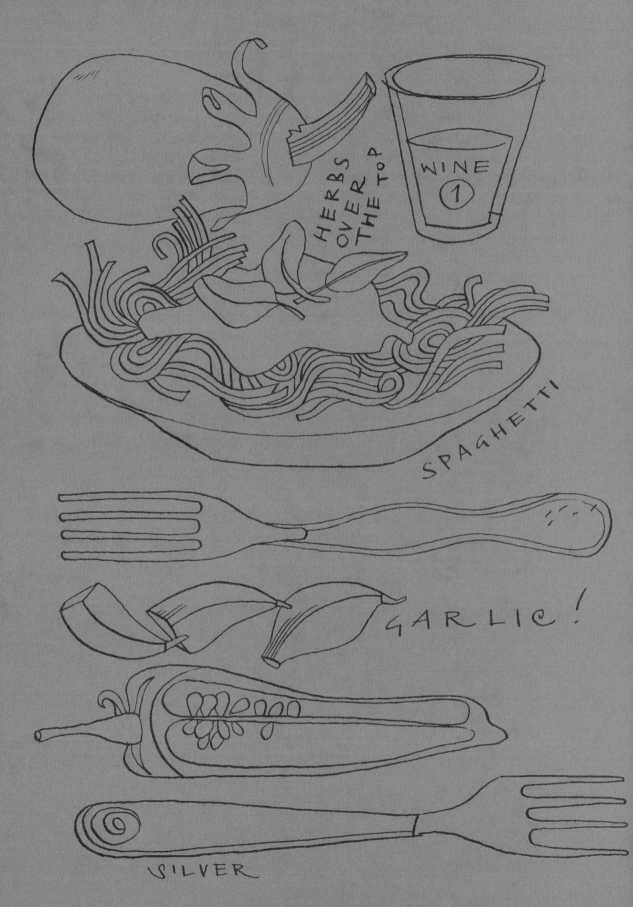

HERBS OVER THE TOP

WINE ①

SPAGHETTI

GARLIC!

SILVER

FIRST
COURSES →

FIRST COURSES

The traditional Italian classification of first courses is minestre in brodo, literally soups in broth, and minestre asciutte, literally dry soups. Besides various kinds of soups, the first group also includes purées. The second group includes fresh and dried pasta, rice, risottos, polenta and gnocchi. This method of classification can lead to confusion among those readers who are approaching the world of Italian cuisine for the first time, particularly in the case of pasta, which is defined as a 'dry soup'. It therefore seemed simpler and clearer to call this chapter First Courses and divide it into two parts: In Broth and Dry. For those new to Italian cooking, it should also be pointed out that first and second courses are considered of equal importance and size, unlike their American namesakes.

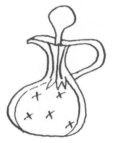

IN BROTH

Soup was once common on Italian dinner tables, but then the habit of serving soup almost died out. Soup tureens were left forgotten in buffets or occasionally exhibited as original center-pieces or collectors' items. The rediscovery of some ancient cereals, such as farro, together with a trend toward a vegetarian diet and the return of soups to the menus of some young restaurateurs who looked to the past for inspiration, has brought the whole soup family back into fashion. The recipes in this section include classic recipes from both Italy and elsewhere as well as traditional and contemporary dishes. The recipes are divided according to type: broths, cream soups, various soups, minestrones and thick soups.

DRY

Dry first courses are always present on Italian dinner tables. Pasta is definitely the most popular dish in Italy, but the word 'pasta' does nothing to describe the number of different varieties that this family contains. Basic fresh pasta is made with eggs and all-purpose flour (preferably Italian type 00). Lasagna is probably the best known; comprising thin sheets of pasta dough, lasagne can be layered within a traditional oven-baked dish or, when they are rolled

up, instantly transformed into cannelloni. Fresh pasta can also be cut into thinner strips: tagliatelle, delicate ribbons which are excellent accompaniments to rich sauces; smaller tagliolini e tagliatelline, suitable for more delicate sauces; and fettucine, larger and thicker shapes, perfect with meat, sausage, mushroom and tomato sauces. In addition to fresh pasta with eggs, others are made with different types of flour. Orecchiette, made with a mixture of flour and semolina, are the most typical pasta shapes from Puglia. Made by hand, orecchiette are shaped like small shells, with a rough outer surface created by the light press of the maker's thumb. Orecchiette are the ideal accompaniment to vegetable sauces. Next come the many different types of filled pasta — ravioli, tortelli, tortellini and tortelloni, each with a different shape and size. These can be stuffed with meat, fish, vegetables or cheese and are perfect either with basic sauces such as butter and sage or more complicated ones, chosen specifically to accompany the flavor of their stuffing. Dried pasta is simpler in its composition: durum wheat flour and water are combined to create the numerous shapes that accompany all different kinds of sauces. First of all comes spaghetti; loved throughout the world, these long strings are the ideal accompaniment for tomato, vegetable, fish and clam sauces. Bucatini, the pasta chosen for an authentic pasta all'amatriciana, are long tubes. Linguine, which are flat, 3 mm wide and around 26 cm long, are common in Liguria, and bavette and trenette are similar to linguine. All three are perfect served with herbs or fish sauce. Among the different types of short pasta, macaroni and penne are probably the most popular. The term 'macaroni' includes a lot of different varieties, such as rigatoni and tortiglioni, but all macaroni and penne are cylindrical and can either be smooth (lisce) or have a coarser 'striped' (rigate) texture. (Pasta shapes such as these, which have a central channel, allow the sauce to be retained.) Farfalle, small rectangles pinched in the center to form the shape of a butterfly, are ideal for tomato, pea, light and cream sauces, while fusilli, with their twisted corkscrew shape, are good for tasty Mediterranean sauces based on vegetables. The recipes here have been selected mainly for their short preparation times and lightness, but the great and more substantial traditional dishes have not been overlooked. This collection of dry first courses is divided into gnocchi, fresh pasta, dried pasta, polenta, rice, rice salads, risottos and timbales.

BROTHS

FIRST COURSES IN BROTHS

The way in which plain water is transformed from a tasteless, colorless and odorless liquid into broth is almost magical. It becomes fine, fragrant and tasty, thanks to the qualities given to it by meat, salt, herbs and spices. Broths may be made from meat (dark, thick or clear), fish and vegetables (single or mixed). There are some basic rules about the stocks used for broths.

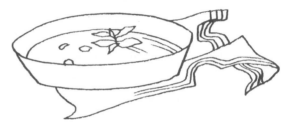

QUANTITIES AND COOKING TIMES

THE PAN

Pans should be made of aluminum or stainless steel to prevent them from tainting the flavor of the broth.

WATER

7 pints per 2½ pounds of beef or veal; 6 pints per 3¼ pounds of chicken.

SALT

¼ teaspoon per 4 cups of water. Otherwise you risk an unpleasantly salty stock; taste and adjust the seasoning at the end of cooking.

HERBS AND VEGETABLES

The water must be brought to a boil gradually and the vegetables and herbs should be added in the right proportions. For every 2¼ pounds meat: 3½ ounces carrots, 3½ ounces onions, 3½ ounces leeks and 1 celery stalk. Parsley is optional and some people like to stick a clove into the onion to give it a slight hint of spice.

DARK

This is the classic meat stock. The most suitable cuts of beef are the shoulder and rump. For veal stock, on the other hand, use the neck and the shank.

CONCENTRATED STOCK OR CONSOMMÉ

The original version dates back to a long and complicated nineteenth-century recipe. Today a more modern recipe insures excellent results.

CLEAR OR DELICATE

Chicken stock. Some people strengthen the flavor by adding a piece of beef to the pan, but this section includes the classic recipe (see page 209) without beef. Ideal for tortellini.

FISH

Fish stock has a delicate flavor. Recommended fish are cod and skate. Cod stock is delicious for rice and parsley soup. An excellent fatless stock may be made from the shells of seafood, including shrimp, plus the heads and tails of various white fish. It is suitable for sauces and soups.

VEGETABLE

Meat is completely replaced by more or less the same quantity of various types of vegetables. The most suitable are carrots, turnips (they give a lot of flavor), onions, leeks and cherry tomatoes. As far as potatoes are concerned, add no more than two. Vegetable stock is excellent for a large number of thin soups and is also pleasant as a simple drink.

STOCK AND BOUILLON CUBES AND POWDERS

These can be used to make almost any type of stock (beef, chicken, vegetable or fish) in a few minutes. They are useful time-savers, but you should check the salt content. Some brands have a much better flavor than others.

RICOTTA DUMPLINGS IN BROTH

BOMBOLINE DI RICOTTA IN BRODO

Serves 4

generous 1 cup ricotta cheese

1 egg

2¹/₂ ounces all-purpose flour, plus extra for coating

pinch of freshly grated nutmeg

4 cups Meat Stock (see page 208)

3 tablespoons olive oil

salt and pepper

Parmesan cheese, freshly grated, to serve

Beat the ricotta with a wooden spoon until smooth, then stir in the egg, flour and nutmeg and season with salt and pepper. Shape the mixture into small dumplings the size of hazelnuts. Coat the dumplings lightly in flour. Meanwhile, bring the stock to a boil over low heat. Heat the oil in a skillet, add the dumplings and cook until golden brown all over. Drain on paper towels. Put the dumplings into a soup tureen and ladle in the stock. Serve with Parmesan.

WATERCRESS BROTH

BRODO AL CRESCIONE

Serves 4

1 bunch of watercress or young spinach

4 cups Chicken Stock (see page 209)

1 celery stalk, chopped

1 fresh flat-leaf parsley sprig, chopped

salt and pepper

toast, to serve

Set 12 watercress or 3 spinach leaves leaves aside and finely chop the remainder. Gradually bring the stock to a boil and add the watercress or spinach, celery and parsley. Cook over low heat, stirring constantly, for a few minutes. Strain the broth and season with salt and pepper to taste. Place the reserved watercress or spinach leaves on the base of bowls or soup plates and ladle the broth over them. Serve with slices of toast.

SPICED WINE BROTH

BRODO AL VINO AROMATIZZATO

Serves 4

4 cups Meat Stock (see page 208)

2 cloves

scant 1 cup dry white wine

3 egg yolks

pinch of ground cinnamon

pinch of freshly grated nutmeg

Place the pan of stock over low heat, add the cloves and bring to a boil. Heat the wine in another pan. Whisk the egg yolks in a soup tureen, then pour in the stock and warm wine and stir in the cinnamon and nutmeg. Serve immediately.

SMALL CHEESE GNOCCHI IN CLEAR BROTH

BRODO CON GNOCCHETTI DI FORMAGGIO

Serves 4

3 tablespoons butter, softened

1 egg, separated

1¹/₂ tablespoons Parmesan cheese, freshly grated, plus extra for serving

1 tablespoon all-purpose flour

6¹/₄ cups Meat or Chicken Stock (see pages 208–209)

salt

Cream the butter in a bowl, then stir in the egg yolk, Parmesan and flour. Mix well. Beat the egg white in another bowl, then add to the mixture with a pinch of salt. Bring the stock to a boil. Add the cheese mixture, 1 teaspoon at a time. When the gnocchi float to the surface, they are cooked. Ladle into a soup tureen and serve with plenty of Parmesan.

BREAD GNOCCHI IN BROTH

For the stock, place all the vegetables in a pan, pour in 6¼ cups water, season with salt and bring to a boil. Lower the heat and simmer for 45 minutes. Meanwhile, prepare the gnocchi. Combine the bread crumbs, Parmesan, eggs and half the chive in a bowl and season with salt and pepper. The mixture should be medium-thick so, if necessary, add more bread crumbs. Shape the mixture into ½-inch rolls. Cut into short lengths and flatten the middles slightly with your finger. Strain the stock into a clean pan and return to the heat. (The vegetables can be eaten cold as a salad or baked au gratin in the oven.) Add the gnocchi to the stock. When they float to the surface they are ready. Ladle into a soup tureen, sprinkle with the remaining chive and serve with Parmesan.

BRODO CON GNOCCHETTI DI PANE

Serves 4

For the stock

1 leek, trimmed and chopped

1 onion, chopped

2 celery stalks, chopped

2 carrots, chopped

salt

For the gnocchi

2 cups bread crumbs

⅔ cup Parmesan cheese, freshly grated, plus extra for serving

2 eggs • 1 small fresh chive, chopped

salt and pepper

BROTH À LA ROYALE

This is a basic recipe for various different royales – soup garnishes – each named according to the type of cream of vegetable soup chosen (pea, asparagus, carrot, etc.). Beat the eggs with salt and pepper to taste. Add scant 1 cup of stock, a little at a time, followed by the cream of vegetable soup chosen. Grease a heatproof dish or several small molds with plenty of butter. Pour in the mixture, place in a large shallow pan, pour in boiling water to come about halfway up the sides and cook over low heat for 12–15 minutes until the mixture sets, making sure the water barely simmers. Remove from the heat, let cool, then turn out the royale and cut into squares. Heat the remaining stock, then ladle into a soup tureen and garnish with the royales.

BRODO CON ROYALE

Serves 4

2 eggs

4 cups Vegetable Stock (see page 209)

cream of vegetable soup (for recipes, see pages 212–224)

butter, for greasing

salt and pepper

HOMEMADE BROTH À LA ROYALE

Beat the eggs, then beat in the flour and Parmesan and season with salt and a little pepper. Stir in just enough milk to give the texture of cream. Grease several small molds with butter and pour in the mixture. Place in a large shallow pan, pour in boiling water to come about halfway up the sides and cook for 12–15 minutes until the mixture sets, making sure the water barely simmers. Remove from the heat, let cool, then turn out and cut into cubes. Heat the remaining stock in a pan, then ladle into a soup tureen and add the royales.

BRODO CON ROYALE ALLA CASALINGA

Serves 4

4 eggs

1 tablespoon all-purpose flour

2 tablespoons Parmesan cheese, freshly grated

3–5 tablespoons milk

butter, for greasing

4 cups Vegetable Stock (see page 209)

salt and pepper

BROTH WITH CRÊPE STRIPS

BRODO CON TAGLIOLINI DI CRÊPES

Serves 4

1 cup all-purpose flour

1 egg

1 egg yolk

scant 1 cup milk

1 tablespoon butter

4 cups Chicken Stock (see opposite)

salt

Combine the flour, egg and egg yolk in a bowl and gradually stir in the milk – the batter should be quite thin. Melt 1 tablespoon of the butter, stir into the batter with a pinch of salt and set aside for 1 hour. Heat a pat of the butter in a small skillet and pour in 1 tablespoon of the batter. Cook for 4–5 minutes until the underside is browned, then flip over and cook for 2 minutes more until the second side is browned. Slide out onto a plate and continue making crêpes in the same way, adding more butter as required, until the batter is used up. Meanwhile, heat the stock in a large pan. Cut the crêpes into thin strips, divide among individual soup bowls and ladle the hot stock over them.

MEAT STOCK

BRODO DI CARNE

Serves 4

1³/₄ pounds lean beef, cut into cubes

1 pound 5 ounces veal, cut into cubes

1 onion, coarsely chopped

1 carrot, coarsely chopped

1 leek, trimmed and coarsely chopped

1 celery stalk, coarsely chopped

salt

Place the meat in a large pan, add cold water to cover and bring to a boil, bearing in mind that slow cooking and gentle simmering are essential for successful stock. Skim off any scum that rises to the surface and add the onion, carrot, leek and celery and season with salt. Lower the heat and simmer for about 3¹/₂ hours. Remove from the heat, strain into a bowl, let cool, then chill in the refrigerator. When the fat has solidified on the surface carefully remove and discard. The stock may be used for soups, risottos and making gravy.

FISH STOCK (1)

BRODO DI PESCE (1)

Serves 4–6

1 fresh flat-leaf parsley sprig

1 fresh thyme sprig

1 onion, chopped

1 carrot, sliced

1 celery stalk, sliced

1 tablespoon black peppercorns, lightly crushed

2¹/₄ pounds white fish or white fish bones and heads, gills removed

salt

Pour 8³/₄ cups water into a large pan, add the herbs, onion, carrot, celery and peppercorns and season with salt. Gradually bring to a boil, then lower the heat and simmer for 30 minutes. Remove from the heat, let cool, then add the fish (the water should just cover). Return to the heat, bring just to a boil, then lower the heat and simmer for 20 minutes. Remove from the heat and leave the fish to cool in the stock for a stronger flavor. Strain the stock and use for a rice soup or Seafood Risotto (see page 328). If using only bones and heads, add to the pan with the herbs and vegetables and simmer for 30 minutes. Let cool slightly, then strain.

FISH STOCK (2)

Pour 8³/₄ cups water into a pan and add the vegetables, parsley and wine. Season with salt and pepper and bring just to a boil. Lower the heat and simmer for 30 minutes. Add the skate and simmer for 20 minutes. Remove the fish and strain the stock into a bowl, pressing down well on the vegetables with a spoon. If a very clear stock is required, dampen and squeeze out a square of cheese-cloth and use as a filter in the strainer.

BRODO DI PESCE (2)

Serves 4–6

1 onion

1 cherry tomato

1 celery stalk

fresh flat-leaf parsley

¹/₃ cup dry white wine

2¹/₄ pounds skate wings

salt and pepper

CHICKEN STOCK

It is best to use a boiling fowl, if you can find one, as it produces a more delicate flavor than a chicken and is less likely to be intensively raised. Place the bird and vegetables in a large pan and add a pinch of salt and water to cover. Bring to a boil over medium-high heat, then lower the heat and simmer for at least 2 hours, occasionally skimming off any scum that rises to the surface. Strain through a wire mesh strainer into a bowl, let cool, then chill in the refrigerator. When the fat has solidified on the surface, remove and discard it. Chicken stock may be served as a broth with small gnocchi, julienne vegetables or small omelets cut into thin strips.

BRODO DI POLLO

Serves 4–6

1 chicken or boiling fowl, skinned and trimmed of visible fat

1 onion

1 carrot

1 celery stalk

salt

VEGETABLE STOCK

Place all the vegetables in a large pan, pour in 6¹/₄ cups water, add a pinch of salt and bring to a boil. Lower the heat and simmer gently for about 20 minutes. Remove from the heat and let cool slightly, then strain into a bowl pressing down well on the vegetables with a spoon.

BRODO DI VERDURE

Serves 4–6

2 potatoes, coarsely chopped

2 onions, coarsely chopped

2 leeks, trimmed and coarsely chopped

2 carrots, coarsely chopped

2 turnips, coarsely chopped

1 celery stalk, coarsely chopped

3 cherry tomatoes, coarsely chopped

salt

AROMATIC COLD BROTH

BRODO FREDDO AROMATICO

Serves 4

3 cups Meat Stock (see page 208)

4 fresh basil leaves, chopped

1 fresh chervil sprig, chopped

1 fresh flat-leaf parsley sprig, chopped

4 mint leaves, chopped

2 teaspoons chopped fresh thyme

salt

Prepare a fairly thick meat stock, let cool, then strain through a fine strainer into a pan to remove the fat. Bring to a boil over low heat. Place all the herbs in a soup tureen, remove the stock from the heat and ladle it over them. Season lightly with salt and let infuse for at least 2 hours, then serve.

CONSOMMÉ

CONSOMMÉ

Serves 4

11 ounces ground beef

1 leek, trimmed and chopped

1 carrot, chopped

1 celery stalk, chopped

2 egg whites

10²/₃ cups Meat Stock (see page 208)

4 tablespoons dry sherry (optional)

Put the beef, vegetables and egg whites into a pan. Pour in the stock and mix well. Gradually bring to a boil, stirring constantly. Lower the heat and simmer for about 1 hour. Strain through a cheesecloth-lined strainer into a bowl, then ladle into soup bowls. If you want to add extra fragrance, stir 1 tablespoon dry sherry into each bowl.

CONCENTRATED FISH STOCK

FUMETTO DI PESCE

2 tablespoons olive oil or butter

1 carrot, chopped

1 celery stalk, chopped

1 small onion, chopped

6 black peppercorns, lightly crushed

2¹/₄ pounds white fish heads, gills and bones removed

salt

Heat the oil or butter in a pan, add the vegetables and cook over low heat, stirring occasionally, for 5 minutes. Season with salt and add the peppercorns. Pour in 4 cups warm water, add the fish bones and heads, cover and bring to a boil. Skim off any scum that rises to the surface. Lower the heat and simmer for about 45 minutes until the liquid has reduced by half. Remove from the heat, let cool slightly, then strain. Concentrated fish stock is used to enhance the taste of poached fish, seafood risottos and fish sauces and soups.

ASPIC

Put the bones, calf's foot, ground beef, leek, carrots, celery and egg whites into a large pan. Pour in the stock and bring to a boil, stirring occasionally and skimming off any scum that rises to the surface. Lower the heat and simmer for about 2 hours, then season with salt to taste. Strain into a bowl and let cool. If the mixture is not completely translucent, return to the heat, add a beaten egg white and boil for 5 minutes. Strain again and let cool. Chill in the refrigerator. Aspic does not have to set completely: a jelly-like consistency is adequate. Just before serving, place in appropriate bowls. Although it has fallen out of fashion, aspic makes an elegant start to a meal.

GELATINA

Makes 4 cups of aspic

1 pound 2 ounces beef bones

9 ounces veal shank or knuckle bones

1 calf's foot

11 ounces ground beef

1 leek, trimmed and chopped

2 carrots, chopped

1 celery stalk, chopped

2 egg whites, lightly beaten

11¼ cups Meat Stock (see page 208)

salt

CREAM SOUPS

Cream soups are light, delicate and easy to prepare. They are always delightful served to mark the start of an elegant and sophisticated dinner. They may be made from vegetables, legumes or puréed meat. To give them the right consistency, just add béchamel sauce or a few tablespoonfuls of mashed potato. To make them more velvety, add a little cream, perhaps mixed with one or two egg yolks. For a little more flavor, try adding a few curls of extremely fresh butter just before serving. Cream soups are classically served with small triangles of bread fried in butter. If they are served in individual soup plates, the surface may be decorated with a swirl of whipped cream (particularly good with Cream of Lettuce Soup), a hard-cooked quail's egg (with Cream of Tomato Soup) or balls of carrot fried in butter (with Cream of Bean Soup). Nowadays, the food processor has made their preparation very quick and easy. Cream soups have one great advantage above all – they may be prepared the day before and warmed up just before serving.

CREAM OF PORCINI SOUP

Put the chicken, carrot, celery and onion in a large pan, pour in 8³/₄ cups water, add a pinch of salt and bring to a boil. Lower the heat and simmer for 40 minutes until the chicken is tender. Meanwhile, melt half the butter in a skillet, add the porcini and cook, stirring frequently, for about 7 minutes. Sprinkle with the brandy and cook until it has evaporated. Season with salt and pepper and remove from the heat. Lift the chicken out of the pan and strain the stock. Cut off the breast fillets, slice and set aside. Remove the remaining meat from the bones and place in a food processor with a ladleful of the stock and two-thirds of the porcini. Process to a purée. Melt the remaining butter in a pan, add the leeks and cook over low heat, stirring occasionally, for 5 minutes. Stir in the flour and gradually stir in the stock. Bring to a boil, stirring constantly, then lower the heat and simmer for 10 minutes. Stir in the purée and cook for a further 5 minutes, then pour in the cream. Pour into a soup tureen and garnish with the sliced breast fillets and remaining porcini.

CREMA AI PORCINI

Serves 4

¹/₂ chicken

1 carrot

1 celery stalk

1 onion

¹/₄ cup butter

4³/₄ cups porcini, sliced

¹/₄ cup brandy

2 leeks, trimmed and finely chopped

¹/₄ cup all-purpose flour

scant ¹/₂ cup heavy cream

salt and pepper

CREAM OF JERUSALEM ARTICHOKE SOUP

Heat the olive oil in a pan, add the onion and cook over low heat, stirring occasionally, for 5 minutes until softened. Add the Jerusalem artichokes and cook for 3–4 minutes, then pour in the stock and bring to a boil. Cover and cook over low heat for 30 minutes. Transfer the mixture to a food processor and process until smooth. Season with salt to taste. Stir in the cream and reheat if necessary. Pour into a soup tureen, sprinkle with the parsley and serve.

CREMA AI TOPINAMBUR

Serves 4

2 tablespoons olive oil

1 onion, thinly sliced

2 cups Jerusalem artichokes, chopped

³/₄ quantity Meat Stock (see page 208)

scant 1 cup heavy cream

1 fresh flat-leaf parsley sprig, chopped

salt

CREAM OF TRUFFLE SOUP

CREMA AL TARTUFO

Serves 4

3 tablespoons olive oil

2 leeks, trimmed and chopped

1 pound 2 ounces potatoes, about 4 medium, sliced

³/₄ quantity Vegetable Stock (see page 209)

1¹/₄ cups milk

¹/₂ cup heavy cream

12 bread slices, crusts removed

3 ¹/₂ ounces fontina cheese, sliced

salt

1 black truffle, shaved, to garnish

Heat the oil in a pan, add the leeks and cook over low heat, stirring occasionally, for 5 minutes until softened. Add the potatoes and cook for 5 minutes more until lightly browned, then pour in the stock and milk. Season with salt, cover and cook over medium heat for 45 minutes. Transfer to a food processor and process to a purée, add the cream and process again. Return to the pan and keep warm over a very low heat. Toast the bread on one side under a preheated broiler, then turn over, top with the slices of fontina and broil until the cheese melts. Taste the soup and adjust the seasoning if necessary. If it requires thickening, place it on the heat for a little longer. Ladle into individual soup plates and garnish with the truffle. Serve with the fontina toast.

CREAM OF ASPARAGUS SOUP

CREMA DI ASPARAGI

Serves 4

1 pound 5 ounces green asparagus, spears trimmed

¹/₄ cup butter

1 onion, thinly sliced

2 tablespoons all-purpose flour

scant ¹/₂ cup white wine

4 cups Vegetable Stock (see page 209)

2–3 tablespoons heavy cream

salt and pepper

Cut off and reserve the asparagus spears and chop the stems. Melt the butter in a pan, add the onion and cook over low heat, stirring occasionally, for 5 minutes until softened. Add the asparagus stems and cook for a few minutes, then sprinkle with the flour, stir well and pour in the wine and stock. Season with salt and pepper and cook over low heat, stirring frequently, for 30 minutes. Transfer to a food processor and process to a purée. Bring 1¹/₂ cups water to a boil in a pan and parboil the asparagus spears for 2 minutes. Pour the purée into a clean pan and reheat. Drain the asparagus spears and add to the soup with the cream. Serve in individual soup plates.

CREAM OF ARTICHOKE SOUP

CREMA DI CARCIOFI

Serves 4

2 tablespoons lemon juice, strained

6 globe artichokes

5 tablespoons butter

1 onion, thinly sliced

1 celery stalk, chopped

7 ounces potatoes, cut into wedges

6¹/₄ cups Chicken Stock (see page 209)

1 egg yolk

salt and pepper

Parmesan cheese, freshly grated, to serve

Half-fill a bowl with water and stir in the lemon juice. Working on one artichoke at a time, break off the stems, cut off all the leaves and remove the chokes. Drop the hearts into the acidulated water. Melt 3 tablespoons of the butter in a pan, add the onion and celery and cook over low heat, stirring occasionally, for 5 minutes until softened. Drain the artichoke hearts, add to the pan with the potatoes and cook for 5 minutes. Pour in the stock, season with salt and pepper to taste, cover and simmer for about 40 minutes. Transfer to a food processor and process to a purée. Pour into a clean pan, taste and adjust the seasoning if necessary and reheat. Beat the egg yolk with the remaining butter. Remove the soup from the heat and stir in the egg yolk mixture to thicken. Serve in individual soup plates with plenty of Parmesan.

CREAM OF CARROT SOUP

Put the carrots and garlic in a pan, pour in water to cover and add a pinch of salt. Bring to a boil over medium heat and cook until almost all the liquid is absorbed. Transfer to a food processor and process to a purée. Pour the mixture back into the pan. Warm the milk in another pan, then stir it into the carrot purée with the stock and mix well. Cook for 10 minutes until fairly thick. Taste and adjust the seasoning according to your preference. Ladle the soup into individual flameproof soup plates. Sprinkle with the fontina, nutmeg and a pinch of pepper. Put the plates under a preheated broiler to melt the cheese, then serve.

CREMA DI CAROTE

Serves 4

$4^{1}/_{3}$ cups carrots, chopped

1 garlic clove

$2^{1}/_{4}$ cups milk

$1^{3}/_{4}$ cups Meat Stock (see page 208)

$^{1}/_{3}$ cup fontina cheese, grated

pinch of freshly grated nutmeg

salt and pepper

CREAM OF CARROT AND MUSSEL SOUP

Dice two carrots and slice the remainder. Melt 2 tablespoons of the butter in a pan, add the diced carrots, a pinch of salt and a pinch of sugar and cook over low heat, stirring occasionally, for 5 minutes. Remove from the heat and set aside. Melt the remaining butter in another pan, add the sliced carrots, a pinch of salt and a pinch of sugar and cook over low heat, stirring occasionally, for 5 minutes. Pour in the stock and simmer for about 20 minutes. Transfer to a food processor and process to a purée. Discard any mussels with broken shells or that do not shut immediately when sharply tapped. Heat the mussels in a skillet with the wine and garlic for 5 minutes until they open. Discard any that remain closed. Remove the mussels from their shells. Reheat the carrot purée, then pour into a soup tureen and add the diced carrots and the mussels. Sprinkle with the parsley and serve immediately.

CREMA DI CAROTE CON LE COZZE

Serves 4

$1^{1}/_{2}$ pounds carrots

5 tablespoons butter

2 pinches of sugar

4 cups Chicken Stock (see page 209)

32 mussels, scrubbed and beards removed

scant 1 cup white wine

$^{1}/_{2}$ garlic clove

1 tablespoon chopped fresh flat-leaf parsley

salt

CREAM OF CAULIFLOWER SOUP WITH MUSSELS

Melt the butter in a pan, add the shallot and cook over low heat, stirring occasionally, for 5 minutes. Add the parsley and lemon juice. Discard any mussels with broken shells or that do not shut immediately when sharply tapped. Add the mussels to the pan and cook for about 5 minutes until the shells open. Strain the mussels, reserving the cooking liquid. Discard any mussels that remain closed and remove the rest from their shells. Strain the cooking liquid into a pan, add 4 cups water and bring to a boil. Add the cauliflower flowerets and cook for 15 minutes. Transfer the mixture to a food processor and process to a purée. Pour into a clean pan, add the cream and mussels and season with salt and pepper. Reheat for 5 minutes, pour into a soup tureen and serve with croûtons.

CREMA DI CAVOLFIORE CON LE COZZE

Serves 4

2 tablespoons butter

1 shallot, thinly sliced

2 tablespoons chopped fresh flat-leaf parsley

juice of 1 lemon, strained

2$^1/_4$ pounds mussels, scrubbed and beards removed

1 small cauliflower, cut into flowerets

scant $^1/_2$ cup heavy cream

salt and pepper

croûtons, to serve

CREAM OF GARBANZO BEANS AU GRATIN

Place the garbanzo beans in a pan with 6$^1/_4$ cups cold water and the onion. Bring to a boil, cover and cook over medium heat for 2 hours. Transfer the mixture to a food processor and process to a purée. Heat the oil in a pan, add the garlic and rosemary and cook for a few minutes, then season with salt and pepper. Remove and discard the garlic and rosemary and pour the flavored oil onto the bean purée. Ladle into individual flameproof soup plates, place the toast on top, sprinkle with the fontina and melt the cheese under a preheated broiler.

CREMA DI CECI AL GRATIN

Serves 4

scant 1 cup garbanzo beans, soaked overnight in cold water to cover and drained

1 onion, sliced

2 tablespoons olive oil

1 garlic clove

1 fresh rosemary sprig

4 bread slices, toasted

$^1/_2$ cup fontina cheese, grated

salt and pepper

CREAM OF BEAN SOUP

Put the beans, potatoes, onion and carrot into a pan, add 6$^1/_4$ cups water, bring to a boil and simmer for 20 minutes. Transfer to a food processor and process to a purée. Season with salt and pepper and pour into a pan. Add the milk, butter, basil and Parmesan and bring back to a boil for 1 minute. Pour into a soup tureen and serve with croûtons.

CREMA DI FAVE

Serves 4

1 pound 2 ounces shelled fava beans

3 potatoes, sliced

1 onion, sliced

1 carrot, sliced

3 tablespoons milk

2 tablespoons butter

1 tablespoon chopped fresh basil

1 tablespoon Parmesan cheese, freshly grated

salt and pepper

croûtons, to serve

CREAM OF FENNEL SOUP WITH SMOKED SALMON

CREMA DI FINOCCHI AL SALMONE AFFUMICATO

Serves 4

2 tablespoons butter
3 fennel bulbs, sliced
1 tablespoon heavy cream
3 ounces smoked salmon, chopped
pinch of dill
salt and pepper

Melt the butter in a pan, add the fennel and 5 tablespoons water and cook over low heat for about 20 minutes. Stir in another 5 tablespoons water, transfer the mixture to a food processor and process to a purée. Pour into a soup tureen, stir in the cream and season with salt and pepper to taste. Add the salmon and dill and serve.

CREAM OF SHRIMP AND BEAN SOUP

CREMA DI GAMBERETTI E FAGIOLI

Serves 4

scant 1¹/₂ cups fresh cannellini beans
6 tablespoons butter
1 shallot, chopped
1³/₄ cups raw shrimp, peeled and deveined
scant ¹/₂ cup dry white wine
4 cups Vegetable Stock (see page 209)
¹/₂ cup all-purpose flour
¹/₃ cup heavy cream
1 fresh thyme sprig, leaves only
salt and pepper

Cook the beans in boiling water until tender, then drain and pass through a food mill. Melt 2 tablespoons of the butter in a pan, add the shallot and cook over low heat, stirring occasionally, for 5 minutes. Add the shrimp and cook for 2 minutes, then add the wine and cook until it has evaporated. Season with salt and pepper, transfer to a food processor and process to a purée. Bring the stock to a boil in a pan. Melt the remaining butter in another pan and stir in the flour. Pour in the bean purée, gradually stir in the boiling stock and cook over low heat for about 15 minutes. Add the cream and thyme to the shrimp purée, then pour into the bean mixture. Pour into a soup tureen and serve.

CREAM OF SHRIMP AND TOMATO SOUP

CREMA DI GAMBERI E POMODORI

Serves 4

4 cups Vegetable Stock (see page 209)
2¹/₄ pounds large shrimp
3 tablespoons butter
¹/₃ cup all-purpose flour
5 ripe tomatoes, peeled, seeded and chopped
2 teaspoons curry powder
salt

Bring the stock to a boil in a pan, add the shrimp and cook for 3 minutes. Drain, reserving the stock. Peel and devein the shrimp, set 10 aside for the garnish and finely chop the remainder. Strain the stock. Melt the butter in a pan, stir in the flour and cook, stirring constantly, for 2–4 minutes, then gradually stir in the stock. Bring to a boil, stirring constantly, lower the heat and simmer, stirring constantly, for 10 minutes. Add the chopped shrimp. Process the tomatoes in a food processor to a purée, add the curry powder, process briefly again and add to the soup. Bring to a boil for a few minutes and season with salt to taste. Pour into a soup tureen, garnish with the reserved shrimp and serve.

CREAM OF BELGIAN ENDIVE SOUP

Bring the stock to a boil in a pan. Melt 2 tablespoons of the butter in another pan, add the peas, cover and cook over low heat for 5 minutes. Season with salt, pour in the stock and cook for about 20 minutes. Meanwhile, melt the remaining butter in another pan, stir in the flour and gradually stir in the milk. Cook, stirring constantly, until thickened, then season with salt and pepper. Add the Belgian endive, cover and cook over low heat for 15 minutes. Transfer to a food processor and process to a purée. Pour into a soup tureen and sprinkle with the parsley. Serve with Parmesan.

CREMA DI INDIVIA BELGA

Serves 4

$2^1/_4$ cups Meat Stock (see page 208)

6 tablespoons butter

scant 1 cup shelled peas

$^1/_2$ cup all-purpose flour

$2^1/_4$ cups milk

1 pound 2 ounces Belgian endive, chopped

1 tablespoon chopped fresh flat-leaf parsley

salt and pepper

Parmesan cheese, freshly grated, to serve

CREAM OF LETTUCE SOUP

Bring the milk and stock to a boil, season with salt, add the lettuces and cook for 5 minutes. Transfer to a food processor and process to a purée, then pour into a clean pan. Melt the butter in another pan, stir in the flour and cook, stirring constantly, for 3–5 minutes, then stir into the purée and season with salt and pepper to taste. Simmer for 15 minutes. Lightly beat the egg yolk with the Parmesan in a soup tureen, then gradually ladle in the soup, stirring constantly.

CREMA DI LATTUGA

Serves 4

$2^1/_4$ cups milk

$2^1/_4$ cups Meat Stock (see page 208)

3 lettuces, coarsely shredded

2 tablespoons butter

2 tablespoons all-purpose flour

1 egg yolk

1 tablespoon Parmesan cheese, freshly grated

salt and pepper

CREAM OF DRIED LEGUMES SOUP

Put the legumes in a pan with the carrot, celery, onion and potatoes, add water to cover and bring to a boil. Lower the heat and simmer until tender. Transfer to a food processor and process to a purée. Add the cream and process briefly again, then season with salt and pepper to taste. Pour into a soup tureen and serve with the grated Parmesan.

CREMA DI LEGUMI

Serves 4

$1^1/_2$ cups mixed dried legumes, such as beans, lentils and peas, soaked overnight in cold water and drained

1 carrot, chopped

1 celery stalk, chopped

1 onion, chopped

2 potatoes, sliced

2 tablespoons heavy cream

salt and pepper

Parmesan cheese, freshly grated to serve

CREAM OF POTATO SOUP

CREMA DI PATATE

Serves 4

4 cups Vegetable Stock (see page 209)
¹/₄ cup butter
2 leeks, trimmed and chopped
generous 2 cups potatoes, diced
4 bread slices, crusts removed, diced
scant ¹/₂ cup heavy cream
salt
croûtons, to serve

Bring the stock to a boil. Melt 2 tablespoons of the butter in another pan, add the leeks and cook over low heat, stirring occasionally, for 5 minutes until softened. Add the potatoes and cook for a few minutes, then pour in the stock, season with salt to taste and cook over medium heat for about 20 minutes. Meanwhile, melt the remaining butter in a skillet, add the bread cubes and cook, stirring frequently, until golden brown all over. Drain on paper towels. Transfer the potato mixture to a food processor and process to a purée. Return to the pan and bring back to a boil, then stir in the cream. Pour into a soup tureen and serve with the croûtons.

CREAM OF PEA AND POTATO SOUP

CREMA DI PISELLI E PATATE

Serves 4

2 tablespoons olive oil
5¹/₄ cups shelled peas
3 potatoes, diced
2 leeks, trimmed and chopped
2 tablespoons plain yogurt
6 fresh mint leaves
4 thin bread slices, crusts removed, toasted
juice of ¹/₂ lemon, strained
salt

Heat the oil in a pan, add the peas, potatoes and leeks and cook for 1 minute. Pour in 4 cups water and cook for 20 minutes until the vegetables are tender. Reserve 1 tablespoon of the peas. Transfer the rest of the mixture to a food processor and process to a purée, then return to the pan and reheat. Add the reserved peas and season with salt to taste. Stir in the yogurt, add the mint leaves and pour into a soup tureen. Serve with the slices of toast sprinkled with the lemon juice.

CREAM OF TOMATO SOUP

CREMA DI POMODORO

Serves 4

2 tablespoons butter
1 onion, thinly sliced
2¹/₄ pounds plum tomatoes, peeled, seeded and sliced
2 potatoes, diced
scant ¹/₂ cup heavy cream
salt and pepper
Parmesan cheese, freshly grated, to serve
croûtons, to serve

Melt the butter in a pan, add the onion and cook over low heat, stirring occasionally, for 5 minutes until softened. Add the tomatoes and cook for 15 minutes. Season with salt and pepper to taste, pour in 3 cups water, add the potatoes and bring to a boil. Lower the heat and simmer for 1 hour. Transfer to a food processor and process to a purée, then pour into a pan. Reheat, then stir in the cream. Pour into a soup tureen and serve with Parmesan and croûtons.

CREAM OF LEEK SOUP

Heat the oil in pan, add the leeks and cook over low heat, stirring occasionally, for 5 minutes. Stir together the tomato paste and milk, add to the pan and heat gently. Transfer to a food processor and process to a purée. Melt the butter in a pan, stir in the flour, then gradually stir in the stock. Cook, stirring constantly, for 20 minutes, then add the leek purée and cook over very low heat for 15 minutes more. Season lightly with salt. Beat together the egg yolk, cream and Parmesan in a bowl, then whisk into the soup. Pour the soup into a soup tureen and serve.

CREMA DI PORRI

Serves 4

3 tablespoons olive oil

6 leeks, white parts only thinly sliced

1 tablespoon tomato paste

³/₄ cup milk

2 tablespoons butter

¹/₃ cup all-purpose flour

4 cups Vegetable Stock (see page 209)

1 egg yolk

2 tablespoons heavy cream

¹/₄ cup Parmesan cheese, freshly grated

salt and pepper

CREAM OF CELERY SOUP

Bring the stock to a boil. Heat the butter and oil in another pan, add the onion and celery and cook, stirring occasionally, for 4 minutes. Pour in the stock, add the potatoes, cover and simmer for 40 minutes. Transfer to a food processor and process to a purée, then pour into a pan and reheat. Meanwhile, heat the milk to simmering point. Remove the soup from the heat, stir in the hot milk and season with salt. Pour into a soup tureen and serve with Parmesan.

CREMA DI SEDANO

Serves 4

4 cups Meat Stock (see page 208)

2 tablespoons butter

1 tablespoon olive oil

1 onion, chopped

3¹/₂ cups celery, chopped

3 potatoes, diced

¹/₃ cup milk

salt

Parmesan cheese, freshly grated, to serve

CREAM OF SPINACH SOUP

Bring the stock to a boil. Melt the butter in another pan, add the onions and cook over low heat, stirring occasionally, for 5 minutes until softened. Stir in the flour and cook, stirring constantly, for 2 minutes, then gradually stir in the hot stock. Add the spinach and simmer for about 20 minutes. Stir in the lemon juice, then transfer to a food processor and process to a purée. Pour into a pan, season with salt and pepper to taste, stir in the cream and simmer briefly. Remove from the heat, cover and let stand for 5 minutes. Pour into individual soup plates and garnish with a swirl of cream sprinkled with a pinch of hot paprika.

CREMA DI SPINACI

Serves 4

4 cups Meat Stock (see page 208)

3 tablespoons butter

2 onions, finely chopped

¹/₃ cup all-purpose flour

6 cups frozen chopped spinach, thawed

3 tablespoons lemon juice, strained

2 tablespoons heavy cream, plus extra to garnish

salt and pepper

hot paprika, to garnish

CREAM OF PUMPKIN SOUP AU GRATIN

CREMA DI ZUCCA GRATINATA

Serves 4

4 cups milk

3 potatoes, cut into wedges

4 cups peeled, seeded and chopped pumpkin

1 fresh sage leaf

scant 1/2 cup heavy cream

4 country-style bread slices

2 tablespoons Parmesan cheese, freshly grated

salt and pepper

Pour the milk and 1 1/2 cups water into a pan and bring to a boil. Add the potatoes, pumpkin and sage, season with salt and pepper and bring back to a boil. Lower the heat to medium and cook for 40 minutes. Remove the sage leaf, transfer the mixture to a food processor and process to a purée. Pour into a pan, stir in the cream, season with salt and pepper to taste and reheat for a few minutes. Pour into individual flameproof soup plates. Top with a slice of bread, sprinkle with the Parmesan and melt the cheese under a preheated broiler.

CREAM OF ZUCCHINI SOUP

CREMA DI ZUCCHINE

Serves 4

2 tablespoons butter

6 cups zucchini, sliced

1 onion, thinly sliced

1 garlic clove, crushed

2 1/4 cups Chicken Stock (see page 209)

2 1/4 cups milk

1 fresh flat-leaf parsley sprig, chopped

salt and pepper

Melt the butter in a pan, add the zucchini, onion and garlic and cook over low heat for 15 minutes. Pour in the stock and cook for 15 minutes more. Transfer to a food processor and process to a purée, then pour into a pan. Heat the milk to simmering point in another pan, then stir it into the purée and season with salt and pepper to taste. Reheat to simmering point, pour into a soup tureen, sprinkle with the parsley and serve.

COLD CUCUMBER CREAM SOUP

CREMA FREDDA DI CETRIOLI

Serves 4

2 1/4 cups Meat Stock (see page 208)

3 tablespoons olive oil

1 onion, chopped

1 3/4 cups cucumbers, chopped

scant 1 cup potatoes, diced

1/2 cup lettuce, chopped

6 fresh mint leaves, plus extra to garnish

1/4 cup heavy cream

salt and pepper

Bring the stock to a boil. Heat the oil in another pan, add the onion and cook over low heat, stirring occasionally, for 5 minutes until softened. Add the cucumbers, potatoes, lettuce and mint and cook for 5 minutes more. Season with salt and pepper to taste, pour in the hot stock and cook for about 15 minutes. Transfer to a food processor and process to a purée. Pour into a pan and reheat. Stir in the cream and heat for 5 minutes more. Remove from the heat, let cool to room temperature, then chill in the refrigerator for several hours. To serve, pour into a soup tureen and garnish with mint leaves.

VELVETY LENTIL SOUP

VELLUTATA DI LENTICCHIE

Serves 4

scant 1 cup green lentils,
soaked in cold water for 3 hours and drained
scant 1/2 cup red lentils,
soaked in cold water for 3 hours and drained
2 pearl onions, halved
1 garlic clove, crushed
1 fresh thyme sprig
scant 1 cup heavy cream
pinch of freshly grated nutmeg
salt and pepper

Put the lentils, onions, garlic and thyme in a pan, pour in 4 cups water, bring to a boil, then cover and cook over medium heat, stirring occasionally, for 30–40 minutes. Remove the thyme. Reserve 3 tablespoons of the lentils, then transfer the mixture to a food processor and process to a purée. Pour into a soup tureen and whisk in the cream. Season with the nutmeg and salt and pepper, stir in the reserved lentils and serve.

GREEN CREAM SOUP

CREMA VERDE

Serves 4

2 tablespoons butter
2 leeks, white part only, thinly sliced
3 potatoes, diced
4 cups Vegetable Stock (see page 209)
3 cups watercress or
young spinach leaves, chopped
pinch of freshly grated nutmeg
2/3 cup heavy cream • salt and pepper
buttered toasted croûtons, to serve

Melt the butter in a pan, add the leeks and cook over low heat, stirring occasionally, for 5 minutes until softened. Add the potatoes, pour in the stock and cook over low heat for 10 minutes. Add the watercress or spinach and nutmeg, season with salt and pepper and cook for 10 minutes more. Transfer to a food processor and process to a purée. Pour into a pan, stir in the cream and reheat briefly. Serve with toasted croûtons lightly spread with butter.

VICHYSSOISE

VICHYSSOISE

Serves 4

2 celery hearts, chopped
2 leeks, white parts only, chopped
2 potatoes, diced
4 cups Chicken Stock (see page 209)
scant 1 cup heavy cream
salt and pepper
fresh flat-leaf parsley, chopped, to garnish

Put the celery hearts, leeks and potatoes in a pan, pour in the stock, season with salt and pepper to taste and bring to a boil. Lower the heat and simmer for about 45 minutes. Transfer to a food processor and process to a purée. Pour into a pan, stir in the cream and reheat. Pour into individual soup plates, let cool, then chill in the refrigerator. Serve garnished with parsley.

VARIOUS SOUPS

The soups in this section range from simple, thin soups suitable for dinner – clear broths with a few star-, ring- or seed-shaped pasta specks – to substantial rice, pasta, tapioca and semolina soups. These are often enriched with liver, vegetables or legumes and served with grated cheese as a final touch. Soups may be made from homemade meat stock or stock cubes or bouillon cubes powder; be thick or thin and be served hot, warm or even cold.

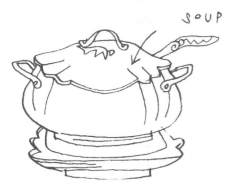

FARFALLINE WITH PESTO

Heat the oil in a pan, add the onion, carrots and potatoes and cook over low heat, stirring occasionally, for 5 minutes. Add 6¼ cups water, bring to a boil and simmer for 20 minutes. Add the pesto and beans and cook for 10 minutes until tender. Add the pasta and cook until al dente. Remove the pan from the heat and sprinkle the soup with the Parmesan, stir well and let stand for a few minutes before ladling into a soup tureen and serving. This is a fresh aromatic soup. Salt is not required because the pesto gives it a strong flavor, but you can season to taste if you like. If you wish to use fresh pesto, see page 68.

see page 68.

FARFALLINE AL PESTO

Serves 4

3 tablespoons olive oil

1 onion, chopped

2 carrots, chopped

2 potatoes, diced

1 jar bottled pesto

²/₃ cup green beans, trimmed

1³/₄ cup farfalline pasta

¹/₃ cup Parmesan cheese, freshly grated

salt

GAZPACHO

GAZPACHO

Serves 4

5 ounces white bread slices, about 5 thick slices,
crusts removed

1³/₄ pounds tomatoes

2 red bell peppers, halved and seeded

2 cucumbers

1 garlic clove

2 scallions

3–4 tablespoons olive oil

juice of 1 lemon, strained

ice cubes

salt and pepper

Tear the bread into pieces, place in a bowl, add water to cover and let soak. Coarsely chop half the tomatoes, 1 bell pepper, 1 cucumber and the garlic and place in a food processor. Add the bread and process to a purée. Pour into a large bowl and add up to 4 cups water to obtain the desired consistency. Chill in the refrigerator. Meanwhile, cut the remaining bell pepper into strips and slice the remaining cucumber, the remaining tomatoes and the scallions and place in separate bowls. Whisk together the olive oil and lemon juice. Just before serving, season the soup with salt and pepper and stir in the oil and lemon juice dressing. Pour into a soup tureen, add a few ice cubes and serve with the bowls of raw vegetables.

SIMPLE GAZPACHO

GAZPACHO SEMPLICE

Serves 4

1 large cucumber, peeled and thinly sliced

3¹/₄ pounds tomatoes, peeled and seeded

2 scallions, finely chopped

6 fresh basil leaves, finely chopped

1 tablespoon chopped fresh flat-leaf parsley

3 tablespoons olive oil

juice of 1 lemon, strained

ice cubes

salt and pepper

Put the cucumber in a colander, sprinkle with salt and set aside to drain for 20 minutes. Put the tomatoes in a food processor and process to a purée, then scrape into a bowl. Rinse the cucumber and pat dry with paper towels, then add to the tomato paste along with the scallions, parsley and basil. Season with salt and pepper to taste. Beat the oil with the lemon juice and stir into the soup. Chill in the refrigerator for a few hours, then ladle into a soup tureen and add a few ice cubes.

LENTIL AND SQUID SOUP

LENTICCHIE E CALAMERETTI

Serves 4

scant 1 cup lentils, soaked in cold water for 3 hours and drained

1 pound 2 ounces small squid, cleaned and chopped

9 ounces leafy green vegetables, such as Swiss chard or beet tops, coarsely chopped

pinch of chili powder

salt

Put the lentils into a pan, add 6¹/₄ cups water and bring to a boil. Add the squid, lower the heat, cover and simmer for 30 minutes. Add the green vegetables, cover the pan again and cook for 30 minutes more. Add the chili powder and season with salt to taste, then ladle into a soup tureen.

MESC–IUÀ

Put the cannellini beans, garbanzo beans and farro into a pan, add 6$\frac{1}{4}$ cups water, bring to a boil, then lower the heat and simmer for about 3 hours. Ladle into a soup tureen, drizzle with oil and season with salt and pepper. This is one of the most ancient Ligurian soups and is very common in La Spezia. It seems to date back to the time of the Saracens.

MESC–IUÀ

Serves 4

1 cup dried cannellini beans, soaked in cold water overnight and drained

scant 1 cup garbanzo beans, soaked in cold water overnight and drained

$\frac{1}{2}$ cup pearl farro, soaked in cold water overnight and drained

olive oil, for drizzling

salt and pepper

ZUCCHINI FLOWER SOUP

Bring the stock to a boil. Heat the butter and olive oil in another pan, add the onion, carrot and celery and cook over low heat, stirring occasionally, for 10 minutes. Add the zucchini and zucchini flowers and cook for 2 minutes, then pour in the hot stock. Bring to a boil, add the pasta and cook until al dente. Season with salt and pepper to taste, ladle into a soup tureen and serve with Parmesan.

MINESTRA AI FIORI DI ZUCCHINE

Serves 4

4 cups Meat Stock (see page 208)

2 tablespoons butter

1 tablespoon olive oil

1 onion, chopped

1 carrot, chopped

1 celery stalk, chopped

4 zucchini, finely diced

11 ounces zucchini flowers, cut into strips

1 cup soup pasta, such as ditalini

salt and pepper

Parmesan cheese, freshly grated, to serve

WHEAT GERM SOUP

Soak the wheat germ and beans in the stock overnight. Pour into a pan, add 4 cups water and bring to a boil over low heat. Heat the oil in another pan, add the onion, celery and tomatoes and cook over low heat, stirring occasionally, for 5 minutes. Add a ladleful of the boiling stock, then pour the mixture into the pan of beans. Simmer for about 2 hours until the beans are tender. Season with salt and pepper and stir in the basil. Leave the soup to stand in a warm place for 10 minutes before ladling into a soup tureen and serving.

MINESTRA AL GERME DI GRANO

Serves 4

scant 1 cup wheat germ

$\frac{1}{3}$ cup dried toscanelli or cannellini beans

4 cups Meat Stock (see page 208)

2 tablespoons olive oil

1 onion, chopped

1 celery stalk, chopped

2 ripe tomatoes, chopped

1 bunch of fresh basil, chopped

salt and pepper

HERB SOUP

Bring the stock to a boil. Melt the butter in another pan, add the onion and potatoes and cook over low heat, stirring occasionally, for about 5 minutes until the onion is translucent and the potatoes are soft. Sprinkle with the oregano, season with salt and pepper to taste and cook for a further 10 minutes. Pour in the boiling stock and simmer for about 20 minutes until the potatoes have almost disintegrated. Stir in the basil and parsley, then ladle into a soup tureen and serve.

MINESTRA AROMATICA

Serves 4

6$\frac{1}{4}$ cups Meat Stock (see page 208)

2 tablespoons butter • 1 onion, thinly sliced

2$\frac{3}{4}$ cups potatoes, diced

1 teaspoon dried oregano

10 fresh basil leaves, chopped

1 tablespoon chopped fresh flat-leaf parsley

salt and pepper

CORN SOUP

Bring the stock to a boil. Melt the butter in another pan, add the onion and cook over low heat, stirring occasionally, for 5 minutes until translucent. Add the corn and zucchini, cook for 2 minutes, then add the mushrooms and zucchini flowers and cook for a few minutes more. Pour in the hot stock and simmer for about 20 minutes. Season lightly with salt, ladle into a soup tureen, add the chile and serve.

MINESTRA CON IL MAIS

Serves 4

6$\frac{1}{4}$ cups Chicken Stock (see page 209)

3 tablespoons butter • 1 onion, thinly sliced

1$\frac{1}{2}$ cups canned corn, drained

1 cup coarsely chopped zucchini

2 cups sliced mushrooms

16 zucchini flowers, cut into strips

$\frac{1}{2}$ fresh chile, seeded and finely chopped

salt

LEEK SOUP

Put the leeks, carrot, celery and olive oil in a pan and add 2 tablespoons water. Cook over low heat for about 5 minutes. Add 6$\frac{1}{4}$ cups water, increase the heat to medium and bring to a boil. Stir in the rice and a pinch of salt and bring back to a boil. Lower the heat to medium-low and cook, stirring occasionally, for about 20 minutes until the rice is tender. Ladle into a soup tureen and serve with plenty of Parmesan.

MINESTRA CON I PORRI

Serves 4

4 leeks, white parts only, sliced

1 carrot, chopped • 1 celery stalk, chopped

2 tablespoons olive oil

$\frac{3}{4}$ cup long-grain rice

salt

Parmesan cheese, freshly grated, to serve

SOUP WITH MEATBALLS

Tear the bread into pieces, place in a bowl and add 3 tablespoons water. Set aside to soak. Combine the veal, egg yolk and Parmesan in another bowl. Squeeze out the bread, add to the veal mixture with the ham and season with salt and pepper. Bring the stock to a boil. Shape the veal mixture into small balls, add to the stock and simmer over medium heat for 15 minutes. Ladle into a soup tureen and serve. Leftover boiled or roast meat may be used to make the meatballs.

MINESTRA CON NOCCIOLINE DI CARNE

Serves 4

1 bread slice, crusts removed

1$\frac{1}{4}$ cups ground veal

1 egg yolk

$\frac{2}{3}$ cup Parmesan cheese, freshly grated

1 slice cured ham, chopped

6$\frac{1}{4}$ cups Meat Stock (see page 208)

salt and pepper

BARLEY AND LEGUME SOUP

MINESTRA CON ORZO E LEGUMI
Serves 4

MINESTRA CON ORZO E LEGUMI

Serves 4

8³/₄ cups Meat Stock (see page 208)

4 tablespoons olive oil

1 onion, chopped

1 garlic clove, chopped

¹/₂ cup dried borlotti beans, soaked in cold water overnight and drained

¹/₃ cup dried green soya beans, soaked in cold water overnight and drained

¹/₄ cup dried garbanzo beans, soaked in cold water overnight and drained

¹/₄ cup lentils

¹/₂ cup barley

salt and pepper

Bring the stock to a boil. Heat 3 tablespoons of the olive oil in another pan, add the onion and garlic and cook over low heat, stirring occasionally, for 10 minutes until lightly browned being careful not to burn the onion and garlic. Add the beans, garbanzo beans, lentils and barley and cook for a few minutes. Pour in the stock, bring to a boil and boil vigorously for 15 minutes. Lower the heat to medium and cook for 1¹/₂hours. Season with salt and pepper according to taste and stir in the remaining oil, then ladle into a soup tureen and serve.

WHITEBAIT SOUP

MINESTRA DI BIANCHETTI

Serves 4

3¹/₂ ounces whitebait or smelt

6¹/₄ cups Fish Stock (see page 208)

3¹/₂ ounces capelli d'angelo pasta

1 tablespoon extra virgin olive oil

salt and pepper

Rinse the fish. Bring the stock to a boil and add the fish and 'angel-hair' pasta. Cook for just under 2 minutes. Stir in the olive oil, season with salt and pepper, ladle into a soup tureen and serve immediately.

GARBANZO BEAN AND SPINACH SOUP

MINESTRA DI CECI E SPINACI

Serves 4

6¹/₄ cups Meat Stock (see page 208)

3 tablespoons olive oil, plus extra for drizzling

1 onion, chopped

1 carrot, chopped

1 celery stalk, chopped

3 cups spinach, chopped

scant 1 cup canned or cooked garbanzo beans, drained

scant 1 cup soup pasta

salt and pepper

Bring the stock to a boil in a pan. Heat the oil in another pan, add the onion, carrot and celery and cook over low heat, stirring occasionally, for 5 minutes until softened. Add the spinach, season with salt and cook for a few minutes more. Add the garbanzo beans and stock and simmer for 30 minutes. Add the pasta and cook until al dente. Season with pepper, ladle into a soup tureen, drizzle with olive oil and serve.

SWISS CHARD AND LENTIL SOUP

Bring the stock to a boil. Heat the oil in another pan, add the onion, garlic, celery and carrot and cook over low heat, stirring occasionally, for 10 minutes until lightly browned. Stir in the Swiss chard and cook for 2–3 minutes, then add the lentils and tomato paste and stir well. Pour in the stock, bring back to a boil and add the rice. Cook for 15 minutes or until the rice is tender. Season with salt and pepper, ladle into a soup tureen, drizzle with olive oil and serve with Parmesan.

MINESTRA DI COSTE E LENTICCHIE

Serves 4–6

$6^1/_4$ cups Meat Stock (see page 208)

3 tablespoons olive oil, plus extra for drizzling

1 onion, finely chopped

1 garlic clove, finely chopped

1 celery stalk, finely chopped

1 carrot, finely chopped

12 ounces Swiss chard, coarsely chopped

$^2/_3$ cup lentils, soaked in cold water

for 3 hours and drained

2 tablespoons tomato paste

$^1/_2$ cup long-grain rice

salt and pepper

Parmesan cheese, freshly grated, to serve

FARRO AND LEEK SOUP

Heat the oil in pan, add the leeks and cook over low heat, stirring occasionally, for 10 minutes until golden brown. Add the farro, pour in the stock, season with salt and simmer over low heat for $1^1/_2$ hours or until the farro is tender. Season with pepper, ladle into a soup tureen and sprinkle with the Parmesan.

MINESTRA DI FARRO E PORRI

Serves 4

2 tablespoons olive oil

2 leeks, white parts only sliced

$1^1/_2$ cups pearl farro

$6^1/_4$ cups Meat Stock (see page 208)

2 tablespoons Parmesan cheese, freshly grated

salt and pepper

MILLET SOUP

Pour $6^1/_4$ cups water into a pan, add the onion, carrot and celery and bring to a boil. Stir in the millet flour, season with salt and pepper and cook over medium heat for about 1 hour. Ladle into a soup tureen, stir in the olive oil and sprinkle with the parsley.

MINESTRA DI MIGLIO

Serves 4

1 onion, chopped

1 carrot, chopped

1 celery stalk, chopped

scant 1 cup toasted millet flour

2 tablespoons extra virgin olive oil

1 fresh flat-leaf parsley sprig, chopped

salt and pepper

NETTLE SOUP

MINESTRA DI ORTICHE

Serves 4

1 pound 5 ounces fresh nettles

6¹/₄ cups Meat Stock (see page 208)

3 tablespoons olive oil

¹/₃ cup pancetta, diced

1 garlic clove, chopped

2 ripe tomatoes, peeled, seeded and chopped

³/₄ cup long-grain rice

salt

Wearing a pair of gloves, remove all the nettle leaves and strings that cling to the stems. Wash and drain well and chop coarsely. Bring the stock to a boil. Heat the oil in another pan, add the pancetta and garlic and cook for 5 minutes. Add the tomatoes and cook for 10 minutes more, then season with salt and stir in the nettles. Cook for a few minutes more, then pour in the stock, bring back to a boil and add the rice. Cook for 15–20 minutes until the rice is tender. Ladle into a soup tureen and serve immediately.

BARLEY AND CHICKEN SOUP

MINESTRA DI ORZO E POLLO

Serves 4

2 chicken portions

2 onions, chopped

1 carrot, chopped

1 celery stalk, chopped

generous ¹/₂ cup barley

2 tablespoons butter

scant ¹/₂ cup dry white wine

¹/₂ teaspoon ground cumin

salt and pepper

Put the chicken, one of the onions, the carrot and celery in a pan, add 8³/₄ cups water and bring to a boil. Lower the heat and simmer for 1 hour, skimming the surface occasionally. Meanwhile, cook the barley in salted, boiling water for 30 minutes, then drain well. Melt the butter in a skillet, add the barley and the remaining onion and cook over low heat, stirring occasionally, for 5 minutes. Sprinkle with the wine and cook until it has evaporated. When the chicken is cooked through, lift it out of the stock with a slotted spoon. Remove and discard the skin and cut the meat off the bones. Return the meat to the stock, add the barley mixture and cook for a further 10 minutes. Stir in the cumin and season with salt and pepper to taste. Ladle into a soup tureen and serve.

CAESAR'S MUSHROOM SOUP

MINESTRA DI OVOLI

Serves 4

3 tablespoons butter

4¹/₂ cups Caesar's mushrooms, sliced

6¹/₄ cups Meat Stock (see page 208)

1 egg

1 tablespoon Parmesan cheese, freshly grated

salt

Melt the butter in a pan, add the mushrooms and season with salt, then cover and cook over high heat for about 15 minutes until a thick, yellowish sauce has formed. Meanwhile, bring the stock to a boil in another pan. Pour the stock into the pan of mushrooms and simmer over low heat for 15 minutes. Beat the egg with the Parmesan, then stir into the soup. Ladle into a soup tureen and serve immediately.

LEEK AND POTATO SOUP

Put the leeks, potatoes, onion and a pinch of salt into a pan, pour in ⅔ cup water and cook for about 10 minutes. Add 2¼ cups warm water, cover and cook over low heat for 30 minutes. Ladle half the soup into a food processor and process to a purée, then return to the pan. Cook over low heat for a further 20 minutes. Drizzle with olive oil, sprinkle with the parsley and serve with Parmesan.

MINESTRA DI PORRI E PATATE

Serves 4

5¼ cups leeks, white parts only sliced

3 potatoes, diced • 1 onion, sliced

olive oil, for drizzling

1 fresh flat-leaf parsley sprig, chopped

salt

Parmesan cheese, freshly grated, to serve

FLEMISH SOUP

Put the Belgian endive, chicken, mushrooms, carrot, potato, celery and leeks into a pan, add 6¼ cups water and bring to a boil. Cover and simmer over low heat for 1 hour. Season with salt to taste. Beat the egg yolk with the cream in a soup tureen, ladle in the soup, stirring, and serve.

MINESTRA FIAMMINGA

Serves 4

4 Belgian endive heads, thinly sliced

7-ounce skinless, boneless chicken breast, cut into thin strips

2¾ cups white mushrooms, thinly sliced

1 carrot, cut into thin batons • 1 potato, cut into thin batons • 1 celery stalk, cut into thin batons

2 leeks, trimmed and thinly sliced

1 egg yolk • scant 1 cup heavy cream • salt

THREE–COLOR SOUP

Beat the eggs with the Parmesan and a pinch of salt. Heat a little of the olive oil in a small omelet pan, add a little of the egg mixture and tilt the pan to coat the base. Cook over low heat, drawing the cooked egg toward the center to allow the raw egg to flow underneath. When the underside is set, slide the omelet out of the pan. Make one or two more omelets in the same way, adding more oil as necessary. Roll up the omelets and cut into strips. Cook the peas in salted, boiling water for 8–10 minutes until tender, then drain. Bring the stock to a boil. Put the tongue, omelet strips and peas in a soup tureen. Pour in the stock and serve immediately.

MINESTRA TRICOLORE

Serves 4

2 eggs

⅓ cup Parmesan cheese, freshly grated

1 tablespoon olive oil

¾ cup shelled peas

4 cups Meat Stock (see page 208)

3½ ounces pickled tongue, cut into strips

salt

GREEN SOUP

Cook the Swiss chard in salted, boiling water until tender, then drain and let cool. Squeeze out as much liquid as possible and shred. Combine the chard, Parmesan, eggs, a pinch of salt and a ladleful of stock. Bring the remaining stock to a boil, then whisk in the chard mixture. Simmer gently for 5 minutes, then ladle into a soup tureen. Serve with Parmesan.

MINESTRA VERDE

Serves 4

14 ounces Swiss chard

½ cups Parmesan cheese, freshly grated, plus extra for serving • 3 eggs, lightly beaten

6¼ cups Meat Stock (see page 208)

salt

BREAD SOUP

PANCOTTO

Serves 4

4 tablespoons olive oil, plus extra for drizzling

3 ripe tomatoes, peeled, seeded and chopped

1 garlic clove, chopped

14 ounces day-old bread, crusts removed, diced

1/3 cup Parmesan cheese, freshly grated

salt and pepper

Heat the oil in a pan, add the tomatoes and garlic and cook over low heat, stirring frequently, for 10 minutes. Pour in 1 cup boiling water, add the bread and mix well. Pour in 4 cups water and season with salt. Cook over medium heat until the soup is fairly thick. Remove from the heat and let stand for a few minutes. Drizzle with oil and stir, then ladle into a soup tureen, sprinkle with Parmesan, season with pepper and serve.

BREAD SOUP WITH TOMATO

PAPPA AL POMODORO

Serves 4

1 tablespoon olive oil

11 ounces ripe tomatoes, peeled, seeded and coarsely chopped

1 garlic clove, chopped

1 celery stalk, chopped

2 day-old country-style bread slices, cubed

6 fresh basil leaves, chopped

1/3 cup Parmesan cheese, freshly grated

salt and pepper

Put the olive oil, tomatoes, garlic, celery and a pinch each of salt and pepper into a pan, add 5 cups water and bring to a boil. Lower the heat and simmer for about 1 hour. Remove the pan from the heat and let stand. About 30 minutes before serving, stir in the bread and simmer the soup over low heat. Ladle into a soup tureen, sprinkle with the basil and Parmesan and serve.

PASSATELLI

PASSATELLI

Serves 4

1³/₄ cups bread crumbs

generous 1 cup Parmesan cheese, freshly grated, plus extra to serve

2 tablespoons butter, melted

pinch of freshly grated nutmeg

3 eggs, lightly beaten

4 cups Meat Stock (see page 208)

salt

Combine the bread crumbs, Parmesan, melted butter, nutmeg, eggs and a large pinch of salt in a bowl. The mixture should be fairly firm; if it is too soft, add more bread crumbs. Bring the stock to a boil in a pan. Hold a potato masher with fairly large holes over the pan and press the bread crumb mixture through it to form short, worm-shaped dumplings. Serve with Parmesan.

PASTA AND GARBANZO BEANS

Put the garbanzo beans in a pan, add 4 cups water and bring to a boil. Lower the heat, cover and cook for about 1½ hours. Remove about 3 ladlefuls of the garbanzo beans, place in a food processor and process to a purée. Scrape the purée into the pan, re-cover and cook for a further 1½ hours. Heat the olive oil in a skillet, add the garlic, rosemary and tomatoes and cook, stirring occasionally, for 10 minutes. Stir the tomato mixture into the garbanzo beans and season with salt. Add the tagliatelle and cook until al dente. Season with pepper, ladle into a soup tureen, drizzle with oil and sprinkle with the Parmesan.

PASTA E CECI ALLA TOSCANA

Serves 4

generous 1 cup dried garbanzo beans, soaked in cold water overnight and drained

1 tablespoon olive oil, plus extra for drizzling

1 garlic clove, crushed

1 fresh rosemary sprig, chopped

9 ounces tomatoes, peeled and chopped

5 ounces fresh tagliatelle, cut into short lengths

⅓ cup Parmesan cheese, freshly grated

salt and pepper

PASTA AND WHITE BEAN

Put the beans into a pan, add cold water to cover and bring to a boil. Lower the heat and simmer for about 2 hours. Transfer half the beans to a food processor and process to a purée. Heat the oil in a pan, add the sage leaves and garlic and cook for a few minutes. Pour in the bean purée and 6¼ cups water, season with salt and pepper and stir in the strained tomatoes. Finally, add the whole beans. Bring to a boil, add the pasta and cook for 10 minutes or until al dente, then ladle into a soup tureen. This is excellent hot, cold or even warm.

PASTA E FAGIOLI

Serves 4

2 cups dried white beans, soaked in cold water overnight and drained

3 tablespoons olive oil

4 sage leaves

1 garlic clove, crushed

3 tablespoons bottled strained tomatoes

¾ cup maltagliati pasta

salt and pepper

PASTA, POTATOES AND CELERY

Heat the olive oil in pan, add the carrot and celery hearts and cook over low heat, stirring occasionally, for 5 minutes. Stir in the pancetta, add the potatoes and pour in 4 cups hot water. Cover and simmer for 30 minutes. Stir in the tomato paste, season with salt and pepper and add more water if necessary. Add the pasta and cook until al dente. Ladle into a soup tureen and serve with Parmesan.

PASTA, PATATE E SEDANO

Serves 4

3 tablespoons olive oil

1 carrot, chopped

2 celery hearts, chopped

⅓ cup pancetta, diced

3⅔ cups potatoes, diced

1 tablespoon concentrated tomato paste

1¾ cups ditalini pasta

salt and pepper

Parmesan cheese, freshly grated, to serve

PORRIDGE

PORRIDGE

Serves 4

1 cup oat flakes • salt

sugar (optional)

cold milk or light cream, to serve

Bring 2¹/₄ cups water to a boil. Add a pinch of salt, sprinkle in the oat flakes and stir until thickened. Simmer for 15 minutes. Serve hot with milk or light cream handed separately. Porridge may be sweetened with sugar.

POT–AU–FEU

POT–AU–FEU

Serves 6

4 potatoes

1³/₄ pounds lean beef

1 pound 2 ounces veal

1 marrow bone

2 turnips, chopped • 1 leek, chopped

3 carrots, chopped

1 onion, chopped

1 celery stalk, chopped • 1 garlic clove, chopped

salt

Cook the potatoes in lightly salted, boiling water for 20 minutes until tender. Meanwhile, put the beef and veal into a large pan and add plenty of water to cover and a pinch of salt. Wrap the marrow bone in cheesecloth, add to the pan and bring to a boil. Skim off any scum that rises to the surface, then add the chopped vegetables and the garlic. Simmer over low heat for 3¹/₂ hours. Meanwhile, peel and dice the potatoes. Remove the meat and vegetables from the pan and arrange on a warm serving dish. Add the potatoes to the soup, heat through briefly, then ladle into a soup tureen. Serve the two dishes at the same time.

QUADRUCCI WITH VEGETABLES

QUADRUCCI CON VERDURE

Serves 4

6¹/₄ cups Meat Stock (see page 208)

3 tablespoons olive oil

1 onion, chopped • 1 carrot, chopped

1 celery stalk, chopped

³/₄ cup potatoes, diced

³/₄ cup turnips, diced

5 ounces quadrucci pasta

salt and pepper

Bring the stock to a boil. Heat the oil in another pan, add the onion, carrot and celery and cook over low heat, stirring occasionally, for 10 minutes until lightly browned. Add the potatoes and turnips, mix well and pour in the stock. Bring back to a boil, then lower the heat and cook for about 45 minutes. Add the pasta and cook for a further 8 minutes until al dente. Season with salt and pepper to taste. Ladle into a soup tureen and serve.

RICE AND PEAS

RISI E BISI

Serves 4

5 cups Meat Stock (see page208)

3 tablespoons olive oil • ¹/₄ cup butter

1 onion, chopped

1 garlic clove • 1 celery stalk, chopped

2¹/₄ cups peas, shelled

1 cup risotto rice

¹/₃ cup Parmesan cheese, freshly grated

salt

Bring the stock to a boil. Heat the oil and half the butter in another pan, add the onion, garlic and celery and cook over low heat, stirring occasionally, for 5 minutes. Remove and discard the garlic. Add the peas followed by the rice. Stir for about 1 minute, then stir in a ladleful of the stock. Cook, adding the stock a ladleful at a time, for about 20 minutes until the rice is tender and all the stock has been used. Season with salt to taste, stir in the remaining butter and the Parmesan, ladle into a soup tureen and serve.

RICE AND POTATOES

RISO E PATATE

Serves 4

2 tablespoons butter

1 onion, chopped

1/3 cup prosciutto, diced

1 cup risotto rice

generous 1 cup potatoes, diced

6 1/4 cups Meat Stock (see page 208)

1 fresh flat-leaf parsley sprig, chopped

salt

Melt the butter in a pan, add the onion and prosciutto and cook over low heat, stirring occasionally, for 10 minutes until lightly browned. Add the rice and stir well to coat with the butter. Season with salt, add the potatoes and stir in a ladleful of the stock. Cook, adding the stock a ladleful at a time, for about 20 minutes until the rice is tender and all the stock has been used. Ladle into a soup tureen, sprinkle with the parsley and serve.

SEMOLINA

SEMOLINO

Serves 4

6 1/4 cups Meat Stock (see page 208)

1/2 cup semolina

2 tablespoons butter

2 egg yolks, lightly beaten

Parmesan cheese, freshly grated, to serve

Bring the stock to a boil and sprinkle in the semolina, stirring constantly. Cook for 10 minutes, then stir in the butter and remove the pan from the heat. Ladle into a soup tureen and stir in the egg yolks. Serve with Parmesan. You can make this soup thicker or thinner according to taste.

STRACCIATELLA

STRACCIATELLA

Serves 4

1/2 cup bread crumbs

1/2 cup Parmesan cheese, freshly grated

3 eggs, lightly beaten

6 1/4 cups Meat Stock (see page 208)

1 1/2 teaspoons chopped fresh flat-leaf parsley

salt

Combine the bread crumbs, Parmesan, eggs and a pinch of salt in a bowl. Heat the stock, add a ladleful to the egg mixture and mix until smooth. Bring the stock to a boil and add the egg mixture, which will float up to the surface in a clump. Break up slightly with the prongs of a fork. Ladle the soup into a tureen, sprinkle with the parsley and serve.

TAPIOCA

TAPIOCA

Serves 4

6 1/4 cups Meat Stock (see page 208)

1/2 cup tapioca

1/3 cup Parmesan cheese, freshly grated

heavy cream, whipped (optional)

lettuce (optional)

salt

Bring the stock to a boil and pour in the tapioca, stirring constantly. Add a pinch of salt and cook, stirring constantly, for about 10 minutes. Ladle into a soup tureen and serve with Parmesan. If you like, stir in a few tablespoonfuls of cream before serving. Another alternative is to add lettuce: cut 3–4 lettuce leaves into strips, soften with a pat of butter on low heat for a few minutes and add to the tapioca halfway through cooking.

MINESTRONES

Cream soups, soups and now minestrones – a true crescendo. Fresh garden vegetables and herbs go into a minestrone, along with pasta, rice and legumes (according to taste) and the essential butter, bacon fat, oil or lard. For a lighter version, the oil or butter may be added when the soup has been cooked. In the case of lard or bacon fat, which are necessarily added at the beginning to give flavor to the ingredients, it is advisable to limit their frying time. Almost every Italian region has its own exclusive recipe and this chapter lists the most famous. Hot minestrone is a pleasant winter dish, and the cold version is a true delicacy, provided it is not served straight from the refrigerator.

GENOESE PESTO MINESTRONE

Put the dried mushrooms in a bowl, add hot water to cover and let soak for 20 minutes, then drain and chop. Put the mushrooms, fava beans, cabbage, green beans, tomatoes, zucchini, eggplant and a pinch of salt into a pan, pour in 8³/₄ cups water and the olive oil and bring to a boil. Lower the heat and simmer for 2 hours. Add the rice or pasta and cook until al dente. Remove from the heat and stir in the pesto. Ladle into a soup tureen and serve very hot with Parmesan. This minestrone is also good cold. In this case do not add oil during cooking, and let cool to room temperature. Just before serving, drizzle with a little oil.

MINESTRONE ALLA GENOVESE COL PESTO

Serves 4–6

¹/₄ cup dried mushrooms

³/₄ cup fava beans, shelled

¹/₂ cabbage, shredded

scant 1¹/₂ cups green beans, cut into short lengths

3 tomatoes, chopped

3 zucchini, chopped

1 eggplant, chopped

3 tablespoons olive oil

scant ¹/₂ cup long-grain rice or short pasta

Pesto (see page 68), to taste

salt

Parmesan cheese, freshly grated, to serve

MILANESE MINESTRONE

Finely chop the lardons with the garlic and onion. When the mixture is quite fine, add the parsley and celery and chop. Put the mixture into a pan, add the tomatoes, carrots, potatoes, zucchini and oil and pour in 8³/₄ cups water. Season with salt and bring to a boil over high heat. Lower the heat and cook for at least 2 hours. Add the peas and cabbage, simmer for 15 minutes, then add the rice and simmer, stirring occasionally, for a further 18 minutes until it is tender. Stir in the herbs, ladle into a soup tureen and serve with plenty of Parmesan. This minestrone should be fairly thick. It is excellent hot, but it is also good served warm or cold in the summer.

MINESTRONE ALLA MILANESE

Serves 4–6

¹/₄ cup lardons

¹/₂ garlic clove

¹/₂ onion

1 fresh flat-leaf parsley sprig

1 celery stalk

3 tomatoes, peeled, seeded and diced

2 carrots, chopped • 3 potatoes, chopped

2 zucchini, chopped

2 tablespoons olive oil

1³/₄ cups peas, shelled

¹/₂ Savoy cabbage, shredded

³/₄ cup fresh shelled borlotti beans

¹/₂ cup long-grain rice

4 fresh sage leaves, chopped

6 fresh basil leaves, chopped

salt

Parmesan cheese, freshly grated, to serve

MINESTRONE NAPOLETANA

Place the bell pepper under a preheated broiler and cook, turning frequently, until the skin is charred and blistered. Place in a plastic bag and tie the top. When cool enough to handle, peel off the skin, halve and seed the pepper and dice the flesh. Finely chop the pancetta with the onion, carrot and garlic. Heat the oil, add the pancetta mixture and cook over low heat for a few minutes until lightly browned. Add the tomatoes and cook for about 10 minutes. Add 8³/₄ cups water and season with salt and pepper. Bring to a boil, add the potatoes and beans and simmer for 1 hour. Add the zucchini, peas, cabbage, Belgian endive, eggplants and yellow pepper. Simmer for a further 30 minutes. Add the pasta and cook for 10 minutes until al dente. Season with salt if necessary. Ladle the minestrone into a soup tureen, sprinkle with the basil and serve with provolone.

MINESTRONE ALLA NAPOLETANA

Serves 4–6

1 yellow bell pepper

2 ounces pancetta

¹/₂ onion

¹/₂ carrot

¹/₂ garlic clove

2 tablespoons olive oil

3 tomatoes, peeled, seeded and chopped

1 fresh flat-leaf parsley sprig, chopped

2 potatoes, diced

³/₄ cup fava beans, shelled

2 zucchini, sliced

scant 1 cup peas, shelled

¹/₄ cabbage, coarsely shredded

1 Belgian endive head, cut into strips

2 eggplants, diced

scant 1 cup cannolicchi pasta

2 teaspoons chopped fresh basil

salt and pepper

provolone cheese, freshly grated, to serve

PUGLIAN MINESTRONE

MINESTRONE ALLA PUGLIESE

Serves 4–6

2 pounds turnip greens
2 onions, chopped
5 tablespoons olive oil
pinch of chili powder
1 1/4 cups tortiglioni pasta
1/3 cup romano cheese, freshly grated
salt and pepper

If possible choose turnip greens in flower since they are tastier. Cook in salted, boiling water for about 10 minutes, then separate the stems from the flowers. Chop the stems and put in a pan with the onions, 3 tablespoons of the olive oil, the chili powder and a pinch of pepper. Cook over low heat, stirring frequently, for 5 minutes, then pour in 1 3/4 cups hot water and simmer for 1 3/4 hours. Stir in the pasta, then stir in the turnip flowers and cook until the pasta is al dente. Remove the pan from the heat, stir in the romano and let stand for a few minutes. Season with a little more pepper and chili powder, stir in the remaining oil, ladle into a soup tureen and serve.

BORSCH

MINESTRONE ALLA RUSSA

Serves 4–6

3 tablespoons butter
1 white onion, finely chopped
2 garlic cloves, finely chopped
1 3/4 cups raw beets, diced
1 celery heart, chopped
3 tomatoes, peeled, seeded and chopped
pinch of sugar
2 tablespoons white wine vinegar
6 1/4 cups Meat Stock (see page 208)
14 ounces potatoes, cut into wedges
4 1/3 cups white cabbage, shredded
1 pound 2 ounces boiled beef, diced
2 tablespoons chopped fresh flat-leaf parsley
salt
1 cup sour cream, to serve

Melt the butter in a large pan, add the onion and garlic and cook over low heat, stirring occasionally, for 5 minutes until soft. Add the beets, celery, half the tomatoes, sugar, a pinch of salt and 3/4 cups of the stock and cook over medium heat for 30 minutes. Meanwhile, cook the potatoes and cabbage in the remaining stock in another pan for about 20 minutes, but do not let the potatoes overcook. Add the remaining tomatoes, the beef and the beets mixture, stir and simmer for a further 10 minutes. Season with salt if necessary, sprinkle with the parsley and remove the pan from the heat. Pour the minestrone into a soup tureen and serve with sour cream. This Russian version of minestrone is immediately recognizable owing to the red color of the beets. There are other versions, but this is the most common.

TUSCAN MINESTRONE

Put the beans, rosemary and bay leaf into a pan, add cold water to cover, bring to a boil and simmer for about 2 hours. Remove and discard the herbs, then transfer half the beans to a food processor and process to a purée. Scrape the purée back into the pan. Heat the oil in another pan, add the onion, celery, carrot and parsley and cook over low heat, stirring occasionally, for 5 minutes. Add the escarole, tomato, zucchini and leek and cook for a further 10 minutes. Stir the vegetable mixture into the beans, season with salt and pepper to taste and add more hot water if necessary. Bring to a boil, add the rice and cook for 15–20 minutes until tender. Ladle into a soup tureen and serve with Parmesan.

MINESTRONE ALLA TOSCANA

Serves 4–6

$^1/_2$ cup toscanelli or cannellini beans,
soaked overnight in cold water and drained
1 fresh rosemary sprig • 1 bay leaf
4 tablespoons olive oil
1 onion, chopped • 1 celery stalk, chopped
1 carrot, chopped
1 tablespoon chopped fresh flat-leaf parsley
1 escarole head, chopped
1 tomato, peeled, seeded and chopped
1 zucchini, chopped
1 leek, white part only chopped
scant $^1/_2$ cup long-grain rice • salt and pepper
Parmesan cheese, freshly grated, to serve

FARRO AND BEAN MINESTRONE

Heat the olive oil in a pan, add the onion, carrot, celery and garlic and cook over low heat, stirring occasionally, for 5 minutes. Sprinkle with the wine and cook until it has evaporated. Add the tomatoes and sage leaves and simmer, stirring occasionally, for 15 minutes. Add the beans and 4 cups water, bring to a boil, then lower the heat and simmer for 1 hour. Transfer to a food processor and process to a purée. Pour into a clean pan, bring to a boil, season with salt and pepper to taste and add the farro. Lower the heat and simmer for 1$^1/_2$ hours. Ladle into a soup tureen, drizzle with olive oil and serve.

MINESTRONE DI FARRO E FAGIOLI

Serves 4

2 tablespoons olive oil, plus extra for drizzling
1 onion, chopped • 1 carrot, chopped
1 celery stalk, chopped • 1 garlic clove, chopped
scant $^1/_2$ cup white wine
2 tomatoes, peeled and chopped
2 fresh sage leaves
$^3/_4$ cup dried white beans,
soaked in cold water overnight and drained
1 cup pearl farro,
soaked in cold water overnight and drained
salt and pepper

WINTER MINESTRONE

Put the potatoes, carrots, turnip, leeks, cabbage, celery and chard stalks into a pan, pour in 6$^1/_4$ cups water, add a pinch of salt and bring to a boil. Lower the heat and simmer for 1 hour. Season with salt. Transfer 2 ladlefuls of the mixture to a food processor, process to a purée and return to the pan. Mix well and cook for a few minutes more. Stir in the parsley and oil, ladle into a soup tureen and serve.

MINESTRONE D'INVERNO

Serves 4

2 potatoes, chopped • 2 carrots, chopped
1 turnip, chopped • 2 leeks, trimmed and chopped
1 small Savoy cabbage, shredded
1 celery stalk, chopped
bunch of Swiss chard stalks, chopped
1 tablespoon chopped fresh flat-leaf parsley
1 tablespoon olive oil
salt

SEASONAL MINESTRONE

Put the mushrooms in a bowl, pour in warm water to cover and let soak for 20 minutes, then drain. Cook the fava beans in lightly salted, boiling water for 10 minutes, then add the potatoes, green beans, zucchini and mushrooms. Stir in 3 tablespoons of the oil and cook 15 minutes more until the vegetables are tender. Add the pasta and cook for 15 minutes. Meanwhile, heat the remaining oil with the garlic in a small pan, add the tomatoes and tomato paste, season with salt and pepper and cook over low heat, stirring occasionally, for 10–15 minutes. Stir the tomato mixture into the soup and serve.

MINESTRONE DI STAGIONE

Serves 4

$1/3$ cup dried mushrooms

scant $1^1/2$ cups fava beans, shelled

2 potatoes, sliced

scant $1^1/2$ cups green beans, chopped

$1^1/2$ cups zucchini, sliced

5 tablespoons olive oil

scant 1 cup ditalini pasta

1 garlic clove, chopped

3 tomatoes, peeled and chopped

1 teaspoon concentrated tomato paste

salt and pepper

SAVOY CABBAGE AND RICE MINESTRONE

Heat 1 tablespoon of the oil in a pan with $1/2$ cup water, add the leeks, prosciutto and rosemary and cook over low heat for 10 minutes until the leeks have softened. Add the tomatoes, season with salt and pepper and cook for a further 10 minutes. Stir in the cabbage, add 4 cups warm water, increase the heat to medium and simmer for 15 minutes. Bring to a boil, add the rice and stir and cook for about 18 minutes until tender. Ladle into a soup tureen, stir in the remaining oil and the Parmesan and serve.

MINESTRONE DI VERZA E RISO

Serves 4–6

4 tablespoons olive oil

2 leeks, trimmed and chopped

1 thick prosciutto slice, chopped

1 fresh rosemary sprig

2 tomatoes, peeled, seeded and coarsely chopped

$6^1/2$ cups Savoy cabbage, cut into strips

$1/2$ cup long-grain rice

1 tablespoon Parmesan cheese, freshly grated

salt and pepper

THICK SOUPS

The distinctive characteristic of most Italian thick soups is the immersion of one or more slices of bread in the stock with no additional pasta or rice. Other typical ingredients include legumes, fish and vegetables. Thick soups are tasty and aromatic and are often cooked au gratin in the oven. Onion Soup (see page 249) is particularly delicious and famous, while Pavian Soup (see page 248), served with an egg lying on golden fried bread, is especially attractive.

RIBOLLITA

RIBOLLITA

Serves 4

¹/₄ cup olive oil, plus extra for drizzling

1 carrot, chopped

1 onion, chopped

1 celery stalk, chopped

3 fresh or canned tomatoes, peeled

1 fresh thyme sprig

2 potatoes, coarsely diced

7¹/₂ cups cavolo nero
(Tuscan cabbage), shredded

1 cup fresh white beans,
or ¹/₂ cup dried white beans,
soaked in cold water overnight and drained

4 country-style bread slices

salt and pepper

This soup is called ribollita (reboiled) because it was originally made using the previous day's leftover vegetable soup heated in an earthenware pot with thinly sliced onion, black pepper and olive oil sprinkled on the surface. It was taken off the heat and served when the onion had turned golden brown. Today, however, it is normally made as follows. Heat the oil in a pan, add the carrot, onion and celery and cook over low heat, stirring occasionally, for 5 minutes until softened. Add the tomatoes, thyme and potatoes and cook for a few minutes, then add the cavolo nero and beans. Pour in 8³/₄ cups water and season with salt. Bring to a boil, lower the heat, cover and simmer for about 2 hours. Preheat the oven to 350°F. Place the bread on the base of a large earthenware casserole and ladle in the soup. Cook in the oven for about 10 minutes. Sprinkle with pepper and drizzle with oil.

PAVIAN SOUP

ZUPPA ALLA PAVESE

Serves 4

3 cups Meat Stock (see page 208)

2 tablespoons butter

8 bread slices, crusts removed

4 eggs

4 tablespoons Parmesan cheese, freshly grated

salt

Preheat the oven to 400°F. Bring the stock to a boil. Meanwhile, melt the butter in a skillet, add the bread, in batches, and fry until golden on both sides. Drain on paper towels. Place the fried bread on the base of four ovenproof soup bowls. Break an egg on top of each, ladle in the boiling stock and sprinkle with the Parmesan. Place the bowls on a cookie sheet in the oven for a few minutes until the cheese melts. Alternatively, you can serve the soup immediately after adding the cheese. This soup is substantial, but delicate at the same time.

BARLEY SOUP AL VERDE

ZUPPA CON ORZO AL VERDE

Serves 4

6¼ cups Meat Stock (see page 208)

3 tablespoons olive oil

1 onion, chopped

1 fresh sage leaf

1 cup Savoy cabbage, cut into strips

3 cups spinach, chopped

¾ cup pearl barley

⅓ cup Parmesan cheese, freshly grated

salt

croûtons, to serve

Bring the stock to a boil. Heat the oil in another pan, add the onion and sage leaf and cook over low heat, stirring occasionally, for 5 minutes. Stir in the cabbage and spinach and cook for a few minutes more. Pour in the hot stock, cover and cook on a medium heat for 15 minutes. Add the barley, season with salt and cook for a further 30 minutes. Remove from the heat, ladle into a soup tureen, sprinkle with the Parmesan and serve with croûtons.

BARLEY AND PEA SOUP

ZUPPA CON ORZO E PISELLI

Serves 4

2¼ cups milk

generous 1 cup barley

1¼ cups fresh peas or frozen peas, shelled

pinch of chili powder

salt and pepper

Bring the milk and 4 cups water to a boil. Add the barley and peas, season with salt, pepper and chili powder to taste and cook over low heat for about 30 minutes, stirring occasionally. Ladle into a soup tureen. This is a very simple soup, but is nutritious and tasty. It may be enriched by adding diced chicken breast.

CABBAGE SOUP

Heat the oil in a pan, add the onion, carrot and celery and cook over low heat, stirring occasionally, for 10 minutes until lightly browned. Add both kinds of cabbage, season with salt and cook for 10 minutes. Pour in 6¼ cups water and bring to a boil. Lower the heat, cover and simmer for 1 hour. If the soup is too watery, remove the lid and cook for a few minutes more. Preheat the oven to 400°F. Toast the bread on both sides under a preheated broiler and place in four ovenproof soup bowls. Ladle the soup over it, sprinkle with the Parmesan and place on a cookie sheet in the oven for a few minutes until the cheese melts.

ZUPPA DI CAVOLI

Serves 4

3 tablespoons olive oil

1 onion, chopped

1 carrot, chopped

1 celery stalk, chopped

2 cups Savoy cabbage, cut into strips

2 cups white cabbage, cut into strips

4 country-style bread slices

4 tablespoons Parmesan cheese, freshly grated

salt and pepper

BELGIAN ENDIVE SOUP

Bring the stock to a boil. Meanwhile, parboil the Belgian endive in boiling water for 5 minutes. Drain, squeezing out as much liquid as possible, and chop coarsely. Melt the butter in a pan, add the belgian endive and cook over high heat for about 10 minutes, then add the stock. Beat the eggs with the Parmesan, season with salt and pepper and whisk into the soup. Lightly toast the bread on both sides under a preheated broiler, put one slice in each of four soup bowls and ladle in the soup.

ZUPPA DI CICORIA

Serves 4

5 cups Meat Stock (see page 208)

1½ pounds Belgian endive

2 tablespoons butter

2 eggs

⅓ cup Parmesan cheese, freshly grated

4 country-style bread slices

salt and pepper

MILK AND ONION SOUP

Melt the butter in a pan, add the onions, cover and cook, stirring occasionally, over very low heat for about 30 minutes until very soft and lightly browned. Meanwhile, bring the milk to just below simmering point in another pan. Add the milk to the onions, season with salt, increase the heat to medium and cook for 30 minutes more, making sure that the soup does not boil over. Ladle into a soup tureen and serve with plenty of Parmesan and croûtons.

ZUPPA DI CIPOLLE AL LATTE

Serves 4

2 tablespoons butter

14 ounces onions, very thinly sliced

4 cups milk

salt

To serve

Parmesan cheese, freshly grated

croûtons

ONION SOUP AU GRATIN

ZUPPA DI CIPOLLE GRATINATA

Serves 4

1/4 cup butter

14 ounces onions, sliced

5 cups Meat Stock (see page 208)

pinch of all-purpose flour

8 toast slices

3/4 cup Emmenthal cheese, freshly grated

salt and pepper

Melt 3 tablespoons of the butter in a pan, add the onions, cover and cook over very low heat, stirring occasionally, for about 30 minutes until very soft and lightly browned. Meanwhile, bring the stock to a boil. Sprinkle the onions with the flour, season with salt and pepper, pour in the stock and cook for a further 15 minutes. Meanwhile, preheat the oven to 400°F. Ladle the soup into four ovenproof soup bowls, place two slices of toast in each and sprinkle with the Emmenthal. Dot with the remaining butter, season with pepper and place on a cookie sheet in the oven for a few minutes until the cheese has melted.

MUSSEL SOUP

ZUPPA DI COZZE

Serves 4

20 mussels, scrubbed and beards removed

2 tablespoons olive oil

1 onion, chopped

pinch of saffron threads

2 tomatoes, peeled, seeded and chopped

6 1/4 cups Fish Stock (see page 208)

4 country-style bread slices

1 garlic clove, halved

1 tablespoon chopped fresh flat-leaf parsley

salt and pepper

Discard any mussels with broken shells or that do not shut immediately when sharply tapped. Put the mussels in a dry skillet, place over high heat and cook for about 5 minutes until the shells open. Discard any mussels that remain closed. Remove the mussels from the shells and set aside. Heat the olive oil in a pan, add the onion and saffron and cook over low heat, stirring occasionally, for 5 minutes. Add the tomatoes and stock, season with salt and pepper and cook for 20 minutes. Add the mussels. Toast the bread on both sides under a preheated broiler, then rub with the garlic and place a slice in each of four soup bowls. Ladle in the soup and sprinkle with the parsley.

BEAN AND BARLEY SOUP

ZUPPA DI FAGIOLI E ORZO

Serves 4

3/4 cup dried red kidney beans, soaked in cold water overnight and drained

2 tablespoons olive oil, plus extra for drizzling

1/3 cup pancetta, diced

1 garlic clove, chopped

1 small onion, chopped

scant 1 cup barley

3 potatoes, diced

2 tablespoons tomato paste

salt and pepper

Put the beans in a pan, pour in 4 cups water, bring to a boil and boil vigorously for 15 minutes, then lower the heat and simmer for 2 hours. Heat the oil in another pan, add the pancetta, garlic and onion and cook over low heat, stirring occasionally, for 5 minutes. Add the barley and 4 cups water, bring to a boil, then simmer for 2 hours. Add the beans, with their cooking liquid, the potatoes and tomato paste and season with salt and pepper to taste. Cook for 1 hour, then ladle into a soup tureen, drizzle with oil and serve.

OATMEAL SOUP

Put the potatoes, onion and pancetta into a pan, add 6¼ cups water and the oil, bring to a boil and cook for 15 minutes until the potatoes are tender. Season with salt to taste, stir in the rolled oats and cook for 10 minutes; this soup should be fairly thick. Ladle into a soup tureen and serve with Parmesan and croûtons.

ZUPPA DI FIOCCHI D'AVENA

Serves 4

4 potatoes, diced

1 onion, thinly sliced

1 pancetta slice, diced

1 tablespoon olive oil

¼ cup rolled oats

salt

To serve

Parmesan cheese, freshly grated

croûtons

CHEESE AND LEEK SOUP

Bring the stock to a boil. Meanwhile, heat the butter and olive oil in another pan, add the leeks and cook over low heat, stirring occasionally, for 5 minutes. Sprinkle with the nutmeg, season with salt and pepper, pour in the stock and cook for about 10 minutes. Preheat the oven to 350°F. Place the bread in each of four ovenproof soup bowls, top with the fontina and sprinkle with the brandy and Emmenthal, then ladle in the soup. Place on a cookie sheet in the oven for about 10 minutes, then let stand for a few minutes before serving.

ZUPPA DI FORMAGGI E PORRI

Serves 4

6¼ cups Meat Stock (see page 208)

¼ cup butter

1 tablespoon olive oil

3 leeks, sliced

pinch of freshly grated nutmeg

4 country-style bread slices

3½ ounces fontina cheese, sliced

scant 1 cup Emmenthal cheese, freshly grated

¼ cup brandy

salt and pepper

BEAN AND MUSHROOM SOUP

Put the beans in a pan, add 6¼ cups water, one of the garlic cloves and 1 tablespoon of the oil and bring to a boil, then lower the heat and simmer for 2 hours. Heat the remaining oil in a skillet, add the onion and cook over low heat, stirring occasionally, for 10 minutes until lightly browned. Add the porcini, increase the heat to high and cook for a few minutes more, then season with salt and pepper and tip the contents of the skillet into the pan with the beans. Cook for a few more minutes, then add the parsley and taste and adjust the seasoning. Gently rub the bread with the remaining garlic, spread with a little butter, toast lightly and serve with the soup.

ZUPPA DI FUNGHI E FAGIOLI

Serves 4

1¾ cups dried cannellini beans, soaked in cold water overnight and drained

2 garlic cloves

3 tablespoons olive oil

1 onion

7¼ cups porcini, thinly sliced

1 tablespoon chopped fresh flat–leaf parsley

8 country-style bread slices

butter, for spreading

salt and pepper

CRAB SOUP

ZUPPA DI GRANCHI

Serves 4

1 onion

1 fresh thyme sprig

1 clove

2¼ pounds live crabs

2 tomatoes, peeled, seeded and chopped

scant ½ cup dry white wine

1 egg yolk

½ tablespoon cornstarch

pinch of saffron threads

salt and pepper

thick bread slices, lightly toasted, to serve

Cook the onion in boiling water for about 20 minutes until soft, then drain. Bring 5 cups lightly salted water to a boil, add the thyme and clove and plunge in the crabs. Cover and cook for 5 minutes, then drain, reserving the cooking liquid. Stand each crab on one edge, then prize the shell apart with your thumbs. Break off the legs and claws, crack them open and pick out the meat. Pull off and discard the gills from the sides of the body, split open the body and prize out the meat. Chop the crab meat and the boiled onion and combine them with the tomatoes. Add the mixture to the reserved cooking liquid, pour in the wine and cook over medium heat for about 15 minutes. Beat the egg yolk with the cornstarch in a bowl, then stir into the soup. Season with salt and pepper and stir in the saffron just before ladling into a soup tureen. Serve the soup very hot with toast.

LETTUCE SOUP AU GRATIN

ZUPPA DI LATTUGHE GRATINATA

Serves 4

5 tablespoons butter, plus extra for greasing

4 lettuces, shredded

1 tablespoon all-purpose flour

4 cups Meat Stock (see page 208)

4 homemade bread slices, toasted

scant 1 cup Emmenthal cheese, freshly grated

1 tablespoon chopped fresh flat-leaf parsley

salt and pepper

Melt the butter in a small pan, add the lettuces and cook over low heat, stirring occasionally, for 30 minutes. Season with salt and pepper and stir in the flour. Gradually stir in the stock and simmer for 40 minutes over low heat. Preheat the oven to 350°F. Grease an ovenproof soup tureen or dish with butter. Place the toast in the prepared dish, sprinkle with the Emmenthal and ladle in the soup. Cook in the oven for 10 minutes. Sprinkle with the parsley and serve.

ZUPPA DI PANE

Serves 4

scant 1¹/₂ cups dried cannellini beans,
soaked in cold water overnight and drained

4 tablespoons olive oil, plus extra for drizzling

¹/₂ onion, chopped

2 garlic cloves, chopped

1 carrot, chopped

1 celery stalk, chopped

1 fresh flat-leaf parsley sprig, chopped

2 ounces prosciutto

¹/₂ Savoy cabbage, shredded

1 bunch of Swiss chard, chopped

2 potatoes, coarsely chopped

2 tablespoons tomato paste

14 ounces day-old bread, thinly sliced

salt and pepper

THICK BREAD SOUP

Put the beans in a pan, add cold water to cover and bring to a boil, then lower the heat and simmer for about 2 hours until tender. Heat the oil in another pan, add the onion, garlic, carrot, celery, parsley and prosciutto and cook over low heat, stirring occasionally, for 10 minutes until lightly browned. Add the cabbage, Swiss chard and potatoes and season with salt and pepper to taste. Stir the tomato paste with 1¹/₄ cups of the bean cooking liquid in a bowl, then stir into the pan of vegetables and prosciutto. Cover and cook over medium heat for 15–20 minutes until all the vegetables are tender. Meanwhile, drain the beans, pass them through a food mill, then stir them into the vegetable mixture and simmer for a further 10 minutes. Place the bread in a soup tureen, ladle in the soup and let stand in a warm place for about 20 minutes so that most of the liquid soaks into the bread. Drizzle with olive oil before serving.

ZUPPA DI PANE E LENTICCHIE

Serves 4

scant 1 cup lentils, soaked in cold water
for 2 hours and drained

2 garlic cloves, chopped

1 leek, white part only, thinly sliced

1 fresh thyme sprig, chopped

6¹/₄ cups Meat Stock (see page 208)

2 eggs

4 day-old bread slices

3 tablespoons olive oil, plus extra for drizzling

salt and pepper

BREAD AND LENTIL SOUP

Put the lentils, garlic, leek and thyme into a pan, pour in the stock and bring to a boil, then lower the heat and simmer for 2 hours. If necessary, add a little hot water during cooking. Beat the eggs with a pinch of salt in a shallow dish and dip in the bread. Heat the oil in a skillet, add the egg-coated bread and fry until golden on both sides. Drain on paper towels and place a slice in each of four soup bowls. Ladle in the lentils, season with salt and pepper and drizzle with oil.

ZUPPA DI PATATE

Serves 4

2 tablespoons olive oil

4 pancetta slices, chopped

6 potatoes, sliced

1 onion, sliced

2 small carrots, grated

salt and pepper

fresh flat-leaf parsley, chopped, to garnish

POTATO SOUP

Heat the oil in a pan, add the pancetta and cook, stirring occasionally, for 5 minutes. Add the potatoes, onion and carrots and cook, stirring frequently, for 10 minutes until golden brown. Season with salt and pepper. Pour in 6¹/₄ cups water and bring to a boil. Lower the heat and simmer for about 1 hour until thickened. Serve garnished with parsley.

POTATO AND CLAM SOUP

Discard any clams with broken shells or that do not shut immediately when sharply tapped. Place the clams in a large skillet, add the wine and cook over high heat for about 5 minutes until the shells open. Drain the clams, reserving the cooking liquid, and discard any that remain closed. Remove the clams from their shells and strain the cooking liquid through a fine strainer. Heat the oil in a pan, add the celery, onion and carrot and cook over low heat, stirring occasionally, for 10 minutes until lightly browned. Add the tomatoes, potatoes, reserved cooking liquid and 5 cups water. Bring to a boil and add the rosemary and chervil, then lower the heat and simmer for about 1 hour. Add the clams and season with salt and pepper to taste. Remove and discard the rosemary sprig. Put a slice of bread on the base of each of four soup bowls and ladle in the soup. .

ZUPPA DI PATATE E VONGOLE

Serves 4

3¼ pounds clams, scrubbed

scant ½ cup dry white wine

3 tablespoons olive oil

1 celery stalk, chopped

1 onion, chopped

1 carrot, chopped

4 tomatoes, peeled, seeded and chopped

2 potatoes, diced

1 fresh rosemary sprig

1 tablespoon fresh chervil leaves

4 country-style bread slices

salt and pepper

LEEK AND LENTIL SOUP

Put the pancetta into a pan and cook over a low heat until tender, add the lentils and cook for a further 10 minutes. Transfer half the mixture to a food processor and process to a purée. Heat the oil in a skillet, add the leek and cook over low heat for about 10 minutes until lightly browned. Remove the leek from the skillet and add the slices of bread. Cook until golden brown on both sides. Put the slices of bread and the leek into four soup plates and ladle in the purée and the whole lentils. Season with a pinch of white pepper and serve.

ZUPPA DI PORRI E LENTICCHIE

Serves 4

3 slices pancetta, cut into strips

2¾ cups cooked or canned lentils, drained

2 tablespoons olive oil

1 leek, white part only, thinly sliced

8 milk bread slices

white pepper

RADICCHIO SOUP

Melt the butter in a pan, add the leeks and cook over low heat, stirring occasionally, for 5 minutes until softened. Add the radicchio, stir in the flour and season with salt and pepper to taste. Pour in the stock, bring to a boil, then lower the heat and simmer for 1 hour. Preheat the oven to 400°F. Place the slices of bread on the base of an ovenproof soup tureen or dish, sprinkle with the Parmesan and ladle in the soup. Cook in the oven for about 10 minutes.

ZUPPA DI RADICCHIO

Serves 4

¼ cup butter

2 leeks, white parts only, thinly sliced

4 heads radicchio, shredded

½ cup all-purpose flour

4 cups Meat Stock (see page 208)

4 homemade bread slices, toasted

4 tablespoons Parmesan cheese, freshly grated

salt and pepper

FROG SOUP

ZUPPA DI RANE

Serves 4

24 frogs

3 tablespoons olive oil

1 onion, sliced

1 carrot, sliced

1 celery stalk, chopped

1 garlic clove

3 tomatoes, peeled and chopped

6¼ cups Meat Stock (see page 208)

1 tablespoon chopped fresh flat-leaf parsley

salt and pepper

4 country-style bread slices, toasted, to serve

Remove the frogs' legs and set aside. Heat the oil in a pan, add the onion, carrot, celery and garlic and cook over low heat, stirring occasionally, for 10 minutes until lightly browned. Add the frogs and mix well, then add the tomatoes and stock and season with salt and pepper. Bring to a boil, then lower the heat and simmer until the frogs have almost disintegrated. Transfer to a food processor and process to a purée. Return the purée to the pan, add the frogs' legs and cook for a further 15 minutes. Ladle into a soup tureen, sprinkle with the parsley and serve with toast.

PUMPKIN SOUP

ZUPPA DI ZUCCA

Serves 4

7¾ cups pumpkin, peeled, seeded and chopped

6¼ cups Meat Stock (see page 208)

3 tablespoons butter

2 onions, chopped

2 potatoes, diced

1 garlic clove, chopped

3 day-old bread slices

1¼ cups Swiss cheese, freshly grated

scant 1 cup heavy cream

salt and pepper

Steam the pumpkin for about 20 minutes. Bring the stock to a boil. Melt the butter in another pan, add the onions and cook over low heat, stirring occasionally, for 5 minutes until softened. Add the potatoes, pumpkin and garlic, season with salt and pepper to taste, pour in the hot stock and simmer for about 30 minutes. Lightly toast the bread, then dice it. Combine the Swiss cheese, cream, bread and a pinch of pepper in a bowl. Divide the mixture between four individual soup bowls and ladle in the soup.

ZUCCHINI SOUP

ZUPPA DI ZUCCHINE

Serves 4

6 zucchini, cut into thin batons

3 onions, thinly sliced

1 pound 2 ounces tomatoes, peeled, seeded and chopped

3 tablespoons olive oil

4 cups Meat Stock (see page 208)

1 egg

½ cup Parmesan cheese, freshly grated

4 country-style bread slices, lightly toasted

salt

Put the zucchini, onions, tomatoes and olive oil into a pan and cook over medium heat, stirring occasionally, for 20 minutes. Pour in the stock, season with salt and bring to a boil. Lower the heat and simmer for about 20 minutes until the zucchini are falling apart. Beat the egg with the Parmesan and a pinch of salt. Remove the pan from the heat and stir in the egg mixture. Put a slice of toast in each of four soup bowls and ladle in the soup.

GNOCCHI

Potato gnocchi take pride of place as an all-Italian classic. When making them it is better to steam the potatoes rather than boil them, so that the gnocchi are lighter and, at the same time, tastier and firmer. In either case, the potatoes must always be mashed with a potato masher while they are still hot. This makes the dough easier to knead, and smoother. Gnocchi should be cooked in lightly salted water to prevent them disintegrating. They should be added to the boiling water a few at a time and lifted out gradually with a slotted spoon as they rise to the surface. To cook ricotta, pumpkin, Parmesan or other types of gnocchi, follow the methods shown in the various recipes. Semolina or ricotta gnocchi are particularly suitable for serving at the start of a formal luncheon.

DRY FIRST COURSES

PARISIAN GNOCCHI

Preheat the oven to 400°F and grease an ovenproof dish with butter. Heat the milk with a pinch of salt in a fairly deep pan and add the butter. When it has melted, tip in all the flour at once, stirring constantly. Lower the heat and stir constantly for about 10 minutes until the mixture comes away from the sides of the pan. Remove the pan from the heat, let cool slightly, then stir in the eggs, one at a time. Season with salt and pepper. Bring a large pan of lightly salted water to a boil. Using a piping bag with a ²/₃-inch tip drop small pieces of the mixture into the boiling water. The gnocchi rise to the surface when they are ready. Remove with a slotted spoon and spread out in the prepared dish. Spoon the béchamel sauce over them, sprinkle with the Parmesan and bake for about 20 minutes until golden and bubbling.

GNOCCHI ALLA PARIGINA

Serves 4–6

scant ¹/₂ cup butter, plus extra for greasing

4 cups milk

2¹/₂ cups all-purpose flour

6 eggs

1 quantity Béchamel Sauce (see page 50)

1 cup Parmesan cheese, freshly grated

salt and pepper

ROMAN GNOCCHI

GNOCCHI ALLA ROMANA

Serves 4–6

²/₃ cup butter, plus extra for greasing

4 cups milk

1¹/₂ cups semolina

2 egg yolks

1²/₃ cups romano cheese, freshly grated

salt

Preheat the oven to 400°F. Grease an ovenproof dish with butter. Pour the milk into a pan, add a pinch of salt and bring to a boil. Sprinkle in the semolina, stirring constantly, and cook, stirring, for 10 minutes. Let cool slightly, then stir in the egg yolks, one at a time, followed by ¹/₂ cup of the romano cheese and ¹/₄ cup of the butter. Pour the semolina onto a counter and spread it out to a depth of about ¹/₂ inch with a damp knife. Stamp out rounds with a 1¹/₂-inch cookie cutter and place a layer of these rounds in the prepared dish. Sprinkle them with some of the remaining romano and dot with a little of the remaining butter. Continue making layers of rounds in this way until all the ingredients are used up. Bake for 15 minutes until golden brown.

BREAD GNOCCHI

GNOCCHI DI PANE

Serves 4

9 ounces day-old bread

2¹/₄ cups milk

2 eggs

1³/₄ cups all-purpose flour

pinch of freshly grated nutmeg

¹/₄ cup butter

1 garlic clove

2 fresh sage leaves

²/₃ cup Parmesan cheese, freshly grated

salt and pepper

Tear the bread into small pieces. Pour the milk into a pan and bring to just below boiling point, add a pinch of salt and remove from the heat. Add the bread, let soften, then beat with a wooden spoon to a smooth mixture. Beat in the eggs and stir in the flour a little at a time. Stir in the nutmeg and season with salt and pepper. The mixture should have the consistency of a thick purée. Cover and leave in a cool place for about 2 hours. Bring a large pan of water to a boil and add a pinch of salt. Drop in tablespoonfuls of the mixture, a few at a time, and cook for about 5 minutes, then remove with a slotted spoon and keep warm while you cook the remaining gnocchi. Meanwhile, melt the butter in a small pan, add the garlic and sage and cook for a few minutes. Place the gnocchi on a warm serving dish, discard the garlic clove and pour the sage butter over them. Sprinkle with Parmesan and serve.

BREAD AND SPINACH GNOCCHI

Tear the bread into pieces, place in a large bowl, add the milk and leave until it has been completely absorbed. Meanwhile, cook the spinach, in just the water clinging to the leaves after washing, for about 5 minutes until tender. Drain, squeezing out as much liquid as possible, and chop. Melt 1 1/2 tablespoons of the butter in a skillet, add the spinach and 1/2 cup of the Parmesan and cook, stirring frequently, for 5 minutes. Remove the skillet from the heat and stir into the bowl of bread, then stir in the egg and flour. Make long rolls with the mixture, cut them into pieces the same length, dust lightly with flour and shake off any excess. Bring a large pan of lightly salted water to a boil, add the gnocchi, and when they rise to the surface remove with a slotted spoon. Meanwhile, melt the remaining butter. Drain the gnocchi well, arrange on a warm serving dish and pour the melted butter over them. Sprinkle with the remaining Parmesan, mix gently and serve.

GNOCCHI DI PANE E SPINACI

Serves 4

12 ounces day-old bread

scant 1 cup milk

1 1/2 pounds spinach

scant 1/2 cup butter

1 cup Parmesan cheese, freshly grated

1 egg

scant 1 cup all-purpose flour, plus extra for dusting

salt

PARMESAN GNOCCHI

Grease a broad, shallow ovenproof dish with butter. Melt 1/2 cup of the butter in a double boiler. Pour the milk into a pan, add the melted butter, then tip in all the flour at once, stirring constantly. Beat in the eggs, one at a time. Before adding the next egg, make sure that the previous one has been thoroughly incorporated. Add half the Parmesan and the nutmeg and season with salt and pepper. Place the pan over medium heat and bring to a boil, whisking constantly. Simmer, whisking constantly, for 10 minutes, then pour the mixture onto a counter and spread out evenly to a depth of 1/2 inch using a damp knife. Let cool. Preheat the oven to 400°F. Stamp out rounds of the mixture with a cookie cutter, place the trimmings on the base of the prepared dish and cover with concentric circles of rounds to form a sort of dome. Sprinkle with the remaining Parmesan, dot with the remaining butter and bake for about 30 minutes until light golden brown. Let stand for 5 minutes before serving.

GNOCCHI DI PARMIGIANO

Serves 4

2/3 cup butter, plus extra for greasing

4 cups milk

2 1/4 cups all-purpose flour

4 eggs

generous 1 cup Parmesan cheese, freshly grated

pinch of freshly grated nutmeg

salt and pepper

GNOCCHI DI PATATE (RICETTA BASE)

Serves 4

2¼ pounds potatoes

1¾ cups all-purpose flour, plus extra for dusting

1 egg, lightly beaten

salt

choice of sauce, to serve

POTATO GNOCCHI (BASIC RECIPE)

Steam the potatoes for 25 minutes or until tender, then mash with a potato masher while they are still hot. Stir in the flour, egg and a pinch of salt and knead to a soft, elastic dough. Be careful with the ratio of potato to flour: if there is too much flour, the gnocchi will be hard; if there is too much potato, they tend to disintegrate while cooking. Shape the dough into long rolls just over ⅔ inch in diameter and cut into ¾-inch lengths. Press them gently against the underside of a grater and arrange on a dish towel dusted with flour. Bring a large pan of lightly salted water to a boil, add the gnocchi, a few at a time, and remove with a slotted spoon as they rise to the surface. Drain, put on a warm serving dish and pour your chosen sauce over them.

GNOCCHI DI PATATE ALLA BAVA

Serves 4

1 quantity Potato Gnocchi (see above)

6 tablespoons butter

4 ounces fontina cheese, diced

salt

Parmesan cheese, freshly grated, to serve

GNOCCHI ALLA BAVA

Cook the gnocchi, a few at a time, in lightly salted, boiling water. As they rise to the surface, remove with a slotted spoon, drain well and place on a warm serving dish. Dot with the butter, sprinkle with the fontina, mix gently and serve immediately with Parmesan.

GNOCCHI DI PATATE ALLE NOCI

Serves 4

1¾ pounds potatoes

1¾ cups Parmesan cheese, freshly grated

12 shelled walnuts, finely chopped

2 eggs, lightly beaten

1 tablespoon semolina

3 tablespoons butter, melted

salt and pepper

WALNUT GNOCCHI

Steam the potatoes for 25 minutes until tender, then mash with a potato masher while still hot and knead with 1 cup of the Parmesan, and the walnuts and eggs. Season with salt to taste, then add the semolina. The dough should be well mixed and the right consistency. If necessary, add more semolina. Shape into long rolls, cut into shorter lengths and press them gently against the underside of a grater. Bring a large pan of lightly salted water to a boil, add the gnocchi, a few at a time, and remove with a slotted spoon as they rise to the surface. Place on a warm serving dish, pour the melted butter over them, sprinkle with the remaining Parmesan and season with pepper.

GNOCCHI DI PATATE ALLE ORTICHE

Serves 4

2¹/₄ pounds potatoes

2¹/₃ cups stinging nettles, finely chopped

1³/₄ cups all-purpose flour

1 egg, lightly beaten

6 tablespoons butter

1 garlic clove

4 fresh sage leaves

²/₃ cup Parmesan cheese, freshly grated

salt

POTATO AND NETTLE GNOCCHI

Steam or boil the potatoes for 25 minutes until tender, then mash with a potato masher while still hot. Stir in the nettles, followed by the flour. Beat in the egg, season with salt and knead. Divide the dough into several pieces and shape each into a roll about ²/₃ inch in diameter. Cut into ³/₄-inch lengths and press them gently against the underside of a grater. Bring a large pan of lightly salted water to a boil, add the gnocchi, a few at a time, and remove with a slotted spoon as they rise to the surface. Meanwhile, melt the butter in a small skillet, add the garlic and sage leaves and cook for a few minutes until the garlic is lightly browned. Remove and discard the garlic. Place the gnocchi on a warm serving dish, pour the sage butter over them, sprinkle with the Parmesan and mix gently.

GNOCCHI DI PATATE CON GLI SCAMPI

Serves 4

2¹/₄ pounds potatoes

1³/₄ cups all-purpose flour

1 egg, lightly beaten

²/₃ cup Parmesan cheese, freshly grated

salt

For the sauce

4 tablespoons olive oil

14 ounces langoustines or jumbo shrimp, peeled and chopped

1 tablespoon chopped fresh flat-leaf parsley

4 tablespoons dry white wine

scant ¹/₂ cup heavy cream

2 tomatoes, peeled and diced

salt and pepper

POTATO GNOCCHI WITH LANGOUSTINES

Cook the potatoes in lightly salted, boiling water for 25 minutes until tender, then mash with a potato masher while still hot. Add the flour, egg, Parmesan and a pinch of salt and knead to a soft, elastic dough. Divide into several pieces and shape into long rolls about ²/₃ inch in diameter. Cut into ³/₄-inch lengths and press them gently against the underside of a grater. To make the sauce, heat the oil in a skillet, add the langoustines or jumbo shrimp and parsley and cook for 2 minutes. Sprinkle with the wine and cook until it has evaporated, then stir in the cream and tomatoes. Cook for 5 minutes, then remove from the heat. Meanwhile, bring a large pan of lightly salted water to a boil. Add the gnocchi, a few at a time, and remove with a slotted spoon as they rise to the surface. Place the gnocchi on a warm serving dish and pour the langoustine sauce over them.

POTATO GNOCCHI FILLED WITH FONDUE

Put the fontina for the fondue in a heatproof bowl, add milk to cover and set aside to soak overnight. The next day, cook the potatoes in lightly salted, boiling water, then drain and mash while still hot. Beat in the flour, egg and a pinch of salt and let stand. Meanwhile, prepare the fondue. Add the butter and egg yolks to the fontina and mix well. Set the bowl over a pan of barely simmering water and cook, stirring constantly, to a smooth, thick cream. Season with salt to taste and let cool. Halve the potato dough, roll out one piece and arrange small heaps of fondue on top as if making ravioli. Roll out the second piece of dough and cover the first, pressing the edges down well, then cut out with a pastry wheel. Bring a large pan of lightly salted water to a boil, add the gnocchi, a few at a time, and remove with a slotted spoon as they rise to the surface. Meanwhile, melt the butter in a small skillet, add the sage leaves and cook for a few minutes. Place the gnocchi on a warm serving dish and pour the sage butter over them. Serve with Parmesan.

GNOCCHI DI PATATE
CON RIPIENO DI FONDUTA

Serves 4

2¼ pounds potatoes

1¾ cups all-purpose flour, plus extra for dusting

1 egg, lightly beaten

¼ cup butter

8 fresh sage leaves

salt

Parmesan cheese, freshly grated

For the fondue

14 ounces fontina cheese, thinly sliced

1¼–2 cups milk

4 egg yolks

2 tablespoons butter

salt

TRIESTIAN POTATO GNOCCHI WITH PRUNES

This regional recipe is traditionally made with fresh plums, blanched for 5–7 minutes, then split, pitted, stuffed with half a sugar cube and put back into shape again. However, when plums are out of season, prunes are often used. Split the prunes and remove the pits, if this has not already been done, and fill the cavity with a pinch of sugar. Cook the potatoes in lightly salted, boiling water for 25 minutes until tender, then mash while still hot. Spoon into a mound on a counter, add the flour, egg and a pinch of salt and knead to a smooth dough. Make 12 egg sized gnocchi and press a prune into each one. Bring a large pan of lightly salted water to a boil, add the gnocchi, a few at a time, and remove with a slotted spoon as they rise to the surface. Meanwhile, melt the butter in a small skillet, add the bread crumbs, cinnamon and a sprinkling of sugar and cook, stirring frequently, until golden. Place the gnocchi on a warm serving dish and garnish with the bread crumbs.

GNOCCHI DI PATATE
CON SUSINE ALLA TRIESTINA

Serves 4

12 ready-to-eat prunes

1½ teaspoons sugar, plus extra for sprinkling

2¼ pounds potatoes

1¾ cups all-purpose flour

1 egg

3 tablespoons butter

4 tablespoons bread crumbs

pinch of ground cinnamon

salt

POTATO AND SPINACH GNOCCHI

GNOCCHI DI PATATE E SPINACI

Serves 4

1¹/₂ pounds spinach

1³/₄ pounds potatoes

1³/₄ cups all-purpose flour, plus extra for dusting

2 egg yolks, lightly beaten

¹/₄ cup butter, melted

²/₃ cup Parmesan cheese, freshly grated

salt

Cook the spinach, in just the water clinging to the leaves after washing, for 5 minutes, then drain, squeezing out as much liquid as possible, and chop. Cook the potatoes in lightly salted, boiling water for 25 minutes until tender, then mash while still hot. Combine the potato, spinach and flour. Season with salt, beat in the egg yolks and knead the dough for a few minutes. Shape the dough into several long rolls, about ²/₃ inch in diameter. Cut into ³/₄ inch lengths and press them gently against the underside of a grater. Dust lightly with flour. Bring a large pan of lightly salted water to a boil, add the gnocchi, a few at a time, and remove with a slotted spoon as they rise to the surface. Drain well and arrange on a warm serving dish. Pour the butter over them and sprinkle with the Parmesan. You could use the cooking juices from a roast instead.

RICOTTA AND SPINACH GNOCCHI

GNOCCHI DI RICOTTA E SPINACI

Serves 4

2¹/₄ pounds spinach

1¹/₂ cups ricotta cheese

4 tablespoons Parmesan cheese, freshly grated

2 egg yolks, lightly beaten

all-purpose flour, for dusting

¹/₄ cup butter, melted

salt and pepper

Cook the spinach, in just the water clinging to the leaves after washing, for 5 minutes, then drain, squeezing out as much liquid as possible, chop finely and put in a bowl. Add the ricotta, half the Parmesan and the egg yolks and season with salt and pepper. Shape the mixture into balls and dust lightly with flour. Bring a large pan of lightly salted water to a boil, add the gnocchi, a few at a time, and remove with a slotted spoon as they rise to the surface. Place the gnocchi on a warm serving dish, pour the melted butter over them and sprinkle with the remaining Parmesan. You could also serve them with a light Béchamel Sauce (see page 50).

RICE GNOCCHI

GNOCCHI DI RISO

Serves 4

2 cups long-grain rice

4 eggs, lightly beaten

2–3 cups bread crumbs

4 cups Meat Stock (see page 208)

¹/₄ cup butter, melted

¹/₂ cup Swiss cheese, freshly grated

²/₃ cup Parmesan cheese, freshly grated

salt and pepper

Bring a large pan of salted water to a boil, add the rice and cook for 15–18 minutes until tender. Drain well and place in a bowl. Stir in the eggs and enough bread crumbs to make a thick mixture and season with salt and pepper. Bring the stock to a boil. Shape the rice mixture into small gnocchi and add to the stock, a few at a time, and cook for a few minutes. Remove with a slotted spoon, drain well and arrange on a warm serving dish. Pour the butter over them and sprinkle with the cheeses.

SEMOLINA AND HAM GNOCCHI

GNOCCHI DI SEMOLINO AL PROSCIUTTO

Serves 4

2 tablespoons butter, plus extra for greasing
4 cups milk
1 1/2 cups semolina
2 egg yolks, lightly beaten
1 cup Parmesan cheese, freshly grated
generous 1/2 cup cooked, cured ham, chopped
salt

Preheat the oven to 400°F. Grease an ovenproof dish with butter. Bring the milk to a boil and add a pinch of salt. Sprinkle in the semolina, stirring constantly, and simmer, stirring, for 10 minutes. Remove the pan from the heat, let cool slightly, then stir in the egg yolks, 2/3 cup of the Parmesan and the ham. Shape the mixture into slightly squashed gnocchi, arrange in the prepared dish, sprinkle with the remaining Parmesan and dot with the butter. Bake for 30 minutes until golden brown.

PUMPKIN AND AMARETTI GNOCCHI

GNOCCHI DI ZUCCA E AMARETTI

Serves 4

7 3/4 cups pumpkin, peeled, seeded and cut into chunks
4 eggs, lightly beaten
1 3/4 cups amaretti, crushed
1 3/4 cups all-purpose flour
1/4 cup butter
8 fresh sage leaves
2/3 cup Parmesan cheese, freshly grated
salt and pepper

Preheat the oven to 400°F. Place the pumpkin in an ovenproof dish and bake for about 45 minutes until softened. Mash the pumpkin with a potato masher while still hot. Stir in the eggs, amaretti and flour and season with salt and pepper. Knead well and let rest for 30 minutes. Melt the butter in a skillet, add the sage leaves and cook for a few minutes. Bring a large pan of lightly salted water to a boil, add teaspoonfuls of the pumpkin mixture, a few at a time, and remove with a slotted spoon as they rise to the surface. Place on a warm serving dish, pour the sage butter over them and sprinkle with the Parmesan.

WHOLE–WHEAT GNOCCHI

GNOCCHI INTEGRALI

Serves 4

scant 1 cup milk
1/2 cup whole-wheat flour, plus extra for dusting
1 1/4 cups oat flakes
1/2 cup barley flakes
1 2/3 cups Parmesan cheese, freshly grated
1 tablespoon chopped fresh flat-leaf parsley
1 egg, lightly beaten
1/4 cup butter, melted
salt

Heat the milk in a small pan to just below simmering point, then remove from the heat. Combine the flour, oat and barley flakes, generous 1 cup of the Parmesan, the parsley, egg and warm milk. This should produce a soft but thick dough. If necessary, add a few more oat or barley flakes and let rest for 30 minutes. Shape into several long rolls about 2/3 inch in diameter and cut into 3/4-inch lengths. Place on a dish towel and sprinkle with flour. Bring a large pan of lightly salted water to a boil, add the gnocchi and cook for about 15 minutes. Drain, pour on the butter and sprinkle with the remaining Parmesan.

FRESH PASTA

Nowadays, in Italy fresh pasta is usually called egg pasta. It was once known as homemade pasta and was mostly prepared at vacation times. In those days, cappelletti, tortellini, lasagne, timbales, ravioli, pappardelle, tagliatelle, quadretti and agnolotti were invariably made by hand, but today it is more usual to use a pasta machine and other such kitchen appliances that halve the preparation time – or even to buy ready-made egg pasta and egg pasta products. For more information, see page 202.

QUANTITY

For four people, the recommended amounts are 1³/₄ cups flour, 2 eggs and a pinch of salt, which yield 10 ounces fresh pasta, equivalent to about 2¹/₂ ounces per person.

COOKING

Fresh pasta cooks more quickly than dried pasta. When boiling filled pasta, remember that the filing adds extra flavor, so reduce the quantity of salt in the water.

OIL

When boiling sheets of pasta for lasagne, add 1 tablespoon olive oil to the cooking water to prevent them from sticking.

SAUCE AND CHEESE

Fresh pasta is more absorbent than dried pasta, but otherwise the same recommendations apply: the grated cheese should be sprinkled on the pasta before the sauce and serving dish should be warm.

QUANTITIES
AND COOKING TIMES

PASTA ALL'UOVO (RICETTA BASE)

Serves 4

1³/₄ cups all-purpose flour, preferably Italian type 00,
plus extra for dusting

2 eggs, lightly beaten

salt

FRESH PASTA DOUGH (BASIC RECIPE)

Sift the flour and a pinch of salt into a mound on a counter. Make a well in the center and add the eggs. Using your fingers, gradually incorporate the flour, then knead for about 10 minutes. If the mixture is too soft, add a little extra flour; if it is too firm, add a little water. Shape the dough into a ball and let rest for 15 minutes. Roll out on a lightly floured surface or use a pasta machine to make a thin sheet, and cut out tagliatelle, lasagne, etc.

PASTA VERDE (RICETTA BASE)

Serves 4

1³/₄ cups all-purpose flour, preferably Italian type 00,
plus extra for dusting

2 eggs, lightly beaten

generous 1 cup spinach, cooked,
well drained and chopped

salt

GREEN PASTA DOUGH (BASIC RECIPE)

Sift the flour and a pinch of salt into a mound on a counter. Make a well in the center and add the eggs and spinach. Using your fingers, gradually incorporate the flour, then knead for a few minutes. If the spinach is very damp, add more flour, a little at a time. Shape the dough into a ball and let rest for 15 minutes, then roll out on a lightly floured surface or use a pasta machine to make a fairly thick sheet. This pasta may be used for lasagne, tagliatelle, tortellini and ravioli. A dish of green tagliatelle mixed with ordinary tagliatelle is called paglia e fieno, that is, straw and hay. The most suitable seasonings are classic sauces: ragù (meat sauce, see page 52) or butter and cheese.

AGNOLOTTI ALLA PIEMONTESE

Serves 6

generous 2¹/₂ cups all-purpose flour,
preferably Italian type 00, plus extra for dusting

3 eggs, lightly beaten

salt

For the filling

9 ounces spinach

14 ounces braised beef, ground

2 egg yolks, lightly beaten • 1 egg, lightly beaten

²/₃ cup Parmesan cheese, freshly grated

scant 1 cup cooked, cured ham, chopped

salt and pepper

AGNOLOTTI PIEDMONTESE

Make the pasta dough (see Fresh Pasta Dough, above) with the quantities specified. Blanch the spinach in boiling water, drain, chop and combine with the beef in a bowl. Stir in the egg yolks, whole egg, Parmesan and ham and season with salt and pepper. If the mixture is a little dry, soften with a few tablespoons of gravy from the braised beef. Roll out the pasta dough into strips. Put mounds of filling at regular intervals along one strip, place another strip on top and press down well around the filling. Cut square agnolotti with a pasta or pastry wheel. Cook in salted, boiling water for about 10 minutes. Drain and dress with gravy from the braised beef or melted butter and grated Parmesan.

BIGOLI WITH ANCHOVIES

Sift the flour with a pinch of salt into a mound on a counter and make a well in the center. Add the eggs and enough water to make an elastic dough. Make the bigoli by pressing the dough through the bigolaro, a little at a time. Heat the oil in a pan, add the onions and parsley and cook over low heat, stirring occasionally, for 5 minutes until the onions are softened. Add the anchovies and cook, mashing with a wooden spoon until they disintegrate. Cook the bigoli in salted, boiling water for 2–3 minutes until al dente. Drain and toss with the onion mixture.

BIGOLI ALLE ACCIUGHE

To make bigoli (thick spaghetti),

you need a small tool called bigolaro which

may be found in specialist kitchenware stores.

Serves 4–6

$3^{1}/_{2}$ cups all-purpose flour, preferably Italian type 00

3 eggs, lightly beaten • 4 tablespoons olive oil

2 onions, chopped

1 tablespoon chopped fresh flat-leaf parsley

3 canned anchovy fillets, drained • salt

CANNELLONI WITH BÉCHAMEL SAUCE

Preheat the oven to 400°F. Grease an ovenproof dish with butter. Cook the spinach, in just the water clinging to the leaves after washing, for five minutes. Drain well and pass through a vegetable mill, then combine with the veal, ham, Parmesan and egg and season to taste. Roll out the pasta dough into a thin sheet and cut into large rectangles. Cook the rectangles, a few at a time, in a large pan of salted, boiling water for 6–7 minutes. Drain on a damp dish towel. Put some of the spinach mixture and a little béchamel sauce on each rectangle and roll up from one long side. Arrange the cannelloni in a single layer in the prepared dish, pour the remaining béchamel sauce over them and dot with the butter. Bake for 20 minutes, then let rest for 5 minutes before serving.

CANNELLONI ALLA BESCIAMELLA

Serves 4

2 tablespoons butter, plus extra for greasing

11 ounces spinach

7 ounces roast veal, chopped

1 slice cooked, cured ham, chopped

2 tablespoons Parmesan cheese, freshly grated

1 egg, lightly beaten

1 quantity Fresh Pasta Dough (see opposite)

1 quantity Béchamel Sauce (see page 50)

salt and pepper

CHEESE AND PROSCIUTTO CRÊPES

Whisk together the eggs, flour, milk and a pinch of salt to make a smooth batter. Let rest for 30 minutes. Brush a 6-inch crêpe pan with a little of the melted butter and heat the pan. Pour in 1 tablespoon batter, tilt the pan so that the batter covers the base and cook until the underside is set and golden. Turn over and cook the other side, then slide out of the pan. Continue making crêpes until the batter is used up, bearing in mind that about two crêpes per serving is usual. Preheat the oven to 400°F. Grease an ovenproof dish with butter. Lay a slice of prosciutto on each crêpe and top with a slice of cheese. Roll up the crêpes like cannelloni and arrange in layers in the prepared dish. Stir the grated Swiss cheese and the nutmeg into the béchamel sauce and season with salt and pepper. Pour over the crêpes and bake for 20 minutes. Let stand for 5 minutes before serving.

CRESPELLE DI FORMAGGIO E PROSCIUTTO

Serves 4

2 eggs, lightly beaten

scant 1 cup all-purpose flour

1 cup milk

1 teaspoon butter, melted, plus extra for greasing

$3^{1}/_{2}$ ounces prosciutto slices

$^{3}/_{4}$ cup Swiss cheese, sliced, or Italian sottilette

$^{3}/_{4}$ cup Swiss cheese, freshly grated

pinch of freshly grated nutmeg

1 quantity Béchamel Sauce (see page 50)

salt and pepper

FETTUCCINE IN BROWN BUTTER

FETTUCCINE AL BURRO BRUNO

Serves 4

10 ounces fettuccine

¹/₄ cup butter

4–5 tablespoons pan juices

²/₃ cup Parmesan cheese, freshly grated

salt

Cook the fettuccine in a large pan of salted, boiling water for 2–3 minutes until al dente. Meanwhile, melt the butter in a skillet over low heat and stir in the pan juices, which should be fairly concentrated. Drain the pasta, add to the skillet, toss well and transfer to a warm serving dish. Sprinkle with the Parmesan and serve.

FETTUCCINE IN WHITE SAUCE

FETTUCCINE IN SALSA BIANCA

Serves 4

1 quantity Fresh Pasta Dough (see page 268)

¹/₄ cup butter

1 cup Parmesan cheese, freshly grated

4 tablespoons heavy cream

salt and pepper

Roll out the pasta dough into a sheet, fold over and cut into fettuccine. Melt the butter in a small pan over low heat and add half the Parmesan and a little pepper. Cook the fettuccine in a large pan of salted, boiling water for 2–3 minutes until al dente. Drain, return to the pan and toss with the cream and remaining Parmesan. Transfer to a warm serving dish, add the Parmesan and melted butter mixture, season with pepper and serve.

LASAGNE BOLOGNESE

LASAGNE ALLA BOLOGNESE

Serves 4

3 tablespoons olive oil

1 carrot, chopped

1 onion, chopped

2³/₄ cups ground meat

scant ¹/₂ cup dry white wine

generous 1 cup bottled strained tomatoes

2 tablespoons butter, plus extra for greasing

1 quantity Fresh Pasta Dough (see page 268)

1 quantity Béchamel Sauce (see page 50)

scant 1 cup Parmesan cheese, freshly grated

salt and pepper

Heat the olive oil in a pan, add the carrot and onion and cook over low heat, stirring occasionally, for 5 minutes. Add the meat and cook until browned, then pour in the wine and cook until it has evaporated. Season with salt, add the strained tomatoes and simmer for 30 minutes, then season with pepper. Preheat the oven to 400°F. Grease an ovenproof dish with butter. Roll out the pasta dough into a sheet. Cut into 4-inch squares and cook, a few at a time, in plenty of lightly salted, boiling water for a few minutes. Drain and place on a damp dish towel. Arrange a layer of lasagne on the base of the prepared dish, spoon some of the meat sauce, then some of the béchamel sauce on top, sprinkle with some of the Parmesan and dot with some of the butter. Repeat the alternating layers until all the ingredients have been used, ending with a layer of béchamel sauce. Bake for 30 minutes.

LASAGNE ALLA NAPOLETANA

Serves 6

2³/₄ cups all-purpose flour,
preferably Italian type 00, plus extra for dusting

3 eggs, lightly beaten

salt

For the filling

5 tablespoons olive oil

1 onion, chopped

1 carrot, chopped

1 celery stalk, chopped

¹/₂ garlic clove, chopped

4 cups bottled strained tomatoes

5 eggs

2³/₄ cups ground beef

²/₃ cup Parmesan cheese, freshly grated

3 tablespoons butter, plus extra for greasing

1 mozzarella cheese, sliced

salt and pepper

LASAGNE NAPOLETANA

For the filling, heat 3 tablespoons of the oil in a pan, add the onion, carrot, celery and garlic and cook over low heat, stirring occasionally, for 5 minutes, then add the strained tomatoes. Season with salt and pepper and simmer for about 1 hour. Meanwhile, boil four of the eggs for 12 minutes, then refresh in cold water, shell and slice. Combine the ground beef, Parmesan and remaining egg in a bowl and season with salt. Shape the mixture into small balls. Heat 2 tablespoons of the butter and the remaining oil in a skillet, add the meatballs and cook until browned all over, then add them to the tomato sauce. Make the pasta (see Fresh Pasta Dough, page 268) with the quantities specified and roll out into two thin sheets. Cut into 4-inch squares and cook, a few at a time, in plenty of lightly salted, boiling water for a few minutes. Drain and place on a damp dish towel. Preheat the oven to 325°F. Grease a large ovenproof dish with butter, arrange a layer of pasta on the base and cover with the tomato sauce with meatballs, then the mozzarella and a few slices of eggs, hard-cooked. Repeat the layers until all the ingredients are used, ending with a layer of tomato sauce. Dot the top with the remaining butter, cover the dish with foil or baking parchment and bake for about 1 hour. Let stand for 10 minutes before serving.

LASAGNE CON MELANZANE E RICOTTA

Serves 4

1 large eggplant, sliced

butter, for greasing

11 ounces lasagne sheets, or made with

2³/₄ cups all-purpose flour,
preferably Italian type 00, plus extra for dusting
(see Lasagne Napoletana, above)

¹/₂ cup pine nuts, chopped

²/₃ cup ricotta cheese, crumbled

¹/₂ cup tomato paste

12 fresh basil leaves

olive oil, for drizzling • 4 tablespoons Parmesan
cheese, freshly grated • salt

EGGPLANT AND RICOTTA LASAGNE

Place the eggplant slices in a colander, sprinkle with salt and let drain for 2 hours. Rinse, pat dry and cook under a preheated broiler until tender. Preheat the oven to 350°F. Grease an ovenproof dish with butter. Cook the lasagne sheets in a large pan of salted, boiling water for 6–7 minutes until al dente, then drain and place on a damp dish towel. Arrange a layer of pasta on the base of the prepared dish, place half the eggplant slices on top and sprinkle with half the pine nuts, half the ricotta, 4 tablespoons of the tomato paste and six of the basil leaves. Drizzle with olive oil and repeat the layers. Sprinkle with the Parmesan and bake for about 40 minutes.

RADICCHIO LASAGNE

Make the pasta (see Fresh Pasta Dough, page 268) with the quantities specified. Heat the cream in a pan over low heat, stir in the radicchio, add the butter and cook until the radicchio is soft. Stir in the béchamel sauce and season with salt and pepper to taste. Preheat the oven to 300°F. Grease an ovenproof dish with butter. Cook the lasagne, a few at a time, in a large pan of salted, boiling water, for 6–7 minutes until al dente, drain and place on a damp dish towel to cool. Place a layer of pasta on the base of the prepared dish and top with a layer of radicchio sauce. Continue making alternate layers until all the ingredients are used, ending with a layer of radicchio sauce. Bake for 30 minutes, then serve.

LASAGNE DI RADICCHIO

Serves 6

2³/₄ cups all-purpose flour, preferably Italian type 00, plus extra for dusting (see Lasagne Napoletana, above) • 3 eggs, lightly beaten

salt

For the sauce

3 tablespoons heavy cream

3¹/₂ cups radicchio, cut into strips

2 tablespoons butter, plus extra for greasing

1 quantity Béchamel Sauce (see page 50)

salt and pepper

MACCHERONI ALLA CHITARRA

Make the pasta (see Fresh Pasta Dough, page 268) with the quantities specified and then roll out into a sheet ¹/₈ inch thick on a lightly floured surface. Place on the chitarra and roll over it with a rolling pin so that the wires cut the pasta into long square-section ribbons. Heat the olive oil in a skillet, add the tomatoes and cook, stirring occasionally, for 10 minutes. Season with salt and chili powder. Cook the maccheroni in a large pan of salted, boiling water for 2–3 minutes until al dente, drain, toss with the tomato sauce and serve immediately.

MACCHERONI ALLA CHITARRA

A speciality of Abruzzo, this ribbon pasta is made with a chitarra, a special utensil that consists of steel wires on a wooden frame.

Serves 6

3¹/₂ cups all-purpose flour, preferably Italian type 00, plus extra for dusting

4 eggs, lightly beaten

salt

For the sauce

6 tablespoons olive oil

1 pound 2 ounces plum tomatoes, peeled and diced

pinch of chili powder

salt

MACCHERONI ALLA CHITARRA
WITH CHICKEN LIVERS

Heat the butter and oil in a skillet, add the onion and cook over low heat, stirring occasionally, for 5 minutes. Add the chicken livers and cook, stirring occasionally until browned. Add the stock and cook until it has evaporated, then season with salt. Cook the maccheroni in a large pan of salted, boiling water for 2–3 minutes until al dente, drain and toss with the sauce. Sprinkle with the Parmesan and serve.

MACCHERONI ALLA CHITARRA
CON FEGATINI

Serves 6

3 tablespoons butter

3 tablespoons olive oil • 1 onion, chopped

12 ounces chicken livers, trimmed and chopped

4 tablespoons Meat Stock (see page 208)

1 quantity Maccheroni (see above)

3 tablespoons Parmesan cheese, freshly grated

salt

MALTAGLIATI WITH PUMPKIN

MALTAGLIATI CON LA ZUCCA

Serves 6

3 tablespoons olive oil

scant 1/2 cup butter

4 cups pumpkin, peeled, seeded and diced

14 ounces fresh maltagliati

pinch of freshly grated nutmeg

2/3 cup Parmesan cheese, freshly grated

salt and pepper

Heat the oil and 6 tablespoons of the butter in a pan, add the pumpkin and cook over low heat, stirring occasionally, for 5 minutes. Add a little water, season with salt and simmer, stirring frequently, until the pumpkin is tender. Meanwhile, cook the pasta in a large pan of salted, boiling water for 2–3 minutes until just al dente. Drain, stir into the pumpkin and add the remaining butter, the nutmeg and a little pepper. Mix well, sprinkle with the Parmesan and serve.

ORECCHIETTE (BASIC RECIPE)

ORECCHIETTE (RICETTA BASE)

Serves 4

1 3/4 cups all-purpose flour, preferably Italian type 00

generous 1/2 cup semolina

salt

Combine the flour, semolina and a pinch of salt and heap into a mound on the counter. Make a well in the center, add a little warm water and mix to a firm, elastic dough. Knead well, then shape into long rolls 1 inch in diameter. Cut into sections and drag them, one at a time, slowly over the counter using the tip of a knife to form small shells. Put each shell upside down on the tip of your thumb and press it down on the counter to accentuate its curvature.

ORECCHIETTE WITH BROCCOLI

ORECCHIETTE CON BROCCOLI

Serves 4

1 3/4 pounds broccoli, cut into flowerets

2 tablespoons olive oil

1 garlic clove, chopped

1 fresh chile, seeded and chopped

11 ounces Orecchiette (see above)

salt

Parmesan or romano cheese, freshly grated, to serve

Cook the broccoli in salted, boiling water for 5 minutes, then drain. Heat the olive oil in a pan, add the garlic and chile and cook for 3 minutes, then add the broccoli and cook over low heat, stirring occasionally, for 5 minutes until tender. Meanwhile, cook the orecchiette in a large pan of salted, boiling water for 10 minutes until al dente, then drain and toss with the broccoli. Serve with Parmesan or romano. Alternatively, the broccoli may be cooked with the orecchiette. In this case, drain everything, then drizzle with olive oil and sprinkle with grated romano.

ORECCHIETTE WITH TURNIP GREENS

ORECCHIETTE CON CIME DI RAPA

Serves 4

12 1/2 ounces Orecchiette (see above)

14 ounces turnip greens

olive oil, for drizzling

salt and pepper

Cook the orecchiette in a large pan of salted, boiling water for 10 minutes until al dente, then add the turnip greens and cook for a further 5 minutes until tender. Drain, transfer to a warm serving dish, drizzle with plenty of olive oil and season with pepper. Alternatively, heat 4 tablespoons olive oil with 2 garlic cloves, add the drained orecchiette mixture, cook for a few minutes, then discard the garlic and serve immediately.

ORECCHIETTE CON POMODORO
E RICOTTA

Serves 4

4 tablespoons olive oil

9 ounces canned tomatoes

6 fresh basil leaves

12$^1/_2$ ounces Orecchiette (see page 274)

$^1/_2$ cup firm ricotta cheese, freshly grated

salt

ORECCHIETTE WITH TOMATO AND RICOTTA

Heat the oil in a small pan, add the tomatoes and a pinch of salt and simmer for about 30 minutes. Mash the tomatoes with a fork, add the basil, turn off the heat and cover. Cook the orecchiette in a large pan of salted, boiling water for 10 minutes until al dente, drain well and transfer to a warm serving dish. Pour the tomato sauce over the pasta and sprinkle with the ricotta.

PANSOTTI ALLA GENOVESE

Serves 6

3$^1/_2$ cups all-purpose flour, preferably Italian type 00, plus extra for dusting

1 tablespoon dry white wine

2 tablespoons butter, diced

$^2/_3$ cup Parmesan cheese, freshly grated

salt

For the filling

2$^1/_4$ pounds borage, belgian endive, Swiss chard or turnip greens

$^1/_2$ garlic clove

scant 1 cup ricotta cheese

2 eggs, lightly beaten

4–6 tablespoons Parmesan cheese, freshly grated

For the sauce

1 bread slice, crusts removed

2 tablespoons milk

1$^3/_4$ cups shelled walnuts

$^1/_2$ garlic clove

$^2/_3$ cup olive oil

GENOESE PANSOTTI

Make the pasta dough (see Fresh Pasta Dough, page 268) with the flour, 5 tablespoons water, the wine and a pinch of salt. Cook the greens in salted, boiling water for 5 minutes or until tender. Drain, reserve some of the water and chop the greens with the garlic, then combine with the ricotta, eggs and enough Parmesan to thicken the mixture. Roll out the pasta dough into a thin sheet and place mounds of the filling at regular intervals on top. Cut the dough into squares around each mound, then fold them in half. To make the sauce, tear the bread into pieces, place in a bowl, add the milk and let soak. Blanch the walnuts in boiling water and peel off the skins. Squeeze out the bread. Pound the walnuts, garlic and bread in a mortar and gradually whisk in the oil to make a runny sauce. If necessary, add 1–2 tablespoons of the cooking water from the greens. Cook the pansotti in a large pan of salted, boiling water until al dente, then drain and place in a warm serving dish. Add the walnut sauce, the butter and Parmesan, mix well and serve.

VALTELLINA PIZZOCCHERI

Sift together both flours and a pinch of salt into a mound on the counter and make a well in the center. Add the egg, 1 tablespoon warm water and milk and gradually incorporate the flour with your fingers, adding more warm water if necessary. Knead until smooth. Roll in a damp dish towel and let stand for 30 minutes. Meanwhile, put the cabbage and potato into a pan, add water to cover and season with salt and pepper. Bring to a boil, then lower the heat and simmer for 20 minutes until the cabbage is tender and the potato is almost disintegrating. Divide the butter between three small pans and cook the onion, garlic and sage in the separate pans until soft and golden brown. Roll out the pasta dough into a fairly thick sheet on a lightly floured surface and cut into $^1/_2$-inch wide ribbons about 8 inches long. Add to the pan of vegetables, cook for 5 minutes, then drain and transfer to a large dish. Pour the hot butters over the mixture and toss lightly. Arrange a layer of vegetables and pizzoccheri on the base of a soup tureen, place a layer of cheese slices on top and sprinkle with the Parmesan. Continue making alternating layers until all the ingredients are used. Serve hot.

PIZZOCCHERI DELLA VALTELLINA

Serves 6

1$^1/_4$ cups buckwheat flour

$^2/_3$ cup all-purpose flour, preferably Italian type 00, plus extra for dusting

1 egg, lightly beaten

2 tablespoons milk

4$^1/_3$ cups Savoy cabbage, shredded

1 potato, chopped

scant $^1/_2$ cup butter

1 onion, thinly sliced

1 garlic clove, thinly sliced

4 fresh sage leaves, shredded

5 ounces low-fat cheese, sliced

1 cup Parmesan cheese, freshly grated

salt and pepper

RAVIOLI NAPOLETANA

Make the pasta dough (see Fresh Pasta Dough, page 268) with the quantities specified, cover with a damp dish towel and let stand for 30 minutes. Meanwhile, beat the ricotta in a bowl with a wooden spoon, then stir in the egg, parsley, Parmesan, ham and mozzarella. Roll out the pasta dough into a fairly thick sheet and place mounds of the filling at regular intervals on half the sheet. Fold over the dough and cut out ravioli, pressing the edges firmly to seal. Cook the ravioli in a large pan of salted, boiling water for 15–20 minutes. Drain, toss with the tomato sauce, transfer to a warm serving dish and serve with Parmesan.

RAVIOLI ALLA NAPOLETANA

Serves 6

2$^3/_4$ cups all-purpose flour, preferably Italian type 00, plus extra for dusting

3 eggs, lightly beaten

salt

For the filling

scant $^1/_2$ cup ricotta cheese

1 egg, lightly beaten

1 tablespoon chopped fresh flat-leaf parsley

generous 1 cup Parmesan cheese, freshly grated, plus extra to serve

generous $^1/_2$ cup cooked, cured ham, finely chopped

3$^1/_2$ ounces mozzarella cheese, diced

1 quantity Tomato Sauce (see page 57)

VEGETABLE AND CHEESE FILLED RAVIOLI

For the filling, cook the spinach, in just the water clinging to the leaves after washing, for 5 minutes, then drain well and chop. Beat the ricotta in a bowl with a wooden spoon and stir in the spinach. Stir in the eggs and Parmesan and season with salt and pepper to taste, stirring until very smooth. Make the pasta dough (see Fresh Pasta Dough, page 268) with the flour, eggs and a pinch of salt. Roll out into a sheet, place mounds of the filling at regular intervals on half the sheet, fold over and cut out ravioli (a little larger than normal). Press the edges to seal. Cook in a large pan of salted, boiling water for about 10 minutes, then drain and place in a warm serving dish. Meanwhile melt the butter in a small pan and cook the sage leaves until golden. Sprinkle the ravioli with the ricotta and Parmesan, pour the sage butter over them and serve.

RAVIOLI DI MAGRO

Serves 6

2³/₄ cups all-purpose flour
plus extra for dusting

3 eggs • ¹/₄ cup butter

8 fresh sage leaves

¹/₂ cup ricotta cheese, crumbled

²/₃ cup Parmesan cheese, freshly grated

salt

For the filling

3¹/₄ pounds spinach

2¹/₄ cups ricotta cheese • 2 eggs, lightly beaten

2 tablespoons Parmesan cheese, freshly grated

salt and pepper

STRACCI WITH LOBSTER

Melt the butter in a pan, add the onion and cook over low heat, stirring occasionally, for 5 minutes until softened. Parboil the celery for a few minutes, then drain. Heat 3 tablespoons of the oil in a pan, add the garlic and parsley and cook for a few minutes. Add the onion, zucchini, eggplant, celery and fennel, season and cook, stirring frequently, for about 10 minutes until tender. Meanwhile, plunge the lobsters into a pan of salted water, cover and cook for 8 minutes, drain and extract the meat. Heat the remaining oil in a pan, add the lobster meat and tomatoes and cook for 5 minutes. Cook the stracci in a pan of salted, boiling water for 2–3 minutes until al dente, drain and add to the vegetables. Mix well, add the lobster mixture and transfer to a warm serving dish.

'STRACCI' AGLI ASTICI

Serves 6

2 tablespoons butter • 1 onion, chopped

1 celery stalk, cut into 1¹/₄-inch batons

5 tablespoons olive oil • 1 garlic clove

2 fresh flat-leaf parsley sprigs

1 zucchini, cut into 1¹/₄-inch batons

¹/₂ eggplant, cut into 1¹/₄-inch batons

¹/₂ cooked fennel bulb, cut into 1¹/₄-inch batons

2 live lobsters

3 plum tomatoes, peeled and diced

12 ounces stracci pasta (fresh pasta squares)

salt and pepper

TAGLIATELLE WITH MUSHROOMS

Place the mushrooms in a bowl, add warm water to cover and let soak for 1 hour. Drain, squeeze out the liquid and chop finely with the onion. Heat the oil in a pan, add the mushrooms and onion and cook over low heat, stirring occasionally, for 5 minutes. Stir in ¹/₂ cup water and season lightly with salt. Add the white wine and cook until it has evaporated, then stir in the tomato paste. Simmer over medium heat for 30 minutes. Cook the tagliatelle in a large pan of salted, boiling water for 2–3 minutes until al dente. Sprinkle with the Parmesan and toss with the mushroom sauce.

TAGLIATELLE AI FUNGHI

Serves 4

¹/₂ cup dried mushrooms

1 small onion

2 tablespoons olive oil

5 tablespoons dry white wine

3 tablespoons concentrated tomato paste

10 ounces fresh tagliatelle

¹/₂ cup Parmesan cheese, freshly grated

salt

TAGLIATELLE ALLE MELANZANE

Serves 4

6 tablespoons olive oil

2 eggplants, thinly sliced

1 garlic clove

approximately 2 tomatoes, peeled and chopped

10 fresh basil leaves

10 ounces fresh tagliatelle

scant 1 cup firm ricotta cheese, freshly grated

salt and pepper

TAGLIATELLE WITH EGGPLANT

Heat 4 tablespoons of the olive oil in a skillet, add the eggplant slices and cook over medium heat for 8–10 minutes until golden brown all over. Heat the remaining oil in a pan, add the garlic and the tomatoes and cook over low heat for 10 minutes, then remove and discard the garlic. Remove the pan from the heat and season with salt and pepper, then chop one of the basil leaves and stir in. Cook the tagliatelle in a large pan of salted, boiling water until al dente, then drain and place in a warm serving dish. Cover with the ricotta, then spoon the tomato sauce over it. Top with the eggplant slices and sprinkle with the remaining basil.

TAGLIATELLE AL NERO DI SEPPIA

Serves 4

1³/₄ cups all-purpose flour, preferably Italian type 00, plus extra for dusting

2 eggs, lightly beaten

1 or 2 cuttlefish ink sacs

5 ounces canned tuna in oil, drained and flaked

1 tablespoon capers, rinsed

3 tablespoons olive oil

salt

CUTTLEFISH INK TAGLIATELLE

Sift the flour with a pinch of salt into a mound on the counter and make a well in the center. Add the eggs and cuttlefish ink and gradually incorporate the flour with your fingers. Knead the dough until soft and smooth, then roll out into a sheet, on a lightly floured surface, fold over several times and cut into ¹/₄-inch wide tagliatelle. Combine the tuna, capers and olive oil in a bowl. Cook the tagliatelle in a large pan of salted, boiling water until al dente, then drain and toss with the tuna sauce. Transfer to a warm serving dish.

TAGLIATELLE AL SALMONE

Serves 4

¹/₄ cup butter

generous ¹/₂ cup smoked salmon, chopped

juice of ¹/₂ lemon, strained

scant ¹/₂ cup heavy cream

5 tablespoons whisky

10 ounces fresh tagliatelle

salt and pepper

TAGLIATELLE WITH SALMON

Melt the butter in a pan, add the salmon, stir and sprinkle with the lemon juice. Cook for a few minutes, then add the cream and whisky and season with salt and pepper. Cook over low heat for 5 minutes. Cook the tagliatelle in a large pan of salted, boiling water until al dente, drain, add to the sauce and cook for a few minutes. Toss gently and transfer to a warm serving dish.

TAGLIATELLE WITH ARTICHOKES

Break off the artichoke stalks and remove the tough outer leaves and the chokes. Rub all over with lemon juice to prevent discoloration. Cook in lightly salted, boiling water for 7 minutes, then drain and slice thinly. Heat the oil in a skillet, add the garlic and cook for a few minutes until browned. Remove and discard the garlic and add the artichokes, basil, parsley and tomatoes to the skillet. Season with salt and cook over low heat for 10 minutes. Cook the tagliatelle in a large pan of salted, boiling water until al dente, then drain and add to the skillet. If necessary, add a few tablespoonfuls of the pasta cooking water to thin the sauce. Drizzle with olive oil and sprinkle with the Parmesan. Remove and discard the parsley, transfer to a warm serving dish and serve.

TAGLIATELLE CON CARCIOFI

Serves 4

4 globe artichokes

juice of 1 lemon, strained

4 tablespoons olive oil, plus extra for drizzling

1 garlic clove

6 fresh basil leaves

1 fresh flat-leaf parsley sprig

5 canned tomatoes, drained and chopped

10 ounces fresh tagliatelle

4 tablespoons Parmesan cheese, freshly grated

salt

TAGLIATELLE WITH SPINACH

Preheat the oven to 400°F and grease an ovenproof dish with butter. Cook the spinach, in just the water clinging to the leaves after washing, for 5 minutes, then drain and chop. Heat half the butter in a pan, add the onion and cook over low heat, stirring occasionally, for 5 minutes until softened. Add the spinach and cook for a few minutes more. Season with salt and pepper and sprinkle with half the Parmesan. Cook the tagliatelle in a large pan of salted, boiling water for 2–3 minutes until al dente, then drain, return to the pan and toss with the remaining butter. Make layers of tagliatelle, most of the remaining Parmesan and the spinach in the prepared dish, ending with a layer of spinach. Pour the cream on top, sprinkle with the rest of the Parmesan and bake for 10 minutes until golden and bubbling.

TAGLIATELLE CON SPINACI

Serves 4

5 tablespoons butter, plus extra for greasing

1^1/$_2$ pounds spinach

1 onion, finely chopped

^{1}/$_3$ cup Parmesan cheese, freshly grated

10 ounces fresh tagliatelle

scant 1 cup heavy cream

salt and pepper

TAGLIATELLE WITH CREAM, PEAS AND HAM

Heat the butter and oil in a pan, add the onion and cook over low heat, stirring occasionally, for 5 minutes until softened. Add the peas and cook, stirring occasionally, for 20 minutes, then stir in the cream. Cook for 5 minutes, then add the ham. Cook the tagliatelle in a large pan of salted, boiling water until al dente, then drain and toss with the Parmesan and hot sauce. Transfer to a warm serving dish.

TAGLIATELLE PANNA,
PISELLI E PROSCIUTTO

Serves 4

2 tablespoons butter • 2 tablespoons olive oil

1 onion, very thinly sliced

1^3/$_4$ cups peas, shelled

scant ^{1}/$_2$ cup heavy cream

2 cooked, cured ham slices, diced

10 ounces fresh tagliatelle

^{2}/$_3$ cup Parmesan cheese, freshly grated • salt

281

TAGLIATELLINE WITH ONIONS

TAGLIATELLINE ALLE CIPOLLE

Serves 4

3 tablespoons butter • 4 tablespoons olive oil

14 ounces white onions, thinly sliced

10 ounces fresh tagliatelline

²/₃ cup Parmesan cheese, freshly grated

salt and pepper

Heat the butter and oil in a flameproof casserole. Add the onions and cook over low heat, stirring occasionally, for 5–10 minutes until translucent, then season with salt. Meanwhile, cook the tagliatelline in a large pan of salted, boiling water until al dente, then drain and tip into the casserole. Season lightly with pepper and toss. Remove from the heat and sprinkle with the Parmesan.

TAGLIOLINI WITH LANGOUSTINES

TAGLIOLINI AGLI SCAMPI

Serves 4

14 ounces langoustines or jumbo shrimp

1 onion

1 carrot

1 celery stalk

3 tablespoons olive oil

1 tablespoon chopped fresh flat-leaf parsley

1 teaspoon concentrated tomato paste

10 ounces fresh tagliolini

salt

Peel the langoustines or shrimp, reserving the shells. Put the shells in a pan with the onion, carrot and celery, add water to cover and a pinch of salt. Bring to a boil, lower the heat and simmer for 15 minutes, then strain into a bowl. Reserve some of the stock. Heat the oil in a skillet, add the langoustines or shrimp and cook for 3 minutes, then sprinkle with the parsley. Stir the tomato paste with a little of the shellfish stock in a bowl and add to the pan. Cook the tagliolini in a large pan of salted, boiling water until al dente, then drain, toss with the sauce and transfer to a warm serving dish.

TAGLIOLINI WITH BUTTER AND TRUFFLE

TAGLIOLINI AL BURRO E TARTUFO

Serves 4

6 tablespoons butter

pinch of freshly grated nutmeg

10 ounces fresh tagliolini

1 cup Parmesan cheese, freshly grated

1 small white truffle

salt and pepper

Melt the butter in a small pan and season with the nutmeg and a pinch each of salt and pepper. Cook the tagliolini in a large pan of salted, boiling water until al dente, then drain and tip into a warm serving dish. Pour the melted butter over the pasta, sprinkle with the Parmesan and then shave the truffle over the top.

TAGLIOLINI WITH SCALLOPS AND LETTUCE

TAGLIOLINI ALLE CAPPESANTE E LATTUGA

Serves 4

2 garlic cloves • 3 tablespoons olive oil

7 ounces shelled scallops with coral

scant ¹/₂ cup white wine

2¹/₂ cup lettuce, shredded

2 tablespoons butter • pinch of chili powder

1 tablespoon chopped fresh flat-leaf parsley

10 ounces fresh tagliolini • salt

Heat the oil in a pan, add the garlic and cook for 30 seconds. Remove and discard the garlic and add the scallops to the pan. Sprinkle in the wine, cook until it has evaporated, then season with salt. Add the lettuce and butter and stir well. Stir in the chili powder and parsley. Cook the tagliolini in a large pan of salted, boiling water until al dente, then drain and add to the sauce. Toss gently and transfer to a warm serving dish.

PUMPKIN TORTELLI

Preheat the oven to 350°F. Put the pumpkin in a roasting pan, drizzle with the oil, cover with foil and bake for about 1 hour. Pass the pumpkin through a food mill into a bowl, add the Parmesan and eggs and season with salt and pepper. Stir in enough bread crumbs to make a fairly firm mixture. Roll out the pasta dough into a sheet and stamp out 3-inch rounds with a cookie cutter. Spoon a little of the pumpkin filling into the center of each round, fold in half and crimp the edges. Cook the tortelli in a large pan of salted, boiling water for 10 minutes. Meanwhile, melt the butter in a skillet, add the sage and cook for a few minutes. Drain the tortelli, place in a warm serving dish and sprinkle with the sage butter and extra Parmesan.

TORTELLI DI ZUCCA

Serves 4

4 cups pumpkin, peeled, seeded and chopped

2 tablespoons olive oil

$2^1/_3$ cup Parmesan cheese,

freshly grated, plus extra to serve

2 eggs, lightly beaten

$1^1/_2$–2 cups bread crumbs

7 ounces Fresh Pasta Dough (see page 268)

$^1/_4$ cup butter

8 fresh sage leaves

salt and pepper

CURRIED TORTELLINI

Melt half the butter in a pan, add the peas and ham and cook over low heat, stirring occasionally, for 10 minutes. Stir in the curry powder and cook for a further 10 minutes. Cook the tortellini in a large pan of salted, boiling water until al dente. Drain and toss with the remaining butter, the Parmesan and cream, and then with the curry sauce. Transfer to a warm serving dish.

TORTELLINI AL CURRY

Serves 4

$^1/_4$ cup butter

$1^3/_4$ cups peas, shelled

$^1/_3$ cup cooked, cured ham, diced

2 teaspoons curry powder

14 ounces fresh tortellini

$^2/_3$ cup Parmesan cheese, freshly grated

scant 1 cup heavy cream

salt

TORTELLINI BOLOGNESE

Melt the butter in a small pan, add the veal and cook over high heat, stirring frequently, until browned. Transfer to a bowl, let cool, then stir in the Parmesan, prosciutto, mortadella and egg. Roll out the pasta dough into a thin sheet, put small mounds of the filling at regular intervals on the sheet and cut it into squares. Fold the squares corner to corner into triangles, then wrap each triangle around your index finger, press the points together and gently push the rest of the dough backwards to make the classic tortellini shape. Make 20 tortellini per person. Serve with tomato sauce.

TORTELLINI ALLA BOLOGNESE

Serves 4

2 tablespoons butter

$^1/_2$ cup ground veal

2 tablespoons Parmesan cheese, freshly grated

$^1/_2$ cup prosciutto, diced

$^1/_4$ cup mortadella, diced

1 egg, lightly beaten

1 quantity Fresh Pasta Dough (see page 268)

Tomato Sauce (see page 57), to serve.

MUSHROOM TORTELLONI

Prepare the pasta dough and let rest covered with a damp dish towel for 30 minutes. Heat the oil in a pan, add the onion and porcini and cook over low heat, stirring occasionally, for 5 minutes. Season with salt and cook for a further 15 minutes. Transfer the mixture to a food processor, add the ricotta, Parmesan and parsley and process to a purée. Season with salt and pepper to taste. Roll out the pasta dough to make a thin sheet and cut out 2-inch squares. Put a little ricotta mixture into the center of each square. Fold the squares corner to corner into triangles, then wrap each triangle around your index finger, press the points together and gently push the rest of the dough backwards to make the classic tortellini shape. Melt the butter in a large skillet, add the sage leaves and cook for a few minutes. Cook the tortelloni in a large pan of salted, boiling water until al dente. Drain, add to the skillet and stir over high heat. Transfer to a warm serving dish, sprinkle with Parmesan and serve.

TORTELLONI DI FUNGHI

Serves 4

1 quantity Fresh Pasta Dough (see page 268)

4 tablespoons olive oil

1 small onion, chopped

$4^1/_2$ cups porcini, thinly sliced

generous 1 cup ricotta cheese, crumbled

$^2/_3$ cup Parmesan cheese,

freshly grated, plus extra to serve

1 fresh flat-leaf parsley sprig, chopped

3 tablespoons butter

10 fresh sage leaves

salt and pepper

PESTO TORTELLONI WITH SQUID

Make the pasta dough (see Fresh Pasta Dough, page 268) with the flour, eggs and a pinch of salt. For the pesto, put the basil, parsley, pine nuts, walnuts and olive oil into a food processor and process until combined, then scrape into a bowl. Season with salt and stir in the ricotta. Roll out the pasta dough into a sheet and make pesto-filled tortelloni (for method of making tortelloni, see above). For the sauce, heat 3 tablespoons of the oil in a skillet, add the squid and garlic and cook, stirring frequently, for a few minutes until the squid are light golden brown. Season with salt and pepper to taste, sprinkle with the wine and cook until it has evaporated. Remove the squid from the pan, leaving the cooking juices in the pan.and slice into fairly thin rounds. Cook the pasta in a large pan of salted, boiling water until al dente, drain and tip into the skillet. Remove and discard the garlic, add the remaining oil, the tomatoes and squid rounds and mix well. Sprinkle with the parsley and basil and mix again. Transfer to a warm serving dish.

TORTELLONI DI PESTO CON CALAMARETTI

Serves 4

$2^3/_4$ cups all-purpose flour, preferably Italian type 00,

plus extra for dusting

3 eggs, lightly beaten • salt

For the pesto

$1^3/_4$ cups fresh basil leaves

$^3/_4$ cup fresh flat-leaf parsley

3 tablespoons pine nuts

1 tablespoon walnuts

$^1/_2$ cup olive oil

scant 1 cup ricotta cheese • salt

For the sauce

4 tablespoons olive oil

7 ounces small squid, cleaned

1 garlic clove

5 tablespoons dry white wine

2 tomatoes, peeled and diced

1 tablespoon chopped fresh flat-leaf parsley

6 fresh basil leaves, torn

salt and pepper

DRIED PASTA

Pasta is a truly Italian passion that never fades or becomes jaded. It is a wholly Italian speciality made, by law, exclusively from durum wheat flour. In Italy it can be sold only in sealed boxes showing the net weight, producer, type and name (bucatini, fusilli, farfalle, rigatoni, etc.). For more information about the different types and shapes of pasta, see page 202.

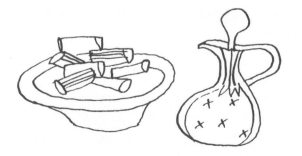

QUANTITY

On average use 2$\frac{1}{2}$–3$\frac{1}{2}$ ounces or $\frac{1}{2}$–scant $\frac{2}{3}$ cup per person.

PAN

This should be large and also deeper than it is wide. It is best to choose an aluminum or steel pan (special pans with removable metal colanders inside are available).

WATER AND SALT

The right proportion to use is 4 cups water and 1$\frac{1}{2}$ teaspoons salt for every 3$\frac{1}{2}$ ounces of pasta.

WATER

Add the pasta only when the water has come to a rolling boil and, in the case of spaghetti, fan out the strands. Stir immediately. As soon as the water begins to boil again, put the lid on. When the water reaches a rolling boil once more, remove the lid. Stir occasionally so that the pasta does not stick.

TIMING

Follow the packet instructions but check the pasta at least twice to make sure that it does not overcook.

COLD WATER

When the pasta is al dente, some people pour in about $\frac{2}{3}$ cup cold water to stop it from overcooking. This is useful if, for some unexpected reason, the pasta is not drained immediately. Otherwise it is unnecessary.

SAUCE AND CHEESE

Grated cheese, if required, should always be sprinkled on the pasta before the sauce and it should always be freshly grated. Do not overdo the quantity. Those who wish may add more at the table from the cheese dish. It is worth pointing out that metal spoons may rust on contact with fatty particles, so you should serve the cheese with a spoon made from another material.

QUANTITIES AND COOKING TIMES

BAVETTE WITH CLAMS AND ZUCCHINI

BAVETTE ALLE VONGOLE E ZUCCHINE

Serves 4

1³/₄ pounds clams, scrubbed

3 tablespoons olive oil

1 shallot

1 garlic clove

¹/₂ fresh chile, seeded and chopped

11 ounces zucchini, cut into strips

1 tablespoon chopped fresh flat-leaf parsley

scant ¹/₂ cup dry white wine

3 tomatoes, peeled and diced

12 ounces bavette

salt

Discard any clams with broken shells or that do not shut immediately when sharply tapped. Put the clams in a dry skillet and cook over high heat for about 5 minutes until they open. Discard any that remain closed. Remove the clams from their shells and set aside. Heat the oil in a pan, add the shallot, garlic and chile and cook over low heat, stirring occasionally, for 5 minutes until soft. Remove and discard the garlic, add the clams, zucchini and parsley and cook for 5 minutes. Sprinkle in the wine and cook until it has evaporated. Add the tomatoes, season with salt and cook for 20–30 minutes until thickened. Cook the bavette in a large pan of salted, boiling water until al dente, then drain, add to the zucchini and clam mixture and toss.

BUCATINI WITH GREEN TOMATOES

BUCATINI AI POMODORI VERDI

Serves 4

2 tablespoons olive oil

generous ¹/₂ cup pancetta, diced

¹/₂ garlic clove, chopped

1 fresh flat-leaf parsley sprig, chopped

4 green tomatoes, seeded and chopped

3 ounces canned tuna in oil, drained and flaked

12 ounces bucatini • salt

Heat the oil in a pan, add the pancetta, garlic and parsley and cook over medium heat for 5 minutes until lightly browned. Add the tomatoes and tuna, season with salt if necessary and cook over low heat for 40 minutes. Cook the bucatini in a large pan of salted, boiling water until al dente, then drain and tip into the pan of sauce. Mix well and serve.

BUCATINI WITH MUSHROOM SAUCE

BUCATINI ALLA SALSA DI FUNGHI

Serves 4

¹/₂ cup dried mushrooms

7 ounces fresh porcini

4 tablespoons olive oil

1¹/₂ garlic cloves

¹/₄ cup ricotta cheese

1 tablespoon concentrated tomato paste

12 ounces bucatini

salt and pepper

Place the dried mushrooms in a bowl, add warm water to cover and let soak for 20 minutes, then drain and squeeze out. Chop half the fresh porcini and thinly slice the rest. Heat 3 tablespoons of the oil with the whole garlic clove in a pan, add the drained mushrooms and chopped porcini and cook for about 10 minutes until the mushrooms have given up their liquid. Remove and discard the garlic. Add ²/₃ cup water and cook for 20 minutes. Transfer the mixture to a food processor and process to a purée, then stir into the ricotta. Put the sliced porcini into a pan with the remaining oil, the remaining garlic and the tomato paste. Mix well, add 2 tablespoons water and cook for 15 minutes. Season with salt and pepper. Meanwhile, cook the bucatini in a large pan of salted, boiling water until al dente. Drain, place in a warm serving dish and spoon the ricotta mixture and fried mushrooms on top.

BUCATINI WITH BELL PEPPER SAUCE

Heat the oil in a pan, add the onion and garlic and cook over low heat, stirring occasionally, for 10 minutes until lightly browned. Add the bell peppers, mix well and cook for a further 10 minutes until tender. Transfer to a food processor and process to a purée. Return to the pan, stir in the cream and season with salt and pepper according to taste. Keep warm over a very low heat. Cook the bucatini in a large pan of salted, boiling water until al dente, then drain and tip into the sauce. Cook for 1 minute, stir in the marjoram and serve.

BUCATINI CON SALSA AI PEPERONI

Serves 4

2 tablespoons olive oil

1 pearl onion, chopped

1/2 garlic clove, chopped

3 red or yellow bell peppers, halved, seeded and sliced

scant 1/2 cup heavy cream

12 ounces bucatini

2 teaspoons chopped fresh marjoram

salt and pepper

FARFALLE WITH SMOKED PANCETTA

Heat the oil in a pan, add the pancetta and chile and cook over medium heat for 5 minutes until lightly browned. Add the tomatoes, season with salt and cook over low heat for 25 minutes. Stir in the cream and cook over very low heat for 5 minutes until thickened. Meanwhile, cook the farfalle in a large pan of salted, boiling water until al dente, then drain, tip into the sauce and cook, stirring constantly, for 30 seconds. Sprinkle with the Parmesan and serve.

FARFALLE ALLA PANCETTA AFFUMICATA

Serves 4

1 tablespoon olive oil

generous 1/2 cup smoked pancetta, diced

1 fresh chile, seeded and chopped

2 tomatoes, peeled and chopped

scant 1 cup heavy cream

3 cups farfalle

1/3 cup Parmesan cheese, freshly grated

salt

FUSILLI WITH MUSHROOMS

Heat the oil in a pan, add the onion and mushrooms and cook over low heat, stirring occasionally, for 10 minutes. Season with salt and pepper and add the tomatoes with their can juices. Simmer for 45 minutes, then remove the pan from the heat and add the parsley. Meanwhile, cook the fusilli in a large pan of salted, boiling water until al dente, drain and tip onto a warm serving dish. Sprinkle with the Parmesan, add the butter and toss. Spoon the mushroom sauce on top and serve.

FUSILLI AI FUNGHI

Serves 4

3 tablespoons olive oil

1 onion, chopped

1 1/4 cups chanterelle mushrooms or honey fungus, chopped

9 ounces canned tomatoes

1 tablespoon chopped fresh flat-leaf parsley

3 cups fusilli

1/3 cup Parmesan cheese, freshly grated

2 tablespoons butter

salt and pepper

FUSILLI IN CUTTLEFISH INK

FUSILLI AL NERO DI SEPPIA

Serves 4

1¹/₂ pounds prepared cuttlefish, ink sacs reserved

2 tablespoons olive oil

1 onion, very thinly sliced

scant 1 cup dry white wine

2 tablespoons tomato paste

3 cups fusilli

1 tablespoon chopped fresh flat-leaf parsley

salt and pepper

Cut the cuttlefish into strips. Heat the oil in a pan, add the onion and cook over low heat, stirring occasionally, until softened. Add the cuttlefish and cook over medium heat, stirring occasionally, until lightly browned. Add the wine and cook until it has evaporated. Stir in the tomato paste, season with salt and pepper, lower the heat, cover and cook for 1 hour. Cook the fusilli in a large pan of salted, boiling water until al dente. Pour the cuttlefish ink into the sauce and stir in the parsley. Drain the pasta, tip it into the sauce, mix well and transfer to a warm serving dish.

FUSILLI SALAD

FUSILLI IN INSALATA

Serves 4

4 tomatoes, peeled, seeded and diced

16 fresh basil leaves

1 garlic clove

olive oil, for drizzling

3 cups fusilli

3 ounces canned tuna in oil, drained and flaked

12 black olives, pitted and halved

4 ounces mozzarella cheese, diced

salt

Put the tomatoes, basil and garlic in a serving bowl, drizzle with oil and season with salt. Cook the pasta in a large pan of salted, boiling water until al dente, then drain. Remove and discard the garlic, then tip the fusilli into the bowl. Add the tuna, olives and mozzarella, toss and serve.

LINGUINE WITH GENOESE PESTO

LINGUINE AL PESTO GENOVESE

Serves 4

12 ounces linguine

2 potatoes, cut into thin batons

¹/₃ cup green beans

For the pesto

25 fresh basil leaves

2 garlic cloves, chopped

5 tablespoons olive oil

¹/₃ cup romano cheese, freshly grated

¹/₃ cup Parmesan cheese, freshly grated

salt

To make the pesto, put the basil, garlic, a pinch of salt and the olive oil in a food processor and process briefly at medium speed. Add both cheeses and process again until blended. Cook the linguine, potatoes and beans together in a large pan of salted, boiling water until al dente, then drain. Toss with the pesto and serve.

MACARONI WITH MUSHROOMS

MACCHERONI AI FUNGHI PORCINI

Serves 4

2 tablespoons butter

3 tablespoons olive oil

1 garlic clove

3²/₃ cups porcini, sliced

5 ounces canned chopped tomatoes, drained

1 tablespoon chopped fresh flat-leaf parsley

3 cups macaroni

salt and pepper

Heat the butter and oil in a pan, add the garlic clove and porcini and cook, stirring occasionally, for 5 minutes. Add the tomatoes, season with salt and pepper to taste, cover and cook over low heat for about 20 minutes. Remove and discard the garlic and stir in the parsley. Cook the macaroni in a large pan of salted, boiling water until al dente, then drain, toss with the porcini sauce and serve. This sauce can also be made without tomatoes, in which case use 3 tablespoons butter.

MACARONI WITH CUTTLEFISH

MACCHERONI CON LE SEPPIOLINE

Serves 4

1 pound 5 ounces cleaned cuttlefish

9 ounces canned chopped tomatoes

1 onion, finely chopped

2 garlic cloves

1 large potato, sliced

1³/₄ cups baby peas, shelled

2 tablespoons chopped fresh flat-leaf parsley

4 tablespoons olive oil

3 cups macaroni

salt and pepper

Put the cuttlefish, tomatoes with their can juices, onion, garlic, potato, baby peas, parsley and oil in a large pan and cook over medium heat, stirring frequently, for 10 minutes. Lower the heat, cover and cook for a further 30 minutes. Season with salt and pepper to taste. Cook the macaroni in a large pan of salted, boiling water until al dente, then drain and tip into the sauce. Mix well, transfer to a serving dish and serve.

MACARONI AU GRATIN

MACCHERONI GRATINATI

Serves 4

2 tablespoons butter, plus extra for greasing

1 quantity Béchamel Sauce (see page 50)

²/₃ cup Parmesan cheese, freshly grated

2 egg yolks

3 cups macaroni

salt

Preheat the oven to 475°F. Grease an ovenproof dish with butter. Combine the béchamel sauce, Parmesan, butter and egg yolks. Cook the macaroni in a large pan of salted, boiling water until just al dente, then drain and tip into a bowl. Gently stir in half the béchamel sauce mixture and put in the prepared dish, then spoon the remaining béchamel sauce mixture on top. Bake for 15–20 minutes until golden brown.

PASTA WITH SARDINES

Place the raisins in a bowl, add hot water to cover and let soak. Cook the fennel in lightly salted, boiling water for 15–20 minutes, then drain, reserving the cooking liquid, and chop. Heat the oil in a pan, add the onion and cook over low heat, stirring occasionally, for 5 minutes. Drain the anchovies, add the filleted fish to the pan and mash with a wooden spoon. Drain the raisins, squeezing out the excess liquid, and add to the pan with the fennel and pine nuts. Sprinkle with the saffron, cover and cook over low heat for 15 minutes. Open the sardines out like the pages of a book, leaving them attached along their backs. Rinse well, pat dry and dust with flour, shaking off any excess. Heat the vegetable oil in a deep-fryer or large pan to 350–375°F or until a cube of day-old bread browns in 30 seconds. Add the sardines and deep-fry until golden brown, then remove and drain on paper towels. Season with a little salt. Preheat the oven to 400°F and brush an ovenproof dish with oil. Cook the zite in a large pan of salted, boiling water mixed with the reserved fennel cooking water until al dente, then drain, return to the pan and stir in half the sauce. Spoon a layer of pasta onto the base of the prepared dish and place a layer of sardines on top. Add a layer of the sauce and continue making layers until all the ingredients are used, ending with a layer of sauce. Bake for 10 minutes.

PASTA CON LE SARDE

Serves 4

scant 1 cup golden raisins

4 salted anchovy fillets, heads removed, cleaned and filleted (see page 596), soaked in cold water for 10 minutes and drained

7 ounces wild fennel

2 tablespoons olive oil, plus extra for brushing

1 onion, chopped

¼ cup pine nuts

½ envelope saffron powder

12 ounces fresh sardines, scaled and cleaned

all-purpose flour, for dusting

vegetable oil, for deep-frying

11 ounces zite (long tubes of dried pasta)

salt

PENNE WITH LETTUCE

Preheat the oven to 350°F and grease an ovenproof dish with butter. Place the lettuce in a bowl, add the oil and season with salt and pepper. Cook the penne in a large pan of salted, boiling water until al dente, then drain and tip into the prepared dish. Cover with the lettuce, sprinkle with the Swiss cheese and dot with the butter. Bake for about 20 minutes.

PENNE ALLA LATTUGA

Serves 4

2 tablespoons butter, plus extra for greasing

14 cups lettuce, shredded

3 tablespoons olive oil

3 cups penne

scant 1 cup Swiss cheese, freshly grated

salt and pepper

PENNE ARRABBIATA

Heat the oil in a skillet, add the garlic cloves and chile and cook until the garlic browns, then remove the cloves from the skillet. Add the tomatoes to the pan, season with salt and cook for about 15 minutes. Cook the penne in a large pan of salted, boiling water until al dente, then drain and tip into the skillet. Toss over high heat for a few minutes, then transfer to a warm serving dish, sprinkle with the parsley.

PENNE ALL'ARRABBIATA

Serves 4

6 tablespoons oil

2 garlic cloves

$^1/_2$ fresh chile, seeded and chopped

1 pound 2 ounces canned chopped tomatoes, drained

3 cups penne lisce

1 tablespoon chopped fresh flat-leaf parsley

salt

PENNE WITH BLACK OLIVES

Put the olives and cream in a pan and cook over low heat for about 15 minutes. Cook the penne in a large pan of salted, boiling water until al dente, then drain. Spoon half the olive sauce onto the base of a warm serving dish and top with the pasta. Sprinkle with the Parmesan, then spoon the remaining sauce on top. Mix well and serve.

PENNE ALLE OLIVE NERE

Serves 4

$1^1/_4$ cups black olives, pitted and finely chopped

$^3/_4$ cup heavy cream

3 cups penne lisce

$^1/_3$ cup Parmesan cheese, freshly grated

salt

PENNE WITH TURNIP GREENS

Cook the turnip greens in salted, boiling water for 10 minutes, then drain and chop. Put the anchovy fillets and the oil in a food processor and process to a purée. Cook the penne in a large pan of salted, boiling water until al dente, then drain and tip into a fairly deep warm serving dish. Add the turnip greens, drizzle with oil, season with pepper and stir. Pour in the anchovy purée, mix again and serve.

PENNE CON CIME DI RAPA

Serves 4

1 pound 2 ounces turnip greens

4 anchovy fillets (see page 596)

3 tablespoons olive oil, plus extra for drizzling

scant 3 cups penne

salt and pepper

PENNE WITH SAFFRON

Bring the stock to a boil. Heat the butter and oil in another large pan, add the onion and cook over low heat, stirring occasionally, for 5 minutes until softened. Add the penne and stir until it is shiny and coated with fat. Add a ladleful of hot stock and stir until it has been absorbed. Continue adding stock, a ladleful at a time, as if making risotto, until the pasta is completely cooked. Stir the saffron into the last ladleful of stock before adding it to the pan. Mix well until the dish is an even yellow color. Remove the pan from the heat, sprinkle with the Parmesan, mix well and stir in a pat of butter if you like. Transfer to a warm serving dish and serve. Saffron threads may be used instead of saffron powder.

PENNE GIALLE

Serves 4

1 quantity Meat Stock (see page 208)

3 tablespoons butter, plus extra for serving (optional)

1 tablespoon olive oil

1 onion, thinly sliced

scant 3 cups penne lisce

1 envelope saffron powder

$^1/_2$ cup Parmesan cheese, freshly grated

CURRIED PENNE SALAD

PENNE IN INSALATA AL CURRY

Serves 4

2 tablespoons olive oil

1 onion, thinly sliced

2 tablespoons curry powder

1 tablespoon all-purpose flour

scant 1 cup Meat Stock (see page 208)

3 cups penne

scant ¹/₂ cup heavy cream

1 small cucumber, peeled and finely diced

salt

Heat the oil in a pan, add 1 tablespoon water, a pinch of salt and the onion and cook for 5–6 minutes until softened and translucent. Stir in the curry powder and cook for a few seconds, then stir in the flour and cook for a few seconds more. Gradually stir in the stock, bring to a boil, stirring constantly, then lower the heat and simmer, stirring frequently, for 15 minutes. Remove the pan from the heat and let cool. Cook the penne in a large pan of salted, boiling water until al dente, then drain, tip into a serving dish and mix with the cream. Let cool, but do not chill in the refrigerator. To serve, spoon the curry sauce over the pasta and sprinkle with the cucumber.

FRIED PENNE

PENNE IN TEGAME

Serves 4

¹/₄ cup butter

1 onion, thinly sliced

3 cups penne

¹/₂ cup Parmesan cheese, freshly grated

salt and pepper

Melt the butter in a pan, add the onion, then add the penne. Mix well to coat the pasta with butter, then pour in enough boiling water to cover. Add salt and cook until the pasta is al dente, adding more boiling water if necessary. Season with pepper, transfer to a warm serving dish and sprinkle with the Parmesan.

PENNE RIGATE WITH ARTICHOKES

PENNE RIGATE AI CARCIOFI

Serves 4

juice of ¹/₂ lemon, strained

4 globe artichokes

4 tablespoons olive oil

1 garlic clove, chopped

1 tablespoon chopped fresh flat-leaf parsley

3 cups penne rigate

salt and pepper

Half-fill a bowl with water and stir in the lemon juice. Working on one artichoke at a time, break off the stem, remove the coarse, outer leaves and choke, if necessary. Cut into fourths, then slice thinly and drop into the acidulated water to prevent discoloration. Heat the oil in a pan, add the garlic and parsley and cook over low heat for 2 minutes. Drain the artichokes, add to the pan and mix well. Cover and cook over low heat for a few minutes, then add 2–3 tablespoons water, season with salt and re-cover the pan so that the artichokes cook in their own steam. Meanwhile, cook the penne in a large pan of salted, boiling water until al dente, then drain and tip into a serving dish. Pour the artichoke sauce, which should not be too runny, over the pasta, season with pepper and serve.

PENNE RIGATE ALLA VODKA

Serves 4

¹/₄ cup butter

1 thick slice cooked, cured ham, diced

2 tablespoons tomato paste

1 tablespoon chopped fresh flat-leaf parsley

5 tablespoons heavy cream

¹/₄ cup vodka

3 cups penne rigate

salt and pepper

PENNE RIGATE IN VODKA

Melt the butter in a pan, add the ham, tomato paste and parsley, season with salt and pepper and cook, stirring occasionally, for about 10 minutes. Stir in the cream and vodka and cook until the vodka has evaporated. Cook the penne in a large pan of salted, boiling water until al dente, then drain and tip into a warm serving dish. Pour the sauce over the pasta.

RIGATONI CON POLPETTINE

Serves 4

2³/₄ cups ground meat

1 fresh flat-leaf parsley sprig, chopped

¹/₂ garlic clove, chopped

1 egg, lightly beaten

all-purpose flour, for dusting

3 tablespoons olive oil

1 onion, thinly sliced

1 celery stalk, chopped

1 carrot, chopped

1 small fresh rosemary sprig, chopped

1³/₄ cups bottled strained tomatoes

4 cups rigatoni

¹/₃ cup Parmesan cheese, freshly grated

salt and pepper

RIGATONI WITH MEATBALLS

Combine the ground meat, parsley and garlic in a bowl, then stir in the egg and season with salt and pepper. Shape the mixture into small meatballs, dust with flour and set aside. Heat the oil in a pan, add the onion, celery, carrot and rosemary and cook over low heat, stirring occasionally, for 5 minutes, then add the meatballs and increase the heat to medium. Cook until the meatballs are lightly browned all over, then add the strained tomatoes and season with salt. Lower the heat, cover and simmer, stirring occasionally, for about 40 minutes. Cook the rigatoni in a large pan of salted, boiling water until al dente, then drain and tip into the pan with the meatballs. Mix well and heat through for 2 minutes. Transfer to a warm serving dish and sprinkle with the Parmesan.

RIGATONI INTEGRALI AL FORNO

Serves 4

butter, for greasing

1 quantity Béchamel Sauce (see page 50)

7 ounces caciotta

or other semi-hard mild cheese, diced

3 cups wholewheat rigatoni

¹/₂ cup Parmesan cheese, freshly grated

salt

BAKED WHOLE-WHEAT RIGATONI

Preheat the oven to 350°F. Grease an ovenproof dish with butter. Combine the béchamel sauce and diced cheese. Cook the rigatoni in a large pan of salted, boiling water until al dente, then drain and tip into the prepared dish. Spoon the béchamel mixture over the pasta, sprinkle with the Parmesan and bake for about 20 minutes. Let stand for 5 minutes before serving.

RIGATONI WITH CREAM, PESTO AND TOMATOES

Pour the cream into a pan, add the tomatoes and cook over low heat for 10 minutes. Remove the pan from the heat and stir in the pesto. Meanwhile, cook the rigatoni in a large pan of salted, boiling water until al dente, then drain and tip into a warm serving dish. Sprinkle the pasta with the Parmesan and spoon the sauce over it.

RIGATONI PANNA, PESTO E POMODORO

Serves 4

scant 1 cup heavy cream

11 ounces fresh tomatoes, thinly sliced, or canned chopped tomatoes, drained

2 tablespoons Pesto (see page 68)

4 cups rigatoni

$^1/_2$ cup Parmesan cheese, freshly grated

salt

SPAGHETTI WITH GARLIC AND CHILE OIL

Heat the oil in a small pan, add the garlic and chile and cook over low heat for a few minutes until the garlic is golden brown. Season lightly with salt, remove the pan from the heat and add the parsley. Cook the spaghetti in a large pan of salted, boiling water until al dente, then drain, toss with the garlic and chile oil, and serve.

SPAGHETTI AGLIO, OLIO E PEPERONCINO

Serves 4

5 tablespoons olive oil

2 garlic cloves, thinly sliced

$^1/_2$ fresh chile, seeded and chopped

1 fresh flat-leaf parsley sprig, chopped

12 ounces spaghetti

salt

SPAGHETTI WITH BROCCOLI

Parboil the broccoli in salted water for 10 minutes. Heat the oil and butter in a skillet, add the onion and cook over low heat, stirring occasionally, for 5 minutes until softened. Drain the broccoli, add to the skillet and mix well. Stir in the cream and simmer gently for 10 minutes. Transfer the mixture to a food processor and process to a purée. Season with salt and pepper to taste. Meanwhile, cook the spaghetti in a large pan of salted, boiling water until al dente, then drain, toss with the broccoli and cream mixture, sprinkle with the Parmesan and serve.

SPAGHETTI AI BROCCOLETTI

Serves 4

1 pound 2 ounces frozen broccoli

3 tablespoons olive oil

2 tablespoons butter

1 onion, chopped

4 tablespoons heavy cream

12 ounces spaghetti

$^1/_3$ cup Parmesan cheese, freshly grated

salt and pepper

SPAGHETTI WITH CAPERS

Heat the oil in a pan, add the anchovy and garlic and cook over low heat, stirring frequently, until the anchovy has disintegrated and the garlic has turned golden brown. Remove the pan from the heat, discard the garlic and add the capers. Meanwhile, cook the spaghetti in a large pan of salted, boiling water until al dente, then drain, toss with the sauce and serve.

SPAGHETTI AI CAPPERI

Serves 4

1 salted anchovy, head removed, cleaned and filleted (see page 596), soaked in cold water for 10 minutes and drained

4 tablespoons olive oil • 2 garlic cloves

2 tablespoons capers, rinsed

12 ounces spaghetti

salt

SPAGHETTI CARBONARA

SPAGHETTI ALLA CARBONARA

Serves 4

2 tablespoons butter

generous $1/2$ cup pancetta, diced

1 garlic clove

12 ounces spaghetti

2 eggs, beaten

$1/2$ cup Parmesan cheese, freshly grated

$1/2$ cup romano cheese, freshly grated

salt and pepper

Melt the butter in a pan, add the pancetta and garlic and cook until the garlic turns brown. Remove and discard the garlic. Meanwhile, cook the spaghetti in a large pan of salted, boiling water until al dente, then drain and add to the pancetta. Remove the pan from the heat, pour in the eggs, add half the Parmesan and half the romano and season with pepper. Mix well so that the egg coats the pasta. Add the remaining cheese, mix again and serve.

SPAGHETTI AMATRICIANA

SPAGHETTI ALL'AMATRICIANA

Serves 4

olive oil, for brushing

generous $1/2$ cup pancetta, diced

1 onion, thinly sliced

1 pound 2 ounces tomatoes, peeled, seeded and diced

1 fresh chile, seeded and chopped

12 ounces spaghetti

salt and pepper

Brush a flameproof casserole with oil, add the pancetta and cook over low heat until the fat runs. Add the onion and cook, stirring occasionally, for 10 minutes until lightly browned. Add the tomatoes and chile, season with salt and pepper, cover and cook for about 40 minutes, adding a little warm water if necessary. Cook the spaghetti in a large pan of salted, boiling water until al dente, then drain and toss with the sauce in a warm serving dish.

SPAGHETTI WITH RAW TOMATO

SPAGHETTI AL POMODORO CRUDO

Serves 4

1 pound 2 ounces ripe vine tomatoes, peeled, seeded and chopped

4 tablespoons olive oil

10 fresh basil leaves, chopped

2 garlic cloves

12 ounces spaghetti

salt and pepper

Put the tomatoes into a salad bowl, add the oil, basil and garlic and season with salt and pepper. Mix well, cover and set aside in a cool place for 30 minutes to allow the flavors to mingle, then remove and discard the garlic. Cook the spaghetti in a large pan of salted, boiling water until al dente, then drain and toss with the raw tomato sauce and serve.

SPAGHETTI WITH ROSEMARY

SPAGHETTI AL ROSMARINO

Serves 4

2 tablespoons olive oil

2 tablespoons fresh rosemary needles, finely chopped

1 garlic clove, finely chopped

$^1/_2$ fresh chile, seeded and finely chopped

9 ounces canned chopped tomatoes

1 tablespoon all-purpose flour

1 tablespoon milk

12 ounces spaghetti

$^1/_2$ cup Parmesan cheese, freshly grated

salt

Heat the oil in a pan, add the rosemary, garlic and chile and cook for about 2 minutes. Stir in the tomatoes with their can juices and bring to a boil, then lower the heat, cover and simmer for 30 minutes. Stir the flour with 1–2 tablespoons warm water. Season the rosemary sauce with salt, stir in the flour mixture and milk and cook for a further 5 minutes. Cook the spaghetti in a large pan of salted, boiling water until al dente, then drain and transfer to a warm serving dish. Sprinkle with the Parmesan and pour on the sauce.

SPAGHETTI WITH ANCHOVIES

SPAGHETTI CON ACCIUGHE

Serves 4

5 ounces salted anchovies, heads removed, cleaned and filleted (see page 596), soaked in cold water for 10 minutes and drained

1 fresh flat-leaf parsley sprig

$^1/_2$ garlic clove

2 tablespoons olive oil

12 ounces spaghetti

salt and pepper

Chop the anchovies very finely with the parsley and garlic, then put the mixture in a salad bowl and stir in the olive oil. Cook the spaghetti in a large pan of salted, boiling water until al dente, then drain and tip into the salad bowl. Toss well and season with pepper.

SPAGHETTI WITH TUNA

SPAGHETTI CON IL TONNO

Serves 4

3 tablespoons olive oil

1 garlic clove

$2^1/_2$ ounces canned tuna in oil, drained and flaked

3 tablespoons tomato paste

1 tablespoon finely chopped fresh flat-leaf parsley

12 ounces spaghetti

salt and pepper

Heat the oil in a pan, add the garlic, cook until it has browned, then remove it from the pan. Add the tuna and mix well. Stir the tomato paste with 1–2 tablespoons warm water in a bowl, then stir into the pan and cook over low heat for 15 minutes. Remove the pan from the heat, stir in the parsley and season with salt and pepper. Meanwhile, cook the spaghetti in a large pan of salted, boiling water until al dente, then drain, toss with the sauce and serve.

SPAGHETTI WITH BREAD CRUMBS

Heat 2 tablespoons of the oil in a pan, add the anchovies and cook, mashing with a wooden spoon until they have almost disintegrated, then season with pepper according to taste and add the capers and olives. Combine the bread crumbs, garlic and a pinch of salt in a bowl. Heat the remaining oil in a small skillet, add the bread crumb mixture and cook, stirring frequently, until golden. Cook the spaghetti in a large pan of salted, boiling water until al dente, then drain and return to the pan. Add the anchovy sauce and stir. Transfer to a warm serving dish and sprinkle with the fried bread crumbs.

SPAGHETTI CON LA MOLLICA

Serves 4

2 salted anchovies, heads removed, cleaned and filleted (see page 596), soaked in cold water for 10 minutes and drained

5 tablespoons olive oil

1 tablespoon capers, rinsed

8 black olives, pitted and halved

1 1/2 cups bread crumbs

1/2 garlic clove chopped

12 ounces spaghetti

salt and pepper

SPAGHETTI WITH ZUCCHINI

Heat the oil in a pan, add the garlic clove, whole onion, sage leaves and celery stalk and cook over low heat for 5 minutes. Add the tomatoes and bring to a boil over medium heat, then add the zucchini. Season with salt and pepper, cover and cook for 15 minutes, then remove the onion, garlic, celery and sage. Meanwhile, cook the spaghetti in a large pan of salted water until al dente, then drain and return to the pan. Toss with the sauce, mozzarella and Parmesan and serve.

SPAGHETTI CON LE ZUCCHINE

Serves 4

3 tablespoons olive oil

1 garlic clove

1 small onion

2 fresh sage leaves

1 celery stalk

3 plum tomatoes, peeled, seeded and chopped

2 2/3 cups zucchini, thinly sliced

12 ounces spaghetti

1 mozzarella cheese, diced

1/3 cup Parmesan cheese, freshly grated

salt and pepper

SPAGHETTINI WITH BOTTARGA

Crumble half the bottarga and slice the remainder very thinly. Heat the oil in a small pan, add the bottarga and cook over low heat. Meanwhile, cook the spaghettini in a large pan of salted, boiling water until al dente, then drain and tip into the pan of sauce and mix well. Transfer to a warm serving dish.

SPAGHETTINI ALLA BOTTARGA

Serves 4

3 1/2 ounces bottarga

2 tablespoons olive oil

12 ounces spaghettini

salt

TORTIGLIONI WITH MUSHROOM AND EGGPLANT

TORTIGLIONI CON FUNGHI E MELANZANE

Serves 4

2 tablespoons olive oil

1 onion, thinly sliced

1 garlic clove

2³/₄ cups mushrooms, chopped

1 eggplant, diced

scant ¹/₂ cup heavy cream

3 cups tortiglioni

¹/₂ cup Parmesan cheese, freshly grated

salt and pepper

Heat the oil in a pan, add the onion and garlic and cook over low heat until the garlic has browned. Remove and discard the garlic, add the mushrooms and eggplant to the pan and cook, stirring frequently, until light golden brown. Stir in the cream, season with salt and pepper, cover and cook over low heat for a further 10 minutes. Meanwhile, cook the tortiglioni in a large pan of salted, boiling water until al dente, then drain, tip into the pan of sauce and cook for 1 minute. Transfer to a warm serving dish and sprinkle with the Parmesan.

VERMICELLI WITH CLAMS

VERMICELLI CON LE VONGOLE

Serves 4

2¹/₄ pounds clams, scrubbed

²/₃ cup olive oil

2 garlic cloves

12 ounces vermicelli

1 tablespoon fresh flat-leaf parsley

salt and pepper

Discard any clams with broken shells or that do not shut immediately when sharply tapped. Heat the oil in a pan, add the garlic and clams and cook for about 5 minutes until the shells open. Remove the pan from the heat and lift out the clams with a slotted spoon. Discard any that remain closed. Remove the clams from their shells. Strain the cooking liquid into a skillet and add the clams. Meanwhile, cook the vermicelli in a large pan of salted, boiling water until al dente, then drain and tip into the skillet. Cook for 2 minutes, tossing frequently, then season with salt and pepper to taste and sprinkle with the parsley. Tip onto a warm serving dish.

POLENTA

There are two common types of polenta: fine-grained, pale straw-colored Veneto polenta and large-grained, bright golden-yellow Lombard or Piedmontese polenta. The former is almost always served all'onda (literally 'with wave', meaning with a consistency similar to mashed potato), while the latter is almost always firm. Both, however, are stirred and stirred again in a copper pot with a softwood stick, traditionally over the flames of an open fire. At least, once upon a time it was like that. Today, polenta has caught up with the times and modern kitchen appliances. In fact it can even 'cook itself' in an electric, copper polenta pot or be purchased ready-made at some Italian delicatessens. There is also a third kind of polenta flour, buckwheat flour, which is used to make polenta taragna.

TO SERVE 6

About 3²/₃ cups polenta flour and 7¹/₂ cups water; the proportions vary according to how firm the polenta must be for the recipe.

WATER

Bring salted water to a boil and keep another pan of water boiling in case it is needed.

POLENTA FLOUR

Sprinkle it into the pan while stirring constantly.

ADDITIONS

As soon as the polenta thickens, soften it with a drop of the reserved hot water. This is the secret to cooking polenta successfully, as polenta thickens with heat and softens with water.

COOKING TIME

This ranges from 45 minutes to 1 hour; the longer the cooking time, the more easily the polenta is digested.

SAUCES

Simple cold milk, fresh or melted butter, tomato sauce and cheese such as Gorgonzola or fontina. Polenta can also be served with stews and braised meat, or baked with cheese, butter and ragù (meat sauce).

STORAGE

Polenta flour must be kept dry, otherwise it goes moldy. Cooked polenta should be stored wrapped in a dish towel in the bottom of the refrigerator.

QUANTITIES
AND COOKING METHOD

POLENTA GNOCCHI

GNOCCHI DI POLENTA

Serves 4

scant 2¹/₂ cups coarse polenta flour

¹/₄ cup butter, plus extra for greasing

¹/₂ cup Parmesan cheese, freshly grated

salt and pepper

Make a fairly soft polenta (see page 305). When it is ready, pour it onto a counter or tray, spread out to a layer ¹/₂ inch thick and let cool and set. When it is cold, stamp out rounds using a wet glass or a cookie cutter. Preheat the oven to 350°F. Grease a wide cookie sheet with butter and arrange the polenta rounds on it in concentric circles. Top with another layer of polenta rounds, omitting the outer circle, and continue in the same way until a pyramid is formed. Sprinkle with the Parmesan, season with pepper and dot with the butter. Bake for about 20 minutes until golden brown.

POLENTA SOUP

MINESTRA DI POLENTA

Serves 4

6 tablespoons butter

1 onion, chopped

4 cups milk

1³/₄ cups coarse polenta flour

scant ¹/₂ cup heavy cream

¹/₂ cup Parmesan cheese, freshly grated

salt and pepper

Melt 3 tablespoons of the butter in a pan, add the onion and cook over low heat, stirring occasionally, for 10 minutes until lightly browned. Meanwhile, bring the milk to just below simmering point in another pan, then remove from the heat. Stir the polenta flour into the onion and cook, stirring constantly, for 2–3 minutes. Gradually stir in the warm milk and 2¹/₄ cups warm water. Season with salt and pepper to taste and cook for 1 hour. Stir in the cream, the remaining butter and the Parmesan and serve.

POLENTA WITH GORGONZOLA

POLENTA AL GORGONZOLA

Serves 4

scant 2¹/₂ cups coarse polenta flour

²/₃ cup butter, cut into 4 pieces

5 ounces Gorgonzola cheese, sliced

salt

Parmesan cheese, freshly grated, to serve

Make a fairly stiff polenta with 5 cups salted water (see page 305). Preheat the oven to 350°F. Pour the polenta into soup plates or individual ovenproof dishes while it is still hot. Put a piece of butter in the middle of each, pushing it down slightly into the polenta, and lay a small slice of Gorgonzola on top. Bake until the butter and Gorgonzola have completely melted. Serve with Parmesan.

POLENTA WITH LANGOUSTINES AND RADICCHIO

Make a soft polenta (see page 305). Meanwhile, place the radicchio strips in a large salad bowl. Heat the oil and garlic in a pan and cook for a few minutes until the garlic browns, then remove it from the pan. Add the langoustines or shrimp and cook for a few minutes over high heat. Season with salt and pepper and stir in the lemon juice. Tip into the salad bowl and mix well. When the polenta is ready, pour it over the langoustines or shrimp and radicchio, let stand for a few minutes, then serve.

POLENTA CON GLI SCAMPI E LA CICORIA

Serves 4

scant 2^1/$_2$ cups coarse polenta flour

2 heads radicchio, cut into strips

2 tablespoons olive oil

1 garlic clove

11 ounces langoustines

or jumbo shrimp, peeled

juice of ^{1}/$_2$ lemon, strained

salt and pepper

POLENTA WITH COD

Heat the oil in a pan, add the onion and cook over low heat, stirring occasionally, for 10 minutes until lightly browned. Add the anchovies, garlic and walnuts, cook for a few minutes, then add the tomatoes, rosemary and parsley and cook for a further 10 minutes. Add the cod and potatoes, season with salt and pepper and cook for about 1 hour or until the potatoes have almost disintegrated and the sauce has thickened. Meanwhile, make the polenta (see page 305). Turn it out onto a warm serving dish, place the cod and sauce in the middle and serve.

POLENTA CON IL MERLUZZO

Serves 4

4 salted anchovies, heads removed, cleaned and filleted (see page 596), soaked in cold water for 10 minutes and drained

3 tablespoons olive oil

1 onion, chopped

1 garlic clove, chopped

8 walnuts, chopped

3 tomatoes, peeled, seeded and chopped

pinch of chopped fresh rosemary

1 fresh flat-leaf parsley sprig, chopped

1^3/$_4$ pounds cod fillet, skinned and diced

2 potatoes, diced

2^1/$_4$ cups coarse polenta flour

salt and pepper

POLENTA WITH MEAT SAUCE

Heat the oil and butter in a pan, add the onion, carrot and celery and cook over low heat, stirring occasionally, for 10 minutes until browned. Add the meat, season with salt and pepper and cook for a few minutes more. Mix the tomato sauce with 1–2 tablespoons warm water in a bowl, add to the pan and cook over low heat for about 1 hour, adding more water if necessary. Meanwhile, prepare the polenta (see page 305). When it is ready, pour it into a nonstick ring mold, rinsed out with cold water, let stand for 2–3 minutes, then turn it out onto a warm serving dish. Pour the hot meat sauce into the middle and serve with Parmesan.

POLENTA CON IL RAGÙ

Serves 4

2 tablespoons olive oil

2 tablespoons butter

1 onion, chopped

1 carrot, chopped

1 celery stalk, chopped

1^3/$_4$ cups ground beef

3 tablespoons Tomato Sauce (see page 57)

scant 2^1/$_2$ cups coarse polenta flour

salt and pepper

Parmesan cheese, freshly grated, to serve

POLENTA WITH FONDUE

POLENTA CON LA FONDUTA

Serves 4

scant 2¹/₂ cups coarse polenta flour

3 tablespoons butter

1 quantity Piedmontese Fondue (see page 995)

1 black truffle, thinly sliced

salt

Make a fairly firm polenta (see page 305). When it is ready, beat in the butter. Rinse a nonstick ring mold with cold water, pour in the polenta and smooth the surface. Turn out onto a serving dish. Pour the fondue into the middle of the ring so that it flows over the sides. Sprinkle with the slices of truffle and serve.

POLENTA WITH RICOTTA

POLENTA CON LA RICOTTA

Serves 4

scant 2¹/₂ cups coarse polenta flour

1¹/₃ cups ricotta cheese

3 tablespoons olive oil

1 onion, chopped

¹/₃ cup pancetta, diced

11 ounces tomatoes, peeled and diced

2 tablespoons butter, plus extra for greasing

²/₃ cup Parmesan cheese, freshly grated

salt and pepper

Prepare the polenta (see page 305), pour it onto a counter or tray and let cool and set, then cut it into slices. Beat the ricotta in a bowl until smooth. Heat the oil in a small pan, add the onion and pancetta and cook over low heat, stirring occasionally, for 5 minutes. Add the tomatoes, season with salt and pepper according to taste and simmer for 30 minutes. Preheat the oven to 350°F. Grease an oven-proof dish with butter. Arrange the polenta, ricotta, Parmesan and tomato sauce in layers in the prepared dish, finishing with a layer of polenta. Dot with the butter and bake for 20–25 minutes.

POLENTA WITH SAUSAGE

POLENTA CON LA SALCICCIA

Serves 4

7 ounces Italian sausages, cut into short lengths

2 tablespoons olive oil

1 onion, chopped

1 carrot, chopped

1 celery stalk, chopped

2¹/₄ cups bottled strained tomatoes

scant 2¹/₄ cups coarse polenta flour

salt and pepper

Prick the sausages, place in a dry skillet and cook over medium heat for 5–6 minutes until the fat runs, then remove with a slotted spoon. Heat the oil in a pan, add the onion, carrot and celery and cook for 2 minutes. Pour in the strained tomatoes, season with salt and pepper to taste and cook for 20 minutes. Add the sausages and continue cooking for a further 10 minutes. Meanwhile, make the polenta (see page 305). When it is ready, turn it out onto a warm serving dish, spoon the sausage and tomato sauce all around and serve.

POLENTA WITH EGGS

Make the polenta (see page 305). Preheat the oven to 350°F. A few minutes before the polenta is ready, beat in the butter. Make shirred eggs (see page 359). Pour the polenta onto a warm serving dish and lay the shirred eggs on top.

POLENTA CON LE UOVA

Serves 4

scant 2¹/₂ cups coarse polenta flour

3 tablespoons butter, plus extra for the eggs

8 eggs

salt

VALLE D'AOSTA POLENTA PASTICCIATA

Prepare a fairly stiff polenta (see page 305). Pour it onto a counter or tray and let cool and set, then cut into slices. Preheat the oven to 350°F and grease an ovenproof dish with butter. Arrange a layer of polenta in the prepared dish, place the slices of fontina on top, sprinkle with the Parmesan and dot with the butter. Continue making alternate layers, ending with a layer of polenta dotted with the butter. Season with pepper and bake for about 20 minutes.

POLENTA PASTICCIATA ALLA VALDOSTANA

Serves 4

2¹/₄ cups coarse polenta flour

6 tablespoons butter, plus extra for greasing

11 ounces fontina cheese, thinly sliced

1 cup Parmesan cheese, freshly grated

salt and pepper

POLENTA PASTICCIATA WITH MUSHROOMS

Place the mushrooms in a bowl, add warm water to cover and let soak for 20 minutes. Make a fairly stiff polenta (see page 305). When it is ready, pour it onto a counter or tray and let cool and set. Meanwhile, melt half the butter in a pan, add the garlic and cook until it turns golden brown, then discard it. Drain the mushrooms, squeezing out as much liquid as possible, and add to the pan. Season with salt and pepper and cook for 10 minutes. Stir the mushrooms and their cooking juices into the béchamel sauce with half the Parmesan. Preheat the oven to 350°F and grease an ovenproof dish with butter. Cut the cold polenta into slices and arrange in alternating layers with the mushroom mixture in the prepared dish, ending with a layer of polenta. Dot with the remaining butter, sprinkle with the remaining Parmesan and bake for about 1 hour.

POLENTA PASTICCIATA CON I FUNGHI

Serves 4

1³/₄ cups dried mushrooms

2¹/₂ cups coarse polenta flour

¹/₄ cup butter, plus extra for greasing

1 garlic clove

1 quantity Béchamel Sauce (see page 50)

²/₃ cup Parmesan cheese, freshly grated

salt and pepper

POLENTA PASTICCIATA WITH ANCHOVIES

Prepare a fairly stiff polenta (see page 305) using 2¼ cups salted water and the wine. When it is ready, pour it onto a counter or tray and let cool and set, then cut into slices. Preheat the oven to 350°F and grease an ovenproof dish with butter. Melt 4 tablespoons of the butter in a pan, add the garlic and cook for 1 minute. Lower the heat, add the anchovies and cook, mashing with a wooden spoon until they have almost completely disintegrated. Remove the garlic, pour in the cream, season with pepper and cook for a few minutes more. Make alternate layers of polenta and anchovy sauce in the prepared dish, ending with a layer of polenta. Sprinkle with the Parmesan, dot with the remaining butter and bake until golden brown.

POLENTA PASTICCIATA
CON LE ACCIUGHE

Serves 4

2¼ cups coarse polenta flour

2¼ cups dry white wine

3½ ounces salted anchovies, heads removed, cleaned and filleted (see page 596), soaked in cold water for 10 minutes and drained

6 tablespoons butter, plus extra for greasing

1 garlic clove

scant 1 cup heavy cream

⅓ cup Parmesan cheese, freshly grated

salt and pepper

POLENTA TARAGNA

Pour 6¼ cups water into a pan and add salt. Bring to a boil and sprinkle in both types of flour together, stirring constantly. Cook, stirring constantly, for 30 minutes, then gradually beat in the butter. When the polenta has absorbed all the butter, add the cheese. Continue to stir for a few minutes more, then serve while hot. Fried sausages may be added if you like.

POLENTA TARAGNA

Serves 4

2¼ cups buckwheat flour

¾ cup coarse polenta flour

⅔ cup butter, cut into pieces

7 ounces soft cheese, thinly sliced

salt

RICE

Luckily, there is a lot of rice – some 450 million tons are harvested every year throughout the world. Rice belongs to the family Gramineae and contains protein, fats, carbohydrates, sodium, potassium, calcium, phosphorus, iron and other nutritional essentials; and ¹/₂ cup provides 350 calories. It is a highly recommended food because it cannot be adulterated and is easy to digest. Furthermore, it goes well with meat, legumes, vegetables, fruit and milk.

TYPES OF RICE AND COOKING METHODS

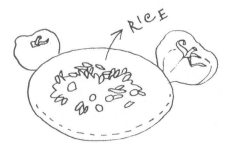

QUANTITIES

Allow ¹/₃ cup per serving in broth, ¹/₂ cup for risotto and scant ¹/₂ cup as a side dish. The quantity also depends on the other ingredients with which it is served.

ORDINARY

These include Originario and Balilla for soups and desserts; 12–13 minutes cooking time.

SEMI–FINE

These include Maratelli and Ardizzone for antipasti, timbales and croquettes; 13–15 minutes cooking time.

FINE

These include Rizzotto and Vialone for risottos, salads and pilafs; 16 minutes cooking time.

SUPERFINE

These include Arborio, Sesia and Carnaroli for risottos and side dishes; about 18 minutes cooking time.

EASY COOK

This is a factory-produced, parboiled rice that does not overcook and can be stored in the refrigerator for three days after cooking.

FOREIGN

Basmati, an Indian rice which goes well with shrimp and crab meat; Jasmine and Thai, which are excellent boiled with red beans or cooked in coconut milk as a side dish; Patna and Carolina rice with a slightly nutty taste, which is stronger when whole-grain; Tilda rices, which are excellent steamed; Giant Canadian Wild, a long black thin rice 'discovered' by Native Americans and currently very fashionable.

BAKED RICE (BASIC RECIPE)

Cook the rice in a pan with plenty of salted, boiling water for no longer than 7–8 minutes. Drain well until the rice is dry. Melt some butter in an ovenproof dish and add the rice. Bake in a preheated oven, 225°F, for about 45 minutes. Baked rice may be served with various delicately flavored or fiery hot sauces, or meat, liver or mushroom ragù. It may also be served with several types of vegetables seasoned in a variety of ways.

COTTURA AL FORNO (RICETTA BASE)

Quantities of rice and water will vary according to requirements (see opposite)

CREOLE RICE (BASIC RECIPE)

Allow 4 cups water, about ¼ cup butter and a pinch of salt per 2½ cups rice. Bring the salted water to a boil in a pan, add the butter and when it has melted add the rice. Cook for just under 20 minutes until the rice has absorbed all the liquid. Drain, fluff up the grains with a fork and dot with a little butter. Alternatively, it may be served with light or medium meat, mushroom, liver or vegetable ragù.

*COTTURA ALLA CREOLA
(RICETTA BASE)*

Quantities of rice and water will vary according to requirements (see opposite)

RICE COOKED IN MILK (BASIC RECIPE)

This dish may be sweet or savory. In both cases, allow 2¼ cups milk per ½ cup rice. Bear in mind that rice absorbs less milk if it is first par-boiled in lightly salted water for 2–3 minutes. When used as a garnish, for making croquettes or as a pudding, use the following proportions: put ¾ cup rice in 4 cups milk and add 2 tablespoons butter and a pinch of salt. Cook on the stovetop for the first 10 minutes, then continue in a medium oven, 350°F, for about 20 minutes, without stirring. When the rice is tender, beat 2 eggs with a pinch of salt and stir in. Even without eggs, this dish has a delicious, delicate taste. To make dessert rice, proceed in the same way, but add ½ cup superfine sugar and a dash of vanilla essence at the end.

COTTURA AL LATTE (RICETTA BASE)

Quantities of rice and water will vary according to requirements (see opposite)

313

INDIAN RICE (BASIC RECIPE)

COTTURA ALL'INDIANA (RICETTA BASE)

Quantities of rice and water will vary according to requirements (see page 312)

Cook the rice in plenty of salted, boiling water. When it is tender, drain and refresh under cold running water. Drain again, spread out on a cookie sheet or in a roasting pan and put in a warm oven for 10–15 minutes, separating the grains occasionally with a fork. All curries call for rice cooked in this way.

BOILED RICE (BASIC RECIPE)

COTTURA PER RISO BOLLITO (RICETTA BASE)

Quantities of rice and water will vary according to requirements (see page 312)

This is the simplest way of cooking rice. Pour the rice slowly into salted, boiling water and cook over high heat for 15–18 minutes according to type. It may be seasoned with melted butter or simply with olive oil and cheese. The same method is used for rice salads. In this case the rice should be a superfine variety, and is drained when tender and rinsed under cold running water before dressing.

WHOLE–GRAIN RICE (BASIC RECIPE)

COTTURA PER RISO INTEGRALE (RICETTA BASE)

Quantities of rice and water will vary according to requirements (see page 312)

Dark whole-grain rice takes a long time to cook. Allow $2^1/_4$ cups water per 1 cup rice. Put the required quantity of rice and cold water in a pan with a little salt, bring to a boil and cook for about 30 minutes. When it is tender, the rice should be dry and the water should be completely absorbed. Season according to taste.

PILAF RICE (BASIC RECIPE)

COTTURA PER RISO PILAF (RICETTA BASE)

Quantities of rice and water will vary according to requirements (see page 312)

Preheat the oven to 350°F. Pilaf means rice in Turkish, so obviously this is Turkish-style rice. Melt the butter in a fairly shallow, ovenproof pan, add the chopped onion and cook over low heat for 5 minutes until softened. Add the rice and a pinch of salt and stir until the rice is thoroughly coated in the butter. Pour boiling water or stock to cover, 4 cups per $2^1/_2$ cups rice, bring back to a boil, then cover the pan and place in the oven. Bake without uncovering or stirring for 18–20 minutes. Before serving, stir in a pat of butter. Pilaf is usually served with shellfish, shrimp, langoustines, chicken in egg sauce, mushrooms, etc.

SICILIAN CROQUETTES

Cook the rice in plenty of salted, boiling water for 15–18 minutes until tender. Drain, tip into a bowl and stir in half the butter and the Parmesan, then spread the rice out on the counter and let cool. Melt the remaining butter in a pan, add the beef and cook, stirring frequently, until browned all over. Sprinkle with the wine and cook until it has evaporated. Stir in the tomato paste, cover and cook over low heat for 15 minutes, then season with salt and remove from the heat. Shape the cooled rice into croquettes as large as small oranges – hence the name arancini – and hollow out the centers. Fill with a little meat sauce and a cube of mozzarella and seal with more rice. Beat the eggs with a pinch of salt in a shallow dish and spread out the flour in another shallow dish. Dip the croquettes in the beaten eggs, then in the flour and shake off any excess. Heat the oil in a deep-fryer or pan to 350–375°F or until a cube of day-old bread browns in 30 seconds. Deep-fry the croquettes in the hot oil until golden brown all over. Drain on paper towels and serve.

ARANCINI ALLA SICILIANA

Serves 4

1¹/₂ cups long-grain rice

¹/₄ cup butter

2 tablespoons Parmesan cheese, freshly grated

scant ¹/₂ cup ground lean beef

scant ¹/₂ cup dry white wine

2 tablespoons tomato paste

3¹/₂ ounces mozzarella cheese, diced

2 eggs

¹/₂ cup all-purpose flour

vegetable oil, for deep-frying

salt

RICE WITH CURRY SAUCE AND SHRIMP

Preheat the oven to 425°F and grease a ring mold with butter. Bring the stock to a boil. Melt the butter in a roasting pan, add the onion and cook over low heat, stirring occasionally, for 5 minutes until softened. Add the rice and stir until it is thoroughly coated in the butter. Add the stock, cover the pan with foil and place in the oven for about 17 minutes. Meanwhile, cook the shrimp in salted, boiling water for 2 minutes, then drain. Take the rice out of the oven, spoon into the prepared mold and tap the mold on the counter to get rid of any air pockets. Gently turn the molds out onto a warm serving dish and garnish it with the shrimp. Spoon the curry sauce over the rice and serve immediately.

RISO AL CURRY CON GAMBERI

Serves 4

3 tablespoons butter, plus extra for greasing

3 cups Fish or Chicken Stock
(see pages 208–209)

1 onion, sliced

1³/₄ cups long-grain rice

12 ounces large raw shrimp, peeled

1 quantity Curry Sauce (see page 54)

salt

CANTONESE RICE

Melt half the butter in a pan, add the rice and stir until it is thoroughly coated in the butter. Add the stock and season with salt and pepper. Cover and simmer for 15 minutes without stirring. Melt the remaining butter in another pan, add the onions and cook over low heat, stirring occasionally, for 5 minutes. Add the chicken, season with salt and cook, stirring occasionally, for a further 15 minutes. Just before the rice is ready, stir the almonds into it. Spoon the rice and almonds onto a warm serving dish and top with the chicken mixture. Serve with soy sauce.

RISO ALLA CANTONESE

Serves 4

generous $1/2$ cup butter

$1^1/2$ cups long-grain rice

4 cups Chicken Stock (see page 209)

2 onions, chopped

2 skinless, boneless chicken breasts, diced

$1/4$ cup blanched almonds, coarsely chopped

salt and pepper

soy sauce, to serve

RICE WITH MINT

Combine the mint, leek, lemon juice and olive oil in a bowl and season with salt and pepper. Cook the rice in plenty of salted, boiling water until tender. Drain well and season with the fresh mint sauce. Be aware that the taste of mint does not go well with wine.

RISO ALLA MENTA

serves 4

8 fresh mint leaves, chopped

1 leek, white part only finely chopped

juice of 1 lemon, strained

$2/3$ cup pint olive oil

$1^3/4$ cups long-grain rice

salt and pepper

RICE WITH CARROTS AND WALNUTS

Preheat the oven to 350°F. Rinse the rice under cold running water, then put in a pan with 3 cups water. Add a pinch of salt, bring to a boil and cook over low heat for 15 minutes. Stir in the carrots, cover and cook for a further 15 minutes until all the water has been absorbed and the rice is tender. Meanwhile, spread out the walnuts on a cookie sheet and toast in the oven for a few minutes until golden. When cool enough to handle, chop the nuts. When the rice is tender, stir in the walnuts and corn oil and heat through for a few minutes, then transfer to a warm serving dish.

RISO ALLE CAROTE E NOCI

Serves 4

$1^3/4$ cups whole-grain rice

7 ounces carrots, sliced

$1/2$ cup shelled walnuts

2 tablespoons corn oil

salt

INDONESIAN RICE

RISO ALL'INDONESIANA

Serves 4

1 chicken, weighing about 1 pound 2 ounces

1¹/₄ cups peas, shelled

3 tablespoons olive oil

1¹/₃ cups long-grain rice

4 cups Chicken Stock (see page 209)

scant 1 cup cooked, cured ham, diced

1¹/₄ teaspoons curry powder

salt and pepper

Remove and discard the chicken skin and cut the meat off the bones into fairly neat pieces. Place the chicken meat in a pan, add 6¹/₄ cups water and bring to a boil, then lower the heat and simmer for 40 minutes. Add the peas and season lightly with salt and pepper. Heat the oil in another pan, add the rice and cook, stirring constantly, until it has changed color. Stir in a ladleful of stock, and the ham and curry powder. Gradually add more stock as each ladleful is absorbed. Add the chicken and peas to the rice and cook until the rice is tender. Season with salt and pepper to taste and serve in individual bowls or soup plates.

RICE WITH RAW EGG

RISO ALL'UOVO CRUDO

Serves 4

1³/₄ cups long-grain rice • 4 egg yolks

3¹/₂ ounces fontina cheese, thinly sliced

2 tablespoons butter

¹/₂ cup Parmesan cheese,

freshly grated, plus extra to serve • salt

Cook the rice in plenty of salted, boiling water for 15–18 minutes until tender. Meanwhile, beat the egg yolks in a large bowl and add a pinch of salt and the fontina. Drain the rice, spoon it into the bowl and mix quickly so that the egg coats the rice like a cream. Stir in the butter and Parmesan, transfer to a warm serving dish and serve with extra Parmesan.

CURRIED RICE AND LENTILS

RISO CON LENTICCHIE AL CURRY

Serves 4

²/₃ cup lentils

1³/₄ cups long-grain rice

2 teaspoons curry powder

3 tablespoons butter

salt

Put the lentils in a pan, add water to cover, bring to a boil and simmer for 30 minutes. Drain, reserving 2¹/₄ cups of the cooking liquid. Put the rice in a pan, add the reserved cooking liquid, the curry powder, butter and a pinch of salt. Bring to a boil and simmer for 15–20 minutes until the rice is tender and all the liquid has been absorbed. Stir in the lentils and transfer to a warm serving dish.

RICE WITH SPINACH

RISO CON SPINACI

Serves 4

1 pound 5 ounces spinach

3 tablespoons butter

1³/₄ cups long-grain rice

¹/₂ cup Parmesan cheese, freshly grated

salt

Cook the spinach in 2¹/₄ cups lightly salted, boiling water for 5 minutes, then drain, reserving the cooking liquid. Squeeze out as much liquid as possible and chop. Melt half the butter in a skillet, add the spinach and cook over low heat for 5 minutes. Cook the rice in the reserved cooking liquid for 15–18 minutes until tender, then drain, tip into a warm serving dish and stir in the remaining butter. Top the rice with the spinach and sprinkle with the Parmesan.

SEASONED BOILED RICE

RISO IN CAGNONE

Serves 4

1³/₄ cups long-grain rice

2 tablespoons butter

8 fresh sage leaves

¹/₂ cup Parmesan cheese, freshly grated

salt

Cook the rice in plenty of salted, boiling water for 15–18 minutes until tender, then drain. Meanwhile, melt the butter in a small pan, add the sage leaves and cook for a few minutes until lightly browned. While the rice is still very hot, pour the sage butter over it, sprinkle with the Parmesan and serve.

MOLDED RICE WITH HAM AND PEAS

RISO IN FORMA CON PROSCIUTTO E PISELLI

Serves 4

¹/₄ cup butter, plus extra for greasing

¹/₂ onion, chopped

2¹/₄ cups frozen peas

²/₃ cup Meat Stock (see page 208)

3¹/₂ ounces fontina cheese, diced

3¹/₂ ounces mozzarella cheese, diced

3¹/₂ ounces Emmenthal cheese, diced

scant 1 cup milk

1¹/₂ cups long-grain rice

7 ounces cooked, cured ham, sliced

salt

Preheat the oven to 400°F. Grease a ring mold with butter. Melt the butter in a small pan, add the onion and cook over low heat, stirring occasionally, for 10 minutes until golden brown. Add the peas, a pinch of salt and the stock, bring to a boil and simmer, uncovered, for 8 minutes or until the peas are tender. Place the cheeses in a bowl, add the milk and set aside. Cook the rice in plenty of salted, boiling water for 15–18 minutes until tender, then drain and tip into a bowl. Drain the cheeses and stir them into the rice. Line the prepared mold with slices of ham, spoon in the rice and press down well. Bake for 5 minutes, then turn out onto a warm serving dish and spoon the peas into the center.

BAKED RICE WITH PARSLEY

RISO IN FORNO AL PREZZEMOLO

Serves 4

1³/₄ cups long-grain rice

4 tablespoons olive oil

1 shallot, chopped

2 fresh flat-leaf parsley sprigs, chopped

salt and pepper

Parmesan cheese, freshly grated, to serve

Preheat the oven to 350°F. Cook the rice in plenty of salted, boiling water for 7–8 minutes, then drain until very dry. Tip it into an ovenproof dish, stir in half the oil, cover with foil and put in the oven for about 20 minutes. Meanwhile, heat the remaining oil in a skillet, add the shallot and parsley and cook over low heat, stirring occasionally for 5 minutes until softened. Season with salt and pepper according to taste and stir into the rice. Serve with Parmesan.

MINI RICE CROQUETTES WITH MOZZARELLA

Cook the rice in plenty of salted, boiling water for 7–8 minutes, then drain and tip into a large bowl. Add the mozzarella, ham and egg yolks, mix well, then stir in the Parmesan. Shape the mixture into oval croquettes the size of walnuts. Place the flour in a shallow dish, beat the egg with salt and pepper in another shallow dish and place the bread crumbs in a third shallow dish. Dip the croquettes first in the flour, then in the beaten egg and finally in the bread crumbs. Heat the oil in a deep-fryer or pan to 350–375°F or until a cube of day-old bread browns in 30 seconds. Add the croquettes, in batches, and cook until golden brown. Remove with a slotted spoon and drain on paper towels. Serve while still very hot.

MINI SUPPLÌ DI RISO CON MOZZARELLA

Serves 4

1¼ cups long-grain rice

7 ounces mozzarella cheese, diced

generous ½ cup cooked, cured ham, finely diced

2 egg yolks

1 cup Parmesan cheese, freshly grated

½ cup all-purpose flour

1 egg

1 cup bread crumbs

vegetable oil, for deep-frying

salt and pepper

PAELLA

Preheat the oven to 425°F. Discard any shellfish with broken shells or that do not shut immediately when sharply tapped. Cut the fish into chunks. Heat 4 tablespoons of the oil in a flameproof casserole, add the fish and cook over medium heat, stirring occasionally, for 5 minutes, then add the bell peppers and shellfish, lower the heat, cover and cook until the shells open. Discard any shellfish that remain closed. Meanwhile, heat the remaining oil in a pan, add the onion and cook over low heat, stirring occasionally, for 5 minutes until softened, then stir in the rice. When the rice has changed color, pour in the stock, stir in the garlic and cook for 12 minutes. Pour the rice into the casserole, mix well, increase the heat and cook for a few minutes more. Drizzle with oil and season with salt and pepper. Transfer the casserole to the oven and bake for 5 minutes. Serve straight from the casserole. There are numerous versions of this classic Spanish dish. Some recipes include artichoke wedges, chicken, pork, turkey, smoked bacon or saffron, depending on the region.

PAELLA

Serves 4

12 ounces shellfish, such as clams and mussels, scrubbed and beards removed

1 pound 5 ounces mixed fish, such as sea bass, hake and red mullet, filleted

7 tablespoons olive oil, plus extra for drizzling

1 red bell pepper, halved seeded and cut into strips

1 yellow bell pepper, halved seeded and cut into strips

1 onion, sliced

1¾ cups long-grain rice

2½ cups Chicken or Vegetable Stock (see page 209)

2 garlic cloves, crushed

salt and pepper

RICE
SALADS

Serves 4

1³/₄ cups long-grain rice

3 tablespoons olive oil

juice of 1 lemon, strained

1³/₄ cups cooked, peeled shrimp

3 tablespoons chopped fresh flat-leaf parsley

8 fresh basil leaves, torn

butter, for greasing

salt and pepper

RICE AND SHRIMP SALAD

Cook the rice in plenty of salted, boiling water for about 18 minutes until tender, then drain, rinse under cold running water and drain again. Tip into a bowl. Whisk together the olive oil and lemon juice in a pitcher and season with salt and pepper. Add the shrimp, parsley and basil to the rice, pour the dressing on top and toss gently. Grease a dome-shaped mold with butter and spoon in the rice mixture, pressing it down well. Turn out onto a serving dish and store in a cool place, but not the refrigerator, until ready to serve.

RISO IN INSALATA AL CURRY

Serves 4

1 1/2 cups long-grain rice

1/3 cup green beans

1 zucchini • 2 eggs, hard-cooked

1 celery stalk, finely chopped

2 tomatoes, peeled, seeded and diced

1 red bell pepper,

halved, seeded and finely chopped

4 radishes, thinly sliced • 3 tablespoons olive oil

1 tablespoon white wine vinegar

2 teaspoons curry powder

1 teaspoon Dijon mustard • salt

CURRIED RICE SALAD

Cook the rice in plenty of salted, boiling water for about 18 minutes until tender, then drain, rinse under cold running water and drain again. Tip into a salad bowl. Meanwhile, cook the green beans and zucchini in salted, boiling water for 8–10 minutes until tender, then drain and chop. Shell the eggs, cut in half and scoop out the yolks with a teaspoon. Finely chop the egg whites. Gently stir the beans, zucchini, celery, tomatoes, bell pepper, radishes and egg white into the rice. Whisk together the olive oil and vinegar in a bowl, crumble in the egg yolks, stir in the curry powder and mustard and season with salt. Pour the dressing over the rice, toss gently and serve immediately.

RISO IN INSALATA AL FORMAGGIO

Serves 4

1 1/2 cups long-grain rice

4 tablespoons olive oil • 1 apple

5 ounces Emmenthal cheese, diced

2 celery hearts including leaves, chopped

1/2 cup shelled walnuts, chopped

salt and pepper

RICE SALAD WITH CHEESE

Cook the rice in plenty of salted, boiling water for about 18 minutes until tender, then drain, rinse under cold running water and drain again. Tip into a salad bowl and stir in 3 tablespoons of the olive oil. Core and dice the apple and add to the rice with the Emmenthal, celery and walnuts. Stir in the remaining olive oil and season with salt and pepper to taste. Store in a cool place, but not the refrigerator, until ready to serve.

RISO IN INSALATA ALLA MARINARA

Serves 4

1 pound 2 ounces clams, scrubbed

1 pound 2 ounces mussels, scrubbed and

beards removed

11 ounces baby octopuses

1 1/4 cups long-grain rice

2 eggs, hard-cooked

3 tablespoons olive oil

1–2 teaspoons lemon juice, strained

salt

SEAFOOD RICE SALAD

Discard any clams and mussels with broken shells or that do not shut immediately when sharply tapped. Put the shellfish in two separate skillets and cook on high heat for 5 minutes until they have opened. Remove from the heat and discard any that remain closed. Remove the clams and mussels from their shells and set aside. Cook the baby octopuses in salted, boiling water for about 10 minutes, remove from the heat and let cool, then cut in half. Cook the rice in plenty of salted, boiling water for about 18 minutes until tender, then drain, rinse under cold running water and drain again. Tip into a salad bowl and add the clams, mussels and octopuses. Shell the eggs, cut in half and scoop out the yolks. Crumble the yolks into a bowl and gradually whisk in the olive oil a drop at a time. When the dressing has the desired consistency (you may not need all the oil), whisk in lemon juice to taste and season with salt. Sprinkle the dressing over the rice salad and store in a cool place, but not the refrigerator, until ready to serve.

RICE AND BEETS SALAD

Cook the rice in plenty of salted, boiling water for about 18 minutes until tender, then drain, rinse under cold running water and drain again. Tip into a salad bowl and add the cheese and capers. Shell and chop two of the eggs and add to the rice. Whisk together the oil, vinegar and mustard in a pitcher, season with salt and pepper and pour over the salad. Toss well and sprinkle the beet and parsley on top. Shell and slice the remaining egg and arrange over the salad.

RISO IN INSALATA CON BARBABIETOLE

Serves 4

1½ cups long-grain rice

3½ ounces Emmenthal cheese, diced

16 capers, rinsed • 3 eggs, hard-cooked

6 tablespoons olive oil

2 tablespoons white wine vinegar

1 teaspoon Dijon mustard

1 cooked beet, peeled and diced

1 fresh flat-leaf parsley sprig, finely chopped

salt and pepper

RICE SALAD WITH PICKLED BELL PEPPERS

Cook the rice in plenty of salted, boiling water for about 18 minutes until tender, then drain, rinse under cold running water and drain again. Tip into a bowl and stir in 2 tablespoons of the olive oil. Stir in the bell peppers and cornichons or dill pickles, then mix in the remaining oil and season with salt and pepper to taste. Spoon the rice into a round mold and press down well, then turn out onto a serving dish and cover completely with Parmesan shavings.

RISO IN INSALATA
CON PEPERONI SOTTACETO

Serves 4

1½ cups long-grain rice

3 tablespoons olive oil

1 jar (6¼ ounces) pickled bell peppers, drained and cut into strips

1 jar (6¼ ounces) cornichons or dill pickles, drained and chopped

1½ cups Parmesan cheese, shaved

salt and pepper

RICE AND CRAB MEAT SALAD

Cook the rice in plenty of salted, boiling water for about 18 minutes until tender, then drain, rinse under cold running water and drain again. Tip into a salad bowl and stir in 1 tablespoon of the oil and a pinch of pepper. Heat 2 tablespoons of the remaining oil in a pan, add the leeks and cook, stirring occasionally, for 5 minutes until soft. Add the peas, season with salt and cook over medium heat for 10 minutes until tender. Beat the eggs with a pinch of salt. Heat the remaining oil in a skillet, pour in the eggs, tilt the pan to spread them evenly over the base and cook until the underside is set. Flip the omelet over and cook until the second side is set. Slide out of the skillet and cut into strips. Pick over the crab meat and remove any pieces of cartilage or shell, then stir the meat into the rice with the leeks and peas and strips of omelet. Taste and adjust the seasoning if necessary. Store in a cool place, but not the refrigerator, until ready to serve.

RISO IN INSALATA
CON POLPA DI GRANCHIO

Serves 4

1½ cups long-grain rice

4 tablespoons olive oil

2 leeks, trimmed and sliced

1¾ cups peas, shelled

2 eggs

11 ounces crab meat, drained if canned

salt and pepper

LOW–FAT RICE SALAD

Cook the rice in plenty of salted, boiling water for about 18 minutes until tender, then drain and tip into a wide salad bowl while still warm. Arrange the tuna on top, followed by the corn, then the salmon, then the shrimp. Finally, sprinkle the capers on top. Drizzle with olive oil and season with salt and white pepper to taste. Mix thoroughly but gently so that the flavors blend.

RISO IN INSALATA DI MAGRO

Serves 4

1¼ cups long-grain rice

5 ounces canned tuna in oil, drained and flaked

scant 1 cup canned corn, drained

scant 1 cup smoked salmon, diced

1¾ cups shrimp, cooked and peeled

1 tablespoon capers, rinsed

olive oil, for drizzling

salt and white pepper

SMOKED FISH AND RICE SALAD

Bring the fish stock to a boil in a pan. Add the rice and cook for about 18 minutes until tender, then drain and let cool. Put the radishes, horseradish, salmon and swordfish into a salad bowl. Whisk together the olive oil, walnut oil, lemon juice and lime juice in a bowl and season with salt and pepper. Pour the dressing over the rice salad, toss and sprinkle with the dill. Store in a cool place, but not the refrigerator, until ready to serve.

RISO IN INSALATA DI PESCE AFFUMICATO

Serves 4

2¼ cups Concentrated Fish Stock
 (see page 210)

1½ cups long-grain rice

4 radishes, sliced

½-inch piece of fresh
horseradish root, chopped

1 smoked salmon slice, cut into strips

1 smoked swordfish slice, cut into strips

2 tablespoons olive oil

1 tablespoon walnut oil

juice of 1 lemon, strained

juice of 1 lime, strained

1 tablespoon chopped fresh dill

salt and pepper

SUMMER RICE SALAD

Cook the rice in plenty of salted, boiling water until tender, then drain, rinse under cold running water and drain again. Meanwhile, put the tuna, cheese, tomatoes and capers into a salad bowl. Add the rice and mix well so that it soaks up the flavors. Whisk together the olive oil and lemon juice in a bowl, then pour the dressing over the salad and toss. Finally, mix in the onions and artichokes.

RISO IN INSALATA ESTIVO

Serves 4

1½ cups easy cook rice

9 ounces canned tuna in oil, drained and flaked

7 ounces Swiss cheese, diced

4 tomatoes, seeded and diced

2 tablespoons capers, rinsed

3 tablespoons olive oil

juice of 1 lemon, strained

8 pickled pearl onions

8 baby artichokes in oil

salt

RISOTTOS

Rice is the most popular grain in the world but the way of cooking risotto is quintessentially Italian. Its texture varies in relation to regional tastes but the method of its preparation always remains the same. Despite variations in many recipes, the general rule is that, after 'toasting' the rice in a pan with a little oil or butter over low heat, you need to add hot stock, spoonful by spoonful. It is essential that you choose the right type of rice, such as Arborio or Carnaroli, as these will release starch and create a perfect, creamy mixture.

GARLIC

SEAFOOD RISOTTO

RISOTTO AI FRUTTI DI MARE

Serves 4

4 tablespoons olive oil
1 onion, chopped
1 garlic clove
1 pound 5 ounces cleaned mixed seafood, such as small octopus, cuttlefish and small squid
about 5 cups Fish Stock (see page 208)
³/₄ cup dry white wine
2 tablespoons tomato paste
scant 2 cups risotto rice
7 ounces shelled mussels
1 tablespoon chopped fresh flat-leaf parsley
salt and pepper

Heat the oil in a pan, add the onion and garlic and cook over low heat for 10 minutes until lightly browned. Remove and discard the garlic, add the seafood to the pan and cook for a few minutes more. Meanwhile, bring the stock to a boil in another pan. Sprinkle the wine over the seafood and cook until it has evaporated, then season to taste. Pour in 3 tablespoons water, add the tomato paste and cook for a further 10 minutes. Add the rice and cook, stirring constantly, until it has absorbed all the liquid. Add a ladleful of the hot stock and cook, stirring, until it has been absorbed. Continue adding the stock, a ladleful at a time, and stirring until each addition has been absorbed. This will take 18–20 minutes. When the rice is almost tender, add the mussels and mix gently. Sprinkle with the parsley and serve.

BLUEBERRY RISOTTO

Bring the stock to a boil. Meanwhile, melt the butter in another pan, add the onion and cook over low heat, stirring occasionally, for 5 minutes until softened. Add the rice and cook, stirring constantly, until the grains are coated in butter. Sprinkle in the wine and cook until it has evaporated. Set aside 2 tablespoons of the blueberries and add the remainder to the pan. Add a ladleful of the hot stock and cook, stirring, until it has been absorbed. Continue adding the stock, a ladleful at a time, and stirring until each addition has been absorbed. This will take 18–20 minutes. When the rice is tender, stir in the cream and transfer to a warm serving dish. Garnish with the reserved blueberries and serve with Parmesan.

RISOTTO AI MIRTILLI

Serves 4

about 6$\frac{1}{4}$ cups Vegetable
Stock (see page 209)

3 tablespoons butter

1 onion, finely chopped

2 cups risotto rice

$\frac{3}{4}$ cup white wine

1$\frac{3}{4}$ cups blueberries

scant $\frac{1}{2}$ cup light cream

Parmesan cheese, freshly grated, to serve

JERUSALEM ARTICHOKE RISOTTO

Bring the stock to a boil. Meanwhile, melt the butter in another pan, add the onion and cook over low heat, stirring occasionally, for 5 minutes until softened. Add the artichokes and cook, stirring occasionally, for a further 5 minutes. Add a ladleful of the stock and simmer for 20 minutes, then mash with a fork. Stir in the rice. Add a ladleful of the hot stock and cook, stirring, until it has been absorbed. Continue adding the stock, a ladleful at a time, and stirring until each addition has been absorbed. This will take 18–20 minutes. When the rice is tender, season with salt to taste and stir in the cream. Serve with Parmesan.

RISOTTO AI TOPINAMBUR

Serves 4

about 6$\frac{1}{4}$ cups Vegetable
Stock (see page 209)

3 tablespoons butter

1 onion, chopped

6 Jerusalem artichokes, sliced

2 cups risotto rice

1 tablespoon light cream

salt

Parmesan cheese, freshly grated, to serve

BAROLO AND MUSHROOM RISOTTO

Place the mushrooms in a bowl, add hot water to cover and let soak for 20 minutes, then drain and squeeze out. Melt the butter with the oil in another pan, add the garlic, onion, rosemary, sage and basil and cook over low heat, stirring occasionally, for 5 minutes. Add the tomatoes and cook for a further 15 minutes. Add the mushrooms, season with salt and pepper to taste, then cover and simmer for 15 minutes. Meanwhile, bring the stock to a boil. Stir the parsley and rice into the pan of vegetables and cook, stirring constantly, until the grains are coated in fat. Sprinkle in the wine and cook until it has evaporated. Add a ladleful of the hot stock and cook, stirring, until it has been absorbed. Continue adding the stock, a ladleful at a time, and stirring until each addition has been absorbed. This will take 18–20 minutes. When the rice is tender, sprinkle with the Parmesan and serve.

RISOTTO AL BAROLO CON FUNGHI

Serves 4

1$\frac{3}{4}$ cups dried mushrooms

3 tablespoons butter • 2 tablespoons olive oil

1 garlic clove, finely chopped

1 onion, finely chopped • 1 fresh rosemary sprig, finely chopped • 1 fresh sage sprig, finely chopped

1 fresh basil sprig, finely chopped

4 tomatoes, peeled and chopped

about 6$\frac{1}{4}$ cups Vegetable
Stock (see page 209)

1 fresh flat-leaf parsley sprig, finely chopped

2 cups risotto rice • scant 1 cup Barolo

1$\frac{1}{2}$ cups Parmesan cheese, freshly grated

salt and pepper

CAVIAR RISOTTO

RISOTTO AL CAVIALE

Serves 4

6 tablespoons butter

1 onion, chopped

2 cups risotto rice

1$\frac{1}{2}$ cups dry white wine

1 cup heavy cream

3 tablespoons caviar

salt and pepper

Melt the butter in a pan, add the onion and cook over low heat, stirring occasionally, for 5 minutes. Stir in the rice, then pour in the wine and bring just to a boil over low heat. Gradually, stir in the cream and cook, stirring, until the rice is tender, adding a little boiling water if necessary. Season with salt and pepper, remove the pan from the heat and add the caviar. Stir vigorously until the risotto is an even color, then serve.

MILANESE RISOTTO

RISOTTO ALLA MILANESE

Serves 4

about 6$\frac{1}{4}$ cups Meat Stock (see page 208)

$\frac{3}{4}$ ounces beef bone marrow

6 tablespoons butter

1 small onion, chopped

2 cups risotto rice

$\frac{1}{2}$ teaspoon saffron threads

1 cup Parmesan cheese, freshly grated

salt

Bring the stock to a boil. Heat the beef marrow with 4 tablespoons of the butter in another pan. Add the onion and cook over low heat, stirring occasionally, for 5 minutes. Stir in the rice and cook, stirring, until the grains are coated in butter. Add a ladleful of the hot stock and cook, stirring, until it has been absorbed. Continue adding the stock, a ladleful at a time, and stirring until each addition has been absorbed. This will take 18–20 minutes. Before adding the final ladleful of stock, stir the saffron into it. When the rice is tender, season with salt to taste, then remove the pan from the heat, stir in the remaining butter and the Parmesan and serve.

SALMON AND WINE RISOTTO

RISOTTO ALLA SALSA DI SALMONE E SPUMANTE

Serves 4

about 6$\frac{1}{4}$ cups Vegetable Stock (see page 209)

3 tablespoons butter

2 cups risotto rice

1$\frac{1}{2}$ cups sparkling white wine

3 ounces smoked salmon

Bring the stock to a boil. Melt half the butter in another pan, stir in the rice and cook, stirring, until the grains are coated in butter. Pour in the wine and cook until it has evaporated. Add a ladleful of the hot stock and cook, stirring, until it has been absorbed. Continue adding the stock, a ladleful at a time, and stirring until each addition has been absorbed. This will take 18–20 minutes. Meanwhile, finely chop half the salmon and coarsely chop the other half. Cream the remaining butter in a bowl and beat in the finely chopped salmon. About 2 minutes before the rice has finished cooking, stir in the butter mixture and coarsely chopped salmon.

CARROT RISOTTO

RISOTTO ALLE CAROTE

Serves 4

about 6¼ cups Vegetable
Stock (see page 209)

4 young carrots, chopped

¾ cup dry white wine

¼ cup butter

1 small onion, chopped

2 cups risotto rice

2 ounces Emmenthal cheese, shaved

2 tablespoons light cream

salt and pepper

Bring the stock to a boil. Meanwhile, put the carrots and wine in a food processor and process to a purée. Melt the butter in another pan, add the onion and cook over low heat, stirring occasionally, for 5 minutes. Add the carrot purée to the pan, increase the heat to medium and cook for a few seconds, then stir in the rice. Add a ladleful of the hot stock and cook, stirring, until it has been absorbed. Continue adding the stock, a ladleful at a time, and stirring until each addition has been absorbed. This will take 18–20 minutes. About 5 minutes before the rice is tender, season with salt and pepper to taste and stir in the Emmenthal and cream. Remove the pan from the heat, cover and let stand for 2 minutes before serving.

STRAWBERRY RISOTTO

RISOTTO ALLE FRAGOLE

Serves 4

about 6¼ cups Vegetable
Stock (see page 209)

7 tablespoons butter

1 onion, chopped

2 cups risotto rice

1½ cups dry white wine

2¾ cups strawberries, hulled

1 cup light cream

salt and pepper

Bring the stock to a boil. Melt half the butter in another pan, add the onion and cook over low heat, stirring occasionally, for 5 minutes. Add the rice and cook, stirring, until the grains are coated in butter. Pour in the wine and cook until it has evaporated. Add a ladleful of the hot stock and cook, stirring, until it has been absorbed. Continue adding the stock, a ladleful at a time, and stirring until each addition has been absorbed. This will take 18–20 minutes. Meanwhile, set a few whole strawberries aside, mash the remainder and add to the risotto about halfway through the cooking time. When the rice is almost tender, stir in the cream and season with salt and pepper. Serve garnished with the reserved strawberries.

EGGPLANT RISOTTO

Place the eggplant slices in a colander, sprinkle with salt and let drain in the sink for 30 minutes, then rinse well, pat dry with paper towels and chop. Bring the stock to a boil. Meanwhile, heat the olive oil in another pan, add the garlic and cook for a few minutes until browned, then remove and discard. Add the eggplants, stir in the tomato and oregano, increase the heat to high and cook for a few minutes. Stir in the rice. Add a ladleful of the hot stock and cook, stirring, until it has been absorbed. Continue adding the stock, a ladleful at a time, and stirring until each addition has been absorbed. This will take 18–20 minutes. About 5 minutes before the end of the cooking time, season with salt and pepper to taste and stir in the mozzarella. When the rice is tender, transfer to a warm serving dish.

RISOTTO ALLE MELANZANE

Serves 4

2 eggplants, sliced

about 6¼ cups Vegetable
Stock (see page 209)

2 tablespoons olive oil

1 garlic clove

1 ripe tomato, peeled, seeded and diced

pinch of dried oregano

2 cups risotto rice

7 ounces mozzarella cheese, diced

salt and pepper

NETTLE RISOTTO

Bring the stock to a boil. Meanwhile, melt the butter with the oil in another pan, add the nettles and cook over low heat, stirring occasionally, for a few minutes. Stir in the rice and cook, stirring, until the grains are coated in fat. Add the wine and cook until it has evaporated. Add a ladleful of the hot stock and cook, stirring, until it has been absorbed. Continue adding the stock, a ladleful at a time, and stirring until each addition has been absorbed. This will take 18–20 minutes. When the rice is almost tender, stir in the cream. When the rice is tender, remove the pan from the heat, stir in the Parmesan, cover and let stand for 2 minutes before serving.

RISOTTO ALLE ORTICHE

Serves 4

about 6¼ cups Vegetable
Stock (see page 209)

2 tablespoons butter

3 tablespoons olive oil

3²/₃ cups fresh young nettles, coarsely chopped

2 cups risotto rice

5 tablespoons dry white wine

scant 1 cup light cream

½ cup Parmesan cheese, freshly grated

RADICCHIO RISOTTO

Bring the stock to a boil. Meanwhile, melt half the butter in another pan, add the onion and cook over low heat, stirring occasionally, for 5 minutes. Stir in the radicchio, then stir in the rice and cook, stirring, until the grains are coated in butter. Pour in the wine and cook until it has evaporated. Add a ladleful of the hot stock and cook, stirring, until it has been absorbed. Continue adding the stock, a ladleful at a time, and stirring until each addition has been absorbed. This will take 18–20 minutes. When the rice is tender, season with salt to taste, stir in the remaining butter and the Parmesan and serve.

RISOTTO AL RADICCHIO TREVIGIANO

Serves 4

about 6¼ cups Vegetable
Stock (see page 209)

6 tablespoons butter

1 onion, chopped

7 ounces radicchio, cut into strips

2 cups risotto rice

5 tablespoons white wine

2 tablespoons Parmesan cheese, freshly grated

salt

SHRIMP RISOTTO

Bring 4 cups salted water to a boil, add the shrimp and cook for 2–3 minutes. Remove with a slotted spoon and peel and devein when cool enough to handle, reserving the shells. Crush the shells in a mortar with a pestle. Stick the onion with the cloves and add to the shrimp cooking liquid with the celery and carrot, then bring to a boil and simmer for 30 minutes. Remove and discard the cloves, transfer the contents of the pan to a food processor, add the crushed shells and process to a purée. Melt 4 tablespoons of the butter in a pan, stir in the rice and cook, stirring, until the grains are coated in butter. Add a ladleful of the purée and cook, stirring, until it has been absorbed. Continue adding the purée, a ladleful at a time, and stirring until each addition has been absorbed. This will take 18–20 minutes. Meanwhile, melt the remaining butter in a skillet. Add the shrimp and cook, stirring occasionally, for 4–5 minutes. When the rice is tender, transfer to a warm serving dish, arrange the shrimp around it and serve.

RISOTTO CON I GAMBERI

Serves 4

11 ounces large raw shrimp

1 onion

2 cloves

1 celery heart

1 carrot

6 tablespoons butter

2 cups risotto rice

salt

APPLE RISOTTO

Bring a pan of water to a boil, add the lemon rind and apples and parboil for 4–5 minutes. Drain well, discarding the lemon rind, and pat dry with paper towels. Melt 1 tablespoon of the butter in a skillet over high heat, add the apples and cook, stirring frequently, for 5 minutes. Meanwhile, bring the stock to a boil. Heat the olive oil in another pan, stir in the rice and cook, stirring, until the grains are coated in oil. Sprinkle in the wine and cook until it has evaporated. Add a ladleful of the hot stock and cook, stirring, until it has been absorbed. Continue adding the stock, a ladleful at a time, and stirring until each addition has been absorbed. This will take 18–20 minutes. After about 6 minutes of the cooking time, add the apples. When the rice is almost tender, stir in the Parmesan, Worcestershire sauce and remaining butter and season with salt and pepper to taste.

RISOTTO CON LE MELE

Serves 4

thinly pared strip of lemon rind

2 apples, peeled and diced

3 tablespoons butter

about 6$\frac{1}{4}$ cups Vegetable

Stock (see page 209)

2 tablespoons olive oil

2 cups risotto rice

5 tablespoons dry white wine

2 tablespoons, Parmesan cheese, freshly grated

1 tablespoon Worcestershire sauce

salt and pepper

CREAM AND ARUGULA RISOTTO

RISOTTO CON PANNA E RUCOLA

Serves 4

about 6¹/₄ cups Vegetable
Stock (see page 209)

3 tablespoons butter • 1 onion, finely chopped

2 cups risotto rice

5 tablespoons dry white wine

1¹/₂ tablespoons Parmesan cheese, freshly grated
plus extra to serve

³/₄ cup light cream

small bunch of arugula, chopped

salt and pepper

Bring the stock to a boil. Meanwhile, melt the butter in another pan, add the onion and cook over low heat, stirring occasionally, for 5 minutes. Stir in the rice and cook, stirring, until the grains are coated in butter. Sprinkle in the wine and cook until it has evaporated. Add a ladleful of the hot stock and cook, stirring, until it has been absorbed. Continue adding the stock, a ladleful at a time, and stirring until each addition has been absorbed. This will take 18–20 minutes. Just before the rice is tender, stir in the Parmesan and cream, sprinkle with the arugula and season with salt and pepper to taste. Transfer to a warm serving dish and serve with extra Parmesan.

BELL PEPPER RISOTTO

RISOTTO CON PEPERONI

Serves 4

about 6¹/₄ cups Vegetable
Stock (see page 209)

4 tablespoons olive oil • 1 onion, finely chopped

3 tomatoes, peeled, seeded and diced

3 red bell peppers, halved, seeded and cut into strips

1 fresh rosemary sprig, finely chopped

2 cups risotto rice

4 tablespoons Parmesan cheese, freshly grated

Bring the stock to a boil. Meanwhile, heat the oil in another pan, add the onion and cook over low heat, stirring occasionally, for 5 minutes. Add the tomatoes, bell peppers and rosemary and cook, stirring occasionally for a further 5 minutes. Stir in the rice and cook, stirring, until the grains are coated in oil. Add a ladleful of the hot stock and cook, stirring, until it has been absorbed. Continue adding the stock, a ladleful at a time, and stirring until each addition has been absorbed. This will take 18–20 minutes. When the rice is tender, stir in the Parmesan and serve.

ASPARAGUS RISOTTO

RISOTTO CON PUNTE DI ASPARAGI

Serves 4

1 pound 2 ounces asparagus, spears trimmed

about 6¹/₄ cups Vegetable
Stock (see page 209)

5 tablespoons butter

3 tablespoons olive oil

¹/₂ onion, chopped

2 cups risotto rice

salt

Parmesan cheese, freshly grated, to serve

Cook the asparagus in a pan of salted, boiling water for 10–12 minutes until tender, then drain and cut off and reserve the spears. Chop the stems and set aside. Bring the stock to a boil. Meanwhile, melt 1 tablespoon of the butter in a skillet, add the asparagus spears and cook over low heat, stirring occasionally, for 5 minutes, then remove from the heat and set aside. Melt 2 tablespoons of the remaining butter with the oil in a pan, add the onion and cook over low heat, stirring occasionally, for 5 minutes. Stir in the rice and cook, stirring, until the grains are coated in fat, then add the chopped asparagus stems. Add a ladleful of the hot stock and cook, stirring, until it has been absorbed. Continue adding the stock, a ladleful at a time, and stirring until it has been absorbed. This will take 18–20 minutes. When the rice is tender, stir in the remaining butter and the asparagus spears. Serve with Parmesan.

RISOTTO WITH SAUSAGES

Bring the stock to a boil. Meanwhile, melt 2 tablespoons of the butter in another pan, add the onion and crumbled sausages and cook over low heat, stirring occasionally, for 5 minutes. Stir in the rice and cook, stirring, until the grains are coated in butter. Pour in the wine and cook until it has evaporated. Add a ladleful of the hot stock and cook, stirring, until it has been absorbed. Continue adding the stock, a ladleful at a time, and stirring until each addition has been absorbed. This will take 18–20 minutes. When the rice is tender, remove the pan from the heat, stir in the Parmesan and remaining butter, transfer to a warm serving dish and serve.

RISOTTO CON SALSICCIA

Serves 4

about 6¼ cups Meat Stock (see page 208)

3 tablespoons butter

1 onion, chopped

9 ounces Italian sausages, skinned and crumbled

2 cups risotto rice

¾ cup red wine

4 tablespoons Parmesan cheese, freshly grated

PUMPKIN AND ARTICHOKE RISOTTO

Melt half the butter in a pan, add the pumpkin and cook, stirring occasionally, for 5 minutes. Season with salt, stir in 5 tablespoons water and simmer for 20 minutes. Meanwhile, break off the artichoke stems and discard the outer coarse leaves and the chokes, then cut into thin wedges. Add to the pan and cook for a further 15 minutes. Meanwhile, bring the stock to a boil in another pan. Mash the pumpkin with a fork, then stir in the rice and season with salt and pepper. Add a ladleful of the hot stock and cook, stirring, until it has been absorbed. Continue adding the stock, a ladleful at a time, and stirring until each addition has been absorbed. This will take 18–20 minutes. When the rice is tender, stir in the remaining butter and serve with Parmesan.

RISOTTO CON ZUCCA E CARCIOFI

Serves 4

3 tablespoons butter

1½ cups pumpkin flesh, chopped

3 globe artichokes

about 6¼ cups Vegetable Stock (see page 209)

2 cups risotto rice

salt and pepper

Parmesan cheese, freshly grated, to serve

FOUR CHEESE RISOTTO

Bring the stock to a boil. Meanwhile, melt 2 tablespoons of the butter in another pan, add the onion and cook, stirring occasionally, for 5 minutes. Stir in the rice and cook, stirring, until the grains are coated in butter. Add a ladleful of the hot stock and cook, stirring, until it has been absorbed. Continue adding the stock, a ladleful at a time, and stirring until each addition has been absorbed. This will take 18–20 minutes. About 5 minutes before the rice is cooked, stir in the cheeses. When the rice is tender and the cheeses have melted, remove the pan from the heat, stir in the remaining butter and serve.

RISOTTO MANTECATO
AI QUATTRO FORMAGGI

Serves 4

about 6¼ cups Vegetable Stock (see page 209)

3 tablespoons butter

1 onion, thinly sliced

2 cups risotto rice

2 ounces fontina cheese, diced

2 ounces Emmenthal cheese, diced

2 ounces Gorgonzola cheese, diced

⅔ cup Parmesan cheese, freshly grated

BLACK RISOTTO WITH CUTTLEFISH

Cut the cuttlefish into strips. Bring the stock to a boil. Meanwhile, heat the oil in another pan, add the onion and garlic and cook over low heat, stirring occasionally, for 5 minutes. Add the cuttlefish, season with salt and pepper to taste and cook for a few minutes. Pour in the wine and 2/3 cup water and simmer over low heat for about 20 minutes. Stir in the rice and cook for a few minutes, then add the hot stock and the cuttlefish ink and cook for a further 20 minutes until the rice and cuttlefish are tender and the liquid has been absorbed. Stir in the butter and serve.

RISOTTO NERO CON LE SEPPIE

Serves 4

2¼ pounds cuttlefish, cleaned and ink sacs reserved

4 cups Fish Stock (see page 208)

3 tablespoons olive oil

1 small onion, chopped • ½ garlic clove, chopped

3¼ cups dry white wine

2 cups risotto rice

2 tablespoons butter

salt and pepper

CREAM AND LEEK RISOTTO

Melt the butter in a pan, add the leeks and cook, stirring occasionally, for 5 minutes. Add 1 tablespoon water and simmer for 20 minutes, adding more water if necessary. Meanwhile bring the stock to a boil in another pan. Stir the rice into the leeks. Add a ladleful of the hot stock and cook, stirring, until it has been absorbed. Continue adding the stock, a ladleful at a time, and stirring until each addition has been absorbed. This will take 18–20 minutes. When the rice is tender, stir in the cream and season with salt and pepper to taste. Serve with Parmesan.

RISOTTO PANNA E PORRI

Serves 4

2 tablespoons butter

4 small leeks, white parts only, thinly sliced

about 6¼ cups Vegetable

Stock (see page 209)

2 cups risotto rice

¾ cup light cream

salt and pepper

Parmesan cheese, freshly grated, to serve

GREEN RISOTTO

Melt 2 tablespoons of the butter with the oil in a pan, add the spinach, carrot, onion, celery and celery leaves and cook over medium heat for 5 minutes, then lower the heat and cook for a further 10 minutes. Meanwhile, bring the stock to a boil in another pan. Season the vegetables with salt to taste and stir in the rice. Add a ladleful of the hot stock and cook, stirring, until it has been absorbed. Continue adding the stock, a ladleful at a time, and stirring until each addition has been absorbed. This will take 18–20 minutes. When the rice is tender, stir in the remaining butter and serve with Parmesan.

RISOTTO VERDE

Serves 4

3 tablespoons butter • 3 tablespoons olive oil

1⅔ cups spinach, chopped • 1 carrot, chopped

1 onion, chopped

1 celery stalk including leaves, chopped

about 6¼ cups Vegetable

Stock (see page 209)

2 cups risotto rice • salt

Parmesan cheese, freshly grated, to serve

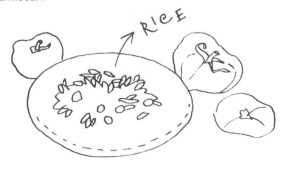

TIMBALES

According to the dictionary a timbale is a puff pastry shell filled with cooked ingredients, such as chicken giblets, mushrooms or pasta. Other definitions state that timbale is the name of a cone-shaped mold whose height is equal to its diameter (8 inches), made of tin-plated iron or stainless steel and at one time called a dariola in Italian. A timbale is usually a cylindrical baked pie. It may be filled with rice or pasta, together with meat, chicken giblets, meatballs, mushrooms or truffles. The timbale is, in any case, a demanding dish – as dishes with fillings often are – which immediately gives the impression of being a rich one. Timbales are, in fact, very rich since they were born from the imagination of chefs who were expected to excel on special occasions, such as princely weddings and royal dinners, and summit meetings as we would say today, and who invented the timbale in order to surprise, intrigue and tempt. On those occasions their golden brown casing made of various types of pastry (puff, pie dough, pâte brisée, etc.) concealed sophisticated sauces, aromatic spices, delicate meats, rare mushrooms and precious truffles. Even today, timbales mark the most important moment of a formal luncheon.

A FEW RULES

FILLING
Do not overdo the quantity.

BECHAMEL SAUCE
It should be runny and well cooked, otherwise it sticks the pastry together and makes it soggy.

RAGÙ (MEAT SAUCE)
It should be neither too thick nor too thin.

SPICES
Give priority to only one, such as nutmeg or saffron, and do not overdo it.

CHEESE
Cheese should always be freshly grated.

PORTIONS
Timbales should be cut using a special slicer with one sharpened edge or, if you do not have one, with a knife with a broad blade. To serve the slices lay them on a plate using the same utensil.

PHEASANT PIE

PASTICCIO DI FAGIANO

Serves 6

¹/₄ cup butter, plus extra for greasing

7 ounces chicken livers, thawed if frozen and trimmed

2 garlic cloves

2 bay leaves

¹/₂ pheasant, skinned, boned and chopped

5 ounces lean pork, finely chopped

¹/₄ cup Marsala

2 tablespoons brandy

scant ¹/₂ cup heavy cream

12 ounces puff pastry dough, thawed if frozen

all-purpose flour, for dusting

1 egg yolk, lightly beaten

salt and pepper

Preheat the oven to 350°F. Grease six individual molds with butter. Melt half the butter in a skillet, add the chicken livers, garlic and bay leaves and cook, stirring frequently, for 5 minutes. Add the pheasant meat and pork, season with salt and pepper and cook over medium heat, stirring occasionally, for 15 minutes. Pour in the Marsala and brandy and cook until they have evaporated. Remove and discard the garlic and bay leaves and transfer the mixture to a food processor. Melt the remaining butter. Process the mixture and, with the motor running, gradually add the melted butter and the cream. Roll out the pastry on a lightly floured surface into a thin sheet and use to line the prepared molds. Fill with the meat mixture, cover with rounds of pastry and crimp the edges to seal. Make a hole in the center of each pie and prick lines of little holes radiating out from the center with a fork. Brush the surface with the egg yolk and bake for about 15 minutes. Remove from the oven and let stand for 5 minutes before turning out and serving.

PUMPKIN PIE

PASTICCIO DI PASTA DI ZUCCA

Serves 4

1 cup dried mushrooms

2 tablespoons butter, plus extra for greasing

¹/₂ shallot, chopped

¹/₂ carrot, chopped

1 cup Béchamel Sauce (see page 50)

1¹/₂ cups cooked pumpkin

2³/₄ cups all-purpose flour, plus extra for dusting

1 egg, lightly beaten

salt and pepper

Put the mushrooms in a bowl, add hot water to cover and let soak for 20 minutes, then drain, squeeze out and chop. Melt the butter in a skillet, add the shallot and carrot and cook over low heat until softened, then add the mushrooms. Cover and cook for 15 minutes until tender, then stir into the béchamel sauce. Preheat the oven to 400°F. Grease an ovenproof dish with butter. Meanwhile, process the pumpkin with a pinch of salt in a food processor. Transfer to a bowl and combine with the flour, then stir in the egg to bind into a dough. Knead quickly and roll out on a lightly floured surface into a fairly thin sheet. Cut out 10–12 rectangles. Bring a pan of salted water to a boil, add the pumpkin rectangles and cook for a few minutes, then drain. Arrange the rectangles in alternate layers with the mushroom sauce and bake for a few minutes.

PENNE AND MUSHROOM PIE

Preheat the oven to 350°F. Grease an ovenproof timbale mold with butter. Melt half the butter with the oil in a pan. Add the garlic and cook over low heat for 2–3 minutes until golden brown, then remove and discard. Add the porcini to the pan and sprinkle with a ladleful of stock. Cover and cook over medium heat for about 10 minutes until soft, sprinkling with a little more stock if necessary. Beat the egg in a bowl with 1 teaspoon of the stock. Season the mushrooms with salt and pepper to taste, stir in the cream and cook for a few minutes more. Remove the pan from the heat and stir in the parsley and egg yolk mixture, making sure that the porcini are evenly coated with the sauce. Cook the pennette in a large pan of salted, boiling water until al dente, then drain. Arrange half the pennette in a layer on the base of the prepared mold, sprinkle with half the Parmesan and dot with half the remaining butter. Place half the porcini on top, spoon on the remaining pasta, sprinkle with the remaining Parmesan and dot with the remaining butter. Top with the remaining porcini. Roll out the pie crust dough on a lightly floured surface to make a round 1/4 inch thick. Cover the mushrooms with the pasta frolla, trimming to fit. Bake for 15 minutes or until light golden brown.

PASTICCIO DI PENNE AI FUNGHI
Serves 6

1/4 cup butter, plus extra for greasing

1 tablespoon olive oil

1 garlic clove

11 1/4 cups porcini, thinly sliced

3/4–1 cup Vegetable Stock

(see page 209)

1 egg

5 tablespoons heavy cream

1 tablespoon chopped fresh flat-leaf parsley

2 3/4 cups pennette lisce

4 tablespoons Parmesan cheese, freshly grated

1 quantity Pie Crust Dough,

made with half quantity sugar (see page 1008)

all-purpose flour, for dusting

salt and pepper

TAGLIATELLE PIE

Preheat the oven to 350°F. Grease an ovenproof dish with butter. Roll out the dough on a lightly floured surface to a sheet 1/8 inch thick and use to line the prepared dish. Cook the spinach, in just the water clinging to its leaves after washing, for 5 minutes then drain, squeezing out as much liquid as possible, and chop. Melt the butter in a skillet, add the spinach and cook over low heat for 5 minutes. Add the milk and season with salt. Stir in the cream and season with pepper. Cook the tagliatelle in a large pan of salted, boiling water until al dente, drain, tip into a bowl and mix with the spinach and ham. Spoon the mixture into the dough-lined dish. Beat the eggs with the Parmesan and a small pinch of salt in a bowl, then pour onto the hot tagliatelle. Bake for 30–40 minutes or until the surface is well browned.

PASTICCIO DI TAGLIATELLE
Serves 6

7 tablespoons butter, plus extra for greasing

11 ounces Pizza Dough (see page 193)

all-purpose flour, for dusting

7 ounces spinach

5 tablespoons milk

1/4 cup heavy cream

12 ounces tagliatelle

scant 1 cup cooked, cured ham, diced

3 eggs

2/3 cup Parmesan cheese, freshly grated

salt and pepper

SARTÙ

Serves 6

7 tablespoons butter, plus extra for greasing

1½ cups bread crumbs

⅓ cup dried mushrooms

1 thick bread slice, crusts removed

¾ cup milk

scant 1 cup ground beef

all-purpose flour, for coating

3 tablespoons olive oil

3½ ounces chicken livers, thawed if frozen, trimmed and chopped

2 ounces Italian sausage, peeled and crumbled

2½ ounces mozzarella cheese, diced

3 cups Meat Stock (see page 208)

½ onion, chopped

¼ cup bottled strained tomatoes

scant 2 cups risotto rice

2 eggs, lightly beaten

salt and pepper

SARTÙ

Preheat the oven to 350°F. Grease an ovenproof dish with butter and sprinkle with the bread crumbs, turning to coat. Tip out any excess. Put the mushrooms in a bowl, add hot water to cover and let soak for 20 minutes, then drain, squeeze and chop coarsely. Tear the bread into pieces, place in a bowl, add the milk and a pinch of salt and let soak for 10 minutes, then squeeze out. Combine the ground beef and soaked bread, then roll the mixture into hazelnut-size balls and coat with flour. Heat 2 tablespoons of the butter with the oil in a skillet, add the meatballs and cook until golden brown all over. Remove with a slotted spoon, drain on paper towels and set aside. Heat 2 tablespoons of the remaining butter in another pan, add the mushrooms and a pinch of salt, cover and cook over low heat for 20 minutes. Melt 2 tablespoons of the remaining butter in another skillet. Add the chicken livers and cook over medium heat, stirring frequently, for about 5 minutes until lightly browned. Remove from the heat and season with salt. Heat the sausage and mozzarella in a small pan until the cheese has melted. Bring the stock to a boil. Meanwhile, melt the remaining butter in another pan, add the onion and cook over low heat, stirring occasionally, for 5 minutes, then add the strained tomatoes and stir in the rice. Add a ladleful of the hot stock and cook, stirring, until it has been absorbed. Continue adding the stock, a ladleful at a time, and stirring until each addition has been absorbed. This will take 18–20 minutes. Cover the base and sides of the prepared dish with a layer of risotto. Combine all the filling ingredients and spoon them into the dish, pour the eggs over the filling and cover with the remaining risotto. Bake for about 45 minutes. Remove from the oven, let stand for 10 minutes, then turn out onto a serving dish and serve.

FUSILLI TIMBALE

TIMBALLO DI FUSILLI

Serves 6

¹/₄ cup butter, plus extra for greasing

4 leeks, white parts only, thinly sliced

³/₄ cup dry white wine

5 tablespoons milk

3 cups fusilli

1 cup Parmesan cheese, freshly grated

2 eggs

6 fresh sage leaves

salt and pepper

Preheat the oven to 350°F. Grease an ovenproof dish with butter. Melt half the butter in a pan, add the leeks, pour in water to a depth of ²/₃ inch and cook over low heat for 10 minutes until softened. Add the wine, increase the heat to medium and cook until it has evaporated. Pour in the milk and cook until it has evaporated, then season with salt and pepper to taste. Cook the fusilli in a large pan of salted, boiling water until al dente, then drain. Cover the base of the prepared dish with a thick layer of fusilli, spoon a little of the leek mixture on top, sprinkle with some of the Parmesan and dot with some of the remaining butter. Repeat these layers until all the ingredients are used, ending with a layer of fusilli. Beat the eggs with a pinch of salt and a pinch of pepper, pour them over the fusilli and dot with butter. Garnish with the sage and bake for 40 minutes. Remove the timbale from the oven and let stand for 10 minutes before serving.

MACARONI NAPOLETANA TIMBALE

TIMBALLO DI MACCHERONI
ALLA NAPOLETANA

Serves 6

¹/₂ cup dried mushrooms

¹/₄ cup butter, plus extra for greasing

1 garlic clove, chopped

¹/₂ onion, chopped

9 ounces chicken giblets, trimmed and chopped

3¹/₂ ounces Italian sausages, peeled and crumbled

14 ounces ripe tomatoes, peeled, seeded and diced

1¹/₂ cups bread crumbs

3 cups macaroni

1 mozzarella cheese, diced

²/₃ cup Parmesan cheese, freshly grated

salt

Preheat the oven to 350°F. Put the mushrooms in a bowl, add hot water to cover and let soak for 20 minutes, then drain and squeeze out. Melt the butter in a pan, add the garlic and onion and cook over low heat, stirring occasionally, for 10 minutes until lightly browned. Add the chicken giblets, sausages and mushrooms, season with salt, stir well and cook for a few minutes. Add the tomatoes, cover and cook over medium heat for 30 minutes. Meanwhile, grease a high-sided cake pan with butter, sprinkle with the bread crumbs and turn to coat. Tip out and reserve the excess. Cook the macaroni in a large pan of salted, boiling water until al dente, then drain and tip into a bowl. Add the meat sauce and let cool. When cold, stir in the mozzarella and Parmesan and spoon into the prepared tin. Smooth the surface and sprinkle with the reserved bread crumbs. Bake for about 40 minutes until golden brown. Remove from the oven and let stand for 5 minutes, then turn out onto a serving dish and serve.

RICE TIMBALE

Preheat the oven to 350°F. Cook the rice in a large pan of lightly salted, boiling water for 15–18 minutes until tender, then drain and stir in 2 tablespoons of the butter, the egg yolks and 4 tablespoons of the Parmesan. Spread out on a large plate or cookie sheet and let cool. Meanwhile, put the mushrooms in a bowl, add hot water to cover and let soak for 20 minutes, then drain, squeeze out and chop. Melt 2 tablespoons of the remaining butter with the oil, add the garlic and cook for 2–3 minutes, then remove and discard. Add the mushrooms to the pan and cook for 5 minutes. Melt 3 tablespoons of the remaining butter in another pan, add the chicken giblets and livers, sweetbreads and sausage. Season with a pinch of salt and a pinch of pepper, stir well and cook for about 5 minutes. Grease an ovenproof dish with plenty of butter and sprinkle with the bread crumbs, turning to coat. Tip out and reserve the excess. Spoon half the rice mixture onto the base of the dish, cover with the mushrooms and top with the liver and sweetbread mixture. Cover with the remaining rice, dot with the remaining butter and sprinkle with the remaining Parmesan and reserved bread crumbs. Bake for about 15 minutes.

TIMBALLO DI RISO

Serves 6

1³/₄ cups long-grain rice
¹/₂ cup butter, plus extra for greasing
2 egg yolks, lightly beaten
6 tablespoons Parmesan cheese, freshly grated
¹/₂ cup dried mushrooms
2 tablespoons olive oil
1 garlic clove
9 ounces chicken giblets and livers, thawed if frozen, trimmed and chopped
7 ounces sweetbreads, chopped
2 ¹/₂ ounces Italian sausage, peeled and crumbled
1¹/₂ cups bread crumbs
salt and pepper

CHEESE PIE

Preheat the oven to 350°F. Lightly grease an ovenproof dish with butter. Roll out the dough on a lightly floured surface to a sheet ¹/₈ inch thick and use to line the prepared dish. Crumble the ricotta into a bowl and add the robiola, Gorgonzola and a pinch of pepper. Cook the tagliatelle in a large pan of salted, boiling water until al dente, then drain and tip onto the cheeses. Toss the pasta with two forks until it is completely covered with cheese and tip into the dough-lined dish. Beat the eggs with the Parmesan, a pinch of salt and a pinch of pepper in a bowl and pour the mixture over the tagliatelle. Bake for 15–20 minutes.

TORTA AI FORMAGGI

Serves 6

butter, for greasing
7 ounces Pizza Dough (see page 193)
all-purpose flour, for dusting
²/₃ cup ricotta cheese
5 ounces robiola cheese, diced
3¹/₂ ounces mild Gorgonzola cheese, diced
9 ounces tagliatelle
2 eggs
4 tablespoons Parmesan cheese, freshly grated
salt and pepper

VINCISGRASSI

VINCISGRASSI

Serves 6–8

butter, for greasing

For the Pasta dough
3 cups all-purpose flour, preferably Italian type 00, plus extra for dusting
generous 1 cup semolina
3 tablespoons Vin Santo or Marsala
3 eggs, lightly beaten
salt

For the filling
$^1/_2$ cup dried mushrooms
$3^1/_2$ ounces sweetbread
$^1/_4$ cup butter
2 tablespoons olive oil
$^1/_2$ onion, chopped
1 black truffle, diced
2 tablespoons Chicken Stock (see page 209)
1 skinless, boneless chicken breast, cut into strips
7 ounces chicken giblets, trimmed and chopped
5 tablespoons dry Marsala
1 cup Parmesan cheese, freshly grated
1 quantity Béchamel Sauce (see page 50)
salt and pepper

Preheat the oven to 350°F. Grease an ovenproof dish with butter. For the filling, put the mushrooms in a bowl, add hot water to cover and let soak for 20 minutes, then drain, squeeze dry and chop. Blanch the sweetbread in boiling water for a few minutes, drain and let cool, then dice. Melt half the butter in a skillet, add the sweetbread and cook, stirring occasionally, for a few minutes. Heat the remaining butter with the oil in a pan, add the onion and cook over low heat, stirring occasionally, for 5 minutes, then stir in the mushrooms, truffle and stock. Add the chicken strips and cook over high heat until browned, then add the giblets and cook for a few minutes more. Pour in the Marsala, lower the heat and cook until half the wine has evaporated. Pour in just enough hot water to cover, season with salt and pepper, cover and cook over low heat for about 30 minutes. Add the sweetbread. Make the pasta dough (see Fresh Pasta Dough, page 268) using the ingredients specified, then roll out into a sheet and cut into strips about 4 inches wide and 20 inches long. Bring a large pan of salted water to a boil, add the pasta strips and boil for a few minutes until half-cooked, then remove and refresh in a bowl of cold water. Drain the pasta and spread out on a damp dish towel. Arrange pasta strips in the base of the prepared dish so that they cross to cover the base, allowing the excess to overhang the sides. Cut the remaining strips into rectangles. Fill the dish with alternate layers of filling and pasta, sprinkled with Parmesan and tablespoonfuls of béchamel sauce, ending with a layer of béchamel sauce. Fold over the overhanging ends of the pasta strips to make a pie. Place the dish in a roasting pan, add hot water to come about halfway up the sides and bake for 30 minutes.

RAVIOLINI PATTY SHELL

VOL–AU–VENT CON RAVIOLINI

Serves 6

$^1/_4$ cup butter
scant1 cup peas, shelled
1 pound 2 ounces small ravioli
$^1/_2$ cup Parmesan cheese, freshly grated
1 large, ready-made patty shells, about 6–8 inches
1 quantity Béchamel Sauce (see page 50)
salt

Preheat the oven to 300°F. Line a cookie sheet with baking parchment. Melt half the butter in a pan, add the peas and 2 tablespoons warm water and cook for about 10 minutes until tender. Season with salt, drain and set aside. Cook the ravioli in a large pan of salted, boiling water until al dente, then drain, tip into a bowl and gently toss with the remaining butter, $^1/_3$ cup of the Parmesan and the peas. Fill the patty shell with the ravioli and spoon in the béchamel sauce. Sprinkle with the remaining Parmesan, place on the cookie sheet and heat through in the oven.

SEAFOOD PATTY SHELL

Pour 8³/₄ cups water into a large pan, add the wine, bay leaf, garlic, clove, parsley, celery, onion and carrot and bring to a boil. Lower the heat and simmer for 15 minutes, then season with salt and pepper and add the hake or cod. Cover and simmer for 20 minutes, then remove from the heat and let cool in the stock. Preheat the oven to 300°F. Tear the bread into pieces, place in a bowl, add the milk and let soak for 10 minutes, then squeeze out. Melt the butter in a skillet, add the shrimp and cook for 2 minutes. Sprinkle in the sherry and cook until it has evaporated. Season with salt and pepper, remove the pan from the heat and keep warm. Place the patty shell on a cookie sheet in the oven to warm through. Drain the fish, reserving the stock, flake coarsely and pass through a food mill into a bowl. Add the soaked bread and the egg, season with salt and pepper and mix well. Shape the mixture into balls and dust lightly with flour, shaking off any excess. Strain the fish stock into a clean pan and bring to a boil. Add the fish balls and remove with a slotted spoon as they float to the surface. Drain, dry on paper towels and arrange in the patty shell. Top with the shrimp and spoon in the béchamel sauce. Serve immediately.

VOL–AU–VENT DI MARE

Serves 6

1¹/₂ cups dry white wine

1 bay leaf

1 garlic clove

1 clove

1 fresh flat-leaf parsley sprig

1 celery stalk

1 onion, sliced

1 carrot, sliced

1¹/₂ pounds hake or cod fillet

2 ounces bread, crusts removed

³/₄ cup milk

2 tablespoons butter

2³/₄ cups small raw shrimp, peeled

¹/₄ cup sherry

1 large patty shell, about 6–8 inches

scant 1 cup Béchamel Sauce (see page 50)

1 egg, lightly beaten

all-purpose flour, for dusting

salt and pepper

EGG

EGG CUP

TURNER

SALT

PEPPER

ALUMINUM FRY PAN

1

2

N-11

EGGS →

FRITTATA →

EGGS

Hardly a day goes by in any kitchen without at least one egg being needed – on its own for breakfast or as a snack, as the basis of a sauce such as a wonderful mayonnaise, to thicken a cream, as 'glue' for all fried dishes that need coating in bread crumbs, or to complete and enrich a salad. Eggs are required for desserts, flans, home-made pasta and even cocktails. They are also the main constituent of a famous tonic. Their nutritional value (156 calories per 2-ounce egg) is more or less equivalent to 1 cup milk or 3¹/₂ ounces meat. However, their proteins are higher quality and more easily assimilated by the human digestive system than those of any other food. Altogether, this small, white or brown, 2¹/₂-inch tall object, weighing 2–2¹/₂ ounces, is also a concentrated source of vitamins and minerals. Yet the Italians are among the peoples in the world who consume them the least: only 200 eggs per year per person, compared to 280 for the French, 300 for the Spanish and 400 for the Israelis. On the other hand, Italy exports eggs in large numbers: the most recent figures quote about 70 million eggs in shells and more than 3,000 tons of egg-containing products (pasta, desserts, etc.), plus 8,000 tons of egg whites for use in the pharmaceutical industry. Soft-cooked or poached eggs, i.e. ones that are briefly cooked, are digested in an hour and a half; whereas fried and hard-cooked eggs take three hours.

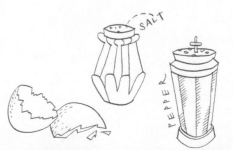

USEFUL TIPS

→ When buying eggs, always check the 'use by' date on the box.

→ The box should also show the size of the eggs, such as medium or large. Differences in size do not affect quality, but do justify the differences in price.

→ Eggs should always be stored in the refrigerator to retain their flavor and keep them fit for consumption. They are best stored in their box with their pointed ends downwards. It is not advisable to store eggs near strong-smelling food as their shells are porous and tend to absorb odors easily.

→ Once shelled, whites will keep in the refrigerator for 2–3 days and yolks for 1–2 days.

→ Remove eggs from the refrigerator 30 minutes before use. This helps to prevent mayonnaise from curdling, egg whites will whisk to a greater volume, and shells are less likely to crack during boiling.

→ Break eggs on to a plate to check their freshness: the yolk should be a bright color and firm, while the white should be thick, viscous and adhere to the yolk. There is no significance in the precise color of the yolk, which may range from pale yellow to almost orange – the shade depends on what the hen has eaten. On the other hand the color of the shell, usually white or brown and sometimes speckled, depends on the breed of bird.

FRITTATA

In Italian cuisine, the frittata family is quite varied and includes omelets and crêpes. The classic frittata does not include any ingredient other than eggs, salt and, if liked, pepper, along with the oil needed to cook it. Ingredients for other frittata include vegetables or legumes or any other ingredient which may be 'held together' by one or more eggs and fried in a skillet. It is advisable to use an ordinary nonstick skillet, which ensures perfect results. Separate sections are devoted to omelets and crêpes. Both – besides being delicious dishes – may also be served as desserts.

POACHED

Bring a pan of salted water to a boil with 2 tablespoons white wine vinegar – don't use red wine vinegar as it discolors the egg white. Break the eggs into a small bowl, one at a time, and make sure that they are fresh. Plunge each egg into the boiling water and poach for 3–4 minutes. Remove with a slotted spoon and trim the white neatly. If you are poaching several eggs in the same pan, make sure that they do not touch.

UOVA AFFOGATE AI CARCIOFI

Serves 4

4 artichoke hearts

1 tablespoon olive oil

scant 1¼ cups smoked pancetta, chopped

2 tablespoons white wine vinegar

4 eggs

salt and pepper

For the sauce

3 tablespoons butter

1 teaspoon Dijon mustard

1 teaspoon all-purpose flour

2 tablespoons white wine vinegar

salt and pepper

POACHED EGGS WITH ARTICHOKE HEARTS

To make the sauce, melt the butter in a pan, stir in the mustard and flour and cook for a few seconds. Gradually stir in 1 cup water, alternating with the vinegar, and season with salt and pepper to taste. Cook, stirring constantly, for 5 minutes. Blanch the artichoke hearts in boiling water for a few minutes, then drain and slice into eight rounds. Arrange in a ring on a warm serving dish. Heat the oil in a skillet, add the pancetta and cook, stirring occasionally, for 5 minutes until tender. Drain and sprinkle in the middle of the dish. Bring a pan of salted water to a boil, add the vinegar and poach the eggs for 3–4 minutes. Remove with a slotted spoon, place on top of the pancetta and spoon the sauce over them.

UOVA AFFOGATE AL FORMAGGIO

Serves 4

4 bread slices, crusts removed

3 tablespoons butter, softened

2 tablespoons white wine vinegar

4 eggs

$^1/_2$ cup Emmenthal cheese, freshly grated

salt

POACHED EGGS WITH CHEESE

Preheat the oven to 350°F. Spread the bread with the butter and place on an ovenproof dish. Bring a pan of salted water to a boil, add the vinegar and poach the eggs for 3 minutes. Remove with a slotted spoon, place on the bread, sprinkle with the Emmenthal and bake until the cheese has melted.

UOVA AFFOGATE CON CROCCHETTE DI ASPARAGI

Serves 4

11 ounces asparagus tips

1 quantity thick Béchamel Sauce made with only $^3/_4$ cups milk (see page 50)

4 tablespoons Parmesan cheese, freshly grated

6 eggs

all-purpose flour, for dusting

1$^1/_2$ cups bread crumbs

$^1/_4$ cup butter

2 tablespoons white wine vinegar

salt

POACHED EGGS WITH ASPARAGUS CROQUETTES

Cook the asparagus tips in salted, boiling water for about 10 minutes, then drain and pass through a food mill. Stir them into the béchamel sauce with the Parmesan and let cool slightly. Separate one egg and stir the yolk into the béchamel, then let stand in a cool place for about 1 hour. Divide the béchamel mixture into four and shape into four croquettes with a hollow in the centre of each. Dust lightly with flour. Beat one of the remaining eggs in a shallow dish and spread out the bread crumbs in another shallow dish. Dip each croquette into the beaten egg and then into the bread crumbs. Melt 3 tablespoons of the butter in a skillet, add the croquettes and cook over medium heat until golden brown all over. Meanwhile, bring a pan of salted water to a boil, add the vinegar and poach the remaining eggs for 3–4 minutes. Remove with a slotted spoon and place a poached egg in the middle of each croquette. Dot with the remaining butter, transfer to a warm serving dish and serve.

POACHED EGGS WITH MIXED VEGETABLES

Heat the oil in a skillet, add the onion and eggplants and cook over low heat, stirring occasionally, for 5 minutes. Add the tomatoes and zucchini and cook over low heat for about 30 minutes. Meanwhile, bring a pan of salted water to a boil, add the vinegar and poach the eggs for 3–4 minutes. Remove with a slotted spoon, pat dry with a dish towel and arrange on a warm serving dish. Surround with the hot vegetables and serve.

UOVA AFFOGATE CON VERDURE MISTE

Serves 4

3 tablespoons olive oil

1 onion, chopped

3 eggplants, diced

3 tomatoes, peeled, seeded and diced

3 zucchini, sliced

2 tablespoons white wine vinegar

4 eggs

salt

POACHED EGGS IN GELATIN

Dissolve the gelatin in 2$\frac{1}{4}$ cups according to the packet instructions and let cool, but do not chill. Bring a pan of salted water to a boil, add the vinegar and poach the eggs for 3–4 minutes. Remove with a slotted spoon and let cool. Put each egg in the middle of a slice of ham and roll up. Arrange them on a slightly concave serving dish and garnish with the anchovy fillets, capers and cornichons or dill pickles. Spoon the gelatin over the eggs so that it covers the surface and chill in the refrigerator for 3 hours until set.

UOVA AFFOGATE IN GELATINA

Serves 4

2$\frac{1}{4}$ cups prepared gelatin

2 tablespoons white wine vinegar

4 eggs

4 cooked ham slices

4 canned anchovy fillets in oil, drained

1 tablespoon capers, drained and rinsed

4 cornichons or dill pickles, thinly sliced

salt

SOFT COOKED

Soft-cooked eggs may be cooked in three different ways:
→ *Immerse the eggs in a pan of boiling water. Lower the heat to a simmer and cook for 3–4 minutes.* → *Immerse the eggs in a pan of boiling water and boil for 1 minute. Remove the pan from the heat and leave the eggs to stand in the hot water for 3–4 minutes.* → *Immerse the eggs in a pan of cold water and bring to a boil over a medium heat. Turn off the heat as soon as the water comes to a boil. The cooking time varies according to taste, as some people prefer the white quite firm and others like it more runny. In either case, it is important for the egg yolk to be runny.*

UOVA ALLA COQUE CON ASPARAGI

Serves 4

1³/₄ pounds asparagus, spears trimmed

4 eggs

salt

lightly salted butter, melted, to serve

EGGS WITH ASPARAGUS

Cook the asparagus in salted, boiling water for 20 minutes, then drain. Soft-cook the eggs, place in egg cups and serve with the hot asparagus and individual bowls of melted butter. To eat, dip the asparagus tip into the butter and then into the soft-cooked egg.

UOVA ALLA COQUE CON KETCHUP

Serves 4

4 eggs

4 teaspoons ketchup

sesame-seed bread sticks

salt

EGGS WITH KETCHUP

Soft-cook the eggs according to taste. Place them in egg cups, cut off the tops and season with a teaspoonful of ketchup and a pinch of salt. Mix, using a teaspoon or the bread sticks. The sesame seed flavor of the bread sticks goes well with egg yolk.

SHIRRED

Break the eggs on to a plate to make sure they are fresh. Melt a pat of butter in an ovenproof dish or stainless steel pan over a medium heat and slide in the eggs, one at a time. Season with salt and pepper to taste. Bake in a medium oven (325°F) for 5–6 minutes without stirring. In this way, the whites set perfectly and the yolks remain soft and runny. Shirred eggs can also be cooked on the stovetop, but are more successful using the method described above.

EGGS WITH MUSHROOMS

Preheat the oven to 325°F. Remove the mushroom stems (they may be retained and used for a sauce) and thinly slice the caps. Melt ¼ cup of the butter in a skillet, add the mushrooms and cook, stirring occasionally, for about 10 minutes until lightly browned, then season with salt and pepper to taste. Grease four individual ovenproof dishes with the remaining butter, divide the mushrooms among them and break an egg on top of each. Season the egg whites with a little salt and bake for about 10 minutes until the egg whites have set. Serve immediately in the same dishes.

UOVA AL PIATTO AI FUNGHI

Serves 4

3²/₃ white mushrooms

3 ounces butter

4 eggs

salt and pepper

EGGS WITH PARSLEY

Combine the parsley and ¼ cup of the butter and season lightly with salt. Melt the remaining butter in a skillet without letting it brown, break in the eggs and season lightly with salt. Cook for a few minutes until the whites have set but the yolks are still soft. Dot with the parsley butter, remove the pan from the heat and serve immediately on the bread.

UOVA AL PIATTO AL PREZZEMOLO

Serves 4

2 fresh flat-leaf parsley sprigs, chopped

scant ½ cup butter

8 eggs

8 thick bread slices

salt

359

EGGS WITH TRUFFLE

UOVA AL PIATTO AL TARTUFO

Serves 4

¼ cup butter

8 eggs

2 ounces black truffle

salt and pepper

Melt the butter in a skillet. When frothy, but not brown, break in the eggs and combine. Season with salt and pepper and cook over medium heat for 5–6 minutes. Transfer to a warm serving dish, shave the black truffle over the top and serve immediately.

EGGS WITH ASPARAGUS

UOVA AL PIATTO CON ASPARAGI

Serves 4

1¾ pounds asparagus, spears trimmed

4 tablespoons Parmesan cheese, freshly grated

6 tablespoons butter

4 eggs

salt

Tie the asparagus together in a bunch. Fill a tall, narrow pan or asparagus pan with water, bring to a boil and add the bunch of asparagus so that the tips are above the waterline. Steam for about 20 minutes until tender, then drain and arrange on a warm serving dish, half on one side and half on the other with their tips touching. Sprinkle with the Parmesan, then melt 3 tablespoons of the butter and spoon it over the asparagus. Melt the remaining butter in a pan, break in the eggs, one at a time, season with salt and cook until the whites have set. Lift out with a spatula and place on the asparagus on top of the tips.

EGGS WITH FENNEL AND MOZZARELLA

UOVA AL PIATTO CON FINOCCHI E MOZZARELLA

Serves 4

1¾ pounds fennel bulbs

¼ cup butter, plus extra for greasing

7 ounces mozzarella cheese, thinly sliced

4 eggs

4 tablespoons Parmesan cheese, freshly grated

salt and pepper

Cook the fennel in salted, boiling water for about 15 minutes until tender, then drain and chop. Meanwhile, preheat the oven to 325°F. Grease an ovenproof dish with butter. Melt the butter in a skillet, add the fennel, season with salt and pepper and cook over medium heat until light golden brown. Spoon the fennel into the prepared dish, cover with slices of mozzarella and break the eggs on top. Sprinkle with the Parmesan and bake until the cheeses have melted.

EGGS WITH EGGPLANT

Preheat the oven to 325°F. Grease an oven-proof dish with butter. Dust the eggplants with flour. Heat the oil with the butter in a skillet, add the eggplants and cook over medium heat until golden brown. Drain on paper towels and season with salt and pepper. Arrange the eggplants in the prepared dish, dot with the tomato paste and break the eggs on top. Bake until the egg whites have set.

UOVA AL PIATTO CON MELANZANE

Serves 4

2 tablespoons butter, plus extra for greasing

2 eggplants, sliced

all-purpose flour, for dusting

scant $1/2$ cup olive oil

3 tablespoons tomato paste

4 eggs

salt and pepper

EGGS WITH POLENTA

Preheat the oven to 325°F. Grease an oven-proof dish with butter. Melt 3 tablespoons of the butter in a skillet, add the polenta slices and cook over medium heat until golden brown on both sides. Drain on paper towels and arrange in the prepared dish. Break an egg on top of each slice, season with salt and dot with the remaining butter. Bake until the egg whites have set and serve immediately.

UOVA AL PIATTO CON POLENTA

Serves 4

$1/4$ cup butter

4 thick slices ready-made

or home-cooked set polenta (see page 305)

4 eggs

salt

EGGS WITH TOMATOES

Preheat oven to 350°F. Brush an ovenproof dish with olive oil. Cut the tops off the tomatoes and scoop out the seeds and some of the flesh. Sprinkle the insides with a little salt and place upside down on paper towels for 10 minutes to drain. Season the insides of the tomatoes with oregano and pepper and divide the olive oil among them. Place the tomatoes in the prepared dish and bake for 20 minutes. Remove the dish from the oven, break an egg into each tomato, return the dish to the oven and bake for a further 5 minutes. Garnish with parsley and serve.

UOVA AL PIATTO CON POMODORI

Serves 4

2 teaspoons olive oil, plus extra for brushing

4 large tomatoes

pinch of dried oregano

4 eggs

1 fresh flat-leaf parsley sprig, chopped

salt and pepper

EGGS WITH SAUSAGE

Preheat the oven to 350°F. Grease four individual ovenproof dishes with butter. Heat a skillet, add the sausages and cook over medium heat without added oil or fat until well browned. Sprinkle in the wine and cook until it has evaporated. Divide the sausages among the prepared dishes and break an egg on top of each. Season lightly with salt and bake until the egg whites have set. Serve immediately.

UOVA AL PIATTO CON SALSICCIA

Serves 4

butter, for greasing

11 ounces Italian sausages, coarsely chopped

scant ½ cup dry white wine

4 eggs

salt

EGGS ON MILK SOAKED BREAD

Preheat oven to 350°F. Grease an ovenproof dish with butter and place the bread in it in a single layer. Bring the milk to just below boiling point, then pour it over the bread and let soak. Heat the oil in a skillet, add the onion and cook over low heat, stirring occasionally, for 10 minutes. Set aside and keep warm. Break an egg on top of each piece of bread, season with salt and bake until the egg whites have set and the bread is light golden brown. Sprinkle the onion on top and serve.

UOVA AL PIATTO
SUI CROSTONI AL LATTE

Serves 4

butter, for greasing

4 slices day-old bread, crusts removed

2¼ cup milk

3 tablespoons olive oil

1 onion, chopped

4 eggs

salt

FRIED

Break eggs on to a plate one at a time and season with salt. Heat a pat of butter and a teaspoon of oil in a skillet and slide in the eggs. Gather the whites around the yolks immediately, using a slotted spoon, so that the eggs remain neat and separated. When done, the whites should be a light golden brown and the yolks soft. Lift out the eggs with a spatula, drain on paper towels and arrange on a warm serving dish.

EGGS WITH ANCHOVY BUTTER

UOVA FRITTE AL BURRO D'ACCIUGA

Serves 4

scant ¹/₂ cup butter

4 bread slices, crusts removed

1 tablespoon anchovy paste

4 eggs

salt

4 canned anchovy fillets in oil, drained, to garnish

Melt 3 tablespoons of the butter in a skillet, add the bread and fry until golden brown on both sides. Remove from the pan and drain on paper towels. Beat 2 tablespoons of the remaining butter with the anchovy paste in a bowl and spread the mixture on one side of each fried bread slice. Fry the eggs in the remaining butter and sprinkle a little salt on the whites. Lift out with a spatula and place one on each slice of fried bread. Garnish with the anchovy fillets and serve while hot.

EGGS IN RED WINE

UOVA FRITTE AL CIVET

Serves 4

4 tablespoons olive oil

14 ounces onions, thinly sliced

1 teaspoon sugar

2 tablespoons balsamic vinegar

1 tablespoon sherry vinegar

5 tablespoons red wine

8 eggs

salt and pepper

toast, to serve

Heat the oil in a skillet, add the onions and stir-fry over a high heat until lightly browned. Add 2 tablespoons water and the sugar, lower the heat and cook for 20–30 minutes until the onions are very soft and caramelized. Sprinkle in the vinegars and cook until they have evaporated. Pour in the wine and cook until about half has evaporated. Season with salt and pepper, then break the eggs into the pan, one at a time, and cook for a few minutes over medium heat. Transfer the eggs and their sauce to a warm serving dish and serve with toast.

EGGS WITH VINEGAR

Melt ¼ cup of the butter in a skillet and break in one egg at a time. Season lightly with salt and fry for a few minutes. Transfer to a warm serving dish. Melt the remaining butter in the same skillet. When it starts to brown, sprinkle in the vinegar, add the sage and parsley and cook for a few minutes, then pour the sauce over the eggs.

UOVA FRITTE ALL'ACETO

Serves 4

scant ½ cup butter

8 eggs

4 tablespoons white wine vinegar

4 fresh sage leaves, chopped

1 fresh flat-leaf parsley sprig, chopped

salt

AMERICAN—STYLE EGGS

Heat the oil and butter in a skillet, add the pancetta and cook for 5 minutes until tender, then remove and drain on paper towels. Break the eggs into the pan, one at a time, and season with salt and pepper. Using a wooden spoon, flip the egg whites over the yolks to cover. When the whites are set, remove the eggs from the skillet using a spatula and arrange on a warm serving dish. Surround with pancetta and serve with broiled tomatoes.

UOVA FRITTE ALL'AMERICANA

Serves 4

2 tablespoons olive oil

2 tablespoons butter

3½ ounces smoked pancetta, cut into strips

4 eggs

salt and pepper

broiled tomatoes, to serve

EGGS ROSSINI

Melt the pâté in a small pan with ¼ cup of the butter. Melt the remaining butter in a skillet, break in the eggs, one at a time, and cook until the whites start to set. Pour the pâté butter on top and cook for a further 2 minutes, then serve.

UOVA FRITTE ALLA ROSSINI

For 4

5 ounces pâté de foie gras

scant ½ cup butter

8 eggs

EGGS WITH BRUSSELS SPROUTS

Bring a large pan of salted water to a boil, add the Brussels sprouts and simmer for 15 minutes, then drain well. Melt 2 tablespoons of the butter in a skillet, add the ham and onion and cook over low heat, stirring occasionally, for 5 minutes. Sprinkle in the flour and cook, stirring, for 1 minute, then stir in ⅔ cup warm water and simmer for a further 10 minutes. Stir in the cream, season with salt and pepper and heat through. Meanwhile, melt the remaining butter in another skillet, break in the eggs, one at a time, and fry for a few minutes over a medium heat. Season with salt to taste. Arrange the Brussels sprouts on a warm serving dish, cover with the hot ham sauce, top with the eggs and serve.

UOVA FRITTE CON CAVOLINI DI BRUXELLES

Serves 4

1 pound 2 ounces Brussels sprouts

scant ½ cup butter

1 thick ham slice, diced

1 onion, finely chopped

1 tablespoon all-purpose flour

scant 1 cup heavy cream

6 eggs

salt and pepper

EN COCOTTE

Eggs en cocotte can be cooked in a double boiler, on the stovetop or in the oven. Arrange a layer of chicken livers, ham or similar ingredients in a lightly buttered ramekin and break an egg on top. Add salt and pepper to taste and a pat of butter. Cooking in a double boiler with barely simmering water takes 6–8 minutes. The white must set softly and the yolk remain runny.

UOVA IN COCOTTE AI PORRI

Serves 4

1 pound 5 ounces leeks, trimmed

¼ cup butter, plus extra for greasing

pinch of freshly grated nutmeg

4 eggs

salt and pepper

EGGS EN COCOTTE WITH LEEKS

Halve the leeks lengthwise, then slice very thinly. Melt the butter in a small skillet, add the leeks and cook over low heat, stirring occasionally, for 5 minutes until softened. Season with salt and pepper to taste and sprinkle with the nutmeg. Stir well and add 3 tablespoons warm water, then cover and cook over low heat for about 20 minutes. Meanwhile, preheat the oven to 350°F and grease four ramekins with butter. Divide the leeks among the ramekins, break an egg into each dish and bake for 4 minutes. Turn off the heat, cover the ramekins with a sheet of foil and return to the oven for 2 minutes. Remove the foil, season lightly with pepper and serve.

UOVA IN COCOTTE ALLA PESCATORA

Serves 4

1 tablespoon butter, plus extra for greasing

3 ounces canned sardines in oil, drained

4 eggs

1 fresh flat-leaf parsley sprig, chopped

salt and pepper

FISHERMAN'S EGGS EN COCOTTE

Preheat the oven to 350°F if you wish to bake the eggs. Grease four ramekins with butter. Remove the bones from the sardines and chop the flesh. Divide the flesh among the ramekins, break an egg into each dish, season with salt and pepper to taste and dot with the butter. Place the ramekins in a roasting pan, add boiling water to come about halfway up the sides and bake for 8–10 minutes or until the egg whites are lightly set. Alternatively, place the roasting pan over low heat for 8–10 minutes. Sprinkle with the parsley and serve.

EGGS EN COCOTTE WITH BACON FAT

UOVA IN COCOTTE AL LARDO

Serves 4

4 small slices bacon fat

4 tablespoons heavy cream

4 eggs

2 tablespoons Parmesan cheese, freshly grated

Preheat the oven to 350°F if you wish to bake the eggs. Parboil the bacon fat in boiling water for about 1 minute, then drain. Put 1 tablespoon cream and a slice of bacon fat in each of four ramekins, break an egg into each and sprinkle with the Parmesan. Place the ramekins in a roasting pan, add boiling water to come about halfway up the sides and bake for 6–8 minutes or until the egg whites are lightly set. Alternatively, place the roasting pan over low heat for 6–8 minutes. The combination of bacon fat and cream – a strong savory taste and a milder flavor – gives the eggs a very delicate flavor.

EGGS EN COCOTTE WITH BOLOGNESE MEAT SAUCE

UOVA IN COCOTTE AL RAGÙ

Serves 4

butter, for greasing

1 quantity Bolognese Meat Sauce (see page 52)

8 eggs

salt

Preheat the oven to 350° if you wish to bake the eggs. Grease four ramekins with butter and pour a layer of meat sauce into each. Break the eggs on top, season lightly with salt and cover with another layer of meat sauce. Place the ramekins in a roasting pan, add boiling water to come about halfway up the sides and bake for 8–10 minutes. Alternatively, place the roasting pan over low heat for 8–10 minutes. Serve hot.

FRAGRANT EGGS EN COCOTTE

UOVA IN COCOTTE AROMATICHE

Serves 4

butter, plus extra for greasing

8 fresh basil leaves, chopped

pinch of dried oregano

4 plum tomatoes, thinly sliced

4 eggs

salt and pepper

Preheat the oven to 350°F if you wish to bake the eggs. Grease four ramekins with plenty of butter, sprinkle with half the basil and the oregano, add a few slices of tomato and break an egg into each. Season lightly with salt and pepper and dot with butter, then top with the remaining tomato slices and basil. Place the ramekins in a roasting pan, add boiling water to come about halfway up the sides and bake for 6–8 minutes or until the egg whites are lightly set. Alternatively, place the roasting pan over low heat for 6–8 minutes.

MEDIUM COOKED

Immerse the eggs in a pan of boiling water, bring back to a boil and cook for 5 minutes. Remove from the pan and refresh under cold running water to prevent any further cooking and to make shelling them without damaging the white easier. Handle them very gently. Medium-cooked eggs are very tasty sprinkled with sauce or with vegetables seasoned in various ways.

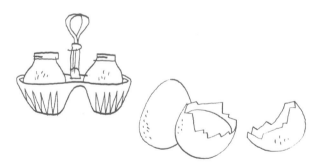

BOILED EGGS WITH SPINACH

Cook the spinach, in just the water clinging to the leaves after washing, for 5 minutes, then drain, squeeze out as much liquid as possible and chop finely. Melt the butter in a skillet, add the spinach and cook over low heat, stirring occasionally, for 5 minutes. Stir in the cream and season with salt and pepper. Meanwhile, cook the eggs in boiling water for 4–5 minutes, then remove from the pan, refresh under cold water and shell. Place the spinach on a warm serving dish, top with the eggs and serve.

UOVA MOLLETTE AGLI SPINACI

Serves 4

1 ¹/₂ pounds spinach

¹/₄ cup butter

2 tablespoons heavy cream

4 eggs

salt and pepper

BOILED EGGS WITH MUSHROOMS

UOVA MOLLETTE AI FUNGHI

Serves 4

4 large porcini

olive oil, for brushing

6 tablespoons butter

1 tablespoon chopped fresh flat-leaf parsley

1 teaspoon lemon juice, strained

4 eggs

salt and pepper

Preheat the broiler to medium. Remove the mushroom stems, season the caps with salt and pepper, brush with oil and broil for about 15 minutes. Cream the butter in a bowl and beat in the parsley, lemon juice and salt to taste. Cook the eggs in boiling water for 4–5 minutes, then remove from the pan, refresh under cold water and shell. Place an egg in the hollow of each mushroom cap and add a little parsley butter. Arrange on a warm serving dish and serve immediately.

BOILED EGGS WITH HERBED MUSTARD

UOVA MOLLETTE ALLA SENAPE AROMATICA

Serves 4

$^1/_4$ cup butter

1 shallot, finely chopped

1 tablespoon all-purpose flour

8 eggs

1 tablespoon herbed mustard or flavored mustard of choice

1 tablespoon finely chopped fresh chives

salt and pepper

Melt the butter in a pan, add the shallot and cook over low heat, stirring occasionally, for 8–10 minutes until lightly browned. Sprinkle in the flour and cook, stirring constantly, for 1 minute, then stir in $^2/_3$ cup warm water, season with salt and pepper and simmer gently for about 20 minutes. Meanwhile, cook the eggs in boiling water for 5 minutes, then remove from the pan, refresh under cold water and shell. Stir the mustard into the sauce and spoon on to a warm serving dish. Place the eggs on top, sprinkle with the chives and serve immediately.

BOILED EGGS WITH TOMATO

UOVA MOLLETTE AL POMODORO

Serves 4

scant 1 cup bottled Italian tomato sauce

1 onion, chopped

1 celery stalk, chopped

1 carrot, chopped

1 tablespoon chopped fresh flat-leaf parsley

8 eggs

salt

Heat the tomato sauce in a pan, add the onion, celery, carrot and parsley, season with salt and simmer over low heat for 20 minutes. Cook the eggs in boiling water for 4–5 minutes, then remove from the pan, refresh under cold water and shell. Spoon half the sauce on to the base of a warm serving dish, place the eggs on top and spoon the remaining sauce over them.

BOILED EGGS WITH BROCCOLI

Cook the broccoli in a pan of salted, boiling water for 10 minutes, then drain. Heat the oil in a skillet, add the garlic clove and cook until golden brown. Remove and discard the garlic, add the broccoli to the skillet and cook over low heat for a few minutes. Meanwhile, cook the eggs in boiling water for 4–5 minutes, then remove from the pan, refresh under cold water and shell. Arrange the eggs on a warm serving dish, spoon the broccoli around them and serve.

UOVA MOLLETTE CON I BROCCOLI

Serves 4

1³/₄ pounds broccoli, cut into flowerets

3 tablespoons olive oil

1 garlic clove

4 eggs

salt

BOILED EGGS WITH ARTICHOKE HEARTS

Cook the artichoke hearts in salted, boiling water until just tender, then drain and arrange on a warm serving dish. Melt the butter in a skillet, add the shallot, thyme and a pinch of pepper and cook over low heat, stirring occasionally, for 5 minutes Pour in the wine and cook until it has almost completely evaporated. Sprinkle with the flour, stir in scant 1 cup warm water and simmer for 5 minutes. Cook the eggs in boiling water for 4–5 minutes, then remove from the pan, refresh under cold water and shell. Place the eggs on the artichoke hearts and pour the sauce over them. Garnish with the ham and serve.

UOVA MOLLETTE CON I CARCIOFI

Serves 4

4 artichoke hearts

2 tablespoons butter

1 shallot, chopped

1 fresh thyme sprig, chopped

scant 1 cup dry white wine

pinch of all-purpose flour

4 eggs

salt and pepper

2 cooked cured ham slices, cut into strips, to garnish

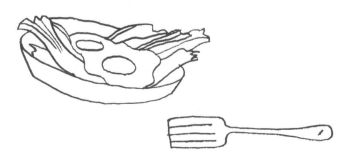

HARD
COOKED

Add salt to the water to prevent the shells from breaking and bring to a boil. Immerse the eggs and cook over a high heat for about 8 minutes. If the recipe calls for very hard-cooked eggs, cook them for 10 minutes. Refresh the eggs under cold running water to make shelling easier.

N° 11

HARD—COOKED EGGS IN ASPIC

ASPIC DI UOVA SODE

Serves 4–6

4 eggs, hard-cooked
5 ounces roast chicken breast, skinned and cut into strips
3 ounces pickled ox tongue, cut into strips
5 ounces cooked ham, trimmed of fat and diced
1 quantity Mayonnaise made with lemon juice (see page 65)
2 gelatin leaves
salt and pepper
radishes, thinly sliced or cut into flowers, to garnish

Shell the eggs and cut three of them into equally thick round slices. Chop the remaining egg, place in a bowl with the chicken, tongue and ham and gently stir in the mayonnaise. Prepare the gelatin according to the packet instructions and let cool but do not chill in the refrigerator. Pour a little cooled gelatin on to the base of a mold, brush the sides with a generous amount and chill in the refrigerator until set. Arrange some slices of hard-cooked egg on the base, pour a thin layer of gelatin on top and return to the refrigerator until set. Make a layer of the meat mixture in the mold and place a few slices of egg on top. Cover with another layer of gelatin and return to the refrigerator until set. Continue making alternating layers of the meat mixture, egg slices and gelatin until all the ingredients are used, ending with a layer of gelatin. Chill in the refrigerator for 3 hours. To serve, immerse the mold in hot water for a few seconds, then turn out on to a serving dish and garnish with the radishes.

HARD—COOKED EGGS IN CURRY SAUCE

UOVA SODE AL CURRY

Serves 4

butter, for greasing

1 teaspoon curry powder

1 quantity Béchamel Sauce (see page 50)

6 eggs

1 tablespoon Parmesan cheese, freshly grated

salt

Preheat the oven to 350°F. Grease an oven-proof dish with butter. Stir the curry powder and a pinch of salt into the béchamel sauce. Hard-cook the eggs in salted water, shell and halve lengthwise. Scoop out the yolks into a bowl and mash with 2 tablespoons of the curry sauce. Spoon the mixture into the egg whites, arrange them in the prepared dish, spoon the remaining curry sauce over them and sprinkle with the Parmesan. Bake until golden and bubbling.

HARD—COOKED EGGS NAPOLETANA

UOVA SODE ALLA NAPOLETANA

Serves 4

8 eggs

4 tomatoes, peeled, seeded and diced

1/2 cup green and black olives, pitted and chopped

4 canned anchovy fillets in oil, drained and finely chopped

4–6 tablespoons Mayonnaise (see page 65)

salt

lettuce leaves, to serve

Hard-cook the eggs in salted water, refresh in cold water and shell. Halve lengthwise and scoop out the yolks into a bowl. Mash with a fork and add 1 tablespoon of the tomatoes, and the olives, anchovy fillets and enough mayonnaise to combine. Fill the egg whites with the mixture, doming it up well. Make a bed of lettuce leaves on a serving dish, place the stuffed eggs on top and surround with the remaining tomatoes.

HARD—COOKED EGGS WITH WALNUTS

UOVA SODE ALLE NOCI

Serves 4

4 eggs

10 shelled walnuts

1 tablespoon anchovy paste

3 tablespoons butter, softened

juice of 1/2 lemon, strained

salt and pepper

1 tablespoon chopped fresh flat-leaf parsley, to garnish

Hard-cook the eggs in salted water, refresh in cold water, then shell. Halve lengthwise, scoop out the yolks into a bowl and mash with a fork. Finely chop two of the walnuts. Add the chopped walnuts, anchovy paste, butter and lemon juice to the egg yolks and mix well. Season with salt and pepper to taste. Fill the egg whites with the mixture and put a shelled walnut in the centre of each. Arrange on a serving dish and garnish with the parsley.

HARD—COOKED EGGS WITH HATS

Hard-cook the eggs in salted water, refresh in cold water and shell. Whisk together the oil and vinegar in a bowl, and season with salt and pepper. Add the salad leaves and toss then arrange on a serving dish. Cut the bottom off each egg so that it stands upright and place the eggs on top of the salad. Cut the top third off the tomatoes, scoop out the seeds and place the thirds on top of the eggs like hats. Slice the remaining parts of the tomatoes and use to garnish the dish. Serve with caper mayonnaise.

UOVA SODE COL CAPELLO

Serves 4

8 eggs

6 tablespoons olive oil

2 tablespoons white wine vinegar

1 bunch of Belgian endive or frisée, cut into strips

1 bunch of arugula, cut into strips

4 tomatoes

salt and pepper

caper mayonnaise, to serve

HARD—COOKED EGGS WITH SHRIMP

Hard-cook the eggs in salted water, refresh under cold running water and shell. Halve lengthwise and scoop out the yolks into a bowl. Mash with a fork, add the butter and anchovy paste and mix well. Fill the egg whites with the mixture and sprinkle with the parsley. Arrange the shrimp on top.

UOVA SODE CON I GAMBERETTI

Serves 4

4 eggs

2 tablespoons butter, softened

1 teaspoon anchovy paste

1 fresh flat-leaf parsley sprig, finely chopped

8 cooked, peeled shrimp • salt

HARD—COOKED EGGS WITH SMOKED SALMON

Hard-cook the eggs in salted water, refresh in cold water and shell. Halve lengthwise, scoop out the yolks into a blender, add the salmon and cream and season with salt and pepper. Process to a thick purée and use to fill the egg whites, doming the mixture on top. Fan out the lettuce leaves on a serving dish, and arrange two half-eggs on each leaf.

UOVA SODE CON IL SALMONE

Serves 4

4 eggs

5 ounces smoked salmon, chopped

3 tablespoons heavy cream

4 lettuce leaves

salt and pepper

HARD—COOKED EGGS WITH OYSTERS

Hard-cook the eggs in salted water, refresh in cold water and shell. Halve lengthwise, scoop out the yolks into a bowl and mash with a fork. Stir in the olive oil and lemon juice to make a smooth sauce and season with salt and pepper. Melt the butter in a skillet, add the oysters and parsley and cook over low heat for a few minutes, then spoon into the egg whites. Lightly toast the bread on both sides and spread with a little butter while still hot. Put a small slice of lemon on each slice and top with the oyster-filled eggs. Spoon the egg yolk sauce over them.

UOVA SODE CON LE OSTRICHE

Serves 4

4 eggs

2–3 tablespoons olive oil

2–3 tablespoons lemon juice, strained

2 tablespoons butter, plus extra for spreading

8 oysters, shucked

1 fresh flat-leaf parsley sprig, chopped

8 bread slices, crusts removed

1 lemon, peeled and thinly sliced

salt and pepper

UOVA SODE IN GELATINA

Serves 4

6 eggs

4 cups gelatin

6–7 cooked ham slices

$^{1}/_{2}$ cup capers, drained and rinsed

12 black olives

salt and pepper

HARD—COOKED EGGS AND HAM IN ASPIC

Hard-cook the eggs in salted water, refresh under cold water and shell. Halve the eggs crosswise. Prepare the gelatin according to the packet instructions, let cool slightly, then pour a thin layer on to the base of a serving dish and chill in the refrigerator until set. Using a cookie cutter or the rim of a glass, cut out 24 rounds of ham a little larger than the maximum diameter of the eggs. Place 12 ham rounds on the layer of set gelatin. Cut the tip off each half-egg so that it stands upright and place one on each ham round. Garnish each egg yolk with capers, a pinch of pepper and an olive and cover with another ham round. Pour the remaining gelatin over the eggs and chill in the refrigerator until set. Remove from the refrigerator 15 minutes before serving.

UOVA SODE RIPIENE E FRITTE

Serves 4

5 eggs

$^{1}/_{2}$ cup ricotta cheese

$^{1}/_{2}$ cup Parmesan cheese, freshly grated

2–3 tablespoons heavy cream

1 tablespoon chopped fresh flat-leaf parsley

1 tablespoon bread crumbs

all-purpose flour, for dusting

2 tablespoons butter

salt and pepper

FRIED STUFFED HARD—COOKED EGGS

Hard-cook four of the eggs in salted water, refresh under cold running water and shell. Halve lengthwise, scoop out the yolks into a bowl and mash with a fork. Add the ricotta, Parmesan, 2 tablespoons of the cream and the parsley, season with salt and pepper and mix well. If the mixture is too soft, add 1 tablespoon of the bread crumbs; if it is too firm, add the remaining cream. Fill the egg whites with the mixture and dust lightly with flour. Beat the remaining egg in a shallow dish and place the bread crumbs in another shallow dish. Dip the filled eggs first in beaten egg, then in bread crumbs. Melt the butter in a skillet, add the filled eggs and cook until lightly browned. Drain on paper towels, arrange on a serving dish and serve immediately.

SCRAMBLED

Melt scant ¹/₂ cup butter in a skillet for every 6 eggs. Lightly beat the eggs with a pinch of salt and pour into the skillet. Stir over medium heat until creamy, then stir in 2 tablespoons butter and transfer to to a serving dish. Take care not to overcook the eggs. To be sure that scrambled eggs will be soft, set aside 1 tablespoon beaten egg and add it once the skillet has been removed from the heat.

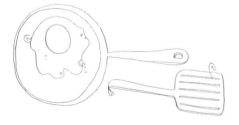

SCRAMBLED EGGS WITH ARTICHOKES

Break off the artichoke stalks, remove the tough, outer leaves and chokes and slice thinly. Melt the butter in a skillet, add the artichokes and season lightly with salt and pepper. Add 4 tablespoons water, cover and cook for 15 minutes, adding a little more water if necessary. Break the eggs, one at a time, onto a small plate and slide into the skillet. Scramble the eggs by stirring them with the artichokes, and remove from the heat as soon as the mixture starts to set. Serve hot.

UOVA STRAPAZZATE AI CARCIOFI

Serves 4

3 artichokes

¹/₄ cup butter

4 eggs

salt and pepper

UOVA STRAPAZZATE ALL'ABRUZZESE

Serves 4

3 tablespoons olive oil

1 onion, finely chopped

1 garlic clove, finely chopped

4 tomatoes, peeled, seeded and diced

1 fresh basil sprig, finely chopped

1 fresh marjoram sprig, finely chopped

1 fresh red chile, seeded and finely chopped

8 eggs, lightly beaten

scant 1 cup black olives, pitted

salt and pepper

ABRUZZO SCRAMBLED EGGS

Heat the oil in a skillet, add the onion and garlic and cook over low heat, stirring occasionally, for 5 minutes. Add the tomatoes, herbs and chile and cook, stirring occasionally, for 10 minutes. Pour in the eggs and mix with a fork to scramble When the mixture is soft, add the olives and season lightly with salt and pepper. Turn off the heat, cover and let stand for a few minutes before serving.

UOVA STRAPAZZATE ALLA FONTINA

Serves 4

5 eggs

6 tablespoons butter

³/₄ cup fontina cheese, freshly grated

salt and pepper

SCRAMBLED EGGS WITH FONTINA

Break one egg into a small bowl, beat lightly with a fork and set aside. Break the remaining eggs into another bowl and beat lightly with a fork. Melt 5 tablespoons of the butter in a skillet over medium heat, pour in the larger bowl of eggs and scramble. Sprinkle in the cheese, season with salt and pepper and continue scrambling. Add the remaining butter, small pieces at a time. When the mixture is soft and creamy, remove the skillet from the heat and immediately stir in the reserved beaten egg. Mix well and serve immediately.

UOVA STRAPAZZATE AL TARTUFO

Serves 4

4 bread slices, crusts removed

8 eggs

3 tablespoons butter, softened, plus extra for spreading

scant ¹/₂ cup truffle paste

2 tablespoons heavy cream

salt and pepper

SCRAMBLED EGGS WITH TRUFFLE

Lightly toast the bread on both sides. Lightly beat the eggs with a pinch of salt and pepper. Cream the butter with the truffle paste in another bowl, then melt in a skillet over a low heat. Pour in the eggs and as soon as the mixture starts to thicken, add the cream, mix well and remove the skillet from the heat. Thinly spread the toast with butter and arrange on a warm serving dish. Spoon the truffled eggs on top and serve immediately.

SCRAMBLED EGGS WITH SPINACH

Cook the spinach, in just the water clinging to the leaves after washing, for 5 minutes, then drain well, squeezing out as much liquid as possible, and chop. Place in a clean pan over low heat for 1–2 minutes to drive off excess water, then remove from the heat and add the parsley, basil and shallot. Lightly beat the eggs in a bowl with 1 tablespoon water and season with salt and pepper. Stir in the spinach mixture. Heat the oil in a nonstick skillet, pour in the egg mixture and cook over medium heat, stirring constantly. When the mixture is green and soft, remove the pan from the heat, let stand for 2 minutes, then transfer to a warm serving dish and serve immediately.

UOVA STRAPAZZATE AL VERDE

Serves 4

14 ounces spinach

1 fresh flat-leaf parsley sprig, chopped

6 fresh basil leaves, chopped

1 shallot, chopped

6 eggs

2 tablespoons olive oil

salt and pepper

SCRAMBLED EGGS WITH BEANS

Heat the oil in a skillet, add the onion and beans and cook over low heat, stirring occasionally, for 10 minutes. Add the eggs, season with salt and pepper and stir with a fork to scramble. As soon as the eggs become creamy, remove the skillet from the heat and serve immediately.

UOVA STRAPAZZATE CON I FAGIOLI

Serves 4

2 tablespoons olive oil

1 onion, cut into thin rings

11 ounces canned borlotti beans,

drained and rinsed

4 eggs, lightly beaten

salt and pepper

SCRAMBLED EGGS WITH CHICKEN LIVERS

Melt half the butter in a skillet over a high heat, add the chicken livers and cook, stirring frequently, for 5 minutes. Season with salt and pepper and stir in the tomato paste. Add the liver mixture to the eggs. Melt the remaining butter in a clean skillet, pour in the egg mixture and stir with a fork to scramble until creamy. Remove the skillet from the heat and serve immediately.

UOVA STRAPAZZATE CON I FEGATINI

Serves 4

$1/4$ cup butter

7 ounces chicken livers, thawed if frozen, trimmed and coarsely chopped

1 tablespoon tomato paste

4 eggs, lightly beaten

salt and pepper

SCRAMBLED EGGS WITH SAUSAGE

Put the sausages, garlic and half the butter in a skillet and cook over low heat, stirring frequently, until browned, then remove the skillet from the heart. Discard the garlic. Lightly beat the eggs with a pinch of salt. Melt the remaining butter in another skillet and pour in the eggs. Remove the crumbled sausages with a slotted spoon, draining well, and add to the eggs. Stir with a fork until creamy, then remove from the heat and serve immediately.

UOVA STRAPAZZATE CON LA SALSICCIA

Serves 4

7 ounces Italian sausages, skinned and crumbled

1 garlic clove

2 tablespoons butter

5 eggs

salt

SCRAMBLED EGGS IN THEIR NESTS

Cook the potatoes in salted, boiling water for 20–30 minutes until tender. Drain, peel and mash in a bowl, then add 2 tablespoons of the butter, 2–3 tablespoons of the cream, one egg and the Parmesan. Mix well and season with salt. Preheat the oven to 350°F. Grease a cookie sheet with butter. Make four spirals with the potato mixture on the cookie sheet and surround each with another higher ring of the mixture. Bake for 20 minutes until golden. Meanwhile, lightly beat the remaining eggs with salt and pepper. Melt the remaining butter in a skillet, pour in eggs and cook over a low heat for 2 minutes. Stir in the remaining cream and cook, stirring, until thick. Spoon the eggs into the potato 'nests' and serve.

UOVA STRAPAZZATE NEL NIDO

Serves 4

1 pound 2 ounces potatoes

6 tablespoons butter, plus extra for greasing

$^1/_4$ cup heavy cream

6 eggs

$^2/_3$ cup Parmesan cheese, freshly grated

salt and pepper

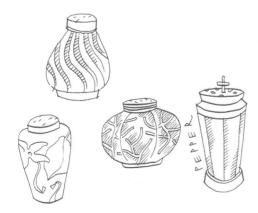

THE FRITTATA FAMILY

Italian omelets – frittate – are economical and quick and are among the tastiest dishes that can be made with eggs. They are also very versatile, as the basic recipe may be enriched and flavored with a wide range of other ingredients, including herbs, vegetables, fish, cheeses, salami, ham and fruit. As regards quantities, in general allow two eggs per person if the frittata is served as a main course and one if it is an antipasto. As a general rule, $1^1/_2$ teaspoons butter or olive oil is required to cook every two eggs.

COOKING

A SKILLET IS ESSENTIAL

No other pan produces the same result. The choice of material, on the other hand, may vary – classic black cast iron, nonstick which does not need butter or oil, or a double pan which may be closed and turned over to brown both sides perfectly. The perfect frittata should be dry and golden brown on the outside, while still slightly soft inside.

THE METHOD IS AS FOLLOWS

Lightly beat the eggs in a bowl, season with salt (pepper is optional) and immediately pour into a skillet with butter or oil at just the right temperature. Lower the heat and, after 1–2 minutes when the egg starts to set, shake the skillet slightly to loosen the frittata and then turn it over. The easiest way to do this is to cover the skillet with a flat plate and, holding it tightly, invert the skillet then slide the frittata back into the pan and cook it on the other side. Keep the skillet over the heat for the necessary time: 2–3 minutes if there are more than four eggs. Although the degree of cooking depends on individual taste, very dry frittata are not recommended.

SAVOURY CRÊPES

Basically, crêpes are only fried eggs, but so many versions exist that you could offer filled crêpes for months without repeating yourself. They may also be used to make timbales, gratins and cannelloni, according to how they are arranged or folded. They may be served as a first course or main course, or as a one-course meal. What is important is that they are thin.

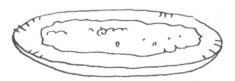

SMOKED SALMON CRÊPES

Prepare the crêpes and while still warm spread lightly with the butter and place 1–2 slices of smoked salmon on top of each. Fold each crêpe into four, arrange on a warm serving dish and sprinkle with the lemon juice. Serve immediately.

CRÊPES AL SALMONE AFFUMICATO

Serves 4

12 crêpes (see page 155)

3 tablespoons butter, softened

5 ounces smoked salmon, thinly sliced

juice of 1 lemon, strained

PICKLED SALMON CRÊPES

Put the slices of raw salmon in a soup plate, pour in the lemon juice, sprinkle with the peppercorns and let marinate for 1 hour. Prepare the crêpes and let cool. Place two slices of salmon on each crêpe, fold into four and arrange on a serving dish.

CRÊPES AL SALMONE MARINATO

Serves 4

8 thin slices raw salmon

juice of 2 lemons, strained

1 tablespoon green peppercorns

12 crêpes (see page 155)

383

CHEESE AND WALNUT CRÊPES

CRÊPES CON FORMAGGIO E NOCI

Serves 4

12 crêpes (see page 155)

butter, for greasing

5 ounces mild Gorgonzola cheese, crumbled

scant ½ cup mascarpone cheese

12 shelled walnuts, chopped

4 tablespoons heavy cream

Prepare the crêpes and let cool. Preheat the oven to 350°F. Grease an ovenproof dish with butter. Combine together the Gorgonzola and mascarpone in a bowl and add the walnuts. Spread the mixture over the crêpes, fold into four and arrange in the prepared dish. Sprinkle with the cream and bake until the cream is absorbed.

CARDOON CRÊPES

CRÊPES CON I CARDI

Serves 4

1 pound 2 ounces cardoons, trimmed

3 tablespoons butter, plus extra for greasing

12 crêpes (see page 155)

¾ quantity Béchamel Sauce (see page 50)

salt

Cook the cardoons in salted, boiling water for 1 hour, then drain well and chop. Melt 2 tablespoons of the butter in a skillet, add the cardoons and cook over low heat, stirring occasionally, for 5 minutes. Prepare the crêpes and let cool. Preheat the oven to 350°F. Grease an ovenproof dish with butter. Spread a little béchamel sauce on each crêpe and arrange a little chopped cardoon on top, then cover with more béchamel sauce and roll up. Place the crêpes in the prepared dish, dot with the remaining butter and bake for 15 minutes. Remove from the oven and let stand for about 10 minutes, then serve.

RICOTTA AND SPINACH CRÊPES

CRÊPES CON RICOTTA E SPINACI

Serves 4

12 crêpes (see page 155)

3 tablespoons butter, plus extra for greasing

1 pound 2 ounces spinach

1 tablespoon olive oil

scant 1 cup ricotta cheese

1 egg yolk

2 tablespoons Parmesan cheese, freshly grated

Prepare the crêpes and let cool. Preheat the oven to 350°F. Grease an ovenproof dish with butter. Cook the spinach, in just the water clinging to the leaves after washing, for 5 minutes, then drain, squeeze out as much liquid as possible and chop. Melt 2 tablespoons of the butter with the oil in a skillet, add the spinach and cook over low heat, stirring frequently, for 5 minutes. Transfer to a bowl and mix with the ricotta and egg yolk. Spread the mixture on the crêpes, fold in half and arrange in the prepared dish. Sprinkle with the Parmesan and dot with the remaining butter. Bake for 15 minutes, then remove from the oven and let stand for a few minutes before serving.

FRITTATA

FRITTATA AI PEPERONI

Serves 4

3 tablespoons butter

4 tablespoons olive oil

2 yellow bell peppers, halved, seeded and diced

3 tomatoes, peeled, seeded and diced

6 eggs, lightly beaten

salt and pepper

BELL PEPPER FRITTATA

Heat half the butter and the oil in a skillet, add the bell peppers and cook, stirring, for 2 minutes. Add the tomatoes, season with salt and pepper, cover and cook over low heat for 15–20 minutes. Add the eggs. Melt the remaining butter in another skillet and pour the entire mixture into it. Cook the frittata on both sides and serve.

FRITTATA AL FORMAGGIO

Serves 4

8 eggs

3 ounces fontina cheese, diced

1 small cooked ham slice, diced

1 tablespoon Parmesan cheese, freshly grated

olive oil, for brushing

salt

CHEESE FRITTATA

Lightly beat the eggs with a pinch of salt and stir in the fontina, ham and Parmesan. Heat a skillet and brush lightly with oil. Pour in the egg mixture and cook over low heat until browned on both sides. When the frittata is ready, it should be soft and the cheese in the middle should form strings. Transfer to a warm serving dish.

BORAGE FRITTATA

Tear the bread into pieces, place in a bowl, add water to cover and let soak, then squeeze out. Heat 3 tablespoons of the oil in a pan, add the borage, cover and cook over low heat until wilted. Lightly beat the eggs with the Parmesan, soaked bread, marjoram and garlic, then stir in the borage and season with salt and pepper. Heat the remaining oil in a skillet, pour in the mixture and smooth the surface by pressing lightly with a spatula. Cook over low heat on both sides. This frittata should be very thick and quite soft inside.

FRITTATA ALLA BORRAGINE

Serves 4

2 ounces bread slices, crusts removed

5 tablespoons olive oil

7 cups borage, finely chopped

4 eggs

2 tablespoons Parmesan cheese, freshly grated

6 fresh marjoram leaves, chopped

1/2 garlic clove, finely chopped

salt and pepper

HAM FRITTATA

Lightly beat the eggs and stir in the ham, parsley, Parmesan and cream. Season lightly with salt and pepper. Melt the butter in a skillet, pour in the mixture and cook until golden brown on both sides. Serve hot.

FRITTATA AL PROSCIUTTO COTTO

Serves 4

6 eggs

4 ounces cooked ham, chopped

1 fresh flat-leaf parsley sprig, chopped

1 tablespoon Parmesan cheese, freshly grated

2 tablespoons heavy cream

1 ounces butter

salt and pepper

HAM AND SAGE FRITTATA

Lightly beat the eggs, stir in the ham, sage, Parmesan and cream and season with salt and pepper. Melt the butter in a skillet, pour in the mixture and cook until light golden brown on both sides. The frittata should be dry outside and soft inside.

FRITTATA AL PROSCIUTTO COTTO E SALVIA

Serves 4

6 eggs

2/3 cup cooked ham, chopped

6 fresh sage leaves, chopped

1 tablespoon Parmesan cheese, freshly grated

2 tablespoons heavy cream

2 tablespoons butter

salt and pepper

CELERY AND SAUSAGE FRITTATA

Lightly beat the eggs, stir in the sausage and celery and season lightly with salt and pepper. Heat the olive oil in a skillet, pour in the mixture and cook until browned on both sides. This frittata is good eaten both hot or cold.

FRITTATA AL SEDANO E SALSICCIA

Serves 4

6 eggs

5 ounces Italian sausage, skinned and crumbled

1 celery heart, chopped

2 tablespoons olive oil

salt and pepper

TUNA FRITTATA

FRITTATA AL TONNO

Serves 4

2 tablespoons butter

1 scallion, thinly sliced

3¹/₂ ounces canned tuna in oil, drained and flaked

6 eggs

1 tablespoon chopped fresh flat-leaf parsley

salt

Melt the butter in a skillet over very low heat, add the scallion and cook, stirring frequently, for 5 minutes until translucent. Stir in the tuna. Lightly beat the eggs, stir in the parsley and a pinch of salt and pour the mixture over the tuna. Cook until the frittata is browned on both sides. Serve warm.

ONION AND THYME FRITTATA

FRITTATA CON CIPOLLE E TIMO

Serves 4

2 tablespoons olive oil

2 tablespoons butter

11 ounces onions, thinly sliced

2 fresh thyme sprigs, leaves only

6 eggs • salt

Heat the oil and butter in a skillet, add the onions and cook over low heat, stirring occasionally, for 5 minutes. Stir in the thyme and cook for a few minutes more. Meanwhile, lightly beat the eggs with a pinch of salt, then pour into the skillet. Cook until lightly browned on both sides.

BREAD FRITTATA

FRITTATA CON IL PANE

Serves 4

2 day-old bread slices, crusts removed

scant 1 cup milk

6 eggs

2 tablespoons Parmesan cheese, freshly grated

1 tablespoon chopped fresh flat-leaf parsley

2 tablespoons olive oil

2 tablespoons butter

salt and pepper

Tear the bread into pieces, place in a bowl, add the milk and let soak for 10 minutes, then squeeze out. Lightly beat the eggs, stir in the bread, Parmesan and parsley and season with salt and pepper. Mix until the bread softens and is incorporated. Heat the oil and butter in a skillet, pour in the mixture and cook until browned on both sides. This frittata has a simple but delicate taste.

OLIVE FRITTATA

FRITTATA CON LE OLIVE

Serves 4

1¹/₂ tablespoons butter

1 shallot, thinly sliced

2 ounces pancetta, cut into strips

5 eggs

2 tablespoons Parmesan cheese, freshly grated

¹/₄ cup green olives, pitted and chopped

¹/₄ cup black olives, pitted and chopped

2 tablespoons olive oil

salt and pepper

Melt the butter in a skillet, add the shallot and cook over low heat, stirring occasionally, for 5 minutes until soft. Stir in the pancetta and cook for a few minutes more, then remove the skillet from the heat and let cool slightly. Lightly beat the eggs with the Parmesan and season with salt and pepper. Stir in the olives and the shallot and pancetta mixture. Heat the oil in a skillet, pour in the mixture and cook until browned on both sides, but do not let the frittata dry out too much. Serve immediately.

ZUCCHINI FRITTATA

Heat the oil and half the butter in a pan, add the zucchini and cook, stirring occasionally, for 10 minutes. Season with salt and pepper and remove from the heat. Lightly beat the eggs with a pinch of salt and stir in the zucchini. Melt the remaining butter in a skillet, pour in the mixture and cook until lightly browned on both sides. This frittata may be served hot or cold.

FRITTATA CON LE ZUCCHINE

Serves 4

2 tablespoons olive oil

1/4 cup butter

2 1/2 cups zucchini, thinly sliced

6 eggs

salt and pepper

POTATO AND CINNAMON FRITTATA

Cook the potatoes in salted, boiling water for 20 minutes or until tender, then drain, tip into a large bowl and mash. Add the milk, 3 tablespoons of the butter and a pinch of salt and beat to a purée with a wooden spoon. Stir in the egg yolks, one at a time. Whisk two egg whites in a separate grease-free bowl until stiff, then fold into the potato mixture. Add a pinch of cinnamon, season with salt to taste and mix very gently to avoid knocking out the air. Melt the remaining butter with the oil in a skillet, pour in the potato mixture and cook over medium heat until browned on both sides.

FRITTATA CON PATATE E CANNELLA

Serves 4

2 potatoes

scant 1/2 cup milk

5 tablespoons butter

4 eggs, separated

pinch of ground cinnamon

2 tablespoons olive oil

salt

MEAT FRITTATA

Melt half the butter in a small pan, add the meat and a pinch of salt and cook over medium heat, stirring frequently, until browned. Lightly beat the eggs, season with salt and pepper and stir in the meat and parsley. If the mixture seems too dry, stir in a little milk. Melt the remaining butter with the oil in a skillet, pour in the mixture and cook until golden brown on both sides. Serve hot or cold. It is also possible to use leftover cooked meat, but in this case sautéing is unnecessary.

FRITTATA DI CARNE

Serves 4

1/4 cup butter

1 1/4 cups ground meat

4 eggs

1 fresh flat-leaf parsley sprig, chopped

2–3 tablespoons milk (optional)

1 tablespoon olive oil

salt and pepper

FILLED FRITTATA

FRITTATA RIPIENA

Serves 4

4 eggs

5 tablespoons butter

generous 2¾ cups mushrooms, cut into thin strips

⅓ cup cooked ham, diced

½ cup tongue, diced

2 ounces Swiss cheese, diced

salt and pepper

Preheat the oven to 350°F. Lightly beat the eggs with salt and pepper. Melt 2 tablespoons of the butter in a large skillet, pour in the eggs and fry a very thin frittata on both sides. Melt 2 tablespoons of the remaining butter in a small pan, add the mushrooms and cook, stirring occasionally, for about 10 minutes. Add the ham, tongue and cheese to the mushrooms and remove from the heat. Melt the remaining butter. Arrange the mushroom filling on one half of the frittata, brush the other half with melted butter and fold over. Place the frittata on an ovenproof plate and put in the oven for a few minutes until the cheese has melted. Serve immediately while hot.

FRITTATA CAKE

TORTA DI FRITTATE

Serves 6

7 ounces eggplants, sliced

7 ounces red or yellow bell peppers

6 eggs

1 fresh flat-leaf parsley sprig, chopped

1 tablespoon Parmesan cheese, freshly grated

2 tablespoons butter

3½ ounces fontina cheese, sliced

olive oil

salt and pepper

Preheat the oven to 400°F, and preheat the broiler. Broil the eggplants until soft and golden brown. Roast the bell peppers in the oven until blackened and charred, then transfer to a plastic bag and seal the top. Increase the oven temperature to 475°F. When cool enough to handle, peel and seed the peppers and cut the flesh into strips. Beat two eggs in one bowl and two eggs in another bowl, season both with salt and pepper and divide the parsley between them. Beat the remaining eggs in a third bowl, season with salt and pepper and stir in the Parmesan. Heat the oil and butter in a skillet, pour in one bowl of the egg and parsley mixture and cook until set on one side, but still quite soft on the other. Slide the frittata out of the skillet and cook two more in the same way, with the remaining egg and parsley mixture and the egg and Parmesan mixture. Line a cake pan with baking parchment and place one of the parsley frittatas, soft side up, in it. Cover with the eggplant and half the fontina. Place the Parmesan frittata on top of them, soft side up, and cover with the strips of bell pepper and the remaining fontina. Finally, place the second parsley frittata on top, soft side down. Bake for 10 minutes. Serve hot or cold.

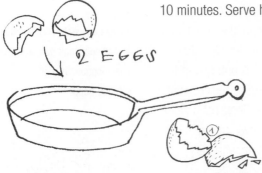

OMELETS

SET

BELL PEPPER OMELET

OMELETTE AI PEPERONI

Serves 4

3 tablespoons butter

2 tablespoons olive oil

1 onion, chopped

2 small bell green peppers, halved, seeded and cut into thick strips

3 tomatoes, peeled, seeded and diced

⅓ cup cooked ham, diced

4 eggs • salt and pepper

Melt the butter with the oil in a skillet, add the onion and cook over low heat, stirring occasionally, for 10 minutes until lightly browned. Add the bell peppers and cook for 5 minutes, then add the tomatoes and ham. Cook over medium heat for about 30 minutes. Lightly beat the eggs with salt and pepper, pour the mixture over the vegetables and increase the heat so that the omelet cooks quickly. This omelet should be soft and puffy; do not turn or fold, but slide whole on to a warm serving dish.

CRABMEAT OMELET

OMELETTE ALLA POLPA DI GRANCHIO

Serves 4

¼ cup butter

2 ounces crabmeat, drained if canned, and finely chopped

2 tablespoons heavy cream

6 eggs

salt and pepper

Melt half the butter in a small pan, add the crabmeat and cook, stirring occasionally, for 5 minutes. Season with salt and plenty of pepper, add the cream and cook over low heat for 15 minutes without letting the butter turn brown. Lightly beat the eggs with a pinch of salt, a pinch of pepper and 1 tablespoon cold water. Melt the remaining butter in a skillet, pour in the eggs and cook until set on the underside and soft on top. Spoon the crabmeat on to one half of the omelet, fold over and serve.

PROVENÇAL OMELET

OMELETTE ALLA PROVENZALE

Serves 4

2 tablespoons olive oil

2 tomatoes, peeled, seeded and diced

1 garlic clove, finely chopped

3½ ounces Italian sausages, skinned and crumbled

4 eggs

2 tablespoons butter

1 fresh flat-leaf parsley sprig, chopped

salt and pepper

Heat the oil in a skillet, add the tomatoes and garlic and cook, stirring occasionally, until the tomatoes are softened. Meanwhile, pour 1 tablespoon water into another pan, add the sausages and cook over low heat for 15 minutes, then add to the pan of tomatoes. Lightly beat the eggs with 1 tablespoon water and season lightly with salt and pepper. Melt the butter in a skillet, pour in the eggs and cook until set on the underside and soft on top. Place the sausage mixture on one half of the omelet, sprinkle with the parsley and fold over. Slide on to a warm serving dish.

OMELET WITH SNAILS

Prepare the snails (see page 730). Heat the oil in a pan over medium heat, add the garlic and cook for a few minutes until browned, then remove and discard. Stir in the parsley, add the snails and season with salt and pepper. Stir gently and sprinkle with the vinegar. Lightly beat the eggs with 1 tablespoon water and a pinch of salt and pepper. Melt the butter in a skillet, pour in the eggs and cook until set on the underside and soft on top. Spoon the snails, together with their hot cooking juices, on to one half of the omelet, fold over and slide on to a warm serving dish.

OMELETTE ALLE LUMACHE

Serves 4

12 fresh, canned or frozen snails

1 tablespoon olive oil

1 garlic clove

1 tablespoon finely chopped fresh flat-leaf parsley

1 tablespoon white wine vinegar

6 eggs

2 tablespoons butter

salt and pepper

ZUCCHINI OMELET

Put the zucchini into a nonstick skillet and place over high heat for a few minutes so that they dry a little. Sprinkle with salt and pepper and set aside in warm place. Lightly beat the eggs with salt and pepper and stir in the parsley. Heat the oil and butter in a skillet, pour in the eggs and cook until set on the underside and soft on top. Spoon the zucchini on to one half of the omelet, fold over and leave on the heat for 1 minute. Slide the omelet on to a warm serving dish.

OMELETTE ALLE ZUCCHINE

Serves 4

3 zucchini, cut into thin batons

6 eggs

1 fresh flat-leaf parsley sprig, finely chopped

1 tablespoon olive oil

2 tablespoons butter

salt and pepper

RADICCHIO OMELET

Melt half the butter in a pan, add the radicchio and cook over low heat until softened. Season with salt and pepper to taste, add the cream and flour and cook over low heat for about 20 minutes. Remove the pan from the heat and set aside in a warm place. Lightly beat the eggs with 1 tablespoon water, salt and pepper. Melt the remaining butter in a skillet, pour in the eggs and cook until set on the underside and soft on top. Spoon the radicchio on to one half of the omelet and fold over. Slide on to a warm serving dish.

OMELETTE AL RADICCHIO

Serves 4

2 ounces butter

2 radicchio, cut into thin strips

$3^1/_2$ fl ounces heavy cream

pinch of all-purpose flour

4 eggs

salt and pepper

AROMATIC OMELET

Lightly beat the eggs with salt, pepper and 1 tablespoon water. Combine herbs together and stir into the eggs. Heat the butter and oil in a skillet over medium heat, pour in the egg mixture and cook until set on the underside and soft on top. Slide the omelet on to a warm serving dish. Serve.

OMELETTE AROMATICA

Serves 4

6 eggs • 1 fresh flat-leaf parsley sprig, chopped

6 fresh basil leaves, chopped • 2 fresh mint leaves, chopped • 1 tablespoon chopped fresh chives

2 tablespoons butter • 1 tablespoon olive oil

salt and pepper

CURRIED MUSHROOM OMELET

Melt half the butter in a skillet, add the onion and cook over low heat, stirring occasionally, for 5 minutes. Add the mushrooms and cook for a few minutes, then season with salt and pepper to taste and add the flour, curry powder and cream. Mix well and cook over medium heat for about 30 minutes. Lightly beat the eggs with 1 tablespoon water, a pinch of salt and a pinch of pepper. Melt the remaining butter in a skillet, pour in the eggs and cook until set on the underside and soft on top. Sprinkle the mushrooms on one half of the omelet, fold over and slide on to a warm serving dish. If you like, this omelet may be served with Curry Sauce (see page 54) or very runny Béchamel Sauce (see page 50).

OMELETTE CON FUNGHI AL CURRY

Serves 4

$1/4$ cup butter

1 onion, thinly sliced

2 cups white mushrooms, sliced

pinch of all-purpose flour

pinch of curry powder

scant $1/2$ cup heavy cream

6 eggs

salt and pepper

FOUR CHEESE OMELET

Preheat the oven to 325°F. This is a variation on the classic omelet since milk and different types of cheese are added. Lightly beat the eggs with a little salt and add the Parmesan, milk, salt and pepper. Melt the butter in a small skillet, pour in the eggs and cook until set on the underside and soft on top. Sprinkle the diced cheeses on one half of the omelet and fold over. Gently slide on to an ovenproof serving dish. Turn off the oven and cook until the cheeses have melted.

OMELETTE VARIANTE
AI QUATTRO FORMAGGI

Serves 4

6 eggs

3 tablespoons Parmesan cheese, freshly grated

scant $1/2$ cup milk

2 tablespoons butter

1 ounces Emmenthal cheese, finely diced

$1 1/2$ ounces mozzarella cheese, finely diced

1 ounces fontina cheese, finely diced

salt and pepper

RICOTTA OMELET

Combine the flour and 1 tablespoon water in a bowl. Add the eggs and beat lightly, then season lightly with salt and pepper. Melt the butter in a skillet, pour in a ladleful of the mixture and cook until set on the underside and soft on top. Continue making omelets in the same way until the egg mixture is used. Combine the ricotta and ham in a bowl, season with salt and, if necessary, dilute with one or more tablespoons warm water. Sprinkle a little of the Parmesan over each omelet, spoon on the ricotta mixture and fold. Arrange on a warm serving dish and serve with tomato sauce.

OMELETTE VARIANTE ALLA RICOTTA

Serves 4

2 tablespoons all-purpose flour

4 eggs

2 tablespoons butter

scant 1 cup ricotta cheese

$1/3$ cup cooked ham, chopped

$1/3$ cup Parmesan cheese, freshly grated

salt and pepper

Tomato Sauce (see page 57), to serve

LEMON

OIL BOTTLE

FINE IMITATION OF CUT GLASS

MMM...

VEGETABLES →

VEGETABLES

Italy was once called the garden of Europe. Perhaps this description included the idea of the vegetable garden, given the abundance of salad vegetables, greens, potatoes, bell peppers, artichokes, mushrooms, tubers, roots, cereals and all the other components that make up the enormous and prolific Italian vegetable family. At one time vegetables were considered a side dish and legumes a poor food – or even food for the poor. Today things are very different. Recently, raw and cooked vegetables have also become first courses, and legumes have been promoted with honor to the highest ranks owing to their high nutritional value. We were once used to eating asparagus and peas in the spring, and cabbages and turnips in the winter. Today, with greenhouse cultivation and international trade, we can find every kind of vegetable all year round. Of course, the taste is not what it was: out-of-season vegetables are often either tasteless or so strongly flavored that they almost seem chemically synthesized. Nevertheless, whether they are fresh, frozen, canned or bottled, there is no lack of vegetables and they can be prepared in hundreds of ways. Vegetables form an essential part of the healthy diet and nutritionists recommend that we should eat at least five portions a day. While vegetables in general are available fresh and may be eaten either raw or cooked, legumes may be fresh or dried and must always be cooked. Specific cooking times and advice regarding the various recipes are given in the introductions to individual vegetables.

OIL VINEGAR

STEAMING

This is the best way to cook all vegetables as they absorb less water, retain more taste and, above all, lose fewer nutrients.

BOILING

To retain the bright color of vegetables when cooking in boiling salted water, do not cover the pan. When boiling some vegetables, it is advisable to add a 'blanching mixture', consisting of 1 tablespoon all-purpose flour, 1 tablespoon olive oil and the juice of 1 lemon. This prevents vegetables such as artichokes, cardoons and scorzonera from turning black and helps retain the bright green color of green beans, peas, etc.

PARBOILING

This means boiling vegetables for a few minutes before cooking them by the method described in the recipe or before adding them to another dish.

MARINATING

This means leaving ingredients in an aromatic liquid to soak up its flavor. Put scant $^1/_2$ cup oil, $2^1/_2$ cups water, a bouquet garni, consisting of parsley, thyme, a bay leaf and a celery stalk, 1 teaspoon black pepper-

corns and 1 teaspoon cilantro in a pan and bring to a boil. Lower the heat and simmer for 20 minutes, then pour the hot or warm marinade (according to the instructions in the recipe) into a bowl, immerse the raw, broiled or fried vegetables (asparagus spears, artichoke hearts, zucchini or eggplants) and let marinate for at least 20 minutes or more according to the recipe. Remember to leave vegetables to marinate in a cool place, but not in the refrigerator unless otherwise specified.

FRYING

This is a method of cooking some vegetables – which may be dredged with flour or coated in bread crumbs or batter – in hot oil. To make a batter, sift 9 tablespoons all-purpose flour into a bowl, break an egg into the middle and add 1 tablespoon olive oil and a pinch of salt. Mix thoroughly with a wooden spoon to prevent lumps from forming, then stir in scant $^1/_2$ cup milk. Cover and let stand for at least 30 minutes, then fold in a stiffly whisked egg white. Dip only a few pieces of vegetable in the batter at a time, then fry in hot oil.

ASPARAGUS

Asparagus is elegant, expensive and delicate. Its short season runs from April to June, but it has its best fragrance, firmness and flavor in May. Thanks to imports, however, it can now be found almost all year round. The most widely available types are white, green and violet and there are different varieties for each color. Choice is a matter of personal taste. Asparagus must be bought fresh. The spears should be straight and green, the stems should be shiny, plump and smooth without blemishes and the bunches should be compact. Asparagus has few calories, but has diuretic properties and is rich in vitamins A and C. Its particularly delicate taste goes well with eggs, shrimp, chicken, rabbit and veal. Cream of asparagus soup makes a delicious and sophisticated start to any formal meal. So, too, does a savory pie containing asparagus among its ingredients. Lastly, on the subject of etiquette, although modern manners allow us to use our fingers to dip asparagus stems in egg yolk or sauces, at least among family and friends, it is more correct to use a fork.

QUANTITIES AND COOKING TIMES

QUANTITIES

Allow 9–11 ounces per serving.

BOILING

Cut off the toughest part of the stems and peel the rest if necessary. Rinse and cut the stems to more or less the same length, then tie together in bunches. Place them upright in salted, boiling water with the spears protruding above the waterline and cook for 15–20 minutes.

STEAMING

This is the best cooking method. Bring about 2 inches salted water to a boil, add the asparagus and steam for about 10 minutes. Just 3 minutes is long enough for blanching.

ASPARAGUS AU GRATIN

Cook the asparagus in salted, boiling water for approximately 15 minutes, then drain and pat dry. Meanwhile, preheat the oven to 350°F. Grease an ovenproof dish with butter. Arrange half the asparagus spears with the tips pointing inwards in the prepared dish and dot with half the butter. Sprinkle with the Parmesan, cover with the Emmenthal and pour the béchamel sauce over the cheeses while it is still hot. Place the remaining asparagus on top and dot with the remaining butter. Bake for 15 minutes.

ASPARAGI AL GRATIN

Serves 4

2¼ pounds asparagus, spears trimmed

¼ cup butter, plus extra for greasing

½ cup Parmesan cheese, freshly grated

2½ ounces Emmenthal cheese, thinly sliced

1¼ cups Béchamel Sauce (see page 50)

salt

ASPARAGUS BELLA ELENA

Cook the asparagus in salted, boiling water for 15 minutes. Meanwhile, tear the bread into pieces, place in a bowl, pour in the milk and let soak. Drain the asparagus, cut off the spears and set aside. Place the stems in a food processor and process to a purée, then scrape into a bowl. Squeeze out the bread and stir it into the purée with the Parmesan. Separate one of the eggs and stir the yolk, together with two whole eggs, into the purée. Season with salt and pepper and stir in the asparagus spears. If the mixture is too runny, add some of the bread crumbs or more Parmesan. Shape the mixture into balls. Spread out the flour in a shallow dish, beat the remaining egg in another shallow dish and spread out the bread crumbs in a third. Dip the asparagus balls first in the flour, then in the beaten egg and, finally, in the bread crumbs. Heat the oil in a skillet, add the asparagus balls, in batches if necessary, and fry until golden brown all over. Remove with a slotted spatula and drain on paper towels. Serve immediately.

ASPARAGI ALLA BELLA ELENA

Serves 4

2¼ pounds asparagus, spears trimmed

2 ounces bread, crusts removed

scant ½ cup milk

½ cup Parmesan cheese, freshly grated

4 eggs

1⅔ cups dried bread crumbs

4 tablespoons all-purpose flour

vegetable oil, for deep-frying

salt and pepper

ASPARAGUS WITH PANCETTA

Cook the asparagus in salted, boiling water for 15 minutes. Meanwhile, preheat the oven to 350°F. Grease an ovenproof dish with butter. Drain the asparagus and place it in the prepared dish. Stir the Parmesan and egg yolks into the pan of béchamel sauce and season with salt and pepper. Set over medium heat, stir in the wine and cook until it has evaporated. Remove the pan from the heat and stir in the nutmeg. Place the pancetta slices on top of the asparagus and spoon the sauce over them. Dot with the butter and bake for 15 minutes until golden and bubbling.

ASPARAGI ALLA PANCETTA

Serves 4

2¼ pounds asparagus, spears trimmed

2 tablespoons butter, plus extra for greasing

½ cup Parmesan cheese, freshly grated

2 egg yolks

1¼ cups Béchamel Sauce (see page 50)

scant ½ cup dry white wine

pinch of freshly grated nutmeg

7 ounces pancetta, sliced

salt and pepper

PARMESAN ASPARAGUS

ASPARAGI ALLA PARMIGIANA

Serves 4

2¹/₄ pounds asparagus, spears trimmed
1 cup Parmesan cheese, freshly grated
2 tablespoons butter
salt

Cook the asparagus in salted, boiling water for 15 minutes. Drain and pat dry gently. Arrange on a warm serving dish with the spears pointing inwards. Sprinkle with the Parmesan. Melt the butter, season with a little salt and pour onto the asparagus. Serve immediately.

ASPARAGUS WITH ORANGE

ASPARAGI ALL'ARANCIA

Serves 4

2¹/₄ pounds asparagus, spears trimmed
1 quantity Mayonnaise (see page 65)
1 teaspoon Dijon mustard
juice of ¹/₂ orange, strained
salt

Cook the asparagus in salted, boiling water for 15 minutes. Drain and arrange on a serving dish. Combine the mayonnaise, mustard and orange juice in a bowl. Spoon a few table-spoons of the dressing onto the asparagus spears and serve the remainder separately in a sauce boat. A few thin slices of orange rind may be added to the sauce if you like.

VALLE D'AOSTA ASPARAGUS

ASPARAGI ALLA VALDOSTANA

Serves 4

butter, for greasing
2¹/₄ pounds asparagus, spears trimmed
2 cooked, cured ham slices, cut into strips
4 ounces fontina cheese, sliced
2 eggs
2 tablespoons Parmesan cheese, freshly grated
salt and pepper

Preheat the oven to 350°F. Grease an oven-proof dish with butter. Cook the asparagus in salted, boiling water for 10 minutes. Drain and place in the prepared dish and top with the ham and fontina. Beat the eggs with the Parmesan, season with salt and pepper and pour over the asparagus. Bake for 15–20 minutes until the Parmesan has melted and the eggs have set.

ASPARAGUS MIMOSA

ASPARAGI MIMOSA

Serves 4

2¹/₄ pounds asparagus, spears trimmed
4 eggs, hard-cooked
1 fresh flat-leaf parsley sprig
1 tablespoon olive oil
salt

Cook the asparagus in salted, boiling water for 15 minutes. Drain and arrange on a serving dish. Shell the eggs and chop with the parsley, place in a bowl and stir in the oil. Sprinkle the egg mixture over the asparagus and serve.

ASPARAGUS MOUSSE

MOUSSE DI ASPARAGI

Serves 4

1 pounds 2 ounces asparagus, spears trimmed

3 eggs

2 tablespoons olive oil

generous 1 cup cream cheese

juice of ¹/₂ lemon, strained

1 egg white

salt and pepper

Cook the asparagus in salted, boiling water for 10 minutes. Drain, set aside the most attractive spears for the garnish and process the remainder to a purée in a blender. Scrape the purée into a pan and heat gently to dry slightly. Meanwhile, hard-cook the eggs, refresh under cold water and shell. Halve the eggs, scoop out the yolks and crumble them into a bowl. Season with salt and pepper and stir in the olive oil. Beat in the cheese, then stir in the asparagus purée and lemon juice. Stiffly whisk the raw egg white in a grease-free bowl and gently fold it into the asparagus mixture. Season with salt and pepper to taste. Spoon the mixture into individual dishes and garnish with the reserved asparagus spears. Serve the mousse cold.

ASPARAGUS ROLLS

ROTOLINI DI ASPARAGI

Serves 4

2¹/₄ pounds asparagus, spears trimmed

¹/₄ cup butter, plus extra for greasing

3¹/₂ ounces prosciutto, sliced

scant 1 cup Parmesan cheese, freshly grated

salt

Cook the asparagus in salted, boiling water for 15 minutes. Meanwhile, preheat the oven to 350°F. Grease an ovenproof dish with butter. Drain the asparagus and gently pat dry. Spread out the prosciutto on the counter, lay two large or three small asparagus spears on each slice, roll up and fasten each roulade with a toothpick. Place the rolls in the prepared dish, sprinkle with the Parmesan, dot with the butter and bake for 10 minutes. Serve immediately.

BEET

Raging and bloodthirsty are two strong adjectives that have been used to describe beets because of their brilliant red coloring, which derives from a pigment in their leaves and roots. Quite the opposite is true – their flesh is soft and sweet. In fact, the sugar beet belongs to the same family. As well as the widely available red beet, there are also cream-colored and lighter-pink beets, all rich in potassium, calcium, sodium and phosphorus, among other nutrients. It has been suggested that eating them regularly helps to prevent cancer. In Italy, beets are usually sold ready cooked, but they are also available raw. When choosing them, make sure they are firm and without blemishes or traces of mold. They may be eaten raw – peeled, grated and dressed with oil and lemon juice or sprinkled on salads. When boiled, they go well with sour cream, mayonnaise and mustard. When included in Russian salad, they must be added at the last minute, otherwise they dye the other vegetables red. Lastly, do not worry if the flesh has concentric paler circles, as this is characteristic of a variety that came on the market a few years ago. On the other hand, pay attention to the juice, but only because it stains.

QUANTITIES
Allow about 5 ounces per serving.

BAKING
Wrap each beet separately in foil and bake in a preheated oven, 400°F, for about 2 hours.

STEAMING
Arrange whole or halved beet in a steamer and steam until tender. Test by piercing with the prongs of a fork.

QUANTITIES AND COOKING TIMES

Serves 4

2 tablespoons butter, melted, plus extra for greasing

1 pound 5 ounces cooked beet, peeled and cut into ¼-inch thick slices

1¼ cups Béchamel Sauce (see page 50)

salt

BEET WITH BÉCHAMEL SAUCE

Preheat the oven to 350°F. Grease an ovenproof dish with butter. Arrange the beet slices in the prepared dish and drizzle with the melted butter. Season with salt, spoon the béchamel sauce over the beet and bake until hot and bubbling. Serve immediately.

Serves 4

4 salted anchovies, heads removed, cleaned and filleted (see page 596), soaked in cold water for 10 minutes and drained

1 pound 5 ounces cooked beet, peeled and diced

1 fresh flat-leaf parsley sprig, chopped

½ garlic clove, chopped

4 tablespoons olive oil

1 tablespoon red wine vinegar

BEET WITH ANCHOVIES

Chop the anchovy fillets. Put the beet in a salad bowl and sprinkle with the parsley and garlic. Heat the oil and vinegar in a pan, add the anchovies and cook, mashing with a wooden spoon until they have almost disintegrated. Spoon the mixture over the beet, mix well and let stand for 15 minutes before serving.

Serves 4

2 tablespoons butter

1 onion, chopped

1 pound 5 ounces cooked beet, peeled and cut into thin batons

salt

BEET WITH ONIONS

Heat the butter in a pan, add the onion and cook over low heat, stirring occasionally, for 5 minutes until softened. Add the beet, mix well and season with salt. Cook for a few minutes more, then remove the pan from the heat and serve.

BUCK'S HORN PLANTAIN

This almost uniquely Italian vegetable consists of small sprigs of short, fairly thin green shoots, held together by a root which should be trimmed off before cooking. It is not a common vegetable in other countries and is difficult to obtain outside Italy. It is boiled after being washed several times in cold water. Barba di frate – 'friar's beard' – has a mouth-puckeringly sharp taste, rather like samphire, when served sprinkled with olive oil, salt and lemon juice, which makes it an excellent side dish for boiled meat.

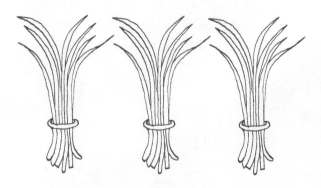

QUANTITIES AND COOKING TIMES

QUANTITIES
Allow about 5 ounces per serving.

BOILING
Cook in salted, boiling water for 10 minutes.

BUCK'S HORN PLANTAIN WITH PANCETTA

Cook the buck's horn plantain or samphire in lightly salted, boiling water for 10 minutes (don't add salt if using samphire). Drain and pat dry with paper towels. Heat the butter in a skillet, add the onion, pancetta and parsley and cook over low heat, stirring occasionally, for 10 minutes until very lightly browned. Add the buck's horn plantain or samphire, increase the heat to medium and cook for 15 minutes, gradually adding the cream. Season with salt and pepper to taste and serve immediately.

BARBA DI FRATE ALLA PANCETTA

Serves 4

2 bunches of buck's horn plantain or samphire

¹/₄ cup butter

1 onion, finely chopped

generous ¹/₂ cup pancetta, finely chopped

1 fresh flat-leaf parsley sprig, chopped

4–5 tablespoons heavy cream

salt and pepper

TASTY BUCK'S HORN PLANTAIN

Cook the buck's horn plantain or samphire in lightly salted, boiling water for 10 minutes (don't add salt if using samphire), then drain. Meanwhile, chop the anchovy fillets. Heat the oil in a pan, add the garlic and cook over low heat for a few minutes until golden brown. Remove and discard the garlic and add the anchovies and buck's horn plantain or samphire to the pan. Season with salt and pepper to taste and cook for about 15 minutes more.

BARBA DI FRATE SAPORITA

Serves 4

2 bunches of buck's horn plantain or samphire

4 salted anchovies, heads removed, cleaned and filleted (see page 596), soaked in cold water for 10 minutes and drained

4 tablespoons olive oil

1 garlic clove

salt and pepper

SWISS CHARD

Beet tops and true Swiss chard are both widely used in Italy. The former offer a tasty alternative to spinach and are prepared in the same way. Swiss chard, on the other hand, has a sweeter taste and is larger. It is rich in calcium, provides plenty of dietary fiber and has a fair amount of vitamin A. When buying Swiss chard look for brightly colored, almost shiny green leaves, and fleshy white stems that snap rather than bend.

QUANTITIES AND COOKING TIMES

QUANTITIES

Allow about 5 ounces per serving.

BOILING

Cook 2¼ pounds Swiss chard in a large pan of lightly salted, boiling water for 10–15 minutes. If the stems are very thick, separate them from the leaves, chop into 2–2½-inch pieces, remove the fibrous parts and boil for 15–20 minutes. The stems are usually then sautéed in butter and sprinkled with grated Parmesan. The boiled leaves are served dressed with olive oil, lemon and salt.

SWISS CHARD WITH PARMESAN

Serves 4

2¼ pounds Swiss chard

scant ½ cup milk

3 tablespoons butter

generous 1 cup Parmesan cheese, freshly grated

salt and pepper

Separate the chard leaves from the stems using kitchen scissors or a sharp knife. (Set the leaves aside to make soup.) Cut the stems into 2-inch pieces and cook in lightly salted, boiling water for 10–15 minutes until tender, then drain well. Heat the milk to just below simmering point, then remove the pan from the heat. Melt the butter in a pan, add the chard stems and cook over high heat, stirring frequently, for a few minutes. Pour in the hot milk, lower the heat to medium and simmer for 5–10 minutes. Sprinkle with the Parmesan, season with salt and pepper, and transfer to a warm serving dish.

SWISS CHARD WITH ANCHOVIES

Serves 4

2¼ pounds Swiss chard

4 salted anchovies, heads removed, cleaned and filleted (see page 596), soaked in cold water for 10 minutes and drained

2 tablespoons olive oil, plus extra for drizzling

1 garlic clove, chopped

½ cup Parmesan cheese, freshly grated

salt and pepper

Separate the chard leaves from the stems using kitchen scissors or a sharp knife. (Set the leaves aside to make soup.) Cut the stems into 2-inch pieces and cook in lightly salted, boiling water for 10–15 minutes until tender, then drain well. Meanwhile, chop the anchovies. Heat the olive oil in a skillet, add the garlic and anchovies and cook over low heat, mashing with a wooden spoon until the anchovies have almost disintegrated. Add the chard stems, increase the heat to high and cook, stirring frequently, for a few minutes. Lower the heat to medium, season with salt and pepper and drizzle with olive oil. Mix well and cook for a further 10 minutes. Remove the pan from the heat, sprinkle with the Parmesan and serve.

SWISS CHARD AU GRATIN

Serves 4

butter, for greasing

2¼ pounds Swiss chard

1 quantity Béchamel Sauce (see page 50)

1 cup Parmesan cheese, freshly grated

salt

Preheat the oven to 350°F. Grease an ovenproof dish with butter. Separate the chard leaves from the stems using kitchen scissors or a sharp knife. (Set the leaves aside to make soup.) Cook the stems in lightly salted, boiling water for 10–15 minutes until tender, then drain well and cut into small pieces. Make alternate layers of Swiss chard stems, béchamel sauce and Parmesan, ending with a layer of Parmesan. Bake for about 15 minutes.

BROCCOLI

There are two different types of broccoli: calabrese with a single, compact, dense head similar to a cauliflower but colored; and sprouting broccoli with lots of small flowerets, commonly known in Italy as broccoletti. Both are rich in calcium, iron and vitamin C. Fresh broccoli should have bright green leaves and compact firm flowerets. Prepare it by removing the toughest leaves, cutting the stems into 2¹/₂-inch long pieces and removing the most fibrous parts. Cut the flowerets in half lengthwise.

QUANTITIES AND COOKING TIMES

QUANTITIES
Allow about 9 ounces per serving.

BOILING
Cook in salted, boiling water for 8–10 minutes.

BROCCOLETTI ALLA BOTTARGA

Serves 4

2¹/₄ pounds sprouting broccoli, cut into flowerets

3¹/₂ ounces bottarga (dried gray mullet or tuna roe)

juice of 1 lemon, strained

1 garlic clove, chopped

1 fresh flat-leaf parsley sprig, chopped

8 fresh basil leaves, torn

3 tomatoes peeled, seeded and chopped

olive oil, for drizzling

salt and pepper

thin lemon slices, to garnish

BROCCOLI WITH BOTTARGA

Cook the broccoli in salted, boiling water for 15 minutes, then drain and let cool slightly. Pound the bottarga in a mortar with the lemon juice, then gradually pound in the garlic, parsley, basil and tomatoes. Season with salt and pepper and, when the sauce is fairly thick, drizzle with olive oil. Mix well and pour into a sauce boat. Place the broccoli on a warm serving dish, garnish with the lemon slices and serve with the sauce.

BROCCOLI WITH ANCHOVIES

BROCCOLETTI ALLE ACCIUGHE

Serves 4

2¹/₄ pounds sprouting broccoli, cut into flowerets
3 ounces salted anchovies, heads removed, cleaned
and filleted (see page 596), soaked
in cold water for 10 minutes and drained
3 tablespoons olive oil • 2 garlic cloves
¹/₂ fresh chile, seeded and chopped • salt

Cook the broccoli in salted, boiling water for 15 minutes. Meanwhile, chop the anchovy fillets. Heat the olive oil in a pan, add the garlic and chile and cook for 1 minute. Add the anchovies and cook, mashing with a wooden spoon until they have almost completely disintegrated. Remove and discard the garlic. Drain the broccoli, add to the pan, mix well and cook over low heat, stirring occasionally, for about 15 minutes. Serve immediately.

SPICY BROCCOLI WITH YOGURT

BROCCOLETTI PICCANTI ALLO YOGURT

Serves 4

2¹/₄ pounds sprouting broccoli, cut into flowerets
1 fresh flat-leaf parsley sprig, chopped
1 garlic clove, chopped
1 fresh chile, seeded and chopped
scant ¹/₂ cup low-fat plain yogurt
pinch of mustard powder • salt

Parboil the broccoli in salted, boiling water for a few minutes until just tender, then drain well and place in a large salad bowl. Combine the parsley, garlic, chile and yogurt in a bowl, stir in the mustard and season with salt to taste. Pour the sauce over the broccoli and serve warm.

BRAISED BROCCOLI

BROCCOLETTI STUFATI

Serves 4

2 tablespoons olive oil
2 garlic cloves, chopped
2¹/₄ pounds sprouting broccoli, cut into flowerets
salt and pepper

Heat the olive oil in a pan, add the garlic and broccoli and cook over low heat, stirring occasionally, for 5 minutes. Season with salt and pepper, add ²/₃ cup water, cover and simmer gently for about 15 minutes until tender. Remove the lid, increase the heat to medium and reduce any excess cooking liquid before serving.

FABULOUS BROCCOLI

BROCCOLI FANTASIA

Serves 4

2¹/₄ pounds calabrese broccoli, cut into flowerets
2 tablespoons olive oil
2 garlic cloves,
2 leeks, trimmed and sliced
1 tablespoon all-purpose flour
scant ¹/₂ cup heavy cream
scant ¹/₂ cup dry white wine
2 tablespoons butter, plus extra for greasing
6 tablespoons Parmesan cheese, freshly grated
salt and pepper

Parboil the broccoli in salted, boiling water for a few minutes, then drain and let cool slightly. Meanwhile, heat the olive oil in a large pan, add the garlic and leeks and cook over low heat, stirring occasionally, until softened. Remove and discard the garlic. Stir in the flour and cook, stirring constantly, for 2 minutes until lightly browned. Stir in the cream, season with salt and pepper and mix well. Add the broccoli, pour in the wine and simmer for about 10 minutes. Meanwhile, preheat the oven to 400°F. Grease an ovenproof dish with butter. Remove the pan from the heat and transfer the mixture to the prepared dish. Sprinkle with the Parmesan, dot with the butter and bake until golden and bubbling.

GLOBE ARTICHOKES

Globe artichokes may be tapered with thorns or round without thorns. The former are Ligurian and have shiny, firm leaves, and the latter, which are cultivated in central southern Italy, are ball-shaped and known as mammole in Lazio. The artichoke season runs from September to May. Artichokes are rich in iron, phosphorus and calcium, and their considerable fiber content makes them useful for the digestive system. They have another beneficial effect on the digestion because they contain cynarine, a substance which stimulates bile production. Fresh artichokes can be recognized by the compactness and firmness of their leaves, which should break with a sharp crack when folded. They should be prepared by shortening the stem to $1^1/_2$–2 inches and removing the fibrous part. Discard the toughest and darkest leaves until the lightest and most tender are revealed. Remove the tips by cutting the artichoke a little above its maximum circumference, and scoop out the choke from inside using a teaspoon. As you prepare the artickokes, open out the central leaves and put them in a bowl of water mixed with lemon juice to prevent them going black.

QUANTITIES

If globe artichokes are served whole and alone, allow 2 per person.

COOKING

Cook in salted, boiling water for 30 minutes if whole and 15 minutes if cut into wedges.

QUANTITIES
AND COOKING TIMES

ARTICHOKES IN GARLIC AND OLIVE OIL

CARCIOFI AGLIO E OLIO

Serves 4

8 globe artichokes, trimmed
1–2 garlic cloves
olive oil (see method)
salt and pepper

Place the artichokes in a fairly tall pan. Add the garlic and pour in a mixture of two parts olive oil and one part water until the artichokes are two-thirds covered. Season with salt and pepper to taste, cover and cook over low heat for about 30 minutes.

ARTICHOKES WITH CHEESE

CARCIOFI AL FORMAGGIO

Serves 4

2 tablespoons butter, plus extra for greasing
8 globe artichokes, trimmed
1 cup milk
3 tablespoons rice flour
pinch of saffron threads
pinch of curry powder
1¼ cups Emmenthal cheese, freshly grated
1 egg, separated
1 fresh thyme sprig, leaves only
salt

Preheat the oven to 350°F. Grease an ovenproof dish with butter. Parboil the artichokes for about 10 minutes, then drain well. Meanwhile, heat the milk to just below boiling point, then remove from the heat. Melt the butter in another pan, stir in the flour and cook over low heat, stirring constantly, for 2–3 minutes until lightly browned. Gradually stir in the hot milk, then season with salt and add the saffron and curry powder. Remove the pan from the heat and stir in the Emmenthal, egg yolk and thyme. Stiffly whisk the egg white in a grease-free bowl and fold into the sauce. Fill the artichokes with the sauce and arrange in the prepared dish. Bake for 30 minutes, then remove them from the oven and let stand for about 5 minutes before serving.

JEWISH ARTICHOKES

CARCIOFI ALLA GIUDIA

Serves 4

8 Roman artichokes
olive oil (see method)
salt

Young, whole, round (if possible), thornless artichokes are required for this dish. Break off the stems, discard the tough outer leaves and cut the tips off the others with a small sharp knife while holding the artichokes horizontally on a cutting board. They will be wide at the base and rounded at the top. Fill a wide, high-sided, cast-iron skillet with enough olive oil to half-cover the artichokes and heat gently. Open out the leaves slightly and place the artichokes upright in the oil. Cook over medium heat for 10–12 minutes, then increase the heat and turn the artichokes upside down. Cook for a further 10 minutes until they have turned golden brown and are crisp at the tips. Remove with a slotted spatula, taking care not to break them. Serve immediately, sprinkled with a pinch of salt.

ARTICHOKES WITH CHICKEN LIVER MOUSSE

CARCIOFI ALLA MOUSSE DI FEGATINI

Serves 4

juice of ¹/₂ lemon, strained

8 globe artichokes, trimmed

¹/₂ cup butter

²/₃ cup dry white wine

1 shallot, finely chopped

7 ounces chicken livers, thawed if frozen, trimmed

¹/₄ cup brandy

¹/₄ cup Madeira

scant ¹/₂ cup heavy cream

salt and pepper

fresh chervil sprigs, to garnish

Half-fill a bowl with water and add the lemon juice. Open out the central leaves of the artichokes slightly and place in the acidulated water. Drain and parboil in salted, boiling water for 10–15 minutes, then drain and leave upside down on a dish towel to dry. Preheat the oven to 350°F. Place the artichokes upright in an ovenproof dish, dot with 1 tablespoon of the butter and sprinkle with the wine. Season with salt and pepper, cover with foil and bake for 30 minutes. Meanwhile, melt 2 tablespoons of the remaining butter in a skillet, add the shallot and cook over low heat, stirring occasionally, for 10 minutes until lightly browned. Add the chicken livers, increase the heat to high and cook, stirring frequently, for a few minutes until lightly browned all over. Remove the shallot and livers from the skillet and set aside. Pour the brandy into the skillet and cook, scraping up the residue from the base, until it has evaporated. Pour in the Madeira and season with salt and pepper. Put the chicken liver mixture in a food processor and process to a purée, then pass through a strainer into a bowl. Stand the bowl in a pan full of ice and beat in the remaining butter and the juices from the skillet. Finally, beat in the cream. Fill the artichokes with the mousse using a tablespoon or pastry bag. Arrange the artichokes on a serving dish and garnish with the chervil.

ARTICHOKES NAPOLETANA

CARCIOFI ALLA NAPOLETANA

Serves 4

juice of ¹/₂ lemon, strained

8 globe artichokes, trimmed and cut into wedges

3–4 tablespoons olive oil

2 garlic cloves

1 tablespoon capers, drained and rinsed

scant 1 cup green olives, pitted and chopped

1 tablespoon fresh flat-leaf parsley, chopped

1 lemon, cut into wedges

salt and pepper

Half-fill a bowl with water, stir in the lemon juice, add the artichokes and let soak for 10 minutes, then drain and pat dry. Heat the olive oil in a pan, add the garlic and cook for a few minutes until golden brown, then remove and discard. Add the artichoke wedges to the pan and cook over high heat for 5 minutes, then add the capers and olives. Season with salt and pepper to taste and add ²/₃ cup warm water. Mix well, cover and simmer for about 30 minutes until tender. Remove the lid and boil off any excess liquid. Transfer the artichokes to a warm serving dish, sprinkle with the parsley and garnish with the lemon wedges.

PROVENÇAL ARTICHOKES

Half-fill a bowl with water, stir in the lemon juice, add the artichokes and let soak for 10 minutes. Heat the olive oil in a skillet, add the scallions and pancetta and cook over low heat, stirring occasionally, for about 8 minutes until lightly browned. Drain the artichokes, add to the skillet, increase the heat to high and cook for 5 minutes. Add the basil and thyme, sprinkle in the wine and cook until it has evaporated. Lower the heat, pour in the stock, cover and simmer for 15 minutes. Add the tomatoes, re-cover the skillet and cook for a further 5 minutes. Remove the lid, season with salt and pepper and boil off the excess liquid before serving.

CARCIOFI ALLA PROVENZALE

Serves 4

juice of ¹/₂ lemon, strained

4 violet globe artichokes, trimmed and cut into wedges

3 tablespoons olive oil

3 scallions, chopped

¹/₂ cup pancetta, diced

1 fresh basil sprig, chopped

1 fresh thyme sprig, chopped

scant ¹/₂ cup dry white wine

5 tablespoons Vegetable Stock (see page 209)

3 tomatoes, peeled and sliced

salt and pepper

ROMAN ARTICHOKES

Half-fill a bowl with water and stir in the lemon juice. Trim the artichokes, reserving the stems, and place in the acidulated water. Remove the tough strings from the stems and chop them with the garlic and parsley, then season with salt and pepper. Drain the artichokes well and fill with the mixture. Place in a pan or flameproof casserole, pour in 1¹/₂ cups water, drizzle with olive oil, cover and cook over a medium-low heat for 1 hour. Serve warm, garnished with the mint leaves.

CARCIOFI ALLA ROMANA

Serves 4

juice of ¹/₂ lemon, strained

8 globe artichokes

2 garlic cloves

1 fresh flat-leaf parsley sprig

olive oil, for drizzling

salt and pepper

fresh mint leaves, to garnish

SARDINIAN ARTICHOKES

Half-fill a bowl with water, stir in the lemon juice, add the artichokes and let soak. Heat the olive oil in a pan, add the onion and garlic and cook over low heat, stirring occasionally, for 10 minutes until lightly browned. Drain the artichokes and add to the pan with the potatoes, season with salt, pour in the stock and simmer for 30 minutes. Sprinkle with the parsley and serve.

CARCIOFI ALLA SARDA

Serves 4

juice of ¹/₂ lemon, strained

4 globe artichokes, trimmed and sliced

3 tablespoons olive oil

1 onion, chopped

1 garlic clove, chopped

1³/₄ cups potatoes, diced

²/₃ cup Vegetable Stock (see page 209)

1 fresh flat-leaf parsley sprig, chopped

salt

CARCIOFI AL PECORINO

Serves 4

juice of $\frac{1}{2}$ lemon, strained

8 globe artichokes, trimmed and cut into wedges

3 tablespoons olive oil

2 garlic cloves

1 fresh flat-leaf parsley sprig, chopped

$3\frac{1}{2}$ ounces romano cheese, shaved

generous 1 cup bread crumbs

salt

ARTICHOKES WITH ROMANO

Half-fill a bowl with water, stir in the lemon juice, add the artichokes and let soak for 10 minutes. Heat the olive oil in a pan, add the garlic and cook over low heat for 2 minutes, then remove and discard. Drain the artichokes and add to the pan, season with salt, cover and cook over low heat for 30 minutes. If necessary, add a little hot water. Arrange the artichokes on a warm serving dish and sprinkle with the parsley, romano and bread crumbs. Mix well and serve.

CARCIOFI AL TONNO

Serves 4

3 tablespoons olive oil, plus extra for brushing

4 large globe artichokes, trimmed

juice of 1 lemon, strained

2 eggs

2 tablespoons light cream

1 fresh flat-leaf parsley sprig, chopped

$\frac{1}{3}$ cup Parmesan cheese, freshly grated

9 ounces canned tuna in oil, drained and flaked

salt

ARTICHOKES WITH TUNA

Preheat the oven to 350°F. Brush an ovenproof dish with olive oil. Sprinkle the artichokes with the lemon juice to prevent discoloration and cook in salted boiling water for 10–15 minutes. Drain, open out the central leaves slightly and place in the prepared dish. Season with salt, drizzle with the olive oil, cover with foil and bake for 10 minutes. Meanwhile, beat the eggs with the cream in a bowl and add the parsley, Parmesan and tuna. Fill the artichokes with the tuna mixture. Cover with foil return to the oven and bake for a further 30 minutes.

CARCIOFI FRITTI

Serves 4

juice of 3 lemons, strained

6 globe artichokes

pinch of dried oregano

1 garlic clove, chopped

vegetable oil, for deep-frying

5 tablespoons all-purpose flour

1 egg

salt and pepper

To garnish

lemon slices

fresh flat-leaf parsley sprigs

FRIED ARTICHOKES

Bring a large pan of water to a boil and add a pinch of salt and the juice of one of the lemons. Trim the artichokes, reserving the stems. Cut the heads into wedges and chop the stems, then add to the pan of boiling water and simmer for 4–5 minutes. Drain and tip into a bowl. Season with salt and pepper, sprinkle with the oregano and garlic and pour in the remaining lemon juice. Mix well, cover and let marinate for 2 hours. Heat the oil in a pan. Place the flour in a shallow dish and beat the egg with a pinch of salt and pepper in another shallow dish. Drain the artichokes, then dip them first in the flour and then in the egg. Fry them, in batches, until golden brown and crisp. Remove with a slotted spatula and drain on paper towels. Arrange on a warm serving dish and garnish with lemon slices and sprigs of parsley.

ARTICHOKES IN HOLLANDAISE SAUCE

Bring a large pan of water to a boil, add a pinch of salt and the lemon juice, then add the artichokes and cook for about 20 minutes. Drain, let cool slightly, then cut into wedges. Place on a serving dish and pour the hollandaise sauce over them. Garnish with a few sprigs of parsley and serve.

CARCIOFI IN SALSA OLANDESE

Serves 4

juice of 1 lemon, strained

8 globe artichokes, trimmed

1 quantity Hollandaise Sauce (see page 59)

salt

fresh flat-leaf parsley sprigs, to garnish

ARTICHOKES STUFFED WITH SAUSAGE

Preheat the oven to 350°F. Half-fill a bowl with water and stir in the lemon juice. Trim the artichokes, reserving the stems, open out the leaves slightly and place in the acidulated water. Remove the tough stringy parts from the stems and chop. Heat the olive oil in a skillet, add the pancetta, garlic, parsley, onion and artichoke stems and cook over low heat, stirring occasionally, for 5 minutes. Add the sausages, season with salt and pepper and cook over very low heat for 5 minutes. Drain the artichokes, place upright in an ovenproof dish and stuff with the sausage mixture. Drizzle with olive oil and pour in the wine. Cover with foil and bake for about 1 hour, basting occasionally.

CARCIOFI RIPIENI ALLA SALSICCIA

Serves 4

juice of 2 lemons, strained

8 globe artichokes

3 tablespoons olive oil, plus extra for drizzling

generous $^2/_3$ cup pancetta, diced

2 garlic cloves, chopped

1 fresh flat-leaf parsley sprig, chopped

1 onion, chopped

3$^1/_2$ ounces Italian sausages, skinned and crumbled

scant 1 cup dry white wine

salt and pepper

ARTICHOKES STUFFED WITH BELL PEPPERS

Bring a pan of water to a boil, add half the lemon juice and a pinch of salt, then add the artichokes and cook for 30 minutes. Drain and let cool. Combine the bell peppers and parsley in a bowl and drizzle with olive oil. Stuff the artichokes with the bell pepper mixture, arrange on a dish, sprinkle with the remaining lemon juice and season with salt and pepper. Garnish with mushrooms in oil if you like.

CARCIOFI RIPIENI CON PEPERONI

Serves 4

juice of 2 lemons, strained

8 globe artichokes, trimmed

2 yellow bell peppers, halved seeded and chopped

1 fresh flat-leaf parsley sprig, chopped

olive oil, for drizzling

salt and pepper

mushrooms in oil, to garnish (optional)

ARTICHOKE CLAFOUTIS

CLAFOUTIS DI CARCIOFI
Serves 4
butter, for greasing
juice of ¹/₂ lemon, strained
6 globe artichokes, trimmed • ²/₃ cup all-purpose flour
3 eggs • 1³/₄ cups milk
1 fresh flat-leaf parsley sprig, chopped
salt and pepper

Preheat the oven to 350°F. Grease an ovenproof dish with butter. Half-fill a bowl with water, stir in the lemon juice, add the artichokes and let soak for 10 minutes. Sift the flour into a bowl, stir in the eggs, one at a time, and gradually whisk in the milk. Season with salt and pepper and stir in the parsley. Drain the artichokes, pat dry and place in the prepared dish. Pour the batter over them and bake for 30 minutes.

ARTICHOKE MOLDS

SFORMATINI DI CARCIOFI
Serves 4
juice of 1 lemon, strained
5 globe artichokes, trimmed and thinly sliced
2 tablespoons butter, plus extra for greasing
¹/₂ onion, chopped
3 tablespoons Parmesan cheese, freshly grated
scant 1 cup heavy cream
pinch of freshly grated nutmeg
3 eggs, lightly beaten
salt and pepper

Half-fill a bowl with water, stir in the lemon juice, add the artichokes and let soak for 15 minutes. Preheat the oven to 350°F. Grease four molds with butter. Melt the butter in a skillet, add the onion and cook over low heat, stirring occasionally, for 5 minutes. Drain the artichokes, add to the pan, season with salt and pepper and mix well. Cover and cook for 15 minutes. Add the Parmesan, cream and nutmeg to the eggs and season with salt, then add the artichokes. Pour into the prepared molds and place them in a roasting pan. Add hot water to come about halfway up the sides and bake for about 30 minutes until set. Turn out and serve.

SAVORY ARTICHOKE AND POTATO PIE

TORTA RUSTICA DI CARCIOFI E PATATE
Serves 4
butter, for greasing • juice of ¹/₂ lemon, strained
4–5 globe artichokes, trimmed and cut into thin wedges
1 pound 2 ounces potatoes, thinly sliced
4 tablespoons romano cheese, freshly grated
1 fresh thyme sprig, leaves only
5 tablespoons olive oil • salt and pepper

Preheat the oven to 350°F. Grease an ovenproof dish with butter. Half-fill a bowl with water, stir in the lemon juice, add the artichokes and let soak for 10 minutes. Place the potato slices in the prepared dish, then drain the artichokes and place them on top of the potatoes. Sprinkle with the romano and thyme, season with salt and pepper and drizzle with the olive oil. Bake for 1 hour. Serve warm.

ARTICHOKE PIE

TORTINO AI CARCIOFI
Serves 4
3 tablespoons butter, plus extra for greasing
5 globe artichokes, trimmed and cut into wedges
¹/₄ cup milk
6 eggs
salt

Preheat the oven to 400°F. Grease an ovenproof dish with butter. Melt the butter in a skillet, add the artichokes and cook over medium heat for a few minutes. Meanwhile, heat the milk in a pan. Season the artichokes with salt, pour in the warm milk and simmer for 10 minutes, then transfer the mixture to the prepared dish. Beat the eggs with a pinch of salt and pour them over the artichokes. Bake for about 30 minutes until the eggs have set.

CARDOONS

A member of the globe artichoke family, cardoons are tiresome to clean and take a long time to cook. Even in Italy, they are not as popular as they deserve to be, as is confirmed by the patient gourmets who wait every year for the return of winter, the only season when these delicate vegetables can be found. They are an extremely rare treat outside southern Europe. Cardoons are not so much appreciated for their nutritional value (they are rich in cellulose) as for their delicate, unexpected flavor, which is reminiscent of globe artichokes. Good-quality cardoons have white stems with pale green tints. If they are not fresh, they have a slightly reddish color. To prepare them, remove the tough, outer stems until you reach the tender inner ones. Remove the tips, cut the stems into 2–3-inch long pieces and place in water acidulated with lemon juice to prevent them from turning black. The woody covering of the heart should also be removed before chopping. One of the most mouthwatering dishes that includes raw cardoons in its ingredients is the tasty Piedmontese bagna cauda (see page 424).

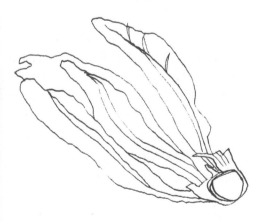

QUANTITIES

Allow about 5 ounces per serving.

BOILING

Almost all recipes involve pre-cooking cardoons in salted, boiling water for over 2 hours.

**QUANTITIES
AND COOKING TIMES**

CARDOONS WITH CHEESE

CARDI AI FORMAGGI

Serves 4

juice of 1 lemon, strained

1 tablespoon olive oil

1 teaspoon all-purpose flour

2$\frac{1}{4}$ pounds cardoons

2 tablespoons butter, melted, plus extra for greasing

$\frac{2}{3}$ cup Parmesan cheese, freshly grated

2$\frac{1}{2}$ ounces fontina cheese, shaved

2$\frac{1}{2}$ ounces Emmenthal cheese, thinly sliced

scant $\frac{1}{2}$ cup milk

scant 1 cup heavy cream

salt

Pour plenty of water into a pan and add the lemon juice, olive oil, flour and a pinch of salt. Trim the cardoons, cut the inner stems into 2-inch lengths and remove all strings, immediately dropping the stem pieces into the pan. Bring to a boil, then lower the heat and simmer for about 45 minutes. Meanwhile, preheat the oven to 350°F. Grease an ovenproof dish with butter. Drain the cardoons well, tip into the prepared dish, pour the melted butter on top and sprinkle with the Parmesan and fontina. Cover with a layer of the Emmenthal. Combine the milk and cream in a pitcher and carefully pour the mixture over the top. Bake for about 30 minutes and serve.

CARDOONS WITH BAGNA CAUDA

CARDI ALLA BAGNA CAUDA

Serves 4

juice of 1 lemon, strained

2$\frac{1}{4}$ pounds cardoons

$\frac{2}{3}$ cup butter, plus extra for greasing

2 garlic cloves

10 canned anchovy fillets in oil, drained

$\frac{1}{2}$ cup Parmesan cheese, freshly grated

salt

Pour 8$\frac{3}{4}$ cups water into a large pan and add the lemon juice and a pinch of salt. Trim the cardoons, cut the inner stems into 3-inch lengths and remove all strings, immediately dropping the stem pieces into the pan. Bring to a boil, lower the heat and simmer for 30 minutes. Meanwhile, preheat the oven to 350°F. Grease an ovenproof dish with butter. Drain the cardoons well, then tip into the prepared dish. Melt the butter in a small pan, add the garlic and cook for a few minutes until lightly browned, then remove and discard. Add the anchovies to the pan and cook, mashing with a fork until smooth. Pour the anchovy-flavored butter over the cardoons and sprinkle with the Parmesan. Bake for 30 minutes and serve.

DELICATE CARDOONS

CARDI DELICATI

Serves 4

juice of 1 lemon, strained

2$\frac{1}{4}$ pounds cardoons

2 tablespoons butter, plus extra for greasing

scant $\frac{1}{2}$ cup milk

scant $\frac{1}{2}$ cup heavy cream

$\frac{1}{2}$ cup Parmesan cheese, freshly grated

salt

Pour plenty of water into a pan and add the lemon juice and a pinch of salt. Trim the cardoons, cut the inner stems into 2-inch lengths and remove all strings, immediately dropping the stem pieces into the pan. Bring to a boil, lower the heat and simmer for about 45 minutes. Meanwhile, grease a flameproof dish with butter. Drain the cardoons well and tip into the prepared dish. Dot the surface with butter, pour in the milk and cook over low heat for about 30 minutes. Add the cream and cook for about 10 minutes until thickened. Remove from the heat, transfer to a warm serving dish, sprinkle with the Parmesan and serve.

FRIED CARDOONS

Pour plenty of water into a pan and add the lemon juice and a pinch of salt. Trim the cardoons, cut the inner stems into 2-inch lengths and remove all strings, immediately dropping the stem pieces into the pan. Bring to a boil, then lower the heat and simmer for about 1 hour. Drain well and spread out on a dish towel to cool. Meanwhile, sift the flour into a bowl, break the egg in to the middle of the flour and add the olive oil and a pinch of salt. Mix thoroughly with a wooden spoon, then stir in $^{1}/_{2}$ cup water. Cover and let stand for at least 30 minutes. Stiffly whisk the egg white in a grease-free bowl and fold it into the batter. Heat the oil for deep-frying. Dip the cardoons, a few at a time, into the batter and fry in the hot oil. Remove with a slotted spatula, drain on paper towels and serve as soon as all the cardoons are cooked.

CARDI FRITTI

Serves 4

juice of 1 lemon, strained

2$^{1}/_{4}$ pounds cardoons

9 tablespoons all-purpose flour

1 egg

1 tablespoon olive oil

1 egg white

vegetable oil, for deep-frying

salt

CARDOON SALAD

Pour plenty of water into a pan and add the lemon juice and a pinch of salt. Trim the cardoon, cut the inner stalk into 2-inch lengths and remove all strings, immediately dropping the stem pieces into the pan. Bring to a boil, then lower the heat and simmer for about 45 minutes. Meanwhile, hard-cook the eggs, refresh in cold water, shell and chop finely. Drain the cardoon well, dry on a dish towel and put in a salad bowl. Sprinkle with the chopped eggs and the parsley. Heat the olive oil in a small pan, add the bread crumbs and cook, stirring constantly, for a few minutes until golden brown and crisp. Spoon the bread crumbs over the cardoon mixture, let stand for a few minutes, then serve.

CARDI IN INSALATA

Serves 4

juice of 1 lemon, strained

1 cardoon

4 eggs

1 fresh flat-leaf parsley sprig, chopped

3 tablespoons olive oil

1 tablespoon bread crumbs

salt

CARDOON MOLDS WITH MUSHROOMS

SAVARIN DI CARDI AI FUNGHI

Serves 4

juice of 1 lemon, strained

14 ounces cardoons

¹/₄ cup butter, plus extra for greasing

2–3 tablespoons bread crumbs

1 quantity Béchamel Sauce (see page 50)

¹/₂ cup Parmesan cheese, freshly grated

1 egg, lightly beaten

1 small shallot, chopped

scant 1¹/₂ cups mushrooms, chopped

4 fresh mint leaves, chopped

1 fresh flat-leaf parsley sprig, chopped

salt and pepper

Pour plenty of water into a pan and add the lemon juice and a pinch of salt. Trim the cardoons, cut the inner stems into 2-inch lengths and remove all strings, immediately dropping the stem pieces into the pan. Bring to a boil, then lower the heat and simmer for about 45 minutes, then drain well. Meanwhile, preheat the oven to 350°F. Grease four individual ring molds with butter, sprinkle with the bread crumbs, turning to coat, and tip out any excess. Melt 1¹/₂ teaspoons of the butter in a skillet, add the cardoons and cook over low heat, stirring occasionally, for 5 minutes. Tip into a food processor and process to a purée. Stir the cardoon purée, béchamel sauce and Parmesan into the beaten egg. Spoon the mixture into the prepared molds. Place on a cookie sheet and bake for about 30 minutes. Meanwhile, melt the remaining butter in a skillet, add the shallot and cook over low heat, stirring occasionally, for 5 minutes. Add the mushrooms, mint and parsley, season with salt and pepper and cook for about 10 minutes until all the liquid has evaporated and the mushrooms are very tender. Remove the molds from the oven and turn out in a circle on a warm serving dish. Spoon the hot mushroom sauce over them and serve.

CARROTS

Carrots grow throughout Italy and are harvested in every season of the year. They are eaten in all sorts of ways, both cooked and raw. They are rich in carotene, which the human metabolism transforms into vitamin A, and in sugars, phosphorus, calcium, sodium, potassium, magnesium and other nutrients. They are good for the skin and essential for good eyesight in poor light conditions. When fresh they have a bright orange color and fragrant flesh. To prevent them from discoloration, carrots should be washed before they are peeled. It is best not to buy ready-prepared carrots since pro-vitamin A oxidizes quickly. One of the simplest and most refreshing raw carrot recipes is a salad consisting of thinly sliced, shaved or grated carrots dressed with olive oil, lemon juice and salt. One of the tastiest side dishes is glazed carrots, which makes even the simplest roast seem more spectacular.

QUANTITIES

Allow 2 per person.

BOILING

Wash and scrape young carrots under cold running water, then cook in salted, boiling water for just a few minutes. Peel older carrots with a knife and remove the woody part in the center. Whole carrots cook in about 40 minutes but if cut into thin strips, they cook in 15 minutes. In both cases, slightly salt the water and add a pinch of sugar which brings out their flavor.

**QUANTITIES
AND COOKING TIMES**

CARROTS WITH ROQUEFORT

CAROTE AL ROQUEFORT

Serves 4

3 ounces Roquefort cheese, diced

²/₃ cup milk

1 fresh flat-leaf parsley sprig, chopped

1 pound 5 ounces carrots, cut into thin batons

Put the Roquefort into a pan and melt over low heat. Add the milk and stir to make a smooth, runny sauce. Remove the pan from the heat. Do not let the mixture boil. Stir in the parsley, pour the sauce over the carrots and serve.

CARROTS WITH ROSEMARY

CAROTE AL ROSMARINO

Serves 4

1 pound 10 ounces carrots, cut into thin batons

1¹/₄ cups Vegetable Stock (see page 209)

olive oil, for drizzling

1 teaspoon chopped fresh rosemary

salt and pepper

Put the carrots and stock into a pan, bring to a boil over medium heat, then cover and simmer for about 15 minutes. Remove the lid and season with salt and pepper to taste. If the mixture is too runny, continue cooking until it has reduced to the desired consistency. Drizzle with olive oil, sprinkle with the rosemary and cook for a few minutes more. Transfer to a warm serving dish.

SURPRISE RAW CARROTS

CAROTE CRUDE AL RAFANO

Serves 4

¹/₂ horseradish root

juice of 1 lemon, strained

1 tablespoon white wine vinegar

1 teaspoon Dijon mustard

pinch of sugar

2 tablespoons olive oil

14 ounces carrots, cut into thin batons

salt and pepper

Scrape the horseradish root under cold running water, chop finely and place in a bowl. Stir in the lemon juice, vinegar, mustard, sugar and olive oil and season with salt and pepper. Beat the mixture until thoroughly combined and creamy. Put the carrots in a salad bowl, spoon the horseradish sauce over them and mix well. Let stand for 10 minutes, then serve.

GLAZED CARROTS WITH LEMON

CAROTE GLASSATE AL LIMONE

Serves 4

1³/₄ pounds carrots, fairly thickly sliced

3 tablespoons butter

2 pearl onions, chopped

strained juice and grated rind of ¹/₂ lemon

1 teaspoon sesame seeds

1 fresh flat-leaf parsley sprig, chopped

olive oil, for drizzling

salt and pepper

Put the carrots in a bowl, add water to cover and a pinch of salt and let soak for 15 minutes, then drain. Melt the butter in a pan, add the onions and cook over low heat, stirring occasionally, for 5 minutes. Add the lemon juice and rind and cook for a few minutes more, then add the carrots, season with salt and pepper and cook for a further 10 minutes. Meanwhile, dry-fry the sesame seeds in a heavy skillet for a few seconds until they give off their aroma. Remove the pan of carrots from the heat, transfer to a warm serving dish and sprinkle with the parsley and sesame seeds. Drizzle with olive oil and serve.

CARROTS IN FRENCH SAUCE

CAROTE IN SALSA FRANCESE

Serves 4

2 tablespoons olive oil, plus extra for brushing

1 pound 5 ounces baby carrots

1 egg

1 tablespoon Dijon mustard

1 tablespoon white wine vinegar

salt

Brush a flameproof dish with olive oil. Steam the carrots for about 15 minutes, then drain and pat dry with a dish towel. Cut them into thin batons and place in the prepared dish. Beat the egg with the oil, mustard, vinegar and a pinch of salt in a bowl, then pour the mixture over the carrots and cook over low heat, stirring constantly, for 10 minutes.

MARINATED CARROTS

CAROTE MARINATE

Serves 4

1 pound 2 ounces small carrots

2 garlic cloves

1 fresh flat-leaf parsley sprig, chopped

pinch of dried oregano

6 tablespoons olive oil

2 tablespoons white wine vinegar

1 small chile, seeded and chopped

salt

Cook the carrots in salted, boiling water for about 15 minutes until just tender, then drain and dry thoroughly with a dish towel. Cut into thin batons and place in a salad bowl. Rub the garlic around the sides of another bowl, add the parsley, oregano, olive oil, vinegar and chile, season with salt and mix well. Pour the dressing over the carrots, mix well and let marinate in a cool place for 24 hours before serving.

BABY CARROTS IN CREAM

CAROTINE NOVELLE ALLA PANNA

Serves 4

1³/₄ pounds baby carrots

2 tablespoons butter

²/₃ cup heavy cream

pinch of freshly grated nutmeg

1 fresh flat-leaf parsley sprig, chopped

4 fresh chives, chopped

salt and pepper

Cook the carrots in salted, boiling water for about 10 minutes, then drain and let cool. When cold, cut into thin batons. Melt the butter in a pan over low heat, pour in the cream, add the nutmeg and season with salt and pepper. Bring to a boil, add the carrots and cook for a few minutes, then add the parsley and chives. Mix well and cook for a further 2 minutes. Serve while hot.

SURPRISE CARROT CROQUETTES

Cook the carrots in salted, boiling water for 15 minutes, then drain and chop. Melt the butter in a pan, add the carrots and cook over low heat, stirring occasionally, for 15 minutes. Remove the pan from the heat and pass the carrots through a strainer into a bowl. Stir in one of the eggs, and the Parmesan and nutmeg, season to taste with salt and pepper and add as many bread crumbs as needed to obtain a fairly firm mixture. Shape the mixture into small croquettes, make a well in the center of each and fill with a cube of Emmenthal, then reshape. Spread out the flour in a shallow dish, beat the remaining egg with a pinch of salt in another shallow dish and spread out the remaining bread crumbs in the third. Heat the oil for deep-frying. Dip the croquettes first in the flour, then in the egg and, finally, in the bread crumbs. Cook in the hot oil until golden brown on all sides. Arrange the croquettes in a pyramid on a warm serving dish and serve while hot.

CROCCHETTE A SORPRESA

Serves 4

2¹/₄ pounds carrots

3 tablespoons butter

2 eggs

5 tablespoons Parmesan cheese, freshly grated

pinch of freshly grated nutmeg

2–2¹/₂ cups bread crumbs

2¹/₂ ounces Emmenthal cheese, diced

4 tablespoons all-purpose flour

vegetable oil, for deep-frying

salt and pepper

CHESTNUTS

Chestnuts are included in this chapter because, when they are not used for desserts, they make an excellent savory side dish. It is important to distinguish between the cultivated variety and wild chestnuts. The former has a paler skin with longitudinal streaks and contains a higher percentage of fat. Both types require quite long cooking times. All chestnuts go well with pork, turkey and goose.

QUANTITIES AND COOKING TIMES

QUANTITIES
Allow about 3½ ounces unpeeled chestnuts per serving.

BOILING
Cut a slit in the flat side of each nut and boil for 45 minutes.

ROASTING
Cut a slit in the flat side of each nut and roast in a preheated oven, 350°F, for 30 minutes.

ROAST CHESTNUTS

CASTAGNE ARROSTITE

Serves 4

1 pound 5 ounces chestnuts

Preheat the oven to 350°F. Cut a slit in each chestnut with a small sharp knife. Spread out on a cookie sheet and roast for 30 minutes. Alternatively, if you have a chestnut roasting pan, put the chestnuts in it and cook over high heat. Chestnuts are ready when the shells are begin to char. Remove the shells and inner skins and use either whole or mashed chestnuts to stuff roast chicken or turkey. They may also be mashed with melted butter, a bay leaf and a pinch of salt and pepper and served as a side dish.

ROAST CHESTNUTS WITH BRUSSELS SPROUTS

Cut a slit in each chestnut with a small knife, place in a pan and add water to cover. Bring to a boil and cook for 20 minutes. Melt half the butter in a pan, add the shallot and cook over low heat, stirring occasionally, for 5 minutes. Add the Brussels sprouts, lemon juice and 1/2 cup water. Season with salt and pepper and add the nutmeg. Cover and simmer for about 10 minutes. Meanwhile, preheat the oven to 400°F. Grease an ovenproof dish with butter. Drain the chestnuts, refresh under cold running water, peel off the shells and inner skins and place in the prepared dish. Add the Brussels sprouts with a little of their cooking liquid. Sprinkle the fontina on top and dot with the remaining butter. Bake for 30 minutes.

CASTAGNE CON CAVOLINI AL FORNO

Serves 4

1 pound 2 ounces chestnuts

1/4 cup butter, plus extra for greasing

1 shallot, chopped

1 pound 2 ounces Brussels sprouts, trimmed

juice of 1 lemon, strained

pinch of freshly grated nutmeg

1 cup fontina cheese, freshly grated

salt and pepper

BRAISED CHESTNUTS

Preheat the oven to 425°F. Melt the butter in a small, flameproof casserole, add the chestnuts and cook for 1 minute, then pour in the stock. Add the bay leaf, thyme and celery. Cover and cook in the oven for 45 minutes, gently shaking the casserole occasionally. Do not stir as this can break up the nuts. Season with salt and pepper and serve as a side dish with guinea fowl, duck, goose or roast meat.

MARRONI BRASATI

Serves 4

1 1/2 tablespoons butter

1 pound 5 ounces cultivated chestnuts, peeled

6 1/4 cups Meat Stock (see page 208)

1 bay leaf

1 fresh thyme sprig

1 celery stalk

salt and pepper

CHESTNUT PURÉE

Put the chestnuts in a pan, add water to cover, bring to a boil and cook for 45 minutes. Drain and pass through a food mill into a clean pan. Set the pan over low heat and stir in the cream, followed by the butter, and season with salt and pepper, still stirring constantly. Remove the pan from the heat and serve the hot purée as a side dish with meat or game.

PURÉ DI MARRONI

Serves 4

1 pound 2 ounces cultivated chestnuts, peeled

5 tablespoons heavy cream

2 tablespoons butter

salt and pepper

DANDELION

Catalogna (Italian dandelion) is cultivated in southern Italy and is only ever eaten cooked. It does not have great nutritional properties, but thanks to the bitter substances it contains it acts as a diuretic, and is thought to help purify the system, protect the liver and act as a tonic. The large heads have fairly long leaves. Remove the toughest ones, leaving the hearts intact. Cut off the tops of the remaining leaves and cut into strips. Catalogna has a light but pleasant, slightly bitter taste and is served hot dressed with salt, oil and vinegar or lemon juice. The hearts of the smaller varieties, known as puntarelle, are served raw with pinzimonio (olive oil, salt and pepper). Their leaves are cut into strips and left to soak in cold water where they curl up attractively. They are eaten in salads dressed with oil, vinegar and chopped anchovy. You can substitute other types of dandelion. Pick them while they are young from an unpolluted source well away from the roadside.

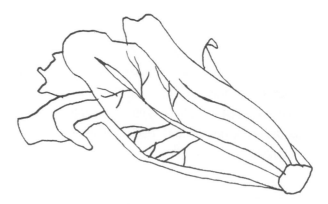

QUANTITIES AND COOKING TIMES

QUANTITIES
Allow about 7 ounces per serving.

BOILING
Cook in salted, boiling water for 15–20 minutes. If the recipe specifies parboiling, a few minutes is sufficient.

DANDELION WITH GARLIC AND OLIVE OIL

Cook the dandelion strips in salted, boiling water for 15 minutes, then drain and squeeze out as much liquid as possible. Heat the oil in a skillet, add the garlic and cook over low heat, stirring frequently, until golden brown, then remove and discard. Add the dandelion strips to the skillet, increase the heat and cook, stirring occasionally, for about 15 minutes. Season to taste with chili powder, if you like, or pepper.

CATALOGNA ALL'AGLIO E OLIO
Serves 4
2$^{1}/_{4}$ pounds Italian dandelion, leaves cut into strips
olive oil
4 garlic cloves
pinch of chili powder (optional)
salt and pepper

DANDELION WITH PARMESAN

Cook the dandelion strips in salted, boiling water for 15 minutes, then drain, squeeze out as much liquid as possible, chop coarsely and place on a warm serving dish. Melt the butter in a small pan and, when it turns slightly golden in color, pour it over the dandelions. Sprinkle with the Parmesan and serve.

CATALOGNA AL PARMIGIANO
Serves 4
1 pound 10 ounces Italian dandelion, leaves cut into strips • 5 tablespoons butter
4 tablespoons Parmesan cheese, freshly grated
salt

DANDELION TIP SALAD

Chop the anchovy fillets. Put the dandelion tips in a salad bowl. Combine the garlic, anchovies, lemon juice and olive oil in another bowl and season lightly with salt. Pour the dressing over the salad, let stand for 15 minutes, then serve.

PUNTE DI CATALOGNA IN INSALATA
Serves 4
3 salted anchovies, heads removed,
cleaned and filleted (see page 596),
soaked in cold water for 10 minutes and drained
1 pound 2 ounces Italian dandelion tips
$^{1}/_{2}$ garlic clove, chopped
juice of 1 lemon, strained
6 tablespoons olive oil
salt

OIL

CAULIFLOWER

In Fano, in the region called Marche in eastern central Italy, they produce some of the very best cauliflowers. There are both all-year-round varieties and ones that are in season only from October to May. For several years now, cross-breeding techniques have produced a 'ball' cauliflower, consisting of white flowerets, each one shorter than the next, encircled by leaves, which transforms the vegetable into a sort of bouquet. Cauliflower is an attractive vegetable, has a delicate flavor and contains calcium, potassium and magnesium salts, but it's not always easy to digest. When buying cauliflower, make sure it is firm, with white compact flowerets and whole leaves. To prepare, remove the toughest, outer leaves, cut the stem at the base and either split the flowerets away from the stem one at a time or leave the cauliflower whole, according to the recipe. To reduce its slightly unpleasant smell during cooking, soak a slice of bread, without crusts, in vinegar and add it to the pan. Boiled cauliflower may be served hot or cold dressed with oil, vinegar or lemon juice, salt and pepper. It may also be sautéed in a skillet with oil and garlic.

QUANTITIES AND COOKING TIMES

QUANTITIES
Allow about 7 ounces per serving.

BOILING
To cook whole, place the cauliflower upright in a pan and add sufficient cold water to come about three-fourths of the way up the sides. Add a pinch of salt, bring to a boil and simmer for 30–40 minutes. If divided into flowerets, cook for 15–20 minutes.

CAULIFLOWER WITH GORGONZOLA

Put the cauliflower in a pan, add cold water, the flour and a pinch of salt and bring to a boil, then simmer for 15 minutes until just tender. Drain and place on a warm serving dish. Meanwhile, put the Gorgonzola, milk, butter and brandy in a blender, add salt and pepper to taste and process until smooth and combined. Spoon the mixture over the cauliflower, sprinkle with the cumin and serve immediately.

CAVOLFIORE AL GORGONZOLA

Serves 4

2¼-pound cauliflower, cut into flowerets

1 teaspoon all-purpose flour

9 ounces strong Gorgonzola cheese, diced

scant ½ cup milk

2 tablespoons butter, softened

2 tablespoons brandy

1 tablespoon cumin seeds

salt and pepper

CAULIFLOWER WITH HAM

Put the cauliflower in a pan, add cold water and a pinch of salt and bring to a boil, then simmer for 20 minutes until tender. Drain thoroughly and tip into a bowl. Preheat the oven to 350°F. Grease an oven-proof dish with butter. Meanwhile, hard-cook the eggs, refresh in cold water, then shell and halve lengthwise. Scoop out the yolks and mash in a bowl with a fork. Chop the whites, then add the yolks and whites to the cauliflower. Melt half the butter in a small pan, add the bread crumbs and cook, stirring frequently, until crisp and golden. Spoon the bread crumbs over the cauli-flower, add the ham and Parmesan, season with salt and pepper to taste and mix gently. Spoon the mixture into the prepared dish, dot with the remaining butter and bake for 20 minutes.

CAVOLFIORE AL PROSCIUTTO

Serves 4

2¼-pound cauliflower, cut into flowerets

2 tablespoons butter, plus extra for greasing

2 eggs

2 tablespoons bread crumbs

scant 1 cup cooked, cured ham, diced

4 tablespoons Parmesan cheese, freshly grated

salt and pepper

TWO-COLOR CAULIFLOWER WITH BELL PEPPER

Parboil the cauliflowers in separate pans of salted water for 5–8 minutes. Drain well and arrange in alternate colored layers on a serving dish. Mix together the lemon juice, lemon rind, olive oil, red bell pepper, chili powder, oregano and garlic in a bowl and season with salt and pepper to taste. Pour the dressing over the cauliflower and leave in a cool place for 1 hour to allow the flavors to mingle, then mix and serve.

CAVOLFIORE BICOLORE AL PEPERONE

Serves 4

1 small white cauliflower, cut into flowerets

1 small green cauliflower, cut into flowerets

juice of 1 lemon, strained

2 teaspoons finely grated lemon rind

6 tablespoons olive oil

1 red bell pepper preserved in brine,

drained and finely chopped

pinch of chili powder • pinch of dried oregano

1 garlic clove, chopped

salt and pepper

CAULIFLOWER CROQUETTES

Put the cauliflower in a pan, add cold water and a pinch of salt and bring to a boil, then simmer for 10 minutes until just tender. Drain thoroughly. Melt the butter in a skillet, add the cauliflower and cook over medium heat, stirring occasionally, for 5 minutes. Remove the skillet from the heat and let cool slightly, then pass through a food mill into a bowl. Add one of the eggs, and the Parmesan, parsley and nutmeg, mix well and season with salt and pepper. Stir in as many bread crumbs as required to obtain a fairly firm consistency. Shape the mixture into croquettes. Beat the remaining egg with a pinch of salt in a shallow dish. Spread out the flour in another shallow dish and spread out the remaining bread crumbs in a third. Heat the oil in a large pan. Dip the croquettes first in the flour, then in beaten egg and, finally, in bread crumbs. Fry in the hot oil, then remove with a slotted spatula or slotted spatula and drain on paper towels. Place on a warm serving dish.

CROCCHETTE DI CAVOLFIORE

Serves 4

1 cauliflower, cut into flowerets

2 tablespoons butter

2 eggs

$1/2$ cup Parmesan cheese, freshly grated

1 fresh flat-leaf parsley sprig, chopped

pinch of freshly grated nutmeg

$1^1/_2$–$1^3/_4$ cups bread crumbs

3–4 tablespoons all-purpose flour

vegetable oil, for deep-frying

salt and pepper

FRENCH–STYLE CAULIFLOWER

Parboil the cauliflower in salted water for a few minutes, then drain thoroughly. Beat the egg with the flour and milk in a bowl and add enough water to make a slightly runny batter. Heat plenty of oil in a pan over high heat. Dip the flowerets in the batter and cook in the hot oil, a few at a time, until golden brown. Remove with a slotted spatula, drain on paper towels and place on a warm serving dish. Heat the tomato sauce in a small skillet and add the basil. Pour the sauce into a sauce boat and serve separately with the cauliflower.

CAVOLFIORE FRITTO ALLA FRANCESE

Serves 4

$2^1/_4$-pounds cauliflower, cut into flowerets

1 egg

scant 1 cup all-purpose flour

scant 1 cup milk

vegetable oil, for deep-frying

1 quantity Tomato Sauce (see page 57)

4 fresh basil leaves, torn

salt

CAULIFLOWER SALAD

Put the cauliflower in a pan, add cold water and a pinch of salt and bring to a boil, then simmer for 15 minutes until just tender. Drain well, tip into a salad bowl and let cool. Hard-cook the eggs, refresh briefly in cold water, then shell and chop while warm. Chop the anchovy fillets. Add the anchovies, eggs, capers and olives to the salad bowl and mix gently. Mix the vinaigrette with the parsley, pour it over the salad and let stand for 10 minutes.

CAVOLFIORE IN INSALATA

Serves 4

1 small cauliflower • 2 eggs

4 salted anchovies, heads removed, cleaned and filleted (see page 596), soaked in cold water for 10 minutes and drained

1 tablespoon capers, drained and rinsed

10 black olives, pitted and quartered

1 quantity Vinaigrette (see page 76)

1 fresh flat-leaf parsley sprig, chopped

salt

CAVOLFIORE IN SALSA D'UOVA

Serves 4

2¼-pound cauliflower, cut into flowerets

¼ cup butter

1½ garlic cloves, finely chopped

3 eggs

1 tablespoon all-purpose flour

1 tablespoon white wine vinegar

salt and pepper

CAULIFLOWER IN EGG SAUCE

Put the cauliflower in a pan, add cold water and a pinch of salt and bring to a boil, then simmer for 15–20 minutes until tender. Drain well, pile into a heap on a serving dish and keep warm. Melt the butter in a small pan, add the garlic and cook, stirring occasionally, for a few minutes. Meanwhile, beat the eggs with the flour in a bowl, season with salt, pepper and whisk in the vinegar. Add the mixture to the garlic and mix well, then immediately remove the pan from the heat. Continue stirring until the sauce is thick and creamy, then pour in a continuous thin stream over the cauliflower and serve.

CAVOLFIORE IN SALSA VERDE

Serves 4

1¾-pound cauliflower, cut into flowerets

1 egg

2 salted anchovies, heads removed, cleaned and filleted (see page 596), soaked in cold water for 10 minutes and drained

1 fresh flat-leaf parsley sprig

1 tablespoon capers, drained and rinsed

3 cornichons or small dill pickles, drained

⅔ cup olive oil

2 tablespoons white wine vinegar

salt

CAULIFLOWER IN GREEN SAUCE

Put the cauliflower in a pan, add cold water and a pinch of salt and bring to a boil, then simmer for 20 minutes until tender. Meanwhile, hard-cook the egg, refresh in cold water, shell and chop coarsely. Chop the anchovy fillets. Drain the cauliflower well, pile into a heap on a serving dish and keep warm. Put the egg, parsley, anchovies, capers and cornichons or dill pickles in a food processor and process to a purée. Transfer to a bowl and stir in the olive oil and vinegar until thickened and creamy. Pour the sauce over the cauliflower in a continuous thin stream and serve.

CAVOLFIORE SPEZIATO

Serves 4

1 small cauliflower

2 carrots, cut into thin strips

1 garlic clove, finely chopped

juice of 1 lemon, strained

1 tablespoon dry white wine

3 tablespoons olive oil

½ teaspoon cumin seeds

pinch of paprika

salt

SPICED CAULIFLOWER

Cut only the most tender flowerets from the cauliflower and put into a salad bowl. Add the carrots and garlic. Combine the lemon juice, wine, olive oil, cumin seeds, paprika and a pinch of salt in a pitcher. Pour the dressing over the flowerets and mix well.

CABBAGE

The cabbage family is a large one and includes the Savoy cabbage, collard greens, summer and winter cabbages, Chinese cabbages, green and red cabbages, broccoli, cauliflower and Brussels sprouts. All, apart from the Chinese varieties, love the cold weather which even improves their flavor. Because they are so numerous, cabbages can be found all year round, although they are at their best in autumn and winter. The most popular varieties in Italy are the green and Savoy cabbages, both rich in vitamin A, iron and calcium. Green and Savoy cabbages should be firm, compact and without any signs of yellowing. To prepare them, remove the outer, coarse leaves and any damaged ones, cut out the core, split them in half or into segments and wash. They may then be steamed, boiled or braised. Savoy cabbage cut into strips and preserved in brine is called sauerkraut, but as it takes a long time to prepare, it is generally bought ready made.

QUANTITIES AND COOKING TIMES

QUANTITIES
Allow about 5 ounces per serving.

BOILING
Immerse green and Savoy cabbages in salted, boiling water and remove as soon as the water comes back to a boil.

FOR ROULADES
Blanch whole leaves in boiling water, refresh in iced water and spread out on a dish towel.

CABBAGE WITH PAPRIKA

CAVOLO ALLA PAPRICA

Serves 4

3 tablespoons butter

3 onions, chopped

1³/₄-pound white cabbage, shredded

1 apple, peeled, cored and thinly sliced

1¹/₄ cups light cream

pinch of sugar

large pinch of paprika

salt

fresh marjoram leaves, to garnish

Melt the butter in a pan, add the onions and cook over low heat, stirring occasionally, for 5 minutes until softened. Add the cabbage, increase the heat to high and cook for a few minutes. Lower the heat, pour in ²/₃ cup water, cover and cook for 20 minutes. Add the apple to the pan, mix well and cook for a few minutes more, then remove the pan from the heat. Put the cream into a bowl and season with salt, sugar and paprika. Transfer the cabbage mixture to a warm serving dish and spoon the cream mixture over it. Garnish with the marjoram leaves.

BAKED SAVOY CABBAGE

CAVOLO VERZA AL FORNO

Serves 6

2¹/₄-pound Savoy cabbage, cored and cut into strips

3 tablespoons olive oil, plus extra for brushing

9 ounces Italian sausages, skinned and crumbled

2 tablespoons tomato paste

11 ounces mozzarella cheese, sliced

scant 1 cup heavy cream

¹/₂ cup Parmesan cheese, freshly grated

salt and pepper

Bring a large pan of water to a boil, plunge in the cabbage and cook for 5 minutes, then drain and refresh in iced water. Drain well again and spread out on a dish towel. Preheat the oven to 350°F. Brush an ovenproof dish with olive oil. Put the sausages in a pan with the olive oil and heat gently. Stir in the tomato paste and 5 tablespoons water. Season with salt and pepper to taste and cook over medium heat for 10 minutes. Make a layer of cabbage in the prepared dish, season with salt and pepper, cover with a layer of mozzarella, add a layer of sausage, top with another layer of cabbage and season with salt and pepper. Continue making layers, seasoning each layer of cabbage with salt and pepper, until all the ingredients are used, ending with a layer of cabbage. Pour the cream over the top, sprinkle with the Parmesan and bake for about 40 minutes.

CAPUCHIN SAVOY CABBAGE

CAVOLO VERZA ALLA CAPPUCINA

Serves 4

¹/₂ Savoy cabbage, cored and cut into strips

2 salted anchovies, heads removed, cleaned and filleted (see page 596), soaked in cold water for 10 minutes and drained

2 tablespoons olive oil

2 garlic cloves

1 tablespoon fresh flat-leaf parsley, chopped

salt and pepper

Parboil the cabbage in salted, boiling water for 5 minutes, then drain well. Chop the anchovy fillets. Heat the oil in a pan, add the garlic and cook for a few minutes until browned, then remove and discard. Add the anchovies to the pan and cook, mashing with a wooden spoon until they have almost completely disintegrated. Add the cabbage and parsley, season with salt and pepper, cover and cook, stirring occasionally, for about 50 minutes.

PAN–COOKED SAVOY CABBAGE

Melt half the butter in a large skillet and make a layer of half the potato slices on the base, then top with the cabbage and sprinkle with the Parmesan. Beat the eggs with the milk and a pinch of salt and pour into the pan. Make a layer of the remaining potato slices on top, season with salt and pepper and dot with the remaining butter. Cover the pan with a tight-fitting lid and cook over low heat for 1 hour.

CAVOLO VERZA IN PADELLA

Serves 4

1/4 cup butter

3 potatoes, thinly sliced

1/2 Savoy cabbage, cored and cut into thin strips

1 tablespoon Parmesan cheese, freshly grated

2 eggs

scant 1/2 cup milk

salt and pepper

SAUERKRAUT WITH MUSHROOMS AND POTATOES

Melt the butter in pan, add the onion and cook over low heat, stirring occasionally, for 10 minutes until lightly browned. Add the sauerkraut and mushrooms, increase the heat to high and cook, stirring frequently, for about 8 minutes. Add the potatoes, season with salt, lower the heat, cover and cook for 45 minutes, adding a little water if necessary.

CRAUTI CON FUNGHI E PATATE

Serves 4

2 tablespoons butter

1 onion, chopped

2 1/4 cups sauerkraut, drained and rinsed

2 3/4 cups mushroom caps, sliced

11 ounces potatoes, thinly sliced

salt

BRAISED SAUERKRAUT

Heat the butter and olive oil in a large pan, add the onion and pancetta and cook over low heat, stirring occasionally, for 5 minutes. Sprinkle in the wine and vinegar and cook until reduced by half. Add the cabbage, thyme and juniper berries, mix well and pour in enough hot stock to cover. Cook over a very low heat, stirring occasionally and adding more hot stock if necessary, for about 2 hours. Season with salt and pepper to taste and serve hot with pork, cotechino (large spiced pork sausage) or zampone (stuffed pig's foot).

CRAUTI IN UMIDO

Serves 6

2 tablespoons butter

4 tablespoons olive oil

1 onion, chopped

scant 1 cup pancetta, chopped

scant 1/2 cup dry white wine

2 tablespoons white wine vinegar

3 1/4-pound white cabbage, cored and cut into strips

1 fresh thyme sprig, leaves only

6 juniper berries

about 1 1/4 cups hot Meat Stock (see page 208)

salt and pepper

RICOTTA AND
SAVOY CABBAGE ROLLS

INVOLTINI DI CAVOLO ALLA RICOTTA

Serves 4

8 Savoy cabbage leaves

11 ounces Swiss chard, stems removed

scant 1 cup ricotta cheese

4 tablespoons Parmesan cheese, freshly grated

2 eggs, lightly beaten

1 quantity Tomato Sauce (see page 57)

salt and pepper

Blanch the cabbage leaves in salted, boiling water for 5 minutes, then drain and refresh in iced water. Drain again and spread out on a dish towel. Cook the Swiss chard in salted, boiling water for 10–15 minutes, then drain, squeezing out as much liquid as possible. Chop finely, put in a bowl and stir in the ricotta, Parmesan and eggs. Season with salt and pepper, mix well and divide the mixture among the cabbage leaves. Roll up each leaf and tie with kitchen string. Place the cabbage rolls in a wide pan or flameproof casserole, pour in the tomato sauce, cover and simmer for about 20 minutes.

BRUSSELS SPROUTS

The best Brussels sprouts are about the size of walnuts. They come into season in midwinter and make an easy, quick and convenient side dish, as there is very little waste. Like cabbages, to which family they belong, they contain protein, iron and vitamin A, but they are easier to digest as they are not so rich in calcium and vitamin C. When fresh, they should be compact and firm, without any blemished leaves. Brussels sprouts that have opened a little are almost tasteless. Prepare them by washing them in plenty of water, trimming the stems and cutting a cross in their bases. They are good sautéed in the juices of a pork roast, as a side dish with zampone (stuffed pig's foot) or simply fried in butter.

QUANTITIES AND COOKING TIMES

QUANTITIES
Allow about 6 per person.
BOILING
Plunge them into plenty of salted, boiling water and cook, uncovered, for about 15 minutes.

STEAMING
Place in a steamer, sprinkle with salt, cover and cook for 15 minutes.

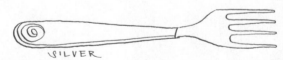

PARMESAN BRUSSELS SPROUTS

Serves 4

1³/₄ pounds Brussels sprouts, trimmed
2 tablespoons butter
pinch of freshly grated nutmeg
6 tablespoons Parmesan cheese, freshly grated
salt and pepper

Cook the Brussels sprouts in salted, boiling water for 15 minutes, then drain. Melt the butter in a pan and, when golden brown, add the sprouts and cook over low heat for a few minutes. Season with salt and pepper to taste and add the nutmeg. Transfer to a warm serving dish, sprinkle with the Parmesan and serve.

Serves 4

1¹/₂ pounds Brussels sprouts, trimmed

¹/₄ cup butter

¹/₄ cup blanched almonds

1 garlic clove

thinly pared rind of 1 lemon, chopped

1¹/₂ teaspoons bread crumbs

salt and pepper

BRUSSELS SPROUTS WITH ALMONDS

Cook the Brussels sprouts in salted, boiling water for 5 minutes, then drain thoroughly, place on a serving dish and keep warm. Heat half the butter in a skillet, add the almonds and the garlic and stir-fry for a few minutes. Add the lemon rind, season with salt and pepper and remove from the heat. Remove and discard the garlic. Melt the remaining butter in a small pan and stir-fry the bread crumbs until golden, then stir into the almond mixture, spoon over the Brussels sprouts and serve.

Serves 4

¹/₄ cup butter, plus extra for greasing

1¹/₂ pounds Brussels sprouts, trimmed

2 tablespoons olive oil

generous ¹/₂ cup pancetta, diced

scant 1 cup Swiss cheese, freshly grated

1 quantity Béchamel Sauce (see page 50)

salt and pepper

BRUSSELS SPROUTS AU GRATIN

Preheat the oven to 350°F. Grease an ovenproof dish with butter. Cook the Brussels sprouts in salted, boiling water for about 10 minutes, then drain, set aside and keep warm. Heat the butter and olive oil in a pan, add the pancetta and cook, stirring occasionally, until lightly browned. Add the Brussels sprouts and 1 tablespoon hot water and cook, stirring occasionally, for about 5 minutes. Stir half the Swiss cheese into the béchamel sauce and season with salt and pepper. Place the Brussels sprouts in the prepared dish and sprinkle with half the remaining Swiss cheese. Spoon the béchamel sauce on top and sprinkle with the remaining Swiss cheese. Bake for about 20 minutes.

Serves 4

8 black peppercorns

1 lemon, sliced

1¹/₂ cups dry white wine

1¹/₂ pounds Brussels sprouts, trimmed

2–3 fresh chives, chopped

1 quantity Velouté Sauce (see page 61)

4 tablespoons Parmesan cheese, freshly grated

salt

VELOUTÉ BRUSSELS SPROUTS

Bring a large pan of water to a boil and add the peppercorns, lemon slices, wine and a pinch of salt. Place the Brussels sprouts in a steamer on top, cover and cook for 15 minutes until tender. Transfer the sprouts to a serving dish and keep warm. Stir the chives into the velouté sauce. Sprinkle the Parmesan over the Brussels sprouts, spoon the velouté sauce over them and serve.

GARBANZO BEANS

Garbanzo beans come third on the list of the world's most popular legumes. Because of their mouthwatering flavor, they form the main ingredient in a number of rustic dishes, including a traditional soup with rosemary. As dried garbanzo beans need to be soaked and boiled for an extremely long time, canned ones have become popular. If dried garbanzo beans are used, either in soups or salads, they must be boiled first in any case and the best way to cook them is in an earthenware pot. Nutritionally, they are rich in protein, calcium, phosphorus and potassium. Garbanzo bean flour is the essential basic ingredient of Ligurian panissa, a kind of polenta, where it is mixed with oil, pearl onions, salt and pepper. This may be served hot or cold, but is tastiest when fried and cut into squares or strips.

BOILING

Soak in cold water for 24 hours, then drain and cook for 3–4 hours in plenty of boiling water over medium heat.

QUANTITIES

Allow about ¼ cup per serving.

QUANTITIES AND COOKING TIMES

GARBANZO BEANS WITH ANCHOVIES

Put the garbanzo beans in a large pan, add cold water to cover, bring to a boil and cook over medium heat for 3–4 hours until tender. Meanwhile, chop the anchovy fillets. Heat the olive oil in a small pan, add the anchovies and cook, mashing with a wooden spoon for about 10 minutes until they have almost completely disintegrated. Add the parsley, season with pepper and mix well. Drain the garbanzo beans, tip into a warm serving dish, add the hot sauce and season with salt to taste.

CECI ALLE ACCIUGHE

Serves 4

scant 1 cup garbanzo beans,
soaked in cold water for 24 hours and drained
3 ounces salted anchovies, heads removed,
cleaned and filleted (see page 596),
soaked in cold water for 10 minutes and drained
scant ½ cup olive oil
1 fresh flat-leaf parsley sprig, chopped
salt and pepper

GARBANZO BEANS WITH TUNA

CECI CON IL TONNO

Serves 4

scant 1 cup garbanzo beans

pinch of baking soda

5 ounces canned tuna in oil, drained and flaked

6 tablespoons olive oil

2 tablespoons white wine vinegar

salt and pepper

Put the garbanzo beans in a bowl, add warm water to cover and the baking soda and let soak for 24 hours. Rinse, drain and tip into a pan. Add water to cover, bring to a boil, then lower the heat and simmer gently for 4–5 hours. Drain and refresh under cold running water. Drain well again, tip into a salad bowl and add the tuna. Whisk together the olive oil and vinegar in a pitcher, season with salt and pepper and pour the dressing over the salad. Serve immediately.

LIGURIAN PANCAKES

CECINA O FARINATA

Serves 6

2³/₄ cups garbanzo bean flour

scant ¹/₂ cup olive oil, plus extra for brushing

salt and pepper

Pour 6¹/₄ cups cold water into a large bowl. Gradually add the flour, whisking constantly to prevent lumps from forming. Add the olive oil and 1 teaspoon salt and mix well. Let stand for 30 minutes. Preheat the oven to 425°F. Brush an ovenproof dish with oil. Pour the garbanzo bean mixture into the prepared dish and bake until the top is crisp and golden. Sprinkle with pepper, cut into wedges and serve either hot or warm.

LIGURIAN POLENTA

PANISSA

Serves 4

2³/₄ cups garbanzo beans flour

6 tablespoons olive oil

salt

Pour 4 cups water into a large pan and heat until warm, then remove the pan from the heat. Pour in the flour, stirring constantly to prevent lumps from forming. Return the pan to the heat and cook, stirring constantly, for about 1¹/₄ hours. Rinse several dishes with iced water, ladle the mixture into them and let cool and set. When set, cut into thin strips. Heat the olive oil in a heavy skillet, add the strips, in batches if necessary, and fry until golden brown. Remove with a slotted spatula, drain on paper towels, sprinkle with salt and serve hot.

CUCUMBERS

Raw cucumbers have a pleasant aroma, but are not very easy to digest. To reduce this problem, cut them into slices, sprinkle with salt and let drain. Any bitter flavor can be eliminated by cutting off the ends and gently rubbing the cut surfaces. This produces a light foam that can then be rinsed off under running water. There are very few recipes for cooked cucumbers. Cucumbers may be green or yellowish, but in both cases they must be firm and compact to the touch. The biggest ones should be cut in half lengthwise and the seeds removed with a teaspoon. Small gherkin cucumbers are picked when unripe and pickled in vinegar. They are particularly tasty and mouthwatering.

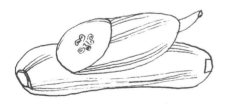

CUCUMBERS IN MAYONNAISE

Put the cucumber slices in a colander, sprinkle with salt and let drain for 30 minutes. Rinse, drain, pat dry and put in a salad bowl. Mix with the mayonnaise and sprinkle with the parsley.

CETRIOLI ALLA MAIONESE

Serves 4

3 cucumbers, peeled and thinly sliced

6 tablespoons Mayonnaise (see page 65)

1 fresh flat-leaf parsley sprig, chopped

salt

451

CUCUMBERS WITH CREAM

CETRIOLI ALLA PANNA

Serves 4

5 cucumbers, peeled

3 tablespoons butter

3 tablespoons heavy cream

salt

Remove the cucumber seeds with a teaspoon, and scoop out balls of the flesh using a melon baller. Blanch the balls in salted, boiling water for a few minutes, then drain. Melt the butter in a pan, add the balls and cook over low heat for a few minutes, then stir, season with salt to taste and cook gently for 15 minutes. Pour in the cream and cook until it has been absorbed. Transfer to a warm serving dish.

PARISIAN CUCUMBERS

CETRIOLI ALLA PARIGINA

Serves 4

3 cucumbers, peeled and thinly sliced

1 fresh flat-leaf parsley sprig, chopped

1 fresh chervil, sprig, chopped

1 garlic clove, finely chopped

juice of 1 lemon, strained

1 teaspoon Dijon mustard

$1/2$ cup olive oil

salt and pepper

Put the cucumber slices in a colander, sprinkle with salt and let drain for 30 minutes. Rinse, drain, pat dry and put in a salad bowl. Add the parsley, chervil and garlic. Combine the lemon juice, mustard and olive oil in a bowl, season with salt and pepper and pour the dressing over the cucumbers. Toss well and serve.

CUCUMBERS WITH OLIVES

CETRIOLI ALLE OLIVE

Serves 4

2 cucumbers, peeled and thinly sliced

1 tablespoon chopped fresh dill

1 tablespoon lemon juice, strained

1 tablespoon olive oil

20 black olives, pitted and quartered

salt

Put the cucumber slices in a colander, sprinkle with salt and let drain for 30 minutes. Rinse, drain, pat dry and put in a salad bowl. Sprinkle with the dill and drizzle with the lemon juice and olive oil. Add the olives, season with salt if necessary and toss. Let stand for a few minutes, then serve.

SLICES

CHICORY FAMILY

The chicory family includes various types of radicchio, curly chicory, also known as frisée, and escarole, also known as Batavian or broad-leaf chicory. They are all very versatile vegetables which – eaten both raw in various salads and cooked – add a distinctive flavor to several recipes. Loose-leaf chicories are prepared by gathering the leaves in bunches so that the stems are aligned at the point where the leaves start, then cutting all of them at the same height. The leaves are then cut into strips. Chicories with firm heads must be cleaned by removing the most damaged and toughest leaves. Other chicories, if eaten raw, are cut into large slices of the right size for salads. If they are cooked, the heads should be cut in half or in four. The toughest leaves may be used in minestrones. The pleasantly bitter taste of chicory aids digestion. The chicory family includes several vegetables that are not commonly found outside Italy.

QUANTITIES

Allow about 6¹/₂ ounces per serving.

BOILING

Cook in salted, boiling water for 20–30 minutes.

QUANTITIES
AND COOKING TIMES

453

CHICORY WITH BÉCHAMEL SAUCE

CICORIA ALLA BESCIAMELLA

Serves 4

2¹/₄ pounds white chicory heads

2 tablespoons butter, plus extra for greasing

generous ¹/₂ cup cooked, cured ham, coarsely chopped

1¹/₄ cups Béchamel Sauce (see page 50)

salt

Cook the chicory in salted, boiling water for 15 minutes. Drain, squeeze out the excess liquid and chop coarsely. Preheat the oven to 350°F. Grease an ovenproof dish with butter. Heat the butter in a skillet, add the chicory and cook over low heat, stirring occasionally, for about 10 minutes. Place the chicory in the prepared dish, sprinkle the ham over the top and spoon on the béchamel sauce to cover. Bake for 10 minutes.

CHICORY WITH CHILE

CICORIA AL PEPERONCINO

Serves 4

2¹/₄ pounds white chicory heads

3 tablespoons olive oil

3 garlic cloves

1 fresh red chile, seeded and chopped

salt and pepper

Cook the chicory in salted, boiling water for 15 minutes, then drain and squeeze out the excess liquid. Heat the olive oil in a skillet, add the garlic and chile and cook until the garlic is browned. Remove and discard the garlic, add the chicory to the skillet, season with salt and pepper and cook for a further 10 minutes.

CHICORY PURÉE

PURÉ DI CICORIA

Serves 4

4¹/₂ pounds white chicory

¹/₄ cup butter, plus extra for greasing

scant ¹/₂ cup heavy cream

pinch of sugar

pinch of freshly grated nutmeg

scant 1 cup Swiss cheese, freshly grated

salt and pepper

Cook the chicory in salted, boiling water for 15 minutes. Preheat the oven to 350°F. Grease an ovenproof dish with butter. Drain the chicory and squeeze out the excess liquid, then put into a blender. Add the cream and sugar and process to a purée. Add the nutmeg, season with salt and pepper to taste and process briefly again to mix. Spoon the purée into the prepared dish, dot with butter, sprinkle with the Swiss cheese and bake until golden brown.

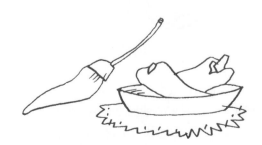

TURNIP GREENS

Turnip greens are the leaves and flowerets of turnips, sometimes also called broccoletti in Italian (as, somewhat confusingly, are the flowerets of sprouting broccoli). They are available in autumn and winter and are only eaten cooked. They are exceptionally rich in vitamin C and also contain calcium and phosphorus. To prepare, remove the leaves one at a time, discarding the damaged or very coarse ones and the thickest stems. The flowery tops are left whole. Boiled turnip greens are served hot, warm or cold, dressed with oil, lemon juice or vinegar and salt. They are very tasty sautéed with oil and garlic.

QUANTITIES

Allow about 2 ounces per serving.

BOILING

Immerse in salted, boiling water and press down with a ladle so that they stay under the surface. Once the water comes back to a boil, lower the heat and simmer for 15 minutes.

QUANTITIES
AND COOKING TIMES

TURNIP GREENS BAKED IN A PACKET

CIME DI RAPA AL CARTOCCIO

Serves 4

olive oil, for brushing and drizzling

2¼ pounds turnip greens

½ garlic clove, sliced

juice of ½ lemon, strained

salt and pepper

Preheat the oven to 400°F. Cut four sheets of foil and brush generously with olive oil. Divide the turnip greens among them and put a small slice of garlic in the middle of each. Sprinkle with the lemon juice, drizzle with oil, season with salt and pepper and fold the foil over to enclose. Place on a cookie sheet and bake for about 40 minutes. Remove from the oven, let stand for a few minutes, then place on a warm serving dish.

PARMESAN TURNIP GREENS

CIME DI RAPA ALLA PARMIGIANA

Serves 4

2¼ pounds turnip tops

¼ cup butter

½ cup Parmesan cheese, freshly grated

salt and pepper

Cook the turnip tops in salted, boiling water for 10 minutes, then drain. Melt the butter in a pan, add the turnip tops and cook over high heat, stirring frequently with a fork, for 10 minutes. Season with salt and pepper to taste, transfer to a warm serving dish and sprinkle with the Parmesan.

TURNIP GREENS WITH HAM

CIME DI RAPA AL PROSCIUTTO

Serves 4

2¼ pounds turnip tops

2 tablespoons olive oil

2 garlic cloves

½ fresh chile, seeded and chopped

3½ ounces cooked, cured ham, cut into strips

½ cup bread crumbs

salt

Cook the turnip tops in salted, boiling water for 10 minutes, then drain well, place on a serving dish and keep warm. Heat the olive oil in a pan, add the garlic and cook until lightly browned, then remove and discard. Add the chile, ham and bread crumbs to the pan and cook, stirring occasionally, for a few minutes. Spoon the ham mixture over the turnip greens and serve.

SPICY TURNIP GREENS

CIME DI RAPA PICCANTINE

Serves 4

2¼ pounds turnip tops

3½ ounces salted anchovies, heads removed, cleaned and filleted (see page 596), soaked in cold water for 10 minutes and drained

2 tablespoons olive oil

1 garlic clove

2 tablespoons capers, drained, rinsed and chopped

salt

Cook the turnip greens in salted, boiling water for 5 minutes, then drain well. Meanwhile, chop the anchovy fillets. Heat the oil in a pan, add the garlic and cook until lightly browned, then remove and discard it. Add the anchovies and cook over low heat, mashing with a wooden spoon until they have almost completely disintegrated. Add the turnip tops, mix well and cook over medium heat for about 20 minutes. Stir in the capers, then remove from the heat and serve.

ONIONS

Onions are invaluable for flavoring broths, meat, vegetable dishes and marinades. To prevent them from making your eyes water excessively when peeling them, hold them under running water while you do so. There are different kinds and colors – round, flat and onion-shaped, and white, red and golden brown. Purple ones have the strongest taste, white ones are the most delicate and red Tropea onions are the sweetest. Pearl onions, often sold ready cleaned in bags, are delicate. To make the flavor of onions less intense, blanch them briefly in boiling water.

QUANTITIES AND COOKING TIMES

QUANTITIES

Allow a minimum of 4 ounces (1 medium onion) per serving.

BOILING

Cook standard onions for 30 minutes in boiling water and pearl onions for 10 minutes.

FRIED ONION RINGS

To make the batter, sift the flour and a pinch of salt into a bowl, make a well in the center, break the egg into the well and add the olive oil and a pinch of pepper. Mix well until the batter is smooth and even. Let rest for 1 hour. Meanwhile, put the onion rings in a dish, add cold water to cover and set aside for about 30 minutes. Drain and pat dry with paper towels. Heat the oil for deep-frying in a large pan. Dip the onion rings in the batter and fry, in batches, in the hot oil until golden brown. Remove with a slotted spatula, drain on paper towels and sprinkle with salt and pepper. Serve immediately.

ANELLI FRITTI

Serves 4

2 large onions, cut into thick rings

vegetable oil, for deep-frying

salt and white pepper

For the batter

3 tablespoons all-purpose flour

1 egg

3 tablespoons olive oil

salt and pepper

PEARL ONION OMELET

Heat the olive oil in a skillet, add the garlic and cook for a few minutes until browned, then remove and discard it. Add the onions to the skillet and cook over low heat, stirring occasionally, for 5 minutes. Beat the eggs with the Parmesan in a bowl and season with salt and pepper. Pour the mixture into the skillet and cook, stirring occasionally with a fork, until the eggs are lightly set. Transfer to a warm serving dish and serve with homemade bread.

CIPOLLATA

Serves 4

4 tablespoons olive oil

1 garlic clove

1 pound 5 ounces pearl onions, thinly sliced

6 eggs

$^1/_2$ cup Parmesan cheese, freshly grated

1 fresh flat-leaf parsley sprig, chopped

salt and pepper

homemade bread, to serve

GROSSETO ONIONS

Cook the onions in salted, boiling water for 15 minutes. Drain and let cool. Scoop out the flesh from the centers using a small sharp knife, leaving hollow 'shells'. Chop the scooped-out flesh and mix with the veal, sausage, Parmesan, olive oil, egg and nutmeg, then season with salt and pepper. Fill the onion shells with the mixture. Place the onions in a large pan in a single layer and pour in the stock. Cover and simmer for about 30 minutes until the sauce thickens. Place on a warm serving dish.

CIPOLLE ALLA GROSSETANA

Serves 4

4 large onions

1$^1/_4$ cups ground lean veal

1 small Italian sausage, skinned and crumbled

2 tablespoons Parmesan cheese, freshly grated

2 tablespoons olive oil

1 egg, lightly beaten

pinch of freshly grated nutmeg

scant $^1/_2$ cup Meat Stock (see page 208)

salt and pepper

STUFFED ONIONS

Tear the bread into pieces, place in a bowl, add the milk and let soak. Preheat the oven to 350°F. Grease an ovenproof dish with butter. Parboil the onions in salted, boiling water for a few minutes, then drain well and let cool slightly. Carefully cut them in half without breaking them up. Scoop out the flesh from the centers, leaving the 'shells' intact. Chop the scooped-out flesh and mix it with the meat in a bowl. Squeeze out the bread, add it to the bowl with the parsley, grated Swiss cheese and egg, season with salt and pepper and mix well. Fill the onion shells with this mixture, top each with a slice of Swiss cheese and dot with the butter. Arrange the onions in a single layer in the prepared dish, pour in $^2/_3$ cup water and bake for about 30 minutes or until golden brown.

CIPOLLE RIPIENE

Serves 4

1 bread slice, crusts removed

4 tablespoons milk

3 tablespoons butter, plus extra for greasing

4 large onions

$1^1/_4$ cups ground meat, cooked

1 fresh flat-leaf parsley sprig, chopped

1 tablespoon Swiss cheese, freshly grated

1 egg, lightly beaten

8 small Swiss cheese slices

salt and pepper

PEARL ONIONS WITH SAGE

Heat the oil in a pan, add the pancetta and cook, stirring occasionally, for 5 minutes. Add the onions and sage, season with salt and cook over high heat until lightly browned all over. Lower the heat, add 5 tablespoons water, cover and cook for about 30 minutes.

CIPOLLINE ALLA SALVIA

Serves 4

1 tablespoon olive oil

$^1/_3$ cup pancetta, chopped

1 pound 2 ounces pearl onions

5 fresh sage leaves

salt

THE SULTAN'S ONIONS

Blanch the onions in salted, boiling water for a few minutes, then drain well and put in a clean pan. Season with salt and pepper, sprinkle with the thyme, then pour in the wine and cook over high heat until it has evaporated. Meanwhile, heat the stock in another pan. Lower the heat under the pan of onions, pour in the hot stock, cover and cook for 30 minutes. Meanwhile, put the golden raisins in a bowl, add lukewarm water to cover and let soak. When the onions are tender, drain the raisins and squeeze out the excess liquid, then stir them into the pan and cook for 5 minutes. Transfer to a warm serving dish.

CIPOLLINE DEL SULTANO

Serves 4

1 pound 2 ounces pearl onions

1 fresh thyme sprig, chopped

5 tablespoons dry white wine

$^3/_4$ cup Vegetable Stock (see page 209)

3 tablespoons golden raisins

salt and pepper

CIPOLLINE GLASSATE

Serves 4

6 tablespoons butter

1 pound 2 ounces pearl onions

1½ teaspoons sugar

salt

GLAZED PEARL ONIONS

Melt the butter in a pan, add the onions and a pinch of salt and cook over low heat, stirring with a wooden spoon, until the onions have absorbed some of the butter. Sprinkle with the sugar and add just enough warm water to cover. Cover and cook over low heat until the liquid has completely evaporated and the onions are lightly caramelized. Transfer to a warm serving dish. This delicious dish is an ideal accompaniment to roast meat.

CIPOLLINE STUFATE

Serves 4

1¾ pounds pearl onions

6 tablespoons butter

1 tablespoon all-purpose flour

scant ½ cup Vegetable Stock (see page 209)

salt and pepper

BRAISED PEARL ONIONS

Parboil the onions in salted, boiling water for about 10 minutes, then drain. Melt half the butter in a pan, add the onions, season with salt and pepper and cook, stirring halfway through cooking, for 20 minutes until golden brown all over. Mix the remaining butter with the flour to a paste and add to the pan with the stock. Increase the heat and cook for a further 10 minutes or until the cooking juices thicken. Place the onions on a warm serving dish and spoon the juices over them.

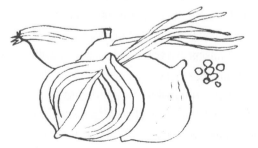

BEANS

There are at least 400 different types of beans. Among the most common in Italy are speckled, red borlotti beans, which are delicious in minestrones and with pasta, thin-skinned cannellini or toscanelli beans, which are tasty in salads and stews, black-eyed peas, which are dark with a small black 'eye' and are excellent boiled or stewed, and large, white kidney beans. Fresh beans are harvested from June to October; dried beans keep for up to three years but are best eaten within 12 months of harvesting. In both cases, their nutritional value is very high and they are rich in protein, potassium, sodium, iron, magnesium and phosphorus.

QUANTITIES

Allow $2^1/_2$–3 ounces dried beans per serving, 3–$3^1/_2$ ounces fresh beans per serving.

FRESH

The pods should be undamaged and without blemishes. They must be cooked as soon as they are shelled, for 40 min-utes –$1^1/_2$ hours depend-ing on the variety.

DRIED

The beans should not be broken or damaged. Before cooking, soak in cold water to cover for at least 12 hours and remove and discard any that float to the surface. They take 2–3 hours to cook, depending on the variety.

BOILING

Put the beans in a pan of cold water with celery, garlic and sage. Bring to a boil, then cover and sim-mer. To prevent their skins becoming tough do not interrupt the cooking, and add more hot water when necessary. Some beans, including borlotti, black-eyed peas and all colors of kidney beans, contain a naturally occurring toxin. This can be destroyed by pre-cooking the beans vigorously for 15 minutes. Drain and then cook in the usual way in fresh water.

QUANTITIES
AND COOKING TIMES

THREE BEAN SALAD

FAGIOLI AI TRE LEGUMI

Serves 4

9 ounces canned white beans, drained and rinsed

4$\frac{1}{2}$ ounces canned lentils, drained and rinsed

4$\frac{1}{2}$ ounces canned garbanzo beans, drained and rinsed

7 tablespoons olive oil

2 tablespoons white wine vinegar

1 tablespoon lemon juice, strained

1 bunch of fresh chives, chopped

salt and white pepper

This is a tasty mixed salad of beans, lentils and garbanzo beans which is traditionally prepared with freshly cooked legumes boiled in separate pans. However, to speed things up, canned legumes may be used. Tip the beans, lentils and garbanzo beans into a large salad bowl and drizzle with the olive oil. Combine the vinegar and lemon juice, season with salt and pepper and add to the salad. Sprinkle with the chives and toss lightly. Transfer to a serving dish and serve immediately.

BEANS PIZZAIOLA

FAGIOLI ALLA PIZZAIOLA

Serves 4

2$\frac{1}{4}$ pounds fresh beans, shelled

2 celery stalks

3 fresh sage leaves

1 garlic clove

2 tablespoons butter

4 tablespoons bottled strained tomatoes

4 fresh basil leaves, torn

1 fresh flat-leaf parsley sprig, chopped

salt and pepper

Put the beans in a pan, pour in enough water to cover them by at least 2 inches and add one of the celery stalks, the sage and garlic. Bring to a boil, then lower the heat and simmer for 1 hour or until tender. Drain, remove and discard the sage and garlic, place the beans in a serving dish and keep warm. Meanwhile, thinly slice the remaining celery. Melt the butter in a pan, add the strained tomatoes, celery and basil and cook until slightly reduced. Pour the sauce over the beans, season with salt and pepper according to taste and mix well. Sprinkle with the parsley and serve.

BEANS UCCELLETTO

FAGIOLI ALL'UCCELLETTO

Serves 4

1$\frac{3}{4}$ cups dried beans, soaked in cold water for 12 hours and drained

3 tablespoons olive oil

2 garlic cloves

4–5 fresh sage leaves

14 ounces canned tomatoes

salt and pepper

Place the beans in a pan, add water to cover, bring to a boil, then lower the heat and simmer for 2 hours until tender. Meanwhile, heat the oil in a skillet, add the garlic and sage and cook for a few minutes. Remove and discard the garlic when it turns golden brown. Drain the beans, add to the skillet and cook over medium heat for about 10 minutes. Add the tomatoes, season with salt and pepper and cook, stirring frequently for a further 15 minutes until the sauce starts to thicken. Remove the skillet from the heat, and transfer the beans to a warm serving dish.

BEANS WITH SAUSAGES

FAGIOLI CON SALSICCIA

Serves 4

1 cup dried beans,
soaked in cold water for 12 hours and drained

1 celery stalk

2 garlic cloves

2 fresh sage leaves

2 tablespoons olive oil

8 small Italian sausages

scant 1/2 cup dry white wine

salt and pepper

Place the beans in a pan, pour in water to cover and add the celery, one of the garlic cloves and one of the sage leaves. Cover, bring to a boil, then lower the heat and simmer for 2–3 hours, adding more hot water if necessary. Drain well and keep warm. Heat the oil in a skillet. Crush the remaining garlic clove, add to the skillet with the remaining sage leaf and cook for a few minutes. Prick the sausages with a fork, add to the skillet and cook until lightly browned all over. Sprinkle in the wine and cook until it has evaporated. Drain the beans and add to the pan, then cover and cook over medium heat for 30 minutes. Remove the lid and cook until the excess liquid has boiled off. Season with salt and pepper, mix well and transfer to a warm serving dish.

EXOTIC BEANS

FAGIOLI ESOTICI

Serves 4

1/2 avocado, peeled, pitted and sliced

juice of 1/2 lemon, strained

2 tablespoons butter

scant 1 cup cooked, cured ham, diced

1/2 pineapple, peeled, cored and diced

1 pound 5 ounces canned beans,
drained and rinsed

2 teaspoons mustard

salt

Sprinkle the avocado with the lemon juice to prevent it going brown. Melt the butter in a pan, add the ham, pineapple and beans and mix gently. Season lightly with salt and cook over medium heat for a few minutes. Mix the mustard with 1–2 tablespoons of the cooking juices in a small bowl and stir into the pan. Add the avocado, cook for a few minutes more and serve.

SUMMER CANNELLINI BEANS

CANNELLINI ESTIVI

Serves 4

3 tablespoons olive oil

1 garlic clove

1 eggplant, diced

1 yellow bell pepper, halved, seeded and diced

2 fresh tomatoes, peeled, seeded and chopped

12 ounces canned cannellini beans,
drained and rinsed

grated rind of 1/2 lemon

4 fresh basil leaves, chopped

1 fresh flat-leaf parsley sprig, chopped

salt and pepper

Heat the oil in a pan, add the garlic and cook until browned, then remove and discard. Add the eggplant and bell pepper to the pan and cook over high heat for a few minutes, then add the tomatoes and beans, cover and cook for 5 minutes. Season with salt and pepper and cook, uncovered, for a further 5 minutes. Remove the pan from the heat, transfer the beans to a warm serving dish and sprinkle with the lemon rind, basil and parsley. Mix well and serve.

MIXED BEAN SALAD

Cook the beans and shallot in salted, boiling water for 1–1½ hours until tender. Cook the green beans in a separate pan of salted, boiling water for 10–15 minutes. Drain all the beans and combine in a salad bowl with the garlic, olive oil and a pinch of salt. Crumble in the chile and mix again. Don't dress this mixed bean salad more than 10 minutes before serving.

FAGIOLI MISTI IN INSALATA

Serves 4

1 pound mixed fresh beans

such as borlotti and cannellini, shelled

1 shallot, chopped

⅓ cup green beans, trimmed

½ garlic clove, chopped

4 tablespoons olive oil

1 dried red chile

salt

BEAN PURÉE

Put the beans, celery, garlic and sage in a pan, add cold water to cover, cover the pan, bring to a boil and simmer for 2–3 hours, adding more hot water if necessary. Drain, discard the herbs and vegetables and pass through a food mill into a clean pan. Season lightly with salt, add the butter and heat gently, stirring constantly. Gradually stir in the stock until the mixture has the desired consistency; you may not need all the stock. Mix well, remove the pan from the heat and season with pepper. This purée is an excellent side dish for roast pork.

FAGIOLI IN PURÉ

Serves 4

scant ½ cup dried beans,

soaked in cold water for 12 hours and drained

1 celery stalk

1 garlic clove

1 fresh sage sprig

3 tablespoons butter

1½ cups Vegetable Stock (see page 209)

salt and white pepper

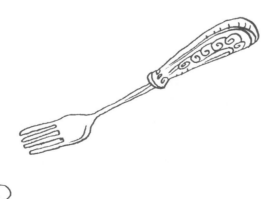

467

GREEN BEANS

Green beans, whether string beans, plain green, wax or any other variety, are best if they have been harvested when young before any strings form. Their color ranges from yellow to pale or dark green and most varieties are long and thin, but there are also some flat types, and even a miniature one known as fagiolini dall'occhio. As for nutritional value, green beans contain some vitamins A and C, calcium and potassium. When buying, reject any that look withered or are floppy when touched, and choose firm, brightly colored ones. Green beans cannot be eaten raw and should always be boiled or at least parboiled. Some people prefer to trim the ends and remove any strings before cooking and others prefer to do it afterwards. The latter practice is less widespread, but does mean that the beans absorb less water. The various types of green beans are mostly interchangeable.

QUANTITIES AND COOKING TIMES

QUANTITIES

Allow about 1 cup per serving as a side dish.

COOKING

Always cook in an uncovered pan to prevent the beans going yellow. The proportions are 4 cups water, 1$^1/_2$ cups beans and 1$^1/_2$ teaspoons salt. For al dente beans, simmer for 10 minutes; for very tender beans, simmer for 15–20 minutes. Do not overcook or they will become mushy.

GREEN BEANS IN EGG CREAM

Cook the beans in salted, boiling water for 15 minutes, then drain and chop. Melt the butter in a pan over low heat, add the onions and cook, stirring occasionally, for 5 minutes. Add the beans, mix well and cook for a few minutes more. Meanwhile, beat the eggs in a bowl, stir in the Parmesan and season with salt and pepper. Pour the egg mixture into the pan, stirring constantly, then remove from the heat. The beans should be pleasantly creamy. This is an elegant side dish.

FAGIOLINI ALLA CREMA D'UOVA

Serves 4

$4^1/_4$ cups green beans, trimmed

3 tablespoons butter

2 small mild onions, chopped

2 eggs

$^1/_3$ cup Parmesan cheese, freshly grated

salt and pepper

POLISH BEANS

Cook the beans in salted, boiling water for 15 minutes, then drain and tip into a salad bowl. Add the cannellini beans, scallion and anchovies, season lightly with salt and pepper and add the frankfurters. Shell and chop the eggs, place in a bowl, mix with the paprika and season with salt and pepper. Sprinkle with the vinegar and drizzle generously with olive oil. Dress the beans with this sauce.

FAGIOLINI ALLA POLACCA

Serves 4

generous $2^3/_4$ cups green beans, trimmed

9 ounces canned cannellini beans, drained and rinsed

1 scallion, finely chopped

3 canned anchovy fillets, drained and chopped

4 frankfurters, parboiled, skinned and sliced

2 eggs, hard-cooked • pinch of paprika

1 tablespoon white wine vinegar

olive oil, for drizzling

salt and pepper

GREEN BEANS WITH PARMESAN

Preheat the oven to 350°F. Grease an ovenproof dish with butter. Cook the beans in salted, boiling water for 15 minutes, then drain and place in the prepared dish. Beat the eggs with the milk and Parmesan and season with salt and pepper. Pour the egg mixture over the beans and bake until just set. Serve immediately.

FAGIOLINI AL PARMIGIANO

Serves 4

butter, for greasing

$5^2/_3$ cups green beans, trimmed

3 eggs • 5 tablespoons milk

generous 1 cup Parmesan cheese, freshly grated

salt and pepper

GREEN BEANS WITH TOMATO

Cook the beans in salted, boiling water for 10 minutes. Meanwhile, heat the oil in another pan, add the onion and garlic and cook over low heat, stirring occasionally, for 5 minutes. Drain the beans, add to the pan and mix well. Stir in the tomatoes, season with salt and pepper, then remove and discard the garlic. Simmer over low heat for about 10 minutes, then stir in the olives and basil and cook for a further 5 minutes. Serve warm.

FAGIOLINI AL POMODORO

Serves 4

$4^1/_4$ cups green beans, trimmed

2 tablespoons olive oil

1 onion, chopped • 1 garlic clove

5 tomatoes, peeled, seeded and chopped

6 green olives, pitted and quartered

6 fresh basil leaves, chopped

salt and pepper

FROSTED GREEN BEANS WITH SESAME

FAGIOLINI GLASSATI AL SESAMO

Serves 4

4¹/₄ cups green beans, trimmed
2 tablespoons butter
2 scallions, thinly sliced
strained juice and grated rind of ¹/₂ lemon
1 tablespoon sesame seeds
olive oil, for drizzling
salt and pepper

Cook the beans in salted, boiling water for 10 minutes, then drain and set aside. Melt the butter in a pan, add the scallions and cook over low heat, stirring occasionally, for about 5 minutes until softened. Stir in the lemon juice and rind, add the beans, season with salt and pepper and simmer for a further 10 minutes. Meanwhile, dry-fry the sesame seeds, stirring frequently, for about 1 minute until they give off their aroma, then remove from the heat. Transfer the bean mixture to a warm serving dish, sprinkle with the sesame seeds and drizzle with olive oil. Mix well and serve.

STRING BEANS AU GRATIN

FAGIOLINI GRATINATI

Serves 4

4¹/₄ cups string beans, trimmed
2 tablespoons olive oil
1 garlic clove
2 leeks, trimmed and sliced
1 tablespoon all-purpose flour
scant ¹/₂ cup milk
scant 1 cup dry white wine
2 tablespoons butter, plus extra for greasing
4 tablespoons Parmesan cheese, freshly grated
salt and pepper

Cook the beans in salted, boiling water for about 10 minutes, then drain and let cool slightly. Heat the oil in a large pan, add the garlic and leeks and cook over low heat, stirring occasionally, for 5 minutes. Remove and discard the garlic and stir in the flour. Gradually stir in the milk and season with salt and pepper. Add the beans, pour in the wine, cover and simmer for about 10 minutes. Meanwhile, preheat the oven to 350°F. Grease an ovenproof dish with butter. Remove the pan from the heat and tip the mixture into the prepared dish. Sprinkle with the Parmesan, dot with the butter and bake for 15 minutes or until golden and bubbling. Remove from the oven and let stand for 10 minutes before serving.

GREEN BEANS IN BÉCHAMEL SAUCE AU GRATIN

FAGIOLINI GRATINATI ALLA BESCIAMELLA

Serves 4

¹/₄ cup butter, plus extra for greasing
2 tablespoons olive oil
1 onion, chopped
generous 2³/₄ cups green beans, trimmed and halved
2³/₄ cups white or cremini mushrooms, thinly sliced
1 quantity Béchamel Sauce (see page 50)
generous ¹/₂ cup cooked, cured ham, diced
1 egg
1 egg yolk
salt and pepper

Divide the butter and olive oil between two small pans and heat. Add half the onion to each pan and cook over low heat, stirring occasionally, for 5 minutes until softened. Add the beans to one pan and the mushrooms to the other and cook over low heat, stirring occasionally, for 15 minutes. Meanwhile, preheat the oven to 350°F. Grease a mold with butter. Season the bean and mushroom mixtures with salt and pepper, then stir both into the béchamel sauce with the ham, whole egg and egg yolk. Spoon the mixture into the prepared mold and bake for about 40 minutes. Turn out onto a serving dish.

GREEN BEAN SALAD

FAGIOLINI IN INSALATA

Serves 4

4¹/₄ cups green
and yellow beans, trimmed

1 onion, thinly sliced

1 garlic clove, thinly sliced

1 teaspoon mustard seeds

juice of ¹/₂ lemon, strained

1 fresh flat-leaf parsley sprig, chopped

olive oil, for drizzling

salt and pepper

Cook the beans in salted, boiling water for 15 minutes, then drain and tip into a salad bowl. Add the onion, garlic, mustard seeds, lemon juice and parsley, drizzle with olive oil and season with salt and pepper. Toss and set aside in a cool place for 30 minutes for the flavors to mingle before serving.

BEANS IN GARLIC SAUCE

FAGIOLINI IN SALSA D'AGLIO

Serves 4

1 thick bread slice, crusts removed

scant ¹/₂ cup white wine vinegar

2¹/₄ cups yellow wax beans

2¹/₄ cups green beans

2 garlic cloves

¹/₂ cup olive oil

salt and pepper

Tear the bread into pieces, place in a bowl, add the vinegar and let soak. Cook the beans in salted, boiling water for about 10 minutes, then drain and place on a serving dish. Crush the garlic in a mortar with a pestle, then gradually stir in the olive oil until thick and smooth. Squeeze out the bread, stir it into the sauce and season with salt and pepper. Spoon the sauce over the warm beans and serve.

GREEN BEANS IN EGG SAUCE

FAGIOLINI IN SALSA D'UOVA

Serves 4

4¹/₄ cups green beans

¹/₄ cup butter

1 fresh flat-leaf parsley sprig, chopped

2 egg yolks

juice of 1 lemon, strained

salt

Cook the beans in salted, boiling water for 15 minutes, then drain. Melt the butter in a pan, add the beans and cook over medium heat, stirring occasionally, for 10 minutes. Stir in the parsley and lower the heat. Beat the egg yolks with the lemon juice, pour the mixture over the beans and stir over very low heat until slightly thickened. Serve immediately.

FAVA BEANS

The very distinctive flavor of fava beans is more noticeable when they are fresh, small and so young that you need only shell them without peeling off their skins, which are still tender and sweet at this stage. They are delicious eaten raw in the spring with romano cheese. Larger, older beans, on the other hand, must be peeled and cooked. These are perfect in minestrones, barley soups or puréed. Deciding whether it is best to remove the skin depends a lot on the recipe. Mostly, however, it is recommended to do so, as the resulting dish will be lighter and tastier. Dried beans, whether with or without skins, should be soaked in cold water for a long period – as much as a whole day. In Calabria, fava beans are used to make an ancient, traditional dish called macco. It is a thick soup seasoned with oil and freshly ground pepper. As for their nutritional value, both dried and fresh fava beans are rich in phosphorus, calcium and potassium.

FRESH

Allow ³/₄ cup shelled fava beans per serving as a side dish. Note that 6¹/₂ pounds unshelled fava beans correspond to about 4¹/₂ cups shelled ones.

DRIED

Allow about ¹/₂ cup per serving as a side dish.

BOILING

Cook fresh fava beans in salted, boiling water for 20–30 minutes. Cook dried beans without salt for 2–3 hours.

QUANTITIES AND COOKING TIMES

473

PIEDMONTESE FAVA BEANS

FAVE ALLA PIEMONTESE

Serves 4

4 1/2 pounds fresh fava beans, shelled

scant 1 cup heavy cream

2 ounces fontina cheese, sliced

salt

Cook the beans in salted, boiling water for 10 minutes, then drain and tip into a skillet. Stir in the cream and simmer gently for about 10 minutes until thickened. Stir in the fontina and cook until it is just starting to melt.

FAVA BEANS WITH HAM

FAVE AL PROSCIUTTO

Serves 4

4 1/2 pounds fresh fava beans, shelled

3 tablespoons butter

generous 1/2 cup cooked, cured ham, diced

1 onion, chopped

1 carrot, chopped

scant 1 cup Meat Stock (see page 208)

1 fresh flat-leaf parsley sprig, chopped

salt and pepper

Put the beans in a pan, add cold water to cover, bring to a boil and cook for 10 minutes. Meanwhile, melt half the butter in another pan, add the ham, onion and carrot and cook, stirring occasionally, for 5 minutes. Drain the beans and add to the ham mixture, then pour in the stock and season with salt and pepper. Simmer until the sauce is very thick, then stir in the remaining butter, transfer to a warm serving dish and sprinkle with the parsley.

FRESH FAVA BEAN PURÉE

PURÉ DI FAVE FRESCHE

Serves 4

6 1/2 pounds fresh fava beans, shelled

2 small potatoes, diced

scant 1/2 cup Vegetable Stock (see page 209)

olive oil, for drizzling

salt and pepper

Soak the beans in cold water for 30 minutes, then drain, peel and put into a pan. Add enough cold water just to cover and bring to a boil over low heat. As soon as the water begins to boil, remove the pan from the heat, drain the beans, return to the pan and mash. Season with salt, add the potatoes and stock and cook until soft and creamy. Remove the pan from the heat, drizzle generously with olive oil, then taste and adjust the seasoning if necessary. Serve hot or cold.

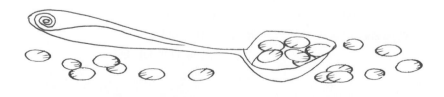

FENNEL

Fennel bulbs are attractive, tasty and aid digestion. They are also the leanest vegetable. Florence fennel bulbs contain no fat and have just 9 calories per 3¹⁄₂ ounces. On the other hand, they are rich in minerals, including calcium, phosphorus, sodium and potassium. Their delicate aroma is reminiscent of aniseed. When buying fennel, bear in mind that the division into male (round) and female (elongated) bulbs has no scientific basis, but it is worth knowing that the former are better for eating raw – on their own or with other types of salad – while the latter are better cooked. To prepare fennel, rinse very thoroughly under cold running water, remove the outer leaves, which may be very hard, and trim the base. Leave the bulbs whole, or cut them in half or into fourths according to the recipe. Cut surfaces turn brown on exposure to air so fennel should be cooked immediately or dropped into a bowl of acidulated water. Sweet fennel is a highly aromatic herb and is used in roasts as it brings out their fragrance and flavor. Fennel seeds, from both sweet and Florence fennel, are aromatic spices. Fennel also has a noble relative: dill. This light herb has an aroma very like that of fennel and is a favorite with professional and experienced cooks alike. However, it should always be used sparingly.

QUANTITIES AND COOKING TIMES

QUANTITIES

Allow 1 raw Florence fennel bulb per serving and 1¹⁄₂ bulbs if cooked.

BOILING

Whole fennel bulbs take about 45 minutes to cook. If halved, they take 30 minutes or less.

DEVIL'S FENNEL

Chop the anchovy fillets. Heat the oil in a pan, add the anchovies and cook, mashing with a wooden spoon until they have almost completely disintegrated, then add the fennel. Combine the mustard and vinegar, season with salt and pepper and sprinkle the mixture over the fennel. Cover and cook over very low heat, stirring frequently and adding a little water if necessary, until tender. Remove the fennel with a slotted spatula and place on a warm serving dish. Stir the lemon juice into the cooking juices and cook, stirring, until thickened. Pour the sauce in a continuous stream over the fennel and serve.

FINOCCHI ALLA DIAVOLA

Serves 4

4 salted anchovies, heads removed,
cleaned and filleted (see page 596),
soaked in cold water for 10 minutes
rinsed and drained
scant 1/2 cup olive oil
4 fennel bulbs, trimmed and cut into wedges
1 teaspoon Dijon mustard
1 tablespoon white wine vinegar
juice of 1 lemon, strained
salt and pepper

FENNEL WITH MOZZARELLA

Cook the fennel in salted, boiling water for about 45 minutes until tender. Drain, pat dry and let cool slightly, then cut into thin wedges while still warm Preheat the oven to 325°F. Melt the butter in a flameproof dish, add the fennel and cook, stirring constantly, until lightly browned. Remove from the heat, cover with the mozzarella slices and sprinkle with the parsley. Beat together the eggs, cream and Parmesan in a bowl, season with salt and pepper and pour the mixture over the fennel. Bake until the eggs are just set. Serve immediately.

FINOCCHI ALLA MOZZARELLA

Serves 4

2 1/4 pounds fennel bulbs, trimmed
2 tablespoons butter
7 ounces mozzarella cheese, sliced
1 fresh flat-leaf parsley sprig, chopped
4 eggs
scant 1 cup heavy cream
1/2 cup Parmesan cheese, freshly grated
salt and pepper

FENNEL WITH WHITE WINE

Put the fennel in a pan with the garlic and olive oil and sprinkle with the white wine. Cover and cook for 20 minutes or until the fennel is very tender. Remove the pan from the heat, season with salt and pepper and sprinkle with the parsley.

FINOCCHI AL VINO BIANCO

Serves 4

2 1/4 pounds fennel bulbs,
trimmed and cut into wedges
1 garlic clove, chopped • 2 tablespoons olive oil
scant 1 cup dry white wine
1 fresh flat-leaf parsley sprig, chopped
salt and pepper

FENNEL WITH WALNUTS AND ORANGES

Place the fennel slices in a salad bowl, drizzle with olive oil and season with salt and pepper. Peel the oranges and cut off all traces of pith, then slice and add to the fennel. Add the walnuts, mix and serve.

FINOCCHI CON NOCI E ARANCE

Serves 4

4 tender, round fennel bulbs, trimmed and thinly sliced
olive oil, for drizzling
2 oranges • 6 shelled walnuts, chopped
salt and pepper

FRIED FENNEL

FINOCCHI FRITTI
Serves 4
4 fennel bulbs, trimmed
1 egg
$1/2$ cup Parmesan cheese, freshly grated
$1/4$ cup butter
salt

Cook the fennel in salted, boiling water for about 45 minutes until tender. Thinly slice crosswise and pat dry on paper towels. Beat the egg with a pinch of salt in a shallow dish and spread out the Parmesan in another shallow dish. Melt the butter in a nonstick pan. Dip the fennel slices first in the beaten egg and then in the Parmesan. Add to the pan and cook until golden brown on both sides. Serve hot.

FENNEL EN CROÛTE

FINOCCHI IN CROSTA
Serves 8
$2^3/4$ cups all-purpose flour, plus extra for dusting
scant $1/2$ cup butter, softened
$2^1/4$ pounds fennel bulbs, trimmed
4 salted anchovies, heads removed, cleaned and filleted (see page 596), soaked in cold water for 10 minutes rinsed and drained
scant 1 cup Swiss cheese, freshly grated
1 egg, separated
salt and pepper

Sift the flour and a pinch of salt into a mound on the counter, make a well in the center and add $1/4$ cup of the butter. Knead to incorporate the flour, adding cold water, 1 tablespoon at a time, to make a smooth dough. Shape the dough into a ball, wrap in plastic wrap and chill in the refrigerator. Meanwhile, melt the remaining butter in a pan, add the fennel and cook over low heat until softened. Season with salt and remove from the heat. Chop the anchovy fillets and put them, with the Swiss cheese, egg yolk and fennel in a food processor and process to a purée. Season with salt and pepper to taste. Preheat the oven to 400°F. Remove the dough from the refrigerator and roll out thinly on a lightly floured surface. Stamp out an even number of rounds using a cookie cutter or the rim of a glass. Put 1 tablespoon of fennel purée in the centers of half the rounds, place another round on top and crimp the edges to seal. Brush with the lightly beaten egg white, place on a cookie sheet and bake for 5 minutes. Serve hot.

FENNEL PIE

TORTINO DI FINOCCHI
Serves 6
7 small fennel bulbs, trimmed
3 eggs
$1/4$ cup butter, plus extra for greasing
5 wholemeal bread slices, crusts removed
6 tablespoons milk
7 ounces taleggio cheese, sliced
4 tablespoons Parmesan cheese, freshly grated
salt

Cook the fennel in salted, boiling water for 45 minutes. Meanwhile hard-cook the eggs, refresh under cold water, then shell and slice thinly. Drain the fennel, pat dry with paper towels and cut into crosswise slices. Preheat the oven to 350°F. Grease an ovenproof dish with butter. Sprinkle the slices of bread with milk and make a layer in the base of the prepared dish. Place a layer of fennel on top, followed by a layer of hard-cooked egg and then a layer of taleggio. Continue making layers until all the ingredients are used, then sprinkle with the Parmesan and dot with the butter. Bake until golden, remove from the oven and serve warm.

MUSHROOMS

Honey fungus, chanterelles, black poplar, porcini, also known as ceps, oyster, morels and Caesar's mushrooms are just some of the best-known and most popular wild mushrooms. For some types you have to wait for the right season, while others are available all year round. Do not pick wild mushrooms unless you are absolutely sure that you can identify the species; and check whether there are restrictions on the quantity you can take. Instead, buy from a reliable supplier to be certain they are safe to eat. From the nutritional point of view, mushrooms contain 90 per cent water and are mainly rich in minerals and phosphorus. They are low in fat and calories and are often included in weight-loss diets. Their main characteristic is their fragrance, which is the product of 38 different substances that remain even after drying. As fresh mushrooms are highly perishable, they should be eaten within a day or two of purchase. When choosing, select the smallest, as these are the most tender, and those with large caps in comparison with their stems. They should be firm to the touch with no trace of an unpleasant smell or any blemishes. They should not look dry or swollen with water or conceal insects. To clean them, wipe gently with a damp cloth, pass them quickly under cold running water and dry them immediately. When cooking, don't cover the pan until all the liquid they give off has evaporated. The time this takes varies according to type but some mushrooms need at least 30 minutes to cook completely. Porcini have a wonderful aroma and are ideal for all methods of preparation. Black poplar mushrooms are delicious sliced and sautéed with garlic and parsley (trifolati). The highly prized Caesar's mushrooms are wonderful in salads or baked. Chanterelles are excellent in risottos and sauces. Honey fungus is good stewed. Cultivated mushrooms present no problems. Cremini mushrooms are always available, inexpensive and more or less equivalent to wild mushrooms from a nutritional point of view. There are different types; the white ones stay fresh longer than the brown ones. Lastly, dried mushrooms have more properties and fragrance than fresh ones. Before cooking they should be soaked in warm water. Although some professionals recommend straining the soaking water and adding it to risottos this is not advisable as the liquid may contain invisible traces of soil or dirt which could ruin the final result.

QUANTITIES

Allow about 5–7 ounces or 2 medium-sized caps per serving.

TRIFOLATI

This is a method of cooking in a skillet with olive oil, garlic and fresh flat-leaf parsley. The cooking time depends on the kind of mushroom: porcini and chestnut mushrooms, for example, cook in 10 minutes (see page 486).

MUSHROOMS WITH CREAM

Slice the mushrooms and sprinkle with the lemon juice. Melt the butter in a skillet, add the garlic and cook over low heat for a few minutes. Add the mushrooms, season with salt and pepper to taste and stir. Cover and cook until tender. Meanwhile, heat the stock in a small pan. Remove and discard the garlic from the skillet and, using a slotted spatula, transfer the mushrooms to a dish. Sift the flour into the skillet and cook, stirring constantly, for 2 minutes, then stir in the warm stock. Stir in the cream, mushrooms and egg yolks. Cook for 5 minutes, stirring gently but constantly. Remove the skillet from the heat as soon as the sauce thickens, and serve.

FUNGHI ALLA CREMA

Serves 4

3 ounces mushrooms

juice of 1 lemon, strained

2 tablespoons butter

1 garlic clove

$^2/_3$ cup Vegetable Stock (see page 209)

1 tablespoon all-purpose flour

$^2/_3$ cup heavy cream

2 egg yolks

salt and pepper

MUSHROOMS WITH TOMATO

FUNGHI AL POMODORO

Serves 4

2 tablespoons olive oil

1 shallot, finely chopped

1 garlic clove, finely chopped

2 fresh flat-leaf parsley sprigs, finely chopped

1 pound 5 ounces white
or cremini mushrooms, thinly sliced

scant ¹/₂ cup dry white wine

12 ounces tomatoes, peeled and chopped

1 tablespoon chopped fresh marjoram

salt and pepper

Heat the oil in a pan, add the shallot, garlic and half the parsley and cook over low heat, stirring occasionally, for 5 minutes. Add the mushrooms, increase the heat to high and cook for a few minutes. Pour in the wine and cook until it has evaporated. Lower the heat, add the tomatoes and season with salt and pepper, then cover and cook, stirring frequently, for about 10 minutes. Remove the lid, increase the heat slightly and cook until the excess liquid boils off. Stir in the remaining parsley. Transfer to a warm serving dish, sprinkle with the marjoram and serve immediately.

MUSHROOMS WITH PUMPKIN

FUNGHI CON LA ZUCCA

Serves 4

2 tablespoons butter

2 tablespoons olive oil

1 onion, thinly sliced

2¹/₂ cups pumpkin flesh, diced

1 pound 5 ounces mixed mushrooms,
cut into thick slices if large

²/₃ cup Vegetable Stock (see page 209)

3 tablespoons fresh flat-leaf parsley, chopped,

1 tablespoon chopped fresh marjoram

salt and pepper

Heat the butter with the oil in a pan, add the onion and cook over low heat, stirring occasionally, for 5 minutes. Add the pumpkin and mushrooms, increase the heat to high and cook for a few minutes. Meanwhile, heat the stock in a small pan. Season the mushroom mixture with salt and pepper, lower the heat, pour in the hot stock and cook until tender. Stir in the parsley and marjoram, and transfer to a warm serving dish.

MELTING BAKED PORCINI

FUNGHI CROGIOLATI AL FORNO

Serves 4

scant ¹/₂ cup olive oil, plus extra for brushing

1³/₄ pounds porcini

1 fresh flat-leaf parsley sprig, chopped

1 garlic clove, chopped

soft part of 2 bread rolls, crumbled

salt and pepper

Preheat the oven to 350°F. Brush an ovenproof dish with oil. Separate the porcini caps and stems and clean, wash and dry both. Pour 5 tablespoons of the olive oil into a bowl and season with salt and pepper. Add the porcini caps and let marinate. Combine the parsley, garlic, bread crumbs and remaining oil in another bowl. Take the porcini caps out of the marinade, place on a rack and put in the oven briefly to dry. Chop the porcini stems, place in the prepared dish, place the caps, gill side up, on top and sprinkle with the bread crumb mixture. Drizzle with a little of the marinade. Bake for 10 minutes.

MUSHROOMS AU GRATIN

Melt 2 tablespoons of the butter in a pan, add the shallot and cook over low heat, stirring occasionally, for 5 minutes. Add the mushrooms, increase the heat to high and cook for a few minutes. Add the ham and parsley, season with salt and pepper, lower the heat to medium and cook, stirring occasionally, for about 10 minutes. Meanwhile, preheat the oven to 350°F. Grease an ovenproof dish with butter. Remove the pan from the heat and transfer the mixture to the prepared dish. Stir the egg yolk, Parmesan and nutmeg into the béchamel sauce and spoon it over the mushrooms. Sprinkle with the bread crumbs, dot with the remaining butter and bake for about 20 minutes. Remove the dish from the oven, let cool slightly, then serve.

FUNGHI GRATINATI

Serves 4

3 tablespoons butter, plus extra for greasing

1 shallot, chopped

1 pound 5 ounces mushrooms,

cut into thick slices if large

1/2 cup cooked, cured ham, diced

1 fresh flat-leaf parsley sprig, chopped

1 egg yolk

2 tablespoons Parmesan cheese, freshly grated

pinch of freshly grated nutmeg

1 quantity Béchamel Sauce (see page 50)

1 tablespoon bread crumbs

salt and pepper

WARM MUSHROOM SALAD

Heat the olive oil in a pan, add the mushrooms, garlic and speck and cook over high heat for 2–3 minutes. Lower the heat, remove and discard the garlic and season with salt and pepper. Remove the pan from the heat and let cool slightly. Divide the corn salad among four plates and add the vinaigrette. Place the mushrooms and speck in the middle of each plate and serve immediately.

FUNGHI IN INSALATA TIEPIDA

Serves 4

2 tablespoons olive oil

14 ounces white or cremini mushrooms, sliced

1 garlic clove

2 ounces speck (Austrian smoked ham), cut into strips

7 ounces corn salad

1 quantity Vinaigrette, made with balsamic vinegar

(see page 76)

salt and pepper

MUSHROOMS WITH AÏOLI

Slice the mushrooms thinly and sprinkle with the lemon juice. Blanch in boiling water for a few minutes, then drain. Heat the oil in a pan, add the mushrooms, herbs and fennel seeds and cook, stirring frequently, for 5 minutes. Lower the heat and cook the mushrooms slowly in their own juices until tender. Season with salt and pepper, remove from the heat and place in a warm serving dish. Serve with the aïoli.

FUNGHI IN SALSA AÏOLI

Serves 4

1 1/2 pounds mushrooms

juice of 1 lemon, strained

2 tablespoons olive oil

1 fresh tarragon sprig, chopped

4 fresh chives, chopped

1 fresh thyme sprig, chopped

1 fresh chervil sprig, chopped

1 teaspoon fennel seeds

1 quantity Aïoli, made with 10 garlic cloves

(see page 64)

salt and pepper

PORCINI WITH TARRAGON

FUNGHI PORCINI AL DRAGONCELLO

Serves 4

8 porcini
¹/₄ cup butter
1 fresh tarragon sprig, chopped,
or 1 teaspoon dried tarragon
juice of 1 lemon, strained
salt and pepper

Preheat the oven to 325°F. Line a roasting pan with foil. Separate the porcini caps and stems and set the stems aside for another dish. Place the caps in the roasting pan and place in the oven until they have dried out. If the caps are very big, make a cut in their tops with a knife. Melt the butter in a pan, add the mushrooms and tarragon, season with salt and pepper and cook over low heat for 20 minutes. Sprinkle with the lemon juice and cook until it has evaporated, then serve.

PORCINI WITH PROSCIUTTO

FUNGHI PORCINI AL PROSCIUTTO

Serves 4

1³/₄ pounds small porcini • 2 tablespoons olive oil
³/₄ cup prosciutto, diced
scant ¹/₂ cup dry white wine
1 garlic clove, chopped
1 fresh marjoram sprig, finely chopped
salt and pepper

Separate the porcini caps and stems and chop the stems. Heat the oil in a pan, add the porcini stems and prosciutto and cook over medium heat for 5 minutes. Add the wine and cook until it has evaporated. Add the garlic and marjoram and cook for a few minutes, then add the porcini caps. Lower the heat, cover and cook, shaking the pan occasionally, for 30 minutes. Season with salt and pepper and serve.

FRIED PORCINI

FUNGHI PORCINI FRITTI

Serves 4

vegetable oil, for deep-frying
all-purpose flour, for dusting
1 pound 5 ounces porcini, chopped
1 egg, lightly beaten
salt

Heat the oil in a large pan. Meanwhile, put the flour in a plastic bag, add the porcini, in batches, and shake to coat, then remove the porcini and dip them in the beaten egg. Deep-fry, in batches, in the hot oil until golden brown. Remove with a slotted spatula, drain on paper towels and transfer to a warm serving dish. Sprinkle with salt and serve immediately.

STUFFED MUSHROOMS

FUNGHI RIPIENI

Serves 4

2 tablespoons olive oil, plus extra
for brushing and drizzling
8 large cremini mushrooms
3 bread slices, crusts removed
5 tablespoons milk
1 garlic clove
1 egg, lightly beaten
2 tablespoons Parmesan cheese, freshly grated
1 fresh flat-leaf parsley sprig, chopped
salt and pepper

Brush a flameproof casserole with oil. Separate the mushroom caps and stems. Place the caps, gill side up, in the prepared casserole and chop the stems. Tear the bread into pieces, place in a bowl, pour in the milk and let soak. Heat the olive oil in a pan, add the garlic and cook for a few minutes, then add the mushroom stems and cook for 5 minutes more. Season with salt and pepper, remove the pan from the heat and discard the garlic. Squeeze out the bread, mix with the mushroom stems, egg, Parmesan and parsley and season with salt and pepper. Fill the mushroom caps with the mixture, drizzle with olive oil, cover and cook over medium heat for 15–20 minutes.

MUSHROOM TRIFOLATI

FUNGHI TRIFOLATI

Serves 4

3 tablespoons olive oil

¹/₄ cup butter

1 garlic clove

2 pounds porcini

1 fresh flat-leaf parsley sprig, chopped

salt and pepper

Heat the olive oil, half the butter and the garlic in a pan until the garlic is browned, then remove and discard it. Add the porcini to the pan and cook over high heat for about 30 minutes until all the liquid they release has evaporated, then lower the heat. Beat the parsley into the remaining butter in a bowl, then add to the pan and season with salt and pepper to taste. Serve immediately or set aside and re-heat gently before serving.

MUSHROOM CAPS MONTANARA

TESTE DI FUNGHI ALLA MONTANARA

Serves 4

4 large porcini

olive oil, for brushing

1¹/₂ cups milk

1 garlic clove

1 teaspoon chopped fresh marjoram

3¹/₂ ounces polenta flour

2 ounces fontina cheese, cut into thin strips

salt and pepper

Preheat the broiler. Separate the porcini caps and stems, brush the caps with olive oil and cook under the broiler for a few minutes, then set aside. Reserve the stems for another recipe. Pour the milk into a pan, add the garlic and cook over low heat until just below simmering point. Remove and discard the garlic and stir in the marjoram. Prepare polenta (see page 305) with the flour, substituting the hot, flavored milk for water. When the polenta is very soft and smooth, season with salt and pepper, remove from the heat and stir in the fontina. Fill the porcini caps with the polenta mixture and arrange on a warm serving dish and serve.

MUSHROOM AND POTATO PIE

TORTINO DI FUNGHI E PATATE

Serves 4

3 tablespoons butter

1 pound 2 ounces potatoes, very thinly sliced

1 pound 2 ounces porcini, sliced

generous 1 cup Parmesan cheese, freshly grated

3 tablespoons fresh flat-leaf parsley, chopped

salt

Preheat the oven to 350°F. Melt the butter in an ovenproof dish and make alternating layers of potato and porcini slices, sprinkling each layer with Parmesan, parsley and a little salt. Add 5 tablespoons water, cover and bake for 1 hour. Remove from the oven, let stand for 5 minutes and serve.

BEAN SPROUTS

Soy beans are legumes and therefore belong to the same family as garbanzo beans, beans and lentils. Outside Italy, soy consumption in the form of flour, sauce, oil and tofu is quite common. However, in Italy soy is best known for its sprouts. There are different varieties of soy beans, including yellow, which are very widespread in the United States, green, which have a more delicate flavor, and red, which are generally considered the best. In the United States, mung bean sprouts are also widely available and popular. Bean sprouts are best bought fresh. They should be white, without any blemishes, and firm enough to snap rather than bend. When they are sold in bags always check the 'use by' date on the packaging. Bean sprouts are best eaten on the day of purchase and should not really be stored in the refrigerator unless this is unavoidable. Even then, the maximum period for storing them is 24–48 hours. If you have to put them in the refrigerator, take them out of their packaging, place them in a glass dish and cover. Bean sprouts have no waste and simply require rinsing in cold water. They are tasty eaten raw, mixed in salads and are also delicious stir-fried or added to risottos. As for their nutritional value, they contain protein, vitamins A, B and C, potassium salts, magnesium, calcium and phosphorus. Bean sprouts are thought to help lower blood cholesterol levels, while the lecithin they contain is considered to have a restorative effect on the central nervous system.

QUANTITIES
According to the recipe.

BOILING
Cook in boiling water for 2 minutes.

QUANTITIES AND COOKING TIMES

487

GERMOGLI DI SOIA AI GAMBERETTI

Serves 4

1 skinless, boneless chicken breast

3¹/₂ cups cooked, peeled shrimp

1 celery stalk, sliced

7 cups bean sprouts

1 tablespoon sesame seeds

1 scallion, green part only, chopped

5 tablespoons dark soy sauce

2 teaspoons sesame oil

salt

BEAN SPROUTS WITH SHRIMP

Poach the chicken in lightly salted, simmering water for about 25 minutes until cooked through. Drain and thinly slice. Arrange the chicken slices, shrimp, celery and bean sprouts on a fairly shallow serving dish and sprinkle with the sesame seeds and scallion. Combine the soy sauce and sesame oil in a bowl and season lightly with salt if necessary. Pour the dressing over the salad and serve immediately.

GERMOGLI DI SOIA AL PARMIGIANO

Serves 4

5 tablespoons butter

14 cups bean sprouts

¹/₂ cup Parmesan cheese, freshly grated

salt

BEAN SPROUTS WITH PARMESAN

Melt the butter in a skillet, add the bean sprouts, season with salt and cook over low heat, stirring frequently, for about 10 minutes. Sprinkle in the Parmesan, cook until the cheese melts, then remove the skillet from the heat. Transfer to a warm serving dish and serve immediately.

GERMOGLI DI SOIA PICCANTI

Serves 4

7 cups bean sprouts

3 salted anchovies, heads removed, cleaned and filleted (see page 596), soaked in cold water for 10 minutes and drained

1 tablespoon capers, drained, rinsed and chopped

3 tablespoons olive oil

juice of 1 lemon, strained

10 green olives, pitted and quartered

1 tablespoon fresh flat-leaf parsley, chopped

salt and pepper

SPICY BEAN SPROUTS

Parboil the bean sprouts for 2 minutes, then drain well and place in a salad bowl. Chop the anchovy fillets and combine with the capers, olive oil and lemon juice in a bowl, season with salt and pepper and spoon the mixture over the bean sprouts. Add the olives, sprinkle with the parsley and serve.

CHICORY

Chicory belong to the same family as Belgian endive and radicchio. There are two types – curly chicory, also called frisée, with curly leaves, and escarole, also called Batavian or broad-leaf chicory, with longer flatter leaves. The base of the head, which gives chicory their characteristic bitter flavor, may be trimmed according to taste. When cooking, the head may be left whole, or cut in half or even in fourths. Cooked or raw, chicory make an excellent side dish for any kind of roast or fried meat.

QUANTITIES

Allow half a head per serving as a raw side dish. When cooking follow the quantity specified in the recipe.

BOILING

Immerse in salted, boiling water for about 10 minutes. Alternatively chicory may be blanched, then sautéed in a skillet with other flavorings.

QUANTITIES AND COOKING TIMES

CURLY CHICORY IN BATTER

To make the batter, combine the flour, a pinch of salt, the egg yolk and the olive oil in a bowl and add as much water as needed to obtain a smooth, runny mixture. Let stand for 30 minutes. Whisk the egg white in a grease-free bowl and fold it into the batter. Heat the vegetable oil in a large pan. Dip the chicory leaves in the batter, one at a time, and fry in the oil until light golden brown. Remove with a slotted spatula and drain on paper towels. Place the leaves on a warm serving dish, and sprinkle with salt.

INDIVIA FRITTA IN PASTELLA

Serves 4

vegetable oil, for deep-frying

1 pound 2 ounces curly chicory, trimmed

For the batter

9 tablespoons all-purpose flour

1 egg, separated

1 tablespoon olive oil

salt

ESCAROLE STUFFED WITH OLIVES AND CAPERS

Serves 4

1½ garlic cloves

2 heads of escarole, trimmed

3 tablespoons olive oil, plus extra for brushing

1 cup bread crumbs

³/₄ cup pitted green olives, sliced

¹/₄ cup capers, drained and rinsed

1 fresh flat-leaf parsley sprig, chopped

salt and pepper

Chop the whole garlic clove. Place the escarole heads, with some of the water from washing still clinging to their leaves, in a skillet with 2 tablespoons of the olive oil and the chopped garlic. Season with salt and pepper according to taste. Cover and cook over low eat for about 15 minutes. Meanwhile, preheat the oven to 350°F. Brush an ovenproof dish with oil. Heat the remaining olive oil in a pan, add the bread crumbs and remaining garlic and cook, stirring the mixture frequently, until the bread crumbs are golden. Remove and discard the garlic and stir in the olives, capers and parsley. Gently open out the escarole leaves, stuff the heads with almost all the bread crumb mixture and press back into their original shapes. Place in the prepared dish and sprinkle with the remaining bread crumbs. Bake for about 20 minutes.

CURLY CHICORY PURÉE

Serves 4

2¹/₄ pounds curly chicory, trimmed

6 tablespoons butter

pinch of sugar (optional)

¹/₄ cup all-purpose flour

2¹/₄ cups milk

salt and pepper

Cook the chicory in salted, boiling water for about 10 minutes until tender, then drain well and chop. Melt half the butter in a pan, add the chicory and cook, stirring occasionally, until they are extremely soft – almost mashed – adding a little water if necessary. Season with salt and pepper, taste and, if the flavor is too bitter, add a pinch of sugar. Meanwhile, make a Béchamel Sauce (see page 50) using the remaining butter, the flour and milk. As soon as the sauce is ready, remove the pan from the heat, stir in the chicory and serve.

BELGIAN ENDIVE

Belgian endive has a characteristic elongated white head with hints of yellow. The leaves have a delicate, quite bitter taste. To reduce the bitterness, plunge into hot water for a few minutes. To prepare Belgian endive, remove coarse or withered leaves and cut out the core with a small, sharp knife. Rinse the heads whole without opening the leaves. Belgian endive may be eaten raw in salads (sliced, then cut into strips), boiled and served with a variety of sauces, braised or baked.

QUANTITIES AND COOKING TIMES

QUANTITIES
Allow 1 medium-sized head per serving as a salad.

BRAISING
Blanch the Belgian endive, then put it in a pan with butter and olive oil, cover and braise over low heat until tender.

RAW
Remove the leaves one at a time. Because they are shaped like little boats they may be filled with tuna or salmon mousse.

BELGIAN ENDIVE WITH PRAGUE HAM

Preheat the oven to 350°F. Grease an ovenproof dish with butter. Wrap each head of Belgian endive in a slice of ham and place in the prepared dish. Season with salt and pepper, spoon in the béchamel sauce and sprinkle with the nutmeg. Add the stock and sprinkle with the Parmesan. Bake for 15 minutes. Remove the dish from the oven, let stand for 5 minutes and serve.

INDIVIA BELGA AL PROSCIUTTO DI PRAGA

Serves 4

butter, for greasing

4 heads of Belgian endive, trimmed

4 large Prague ham or other smoked ham slices

1 cup Béchamel Sauce (see page 50)

pinch of freshly grated nutmeg

$^2/_3$ cup Meat Stock (see page 208)

4 tablespoons Parmesan cheese, freshly grated

salt and pepper

BAKED BELGIAN ENDIVE

Preheat the oven to 350°F. Grease an ovenproof dish with butter. Cut each head of Belgian endive into four and place in the prepared dish. Season with salt and pepper, pour in the milk and stock and bake for 30 minutes or until the liquid has almost completely evaporated.

INDIVIA BELGA IN TEGLIA

Serves 4

butter, for greasing

1³/₄ pounds Belgian endive, trimmed

scant 1 cup milk

scant 1 cup Vegetable Stock (see page 209)

salt and pepper

BAKED BELGIAN ENDIVE WITH NUTMEG

Preheat the oven to 350°F. Grease an ovenproof dish with butter. Place the Belgian endive in a steamer and steam for about 10 minutes. Remove from the heat, cut each head in half and place in the prepared dish. Season with salt and sprinkle with the bread crumbs and nutmeg. Bake for 15 minutes until golden.

INDIVIA BELGA IN TEGLIA
ALLA NOCE MOSCATA

Serves 4

butter, for greasing

1³/₄ pounds Belgian endive, trimmed

1¹/₂ cups bread crumbs

generous pinch of freshly grated nutmeg

salt

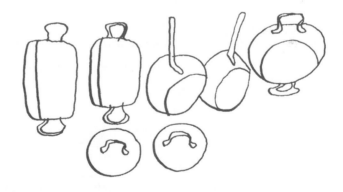

SALADS

Although the following pages are devoted to raw salads, you should not make the mistake of thinking they will cover only lettuce, Belgian endive, radicchio, curly chicory and escarole salads. Here, salad means any food – either raw or cooked – which is dressed with oil, vinegar and salt. Therefore you can have rice, crab, lentil, chicken, asparagus and many other types of salad. Dressing a salad is an art that requires a light hand. Tossing it properly is a culinary skill. Salads should be tossed lightly with the hands, as metal spoons can damage and bruise the leaves. Those who do not want to use their hands should choose wooden utensils. The salad bowl should be fairly large and preferably made of glass or porcelain. The classic dressing is salt, vinegar and oil, used in that order, just before serving so that the salad remains crisp. However, there are many other types of dressing and there are also several different types of oil and vinegar, each with a different aroma and flavor. Lemon juice is also widely used and several variations on the theme are possible.

OIL   VINEGAR

Serves 4

1 head of wild dandelion, trimmed

2 Bibb lettuces, trimmed

1 head of curly Belgian endive, trimmed

1 bunch of radishes, thinly sliced

1 scallion, thinly sliced

5 ounces smoked salmon, cut into strips

juice of 1 lemon, strained

scant $^1/_2$ cup olive oil • $^1/_4$ cup ricotta cheese

1 fresh flat-leaf parsley sprig, chopped

$^1/_2$ teaspoon chopped fresh dill

salt and pepper

SALMON SALAD WITH 'BEADS'

Place all the salad leaves in a salad bowl and add the radishes, scallion and smoked salmon. Whisk together the lemon juice and olive oil in a bowl and season with salt and pepper. Pour the dressing over the salad and toss well. Put the ricotta in another bowl and stir in the parsley and dill. Roll into 'beads' with your fingers, sprinkle them over the salad and serve.

Serves 4

1 pomegranate

2 carrots, cut into thin batons

1 bunch of corn salad, trimmed

1 bunch of arugula, trimmed

1 bunch of young spinach, trimmed

scant ¹/₂ cup olive oil

1–2 tablespoons balsamic vinegar

juice of ¹/₂ orange, strained

salt

MIXED SALAD
WITH POMEGRANATE

Cut a thin slice from one end of the pomegranate, stand it upright and cut down through the skin at intervals. Holding the pomegranate over a bowl, bend the segments backwards and scrape the seeds into the bowl with your fingers. Remove all traces of pith and membranes. Place the carrots, corn salad, arugula and spinach in a salad bowl. Whisk together the oil, vinegar and orange juice in another bowl and season with salt to taste. Pour the dressing over the salad and toss. Sprinkle with the pomegranate seeds and serve.

Serves 4

2 avocados

juice of 1 lemon, strained

2 tangerines

1 romaine lettuce, trimmed

2 tomatoes, sliced

1 scallion, sliced

2 fresh flat-leaf parsley sprigs, chopped

2 teaspoons Dijon mustard

6 tablespoons olive oil

salt and pepper

AVOCADO SALAD

Peel, halve and pit the avocados, then cut into slices and sprinkle with the lemon juice. Peel the tangerines, cut away all traces of pith and slice horizontally. Arrange a bed of lettuce leaves on each of four plates. Make a layer with the tomatoes and scallion, then arrange a ring of avocado slices, top with the tangerine slices and sprinkle with the parsley. Combine the mustard and olive oil in a bowl, season with salt and pepper, pour the dressing over the salad and serve.

Serves 4

5 ounces corn salad

2 round fennel bulbs, trimmed, halved and thinly sliced

5 ounces bresaola, thinly sliced

1 celery stalk, cut into thin batons

1 egg yolk

3 tablespoons balsamic vinegar

scant ¹/₂ cup olive oil

salt and pepper

BRESAOLA WITH
CORN SALAD

Arrange a bed of lettuce leaves on each of four plates and top with a fan of fennel. Place the bresaola on top and sprinkle with the celery. Whisk together the egg yolk, vinegar and olive oil in a bowl and season with salt and pepper, then pour into a sauce boat. Serve the salad with the sauce.

WHITE CABBAGE SALAD

INSALATA DI CAVOLO CAPUCCIO

Serves 4

¹/₂ white cabbage, cored and shredded
2 carrots, cut into thin batons
1 celery stalk, cut into thin batons
1 scallion, thinly sliced
1 fresh flat-leaf parsley sprig, chopped
¹/₂ cup Mayonnaise (see page 65)
1 teaspoon Worcestershire sauce
salt and pepper

Put the cabbage in a salad bowl and add the carrots and celery. Sprinkle the salad with the scallion and parsley, season with salt and pepper and toss. Combine the mayonnaise and Worcestershire sauce in a bowl, add to the salad and toss again.

CUCUMBER SALAD

INSALATA DI CETRIOLI

Serves 4

3 small cucumbers, sliced
2 pears
juice of 1 lemon, strained
7 ounces feta cheese, diced
1 fresh thyme sprig, chopped
4 tablespoons olive oil
1 tablespoon balsamic vinegar
salt and pepper

Blanch the cucumber slices in salted, boiling water for a few minutes, then drain and refresh under cold water. Spread out on a dish towel to dry. Peel and core the pears, then slice thinly and sprinkle with lemon juice. Make a ring of cucumber slices on each of four individual plates. Surround with a ring of pear slices, then another ring of cucumber and, finally, a ring of feta. Sprinkle with the thyme. Whisk together the olive oil and vinegar in a bowl, season with salt and pepper, pour the dressing over the salad and serve.

SWEETCORN AND RADICCHIO SALAD

INSALATA DI MAIS E RADICCHIO

Serves 4

3¹/₂ ounces baby spinach leaves, chopped
3 Treviso radicchio, chopped
generous ¹/₂ cup smoked ham, diced
generous 1 cup canned corn, drained
juice of 1 lemon, strained
scant ¹/₂ cup olive oil
salt

Put the spinach and radicchio in a salad bowl and add the ham and corn. Put a pinch of salt in a bowl, add the lemon juice and stir to dissolve, then whisk in the olive oil. Pour the dressing over the salad and toss.

CAESAR'S MUSHROOM SALAD WITH MARJORAM

INSALATA DI OVOLI CRUDI ALLA MAGGIORANA

Serves 4

14 ounces Caesar's mushrooms, trimmed
juice of ¹/₂ lemon, strained
1 small fresh marjoram sprig, chopped
olive oil, for drizzling • salt

Thinly slice the mushrooms, place in a bowl and sprinkle with the lemon juice and marjoram. Season with salt and drizzle with olive oil. Toss and serve.

SPINACH AND SEA SCALLOP SALAD

Holding the shell flat side up, open each sea scallop by inserting a strong knife between the shells and cutting through the upper muscle. Separate the shells and slide the blade under the scallop to cut the lower muscle. Remove the white flesh and discard the remainder. Heat 1 tablespoon of the olive oil in a small pan, add the scallops, then pour in the wine and cook until it has evaporated. Season with salt and pepper and remove from the heat. Place the spinach and tomatoes in a salad bowl. Peel the lemon, remove all traces of pith and dice the flesh, then add to the salad. Combine the shallot, parsley, vinegar, and remaining olive oil in a bowl and season with salt and pepper. Pour the dressing over the salad and toss. Add the scallops and serve.

INSALATA DI SPINACI E CAPPESANTE

Serves 4

8 scallops

6 tablespoons olive oil

scant $^1\!/_2$ cup white wine

11 ounces young spinach leaves,

tough stems removed

8 cherry tomatoes, halved

1 lemon

1 shallot, chopped

1 fresh flat-leaf parsley sprig, chopped

2 tablespoons red wine vinegar

salt and pepper

SPINACH AND MUSHROOM SALAD

Sprinkle the mushrooms with a little of the lemon juice and place in a salad bowl. Add the spinach and pine nuts. Whisk together the olive oil and remaining lemon juice in a bowl and season with salt and pepper. Pour the dressing over the salad, toss and serve.

INSALATA DI SPINACI E FUNGHI

Serves 4

2 cups mushrooms, thinly sliced

juice of 1 lemon, strained

11 ounces spinach, coarse stems removed

$^1\!/_4$ cup pine nuts

4 tablespoons olive oil

salt and pepper

TURKEY AND BEAN SALAD

Heat 3 tablespoons of the olive oil in a skillet, add the turkey breast and cook over medium heat, stirring frequently, until golden brown all over. Season with salt and pepper and remove from the heat. Chop the capers with the parsley, put them in a salad bowl and add the turkey, scallion and beans. Combine the mustard, the remaining olive oil and the vinegar in a bowl and season with salt and pepper. Pour the dressing over the salad, toss and serve.

INSALATA DI TACCHINO E FAGIOLI

Serves 4

7 tablespoons olive oil, plus extra for dressing

9 ounces skinless turkey breast fillet, cut into strips

1 tablespoon capers, drained and rinsed

1 fresh flat-leaf parsley sprig

1 scallion, thinly sliced

12 ounces canned borlotti beans,

drained and rinsed

$1^1\!/_2$ teaspoons Dijon mustard

1 tablespoon red wine vinegar

salt and pepper

INSALATA DI TREVISANA AI FUNGHI

Serves 4

3 Treviso radicchio, trimmed

11 ounces mushrooms

juice of 1 lemon, strained

7 ounces corn salad, trimmed

1 bunch of dandelion leaves, trimmed

4 tablespoons olive oil

salt and pepper

TREVISO RADICCHIO SALAD WITH MUSHROOMS

Make a bed of radicchio leaves on each of four plates. Slice the mushrooms, sprinkle with a little of the lemon juice and fan out on top of the radicchio. Add the corn salad and dandelion leaves. Whisk together the olive oil and 2 tablespoons of the remaining lemon juice in a bowl and season with salt and pepper. Gently pour the dressing over the salad and serve.

INSALATA DI TREVISANA AI GAMBERETTI

Serves 4

3 Treviso radicchio, trimmed

2 avocados

juice of 1 lemon, strained

11 ounces cooked shrimp, peeled and deveined

7 ounces canned palm hearts, drained, rinsed and sliced

2 tablespoons olive oil

1 fresh thyme sprig, chopped

1 fresh marjoram sprig, chopped

1 fresh flat-leaf parsley sprig, chopped

salt and pepper

TREVISO RADICCHIO AND SHRIMP SALAD

Make a bed of radicchio leaves on each of four plates. Peel, halve, pit and slice the avocados, sprinkle with a little of the lemon juice to prevent discoloration and arrange in rings on top of the radicchio. Top with the shrimp and complete with the palm hearts. Whisk together 2 tablespoons of the remaining lemon juice and the olive oil in a bowl, season with salt and pepper and stir in the thyme, marjoram and parsley. Pour the dressing over the salad and serve.

INSALATA GIALLA AL MAIS

Serves 4

1/2 Golden Delicious apple

juice of 1 lemon, strained

2 ounces mature romano cheese, diced

2 carrots, cut into thin batons

1 1/2 cups canned corn, drained

3 1/2 cups bean sprouts

5 radishes, thinly sliced

2 tablespoons olive oil

salt and white pepper

YELLOW SALAD WITH SWEETCORN

Peel, core and dice the apple, sprinkle with half the lemon juice and put in a salad bowl. Add the romano, carrots, corn, bean sprouts and radishes. Whisk together the olive oil and the remaining lemon juice in a bowl and season with salt and pepper. Pour the dressing over the salad, toss very gently and let stand in a cool place for about 30 minutes before serving.

HAWAIIAN SALAD

Put the shrimp, corn and bell peppers in a salad bowl. Halve the pineapples, lengthwise, keeping the leaves attached. Using a small sharp knife, scoop out the insides, leaving about ¼ inch around the sides of the 'shells'. Reserve the shells. Discard the core and dice the flesh of one pineapple. Add to the salad and let stand in a cool place. Whisk together the lemon juice, olive oil and Tabasco in a bowl and season with salt and pepper. Just before serving, pour the dressing over the salad, toss well and spoon into the pineapple shells. Place on individual plates, garnish with a few arugula leaves and serve.

INSALATA HAWAIANA

Serves 4

7 ounces cooked shrimp, peeled and deveined

generous 1 cup canned corn, drained

1 red bell pepper, halved, seeded and diced

½ green bell pepper, halved, seeded and diced

2 small pineapples

juice of 1 lemon, strained

4 tablespoons olive oil

dash of Tabasco sauce

salt and pepper

arugula leaves, to garnish

MIXED TUNA SALAD

Put the beans, arugula, radicchio, bell pepper, celery, fennel and tomatoes in a salad bowl. Add the tuna and olives. Whisk together the olive oil, oregano and a pinch each of salt and pepper in a bowl. Pour the dressing over the salad, toss and serve.

INSALATA MISTA AL TONNO

Serves 4

9 ounces canned cannellini beans, drained and rinsed

1 bunch of arugula, trimmed

1 radicchio, trimmed

1 red bell pepper, halved seeded and cut into strips

1 celery stalk, cut into thin batons

1 round fennel bulb, trimmed and thinly sliced

2 tomatoes, cut into wedges

9 ounces canned tuna in oil, drained and flaked

½ cup pitted black olives

4 tablespoons olive oil

pinch of dried oregano

salt and pepper

RICH SALAD

Peel, halve and pit the avocado, then slice thinly and sprinkle with a little of the lemon juice. Put the avocado slices, chicory, radicchio, pine nuts and palm hearts in a salad bowl. Whisk together the olive oil, Worcestershire sauce and remaining lemon juice in a bowl and season with salt and pepper. Pour the dressing over the salad, toss and serve.

INSALATA RICCA

Serves 4

1 avocado

juice of 1 lemon, strained

1 head of curly chicory, chopped

1 radicchio, cut into strips

⅓ cup pine nuts

11 ounces canned palm hearts,

drained, rinsed and sliced

4 tablespoons olive oil

1 teaspoon Worcestershire sauce

salt and pepper

INSALATA SICILIANA

Serves 4

1 scallion, trimmed and soaked in cold water

4 radishes, trimmed and soaked in cold water

2 citrons

2 bunches of arugula, trimmed

2 heads of escarole, trimmed

2 bunches of corn salad, trimmed

1 cup bean sprouts

juice of 1 lemon, strained

4 tablespoons olive oil

1 fresh flat-leaf parsley sprig, chopped

salt and pepper

SICILIAN SALAD

Drain the scallion and radishes and slice thinly. Cut off all the peel and pith from the citrons and slice crosswise. Put the scallion, radishes, citrons, arugula, escarole, corn salad and bean sprouts in a salad bowl. Whisk the lemon juice with a pinch of salt and pepper in a bowl, then gradually whisk in the olive oil. Stir in the parsley, pour the dressing over the salad, toss gently and serve immediately.

INSALATINA AI CAPPERI

Serves 4

1 bunch of dandelion leaves, trimmed

1 curly lettuce, such as lollo rosso, trimmed

1 carrot, cut into thin batons

1 round fennel bulb, thinly sliced

4 tablespoons olive oil

2 tablespoons red wine vinegar

2 tablespoons capers, drained and rinsed

6 fresh basil leaves, chopped

salt

CAPER SALAD

Cut the dandelion and lettuce leaves into thin strips and put in a salad bowl. Add the carrot and fennel. Whisk together the olive oil and vinegar in a bowl and season with salt. Add the capers and basil to the salad, pour the dressing over it, toss and serve.

LETTUCE

Lettuce is one of the best-known and most delightful vegetable families. Butterhead lettuces, with soft, light leaves, have a nearly ball-shaped head. Long lettuces, such as romaine, with long crispy leaves, have very large heads. Loose-leaf varieties are early lettuces that grow back after cutting. Their aroma is best appreciated in refreshing salads and, when cooked, they are said to alleviate digestive disorders and induce sleep. Lettuce's reputation for reducing libido, if it is based on the properties of the plant's sap, is undeserved in the light of normal sized portions. Lettuce's true gift is that it is low in calories and at the same time provides plenty of vitamins and minerals. Its juice is said to calm coughing. Cream of lettuce soup is very delicate, and lettuce fried with peas, makes a delicious side dish. Adding lettuce to soups, cutting it into strips or puréeing it enhances their flavor.

QUANTITIES

A medium head is sufficient for 2–3 servings of raw salad.

BOILING

Cook for 20 minutes in salted, boiling water.

**QUANTITIES
AND COOKING TIMES**

LETTUCE HEARTS WITH HERBS

CUORI DI LATTUGA ALLE ERBE

Serves 4

4 lettuce hearts

1 tablespoon Dijon mustard

2 tablespoons balsamic vinegar

5–6 tablespoons olive oil

1 fresh tarragon sprig, chopped

4 fresh chives, chopped

1 fresh chervil sprig, chopped

salt and pepper

Cut each lettuce heart into four and place in a salad bowl. Combine the mustard and vinegar in a bowl and season with salt and pepper. Gradually whisk in the olive oil. Sprinkle the lettuce with the herbs and pour the dressing over the salad. Toss and let stand for 10 minutes before serving.

BRAISED LETTUCE WITH PANCETTA COPPATA

LATTUGA BRASATA CON PANCETTA

Serves 4

4 heads of lettuce, trimmed

7 ounces pancetta coppata

(unsmoked pancetta stuffed with shoulder ham)

3 tablespoons butter

1 shallot, sliced

1 carrot, chopped

²/₃ cup Meat Stock (see page 208)

salt

Parboil the lettuce in salted, boiling water for a few minutes, then drain, pat dry with paper towels and chop finely. Cut 12 slices of pancetta coppata and place a mound of lettuce on each slice, then roll up and secure each with a toothpick. Chop the remaining pancetta coppata. Melt half the butter in a pan, add the shallot, carrot and chopped pancetta coppata. Add the filled rolls and cook, turning occasionally, until lightly browned all over, then pour in the stock and simmer for 10 minutes. Add the remaining butter and a pinch of salt, stir and cook over high heat for a few minutes. Transfer the filled rolls to a warm serving dish and spoon the cooking juices over them.

STUFFED LETTUCE

LATTUGA RIPIENA

Serves 4

1 thick bread slice, crusts removed

scant ¹/₂ cup milk

scant 1 cup ground meat

scant 1 cup bulk sausage

1 tablespoon Parmesan cheese, freshly grated

1 egg, lightly beaten

4 round lettuces

¹/₃ cup lardons

3 tablespoons olive oil

3 tablespoons butter

salt and pepper

Tear the bread into pieces, place in a bowl, add the milk and let soak for 10 minutes, then squeeze out. Combine the meat, bulk sausage, bread and Parmesan in a bowl and season with salt and pepper. Add the egg and mix until combined. Remove and discard the outer leaves and part of the centers of the lettuces, wash the lettuces and blanch in salted, boiling water for 3 minutes. Drain, gently open out the leaves and stuff with the meat mixture. Reshape and tie the tops with kitchen string. Spread out the lardons in a flameproof casserole and place the lettuces on top. Pour in the olive oil and dot the lettuces with the butter. Add scant ¹/₂ cup water, cover and cook over medium heat for about 30 minutes.

LENTILS

Lentils are small but rich in nutrients. They contain a remarkable amount of calcium, phosphorus and iron. There are several different types. In Italy the most famous, owing to their particularly delicate flavor, are Umbrian lentils, which are cultivated on the Castelluccio plateau in the province of Norcia. They are small, dull green in color and keep their shape when cooked. Orange lentils, which cook more quickly than other kinds, are known in Italy as Egyptian lentils. Like all dried legumes, lentils may be soaked in cold water for a few hours before cooking, but not for too long or they begin to sprout. Discard any that float to the surface during soaking. Lentils lend themselves to a variety of dishes, including soups and side dishes. They can be served warm – dressed with salt, vinegar, oil and basil leaves – as a starter for a summer lunch or at any other time of year.

QUANTITIES AND COOKING TIMES

OIL

QUANTITIES

Allow ¹/₃ cup per serving.

BOILING

Soak, drain and rinse the lentils. Put them in a pan, add water to cover, a celery stalk, carrot and small onion and bring to a boil. Lower the heat and simmer for about 1¹/₂ hours, adding hot water if necessary to prevent them drying out. Season with salt once they are cooked.

LENTICCHIE CON SALSICCIA

Serves 4

generous 1 cup lentils, soaked in cold water
for 3 hours and drained
1 celery stalk • 1 carrot
1 small onion
8 small Italian sausages
2 tablespoons olive oil
6 fresh sage leaves
1 garlic clove

LENTILS WITH SAUSAGES

Put the lentils into a pan, add water to cover, and the celery, carrot and onion and bring to a boil. Lower the heat and simmer for about 1¹/₂ hours. Put the sausages in a pan with 2 tablespoons water, prick with a fork and cook for 10 minutes until browned. Meanwhile, heat the olive oil in another pan, add the sage and garlic and cook over low heat until the garlic is golden brown. Remove and discard the garlic. Drain the lentils and add to the flavored oil with the sausages. Mix well and serve.

LENTILS IN TOMATO SAUCE

LENTICCHIE IN UMIDO

Serves 4

generous 1 cup lentils, soaked in cold water
for 3 hours and drained
2 tablespoons olive oil
2 tablespoons butter
1 fresh sage leaf, chopped
2¹/₂ tablespoons pancetta, chopped
1 carrot, chopped
1 celery stalk, chopped
1 onion, chopped
2¹/₄ cups bottled strained tomatoes
salt and pepper

Put the lentils into a pan, add water to cover and bring to a boil. Lower the heat and simmer for about 1¹/₂ hours. Heat the olive oil and butter in a pan, add the sage, pancetta, carrot, celery and onion and cook over low heat, stirring occasionally, for 5 minutes. Add the strained tomatoes, season with salt and pepper to taste and simmer for 15 minutes. Drain the lentils and tip into the pan of vegetables, mix well and simmer for 10 minutes. Transfer to a warm serving dish.

LENTILS WITH BACON

LENTICCHIE STUFATE AL BACON

Serves 4

1¹/₃ cups lentils, soaked in cold water
1 carrot
1 celery stalk
3¹/₂ ounces bacon in a single slice
1 garlic clove
1 onion
salt

Put the lentils into a pan, add water to cover, and the carrot and celery and bring to a boil. Add the bacon, garlic and onion, lower the heat, cover and simmer for about 1¹/₂ hours. Remove and discard the vegetables. Remove the bacon, cut it into strips and return to the pan. Season with salt to taste. This side dish may also be served as a fairly thick soup.

LENTIL PURÉE

PURÉ DI LENTICCHIE

Serves 4

1¹/₃ cups lentils, soaked in cold water
for 3 hours and drained
1 celery stalk
1 carrot
scant 1 cup heavy cream
2 tablespoons butter
salt and white pepper

Put the lentils into a pan, add water to cover, and the celery and carrot and bring to a boil. Lower the heat and simmer for about 1¹/₂ hours. Drain and pass through a food mill into a clean pan, then season with salt. Set the pan over low heat, stir in the cream and cook until the purée has the desired consistency. Remove the pan from the heat, stir in the butter and season with pepper to taste.

EGGPLANT

The round Violetta di Firenze, Violetta Lunga di Napoli, the long Violetta di Rimini, Lunga Nera di Chioggia and Black Beauty are just some of the many varieties of eggplant whose names are inspired by the deep, brilliant color of the skin of this vegetable, originally from India. Lesser known, but equally good, is the white eggplant. When preparing eggplant it is not always necessary to sprinkle them with salt and let drain for 30 minutes. Modern varieties do not usually contain bitter juices. However, salting makes their flavor more delicate and helps to reduce the amount of oil they will absorb. In case of doubt, follow the instructions given in the recipe.

QUANTITIES

Allow about 7 ounces per serving, according to the recipe.

BOILING

Eggplants are not usually boiled, but they are sliced, then blanched in water and vinegar before being preserved in oil.

SWEATING

Cook in a skillet over low heat with garlic, oil, salt and diced tomatoes. This takes about 20 minutes.

QUANTITIES AND COOKING TIMES

EGGPLANT CAVIAR

Slice off and discard the ends of the eggplants, then cook in salted, boiling water until very tender. Tip into a colander and let drain so that they lose as much water as possible, but do not allow them to cool completely. Peel the eggplants, place the flesh in a bowl and mash with a potato masher. Alternatively, pass the flesh through a food mill into a bowl. Stir in the lemon juice and olive oil and season with salt and pepper. Mix well and let cool. Garnish with tomato slices and serve with buttered toast. Eggplant caviar keeps in an airtight container in the refrigerator for several days.

CAVIALE DI MELANZANE

Serves 4

3 eggplants

juice of 1 lemon, strained

6 tablespoons olive oil

salt and pepper

sliced tomatoes, to garnish

buttered toast, to serve

EGGPLANT FRICASSÉE

FRICASSEA DI MELANZANE

Serves 4

5 eggplants, thickly sliced
2 tablespoons butter
3 tablespoons olive oil
1 onion, chopped
1 pound 2 ounces ripe plum tomatoes,
peeled, seeded and chopped
1 fresh flat-leaf parsley sprig, chopped
1 garlic clove, chopped
2 eggs
juice of 1 lemon, strained
salt and pepper

Place the eggplant slices in a colander, sprinkle with salt and let drain for 30 minutes. Meanwhile, melt the butter with the oil in a pan, add the onion and cook over low heat, stirring occasionally, for 5 minutes. Rinse the eggplants, pat dry and add to the pan, then add the tomatoes, parsley and garlic and season with salt and pepper. Mix well and cook over medium heat for about 15 minutes or until the eggplants are tender. Remove the pan from the heat. Beat the eggs with the lemon juice and pour over the eggplant mixture. Stir rapidly so that the egg does not scramble but coats the mixture like a cream. Transfer the fricassée to a warm serving dish and serve immediately.

EGGPLANT WITH CREAM

MELANZANE ALLA PANNA

Serves 4

3 eggplants, cut into $1/4$-inch thick slices
$1/4$ cup butter
1 shallot, chopped
1 fresh flat-leaf parsley sprig, chopped
4 dill pickles, drained and chopped
$1/4$ cup pine nuts, chopped
5 tablespoons white wine vinegar
5 tablespoons heavy cream
salt and pepper

Blanch the eggplant in salted, boiling water for a few minutes, then drain and let cool slightly. Melt half the butter in a pan, add the shallot and cook over low heat, stirring occasionally, for 5 minutes. Add the parsley, dill pickles and pine nuts, stir well, sprinkle in the vinegar and cook until it has evaporated. Pour in the cream, season with salt and pepper and cook over very low heat for 15 minutes. Meanwhile, melt the remaining butter in a skillet, add the eggplant and cook over medium heat until golden brown on both sides. Tip the contents of the skillet into the cream sauce and cook for a further 10 minutes. Transfer to a warm serving dish.

EGGPLANT WITH ANCHOVIES

MELANZANE ALLE ACCIUGHE

Serves 4

$1/2$ cup olive oil
3 eggplants, cut into $1/4$-inch thick slices
1 garlic clove
4 salted anchovies, heads removed,
cleaned and filleted (see page 596),
soaked in cold water for 10 minutes and drained
1 fresh flat-leaf parsley sprig, chopped
1 tablespoon white wine vinegar

Heat half the oil in a skillet, add the eggplant, in batches if necessary, and cook over medium heat until golden brown all over. Remove with a slotted spatula, drain on paper towels and place on a warm serving dish. Heat the remaining oil in a small pan, add the garlic and cook for a few minutes until browned, then remove and discard. Add the anchovies to the pan and cook, mashing with a fork until they have almost disintegrated. Stir in the parsley and vinegar, cook for a few minutes more, then pour over the eggplant and serve.

BROILED EGGPLANT

MELANZANE ARROSTO

Serves 4

3 eggplants, thickly sliced

3 garlic cloves, thinly sliced

18 fresh basil leaves

olive oil, for drizzling

salt and pepper

Place the eggplant slices in a colander, sprinkle with salt and let drain for about 30 minutes. Preheat the broiler. Rinse the eggplant slices and pat dry with paper towels, then broil on both sides for a few minutes. Remove from the heat and let cool. Arrange the eggplant slices in layers on a serving dish, sprinkling each layer with garlic, basil eaves, salt and pepper and drizzling with plenty of olive oil. Set aside in a cool place for at least 1 hour to allow the flavors to mingle before serving.

GRANDMA'S EGGPLANT

MELANZANE DELLA NONNA

Serves 4

4 eggplants, halved

2 tablespoons olive oil

2 onions, thinly sliced

2 garlic cloves

5 tomatoes, peeled, seeded and diced

1 fresh flat-leaf parsley sprig, chopped

1 tablespoon capers, drained, rinsed and chopped

1 tablespoon black olives, pitted and sliced

1 tablespoon white wine vinegar

1 teaspoon sugar

salt and pepper

Scoop out and discard the central, seed-filled part of the eggplants and dice the remaining flesh. Place in a colander, sprinkle with salt and set aside for 30 minutes to drain, then rinse and pat dry with paper towels. Heat the oil in a skillet, add the onions and garlic and cook for 1–2 minutes over low heat until the garlic is light golden brown, then remove and discard it. Add the eggplants to the pan, mix well, then stir in the tomatoes and season with salt and pepper. Cook, stirring frequently, for 15 minutes. Add the parsley, capers, olives, vinegar and sugar and cook for a few minutes more. Taste for the combination of sweet and sour. If the mixture is too sweet, add a little more vinegar; if it is too sour, add a pinch of sugar. After a few minutes, remove the skillet from the heat, and transfer the eggplant to a warm serving dish.

EGGPLANT STUFFED WITH MOZZARELLA

MELANZANE FARCITE ALLA MOZZARELLA

Serves 4

2 tablespoons olive oil, plus extra for drizzling

4 small eggplants, halved lengthwise

7 ounces mòzzarella cheese, diced

2 salted anchovies, heads removed, cleaned and filleted (see page 596), soaked in cold water for 10 minutes and drained

1/2 cup bottled strained tomatoes

salt and pepper

fresh basil sprigs, to garnish (optional)

Preheat the oven to 400°F. Brush an ovenproof dish with oil. Scoop out the eggplant flesh with a small sharp knife leaving the 'shells' intact. Dice the flesh, place in a bowl and add the mozzarella and anchovies. Mix well, season with salt and pepper and stir in the olive oil. Spoon the mixture into the eggplant shells and top each with 1 table-spoon of the tomato sauce. Place in the prepared dish and bake for about 30 minutes. Transfer to a warm serving dish. This dish may be garnished with fresh basil sprigs if you like.

EGGPLANT AU GRATIN

Place the eggplant slices in a colander, sprinkle with salt and let drain for about 30 minutes. Preheat the broiler to high. Rinse the eggplants, pat dry and brush with a little oil. Broil until golden on both sides. Heat the oil in a pan, add the garlic and onions and cook over low heat, stirring occasionally, for 5 minutes. Add the parsley and tomatoes, season with salt and pepper, mix well and simmer for about 15 minutes until thickened. Meanwhile, preheat the oven to 400°F. Brush an ovenproof dish with oil. Make a layer of eggplant slices in the prepared dish, season with salt and pepper and spoon in a layer of the tomato sauce. Continue making alternating layers of eggplant slices and tomato sauce until all the ingredients are used. Combine the Emmenthal and bread crumbs and sprinkle over the top. Dot with the butter and bake for about 20 minutes until golden brown.

MELANZANE GRATINATE

Serves 4

1 pound 5 ounces eggplants,
cut into $1/4$-inch thick slices
2 tablespoons olive oil, plus extra for brushing
2 garlic cloves, chopped
2 onions, chopped
1 fresh flat-leaf parsley sprig, chopped
1 pound 2 ounces canned chopped tomatoes
3 ounces Emmenthal cheese, diced
1 cup bread crumbs
2 tablespoons butter
salt and pepper

SURPRISE EGGPLANT IN BREAD CRUMBS

Place the eggplant slices in a colander, sprinkle with salt and let drain for about 30 minutes. Meanwhile, combine the prosciutto, scamorza or provolone, parsley and Parmesan in a bowl and season with salt and pepper. Preheat the broiler to high. Rinse the eggplant, pat dry carefully and brush with a little oil. Broil until golden brown on both sides. Sandwich the slices together in pairs filled with the prosciutto and cheese mixture. Beat the eggs with a pinch of salt in a shallow dish and spread out the bread crumbs in another shallow dish. Heat the oil in a large skillet. Dip each eggplant sandwich first in the beaten eggs, then in the bread crumbs. Fry in the hot oil until evenly browned all over. Remove with a slotted spatula and drain on paper towels. Arrange on a warm serving dish.

MELANZANE IMPANATE A SORPRESA

Serves 4

1 pound 5 ounces round eggplants,
cut into $1/4$-inch thick slices
generous $1/2$ cup prosciutto, diced
4 ounces smoked scamorza,
provolone or other stretched curd cheese, diced
1 fresh flat-leaf parsley sprig, chopped
2 tablespoons Parmesan cheese, freshly grated
olive oil, for brushing and frying
2 eggs
$1^{1}/2$ cups bread crumbs
salt and pepper

FESTIVE EGGPLANT

Serves 4

olive oil, for brushing and drizzling

4 small round eggplants

4 large ripe tomatoes, seeded and thinly sliced

9 ounces mozzarella cheese, thinly sliced

2 garlic cloves, finely chopped

1 fresh flat-leaf parsley sprig, finely chopped

4 fresh basil leaves, finely chopped

salt and pepper

Preheat the oven to 350°F. Brush an ovenproof dish with oil. Cut off the eggplant stems, then slice lengthwise without cutting all the way through, leaving the slices joined at the base. Place the eggplant in the prepared dish. Carefully place alternate slices of tomato and mozzarella between each eggplant slice and the next. Combine the garlic, parsley and basil in a bowl and sprinkle over the eggplant. Season with salt and pepper to taste and drizzle with olive oil. Cover the dish with foil and bake for 45 minutes. Remove the foil and continue to bake for a further 15–20 minutes. Carefully transfer the eggplant to a warm serving dish and spoon the cooking juices over them.

ROAST EGGPLANT WITH RICOTTA

Serves 4

1 cup dried mushrooms

olive oil, for brushing and drizzling

4 small eggplants, halved lengthwise

2 garlic cloves, chopped

1 fresh flat-leaf parsley sprig, chopped

²/₃ cups ricotta cheese

4 tablespoons Parmesan cheese, freshly grated

1 egg, lightly beaten

pinch of dried oregano

2 salted anchovies, heads removed, cleaned and filleted (see page 596), soaked in cold water for 10 minutes and drained

salt and pepper

Put the mushrooms in a bowl, add hot water to cover and let soak for about 30 minutes. Preheat the oven to 350°F. Brush an ovenproof dish with oil. Scoop out the flesh from the eggplants into a bowl without piercing the 'shells'. Cook the shells in salted, boiling water for 8–9 minutes, then remove with a slotted spatula and place upside down on paper towels to drain. Add half the eggplant flesh to the same water, cook for a few minutes, then drain, squeeze out and mix with the garlic and parsley. Combine the ricotta, Parmesan, egg and oregano in a bowl and season with salt and pepper, then stir in the eggplant and garlic mixture. Drain and squeeze out the mushrooms. Chop the mushrooms and anchovies together and stir into the mixture. Spoon the mixture into the eggplant shells, place in the prepared dish and drizzle with olive oil. Bake for 40–50 minutes, basting occasionally with the cooking juices. Serve hot.

MARINATED EGGPLANT

Place the eggplant slices in a colander, sprinkle with salt and let drain for about 30 minutes. Heat a heavy-based, nonstick skillet. Rinse the eggplants, pat dry and brush with some of the oil. Add the eggplant slices to the skillet, in batches if necessary, and cook over high heat until golden brown on both sides. Combine the chile, garlic, capers and mint in a bowl and season with salt and pepper. Make a layer of eggplant slices in a salad bowl, sprinkle with a tablespoon of the chile dressing and continue making layers until all the ingredients are used. Pour in the remaining olive oil and let marinate in a cool place for at least 6 hours. This dish may be served as a first course in summer.

MELANZANE MARINATE

Serves 4

1 pound 5 ounces eggplants,
cut into ¹/₄-inch thick slices

³/₄ cup olive oil

1 fresh chile, seeded and chopped

3 garlic cloves, finely chopped

1 tablespoon capers, drained, rinsed and chopped

10 fresh mint leaves, chopped

salt and pepper

PARMESAN EGGPLANT

Place the eggplant slices in a colander, sprinkle with salt and let drain for about 1 hour. Meanwhile, put the tomatoes, 4–5 basil leaves in a pan, season with salt and pepper according to taste, and cook over high heat, stirring frequently, for 20 minutes. Remove from the heat and pass through a food mill into a bowl. Preheat the oven to 350°F. Rinse the eggplant slices and pat dry. Heat the oil in a skillet, add the eggplant slices, in batches if necessary, and fry until golden brown on both sides. Remove with a slotted spatula and drain on paper towels. Spoon a little of the tomato sauce into an ovenproof dish and arrange a layer of slightly overlapping eggplant slices on top. Sprinkle with a little of the Parmesan, cover with a few slices of the mozzarella and sprinkle a few basil leaves and 3–4 tablespoons of the beaten eggs on top. Continue making layers until all the ingredients are used, ending with a layer of sliced eggplant sprinkled with tomato sauce. Dot with the butter and bake for 30 minutes. This dish is also good served cold.

PARMIGIANA DI MELANZANE

For 6

4–5 eggplants,
cut lengthwise into ¹/₄-inch thick slices

1 pound 2 ounces tomatoes, peeled,
seeded and diced

¹/₂ bunch of fresh basil

6 tablespoons olive oil

²/₃ cup Parmesan cheese, freshly grated

3¹/₂ ounces mozzarella cheese, sliced

2 eggs, lightly beaten

2 tablespoons butter

salt and pepper

EGGPLANT TERRINE

TERRINA DI MELANZANE

Serves 4

2 tablespoons olive oil,
plus extra for drizzling and brushing
2 yellow bell peppers
1 red bell pepper
3 eggplants, cut into $1/4$-inch thick slices
5 ounces Emmenthal cheese
1 fresh basil sprig, chopped
3 eggs, lightly beaten
3 ripe tomatoes, peeled and chopped
1 garlic clove
salt and pepper

Preheat the broiler and the oven to 350°F. Brush an ovenproof dish with oil. Place the bell peppers on a cookie sheet, drizzle with oil and roast, turning frequently, until charred and blackened all over. Remove from the oven, place in a plastic bag and seal the top. Do not switch off the oven. Meanwhile, brush the eggplant slices with oil and broil until golden brown on both sides. When the bell peppers are cool enough to handle, peel and seed, and chop the flesh. Make a layer of eggplant slices in the prepared dish. Grate $1/2$ cup of the Emmenthal and slice the remainder. Stir the grated Emmenthal, chopped bell peppers and a little basil into the eggs and season with salt and pepper. Arrange a layer of Emmenthal slices on top of the eggplant and spoon in some of the egg mixture. Continue making alternate layers until all the ingredients are used, ending with the egg mixture. Place the dish in a roasting pan, add boiling water to come about halfway up the sides and bake for 1 hour. Meanwhile, put the tomatoes, oil and garlic in a small pan, season with salt and pepper and cook over medium heat, stirring frequently, for 20 minutes. Remove and discard the garlic and pass the mixture through a strainer into a bowl. Remove the terrine from the oven, turn out onto a warm serving dish and serve with the tomato sauce.

COLD EGGPLANT TOWER

TORRE FREDDA DI MELANZANE

Serves 4

1 pound 5 ounces eggplants,
cut into $1/4$-inch thick slices
olive oil, for brushing and drizzling
4 country-style bread slices, crusts removed
12 ounces mozzarella cheese, thinly sliced
1 scallion, thinly sliced
10 fresh basil leaves, plus extra to garnish
4 ripe tomatoes, peeled, seeded and thinly sliced
salt and pepper

Place the eggplant slices in a colander, sprinkle with salt and let drain for about 30 minutes. Preheat the broiler. Rinse the eggplant slices, pat dry, brush with oil and broil until golden brown on both sides. Lightly toast the bread on both sides and place in a deep serving dish. Arrange a layer of eggplant slices on top and season with salt and pepper. Top with a layer of mozzarella, sprinkle with scallion and basil leaves, season with salt and pepper, then make a layer of tomato slices and season with salt and pepper. Continue making layers until all the ingredients are used. Drizzle with olive oil and garnish with a few more basil leaves. Let stand for 15 minutes, then serve.

POTATOES

It is almost impossible to find another vegetable as versatile as the potato. It is suitable for both the simplest and most sophisticated dishes. It can even be said that virtually everyone likes potatoes. They boast a fair amount of sodium, potassium, magnesium, calcium and iron, and new potatoes are rich in vitamins B1, B2 and C. They are less fattening than you might think, as long as they are cooked without excessive oil or other fats. Yellow-fleshed, waxy potatoes are excellent boiled, as they keep their shape well. White-fleshed, mealy potatoes are ideal for purées, gnocchi, soups and molds. Steaming is recommended for both types, as they retain more flavor and lose fewer nutrients. New potatoes don't need to be peeled; simply rub them with a dish towel. To make potato balls, use a melon baller to scoop out the flesh from large potatoes. Dress potato salad 1 hour before serving; wine may be substituted for vinegar in the dressing, but ask your guests first whether they might like this unusual taste. Lastly, it should be remembered that potatoes must not be kept in the refrigerator, but in a cool, dark place.

QUANTITIES AND COOKING TIMES

QUANTITIES

Allow about 7 ounces per serving.

BOILING

Immerse whole, unpeeled potatoes in a pan of lightly salted, cold water and bring to a boil. Lower the heat and simmer for about 45 minutes, then drain and peel. Do not leave them standing in the water as they will lose their flavor.

STEAMING

Peel the potatoes, halve or cut into pieces and place in a steamer over boiling water. Cook for 20–30 minutes.

FRYING

Peel the potatoes, cut to the required shape and keep them immersed in cold water until ready to cook to prevent them turning black. Drain and pat dry before cooking.

POTATO AND CAULIFLOWER RING

Steam the potatoes for 20–25 minutes, then tip into a bowl and mash with a potato masher. Preheat the oven to 375°F. Grease a ring mold with butter. Heat half the butter in a pan, add the shallot and cook over low heat, stirring occasionally, for 5 minutes, then add the potato, ricotta and farmer's cheese. Mix well, then remove from the heat and beat in the egg yolks, one at a time. Add the Parmesan and season with salt and pepper. Stiffly whisk the egg whites in a grease-free bowl and fold into the potato mixture. Spoon the mixture into the prepared mold and bake for about 30 minutes. Meanwhile, cook the cauliflower in salted, boiling water for about 15 minutes until just tender, then drain. Heat the remaining butter and the oil in a skillet, add the cauliflower flowerets and cook over low heat, stirring occasionally, for about 5 minutes. Season with salt and pepper. Turn out the potato ring onto a warm serving dish and spoon the cauliflower into the middle.

ANELLO DI PATATE E CAVOLFIORE

Serves 6

2¹/₄ pounds mealy potatoes, diced

¹/₄ cup butter, plus extra for greasing

1 shallot, chopped

scant 1 cup ricotta cheese, crumbled

scant 1 cup farmer's cheese

3 eggs, separated

¹/₃ cup Parmesan cheese, freshly grated

1 small cauliflower, cut into flowerets

2 tablespoons olive oil

salt and pepper

POTATO BRIOCHES

Cook the whole, unpeeled potatoes in plenty of salted water for about 45 minutes until tender, then drain and peel. Place in a bowl and mash with a potato masher. Preheat the oven to 400°F. Grease a cookie sheet with butter. Heat the milk to just below simmering point, then remove from the heat. Add the butter, Emmenthal and hot milk to the potatoes and mix well, then stir in one of the eggs. Separate the other egg. Stiffly whisk the egg white in a grease-free bowl, fold into the mixture and season with salt. Spoon small, round monds of the mixture onto the cookie sheet and top each with a smaller mound. Lightly beat the remaining egg yolk and brush the monds with it. Bake until golden brown.

BRIOCHE DI PATATE

Serves 4

1¹/₂ pounds potatoes

3 tablespoons butter, softened, plus extra for greasing

1 cup milk

³/₄ cup Emmenthal cheese, freshly grated

2 eggs

salt

POTATO CROQUETTES WITH FONTINA

CROCCHETTE DI PATATE ALLA FONTINA

Serves 4

1³/₄ pounds mealy potatoes

3 eggs

²/₃ cup Parmesan cheese, freshly grated

3¹/₂ ounces fontina cheese, cut into sticks

2-ounce cooked, cured ham slice, cut into sticks

1¹/₂ cups bread crumbs

vegetable oil, for deep-frying

salt and pepper

fresh basil leaves, to garnish

Cook the whole unpeeled potatoes in plenty of salted water for about 45 minutes until tender, then drain, peel and tip into a bowl. Mash with a potato masher. Separate one of the eggs and stir the yolk and one whole egg into the potato with the Parmesan. Mix well and season with salt and pepper. Shape the mixture into croquettes and push a stick of fontina and a stick of ham into each. Beat the remaining egg with a pinch of salt in a shallow dish and spread out the bread crumbs in another shallow dish. Heat the oil for deep-frying in a large pan. Dip the croquettes in the beaten egg, then in the bread crumbs and fry in the hot oil until golden brown. Remove with a slotted spatula, drain on paper towels and pile into a pyramid on a warm serving dish. Garnish with basil leaves.

DELICE OF POTATO WITH VEGETABLE SAUCE

DELIZIA DI PATATE ALLA CREMA DELL'ORTO

Serves 4

1¹/₂ pounds potatoes

¹/₄ cup butter

1 carrot, chopped

1 celery stalk, chopped

1 shallot, chopped

5 tablespoons dry white wine

¹/₂ teaspoon all-purpose flour

1 fresh flat-leaf parsley sprig, chopped

4 fresh basil leaves, chopped

salt and pepper

Cook the whole, unpeeled potatoes in plenty of salted water for 30–40 minutes. Meanwhile, melt 3 tablespoons of the butter in a pan, add the carrot, celery and shallot and cook over high heat, stirring frequently, until browned. Add the wine and cook until it has evaporated. Season with salt and pepper, lower the heat and cook, stirring frequently, until the mixture is creamy. Mix the remaining butter with the flour to a paste, stir into the mixture and simmer for a few minutes. Remove from the heat and stir in the parsley and basil. Drain, peel and thinly slice the potatoes. Arrange the slices like sun rays on a warm serving dish and spoon the sauce over them.

SPICY POTATO SALAD

INSALATA PICCANTE DI PATATE

Serves 4

Cook the whole, unpeeled potatoes in plenty of salted water for about 45 minutes until tender, then drain, peel and slice thinly. Place the slices in a salad bowl and let cool. Hard-cook the egg, refresh under cold water, shell and halve lengthwise. Scoop out the yolk and press through a strainer into a bowl. Chop and add them with the parsley, capers, pickled onions, dill pickles and pickled bell pepper to the egg yolk and mix well. Whisk together the vinegar, olive oil and mustard in another bowl, season with salt and pepper and pour the dressing into the anchovy mixture. Stir well and, if necessary, add a little more olive oil. Pour the anchovy sauce over the potatoes and toss gently.

1½ pounds waxy potatoes

1 egg

2 salted anchovies, heads removed, cleaned and filleted (see page 596), soaked in cold water for 10 minutes and drained

1 fresh flat-leaf parsley sprig, chopped

1 tablespoon capers, drained and rinsed

4 pickled pearl onions, drained

4 dill pickles, drained and chopped

1 pickled bell pepper, drained and finely chopped

3 tablespoons white wine vinegar

3 tablespoons olive oil

½ teaspoon Dijon mustard

salt and pepper

HAM AND POTATO ROLLS

INVOLTINI DI PATATE AL PROSCIUTTO

Serves 4

Cook the whole, unpeeled potatoes in plenty of salted water for about 45 minutes until tender, then drain, peel and put into a bowl. Mash with a potato masher. Add the fontina, bread crumbs and egg, season with salt and pepper and mix well. Preheat the oven to 400°F. Grease an ovenproof dish with butter. Parboil the leek in salted, boiling water for 5 minutes, then drain, let cool and cut into eight strips. Spread out the slices of ham and divide the potato mixture among them. Roll up and tie with the strips of leek. Place the rolls in the prepared dish and bake for 10 minutes.

1½ pounds potatoes

1¼ cups fontina cheese, freshly grated

3 tablespoons bread crumbs

1 egg, lightly beaten

butter, for greasing

1 leek, white part only

8 cooked, cured ham slices

salt and pepper

POTATO NESTS WITH EGGS

NIDI DI PATATE CON LE UOVA

Serves 4

Preheat the oven to 400°F. Cook the potatoes in salted water for about 10 minutes. Drain, cut off the tops and scoop out the flesh with a teaspoon, leaving the 'shells' intact. Place the potato shells in an ovenproof dish and break an egg into each one. Top each with a slice of butter and a little anchovy paste, season with salt and pepper and bake for 10 minutes.

4 potatoes

4 eggs

2 tablespoons butter, cut into 4 slices

1 teaspoon anchovy paste

salt and pepper

POTATOES BAKED IN FOIL WITH YOGURT

PATATE AL CARTOCCIO CON LO YOGURT

Serves 4

8 potatoes

5 tablespoons butter, diced

scant $1/2$ cup low-fat plain yogurt

$2/3$ cup heavy cream

6 fresh chives, chopped

2 fresh flat-leaf parsley sprigs, chopped

juice of 1 lemon, strained

salt and pepper

Preheat the oven to 425°F. Cut a lengthwise slit in the top of each potato with a small sharp knife. Divide the butter among the openings and season with salt and pepper. Wrap each potato in a sheet of foil, place on a cookie sheet and bake for about 40 minutes. Meanwhile, combine the yogurt, cream, chives and parsley in a bowl, stir in the lemon juice and season with salt to taste. Place the potatoes on a warm serving dish and slightly open the foil, top with 1–2 tablespoons of the sauce and serve the remaining sauce separately.

FONTINA POTATOES

PATATE AL FORNO ALLA FONTINA

Serves 6 – 8

$3^1/4$ pounds potatoes

1 garlic clove

butter, for greasing

7 ounces fontina cheese, diced

$3^1/2$ ounces Swiss cheese, diced

$3^1/2$ ounces cooked, cured ham, cut into strips

1 cup heavy cream

salt and pepper

Parboil the unpeeled potatoes in plenty of water for about 20 minutes, then drain, peel and slice thinly. Preheat the oven to 400°F. Rub the garlic around the inside of an ovenproof dish several times, then grease well with butter. Make a layer of potato slices in the prepared dish, then a layer of the cheeses, followed by a layer of ham. Continue making layers until all the ingredients are used, ending with a layer of potato slices. Pour the cream over the potato slices, season with salt and pepper and bake for 30 minutes. Let stand for 5 minutes before serving.

BAKED POTATOES WITH SALMON

PATATE AL FORNO AL SALMONE

Serves 4

8 potatoes

1 smoked salmon slice, coarsely chopped

scant 1 cup heavy cream

juice of $1/2$ lemon, strained

1 bunch of fresh chives, chopped

$1/4$ cup salmon roe

salt and pepper

Preheat the oven to 400°F. Halve the potatoes lengthwise and scoop about one-third of the flesh from the center. Reassemble in pairs, wrap each par in a sheet of foil, place on a cookie sheet and bake for about 40 minutes. Meanwhile, put the smoked salmon, cream and lemon juice in a blender, season with salt and pepper and process until smooth and combined. Remove the potatoes from the oven, fill with the salmon cream and reassemble. Arrange on a warm serving dish, sprinkle with the chives and salmon roe and serve. The contrast between the hot potato and cold salmon cream is delightful. This dish may also be served as a first course.

POTATOES IN BÉCHAMEL SAUCE

Cook the whole, unpeeled potatoes in plenty of salted water for about 45 minutes, then drain, peel and slice. Preheat the oven to 400°F. Grease an ovenproof dish with butter, arrange the potato slices, slightly overlapping, in it and season with salt and pepper. Stir the cream into the béchamel sauce and pour the mixture over the potatoes to cover. Sprinkle with the Parmesan and melted butter. Bake until golden brown and bubbling, then serve. This dish may also be served as a first course.

PATATE ALLA BESCIAMELLA

Serves 6

2¼ pounds potatoes

2 tablespoons butter, melted, plus extra for greasing

scant ½ cup light cream

1 quantity Béchamel Sauce (see page 50)

⅔ cup Parmesan cheese, freshly grated

salt and pepper

NORMANDY POTATOES

Melt the butter in a flameproof dish or casserole, add the onion, leeks and pancetta and cook over low heat, stirring occasionally, for 5 minutes. Add the potatoes and pour in the stock to cover. Season with salt and pepper, increase the heat to high and cook for about 30 minutes. When the liquid has evaporated, pour in the cream, lower the heat and cook until thickened. Remove from the heat and serve.

PATATE ALLA NORMANNA

Serves 4

¼ cup butter

1 onion, thinly sliced

2 leeks, trimmed and sliced

3½ ounces pancetta, sliced

1½ pounds potatoes, thinly sliced

2¼ cups Meat Stock (see page 208)

1¾ cups heavy cream

salt and pepper

POTATOES WITH SCAMORZA

Cook the whole, unpeeled potatoes in plenty of salted water for about 45 minutes until tender, then drain, peel and cut into ¼-inch slices. Grease an ovenproof dish with butter and make alternating layers of potato and cheese slices. Preheat the oven to 350°F. Melt the butter in a pan, stir in the flour and cook, stirring, for a few minutes, then gradually stir in the milk. Cook for 20 minutes, stirring constantly. Add the shallots and curry powder, season with salt and pepper, mix well and simmer for a few minutes. Pour the sauce over the potatoes and bake for 15 minutes.

PATATE ALLA SCAMORZA

Serves 4

1½ pounds potatoes

2 tablespoons butter, plus extra for greasing

7 ounces scamorza

or provolone cheese, thinly sliced

¼ cup all-purpose flour

2¼ cups milk

2 shallots, chopped

1 teaspoon curry powder

salt and pepper

DUCHESSE POTATOES

PATATE DUCHESSA

Serves 4

1³/₄ pounds potatoes

²/₃ cup butter, plus extra for greasing

4 egg yolks

salt

Cook the whole, unpeeled potatoes in plenty of salted water for about 45 minutes, until tender. Preheat the oven to 400°F. Grease a cookie sheet with butter. Drain and peel the potatoes, then put into a bowl and mash with a potato masher. Transfer to a clean pan and place on low heat. Stir in the butter until it is fully incorporated, then remove from the heat, season with salt and stir in three of the egg yolks. Spoon the mixture into a piping bag fitted with a star tip and pipe 'potato meringues' on the prepared cookie sheet. Brush with the remaining egg yolk and bake for a few minutes until golden brown.

POTATOES IN WHITE BUTTER SAUCE

PATATE IN SALSA BIANCA

Serves 4

1¹/₂ pounds potatoes

2 small shallots, chopped

scant ¹/₂ cup dry white wine

²/₃ cup butter, softened

3 tablespoons fresh flat-leaf parsley, chopped

4 fresh chives, finely chopped

salt and pepper

Cook the whole, unpeeled potatoes in plenty of salted water for about 40 minutes until tender, then drain, peel and slice thinly. Put the slices in a serving bowl and keep warm. Put the shallots in a small pan, add the wine and 1 tablespoon water and bring to a boil over medium heat. Lower the heat and simmer until the liquid has reduced by half, then remove from the heat, season with salt and pepper and let cool slightly. Whisk in the butter, return to the heat and whisk until smooth and creamy. Remove from the heat, stir in the parsley and chives and pour the sauce over the hot potatoes.

POTATOES AND ONIONS BAKED IN AN EARTHENWARE DISH

PATATE IN TERRACOTTA CON CIPOLLE

Serves 4

olive oil, for brushing and drizzling

14 ounces potatoes, thinly sliced

11 ounces onions, thinly sliced

7 ounces carrots, thinly sliced

6 fresh basil leaves, torn

¹/₂ cup Emmenthal cheese, freshly grated

salt and pepper

Preheat the oven to 350°F. Brush an earthenware dish with oil. Arrange slightly overlapping slices of the potatoes, carrots and onions in the prepared dish. Sprinkle with the basil, season with salt and pepper and drizzle generously with olive oil. Cover with foil and bake for 40 minutes. Remove the foil, sprinkle the vegetables with the Emmenthal and return to the oven until the cheese melts. Serve hot straight from the dish.

SAUSAGE STUFFED POTATOES

Cook the potatoes in salted water for about 30 minutes until just tender, then drain. Halve lengthwise and scoop out the flesh to make barquettes. Preheat the oven to 350°F. Grease an ovenproof dish with butter. Heat half the butter in a pan with the bay leaf, add the sausage and cook, stirring frequently, until evenly browned. Add the wine and cook until it has evaporated, then season with salt and pepper. Remove and discard the bay leaf and pass the sausage, cooking juices and cooked chicken through a meat grinder into a bowl. Stir in the parsley and Parmesan. Melt the remaining butter and remove from the heat. Fill the potato barquettes with the meat mixture, place in the prepared dish, sprinkle with the bread crumbs and melted butter and bake for about 45 minutes.

PATATE RIPIENE ALLA SALSICCIA

Serves 4

8 small potatoes, peeled

1/4 cup butter, plus extra for greasing

1 bay leaf

1 Italian sausage, skinned and crumbled

1/4 cup dry white wine

3/4 cup cooked chicken, coarsely chopped

1 fresh flat-leaf parsley sprig, chopped

3 tablespoons Parmesan cheese, freshly grated

4 tablespoons bread crumbs

salt and pepper

PROVENÇAL SAUTÉED POTATOES

Heat the oil in a pan, add the unpeeled garlic and potatoes, season with salt and pepper and cook, stirring frequently, for 20 minutes until golden brown. Meanwhile, combine the butter and saffron in a bowl until smooth. Remove the potatoes from the pan with a slotted spatula and drain on paper towels. Place them on a serving dish, sprinkle with the parsley and thyme and dot with the saffron butter.

PATATE SALTATE ALLA PROVENZALE

Serves 6

3 tablespoons olive oil

5 garlic cloves

2 1/4 pounds new potatoes, diced

1/4 cup butter

1/2 envelope saffron

1 fresh flat-leaf parsley sprig, chopped

1 fresh thyme sprig, chopped

salt and pepper

STEWED POTATOES WITH TOMATO

Heat the oil in a pan, add the shallot and garlic and cook over medium heat, stirring occasionally, until golden brown. Add the potatoes and cook over high heat, stirring frequently, for a few minutes. Add the wine and cook until it has evaporated, then lower the heat and add the tomatoes. Sprinkle with the oregano, season with salt and pepper and add 2/3 cup water. Cover and cook over low heat until the potatoes are falling apart. Transfer to a warm serving dish.

PATATE STUFATE AL POMODORO

Serves 4

2 tablespoons olive oil

1 shallot, chopped

1 garlic clove, chopped

1 pound 5 ounces potatoes, diced

5 tablespoons dry white wine

3 tomatoes, peeled, seeded and chopped

pinch of dried oregano

salt and pepper

NEW POTATOES WITH ROSEMARY

PATATINE NOVELLE AL ROSMARINO

Serves 4

2 tablespoons butter

scant ¹/₂ cup olive oil

1 fresh rosemary sprig

1 garlic clove

1¹/₂ pounds new potatoes

salt

Heat the butter and oil in a large pan, add the rosemary, garlic and potatoes, stir and cover. Cook over low heat until golden brown. Remove and discard the garlic and rosemary, sprinkle with salt and serve.

CREAMY MASHED POTATO

PURÉ DI PATATE CREMOSO

Serves 4

1¹/₂ pounds potatoes

¹/₄ cup butter, softened

scant ¹/₂ cup milk

scant ¹/₂ cup mascarpone cheese

¹/₂ cup light cream

6 fresh chives, chopped

salt and pepper

Steam the potatoes for about 20 minutes, then pass through a potato ricer into a bowl. Gently stir in the butter. Heat the milk to just below simmering point, then remove from the heat. Beat together the mascarpone and cream until smooth in another bowl, then stir in the hot milk and pour the mixture over the potatoes. Mix well, season with salt and pepper to taste and press the mixture through a strainer onto a warm serving dish. Sprinkle with the chives and serve.

BELL PEPPERS

Yellow, red and green bell peppers ripen from April to October. They are rich in vitamin C, phosphorus, calcium and potassium. Before using them, the stalk, seeds and white membranes should be removed. Green and red bell peppers are perfect for a peperonata, while yellow bell peppers are delicious broiled or roasted. Stuffed with meat, rice or other ingredients, bell peppers may even be served as a main course.

QUANTITIES AND COOKING TIMES

QUANTITIES
Allow about 7 ounces per serving. If stuffed, allow 1 bell pepper for each person.

ROASTING
Line a roasting pan with foil, lay the bell peppers on top and cook in a preheated oven, 350°F, for 1 hour. Remove from the oven, wrap in the foil and let cool before peeling.

INSALATA DI PEPERONI E FARRO

Serves 4

2 yellow bell peppers, seeded and cut into very thin strips

1 red bell pepper, seeded and cut into very thin strips

1 green bell pepper, seeded and cut into very thin strips

3 scallions, sliced

10 black olives, pitted and sliced

$^1/_2$ garlic clove, chopped

7 ounces farro, boiled

juice of $^1/_2$ lemon, strained

4 fl ounces olive oil

1 tablespoon chopped fresh flat-leaf parsley

salt and ground white pepper

BELL PEPPER AND FARRO SALAD

Put all the bell peppers, the scallions, olives, garlic and farro in a salad bowl. Whisk together the lemon juice and olive oil in another bowl and season with a pinch each of salt and white pepper. Pour the dressing over the bell pepper mixture, sprinkle with the parsley and toss. Place the salad in the refrigerator for 1 hour before serving to allow the flavors to mingle.

BELL PEPPER AND TUNA ROLLS

INVOLTINI DI PEPERONI AL TONNO

Serves 4

1 red bell pepper
1 yellow bell pepper
1 green bell pepper
12 ounces canned tuna in oil, drained and flaked
1 scallion, chopped
3 tablespoons mushrooms in oil, drained
2 teaspoons capers, rinsed
6 canned anchovy fillets in oil, drained, rinsed and chopped
1 fresh flat-leaf parsley sprig, chopped
1 tablespoon white wine vinegar
olive oil, for drizzling

Preheat the oven to 350°F. Line a roasting pan with foil. Prick the bell peppers with a fork, place in the pan and roast for 1 hour. Remove from the oven, wrap in foil and let cool. Peel the bell peppers, cut into fourths, remove the seeds and membranes and pat dry with paper towels. Combine the tuna, scallion, mushrooms, capers, anchovies and parsley in a bowl and stir in the vinegar. Spread the mixture on the pieces of bell pepper, roll up tightly and chill in the refrigerator. To serve, place different colored rolls side by side on a serving dish and drizzle with olive oil.

DELICATE PEPERONATA

PEPERONATA DELICATA

Serves 4

4 mixed bell peppers
4 tablespoons olive oil
1 garlic clove
1 onion, sliced
4 tomatoes, peeled, seeded and chopped
salt

Preheat the oven to 350°F. Line a roasting pan with foil. Prick the bell peppers with a fork, place in the pan and roast for 1 hour. Remove from the oven, wrap in foil and let cool. Peel and halve the bell peppers, remove the seeds and membranes and cut the bell peppers into large pieces. Heat the oil in a pan with the garlic. Add the bell peppers and onion and cook over low heat, stirring occasionally, for 10 minutes. Add the tomatoes, season with salt and cook for 20 minutes until thickened. Remove and discard the garlic before serving.

ROAST BELL PEPPERS

PEPERONI ARROSTO

Serves 4

4 bell peppers
3 garlic cloves, halved
12 fresh basil leaves
olive oil, for drizzling
salt and pepper

Preheat the oven to 350°F. Line a roasting pan with foil. Prick the bell peppers with a fork, place in the pan and roast for 1 hour. Remove from the oven, wrap in foil and let cool. Peel and halve the bell peppers and let drain, cut side down, on paper towels. Remove the seeds and membranes, cut the bell peppers into $2/3$-inch strips and arrange in layers on a fairly deep serving dish, sprinkling each layer with garlic and basil and seasoning with salt and pepper. Drizzle with olive oil and let stand in a cool place for 1 hour before serving.

FANCY BELL PEPPERS

PEPERONI CAPRICCIOSI

Serves 4

3 tablespoons olive oil, plus extra for brushing

4 yellow bell peppers

6 salted anchovies, heads removed, cleaned and filleted (see page 596), soaked in cold water for 10 minutes and drained

2 garlic cloves, finely chopped

1 fresh flat-leaf parsley sprig, finely chopped

scant 1 cup green olives, pitted and finely chopped

6 fresh basil leaves, finely chopped

9 ounces tomatoes, peeled and diced

9 ounces mozzarella cheese, sliced

salt and pepper

Preheat the oven to 400°F. Brush an ovenproof dish with oil. Halve the bell peppers, including the stems, and remove the seeds and membranes. Place cut side up in the prepared dish and bake for 15–20 minutes. Meanwhile, chop the anchovy fillets. Place them in a bowl, add half the olive oil and mash until smooth. Add the garlic, parsley, olives and basil. Place the tomatoes in another bowl, stir in the remaining olive oil and season with salt and pepper to taste. Remove the bell peppers from the oven but do not switch it off. Fill each bell pepper half with the tomatoes, lay a slice of mozzarella on top and add a tablespoon of the anchovy sauce. Return to the oven and bake for 10 minutes.

SWEET–AND–SOUR BELL PEPPERS

PEPERONI IN AGRODOLCE

Serves 4

3 tablespoons olive oil

4 bell peppers, halved, seeded and thickly sliced

scant 1 cup white wine vinegar

2 tablespoons sugar

salt

Heat the oil in a pan, add the bell peppers and cook over low heat for about 15 minutes. Add salt, then remove from the pan and set aside. Pour the vinegar into the pan juices, stir in the sugar, increase the heat and cook, stirring, until the vinegar has almost completely evaporated. Return the bell peppers to the pan and cook for a further 2 minutes, then transfer to a warm serving dish.

SUMMER STUFFED BELL PEPPERS

PEPERONI RIPIENI D'ESTATE

Serves 6

1 eggplant, diced

2 salted anchovies, heads removed, cleaned and filleted (see page 596), soaked in cold water for 10 minutes and drained

2 tablespoons olive oil, plus extra for brushing

5 ounces Swiss cheese, diced

scant 1 cup olives, pitted and thinly sliced

³/₄ cup fresh flat-leaf parsley, chopped

6 fresh basil leaves, chopped

3 tomatoes, peeled, seeded and chopped

2 potatoes, diced

1 tablespoon capers, drained and rinsed

pinch of dried oregano

6 green bell peppers • salt and pepper

Place the eggplant cubes in a colander, sprinkle with salt and let drain for 30 minutes. Meanwhile, chop the anchovy fillet. Preheat the oven to 350°F. Brush an ovenproof dish with oil. Place the Swiss cheese, olives, parsley, basil, tomatoes and potatoes in a large bowl. Rinse the eggplant, pat dry with paper towels and add to the bowl with the anchovies, capers and oregano. Season with salt and pepper and mix well. Remove the stems from the bell peppers and cut off and reserve the tops. Remove the seeds and membranes using a small sharp knife and a teaspoon. Fill the bell peppers with the stuffing mixture, pour a teaspoon of olive oil into each, replace the tops and secure with a toothpick if necessary. Place the bell peppers in the prepared dish and bake for 1 hour. Serve hot or cold.

PEAS

Fresh, dried, canned and frozen peas are all rich in potassium, phosphorus, protein and B group vitamins. Good quality fresh peas can be recognized by their smooth, elastic, bright green pods. They are perfect for numerous recipes, as side dishes and as an ingredient used with pasta and in risottos. Snow peas are a type of pea with a very thin, edible pod so they do not need shelling. Simply wash them in cold water and gently rub the surface of the pods.

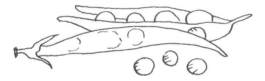

QUANTITIES

Allow about ³/₄ cup shelled peas per serving. After shelling, 2¹/₄ pounds pods yields about 4¹/₂ cups peas.

FRYING

Early peas should be treated with great care. Cook over low heat in butter or oil, but do not allow them to absorb the fat or they will become heavy and indigestible. A high heat makes peas go hard so they should always be cooked over low heat in a covered skillet. The steam formed during cooking prevents the peas from absorbing too much fat. If necessary, add a little hot water during cooking.

BOILING

Cook in salted, boiling water for 15–30 minutes, depending on the size and freshness of the peas.

**QUANTITIES
AND COOKING TIMES**

MATTONELLA TRICOLORE

Serves 6

3¹/₂ cups shelled fresh peas

14 ounces carrots, sliced, plus extra to garnish

7 ounces spinach

butter, for greasing

3 eggs, separated

9 tablespoons heavy cream

2 tablespoons ricotta cheese

salt and pepper

fresh chervil sprigs, to garnish

THREE—COLOUR TERRINE

Cook the peas and carrots in separate pans of salted, boiling water for 15–30 minutes until tender, then drain. Cook the spinach, in just the water clinging to the leaves after washing, for 5–10 minutes, then drain and squeeze out the excess liquid. Preheat the oven to 375°F. Grease a terrine or loaf pan with butter. Separately process each vegetable to a purée and put in three different bowls. Add an egg yolk and 3 tablespoons of the cream to each bowl and season with salt and pepper. Add the ricotta to the spinach and carefully mix the ingredients in each bowl. Stiffly whisk the egg whites in a grease-free bowl, then fold one-third into each vegetable purée. Spoon half the pea mixture into the prepared terrine or loaf pan, smooth the surface with a dampened spatula, spoon in half the carrot mixture and smooth the surface. Spoon all the spinach mixture on top, then the rest of the carrot mixture and the remaining pea mixture, smoothing the surface with a dampened spatula each time. Cover with foil and bake for 40 minutes. Remove from the oven, let cool slightly, then turn out onto a serving dish. Garnish with carrot slices and the chervil sprigs.

PISELLI ALLA MENTA

Serves 4

4¹/₄ cups fresh peas, shelled

¹/₂ teaspoon sugar

10 fresh mint leaves

¹/₄ cup butter

salt and pepper

PEAS WITH MINT

Cook the peas in salted, boiling water with the sugar and five of the mint leaves for 15–30 minutes until tender. Drain and discard the mint. Melt the butter in a pan, add the peas, stir well and cook over low heat for 5 minutes. Season with salt and pepper to taste, add the remaining mint leaves and serve.

PISELLI ALLA PANCETTA

Serves 4

4¹/₄ cups fresh peas, shelled

3 tablespoons butter

3¹/₂ ounces smoked pancetta, cut into strips

salt

PEAS WITH PANCETTA

Cook the peas in salted, boiling water for 15–30 minutes until tender, then drain well. Melt the butter in a pan over a very low heat, add the pancetta and cook until golden brown and tender. Add the peas and cook, stirring occasionally, for 5 minutes. Transfer to a warm serving dish.

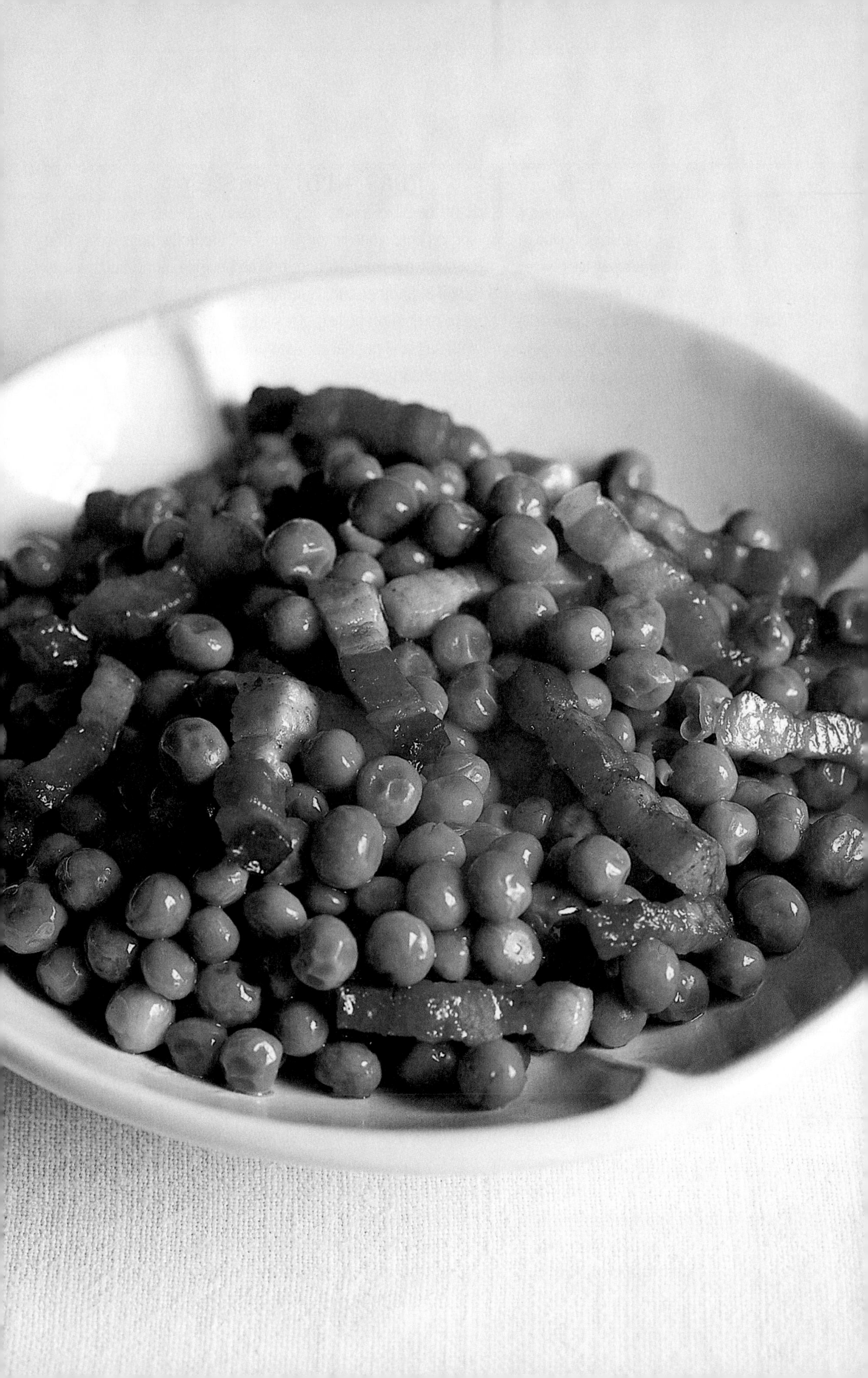

PEAS WITH PARSLEY

PISELLI AL PREZZEMOLO

Serves 4

4 tablespoons olive oil

1 large onion, thinly sliced

4¼ cups fresh peas, shelled

scant ½ cup Vegetable Stock (see page 209)

1 fresh flat-leaf parsley sprig, chopped

pinch of sugar

salt and pepper

Heat the oil in a pan, add the onion and cook over low heat, stirring occasionally, for 5 minutes. Stir in the peas, cover and cook for a further 10 minutes. Meanwhile, bring the stock to a boil in another pan. Sprinkle the parsley over the peas and pour in enough boiling stock to cover. Add the sugar, season with salt and pepper to taste and simmer until the stock has been absorbed.

PEAS WITH CARROTS

PISELLI CON CAROTE

Serves 4

¼ cup butter

7 ounces pearl onions

1 pound 2 ounces baby carrots, sliced

2¼ cups fresh peas, shelled

1½ teaspoons sugar

2 fresh flat-leaf parsley sprigs, chopped

salt and pepper

Melt half the butter in a pan, add the onions and cook over medium heat, stirring occasionally, for 5 minutes. Add the carrots and cook, stirring occasionally, for about 10 minutes. Add the peas, sugar and parsley, season with salt and pepper and mix well. Lower the heat, add 5 tablespoons warm water, cover and simmer for about 40 minutes. Remove the lid and boil off any remaining liquid, then stir in the remaining butter and transfer to a warm serving dish.

PEAS WITH LETTUCE

PISELLI CON LATTUGA

Serves 4

3 tablespoons butter

2 scallions, thinly sliced

1 lettuce, cut into strips

4½ cups fresh peas, shelled

salt

Melt the butter in a pan, add the scallions and cook over low heat, stirring occasionally, for 5 minutes until softened. Add the lettuce and peas, pour in sufficient boiling water to half cover the peas, cover and simmer for 20–30 minutes, making sure the mixture does not dry up too much. Season with salt to taste, remove the pan from the heat and serve. This is a delicate and tasty dish.

HOME—COOKED SNOW PEAS

TACCOLE ALLA CASALINGA

Serves 6

2¼ pounds snow peas, trimmed

4 tablespoons olive oil

1 small onion, thinly sliced

2 garlic cloves

7 ounces tomatoes, peeled, seeded and diced

salt and pepper

fresh basil leaves, to garnish

Cook the snow peas in salted, boiling water for 8–10 minutes until just tender, then drain. Heat the oil in a pan, add the onion and cook over low heat, stirring occasionally, for 5 minutes. Add the garlic and snow peas, increase the heat to high and cook for 5 minutes. Remove and discard the garlic, add the tomatoes to the pan and season with salt and pepper. Lower the heat to medium, cook for 10–15 minutes, taste and adjust the seasoning if necessary, then transfer to a warm serving dish. Garnish with the basil leaves and serve.

TOMATOES

Tomatoes are so rich in vitamins A, B and C that an adult eating a ripe, 3¹/₂-ounce tomato every day would satisfy their daily requirement for these vitamins. Among the many types available, it is enough to be familiar with the two large families: smooth red tomatoes for salads, mixed broils and frying; and plum tomatoes, which are irreplaceable in sauces. Canned tomatoes include simple peeled tomatoes – which are usually drained before being added to the other ingredients, and whose can juices may be used to dilute sauces if they become too thick – chopped peeled tomatoes, bottled strained tomatoes and tomato paste, which may be standard or concentrated. Sliced, seedless green tomatoes coated in bread crumbs and fried are delicious. So, too, are scooped-out green tomatoes filled with Russian salad.

QUANTITIES AND COOKING TIMES

QUANTITIES

Allow 1 pound 2 ounces fresh tomatoes or a 14-ounces can peeled tomatoes for a sauce. Allow ¹/₂–1 medium tomato per serving as an antipasto, 1 large tomato as a first course and 2 medium tomatoes as a main course.

SALAD

Cut tomatoes into slices rather than wedges as they remain firmer for longer. Season lightly with salt just before serving.

STUFFED

Cut the tomatoes in half, scoop out the seeds and sprinkle the insides with salt. Place upside down on paper towels for 10 minutes to drain, then fill.

TOMATO JELLY RING

Put the onion, tomatoes, vinegar, tomato paste and garlic in a large skillet and cook over low heat, stirring occasionally, for 10–15 minutes until softened. Transfer to a food processor and process to a purée, then scrape into a bowl. Prepare the gelatin according to the packet instructions, stir into the purée and season with salt and pepper to taste. Rinse a ring mold in extremely cold water, shake and then pour in the mixture. Chill in the refrigerator for at least 2 hours until set. To serve, dip the base of the mold in boiling water for a few seconds, then invert onto a serving dish. Spoon the tuna into the center and surround the ring with lettuce.

ANELLO DI GELATINA AL POMODORO
Serves 4–6
1 onion, chopped
1 pound 2 ounces plum tomatoes, peeled, seeded and diced
1 tablespoon white wine vinegar
1 teaspoon tomato paste
1 garlic clove • 1 envelope gelatin
9 ounces canned tuna in oil, drained and flaked
loose-leaf lettuce, such as lollo rosso
salt and pepper

TOMATO AND MOZZARELLA PACKETS

Preheat the oven to 400°F. Grease an ovenproof dish with butter. Cut an opening around each tomato stem with a small sharp knife and remove the seeds with a teaspoon without piercing the skins. Put the mozzarella, basil and parsley in a bowl and drizzle with olive oil. Mix well and spoon the mixture into the tomatoes. Season with salt and pepper. Lightly beat the egg white and yolk in separate bowls. Roll out the dough on a lightly floured surface and cut into eight squares. Wrap each tomato in a slice of pancetta and place in the middle of each square. Brush the edges with the egg white and enclose the tomatoes in the pastry by pinching together the corners, then brush the packets with the egg yolk. Place the packets in the prepared dish and bake for about 20 minutes.

FAGOTTINI DI POMODORI E MOZZARELLA
Serves 4
butter, for greasing
8 cherry tomatoes
7 ounces mozzarella cheese, finely diced
4 fresh basil leaves, chopped
1 fresh flat-leaf parsley sprig, chopped
olive oil, for drizzling
1 egg, separated
11 ounces puff pastry dough, thawed if frozen
all-purpose flour, for dusting
8 pancetta slices
salt and pepper

TOMATO AND CHEESE MOLD

Preheat the oven to 350°F. Brush a mold with oil. Heat the oil in a small pan, add the shallots and cook over low heat, stirring occasionally, for 5 minutes. Add the bottled strained tomatoes and cook for a few minutes more, then remove the pan from the heat. Beat the eggs with the cream in a bowl, then stir into the tomato sauce with the herbs and season with salt. Pour the tomato mixture into the mold, place in a roasting pan and add boiling water to come about halfway up the sides. Bake for about 1 hour. Remove from the oven and switch the oven off. Leave the mold to cool for a few minutes, then turn out onto an ovenproof serving dish. Sprinkle with the Swiss cheese and place in the warm oven until the cheese has melted. Serve immediately.

FLAN DI POMODORI ALLA GROVIERA
Serves 4
3 tablespoons olive oil, plus extra for brushing
2 shallots, finely chopped
2 1/4 cups bottled strained tomatoes
4 eggs
1 tablespoon heavy cream
6 fresh basil leaves, chopped
1 fresh flat-leaf parsley sprig, chopped
4 fresh chives, chopped
3/4 cup Swiss cheese, freshly grated
salt

RED TOMATO FRITTATA

FRITTATA ROSSA DI POMODORI

Serves 4

3 tablespoons olive oil

1 shallot, chopped

$1/2$ garlic clove, chopped

11 ounces plum tomatoes, peeled, seeded and chopped

6 eggs

4 fresh basil leaves, chopped

salt and pepper

Heat the oil in a skillet, add the shallot and garlic and cook over low heat, stirring occasionally, for 5 minutes. Add the tomatoes, increase the heat to medium and cook for 5 minutes. Lower the heat and simmer for 15 minutes. Beat the eggs with salt, pepper and the basil leaves in a bowl. Pour the eggs over the tomatoes and cook until evenly set. Do not turn the frittata over. Slide it out of the pan and serve.

TOMATO FRITTERS

FRITTELLINE ROSA DI POMODORO

Serves 4

generous 1 cup all-purpose flour

1 egg, lightly beaten

$1/2$ teaspoon melted butter

4 ripe but firm tomatoes

6 fresh basil leaves, chopped

vegetable oil, for deep-frying

salt and pepper

Sift the flour with a pinch of salt into a bowl and add the egg, melted butter and enough water to make a smooth batter. Let stand for about 1 hour. Meanwhile, slice the tomatoes, remove the seeds and sprinkle with pepper and the basil on both sides. Heat the oil for deep-frying in a large pan. Dip the tomato slices in the batter and fry in the hot oil until golden brown. Remove with a slotted spatula and drain on paper towels. Sprinkle with salt and serve.

BAKED TOMATOES

POMODORI AL FORNO

Serves 4

8 tomatoes, halved

1 thick bread slice, crusts removed

4 tablespoons milk

olive oil, for brushing

$1 1/2$ cups cooked meat, coarsely chopped

3 frankfurters, skinned and coarsely chopped

$1/2$ cup Parmesan cheese, freshly grated

1 egg

1 egg white

1 fresh flat-leaf parsley sprig, coarsely chopped

1 fresh basil sprig, coarsely chopped

1 garlic clove, coarsely chopped

salt and pepper

Scoop out the tomato seeds and some of the flesh, sprinkle with salt and turn upside down on paper towels to drain for 1 hour. Tear the bread into pieces, place in a bowl, add the milk and let soak for 10 minutes. Preheat the oven to 350°F. Brush an ovenproof dish with oil. Put the meat, frankfurters, Parmesan, the bread and milk mixture, the whole egg, the egg white, and the parsley, basil and garlic in a food processor and process until combined. Season with salt and pepper to taste, process briefly again to mix and use to stuff the tomato halves. Place them in the prepared dish and bake for 20 minutes or until golden brown.

TOMATOES AU GRATIN

POMODORI AL GRATIN

Serves 4

4 tomatoes, halved

3 tablespoons olive oil,

plus extra for brushing and drizzling

scant 2 cups bread crumbs

1 onion, chopped

3 canned anchovy fillets in oil,

drained and chopped

1 fresh flat-leaf parsley sprig, chopped

1 tablespoon capers, drained, rinsed and chopped

salt

Scoop out the tomato seeds and some of the flesh, sprinkle with salt and turn upside down on paper towels to drain for 1 hour. Preheat the oven to 325°F. Brush an ovenproof dish with oil. Heat 1 tablespoon of the olive oil in a small pan, add 1 cup of the bread crumbs and cook, stirring frequently, until golden brown. Remove from the heat and set aside. Heat the remaining oil in another small pan, add the onion and cook over low heat, stirring occasionally, for 5 minutes. Add the anchovies and parsley, mix well and remove from the heat. Stir in the capers and fried bread crumbs. Fill the tomato halves with the mixture and place in the prepared dish. Sprinkle with the remaining bread crumbs, drizzle with olive oil and bake for 40 minutes until golden brown.

TOMATOES WITH CUCUMBER MOUSSE

POMODORI ALLA MOUSSE DI CETRIOLI

Serves 4

4 tomatoes

2 small cucumbers, peeled and coarsely chopped

scant 1 cup ricotta cheese

4 fresh mint leaves

2 tablespoons milk

2 egg whites

4 fresh chives, finely chopped

salt

Cut off the tops of the tomatoes and reserve. Scoop out the tomato seeds and some of the flesh, sprinkle with salt and turn upside down on paper towels to drain for 1 hour. Meanwhile, put the cucumbers, ricotta, mint and milk in a food processor and process to a purée, then scrape into a bowl. Stiffly whisk the egg whites in a grease-free bowl, then fold into the mixture. Fill the tomatoes with the mixture, sprinkle with the chives, replace the tomato tops and chill in the refrigerator for 2–3 hours. Remove the tomatoes from the refrigerator 15 minutes before serving.

TOMATOES WITH EGGPLANT

POMODORI ALLE MELANZANE

Serves 4

4 tomatoes

2 tablespoons olive oil

1 eggplant, peeled and diced

1 garlic clove, chopped

1 scallion, finely chopped

1 tablespoon capers, drained, rinsed and chopped

1 fresh basil sprig, chopped

3 tablespoons white wine vinegar

salt and pepper

Cut off the tops of the tomatoes and reserve. Scoop out the tomato seeds and some of the flesh, sprinkle with salt and turn upside down on paper towels to drain for 1 hour. Heat the oil in a pan, add the eggplant and garlic and cook over high heat, stirring frequently, until the eggplant is lightly browned all over. Add the scallion, capers and basil and season with salt and pepper. Pour in the vinegar and cook until it has evaporated. Remove from the heat and let cool. Fill the tomatoes with the eggplant mixture, replace the tops and serve.

TOMATOES WITH ZUCCHINI

POMODORI ALLE ZUCCHINE

Serves 4

olive oil, for brushing and drizzling

8 tomatoes

2 zucchini, trimmed

1 fresh flat-leaf parsley sprig, chopped

1 garlic clove, chopped

7 ounces mozzarella cheese, sliced

1/2 teaspoon dried oregano

salt and pepper

Preheat the oven to 350°F. Brush an ovenproof dish with oil. Thinly slice the tomatoes without cutting all the way through, leaving them joined at the base. Halve the zucchini lengthwise, then slice into thin strips. Slip the strips of zucchini between the slices of tomato. Place the tomatoes in the prepared dish, sprinkle with the parsley and garlic, season with salt and pepper and drizzle with olive oil. Bake for 30 minutes. Remove the dish from the oven but do not switch the oven off. Carefully slip slices of mozzarella between the slices of tomato and zucchini, sprinkle with the oregano and return to the oven for 10 minutes until the mozzarella starts to form strings. Transfer to a warm serving dish and serve immediately.

TOMATOES WITH ROBIOLA

POMODORI CON ROBIOLA

Serves 4

4 round tomatoes, halved

3 1/2 ounces robiola cheese, diced

2 ounces mild Gorgonzola cheese, crumbled

2 tablespoons butter, softened

4 plum tomatoes, peeled and chopped

pinch of paprika

4 fresh chives, chopped

2 tablespoons vodka

salt and pepper

Scoop out the seeds and some of the flesh from the halved tomatoes, sprinkle with salt and turn upside down on paper towels to drain for 1 hour. Put the robiola, Gorgonzola and butter in a bowl, season with salt and pepper and beat until smooth and combined. Add the plum tomatoes, paprika and chives, mix well and sprinkle with the vodka. Fill the tomato halves with the mixture, arrange on a serving dish and keep in a cool place until ready to serve. Serve as a tasty summer first course.

TOMATOES WITH BACON AU GRATIN

POMODORI GRATINATI AL BACON

Serves 4

4 tomatoes, halved

3 tablespoons olive oil, plus extra for brushing and drizzling

2 cups mushrooms, finely chopped

1 onion, finely chopped

scant 1 cup bacon, finely chopped

1 fresh thyme sprig, chopped

1 fresh flat-leaf parsley sprig, chopped

1 fresh marjoram sprig, chopped

1 egg, lightly beaten

1 cup bread crumbs

salt and pepper

Scoop out the tomato seeds and flesh without damaging the 'shells'. Sprinkle the insides with salt and place upside down on paper towels to drain for 1 hour. Preheat the oven to 350°F. Brush an ovenproof dish with oil. Heat the oil in a skillet, add the mushrooms, onion and bacon and cook over high heat, stirring frequently, for about 10 minutes. Add the thyme, parsley and marjoram, season with salt and pepper, mix well and remove the pan from the heat. Stir in the egg and spoon the mixture into the tomato shells. Sprinkle with the bread crumbs, place in the prepared dish and drizzle with olive oil. Bake for 45 minutes.

TOMATOES STUFFED WITH ROMANO

Cut off the tops of the tomatoes. Scoop out the tomato seeds and some of the flesh, sprinkle with salt and turn upside down on paper towels to drain for 30 minutes. Preheat the oven to 400°F. Brush an ovenproof dish with oil. Put both the cheeses in a bowl and stir in the olive oil. Add the oregano, a pinch of pepper and salt to taste if necessary. Spoon the mixture into the tomato 'shells', place in the prepared dish and bake for about 20 minutes. Serve warm.

POMODORI RIPIENI AL PECORINO

Serves 4

8 tomatoes

3 tablespoons olive oil, plus extra for brushing

7 ounces mild romano cheese, crumbled

generous 1 cup sharp romano cheese, freshly grated

large pinch of dried oregano

salt and pepper

TOMATOES STUFFED WITH RUSSIAN SALAD

Scoop out the tomato seeds and some of the flesh, sprinkle with salt and turn upside down on paper towels to drain for at least 30 minutes. Meanwhile, hard-cook the eggs, refresh under cold water, shell and cut each one into four wedges. Pat the tomato 'shells' dry and spoon in the Russian salad, doming it up in the center. Top each filled tomato shell with a wedge of hard-cooked egg. Place in the refrigerator until 15 minutes before you are ready to serve. Arrange the tomatoes on a serving dish and garnish with lettuce leaves. Do not choose overripe tomatoes — delicately flavored, green-red tomatoes are ideal for this dish.

POMODORI RIPIENI D'INSALATA RUSSA

Serves 4

4 round tomatoes, halved

2 eggs

1 quantity Russian Salad (see page 116)

salt

lettuce leaves, to garnish

TOMATOES STUFFED WITH RICE

Preheat the oven to 350°F. Brush an ovenproof dish with oil. Cut off the tops of the tomatoes and reserve. Scoop out the tomato seeds and flesh, reserving the flesh and 'shells'. Pass the tomato flesh through a food mill into a bowl. Parboil the rice for 5 minutes in plenty of salted water, then drain and stir into the tomato flesh. Add the parsley, basil, oregano and olive oil, season with salt and pepper and mix well. Spoon the mixture into the tomato shells, replace the tops and place in the prepared dish. Drizzle with olive oil and bake for about 30 minutes. Serve hot or cold.

POMODORI RIPIENI DI RISO

Serves 6

4 tablespoons olive oil,

plus extra for brushing and drizzling

6 large tomatoes

6 tablespoons long-grain rice

1 fresh flat-leaf parsley sprig, chopped

6 fresh basil leaves chopped

pinch of dried oregano

salt and pepper

TOMATOES STUFFED WITH TUNA

Cut off the tops of the tomatoes and scoop out the tomato seeds and flesh, reserving the flesh. Sprinkle the 'shells' with salt and turn upside down on paper towels to drain for 1 hour. Place the tomato flesh in a strainer and let drain. Chop the anchovy fillets and put them with the tuna, capers, yogurt, parsley, chives and lemon juice in a blender. Process, then add the tomato flesh, season with salt and pepper and process again until thoroughly combined. Spoon the mixture into the tomato shells, garnish with basil leaves and keep in the refrigerator until ready to serve.

POMODORI RIPIENI DI TONNO

Serves 4

4 tomatoes

4 salted anchovies, heads removed, cleaned and filleted (see page 596), soaked in cold water for 10 minutes and drained

7 ounces canned tuna in oil, drained

1 tablespoon capers, drained and rinsed

scant 1 cup low-fat plain yogurt

1 tablespoon fresh flat-leaf parsley, chopped

5–6 fresh chives, coarsely chopped

juice of 1 lemon, strained

salt and pepper

fresh basil leaves, to garnish

RUSTIC TOMATO PIE

Preheat the oven to 350°F. Grease a rectangular mold with butter. Heat the oil in a pan, add the scallions and cook over low heat, stirring occasionally, for 5 minutes. Lightly season with salt and remove from the heat. Cover the base of the prepared mold with half the bread and spoon the scallions on top. Place the tomato slices on top, sprinkle with the oregano and cover with remaining the bread. Beat the egg with the milk in a bowl and season with salt and pepper. Pour the mixture over the bread, cover with the romano and bake for 30 minutes or until the cheese has melted and turned golden brown. Let cool slightly, then turn out onto a serving dish.

TORTINO RUSTICO DI POMODORI

Serves 6

butter, for greasing

3 tablespoons olive oil

3 scallions, finely chopped

12 thin whole-wheat bread slices, crusts removed

1 pound 2 ounces tomatoes, sliced

pinch of dried oregano

1 egg

²/₃ cup milk

2 ounces romano cheese, very thinly sliced

salt and pepper

LEEKS

Leeks belong to the same family as garlic and onion, but have a much more delicate flavor. Generally, only the white part of the leek is eaten, so the whole outer leaf and all the green part should be removed. Leeks are mainly used to add flavor to other vegetables. They are also pleasant cut into very thin slices and used raw in mixed salads, or baked or boiled and smothered with melted butter and cheese.

QUANTITIES AND COOKING TIMES

QUANTITIES

2¼ pounds leeks is sufficient for a side dish for 4; the same amount is enough for a main course if the leeks are combined with other ingredients such as cheese and béchamel sauce.

BOILING

As leeks are very delicate, 15 minutes simmering is enough.

PORRI AL POMODORO

Serves 4

1 shallot, chopped

3 tablespoons olive oil

4 tomatoes, peeled and chopped

1 garlic clove, chopped

1 fresh thyme sprig, chopped

¾ cup dry white wine

2¼ pounds leeks, white part only, sliced

salt and pepper

LEEKS WITH TOMATO

Cook the shallot in a pan with the oil and ½ cup water over medium heat for about 5 minutes until soft. Add the tomatoes, garlic and thyme, season with salt and pepper and cook over high heat for a few minutes. Sprinkle in the wine and cook until it has evaporated, then lower the heat and simmer for 15 minutes. Parboil the leeks in salted water for 5 minutes, then drain well, add to the tomato mixture, cover and simmer for 15 minutes. Remove the lid, boil off any remaining liquid and transfer to a warm serving dish.

LEEKS WITH HAM

PORRI AL PROSCIUTTO

Serves 4

2¼ pounds leeks, white parts only
3½ ounces cooked, cured ham, sliced
7 tablespoons butter
½ cup all-purpose flour
2¼ cups milk
scant 1 cup Swiss cheese, freshly grated
2 tablespoons Parmesan cheese, freshly grated
salt and pepper

Parboil the leeks in salted water for 5 minutes, then drain well. Preheat the oven to 350°F. Trim the fat from the ham and place the fat in an ovenproof dish with 2 tablespoons of the butter. Melt over medium heat, then add the leeks in two layers and cook, basting frequently, until lightly browned. Season with salt and pepper. Meanwhile, make a Béchamel Sauce (see page 50), using 2 tablespoons of the remaining butter, the flour and milk. Stir the Swiss cheese into the sauce. Remove the dish of leeks from the heat, lay the slices of ham on top and spoon the béchamel sauce over them. Dot with the remaining butter, sprinkle with the Parmesan and bake for about 10 minutes.

LEEKS AU GRATIN

PORRI GRATINATI

Serves 4

2¼ pounds leeks, white parts only
5 tablespoons butter, plus extra for greasing
¼ cup all-purpose flour
1½ cups milk
2 egg yolks
½ cup Emmenthal cheese, freshly grated
pinch of freshly grated nutmeg
⅔ cup Parmesan cheese, freshly grated
4 tablespoons bread crumbs
salt and pepper

Cook the leeks in salted, boiling water for about 15 minutes, then drain well, spread out on a dish towel and let dry. Preheat the oven to 350°F. Grease an ovenproof dish with butter. Melt 3 tablespoons of the butter in a pan, add the leeks and cook over low heat, turning occasionally, for a few minutes, then transfer to the prepared dish. Make a Béchamel Sauce (see page 50) with the remaining butter, the flour and milk. Remove the pan of sauce from the heat, beat in the egg yolks, Emmenthal and nutmeg and season with salt and pepper. Pour the sauce over the leeks, sprinkle with the Parmesan and bread crumbs, dot with the remaining butter and bake for about 20 minutes until golden brown and bubbling.

LEEKS IN HOLLANDAISE SAUCE

PORRI IN SALSA OLANDESE

Serves 4

2¼ pounds leeks, white parts only
½ cup butter
3 egg yolks
juice of ½ lemon, strained
salt and pepper

Cook the leeks in salted, boiling water for about 15 minutes, then drain well, spread out on a dish towel and let dry. Meanwhile, prepare a Hollandaise Sauce (see page 59) with the butter, egg yolks and lemon juice and season with salt and pepper. Arrange the leeks on a serving dish, spoon the sauce over them.

RADICCHIO

Radicchio is the generic name of a few types of chicory, a prolific extended family of vegetables. The best-known varieties are the long, red Treviso radicchio, the red Verona radicchio, the variegated red and white Castelfranco Veneto radicchio and the red Chioggia radicchio. Their distinctive features depend on the method of cultivation. Some types are grown in the open and others are grown under glass, which gives them their typically red, white or variegated leaves. The best-known kinds are also the tastiest and most frequently used. As well as being used in classic salads, almost all types of radicchio can be baked or broiled. However, they are no less tasty when used in risottos or for pasta.

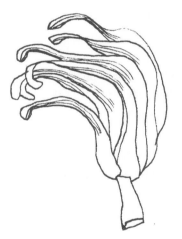

RADICCHIO AND WALNUT ROLLS

Preheat the oven to 350°F. Grease an ovenproof dish with butter. Blanch the radicchio leaves in boiling water for 2 minutes, then remove and drain on paper towels. Combine the ricotta, walnuts, egg yolk and Parmesan in a bowl and season with salt and pepper. Divide the mixture among the radicchio leaves, roll up and place in the prepared dish. Bake for about 15 minutes.

INVOLTINI DI RADICCHIO ALLE NOCI

Serves 4

butter, for greasing

10 Castelfranco radicchio leaves

scant ¹/₂ cup ricotta cheese

10 shelled walnuts, chopped

1 egg yolk

2 tablespoons Parmesan cheese, freshly grated

salt and pepper

BAKED RADICCHIO

RADICCHIO AL FORNO

Serves 4

4 tablespoons olive oil

1¹/₂ pounds Treviso radicchio, trimmed

juice of ¹/₂ lemon, strained

salt and pepper

Preheat the oven to 350°F. Pour half the oil into an ovenproof dish, add the radicchio, sprinkle with the remaining oil and season with salt and pepper. Cover with foil and bake for about 20 minutes. Remove from the oven, transfer to a warm serving dish and sprinkle with the lemon juice.

RADICCHIO WITH PARMESAN

RADICCHIO AL PARMIGIANO

Serves 4

2 tablespoons butter, plus extra for greasing

8–10 Castelfranco radicchio hearts

2 tablespoons Parmesan cheese, freshly grated

¹/₂ cup Parmesan cheese, shaved

salt and pepper

Preheat the oven to 350°F. Grease an ovenproof dish with butter. Blanch the radicchio in boiling water for a few minutes, then remove from the pan and drain on a dish towel. Place the radicchio in the prepared dish, season with salt and pepper and sprinkle with the grated Parmesan and Parmesan shavings. Dot with the butter and bake for 10–15 minutes.

RADICCHIO MIMOSA

RADICCHIO MIMOSA

Serves 4

4 Castelfranco radicchio, cut into strips

5 tablespoons olive oil

2 tablespoons white wine vinegar

4 hard-cooked egg yolks

salt and white pepper

Place the radicchio strips in a salad bowl. Whisk together the olive oil and vinegar in a bowl and season with salt and pepper. Pour the dressing over the radicchio. Press the egg yolks through a strainer over the salad, toss and serve.

TREVISO RADICCHIO SALAD WITH ORANGE

RADICCHIO ROSSO ALL'ARANCIA

Serves 4

juice of 2 oranges, strained

3–4 tablespoons olive oil

1 teaspoon lemon juice (optional)

4 Treviso radicchio, cut into thin wedges

salt and pepper

Whisk together the orange juice and oil in a bowl and season with salt and pepper to taste. Add a few drops of lemon juice to sharpen the taste if the orange juice is too sweet. Place the radicchio in a bowl and pour the orange dressing over it in a continuous stream, then toss gently and serve. The unusual sweet and sour combination of this salad makes it a suitable side dish for boiled fish or mixed boiled meats.

FRIED RADICCHIO

To make the batter, sift the flour with a pinch of salt into a bowl, break the egg into the middle and add the olive oil. Mix thoroughly with a wooden spoon to prevent lumps from forming, then stir in the beer. Cover and let stand for at least 30 minutes. Stiffly whisk the egg white in a grease-free bowl, then fold into the batter. Remove the largest outer leaves individually from the radicchio and cut the hearts into thin wedges. Heat the oil for deep-frying in a large pan. Immerse each leaf in the batter and fry in the hot oil, turning frequently so that it browns evenly. Repeat with the radicchio wedges. Drain on paper towels, sprinkle with salt and serve immediately.

RADICCHIO ROSSO FRITTO

Serves 4

2–3 Treviso radicchio, trimmed

vegetable oil, for deep-frying

salt

For the batter

9 tablespoons all-purpose flour

1 egg

1 tablespoon olive oil

scant ½ cup beer

1 egg white

salt

RADICCHIO EN CROÛTE

Preheat the oven to 350°F, and preheat the broiler. Grease a cookie sheet with butter. Brush the radicchio heads with oil and broil until they wilt slightly, then season with salt and pepper. Roll out the pastry on a lightly floured surface and cut into rectangles (one for each head of radicchio). Lay one head of radicchio on each rectangle and fold over the pastry to enclose it completely. Beat the egg yolk with 1 teaspoon water in a bowl and brush the packets with it. Place the packet on the prepared cookie sheet and bake for 15–20 minutes until golden brown.

RADICCHIO ROSSO IN CROSTA

Serves 4

butter, for greasing

4–6 Treviso radicchio, trimmed

olive oil, for brushing

9 ounces–1 pound 2 ounces puff pastry dough, thawed if frozen

all-purpose flour, for dusting

1 egg yolk

salt and pepper

TURNIPS

To enjoy their pleasant flavor at its best, choose small, heavy, very firm and slightly violet-colored turnips, otherwise they may turn out to be bitter. Turnip stock is fresh and pleasant. When boiled and dressed with oil, vinegar and salt, turnips make a perfect side dish for pork. To prepare, remove the leaves and cut a slice off the top.

QUANTITIES
AND COOKING TIMES

QUANTITIES
Allow 2 small turnips per serving as a side dish, otherwise the quantity is specified in the recipe.

BOILING
Immerse turnips whole, if small, or sliced, if large, in salted, boiling water and cook for 20–40 minutes, depending on their size.

TURNIPS WITH BACON

Scoop out a hole in the middle of each turnip with a small sharp knife. Push 1 tablespoon of the butter into each hole, season with salt and pepper and place in a deep pan. Pour 5 tablespoons water into the pan, cover and bring to a boil, then lower the heat and cook until the turnips are tender, adding more boiling water if necessary. Put the bacon in a skillet and cook over low heat until the fat runs, then remove and drain on paper towels. Make a Béchamel Sauce (see page 50) with the remaining butter, the flour and milk and season with salt and pepper. Stir in the bacon. Remove the turnips from the pan, cut into slices, place on a warm serving dish and cover with the sauce.

RAPE AL BACON

Serves 4

8 small turnips, trimmed

scant $^3/_4$ cup butter

3 ounces bacon, cut into strips

$^1/_3$ cup all-purpose flour

$^1/_3$ cup milk

salt and pepper

TURNIPS IN CREAM

Preheat the oven to 350°F. Line a roasting pan with foil. Pour the cream into a pan and bring to a boil, then add the turnip slices and cook for 2 minutes. Remove the turnip slices with a slotted spatula, drain and arrange in over-lapping concentric circles in the roasting pan. Sprinkle with the Parmesan and chives, season with salt and pep-per and bake until lightly browned. Transfer to a warm serving dish.

RAPE ALLA PANNA

Serves 4

1 cup heavy cream

10 turnips, trimmed and thinly sliced

$^1/_3$ cup Parmesan cheese, freshly grated

6 fresh chives, chopped

salt and white pepper

STUFFED TURNIPS

Cook the turnips in salted, boiling water until tender, then drain. Meanwhile, heat the oil in a small skillet, add the chicken and cook over medium heat, stirring frequently, until golden brown all over, then season with salt and remove from the heat. Preheat the oven to 350°F. Grease an oven-proof dish with butter. Chop the speck together with the sage. Scoop out the centers of the turnips to make 'bowls' and reserve the flesh. Fill each bowl with chicken and speck and dot the tops with the butter. Place in the prepared dish and bake for about 40 minutes. Put the scooped-out turnip flesh in a double boiler or in a heatproof bowl set over a pan of barely simmering water. Add the egg yolks and cream, season with salt and pepper and cook, stirring constantly, until the sauce has thickened. Serve the stuffed turnips with the sauce.

RAPE FARCITE

Serves 6

12 medium turnips, trimmed

2 tablespoons olive oil

1 small skinless, boneless chicken breast, chopped

3 tablespoons butter, plus extra for greasing

5 speck (Austrian smoked ham) slices

5 fresh sage leaves

3 egg yolks

2 tablespoons heavy cream

salt and white pepper

ROAST TURNIPS
WITH POTATOES

RAPE IN TEGLIA CON PATATE

Serves 4

4 tablespoons olive oil

1 onion, thinly sliced

14 ounces turnips, trimmed and sliced

12 ounces potatoes, sliced

²/₃ cup Vegetable Stock (see page 209)

7 ounces mozzarella cheese, diced

pinch of dried oregano

salt and pepper

Preheat the oven to 400°F. Heat the oil in a roasting pan, add the onion and cook over low heat, stirring occasionally, for 5 minutes. Add the turnips and potatoes, season with salt and pepper, mix well and pour in the stock. Roast for 30 minutes until the liquid has been completely absorbed. Sprinkle the mozzarella and oregano over the vegetables, return the pan to the oven and cook for a further 10 minutes.

ROAST TURNIPS
WITH LEEKS AND PUMPKIN

RAPE IN TEGLIA CON PORRI E ZUCCA

Serves 4

7 ounces pumpkin flesh, sliced

1 teaspoon fresh thyme leaves

3 tablespoons olive oil, plus extra for drizzling

7 ounces leeks, white parts only, sliced

11 ounces turnips, trimmed and sliced

2 tablespoons sesame seeds

salt

Preheat the oven to 400°F. Place the pumpkin slices on a sheet of foil, season with salt and sprinkle with the thyme leaves. Fold over the foil to enclose the pumpkin completely, place on a cookie sheet and bake for 30 minutes. Heat the oil in a large pan, add the leeks and turnips and cook over medium heat, stirring occasionally, until tender. Add the pumpkin and cook for a few minutes more. Sprinkle with the sesame seeds and drizzle with olive oil, then serve.

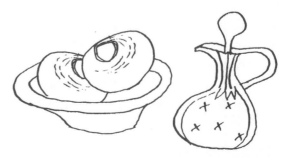

RADISHES

The most common types of radish are red or white, round or elongated. They are eaten raw after they have been trimmed and any blemishes scraped away with a small knife. They may be sliced and added to salads or left whole as a garnish. When served as a dish in their own right, they are simply seasoned with a little salt or served together with thin slices of lightly buttered white or whole-wheat bread.

RADISHES WITH CHEESE

RAVANELLI CON FORMAGGIO

Serves 4

9 ounces crescenza or other stracchino cheese

1 bunch of radishes, trimmed

white pepper

toast slices, to serve

Beat the cheese in a bowl with a wooden spoon until smooth and creamy. Cut the radishes into slices and then into thin batons. Add to the cheese with a pinch of pepper, stir and serve with slices of toast.

GLAZED RADISHES

RAVANELLI GLASSATI

Serves 4

1 pound 5 ounces radishes, trimmed

6 tablespoons butter

2 tablespoons sugar

salt

Halve the radishes, place in a pan, add water to cover, and the butter, sugar and a pinch of salt. Bring to a boil, then lower the heat, cover and simmer very gently until the liquid is thick and syrupy. Mix well so that the radishes are evenly coated with syrup. This unusual side dish goes well with roast pork or veal.

RAVANELLI IN INSALATA CON LE OLIVE

Serves 4

6 red radishes, trimmed

juice of 1 lemon, strained

3¹/₂ ounces corn salad

10 pitted black olives

olive oil, for drizzling

salt

RADISH SALAD WITH OLIVES

Cut the radishes into very thin horizontal slices, put in a salad bowl and sprinkle with the lemon juice. Add the corn salad and olives, drizzle with olive oil and season with salt to taste. Mix gently and let stand for 10 minutes before serving.

RAVANELLI IN INSALATA CON LO YOGURT

Serves 4

2 large white radishes, thinly sliced

1 green apple

scant ¹/₂ cup plain yogurt

salt and white pepper

RADISH SALAD WITH YOGURT

Put the radishes in a salad bowl, sprinkle with a pinch of salt, stir and let stand for 10 minutes. Peel and core the apple and cut into wedges. Using a very sharp knife, cut the wedges into wafer-thin slices and add to the radishes. Combine the yogurt and a pinch of pepper in a bowl, add to the salad, toss and serve.

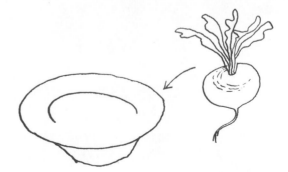

SALSIFY

Black salsify is a winter root vegetable with butter-colored flesh covered with a dark-brown skin. It is also known as scorzonera. However, true salsify, also known as oyster plant, is lighter in color and slightly more difficult to peel. All these recipes can be used for both black salsify and true salsify. To prepare, cut off both ends, scrape off the skin and cut the flesh into short pieces or leave whole, depending on the recipe. If there is a woody core in the middle, remove it. As the pieces are prepared, immerse them in cold water mixed with a little vinegar or lemon juice to prevent discoloration. Salsify may also be grated and served dressed with olive oil and lemon juice.

QUANTITIES

Allow about 5 ounces per serving.

BOILING

Cook in lightly salted, boiling water with a little vinegar or lemon juice for about 30 minutes.

QUANTITIES AND COOKING TIMES

SALSIFY WITH HORSERADISH

SCORZONERA AL CREN

Serves 4

juice of 1 lemon, strained

1 pound 5 ounces salsify

1 tablespoon all-purpose flour

scant 1 cup heavy cream

2 tablespoons white wine vinegar

2 tablespoons finely grated horseradish

salt and pepper

Half-fill a bowl with water and add half the lemon juice. Peel and chop the salsify, then immerse in the acidulated water. Fill a large pan with water, add the flour, a pinch of salt, the salsify and the remaining lemon juice and bring to a boil. Lower the heat and simmer for about 30 minutes. Drain and let cool. Meanwhile, stiffly whip cream, season with salt and pepper and gently stir in the vinegar and horseradish. Place the salsify on a serving dish and spoon the horseradish cream over it.

SALSIFY WITH ANCHOVIES

SCORZONERA ALLE ACCIUGHE

Serves 4

juice of 1 lemon, strained

1¹/₂ pounds salsify, trimmed and peeled

4 ounces salted anchovies, heads removed, cleaned and filleted (see page 596), soaked in cold water for 10 minutes and drained

2 tablespoons olive oil

1 tablespoon capers, drained, rinsed and chopped

1 tablespoon white wine vinegar

1 fresh flat-leaf parsley sprig, chopped

salt

Fill a large pan with water, add the lemon juice, a pinch of salt and the salsify and bring to a boil. Lower the heat and simmer for 30 minutes. Meanwhile, Chop the anchovy fillets. Heat the oil in a skillet, add the anchovies and cook over low heat, mashing with a wooden spoon until they have almost disintegrated. Add the capers and vinegar and cook until the vinegar has evaporated, then remove the skillet from the heat. Drain then chop the salsify, and place it on a warm serving dish. Spoon the anchovy sauce over it, sprinkle with the parsley and serve.

SALSIFY FRICASSÉE

SCORZONERA IN FRICASSEA

Serves 4

juice of 2 lemons, strained

1¹/₂ pounds salsify, trimmed and peeled

2 tablespoons butter

2 egg yolks

1 fresh flat-leaf parsley sprig, chopped

salt

Fill a large pan with water, add half the lemon juice, a pinch of salt and the salsify and bring to a boil. Lower the heat and simmer for 30 minutes, then drain and slice. Melt the butter in a pan, add the salsify and cook over low heat, stirring occasionally, for 5 minutes. Meanwhile, beat the egg yolks with the remaining lemon juice and a pinch of salt in a bowl. Remove the pan from the heat, stir in the egg yolks, return to the heat and cook, stirring constantly until the eggs are lightly cooked. Remove from the heat, sprinkle with the parsley and serve.

CELERY

Green celery is cooked to flavor broths, stews, sauces and boiled meat. White celery is added raw to salads or eaten with pinzimonio (olive oil with pepper and salt). To prepare celery, remove and discard the coarsest stalks and strings. Celery is delicious served raw with creamy cheeses such as Gorgonzola. Recipes for celery may also be used for celery root. The best months to eat this vegetable are from November to April.

QUANTITIES

Allow 1 celery heart per serving.

BOILING

Halve the stalks lengthwise, immerse in salted, boiling water and cook for about 20 minutes.

QUANTITIES AND COOKING TIMES

CELERY ROOT CARPACCIO WITH ANCHOVIES

Put the celery root in a bowl. Combine the lemon juice and 4 tablespoons of the oil, then pour the mixture over the celery root and let marinate for 30 minutes. Combine the remaining oil and the vinegar in a bowl, season with salt and pepper and add the anchovies and capers. Arrange a bed of arugula on each of four plates, place slices of celery root on top, drizzle the dressing over them and sprinkle with the Parmesan.

CARPACCIO DI SEDANO ALLE ACCIUGHE

Serves 4

2 small celery roots, peeled and thinly sliced

juice of 1 lemon, strained

$^2/_3$ cup olive oil

2 tablespoons white wine vinegar

3 canned anchovies in oil, drained and chopped

1 tablespoon capers, drained, rinsed and chopped

1 bunch of arugula, chopped

2 ounces Parmesan cheese, shaved

salt and pepper

CELERY WITH GORGONZOLA

Halve the celery stalks lengthwise and arrange on a serving dish. Beat the Gorgonzola in a bowl until smooth and season with a few drops of vinegar, salt and pepper. Fill the celery stalks with the mixture.

SEDANO AL GORGONZOLA

Serves 4

2 heads of white celery, trimmed

3 ounces Gorgonzola cheese, crumbled

white wine vinegar, to taste

salt and pepper

CELERY IN BÉCHAMEL SAUCE

SEDANO ALLA BESCIAMELLA

Serves 4

2 tablespoons butter, plus extra for greasing

3 heads of white celery, trimmed

1 quantity Béchamel Sauce (see page 50)

1/2 cup Parmesan cheese, freshly grated

salt

Preheat the oven to 400°F. Grease an ovenproof dish with butter. Halve the celery stalks lengthwise and cook in salted, boiling water for 10 minutes, then drain and place in the prepared dish. Spoon the béchamel sauce over them, dot with the butter and sprinkle with the Parmesan. Bake for about 15 minutes until golden and bubbling.

GREEK–STYLE CELERY

SEDANO ALLA GRECA

Serves 4

2 tablespoons golden raisins

2 tablespoons olive oil

1 head of white celery, trimmed and sliced

3 small onions, chopped

3 zucchini, sliced

scant 1 cup dry white wine

2 teaspoons tomato paste

juice of 1 lemon, strained, plus extra to serve

6 fresh basil leaves

salt and pepper

Put the golden raisins in a bowl, cover with warm water and let soak for 10 minutes, then drain and squeeze out the excess liquid. Heat the oil in a pan, add the celery and cook over high heat, stirring frequently, for 5 minutes. Add the onions and zucchini, mix well and pour in the wine. Cook until it has evaporated, lower the heat and add the raisins. Combine the tomato paste and 1 tablespoon water in a small bowl, add to the pan and simmer for about 20 minutes. Stir in the lemon juice, season with salt and pepper and cook for a few minutes more. Transfer the mixture to a salad bowl, add the basil and let cool, then chill in the refrigerator for 3–4 hours. Serve cold with a little extra lemon juice.

MOLISE CELERY

SEDANO ALLA MOLISANA

Serves 4

2 tablespoons olive oil, plus extra for brushing

1 head of green celery, trimmed and sliced

8 scallions, thinly sliced

scant 1 cup pitted black olives

3 tablespoons bread crumbs

salt and pepper

Preheat the oven to 400°F. Brush an ovenproof dish with oil. Cook the celery in salted, boiling water for 10 minutes, then drain, tip into a bowl and let cool slightly. Meanwhile, heat the oil and 1 tablespoon water in a pan, add the scallions and cook over low heat for 5 minutes until softened, then season with salt and pepper. Place the celery in the prepared dish, top with the scallions and olives, sprinkle with the bread crumbs and bake for 15 minutes.

CELERY AND WALNUT SALAD

SEDANO ALLE NOCI

Serves 4

4 ounces white celery, trimmed • 1 green apple, peeled, cored and diced • juice of 1 lemon, strained

4 ounces low-fat tomino or other semi-hard cheese, diced • 1 tablespoon fresh flat-leaf parsley, chopped • 1/2 cup shelled walnuts, chopped

5 tablespoons olive oil • salt and pepper

Halve the celery stalks lengthwise and cut into thin strips. Place the celery and apple in a salad bowl and stir in half the lemon juice. Add the cheese, parsley and half the walnuts. Whisk together the olive oil and remaining lemon juice in a pitcher and season with salt and pepper. Stir in the remaining walnuts and pour the dressing over the salad.

CELERY IN TOMATO SAUCE

SEDANO AL POMODORO

Serves 4

3 tablespoons olive oil

3 heads of white celery, trimmed and sliced

3 tablespoons Tomato Sauce (see page 57)

pinch of sugar

salt and pepper

Heat the oil in a pan, add the celery and cook over medium heat, stirring occasionally, for 5 minutes. Add the tomato sauce and sugar, season with salt and pepper and mix well. Lower the heat and simmer for 15 minutes, then transfer to a warm serving dish.

FRIED CELERY ROOT

SEDANO FRITTO

Serves 4

1 large celery root, peeled

1 egg

1^1/$_2$ cups bread crumbs

3 tablespoons olive oil

2 tablespoons butter

salt

Cook the celery root in salted, boiling water for 10 minutes, then drain and let cool slightly. Meanwhile, beat the egg with a pinch of salt in a shallow dish and spread out the bread crumbs in another shallow dish. Cut the celery root into ^{1}/$_4$-inch slices and dip them first in the beaten egg and then in the bread crumbs. Heat the oil and butter in a skillet, add the celery root and fry until light golden brown all over. Remove with a slotted spatula and drain on paper towels, then sprinkle with a little salt and serve.

CELERY ROOT AU GRATIN

SEDANO GRATINATO

Serves 4

4 celery roots, peeled and thinly sliced

3 tablespoons butter, plus extra for greasing

2 tablespoons olive oil

1 pearl onion, thinly sliced

1 pound 2 ounces canned tomatoes

^{1}/$_2$ cup Parmesan cheese, freshly grated

1 quantity Béchamel Sauce (see page 50)

salt and pepper

Sprinkle the celery root slices with salt. Melt half the butter in a large pan, add the celery root and cook over medium heat, stirring occasionally, for 5 minutes. Add scant ^{1}/$_2$ cup water, cover and cook, stirring occasionally, until tender. Meanwhile, heat the oil in a small pan, add the onion and cook over low heat, stirring occasionally, for 5 minutes until softened. Add the tomatoes, season with salt and pepper, cover and simmer for about 30 minutes. Preheat the oven to 400°F. Grease an ovenproof dish with butter. Stir 1 tablespoon of the Parmesan into the béchamel sauce. Drain the celery root and arrange a layer of the slices in the prepared dish. Spoon some of the tomato sauce on top, sprinkle with some of the remaining Parmesan and top with a layer of béchamel sauce. Continue making layers until all the ingredients are used, ending with a layer of béchamel sauce. Bake for about 20 minutes.

SPINACH

Since several varieties are cultivated, spinach is available all year round. The leaves should be firm, fleshy and green with no signs of yellowing. To check for freshness, look at the stems, which should be firm without any signs of floppiness (although, clearly, they should be removed before using). Spinach should be eaten on the day of purchase but if you must store it, keep it in the salad drawer of the refrigerator for no more than 24 hours. Similarly, leftover cooked spinach should not be kept, as the nitrites absorbed from chemical fertilizers are oxidized into nitrates. Spinach is very rich in vitamin A, calcium, phosphorus and iron. However, there is less iron than is commonly believed and most of it cannot be absorbed by the human digestive system. Raw spinach is very tasty, but in this case choose baby spinach with small, tender leaves. Cream of spinach soup and spinach croquettes are delicious, puréed spinach is flavorsome and spinach molds look impressive.

QUANTITIES

Spinach shrinks considerably during cooking, so allow about 9 ounces raw leaves per serving.

BOILING

Cook spinach, in just the water clinging to its leaves after washing, in a covered pan for 5–8 minutes. Drain well and press out as much liquid as possible with the back of a spoon.

QUANTITIES
AND COOKING TIMES

SPINACH CROQUETTES

CROCCHETTE DI SPINACI

Serves 6

generous 1/3 cup golden raisins

2 1/4 pounds spinach

3 tablespoons butter

1 1/4 cups all-purpose flour, plus extra for dusting

2 1/4 cups milk

pinch of freshly grated nutmeg

4 ounces fontina cheese, thinly sliced

4 tablespoons Parmesan cheese, freshly grated

3 egg yolks

olive oil, for brushing

1 egg

1 1/2 cups bread crumbs

vegetable oil, for deep-frying

salt and pepper

Put the golden raisins in a bowl, add warm water to cover and let soak. Cook the spinach, in just the water clinging to the leaves after washing, for about 5 minutes until tender. Drain well, squeeze out the excess liquid and chop finely. Melt the butter in a pan, stir in the flour, then gradually stir in the milk. Bring just to a boil, stirring constantly, then season with salt and pepper and add the nutmeg. Remove the pan from the heat, add the fontina and Parmesan and stir until smooth and creamy. Stir in the egg yolks, one at a time. Drain the raisins, squeeze out and add to the mixture with the chopped spinach. Brush a marble slab or large tray with olive oil, pour the spinach mixture onto it and smooth the surface with a dampened spatula. Let cool. Spread out a little flour in a shallow dish, beat the egg in another shallow dish and spread out the bread crumbs in a third. Cut the cooled spinach mixture into squares and dip first in the flour, then in the beaten egg and, finally, in the bread crumbs. Heat the oil for deep-frying in a large pan, add the spinach croquettes and cook until golden brown. Remove with a slotted spatula, drain on paper towels and serve hot.

SPINACH IN CREAM

SPINACI ALLA CREMA

Serves 4

2 1/4 pounds spinach

scant 1 cup heavy cream

1 teaspoon all-purpose flour, sifted

3 tablespoons butter

pinch of freshly grated nutmeg

1/2 cup Parmesan cheese, freshly grated

salt and pepper

Cook the spinach, in just the water clinging to the leaves after washing, for about 5 minutes until tender. Drain well and squeeze out the excess liquid. Combine the cream and flour in a bowl. Melt the butter in a pan, add the spinach and cook over low heat, stirring frequently, for a few minutes. Stir in the nutmeg, season with salt and pepper, cover and simmer gently for about 10 minutes. Stir in the cream and simmer gently for a further 20 minutes. Sprinkle with the Parmesan and serve.

GENOESE SPINACH

SPINACI ALLA GENOVESE

Serves 4

generous 1/3 cup golden raisins

4 salted anchovies, heads removed, cleaned and fillleted (see page 596), soaked in cold water for 10 minutes and drained

2 1/4 pounds spinach

4 tablespoons olive oil

1 tablespoon fresh flat-leaf parsley, chopped

1/2 cup pine nuts • salt and pepper

Put the golden raisins in a bowl, add warm water to cover and let soak. Chop the anchovy fillets. Cook the spinach, in just the water clinging to the leaves after washing, for about 5 minutes until tender. Drain well and squeeze out the excess liquid. Heat the oil in a pan, add the anchovies, spinach and parsley and mix well, then add the pine nuts. Drain and squeeze out the raisins, then add to the pan. Season with salt and pepper to taste and cook for about 10 minutes.

SPINACH AND MUSHROOM SALAD

SPINACI IN INSALATA CON CHAMPIGNON

Serves 4

juice of 1 lemon, strained

5 ounces white mushrooms

1 lettuce, trimmed

11 ounces baby spinach leaves,
coarse stems removed

4 tablespoons olive oil

1 tablespoon Dijon mustard

salt

Half-fill a bowl with water and add half the lemon juice. Thinly slice the mushrooms and add to the acidulated water. Tear the lettuce leaves into pieces and put them in a salad bowl with the spinach leaves. Drain the mushrooms and add to the bowl. Whisk together a generous pinch of salt, the olive oil, mustard and the remaining lemon juice in a bowl. Pour the dressing over the salad, toss gently and serve.

SPINACH IN WHITE BUTTER SAUCE

SPINACI IN SALSA BIANCA

Serves 4

1 lemon, sliced

2$^1/_4$ pounds spinach

2 small shallots, chopped

scant $^1/_2$ cup dry white wine

$^2/_3$ cup butter, softened

$^1/_2$ teaspoon fresh thyme leaves

$^1/_3$ cup Parmesan cheese, freshly grated

salt and pepper

Bring a pan of salted water to a boil, add the lemon and spinach and cook for about 5 minutes until the spinach is tender. Remove and discard the lemon, drain the spinach and squeeze out the excess liquid. Place in a serving dish and keep warm. Put the shallots, wine and $^1/_2$ cup water in a small pan and bring to a boil over medium heat. Lower the heat and simmer until the liquid has reduced by half. Remove the pan from the heat, season with salt and pepper and let cool slightly. Stir in the softened butter and return to the heat, whisking constantly until thickened, then add the thyme. Sprinkle the spinach with the Parmesan, and spoon the sauce over it.

TRUFFLES

Two Italian regions are famous for their white truffles –
Piedmont, with Alba in the Langhe (the acknowledged capital
of this prized underground fungus) and other areas of the
Monferrato district (the area around Alessandria and the Po
hills) and Marche, whose most famous truffle-growing centers
are Acqualagna, Sant'Angelo in Vado and Visso in the
province of Pesaro, and Amandola, Comunanza and
Montemonaco in the province of Ascoli Piceno. The most
famous region for the esteemed black truffle is Umbria, with
Norcia, Spoleto, Cascia and Scheggino. Truffles mature from
October to April, but the best and most fragrant are those
gathered in the autumn months. Both white and black truffles
are stored in the same way: wrapped in two layers of damp
paper, with two or three dry sheets on the outside, and kept in
the least cold part of the refrigerator for no more than a
week. To clean them, brush gently, then wipe with a damp
cloth. Black truffles are cooked, but white ones are eaten
raw. White truffles go with egg tagliolini, fondues, raw
meat, agnolotti and risottos. Black truffles go with fried eggs,
crostini and frittata.

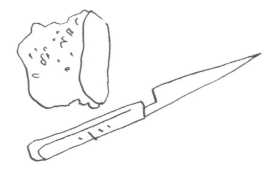

QUANTITIES
Allow about ³/₄ ounces per
serving.

CLASSIC TRUFFLE FRITTATA

FRITTATA CLASSICA DI TARTUFI

Serves 4

5 eggs

3¹/₂ ounces black truffles, chopped

scant ¹/₂ cup heavy cream

juice of ¹/₂–1 lemon, strained

2 tablespoons olive oil

salt

Lightly beat the eggs in a shallow dish and add the truffles, cream, a pinch of salt and lemon juice to taste. Heat the olive oil in a skillet, pour in the mixture and cook over medium heat, stirring occasionally with a wooden spoon, turning once. Cook the frittata until just set, but still soft, and the truffles are lightly cooked.

ROAST TRUFFLES WITH POTATOES

TARTUFI AL FORNO CON PATATE

Serves 4

1¹/₂ pounds potatoes, thinly sliced

2¹/₄ cups milk

2 tablespoons butter, plus extra for greasing

1 shallot, chopped

1 cup heavy cream

3 ounces black truffles, very thinly sliced

¹/₃ cup Parmesan cheese, freshly grated

salt and pepper

Put the potatoes into a pan, pour in the milk and 2¹/₄ cups water, add a pinch of salt and cook for 30–45 minutes until just tender, then drain. Preheat the oven to 350°F. Grease an ovenproof dish with butter. Melt the butter in a pan, add the shallot and cook over low heat, stirring occasionally, for 5 minutes. Add the potatoes and cream, season with salt and pepper and cook for a few minutes more. Remove the potatoes with a slotted spatula and set aside. Reduce the cooking juices over low heat. Arrange slightly overlapping slices of potato and truffle in the prepared dish, spoon the thickened cooking juices over them, sprinkle with the Parmesan and bake until golden brown. Serve hot.

PARMESAN TRUFFLES

TARTUFI ALLA PARMIGIANA

Serves 4

3 tablespoons butter

2 black truffles, thinly sliced

¹/₂ cup Parmesan cheese, freshly grated

Preheat the oven to 425°F. Melt 2 tablespoons of the butter in an ovenproof dish. Remove from the heat and place a layer of the truffle slices in the dish. Sprinkle with the Parmesan and continue making layers until all the ingredients are used. Dot with the remaining butter and bake for a few minutes.

JERUSALEM ARTICHOKES

The Italian name for this vegetable – topinambur – may derive from the name of the Brazilian Topinamba tribe, while the English name is probably a corruption of the Italian for sunflower – girasole – to which family the Jerusalem artichoke belongs. Its shape is similar to that of a knobby potato and its flavor is quite like that of the globe artichoke. There are both white- and violet-skinned varieties, but the former have the better flavor. When buying Jerusalem artichokes choose those with the smoothest surface. They contain very few calories and so are ideal for anyone trying to lose weight. To prepare them, peel them with a small knife, cut them into slices and immerse in cold water to prevent them turning black. Jerusalem artichokes are tasty raw in salads (grated, sliced or cut in strips), and steamed, trifolati (sliced and fried with garlic and parsley) or boiled.

QUANTITIES

Allow 5–7 ounces per serving.

BOILING

Immerse in lightly salted, boiling water and cook for 15–30 minutes or more, according to size.

QUANTITIES
AND COOKING TIMES

INSALATA DI TOPINAMBUR CON CARCIOFI

JERUSALEM ARTICHOKE SALAD

Serves 4

14 ounces Jerusalem artichokes, peeled and thinly sliced
4 globe artichoke hearts
juice of 1 lemon, strained
1 carrot, cut into thin batons
4 tablespoons olive oil
salt and pepper

Put the Jerusalem artichokes into a salad bowl. Thinly slice the artichoke hearts, sprinkle with a little of the lemon juice and add to the bowl. Add the carrot. Beat together the oil and 2 tablespoons of the remaining lemon juice in a bowl and season with salt and pepper. Pour the dressing over the salad in a continuous trickle, mix gently and serve.

PURÉ DI TOPINAMBUR E PATATE

JERUSALEM ARTICHOKE AND POTATO PURÉE

Serves 6

14 ounces Jerusalem artichokes
1³/₄ pounds potatoes
scant ¹/₂ cup butter
scant 1 cup milk
salt

Boil or steam the Jerusalem artichokes and potatoes in separate pans. Drain, if necessary, peel and pass both through a potato ricer into a clean pan. Set the pan over low heat and stir in the butter. Meanwhile, heat the milk in another pan. When the butter has been completely absorbed, gradually pour in the warm milk, stirring constantly. When the purée is soft and creamy, season with salt, mix well and remove the pan from the heat. Serve hot with roast meat.

TOPINAMBUR ALLA PANNA

JERUSALEM ARTICHOKES IN CREAM

Serves 4

2 tablespoons butter
1¹/₂ pounds Jerusalem artichokes, peeled and thinly sliced
1 cup heavy cream
1 fresh flat-leaf parsley sprig, chopped
salt

Melt the butter in a pan, add the artichokes, pour in the cream and cook over low heat for 5 minutes, then season with salt, cover and cook for 10–15 minutes until tender. If necessary, remove the lid and increase the heat slightly towards the end of cooking in order to thicken the sauce. Remove the pan from the heat, sprinkle in the parsley and stir, then transfer the artichokes and cream to a warm serving dish.

PUMPKIN

Two varieties of pumpkin are very popular in Italy. A green, wrinkled pumpkin is grown in the Po delta. It is very common in Chioggia and Venice, where it is baked, sprinkled with sugar and eaten in slices. The other kind, with a smooth yellow rind, can reach exceptional weights and sizes. The thick rind of both encloses plenty of flesh in varying shades of orange, with seeds hidden in a central cavity. Pumpkins are rich in vitamin A, potassium, calcium and phosphorus. They also have diuretic and refreshing properties. Owing to their weight and size, they are usually sold in slices. However, it is worth bearing in mind that about 30 per cent of a pumpkin consists of rind and seeds. Pumpkin gnocchi, tortelli, molds, soups and risottos are delicious. There is also an Indian sweet-and-sour chutney, made with pumpkin, tomatoes, onions, garlic, golden raisins, white and brown sugar, salt, pepper and ginger. It is sold in jars and served with boiled meats.

QUANTITIES AND COOKING TIMES

QUANTITIES

Allow about 5 ounces flesh per person.

BAKING

Cut the flesh into ½-inch slices and bake in a preheated oven, 400°F, for 15 minutes, then increase the temperature to 425°F and bake for a further 5 minutes.

STEAMING

Chop the flesh, place in a steamer and cook for 20–30 minutes.

MOZZARELLA PUMPKIN SANDWICH

Preheat the oven to 400°F. Grease an ovenproof dish with butter. Place the pumpkin slices on a large sheet of foil, season with salt and sprinkle with thyme. Fold over the foil to enclose the pumpkin and seal the edges. Place on a cookie sheet and bake for 30 minutes. Take the pumpkin out of the oven but do not switch the oven off. Sandwich a slice of mozzarella between two slices of pumpkin and place in the prepared dish. Repeat with the remaining mozzarella and pumpkin slices. Sprinkle with the Parmesan, dot with the butter and bake for about 10 minutes.

SANDWICH DI ZUCCA ALLA MOZZARELLA

Serves 4

2 tablespoons butter, plus extra for greasing

1 pound 5 ounces pumpkin flesh,

cut into $2/3$-inch slices

1 fresh thyme sprig, chopped

11 ounces mozzarella cheese, thinly sliced

$1/2$ cup Parmesan cheese, freshly grated

salt

BAKED PUMPKIN WITH POTATOES

Preheat the oven to 350°F. Brush an ovenproof dish with oil. Make alternate layers of potatoes, onion and pumpkin in the prepared dish. Sprinkle the tomato over the top, drizzle with olive oil and season with salt and pepper. Bake for 1 hour. Let stand for 5 minutes before serving.

ZUCCA AL FORNO CON PATATE

Serves 4

olive oil, for brushing and drizzling

4 waxy potatoes, cut into $1/4$-inch slices

1 onion, cut into rings

14 ounces pumpkin flesh,

cut into $1/2$-inch slices

4 ripe tomatoes,

peeled and diced

salt and pepper

PARMESAN PUMPKIN

Heat 2 tablespoons of the oil in a pan, add the shallots and cook over low heat, stirring occasionally, for 5 minutes. Add the tomatoes, season with salt and pepper and cook, stirring occasionally, for 15 minutes. Preheat the oven to 400°F. Brush an ovenproof dish with oil. Dust the pumpkin slices with flour. Heat the remaining oil in a skillet, add the pumpkin slices and cook until lightly browned on both sides. Remove with a slotted spatula and drain on paper towels. Make a layer of pumpkin slices in the prepared dish, sprinkle with a little thyme, spoon some of the tomato sauce on top, add some mozzarella slices and sprinkle with a little Parmesan. Continue making alternating layers until all the ingredients are used. Bake until golden brown and bubbling.

ZUCCA ALLA PARMIGIANA

Serves 6

5 tablespoons olive oil, plus extra for brushing

2 shallots, chopped

14 ounces tomatoes, peeled and diced

1 pound 5 ounces pumpkin flesh, sliced

all-purpose flour, for dusting

2 fresh thyme sprigs, chopped

14 ounces mozzarella cheese, thinly sliced

1 cup Parmesan cheese, freshly grated

salt and pepper

Serves 4

2 tablespoons olive oil

2 garlic cloves

1¹⁄₂ pounds pumpkin flesh, thinly sliced

³⁄₄ cup dry white wine

1¹⁄₂ teaspoons finely chopped fresh rosemary

salt and pepper

PUMPKIN WITH ROSEMARY

Heat the oil in a pan, add the garlic and pumpkin and cook over medium heat, stirring occasionally, until the garlic starts to go brown, then remove and discard it. Pour in the wine and cook until it has evaporated, then lower the heat and simmer until tender. Season with salt and pepper to taste and sprinkle with the rosemary. Cook for a few minutes more, then serve.

ZUCCHINI

Zucchini are refreshing and delicate and can be bought all year round. As well as classic zucchini in varying shades of dark green, there is also a slightly prickly variety. As the vegetable is so easy to digest, it is recommended as a baby food. When choosing zucchini, bear in mind that elongated ones should be no more than 10–12 inches long, while round ones should be no more than 4'/2 inches in diameter. If they grow too big, bitter seeds form inside. Choose zucchini with smooth, bright green skins that are firm to the touch. Before cooking, rinse them under running water and cut off both ends. Zucchini are tasty both raw and cooked. They may be simply boiled, sautéed in a skillet with oil, garlic and parsley or added to rice soups and frittata. Zucchini flowers are also edible. They should be picked as soon as they start to open.

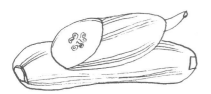

QUANTITIES
Allow about 6 ounces per serving.
BOILING
Cook in boiling water for 15–20 minutes. Be careful not to overcook them.

STEAMING
Small, whole zucchini cook in 15 minutes.
FLOWERS
Gently open the calyx, remove the pistil and rinse quickly under cold water. Stuff and fry in batter or add to frittata or risottos.

QUANTITIES AND COOKING TIMES

STUFFED ZUCCHINI BARQUETTES

BARCHETTE DI ZUCCHINE RIPIENE

Serves 4

generous ¹/₂ cup cooked, cured ham, chopped

2 tablespoons fresh flat-leaf parsley, chopped

1 garlic clove, chopped • ¹/₃ cup pancetta, chopped

scant 1 cup ground lean beef

2 tablespoons Parmesan cheese, freshly grated

1 egg, lightly beaten

4 large zucchini, halved lengthwise

¹/₄ cup butter • 2 tablespoons olive oil

1 onion, chopped

2 tablespoons bottled strained tomato sauce

salt and pepper

Combine the ham, parsley, garlic, half the pancetta, the beef, Parmesan and egg in a bowl and season with salt and pepper. Scoop out the flesh from the zucchini with a small sharp knife, taking care not to pierce the 'shells'. Fill the shells with the meat mixture. Heat the butter and oil in a pan, add the onion and remaining pancetta and cook over low heat, stirring occasionally, for 5 minutes. Add the zucchini and cook for a few minutes more. Mix the bottled strained tomatoes with ³/₄ cup warm water in a bowl and add to the pan. Season with salt, cover and simmer over low heat for 20–30 minutes until the zucchini are tender and the filling is cooked through. Transfer the zucchini to a warm serving dish and spoon the cooking juices over them.

ZUCCHINI AND POTATO CHARLOTTE

CHARLOTTE DI ZUCCHINE E PATATE

Serves 4

1 pound 5 ounces potatoes

3 tablespoons butter, plus extra for greasing

²/₃ cup Parmesan cheese, freshly grated

1 pound 2 ounces zucchini

1 leek, white part only, sliced

scant ¹/₂ cup heavy cream

salt and pepper

Cook the potatoes in salted, boiling water for about 25 minutes until tender. Drain, peel, place in a bowl and mash with a potato masher. Stir in 1 tablespoon of the butter and the Parmesan and let cool slightly. Cut the largest two zucchini into thin strips and parboil the strips in salted water for a few minutes, then drain and spread out on a dish towel. Preheat the oven to 350°F. Grease an ovenproof mold with butter. Dice the remaining zucchini. Melt the remaining butter in a pan, add the diced zucchini and leek and cook over medium heat, stirring occasionally, for 5 minutes. Season with salt and pepper, lower the heat, pour in the cream and cook until it has been absorbed. Remove the pan from the heat and stir the zucchini mixture into the mashed potato. Line the prepared mold with the zucchini strips and pour in the potato mixture. Smooth the surface and bake for about 30 minutes. Let cool slightly before turning out.

FRIED ZUCCHINI FLOWERS

FIORI DI ZUCCHINE FRITTI

Serves 4

scant 1 cup all-purpose flour

2 tablespoons olive oil

5 tablespoons dry white wine

1 egg, separated

vegetable oil, for deep-frying

12 zucchini flowers, trimmed

salt and pepper

Combine the flour, oil, wine and egg yolk in a bowl and season with salt and pepper. Add ²/₃–³/₄ cup warm water to make a fairly runny, smooth batter. Let stand for 1 hour. Whisk the egg white in a grease-free bowl and fold gently into the batter. Heat the oil for deep-frying in a large pan. Dip the flowers in the batter, shake off the excess and fry in the hot oil until golden. Remove with a slotted spatula and drain on paper towels. Sprinkle with salt and serve immediately.

FIORI DI ZUCCHINE RIPIENI

Serves 4

7 ounces robiola cheese, diced

7 ounces Gorgonzola cheese, crumbled

3 dill pickles, drained and chopped

1 egg yolk

12 zucchini flowers, trimmed

salt

STUFFED ZUCCHINI FLOWERS

Put the cheeses in a bowl and beat with a wooden spoon until smooth. Season with salt and stir in the dill pickles and egg yolk. Mix carefully. Fill the zucchini flowers with the cheese mixture, arrange on a serving dish in the shape of a star and serve.

FIORI DI ZUCCHINE RIPIENI E FRITTI

Serves 4

12 zucchini flowers, trimmed

5 ounces mozzarella cheese, cut into sticks

6 canned anchovy fillets in oil, drained and halved

vegetable oil, for deep-frying

For the batter

scant 1 cup all-purpose flour

1 egg, separated

5 tablespoons dry white wine

2 tablespoons olive oil

salt

FRIED STUFFED ZUCCHINI FLOWERS

To make the batter, combine the flour, a pinch of salt, the egg yolk, wine and oil and add $^2/_3$–$^3/_4$ cup warm water to make a fairly runny mixture. Let stand for 30 minutes. Whisk the egg white in a grease-free bowl and fold it into the batter. Fill each zucchini flower with a stick of mozzarella and half an anchovy fillet and seal with a toothpick. Heat the oil for deep-frying in a large pan. Dip the flowers, in the batter and fry in the hot oil until golden brown, then remove with a slotted spatula and drain on paper towels.

INSALATA DI ZUCCHINE NOVELLE

Serves 4

6 baby zucchini, thinly sliced

2 ounces Parmesan cheese, shaved

pinch of dried oregano

3 tablespoons olive oil

2 tomatoes, peeled and sliced

salt and pepper

BABY ZUCCHINI SALAD

Put the zucchini in a salad bowl, add the Parmesan, oregano and olive oil and season with salt and pepper. Mix well and set aside in a cool place for at least 30 minutes to allow the flavors to mingle. Add the tomatoes just before serving.

SWEET AND SOUR ZUCCHINI

Preheat the oven to 350°F. Put the golden raisins in a bowl, add hot water to cover them and let soak. Chop the anchovy fillets. Spread out the pine nuts on a cookie sheet and toast lightly in the oven for 5 minutes. Heat the oil in a skillet, add the zucchini and garlic and cook over high heat, stirring them frequently, for approximately 5 minutes. Drain the raisins and squeeze out the excess liquid. Lower the heat, then add the raisins, pine nuts, vinegar and sugar to the skillet and season with salt according to taste. Mix well and cook for a few minutes, then add the anchovies. Cook for 5–10 minutes more, then serve warm.

ZUCCHINE AGRODOLCI

Serves 4

3 tablespoons golden raisins

2 salted anchovies, heads removed, clean and filleted (see page 596) soaked in cold water for 10 minutes and drained

3 tablespoons pine nuts

2 tablespoons olive oil

6 zucchini, sliced

1 garlic clove, chopped

scant ¹/₂ cup white wine vinegar

¹/₂ tablespoon sugar

salt

ZUCCHINI WITH LEMON

Steam the zucchini for about 15 minutes. Let cool slightly, then place on a serving dish. Sprinkle the herbs on top. Drizzle with olive oil, season with salt and pepper to taste and sprinkle with the lemon juice. Toss, set aside in a cool place for the flavors to mingle, then serve.

ZUCCHINE AL LIMONE

Serves 4

1 pound 5 ounces zucchini, cut into thick strips

1 fresh tarragon sprig, chopped

1 fresh flat-leaf parsley sprig, chopped

4 fresh basil leaves, chopped

4 fresh borage leaves, chopped

olive oil, for drizzling

juice of 1 lemon, strained

salt and pepper

ROAST ZUCCHINI

Preheat the oven to 425°F. Place the zucchini in a roasting pan, add the olive oil, toss to coat and roast for 20–25 minutes, turning occasionally. Make a layer of some of the zucchini slices on a serving dish, sprinkle with some of the garlic, parsley and basil, season with salt and pepper and drizzle with olive oil. Continue making layers until all the ingredients are used. Set aside in a cool place for about 1 hour for the flavors to mingle before serving.

ZUCCHINE ARROSTO

Serves 4

8 zucchini, thickly sliced lengthwise

2 tablespoons olive oil, plus extra for drizzling

3 garlic cloves, thinly sliced

2 tablespoons fresh flat-leaf parsley, chopped

6 fresh basil leaves, chopped

salt and pepper

SURPRISE ZUCCHINI

ZUCCHINE A SORPRESA

Serves 8

6 zucchini, sliced lengthwise

1/2 cup all-purpose flour

2 eggs

1 1/2 cups bread crumbs

1/2 teaspoon dried oregano

7 ounces provolone cheese, sliced

vegetable oil, for deep-frying

salt

Sprinkle the zucchini slices with salt and let stand for about 1 hour, then pat dry with paper towels. Meanwhile, spread out the flour in a shallow dish, beat the eggs with a pinch of salt in another shallow dish and spread out the bread crumbs in a third. Sprinkle a slice of zucchini with a little oregano, place a slice of provolone on top and cover with another slice of zucchini. Press the 'sandwich' down well, dip first in the flour, then in the beaten eggs and, finally, in the bread crumbs. Continue making sandwiches until all the ingredients are used. Heat the oil in a skillet, add the zucchini sandwiches, in batches, and cook until golden brown all over. Remove with a slotted spatula, drain on paper towels and serve.

ZUCCHINI CAPRICCIOSE

ZUCCHINE CAPRICCIOSE

Serves 4

3 tablespoons olive oil, plus extra for brushing

6 zucchini, halved lengthwise

4 salted anchovies, soaked in water and drained

1 garlic clove, chopped

1 fresh flat-leaf parsley sprig, chopped

1 fresh basil sprig, chopped

scant 1 cup green olives, pitted

2 tomatoes, peeled, seeded and chopped

1 mozzarella cheese, diced

salt and pepper

Preheat the oven to 400°F. Brush an oven-proof dish with olive oil. Scoop out the flesh from the zucchini with a small sharp knife, taking care not to pierce the 'shells'. Chop the flesh and set aside. Place the zucchini shells, skin side up, in the prepared dish and bake for 10 minutes. Remove from the oven and set aside. Reduce the oven temperature to 350°F. Meanwhile, place the anchovies skin side up, press along the backbones with your thumb, then turn them over and remove the bones. Chop the flesh, place in a bowl, add 2 tablespoons of the oil and beat with a wooden spoon until smooth. Combine the garlic, parsley, basil, zucchini flesh and olives in another bowl, then stir in the tomatoes. Pour in the remaining oil, add the anchovy mixture and season with salt and pepper. Mix well and spoon the mixture into the zucchini shells. Top with the mozzarella and bake for 20 minutes.

ZUCCHINI CAPRICCIOSE WITH SALMON AND LEEKS

Cook the zucchini in salted, boiling water for about 15 minutes until just tender. Drain, halve lengthwise and scoop out the flesh. Preheat the oven to 350°F. Grease an ovenproof dish with butter. Melt the butter in a skillet, add the leeks and cook over low heat, stirring occasionally, for 5 minutes. Stir in the smoked salmon and remove the pan from the heat. Spoon the mixture into the zucchini 'shells' and place in the prepared dish. Season with salt, spoon the cream over the filled shells and bake for 10 minutes.

ZUCCHINE CAPRICCIOSE
AL SALMONE E PORRI

Serves 4

4 medium zucchini

2 tablespoons butter, plus extra for greasing

2 leeks, white part only, chopped

3 ounces smoked salmon, chopped

$1/2$ cup heavy cream

salt

ZUCCHINI SALAD WITH THYME

Put the zucchini and Belgian endive into a salad bowl. Combine the parsley and thyme and sprinkle them over the vegetables. Whisk together the vinegar and olive oil in a pitcher, season with salt and pepper, pour the dressing over the salad and serve.

ZUCCHINE CON INSALATA BELGA AL TIMO

Serves 4

6 baby zucchini, thinly sliced

2 heads of Belgian endive, cut into $1/2$-inch strips

1 fresh flat-leaf parsley sprig, chopped

3 fresh thyme sprigs, chopped

1 tablespoon white wine vinegar

$2^1/2$ tablespoons olive oil • salt and pepper

ZUCCHINI IN EGG SAUCE

Heat the butter and oil in a pan, add the zucchini and cook over high heat, stirring frequently, for 8–10 minutes until golden brown. Meanwhile, heat the stock in another pan. Pour the hot stock over the zucchini, lower the heat, season with salt and pepper and cook until the liquid has reduced. Beat the egg yolks with the lemon juice and parsley, pour the mixture over the zucchini, mix well and cook until thickened.

ZUCCHINE IN CREMA D'UOVA

Serves 4

3 tablespoons butter

2 tablespoons olive oil

$1^1/2$ pounds baby zucchini, sliced

$2/3$ cup Vegetable Stock (see page 209)

2 egg yolks

juice of 1 lemon, strained

1 fresh flat-leaf parsley sprig, chopped

salt and pepper

SHIP

LEMON

YELLOW

FISH →

CRUSTACEANS →

SHELLFISH →

FISH

The term fish is often used to refer to all seafood, although it may then be sub-divided into finned fish, crustaceans, such as crabs, and shellfish, such as mussels. In this chapter, the sub-divisions are sea fish, freshwater fish, crustaceans and shellfish, which are called mollusks and include octopus, squid and cuttlefish. Generally, a wide variety of most types is available throughout the year. However, with the exception of trout, freshwater fish are not so commonly available commercially outside Italy. Finally, this chapter also includes a section on fish soups, which are often more like substantial stews, and a collection of recipes for preparing and cooking snails and frogs, ingredients that do not readily fit into any other category. Although many types of sea fish are becoming increasingly expensive, you don't have to limit your choice to the rarest and most valued. In fact, some of the most common fish are extremely tasty. For example, the fish known as 'blue-scale fish' in Italy, such as sardines and mackerel, are the perfect choice for a number of truly delicious, yet economical recipes. For some years now, nutritionists have been encouraging the inclusion of fish in the diet in preference to many other foods. They are an excellent source of easily digestible protein, and sea fish also contain iodine, as well as other minerals. The flesh of oily fish contains essential fatty acids and fat soluble vitamins that are vital for good health. White fish, such as cod and skate, are very low in fat and even oily fish, such as salmon and herring, contain less fat than meat or poultry. Fish are so highly regarded that we are advised to eat white fish at least twice a week and oily fish once a week, although there are some provisos for pregnant and nursing mothers and the very young about eating certain species. When choosing between white and oily fish, bear in mind that the nutritional value of the former is slightly lower than that of beef, while the nutritional value of the latter is very high indeed. As for the difference between sea fish and freshwater fish, sea fish are more nutritious, although sometimes less digestible. Mollusks and crustaceans are rich in calcium, magnesium, sodium chloride, iodine and, above all, iron. Other seafood is also rich in minerals. In fact, it can be said that all seafood is good for you provided that it is fresh, properly stored, and prepared correctly.

CRUSTACEANS

In spite of their tough-sounding name, under their shells crustaceans are extremely delicate. The flavor, aroma and quality of their flesh is almost beyond comparison. Langoustines, lobsters, crayfish, shrimp and crabs all have delicious flesh which needs handling with care – simple short cooking and natural dressings, such as extra virgin olive oil or hot or cold sauces made with top-quality ingredients. Otherwise, your considerable investment will be wasted. Crustaceans are expensive, especially the most highly prized varieties, such as lobster. Canned produce, such as crabmeat, is also excellent and may be used in a number of recipes.

SHELLFISH

This group includes mussels, clams, scallops, squid, cuttlefish and many others. Shellfish must be absolutely fresh. While cooking them kills any bacteria, it does not eliminate any toxins that may already have been created if the shellfish have been stored for too long; this may even cause poisoning. This is not intended to be alarmist, but simply to warn you that shellfish require caution. If you are not absolutely sure of their freshness or that they have been stored perfectly in the case of frozen packs, do not buy them. Always buy from a reliable supplier and never gather them from the sea shore yourself. It is advisable to cook shellfish on the day of purchase. Serve them with light sauces, which do not smother their delicate flavor.

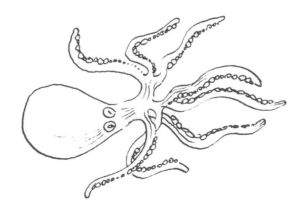

FISH

The quality of fish depends on its freshness. When buying, there are a number of pointers to look for. These include a delicate pleasant smell without any hints of ammonia or strong 'fishiness', a generally healthy appearance, a firm body, close-fitting shiny scales, a naturally colored taut skin, lively non-red eyes, damp, pink or red gills, no trace of blood along the bones and no inadvertent damage to the abdomen.

QUANTITIES

Some fish produce a high proportion of waste, which makes it quite hard to judge the right quantity for each guest. The amount of waste also affects how much value there is for your money. The table below shows the amount of edible flesh that remains after gutting some types of fish.

YIELD PER 2¼ POUNDS FISH

KIND OF FISH	WASTE	YIELD
Sea bass	50%	1 lb 2 oz
Hake	30%	1½ lbs
Porgy	45%	1 lb 7 oz
Halibut	65%	12 oz
Salmon	50%	1 lb 2 oz
Sole	55%	1 lb
Mackerel	35%	12 oz

PER SERVING

Allow an average of 5 ounces per serving for fillets, 7 ounces per serving for steaks or slices and 9–11 ounces per serving (according to the type) for whole fish.

VARIATIONS

If you feel the fish suggested in a recipe is rather too expensive, try replacing it with a more economical but similar one. For example, less expensive flat fish, such as flounder, can be cooked like sole, farmed sea bass may also be used to replace porgy or wild sea bass in some cases, and cod (from a sustainable source) can be used in recipes for salmon.

WASTE

The heads (gills removed) and bones of white fish are valuable for making fish stock. Do not use those of oily fish.

Although the cooking times given in the recipes are as precise as possible, several things may cause them to vary. These include the size and thickness of the fish, the material the pan or dish is made from and the fuel used for cooking (gas, electricity, charcoal, etc.). In addition, how well done the fish should be is a matter of taste. Remember, however, overcooked seafood loses some of its best qualities. For example, shellfish rapidly become rubbery in texture and fish fillets fall apart or become spongy. You can choose from a variety of cooking methods depending on the type of fish, its size and the way it is to be presented. Whole fish are generally better poached or baked, fillets and steaks are good broiled or fried like small fish. To scale fish, use a scaling knife or small round-bladed knife. Hold the fish by the tail and scrape off the scales from tail to head, then rinse well. Small fish, such as sardines, are best scaled under cold, running water.

POACHING

Most fish may be poached in court-bouillon and served with oil and lemon juice, or mayonnaise flavored in various ways.

COURT—BOUILLON

This is an aromatic stock. To prepare it, simmer about $3\frac{3}{4}$ cups water with a small, sliced onion, $\frac{1}{2}$ sliced carrot, a celery stalk, $\frac{1}{2}$ cup white wine vinegar or white wine, a few peppercorns and salt for 45 minutes. Strain through a strainer, discard the vegetables and leave the court-bouillon to cool completely. To poach a fish, immerse it in cold or gently simmering court-bouillon and cook for about 10 minutes per 1 pound 2 ounces.

FISH STOCK

This is a 'by-product' of poaching a fish and is excellent for preparing sauces, risottos and rice soups. If you wish to use the stock for such dishes, do not add vinegar, lemon juice or wine to the court-bouillon.

→ Allow 10–12 minutes per 1 pound 2 ounces of fish.

→ Immerse the fish in cold or gently simmering court-bouillon. In both cases, continue cooking at a very gentle simmer.

→ Both court-bouillon and fish stock should be left to

591

cool before being reused.

CONCENTRATED
FISH STOCK

Also known as fish fumet, this is made using the heads and bones of white fish (see page 210).

LARGE WHOLE FISH

These should be immersed in cold court-bouillon.

FISH PORTIONS AND
SMALL WHOLE FISH

Slices, steaks and fillets, and small fish should be immersed in gently simmering court-bouillon. Remember that they cook very quickly.

FRESHWATER FISH

These require a more highly flavored court-bouillon, so add larger quantities of vegetables.

→ Leave the fish to cool in their cooking liquid, then drain gently to avoid breaking up the flesh.

STEAMING

You will need a combined steamer or a perforated container that can be fitted on an ordinary pan. Steaming enhances the flavor of a number of fish, including red snapper, sea bass and most fillets.

GRILLING

Fish with firm flesh, such as tuna, large fish, such as porgy, and smaller pieces of fish are excellent when barbecued. You can add all sorts of herbs and spices and splash with red or white wine, fish stock, etc. to bring out their aroma. Use a hinged wire rack to make turning the fish easier.

BAKING

All large or medium fish may be baked. They may be flavored with herbs, seasoned butter, stock, wine, or even stuffed in the case of large fish. Small fish, fillets, steaks, etc. are also excellent baked in foil packets. This avoids the problem of lingering smells and has the advantage of concentrating the flavor of the flesh and the added herbs and spices. It is a quick method and results in tender flesh.

BROILING

Do not scale fish before broiling as the scales help to protect the delicate flesh

from the intense heat.

→ Always dry fish before placing on a broiler rack, even if it has been marinated first.

→ Be careful not to overcook. For example: sardines, 1 minute each side; small sea bass, 10 minutes each side; porgy, 15 minutes each side.

→ Cook large fish under a low heat and brush frequently with oil.

SHALLOW—FRYING

This method is suitable for whole flat fish, such as sole, as well as for fillets and sliced fish. Briefly cook in a skillet with a little melted butter over medium-high heat until golden brown on both sides, then lower the heat and cook until the flesh is tender and flakes easily. As a general rule, almost all fish can be lightly sprinkled with salt and flour before cooking. The cooking time varies from 2–3 minutes each side.

DEEP—FRYING

Small whole fish and larger fish cut into small pieces are ideal for deep-frying, as are white fish such as cod and sole. Always dry fish completely first, then coat first with flour, shaking off the excess, and then with a few fine bread crumbs. Heat plenty of oil in a large pan or deep-fat fryer to 350–375°F or until a cube of day-old bread browns in 30 seconds. This is a quick cooking method, so do not leave the fish in the pan too long. After frying, lift out with a slotted spatula and drain on paper towels. Season with salt only after cooking. In Italy, groundnut oil and olive oil (not necessarily extra virgin) are the favorite oils to use. Olive oil would probably be a rather extravagant choice in the United States and, in any case, it does have a low smoke point which makes it more liable to catch fire. One final piece of advice: never reuse the oil, whatever the type, after deep-frying.

MOST SUITABLE SIDE DISHES

Not only do rice, potatoes and other steamed vegetables go well with fish, but so do fresh vegetables in butter.

→ Carrots and green beans go well with sole and cod fillets.

→ Celery root purée is good served with cod.

→ Cucumbers, when peeled and diced, complement mild-flavored fish.

→ Leeks, carrots and baby turnips are an ideal combination with baked or steamed porgy.

→ Mayonnaise is delicious with all poached fish, especially if it is flavored with capers, finely chopped dill pickles, thin tomato sauce (which turns it light pink) or chopped black or green olives.

→ Mixed diced vegetables are perfect with tuna.

→ Rice cooked with a pinch of curry powder in the water is colorful and flavorsome. A similar result may be achieved by dissolving an envelope of saffron in the water.

→ Spinach, Swiss chard, lettuce and sorrel have an affinity with almost all fish.

→ Tomatoes, eggplant and peperonata all go well with baked fish.

→ Zucchini, either sliced or cut into thin batons and steamed or sautéed with a little oil and butter, make a delicious side dish, especially with sole.

RECOMMENDED HERBS, SPICES AND FLAVORINGS

→ Basil, sage and oregano may be added sparingly to sauces, the cooking water of poached fish and the juices of braised fish.

→ Celery may be used together with thyme and bay leaves in a bouquet garni in court-bouillon.

→ Coriander seeds are useful in marinades and court-bouillon.

→ Dill has a fennel-like flavor and goes well with marinated herrings and raw fish carpaccio.

→ Fennel seeds give a lovely flavor to broiled sea bass and other varieties of fish.

→ Garlic is an essential ingredient in fish soup, cod Provençal and with baked fish.

→ Onions, either raw and cut into rings or pickled pearl onions go with almost all steamed fish.

→ Tarragon is used to flavor marinades or broiled fish, especially salmon.

→ Thyme sprinkled generously on baked fish fillets, together with a pinch of salt, brings out their flavor.

→In pans and fish kettles: to prevent or reduce the smell, rub the sides of the pan with a little cooking salt and boil ¹/₂ cup vinegar in it. Keep a pan specially for cooking fish.

→ On hands: when handling fish, rub your hands frequently with lemon juice or very salty water.

→ In the kitchen: put a sugar cube in the middle of a plate and ignite it. This should limit the intensity of fishy smells.

→ Baking in foil: this method is better than ordinary baking because it does not leave unpleasant odors.

To keep cooked fish warm for a short while, cover the dish with foil. Otherwise remember these rules.

→ If the fish is baked, turn off the heat shortly before the end of the cooking time, cover with foil to prevent the fish from drying out and leave in the oven.

→ If the fish is boiled, pan-fried or steamed, put it on a serving dish (covered or uncovered) and set over a pan of freshly boiled water with the heat turned off.

ANCHOVIES

SEA FISH

Anchovies belong to a group of oily fish that the Italians call 'blue-scaled'. In recent years, Italian people have come to appreciate their strong mouthwatering flavor and low price more than they did in the past. Anchovies can be prepared in a variety of ways. Whole ones can be salted and fillets are salted and canned in oil. To fillet a whole salted anchovy, cut off its head and tail, and press along the backbones with your thumb. Turn it over and remove the bones which should come away easily. Anchovies are often used in the kitchen to replace sardines. Fresh ones do not travel well and are not widely available outside the Mediterranean. Slightly larger smelts or considerably larger sardines can be substituted in the following recipes. To clean anchovies, snap the backbones of the anchovies just behind the heads with your fingers, then pull off the heads. Most of the innards will come with them. Slit open the bellies and remove any remaining innards, cut off the tails, then rinse and dry the fish.

COMMON SQUARE PAN

FRIED ANCHOVIES

ACCIUGHE FRITTE

Serves 4

1 1/2 pounds anchovies, cleaned

1 1/4 cups milk • all-purpose flour, for dusting

vegetable oil, for deep-frying • salt

For the garnish

1 lemon, cut into wedges

6 small fresh flat-leaf parsley sprigs

Put the anchovies in a dish, add the milk and let soak for 30 minutes. Spread out the flour in a shallow dish. Heat the oil in a large pan. Drain the anchovies, dip in the flour to coat and deep-fry in the hot oil until golden brown (see page 593). Remove with a slotted spatula, drain on paper towels and season with salt. Transfer to a warm serving dish and garnish with the lemon wedges and parsley sprigs.

ANCHOVIES AU GRATIN

ACCIUGHE GRATINATE

Serves 4

4–5 tablespoons olive oil, plus extra for brushing

1 3/4 pounds anchovies, cleaned

1/4 cup white wine vinegar

1/2 teaspoon dried oregano

1 garlic clove, chopped

salt and pepper

Preheat the oven to 400°F. Brush an ovenproof dish with oil. Place the anchovies skin side up and press along the backbones with your thumb, then turn over and remove the bones, leaving the fish joined along their backs. Place the anchovies in the prepared dish. Combine the vinegar, olive oil, oregano and garlic in a bowl and season with salt and pepper. Pour the mixture over the anchovies and bake for 15 minutes. Arrange on a serving dish and serve hot or cold.

ANCHOVIES WITH TRUFFLES

ACCIUGHE TARTUFATE

Serves 4

1 pound 5 ounces salted anchovies, heads and tails removed, cleaned and filleted (see page 596), rinsed and drained

1 white truffle, thinly sliced

olive oil

Pat the anchovy fillets dry. Arrange a layer of anchovies in a glass jar, cover with a layer of truffle and drizzle with olive oil. Continue making alternate layers until all the ingredients are used, filling the jar with plenty of olive oil. Leave in a cool place for a few days for the flavors to mingle.

MIXED FISH FRY

FRITTO MISTO DI PESCI AZZURRI

Serves 4

all-purpose flour, for dusting

2¼ pounds mixed small oily fish, such as anchovies, sardines and smelts, cleaned

vegetable oil, for deep-frying

4 fresh sage leaves, plus extra to garnish

salt and white pepper

1 lemon, cut into wedges, to garnish

Spread out the flour in a shallow dish. Dip the fish in the flour to coat and shake off any excess. Heat the oil in a large pan with the sage leaves. Remove the sage and fry the larger fish in the hot oil until golden brown, then fry the smaller ones. As the fish are ready, remove with a slotted spoon and drain on paper towels (see page 593). Keep warm while you cook the remaining batches, then arrange on a warm serving dish, garnish with lemon wedges and sage leaves and season with salt and pepper.

LAYERED ANCHOVIES AND POTATOES

TEGLIA D'ACCIUGHE E PATATE

Serves 4

olive oil, for brushing and drizzling

1 pound 5 ounces anchovies, heads and tails removed, cleaned and filleted (see page 596), rinsed and drained

1 fresh flat-leaf parsley sprig, chopped

1 garlic clove, chopped

10 fresh mint leaves, chopped

juice of 2 lemons, strained

1 pound 5 ounces potatoes, peeled and thinly sliced

1 cup bread crumbs

scant 1 cup dry white wine

salt and pepper

Preheat the oven to 350°F. Brush an ovenproof dish with oil. Remove the bones from the anchovies, but leave the fish joined along their backs. Combine the parsley, garlic and half the mint in a bowl. Make a layer of anchovies in the prepared dish, sprinkle with some of the herb mixture, season with salt and pepper, pour in some of the lemon juice and drizzle with olive oil. Cover with a layer of potatoes, sprinkle with more of the herb mixture and season with salt and pepper. Continue making alternate layers until all the ingredients are used. Combine the remaining mint and the bread crumbs in a bowl. Pour the wine over the final layer of potatoes and sprinkle with the bread crumb mixture. Bake for 1 hour.

SHAD

Like salmon, shad are sea fish that swim upstream to spawn. In Italy, they are found in Lake Como, Lake Garda and Lake Maggiore, but in America they are usually taken from estuaries. They may be 10–12 inches long. Their flesh is not among the most highly prized, perhaps because they are extremely bony, but it is tasty, and when fried, soused or broiled, shad are absolutely delicious.

SHAD WITH SAGE

Place the fish in a dish, add the milk and let soak for 10 minutes. Drain, pat dry with paper towels and dust lightly with flour. Heat the olive oil and butter in a skillet, add the sage leaves and cook until lightly browned. Add the shad and cook for 7 minutes on each side. Season with salt, remove from the skillet with a slotted spatula, drain on paper towels and serve.

AGONI ALLA SALVIA

Serves 4

1³/₄ pounds shad, scaled and cleaned

1¹/₄ cups milk

all-purpose flour, for dusting

4 tablespoons olive oil

3 tablespoons butter

6 fresh sage leaves

salt

AGONI AL POMODORO

Serves 4

1³/₄ pounds shad, scaled and cleaned

4 tablespoons olive oil

1 carrot, finely chopped

1 onion, finely chopped

1 garlic clove, finely chopped

1 celery stalk, finely chopped

1 fresh flat-leaf parsley sprig, finely chopped

6 plum tomatoes, peeled, seeded and chopped

1 tablespoon capers, drained and rinsed

salt

SHAD WITH TOMATO SAUCE

Cut each fish into three pieces. Heat the oil in a pan, add the carrot, onion, garlic, celery and parsley and cook over low heat, stirring occasionally, for 10 minutes until lightly browned. Add the tomatoes, cover and simmer for about 10 minutes until slightly thickened. Add the fish and capers, season with salt and cook for about 20 minutes until the flesh flakes easily. This recipe may be used with most kinds of fish.

AGONI FRITTI

Serves 4

1³/₄ pounds shad, scaled and cleaned

1¹/₄ cups milk

all-purpose flour, for dusting

7 tablespoons olive oil

1 lemon, sliced

salt

FRIED SHAD

Place the fish in a dish, add the milk and let soak for 10 minutes. Drain, pat dry with paper towels and dust lightly with flour. Heat the olive oil in a skillet, add the fish and cook for a few minutes on each side until golden brown. Remove with a slotted spatula, drain on paper towels, season with salt, place on a warm serving dish and surround with the slices of lemon.

AGONI IN CARPIONE

Serves 4

1³/₄ pounds shad, scaled and cleaned

all-purpose flour, for dusting

¹/₂ cup olive oil

1 onion, thinly sliced

1 celery stalk, chopped

1 garlic clove, thinly sliced

4 fresh sage leaves

1 bay leaf

1 rosemary sprig

6 peppercorns

1¹/₄ cups red wine vinegar

salt

SOUSED SHAD

Dust the fish with flour, shaking off any excess. Heat 7 tablespoons of the oil in a skillet, add the fish, a few at a time, and cook for a few minutes on each side until golden brown. Remove with a slotted spatula, drain on paper towels, season with salt and place in a dish. Put the onion, celery, garlic, sage leaves, bay leaf, rosemary, peppercorns, vinegar, the remaining olive oil and a pinch of salt in a pan. Bring to a boil, then lower the heat and cook until the mixture comes back to a boil. Remove from the heat and pour the mixture over the fish. Leave in a cool place for 24 hours before serving.

HERRINGS

Herrings live in the waters of the North Atlantic and the Arctic. The most highly prized variety is the Norwegian herring and, of these, the younger ones are the best. Fresh herrings are not available in Italy but preserved herrings are imported. The most common preserved herring is the salted smoked golden herring. To prepare herrings, remove the skins and heads, slit open the backs and remove the bones without disturbing the delicious roe. Soak the fillets in a mixture of water and vinegar for 4 hours to remove the salt, then drain and sprinkle with garlic, oregano and chile or with chopped onion and chopped parsley. If you prefer a more delicate taste, soak the herring fillets in milk and then dress with oil and mixed herbs. Another kind of herring that is easily found in Italy is the pickled herring. The flavor is quite strong so if you are adding it to green salads or potato salads, be careful with the quantities.

SMOKED HERRINGS WITH GRAPEFRUIT

Combine the grapefruit juice, lemon juice, olive oil and mustard in a bowl and season with salt and pepper. Place the fennel slices on a serving dish, top with the smoked herring, pour the grapefruit sauce over them and sprinkle with the dill. Put in the refrigerator to marinate for 15 minutes before serving.

ARINGHE AL POMPELMO

Serves 4

juice of 1 grapefruit, strained

juice of ¹/₂ lemon, strained

4 tablespoons olive oil • ¹/₂ teaspoon herb mustard

1 round fennel bulb, thinly sliced

8 smoked herrings, skinned and filleted

1 teaspoon chopped fresh dill

salt and pepper

HERRING AND CAULIFLOWER SALAD

Cook the cauliflower in a pan of salted, boiling water for 5 minutes. Drain and refresh under cold running water. Roll up the herring fillet halves and secure with a toothpick. Combine the cream, mustard, vinegar, olive oil and pearl onion in a bowl and season with salt and pepper. Place the lettuce and red onion in a large salad bowl and top with the cauliflower and herring rolls. Pour the dressing over the salad and keep in a cool place until ready to serve.

INSALATA D'ARINGHE CON CAVOLFIORI

Serves 4

1 cauliflower, cut into flowerets

1 jar (4 ounces) herring fillets in oil,

drained and halved lengthwise

³/₄ cup heavy cream

1 tablespoon Dijon mustard

1 tablespoon red wine vinegar

3 tablespoons olive oil • 1 pearl onion, chopped

1 loose-leaf lettuce heart, such as lollo rosso, chopped

1 red onion, thinly sliced • salt and pepper

SALT COD

AND STOCKFISH

In Italy, there are two, or rather three, names for the same fish – merluzzo (cod) when it is fresh (see page 627), baccalà (salt cod) when it is cut into small pieces and preserved in salt, and stoccafisso (stockfish) when it is dried and sold whole. Salt cod has white flesh and a black skin. It must be left, skin side uppermost, under cold, running water for 18–24 hours to remove all the salt it has absorbed. Alternatively, soak it in cold water for 24 hours, changing the water frequently. To cook, place it in a pan, add cold water to cover and bring just to a boil over medium heat, then lower the heat, cover and simmer for 10 minutes; do not cook it any longer or the flesh becomes tough. Stockfish is completely rigid. To soften, beat, then soak for 2 days and cook thoroughly for up to 3 hours.

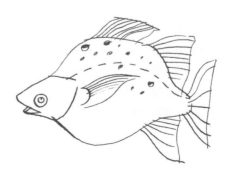

SALT COD AU GRATIN

Preheat the oven to 350°F. Cut the salt cod into fairly large pieces and remove the skin and bones. Heat 4 tablespoons of the olive oil in a roasting pan, add the onion and garlic and cook over low heat, stirring occasionally, for 5 minutes. Add the salt cod and cook until golden brown on both sides, then pour in the milk and season with salt and pepper. Cover the pan with foil, transfer to the oven and bake for about 2 hours or until the milk is completely absorbed. Preheat the broiler. Put the anchovy fillets and the remaining olive oil in a small pan and cook over low heat, mashing with a wooden spoon until the anchovies have almost completely disintegrated. Spoon the anchovy sauce over the salt cod, sprinkle with the parsley and mix gently. Sprinkle with the Parmesan and grill until golden brown.

BACCALÀ AL GRATIN

Serves 4

1³/₄ pounds salt cod, soaked and drained

7 tablespoons olive oil

1 onion, chopped

2 garlic cloves

4 cups milk

4 canned anchovy fillets in oil, drained

1 fresh flat-leaf parsley sprig, chopped

²/₃ cup Parmesan cheese, freshly grated

salt and pepper

SALT COD LIVORNO–STYLE

Place the tomatoes in a food processor and process to a purée. Cut the salt cod into fairly large pieces, pat dry and dust lightly with flour. Heat the oil in a large pan, add the salt cod and cook until lightly browned on both sides. Add the tomatoes, season with salt and pepper and cook over medium heat for a few minutes. Sprinkle with the parsley and garlic and simmer for a further 5 minutes. Serve hot or warm.

BACCALÀ ALLA LIVORNESE

Serves 4

1 pound 2 ounces canned tomatoes

1¹/₂ pounds salt cod, soaked and drained

all-purpose flour, for dusting

scant ¹/₂ cup olive oil

1 fresh flat-leaf parsley sprig, chopped

1 garlic clove, chopped

salt and pepper

SALT COD WITH OLIVES AND CAPERS

Cut the salt cod into fairly large pieces. Chop the anchovy fillets. Heat the olive oil in a pan, add the anchovies and cook over low heat, mashing with a wooden spoon. Add the onion and cook, stirring occasionally, for 5 minutes. Add the salt cod and cook for 5 minutes on each side. Pour in the wine and add the capers and olives. Season with salt if necessary, then simmer, stirring occasionally, for 10–15 minutes and serve.

BACCALÀ CON OLIVE E CAPPERI

Serves 4

1³/₄ pounds salt cod, soaked and drained

2 salted anchovies, heads removed,

cleaned and filleted (see page 596),

soaked in cold water for 10 minutes and drained

2 tablespoons olive oil

1 onion, chopped

³/₄ cup dry white wine

1 tablespoon capers, drained and rinsed

scant 1 cup black olives, pitted and chopped

salt

1³/₄ pounds salt cod, soaked and drained

¹/₂ cup olive oil

1 onion, sliced

1 green bell pepper, halved, seeded and cut into strips

1 red bell pepper, halved, seeded and cut into strips

4 tomatoes, peeled and sliced

11 ounces potatoes, sliced

pinch of cayenne pepper

5 black peppercorns

1 fresh thyme sprig, chopped

1 fresh flat-leaf parsley sprig

1 bay leaf

³/₄ cup dry white wine

scant 1 cup black olives

SALT COD WITH POTATOES AND BELL PEPPERS

Cut the salt cod into large pieces. Heat half the olive oil in a large pan, add the salt cod and cook until lightly browned on both sides. Heat the remaining olive oil in another pan, add the onion and bell peppers and cook, stirring occasionally, for 5 minutes, then add the tomatoes and potatoes and cook for a further 10 minutes. Make alternate layers of salt cod and vegetables in a flameproof casserole. Sprinkle with the cayenne, peppercorns and thyme, add the parsley sprig and bay leaf, pour in the wine and simmer for 50 minutes. Remove and discard the bay leaf and parsley, add the olives and cook for a further 10 minutes.

BACCALÀ FRITTO
Serves 4

1³/₄ pounds salt cod, soaked and drained

vegetable oil, for frying

1 quantity Batter for Frying (see page 1017)

salt

FRIED SALT COD

Cut the salt cod into fairly large pieces and pat dry. Heat plenty of oil in a wide skillet. Dip the pieces of fish in the batter to coat, then fry, in batches, for 5 minutes on each side. Drain on paper towels, season lightly with salt and serve.

STOCCAFISSO ALLA MEDITERRANEA
Serves 4

1³/₄ pounds stockfish, soaked and drained

3 ounces salted anchovies, heads removed, cleaned and filleted (see page 596), soaked in cold water for 10 minutes and drained

scant ¹/₂ cup olive oil

1 onion, chopped

1 garlic clove, chopped

1 fresh flat-leaf parsley sprig, chopped

9 ounces tomatoes, peeled and chopped

1 tablespoon capers, drained and rinsed

salt and pepper

MEDITERRANEAN STOCKFISH

Cut the stockfish into fairly large pieces. Chop the anchovy fillets. Heat the olive oil in a pan, add the onion, garlic and parsley and cook over low heat, stirring occasionally, for 5 minutes. Add the stockfish and cook for 5 minutes on each side. Add the tomatoes, season with salt and pepper and cook for 10 minutes. Add the anchovies, mash them well with a wooden spoon and cook for 5 minutes more. Add the capers, heat through for 1 minute and serve.

VENETO–STYLE CREAMED STOCKFISH

Place the stockfish in a pan, add water to cover and bring to a boil, then lower the heat and simmer for 25–35 minutes. Remove the pan from the heat and let the fish to cool in the liquid. When cold, drain the fish, remove the skin and bones and cut into small pieces. Heat 4 tablespoons of the oil in a pan, add the onion and cook over low heat, stirring occasionally, for 5 minutes. Meanwhile, bring the milk to simmering point in another pan. Add the stockfish to the onion, then gradually add the hot milk and remaining olive oil stirring, vigorously. Simmer for 1 hour until white, frothy and creamy. Season with salt and pepper to taste and serve with polenta.

STOCCAFISSO MANTECATO ALLA VENETA

Serves 4

1 pound 5 ounces stockfish, soaked and drained

²/₃ cup olive oil

¹/₂ onion, chopped

scant ¹/₂ cup milk

salt and pepper

polenta, to serve

WHITEBAIT

In Ligurian cuisine, whitebait refers to anchovy and sardine fry. They are very small, fragile and white, are available in February and March and are appreciated for their delicate flavor. Wash them carefully to get rid of any sand or other impurities. They cook very quickly – a few minutes in boiling water – and are usually eaten dressed with oil and lemon juice. Whitebait are also used in frittata and other simple recipes.

BIANCHETTI ALLA CREMA D'UOVA

Serves 4

4 eggs

5 tablespoons olive oil

1 onion, finely chopped

14 ounces whitebait, washed and drained

juice of 1 lemon, strained

salt and pepper

WHITEBAIT IN EGG CREAM

Lightly beat the eggs with 1 tablespoon hot water and salt and pepper in a bowl. Heat the olive oil in a pan, add the onion and cook over low heat, stirring occasionally, for 5 minutes. Add the whitebait and pour in the egg. Cook, stirring to keep the mixture runny and slightly creamy as it heats. Sprinkle with the lemon juice, mix and serve.

BIANCHETTI ALL'OLIO E LIMONE

Serves 4

11 ounces whitebait, washed and drained

²/₃ cup olive oil

juice of 1 lemon, strained

1 teaspoon Dijon mustard

salt

WHITEBAIT WITH OLIVE OIL AND LEMON

Cook the whitebait in salted, boiling water for 2–3 minutes. Drain and let cool. Whisk together the olive oil, lemon juice and mustard in a bowl, pour the mixture over the fish and serve.

SEA BASS

Sea bass are fairly widespread in the Mediterranean and this large family of fish is found all over the world. Most types are about 16 inches long and weigh about 2¼ pounds, but there are even bigger ones. They are highly prized for their white, lean and delicate flesh. Farmed sea bass are also excellent. The Australian Mulloway is similar in texture to sea bass and a good alternative.

SEA BASS BAKED IN A PACKET

Preheat the oven to 400°F. Cut out a sheet of baking parchment and brush with olive oil. Place the rosemary sprig and one of the garlic cloves in the cavity of the sea bass, season with salt and pepper and place the fish on the baking parchment. Slice the remaining garlic. Sprinkle the fish with the parsley and cover with the lemon slices, onion rings, scallions and garlic slices. Spoon the wine over the fish, fold over the baking parchment to enclose it completely, and seal the edges. Place on a cookie sheet and bake for 15 minutes. Serve with olive oil, lemon slices and salt.

BRANZINO AL CARTOCCIO

Serves 4

olive oil, for brushing and serving

1 fresh rosemary sprig • 2 garlic cloves

2¼-pound sea bass, spines trimmed, scaled and cleaned

1 fresh flat-leaf parsley sprig, chopped

1 lemon, sliced, plus extra for serving

1 onion, sliced into rings

2 scallions, sliced

5 tablespoons dry white wine

salt and pepper

SEA BASS WITH FENNEL

Preheat the oven to 350°F. Sprinkle the dried fennel inside the cavity of the fish. Make several diagonal slashes on each side of the fish, brush it with olive oil and place on a cookie sheet. Bake, turning and brushing with more olive oil occasionally, for about 20 minutes. Season with salt and pepper. Make a bed of fresh fennel slices on a serving dish and place the sea bass on top. Gently warm the brandy in a ladle, then pour it over the fish and ignite. Serve when the flames have died down.

BRANZINO AL FINOCCHIO

Serves 4

large pinch of dried fennel

2¼-pound sea bass, spines trimmed, scaled and cleaned

olive oil, for brushing

¼ cup brandy

salt and pepper

fresh fennel slices, to serve

JELLIED SEA BASS

Put the sea bass in a fish kettle or large pan, pour in the court-bouillon, bring just to a boil, then lower the heat and poach gently for about 20 minutes. Remove from the heat and let cool in the cooking liquid. Prepare the gelatin according to the packet instructions and stir in the sherry or wine. Cook the carrot in salted, boiling water for 15–20 minutes until tender, then drain. Drain the sea bass and pat dry with paper towels. When the gelatin begins to cool, pour a thin layer onto a serving dish and place the fish on top. Garnish with the carrot, egg slices and mayonnaise. Cover carefully with the remaining gelatin, then chill in the refrigerator until set.

BRANZINO IN GELATINA

Serves 4

2¼-pound sea bass, spines trimmed, scaled and cleaned

1 quantity Court-bouillon (see page 591)

2¼ cups dissolved gelatin

1 tablespoon sherry or white wine

1 carrot, sliced

1 egg, hard-cooked, shelled and sliced

1 quantity Mayonnaise (see page 65)

BAKED MARINATED SEA BASS

Pour the olive oil into a dish and add the onion, bay leaf, thyme and parsley. Place the fish in the dish, turning to coat, and let marinate, turning occasionally, for about 1 hour. Preheat the oven to 400°F. Remove and discard the herbs. Transfer the fish to an ovenproof dish or roasting pan, season with salt and pepper and brush with some of the marinade. Bake, basting occasionally with the marinade, for about 20 minutes. Serve with boiled or, better still, steamed potatoes.

BRANZINO MARINATO AL FORNO

Serves 4

5 tablespoons olive oil

1 onion, thinly sliced

1 bay leaf

1 fresh thyme sprig

1 fresh flat-leaf parsley sprig

2¼-pound sea bass, spines trimmed, scaled and cleaned

salt and pepper

boiled or steamed potatoes, to serve

STRIPED MULLET

Striped mullet, also known as gray mullet, are very widespread along Italian coasts and their white flesh has a very pleasant taste, although it is not highly prized. They can reach 20–24 inches in length and weigh as much as 13¹⁄₄ pounds, on average, they weigh 1¹⁄₂–2lb. Striped mullet are usually roasted or grilled whole, but are also good poached. Bottarga is made from their pressed cured roe. It looks like a firm, light-brown sausage and crumbles when cut. It makes a tasty antipasto and is used to season spaghetti (see Spaghettini with Bottarga page 303).

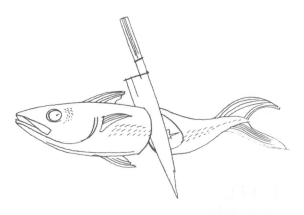

CEFALO ALL'ACETO

Serves 4

3 tablespoons olive oil

1 garlic clove

4 striped mullet, scaled and cleaned

³⁄₄ cup white wine vinegar

2 tablespoons butter

¹⁄₂ teaspoon cornstarch

salt and pepper

STRIPED MULLET IN VINEGAR

Heat the olive oil in a pan, add the garlic clove and cook until it turns brown, then remove and discard it. Add the fish and cook until browned on both sides, then add the vinegar and cook until it has evaporated. Season with salt and pepper and cook over medium heat for 15 minutes. Combine the butter and cornstarch to a paste, add to the pan and stir into the cooking juices to thicken. Cook for a few minutes more and serve.

STRIPED MULLET WITH PARSLEY

Heat the olive oil in a pan, add the garlic and cook until it turns brown, then remove and discard it. Add the fish, season with salt and pepper to taste and cook over medium heat for about 15 minutes. Sprinkle with the parsley, transfer to a warm serving dish, spoon the cooking juices over the fish and garnish with the lemon wedges.

CEFALO AL PREZZEMOLO

Serves 4

3 tablespoons olive oil

1 garlic clove

4 striped mullet, scaled and cleaned

1 fresh flat-leaf parsley sprig, chopped

salt and pepper

1 lemon, cut into wedges, to garnish

STRIPED MULLET AND DILL PACKETS

Preheat the oven to 400°F. Cut four squares of foil, each large enough to hold a fish, and brush with oil. Season the cavities of the fish with salt and pepper and place a dill sprig in each. Put one fish on each foil square and divide the onion and garlic among them. Place a few lemon slices on top of each fish and sprinkle with the wine and brandy. Fold over the foil to enclose the fish completely, place on a cookie sheet and bake for about 10 minutes. Remove from the oven, transfer to a warm serving dish and open the foil packets just before serving.

CEFALO IN CARTOCCIO ALL'ANETO

Serves 4

olive oil, for brushing

4 striped mullet, scaled and cleaned

4 fresh dill sprigs

1 onion, chopped

1 garlic clove, chopped

1 lemon, sliced

$^3/_4$ cup dry white wine

4 teaspoons brandy

salt and pepper

STUFFED STRIPED MULLET IN OLIVE SAUCE

Place a slice of pancetta and a sage leaf in the cavity of each fish and season lightly with salt and pepper. Heat the olive oil in a pan, add the parsley and remaining sage leaves and cook for a few minutes, then remove the pan from the heat and let cool. Place the fish in the pan, return to the heat, cover and cook for 5–6 minutes on each side. Add the wine and cook for about 10 minutes until it has evaporated. Gently stir in the olives, cook for 2 minutes and serve.

CEFALO RIPIENO IN SALSA D'OLIVE

Serves 4

4 pancetta slices

8 fresh sage leaves, chopped

4 striped mullet, scaled and cleaned

5 tablespoons olive oil

1 fresh flat-leaf parsley sprig, chopped

5 tablespoons dry white wine

20 mixed green and black olives, pitted and chopped

salt and pepper

GROUPER

Grouper are among the most highly prized sea fish because their white flesh is tasty and tender. They are best cooked simply; for example, by poaching (their stock is excellent) or baking. Another way to enjoy them and bring out their flavor is to braise them, when they are excellent on spaghetti. Many grouper are more than 31 inches long and some members of the family can reach as much as 5 feet in length and 110 pounds in weight. Large grouper are usually sold as steaks, while smaller grouper, sufficient for two to four servings, are available whole. If you have difficulty finding grouper, you can substitute sea bass or sea trout.

BAKED GROUPER

CERNIA AL FORNO

Serves 4

3 tablespoons olive oil, plus extra for brushing

2¼-pound grouper, fins trimmed and cleaned

2¼ cups white wine

juice of ½ lemon, strained

2 tablespoons capers, drained and rinsed

1 fresh red chile, seeded and chopped

salt and pepper

Preheat the oven to 350°F. Brush an ovenproof dish with olive oil. Season the fish inside and out with salt and pepper and place in the dish. Brush with the oil and pour in the wine and lemon juice. Bake for 15 minutes, then add the capers and chile. Continue to cook, basting occasionally, for a further 30 minutes until cooked through. Transfer to a warm dish, spoon the sauce over the fish and serve.

Serves 4

1 shallot, sliced

1 carrot, sliced

1 celery stalk, chopped

1 garlic clove

1 fresh flat-leaf parsley sprig

1 fresh thyme sprig

juice of 1 lemon, strained

4 black peppercorns

2¼-pound grouper, fins trimmed and cleaned

salt

For the sauce

2 avocados

3 tablespoons olive oil

3–4 tablespoons lemon juice, strained

½ onion, chopped

salt and pepper

For the garnish

lemon slices

fresh flat-leaf parsley leaves

GROUPER WITH AVOCADO

Pour 8¾ cups water into a large pan, add the shallot, carrot, celery, garlic, parsley, thyme, lemon juice, peppercorns and a pinch of salt and bring to a boil. Lower the heat, cover simmer for about 30 minutes. Remove from the heat and let cool. Add the fish to the cooled stock and bring just to a boil, then lower the heat and simmer for 30 minutes. Transfer the fish to a dish, let cool, then chill in the refrigerator for at least 3 hours. Prepare the sauce just before serving. Halve and pit the avocados and scoop out the flesh into a food processor. Add the olive oil, lemon juice and onion, season with salt and pepper and process to a purée. The sauce should have the consistency of mayonnaise, so if it is too thick, thin it with more lemon juice. Place the fish on a serving dish, spread with a little avocado sauce, leaving the head and tail uncovered, and garnish with lemon slices and parsley leaves. Serve with the remaining sauce.

Serves 4

4 grouper steaks

all-purpose flour, for dusting

2 tablespoons olive oil

1 onion, finely chopped

14 ounces plum tomatoes, peeled, seeded and diced

1¼ cups green or black olives, pitted

salt and pepper

GROUPER WITH OLIVES

Lightly dust the fish with flour. Heat the oil in a pan, add the onion and cook over low heat, stirring occasionally, for 5 minutes. Stir in the tomatoes and simmer for 10 minutes. Add the fish, 2 tablespoons hot water and the olives and season with salt and pepper to taste. Cover and simmer gently for about 30 minutes. Remove the lid and, if the cooking juices are too runny, increase the heat to medium and cook for a few more minutes until thickened. Transfer the fish and sauce to a warm serving dish.

MONKFISH

In Italy, monkfish are known as coda di rospo – toad's tail – because only their long fleshy tails are sold, although in Veneto the large, ugly heads, which are sold separately, are used for delicious stocks and jellies. The alternative American name for monkfish is goosefish. Monkfish tails are almost always sold skinned, making them very easy to prepare. However, you may still need to remove the transparent, grayish membrane that covers the flesh. Otherwise, all you need do is rinse quickly and pat dry. The flavorsome, pink flesh turns white when cooked, and although it has compact fibers it is very tender. In addition, it is nearly completely boneless so there is very little waste. During cooking the volume of monkfish decreases considerably so this must be taken into account when calculating quantities. Monkfish are ideal for a number of fabulous dishes.

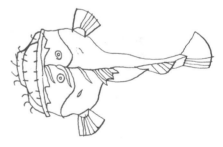

MONKFISH WITH LEMON

Preheat the oven to 425°F. Remove and discard the membrane from the monkfish and snap the backbone in a few places. Make small slits in the flesh and insert the garlic slivers. Season with salt and place in an ovenproof dish. Halve one of the lemons and squeeze the juice from one of the halves. Peel the remaining lemon and lemon half, removing all traces of pith, and slice thinly. Cover the fish with the lemon slices. Pour in half the olive oil and put the dish in the oven. When quite a lot of liquid has formed on the base of the dish, carefully pour it off. Add the remaining olive oil and the lemon juice. Lower the oven temperature to 350°F and bake for about 40 minutes. Transfer to a warm serving dish.

CODA DI ROSPO AL LIMONE

Serves 4

2¹/₄ pounds monkfish

1 garlic clove, very thinly sliced

2 lemons

³/₄ cup olive oil

salt

615

CODA DI ROSPO AL VINO ROSSO

Serves 4

$^1/_4$ cup butter

1 shallot, chopped

1 carrot, chopped

2 tablespoons brandy

1$^1/_2$ cups red wine

4 fresh sage leaves

1 fresh thyme sprig, leaves only

1 tablespoon red wine vinegar

2$^1/_4$ pounds monkfish fillets, cut into chunks

1 tablespoon all-purpose flour

2 tablespoons olive oil

3$^1/_2$ ounces pearl onions, chopped

3$^1/_2$ ounces mushrooms

salt and pepper

MONKFISH IN RED WINE

Melt half the butter in a pan, add the shallot and carrot and cook over low heat, stirring occasionally, for 10 minutes until lightly browned. Add the brandy and cook until it has evaporated. Add the red wine, sage, thyme and vinegar and season with salt and pepper. Cover and simmer very gently for about 20 minutes. Strain the sauce, return it to the pan and reheat thoroughly. Add the fish and cook for 10 minutes. Remove the fish from the pan with a slotted spoon and keep warm. Increase the heat under the sauce to high and cook until reduced. Meanwhile, combine the remaining butter and the flour to a paste, then stir it into the sauce to thicken. Cook, stirring constantly, for 10 minutes. Heat the olive oil in another pan, add the onions and cook, stirring frequently, until softened. Add the mushrooms and stir in the sauce, then add the fish and cook over low heat for 5 minutes. Transfer to a warm serving dish.

CODA DI ROSPO
CON CAVOLFIORE E CIPOLLE

Serves 4

1 bunch of scallions

1 cauliflower, cut into flowerets

scant $^1/_2$ cup butter

juice of $^1/_2$ lemon, strained

2$^1/_4$ pounds monkfish fillets, thickly sliced

1$^1/_2$ cups dry white wine

3 tablespoons heavy cream

1 tablespoon fresh flat-leaf parsley, chopped

salt and pepper

MONKFISH WITH CAULIFLOWER AND SCALLIONS

Chop the white and green parts of the scallions separately. Blanch the cauliflower in salted, boiling water for 5 minutes, then drain and refresh under cold, running water. Melt half the butter in a pan, add the white parts of the scallions and cook over low heat, stirring occasionally, until softened. Add the cauliflower, lemon juice and the green parts of the scallions and cook over low heat for 10 minutes. Melt the remaining butter in another pan, add the fish and cook for 3 minutes on each side. Pour in the wine, cover and cook over medium heat for about 15 minutes. Gently stir in the cream, season with salt and pepper and cook for a few minutes more until thickened. Transfer the fish to a warm serving dish, surround with the cauliflower and scallions and sprinkle with the cooking juices and parsley.

MONKFISH WITH ANCHOVY SAUCE

Preheat the oven to 400°F. Grease an ovenproof dish with butter and place the fish in it. Thinly pare the lemon rind and sprinkle it over the fish with the shallot and parsley. Add 2 tablespoons of the olive oil and the wine, season with salt and pepper and bake for 30 minutes. Chop the anchovy fillets. Place the flesh in a bowl and mash. Squeeze the juice from half the lemon and strain. Hard-cook the eggs, refresh under cold water and shell, then halve lengthwise and scoop out the yolks. Add the egg yolks and lemon juice to the anchovies, mix well and gradually stir in the remaining olive oil to make a fairly thick sauce. Transfer the slices of monkfish to a warm serving dish and spoon the sauce over them. Serve with steamed potatoes.

CODA DI ROSPO CON SALSA D'ACCIUGHE

Serves 4

butter, for greasing

4 monkfish slices

1 lemon

1 shallot, finely chopped

1 fresh flat-leaf parsley sprig, chopped

7 tablespoons olive oil

5 tablespoons white wine

4 salted anchovies, heads removed,
cleaned and filleted (see page 596),
soaked in cold water for 10 minutes and drained

2 eggs

salt and pepper

steamed potato wedges, to serve

MONKFISH AND SHRIMP ROULADES

Preheat the oven to 350°F. Slice the monkfish fillets, make incisions in the flesh and insert the shrimp. Heat half the olive oil in a small, nonstick skillet, add the eggplant slices and cook over medium heat until light golden brown on both sides, then remove from the skillet. Place the monkfish slices on the eggplant slices, roll up and tie with kitchen string. Place the rolls in a roasting pan and bake for 25 minutes. Remove the pan from the oven and prick the roulades all over with a fork. Let stand for 5 minutes, then transfer to a plate and keep warm. Set the roasting pan over low heat and stir in the flour, then stir in the wine, lemon juice and Worcestershire sauce. Gradually stir in the stock and cook, stirring constantly, until thickened. Heat the remaining olive oil in a small pan, add the shallots and garlic and cook over low heat, stirring occasionally, for 5 minutes. Add the olives, arugula and stock mixture, season with salt and pepper and cook for a further 5 minutes. Cut the roulades into thick slices, place on a warm serving dish and spoon the hot sauce over them.

INVOLTINI DI CODA DI ROSPO
CON GAMBERETTI

Serves 6

2¹/₂ pounds monkfish fillets

7 ounces cooked peeled shrimp

2 tablespoons olive oil

3 long eggplants, thinly sliced lengthwise

¹/₄ cup all-purpose flour

5 tablespoons dry white wine

juice of 1 lemon, strained

dash of Worcestershire sauce

²/₃ cup Concentrated Fish Stock (see page 210)

4 shallots, chopped

1 garlic clove, chopped

¹/₂ cup black olives, pitted and chopped

¹/₂ bunch of arugula, chopped

salt and pepper

MONKFISH STEW
WITH TURMERIC RICE

Lightly dust the monkfish with flour. Heat the olive oil and 2 tablespoons of the butter in a pan, add the onions and cook over low heat, stirring occasionally, for 5 minutes. Add the fish and cook, stirring, for 2 minutes, then add the wine and cook until it has evaporated. Add the orange and lemon rind, ginger and Tabasco, season with salt and pepper and cook for a further 10 minutes, then add the tomato and parsley. Meanwhile, put the rice in a pan, add cold water to cover, a pinch of salt and enough turmeric to turn the water bright yellow. Bring to a boil, cover and simmer for 15 minutes. Drain the rice, spread it out well on a warm serving dish, dot with the remaining butter and serve with the hot fish stew.

SPEZZATINO DI CODA DI ROSPO
CON RISO ALLA CURCUMA

Serves 6

2 pounds monkfish fillets, cut into chunks

all-purpose flour, for dusting

2 tablespoons olive oil

3 tablespoons butter

2 onions, finely chopped

³/₄ cup dry white wine

rind of 1 orange, cut into thin strips

rind of 1 lemon, cut into thin strips

1-inch piece of fresh ginger root,

cut into strips

dash of Tabasco sauce

1 tomato, peeled, seeded and diced

1 fresh flat-leaf parsley sprig, chopped

¹/₂–1¹/₂ cups long-grain rice

¹/₂–1¹/₂ teaspoons ground turmeric

salt and pepper

PORGY AND SEA BREAM

GARLIC

This large family of fish is found in many parts of the world. Red porgy are probably the most commonly available type in the United States (although other varieties are also sold) and can be substituted for other types; sea bass are also a good alternative. The three most popular varieties in Italy are dentex, giltheaded sea bream, and white sea bream. Sheepshead bream and scup are the most highly regarded American family members although they are quite a lot smaller, weighing 12 ounces–3¹/₄ pounds. Red porgy, which is the same fish as the European or Crouch's sea bream, weigh up to 2³/₄ pounds and grow up to 1 foot long. If a larger whole fish is required, substitute red snapper. The Italian recipes in this section are divided into three parts: dentex, giltheaded sea bream, and white sea bream. Dentex, often sold as fillets, can be large – up to 3¹/₄ feet long and up to 26¹/₂ pounds in weight. Their lean, firm flesh is highly prized and dentex stock is ideal for rice soups. Giltheaded sea bream, sometimes known by their French name daurade, are mainly caught in the European waters of the eastern Atlantic coast and the Mediterranean. They are among the most valued sea fish because of their delicate flavor. They vary from 12–24 inches long and their weight may, exceptionally, reach as much as 22 pounds. White sea bream are similar to giltheaded sea bream, but much larger. They can be recognised by the large black ring around the base of the tail. Their richer flesh is particularly suitable for adding flavor to fish soups. White sea bream easily exceed 3¹/₄ pounds in weight, but the best fish for cooking whole weigh about 2¹/₄ pounds.

DENTICE AL SALE

Serves 6

3^1/$_4$-pound porgy, scaled and cleaned

12 cups coarse sea salt

olive oil, for drizzling

juice of 1 lemon, strained

salt and pepper

PORGY BAKED
IN A SALT CRUST

Preheat the oven to 400°F. Season the cavity of the fish with salt and pepper. Line a roasting pan with a sheet of foil, sprinkle 2^2/$_3$ cups of the sea salt on the base and place the fish on top. Cover it completely with the remaining salt and bake for about 45 minutes (allow 15 minutes per 1 pound 2 ounces). Remove the pan from the oven, break the salt crust and lift out the fish. Remove and discard the skin, place the fish on a warm serving dish and drizzle with olive oil and the lemon juice.

DENTICE BRASATO

Serves 4

^{1}/$_2$ onion, chopped

1 carrot, chopped

1 celery stalk, chopped

2^1/$_4$-pound porgy, scaled and cleaned

olive oil, for drizzling

1^1/$_2$ cups white wine

salt and pepper

BRAISED PORGY

Preheat the oven to 350°F. Combine the onion, carrot and celery and spread out the mixture in a roasting pan. Place the fish, whole or sliced, on top and season with salt and pepper to taste. Drizzle with olive oil, pour in the wine and add enough water almost to cover the fish. Bring to a boil over medium heat, then transfer to the oven. Cook, basting frequently, for about 30 minutes (allow about 15 minutes per 1 pound 2 ounces).

DENTICE IN GELATINA

Serves 4

2^1/$_4$-pound porgy, scaled and cleaned

1 quantity Court-bouillon (see page 591)

2^1/$_4$ cups dissolved gelatin

1 tablespoon sherry or dry white wine

1 carrot, sliced

1 egg, hard-cooked, shelled and sliced

1 quantity Mayonnaise (see page 65)

JELLIED PORGY

Put the porgy in a fish kettle or large pan, pour in the court-bouillon, bring just to a boil, then lower the heat and poach gently for about 20 minutes. Remove from the heat and let cool in the cooking liquid. Prepare the gelatin according to the packet instructions and stir in the sherry or wine. Cook the carrot in salted, boiling water for 15–20 minutes until tender, then drain. Drain the fish and pat dry with paper towels. When the gelatin begins to cool, pour a thin layer onto a serving dish and place the fish on top. Garnish with the carrot, egg slices and mayonnaise. Cover carefully with the remaining gelatin, then chill in the refrigerator until set.

BROILED PORGY

Combine the olive oil, lemon juice and parsley in a dish, season with salt and pepper, and add the fish, turning to coat, and leave in a cool place to marinate for 3 hours. Preheat the broiler. Drain the fish, reserving the marinade, and sprinkle with the bread crumbs, pressing them on with your fingers. Cook the fish under the broiler, turning and brushing with the reserved marinade two or three times, for about 15 minutes until the flesh flakes easily.

ORATA AI FERRI

Serves 4

4 tablespoons olive oil

juice of 1 lemon, strained

1 fresh flat-leaf parsley sprig, chopped

4 x 9–11-ounce porgy,
scaled and cleaned

³/₄ cup fine bread crumbs

salt and pepper

PORGY WITH FENNEL BULBS

Preheat the oven to 350°F. Cook the fennel in salted, boiling water for 10 minutes, then drain. Put the thyme sprig in the cavity of the fish and season the cavity with salt and pepper. Place the fish in an ovenproof dish, add the garlic, drizzle with olive oil and season with salt and pepper to taste. Arrange the fennel all round the fish and bake, turning halfway through cooking, for about 30 minutes. Drizzle the fish with the lemon juice and serve.

ORATA AI FINOCCHI

Serves 4

4 fennel bulbs, trimmed and halved

1 fresh thyme sprig

2¹/₄-pound porgy, scaled and cleaned

1 garlic clove

olive oil, for drizzling

juice of 2 lemons, strained

salt and pepper

BAKED PORGY

Preheat the oven to 400°F. Spread out the onions in an ovenproof dish and place the fish on top. Place the tomatoes around the fish and cover it with the lemon slices. Season with salt and pepper, pour in the olive oil and wine and add the bay leaf. Bake for about 20 minutes. Sprinkle with the parsley and thyme before serving.

ORATA AL FORNO

Serves 4

2 onions, thinly sliced

2¹/₄-pound porgy,
scaled and cleaned

3 tomatoes, cut into wedges and seeded

2 lemons, thinly sliced

1 tablespoon olive oil

scant 1 cup dry white wine

1 bay leaf • 1 fresh thyme sprig, chopped

1 fresh flat-leaf parsley sprig, chopped

salt and pepper

623

PORGY WITH OLIVES

ORATA ALLE OLIVE

Serves 4

2 tablespoons butter

2 tablespoons olive oil • 2 shallots, chopped

2 tomatoes, peeled, seeded and chopped

1 yellow bell pepper, halved, seeded and cut into strips

1 fresh thyme sprig, chopped

1 fresh chervil sprig, chopped

1$^1/_2$ cups dry white wine

$^3/_4$ cup pitted green olives

$^3/_4$ cup pitted black olives

2$^1/_4$-pound porgy,

scaled and cleaned

salt and pepper

Preheat the oven to 350°F. Heat the butter and oil in a pan, add the shallots and cook over low heat, stirring occasionally, for 5 minutes. Add the tomatoes, yellow bell pepper and herbs, season with salt and pepper and cook for a few minutes more. Pour in the wine and add the green and black olives. Season the cavity of the fish with salt and pepper, place it in an ovenproof dish and spoon the olive sauce over it. Bake for about 30 minutes.

PORGY WITH ZUCCHINI

SARAGO ALLE ZUCCHINE

Serves 4

1 shallot • 1 carrot

1 bouquet garni

pinch of curry powder

1$^2/_3$ cups dry white wine

4 zucchini

2 egg yolks

1 teaspoon Dijon mustard

scant 1 cup olive oil, plus extra for brushing

scant 1 cup plain yogurt

2$^1/_4$-pound porgy, scaled and cleaned

1 fresh chervil sprig, chopped

salt and pepper

Put the shallot, carrot, bouquet garni and curry powder in a pan, pour in 2$^1/_2$ cups water and the wine and season with salt and pepper. Bring to a boil, then lower the heat and simmer for 30 minutes. Meanwhile, steam the zucchini for about 15 minutes, then cut into fairly thick slices. Preheat the oven to 350°F. Combine the egg yolks, mustard and a pinch of salt in a bowl, then gradually whisk in the olive oil and stir in the yogurt. Brush a sheet of foil with olive oil, place the fish on top and place on a cookie sheet. Bake for 30 minutes, sprinkling with the curry stock as the skin dries. Remove the fish from the oven and let cool slightly. Transfer to a warm serving dish, surround with the zucchini and sprinkle with the chervil. Serve with the yogurt sauce.

AROMATIC PORGY

SARAGO AROMATICO

Serves 4

2 garlic cloves

1 tablespoon fresh rosemary needles

1 fresh flat-leaf parsley sprig

1 small fresh thyme sprig

2$^1/_4$-pound porgy, scaled and cleaned

$^3/_4$ cup bread crumbs • 6 tablespoons olive oil

juice of 1 lemon, strained

salt and pepper

Preheat the oven to 350°F. Chop one of the garlic cloves, the rosemary needles, parsley and thyme together with a pinch of salt. Fill the cavity of the fish with the herbs and place the fish in an ovenproof dish. Season with salt and pepper and sprinkle with the bread crumbs. Combine the olive oil, lemon juice, 2 tablespoons water and the remaining garlic clove in a bowl and pour the mixture over the fish. Bake for 20 minutes.

ROAST PORGY

Preheat the oven to 350°F. Make small incisions in the thickest parts of the fish and insert the strips of bacon fat and strips of anchovy. Brush a sheet of foil with oil, place the fish on top and fold the foil over to enclose it completely. Place on a cookie sheet and bake for 30 minutes. Remove the cookie sheet from the oven, unwrap the fish and pour the cooking juices into a small skillet. Wrap the fish again and keep warm. Add the wine to the pan and cook over high heat until reduced by at least one-third. Remove the pan from the heat and gradually stir in the butter. Place the fish on a warm serving dish and serve with the sauce.

SARAGO ARROSTO
Serves 4
3¼-pound white sea bream, scaled and cleaned
1 ounce bacon fat, cut into strips
2 ounces canned anchovy fillets in oil,
drained and cut into strips
olive oil, for brushing
1½ cups white wine
6 tablespoons butter, cut into pieces

PORGY WITH MUSHROOMS

Pour the wine and 3 cups water into a pan, add the onion, lemon juice, herbs and peppercorns and season with salt. Bring to a boil, then lower the heat and simmer for 15 minutes. Add the fish and cook for 20 minutes, then drain and strain the stock. Preheat the oven to 350°F. Skin the fish, remove and discard the bones and cut the flesh into chunks. Place the fish in an ovenproof dish and surround it with the mushrooms. Mix the cornstarch with 2 tablespoons of the cold stock in a bowl. Bring 2¼ cups of the stock to a boil, pour in the cornstarch mixture and cook, stirring constantly, until thickened. Season with salt and pepper to taste and stir in the cream. Pour the sauce over the fish and mushrooms and bake for about 10 minutes.

SARAGO CON FUNGHI
Serves 4
1½ cups white wine
1 onion, sliced
juice of 1 lemon, strained
1 fresh thyme sprig
6 fresh basil leaves
1 fresh chervil sprig
5 black peppercorns
1¾-pound porgy, scaled and cleaned
9 ounces mushrooms
2 teaspoons cornstarch
1 tablespoon heavy cream
salt and pepper

FISH TARTARE WITH KIWI FRUIT

Combine the lemon juice, lime juice, olive oil and peppercorns in a dish and season with salt. Using a very sharp knife, cut the porgy and sardines into thin slices. Add them to dish with the smoked salmon and mix gently. Let marinate in a cool place, but not in the refrigerator, for 1 hour. Drain the fish and pat dry with paper towels. Put each type of fish in the middle of a separate plate and garnish each with the kiwi slices in the shape of a flower.

TARTARA DI PESCI AI KIWI
Serves 4
juice of 5 lemons, strained
juice of 2 limes, strained
4 tablespoons olive oil
4 black peppercorns, lightly crushed
1¾-pound porgy, filleted
3 sardines, filleted
2 smoked salmon slices, cut into strips
salt
4 kiwi fruits, peeled and sliced, to garnish

625

TRANCE DI DENTICE MARINATE

Serves 4

juice of 3 lemons, strained

6 tablespoons olive oil

1 garlic clove, finely chopped

1 fresh mint sprig, finely chopped

1 fresh thyme sprig, finely chopped

pinch of dried oregano

1 fresh flat-leaf parsley sprig, finely chopped

4 porgy fillets

salt and pepper

MARINATED PORGY

Combine the lemon juice, 2 tablespoons of the olive oil, the garlic, mint, thyme, oregano and parsley in a dish. Add the fish, turning to coat, and let marinate in a cool place for 3 hours. Drain the fish, reserving the marinade. Heat the remaining oil in a skillet, add the fish and cook on both sides over high heat for a few minutes, then sprinkle with 2 tablespoons of the reserved marinade and turn the fish. Cook for a few minutes more until the flesh flakes easily, season with salt and pepper and carefully transfer to a warm serving dish with a slotted spoon.

COD

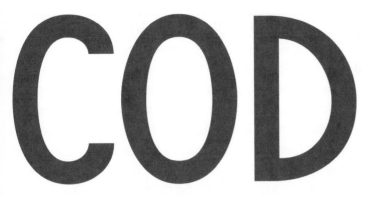

Cod is a tasty, white fish from the North Atlantic. In Italy it is also popular dried, and dried and salted (see Salt Cod – Stockfish page 602). Cod can reach considerable sizes – up to 5 feet – and are usually sold as steaks or fillets. It was once an inexpensive fish, but over-fishing has caused prices to rise. The Australian flathead is a good alternative for all cod recipes.

OIL   VINEGAR

COD WITH LEEKS

Melt the butter in a pan, add the leeks and cook over medium heat, stirring occasionally, for 5 minutes. Lower the heat, cover and cook very gently for 15 minutes, then season with salt and pepper. Meanwhile, spread out the flour in a shallow dish, lightly beat the egg in another shallow dish and spread out the bread crumbs in a third. Heat the oil in a large pan. Dip the cod first in the flour, then in the egg and, finally, in the bread crumbs. Fry in the hot oil, turning occasionally, for about 10 minutes until golden brown and cooked through (see page 593). Remove with a slotted spatula, drain on paper towels and season with salt. Arrange on a warm serving dish and surround with the leeks.

MERLUZZO AI PORRI

Serves 4

1/4 cup butter

4 leeks, white parts only, sliced

1/2 cup all-purpose flour

1 egg

1 cup bread crumbs

vegetable oil, for deep-frying

4 x 5-ounce cod fillets

salt and pepper

COD IN CURRY SAUCE

Put the cod in a pan, add water to cover and a pinch of salt and bring just to a boil, then lower the heat and simmer gently for 15 minutes. Remove with a slotted spatula, drain well and keep warm. Heat the olive oil in a pan, add the onion and cook over low heat, stirring occasionally, for 5 minutes. Add 2/3 cup of the stock, sprinkle with the curry powder and saffron and simmer for 2 minutes. Beat the egg yolk with the remaining stock, pour into the pan and cook until the sauce has thickened. Season with salt and pepper and pour the sauce over the cod.

MERLUZZO AL CURRY

Serves 4

1 3/4 pounds cod fillets

1 tablespoon olive oil

1 onion, thinly sliced

3/4 cup Fish Stock (see page 208)

1 teaspoon curry powder

pinch of saffron powder

1 egg yolk

salt and pepper

BAKED COD WITH VEGETABLES

MERLUZZO AL FORNO CON VERDURE

Serves 4

4 cod fillets

juice of 1 lemon, strained

3 ounces pancetta, sliced

¼ cup butter

4 tomatoes, peeled and chopped

1 leek, white part only, thinly sliced

2 carrots, sliced

1 onion, thinly sliced

scant 1 cup milk

salt and pepper

Preheat the oven to 400°F. Sprinkle the cod with the lemon juice, season with salt and wrap in the pancetta slices. Melt the butter in a flameproof casserole, add the tomatoes, leek, carrots and onion and cook, stirring constantly, for about 10 minutes, then season with salt and pepper. Add the fish, cover and bake for about 25 minutes. Lower the oven temperature to 350°F. Pour the milk into the casserole, return to the oven and bake for a further 15 minutes. Transfer the fish to a serving dish, ladle the hot cooking juices over it and serve.

PROVENÇAL COD

MERLUZZO ALLA PROVENZALE

Serves 4

1¾ pounds cod fillets

1½ cups white wine vinegar

1 fresh thyme sprig

2 potatoes, unpeeled

olive oil, for drizzling

¼ cup milk

2 shallots, chopped

2 tablespoons butter

juice of ½ lemon, strained

1 fresh flat-leaf parsley sprig, chopped

salt and pepper

toasted croûtons, to serve

Put the fish into a pan, pour in water to cover and add a pinch of salt, the vinegar and thyme. Bring just to a boil, then lower the heat and simmer gently for about 10 minutes. Remove the pan from the heat and let the fish to cool in its own stock. Meanwhile, cook the potatoes in lightly salted, boiling water for about 30 minutes until tender, then drain, peel and mash. Drain the fish and flake the flesh, removing any remaining pin bones. Place the fish in a large, heatproof bowl or the top of a double boiler. Season with pepper, drizzle with olive oil, add the milk, potatoes, shallots and butter and mix gently. Set over a pan of barely simmering water and heat through. Sprinkle with the lemon juice and parsley and serve with toasted croûtons.

SICILIAN COD

MERLUZZO ALLA SICILIANA

Serves 4

3 tablespoons olive oil, plus extra for brushing

3½ ounces salted anchovies, heads removed, cleaned and filleted (see page 596), soaked in cold water for 10 minutes and drained

2¼-pound cod, cleaned and boned

1 fresh rosemary sprig, plus extra chopped

2 fresh basil leaves, plus extra chopped

1 cup bread crumbs

salt and pepper

scant 1 cup pitted black olives, to garnish

Preheat the oven to 400°F. Brush an ovenproof dish with oil. Chop the anchovy fillets. Heat 2 tablespoons of the olive oil in a pan, add the anchovies and cook, mashing with a wooden spoon until they have almost completely disintegrated. Spoon a little of the anchovy mixture inside the cavity of the cod and add the rosemary sprig, basil leaves and remaining olive oil. Close the cavity. Spoon the remaining anchovy mixture into the prepared dish, add the fish, sprinkle with chopped rosemary and basil and the bread crumbs, season with salt and pepper to taste and bake for 30 minutes. Serve surrounded by the olives.

COD STEW WITH OLIVES AND CAPERS

Lightly dust the zucchini with flour, shaking off the excess. Heat half the olive oil in a skillet, add the zucchini slices, in batches, and cook until they are golden brown on both sides. Remove with a slotted spoon and drain on paper towels, then sprinkle with salt and keep warm. Heat the remaining olive oil in a pan, add the onion and celery and cook over low heat, stirring occasionally, for 5 minutes. Add the strained tomatoes, capers and olives and simmer for about 10 minutes. Increase the heat to high, add the cod and cook for a few more minutes. Season with salt and pepper, add the zucchini, lower the heat, cover and simmer for 30 minutes.

SPEZZATINO DI MERLUZZO
CON OLIVE E CAPPERI

Serves 4

4 zucchini, thinly sliced

all-purpose flour, for dusting

6 tablespoons olive oil

1 onion, chopped

1 celery stalk, chopped

scant 1 cup bottled strained tomatoes

1 tablespoon capers, drained, rinsed and chopped

scant 1 cup green olives, pitted and chopped

1 pound 5 ounces cod fillets, coarsely chopped

salt and pepper

COD AND WALNUT TERRINE

Preheat the oven to 275°F. Line a terrine or loaf tin with baking parchment. Season the cod with salt and place a layer of the fillets in the terrine or loaf pan. Combine the parsley, chervil and bread crumbs in a bowl. Sprinkle a little of the bread crumb mixture into the terrine or loaf pan, then some walnuts, some capers, a few leaves of arugula and a few thyme leaves. Continue making alternate layers until all the ingredients are used, ending with a layer of cod. Drizzle generously with olive oil, cover with foil and place in a roasting pan. Pour in boiling water to come about halfway up the sides and bake for 40 minutes. Remove the terrine or loaf pan from the oven and set aside, still covered, to cool, then turn out onto a serving dish. To make the sauce, whisk together the vinegar and olive oil in a bowl, stir in the capers and garlic and season with salt and pepper. Serve the cod terrine with the sauce.

TERRINA DI MERLUZZO CON LE NOCI

Serves 4

1 pound 5 ounces cod fillets

1 fresh flat-leaf parsley sprig, chopped

1 fresh chervil sprig, chopped

1³/₄ cups bread crumbs

¹/₂ cup shelled walnuts, chopped

2 tablespoons salted capers, rinsed

1 bunch of arugula

1 fresh thyme sprig

olive oil, for drizzling

salt

For the sauce

1 tablespoon balsamic vinegar

4–5 tablespoons olive oil

1 tablespoon capers, drained and rinsed

¹/₂ garlic clove, chopped

salt and pepper

HAKE

Hake is a similar fish to cod, but, unlike cod, is found in the Mediterranean Sea. It can grow up to 3¹/₄ feet long and is mostly sold in portions. The delicate, easily digestible flesh is excellent poached and seasoned with oil and lemon juice or served with mayonnaise. Hake are easy to bone and may also be bought frozen. If hake is not available, substitute it with cod.

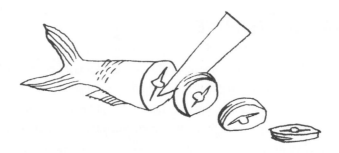

NASELLO CON PATATE

Serves 4

olive oil, for brushing and drizzling

4 potatoes, thinly sliced

1³/₄ pounds hake fillets

1 fresh thyme sprig

1 fresh rosemary sprig

salt and white pepper

HAKE WITH POTATOES

Preheat the oven to 400°F. Brush an ovenproof dish with olive oil and arrange half the potatoes in a layer on the base. Place the fish on top, add the thyme and rosemary and season with salt and pepper. Cover with the remaining potato slices and drizzle with olive oil. Bake for 30 minutes.

NASELLO IN SALSA VERDE

Serves 4

2 tablespoons olive oil, plus extra for brushing

4 hake steaks

1 onion, chopped

1 fresh flat-leaf parsley sprig, chopped

1 celery stalk, chopped plus a few leaves

juice of 1 lemon, strained

salt and pepper

HAKE IN GREEN SAUCE

Preheat the oven to 400°F. Brush an ovenproof dish with oil, place the fish in it and bake for about 10 minutes. Meanwhile, heat the olive oil in a pan, add the onion and cook over low heat, stirring occasionally, for 5 minutes until softened. Season with salt and pepper, remove from the heat and keep warm. Stir in the parsley, celery leaves and lemon juice. Serve the hake with this green sauce.

NASELLO INSAPORITO AGLI SCALOGNI

Serves 4

juice of 2 lemons, strained

2 tablespoons olive oil

1 pound 5 ounces hake fillets, cut into chunks

2 tablespoons butter

2 shallots, finely chopped

scant 1/2 cup dry white wine

salt and pepper

HAKE IN SHALLOT SAUCE

Preheat the broiler. Combine the lemon juice and olive oil. Season the fish with salt and pepper and sprinkle with the lemon and olive oil mixture. Broil for 8 minutes, then transfer to a serving dish and keep warm. Melt the butter in a pan, add the shallots and cook over low heat, stirring occasionally, for 5 minutes. Increase the heat to medium, add the wine and cook for a further 5 minutes. Season with salt and pepper to taste, spoon the sauce over the fish and serve.

NASELLO IN TEGAME

Serves 4

4 tablespoons olive oil

2 shallots, thinly sliced

1 leek, white part only, thinly sliced

1 celery stalk, chopped

2 carrots, chopped

1 garlic clove, chopped

1 fresh flat-leaf parsley sprig, chopped

1 fresh thyme sprig, chopped

scant 1/2 cup dry white wine

7 ounces tomatoes, peeled, seeded and chopped

1 teaspoon tomato paste

1 tablespoon capers, drained and rinsed

10 pitted black olives

2 dill pickles, drained and sliced

1 teaspoon Dijon mustard

2 1/4 pounds hake steaks

salt and pepper

FRIED HAKE

Heat half the olive oil in a pan over medium heat, add the shallots, leek, celery, carrots, garlic and herbs and cook, stirring frequently, for about 10 minutes. Pour in the wine and cook until it has evaporated, then add the tomatoes and season with salt and pepper. Mix the tomato paste with 1 tablespoon hot water in a small bowl and stir into the pan. Cook over medium heat, stirring occasionally, for about 20 minutes. Stir in the capers, olives, dill pickles and mustard and cook for a further 5 minutes. Meanwhile, heat the remaining olive oil in a nonstick skillet, add the fish and cook over medium heat until lightly browned on both sides. Season with salt and pepper, transfer to the pan of vegetables and cook for 10 minutes, then serve.

TOPE
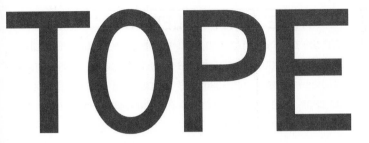

Known as sea veal in some parts of Italy and popularly called rock salmon elsewhere, this fish is actually dogfish and a member of the shark family. It is always sold in fillets and there is no waste. Although tope is nutritious, low in fat and easy to digest, it is not very highly prized. It is good stewed, but also lends itself to the cooking methods used for tuna and swordfish.

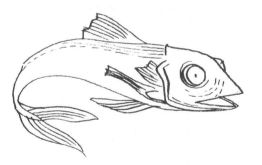

TOPE WITH VEGETABLES

Heat the olive oil in a pan or flameproof casserole. Add the onions, then the eggplant, carrots and zucchini and, finally, the tomatoes and cook for 10 minutes. Place the fish fillets on top of the vegetables, season with salt and pepper and cook for 20 minutes. Arrange the fish and vegetables on a warm serving dish and garnish with basil leaves.

PALOMBO ALLE VERDURE

Serves 4

3 tablespoons olive oil

2 onions, thinly sliced

1 eggplant, diced

3 carrots, diced

3 zucchini, diced

4 tomatoes, diced

4 tope fillets

salt and pepper

fresh basil leaves, to garnish

TOPE WITH CELERY

PALOMBO AL SEDANO

Serves 4

3 tablespoons olive oil

4 tope fillets

4 tomatoes, peeled, seeded and coarsely chopped

1 celery stalk, chopped

pinch of chili powder

4 fresh basil leaves, chopped

$^{1}/_{2}$ cup pitted black olives

salt and pepper

Heat the olive oil in a pan, add the fish and cook until lightly browned on both sides. Add the tomatoes, celery, chili powder and basil, season with salt and pepper and mix gently. Cover and cook for about 30 minutes. Add the olives, cook for a few minutes more and serve.

TOPE WITH POTATOES AU GRATIN

PALOMBO CON PATATE AL GRATIN

Serves 4

$^{1}/_{4}$ cup butter, plus extra for greasing

4 potatoes, thinly sliced

$1^{3}/_{4}$ pounds tope fillets

1 quantity Béchamel Sauce (see page 50)

$^{1}/_{2}$ cup Parmesan cheese, freshly grated

salt and pepper

Preheat the oven to 350°F. Grease an ovenproof dish with butter and arrange half the potatoes on the base. Melt the butter in a skillet, add the fish and cook, turning once, until golden brown on both sides. Using a slotted spatula, place the tope fillets on top of the layer of potatoes, season lightly with salt and pepper and cover with the remaining potatoes. Pour the béchamel sauce over the top, sprinkle with the Parmesan and bake for about 30 minutes.

TOPE WITH GREEN TOMATOES

PALOMBO CON POMODORI VERDI

Serves 4

4 tope fillets

3–4 green tomatoes, peeled, seeded and diced

1 onion, thinly sliced

1 tablespoon chopped fresh oregano

olive oil, for drizzling

1 cup bread crumbs

salt and pepper

Preheat the oven to 350°F. Place the fish in an ovenproof dish, season with salt and pepper, top with the tomatoes, onion and oregano and drizzle with olive oil. Sprinkle the bread crumbs on top, cover with foil and bake for 30 minutes.

SWORDFISH

Swordfish are a feature of Sicilian cuisine. Their firm, tasty flesh, which is sold as steaks, is highly valued in Europe and is ideal for a wide range of recipes, many of which are also suitable for fresh tuna. Swordfish live in temperate seas and can grow up to 13 feet long.

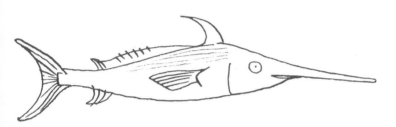

FABULOUS SMOKED SWORDFISH

To make the sauce, put the fennel, mascarpone, olive oil and egg yolk in a food processor and process to a smooth, thick purée. Add 1 tablespoon warm water, the white wine vinegar and the balsamic vinegar, season with salt and pepper and process briefly again. Arrange the radicchio leaves on a serving dish in the shape of a garland. Put the slices of fish in the middle and the celery strips all around. Spoon a little vinegar sauce on top and serve.

PESCE SPADA AFFUMICATO IN FANTASIA

Serves 6

2 Treviso radicchio

12 smoked swords

2 celery stalks, cut into thin strips

For the sauce

7 ounces fennel bulbs, boiled, drained and chopped

$^2/_3$ cup mascarpone cheese

$^1/_4$ cup olive oil

1 egg yolk

1 teaspoon white wine vinegar

1 tablespoon balsamic vinegar

salt and pepper

BAKED SWORDFISH

Preheat the oven to 350°F. Combine the onion, garlic and parsley in a bowl. Place half the mixture in an ovenproof dish and place the fish on top. Season with salt and pepper and cover with the remaining chopped mixture. Pour in the olive oil and white wine. Bake, basting frequently, for 30 minutes.

PESCE SPADA AL FORNO

Serves 4

1 onion, chopped • 1 garlic clove, chopped

3 tablespoons chopped fresh flat-leaf parsley

4 swordfish steaks

$^3/_4$ cup olive oil

$^3/_4$ cup white wine

salt and pepper

SWORDFISH PACKETS

PESCE SPADA IN CARTOCCIO

Serves 4

9 ounces mussels, scrubbed and beards removed

9 ounces clams, scrubbed

²/₃ cup olive oil, plus extra for drizzling

1 garlic clove

5 ounces raw shrimp, peeled and deveined

2 tomatoes, coarsely chopped

1 yellow bell pepper, halved, seeded and cut into large slices

6 fresh basil leaves, chopped

1 fresh chile, seeded and chopped

4 swordfish steaks

1 fresh flat-leaf parsley sprig, chopped

salt and pepper

Preheat the oven to 400°F. Cut four large squares of foil. Discard any mussels or clams that do not shut immediately when sharply tapped, then place the shellfish in a pan with 3 tablespoons of the olive oil and the garlic. Cook over high heat for about 5 minutes until the shells open. Discard any that remain closed. Drain the shellfish, reserving the cooking liquid. Heat 2 tablespoons of the remaining olive oil in another pan, add the shrimp and cook for a few minutes. Add the mussels and clams, still in their shells, the tomatoes, yellow bell pepper, basil, chile and reserved cooking liquid and simmer for 5 minutes. Heat the remaining oil in a skillet, add the swordfish and cook for 5 minutes on each side. Place a swordfish steak on each square of foil, season with salt and pepper and spoon the seafood mixture on top. Sprinkle with the parsley and drizzle with olive oil. Fold the foil over and seal the edges, transfer the packets to a cookie sheet and bake for about 10 minutes. Place the packets on a warm serving dish, opening them slightly.

BRAISED SWORDFISH

PESCE SPADA IN UMIDO

Serves 4

4 swordfish steaks

1 small bay leaf

1 garlic clove

1 fresh chervil sprig, chopped

6 fresh basil leaves, chopped

2 tablespoons olive oil, plus extra for drizzling

¹/₂ cup dry white wine

1 onion, chopped

1 celery stalk, chopped

1 carrot, chopped

11 ounces canned chopped tomatoes

¹/₂ tablespoon capers, drained and rinsed

¹/₂ cup black olives, pitted

1¹/₂ ounces Parmesan cheese, shaved

salt and pepper

Place the fish in a flameproof casserole with the bay leaf and garlic, sprinkle with the chervil and basil, drizzle generously with olive oil and season with salt and pepper. Cook over medium heat, turning the fish occasionally, for 30 minutes. Meanwhile, preheat the oven to 350°F. Transfer the casserole to the oven and cook, sprinkling in the wine during cooking, for just under 15 minutes. Meanwhile, heat the olive oil in a pan, add the onion, celery and carrot and cook over low heat, stirring occasionally, for 5 minutes. Add the tomatoes, capers and olives and simmer for about 10 minutes, adding a little water if necessary. Pour the sauce over the fish, sprinkle with the Parmesan and return to the oven for about 15 minutes. Let stand for a few minutes before serving.

PESCE SPADA MARINATO

Serves 4

11 ounces swordfish, very thinly sliced

olive oil, for drizzling

juice of 2 lemons, strained

3$\frac{1}{2}$ ounces arugula, chopped

3$\frac{1}{2}$ ounces escarole, chopped

leaves from 2 fresh chervil sprigs

salt and pepper

1 lemon, sliced, to garnish

MARINATED SWORDFISH

Place the swordfish on a plate, drizzle with olive oil and the lemon juice and season with salt and pepper. Cover and chill in the refrigerator for about 2 hours. Combine the arugula, escarole and chervil in a bowl. Drain the slices of fish, reserving the marinade, and place in a ring on a serving dish, then put the salad leaves in the center. Spoon the marinade over the dish and garnish with the lemon slices.

TRANCE DI PESCE SPADA
ALL'ACETO BALSAMICO

Serves 4

4 swordfish steaks

scant $\frac{1}{2}$ cup milk

all-purpose flour, for dusting

scant 1 cup butter

$\frac{1}{2}$ teaspoon ground cinnamon

1 clove

scant $\frac{1}{2}$ cup apple vinegar

2 tablespoons balsamic vinegar

salt and pepper

SWORDFISH STEAKS
IN BALSAMIC VINEGAR

Put the fish in a dish, add the milk and set aside for 10 minutes. Drain and dust with flour. Melt half the butter in a skillet, add the fish and cook over medium heat until golden brown on both sides. Season with salt and pepper, remove with a slotted spatula and drain on paper towels. Transfer to a serving dish and keep warm. Melt the remaining butter over low heat, add the cinnamon, clove, apple vinegar and balsamic vinegar and simmer for about 10 minutes or until the sauce is fairly thick. Pour it over the fish and serve.

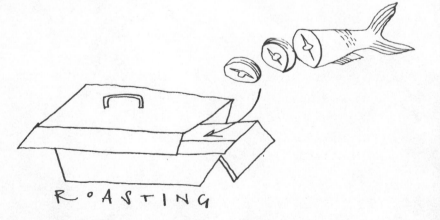

ROASTING

SKATE

Skates and rays are virtually interchangeable. They are kite-shaped, cartilaginous, flat fish with long thin tails. The flesh from the wings is lean with a very subtle flavor. Though it is not highly prized in Italy it is more popular elsewhere.

SKATE WITH CAPERS

Cut the skate wings into fairly large pieces. Heat the olive oil in a pan, add the onion, garlic and parsley and cook over low heat, stirring occasionally, for about 10 minutes until the onion is lightly browned. Add the tomatoes and capers, season with salt and pepper to taste and cook, stirring occasionally, for 10 minutes. Place the skate in the pan, add 2–3 tablespoons warm water, if necessary, and cook for about 30 minutes.

RAZZA AI CAPPERI

Serves 4

2¹/₄ pounds skate wings

4 tablespoons olive oil

1 onion, chopped

1 garlic clove

1 fresh flat-leaf parsley sprig, chopped

1³/₄ pounds tomatoes, peeled and chopped

1 tablespoon capers, drained and rinsed

salt and pepper

SKATE NIÇOISE

Pour 4 cups water into a pan and add one of the onions, the carrot, celery, wine, vinegar and thyme and season with salt. Bring just to a boil, then lower the heat and simmer for 15 minutes. Add the fish and cook over low heat for 5 minutes. Remove the skate, drain and carefully remove the skin. (This may not be necessary, as skate wings are usually sold already skinned.) Place on a serving dish and keep warm. Chop the remaining onion. Heat the olive oil in a pan, add the onion, shallot and parsley and cook over low heat, stirring occasionally, for 5 minutes. Spoon the mixture over the skate and serve.

RAZZA ALLA NIZZARDA

Serves 4

2 onions

1 carrot, sliced

1 celery stalk

scant ¹/₂ cup dry white wine

scant ¹/₂ cup white wine vinegar

1 fresh thyme sprig

1³/₄ pounds skate wings

2 tablespoons olive oil

1 shallot, chopped

1 fresh flat-leaf parsley sprig, chopped

salt

HALIBUT
AND TURBOT

The king of flat fish in Europe is turbot and it is this fish for which these recipes were created. However, turbot is found only on the European side of the Atlantic – and in the Mediterranean Sea – so the recipes have been adapted for preparing halibut, also a very fine fish and one found on both sides of the Atlantic and with a close relation in the Pacific. Halibut may grow as large as 10–13 feet long and weigh as much as 57 pounds, although smaller specimens are more commonly available. The fish is also sold cut into steaks. The flesh is firm, white and flavoursome. Other flat fish that are well suited to these recipes are the winter or blackback flounder and the summer flounder. The latter is usually much larger than the former, but both have sweet-tasting, firm flesh. The Italian recipe titles, incidentally, still refer to turbot – rombo.

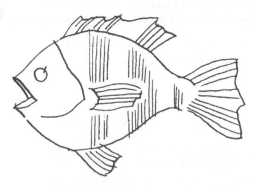

FILETTO DI ROMBO CON VERDURE

Serves 6

1 white onion, thinly sliced

1 carrot, thinly sliced

2 celery stalks, cut into thin strips

2³/₄ cups mushrooms, thinly sliced

³/₄ cup dry white wine

4 halibut or winter flounder fillets

3 tablespoons heavy cream

salt and pepper

HALIBUT FILLETS WITH VEGETABLES

Place the onion, carrot, celery and mushrooms in a large pan, pour in the wine and 1 cup water, cover and simmer for about 15 minutes or until the liquid has reduced. Add the fish fillets, cover and cook for 3–4 minutes. Remove the pan from the heat, transfer the fish to a serving dish and keep warm. Stir the cream into the vegetables, season with salt and pepper and heat gently for a few minutes. Spoon the vegetable sauce over the fish and serve.

HALIBUT FILLETS WITH A POTATO TOPPING

Preheat the oven to 400°F. Grease an ovenproof dish with butter. Cook the potatoes in lightly salted, boiling water for 10–15 minutes until just tender, then drain and refresh under cold, running water. Put the fish in the prepared dish and cover with slightly overlapping slices of potato, like fish scales. Brush with the beaten egg, season with salt and pepper and bake for 15–20 minutes. Meanwhile, pour the wine and stock into a pan, add the shallots and cook over medium heat until the liquid has reduced and the mixture is quite thick. Remove from the heat, let cool slightly, then pour into a food processor, add the basil and process to a purée. Transfer to a bowl and keep warm. Cream the butter in a bowl, then beat in the shallot mixture. Remove the fish from the oven, garnish with the chives and tomatoes and serve with the sauce.

FILETTO DI ROMBO VESTITO DI PATATE

Serves 6

6 tablespoons butter, plus extra for greasing

3 potatoes, thinly sliced

6 halibut or summer flounder fillets

1 egg, lightly beaten

5 tablespoons dry white wine

$^3/_4$ cup Vegetable Stock (see page 209)

6 shallots, chopped

4 fresh basil leaves

salt and pepper

For the garnish

$^1/_2$ bunch of fresh chives, chopped

3 tomatoes, peeled and diced

BAKED HALIBUT WITH LENTIL SAUCE

Put the lentils and one of the bay leaves in a pan, add water to cover and bring to a boil, then lower the heat and simmer for 30–45 minutes until tender. Drain well and discard the bay leaf. Preheat the oven to 350°F. Heat 2 tablespoons of the olive oil in a pan, add one-fourth of the shallots, the bacon and a bay leaf and cook over low heat, stirring frequently, for 5 minutes. Add the lentils, $^1/_4$ cup of the wine and 5 tablespoons of the stock and simmer for about 5 minutes. Remove from the heat, transfer half the mixture to a food processor and process to a purée, then scrape into a clean pan. Heat the remaining olive oil, stock, wine, bay leaf and chopped shallot in a roasting pan. Lightly season the fish fillets with salt, add to the pan and cook for 5 minutes, then transfer to the oven and bake for a further 15 minutes. Remove the pan from the oven, transfer the fish to a serving dish and keep warm. Strain the cooking juices into a bowl and stir in the curry powder. Add the mixture to the lentil purée, heat gently and gradually whisk in the butter. Sprinkle the marjoram over the fish and serve with the lentil mixture and sauce.

ROMBO AL FORNO
CON SUGO DI LENTICCHIE

Serves 6

generous 1 cup lentils

3 bay leaves

$^3/_4$ cup olive oil

2 shallots, chopped

$^1/_3$ cup bacon, diced

$^3/_4$ cup dry white wine

1 cup Concentrated Fish Stock (see page 210)

$4^1/_2$-pound halibut or summer flounder, filleted

pinch of curry powder

3 tablespoons butter, cut into small pieces

1 fresh marjoram sprig, chopped

salt

HALIBUT IN ORANGE SAUCE

ROMBO ALL'ARANCIA

Serves 4

2 oranges

1 tablespoon olive oil

4 halibut or summer flounder fillets

2 tablespoons sugar

salt

orange slices, to garnish

Thinly pare the rind of one of the oranges, discarding all traces of pith, and chop very finely. Squeeze the juice from both oranges and strain into a measuring jug. Heat the olive oil in a pan and add the fish. Season lightly with salt, add half the orange juice and cook over medium heat, turning the fish occasionally, for 15 minutes. Pour 2 tablespoons water into a pan, add the orange rind and sugar, heat for 2–3 minutes and stir in the remaining orange juice. Pour the sauce over the fish and cook for a further 10 minutes. Transfer to a warm serving dish and garnish with orange slices.

HALIBUT IN SPARKLING WINE

ROMBO ALLO SPUMANTE

Serves 4

5 tablespoons butter

1 shallot, chopped

1^1/$_2$ cups mushrooms, finely chopped

4 x 5-ounce halibut or winter flounder fillets

scant 1 cup dry sparkling wine

2 tablespoons heavy cream

1 teaspoon cornstarch

salt and pepper

Heat half the butter in a skillet, add the shallot and cook over low heat, stirring occasionally, for 5 minutes. Stir in the mushrooms and cook until lightly browned. Melt the remaining butter in another skillet, add the fish and cook until lightly browned on both sides. Remove from the skillet with a slotted spatula and add to the other skillet. Add half the wine and cook for 5 minutes, then season with salt and pepper. Using a slotted spatula, transfer the fish to a serving dish and keep warm. Stir the cream into the mushroom mixture over low heat. Mix the cornstarch to a paste with 1 tablespoon warm water, then stir into the skillet. Increase the heat to medium and cook for a few minutes more until thickened. Add the remaining wine and cook, stirring constantly, until piping hot. Spoon the sauce over the fish and serve.

HALIBUT WITH SAFFRON IN CLAM SAUCE

Discard any clams that do not shut immediately when sharply tapped. Heat half the olive oil and half the wine in a skillet, add the garlic and clams and cook over high heat for about 5 minutes until the clams open. Discard any that remain closed. Drain the clams, reserving the cooking liquid, let cool, then remove from their shells. Strain the cooking liquid into a bowl. Heat the remaining olive oil in a pan, add the shallot and cook over low heat, stirring occasionally, for 5 minutes. Add the potatoes, pour in the remaining wine and cook until it has evaporated. Add the stock and about half the reserved cooking liquid and simmer until the potatoes are tender. Meanwhile, preheat the oven to 350°F. Brush an ovenproof dish with oil. Ladle half the potato mixture into a food processor and process to a purée, then return the purée to the pan. Add the clams and tomato and season with salt and pepper to taste. Season the fish fillets with salt and pepper, place them in the prepared dish and bake for 20 minutes. Beat together the butter, saffron and chili powder in a bowl until thoroughly combined. Spoon the saffron butter over the fish, sprinkle with the parsley and serve with the potato and clam mixture.

ROMBO ALLO ZAFFERANO
CON SUGO DI VONGOLE

Serves 6

1 pound 2 ounces clams, scrubbed

4 tablespoons olive oil, plus extra for brushing

1 cup dry white wine

1 garlic clove

1 shallot, chopped

3 potatoes, diced

$^2/_3$ cup Concentrated Fish Stock (see page 210)

1 tomato, peeled, seeded and diced

$4^1/_2$-pound halibut or summer flounder, filleted

6 tablespoons butter, softened

10 saffron threads

pinch of chili powder

1 tablespoon fresh flat-leaf parsley, chopped

salt and pepper

HALIBUT WITH OLIVE SAUCE

Preheat the oven to 400°F. Grease an ovenproof dish with butter. Chop the anchovy fillets. Heat the butter in a skillet, add the pine nuts and cook, stirring frequently, for a few minutes until golden brown. Remove from the skillet and drain on paper towels. Put the anchovy, olives, parsley, shallots and stock in a food processor and process to a purée, then scrape into a bowl and whisk in enough olive oil to make a smooth sauce. Place the fish in the prepared dish, season with salt and pepper, pour the sauce over it and bake for 20 minutes. Transfer to a warm serving dish and sprinkle with the pine nuts. Boiled or steamed potatoes make an excellent side dish.

ROMBO CON SALSA DI OLIVE

Serves 6

2 tablespoons butter, plus extra for greasing

1 salted anchovy, head removed, cleaned and filleted (see page 596), soaked in cold water for 10 minutes and drained

$^1/_4$ cup pine nuts

$2^3/_4$ cups black olives, pitted

$^1/_2$ bunch of fresh flat-leaf parsley, chopped

2 shallots, chopped

1–2 tablespoons Concentrated Fish Stock (see page 210)

$^2/_3$ cup olive oil

$2^1/_2$-pound halibut or summer flounder, filleted

salt and pepper

SALMON

Salmon are among the most highly prized fish. Although they live in the ocean, they swim upstream against the current to reproduce in the rivers in which they were born. Salmon grow up to 5 feet in length and weigh as much as 79 pounds, but they normally range from $3^1/_4$–$19^3/_4$ pounds. Italy imports quite a lot of salmon, usually smoked, but occasionally frozen. However, salmon can also be found fresh, in fillets, steaks or whole in some places. An oily fish, salmon has pink, firm flesh with a delicious flavor.

BOCCONCINI DI SALMONE CON BACON

Serves 4

butter, for greasing

2 fresh sage sprigs

1½ pounds salmon fillets, cut into cubes

5 ounces bacon slices, halved

salt and pepper

SALMON AND BACON BITES

Preheat the oven to 400°F. Grease an ovenproof dish with butter. Pull the sage leaves off the stems and cut them in half. Season the salmon cubes with salt and pepper and wrap each cube in a small slice of bacon with half a sage leaf. Secure with toothpicks and place in the prepared dish. Bake, turning occasionally, for 10–15 minutes.

FAGOTTINI DI SALMONE CON INDIVIA

Serves 4

5 tablespoons olive oil

5 tablespoons dry white wine

4 salmon steaks

1 head of Belgian endive, cut into strips

1 garlic clove, chopped

14 ounces puff pastry dough, thawed if frozen

all-purpose flour, for dusting

1 egg yolk, lightly beaten

salt and pepper

SALMON AND BELGIAN ENDIVE PACKETS

Combine 3 tablespoons of the olive oil and the wine in a dish, season with salt and pepper and add the salmon, turning to coat. Let marinate for 2 hours. Preheat the oven to 400°F. Heat the remaining olive oil in a pan, add the Belgian endive and garlic and cook, stirring occasionally, for 5 minutes. Divide the pastry into four and roll each piece out on a lightly floured surface. Drain the salmon and place a steak on each piece of pastry. Divide the Belgian endive among them, then fold the pastry over and press the edges to seal. Prick with a fork, place on a cookie sheet and brush with the egg yolk. Bake for about 30 minutes.

SALMON PATTIES

SVIZZERE DI SALMONE

Serves 4

3¹/₂ ounces bread, crusts removed

scant 1 cup milk

1 lemon

14 ounces salmon fillet, chopped

5 tablespoons butter, softened

1¹/₂ cups bread crumbs

2 tablespoons Clarified Butter (see page 88)

salt and white pepper

Tear the bread into pieces, place in a bowl, add milk to cover and let soak for 10 minutes, then drain and squeeze out. Grate the rind of half the lemon and peel the other half, removing all traces of pith from both halves, and slice thinly. Combine the salmon, soaked bread and butter in a bowl and season with salt and pepper. Divide the mixture into four, shape into balls, then flatten gently with your hand. Pour the remaining milk into a shallow dish and combine the bread crumbs and lemon rind in another shallow dish. Melt the clarified butter in a skillet. Dip the patties first in the milk, then in the bread crumb mixture and fry for 4 minutes on each side. Remove with a slotted spatula and drain on paper towels. Place on a warm serving dish and garnish with the lemon slices.

SALMON TARTARE

TARTARA DI SALMONE

Serves 4

3 lemons

5 tablespoons olive oil • dash of Tabasco sauce

1 pound 5 ounces salmon fillets, diced

2 yellow bell peppers, halved, seeded and cut into squares

2 tablespoons capers, drained and rinsed

8 green olives, pitted and chopped • 4 egg yolks

salt and pepper

1 tablespoon fresh flat-leaf parsley, chopped, to garnish

Peel one of the lemons, removing all traces of white pith, and chop the flesh. Squeeze the juice from the remaining lemons. Combine the olive oil, lemon juice and Tabasco in a bowl and season with salt and pepper. Combine the salmon, yellow bell peppers, capers, olives and chopped lemon in a dish, add the lemon dressing, mix well and let marinate for 20 minutes. Divide the mixture among four dishes and place an egg yolk in the middle of each. Garnish with the parsley.

SMOKED SALMON TERRINE

TERRINA DI SALMONE AFFUMICATO

Serves 6

7 ounces smoked salmon, coarsely chopped

7 ounces smoked trout, coarsely chopped

scant ¹/₂ cup heavy cream

1 jar (1¹/₂–2 ounces) lumpfish roe

Put the salmon in a food processor, process to a purée and scrape into a bowl. Clean the food processor, add the trout, process to a purée and scrape into another bowl. Whisk the cream and stir half into each purée. Line a rectangular cake pan with plenty of plastic wrap, allowing it to overlap the sides. Spoon the salmon mixture evenly over the base of the pan, sprinkle with the lumpfish roe and cover with the trout mixture. Fold over the overhanging plastic wrap and chill in the refrigerator for about 6 hours. Turn out onto a serving dish.

POMFRET AND JOHN DORY

John Dory are highly-prized, thin-bodied fish with excellent flesh and no pin bones. It is much uglier, but similar in shape, size and flavor to white pomfret, which makes a perfect substitute in these recipes. They are tasty broiled whole. A 3¹/₄-pound fish is sufficient for four servings. The Italian recipe titles still refer to John Dory.

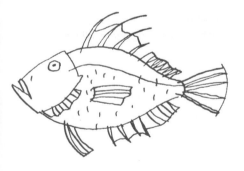

POMFRET FILLETS IN SAUCE

Put the fish fillets in a pan, pour in 4 cups water, add the onion, carrot, parsley and vinegar and season with salt and pepper. Bring just to a boil, then lower the heat and poach for 10 minutes. Combine the ketchup and brandy in a bowl and stir into the mayonnaise. Drain the fish, transfer to a warm serving dish and serve with the sauce.

FILETTI DI SAN PIETRO IN SALSA

Serves 4

1³/₄ pounds white pomfret fillets

1 onion

1 carrot, sliced

1 fresh flat-leaf parsley sprig

1 tablespoon white wine vinegar

1 tablespoon brandy

4 tablespoons ketchup

1 quantity Mayonnaise (see page 65)

salt and pepper

FILETTI DI SAN PIETRO IN SALSA BESCIAMELLA

Serves 4

1 tablespoon olive oil

2 tablespoons butter

1 shallot, chopped

1 celery stalk, chopped • 1 carrot, chopped

4 white pomfret fillets

5 tablespoons dry white wine

1/2 cup dried mushrooms,
soaked in warm water for 30 minutes and drained

1 egg yolk

1 cup Béchamel Sauce (see page 50)

1 fresh flat-leaf parsley sprig, chopped

salt and pepper

POMFRET FILLETS IN BÉCHAMEL SAUCE

Heat the olive oil and butter in a flameproof casserole, add the shallot, celery and carrot and cook over low heat, stirring occasionally, for 5 minutes. Add the fish to the pan and cook until lightly browned on both sides. Pour in the wine, season with salt, add the mushrooms and cook for 15 minutes. Meanwhile, preheat the oven to 350°F. Beat the egg yolk into the béchamel sauce, stir in the parsley and season with pepper. Pour the sauce over the fish, transfer to the oven and bake for about 15 minutes.

INVOLTINI DI SAN PIETRO AL FORNO

Serves 4

1 tablespoon olive oil, plus extra for brushing

2 salted anchovies, heads removed,
cleaned and filleted (see page 596),
soaked in cold water for 10 minutes and drained

2 tablespoons bread crumbs

1 fresh flat-leaf parsley sprig, chopped

1 garlic clove, chopped • 1/2 cup pine nuts

2/3 cup Parmesan cheese, freshly grated

1 pound 5 ounces pomfret fillets

1 fresh thyme sprig, chopped

1 fresh rosemary sprig, chopped

juice of 1 lemon, strained • salt and pepper

BAKED POMFRET ROULADES

Preheat the oven to 350°F. Brush an ovenproof dish with oil. Chop the anchovy fillets. Heat the olive oil in a pan, add the anchovies and cook, mashing with a wooden spoon until they have almost disintegrated. Add the bread crumbs, parsley, garlic, pine nuts and Parmesan, season with salt and pepper and mix well, adding a drop of olive oil if the mixture seems too dry. Season the fillets with salt and pepper, divide the anchovy mixture among them and roll up. Secure with toothpicks and place in the prepared dish, then sprinkle with the thyme, rosemary and lemon juice and bake for about 15 minutes.

SAN PIETRO CON TACCOLE

Serves 4

scant 1/2 cup butter

1 pound 2 ounces snow peas, trimmed

3 1/4-pound white pomfret, filleted

all-purpose flour, for dusting

salt and pepper

fresh fennel fronds, to garnish

POMFRET WITH SNOW PEAS

Melt half the butter in a pan, add the snow peas and cook over low heat, stirring occasionally, for about 5 minutes, then season with salt and pepper to taste. Add 2/3 cup water, cover and simmer for 30 minutes. Lightly dust the fish with flour, shaking off the excess. Melt the remaining butter in a skillet, add the fish and cook over medium heat until golden brown all over and cooked through. Drain the snow peas and transfer them and the fish fillets to a warm serving dish and garnish with fennel fronds.

SARDINES

Sardines are inexpensive, tasty and nutritious, which explains why these fish – common in Italian seas – are so popular. They must be scaled and cleaned before cooking and, in some cases, you will need to cut off their heads and remove the bones. To do this, open them out, place skin side up and press along the backbones with your thumb. Turn them over, cut through the ends of their bones and remove. Rinse well and pat dry with paper towels.

SARDINE ROLLS

Preheat the oven to 350°F. Brush an ovenproof dish with oil. Season the sardines with salt and pepper, wrap each in a slice of pancetta and secure with a toothpick. Place the rolls in the prepared dish, add the bay leaves and thyme and pour in the lemon juice and olive oil. Bake for about 15 minutes.

INVOLTINI DI SARDINE

Serves 4

1–2 tablespoons olive oil, plus extra for brushing

1³/₄ pounds sardines, scaled, cleaned and boned

4 ounces smoked pancetta, thinly sliced

2 bay leaves

1 fresh thyme sprig

juice of 1 lemon, strained

salt and pepper

BROILED SARDINES

Preheat the broiler. Brush the sardines with olive oil. Place them, still opened out, on the broiler rack and grill for 4–5 minutes. Combine the olive oil, lemon juice, chile, garlic and Worcestershire sauce in a bowl and season with salt and pepper. Serve the sardines with the sauce.

SARDINE ALLA GRIGLIA

Serves 4

1³/₄ pounds sardines, scaled, cleaned and boned

5 tablespoons olive oil, plus extra for brushing

juice of 1 lemon, strained

¹/₂ red chile , seeded and chopped

¹/₂ garlic clove, chopped

1 teaspoon Worcestershire sauce

salt and pepper

SARDINES MARINARA

SARDINE ALLA MARINARA

Serves 4

olive oil, for brushing and drizzling

1³/₄ pounds sardines, scaled, cleaned and boned

3 fresh rosemary sprigs, chopped

1 garlic clove, chopped

pinch of dried oregano

1 tablespoon white wine vinegar

salt

Lightly brush a heavy pan with olive oil. Make two layers of the sardines in the pan with the rosemary and garlic between them. Sprinkle with the oregano, season with salt and drizzle generously with olive oil. Cook over medium-low heat for 15 minutes. Sprinkle with the vinegar and cook until the flesh flakes easily. Serve the sardines cold.

SARDINES WITH SHALLOTS

SARDINE ALLO SCALOGNO

Serves 4

all-purpose flour, for dusting

1 egg

³/₄ cup olive oil

1³/₄ pounds sardines, scaled, cleaned and boned

4 shallots, finely chopped

1 fresh flat-leaf parsley sprig, finely chopped

5 tablespoons white wine vinegar

salt and pepper

Spread out the flour in a shallow dish and lightly beat the egg in another shallow dish. Heat the oil in a large skillet. Dip the sardines first in the flour, then in the egg and fry for 5 minutes or longer, depending on their size. Combine the shallots, parsley and vinegar in a bowl and season with salt and pepper. Remove the sardines with a slotted spatula and drain on paper towels. Place them on a warm serving dish and serve with the shallot sauce.

SARDINES IN BREAD CRUMBS

SARDINE IMPANATE

Serves 4

¹/₂ cup all-purpose flour

1 egg

1¹/₂ cups bread crumbs

vegetable oil, for deep-frying

1³/₄ pounds sardines, scaled, cleaned and boned

salt

lemon wedges, to serve

Spread out the flour in a shallow dish, lightly beat the egg with a pinch of salt in another shallow dish and spread out the bread crumbs in a third. Heat the oil for deep-frying. Dip the sardines first in the flour, then in the egg and, finally, in the bread crumbs. Fry in the hot oil for about 7 minutes, turning once (see page 593). Remove from the pan and drain on paper towels. Serve with lemon wedges.

SARDINES BELLAVISTA

SARDINE IN BELLAVISTA

Serves 4

1/4 cup butter

2 tablespoons olive oil, plus extra for brushing

1 onion, chopped

3 2/3 cups porcini, chopped

1 fresh flat-leaf parsley sprig, chopped

2 tablespoons tomato paste

1 pound 5 ounces sardines, boned, scaled and cleaned

2 yellow bell peppers

10 canned anchovy fillets in oil, drained

salt and pepper

Heat the butter and oil in a pan, add the onion and cook over low heat, stirring occasionally, for 5 minutes. Add the porcini and cook, stirring occasionally, until all the liquid they give off has evaporated. Season with salt and pepper, stir in the parsley and tomato paste and cook until thickened. Meanwhile, preheat the oven to 350°F and preheat the broiler. Brush an ovenproof dish with oil. Place the sardines, still opened out, in the prepared dish, spoon the porcini sauce over them and bake for 20 minutes. Meanwhile, broil the bell peppers, peel, seed and cut into strips. Transfer the sardines to a warm serving dish and surround with a ring of alternating anchovy fillets and pepper strips.

STUFFED SARDINES

SARDINE RIPIENE

Serves 4

1/2 bunch of fresh flat-leaf parsley

1 fresh bergamot sprig

1 garlic clove

3 eggs

2 tablespoons bread crumbs

1 tablespoon Parmesan cheese, freshly grated

1 3/4 pounds sardines, scaled, cleaned and boned

all-purpose flour, for dusting

5 tablespoons olive oil

salt and pepper

Chop the parsley, bergamot and garlic together, place in a bowl, add the eggs and mix well. Add the bread crumbs and Parmesan, season with salt and pepper and mix again. Spread the mixture on the inside of the opened-out sardines, fold them back over, dust lightly with flour and shake off any excess. Heat the oil in a skillet, add the sardines and cook for 5–6 minutes, turning once. Remove with a slotted spatula, drain on paper towels, season with salt and serve.

SUCCULENT SARDINES

SARDINE SAPORITE

Serves 4

1 3/4 pounds sardines, scaled, cleaned and boned

all-purpose flour, for dusting

3 tablespoons olive oil

1 garlic clove

1 fresh rosemary sprig

1 bay leaf

3/4 cup white wine

salt and pepper

Preheat the oven to 350°F. Dust the sardines with flour. Heat the olive oil in a pan with the garlic, rosemary and bay leaf, add the sardines and cook for a few minutes until lightly browned on both sides. Season with salt and pepper and transfer the fish to an ovenproof dish. Remove and discard the herbs and garlic and pour the wine into the pan. Mix well and cook over high heat until reduced by half. Pour the sauce over the sardines and bake for about 20 minutes.

SCORPION FISH

There are several types of scorpion fish, which are also known by their French name rascasse. Brown scorpion fish, which are actually gray, have a much better flavor than the much more common red variety. All are proverbially ugly and have thickset bodies and strong spines on their backs that can cause injury. However, their firm, white flesh is tasty and can be prepared in a number of ways, although traditionally it is mainly used in soups and stews. Brown scorpion fish are fairly small – 8–12 inches long – and a lot is wasted because of their big heads. Red scorpion fish are about 20 inches long.

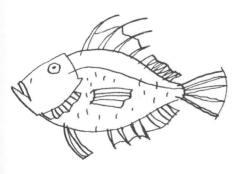

CAPPON MAGRO

Serves 12

6–8 whole-wheat crackers

2 garlic cloves

2–3 tablespoons white wine vinegar

$^3/_4$ cup olive oil, plus extra for drizzling

$3^1/_4$ pounds scorpion fish, spines trimmed, cleaned

1 large live spiny lobster

juice of 1 lemon, strained

7 ounces salted anchovies, heads removed, cleaned and filleted (see page 596), soaked in cold water for 10 minutes and drained

3 egg yolks

4 tablespoons capers, drained and rinsed

$1^3/_4$ cups green olives, pitted

1 fresh flat-leaf parsley sprig, coarsely chopped

$^1/_2$ cup pine nuts

2 bread rolls, crusts removed

12 oysters

5 ounces tuna mosciame (salted and dried tuna fillet)

1 pound 2 ounces green beans, cooked (see page 468)

14 ounces potatoes, cooked (see page 518) and sliced

11 ounces salsify, cooked (see page 561) and sliced

5 globe artichokes, cut into wedges and cooked (see page 415)

4 carrots, sliced and cooked (see page 427)

1 cauliflower, cut into flowerets and cooked (see page 436)

1 beet, cooked (see page 405) and sliced

1 celery heart, cooked (see page 563) and sliced

4 ounces small mushrooms in oil, drained

10 large cooked shrimp, peeled and deveined

6 eggs, hard-cooked, shelled and sliced

salt and pepper

GENOESE SALAD

Rub the crackers with one of the garlic cloves, place in a bowl and add water to cover and 1 tablespoon of the vinegar, then drain and place on the base of a large serving dish. Drizzle with olive oil, season with salt and pepper and set aside. Poach the scorpion fish in gently simmering water for 20–30 minutes until the flesh flakes easily. Drain, then remove and discard the skin and bones. Cut the flesh into chunks, place in a dish, drizzle with olive oil and about half the lemon juice, season with salt and let cool completely. Plunge the lobster into a pan of boiling water, cover and cook for 10–15 minutes, depending on the size. Drain and remove the meat (see page 689), place in a dish, drizzle with olive oil and the remaining lemon juice, season with salt and let cool completely. Meanwhile, chop the anchovy fillets. Put the anchovies, egg yolks, capers, half the olives, the parsley, pine nuts, the remaining garlic and the rolls in a food processor and process to a purée. Scrape into a bowl and stir in the olive oil and remaining vinegar. Open the oysters (see page 716). Place a layer of mosciame on top of the crackers, spoon a little anchovy sauce on top and make alternating layers of the cooked vegetables, most of the anchovy sauce, fish and lobster, piling them up in a pyramid, until all the ingredients are used. Thread the remaining olives, the mushrooms and shrimp alternately onto four or five long wooden skewers and insert them into the top of the pyramid. Garnish with the egg slices, the oysters, any remaining shrimp and any other leftover ingredients. Sprinkle with the remaining sauce and keep in a cool place until just before serving.

SCORPION FISH WITH MUSHROOMS

Preheat the oven to 350°F. Grease an ovenproof dish with butter. Spread out the mushrooms in the dish, season the fish with salt and pepper and place it on top of them. Dot with the butter, top with the lemon slices and pour in the wine. Bake, basting frequently, for 20–30 minutes.

SCORFANO AI FUNGHI

Serves 4

¹/₄ cup butter, plus extra for greasing

3 cups mushrooms, thinly sliced

1³/₄ pounds scorpion fish,

spines trimmed, cleaned

3 lemon slices

³/₄ cup dry white wine

salt and pepper

SCORPION FISH WITH THYME

Preheat the oven to 350°F. Season the cavities of the fish with salt and pepper and fill with some of the thyme. Sprinkle the remainder of the thyme in an ovenproof dish, add the fish and season with salt and pepper. Combine the olive oil and lemon juice and pour the mixture over the fish. Bake, basting frequently, for 20–30 minutes. Meanwhile, chop the anchovy fillets. Pass the anchovies through a strainer into a bowl and combine with the butter. Serve the fish with the anchovy butter.

SCORFANO AL TIMO

Serves 4

4 scorpion fish, spines trimmed, cleaned

¹/₂ bunch of fresh thyme, chopped

4 tablespoons olive oil

juice of 1 lemon, strained

3¹/₂ ounces salted anchovies, heads removed,

cleaned and filleted (see page 596),

soaked in cold water for 10 minutes and drained

scant ¹/₂ cup butter, softened

salt and pepper

SCORPION FISH IN WHITE WINE AND SAFFRON

Put the fish in a flameproof casserole with the olive oil and sprinkle the tomatoes on top of them. Season with salt and pepper, add the garlic and saffron and pour in the wine. Bring to a boil, cover and simmer over medium heat for 15–20 minutes. Remove from the heat and leave the fish to cool in the cooking liquid. Serve cold with the white wine sauce.

SCORFANO AL VINO BIANCO E ZAFFERANO

Serves 4

2 x 11-ounce scorpion fish,

spines trimmed, cleaned

3 tablespoons olive oil

14 ounces tomatoes, peeled, seeded and diced

1 garlic clove

pinch of saffron threads

2¹/₄ cups dry white wine

salt and pepper

MACKEREL

Like sardines, mackerel belong to what is known in Italy as the 'blue-scale' fish family. They vary in length from 10–18 inches. They are plentiful in the Mediterranean and their grayish flesh is not very highly prized. However, it is firm and tasty with a distinctive flavor. Mackerel are excellent grilled or cooked in oil. If they are freshly caught and weigh more than 1 pound 2 ounces, it is best to store them in the refrigerator for a day before cooking.

MACKEREL WITH GREEN BEANS

SGOMBRI AI FAGIOLINI

Serves 4

5 tablespoons olive oil
1 onion, sliced
1 carrot, chopped
1 fresh flat-leaf parsley sprig, chopped
1 fresh thyme sprig, chopped
1 cup green beans, trimmed
1 tomato, peeled seeded and chopped
2 tablespoons capers, drained and rinsed
4 mackerel, cleaned
all-purpose flour, for dusting
salt and pepper

Heat 2 tablespoons of the olive oil in a pan, add the onion, carrot, parsley and thyme and cook over low heat, stirring occasionally, for 5 minutes. Add the beans and cook, stirring frequently, for 15 minutes. Add the tomato and capers, season with salt and pepper and cook for a further 5 minutes. Dust the mackerel with flour, shaking off the excess. Heat the remaining olive oil in a skillet, add the mackerel and cook until golden brown and the flesh flakes easily with a fork. Remove with a slotted spatula, add to the pan of vegetables and cook for a further 5 minutes. Taste and adjust the seasoning if necessary, then serve.

MACKEREL WITH SAGE BUTTER

SGOMBRI AL BURRO

Serves 4

4 mackerel, cleaned
all-purpose flour, for dusting
2 tablespoons butter
1 quantity Sage Butter (see page 87)
juice of ½ lemon, strained
salt

Make several diagonal slashes on each side of the mackerel, then dust lightly with flour, shaking off the excess. Melt the butter in a skillet, add the fish and cook over medium heat for about 5 minutes on each side. Season with salt and transfer to a warm serving dish. Put a little of the sage butter on each fish and sprinkle with the lemon juice.

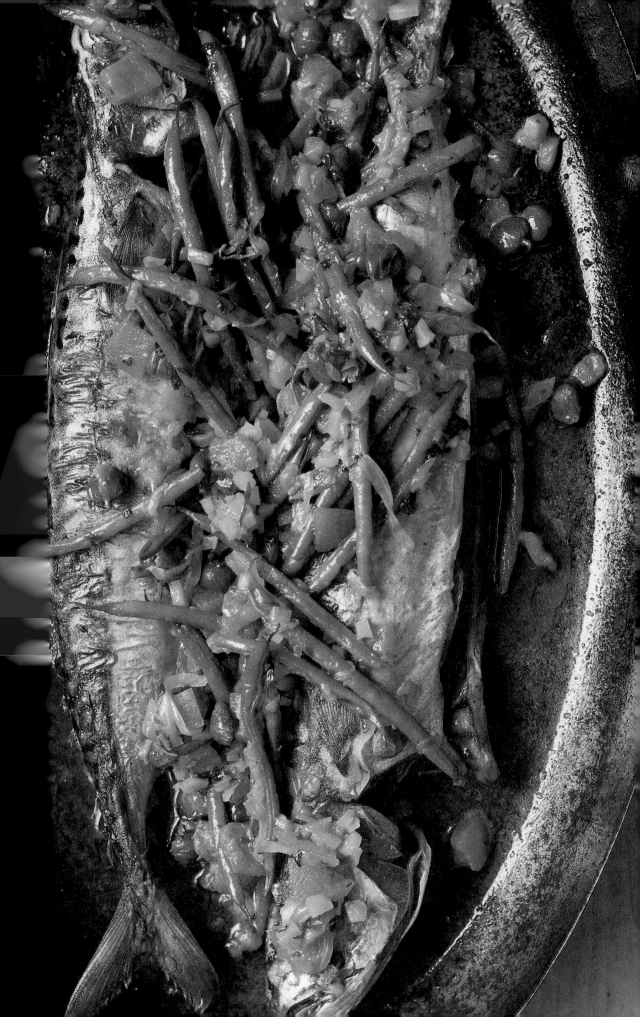

SGOMBRI ALLA GRECA
Serves 4

2 tablespoons olive oil, plus extra

for brushing and drizzling

2 small onions, chopped

4 mackerel, cleaned

2 fresh sage leaves

1 tablespoon fresh flat-leaf parsley, chopped

1 fresh thyme sprig • juice of 1 lemon, strained

scant 1 cup black olives, pitted

salt and pepper

GREEK MACKEREL

Preheat the oven to 350°F. Brush an ovenproof dish with oil. Heat the oil in a small skillet, add the onions and cook over low heat, stirring occasionally, for 5 minutes. Place the mackerel in the prepared dish, sprinkle the onions on top, drizzle with olive oil and add the sage, parsley and thyme. Sprinkle with the lemon juice, season with salt and pepper, add the olives and cover the dish with foil. Bake for 30 minutes.

SGOMBRI AL RIBES
Serves 4

1 1/2 cups currants

4 mackerel, cleaned

2 tablespoons butter

1 onion, chopped

1 garlic clove

3/4 cup dry white wine

1 teaspoon sugar

salt and pepper

MACKEREL WITH CURRANTS

Preheat the oven to 350°F. Place the currants in a bowl, add warm water to cover and let soak. Make several diagonal slashes in each side of the fish and place in an ovenproof dish. Melt the butter in a pan, add the onion and garlic and cook over low heat, stirring occasionally, for about 10 minutes. Drain the currants, reserving the soaking liquid. Set about 3 ounces aside and squeeze the remainder over the bowl of soaking liquid, then discard. Pour the wine and soaking liquid into the pan, add the sugar and season with salt and pepper. Heat through and pour the mixture over the fish. Bake for about 10 minutes. Add the reserved currants and cook the fish for a further 10 minutes. Serve with the sauce.

TERRINA DI SGOMBRI AL VINO BIANCO
Serves 4

1 carrot, sliced

1 onion, sliced

1/2 lemon, sliced

1 fresh flat-leaf parsley sprig, chopped

1 fresh thyme sprig, chopped

1 2/3 cups white wine

scant 1/2 cup white wine vinegar

6 black peppercorns

4 mackerel, cleaned

salt

MACKEREL AND
WHITE WINE TERRINE

Put the carrot, onion, lemon, parsley, thyme, wine, vinegar, peppercorns and a pinch of salt in a pan and bring to a boil. Simmer for a few minutes, then remove from the heat and let stand for 1 hour. Make several diagonal slashes in both sides of the mackerel. Bring the wine mixture back to a boil, lower the heat, add the fish and simmer for 5 minutes. Remove the slices of lemon with tongs and place in a bowl. Remove the mackerel with a slotted spatula and place on top. Boil the cooking juices over high heat for 5 minutes until reduced, then remove and discard the herbs. Pour the mixture into a food processor and process to a purée. Pour the sauce over the fish, let cool and then chill in the refrigerator for about 1 hour.

SOLE

Italian sole are about 8 inches long, whereas sole found in northern seas can reach 16–18 inches. Sole have firm flesh with a delicate flavor and are easy to digest. They are flat fish that live on the seabed. Their bodies are surrounded by a 'frill', which should be cut off. Their upper sides have a characteristic dark skin, which should be removed by making a cut near the tail and tearing it off with one sharp tug. The skin on their undersides is pale and covered with extremely small scales. You can either scale the undersides or remove the skin in the same way as before. If sole are prepared whole, their spines must be snapped in several places so they remain flat during cooking. If you need fillets, on the other hand, it is best to have them cut by the fishmonger.

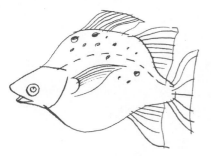

ALMOND–COATED SOLE FILLETS

Lightly dust the fish with flour. Beat the eggs with a little salt and pepper in a shallow dish. Place the almonds in another shallow dish. Melt the butter in a skillet. Dip the sole fillets first in the egg and then in the almonds to coat. Add to the skillet and cook for a few minutes on each side. Transfer to a warm serving dish and garnish with parsley sprigs.

FILETTI DI SOGLIOLE ALLE MANDORLE

Serves 4

8 sole fillets, skinned

all-purpose flour, for dusting

2 eggs

1 cup almonds, coarsely chopped

6 tablespoons butter

salt and pepper

fresh flat-leaf parsley sprigs, to garnish

SOLE SALAD

Put the fillets in a dish, pour the lemon juice over them and cover with plastic wrap. Chill in the refrigerator for 2 hours. Put the bell peppers, carrot, cucumber and tomatoes in a salad bowl. Whisk together the olive oil, rosemary and vinegar in a bowl, season with salt and pepper and pour the dressing over the salad. Drain the fish and dice, then add to the salad and toss. Season lightly with salt and serve.

FILETTI DI SOGLIOLE IN INSALATA

Serves 4

8 large sole fillets, skinned

juice of 2 lemons, strained

2 green bell peppers, halved, seeded and diced

1 yellow bell pepper, halved, seeded and diced

1 carrot, thinly sliced

1 cucumber, thinly sliced

2 tomatoes, peeled, seeded and diced

4–5 tablespoons olive oil

1 tablespoon fresh rosemary needles, chopped

1 tablespoon white wine vinegar

salt and pepper

SOLE AND SHRIMP ROULADES

Melt 2 tablespoons of the butter in a pan, add the shrimp and cook, stirring occasionally, for 2 minutes. Season with salt and pepper and remove from the pan with a slotted spoon. Let cool slightly, then place one of the shrimp on each sole fillet, roll up and secure with a toothpick. Melt the remaining butter in a pan, add the roulades and cook for about 10 minutes, until light golden brown all over. Season lightly with salt, add the wine and cook until it has evaporated. Combine the chives, cream and lemon juice in a bowl. Place the roulades on a warm serving dish and spoon the sauce over them.

INVOLTINI DI SOGLIOLE CON I GAMBERI

Serves 4

6 tablespoons butter

8 raw jumbo shrimp,

peeled and deveined

8 sole fillets, skinned

4 tablespoons dry white wine

$^1/_2$ bunch of fresh chives, chopped

scant $^1/_2$ cup heavy cream

juice of $^1/_2$ lemon, strained

salt and pepper

SOLE WITH MUSHROOMS

Heat 2 tablespoons of the olive oil in a skillet, add the porcini and cook over medium-low heat, stirring occasionally. Meanwhile, place the fish in a pan, pour in the wine and brandy, add the garlic and rosemary and season with salt and pepper to taste. Bring just to a boil, then lower the heat and simmer for 15 minutes. Transfer the fish to the skillet and keep warm. Strain the cooking juices into a clean pan, bring to a boil over high heat and cook until reduced. Lower the heat, add the egg yolks, the remaining olive oil and the lemon juice and mix quickly. As soon as the egg sets, remove the pan from the heat. Place the fish on a warm serving dish, garnish with the porcini and spoon the sauce over them.

SOGLIOLE AI FUNGHI

Serves 4

6 tablespoons olive oil

7 ounces porcini, thinly sliced

8 sole fillets, skinned

scant $^1/_2$ cup dry white wine

$^1/_4$ cup brandy

1 garlic clove

1 fresh rosemary sprig

2 egg yolks

juice of $^1/_2$ lemon, strained

salt and pepper

BROILED SOLE

SOGLIOLE ALLA GRIGLIA

Serves 4

4 sole, cleaned, trimmed and skinned

olive oil, for brushing

salt and pepper

lemon wedges, to serve

Preheat the broiler. Season the fish with salt and pepper and brush with olive oil. Place the fish on the broiler rack and cook under the broiler, brushing frequently with olive oil, for 7–8 minutes on each side. Transfer to a warm serving dish and serve with lemon wedges.

SOLE IN HARD CIDER

SOGLIOLE AL SIDRO

Serves 4

¹/₄ cup butter

1 onion, thinly sliced

1 garlic clove

¹/₂ cup smoked pancetta, cubed

1 tablespoon all-purpose flour

1¹/₂ cups hard cider

1 bay leaf

8 sole fillets, skinned

1 egg yolk, lightly beaten

3 tablespoons heavy cream

salt and pepper

fried bread, to serve

Melt the butter in a pan, add the onion, garlic and pancetta and cook over low heat, stirring occasionally, for 5 minutes. Sprinkle with the flour and cook, stirring, for a few minutes more. Pour in the hard cider, season with salt and pepper, add the bay leaf, increase the heat to medium and cook for 15 minutes until reduced. Lower the heat, place the sole fillets in the pan and simmer gently for 7–8 minutes. Transfer the sole to a warm serving dish. Remove and discard the garlic and bay leaf. Stir the egg yolk and cream into the pan juices, heat through for a few minutes, then pour the sauce over the fish. Serve with thick slices of bread fried in butter.

SOLE WITH THYME

SOGLIOLE AL TIMO

Serves 4

4 sole, cleaned, trimmed and skinned

¹/₂–²/₃ cup olive oil, plus extra for drizzling

juice of ¹/₂ lemon, strained

3 tablespoons fresh thyme leaves

salt and white pepper

This is a very easy recipe. Place the fish in a pan, add water to cover and a pinch of salt and bring just to a boil, then lower the heat and poach until tender. Drain and place on a serving dish. Drizzle with olive oil and sprinkle with the lemon juice. Put the thyme leaves, a pinch of salt and a pinch of pepper in a bowl and gradually stir in the olive oil. Spoon the thyme sauce over the fish and keep in a cool place until ready to serve.

SOLE IN MELTED BUTTER

Put the sole in a dish, add the milk and let soak for at least 15 minutes, then drain, pat dry with paper towels and dust lightly with flour. Melt 4 tablespoons of the butter in a skillet, add the fish and cook over medium-low heat for about 5 minutes on each side until golden brown and tender. Season with salt and transfer to a serving dish. Melt the remaining butter in a double boiler or in a heatproof bowl set over a pan of barely simmering water and continue to heat until it starts to froth, then pour it over the sole. Serve immediately.

SOGLIOLE CON BURRO FUSO

Serves 4

4 sole, cleaned, trimmed and skinned

1¹/₄ cups milk

all-purpose flour, for dusting

²/₃ cup butter

salt

SOLE IN PIQUANT SAUCE

Chop the anchovy fillets. Lightly dust the sole with flour. Melt half the butter in a skillet, add the sole and cook until browned on both sides. Sprinkle with the lemon juice, transfer to a serving dish and keep warm. Melt the remaining butter in a small pan, add the anchovies and capers and cook over medium heat, then pour the sauce over the fish. Sprinkle with the parsley and serve.

SOGLIOLE IN SALSA PICCANTE

Serves 4

2 salted anchovies, heads removed, cleaned and filleted (see page 596), soaked in cold water for 10 minutes and drained

4 sole, cleaned, trimmed and skinned

all-purpose flour, for dusting

6 tablespoons butter

juice of 2 lemons, strained

2 tablespoons capers, drained and rinsed

2 tablespoons chopped fresh flat-leaf parsley

STURGEON

Sturgeon are sea fish that swim up rivers to spawn in early spring. The common sturgeon can reach 10 feet in length. Their roe is used to make caviar and their swim bladders to make gelatin. Their white, firm and tasty flesh is highly prized and is excellent poached, broiled or fried. Sturgeon may be bought as fresh or frozen steaks, dried, smoked or canned. Over-fishing and the destruction of their habitat has severely reduced their numbers. However, white sturgeon have been farmed in Italy for several years. You could substitute a firm white-fleshed fish, such as halibut, for sturgeon in these recipes.

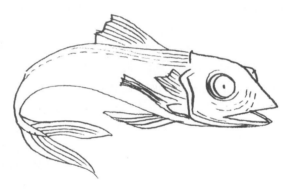

STURGEON IN SWEET-AND-SOUR SAUCE

SCALOPPE DI STORIONE AGRODOLCI

Serves 4

scant 1 cup milk
1 pound 5 ounces sturgeon fillet, thinly sliced
all-purpose flour, for dusting
2 tablespoons butter
2 tablespoons olive oil
salt and pepper

For the sauce
6 tablespoons butter
1 teaspoon sugar
1-inch cinnamon stick
1 clove
scant 1 cup balsamic vinegar
salt

Pour the milk into a dish, season the fish with salt and pepper and add to the milk. Drain and dust with flour. Heat the butter and olive oil in a skillet, add the fish and cook for 4 minutes on each side until evenly browned. Remove with a slotted spatula, drain on paper towels, place on a plate, cover and keep warm. To make the sauce, melt the butter over very low heat, add the sugar, cinnamon, clove and a pinch of salt and mix well. Pour in the vinegar and cook, stirring frequently, until thickened. Remove and discard the cinnamon and clove. Pour the sauce onto a warm serving dish, place the fish on top and serve.

STURGEON IN ANCHOVY SAUCE

SCALOPPE DI STORIONE ALLE ACCIUGHE

Serves 4

scant 1 cup dry white wine

1 bay leaf

4 thin sturgeon fillet slices

salt

For the sauce

3–4 tablespoons olive oil

6 canned anchovy fillets in oil, drained and chopped

1 tablespoon balsamic vinegar

1 tablespoon capers, drained and rinsed

Pour 4 cups water into a pan and add the wine, bay leaf and a little salt. Bring to a boil, add the fish and cook for 10 minutes. Drain, reserving about 1 tablespoon of the cooking liquid, place on a serving dish, cover and keep warm. Meanwhile, heat the olive oil in a small pan, add the anchovies and cook over medium heat, mashing with a fork until they have almost disintegrated. Stir in 1–2 teaspoons of the reserved cooking liquid, add the vinegar and mix well. Remove the pan from the heat and stir in the capers. Spoon the sauce over the fish and serve.

STURGEON IN BALSAMIC VINEGAR

STORIONE ALL'ACETO BALSAMICO

Serves 4

1 onion, chopped

1 celery stalk, chopped

1 1/2 garlic cloves, chopped

4 sturgeon steaks

1 tablespoon balsamic vinegar

4 tablespoons dry white wine

4 salted anchovies, heads removed,

cleaned and filleted (see page 596),

soaked in cold water for 10 minutes and drained

3 tablespoons olive oil

1 fresh flat-leaf parsley sprig, chopped

salt and pepper

Combine the onion, celery and two-thirds of the garlic in a bowl. Place half the mixture in a dish, place the fish on top and sprinkle with the remaining chopped mixture. Season with salt and pepper and sprinkle with the vinegar and wine. Let marinate for about 2 hours. Chop the anchovy fillets. Heat the olive oil in a skillet, add the anchovies and cook, mashing with a wooden spoon until they have almost disintegrated. Stir in the remaining garlic and the parsley, add the fish and cook until golden brown on both sides.

BROILED STURGEON

STORIONE ALLA GRIGLIA

Serves 4

3/4 cup olive oil

5 tablespoons dry white wine

juice of 1 lemon, strained

1 fresh thyme sprig

2 fresh rosemary sprigs

1 fresh flat-leaf parsley sprig

4 sturgeon steaks

1 garlic clove, sliced

salt and pepper

Put the olive oil, wine, lemon juice, thyme, a rosemary sprig and the parsley in a dish, season with salt and pepper and add the fish, turning to coat. Let marinate for 1 hour. Preheat the broiler. Drain the fish, reserving the marinade, and make small incisions in the flesh. Insert pieces of garlic and rosemary needles from the remaining sprig into the cuts. Cook under the broiler, occasionally brushing with the marinade, for 25 minutes.

STORIONE CON CARCIOFI

Serves 4

4 globe artichokes

6 tablespoons olive oil

2 garlic cloves

1 small fresh bergamot sprig

4 sturgeon steaks

4 tomatoes, halved and seeded

salt and pepper

STURGEON WITH ARTICHOKES

Cut off the artichoke stems, remove the coarse outer leaves and trim the remainder. Scoop out and discard the chokes, then place the artichokes upright in a small pan. Pour in enough water to half-cover them and add half the olive oil, one of the garlic cloves, the bergamot, a pinch of salt and a pinch of pepper. Cover and cook over medium-low heat for about 40 minutes until the liquid is almost completely absorbed. Preheat the oven to 350°F. Heat the remaining olive oil in a skillet and cook the fish for 3–4 minutes on each side. Chop the remaining garlic and sprinkle it over the tomatoes. Place on a cookie sheet and bake for 5–6 minutes. Halve the artichokes and arrange in a ring on a warm serving dish, then place the fish in the center, overlapping the steaks slightly, and put the tomato halves between the artichokes.

STORIONE CON SALSA AI PEPERONI

Serves 4

3 tablespoons olive oil, plus extra for brushing

1 onion, chopped

1³/₄ pounds red bell peppers, halved, seeded and sliced

1³/₄-pound sturgeon fillet

1 fresh chervil sprig, chopped

1 fresh tarragon sprig, chopped

1 garlic clove, chopped

1 bay leaf

5 tablespoons dry white wine

salt and pepper

STURGEON WITH RED BELL PEPPER SAUCE

Preheat the oven to 350°F. Brush an ovenproof dish with oil. Heat the olive oil in a pan, add the onion and cook over low heat, stirring occasionally, for 5 minutes. Add the bell peppers, increase the heat to medium, season with salt and pepper, cover and cook for about 30 minutes, adding 2–3 tablespoons hot water during cooking. Meanwhile, put the fish in the prepared dish, brush with olive oil and add the chervil, tarragon, garlic and bay leaf. Season with salt and pepper and bake for about 30 minutes, adding the wine during cooking. When the bell peppers are tender, transfer them to a food processor and process to a purée. If the sauce seems too runny, reduce it over high heat. If it seems too thick, add a little warm water. Pour the sauce over the base of a warm serving dish and place the fish on top.

TUNA

Tuna fishing in the Mediterranean is highly profitable as the fish are greatly appreciated and demand is high. Tuna easily reach 8¹/₄ feet in length, but much bigger ones, up to 14³/₄ feet long and weighing upwards of 1,322 pounds, have also been caught. Canned tuna often appears on Italian tables, but fresh tuna is seen rather less frequently, as it is quite expensive. Tuna steaks can be cooked like meat – stewed, braised or roasted.

TUNA IN VINEGAR

Heat the olive oil in a large, shallow pan, add the garlic and cook for a few minutes, then add the tuna and 2 tablespoons water. Season with salt and pepper to taste and sprinkle with the parsley. Cover and cook over low heat for about 20 minutes. Add the vinegar and cook until it has evaporated, then serve.

TONNO ALL'ACETO

Serves 4

3 tablespoons olive oil

1 garlic clove, sliced

4 tuna steaks

1 fresh flat-leaf parsley sprig, chopped

2 tablespoons white wine vinegar

salt and pepper

TUNA WITH CELERY

TONNO AL SEDANO

Serves 4

2 tablespoons olive oil

2 tablespoons butter

2 pounds tuna steaks, cut into cubes

4 tomatoes, peeled, seeded and diced

4 fresh basil leaves, chopped

1 head of celery, chopped

pinch of chili powder

$^1\!/_2$ cup black olives, pitted

salt and pepper

Heat the olive oil and butter in a pan, add the tuna and cook, stirring frequently, until lightly browned all over. Add the tomatoes, basil, celery and chili powder and season with salt and pepper. Cover and cook over medium heat for 30 minutes. Stir in the olives, heat through briefly and serve.

TUNA AND BEAN SALAD

TONNO IN INSALATA CON FAGIOLINI

Serves 4

$2^1\!/_4$ pounds fresh white beans, shelled

14-ounce tuna steak

olive oil, for brushing and drizzling

1 garlic clove, halved

10 fresh basil leaves, chopped

$^1\!/_3$ cup pine nuts

4 leeks, white parts only, thinly sliced

1 tomato, seeded and sliced

1 head of escarole

salt and pepper

Cook the beans in a pan of boiling water for 40–60 minutes until tender, then drain. Preheat the broiler. Brush the tuna generously with olive oil, place on the hot broiler rack and cook, brushing with more oil occasionally, for 10 minutes on each side. Cut the cooked fish into cubes. Rub the garlic around the inside of a salad bowl and put the basil and pine nuts in the bowl. Season with salt and pepper, drizzle with olive oil and mix well. Add the beans, leeks, tomato, escarole and fish and serve while the tuna is still warm.

SLOW–COOKED TUNA

TONNO STUFATO

Serves 4

2 tablespoons olive oil

4 tuna steaks, halved

1 shallot, chopped

1 carrot, chopped

1 cup turnips, chopped

$1^1\!/_3$ cups green beans, halved

1 fresh thyme sprig

1 fresh rosemary sprig

scant $^1\!/_2$ cup white wine

salt and pepper

Heat the olive oil in a large shallow pan, add the tuna and cook over high heat until browned on both sides. Remove the tuna from the pan, skim off any excess fat, then add the shallot and cook, stirring occasionally, for about 5 minutes. Add the carrots, turnips, beans, thyme and rosemary, season with salt and pepper and cook over medium heat, stirring occasionally, for about 10 minutes. Place the tuna on top of the vegetables, add the wine and $^2\!/_3$ cup warm water, lower the heat, cover and simmer for about 30 minutes. Remove and discard the herbs and transfer the tuna and vegetables to a warm serving dish.

RED SNAPPER AND RED MULLET

Red mullet are highly prized fish with an unmistakable color, but although this fish family is found all over the world, none of the American mullets compares with it for flavor and texture. However, the equally delicious and colorful red snapper is widely available in the United States and is the perfect substitute here. Small snapper are best simply fried, but medium-sized fish can be cooked in a variety of ways. Snapper are also an important ingredient in fish soups. The Italian recipe titles remain unchanged and refer to red mullet.

RED SNAPPER WITH FENNEL

Preheat the oven to 350°F. Sprinkle the fennel over the base of an ovenproof dish. Season the cavities of the fish with salt and pepper, place them on top of the fennel and pour in the lemon juice, wine and 4 tablespoons of the olive oil. Bake, basting occasionally, for about 30 minutes. Meanwhile, combine the shallot, chile, mustard, egg yolk and a pinch of salt in a bowl, then gradually whisk in the remaining olive oil. Serve the red snapper straight from the dish with the sauce handed separately.

TRIGLIE AL FINOCCHIO

Serves 4

2 fresh fennel sprigs, chopped

2¼ pounds red snapper, scaled and cleaned

juice of 2 lemons, strained

³⁄₄ cup dry white wine

scant 1 cup olive oil

1 shallot, chopped

1 dried chile, crushed

1 tablespoon herb mustard

1 hard-cooked egg yolk, mashed

salt and pepper

RED SNAPPER LIVORNO—STYLE

TRIGLIE ALLA LIVORNESE

Serves 4

4 tablespoons olive oil

1 fresh flat-leaf parsley sprig, chopped, plus extra for for sprinkling

½ garlic clove, chopped

scant 1 cup bottled strained tomatoes

2¼ pounds red snapper, scaled and cleaned

salt and pepper

Heat the olive oil in a large skillet, add the parsley and garlic and cook over low heat, stirring frequently, for a few minutes. Add the strained tomatoes, season with salt and pepper and simmer for 5 minutes. Place the fish in the sauce and simmer gently, shaking the pan occasionally, for 20 minutes. Do not turn the fish over, to avoid breaking them. Sprinkle with parsley and serve.

RED SNAPPER WITH HERBS

TRIGLIE ALLE ERBE AROMATICHE

Serves 4

3 tablespoons olive oil

2¼ pounds red snapper, filleted

juice of 1 lemon, strained

2 tablespoons heavy cream

1 fresh flat-leaf parsley sprig, chopped

1 fresh thyme sprig, chopped

1 fresh chervil sprig, chopped

salt and pepper

Heat the olive oil in a skillet, add the fish, skin side down, and cook for 3—4 minutes, then carefully turn them over and cook for 1 minute more. Remove from the skillet with a slotted spatula and keep warm. Skim off the olive oil from the pan juices, stir in the lemon juice and bring to simmering point. Stir in the cream and cook until thickened. Season with salt and pepper and stir in the herbs. Place the fish on a warm serving dish, spoon the hot sauce over them.

RED SNAPPER WITH BEANS

TRIGLIE CON FAGIOLI

Serves 4

1 cup dried cannellini beans, soaked overnight in cold water and drained

1 onion

2 fresh sage leaves

1 fresh tarragon sprig

1 fresh chervil sprig

2¼ pounds red snapper, scaled and cleaned

all-purpose flour, for dusting

6 tablespoons olive oil

1 tablespoon white wine vinegar

1 shallot, finely chopped

salt and pepper

Put the beans in a pan, add water to cover, and the onion, sage, tarragon and chervil and bring to a boil, then lower the heat and simmer for 1—2 hours until tender. Drain the beans and discard the onion and herbs. Lightly dust the fish with flour. Heat half the olive oil in a skillet, add the fish and cook for about 4 minutes on each side. Beat together the remaining olive oil and the vinegar in a bowl, stir in the shallot and season with salt and pepper. Pour the dressing over the beans and mix gently. Arrange the fish on a warm serving dish and surround with the beans.

#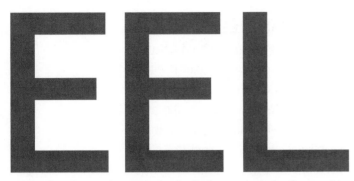

In Italy eels are found in Lake Bolsena and the Comacchio marshes, where they are famously bred and processed. But eel travel enormous distances during migration and can be found all the world over. They look like snakes and are often still slithering when they reach the fishmonger as they are very lively. Young, thin eel fry are called cieche in Italian, meaning blind. When they mature, after four or five years, some are eaten fresh, and others are salted or – and this is the speciality of Comacchio – smoked. The females, called capitoni in central southern Italy and bisati in Veneto, are larger than the males. They sometimes reach 3¼ feet in length and are highly prized. Eels must be skinned for some recipes and it's best to ask the fishmonger to prepare them for you. Otherwise, use a small, sharp, pointed knife and make a T-shaped cut under the head. Take hold of the two flaps and pull the skin inside out. As eels are slippery, it is advisable to hold them firmly with a dish towel.

FRESHWATER FISH

BRETON EEL

Pour the wine and 2¼ cups water into a pan, add the carrot, onion and thyme, season with salt and pepper and bring to a boil. Lower the heat and simmer for 15 minutes. Add the eels and simmer for 10 minutes, then remove from the heat and let cool in the cooking liquid. Heat the olive oil in a pan, add the mushrooms, pancetta and garlic and cook over low heat, stirring frequently, for about 10 minutes until browned. Stir in the tomato paste and ⅔ cup of the eel cooking liquid and season with salt and pepper. Simmer for 20 minutes. Arrange the slices of eel on a warm serving dish and spoon the hot sauce over them.

ANGUILLE ALLA BRETONE

Serves 4

¾ cup dry white wine

1 carrot

1 onion

1 fresh thyme sprig

1¾ pounds eels, skinned, cleaned and sliced and cut into 1½-inch slices

2 tablespoons olive oil

2¾ cups mushrooms, sliced

generous ½ cup smoked pancetta, diced

½ garlic clove, chopped

1 tablespoon tomato paste

salt and pepper

ROAST EEL

ANGUILLE ARROSTO

Serves 4

2¼-pound eels, skinned and cleaned

4 bay leaves

salt

Preheat the oven to 350°F. Make a cut in the back of the eel, coil it into a casserole, add the bay leaves and sprinkle with salt. Cook in the oven for at least 40 minutes, where it will roast in its own fat. Transfer to a warm serving dish.

EEL WITH SAVOY CABBAGE

ANGUILLE CON LE VERZE

Serves 4

1 small Savoy cabbage, cored and quartered

2 tablespoons butter

2 tablespoons olive oil

4 shallots, chopped

2 carrots, sliced

generous ½ cup smoked pancetta, cubed

5 tablespoons dry white wine

5 tablespoons white wine vinegar

1 bay leaf

1¾ pounds eels, skinned, cleaned and sliced

salt and pepper

Parboil the cabbage in salted, boiling water for 10 minutes, then drain. Heat the butter and olive oil in a pan, add the shallots, carrots and pancetta and cook over low heat, stirring occasionally, for 10 minutes. Add the wine, vinegar and bay leaf and season with salt and pepper. Add the cabbage to the pan, cover and cook for 30 minutes. Add the eels to the pan, re-cover and cook, shaking the pan occasionally, for 20 minutes. Remove and discard the bay leaf and transfer the mixture to a warm serving dish.

EEL IN GREEN SAUCE

ANGUILLE IN SALSA VERDE

Serves 4

2–3 tablespoons butter

2 pounds eels, skinned, cleaned and sliced

1 fresh flat-leaf parsley sprig, chopped

1 fresh red sorrel sprig, chopped

1 fresh chervil sprig, chopped

1 tablespoon fresh rosemary needles, chopped

1 onion, chopped

¾ cup dry white wine

1 egg yolk, lightly beaten

pinch of potato flour

juice of 1 lemon, strained

salt and pepper

Melt 2 tablespoons of the butter in a pan, add the eels and cook over medium heat, turning occasionally, for 15 minutes. Season with salt and pepper, remove from the pan and set aside. Add the parsley, sorrel, chervil, rosemary and onion to the pan and cook over low heat, stirring occasionally, for 5 minutes, adding the remaining butter if necessary. Pour in the wine, return the eels to the pan and cook for a further 5 minutes. Stir in the egg yolk, potato flour and lemon juice and cook until the sauce has thickened.

BRAISED EEL

Heat the olive oil in a pan, add the onion, garlic and parsley and cook over low heat, stirring occasionally, for 5 minutes. Add the tomatoes, season with salt and pepper and simmer, stirring occasionally, for 10 minutes. Add the eels and cook for a few minutes more, then pour in the wine. Simmer over very low heat for 30 minutes until the eels are tender, adding a little water if necessary. Sprinkle with parsley and serve.

ANGUILLE IN UMIDO

Serves 4

3 tablespoons olive oil

1 onion, chopped

1 garlic clove

1 fresh flat-leaf parsley sprig, chopped,

plus extra for sprinkling

14 ounces tomatoes, peeled, seeded and chopped

2 pounds eels, skinned, cleaned and thickly sliced

³/₄ cup red or white wine

salt and pepper

EEL KABOBS

Combine the olive oil, vinegar, lemon juice and one of the bay leaves in a dish, season with salt and pepper and add the eels, turning to coat. Leave in a cool place to marinate for 1¹/₂ hours. Preheat the oven to 350°F. Drain the eels, reserving the marinade, and thread onto skewers, alternating with the remaining bay leaves and the bread cubes. Put the kabobs into a roasting pan, sprinkle with the marinade and cook in the oven, turning and brushing with olive oil occasionally, for about 20 minutes.

SPIEDINI D'ANGUILLA

Serves 4

²/₃ cup olive oil, plus extra for brushing

¹/₄ cup red wine vinegar

juice of 1 lemon, strained

17 bay leaves

1³/₄ pounds eels, skinned, cleaned and sliced,

(cut into 1¹/₄-inch slices)

1 white loaf, crusts removed, cut into cubes

salt and pepper

CARP

Carp live in still waters or sluggish rivers with muddy beds. Their flesh is highly prized, but, unfortunately, they have a lot of bones. They easily reach 20–24 inches in length and a weight of 4¹/₂–6¹/₂ pounds. When preparing carp, it is important to leave them under cold, running water or soak them in water acidulated with a little vinegar for several hours, so that their flesh loses any slight muddy taste it may have retained.

CARPA ALLA MAÎTRE D'HÔTEL

Serves 4

¹/₄ cup butter, softened

juice of 1 lemon, strained

1 tablespoon fresh flat-leaf parsley, chopped

4 carp, cleaned and soaked

olive oil, for brushing

salt

CARP WITH MAÎTRE D'HÔTEL BUTTER

Beat the butter with 3 tablespoons of the lemon juice, the parsley and a pinch of salt in a bowl until thoroughly combined. Shape the mixture into cubes and chill in the refrigerator until required. Preheat the broiler. Brush the fish with olive oil and some of the remaining lemon juice and cook under the broiler until the flesh flakes easily. Serve garnished with the butter cubes.

CARP WITH OLIVES

CARPA ALLE OLIVE

Serves 4

olive oil, for brushing

2 garlic cloves, chopped

1 fresh flat-leaf parsley sprig, chopped

4 carp, cleaned and soaked

4 tablespoons white wine vinegar

12 green olives, pitted and chopped

salt and pepper

Preheat the oven to 350°F. Brush an ovenproof dish with olive oil. Combine the garlic and parsley in a bowl, season with salt and pepper and stuff the cavities of the carp with the mixture. Place the carp in the prepared dish, pour 1 tablespoon of the vinegar over each fish and sprinkle with the olives. Bake for about 40 minutes. Transfer the carp to a warm serving dish and spoon the cooking juices over them.

ORIENTAL CARP

CARPA ALL'ORIENTALE

Serves 4

1 1/2 tablespoons raisins

2 1/4-pound carp, cleaned and soaked

cooking salt, for sprinkling

1 1/2 cups onions, chopped

12 almonds, chopped

2 sugar cubes

salt and pepper

Put the raisins in a bowl, add water to cover and let soak for 30 minutes, then drain and squeeze out. Meanwhile, sprinkle the carp with cooking salt and let stand for 30 minutes, then rinse and cut into fairly large slices. Arrange a layer of onions and almonds on the base of a pan, sprinkle with the raisins and place the fish on top. Pour in just enough water to cover, add the sugar cubes and season with salt and pepper. Cover and cook over low heat for 1 hour. Gently lift out the slices of fish and place on a serving dish. Strain the cooking juices into a bowl, pressing down with the back of a spoon. Spoon the contents of the strainer over the slotted spoons and spoon the liquid around them. Let cool.

CARP IN WINE

CARPA AL VINO

Serves 4

2 tablespoons olive oil

1/4 cup butter

2 carrots, finely chopped

2 onions, finely chopped

1 celery stalk, finely chopped

2 1/4-pound carp, cleaned and soaked

2 1/4 cups red wine

salt and pepper

Heat the olive oil and half the butter in a pan, add the carrots, onions and celery and cook over low heat, stirring occasionally, for 15 minutes. Add the carp, season with salt and pepper to taste and pour in the wine and 5 tablespoons water. Bring to a boil, then cover and simmer gently for 45 minutes. Transfer the fish to a serving dish. Pass the vegetables through a food mill and return them to the pan with the cooking juices. Cook until thickened and stir in the remaining butter. Serve the carp with the sauce.

WHITEFISH

Whitefish, a term for a number of different varieties of freshwater fish, are caught in almost all Italian lakes, where they were introduced from northern Europe during the nineteenth century. They are, on average, 6-16 inches long and weigh 1 pound 2 ounces–6¹/₂ pounds. They have firm, white flesh and may be cooked in the same way as trout. (The flesh takes on a pink tinge if they have been feeding on crustaceans.) Cisco are available commercially in the United States, but it's also worth cultivating a friendship with a keen fisherman or becoming one yourself if you want the larger fish from Lake Superior.

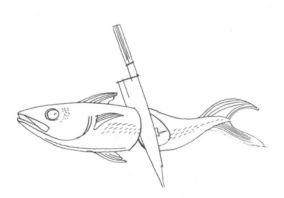

LAVARELLI ALLE ERBE

Serves 4

4 x 7-ounce whitefish, cleaned

1 small fresh bergamot sprig, chopped

1 small fresh marjoram sprig, chopped

1 small fresh rosemary sprig, chopped

1 tablespoon capers, drained and rinsed

5 tablespoons olive oil

juice of ¹/₄ lemon, strained

all-purpose flour, for dusting

5 tablespoons dry white wine

salt and pepper

WHITEFISH WITH HERBS

Open out the fish like a book, place them skin side up and press along the backbones with your thumb. Turn them over and use a knife to prize the backbones away from the flesh, then remove them. Put the bergamot, marjoram, rosemary and capers in a bowl and mix. Add 1 tablespoon of the olive oil and the lemon juice and season with salt and pepper. Sprinkle this mixture onto the insides of the open fish, then close and press firmly together with the palm of your hand. Lightly dust the fish with flour. Heat the remaining olive oil in a skillet, add the fish and cook until browned on both sides. Add the wine and cook until it has evaporated and the fish flakes easily. Lightly season with salt, remove from the heat and serve.

FRIED WHITEFISH

Put the fish in a dish, add the milk and let soak for 15 minutes. Drain, pat dry and dust with flour. Heat the oil in a skillet, add the fish and cook over medium heat for about 8 minutes on each side until browned. Remove the fish with a slotted spatula, drain on paper towels and season with salt. Whitefish fried in a little butter are more delicate.

LAVARELLI FRITTI

Serves 4

4 x 7-ounce whitefish, cleaned

1¼ cups milk

all-purpose flour, for dusting

6 tablespoons olive oil

salt

POACHED WHITEFISH WITH HORSERADISH SAUCE

Put the fish in a fish kettle or large pan, add the court-bouillon and bring just to a boil, then lower the heat and simmer gently for about 20 minutes until the flesh flakes easily. Remove from the heat and let the fish cool in the stock. Combine the mayonnaise, horseradish, mustard, a pinch of salt and 1 tablespoon of the cooled stock. Drain the fish, remove the bones and transfer carefully to a serving dish. Spoon the horseradish sauce over the fish and serve.

LAVARELLI LESSATI
CON SALSA AL RAFANO

Serves 4

2¼-pound whitefish, cleaned

1 quantity Court-bouillon (see page 591)

1 quantity Mayonnaise,

made with 1 egg (see page 65)

2 tablespoons grated horseradish

½ teaspoon English mustard

salt

WHITEFISH AND POTATO PIE

Preheat the oven to 350°F. Brush a roasting pan with oil. Cut several diagonal slashes on each side of each fish. Make layers of the potatoes in the roasting pan, drizzle with olive oil, sprinkle with the garlic and season with salt and pepper. Place the fish on top, sprinkle with the herbs and drizzle with olive oil. Bake for about 30 minutes and transfer to a warm serving dish.

TORTINO DI LAVARELLI CON PATATE

Serves 4

olive oil, for brushing and drizzling

4 x 7-ounce whitefish, cleaned

3–4 potatoes, thinly sliced

1 garlic clove, chopped

1 fresh thyme sprig, chopped

1 fresh marjoram sprig, chopped

salt and pepper

PIKE

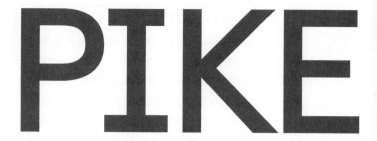

Pike are caught in fresh water in central northern Italy and are appreciated for their firm, white but fairly bony flesh. Female pike may grow to 3¹/₄ feet long. It is best to leave large pike in the refrigerator for 24 hours. Pike roe should be discarded because it is often poisonous.

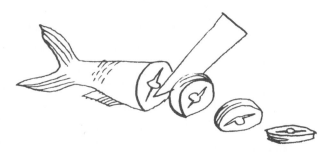

LUCCIO AL BURRO BIANCO

Serves 4

2¹/₄-pound pike, cleaned
1 small onion slice
1 fresh flat-leaf parsley sprig
1 garlic clove
3 tablespoons butter, melted
salt and pepper

For the beurre blanc
3 shallots, finely chopped
1 tablespoon white wine vinegar
1 tablespoon dry white wine
scant 1 cup butter, softened and cut into small pieces
juice of ¹/₂ lemon, strained
salt and white pepper

PIKE IN BEURRE BLANC

Preheat the oven to 350°F. Season the cavity of the pike with salt and pepper and place the onion, parsley and garlic inside it, then season the fish with salt and pepper. Brush the melted butter over the fish, place in an ovenproof dish and bake for 30 minutes, brushing every 5 minutes with the remaining melted butter. Meanwhile, make the beurre blanc. Put the shallots in a pan with the vinegar and wine and cook over medium-high heat until reduced. Remove the pan from the heat and whisk in the butter, a little at a time. Return the pan to the heat for a few seconds after each addition. Stir in the lemon juice and season with salt and pepper to taste. Serve the pike with the beurre blanc handed separately.

OLD-FASHIONED PIKE

Heat the olive oil in a skillet. Season the fish fillets with salt and pepper on both sides, add to the skillet and cook over high heat until golden brown on both sides. Transfer the fish to a plate and keep warm. Pour the wine into the skillet, add the onion and garlic and cook, stirring occasionally, until the liquid has reduced by half. Add the butter, a little at a time, and mix well. Finally, stir in 3 tablespoons warm water and the lemon juice. Keep warm over very low heat. Put the pancetta in another pan and heat until the fat runs, then remove with a slotted spoon. Place the fish in the butter sauce, add the pancetta and simmer gently for 10–15 minutes. Garnish the pike fillets with parsley and serve.

LUCCIO ALL'ANTICA

Serves 4

2 tablespoons olive oil

2$\frac{1}{4}$-pound pike, cleaned and filleted

5 tablespoons dry white wine

1 onion, thinly sliced

$\frac{1}{2}$ garlic clove, chopped

$\frac{1}{4}$ cup butter, softened and cut into pieces

juice of $\frac{1}{2}$ lemon, strained

generous $\frac{1}{2}$ cup smoked pancetta, cubed

salt and pepper

chopped fresh flat-leaf parsley, to garnish

PIKE BLANQUETTE

Lightly dust the fish pieces with flour. Melt the butter in a pan and when it has turned light golden brown, add the fish and cook until evenly browned on both sides. Add the mushrooms, season with salt and pepper to taste and cook over low heat for about 20 minutes. Meanwhile, beat together the egg yolks and cream in a small bowl and season lightly with salt. Remove the pan from the heat and pour the egg mixture over the fish. Return to very low heat and heat through gently. Transfer the fish pieces to a warm serving dish and spoon the sauce over them.

LUCCIO IN BLANQUETTE

Serves 4

2$\frac{1}{4}$-pound pike, cleaned and cut into chunks

all-purpose flour, for dusting

$\frac{1}{4}$ cup butter

2$\frac{3}{4}$ cups mushrooms, thinly sliced

2 egg yolks

scant 1 cup heavy cream

salt and pepper

PERCH

Perch are highly prized freshwater fish. They live along the banks of lakes and slow-flowing rivers in central and northern regions of Italy and Sicily and are found in many other parts of Europe and North America. On average they are 8–14 inches long, but may grow as long as 24 inches. They have firm, white flesh with a delicate flavor and are easy to cut into fillets. They share a number of recipes with trout, and are delicious fried in oil or sautéed in butter.

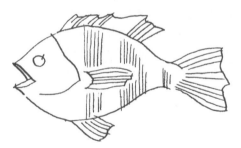

PERCH BAKED IN CREAMY HERB SAUCE

PESCE PERSICO IN TEGLIA
ALLA CREMA VERDE

Serves 4

8 perch fillets

¼ cup butter

3 fresh chervil sprigs, chopped

8 fresh basil leaves, chopped

scant 1 cup dry white wine

scant 1 cup light cream

1 cup bread crumbs

salt and pepper

Preheat the oven to 350°F. Place the perch fillets in an ovenproof dish, dot with the butter, sprinkle with the chervil and basil and season with salt and pepper. Pour in the wine and cream and sprinkle the bread crumbs over the top. Bake for 10–15 minutes, then serve straight from the dish.

MILANESE PERCH

Combine the lemon juice and olive oil in a dish, add the fish, turning to coat, and let marinate for 1 hour. Spread out the flour in a shallow dish, beat the egg with a pinch of salt in another shallow dish and spread out the bread crumbs in a third. Drain the fish, dust lightly with flour, shake off the excess, and dip in the egg and then in the bread crumbs. Melt the butter in a skillet over medium heat, add the fish and fry for 3–4 minutes on each side until light golden brown all over. Remove the fish with a slotted spatula and drain on paper towels. Transfer to a warm serving dish and sprinkle with salt.

PESCE PERSICO ALLA MILANESE

Serves 4

juice of 1 lemon, strained

4 tablespoons olive oil

1 pound 5 ounce perch fillets

1/2 cup all-purpose flour

1 egg

1 1/2 cups bread crumbs

1/4 cup butter

salt

PERCH WITH SAGE

Lightly dust the fish fillets with flour and shake off any excess. Melt the butter with the sage in a skillet, add the fish and cook over medium heat for 3–4 minutes on each side until light golden brown all over. Season with salt and pepper and serve.

PESCE PERSICO ALLA SALVIA

Serves 4

1 pound 5 ounces perch fillets

all-purpose flour, for dusting

1/4 cup butter

8 fresh sage leaves

salt and pepper

PERCH WITH ANCHOVIES

Dice the anchovy fillets. Lightly dust the perch fillets with flour, shaking off any excess. Heat 2 tablespoons of the olive oil in a skillet, add the fish and cook on both sides until lightly browned. Combine the anchovies, garlic, parsley, lemon juice, cayenne, the remaining olive oil and the wine in a bowl and pour the mixture over the perch. Season with salt and cook over low heat for about 15 minutes.

PESCE PERSICO ALLE ACCIUGHE

Serves 4

3 salted anchovies, heads removed, cleaned and filleted (see page 596), soaked in cold water for 10 minutes and drained

1 pound 5 ounces perch fillets

all-purpose flour, for dusting

3 tablespoons olive oil

1 garlic clove, chopped

1 fresh flat-leaf parsley sprig, chopped

juice of 1/2 lemon, strained

pinch of cayenne pepper

5 tablespoons dry white wine

salt

CATFISH AND TENCH

A member of the carp family, tench is a bony freshwater fish. with pleasant-tasting flesh, provided it comes from rivers that are not too muddy. However, it is found only in Europe, but catfish is an excellent substitute and even bears some similarity in appearance. Both tench and catfish should be cleaned and washed, but not scaled. Small tench are excellent simply fried. The Italian recipe titles still refer to tench.

TINCA ALLE ERBE

Serves 4

4 x 9-ounce catfish, cleaned

3 tablespoons olive oil

2 shallots, chopped

1 carrot, chopped

1 celery stalk, chopped

1 fresh flat-leaf parsley sprig, chopped

4 fresh basil leaves, chopped

1 fresh thyme sprig, chopped

1 fresh marjoram sprig, chopped

5 tablespoons dry white wine

$^1/_2$ cup green olives, pitted

juice of 1 lemon, strained

salt and pepper

CATFISH WITH HERBS

Remove as many bones as possible from the fish. Heat the olive oil in a skillet, add the fish and cook until lightly browned on both sides, then remove from the skillet. Add the shallots, carrot, celery and herbs to the pan and cook over low heat for about 10 minutes, then return the fish to the skillet, add the wine and season with salt and pepper. Simmer gently for about 30 minutes, adding a little water if the mixture is drying out. Just before the end of the cooking time, add the olives. Transfer the fish to a serving dish and keep warm. Tip the contents of the pan into a food processor, add the lemon juice and process to a purée. Reheat the mixture briefly, then pour the sauce over the fish and serve.

SOUSED CATFISH WITH HERBS

Dust the fish with flour and shake off any excess. Heat 4 tablespoons of the olive oil in a skillet, add the catfish and cook for 10 minutes, then transfer to a serving dish. Heat the remaining olive oil in another pan, add the onion, carrot, garlic, parsley, sage and rosemary and cook over low heat, stirring the mixture occasionally, for 10 minutes. Season with salt and pepper according to taste, add the vinegar and bring to a boil. Pour the mixture over the fish and let marinate for 6–7 hours in a cool place, but not in the refrigerator.

TINCA IN CARPIONE ALLE ERBE

Serves 4

4 x 9-ounce catfish, cleaned

all-purpose flour, for dusting

$^2/_3$ cup olive oil

1 large onion, chopped

1 carrot, chopped

$^1/_2$ garlic clove, chopped

1 fresh flat-leaf parsley sprig, chopped

4 fresh sage leaves, chopped

1 fresh rosemary sprig, chopped

5 tablespoons white wine vinegar

salt and pepper

CATFISH IN A SALT CRUST

Preheat the oven to 475°F. Fill the cavity of the fish with the mixed herbs. Line a roasting pan with foil and cover with a $^3/_4$-inch thick layer of the coarse salt. Place the catfish on top and cover with the remaining coarse salt. Bake for about 35 minutes, then remove from the oven and let stand for 10 minutes. Meanwhile, combine the garlic, parsley, olive oil and lemon juice in a bowl and season with salt and pepper. To serve, break the salt crust and carefully extract the fish. Remove and discard the skin, cut the fish in half and slice into fillets. Serve with the sauce.

TINCA IN CROSTA DI SALE

Serves 4

$2^1/_4$-pound catfish, cleaned

1 bunch of mixed fresh herbs, chopped

$6^1/_2$–9 pounds coarse sea salt

1 garlic clove, chopped

1 fresh flat-leaf parsley sprig, chopped

scant $^1/_2$ cup olive oil

juice of 1 lemon, strained

salt and pepper

STUFFED CATFISH

Preheat the oven to 350°F. Grease an ovenproof dish with butter. Combine 4 tablespoons of the bread crumbs, the Parmesan, garlic, parsley and olive oil in a bowl and season with salt and plenty of pepper. Fill the cavities of the fish with the mixture. Place the bay leaves in the prepared dish, put the catfish on top and sprinkle with the remaining bread crumbs. Bake, basting occasionally, for 1 hour. When the fish are ready, plenty of tasty sauce should have formed which goes well with polenta or mashed potato.

TINCA RIPIENA

Serves 4

butter, for greasing

1 cup bread crumbs

4 tablespoons Parmesan cheese, freshly grated

2 garlic cloves, chopped

2 tablespoons chopped fresh flat-leaf parsley

1 tablespoon olive oil

4 x 9-ounce catfish, cleaned

3 bay leaves

salt and pepper

TROUT

There are various types of trout. The most commonly caught in Italian lakes and rivers are brown trouts. These average 8–16 inches in length and 1 pound 5 ounces–6¹⁄₂ pounds in weight. Rainbow trout, originally imported from the United States, are farmed. Trout are easy to digest and highly prized, especially sea trout, which are readily identified by their pink flesh. Trout are available both fresh and frozen (the latter are usually farmed).

SEA TROUT ROLL

ROTOLO DI TROTA SALMONATA

Serves 4

4 sea trout fillets
2 gelatin leaves
scant 1 cup heavy cream
2 teaspoons grated horseradish
juice of 1 lemon, strained
1 jar (about 1¹⁄₂ ounces) sea trout roe
salt and white pepper
arugula, to garnish

Remove any remaining pin bones from the fish and place the fillets in a shallow dish. Set the dish over a pan of boiling water and steam for 10 minutes. Put the gelatin in a bowl, add water to cover and let soak for 5 minutes. Pour the cream into a double boiler or heatproof bowl and heat over barely simmering water. Squeeze out the gelatin and stir it into the cream. Flake the fish into a bowl, add the cream mixture, horseradish and lemon juice, season with salt and pepper and mix. Transfer the mixture to a food processor and process until smooth and combined. Scrape out the mixture and shape it into a roll, then wrap tightly in foil and chill in the refrigerator for about 4 hours until set. Thinly slice the roll, place on a serving dish and surround with the roe and garnish with arugula.

SMOKED TROUT WITH MELON

Halve the melon, scoop out and discard the seeds and cut the flesh into thin strips. Thinly slice four of the onions and chop the fifth. Pour the yogurt into a salad bowl, add the chopped onion, cream and vinegar and season with salt and pepper. Mix well and add the sliced onions. Put a trout fillet on each of four plates, add some melon strips, sprinkle with the sauce and garnish with cucumber slices.

TROTA AFFUMICATA AL MELONE

Serves 4

1 small melon
5 baby onions
1³/₄ cups natural yogurt
2 tablespoons heavy cream
1 tablespoon white wine vinegar
4 smoked trout fillets
salt and pepper
¹/₂ cucumber, sliced, to garnish

SEA TROUT WITH JUNIPER BERRIES

Put the bay leaf, carrot, thyme and parsley in a pan, pour in 2¹/₄ cups water and bring to a boil. Place the fish in a steamer over the pan, cover and steam for 10 minutes. Remove the fish from the heat, pat dry and place in a serving dish. Bring the liquid in the pan back to a boil and continue to boil over high heat until reduced, then add the wine, vinegar and juniper and season with salt. Bring back to a boil, then pour the mixture over the fish and let cool to room temperature.

TROTA AL GINEPRO

Serves 4

1 bay leaf
1 carrot, sliced
1 fresh thyme sprig, chopped
1 fresh flat-leaf parsley sprig, chopped
8 sea trout fillets
³/₄ cup dry white wine
³/₄ cup white wine vinegar
4 juniper berries
salt

PROVENÇAL TROUT

Parboil the potatoes in 2¹/₄ cups water and the wine for 10 minutes. Drain and season with salt and pepper. Heat 4 tablespoons of the olive oil in a skillet, add the potatoes and cook, turning occasionally, until tender. Put the tomatoes and red bell pepper in separate pans and heat gently without any additional oil or fat, then divide the butter between them. Heat the remaining olive oil in a skillet, add the trout and cook for 10 minutes on each side. Lift the fish out of the pan with a slotted spatula and remove and discard their skins. Spoon the tomatoes onto a warm serving dish, place the trout in the middle of them and surround with the potatoes, olives and red bell pepper.

TROTA ALLA PROVENZALE

Serves 4

3 potatoes, sliced
1¹/₂ cups dry white wine
6 tablespoons olive oil
4 tomatoes, peeled and chopped
1 red bell pepper, halved, seeded and cut into strips
¹/₄ cup butter
4 small trout, cleaned
scant 1 cup black olives, pitted
salt and pepper

TROUT WITH MUSHROOMS AND MUSSELS

TROTA CON FUNGHI E COZZE

Serves 4

2 tablespoons butter, plus extra for greasing

1/2 cup dried mushrooms

4 small trout, cleaned

1 tablespoon chopped fresh thyme

olive oil, for brushing

1/2 onion, chopped

1 carrot, chopped

1 celery stalk, chopped

1 1/2 cups dry white wine

12 mussels, cooked and shelled (see page 713)

salt and pepper

Preheat the oven to 350°F. Grease an ovenproof dish with butter. Put the mushrooms in a bowl, add warm water to cover and let soak. Season the cavities of the trout with salt and pepper and sprinkle with the thyme. Brush the fish with olive oil, place in the prepared dish and add the onion, carrot and celery. Dot with the butter, cover with foil and bake for 10 minutes. Drain and squeeze out the mushrooms. Remove the foil from the dish, add the wine and mushrooms and bake for a further 10 minutes. Add the mussels and bake for a few more minutes to heat through, then serve.

SMOKED SEA TROUT AND VEGETABLE CASSEROLE

TROTA CON VERDURE

Serves 6

1/4 cup butter, plus extra for greasing

2 eggs, separated

7 ounces smoked sea trout fillet, flaked

1 quantity Béchamel Sauce (see page 50)

1 pound 2 ounces spinach

1 pound 2 ounces red sorrel

4 tablespoons heavy cream

2 tablespoons chopped almonds

salt and pepper

Preheat the oven to 425°F. Grease six ramekins or individual molds with butter. Lightly beat the egg yolks and stiffly whisk the whites in a separate, grease-free bowl. Stir the yolks and fish into the cold béchamel sauce, fold in the egg whites and season with salt and pepper. Pour the mixture into the prepared dishes and place them in a roasting pan. Add boiling water to come about halfway up the sides and bake for 25 minutes. Meanwhile, melt the butter in a pan, add the spinach and sorrel and cook over low heat, stirring frequently, until wilted. Season with salt and pepper, stir in 1 tablespoon of the cream and spoon the mixture over the base of an ovenproof dish. Remove the roasting pan from the oven and lower the temperature to 350°F. Turn out the ramekins or molds on top of the spinach mixture, spoon the remaining cream over them and sprinkle with the almonds. Bake for about 15 minutes.

SEA TROUT ROE WITH POTATOES

UOVA DI TROTA E PATATE

Serves 4

4 potatoes, unpeeled

1/4 cup butter, softened

1 tablespoon chopped fresh chervil

2 tablespoons heavy cream

1 jar (about 1 1/2 ounces) sea trout roe

salt • lemon slices, to garnish

Preheat the oven to 350°F. Wrap each potato in a sheet of foil and bake for about 50 minutes. Unwrap the potatoes and peel them, then cut in half and arrange on a warm serving dish. Cream the butter, beat in the chervil, cream and a pinch of salt and spread the mixture over the potatoes. Divide the roe among and garnish with slices of lemon.

CRUSTACEANS

The crustacean family is quite large especially when you consider how many different species of shrimp there are. However, all crustaceans have relatively elongated bodies covered at the front by a carapace – a shell of varying hardness which protects part of the head and the part of the upper body where the viscera are. They also have eyes, feelers and five pairs of legs. The pair of legs nearest the mouth are often modified into heavy claws or pincers used to grip food and for defence. The end of the body, popularly called the tail, is actually the abdomen. It is the choice part from the culinary point of view and is protected by a segmented shell. The true tail, which opens out like a fan, is technically called the telson. All crustaceans have compact flesh with a mild yet distinctive flavor and a pleasant hint of sweetness. Ideally, they should still be alive when purchased. Traditionally, they are thrown into boiling water where the shell protects the flesh from the fierce heat and keeps it soft and delicate. A more humane alternative is to place crabs and lobsters in the freezer for a couple of hours to induce hypothermia before boiling them. The shell also protects the flesh during frying and broiling. Remember that the most delicate flesh is in the legs and claws. Spiny and American lobsters are both top-ranking crustaceans but no one will ever settle the elegant culinary question of which is the most highly prized. More common crustaceans are also good and tasty.

LOBSTER

Spiny and American lobsters find equal favor with gourmets, although the flesh of the latter is milder and more delicate. Both should be boiled for 15 minutes per 2¹/₄ pounds. Increase the time by 5 minutes for every additional 7 ounces. Small spiny lobsters – 11 ounces – should be boiled for 5 minutes and 1³/₄-pound spiny lobsters should be boiled for 10 minutes. The best spiny lobsters are medium-size females. Given that about 70 per cent is waste, you need a 2¹/₄-pound spiny lobster for two servings. Live lobsters should be immersed in a large pan of boiling water, tightly covered and cooked for 1 minute. To prevent them from jumping out, it is advisable to tie their tails to a wooden stick. To extract the meat, place the lobster on a board, cut it in half lengthwise, open it up and remove the meat from each half of the tail. Remove the dark intestinal tract with the point of a knife and discard. Break off the claws in the case of American lobsters, crack open and remove the meat. The soft green tomalley (liver) and the coral (roe) are considered delicacies. If you're going to use the shells to serve the lobster, remove and discard the stomach sac.

CREOLE SPINY LOBSTER

Bring a large pan of water to a boil with the onions, celery, carrots, herbs, juniper, garlic, peppercorns and a pinch of salt and simmer for 20 minutes. Bring back to a rolling boil, immerse the lobsters, cover tightly and cook for 10 minutes. Remove the pan from the heat and leave the lobsters to cool in the cooking liquid. Drain the lobsters, reserving the cooking liquid, cut open and remove the meat (see above), reserving the coral. Bring the cooking liquid to a boil and boil until reduced to about 2¹/₄ cups, then strain into a bowl. For the dressing melt half the butter in a pan, add the onion and cook over low heat, stirring frequently, for 10 minutes until lightly browned. Pour in the brandy and cook over low heat until the liquid is reduced by half, then strain. Melt the remaining butter in another pan, stir in the flour and curry powder, then gradually stir in the lobster stock. Cook, stirring until thickened and smooth, then add the coral and reduced brandy. Serve the lobsters with the dressing.

ARAGOSTA ALLA CREOLA

Serves 4

2 onions, halved

1 celery stalk, halved • 2 carrots, halved

1 bay leaf

¹/₂ bunch of fresh flat-leaf parsley

8 juniper berries • 1 garlic clove

6 black peppercorns

2 x 1³/₄-pound live spiny lobsters

salt

For the dressing

¹/₄ cup butter

1 onion, chopped

scant ¹/₂ cup brandy

¹/₄ cup all-purpose flour

pinch of curry powder

SPICY LOBSTER

ARAGOSTA ALLE SPEZIE

Serves 4

4 spiny lobster tails, thawed if frozen

6 tablespoons butter

1/2 teaspoon ground ginger • 1/2 teaspoon curry powder

1 teaspoon ground cilantro

juice of 1 lemon, strained

salt and pepper

lemon slices, to garnish

Preheat the broiler. Make a deep cut in the hard outer covering on the undersides of the lobster tails. Melt the butter in a pan, remove from the heat as soon as it has melted, stir in the ginger, curry powder, cilantro and lemon juice and season with salt and pepper. Arrange the lobster tails with the back shells uppermost in a roasting pan and broil for about 3 minutes, then turn over, pour the spiced butter into the cuts in the undersides and broil for a further 3–4 minutes. Season with pepper and garnish with lemon slices.

LOBSTER IN TARRAGON SAUCE

ARAGOSTA IN SALSA DI DRAGONCELLO

Serves 4

2 x 1 3/4-pound spiny lobsters, boiled

scant 1/2 cup butter

1 onion, finely chopped

1 celery stalk, finely chopped

1 carrot, finely chopped

1/4 cup brandy

1 teaspoon herb mustard

1 fresh tarragon sprig, finely chopped

3/4 cup dry white wine

juice of 1/2 lemon, strained

salt and pepper

Cut open the lobsters and remove the meat (see page 689), reserving the tomalley and coral . Melt 1/4 cup of the butter in a pan, add the onion, celery and carrot and cook over low heat, stirring occasionally, for 5 minutes. Add the lobster meat and cook until lightly browned, then season. Add half the brandy and cook until it has evaporated, then add the mustard and tarragon. Pour in the wine, cover and simmer for 10 minutes. Remove the pan from the heat, transfer the lobsters to a plate and keep warm. Strain the cooking liquid into a clean pan. Chop the tomalley and coral and add to the pan with the remaining butter, remaining brandy and the lemon juice. Cook over medium heat until slightly reduced, then season. Serve the lobsters covered with the sauce.

ARMORICAN LOBSTER

ASTICI ALL'ARMORICANA

Serves 4

3 1/4 pounds live American lobsters

2 onions, finely chopped

1/2 garlic clove, finely chopped

1/4 cup butter

2 tablespoons olive oil

5 tablespoons brandy

1 tablespoon fresh flat-leaf parsley, chopped

11 ounces canned chopped tomatoes

1 cup dry white wine

salt and pepper

To garnish

cucumber slices

lemon slices

Bring a large pan of water to a rolling boil, add the lobsters, cover tightly and cook for 2 minutes. Drain, open the lobsters and remove the meat (see page 689), then cut it into fairly large pieces. Cook the onions and garlic in salted, boiling water until soft, then drain, reserving the cooking liquid, place in a food processor and process to a purée. Heat the butter and olive oil in a pan, add the lobster meat and cook until lightly browned all over. Transfer to another pan, add half the brandy and ignite. Scrape the onion back into the pan of reserved cooking liquid, stir in the parsley and tomatoes and heat gently. When the sauce is hot pour it over the lobsters and stir well. Add the wine, season with salt and pepper and cook over medium heat for about 20 minutes. Pour in the remaining brandy, lower the heat, cover and cook for a further 5 minutes. Remove the pan from the heat, transfer the mixture to a warm serving dish and garnish with slices of cucumber and lemon.

LOBSTER AND SHRIMP SALAD

ASTICI IN INSALATA CON MAZZANCOLLE

Serves 6

1 carrot
1 onion
1 lemon
³/₄ cup white wine
1 tablespoon white wine vinegar
5 live American lobsters
40 raw jumbo shrimp,
peeled and deveined
6 fresh basil leaves, chopped
5 vine tomatoes, chopped
1 celery stalk, chopped
³/₄ cup olive oil
juice of ¹/₂ lemon, strained
salt and pepper
¹/₄ cup olives, to garnish

Put the carrot, onion, lemon, wine and vinegar in a large pan, bring to a boil, then lower the heat and simmer for 15 minutes. Bring back to a rolling boil, add the lobsters, cover tightly and cook for 7 minutes, then add the shrimp and cook for 3 minutes more. Drain, open the lobsters and extract the flesh (see page 689), then cut it into large pieces. Put the basil, tomatoes and celery in a bowl and add the lobster meat and shrimp. Whisk together the olive oil and lemon juice in a bowl and season with salt and pepper. Pour the dressing over the salad, toss gently and serve on individual plates garnished with the olives

MAGNIFICENT MEDALLIONS OF LOBSTER

MEDAGLIONI DI ARAGOSTA IN BELLAVISTA

Serves 4

1 quantity Court-bouillon (see page 591)
2¹/₄-pound live spiny lobster
¹/₂ pint dissolved gelatin
1 white loaf of bread, sliced and crusts removed
3 tablespoons butter
1 bunch of arugula
Mayonnaise (see page 65), to serve

Bring the court-bouillon to a rolling boil in a large pan, add the lobster, cover tightly and cook for 15 minutes. Remove the pan from the heat and let the lobster cool in its cooking liquid. Drain, cut open and extract the meat (see page 689), then slice into medallions. Prepare the gelatin according to the packet instructions. Place the lobster medallions on a plate, brush with several coatings of gelatin and chill in the refrigerator until set. Stamp out the same number of rounds of bread as there are lobster medallions. Melt the butter in a skillet, add the bread rounds and fry until golden brown on both sides. Remove with a slotted spatula and drain on paper towels. Place on a serving dish, top with the lobster medallions, surround with arugula leaves and serve with mayonnaise handed separately.

MY KNIFE

SHRIMP

There are many different species, colors and sizes of shrimp. Three types, in particular, feature in Italian cooking. Mediterranean shrimp are 9 inches long, grayish brown in color with stripes and tinges of purple. Their flesh, which turns pink on cooking, has a very delicate flavor. Pink and red shrimp from the Mediterranean Sea grow to about 8'/₂ inches while those from the Atlantic reach as much as 13 inches in length. These vary in color from red to pink, may be variegated and have a delicate but distinctive flavor. Other shrimp, at 4 inches long, may be pink or gray and have a hint of sweetness. It is usually better to peel shrimp after cooking rather than before to protect their delicate flesh. Finally, the freshwater crayfish should also be mentioned. Once these could be found without difficulty in Italian rivers but today they are nearly all imported from Asia.

ASPARAGUS AND SHRIMP

Bring a pan of salted water to a boil, add the vinegar and blanch the shrimp for 2 minutes, then drain. Tie the asparagus into a bunch and cook it, standing upright, in salted, boiling water for 15–20 minutes, then drain and let cool. Put the carrot and celery on a serving dish and top with the shrimp and asparagus. Drizzle with olive oil, season with salt and pepper and sprinkle with the lemon juice. Mix gently and serve immediately.

ASPARAGI E GAMBERI

Serves 4

2 tablespoons white wine vinegar

20 large raw shrimp, peeled and deveined

1³/₄ pounds asparagus, spears trimmed

1 carrot, thinly sliced

1 celery heart, thinly sliced

olive oil, for drizzling

juice of ¹/₂ lemon, strained

salt and pepper

FRIED SHRIMP IN PINK SAUCE

CODE DI GAMBERI FRITTE IN SALSA ROSA

Serves 4

4 tablespoons tomato paste

3 tablespoons heavy cream

juice of ½ lemon, strained

1½ cups dry white wine

1 teaspoon grated fresh root ginger

1 garlic clove

16 large raw shrimp, peeled and deveined

2 egg whites

vegetable oil, for deep-frying

all-purpose flour, for dusting

salt and pepper

Combine the tomato paste, cream and lemon juice in a bowl, season with salt and pepper and set aside. Pour the wine into a dish and add a pinch of salt and the ginger and garlic. Add the shrimp, mix well and let marinate for about 1 hour. Stiffly whisk the egg whites in a grease-free bowl. Drain the shrimp and immerse them in the egg white. Heat the oil for deep frying in a large pan. Spread out the flour in a shallow dish. Holding each shrimp by the tip of its tail, dip it in the flour, then put it in to the hot oil and cook until golden brown. Remove with a slotted spatula and drain on paper towels. Season with salt and serve with the pink sauce handed separately.

SHRIMP WITH SALMON MOUSSE

GAMBERI DI SPUMA DI SALMONE

Serves 4

10 ounces raw shrimp, peeled and deveined

18 fl ounces dissolved gelatin

3 salmon steaks

scant ½ cup heavy cream

2 tablespoons brandy

salt and pepper

Cook the shrimp in salted, boiling water for 4 minutes, then drain. Prepare the gelatin according to the packet instructions. Coat the base of a mold with some of the gelatin and chill in the refrigerator until set. Meanwhile, cook the salmon in a nonstick pan, turning occasionally, for 5 minutes. Remove from the pan with a slotted spatula, flake the flesh, removing any bones, and put it in a food processor with the cream and brandy. Process to a smooth purée and season with salt and pepper to taste. Set aside a few shrimp for the garnish and arrange the remainder on the base of the mold. Spoon the salmon mousse into the mold, cover with a thin layer of gelatin and chill in the refrigerator for 2 hours. To serve, turn out the mold onto a serving dish and garnish with the reserved shrimp.

SHRIMP SALAD WITH BEANS

GAMBERI IN INSALATA CON FAGIOLI

Serves 4

1 lemon slice

1 pound 2 ounces raw shrimp, peeled and deveined

7 ounces cooked (see page 460) or canned cannellini beans, drained and rinsed

2 tablespoons white wine vinegar

5 tablespoons olive oil

1 fresh flat-leaf parsley sprig, chopped

salt and pepper

Bring 4 cups salted water to a boil in a pan with the slice of lemon. Add the shrimp and cook for 5–6 minutes. Drain well, tip into a bowl and let cool. When the shrimp are cold, add the beans. Whisk together the vinegar and olive oil in a bowl and season with salt and pepper. Pour the dressing over the salad, mix gently, sprinkle with the parsley and serve.

GAMBERI IN SALSA DOLCEFORTE

Serves 6

24 large raw shrimp, peeled and deveined

5 tablespoons olive oil

2 carrots, finely chopped

2 celery stalks, finely chopped

$^{1}/_{2}$ onion, finely chopped

1 leek, finely chopped

$^{1}/_{4}$ cup brandy

$^{3}/_{4}$ cup dry white wine

scant 1 cup Concentrated Fish Stock (see page 210)

1 fresh thyme sprig

1 bay leaf

2 ripe tomatoes, peeled, seeded and chopped

2 lemons

1 tablespoon sugar

all-purpose flour, for dusting

$^{1}/_{2}$ teaspoon ground cinnamon

scant $^{1}/_{2}$ cup golden raisins

1 tablespoon pine nuts

salt and pepper

SHRIMP IN STRONG SWEET SAUCE

Pull off the heads and peel the shrimp, reserving the heads and shells. Devein the shrimp. Heat 3 tablespoons of the oil in a pan, add the shrimp heads and shells, carrots, celery, onion and leek and cook over low heat, stirring occasionally, for 5 minutes. Add the brandy and cook until it has evaporated, then pour in the wine and bring to a boil. Add the fish stock, thyme, bay leaf and tomatoes and simmer, stirring occasionally, until thickened. Strain the stock into a clean pan and return to the heat. Simmer until reduced to about 5 tablespoons. Remove from the heat and reserve. Thinly pare the lemons, avoiding all traces of white pith, and cut the rind into very thin batons. Blanch the rind in three separate changes of boiling water, then drain and place in a small pan with the sugar and 2 tablespoons of water. Bring to a boil, stirring until the sugar has dissolved, then boil without stirring until the lemon rind is coated in syrup, then remove from the heat. Meanwhile, squeeze the lemons and strain the juice. Lightly dust the shrimp with flour. Heat the remaining oil in a skillet, add the shrimp, season with salt and pepper and cook, stirring frequently, until lightly browned. Sprinkle in the cinnamon, add the reserved stock, lemon juice, lemon rind, golden raisins and pine nuts and mix well. Season with salt to taste and serve.

ZUCCHINE AI GAMBERETTI

Serves 4

8 zucchini

1 quantity Mayonnaise (see page 65)

1 onion, finely chopped

dash of Tabasco sauce

1 tablespoon ketchup

$1^{3}/_{4}$ cups cooked, peeled shrimp

salt

ZUCCHINI WITH SHRIMP

Cook the zucchini in salted, boiling water for about 8 minutes, then drain and let cool slightly. Combine the mayonnaise, onion, Tabasco and ketchup in a bowl. Halve the zucchini lengthwise and scoop out the flesh without piercing the 'shells'. Fill the shells with the mayonnaise mixture and the shrimp. Serve immediately while warm.

SPIDER CRAB

Spider or spiny crabs are large crabs which are found in the Adriatic (as well as the Atlantic Coast of America), and in Venice they know just how to cook them. Their flavor is delicate and the most prized part is the central body and claws. The roe – known as coral – is delicious. Simply season it with olive oil and lemon juice. Live spider crabs are plunged into boiling water and cooked for about 30 minutes if large or 20 minutes if small. They should be left to cool in the cooking liquid before you open them and extract the flesh. To do this, break off the legs and claws and cut open the body shell in a circle with a knife or scissors. Remove and discard the gills and scoop out the meat, reserving the coral. Crack the claws with a nutcracker or the handle of a heavy knife, but take care not to shatter the cartilage which could then penetrate the flesh. The extracted flesh is usually served in the crab shell, in which case you should also remove the mouth and stomach sac. The snow crab is a suitable substitute if spider crab is unavailable.

SPIDER CRAB IN OLIVE OIL AND LEMON

Bring a large pan of salted water to a rolling boil. Add the spider crabs, cover and cook for just under 10 minutes. Leave in the water to cool a little. Cut open the shells and extract the meat (see above), and coral, if any. Thoroughly wash and dry the insides of the shells and line with one or two lettuce leaves. Fill with crabmeat. Combine the olive oil and lemon juice in a bowl, add the parsley and garlic if using and season with salt and pepper. Drizzle the dressing over the crabs. If there is any coral, mix it with a little olive oil and use as a garnish.

GRANCEOLA ALL'OLIO E LIMONE

Serves 4

4 live spider crabs

4–8 lettuce leaves

4 tablespoons olive oil

juice of 1 lemon, strained

fresh flat-leaf parsley, chopped (optional)

1 garlic clove (optional)

salt and pepper

SPIDER CRAB WITH MAYONNAISE

Bring a large pan of water to a rolling boil with a pinch of salt and pepper, the thyme and marjoram. Add the spider crabs, cover tightly and cook for 10 minutes. Remove the pan from the heat, leave the crabs in the water to cool slightly and then drain. Cut open the shells and extract the meat (see page 697). Thoroughly wash and dry the insides of the shells and line with one or two lettuce leaves. Gently stir the crabmeat into the mayonnaise, then spoon the mixture into the shells and garnish with the shrimp. Keep in a cool place, but not the refrigerator, until ready to serve.

GRANCEOLA CON MAIONESE

Serves 4

1 fresh thyme sprig

1 fresh marjoram sprig

4 live spider crabs

4–8 lettuce leaves

1 quantity Mayonnaise (see page 65)

salt and pepper

scant 1 cup shrimp, cooked and peeled, to garnish

SPIDER CRAB MIMOSA

Bring the court-bouillon to a rolling boil in a large pan, add the spider crabs, cover tightly and cook for about 10 minutes. Remove from the heat and let cool slightly in the cooking liquid. Open the shells and extract the meat (see page 697). Chop the white meat and mix it with the brown meat in a bowl. Press the egg yolks through a fine strainer and add two-thirds to the crab-meat, season with salt and pepper and gently stir in the olive oil and lemon juice. Thoroughly wash and dry the crab shells, then spoon the crabmeat mixture into them. Sprinkle the remaining egg yolk and the parsley on top and serve.

GRANCEOLA MIMOSA

Serves 4

1 quantity Court-bouillon (see page 591)

4 live spider crabs

3 hard-cooked egg yolks

4 tablespoons olive oil

juice of 1 lemon, strained

1 tablespoon fresh flat-leaf parsley, chopped

salt and white pepper

CRAB

There are two well-known and highly popular types of crab in Italy – the green crab (called moleca in Venice), which lives in lagoons and has soft tasty flesh, and the shore crab (known as the granchio di sabbia in Italian), which lives in shallow waters near rivers. The Dungeness, red and sand crabs, as well as the spider crab (see pages 697–99), all make excellent eating. Canned crabmeat from northern seas is widely available. It is very tasty dressed with oil and lemon juice or mixed with tomato sauce and served with spaghetti. To remove the meat from a cooked crab, place it on its back and break off the claws and legs, then break off the tail flap. Insert a heavy-bladed knife between the body shell and the back shell, twist and then prize apart with your thumbs. Remove and discard the 'dead man's fingers' (gills). Using a spoon, scoop the brown meat out into a bowl. Halve the body with a sharp knife and carefully scoop out the remaining white meat from the shell. Crack the claws and legs and carefully pick out the meat. Finally, press on the back shell just behind the eyes, then remove and discard the mouth and stomach sac. Scoop out the remaining brown meat.

CILIEGINE RIPIENE DI GRANCHIO

Serves 4

12 red cherry tomatoes

9 ounces canned crabmeat, drained

4 tablespoons Mayonnaise (see page 65)

salt and pepper

12 black olives, pitted, to garnish

CHERRY TOMATOES STUFFED WITH CRAB

Cut off the tops of the cherry tomatoes, scoop out a little of the flesh without piercing the 'shells' and season the insides with salt. Place upside down on paper towels for 1 hour to drain. Pick over the crabmeat and remove any cartilage. Combine the crabmeat and mayonnaise in a bowl and season with salt and pepper. Fill the cherry tomatoes with the mixture and garnish each with an olive.

CRAB WITH AVOCADO

GRANCHIO CON AVOCADO

Serves 4

2 avocados

juice of 1 lemon, strained

2 tablespoons butter

4 ounces canned crabmeat, drained

scant $1/2$ cup heavy cream

2 tablespoons bottled Marie Rose sauce

dash of Tabasco sauce

salt and pepper

Peel, pit and slice the avocados, then sprinkle with the lemon juice. Melt the butter in a skillet, add the avocado slices and cook over low heat for 10 minutes. Season with salt and pepper and arrange on a serving dish. Pick over the crabmeat and remove any cartilage, then add to the skillet. Stir in the cream, Marie Rose sauce and Tabasco. Heat gently for a few minutes until thickened, then pour the mixture over the slices of avocado.

CRAB SALAD

GRANCHIO IN INSALATA

Serves 4

1 quantity Court-bouillon (see page 591)

1 live crab

1 Treviso radicchio, cut into strips

11 ounces canned palm hearts, drained, rinsed and sliced

olive oil, for drizzling

white wine vinegar, for drizzling

2 dill pickles, drained and coarsely chopped

1 quantity Sauce Aurore (see page 61)

salt and white pepper

Bring the court-bouillon to a rolling boil in a large pan, add the crab, cover tightly and cook for 20 minutes, then drain. Open the crab (see page 700), carefully extract all the meat and chop the white meat. Season the crabmeat, radicchio and palm hearts separately with a drizzle of olive oil, a drizzle of vinegar, a pinch of salt and a pinch of pepper. Line a large salad bowl with a bed of radicchio, arrange the crabmeat and palm hearts on top and sprinkle with the dill pickles. Drizzle the sauce aurore in decorative spirals on top.

CRAB ROLLS

INVOLTINI DI GRANCHIO RIPIENI

Serves 4

1 quantity Court-bouillon (see page 591)

1 live crab

8 large eggplant slices

olive oil, for brushing

$1/4$ cup butter

1 shallot, finely chopped

scant $1/2$ cup dry white wine

salt

Preheat the broiler. Bring the court-bouillon to a rolling boil in a large pan, add the crab, cover tightly and cook for 20 minutes. Meanwhile, brush the eggplant slices with oil and broil on both sides until golden brown. Remove from the broiler and let cool. Drain and open the crab (see page 700), carefully extract all the meat and chop the white meat. Melt the butter in a pan, add the shallot and cook over low heat, stirring occasionally, for 5 minutes. Stir in the chopped crabmeat, add the wine and cook until it has evaporated. Season lightly with salt. Divide the mixture among the eggplant slices, roll up and secure with toothpicks. Brush a pan with olive oil, add the rolls and set over medium heat until warmed through. Transfer to a warm serving dish.

LANGOUSTINES

Italians differentiate between scampi, which are shorter than 8 inches long, and what are called scamponi, which are longer. In the United States, they are known as langoustines, or lobsterettes, although the deep-fried breaded tails are sometimes called scampi. Lobsterettes have a thicker carapace than langoustines, but are otherwise very similar. They should be eaten extremely fresh because their flesh deteriorates very quickly. The only edible part is the flesh in the tail, which has a delicate delicious flavor that some prefer to lobster. Both whole langoustines and just the tails, are cooked, then the tails are shelled and deveined – i.e. the black intestine is removed. The cooking time varies according to size. When added to boiling water, allow 5 minutes from when the water returns to a boil. If added to cold water, allow 3 minutes after it comes to a boil.

LANGOUSTINES WITH TOMATOES

Melt the butter in a pan, add the onion and cook over low heat, stirring occasionally, for 5 minutes, then add the tomatoes. Mix the tomato paste with 2 tablespoons warm water, stir into the pan and simmer for about 10 minutes. Transfer the mixture to a food processor and process to a purée, then return to the pan. Add salt and pepper to taste. Add the langoustines or lobsterettes and cook, stirring constantly, for 2–3 minutes. Stir in the cream and cook until the sauce has thickened. Arrange the langoustines or lobsterettes on a warm serving dish and spoon the sauce over them.

SCAMPI AI POMODORI

Serves 4

¹/₄ cup butter

1 onion, finely chopped

11 ounces tomatoes, peeled, seeded and cubed

1 tablespoon tomato paste

20 langoustines or lobsterettes, peeled

scant ¹/₂ cup heavy cream

salt and pepper

LANGOUSTINES WITH CURRY SAUCE

Bring a large pan of water to a boil with the herbs, and the carrot and onion if using. Add the langoustines or shrimp, bring back to a boil and cook for 5 minutes, then drain, peel and devein. Melt the butter in a pan, add the shallots and cook over low heat, stirring occasionally, for 5 minutes. Stir in the curry powder, then pour in the wine and cook until it has reduced by half. Stir in the cream and season with salt and pepper. Arrange the langoustines or lobsterettes on a warm serving dish, sprinkle with the lemon juice and spoon the sauce over them.

SCAMPI ALLA SALSA DI CURRY

Serves 4

$^1/_2$ bunch of fresh parsley

$^1/_2$ bunch of fresh thyme

1 carrot (optional)

1 onion (optional)

20 langoustines or lobsterettes

3 tablespoons butter

2 shallots, finely chopped

1 teaspoon curry powder

scant $^1/_2$ cup dry white wine

scant $^1/_2$ cup heavy cream

juice of 1 lemon, strained

salt and pepper

LANGOUSTINES WITH SAGE

Put the langoustines or lobsterettes in a bowl, season with salt and pepper, pour in the lemon juice and let marinate for about 1 hour. Preheat the broiler. Drain the langoustines or lobsterettes, reserving the marinade, wrap each in a slice of pancetta together with a sage leaf and secure with a toothpick. Brush lightly with olive oil, arrange on the broiler rack and cook under the broiler, turning twice and occasionally drizzling with the reserved marinade, for 10–12 minutes.

SCAMPI ALLA SALVIA

Serves 4

20 langoustines or lobsterettes, peeled

juice of 2 lemons, strained

20 smoked pancetta slices

20 small fresh sage leaves

olive oil, for brushing

salt and pepper

BROILED LANGOUSTINES

Put the langoustines or lobsterettes in a large bowl, sprinkle with the herbs, add the lemon juice and olive oil and season with salt and pepper. Let marinate for about 45 minutes. Preheat the broiler. Spread out a sheet of foil in a broiler pan and brush with olive oil. Drain the langoustines or lobsterettes, reserving the marinade, place them on the foil and cook under the broiler, turning twice and occasionally drizzling with a little reserved marinade, for about 12 minutes.

SCAMPI GRIGLIATI

Serves 4

20 langoustines or lobsterettes, peeled

1 fresh flat-leaf parsley sprig, finely chopped

1 fresh chervil sprig, finely chopped

1 fresh marjoram sprig, finely chopped

juice of 1 lemon, strained

4 tablespoons olive oil, plus extra for brushing

salt and pepper

SHELLFISH

Quahogs, littleneck clams, mussels, razor clams, surf clams, bay scallops, whelks — and we could go on. Scientifically, mollusks are classified into eight classes with eight thousand different species. However, only three classes are commonly used in the kitchen. These are cephalopods, which do not have external shells, such as octopus and cuttlefish, gastropods, which have a single shell, such as whelks, abalone, and marine snails, and bivalves with two shells, such as clams, scallops and mussels. While the freshness of fish can easily be judged by looking at the liveliness of the eyes, the shininess of the scales and the texture of the flesh, mollusks require more attention and not everyone knows what to look for. Here are the main rules to follow when buying them. The shells should be shiny and completely closed. The more open they are, the longer they have been out of the sea. They should have a mild, pleasant smell — if they have a strong smell, their freshness is at the extreme limit. Shellfish require careful cleaning under plenty of running water. If they are not going to be eaten immediately, they should be cooked anyway and stored in their cooking juices for not longer than 24 hours in the refrigerator.

YELLOW

LEMON

SQUID

The most delicious squid are small, tender ones that are cooked whole. The larger ones are not quite so tender and should be cut into rings. To prepare squid, rinse well and pull the head and body apart. Cut off the tentacles, then squeeze out and discard the beak. Discard the rest of the head. Remove and discard the quill and ink sac from the body and remove any remaining membrane (most of the innards will have come out with the head). Rinse the body sac well and peel off the skin. Some of the ink may be added to risottos and spaghetti sauces to give them an unusual black color and a stronger flavor of the sea.

MARCHE–STYLE SQUID

Chop the anchovy fillets. Heat the olive oil in a pan with the garlic and parsley. Add the squid and anchovies and season lightly with salt and pepper. Cook over low heat for 10 minutes, then stir in the wine and 2–3 tablespoons water. Simmer gently for about 20 minutes until tender.

CALAMARI ALLA MARCHIGIANA

Serves 4

2 salted anchovies, heads removed, cleaned and
filleted (see page 596), soaked in cold water
for 10 minutes and drained

5 tablespoons olive oil

1 garlic clove

1 fresh flat-leaf parsley sprig, chopped

1³/₄ pounds small squid, cleaned

5 tablespoons white wine

salt and pepper

FRIED SQUID

CALAMARI FRITTI

Serves 4

1³/₄ pounds small squid, cleaned

all-purpose flour, for dusting

6 tablespoons olive oil

salt

Dust the squid with flour. Heat the olive oil in a skillet, add the squid and cook until golden brown all over. Remove with a slotted spoon and drain on paper towels, then season lightly with salt. Squid cooked this way are often served with fried langoustines or other delicate fried seafood.

SQUID STUFFED WITH SHRIMP

CALAMARI RIPIENI AI GAMBERETTI

Serves 4

1 potato, unpeeled

4 large squid, cleaned

11 ounces cooked shrimp, peeled and chopped

2 egg yolks, lightly beaten

4 tablespoons olive oil

1 garlic clove

4 tablespoons heavy cream

1 cup bottled strained tomatoes

1 fresh flat-leaf parsley sprig, chopped

salt and pepper

Cook the potato in salted, boiling water for 20–30 minutes until tender, then drain, peel and mash with a potato masher. Cook the squid tentacles in salted, boiling water for 3 minutes, then drain and chop. Combine the mashed potato, tentacles, shrimp and egg yolks in a bowl and season with salt and pepper to taste. Spoon the mixture into the body sacs of the squid, being careful not to overfill them, and secure with toothpicks. Heat the olive oil in a large skillet, add the garlic and cook for a few minutes until browned, then remove and discard it. Add the squid to the pan and cook over low heat for about 30 minutes. Stir the cream into the strained tomatoes, sprinkle with the parsley and pour the mixture over the squid. Heat through briefly, then serve.

BROILED STUFFED SQUID

CALAMARI RIPIENI ALLA GRIGLIA

Serves 4

4 squid, cleaned

1 fresh flat-leaf parsley sprig, plus extra to garnish

¹/₂ garlic clove

1 cup bread crumbs

olive oil, for drizzling and brushing

salt and pepper

lemon wedges, to garnish

Preheat the broiler to hot. Chop the squid tentacles with the parsley and garlic. Put the mixture in a bowl, add the bread crumbs, drizzle with olive oil and season with salt and pepper. Spoon the mixture into the body sacs of the squid and secure with toothpicks. Brush the outside of the squid with olive oil seasoned with salt and pepper, place on the broiler rack and broil, turning frequently, until golden brown and tender. Serve hot with lemon wedges and sprigs of parsley.

SCALLOPS

The scallop has a very flat lower shell and a distinctly convex upper shell. It is off-white and often has shades of pink and hazelnut. Scallops are among the most highly prized shellfish and are sold both alive and shelled. They consist of three parts – a firm white muscle, a yellow or orange coral and a brown bearded part, called the skirt, which is not eaten. In Italy and the rest of Europe, the coral is considered a delicacy, whereas in the United States, it is usually discarded. The best ones are 4–6 inches in diameter. Scallop dishes are often served in the shells, so even if you're buying prepared scallops, it's worth asking the fish store for the upper half-shell. To open a scallop, hold it flat side up, insert the blade of a knife between the shells and cut the muscle attached to the top shell. Carefully remove the top shell, then slide the knife underneath the scallop to sever the lower muscle. Remove and discard the skirt and black stomach sac. The simplest way of enjoying scallops is to poach them. Soak the muscle and coral in cold water for 15 minutes to get rid of any residual sand. Then poach in salted, simmering water for 10 minutes, let cool and slice or leave whole. They may be served with mayonnaise or with oil and lemon juice, or mixed with a lettuce and watercress salad.

BAKED SCALLOPS

CAPPESANTE AL FORNO
Serves 4
12 scallops, shelled (see above)
4 tablespoons olive oil, plus extra for drizzling
1 garlic clove
juice of 1 lemon, strained
6 fresh basil leaves, chopped
salt and white pepper

Scrub the curved half-shells and put in a low oven to keep warm. Heat the oil and garlic in a skillet, add the scallops and cook for 4 minutes. Stir, season with salt, remove the skillet from the heat and put the scallops in the half-shells. Sprinkle each with $1/2$ teaspoon of the cooking juices, a drizzle of olive oil and a pinch of pepper. Sprinkle with the lemon juice and basil and serve.

Serves 4

7 tablespoons olive oil

8 scallops, shelled (see page 710)

3¹/₂ cups lettuce, shredded

1 bunch of arugula

3 tomatoes, peeled, seeded and diced

2 tablespoons white wine vinegar

salt and pepper

SCALLOP SALAD

Heat 2 tablespoons of the olive oil in a skillet, add the scallops and cook for about 2 minutes on each side. Put the lettuce, arugula and tomatoes in a salad bowl. Whisk together the vinegar, a pinch of salt and the remaining olive oil in a bowl, season with pepper and pour the dressing over the salad. Add the scallops and toss.

Serves 4

12 scallops, shelled (see page 710)

1 carrot, diced

1 scallion, thinly sliced

³/₄ cup dry white wine

¹/₄ cup butter, cut into pieces

1 tablespoon heavy cream

pinch of saffron threads

salt

SCALLOPS IN SAFFRON SAUCE

Scrub the curved half-shells and dry with paper towels. Put the carrot, scallion, wine, a pinch of salt and 4 tablespoons water in a pan, bring to a boil and simmer for 10 minutes. Add the scallops and cook for a further 4 minutes. Remove the scallops with a slotted spoon, halve them, place in the half-shells and keep warm. Boil the cooking juices until reduced, then stir in the butter, cream and saffron. Pour the hot sauce over the scallops and serve.

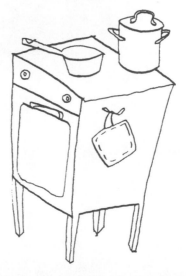

MUSSELS

These mollusks have several different names in Italian — cozze, muscoli, peoci and mitili. Nowadays, most commercially available mussels are farmed, which guarantees a high level of cleanliness. However, they should still be thoroughly scrubbed under cold, running water, but not left to soak in water. Pull off the beards with the help of a short, sharp knife and knock off any barnacles from the shells with the knife handle. Discard any mussels with broken shells or those that do not shut immediately when sharply tapped. To open them, place in a skillet over high heat for a few minutes. Discard any that remain closed. Their tender tasty flesh is very easy to digest and their cooking juices are a delicious addition to soups, sauces and risottos.

CREAMY MUSSELS

Put the mussels in a pan with the olive oil, garlic and lemon juice, cover and cook over high heat, shaking the pan occasionally, for about 5 minutes until the shells open. Drain, reserving the cooking liquid. Discard any mussels that remain shut and the empty half-shells. Place the mussels in their halfshells on a serving dish. Mix the mayonnaise with 1–2 tablespoons of the reserved cooking liquid and spoon the mixture over the mussels. Season with a little pepper and garnish with the basil and diced tomato.

COZZE ALLA CREMA

Serves 4

3¼ mussels,
scrubbed and beards removed
3 tablespoons olive oil
1 garlic clove
juice of ½ lemon, strained
1 quantity Mayonnaise (see page 65)
pepper

For the garnish
8 fresh basil leaves
1 tomato, diced

MUSSELS MARINARA

COZZE ALLA MARINARA

Serves 4

3¹/₄ pounds mussels, scrubbed and beards removed

3 tablespoons finely chopped fresh flat-leaf parsley

pepper

Put the mussels in a pan over high heat with plenty of pepper but no water and cook for about 5 minutes until they open. Discard any that remain closed. Drain, reserving the cooking juices and place in a deep serving dish. Strain the cooking juices thorough a cheesecloth-lined strainer into a bowl. Stir in the parsley, pour the mixture over the mussels and serve.

MUSSELS WITH GREEN BELL PEPPERS

COZZE CON PEPERONI VERDI

Serves 4

2¹/₄ pounds mussels, scrubbed and beards removed

3 tablespoons olive oil

2 garlic cloves

2–3 green bell peppers, halved, seeded and sliced

2 fresh thyme sprigs, chopped

salt

Put the mussels in a skillet with 1 tablespoon of the olive oil and one of the garlic cloves and cook over high heat for about 5 minutes until they open. Discard any that remain closed. Remove the mussels from their shells and set aside. Chop the remaining garlic. Heat the remaining olive oil in a skillet, add the green bell peppers and remaining garlic and cook over medium heat, stirring frequently, for 10 minutes. Season with salt, add the mussels and cook, stirring gently, for a few minutes. Transfer to a warm serving dish and sprinkle with the thyme.

MUSSELS AU GRATIN

COZZE GRATINATE

Serves 4

2¹/₄ pounds mussels, scrubbed and beards removed

3 tablespoons chopped fresh flat-leaf parsley

2 garlic cloves, chopped

large pinch of dried oregano

olive oil, for drizzling

1¹/₂ cups bread crumbs

salt and pepper

1 lemon, cut into wedges, to garnish

Preheat the oven to 400°F. Put the mussels in a skillet and place over high heat for about 5 minutes until they open. As they open, remove from the skillet and place the halfshells containing the mussels in a roasting pan. Discard any that remain closed and the empty halfshells. Sprinkle the mussels with the parsley, garlic and oregano, season with salt, drizzle generously with olive oil and sprinkle with the bread crumbs. Bake for 5 minutes, then transfer to a warm serving dish, season with pepper and garnish with the lemon wedges.

PEPPERED MUSSELS

IMPEPATA DI COZZE

Serves 4

4¹/₂ pounds mussels, scrubbed and beards removed

3 tablespoons chopped fresh flat-leaf parsley

pepper

Put the mussels in a skillet with plenty of pepper and cook over high heat for about 5 minutes until they open. Discard any that remain closed. Sprinkle with the parsley, remove the skillet from the heat and serve.

OYSTERS

Oysters are the favorite antipasto of the most demanding gourmets worldwide, but which type is the best, flat ones or bowl-shaped ones? Flat oysters have smooth, flattened, often rounded shells and come in two varieties: belons with white flesh and marennes with green flesh. The belon is the queen of oysters owing to its plumpness and length, 5–6 inches. Bowl-shaped oysters are longer and deeper. Oysters must reach the kitchen alive. This means that, before they are opened, the shells must be tightly closed and, once opened with a special knife, they must draw away from the slightest touch. To open an oyster, hold it flat side up in the hollow of one hand – it's safest to wrap your hand in a dish towel first to help avoid injury if the knife slips. Insert a strong knife, preferably an oyster knife, into the hinge of the shell and prize the two shells apart. Sever the muscle that holds the oyster to the top shell and lift the shell off, then sever the lower muscle. Pour the liquid out of the bottom halfshell into a bowl and strain. Leave the oysters in their halfshells on a bed of ice for 30 minutes to release their juices, that is what makes their flavor unforgettable. Provide your guests with suitable metal forks to remove the oysters from the halfshells, bearing in mind that silver forks will turn black. According to connoisseurs, oysters should be eaten raw and without any dressing or, at most, with a small dash of lemon juice. Some accept combining them with slices of lightly buttered rye bread. Nevertheless, oysters may also be fried, marinated or prepared American-style. How many oysters per person? Experts vary in recommending between six and nine. We consider six to be the right number when they are served with a simple sauce or dressing. In seafood restaurants, oysters are usually served by the dozen.

GREEK OYSTERS

Open the oysters (see opposite), discard the top shells and arrange the halfshells on a tray. Combine the lemon juice and olive oil in a sauceboat, season with salt and pepper and stir in the parsley. Make a bed of crushed ice on a serving dish and place the oysters on top. Serve with the sauce handed separately.

OSTRICHE ALLA GRECA

Serves 4

24 live oysters

juice of 2 lemons, strained

scant 1/2 cup olive oil

1 small fresh flat-leaf parsley sprig, chopped

crushed ice

salt and pepper

AMERICAN OYSTERS

Preheat the oven to 475°F. Open the oysters (see opposite), discard the top shells and season with a pinch of salt, a few drops of lemon juice and a pinch of cayenne. Crumble the bread over them and drizzle with the melted butter. Bake for 5 minutes and serve.

OSTRICHE ALL'AMERICANA

Serves 4

24 live oysters

dash of lemon juice

pinch of cayenne pepper

2–3 day-old bread slices, crusts removed

3 tablespoons butter, melted

salt

HOT OYSTERS IN BEURRE BLANC

Preheat the oven to 225°F. Put the shallots, half the wine and the vinegar in a pan, season with salt and pepper and set over medium heat until reduced by two-thirds. Add the cream and bring to a boil. Stir in the butter, a little at a time. Remove the pan from the heat, season with salt and pepper to taste and stir in the onion. Return the pan to the heat and keep warm, stirring occasionally, but do not allow the sauce to boil. Open the oysters (see opposite), discard the top shells, tip the juices into a pan and remove the oysters from the halfshells. Add the remaining wine to the juices, season with salt and pepper, bring to a boil and simmer until reduced by two-thirds. Wash the empty halfshells thoroughly, dry and arrange on a bed of sea salt on an ovenproof dish. Place the shells in the oven for 10 minutes. Dip the oysters in the warm juices and wine mixture and place in the hot halfshells. Strain the liquor and wine mixture into the butter sauce, pour it over the oysters and serve.

OSTRICHE CALDE AL BURRO BIANCO

Serves 4

2 shallots, chopped

3 tablespoons dry white wine

1 tablespoon white wine vinegar

1 tablespoon heavy cream

2/3 cup butter, chilled and cut into pieces

1 onion, chopped

24 live oysters

coarse sea salt

salt and pepper

CURRIED OYSTERS

OSTRICHE CALDE AL CURRY

Serves 4

16 live oysters
14 ounces spinach
6 tablespoons heavy cream
scant ¹/₂ cup butter
1 teaspoon curry powder
2 egg yolks
salt and pepper

Open the oysters (see page 716), discard the top shells, tip the liquor into a bowl and remove the oysters from the half-shells. Steam the spinach for about 5 minutes, then drain, pressing out as much liquid as possible, and pass through a food mill. Heat the spinach purée in a pan with 4 tablespoons of the cream and a pinch of salt. Divide the spinach among the half-shells. Strain the oyster liquor into a small pan and heat gently, then add the oysters and simmer for 5 minutes. Drain the oysters and place them on top of the spinach mixture. Combine the butter and curry powder and set aside. Whisk the egg yolks and remaining cream in a double boiler or heatproof bowl set over a pan of barely simmering water until light and fluffy. Stir in the curry butter, cook for a few minutes more and season with salt and pepper to taste. Spoon the sauce over the oysters and serve.

OYSTERS IN SALTED SABAYON SAUCE

OSTRICHE CON LO ZABAIONE SALATO

Serves 4

16 live oysters
1¹/₂ cups zucchini, sliced
¹/₄ cup butter, cut into pieces
4 egg yolks
1 shallot, finely chopped
scant ¹/₂ cup sparkling dry white wine
coarse sea salt
salt and pepper

Preheat the oven to 425°F. Open the oysters (see page 716), remove from the halfshells and place in a dish. Discard the top shells and wash the bottom shells well under cold running water. Cook the zucchini in salted, boiling water for 5 minutes, then drain, tip into a food processor and process to a purée. Gently heat the purée with a pat of the butter and a pinch of salt in a small pan. Beat the egg yolks with the shallot in a double boiler or heatproof bowl, then whisk in the wine. Set the double boiler over medium heat or place the bowl over a pan of barely simmering water and heat, whisking constantly, for about 10 minutes until thickened. Do not let the mixture boil. Remove the sauce from the heat and stir in the remaining butter, a pinch of salt and a pinch of pepper. Make a bed of coarse salt on a cookie sheet and arrange the halfshells on top. Place a tablespoon of the zucchini purée in each shell, top with an oyster and cover with a tablespoon of the sauce. Bake for 4–5 minutes and serve.

OCTOPUS

Octopuses are cephalopods with a highly prized but tough flesh. They require careful preparation to tenderize. Immediately after they are caught, they should be beaten thoroughly, then cooked slowly in a covered pan. Young male octopuses are the tastiest and most tender. To clean an octopus, remove the eyes, beak and only bone, then turn the body sac inside out and empty it. All the rest is edible. Italians also cook very small octopuses. There are two types – musky octopuses, which have a characteristic aroma, and curled octopuses, which are tougher in texture and lack the musky scent. Their Italian name, moscardini, is Ligurian and this is also how they are known in many other Italian regions, but in Naples they are called polpetelli and in Veneto polpetti. They are very small with lean, tender, tasty flesh that is easy to digest. They must be washed well and, if they are really very small, they can be left whole. Otherwise, remove the beak and eyes. Musky octopuses are excellent simply poached and dressed with olive oil and lemon juice. They are often prepared in the same ways as cuttlefish and young squid, which may be substituted for them in the recipes here. Similarly, you could use very small, baby octopuses of another variety.

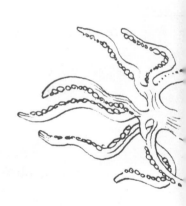

OCTOPUS AND POTATO SALAD

Put the octopus in a large pan and add water to cover and a pinch of salt. Bring to a boil, then lower the heat, cover and simmer for 30 minutes or until tender. Remove from the heat and let cool in the cooking liquid, then drain, skin and cut into pieces. Meanwhile, cook the potatoes in salted, boiling water for about 30 minutes until tender, then drain, peel and dice them. Put them in a salad bowl and sprinkle with the wine. Add the octopus, season with salt and pepper to taste, sprinkle with the rosemary and drizzle with olive oil.

INSALATA DI POLPI E PATATE

Serves 4

2¼-pound octopus, cleaned

4 potatoes, unpeeled

1 tablespoon dry white wine

pinch of fresh rosemary needles

olive oil, for drizzling

salt and pepper

LIGURIAN MUSKY OCTOPUS

Cut the octopuses into pieces unless they are very small. Bring a pan of lightly salted water to a boil, add one of the onions, 2–3 tablespoons of the vinegar and the octopuses and simmer for 10–15 minutes. Drain and set aside. Thinly slice the remaining onions. Heat the olive oil in a pan, add the onions, garlic, sage and bay leaf and cook over low heat, stirring occasionally, for about 10 minutes. Pour in the remaining vinegar, remove and discard the garlic and simmer gently for about 30 minutes. Season with salt and pepper to taste. Pack the octopuses in layers in a jar and pour in the warm vinegar to cover. Close the jar tightly and keep in a cool place. Musky octopuses prepared in this way keep for quite a long time.

MOSCARDINI ALLA LIGURE

Serves 4

3¹/₄ pounds musky octopuses, cleaned

3 onions

4 cups white wine vinegar

4 tablespoons olive oil

1 garlic clove

1 fresh sage sprig

1 bay leaf

salt and pepper

MUSKY OCTOPUS NAPOLETANA

Cook the octopuses in salted, boiling water for 10 minutes or more, depending on their size. Drain, cut into pieces and place in a dish. Combine the olive oil, parsley, garlic and lemon juice in a jug, season with salt and pepper and pour the dressing over the octopuses. Leave in a cool place for 1 hour for the flavors to mingle before serving.

MOSCARDINI ALLA NAPOLETANA

Serves 4

2¹/₄ pounds musky octopuses, cleaned

6 tablespoons olive oil

2 tablespoons chopped fresh flat-leaf parsley

1 garlic clove, chopped

juice of 1 lemon, strained

salt and pepper

BRAISED MUSKY OCTOPUS

Heat the olive oil in a pan with the garlic and chile, add the octopuses and cook, stirring occasionally, until golden brown all over, then remove from the pan. Add the tomatoes to the pan and cook for 5 minutes over low heat. Season with salt and pepper and cook for a further 10 minutes. Return the octopuses to the pan, sprinkle with the parsley, heat through and serve.

MOSCARDINI IN UMIDO

Serves 4

3 tablespoons olive oil

1 garlic clove, chopped

¹/₂ fresh red chile, seeded and chopped

2¹/₄ pounds musky octopuses, cleaned

3 tomatoes, peeled, seeded and chopped

2 tablespoons chopped fresh flat-leaf parsley

salt and pepper

POACHED OCTOPUS

POLPI AFFOGATI

Serves 4

2 pounds small octopuses, cleaned

²/₃ cup olive oil

14 ounces tomatoes, peeled, seeded and sliced

3 tablespoons chopped fresh flat-leaf parsley

1 garlic clove, chopped

salt

Put the octopuses in a flameproof casserole, preferably earthenware, with the olive oil, tomatoes, parsley and garlic. Do not add salt or water. Cover tightly and cook over low heat for 30 minutes. Do not remove the lid during cooking. Season with salt and serve in their sauce, which should be plentiful.

OCTOPUS IN RED WINE

POLPI AL VINO ROSSO

Serves 4

3 tablespoons olive oil

1 onion, chopped

1 garlic clove

1 fresh sage leaf

1 fresh rosemary sprig

2¹/₄-pound octopus, cleaned and cut into pieces

5 tablespoons red wine

2 bay leaves

salt and pepper

Heat the olive oil in a pan, add the onion, garlic, sage and rosemary and cook over low heat, stirring occasionally, for 5 minutes. Add the octopus and cook for a few minutes more, then pour in the wine, add the bay leaves and season with salt and pepper to taste. Simmer over very low heat for 1¹/₂ hours. Serve hot or cold.

MARINER'S OCTOPUS

POLPI DEL MARINAIO

Serves 4

2¹/₄-pound octopus, cleaned

1 garlic clove, crushed

1 onion, thinly sliced

olive oil, for drizzling

1 tomato, peeled, seeded and chopped

5 tablespoons white wine

salt and pepper

Put the octopus into a flameproof casserole, preferably earthenware, add the garlic and onion, season with salt and pepper and drizzle with olive oil. Cover and cook over low heat for 1 hour. Add the tomato and wine and cook for 1 hour more until the octopus is tender. Remove the octopus from the casserole and cut into pieces. Serve with the cooking juices, which should be fairly thick; if they are too thick, add a little lukewarm water.

CUTTLEFISH

Cuttlefish are cephalopods with long tentacles and a character-istic oval bone, called a quill or cuttlebone. The most highly prized cuttlefish are young – 4–4¹/₂ inches long – with tender, easy-to-digest flesh that cooks quickly. Adult cuttlefish are tougher and require longer cooking times. Preparation is simple. Cut off the tentacles just in front of the eyes and discard the beak in their center. Separate and skin the tentacles and pull off the skin from the body. Cut along the back and remove the cuttlebone, then remove the ink sac. Remove and discard the innards and the head. Cut the body in half, unless you're going to stuff it, and wash well. Cuttlefish ink may be used to add flavor and color to spaghetti sauces or risottos.

WARM CUTTLEFISH SALAD WITH GREEN ASPARAGUS

Halve the pieces of asparagus lengthwise, then parboil in salted water for about 5 minutes. Drain and refresh under cold, running water. Heat the olive oil in a skillet, add the cuttlefish and cook, stirring frequently, until lightly browned. Season with salt and pepper, add the parsley, garlic, cilantro and asparagus and mix well. Remove the pan from the heat, transfer to a serving dish and serve warm.

INSALATA TIEPIDA DI SEPPIE CON ASPARAGI VERDI

Serves 6

11 ounces green asparagus,
spears cut into 2-inch lengths
3 tablespoons olive oil
1 pound 2 ounces medium cuttlefish,
cleaned and cut into thin strips
1 tablespoon fresh flat-leaf parsley, chopped
1 garlic clove, chopped
1 teaspoon cilantro seeds • salt and pepper

CUTTLEFISH WITH SPINACH

Cook the spinach, in just the water clinging to the leaves after washing, for about 5 minutes, then drain, squeeze out as much liquid as possible and chop. Heat the olive oil in a pan, add the onion and garlic and cook, stirring occasionally, until the garlic turns brown, then remove and discard it. Add the cuttlefish and mix well, then season and pour in the wine. Cook until it has evaporated, then cover and simmer over low heat for about 10 minutes. Add the spinach and strained tomatoes and simmer for about 30 minutes. Meanwhile, preheat the oven to 325°F. Spread the pine nuts on a cookie sheet and toast in the oven, stirring occasionally, until golden brown. Stir into the cuttlefish for the last few minutes of the cooking time.

SEPPIE AGLI SPINACI

Serves 4

9 ounces spinach
2 tablespoons olive oil
1 onion, thinly sliced
1 garlic clove
1³/₄ pounds small cuttlefish, cleaned and halved
³/₄ cup dry white wine
generous 1 cup bottled strained tomatoes
3 tablespoons pine nuts
salt and pepper

CUTTLEFISH WITH PEAS

SEPPIE AI PISELLI

Serves 4

4 tablespoons olive oil1 garlic clove

1³/₄ pounds cuttlefish, cleaned and cut into strips

3 cups shelled peas

or canned peas, drained and rinsed

³/₄ cup dry white wine

salt and pepper

Heat the oil and garlic in a pan until the garlic turns brown, then remove and discard it. Add the cuttlefish to the pan, season with salt and pepper, stir well and cook for a few minutes. Add the wine and cook until it has evaporated. Pour in just enough water to almost cover the cuttlefish and bring to a boil. Lower the heat, cover and simmer for about 1 hour. Add the peas and cook for about 30 minutes until tender.

CUTTLEFISH WITH ARTICHOKES

SEPPIE CON I CARCIOFI

Serves 4

4 tablespoons olive oil • 1 garlic clove

1³/₄ pounds cuttlefish, cleaned and cut into strips

³/₄ cup dry white wine

6 globe artichokes, trimmed, chokes removed

and cut into wedges

salt and pepper

Heat the oil and garlic in a pan until the garlic turns brown, then remove and discard it. Add the cuttlefish to the pan, season, mix well and cook for a few minutes. Add the wine and cook until it has almost completely evaporated. Pour in just enough water to almost cover the cuttlefish and bring to a boil. Lower the heat, cover and simmer for 30–40 minutes. Add the artichokes and simmer for a further 15 minutes until tender. Season with salt and pepper to taste.

STUFFED CUTTLEFISH

SEPPIE FARCITE

Serves 4

11 ounces baby squid,

cleaned (see page 707) and chopped

1 tablespoon capers, drained, rinsed and chopped

1 tablespoon pine nuts

1 small fresh flat-leaf parsley sprig, chopped

2 eggs, lightly beaten

2–3 bread rolls, crusts removed

4 large cuttlefish, cleaned

3–4 tablespoons olive oil • salt and pepper

Preheat the oven to 350°F. Combine the squid, capers, pine nuts, parsley and eggs in a bowl, crumble in the rolls, mix well and season with salt and pepper. Stuff the cuttlefish with the mixture. Place the cuttlefish in a single layer in an ovenproof dish, drizzle with the olive oil and season with salt and a little pepper. Bake for about 30 minutes.

CUTTLEFISH AU GRATIN

SEPPIE GRATINATE

Serves 6

6 tablespoons olive oil, plus extra for drizzling

2 garlic cloves, chopped

2¹/₄ pounds cuttlefish, cleaned and cut into strips

1 tablespoon capers, drained and rinsed

¹/₂ cup green olives, pitted and chopped

1 fresh flat-leaf parsley sprig, chopped

1 cup bread crumbs • salt and pepper

Heat the olive oil in a flameproof casserole, add the garlic and cuttlefish and cook over high heat until golden brown. Season with salt and pepper, add the capers and olives, lower the heat, cover and simmer gently for about 45 minutes. Preheat the oven to 350°F. Combine the parsley and bread crumbs and sprinkle the mixture over the cuttlefish. Drizzle with olive oil and bake for about 10 minutes.

FISH SOUPS

We have fishermen to thank for fish soups, which were originally created to avoid wasting unsold fish from the day's catch. They simply put everything into a large pot, cooked it and then ate it. To begin with, the poorest and least prized fish were the ones used, but this simple dish gradually developed and improved over the years. Today we have both simple soups and sophisticated stews that often include fine fish, crustaceans and shellfish. Around Italy's 4,350 miles of coastline, there are as many kinds of fish soup as there are region bordering the sea – and they all have different names, such as brodetto, cacciucco, buridda and ciuppin.

→ For 6 servings, allow 5¹/₂–6¹/₂ pounds fish, consisting of five or six different varieties. There are also soups made with only one type of fish. Scorpion fish adds more flavor than almost any other.

→ As a general rule, there should be at least three different types of fish in the soup: one stock-making fish, such as scorpion fish, one sauce-making fish, such as red snapper, and a sliced fish, such as tope.

→ Large fish should be cut into chunks and small ones should be left whole.

→ Add firm-fleshed fish first, then the delicate ones.

→ Cook on high heat for about 20 minutes, then serve immediately. Do not overcook the fish.

→ Add only small quantities of tomato. Pepper, on the other hand, may be used generously. If you like, lightly toasted slices of homemade bread may be gently rubbed with a clove of garlic and served separately. Alternatively, place them in the base of soup plates and ladle the soup over them.

QUANTITIES AND COOKING TIMES

MARCHE—STYLE FISH SOUP

BRODETTO MARCHIGIANO

Serves 8–10

11 ounces mussels, scrubbed and beards removed

11 ounces clams, scrubbed

4–5 tablespoons olive oil

1 onion, finely chopped

11 ounces large cuttlefish, cleaned

1 green bell pepper, halved, seeded and sliced

5 just-ripe tomatoes, peeled, seeded and chopped

1 fresh chile, seeded and finely chopped

scant ¹/₂ cup white wine vinegar

5¹/₂ pounds mixed fish, such as scorpion fish, monkfish fillet, mackerel and red snapper, cleaned and cut into chunks if necessary

11 ounces mantis shrimp, slipper lobsters or langoustines

11 ounces small cuttlefish, cleaned

salt and pepper

There are as many recipes for brodetto as there are regions along the Adriatic coast. This version is traditionally made at San Benedetto del Tronto in Marche. Discard any mussels and clams with broken shells or those that do not shut immediately when sharply tapped. Place them in two separate skillets over high heat until they open. Discard any that remain closed. Remove some of the mussels and clams from their shells and leave the rest in situ. Heat the olive oil in a large flameproof casserole, add the onion and cook over low heat, stirring occasionally, for 5 minutes. Add the large cuttlefish and cook for 10 minutes, then add the green bell pepper, season with salt and pepper and mix well. Cook over low heat for a further 10 minutes. Add the tomatoes, chile and vinegar and cook until the vinegar has evaporated. Gradually add the fish and shellfish in layers, beginning with the least delicate and finishing with the mussels, and the mantis shrimp, slipper lobsters or langoustines. Cover and simmer gently for about 20 minutes.

LIVORNO—STYLE FISH SOUP

CACCIUCCO

Serves 8

³/₄ cup olive oil

1 onion, chopped

1 fresh flat-leaf parsley sprig, chopped

2 garlic cloves, chopped

1 small fresh chile, seeded and chopped

2¹/₄ cups red or white wine

11 ounces tomatoes, peeled, seeded and chopped

5¹/₂ pounds mixed fish (see method), cleaned and cut into chunks if necessary

fish stock (see page 208), optional

1 pound 2 ounces mussels, scrubbed and beards removed

salt and pepper

toast rubbed with garlic, to serve

For this typical Tyrrhenian-coast fish soup, you need a few slices of monkfish, a conger or freshwater eel, a few squid or cuttlefish and some mussels. Heat the olive oil in a flameproof casserole, preferably earthenware, add the onion, parsley, garlic and chile, season with salt and pepper and cook over low heat, stirring occasionally, for about 10 minutes until the onion is golden brown. Add the wine and cook for 10 minutes more, then add the tomatoes and simmer for a further 10 minutes. Add the firmer fish, pour in a little warm water or fish stock, and cook on a high heat for 10 minutes. Gradually add the more delicate fish, finishing with the mussels. (Discard any with broken shells or that do not shut immediately when sharply tapped, and any that remain closed after cooking.) The total cooking time for the fish is about 30 minutes. Serve with slices of toast rubbed with garlic.

FISHERMAN'S SOUP

ZUPPA DI PESCE DEL PESCATORE

Serves 4

1 onion
1 clove
5 carrots
1 celery stalk, chopped
14 ounces sea bass, cleaned
1 pound 2 ounces monkfish fillet
14 ounces gurnard or sea robin, cleaned
1 bunch of fresh mixed herbs
4 potatoes
4 leeks
4 zucchini
2¼ pounds mussels, scrubbed and beards removed
salt and pepper
1 quantity Vinaigrette (see page 76), to serve

Stud the onion with the clove and slice one of the carrots. Put the onion, sliced carrot, celery, any fish trimmings and the herbs in a large pan, season with salt and pepper and add 10⅔ cups water. Bring just to a boil, then lower the heat, cover and simmer for 30 minutes to make a court-bouillon. Meanwhile, put the potatoes in cold salted water and bring to a boil. Add the remaining carrots and other vegetables and cook for about 20 minutes, then drain and slice. Discard any mussels with broken shells or that do not shut immediately when sharply tapped. Place the mussels in a skillet over high heat until the shells open. Discard any that remain closed. Put the fish in a large pan and strain the court-bouillon over them. Bring to a boil and cook over medium heat for about 30 minutes. Transfer the fish to the middle of a warm serving dish and place the mussels on one side and the vegetables on the other. Serve the soup with a vinaigrette.

PIRATE'S FISH SOUP

ZUPPA DI PESCE DEL PIRATA

Serves 6

1 red bell pepper, halved, seeded and sliced
1 green bell pepper, halved, seeded and sliced
2 dried chiles, seeded and crumbled
4 garlic cloves, chopped
1 bunch of fresh mixed herbs, such as marjoram, thyme, basil, sage and chives
scant 1 cup olive oil
scant 1 cup red wine
11 ounces octopuses, cleaned
11 ounces cuttlefish, cleaned and halved if large
11 ounces musky or curled octopuses, cleaned
scant ½ cup white rum
1 pound 2 ounces mussels, scrubbed and beards removed
11 ounces clams, scrubbed
pinch of freshly grated nutmeg (optional)
salt and pepper

Put the bell peppers, chiles, garlic, herbs, olive oil and wine in a flameproof casserole and cook over medium heat for 10 minutes. Add the octopuses and cuttlefish and simmer for 20 minutes. Add the musky or curled octopuses and rum and cook for a further 10 minutes. Discard any mussels and clams with broken shells or that do not shut immediately when sharply tapped. Add the mussels and clams to the casserole, stir well, cover and cook for 5–10 minutes until the shells have opened. Discard any that remain shut. Season with salt and pepper to taste, sprinkle with nutmeg if using, and serve.

MIXED FISH SOUP WITH ORANGE

Put the leek, carrots, wine and any fish trimmings in a large pan, season with salt and add 8³/₄ cups water. Bring to a boil, then lower the heat and simmer for 30 minutes. Strain and reserve 6¹/₄ cups. Heat the olive oil in a flameproof casserole, add the onion and cook over low heat, stirring occasionally, for 5 minutes. Add half the reserved stock and simmer for 20 minutes or until the onion has almost disintegrated. Put the hake, striped mullet, scorpion fish, sole, cod, squid and cuttlefish into a large pan, pour in the remaining reserved stock, season with salt and poach for 30 minutes. Discard any clams with broken shells or that do not shut immediately when sharply tapped. Add the onion mixture, orange juice, langoustines or lobsterettes, clams, tomato and basil, season with salt and pepper, cover and cook for about 3 minutes until the clam shells have opened. Discard any that remain closed. Serve the soup with croûtons.

ZUPPA DI PESCE MISTO ALL'ARANCIA

Serves 6

1 leek
2 carrots
5 tablespoons dry white wine
1 hake, cleaned and cut into chunks
1 striped mullet, cleaned and cut into chunks
1 scorpion fish, cleaned and cut into chunks
1 sole, cleaned and cut into chunks
2 tablespoons olive oil
1 onion, finely chopped
1 pound 2 ounces cod fillet, cut into chunks
3 squid, cleaned
3 cuttlefish, cleaned and halved if large
14 ounces clams, scrubbed
³/₄ cup freshly squeezed orange juice, strained
10 langoustines or lobsterettes
1 tomato, peeled, seeded and cubed
8 fresh basil leaves, chopped
salt and pepper
croûtons, to serve

MIXED SHELLFISH SOUP

Discard any mussels, cockles and clams with broken shells or that do not shut immediately when sharply tapped. Pour the wine into a large pan, add the parsley and celery leaves, onions, lemon rind, scallops and all the other shellfish. Cover and cook over medium-high heat until the shells open. Discard any that remain closed. Season generously with pepper, but taste before adding any salt, as shellfish are already quite salty. Garnish with lemon slices and serve.

ZUPPA DI PESCE MISTO DI CONCHIGLIE

Serves 4

12 mussels, scrubbed and beards removed
12 scallops, shelled
12 cockles, scrubbed
12 littleneck clams, scrubbed
12 medium quahogs clams, scrubbed
²/₃ cup dry white wine
1 fresh flat-leaf parsley sprig, coarsely chopped
leaves of 1 celery stalk, coarsely chopped
2 onions, thinly sliced
grated rind of ¹/₂ lemon
salt and pepper
1 lemon, sliced, to garnish

SNAILS

The most highly prized snails – the ones used for the famous Bourguignonne recipe – are the so-called vineyard snails, widespread in Piedmont and Lombardy. The others are almost all farmed. Cleaned, ready-to-cook, frozen or canned snails are available. If you obtain fresh – that is, live – snails, the task of rendering them edible is long, complicated and requires a ruthlessness that not everyone possesses. However, in order to be comprehensive, an outline of how to prepare live snails is given below.

→ Cover the snails with coarse salt and leave in a fairly large, covered ventilated box for 24 hours.

→ Wash them several times in water, vinegar and salt until there are no traces of sliminess left in the water.

→ Dip them several times in cornmeal and rinse again under cold, running water.

→ Parboil by immersing in boiling water for 5 minutes.

→ Carefully extract the snails from the shells and remove and discard the black end part.

→ Place in a court-bouillon made with carrot, onion, thyme, bay leaf and parsley and simmer for 4 hours.

→ Drain and prepare according to the chosen recipe.

→ Allow 6 per serving as an antipasto and 12 as a main course.

BOURGUIGNONNE SNAILS

Preheat the oven to 375°F. Combine the butter, parsley, garlic and shallots in a bowl, season with salt and pepper and beat until smooth. Put a little of the mixture in the base of each shell, then place the snails on top and spread with a little more of the butter mixture. Place the shells in an ovenproof dish and bake for about 10 minutes.

LUMACHE ALLA BOURGUIGNONNE

Serves 4

1¹/₂ cups butter, softened

1 fresh flat-leaf parsley sprig, finely chopped

2 garlic cloves, finely chopped

2 shallots, finely chopped

48 prepared snails, with shells

salt and pepper

LIGURIAN SNAILS

Place the mushrooms in a bowl, add lukewarm water to cover and let soak for 2 hours. Heat the olive oil in a pan, add the onion, garlic and parsley and cook over low heat, stirring occasionally, for 5 minutes. Drain the mushrooms, squeeze out and chop. Stir the mushrooms, rosemary and oregano into the pan and cook for 5 minutes. Add the snails and cook for a few minutes more, then add the wine and cook until it has evaporated. Pour in the strained tomatoes, season with salt and pepper to taste, cover and simmer over low heat for 45 minutes, adding a little water if the mixture seems to be drying out.

LUMACHE ALLA LIGURE

Serves 4

2 tablespoons dried mushrooms

3 tablespoons olive oil

1 onion, chopped

1 garlic clove, chopped

1 fresh flat-leaf parsley sprig, chopped

1 teaspoon chopped fresh rosemary

¹/₂ teaspoon dried oregano

48 prepared snails

5 tablespoons dry white wine

1³/₄ cups bottled strained tomatoes

salt and pepper

LOMBARD SNAILS

Chop the anchovy. Heat the olive oil with the garlic in a pan until the garlic turns brown, then remove and discard it. Add the anchovies, butter, parsley and onion and cook over low heat, mashing the anchovies until they have almost disintegrated. Stir in the flour, then add the snails and cook for a few minutes. Pour in the wine, season with salt and pepper to taste, cover and simmer for about 1 hour. Serve hot.

LUMACHE ALLA LOMBARDA

Serves 4

2 ounces salted anchovies, heads removed, cleaned and filleted (see page 596), soaked in cold water for 10 minutes and drained

3 tablespoons olive oil

1 garlic clove

¹/₄ cup butter

1 fresh flat-leaf parsley sprig, chopped

¹/₄ onion, chopped

1 tablespoon all-purpose flour

48 prepared snails

³/₄ cup dry white wine

salt and pepper

FROGS

Frog flesh is lean and white, with a delicate flavor that is highly appreciated by connoisseurs. They are mainly found in Piedmont and Lombardy. Frogs are sold cleaned and skinned. Generally, only the legs are cooked, but frog aficionados usually eat them whole, bones and all. A standard portion is a dozen frogs' legs per person.

GENOESE FROG LEGS

RANE ALLA GENOVESE

Serves 4

1 onion, chopped

1 fresh flat-leaf parsley sprig, chopped

pinch of dried oregano

1 bay leaf

³/₄ cup white wine vinegar

2¹/₄ pounds frog legs

all-purpose flour, for dusting

5 tablespoons olive oil

salt and pepper

Combine the onion, parsley, oregano, bay leaf and vinegar in a bowl, season with salt and pepper, add the frogs' legs and let marinate for 30 minutes. Drain the frogs' legs and coat with flour. Heat the olive oil in a skillet, add the frogs' legs and cook, turning occasionally, until golden brown all over. Sprinkle with salt and serve.

FROG LEGS IN WHITE WINE

RANE AL VINO BIANCO

Serves 4

1 cup white wine

1 onion, sliced

1 fresh flat-leaf parsley sprig, chopped

2¹/₄ pounds frog legs

2 tablespoons butter

1 teaspoon all-purpose flour

1 egg yolk

juice of 1 lemon, strained

salt and pepper

Put the wine, onion and parsley in a pan, season with salt and pepper and bring to a boil. Add the frogs' legs and cook over medium heat for 10 minutes. Remove the frogs' legs and boil the cooking liquid until it has reduced by two-thirds. Melt the butter in a small pan, stir in the flour and then stir the mixture into the reduced cooking liquid. Pass through a food mill into another pan, return to the heat and bring to a boil. Add the frogs' legs and cook for a further 5 minutes. Meanwhile, beat together the egg yolk and lemon juice in a bowl. Move the pan to the edge of the stove and stir in the egg yolk mixture.

FRIED FROG LEGS
IN TOMATO SAUCE

Heat 2 tablespoons of the olive oil in a pan, add the tomatoes and a pinch of salt and cook over medium heat, stirring frequently, for 10 minutes. Melt the butter in another pan, add the garlic and cook over low heat, stirring frequently, for a few minutes, then add to the tomatoes. Stir in the lemon juice. Heat the remaining olive oil in a skillet. Dust the frogs' legs with flour, then dip them in the cream and cook in the hot oil until golden brown all over. Transfer to a warm serving dish and spoon the tomato sauce over them.

RANE FRITTE IN SALSA

Serves 4

7 tablespoons olive oil

1 pound 2 ounces tomatoes, peeled, seeded and chopped

2 tablespoons butter

1 garlic clove, chopped

1 tablespoon lemon juice

$2^{1}/_{4}$ pounds frog legs

all-purpose flour, for dusting

scant 1 cup heavy cream

salt

FROG LEGS
IN BREAD CRUMBS

Spread out the flour in a shallow dish, lightly beat the eggs with a pinch of salt in another shallow dish and spread out the bread crumbs in a third. Sprinkle the frogs' legs with salt and pepper. Dip the frogs' legs first in the flour, then in the eggs and, finally, in the bread crumbs. Heat the olive oil and butter in a skillet and cook the frogs' legs, in batches, until golden brown. Remove from the skillet, drain on paper towels and season with salt. Sprinkle with the parsley and surround with the lemon.

RANE IMPANATE

Serves 4

$^{1}/_{2}$ cup all-purpose flour

2 eggs

1 cup bread crumbs

$2^{1}/_{4}$ pounds frog legs

3 tablespoons olive oil

3 tablespoons butter

$^{1}/_{2}$ bunch of fresh flat-leaf parsley, chopped

1 lemon, peeled and sliced

salt and pepper

FROGS IN BATTER

Soak the frogs in cold water for 3 hours. Combine the vinegar, parsley and a generous pinch of pepper in a bowl. Drain the frogs and add them to the bowl so that they are immersed. Combine the flour, egg, egg yolk and a pinch of salt in another bowl and stir in the wine and olive oil to make a smooth batter. Heat the oil for deep-frying in a large pan. Drain the frogs, dip them in the batter and fry in the hot oil. Remove with a slotted spoon, drain on paper towels and season lightly with salt. Serve with the lemon wedges.

RANE IN PASTELLA

Serves 4

$2^{1}/_{4}$ pounds frogs

$2^{1}/_{4}$ cups white wine vinegar

1 fresh flat-leaf parsley sprig, chopped

scant 1 cup all-purpose flour

1 egg

1 egg yolk

5 tablespoons white wine

1 tablespoon olive oil

vegetable oil, for deep-frying

salt and pepper

1 lemon, cut into wedges, to serve

MEAT →

VARIETY
MEATS →

MEAT

Meat? Yes, but always high-quality meat. Since the 1950s, consumption of this superb, protein-rich food has increased in Italy. Today's meat is finer, leaner, more tender and tastier than ever. This has happened in response to the demands of consumers and their determination to obtain the high-quality they expect. The nutritional value of contemporary meat means that, it is even included in some slimming diets. But you need to be choosy. It is certainly possible to identify the quality of meat at a glance, but it is also important to know how to pick the best cut for each recipe. This is also important for the family budget because it does not automatically follow that the most highly prized and expensive cuts are also the most nutritious and tasty. Equally, it would be absurd to ask for porterhouse steak every time. Less expensive cuts for stewing or braising, for example, certainly do not lack flavor.

CLASSIFICATION

In Italy meat is categorized in various ways. It is divided into:

ANIMALI DA MACELLO ('BUTCHERED' ANIMALS)

Beef, kid, lamb, mutton, pork, veal and also horse.

ANIMALI DA CORTILE (FARMYARD ANIMALS)

Chicken, duck, goose, guinea fowl, squab, turkey and rabbit.

SELVAGGINA E CACCIAGIONE (GAME)

Chamois (an Alpine, deer-like animal), hare (the European equivalent of jack rabbit), pheasant, quail, and wild boar. Meat can also divided into: red (beef, horse and mutton); white (kid, lamb, veal and poultry); and black (game). Finally, there are two more categories :

MEAT DERIVATIVES

Meat extract and stock cubes.

SAUSAGES AND CURED MEATS

Whole or ground meat is often mixed with fat, flavored with herbs and seasoned before being used to fill natural or artificial skins. Most sausages and cured meats are made from pork and are divided into cooked (cotechino, ham, etc.) and raw (salami, sausages, etc.).

N.B. For this edition, rabbit is included within Game (see pages 947 to 985) but recipes for all other 'farmyard animals', such as chicken and duck appear in Poultry (see pages 875 to 945).

Time is increasingly precious and today's lifestyles, however relaxed, all attach great importance to health. Therefore, the proper storage of food has become even more vital. As there is usually little time to go shopping and to cook, refrigerators and freezers have become essential. It is always best to wrap meat in foil or plastic wrap or to put it in food bags or glass dishes before placing it in the refrigerator or freezer. This wrapping should, be tight and the meat should be perfectly sealed to avoid contact with the air and protect its flavor and nutritional content. To prevent cross-contamination in the refrigerator, it is essential to store raw meat where the juices cannot drip onto cooked meat or other ingredients. This is usually at the bottom. Many modern refrigerators are multi-temperature. This means that the internal space is divided into various 'compartments' that provide different levels of cold depending on the type of food to be stored. This ranges from 45–46°F for sharp cheeses, salamis and cold pork meats, and 41°F for soft cheeses, yogurt and sauces, to 32°F for meat, fish and delicate foods. Storing food in this way makes sure that it stays fresh for three or four times longer than in traditional refrigerators. This has been made possible by no-frost technology – the best storage temperature is reached through a system of internal air-circulation. This has the additional advantage of preventing the refrigerator from icing up, making defrosting unnecessary.

VARIETY MEATS

Variety meat is delicious and exists in a range of forms which may be prepared in many different ways. In Italy, the most valued variety meat are brains, bone marrow and sweetbreads, followed by liver, kidney, heart and tripe. Also in this category, but with a stronger flavor more suitable for robust dishes, is tongue, calf's head and pig's feet.

LAMB

As tender as a lamb, as they say in Italian to describe something soft. The tenderness of this meat derives from the fact that the animal is not yet one-year-old and has fed only on its mother's milk. Baby lamb, or abbacchio as it is called in Lazio, is even younger – just five or six weeks old. However milk-fed lamb is less common outside Italy and, as a rule, most meat comes from grazing animals of between four months and a year, the younger ones being known as spring lamb. The meat from sheep over a year old is known as yearling lamb and if it comes from animals over two years old it is mutton. Lamb is a pale, tender, fairly fatty meat. It should be eaten fresh and preferably between October and June.

COOKING

→ As lamb tends to shrink during cooking, be generous with the weight when buying and always allow an extra portion.

→ The most common preparation methods are roasting or stewing after marinating in white wine with a drop of vinegar, inserting garlic into incisions in the meat and seasoning with herbs, such as rosemary, thyme, sage and mint.

→ Grilled chops are very tasty and roast leg of lamb en croûte with herbs is an impressive dish for special occasions.

ROASTING

The best cuts for roasting are first of all the leg, especially if it includes half the lamb with the kidney right up to the first rib. Then comes the saddle, then the shoulder. The shoulder is tender and tasty, but rather fatty and difficult to carve neatly. Oven roast-

TOMATO

ing is perfect but pot-roasting also produces excellent results.

BRAISING, STEWING, BLANQUETTES AND CURRIES

The front part of the lamb is particularly suitable for stewing or braising with vegetables and early seasonal produce, such as baby peas, artichokes and pearl onions. It is also ideal for curries, blanquettes (the meat must remain white), and cooking in an egg sauce (mixed with butter and cream) or with lemon juice.

CHOPS

Small lamb chops cut from the loin are particularly tender. They need cooking very quickly – just 2–3 minutes on each side. They are also delicious dipped in egg, then in bread crumbs, and fried in butter, especially clarified butter.

**ITALIAN CUTS
AND COOKING
TECHNIQUES**

1. COLLO
   Stewing and braising
2. SPALLA
   Roasting and stewing
3. CARRÉ
   Ideal for broiling

4. PETTO
   Suitable for stews
5. SELLA
   Excellent for roasting
6. COSCIOTTO
   The best part for roasting

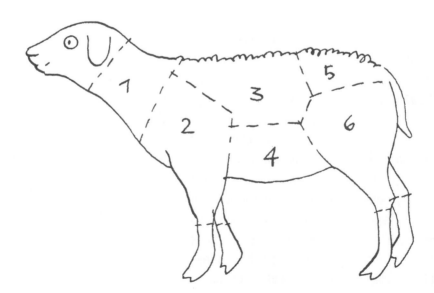

1. **NECK SLICES**
   Stewing
2. **SHOULDER**
   Roasting, stewing, and cut into chops for broiling and frying
3. **RIB**
   Roasting, and cut into chops for broiling and frying
4. **LOIN**
   Roasting, and cut into chops for broiling and frying
5. **LEG**
   Roasting, and cut into chops for broiling and frying
5B. **HIND SHANK**
   Braising and ground meat

6. **BREAST**
   Boned and rolled for roasting and ground meat
7. **FORE SHANK**
   Braising and ground meat

AMERICAN CUTS AND COOKING TECHNIQUES

If you are in doubt over which cut to choose or cannot find one that is listed here, ask a reputable butcher for advice.

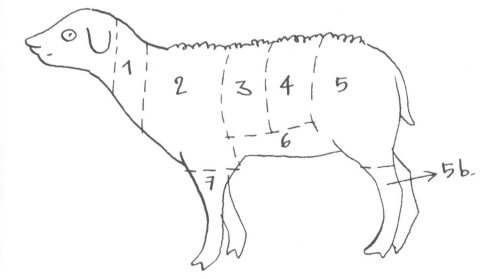

ROMAN SPRING LAMB

ABBACCHIO ALLA ROMANA

Serves 4

2¹/₄-pound leg of lamb
all-purpose flour, for dusting
3 tablespoons olive oil
3 fresh rosemary sprigs
4 fresh sage leaves, chopped
1 garlic clove, crushed
³/₄ cup white wine
5 tablespoons white wine vinegar
4 potatoes, sliced
salt and pepper

Chop the leg into pieces or ask the butcher to do this for you. Preheat the oven to 350°F. Dust the pieces of lamb with flour. Heat the oil in a wide roasting pan, add the lamb and cook over high heat, turning frequently, for about 10 minutes until browned all over. Season with salt and pepper, add the rosemary sprigs and sprinkle with the sage and garlic. Turn the pieces over several times so that they soak up the flavor. Combine the wine and vinegar, add to the roasting pan and cook until the liquid has almost completely evaporated. Add ²/₃ cup boiling water and the potatoes, cover and roast for 30 minutes or until tender. If the gravy seems to be drying out, add a little hot water mixed with white wine vinegar. Transfer the lamb to a warm serving dish and serve while still hot. For an even tastier alternative, omit the potatoes, and when the lamb is nearly ready transfer 2–3 tablespoons of the gravy to a small pan, add three boned and chopped salted anchovies (see page 596) and cook over low heat, mashing the anchovies with a wooden spoon until they have almost disintegrated. Mix well, pour the sauce over the meat and roast for a few minutes more before serving.

LAMB WITH MUSHROOMS

AGNELLO AI FUNGHI

Serves 4

2¹/₄-pound shoulder of lamb, boned and rolled
4 tablespoons olive oil, plus extra for brushing
1 pound 2 ounces porcini
1 cup heavy cream
2 tablespoons butter
2 garlic cloves
1 fresh parsley sprig, chopped
salt and pepper

Preheat the oven to 400°F. Season the meat with salt and pepper and brush it all over with lightly salted olive oil. Place in a roasting pan with the oil and roast for 1 hour. Meanwhile, separate the stalks and caps of the porcini, then slice the caps and chop 1¹/₂ cups of the stalks. Remove the lamb from the pan, cover with foil and keep warm. Pour ³/₄ cup warm water and the cream into a pan, add the chopped porcini stalks and simmer for 15 minutes. Meanwhile, melt the butter in a skillet, add the porcini caps and cook over high heat until lightly browned. Add the garlic, season with salt and pepper, lower the heat to medium and cook for 15 minutes more. Remove and discard the garlic and add the parsley. Carve the lamb into thin slices, place on a warm serving dish, pour the hot sauce over them and serve surrounded by the porcini caps.

ARABIAN LAMB

AGNELLO ALL'ARABA

Serves 4

4 tablespoons olive oil

3 onions, thinly sliced

2¼-pound saddle of lamb,
boned and cut into 2-inch cubes

2 tablespoons honey

1 envelope saffron

pinch of ground cumin

pinch of ground ginger

1 cup hot Meat Stock
(see page 208) or water

¾ cup green olives, pitted

¾ cup almonds

1 bunch of fresh cilantro, finely chopped

salt and pepper

Preheat the oven to 400°F. Heat the oil in a roasting pan, add the onions and cook over low heat, stirring occasionally, for 5 minutes, then remove from the pan. Add the lamb and cook, stirring frequently, for 5 minutes until browned all over. Return the onions to the pan. Combine the honey, saffron, cumin, ginger and stock or water in a pitcher and season with salt and pepper. Pour the mixture over the meat, cover the roasting pan with foil and roast for 1 hour or until tender. Meanwhile, blanch the olives in boiling water for 5 minutes, then drain. Dry-fry the almonds in a heavy skillet, stirring frequently, for a few minutes. About 10 minutes before the end of the roasting time, add the olives and almonds to the roasting pan, mix well and return to the oven to finish cooking. Transfer to a warm serving dish, sprinkle with the cilantro and serve. As a side dish, we suggest fresh fava beans boiled in water for 15 minutes, then tossed with butter.

LEG OF LAMB À LA PÉRIGOURDINE

COSCIOTTO ALLA PERIGORDINA

Serves 6

3 tablespoons olive oil

1½ tablespoons butter

4½-pound leg of lamb, skinned

2 tablespoons brandy

6 garlic cloves

1 onion, chopped

1 leek, trimmed and chopped

1 fresh thyme sprig, chopped

1 fresh flat-leaf parsley sprig, chopped

1 celery stalk, chopped

1 clove

1 bottle (3 cups) dry white wine

salt and pepper

Preheat the oven to 300°F. Heat the oil and butter in a roasting pan, add the lamb and cook over medium heat, turning frequently, until browned all over. Add the brandy, heat for a few seconds, then ignite and cover the pan with a large pan lid or cookie sheet to extinguish the flames. Put the garlic around the lamb, add the onion, leek, thyme, parsley, celery and clove, season with salt and pepper and pour in the wine. Cover tightly and roast for 5 hours. Carefully transfer the lamb to a warm serving dish. Remove and discard the garlic from the roasting pan and pour the gravy into a sauceboat. This dish goes well with zucchini purée or mashed potato.

ROAST LEG OF LAMB

Preheat the oven to 400°F. Grease a roasting pan with the butter. Lard the lamb with the pancetta and, using a small, pointed knife, make small incisions all over it. Insert the sage and some of the rosemary into the incisions. Brush the lamb all over with oil, place in the prepared roasting pan and season with salt and pepper according to taste. Sprinkle the garlic and remaining rosemary on top, pour in the vinegar and wine and roast for 1½ hours. Turn the lamb halfway through the cooking time and baste occasionally with the cooking juices. Serve with baby spinach salad.

COSCIOTTO ARROSTO

Serves 6

6 tablespoons butter

4½-pound leg of lamb

3 ounces pancetta, cut into strips

6 fresh sage leaves, cut into strips

1 tablespoon rosemary needles

olive oil, for brushing

4 garlic cloves, chopped

5 tablespoons white wine vinegar

5 tablespoons white wine

salt and pepper

baby spinach salad, to serve

ROAST LEG OF LAMB IN A HERB CRUST

Preheat the oven to 475°F. Combine the thyme, oregano, parsley and rosemary in a bowl, add the oil and bread crumbs, season with salt and pepper and mix well. Place the lamb in a large roasting pan, spread the herb mixture over it and roast for 15 minutes. Lower the oven temperature to 350°F, add ⅔ cup warm water to the roasting pan and roast for 15 minutes more. Remove the lamb from the roasting pan, cover with foil and let stand for 10 minutes. Carve the meat and place on a warm serving dish. For a side dish, halve and seed some tomatoes, fill with bread crumbs and chopped oregano, drizzle with olive oil, season with salt and pepper and bake for 15 minutes.

COSCIOTTO IN CROSTA D'ERBE

Serves 6

1 tablespoon chopped fresh thyme

1 tablespoon chopped fresh oregano

1 tablespoon fresh flat-leaf parsley, chopped

1 tablespoon chopped fresh rosemary needles

4 tablespoons olive oil

2 tablespoons bread crumbs

4½-pound leg of lamb

salt and pepper

LAMB CHOPS WITH ANCHOVY BUTTER

Preheat the broiler. Brush the chops on both sides with olive oil and broil for 4–6 minutes on each side, depending on how well done you like your lamb. Season with salt, transfer to a serving warm dish and dot with the anchovy butter.

COSTOLETTE AL BURRO D'ACCIUGA

Serves 4

8 lamb rib chop

olive oil

1 quantity Anchovy Butter (see page 85)

salt

LAMB CHOPS COOKED IN VINEGAR

Combine the vinegar, half the oil, the onion, parsley and cloves in a dish and season with salt and pepper according to taste. Add the lamb chops and let marinate for 1 hour. Heat the remaining oil in a skillet, drain the lamb chops, add to the skillet and cook for 2 minutes on each side until golden brown. Transfer to a warm serving dish.

COSTOLETTE ALL'ACETO

Serves 4

³/₄ cup white wine vinegar

6 tablespoons olive oil

1 onion, sliced

1 fresh flat-leaf parsley sprig, chopped

2 cloves

8–12 lamb rib chops

salt and pepper

LAMB CHOPS WITH MINT

Combine the lemon juice, 3 tablespoons of the oil and the mint in a dish, add the lamb chops and let marinate, turning occasionally, for 1–2 hours. Heat the butter and the remaining oil in a skillet. Drain the lamb chops, add to the skillet and cook for 2 minutes on each side. Season with salt and pepper according to taste and serve with peas or zucchini.

COSTOLETTE ALLA MENTA

Serves 4

juice of 1 lemon, strained

plenty of olive oil, for brushing

1 fresh mint sprig, chopped

8 lamb rib chops

1¹/₂ tablespoons butter

salt and pepper

peas or zucchini cooked in butter, to serve

LAMB CHOPS SCOTTADITO

Brush the lamb chops with oil and season with salt and pepper. Cover and let stand in a cool place for 15 minutes. Meanwhile, preheat the broiler to high. Drain the lamb chops carefully to get rid of any excess seasoning, then broil for about 1 minute on each side. Alternatively, brush a non-stick skillet with a little oil and cook the lamb chops over high heat for 1 minute on each side, seasoning with salt and pepper on turning them. Before removing the chops from the heat, sprinkle with lemon juice, if you wish. Transfer to a warm serving dish.

COSTOLETTE A SCOTTADITO

Serves 4

8–12 lamb rib chops

5 tablespoons olive oil

salt and pepper

juice of 1 lemon, strained (optional)

LAMB FRICASSÉE WITH ONIONS

FRICASSEA CON CIPOLLINE

Serves 4

1³/₄-pound leg of lamb
3 tablespoons butter
3 tablespoons olive oil
14 ounces pearl onions
2¹/₄ cups dry white wine
2 egg yolks
juice of 1 lemon, strained
salt and pepper

Ask your butcher to cut the leg into fairly small pieces. Heat the butter and oil in a pan, add the pieces of lamb and cook, turning frequently, until golden brown all over. Remove the lamb from the pan and keep warm. Add the onions to the pan and cook over medium heat, stirring frequently, for about 10 minutes until golden brown. Return the pieces of lamb to the pan, season with salt and pepper and pour in the wine. Cover and cook over medium heat for 40 minutes. Beat the egg yolks with the lemon juice in a bowl. Move the pan to the edge of the hob and pour in the egg yolk mixture. Stir quickly so that the mixture thickens and coats the pieces of lamb without drying out. Transfer to a warm serving dish.

LAMB MEATBALLS WITH EGGPLANT

POLPETTE ALLE MELANZANE

Serves 4

2 eggplants
4¹/₂ cups lean ground lamb
pinch of dried oregano
2 egg yolks
1 fresh flat-leaf parsley sprig, chopped
4 tablespoons olive oil
salt and pepper

Preheat the oven to 350°F. Wrap the eggplants in foil, place on a cookie sheet and bake for about 30 minutes. Unwrap the eggplants and let cool slightly, then cut them in half and scoop out the flesh with a teaspoon. Combine the lamb, eggplant flesh, oregano, egg yolks and parsley in a bowl and season with salt and pepper. Shape the mixture into small meatballs. Heat the oil in a skillet, add the meatballs and cook over medium heat, stirring frequently, until golden brown all over. Transfer to a warm serving dish.

SHOULDER OF LAMB IN A PACKET

SPALLA AL CARTOCCIO

Serves 6

olive oil, for brushing
2¹/₄-pound boneless shoulder of lamb, trimmed of fat
1 fresh flat-leaf parsley sprig, chopped
1 fresh chervil sprig, chopped
1 fresh oregano sprig, chopped
1 bay leaf
³/₄ cup dry white wine
juice of ¹/₂ lemon, strained
salt and pepper

Preheat the oven to 400°F. Brush a large sheet of baking parchment generously with olive oil. Season the top and underside of the lamb with salt and pepper and place it in the middle of the baking parchment. Sprinkle with the herbs and add the bay leaf. Pour the wine and lemon juice on top and wrap carefully so that the liquid does not leak out. Place on a cookie sheet and roast for 1 hour or until cooked through and tender. Open the packet slightly to let the steam escape, then serve.

SPALLA ALLA FORNAIA

Serves 6

2 tablespoons butter, plus extra for greasing

2¼ pounds potatoes, thinly sliced

1 tablespoon chopped fresh thyme

1 pound 2 ounces onions, thinly sliced

2 garlic cloves, thinly sliced

2¼-pound boneless shoulder of lamb

2¼ cups Meat or Vegetable Stock
(see pages 208 and 209)

salt and pepper

SHOULDER OF LAMB À LA BOULANGÈRE

Preheat the oven to 400°F. Grease an ovenproof dish with butter. Make a layer of potatoes on the base of the dish, season with salt and pepper, sprinkle with a little of the thyme and cover with a layer of onions and garlic. Continue making layers until all these ingredients have been used. Make a few incisions in the lamb with a small sharp knife, place it on top of the vegetables and season with salt and pepper. Pour the stock into the dish, dot the lamb with the butter and roast, basting the potatoes occasionally, for 30 minutes. Remove the dish from the oven and cover with a sheet of foil, then return it to the oven and roast for 30–45 minutes more. Let the meat stand, without uncovering it, for about 10 minutes before serving.

SPALLA AL MIRTO

Serves 4

2½-pound shoulder of lamb

3 garlic cloves

2 tablespoons olive oil, plus extra for brushing

5 tablespoons dry white wine

¼ cup mirto (myrtle liqueur) or gin

salt and pepper

SHOULDER OF LAMB WITH MIRTO

Preheat the oven to 400°F. Rub the lamb with the garlic clove, then cut the cloves in half and dip them in salt. Make six fairly deep incisions in the meat with a small knife and insert half a garlic clove in each. Brush the meat with olive oil and season with salt and pepper. Then place the lamb in a roasting pan, add the oil, half the wine and half the mirto or gin and roast for 30 minutes. Turn the shoulder over and spoon the remaining wine and mirto or gin over it, baste well, return to the oven and roast for 30 minutes more.

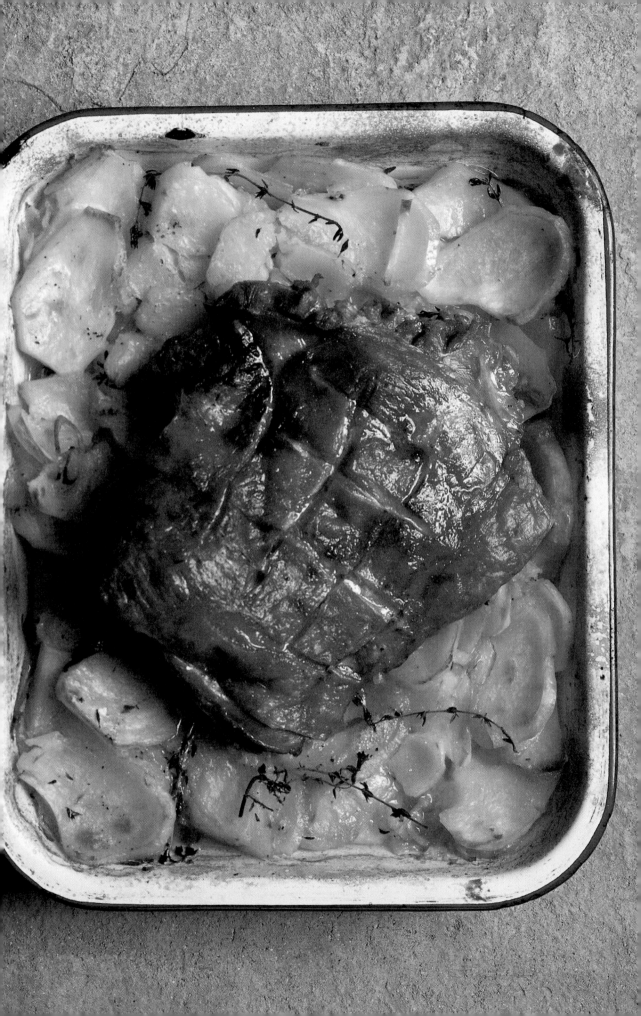

SPEZZATINO ALLE CAROTE

Serves 6

4 tablespoons olive oil

¼ cup butter

1 pound 2 ounces carrots, cut into thin batons

1 shallot, finely chopped

2¼ pounds boneless shoulder of lamb, cut into cubes

1 onion, chopped

1 garlic clove, chopped

pinch of dried oregano

10 celery leaves, chopped

salt and pepper

CHOPPED LAMB AND CARROTS

Heat half the oil and half the butter in a pan, add the carrots and shallot and cook over low heat, stirring occasionally, for 20 minutes. Meanwhile, heat the remaining oil and butter in another pan, add the lamb and cook over high heat, stirring frequently, until browned all over. Season with salt and pepper to taste and continue cooking, stirring constantly, for a few minutes more. Add the onion, garlic, oregano and celery leaves, lower the heat to medium and cook for 10 minutes. When the carrots are almost tender, transfer them to the pan with the lamb and cook for 5 minutes more.

KID

In Italy, the best breeds of goat are the Girgentana, the Alpine, the Apulian and the Sardinian. A suckling kid of 13¹/₂–26¹/₂ pounds in weight is ideal for cooking. The nutritional value of kid is similar to that of lamb, but the beautiful pale pink meat is not as tasty and so requires more seasoning. Consequently, most recipes include herbs and wine. When roasting, allow 1 hour per 2¹/₄ pounds. As kid may be difficult to obtain outside Italy, it is worth noting that many recipes can be used for either lamb or kid, and the best parts of both are the leg, shoulder and loin.

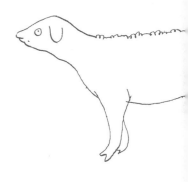

LEG OF KID
WITH TRUFFLE CREAM

Put the rosemary, sage and garlic in a large pan (not aluminum) with the oil, half the brandy and a pinch each of salt and pepper. Add the meat and let marinate overnight. The next day, put the pan over medium heat, add the pieces of butter and cook, turning occasionally, for 1 hour. Pour in the remaining brandy, ignite it and let until the flames die down. Take the kid out of the pan and cut the meat off the bone. Strain the cooking juices and reserve ³/₄ cup. Combine the reserved juices with the truffle paste and cream. Return the meat to the pan, add the sauce and simmer over low heat for about 10 minutes. Transfer to a warm serving dish.

COSCIOTTO ALLA CREMA TARTUFATA

Serves 4

1 tablespoon fresh rosemary needles, chopped

3 fresh sage leaves, chopped

2 garlic cloves, chopped

2 tablespoons olive oil

³/₄ cup brandy

2¹/₄-pound leg of kid

2 tablespoons butter, cut into pieces

1 tablespoon truffle paste

1 cup heavy cream

salt and pepper

PIEDMONTESE LEG OF KID

COSCIOTTO ALLA PIEMONTESE

Serves 4

2¼-pound leg of kid
3½ ounces pancetta, cut into strips
3 tablespoons olive oil
1 onion, chopped
1 garlic clove, chopped
1 carrot, sliced
1 celery stalk, sliced
1 fresh rosemary sprig
2¼ cups dry white wine
3 tablespoons tomato paste
salt and pepper

Lard the kid with the pancetta. Heat the oil in a pan, add the meat and cook over high heat, turning frequently, until browned all over. Season with salt and pepper, add the onion, garlic, carrot, celery and rosemary and cook for a few minutes. Add the wine, tomato paste and 5 tablespoons water and simmer for 1 hour. Remove and discard the rosemary, transfer the vegetables to a food processor and process to a purée. Cut the meat from the bone, place on a warm serving dish and spoon the vegetable purée on top.

EASTER LEG OF KID

COSCIOTTO PASQUALE

Serves 4

2¼-pound leg of kid
1 fresh rosemary sprig, chopped
4 fresh sage leaves, chopped
1 garlic clove, chopped
5 tablespoons olive oil
1¾ pounds new potatoes, diced
1 pound 2 ounces carrots, cut into thin batons
14 ounces pearl onions
1 fresh flat-leaf parsley sprig, chopped
salt and pepper

Preheat the oven to 350°F. Place the leg in a roasting pan, season with salt and pepper and sprinkle with the rosemary, sage and garlic. Pour the oil over the kid and roast, basting occasionally, for about 1 hour. Meanwhile, parboil the potatoes, carrots and onions in separate pans for about 10 minutes, then drain and transfer to the roasting pan with the meat. When the meat is tender, cut it off the bone and place on a warm serving dish. Surround with the vegetables and sprinkle with the parsley.

KID CHOPS WITH CREAM

COSTOLETTE ALLA PANNA

Serves 4

1½ tablespoons butter
1 tablespoon olive oil
12 kid shoulder chops
1 cup heavy cream
juice of 1 lemon, strained
2 fresh flat-leaf parsley sprigs, finely chopped
salt and pepper
lemon slices, to garnish

Heat the butter and oil in a skillet, add the chops and cook over high heat for 2 minutes on each side. Season with salt and pepper, lower the heat, add the cream and simmer for 15 minutes. Pour in the lemon juice and simmer for 5 minutes more. Sprinkle the chops with parsley, place on a warm serving dish and garnish with slices of lemon.

PORK, BACON
HAM

It is well known that no part of the pig is ever thrown away – everything can be successfully transformed into tasty and nutritious foods which delight the taste buds and add flavor to many dishes. In Italy, as in many other countries, so-called lean pork is the favorite choice. It comes from selected breeds that produce meat that is much lower in fat than the breeds of the past. Only some cuts are sold as fresh meat, while the others are used to make salamis, preserved meats, sausages and a variety of other preparations. Good quality fresh pork can be recognized by its fine grain, pink color and slight marbling of white fat.

COOKING

Pork requires rather long cooking times – about 25 minutes per 1 pound 2 ounces.

ROASTING

Loin should be roasted in a preheated low to medium oven so that the heat can penetrate to the center before a crust forms on the outside.

CAUL

Also known as caul fat, this is a lattice-like membrane that encloses the pig's stomach. It is used to wrap and contain other ingredients. In Italy, it can be bought from delicatessens and is used after being soaked in warm water for 3 minutes to soften.

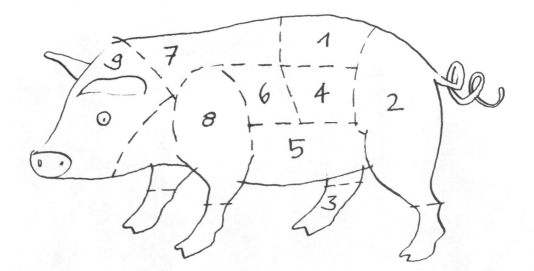

**ITALIAN CUTS
AND COOKING
TECHNIQUES**

1. LONZA
   Ideal for roasting
2. COSCIOTTO
   The part used to make ham
3. PIEDINI
   Boiling and frying
4. PUNTINE COSTINE
   Stewing and braising
5. PANCETTA,
   GUANCIALE
   For forcemeats or for lard-
   ing and wrapping dry meats

6. FILETTO, LOMBO
   Recommended for roasting
   and broiling
7. CARRÉ
   Extremely tasty chops
8. SPALLA
   For roasting and stewing
9. TESTA
   Boiling

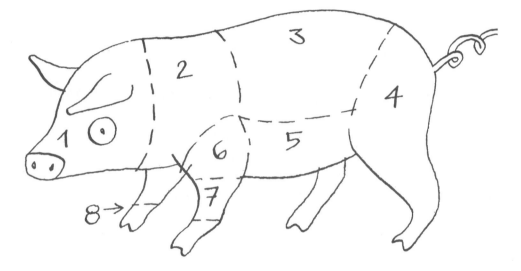

1. HEAD
Head cheese

2. BLADE SHOULDER
Roasting and braising, plus cutting into chops for broiling or frying, and slicing for stir-fries

3. LOIN
Roasting and cut into tenderloin for roasting, frying and medallions and into chops for broiling

4. LEG
Roasting and cut into chops for boiling and braising

5. SIDE
Stuffing and roasting, ground for terrines, adding flavor to casseroles, cut into spare ribs

6. ARM SHOULDER
Braising

7. HOCK
Braising

8. FOOT
Braising

AMERICAN CUTS
AND COOKING
TECHNIQUES

If you are in doubt over which cut to choose or cannot find one that is listed here, ask a reputable butcher for advice.

ROAST LOIN OF PORK

ARISTA AL FORNO

Serves 6

2 tablespoons butter

3 tablespoons olive oil • 1 fresh rosemary sprig

2¼-pound hind loin of pork, chined

¾ cup dry white wine

4–5 tablespoons hot milk

salt and pepper

boiled Tuscan or cannellini beans, to serve

Preheat the oven to 350°F. Heat the butter, oil and rosemary in an oval roasting pan, add the pork and cook, turning frequently, for 5–10 minutes until browned all over. Add the wine and cook until it has evaporated, then season with salt and pepper. Transfer to the oven and roast, turning occasionally and basting with hot milk, for 1 hour or until cooked through. Remove the pork from the oven and let stand for 10 minutes, then carve, serve with a side dish of boiled Tuscan or cannellini beans seasoned with extra-virgin olive oil, salt and pepper.

ROAST PORK WITH ORANGE

ARROSTO ALL'ARANCIA

Serves 6

3 tablespoons butter

1½ cups orange juice, strained

1 teaspoon grated orange rind • 1 garlic clove

pinch of chili powder • pinch of dried oregano

2¼-pound loin of pork, boned • salt and pepper

Preheat the oven to 350°F. Melt the butter in a pan, add the orange juice, grated rind, garlic, chili powder and oregano, season with salt and pepper and mix well. Rub the meat with salt and pepper and place in a roasting pan. Pour in the mixture and roast, basting frequently, for about 1½ hours. Carve and serve with the cooking juices.

ROAST PORK IN GRAPE JUICE

ARROSTO ALL'UVA

Serves 6

2¼-pound tenderloin

6 tablespoons olive oil

1 cup grape juice

salt and pepper

Tie the meat neatly with kitchen string and brush with some of the olive oil. Put the remaining oil in a deep pan, add the pork and cook over high heat, turning frequently, until browned all over. Add the grape juice, lower the heat, cover and simmer for about 1½ hours until the pork is tender and the sauce has thickened. Season with salt and pepper to taste. Lift out the meat, untie it and carve into slices. Place on a warm serving dish and spoon the sauce over them.

BRAISED PORK WITH ROSEMARY

ARROSTO CON IL ROSMARINO

Serves 6

needles from 1–2 rosemary sprigs

2¼-pound loin of pork , boned

2 tablespoons butter

6 tablespoons olive oil

1 garlic clove, crushed • ½ onion, chopped

¾ cup dry white wine

1 tablespoon white wine vinegar

1 teaspoon Dijon mustard

salt and pepper

Push half the rosemary needles into the meat and tie neatly with kitchen string. Heat the butter and 4 tablespoons of the olive oil in a pan, add the pork and cook, turning frequently, until golden brown all over. Add the garlic, onion and remaining rosemary, then pour in the wine and cook until evaporated. Season, cover and simmer for about 1½ hours. Remove the pork from the pan and let stand for 10 minutes, then untie, carve into fairly thick slices and place on a warm serving dish. Meanwhile, stir the vinegar, the remaining oil, the mustard and a pinch of pepper into the cooking juices. Pour into a sauce boat and serve with the meat.

ROAST PORK WITH APPLES

ARROSTO CON LE MELE

Serves 6

2¼-pound loin of pork, boned

2 tablespoons olive oil

1½ cups red wine

¾ cup Vegetable Stock (see page 209)

4 cloves

½ tablespoon mustard powder

2 tablespoons sugar

10 black peppercorns, crushed

2 green apples, peeled, cored and cubed

salt and pepper

Preheat the oven to 400°F. Lightly season the meat with salt and pepper, roll and tie with kitchen string. Heat the oil in a pan, add the meat and cook, turning frequently, until browned all over. Meanwhile, pour the wine and stock into another pan, add the cloves, mustard powder, sugar and peppercorns, season with salt and bring to a boil. Transfer the pork to an ovenproof dish, season with salt and pepper and surround with the apples. Pour the hot wine mixture over it, cover with foil and roast for 20 minutes, then lower the oven temperature to 350°F and roast, basting frequently, for a further 45 minutes. Remove and discard the foil, return the pork to the oven and roast for 15 minutes more until tender. Lift the meat out of the dish and let stand. Strain the sauce into a pan, pressing down the apples with a spoon. Cook over high heat until thickened and caramelized, then season with salt and pepper to taste. Untie the meat and carve into slices. Place on a warm serving dish and spoon the hot sauce over.

ROAST PORK WITH LEMON

ARROSTO CON LIMONE CARAMELLATO

Serves 6

2¼-pound loin of pork, boned

2 tablespoons fresh rosemary needles, chopped

¾ cup dry white wine

¼ cup sugar

5 tablespoons lemon juice, strained

1 tablespoon brandy

1 lemon, sliced

salt and pepper

Make a few incisions in the meat, along the grain, using a small knife. Insert a pinch of rosemary needles in each incision until half have been used. Place the pork in a deep bowl, pour in the wine and sprinkle with the remaining rosemary. Let marinate in a cool place, turning occasionally, for 2 hours. Preheat the oven to 450°F. Drain the pork, reserving the marinade, and tie neatly with kitchen string. Put the meat in a roasting pan and roast for 15 minutes, then lower the temperature to 350°F and roast for a further 30 minutes. Pour the reserved marinade over the pork, season with salt and pepper, return to the oven and roast for about 1 hour more. Meanwhile, dissolve the sugar in the lemon juice and brandy in a bowl. Remove the roasting pan from the oven and skim off the fat with a tablespoon. Pour the lemon mixture over the pork, return to the oven and roast, basting every 10 minutes, until the sauce has thickened and the meat is dark and shiny. Remove the pork and let stand for a few minutes, then untie and carve it into slices. Place on a warm serving dish, surround with the lemon slice and spoon the cooking juices over the meat.

PAN–FRIED PORK FILLET

BISTECCHE DI FILETTO

Serves 4

4 tenderloin slices, ¹/₂ inch thick
all-purpose flour, for dusting
2 tablespoons butter
³/₄ cup dry white wine
1 flat-leaf parsley sprig, chopped
salt

Lightly dust the pork with flour and shake off any excess. Melt the butter in a pan, add the meat and cook over high heat for 2 minutes on each side. Turn the slices several times, then pour in the wine, cover and cook for 5 minutes. Remove the lid, season with salt and, if necessary, cook for a little longer until the pan juices have thickened. Transfer the meat to a warm serving dish, spoon the cooking juices over it and sprinkle with the parsley. Mashed or roast potatoes seasoned with rosemary go well as a side dish.

CASSOEULA

BOTTAGGIO ALLA MILANESE

Serves 8

5 tablespoons olive oil
¹/₄ cup butter
1 onion, chopped
5¹/₂ ounces pork rind
1 pig's foot, chopped
1 quantity Meat Stock (see page 208)
2¹/₄ pounds spare ribs
3 carrots, cut into thin batons
1 celery stalk, chopped
1 Savoy cabbage
4 small mild salamis or Italian sausages
salt and pepper

Heat the oil and butter in a large pan, add the onion and cook over low heat, stirring occasionally, for 10 minutes. Add the pork rind and foot and cook, turning occasionally, until browned all over. Season with salt and pepper to taste, pour in enough stock to cover and cook until the liquid has reduced by half. Add the ribs and cook for about 10 minutes, then add the carrots and celery. Cover and simmer gently for 30 minutes. Meanwhile, briefly blanch the cabbage leaves in boiling water, then refresh under cold water. Add the cabbage to the pan, re-cover and simmer for 20 minutes more, adding more stock if necessary. Prick the salamis or sausages with a fork, add to the pan, re-cover and simmer for 20 minutes more. When the mixture is ready it will have a slightly glutinous consistency owing to the pork rind and foot.

PORK CHOPS WITH BLUEBERRIES

BRACIOLE AI MIRTILLI

Serves 4

4 spare-rib chops
all-purpose flour, for dusting
2 tablespoons butter
3 tablespoons olive oil
³/₄ cup red wine
2³/₄ cups blueberries
scant ¹/₂ cup clear honey
salt

Preheat the oven to 400°F. Dust the chops with flour. Heat the butter and oil in a small flameproof casserole, add the chops and cook, turning occasionally, until browned all over. Pour in the wine and cook until it has partly evaporated, then season with salt. Pass the blueberries through a food mill and mix with the honey in a bowl. Spread this mixture over the chops, then cover the casserole, transfer to the oven and cook for 15 minutes. Let stand for 10 minutes, then serve.

CURRIED PORK CHOPS

BRACIOLE AL CURRY

Serves 4

2 tablespoons butter • 2 tablespoons olive oil

4 rib chops • ¼ cup brandy

1 teaspoon curry powder

1 tablespoon heavy cream

2 tablespoons warm Vegetable Stock (see page 209)

Heat the butter and oil in a pan, add the chops and cook, turning occasionally, until browned all over. Add the brandy and cook until it has evaporated. Combine the curry powder, cream and stock in a bowl and add to the pan. Cover and simmer for 15–20 minutes. Transfer to a warm serving dish.

PORK CHOPS IN GORGONZOLA

BRACIOLE AL GORGONZOLA

Serves 4

2 tablespoons butter

4 rib chops

5 tablespoons dry white wine

3½ ounces mild Gorgonzola cheese

salt

Melt the butter in a skillet, add the chops and cook over high heat for 6 minutes on each side. Transfer to a warm serving dish. Leave the skillet to cool, then pour in the wine and heat gently until half has evaporated, then crumble in the cheese and cook over low heat until melted. Season to taste with salt and pour the sauce over the meat.

PORK CHOPS IN CREAM

BRACIOLE ALLA PANNA

Serves 4

4 rib chops

2 tablespoons butter

1 tablespoon olive oil

¾ cup port

1 cup heavy cream

1 teaspoon all-purpose flour

salt and pepper

Lightly pound the chops. Heat the butter and oil in a skillet, add the chops and cook, turning occasionally, for 6 minutes on each side. Season, then remove from the skillet, drain and keep warm. Pour the port into the skillet and cook over low heat, scraping up any sediment from the base of the skillet, until the liquid has reduced by half. Combine the cream and flour in a bowl, stir into the skillet and season lightly with salt and pepper. Simmer for 5 minutes, then pour the sauce over the chops and serve.

PORK SHOULDER WITH PRUNES

CARRÉ ALLE PRUGNE

Serves 6

2¼-pound shoulder of pork, main bone removed and ribs uncovered

⅔ cup prunes, pitted

¼ cup butter

2 tablespoons olive oil

1 shallot, chopped

2 tablespoons brandy

salt and pepper

Preheat the oven to 400°F. Open out the meat like a book and arrange a row of prunes along the join. Chop the remaining prunes. Roll the pork and tie with kitchen string passed between the ribs, then season. Heat half the butter and the oil in a roasting pan, then remove from the heat, add the pork and roast, basting occasionally, for about 1¼ hours. Melt the remaining butter in a skillet, add the shallot and cook over low heat for 5 minutes. Add the prunes and cook for a further 5 minutes. Pour in the brandy and ignite. Remove the meat from the roasting pan and let stand. Skim off the fat from the cooking juices and strain the juices into the prune sauce. Untie the meat and carve it into slices. Serve with the prune sauce.

PORK SHOULDER WITH CARDOONS

Push the cloves into the meat. Combine the rosemary, sage and a pinch of salt in a bowl and gently rub the mixture over the pork, then tie the meat neatly with kitchen string. Place half the onion in a pan with the peppercorns, half the butter and half the oil and heat gently. Place the pork on top and cook until browned on both sides. Pour in the wine and cook until it has reduced by half. Season with salt and simmer over low heat. Heat the remaining butter and oil in another pan, add the pancetta, garlic and the remaining onion and cook over low heat, stirring occasionally, for 5 minutes. Add the tomatoes and $^2/_3$ cup hot water and cook until the liquid has almost completely evaporated. Cook the cardoons in a pan of salted, boiling water for about 30 minutes until tender but still quite firm to the bite. Drain and add to the sauce. Remove the meat from the pan, untie and carve it into slices. Place on a warm serving dish, spoon the cooking juices over them and serve with the cardoons.

CARRÉ CON I CARDI
Serves 4
3 cloves
1$^3/_4$-pound pork shoulder, boned
pinch of dried rosemary
pinch of dried sage
1 onion, chopped
6 black peppercorns
3 tablespoons butter
2 tablespoons olive oil
$^3/_4$ cup red wine
$^1/_3$ cup pancetta, chopped
1 garlic clove, chopped
7 ounces canned tomatoes
3$^3/_4$ pounds cardoons, trimmed
and chopped (see page 423)
salt

SPARE RIBS WITH POLENTA

Melt the butter in a pan, add the onion and garlic clove and cook over low heat, stirring occasionally, for 10 minutes until golden brown. Remove and discard the garlic. Add the ribs to the pan, pour in the wine and cook until it has evaporated. Add the tomatoes, chile and basil and season with salt and pepper. Simmer over low heat for 1 hour or until the meat starts to fall off the bones. If necessary, add a little warm water and wine to prevent the mixture from drying out during cooking. Serve the spare ribs with soft polenta.

COSTINE CON POLENTA
Serves 4
$^1/_4$ cup butter
1 onion, chopped
1 garlic clove
1$^3/_4$ pounds spare ribs
$^3/_4$ cup red wine
14 ounces canned tomatoes
1 fresh chile, seeded and chopped
6 fresh basil leaves, chopped
salt and pepper
Polenta (see page 305), to serve

PORK CHOPS IN BUTTER AND SAGE

Trim the bones and flatten the chops slightly with a meat mallet. Melt the butter in a pan, add the sage and cook until light golden brown. Add the meat and cook for 5 minutes on each side until tender and cooked through. Season lightly with salt and pepper.

COSTOLETTE AL BURRO E SALVIA
Serves 4
4 loin chops
3 tablespoons butter
6 fresh sage leaves
salt and pepper

PORK CHOPS WITH TUSCAN CABBAGE

COSTOLETTE AL CAVOLO NERO

Serves 4

4¹/₃ cups Tuscan cabbage, shredded

4 tablespoons olive oil

2 garlic cloves

4 loin chops

³/₄ cup red wine

1 fresh flat-leaf parsley sprig, chopped

salt and pepper

Cook the Tuscan cabbage in salted, boiling water for about 30 minutes, then drain. Meanwhile, heat the oil in a skillet, add the garlic and cook until golden brown, then remove and discard it. Add the chops to the skillet, pour in the wine and season with salt and pepper to taste. Simmer over low heat until the wine has evaporated. Remove the chops from the skillet and keep warm. Add the cabbage and parsley to the skillet and cook over low heat for 10 minutes. Return the chops to the skillet and heat through for a few minutes before serving.

PORK CHOPS WITH YELLOW BELL PEPPERS

COSTOLETTE CON PEPERONI

Serves 4

2 tablespoons butter

1 tablespoon olive oil

4 loin chops

4 yellow bell peppers, halved, seeded and cut into strips

1 garlic clove, crushed (optional)

salt

Heat the butter and oil in a skillet, add the chops, season with salt and cook until golden brown on both sides. Add the bell peppers, lower the heat and cook gently for about 15 minutes, adding the garlic, if using, about halfway through the cooking time.

CROÛTES WITH PORK FILLET AND PÂTÉ DE FOIE GRAS

CROSTONI DI FILETTO AL FOIE GRAS

Serves 4

6 tablespoons butter

4 tenderloin slices

4 white bread slices, crusts removed

5 tablespoons Marsala

3¹/₂ ounces pâté de foie gras

salt and pepper

Heat half the butter in a skillet, add the meat and cook for 3 minutes on each side. Season with salt and pepper, remove from the skillet and keep warm. Melt the remaining butter in another skillet, add the slices of bread and cook until golden brown on both sides. Remove with a slotted spatula, drain on paper towels and place on a warm serving dish. Place a slice of pork on each slice of bread. Pour the Marsala into the skillet where the meat was cooked and heat gently, scraping up the sediment from the base with a wooden spoon. Cook until slightly reduced. Lightly spread each slice of meat with the pâté de foie gras and spoon the hot sauce on top.

PORK EN CROÛTE

Heat the butter and oil in a pan, add the onion and cook over low heat, stirring occasionally, for 10 minutes. Stir in the mushrooms and cook for a few minutes, then add 1 tablespoon of the lemon juice, the lemon rind, parsley and crumbled rolls and mix well. Season generously with salt and pepper. Remove the pan from the heat and let cool. Preheat the oven to 400°F. Trim any fat from the meat and make a deep, lengthwise cut in each piece without cutting through completely. Open out each piece of meat like a book and flatten with a meat mallet. Season with salt and pepper and sprinkle with the remaining lemon juice. Spread half the mushroom mixture on each piece of meat, then place one piece on top of the other and press down well so that they form a single block. Roll out the dough on a lightly floured surface into a rectangle 2 inches longer than the meat and three times the width. Place the meat in the middle of the dough, brush the side edges with a little water and fold in towards the middle, then repeat for the two ends. Press down well to seal the packet. Decorate with any dough trimmings and brush with the beaten egg. Place the packet on a cookie sheet and bake for 30 minutes. Lower the oven temperature to 350°F and bake for 45 minutes more. If the pastry begins to brown too much, cover with foil to prevent it from burning. Remove the packet from the oven and let stand for 10 minutes, then slice and reassemble on a serving dish.

FILETTO FARCITO IN CROSTA

Serves 4

2 tablespoons butter

1 tablespoon olive oil

1 onion, chopped

3¼ cups mushrooms

juice and grated rind of ½ lemon

1 fresh flat-leaf parsley sprig, chopped

2 rolls, crusts removed, crumbled

1¾-pound tenderloin, halved

13 ounces puff pastry dough, thawed if frozen

all-purpose flour, for dusting

1 egg, lightly beaten

salt and pepper

PORK ROULADES WITH APRICOTS

If you are not using no-soak apricots, put them in a bowl, add lukewarm water to cover and let soak. Heat the oil and butter in a pan, add the slices of pork and cook until golden brown on both sides. Remove from the pan and set aside. Squeeze out the apricots, if necessary, and chop them. Add the apricots and pancetta to the pan and cook, stirring occasionally, until the pancetta is lightly browned, then season with salt. Divide the apricot mixture equally among the slices of pork, roll up and tie with kitchen string. Put the roulades in the pan, add the brandy and cook until it has evaporated, then serve.

INVOLTINI ALLE ALBICOCCHE

Serves 4

scant ½ cup dried apricots

2 tablespoons olive oil

2 tablespoons butter

8 loin of pork slices

3½ ounces pancetta, cut into strips

¼ cup brandy

salt

LOIN OF PORK WITH TUNA SAUCE

LOMBO TONNATO

Serves 4

1³/₄-pound loin of pork, boned
1 cup dry white wine
2 carrots, cut into thin batons
1 celery stalk, chopped
1 onion
1 tablespoon black peppercorns
1 tablespoon olive oil
salt
1 lemon, sliced, to garnish

For the sauce
3 hard-cooked egg yolks
1 tablespoon Dijon mustard
1 tablespoon white wine vinegar
³/₄ cup olive oil
2 tablespoons capers, drained, rinsed and chopped
4 canned anchovy fillets in oil, drained and chopped
7 ounces canned tuna in oil, drained and flaked
salt

Tie the pork neatly with kitchen string and place in a snug-fitting pan. Pour in the wine and add water to cover. Add the carrots, celery, onion, a pinch of salt, the peppercorns and olive oil, bring to a boil, then lower the heat, cover and simmer gently for 1 hour. Remove the pan from the heat and let the meat cool in the cooking liquid. Drain the pork, reserving the vegetables, place on a plate, cover with plastic wrap and put a weight (such as a couple of cans of tomatoes) on top. Chill in the refrigerator. Meanwhile, make the sauce. Mash the egg yolks in a bowl, then beat in the mustard, a generous pinch of salt and the vinegar until smooth. Gradually beat in the olive oil, adding it in a thin, continuous stream. Stir in the capers, anchovies and tuna. Put the reserved vegetables in a food processor and process to a purée. Stir the purée into the sauce. Uncover the meat and carve it into thin slices. Place the slices, overlapping slightly, in concentric rings on a serving dish. Spoon the sauce over them to cover completely. Garnish with slices of lemon and serve.

LOIN OF PORK WITH JUNIPER

LONZA AL GINEPRO

Serves 4

1³/₄-pound loin of pork, boned
1 shallot, chopped
1 onion, chopped
10–15 juniper berries, lightly crushed
2 bay leaves
5 tablespoons white wine
5 tablespoons oil
3¹/₂ ounces pancetta, sliced
salt and pepper

Make small incisions in the meat and insert pieces of shallot. Put the onion, juniper berries, bay leaves, wine and half the oil in a dish and season with salt and pepper. Add the pork, turning to coat, and let marinate for 2 hours. Preheat the oven to 350°F. Drain the pork, reserving the marinade, wrap it in the slices of pancetta and tie with kitchen string. Put the pork in a roasting pan with the remaining oil and roast, basting occasionally with the reserved marinade, for about 1 hour or until tender and cooked through. Remove the meat from the roasting pan, untie and carve into thin slices. Place them on a warm serving dish and spoon the cooking juices over them.

BACON
AND POTATO PIE

Preheat the oven to 400°F. Combine the bacon and onion in a large bowl, add the potatoes, sprinkle with the flour and mix well. Beat the eggs with a little salt and pepper in another bowl, stir in the milk, pour into the bacon mixture and stir until fully combined. Melt the butter in a roasting pan and when it has turned golden brown, pour in the mixture, then smooth the surface and mark with the prongs of a fork. Bake for about 45 minutes. Slice the pie and serve hot.

PASTICCIO DI BACON E PATATE

Serves 4

8 bacon slices, coarsely chopped

$1/2$ onion, coarsely chopped

11 ounces potatoes, cut into thin batons

1 tablespoon all-purpose flour

2 eggs

5 tablespoons milk

3 tablespoons butter

salt and pepper

BAKED HAM

Preheat the oven to 475°F. Using a sharp knife, score the skin of the ham in a diamond pattern. Combine a generous pinch of sea salt and pepper in a small bowl and rub the mixture into the ham, particularly along the score marks, so that it penetrates well. Put the ham on a rack over a roasting pan and pour the wine and $1^1/2$ cups water into the pan beneath. Bake for 15 minutes, then lower the oven temperature to 300°F and bake for 3 hours, turning the ham halfway through the cooking time. Do not baste as the skin should be crisp when done. Meanwhile, put the butter, $3/4$ cup water, the sugar, vinegar and table salt and pepper in a pan and bring to a boil. Add the cabbage, cover, lower the heat and simmer for 15 minutes. Add the red currant jelly and apples, re-cover and cook for 40 minutes more. If necessary, remove the lid during the end of the cooking period so that any excess liquid boils off. When the ham is cooked, switch off the oven, open the door and leave it in the oven for 20 minutes. Carve the ham into slices, place on a warm serving dish and surround with the cabbage. Stir $2/3$ cup warm water into the cooking juices and serve in a sauce boat with the ham.

PROSCIUTTO AL FORNO

Serves 10

$6^1/2$-pound raw cured ham

1 cup dry white wine

$1/4$ cup butter

2 tablespoons sugar

2 tablespoons red wine vinegar

1 red cabbage, shredded

4 tablespoons red currant jelly

2 apples, peeled, cored and chopped

sea salt

table salt and pepper

SMOKED HAM WITH MARSALA

PROSCIUTTO AL MARSALA

Serves 10

6¹/₂-pound Prague ham or other smoked ham
2¹/₄ cups dry Marsala
6 tablespoons olive oil
6 tablespoons butter
1 onion, diced
2 carrots, diced
2 celery stalks, diced
1 fresh flat-leaf parsley sprig, chopped
salt and pepper

For the sauce
scant 1 cup hot Meat Stock
(see page 208) or hot water
1 teaspoon cornstarch
scant ¹/₂ cup dry Marsala
2 tablespoons butter

Cut off the skin and part of the fat from the ham and place the ham in a snug-fitting pan. Add the Marsala and let marinate for 6 hours. Preheat the oven to 350°F. Drain the ham, reserving the marinade, and tie neatly with kitchen string. Heat the oil and butter in a large roasting pan, add the ham and cook, turning carefully, until lightly browned all over. Add the vegetables, parsley and salt and pepper. Transfer to the oven and roast, basting frequently with the cooking juices and the reserved marinade, for 2 hours. Remove the ham from the roasting pan and keep warm. To make the sauce, pass the vegetable and the ham juices through a food mill into a pan, add any remaining marinade and the stock or water and bring to a boil. Boil until slightly reduced. Mix the cornstarch to a paste with 2 tablespoons cold water in a bowl, stir the mixture into the sauce and cook, stirring constantly, until thickened, then remove from the heat. Whisk in the Marsala and butter. Untie the ham and carve into fairly thick slices. Place on a warm serving dish and serve covered with the sauce.

HAM IN WHITE WINE

PROSCIUTTO AL VINO BIANCO

Serves 4

butter, for greasing
8 thick cooked, cured ham slices
1¹/₂ cups dry white wine
scant 4¹/₂ cups mushrooms, sliced
1 small shallot, chopped
³/₄ cup heavy cream
1 tablespoon white port
salt

Preheat the oven to 300°F. Grease a fairly large, ovenproof dish with butter and place the ham on the base. Pour in half the wine, cover with foil and bake for 3 hours, making sure that the liquid does not come to a boil. Put the mushrooms, shallot and remaining wine in a pan, bring to a boil, then stir in the cream and simmer gently. Add the ham cooking juices and cook until reduced to the required consistency. Stir in the port and season with salt to taste. Place the ham on a warm serving dish and cover with the sauce.

RIBS IN WHITE WINE

PUNTINE AL VINO BIANCO

Serves 4

2 tablespoons olive oil
3 tablespoons butter
4 fresh sage leaves
12 spare ribs
³/₄ cup dry white wine
salt and pepper

Heat the oil, butter and sage leaves in a fairly large pan until the leaves are light golden brown. Add the spare ribs and cook over high heat for a few minutes, turning constantly, until evenly browned. Lower the heat and cook for 20 minutes. Season with salt and pepper and cook, occasionally sprinkling the ribs with the wine, for 40 minutes (do not pour in all the wine at once). Transfer to a warm serving dish.

SWEET–AND–SOUR SPARE RIBS

PUNTINE IN AGRODOLCE

Serves 6

12 spare ribs

3 tablespoons olive oil

1 scallion, sliced

1/2 fresh pineapple, peeled, cored and chopped

1 yellow bell pepper, halved, seeded and cut into squares

1 green bell pepper, halved, seeded and cut into squares

1 red bell pepper, halved, seeded and cut into squares

2 tablespoons sugar

salt and pepper

Preheat the oven to 400°F. Season the spare ribs, put in a roasting pan and roast for 20 minutes, turning them halfway through the cooking time. Meanwhile, preheat the broiler. Place the roasting pan under the broiler and cook for a further 10 minutes. Heat the oil in a pan, add the scallion and cook over low heat, for 5 minutes. Add the pineapple and bell peppers and cook over low heat for about 10 minutes, adding a little water if necessary. Sprinkle with the sugar, season with salt and pepper, mix well and simmer for 10 minutes more. Add the ribs and cook for a few minutes more, then serve.

CHOPPED PORK WITH PRUNES

SPEZZATINO CON LE PRUGNE

Serves 6

1 1/3 cups prunes

2 1/4 cups port or Marsala

1 pound 2 ounces tenderloin, diced

all-purpose flour, for dusting

1/4 cup butter

1 shallot, finely chopped

2 tablespoons heavy cream

salt and pepper

Place the prunes in a bowl, add the port or Marsala and let soak overnight. Preheat the oven to 350°F. Drain the prunes, reserving the port or Marsala, and pit them, then place them in a an ovenproof dish and dry in the oven for 6 minutes. Season the pork with salt and pepper and dust lightly with flour. Melt the butter in a skillet, add the pork and cook, stirring frequently, for 5 minutes. Remove the meat from the skillet and keep warm. Add the shallot to the pan and cook over low heat, stirring occasionally, for 10 minutes until lightly browned. Pour in the reserved port or Marsala and cook until it has evaporated. Whisk in the cream. Place the meat on a warm serving dish, spoon the sauce over it and surround with the prunes.

PORK STEW WITH SMOKED SAUSAGES

SPEZZATINO CON SALSICCIA AFFUMICATA

Serves 4

1 Savoy cabbage, trimmed and separated into leaves

7 ounces carrots, sliced

14 ounces boneless pork blade shoulder, cut into large cubes

14 ounces boneless pork arm shoulder, cut into large cubes

2 Italian smoked sausages

salt and pepper

Blanch the cabbage leaves in salted, boiling water for 5 minutes, then drain and place in a large pan. Add the carrots and all the pork and season with salt and pepper. Cover and cook over low heat for 1 1/4 hours. Prick the sausages with a fork, add to the pan and cook for 10 minutes. Mix well and transfer to a warm serving dish.

SWEET–AND–SOUR PORK STEW

Combine the brandy and soy sauce in a dish, add the pork and let marinate for about 2 hours. Meanwhile, prepare the sauce. Heat half the butter and half the oil in a skillet, add all the vegetables and stir-fry for a few minutes. Add 5 tablespoons water and the vinegar, sprinkle with the sugar and ketchup and season with salt and pepper. Simmer for about 20 minutes. Meanwhile, drain the pork. Heat the remaining butter and the remaining oil in pan, add the pork and cook over medium heat, stirring frequently, until browned all over. Pour the sauce on top of the pork, stir well and simmer for 30 minutes. Serve the stew with boiled rice.

SPEZZATINO IN AGRODOLCE

Serves 4

1/4 cup brandy

4 tablespoons dark soy sauce

1 pound 5 ounces boneless pork shoulder,

cut into cubes

1/4 cup butter

4 tablespoons olive oil

3 green bell peppers, halved, seeded and finely chopped

3 red bell peppers, halved, seeded and finely chopped

1 onion, finely chopped

4 dill pickles, drained and finely chopped

1 tablespoon red wine vinegar

2 tablespoons sugar • 1 tablespoon tomato ketchup

salt and pepper

boiled rice, to serve

PORK STEW WITH PEAS

Tip the tomatoes with their can juices into a food processor and process to a purée. Heat the butter and oil in a pan, add the onion and garlic and cook over low heat, stirring occasionally, for 5 minutes. Add the pork and cook, stirring frequently, until lightly browned all over, then season with salt and pepper. Add the wine and cook until it has evaporated, then add the puréed tomatoes and the peas. Simmer gently for about 1 hour. Transfer the stew to a warm serving dish.

SPEZZATINO CON PISELLI

Serves 4

7 ounces canned tomatoes

3 tablespoons butter

2 tablespoons olive oil

1 onion, chopped

1 garlic clove, chopped

1 pound 5 ounces boneless shoulder of pork,

cut into cubes

3/4 cup red wine

2 1/4 pounds fresh peas, shelled

salt and pepper

SPICY PORK STEW

Melt the butter in a pan, add the pork and cook over high heat, stirring frequently, until browned all over. Pour in half the wine, add the cumin and garlic and season with salt and plenty of pepper. Mix well and bring to a boil, then cover, lower the heat and simmer for 30 minutes until tender. Add the remaining wine and the lemon, increase the heat to medium and cook, stirring constantly, until thickened. Stir in the cilantro and serve.

SPEZZATINO SPEZIATO

Serves 6

1/4 cup butter

2 1/4 pounds boneless shoulder of pork, cut into cubes

1 1/2 cups dry white wine

1 teaspoon ground cumin

1 garlic clove, chopped

5 lemon slices, chopped

2 tablespoons ground cilantro

salt and pepper

PORK KABOBS WITH PRUNES

SPIEDINI ALLE PRUGNE

Serves 4

1 pound 2 ounces boneless loin of pork, cut into 24 cubes
24 no-soak prunes
all-purpose flour, for dusting
2 tablespoons butter
$^1/_4$ cup dry Marsala
$^1/_4$ cup dry white wine
salt and pepper

Thread three cubes of pork alternately with three prunes onto eight skewers, then dust the kabobs with flour. Melt the butter in a skillet, add the kabobs and cook, turning frequently, until browned all over. Season with salt and pepper, pour in the Marsala and cook until it has evaporated. Pour in the wine, lower the heat, cover and simmer gently, basting occasionally, for about 15 minutes.

PORK HOCK WITH VEGETABLES

STINCO CON VERDURE

Serves 4

2 pork hocks
4 carrots, thickly sliced
2 large onions, thinly sliced
4 potatoes, cut into fourths
1 small Savoy cabbage, shredded
salt and pepper

Put the hocks in a wide pan, add water to cover and bring to a boil. Lower the heat, cover and simmer for about 1$^1/_2$ hours. Season with salt and pepper, add the carrots, onions and potatoes and simmer for 15 minutes more. Add the cabbage and cook until the all vegetables are tender, but still slightly firm to the bite.

PORK TENERELLE

TENERELLE

Serves 4

$^1/_3$ cup dried mushrooms
4 tablespoons olive oil
generous $^1/_2$ cup smoked pancetta, diced
1 onion, finely chopped
1 celery stalk, finely chopped
1 carrot, finely chopped
1 pound 5 ounces boneless loin of pork, ground
$^2/_3$ cup hot Meat Stock (see page 208)
1 garlic clove
5 tablespoons dry white wine
2 tablespoons bottled strained tomatoes
fresh flat-leaf parsley, chopped
salt and pepper

Put the mushrooms in a bowl, add hot water to cover and let soak for 20 minutes, then drain and squeeze out. Meanwhile, heat 2 tablespoons of the oil in a pan, add the pancetta and cook over medium heat, stirring frequently, for 5 minutes. Add the onion, celery and carrot, mix well and add the pork, then season with salt and pepper. Cook, stirring frequently, until the meat is evenly browned, occasionally adding a little hot stock, if necessary. Remove from the heat. Heat the remaining oil and the garlic in another pan, then add the mushrooms, wine and strained tomatoes and season with salt and pepper. Simmer gently until reduced by half, then sprinkle with the parsley. Meanwhile, shape the pork mixture into small meatballs and flatten them slightly. Add the meatballs to the mushroom sauce and simmer for a few minutes, then transfer to a warm serving dish.

BEEF

Beef is tasty and nutritious. Its tenderness depends on the age of the animal it comes from, the type of fodder on which it was raised and the length of time it has been hung to mature. For several years, some Italian breeders have issued certificates of origin – a sort of beef identity card which makes the meat traceable and shows its quality. The aim is to provide the consumer with greater guarantees. Certification is voluntary as, currently, no law obliges breeders to give such information. Today, Italian meat stands up handsomely against the famed excellent meat in the rest of the world.

COOKING

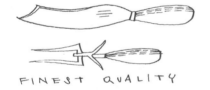

FINEST QUALITY

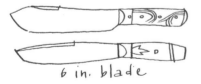

6 in. blade

→ It is important to prevent raw meat from losing its juices during preparation. It is therefore best to put it on a plate, rather than on a wooden board.

→ For the same reason, it is best to salt meat after browning. Avoid "pricking" with a fork during cooking: use a slotted wooden or metal spatula to turn.

→ Meat loses only a small part of its nutritional value in cooking. The only exception is when simmering it in salted water. In this case it "releases" its soluble components (mainly minerals) into the water thus forming a good stock.

→ If water or stock is to be added during cooking, it must be hot. Wine should be poured down the side of the pan to prevent sudden changes in temperature. When butter is stirred into ground meat to make stuffing, it should be melted and cooled slightly first.

ROASTING

The best technique is spit-roasting: the fierce heat of creates a light protective layer around the meat that helps retain the juices.

→ Pot roasts can be cooked in the oven or on the stove-top. They must in any case be cooked briefly on the stove in order to brown and sear the meat to retain the juices. After this, salt may be added and the casserole is placed in a preheated oven. To prevent the meat from drying out during cooking, bast it occasionally with its cooking juices.

→ Medium and large pieces cook better if they are compact: that is why we always suggest tying them neatly in our recipes with a few twists of thin but tough kitchen string which will not leave unsightly marks on the meat.

STEAKS

In general these are large slices of well-hung meat (loin, tenderloin, sirloin, T-bone, shoulder, or round) weighing from 4–5 ounces, which require quick cooking over high heat with oil or butter.

BOILING

Round, flank, short plate, brisket and neck are the ideal cuts. They are cooked in plenty of salted water and flavored with vegetables, such as celery, carrot and onion.

→ If the quality of the stock is important, immerse the meat in slightly salted cold water and gradually bring it to a boil.

→ If the quality of the meat is important, immerse it in

boiling water so that the protein and muscle fibers seal, keeping the meat tender and moist.

→ Since it takes a long time to prepare stock, make more than necessary and pour what is left over into an ice tray. That way you can have excellent tasting stock cubes on hand in the freezer.

BRAISING AND STEWING

The most suitable parts for braising are chuck, flanken-style ribs, round, and neck. After browning and moistening with water or wine, the meat is cooked over low heat for a long time in a pan with a heavy lid.

→ A few vegetables and herbs or spices, such as onions, carrots, celery and cloves, are normally also added to the pot.

→ Stewing and "in umido" are similar techniques to braising, except the latter usually involves adding tomatoes, and contains a very small quantity of liquid.

FRICASSÉE

This is a chopped white meat stew. Cream mixed with egg and lemon juice is added, or just egg and lemon juice are added shortly before cooking is complete.

FRYING

For frying there is nothing better than olive oil, which – when light and very hot – adds flavor to any type of food. Here are a few things to bear in mind:

→ there are two main types of frying: pan-frying and deep-frying;

→ in pan-frying, the oil comes up to about half the thickness of the food which is turned with a slotted spatula so that it browns and cooks evenly and completely;

→ in deep-frying, the food is immersed in plenty of oil which covers it completely

→ while frying, the oil must never smoke;

→ to judge the temperature, put a cube of day-old bread in the pan: if the oil is medium hot, it browns in 40 seconds; if it is very hot, it browns in 30 seconds; if it is extremely hot, it browns in 25 seconds;

→ nonstick pans may be used for foods with long frying times so that the amount of oil needed can be reduced;

→ fried food must be salted after cooking or very lightly salted at the start, otherwise there is a risk (for example with Milanese veal chops) that bread crumbs may come away or crispy

crusts will not form;

→ it is best not to reuse oil after frying;

→ dusting with flour: meat is usually dusted with flour, and any excess flour is shaken off before frying;

→ browning: first of all dust with flour, then dip in lightly salted, beaten egg;

→ bread crumbs: first dust with flour, then dip in beaten egg, then in bread crumbs;

→ batter: batter is made of flour and various liquids; it solidifies on contact with hot oil and forms a crust or puffs up.

STRACOTTO STEW

in this type of stew, the meat is larded, lightly browned all over, then moistened with wine, stock, or water. The liquid is then kept at a gently simmer for 3–4 hours. When cooked the stew will be thickened and rich.

ITALIAN CUTS AND COOKING TECHNIQUES

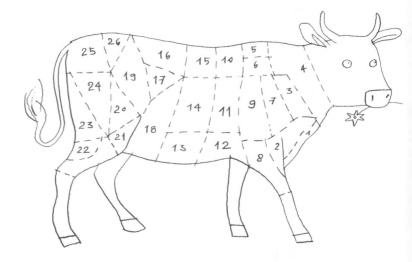

1. FIOCCO
Boiling
2. BRIONE
Stewing and boiling
3. FUSELLO
Fairly lean. Stewing, boiling, roulades and chops
4. COLLO
Boiling and stewing
5. REALE
Boiling and braising
6. BIANCOSTATO
DI REALE
Boiling
7. CAPPELLO DEL PRETE
Its Italian name means priest's hat and derives from its slightly triangular shape. It is soft and gelatinous. Braising, stewing and boiling
8. GERETTO
Boiling, braising and stewing
9. FESONE DI SPALLA
Steaks, boiling, roulades, chops and scallops

10. COSTE DELLA CROCE
Boiling
11. BIANCOSTATO
DI CROCE
Soups
12. PUNTA DI PETTO
Boiling and stewing
13. PANCIA
O BAMBORINO
Soups, stews and meatballs
14. BIANCOSTATO
DI PANCIA
Stocks and boiling
15. COSTATA
16. CONTROFILETTO
(LOMBATA)
Steaks and Florentine steaks
17. FILETTO
The most tender and tastiest cut. Roasting and broiling
18. SCALFO
Stewing
19. SCAMONE
A tender tasty cut. Large roasts

20. NOCE
Very tender. Scallops, slices, steaks and roasting
21. SPINACINO
Stuffed roasts
22. PESCE O PICCIONE
Boiling
23. GIRELLO
O MAGATELLO
Steaks, scallops, roasting, stewing and boiling, and also raw for carpaccio
24. ROSA
Steaks and slices
25. CULACCIO
O SCAMONE
Roasting, boiling, braising and broiling
26. CODONE
Stewing and boiling

AMERICAN CUTS
AND COOKING
TECHNIQUES

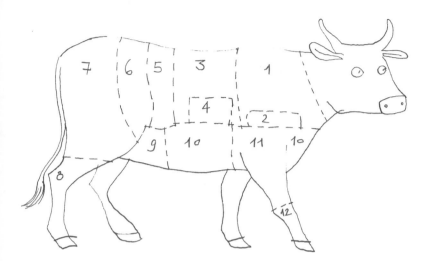

1. CHUCK
Braising, pot-roasting, and casseroles

2. FLANKEN—STYLE RIBS
Braising, occasionally broiling

3. RIB
Roasting

4. BACK RIB
Roasting and cut into Delmonico and Spencer steaks

5. SHORT LOIN
Cut into porterhouse, club, and T-bone steaks

6. SIRLOIN
Roasting, cut into steaks, tenderloin, and New York strip

7. ROUND
Cut into boneless rump for roasting, braising, and pot-roasting, and round steak, suitable for frying

8. HIND SHANK
Stewing and making stock

9. FLANK
Cut into flank steak rolls, broiling (London broil), and frying

10. SHORT PLATE
Braising

11. BRISKET
Braising and corned beef

12. FORE SHANK
Stewing and making stock

If you are in doubt over which cut to choose or cannot find one that is listed here, ask a reputable butcher for advice.

781

POT ROAST BEEF WITH BRANDY AND GRAPEFRUIT

ARROSTO AL BRANDY E POMPELMO

Serves 6

1³/₄ pounds beef round

3 tablespoons butter

3 tablespoons olive oil

³/₄ cup dry white wine

¹/₄ cup brandy

juice of 1 ruby grapefruit, strained

2 yellow grapefruits, peeled and segmented

salt and pepper

Tie the meat neatly with kitchen string. Heat the butter and olive oil in a flameproof casserole, add the meat and cook, turning frequently, until browned on all sides. Combine the wine and brandy in a pitcher and pour the mixture over the meat. Cook until the liquid has evaporated, then season with salt and pepper. Lower the heat and cook for 1¹/₄ hours, gradually adding the grapefruit juice. Transfer 3–4 tablespoons of the cooking juices to a pan, add the grapefruit segments and heat gently. Untie the meat, carve into slices, place on a warm serving dish and surround with the grapefruit segments and gravy.

POT ROAST BEEF IN CREAM

ARROSTO ALLA PANNA

Serves 6

3 tablespoons butter

2 tablespoons olive oil

1 onion, thinly sliced

1³/₄-pound lean beef pot roast or eye of round

3 tablespoons white wine vinegar

scant 1 cup heavy cream

salt and pepper

Heat the butter and olive oil in an oval, flameproof casserole, add the onion and cook, stirring occasionally, for 10 minutes until golden brown. Tie the meat neatly with kitchen string, add to the casserole, increase the heat to high and cook, turning frequently, until browned all over. Season with salt and pepper, add the vinegar, lower the heat, cover and simmer gently for about 2 hours, occasionally adding a little hot water if it seems to be drying out. When the meat is cooked through and tender, remove it from the casserole and let it stand for 10 minutes in a warm place. Stir the cream into the cooking juices and heat until thickened. Untie the beef, carve into slices, place on a warm serving dish and spoon the sauce over them.

POT ROAST BEEF WITH ANCHOVIES AND TOMATO

ARROSTO ALLE ACCIUGHE E POMODORO

Serves 6

4 salted anchovies, heads removed, cleaned and filleted (see page 596), soaked in cold water for 10 minutes and drained

2 tablespoons olive oil

3 tablespoons butter • 1 onion, chopped

5 ounces Italian sausages, skinned and crumbled

1³/₄-pound lean beef pot roast or eye of round

all-purpose flour, for dusting

5 tablespoons dry white wine

4 tomatoes, peeled and diced

salt and pepper

Chop the anchovy fillets. Heat the oil and butter in a pan, add the onion and cook over low heat, stirring occasionally, for 5 minutes. Add the anchovies and cook, mashing with a wooden spoon until they have almost disintegrated, then add the sausages. Tie the meat neatly with kitchen string, dust lightly with flour, and add to the pan. Increase the heat to high and cook, turning frequently, until browned on all sides, then season with salt and pepper. Pour in the wine and cook until it has evaporated. Add the tomatoes, cover, and simmer gently for about 2 hours. Remove the meat from the pan and let it stand for 10 minutes. Untie the meat, carve into slices and serve with the cooking juices.

ROAST BEEF WITH CARROTS

Preheat the oven to 250°F. Cover the base of a roasting pan with two-thirds of the pancetta. Heat the oil in a pan, add the carrots, garlic and thyme and cook over medium-high heat, stirring frequently, until lightly browned. Season with salt and sprinkle with the nutmeg, then transfer to a dish and keep warm. Tie the meat neatly with kitchen string, add to the pan and cook, turning frequently, until browned on both sides. Season with salt, add the brandy and cook until it has evaporated. Transfer the beef to the roasting pan, spoon the carrot mixture and celery leaves around it and sprinkle the remaining pancetta on top. Cover and roast for 2 hours until the carrots have caramelized. Remove the meat from the roasting pan, discard the string, carve into slices and season with pepper. Transfer to a warm serving dish together with the vegetables.

ARROSTO ALLE CAROTE

Serves 6

scant 1 cup pancetta, chopped

3 tablespoons olive oil

2¼ pounds carrots, sliced

1 garlic clove, chopped

1 fresh thyme sprig, chopped

pinch of freshly grated nutmeg

1¾-pound beef round

2 tablespoons brandy

4–5 celery leaves

salt and pepper

POT ROAST MARINATED BEEF

Combine all the marinade ingredients in a dish, add the meat, turning to coat, and let marinate for 6 hours. Drain the meat, reserving the marinade. Heat the oil and half the butter in a flameproof casserole, add the beef and cook, turning frequently, until browned all over. Season with salt and cook over low heat for 1½ hours or until cooked through and tender. Remove the meat from the casserole and let stand. Meanwhile, mix together the remaining butter and the flour and stir the paste into the cooking juices. Cook, stirring until slightly thickened, then strain in a little of the reserved marinade. Carve the beef and serve with the sauce.

ARROSTO MARINATO

Serves 6

2-pound pot roast or eye of round

2 tablespoons olive oil

¼ cup butter • 2 tablespoons all-purpose flour

salt

For the marinade

scant 1 cup olive oil

1 onion, sliced • ½ bunch of mixed fresh herbs, including flat-leaf parsley • 6 black peppercorns

STEAK WITH MUSHROOMS

Melt half the butter in a pan, add the shallot and cook over low heat, stirring occasionally, for 5 minutes. Add the mushrooms, mix well, then add the wine and cook until it has evaporated. Mix the tomato paste with 3 tablespoons warm water, add the mixture to the pan and season lightly with salt. Cover and cook until the sauce is reduced by half. Heat the oil in a skillet, add the slices of bread and cook until brown on both sides. Remove with a slotted spatula and drain on paper towels. Melt the remaining butter in another skillet, add the steaks and cook for 2–3 minutes on each side. Season lightly with salt, place a steak on each slice of bread, spoon the mushroom sauce over them and sprinkle with the parsley.

BISTECCHE AI FUNGHI

Serves 4

¼ cup butter

1 shallot, finely chopped

3⅔ cups mushrooms, sliced

5 tablespoons dry white wine

1 tablespoon tomato paste

3 tablespoons olive oil

4 thick bread slices, crusts removed

4 tenderloin steaks

1 fresh flat-leaf parsley sprig, chopped

salt

BISTECCHE ALL'ACETO BALSAMICO

Serves 4

2 tablespoons butter

2 tablespoons olive oil

4 porterhouse steaks

1 shallot, chopped

2 teaspoons balsamic vinegar

fresh flat-leaf parsley sprig, chopped

salt

STEAK IN BALSAMIC VINEGAR

Heat 1½ tablespoons of the butter and the oil in a skillet. Add the steaks and cook over high heat for 2–4 minutes on each side, depending on how well done you like your steak. Season with salt, transfer to a serving dish and keep warm. Add the shallot to the skillet and cook over low heat, stirring occasionally, for 5 minutes. Add the remaining butter and reduce a little, then stir in the vinegar. Remove the skillet from the heat and pour the sauce over the steaks, sprinkle with the parsley and serve.

BISTECCHE ALLA PIZZAIOLA

Serves 4

2 tablespoons olive oil

2 tablespoons butter

2 garlic cloves

4 round steaks

5 ripe tomatoes, peeled and diced

pinch of dried oregano

salt and pepper

STEAK PIZZAIOLA

Heat the oil and butter in a skillet, add the garlic and cook until it turns brown, then remove and discard it. Add the steaks to the skillet and cook on high heat for 1 minute on each side. Season with salt and pepper, transfer to a plate and keep warm. Add the tomatoes and oregano to the skillet and simmer for 10 minutes until thickened and pulpy. Return the steaks to the skillet and cook until done to your liking.

BISTECCHE ALLA SENAPE

Serves 4

3 tablespoons olive oil

2 tablespoons butter

4 round steaks

1 tablespoon brandy

scant 1 cup heavy cream

4 tablespoons Dijon mustard

salt

STEAK WITH MUSTARD

Heat the oil and butter in a skillet, add the steaks and cook over high heat for 2–4 minutes on each side, depending on how well done you like your steak. Season with salt on both sides, transfer to a serving dish and keep warm. Pour the brandy into the skillet and cook, scraping up the sediment on the base, until the liquid has evaporated. Stir in the cream, season with salt if necessary and cook until thickened. Stir in the mustard, pour the sauce over the steaks and serve.

BEEF PATTIES
WITH CREAM AND MUSHROOMS

Put the mushrooms in a bowl, add warm water to cover and let soak for 1 hour, then drain, squeeze out and chop. Melt 3 tablespoons of the butter in a pan, add the mushrooms and cook over low heat, stirring occasionally, for 20–30 minutes. Meanwhile, tear the bread into pieces, place in a bowl, add milk to cover and let soak. When the mushrooms are cooked, remove with a slotted spatula, pass through a food mill and return to the pan. Stir in the cream and cook until thickened. Drain and squeeze out the bread and mix with the meat in a bowl. Shape the mixture into rounds, flatten gently and dust with flour. Melt the remaining butter in a skillet, add the beef patties and cook, turning once, for 7–8 minutes. Season with salt, transfer the patties to a warm serving dish and pour the sauce over them.

BISTECCHE TRITATE
CON PANNA E FUNGHI

Serves 4

1 cup dried mushrooms

5 tablespoons butter

1–2 bread slices, crusts removed

$2/3$–$3/4$ cup milk

scant 1 cup heavy cream

1 pound 2 ounces lean ground beef

all-purpose flour, for dusting

salt

PIEDMONTESE BOILED MEAT

Bring $5^1/4$ quarts salted water to a boil in a large pan together with the celery, onion and carrot. Add the beef, lower the heat to medium and simmer for 1 hour. Add the veal, boiling fowl and calf's tongue and simmer for 2 hours more. Cook the calf's head separately (see page 870). Meanwhile, prick the cotechino skin with a needle, immerse it in a pan of cold water, bring to a boil and simmer for about 2 hours. Remove the pan from the heat, let the cotechino stand in the cooking liquid for 10 minutes, then lift it out and drain well. Put the various meats together on a large warm serving dish and serve with boiled potatoes and green sauce.

BOLLITO ALLA PIEMONTESE

Serves 8

1 celery stalk

1 onion • 1 carrot

$2^1/4$-pound beef tenderloin

$2^1/4$-pound boneless breast of veal

$1/2$ boiling fowl • 1 small calf's tongue

$2^1/4$ pounds calf's head

1 small cotechino sausage

salt

boiled potatoes and Green Sauce

(see page 74), to serve

MILANESE MIXED BOILED MEAT

Half-fill a large pan with water, add the onion, celery and carrots and bring to a boil. Add the beef and veal and simmer for about 2 hours. If using the cotechino, prick the skin with a needle, place it another pan of water, bring to a boil and simmer for about 2 hours. Place the calf's head in another pan with just enough water to cover, bring to a boil and simmer for $1^1/2$ hours. Drain and slice the beef, veal and calf's head and place on a warm serving dish. Surround with slices of cotechino and serve with green sauce and Cremona mustard. Strain the beef and veal stock and serve with the meats.

BOLLITO MISTO ALLA MILANESE

Serves 6

1 onion • 1 celery stalk

2 carrots

$1^3/4$-pound beef round

1 pound 2-ounce boneless breast of veal

1 pound 2-ounce calf's head

1 cotechino sausage (optional)

Green Sauce (see page 74),

and Cremona mustard to serve

BRAISED BEEF

BRASATO

Serves 6

2¼-pound beef eye of round or another fairly lean cut

¼ cup butter

3 tablespoons olive oil

1 onion, finely chopped

2 carrots, finely chopped

1 celery stalk, finely chopped

¾ cup red wine

1 ripe tomato, peeled and chopped

4 canned tomatoes, chopped

1 tablespoon tomato paste

1 quantity Meat Stock (see page 208)

salt and pepper

Tie the meat neatly with kitchen string. Melt the butter with the oil in a large pan, add the onion, carrots and celery and cook over low heat, stirring occasionally, for 10 minutes. Add the meat and cook, turning frequently, until lightly browned. Season with salt and pepper, add the wine and cook until it has evaporated, then add the fresh and canned tomatoes. Mix the tomato paste with 5 tablespoons warm water in a bowl, add to the pan and cook for a few minutes more. Add enough stock to half-cover the meat, bring to a boil, lower the heat, cover and simmer for about 1½ hours, adding more hot stock as necessary. Remove the meat from the pan, untie and carve into slices. Place the slices on a warm serving dish and strain the cooking juices over them. Hot braised beef may be served with broiled sliced polenta or soft polenta.

BRAISED BEEF WITH BAROLO

BRASATO AL BAROLO

Serves 6

2¼-pound beef eye of round or another fairly lean cut

3 tablespoons olive oil

3 tablespoons butter

3 tablespoons prosciutto fat, chopped

pinch of unsweetened cocoa powder

1 teaspoon rum (optional)

salt

For the marinade

1 bottle (3 cups) Barolo

2 carrots, sliced

2 onions, sliced

1 celery stalk, chopped

4 fresh sage leaves

1 small fresh rosemary sprig

1 bay leaf

10 black peppercorns

salt

Tie the meat neatly with kitchen string, place in a dish and pour in the wine for the marinade. Add the carrots, onions, celery, sage, rosemary, bay leaf, peppercorns and a pinch of salt and let marinate for 6–7 hours. Drain the meat, reserving the marinade, and pat dry with paper towels. Heat the oil, butter and prosciutto fat in a pan, add the meat and cook over high heat, turning frequently, until browned all over. Season with salt, pour in the reserved marinade, lower the heat, cover and simmer for 1½ hours until tender. Remove the meat from the pan, untie and carve. Arrange the slices, slightly overlapping, on a warm serving dish. Discard the herbs from the cooking liquid and pass it through a food mill, then stir in the cocoa and rum if using. Pour the sauce over the meat and serve.

BEEF STROGANOFF

BUE ALLA STROGONOFF

Serves 6

$^1/_2$ cup butter

4 onions, thinly sliced

$1^2/_3$ cups mushrooms, sliced

juice of 1 lemon, strained

3 tablespoons all-purpose flour

1 cup heavy cream

1 teaspoon sugar

1 tablespoon strong mustard

1 tablespoon olive oil

$1^3/_4$ pounds thinly sliced sirloin or round steak, cut into thin strips

salt and pepper

Melt 1 tablespoon of the butter in a pan, add the onions and cook over low heat, stirring occasionally, for 10 minutes until golden brown. Add the mushrooms and lemon juice, cover and simmer gently, shaking the pan occasionally, for 10 minutes. Melt the remaining butter in a skillet, stir in the flour and cook, stirring for 2 minutes. Stir in the cream and sugar and cook, stirring frequently, for 7–8 minutes. Season with salt and pepper, remove from the heat and stir in the mustard. Cut the strips of steak into squares. Heat the oil in a skillet over high heat. Add the steak and cook, stirring frequently, for a few minutes until browned and tender. Stir the steak into the mushroom and onion mixture and spoon the sauce on top, then transfer to a warm serving dish.

BRAISED BEEF WITH ONIONS

BRASATO ALLE CIPOLLE

Serves 6

$2^1/_4$-pound beef eye of round or another fairly lean cut

1 ounce pancetta, cut into thin strips

$2^1/_4$ pounds onions, thickly sliced

salt and pepper

Lard the beef with the pancetta and tie neatly with kitchen string. Put the onions in a large pan, place the meat on top, cover and cook over very low heat for 1 hour. Turn the meat over, season well with salt and pepper, re-cover and cook, stirring occasionally, for 1 hour more or until tender. Remove the meat from the pan, untie and carve into fairly thin slices. Place the slices, slightly overlapping, on a warm serving dish and spoon the onion sauce over them. If you prefer a more even consistency, pass the sauce through a food mill first. This dish is excellent served with soft polenta.

CARPACCIO

CARPACCIO

Serves 4

14 ounces sirloin steak, cut into wafer-thin slices

1 quantity Mayonnaise (see page 65)

1 tablespoon Worcestershire sauce

1 tablespoon lemon juice

3 tablespoons milk

salt and white pepper

Spread out the slices of steak on a serving dish. Combine the mayonnaise, Worcestershire sauce, lemon juice and milk in a bowl, season with salt and pepper and spoon the mixture over the meat. This is the original version of carpaccio invented by Arrigo Cipriani and served in his world-famous Venetian restaurant, but there are several variations. For example, a little mustard may be added to the mayonnaise. The steak may be drizzled with olive oil and lemon juice, seasoned with salt and pepper and then covered with Parmesan shavings and truffle shavings, or even thinly sliced raw mushrooms dressed with oil, pepper and lemon juice. A more exotic version can be made by dressing the meat with olive oil, lemon juice, salt and pepper and covering with sliced palm hearts and Parmesan shavings.

FLORENTINE T–BONE STEAK

COSTATA ALLA FIORENTINA

Serves 4

2 x 1 pound 5-ounce T-bone steaks

olive oil, for drizzling

salt and pepper

Those who wish to serve authentic Florentine T-bone steaks should follow the rules of the Articles of Association of the Florentine T-bone Steak Academy, founded in 1991 by representatives of the Florentine Butchers' Association. For over 200 years, a Florentine steak has been defined as a T-bone steak cut from a chianina calf and hung for 5–6 days. The steak must be cut from the loin through the sirloin with the T-bone in the middle. The meat must be $^3/_4$–$1^1/_4$ inches thick and weigh 1 pound 5 ounces–$1^3/_4$ pounds. It must be cooked for 5 minutes on each side without seasoning over hot charcoal, preferably oak charcoal, about 8 inches above the embers. The steak must be turned once only with a spatula and seasoned only when cooked. The meat should be brown on the outside and slightly rare inside. To serve, lightly drizzle a warm serving dish with olive oil and arrange the seasoned steaks on it.

SALTED T–BONE STEAK IN SAUCE

COSTATA DI BUE AL SALE CON SALSA

Serves 6

$5^1/_2$-pound T-bone steak

6 tablespoons butter

salt and pepper

For the sauce

3 tablespoons butter

2 tablespoons olive oil

6 shallots, chopped

5 tablespoons dry white wine

2 egg yolks

1 tablespoon fresh flat-leaf parsley, chopped

1 tablespoon white wine vinegar

salt and pepper

Preheat the oven to 400°F. Spread the steak with about half the butter and season well with salt and pepper. Generously grease a skillet with the remaining butter, set over medium-high heat, add the steak and cook for 2 minutes on each side. Transfer the skillet to the oven and cook for 15–20 minutes until tender. (If the skillet has a wooden handle, cover it with foil first.) Place the steak on a warm serving dish, tent with foil and let stand for 10 minutes before carving. Meanwhile, prepare the sauce. Heat the butter and oil in a pan, add the shallots and cook over low heat, stirring occasionally, for 5 minutes. Add the wine and cook until it has evaporated, then season with salt and pepper. Remove the pan from the heat and stir in the egg yolks, one at a time. Add the parsley and sprinkle with the vinegar. Return to the heat for a few minutes but do not let the sauce to boil. Slice the steak fairly thickly and serve with the sauce.

BEEF WELLINGTON

Preheat the oven to 425°F. Brush an oval ovenproof dish with oil. Wrap the beef in the pancetta slices and tie with kitchen string, then place in the prepared dish. Cover and cook in the oven for 10 minutes, then remove from the oven and let cool slightly. Lower the oven temperature to 400°F. Meanwhile, roll out the dough on a lightly floured surface. Untie the beef and remove the pancetta. Carefully spread the pâté over the whole roast, then place the meat on the pastry and wrap the dough around to enclose it, crimping the edges to seal. Beat the egg yolk with the milk in a bowl and brush the mixture over the packet. Make two small holes in the dough to let steam to escape during cooking. Place the packet on a cookie sheet and bake for 20 minutes until golden brown. Let stand for 5 minutes, then slice and transfer to a warm serving dish.

FILETTO IN CROSTA AL PÂTÉ

Serves 6

olive oil, for brushing

2¼-pound beef tenderloin

3½ ounces pancetta, sliced

9 ounces puff pastry dough, thawed if frozen

all-purpose flour, for dusting

3½ ounces truffle pâté

1 egg yolk

1 tablespoon milk

FONDUE BOURGUIGNONNE

Dice the meat and place in a serving dish. Place the sauces in small bowls. Place a fondue set on the table, add the oil and a little salt to the pan and keep it hot with a lighted burner. Each guest pierces a piece of meat with a fondue fork and cooks it according to taste in the hot oil. They then dip it in one of the sauces. Provide a selection of sauces with different characteristics and flavors, some hot and some not, such as mayonnaise, curry sauce, tartar sauce, aïoli, hot cream sauce, mustard, etc. (see Sauces, pages 45 to 89).

FONDUE BOURGUIGNONNE

Serves 4

1¾ pounds tender lean beef

various sauces (see method)

2¼ cups olive oil

salt

GOULASH

Heat the butter and oil in a large pan, add the onions and cook over low heat, stirring occasionally, for 5 minutes. Add the meat and stir well. Mix the paprika with ⅔ cup hot water, pour the mixture into the pan and cook for a few minutes, then add the tomatoes. Cook over very low heat until the meat starts to brown, then add ⅔ cup hot water. Cover and simmer gently for about 1 hour. Season with salt to taste, add the potatoes and simmer for 45 minutes more.

GULASCH

Serves 4

3 tablespoons butter

4 tablespoons olive oil

4 onions, thinly sliced

1 pound 5 ounces lean beef, cut into coarse cubes

1 tablespoon hot paprika

1 pound 2 ounces ripe tomatoes,

peeled and chopped or canned chopped tomatoes

generous 2 cups potatoes, diced

salt

HAMBURGERS AMERICAN-STYLE

HAMBURGER ALL'AMERICANA

Serves 4

3½ cups lean ground beef

1 small onion, finely chopped

1 egg, lightly beaten

olive oil, for drizzling

4 soft round rolls

4 small lettuce leaves

8 tomato slices

tomato ketchup, to taste

salt and pepper

Preheat the broiler. Combine the meat and onion in a large bowl, then stir in the egg and season with salt and pepper. Divide the mixture into four, shape into balls and gently flatten into patties. Drizzle with a little oil. Cook the hamburgers under the broiler for 3 minutes on each side, turning them with a slotted spatula. Alternatively, cook in a heavy-based skillet over high heat for 3 minutes on each side. Halve the rolls and place a hamburger on the bottom half of each. Add a lettuce leaf, two tomato slices and a little ketchup to each and replace the tops of the rolls.

HAMBURGERS WITH HAM

HAMBURGER CON PROSCIUTTO

Serves 4

scant 3 cups lean beef, chopped

⅓ cup smoked cooked ham, chopped

4 egg yolks, lightly beaten

1 fresh flat-leaf parsley sprig, chopped

2 tablespoons olive oil

salt and pepper

Combine the beef and ham in a bowl, stir in the egg yolks and parsley and season with a little pepper. Divide the mixture into four, shape into balls and gently flatten into patties. Heat the oil in a skillet, add the hamburgers and cook on medium-high heat for 3 minutes on each side until browned on the outside but rare on the inside. Season with salt and serve.

BEEF AND SPINACH ROULADES

INVOLTINI AGLI SPINACI

Serves 4

14 ounces spinach

¼ cup butter

8 thin lean beef slices

8 thin Swiss cheese slices

3 carrots, chopped

1 tablespoon olive oil

5 tablespoons dry white wine

2 shallots, chopped

1 tomato, peeled and diced

salt and pepper

Cook the spinach, in just the water clinging to the leaves after washing, for about 5 minutes until wilted, then drain and squeeze out as much liquid as possible. Melt half the butter in a skillet, add the spinach and cook over low heat, stirring occasionally, for 5 minutes. Spread out the slices of beef and pound until thin and even. Place a slice of cheese on each and divide two-thirds of the carrots and two-thirds of the spinach among them. Roll up and tie with kitchen string. Heat the oil and the remaining butter in a skillet, add the roulades and cook, turning frequently, until lightly browned all over. Add the wine and cook until it has evaporated, then add the shallots and tomato and season with salt and pepper. Cover and cook over low heat for 20 minutes. Add the remaining carrot and cook for 5 minutes, then add the remaining spinach and cook for 5 minutes more. Remove the string from the roulades and serve in their sauce.

BEEF AND BRESAOLA ROULADES

Pound the meat until it is thin and even and place two slices of bresaola on each piece. Roll up, tie with kitchen string and dust with flour. Melt the butter in a skillet, add the roulades and cook, turning frequently, until browned all over. Add the wine and cook until it has evaporated, then add the stock, cover and simmer over low heat for 15 minutes. Add the cream and juniper berries and cook until thickened. Season with salt if necessary. Remove the string from the roulades, place on a warm serving dish and spoon the sauce over them.

INVOLTINI CON BRESAOLA

Serves 4

14 ounces lean beef, cut into 4 slices

8 bresaola slices

all-purpose flour, for dusting

3 tablespoons butter

$^3/_4$ cup dry white wine

$^2/_3$ cup Meat Stock (see page 208)

4 tablespoons heavy cream

8 juniper berries

salt

TASTY ROULADES

Combine the salami, basil, garlic and butter in a bowl. Spread the mixture on the slices of meat, season with salt and pepper, roll up and tie with kitchen string. Heat the oil in a skillet, add the rosemary, onion and roulades and cook, turning the roulades frequently, until browned all over. Lower the heat, cover and cook for 15 minutes. Remove the string before serving.

INVOLTINI GUSTOSI

Serves 4

generous $^1/_2$ cup salami, chopped

6 fresh basil leaves, chopped

$^1/_2$ garlic clove, chopped

2 tablespoons butter, softened

8 lean beef slices

3 tablespoons olive oil

1 fresh rosemary sprig

$^1/_2$ onion, chopped

salt and pepper

SIMPLE POACHED BEEF

The most suitable cuts of beef for poaching are chuck and blade or brisket. You can also add breast of veal. Although this is a simple, home-cooked dish, it needs a fairly large piece of lean meat. To make sure that the meat is tasty, always add it to hot water in which vegetables have been simmering for about 20 minutes. Season with salt and simmer on a low heat for about 2 hours. Remove the meat from the pan, let stand for 10 minutes, then carve and place on a warm serving dish. Serve with Green Sauce (see page 74) and boiled potatoes if you like. Strain the stock and serve boiling hot in bowls or use for risotto or Stracciatella (see page 238).

LESSO CASALINGO

Serves 6

$2^1/_4$ pounds beef or 1 pound 2 ounces beef and 1 pound 2 ounces veal

1 onion

1 celery stalk

1 carrot

salt

SIMPLE POACHED BEEF SALAD

Let the beef cool, then chop. Put it in a salad bowl, sprinkle with the scallion and parsley and add the capers and dill pickles. Whisk together the olive oil, vinegar, mustard and a pinch of salt in a bowl. Add the dressing to the salad, toss and set aside for 1 hour to let the flavors mingle. Shell the eggs and halve or slice. Garnish the salad with the eggs and put a green bell peppercorn in the middle of each yolk. You can also use leftover beef cooked according to the recipe on page 793 for this salad.

LESSO IN INSALATA

Serves 4

1 pound 2-ounce Simple Poached Beef (see page 793)

1 scallion, finely chopped

1 fresh flat-leaf parsley sprig, chopped

2 tablespoons capers, drained and rinsed

5 dill pickles, drained and sliced

scant $^1/_2$ cup olive oil

3 tablespoons red wine vinegar

1 tablespoon Dijon mustard • salt

2 eggs, hard-cooked, and green bell peppercorns, to garnish

SIMPLE POACHED BEEF WITH ROSEMARY

Heat the oil in a pan, add the meat and cook for a few minutes. Chop the garlic and rosemary together, place in a bowl, stir in the vinegar and pour the mixture over the meat. Cover and simmer for 5–10 minutes. Season with salt to taste. Transfer to a warm serving dish and serve with a side dish of boiled potatoes or beet.

LESSO INSAPORITO AL ROSMARINO

Serves 4

2 tablespoons olive oil

4 slices leftover Simple Poached Beef (see page 793)

1 garlic clove

1 fresh rosemary sprig

5 tablespoons white wine vinegar

salt

boiled potatoes or boiled beet, to serve

STEAK WITH SAGE

Lightly dust the steaks with flour. Melt the butter in a skillet, add the steaks and cook until golden brown on both sides. Add the sage and cook for a few minutes more. Season with salt and serve. Boiled potatoes sautéed with a few tablespoons of oil and a little pepper make a good accompaniment.

LOMBATE ALLA SALVIA

Serves 4

4 sirloin steaks

all-purpose flour, for dusting

2 tablespoons butter • 4 fresh sage leaves

salt

STEAK IN WHITE WINE

Melt the butter in a skillet, add the steaks and cook until lightly browned on both sides. Transfer to a plate and keep warm. Add the onions and carrots to the pan and cook over low heat, stirring occasionally, for 5 minutes. Return the steaks to the pan, add the wine and cook until it has evaporated, then add the strained tomatoes and season with salt and pepper. Cover and cook over low heat for 15 minutes. Switch off the heat and let stand for a few minutes without uncovering. Serve with white turnips in butter.

LOMBATE AL VINO BIANCO

Serves 4

3 tablespoons butter

4 sirloin steaks • 2 onions, thinly sliced

2 carrots, cut into thin strips

$^3/_4$ cup white wine

2 tablespoons bottled strained tomatoes

salt and pepper

white turnips in butter, to serve

POLPETTE AL BRANDY

MEATBALLS IN BRANDY

Serves 4

3¹/₂ cups lean ground beef

¹/₃ cup cooked, cured ham, chopped

2 egg yolks

²/₃ cup Parmesan cheese, freshly grated

1 fresh flat-leaf parsley sprig, chopped

3–4 tablespoons Béchamel Sauce (see page 50)

all-purpose flour, for dusting

¹/₄ cup butter

1 tablespoon olive oil

1 small onion, chopped

1 tablespoon brandy

salt and pepper

Combine the beef, ham, egg yolks, Parmesan, parsley and béchamel sauce in a bowl and season with salt and pepper. Shape the mixture into balls and dust with flour. Heat the butter and oil in a pan. Add the onion and cook over low heat, stirring occasionally, for 5 minutes. Increase the heat to high, add the meatballs and cook for 1 minute on each side, then lower the heat and cook gently for about 15 minutes. Transfer the meatballs to a serving dish and keep warm. Stir 2–3 tablespoons warm water and the brandy into the pan and cook until thickened. Remove the pan from the heat, stir the sauce, pour it over the meatballs and serve immediately.

POLPETTE ALLE ACCIUGHE

MEATBALLS WITH ANCHOVIES

Serves 4

2 rolls, crusts removed

²/₃ cup milk

1 fresh flat-leaf parsley sprig, finely chopped

1 garlic clove, finely chopped

2 canned anchovy fillets in oil, drained and finely chopped

3¹/₂ cups lean ground beef • 1 egg yolk

2 tablespoons Parmesan cheese, freshly grated

1 cup fine bread crumbs

olive oil, for brushing • salt and pepper

spinach in butter, to serve

Tear the rolls into pieces, place in a bowl, add the milk and let soak for 10 minutes, then drain and squeeze out. Combine the parsley, garlic, anchovy fillets and beef in a bowl. Stir in the egg yolk, soaked rolls and Parmesan and season with salt and pepper. Shape the mixture into 8–10 meatballs and flatten slightly. Spread out the bread crumbs in a shallow dish and roll the meatballs in them to coat. Brush the base of a skillet with a little oil, add the meatballs and cook over high heat for 1 minute on each side. Lower the heat, cover and cook gently for about 10 minutes. Serve with spinach in butter.

POLPETTE ALLE PATATE

MEATBALLS WITH POTATO

Serves 4

2 potatoes, boiled and drained

11 ounces lean beef, finely chopped

2 mortadella slices, finely chopped

1 egg, lightly beaten

1 tablespoon Parmesan cheese, freshly grated

1 fresh flat-leaf parsley sprig, chopped

1 cup bread crumbs

2 tablespoons olive oil

salt and pepper

Mash the potatoes in a bowl while they are still hot and stir in the beef, mortadella and egg. Stir in the Parmesan and parsley and season with salt and pepper. Shape the mixture into eight balls. Spread out the bread crumbs in a shallow dish and roll the meatballs in them to coat. Heat the oil in a skillet, add the meatballs and cook, turning frequently, until golden brown all over and cooked through. Remove with a slotted spatula and drain on paper towels.

MEATBALLS IN LEMON

POLPETTE AL LIMONE

Serves 4

3½ cups lean ground beef

⅔ cup Parmesan cheese, freshly grated

4 tablespoons Béchamel Sauce (see page 50)

dash of Worcestershire sauce

3 tablespoons butter

4 tablespoons heavy cream

juice of ½ lemon, strained

1 teaspoon bread crumbs

salt

Combine the ground beef, Parmesan, béchamel sauce and Worcestershire sauce in a bowl and season with salt. Shape the mixture into eight meatballs, then flatten them slightly. Melt the butter in a pan and when it starts to go golden brown, add the meatballs. Cook over medium heat, turning frequently for about 15 minutes. Transfer to a serving dish and keep warm. Pour the cream into a pan, add the lemon juice and bread crumbs and cook, stirring frequently, until slightly thickened. Pour the sauce over the meatballs and serve.

MEATBALLS WITH SPINACH

POLPETTE CON SPINACI

Serves 4

9 ounces spinach

2¼ cups lean ground beef

½ cup Béchamel Sauce (see page 50)

⅓ cup Parmesan cheese, freshly grated

1 egg, lightly beaten

all-purpose flour, for dusting

2 tablespoons butter

2 tablespoons olive oil

salt

Cook the spinach, in just the water clinging to the leaves after washing, for about 5 minutes until wilted, then drain, squeeze out as much liquid as possible and chop. Combine the spinach, beef, béchamel sauce, Parmesan and egg in a bowl and season with salt. Shape the mixture into eight balls and dust with flour. Heat the butter and oil in a skillet, add the meatballs and cook, turning frequently, until browned all over and cooked through. Remove with a slotted spatula, drain on paper towels and serve.

MEATBALLS WITH A TASTY ONION GARNISH

POLPETTE SAPORITE

Serves 4

5 tablespoons butter

1 large onion, sliced

3½ cups lean ground beef

2 egg yolks

salt and pepper

Melt half the butter in a pan, add the onion and cook over low heat, stirring occasionally, for 10 minutes, then season with salt. Combine half the onion, the beef and egg yolks in a bowl and season with salt and pepper. Shape the mixture into eight meatballs. Melt the remaining butter in a skillet, add the meatballs and cook over high heat, turning frequently, until browned all over and cooked through. Transfer to a dish, spoon the cooking juices over them and garnish with the remaining onion.

ROAST BEEF

Preheat the oven to 400°F. Sprinkle the butter and 1 tablespoon of the oil over the base of a roasting pan. Tie the beef neatly with kitchen string, brush with the remaining oil, place in the roasting pan and cook over high heat, turning frequently, until browned all over. Season with salt and pepper. Cover, transfer to the oven and roast for 30 minutes or longer, depending on how well done you like your beef. Test by piercing the meat with a skewer. If the juices are red, it is rare, if they are pink, it is medium and if no juices run, it is well done. Remove from the roasting pan and let stand for 5 minutes before removing the string and carving. Place the roasting pan over low heat and stir in $2/3$ cup hot water, scraping up the sediment on the base. If the gravy is too runny, stir in a pat of butter dipped in flour. Cook, stirring until thickened. Pour the gravy into a sauce boat and serve with the meat.

ROAST—BEEF

Serves 6

3 tablespoons butter, cut into pieces,
plus extra for the gravy (optional)
2 tablespoons oil
$2^{1}/_{4}$-pound fillet of beef
all-purpose flour, for the gravy (optional)
salt and pepper

ROAST BEEF WITH CHESTNUTS

Preheat the oven to 400°F. Tie the meat neatly with kitchen string. Heat the butter and oil in a roasting pan, add the meat and cook, turning frequently, until browned all over. Season with salt and pepper, add the celery, onion, carrot and rosemary to the pan and cook, stirring occasionally, for 10 minutes more. Add the wine and cook until it has evaporated. Cover, transfer to the oven and roast for 30–40 minutes, depending on how well done you like your beef. After 30 minutes the beef will be rare and after 40 minutes it will be medium. Meanwhile, cook the chestnuts in boiling water until tender, then drain and press through a strainer into a bowl. Remove the meat from the roasting pan, let stand for about 10 minutes, then remove the string and carve. Place the roasting pan over low heat, stir in the cream and the chestnut purée and cook, stirring frequently, until slightly thickened. Pour into a sauceboat and serve with the meat.

ROAST—BEEF CON LE CASTAGNE

Serves 4

$2^{1}/_{4}$-pound fillet of beef
2 tablespoons butter
1 tablespoon olive oil
1 celery stalk, chopped
1 onion, chopped
1 carrot, chopped
1 fresh rosemary sprig, chopped
5 tablespoons dry white wine
$3^{1}/_{2}$ ounces dried white chestnuts,
soaked in warm water for 6 hours and drained
3 tablespoons heavy cream
salt and pepper

RAPID ROAST WITH ARUGULA

Preheat the oven to 475°F. Place the beef in an ovenproof dish and cover completely with the arugula. Drizzle with olive oil and season with salt and pepper. Roast for about 1 minute. An alternative version of this simple but tasty recipe uses radicchio instead of arugula, but it has a slightly more bitter flavor.

'SCOTTATA' ALLA RUCOLA

Serves 6

1 pound 5 ounces beef tenderloin, thinly sliced
$1^{1}/_{4}$ cups arugula, coarsely chopped
olive oil, for drizzling
salt and pepper

BEEF STEW

SPEZZATINO DI MANZO

Serves 4

2 tablespoons olive oil

2 tablespoons butter

¹/₂ onion, chopped

1 celery stalk, chopped

1 carrot, chopped

1 pound 5 ounces lean stewing steak, cut into cubes

5 tablespoons dry white wine

2 tomatoes, peeled and diced or

2–3 canned tomatoes

salt and pepper

Heat the oil and butter in a pan, add the onion, celery and carrot and cook over low heat, stirring occasionally, for 10 minutes. Add the meat and cook, stirring constantly, until browned all over. Pour in the wine and cook until it has evaporated, then season with salt and pepper to taste. Put the tomatoes into a food processor and process to a purée, then add to the pan with ²/₃ cup warm water. Cover and simmer over low heat, stirring occasionally, for about 1 hour.

BEEF STEW WITH COFFEE

SPEZZATINO AL CAFFÉ

Serves 4

2 tablespoons olive oil

1 pound 5 ounces lean stewing steak, cut into cubes

2 onions, thinly sliced

1 garlic clove, chopped

2 green bell peppers, halved, seeded and thickly sliced

¹/₄ cup all-purpose flour

5 tablespoons dry white wine

5 tablespoons brewed coffee

salt and pepper

This is a Brazilian recipe. Heat the oil in a pan, add the meat and cook, stirring frequently, until browned all over. Remove the meat with a slotted spatula and keep warm. Add the onions, garlic and bell peppers to the pan and cook over low heat, stirring occasionally, for 10 minutes. Sprinkle in the flour and cook, stirring constantly, for 2–3 minutes. Gradually stir in the wine and coffee and bring to a boil, stirring constantly. Return the meat to the pan, season with salt and pepper to taste, cover and cook for 1 hour or until the meat is tender.

BEEF STEW WITH WINE AND ONIONS

SPEZZATINO AL VINO E CIPOLLE

Serves 4

5 tablespoons butter

1³/₄ pounds onions, finely chopped

scant 1 cup pancetta, diced

1 pound 5 ounces lean stewing steak, cubed

¹/₄ cup all-purpose flour

1²/₃ cups dry white wine

1²/₃ cups red wine

salt and pepper

Melt the butter in a pan, add the onions and pancetta and cook over low heat, stirring occasionally, for 10 minutes. Stir in the meat, sprinkle with the flour and cook, stirring constantly, for 2 minutes. Gradually stir in the white and red wines and cook over low heat until the liquid is almost completely absorbed. Season with salt and pepper to taste and serve.

FLORENTINE BEEF STEW

Cut a few strips from one of the carrots and chop the remainder. Lard the beef with the carrot strips and pancetta and rub with salt and pepper. Tie neatly with kitchen string. Put the celery, onion and chopped carrots into a pan and add the meat and oil. Cook over high heat, turning the meat frequently, until browned all over. Pour in the wine and cook until it has evaporated. Add the tomatoes, lower the heat, cover and simmer gently for about 2 hours. Remove the meat from the pan, cut off the string, carve and place the slices on a warm serving dish. Pass the cooking juices and vegetables through a food mill and pour them over the meat.

STRACOTTO ALLA FIORENTINA

Serves 6

3 carrots

$2^1/_4$-pound lean beef, such as eye of round

$1^1/_2$ ounces pancetta, cut into strips

1 celery stalk, chopped

$^1/_2$ onion, chopped

4 tablespoons olive oil

$^3/_4$ cup red wine

1 pound 2 ounces tomatoes, peeled, seeded and chopped

salt and pepper

BEEF STEW WITH WHITE WINE

Using a larding needle, lard the beef with the strips of pancetta. Put the pork fat, half the onions and three of the carrots in a deep pan, or better still, earthenware casserole and season with salt and pepper. Place the meat on the bed of vegetables and put the remaining onions and carrots on top. Pour in the wine, cover and simmer for 2 hours or until most of the liquid has been absorbed. Serve with mashed potatoes.

STRACOTTO AL VINO BIANCO

Serves 6

$2^1/_4$-pound lean beef, such as eye of round

$3^1/_2$ ounces pancetta, cut into strips

generous $^1/_2$ cup pork fat, chopped

1 pound 2 ounces onions, thinly sliced

$2^1/_4$ pounds carrots, sliced

$2^1/_4$ cups dry white wine

salt and pepper

Creamy Mashed Potato (see page 526), to serve

BEEFBURGERS

Tear the bread into pieces, place in a bowl, add the milk and let soak for 10 minutes, then drain and squeeze out. Combine the beef, soaked bread and parsley in a bowl. Shape the mixture into meatballs, flatten slightly and dust lightly with flour. Heat the oil and butter in a skillet, add the patties and cook for 6—8 minutes until done to your liking. Season with salt and serve.

SVIZZERE

Serves 4

1 bread slice, crusts removed

$^2/_3$ cup milk

4 cups lean ground beef

1 tablespoon fresh flat-leaf parsley, chopped

all-purpose flour, for dusting

2 tablespoons olive oil

2 tablespoons butter

salt

STEAK TARTARE

TARTARA DI MANZO

Serves 4

4 cups lean ground steak

4 egg yolks

1 onion, thinly sliced

1 tablespoon capers, drained and rinsed

2 tablespoons fresh flat-leaf parsley, chopped,

2 canned anchovy fillets in oil, drained and chopped

mild or medium French mustard (optional)

olive oil and lemon wedges, to serve

Divide the steak among four dishes, shaping each portion into a mound. Make a shallow well in the center of each mound and pour in a raw egg yolk. Surround the meat each mound with onion, capers, parsley and anchovies. Serve with olive oil and lemon wedges. Each guest may season the meat to taste and can mix in the surrounding ingredients using a fork. If you like, a little mustard may be used to spice up the dish.

TOURNEDOS ROSSINI

TOURNEDOS ALLA ROSSINI

Serves 6

6 x 1¼-inch thick tournedos, trimmed

3 tablespoons butter

scant ½ cup Madeira or dry Marsala

6 tablespoons heavy cream

¼ cup truffle pâté

salt

For the garnish (optional)

6 black truffle slices

6 white truffle slices

Tournedos are steaks cut from the heart of the tenderloin. They are usually 1¼–2 inches thick and weigh 3½–5 ounces. Tie the tournedos neatly with kitchen string so that they keep their rounded shape while cooking. Melt the butter in a skillet and, when it turns hazel, add the steaks. Cook over high heat for 1 minute on each side, turning with a slotted spatula. Lower the heat and cook for 7–8 minutes for rare or 10 minutes for medium. Pour in the Madeira or Marsala, tilt the skillet and ignite. When the flames die down transfer the tournedos to a warm serving dish and remove the string. Stir the cream into the cooking juices, add the truffle pâté and a pinch of salt and mix well. Cook over medium heat until the sauce has thickened. Pour the sauce over the tournedos and serve. Garnish each steak with a slice each of black and white truffle, if you like.

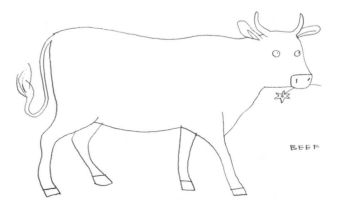

BEEF

MUTTON

Mutton is a highly prized, flavorsome, deep-red meat. It comes from sheep over two years old. Strictly, lambs slaughtered between one and two years old are called yearling lambs but they can be used in mutton recipes and quite often stores make no distinction between yearling lamb and mutton. The best sheep farms in Italy are found in Piedmont, Lazio and Puglia. In the rest of Europe, there are excellent farms in Great Britain and Ireland, where mutton is used to prepare dishes such as tasty mutton chops and the famous Irish stew. New Zealand is the world's largest lamb producer, closely followed by Australia. France, on the other hand, is famous for its pré-salé mutton, reared in pastures near the sea, which makes the meat particularly tasty.

COOKING

Mutton and yearling lamb have a fairly strong flavor, so it is worth marinating them for several hours in wine with a little vinegar, vegetables and herbs (celery, carrot, onion, parsley, thyme and bay leaf), salt and black peppercorns. Don't let marinate in the refrigerator, simply choose a cool place.

→ When choosing the oil or fat to add, remember that mutton is a fatty meat, so avoid making it heavier with excessive quantities of oil and butter.

→ To appreciate the flavor of mutton fully, it should be served rare and very hot.

→ Among the most traditional and fragrant herbs used with mutton are rosemary, mint and fennel, but myrtle and thyme also go well.

ROASTING

It is best to choose the leg for roasting, as this is the most suitable cut and the result is predictable.

→ If it is to be cooked rare, allow 18–20 minutes per 2¼ pounds meat. If you prefer it medium or well done, simply increase the time (but not by too much), according to taste. Italians prefer mutton well done.

BRAISING AND STEWING

These methods of cooking take about 1½ hours, and in the case of large pieces of meat, even 2 hours.

→ The meat should be cut into pieces and cooked with vegetables such as carrots, celery and onion. Other vegetables that go well with mutton are Savoy cabbage and eggplant, as they help to reduce the amount of fat.

CHOPS

The best and tastiest are the double chops cut from the loin. They are excellent brushed well with oil, seasoned with pepper and broiled.

LEG OF MUTTON IN VODKA

Bring the stock to a boil in a large pan, add the mutton and simmer for about 40 minutes. Meanwhile, place the prunes in a bowl, add warm water to cover and let soak for at least 30 minutes, then drain. Melt the butter in a pan and, when it starts to sizzle, stir in the strained tomatoes, then add the onion, garlic, celery and bay leaf. Cook, stirring occasionally, for about 5 minutes, then pour in the vodka, season with salt and paprika and cook, stirring constantly, for a few minutes more. Add the hot stock, a little at a time, stirring constantly, then add the mutton, rice and prunes. Continue to cook, stirring constantly, for about 20 minutes. Remove and discard the bay leaf, transfer the mutton mixture to a warm, fairly deep serving dish and serve with slices of buttered toast.

COSCIOTTO ALLA VODKA

Serves 4

4 cups Meat Stock (see page 208)

1³/₄-pound leg of mutton, cut into pieces

12 prunes, pitted

scant ¹/₂ cup butter

2 tablespoons bottled strained tomatoes

1 onion, chopped

1 garlic clove, chopped

1 celery heart, sliced

1 bay leaf

¹/₄ cup vodka

large pinch of paprika

scant 1 cup risotto rice

salt

buttered toast, to serve

LEG OF MUTTON WITH TURNIPS

Tie the meat neatly with kitchen string, then cook in a heavy pan without adding any fat, turning occasionally, until browned all over. Sprinkle with the flour, turn the meat several times and add the onions, garlic, rosemary, thyme and celery. Pour in ²/₃ cup of the stock or water, lower the heat and simmer. Meanwhile, melt the butter in a skillet, add the turnips and cook over medium heat, stirring frequently, until browned all over. Drain, add to the meat and season with salt and pepper. Cover and cook for 1¹/₂ hours, adding more hot stock or water as required. Remove the meat from the pan, untie and carve into slices. Place on a warm serving dish and surround with the turnips.

COSCIOTTO CON LE RAPE

Serves 6

2¹/₄-pound leg of mutton, boned

2 tablespoons all-purpose flour

2 onions, thinly sliced

1 garlic clove

1 fresh rosemary sprig

1 fresh thyme sprig

1 celery stalk

2¹/₄ cups hot Meat Stock (see page 208) or water

2 tablespoons butter

2¹/₄ pounds turnips, cut into fourths

salt and pepper

ENGLISH MUTTON CHOPS

These famous mutton chops are usually cut fairly thick, the way the English are said to like them. Preheat the broiler to high. Meanwhile, melt the butter. Brush the chops with the butter and broil for 5 or 6 minutes on each side, brushing occasionally with more melted butter. Season with salt and pepper and serve.

COSTOLETTE ALL'INGLESE

Serves 4

3 tablespoons butter

4 mutton chops

salt and pepper

IRISH STEW

Boned shoulder or breast of mutton is ideal for this dish. Arrange alternate layers of meat, potatoes and onions in a flameproof casserole, sprinkling each layer with salt, pepper, thyme and parsley. Add the bay leaf and pour in just enough water to cover. bring to a boil over high heat, cover, lower the heat and simmer for 1¼ hours until tender. In Ireland — famous for its tasty mutton — this stew is considered a national dish. It can also be made with beef.

SPEZZATINO ALL'IRLANDESE

Serves 4

1¾ pounds boneless mutton, sliced or cut into cubes

1¾ pounds potatoes, thinly sliced

3 onions, thinly sliced

1 tablespoon chopped fresh thyme

2 tablespoons fresh flat-leaf parsley, chopped

1 small bay leaf

salt and pepper

MUTTON STEWED IN CITRUS JUICE

Heat the oil and butter in a pan, add the onion and cook over low heat, stirring occasionally, for about 10 minutes. Add the mutton and cook, stirring constantly, until browned all over. Add the potatoes and ⅔ cup warm water. Cook for 20 minutes, then season with salt and pepper and cook for 20 minutes more. Add the romano, cook for 10 minutes more, then pour in the lemon and orange juice and cook until they have evaporated.

SPEZZATINO AL SUCCO DI AGRUMI

Serves 4

2 tablespoons olive oil

2 tablespoons butter

1 onion, thinly sliced

1 pound 5 ounces boneless shoulder

of mutton, coarsely chopped

1 pound 2 ounces new potatoes

3 ounces romano cheese, diced

juice of 1 lemon, strained

juice of 2 oranges, strained

salt and pepper

MUTTON AND BEAN STEW

Melt the butter in a pan, add the meat and cook, stirring frequently, until browned all over. Add the carrots, onions, garlic, thyme and rosemary and season with salt and pepper. Cook, stirring occasionally, for 10 minutes more, then pour in ⅔ cup water, cover and simmer over medium heat for 30 minutes. Add the beans, re-cover the pan and simmer for 45 minutes more. Remove and discard the garlic and rosemary before serving.

SPEZZATINO CON FAGIOLI

Serves 4

2 tablespoons butter

1 pound 5 ounces boneless shoulder of mutton,

cut into cubes

2 carrots, thinly sliced

2 onions, thinly sliced

2 garlic cloves

1 fresh thyme sprig, chopped

1 fresh rosemary sprig

1 pound 5 ounces cooked fresh beans

or canned beans, such as fava beans

salt and pepper

MUTTON AND POTATO STEW

SPEZZATINO CON PATATE

Serves 4

2 tablespoons olive oil

1 pound 5 ounces boneless mutton, cut into cubes

2 onions, thinly sliced

2 garlic cloves, chopped

4 tomatoes, peeled and diced

1 pound 2 ounces potatoes, cut into fourths

1 fresh flat-leaf parsley sprig, chopped

salt and pepper

Heat the oil in a pan, add the mutton and cook, stirring frequently, for a few minutes until browned. Add the onions and garlic, season with salt and pepper and cook, stirring occasionally, for 10 minutes. Stir in the tomatoes. Put the potatoes in another pan, add boiling water to cover and cook over medium heat for 25–30 minutes until tender. Drain, season lightly with salt and sprinkle with the parsley. Bring the mutton cooking juices to a boil and cook over high heat for a few minutes until reduced, then place the meat on a warm serving dish and surround with the potatoes. Spoon the cooking juices over the meat and potatoes.

CHOPPED MUTTON WITH PRUNES

SPEZZATINO CON PRUGNE

Serves 4

scant 1 cup prunes, pitted

1¼ cups dry white wine

1 pound 5 ounces boneless breast of mutton, cut into cubes

1 onion, thinly sliced

1 garlic clove

¼ cup butter

2 tablespoons bottled strained tomatoes

salt and pepper

Place the prunes in a bowl, pour in the wine and set aside. Put the meat in a pan, add cold water to cover and bring to simmering point. Add the onion and garlic, cover and simmer over medium heat for about 1 hour, then season with salt and pepper and drain well, reserving the cooking liquid. Melt the butter in another pan, add the strained tomatoes and meat and cook over high heat, stirring frequently, for a few minutes, then lower the heat, drain the prunes and add them to the pan. Simmer for about 20 minutes. If the meat seems to be drying out, add some of the reserved cooking liquid. Transfer to a warm serving dish.

MARINATED MUTTON KABOBS

SPIEDINI MARINATI

Serves 4

5 tablespoons olive oil

1 garlic clove

1 fresh thyme sprig

6 black peppercorns

1 pound 2 ounces boneless leg of mutton, cut into cubes

salt

Combine the oil, garlic, thyme and peppercorns in a dish, season with salt and add the meat. Stir well and let marinate for 1 hour. Drain the mutton and divide it among four metal skewers. The skewers can be cooked on a barbecue, under the broiler or in a griddle pan – all at a very high heat. Cook, turning frequently, for 3 minutes until almost crisp on the outside, but tender in the middle.

VEAL

Veal is synonymous with tender meat. This is because it comes from animals that are slaughtered when they are very young – 5–7 months or younger – are not very heavy – 300–350 pounds – and are fed exclusively on a milk formula. This also explains the delicate pale-pink color of the meat. Weaned veal is also available and veal is a meat that is gradually gaining popularity, though it can be difficult to obtain and prohibitively expensive in some countries. Chief among veal's benefits are that it is easy to digest and cooks rapidly. As it is dry and rather lean, larding with strips of pancetta or bacon, or pancetta or bacon fat, is an ideal way of cooking it. Some cuts, such as breast, may be prepared with 'pockets' that are then stuffed with other ground meats mixed with eggs, grated cheese and spices. Cooking methods used for beef may also be used for veal.

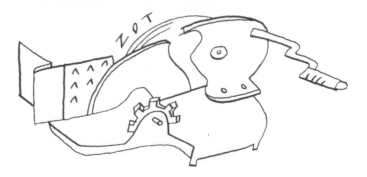

ITALIAN CUTS
AND COOKING
TECHNIQUES

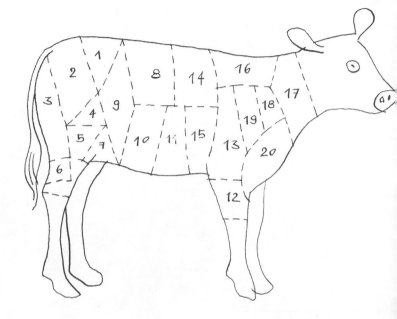

1. CODONE
   O CODONCINO
   Roasting
2. SOTTOFESA
   Roasting, broiling and sliced
   and roulades
3. GIRELLO
   Roasting, and sliced and
   scallops
4. FESA FRANCESE
   Broiling, and sliced, roulades,
   stuffed rolls and scallops
5. NOCE
   Roasting, and chops, sliced
   and scallops
6. PESCE
   O PICCIONE
   Boiling and stewing

7. SPINACINO
   Meat loaves and stuffed
   rolls and pockets
8. NODINI
   Broiling
9. SCAMONE
   Roasting
10. PANCETTA
    Stuffed pockets
11. PUNTA DI PETTO
    Boiling and stewing
12. GERETTO
    Boiling, and chops with
    marrowbone
13. FESA
    DI SPALLA
    Ideal sliced and for stuffed
    rolls

14. COSTOLETTE
    Broiling, and chops and
    scallops
15. FIOCCO
    Stewing and braising
16. REALE
    Roasting, boiling, stewing
    and braising
17. COLLO
    Boiling and stewing
18. FUSELLO
    Roasting, braising, boiling
    and sliced
19. CAPPELLO
    DEL PRETE
    Boiling, stewing and braisin
20. BRIONE
    Boiling, stewing and braising

AMERICAN CUTS
AND COOKING
TECHNIQUES

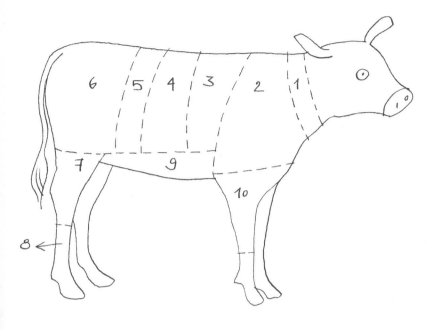

1. **BLADE**
   Braising, stewing, and ground meat
2. **SHOULDER**
   Roasting and diced for kabobs, pies, and meat loaf
3. **RIB**
   Roasting and cut into chops for broiling and frying
4. **LOIN**
   Roasting, and cut into chops or medallions for broiling and frying
5. **SIRLOIN**
   Roasting and cut into steaks

6. **RUMP ROAST**
   Roasting, and cut into round steaks and scallops
7. **LEG**
   Roasting and pot roasting
8. **SHANK**
   Roasting and braising
9. **BREAST**
   Roasting, braising, stewing, and ground meat
10. **FORESHANK**
   Braising

ROASTING

If you are in doubt over which cut to choose or cannot find one that is listed here, ask a reputable butcher for advice.

MILK POT ROAST

ARROSTO AL LATTE

Serves 6

1³/₄-pound boneless breast of veal

all-purpose flour, for dusting

3 tablespoons olive oil

3 tablespoons butter

about 4 cups milk

salt and pepper

Tie the veal neatly with kitchen string and dust lightly with flour. Heat the oil and butter in an oval pan, add the meat and cook, turning frequently, until browned all over. Meanwhile, heat ³/₄ cup of the milk until it is lukewarm. Season the veal with salt and pepper, pour in the warm milk, bring to just below simmering point and add as much of the remaining milk as required to cover the meat completely. Simmer over medium heat for about 1 hour. Remove the veal from the pan, let stand for 10 minutes, then untie and slice. Place on a warm serving dish and spoon the cooking juices over the meat.

VEAL BRAISED IN MILK WITH PROSCIUTTO

ARROSTO AL LATTE E PROSCIUTTO

Serves 6

3 tablespoons butter

2 tablespoons all-purpose flour

2 prosciutto slices, cut into thin strips

1³/₄-pound boneless breast of veal

3³/₄ cups milk

salt

Melt the butter in a pan, stir in the flour, then add the prosciutto and cook, stirring constantly, until browned. Tie the veal neatly with kitchen string, add to the pan and cook over high heat, turning frequently, until browned all over. Season with salt to taste, pour in ³/₄ cup of the milk and cook until it has been absorbed. Repeat this three times without covering the pan. Finally, add the remaining milk and cook until it has been absorbed. Remove the veal from the pan, untie, carve into slices and serve with the cooking juices.

POT ROAST VEAL WITH WALNUTS

ARROSTO ALLE NOCI

Serves 6

¹/₄ cup butter

4 tablespoons olive oil

1³/₄-pound boneless breast of veal

¹/₂ cup shelled walnuts, chopped

juice of 1 lemon, strained

³/₄ cup heavy cream

³/₄ cup Meat Stock (see page 208)

salt and pepper

Melt the butter and oil in a pan, add the veal and cook, turning frequently, for 15 minutes until browned all over. Add the walnuts, lemon juice, cream and stock and season with salt and pepper. Cover and simmer for 45 minutes, making sure that the meat does not stick to the base of the pan. If necessary, add a little more hot stock. Remove the veal and let stand. Tip the cooking juices into a food processor and process to a purée. Carve the veal, place the slices on a warm serving dish and spoon the purée over them.

BRAISED VEAL WITH OLIVES

Make small incisions in the veal with a small, sharp knife, insert the olive halves and tie neatly with kitchen string. Heat the oil and butter in a pan, add the onion, carrot, rosemary and celery and cook over low heat, stirring occasionally, for 10 minutes. Add the meat and cook, turning frequently, until browned all over. Pour in the wine and cook until it has evaporated, then season with salt and pepper. Simmer gently over low heat, turning occasionally and adding a little warm water if necessary, for about 1 hour. Remove the veal from the pan and let stand for 10 minutes. Untie, carve into slices and place on a warm serving dish. Pass the cooking juices through a food mill into a bowl. If they are too thick, thin with a little hot stock; if they are too runny, add a paste of equal quantities of butter and all-purpose flour. Spoon the juices over the meat and serve.

ARROSTO ALLE OLIVE

Serves 6

1³/₄-pound veal round

1³/₄ cups green olives, pitted and halved

2 tablespoons olive oil

¹/₄ cup butter

1 onion, chopped

1 carrot, chopped

1 fresh rosemary sprig, chopped

1 celery stalk, chopped

³/₄ cup dry white wine

salt and pepper

BRAISED VEAL WITH LEMON

Beat together the olive oil and lemon juice in a dish, season with salt and pepper and add the veal, turning to coat. Let marinate, turning occasionally, for 3 hours. Transfer the veal and the marinade to a pan, add ²/₃ cup water and bring to a boil. Lower the heat and simmer for about 1 hour until tender. Remove the veal from the pan, carve into slices and place on a warm serving dish. Boil the cooking juices until slightly reduced, then pour into a sauceboat and serve with the veal.

ARROSTO AL LIMONE

Serves 4

6 tablespoons olive oil

juice of 1 lemon, strained

1³/₄-pound veal round

salt and pepper

POT ROAST VEAL WITH KIDNEY

Make several cuts in the veal and insert a few grains of sea salt, then tie the meat neatly with kitchen string. Melt the butter in a pan, add the veal and cook, turning frequently, until browned all over. Pour in the cream, cover and simmer gently for 1 hour. Remove the veal from the pan and let stand. Add the kidney slices to the pan, cover and cook for 15 minutes. Untie the veal, carve into slices and place on a warm serving dish. Spoon the kidney and sauce on top.

ARROSTO CON ROGNONE

Serves 6

1³/₄-pound boneless breast of veal

3 tablespoons butter

³/₄ cup heavy cream

1 veal kidney, peeled, cored and sliced

sea salt

BRAISED VEAL ROUND

ARROSTO DI GIRELLO

Serves 6

1³/₄-pound veal round
¹/₄ cup butter
1 ounce pancetta, sliced
1 onion, thinly sliced
3 carrots, thinly sliced
1 bunch of fresh herbs, chopped
³/₄ cup dry white wine
salt and pepper

Tie the veal neatly with kitchen string. Melt the butter in a pan, add the veal and cook, turning frequently, for about 10 minutes until browned all over. Season with salt and pepper and remove the veal from the pan. Place the pancetta on the base of the pan, return the veal to the pan, cover with the onion and carrots and add the herbs. Pour in ³/₄ cup warm water and the wine, cover and simmer over low heat for about 1¹/₂ hours. Remove the veal and let stand for about 10 minutes. Pour the cooking juices into a food processor and process to a purée. Untie the veal, carve into slices and place on a warm serving dish. Spoon the cooking juices over the veal.

SIMPLE ROAST VEAL

ARROSTO SEMPLICE

Serves 6

1³/₄-pound veal round
3 tablespoons olive oil
3 tablespoons butter, plus extra for greasing
salt and pepper
²/₃ cup warm meat stock (see page 208)
or water (optional)

Preheat the oven to 250°F. Tie the veal neatly with kitchen string. Heat the oil and butter in a flameproof casserole, add the veal and cook, turning frequently, until brown all over. Season with salt and pepper, cover with greased waxed paper, transfer to the oven and roast, turning occasionally, for 1 hour. If the meat becomes too dry during cooking, add the warm stock or water. Remove the veal from the casserole, let stand for 10 minutes, then untie and carve into slices. Spoon the cooking juices over a warm serving dish and place the slices of meat in a row on top.

BRAISED VEAL WITH TRUFFLE

ARROSTO TARTUFATO

Serves 6

2¹/₄-pound loin of veal, boned
generous ¹/₂ cup pancetta, diced
1 black truffle, sliced
5 tablespoons olive oil
2 tablespoons butter
salt and pepper

Make small incisions in the veal using a sharp knife. Season the incisions with salt and pepper and insert a piece of pancetta and a small slice of truffle into each. Tie the meat neatly with kitchen string. Heat the oil and butter in a pan, add the veal and cook, turning frequently, until browned all over. Lower the heat, cover and cook gently for about 1 hour, adding a little warm water if necessary. Remove the meat and let stand for 10 minutes. Untie and carve into slices. Place the slices on a warm serving dish and spoon the cooking juices over them.

VEAL CHOPS WITH ARTICHOKES

Half-fill a bowl with water and stir in the lemon juice. Cut off the tough outer leaves from the artichokes, remove and discard the chokes, cut into fourths and drop into the acidulated water. Bring a pan of lightly salted water to a boil, drain the artichokes, add to the pan and parboil for 5 minutes, then drain. Combine the ham and 1 tablespoon of the butter in a bowl and spread the mixture over the artichoke wedges. Pound the veal chops with a meat mallet and season with salt and pepper. Place an artichoke wedge on each, roll up and tie with kitchen string. Heat the oil and the remaining butter in a skillet, add the onion and cook over low heat, stirring occasionally, for 5 minutes. Add the roulades and cook, turning frequently, until golden brown all over. Add $2/3$ cup hot water and simmer for about 10 minutes until tender and cooked through, then serve.

BRACIOLINE CON CARCIOFI

Serves 6

juice of 1 lemon, strained

2 tender globe artichokes

$1/3$ cup cooked, cured ham, chopped

$1/4$ cup butter

8 veal rib chops, boned

1 tablespoon olive oil

1 small onion, chopped

salt and pepper

BRAISED VEAL

Lard the veal with the strips of pancetta and tie neatly with kitchen string. Heat the oil in a pan, add the prosciutto fat, onions and carrots and cook over medium heat, stirring occasionally, for 10 minutes until browned. Add the meat, season with salt and pepper and cook, turning frequently, for about 10 minutes until browned all over. Pour in half the wine, increase the heat and cook until it has evaporated. Cook for 10 minutes more, then pour in the remaining wine and cook until it has evaporated. Pour in the hot stock, lower the heat to medium, cover and simmer for $1^1/2$ hours. Remove the veal from the pan, untie and carve into slices. Pass the cooking juices through a food mill. Place the slices of veal on a warm serving dish and spoon the cooking juices over them.

BRASATO

Serves 6

$2^1/4$-pound veal round

$1^1/2$ ounces pancetta, cut into strips

2 tablespoons olive oil

2 ounces prosciutto fat

2 onions, thinly sliced

2 carrots, thinly sliced

$1^1/2$ cups dry white wine

4 cups hot Meat Stock (see page 208)

salt and pepper

SUMMER VEAL

Bring a pan of water to the boil with the celery, carrot and onion. Tie the veal neatly with kitchen string, add to the pan and simmer for 2 hours. Remove the pan from the heat and let the meat cool in its stock. Drain the veal, untie and carve very thinly. Arrange the slices on a serving dish and sprinkle with the capers. Whisk together the oil and lemon juice in a bowl, season with salt and pour the dressing over the meat. Let marinate for 30 minutes, then serve.

CARNE ESTIVA

Serves 6

1 celery stalk

1 carrot • 1 onion

$2^1/4$-pound veal round

$1/3$ cup capers, drained and rinsed

scant $1/2$ cup olive oil

juice of 4 lemons, strained

salt

CIMA ALLA GENOVESE

Serves 6

2¼-pound boneless breast of veal

1 onion

1 carrot

2 bay leaves

salt

For the stuffing

2 thick bread slices, crusts removed

1¾ cups ground veal

3½ ounces sweetbreads

or brains, blanched and diced

¼ cup pork fat, chopped, or lardons

7 ounces Swiss chard, boiled, drained

and coarsely chopped

pinch of freshly grated nutmeg

2 tablespoons chopped fresh marjoram

2 eggs, lightly beaten

2 tablespoons Parmesan cheese, freshly grated

salt and pepper

GENOESE STUFFED BREAST OF VEAL

First prepare the stuffing. Tear the bread into pieces, place in a bowl, add water to cover and let soak for 10 minutes, then drain and squeeze out. Put the ground veal in a bowl and add the sweetbreads or brains and pork fat or lardons, Swiss chard and soaked bread. Mix well, stir in the nutmeg and marjoram and season with salt and pepper. Bind the mixture with the beaten eggs and Parmesan. Make a horizontal cut in the breast of veal along one of the long sides to create a 'pocket'. Fill the pocket with the stuffing, sew up the opening and tie neatly with kitchen string. Bring a large pan of lightly salted water to a boil with the onion, carrot and bay leaves. Add the stuffed breast and simmer gently for about 2 hours. Drain the meat and put on a plate. Cover and place a weight on top. Let cool, then untie and carve into slices. Arrange on a serving dish.

CODINO ARROSTO

Serves 4

1 pound 14-ounce rump

1 tablespoon meat seasoning

2 tablespoons butter

4 tablespoons olive oil

1 fresh flat-leaf parsley sprig, finely chopped

1 fresh rosemary sprig, finely chopped

4 fresh sage leaves, finely chopped

2 scallions, white parts only, chopped

1 carrot, thinly sliced

¾ cup dry white wine

salt and pepper

POT ROAST CODINO OF VEAL

Preheat the oven to 400°F. Gently rub the veal with the meat seasoning and tie neatly with kitchen string. Heat the butter and oil in a flameproof casserole, add the veal and cook, turning frequently, until browned all over. Add the parsley, rosemary and sage to the casserole and mix well, then add the scallions and carrot. Cook until lightly browned, then pour in the wine and cook until it has evaporated. Season with salt and pepper, pour in 5 tablespoons hot water, transfer to the oven and cook for about 1½ hours, adding a few tablespoons of warm water to prevent drying out if necessary. Remove the meat from the casserole and let stand for 10 minutes. Meanwhile, put the cooking juices in a food processor and process until smooth. Untie the veal, carve it into slices, place on a warm serving dish and spoon the sauce over them.

MILANESE VEAL CHOPS

Only chops should be used, but nowadays this dish is often made with slices of thickly cut rump roast. Pound the meat to an even thickness with a meat mallet. Beat the egg with a pinch of salt in a shallow dish. Spread out the bread crumbs in another shallow dish. Melt the clarified butter in a skillet. Dip each chop first in the beaten egg and then in the bread crumbs, pressing them on with your fingers. Fry the chops over low heat for about 10 minutes on each side until golden brown. Remove with a slotted spatula and drain on paper towels, then transfer to a warm serving dish. The chops go well with any vegetables served with butter, or with fresh salads.

COSTOLETTE ALLA MILANESE

Serves 4

4 veal chops, boned

1 egg

1 1/2 cups fine bread crumbs

1/4 cup Clarified Butter (see page 88)

salt

VALLE D'AOSTA VEAL CHOPS

Cut through the center of each chop horizontally, leaving the meat attached to the bone, and open out like a book. Put a slice of fontina and a few truffle shavings between the two halves, then the bring the halves together again, pressing along the edges. Secure with two toothpicks and season with salt and pepper. Beat the eggs with a pinch of salt in a shallow dish. Spread out the bread crumbs in another shallow dish. Dust the chops with flour, then dip them first in the beaten egg and then in the bread crumbs. Heat the butter and oil in a skillet, add the chops and cook for about 10 minutes on each side until browned. Drain, remove the toothpicks and serve.

COSTOLETTE ALLA VALDOSTANA

Serves 4

4 x 5-ounce veal chops

4 slices fontina cheese

1 white truffle, shaved

2 eggs

1 1/2 cups bread crumbs

all-purpose flour, for dusting

3 tablespoons butter

2 tablespoons olive oil

salt and pepper

VILLEROY VEAL CHOPS

Beat the egg with a pinch of salt in a shallow dish. Spread out the bread crumbs in another shallow dish. Lightly dust the chops with flour. Heat half the clarified butter in a skillet, add the chops and cook until lightly browned on both sides. Season with salt and pepper. Stir the egg yolks and nutmeg into the béchamel sauce. Immerse the chops in the béchamel sauce, then remove and drain off the excess. Dust with flour, dip in the beaten egg and then dip in the bread crumbs to coat. Heat the remaining clarified butter in a skillet, add the chops and cook until browned on both sides. Remove with a slotted spatula, drain on paper towels and serve.

COSTOLETTE ALLA VILLEROY

Serves 4

1 egg

1 1/2 cups bread crumbs

4 veal rib chops

all-purpose flour, for dusting

7 tablespoons Clarified Butter (see page 88)

2 egg yolks

pinch of freshly grated nutmeg

1 quantity hot Béchamel Sauce (see page 50)

salt and pepper

VEAL IN 'REDUCED STOCK'

Lightly pound the slices of veal with a meat mallet. Beat the eggs with a pinch of salt in a shallow dish. Spread out the bread crumbs in another shallow dish. Dust the veal slices with flour, dip in the beaten eggs, then dip in the bread crumbs and shake off any excess. Heat the clarified butter in a pan, add the veal and cook until lightly browned on both sides. Pour in the warm stock, cover and cook over low heat until the stock has reduced completely. Increase the heat, pour in the vinegar and cook until it has evaporated. Transfer the veal to a warm serving dish.

COTOLETTE AL 'CONSUMATO DI BRODO'

Serves 4

1 pound 2 ounces veal slices

2 eggs

$1/2$ cup bread crumbs

all-purpose flour, for dusting

3 tablespoons Clarified Butter (see page 88)

scant 1 cup warm Meat Stock (see page 208)

1 tablespoon white wine vinegar

salt

VEAL BOLOGNESE

Beat the egg with a pinch of salt and a pinch of pepper in a shallow dish. Spread out the bread crumbs in another shallow dish. Pound the veal until even with a meat mallet, dip in the beaten egg and then in the bread crumbs. Melt the butter in a skillet, add the veal and cook until golden brown on both sides. Put a slice of prosciutto, grana padano shavings and 2–3 slices of truffle on each slice. Pour in the stock, cover and cook until the prosciutto and cheese are translucent. Just before serving, coat the veal slices with the clarified butter. For a lighter version of this classic recipe, proceed as above but without dipping the meat in bread crumbs.

COTOLETTE ALLA BOLOGNESE

Serves 4

1 egg

$1^1/2$ cups bread crumbs

4 veal slices

6 tablespoons butter

4 prosciutto slices

$3^1/2$ ounces grana padano cheese, shaved

1 small black truffle, sliced

scant 1 cup Meat Stock (see page 208)

2 tablespoons Clarified Butter (see page 88)

salt and pepper

VEAL STEAKS IN VINEGAR

Pound the veal steaks with a meat mallet until even. Whisk together the oil and vinegar in a dish and season with salt and pepper. Add the meat, let marinate for 1 hour, then drain. Melt the butter in a skillet, add the steaks and cook over medium heat for 5 minutes on each side. Season with salt to taste and transfer to a warm serving dish. These steaks have a wonderful aroma and an unusual flavor.

FETTINE ALL'ACETO

Serves 4

14 ounces veal steaks

scant $1/2$ cup olive oil

scant 1 cup white wine vinegar

3 tablespoons butter

salt and pepper

VEAL STEAKS WITH EGG AND LEMON

FETTINE ALL'UOVO E LIMONE

Serves 4

1 pound 2 ounces veal steaks

all-purpose flour, for dusting

3 tablespoons butter

2 egg yolks

juice of 1 lemon, strained

1 fresh flat-leaf parsley sprig, chopped

salt

Dust the steaks with flour. Melt the butter in a skillet, add the steaks and cook for 5 minutes. Season with salt, remove from the skillet and keep warm. Beat together the egg yolks and lemon juice in a bowl. Pour 2 tablespoons water into the pan and heat, scraping up the sediment from the base. Add the egg yolk mixture and mix quickly. Spoon the egg sauce over the meat and sprinkle with the parsley.

VEAL KNOTS

FETTINE ANNODATE

Serves 4

2 tablespoons olive oil

2 tablespoons butter

1 fresh rosemary sprig, chopped

4 fresh sage leaves, chopped

1 garlic clove, chopped

1 onion, chopped

1 pound 2 ounces thin veal slices, cut into strips

all-purpose flour, for dusting

5 tablespoons dry Marsala

1 fresh flat-leaf parsley sprig, chopped

salt and pepper

Heat the oil and butter in a skillet, add the rosemary, sage, garlic and onion and cook over low heat, stirring occasionally, for 5 minutes. Tie a knot in each strip of meat and dust with flour. Add to the skillet and cook, turning occasionally, until browned all over. Season with salt and pepper to taste, cover and cook for 20 minutes. Uncover the pan and increase the heat to reduce the cooking juices, then add the Marsala and cook until it has evaporated. Sprinkle with the parsley and serve.

VEAL STEAKS IN OLIVE SAUCE

FETTINE IN SALSA D'OLIVE

Serves 4

3 tablespoons butter

3 tablespoons olive oil

1 pound 2 ounces veal steaks

all-purpose flour, for dusting

5 tablespoons dry white wine

12 pitted green olives

1 slice bottled red bell pepper in oil, drained and chopped

salt and pepper

Heat the butter and oil in a skillet. Dust the steaks with flour, add to the skillet and cook until browned all over. Season, remove from the skillet and keep warm. Pour the wine into the skillet and cook until it has evaporated. Add 3 tablespoons water and cook, scraping the sediment from the base of the pan with a wooden spoon, then add the olives and bell pepper. Return the meat to the skillet and cook over high heat for a few minutes.

VEAL RIBBONS

Put the veal strips, olive oil and herbs in a pan, season with salt and pepper and cook over low heat, occasionally adding a little hot water, until browned. Cook the onions in salted, boiling water for 10 minutes, then drain and add to the meat. Cook, gradually adding the Marsala, until the meat is tender and cooked through. Stir in the butter and serve.

'FETTUCCINE' DI CARNE

Serves 4

1 pound 2 ounces veal steaks, cut into strips

3 tablespoons olive oil

1 tablespoon fresh flat-leaf parsley, chopped

4 fresh sage leaves, chopped

1 tablespoons chopped fresh thyme

10 pearl onions

scant $1/2$ cup Marsala

2 tablespoons butter

salt and pepper

TENDERLOIN OF VEAL IN CONZA

Cut the tenderloin into extremely thin slices and place in a layer in a bowl. Cover with a layer of rosemary needles, sage, basil, onion slices and strips of lemon rind. Drizzle with olive oil and lemon juice and season with salt and pepper. Continue making alternate layers until all the ingredients are used, ending with a layer of herbs, onion and lemon rind. Drizzle with a little more oil, cover the bowl with plastic wrap and chill in the refrigerator for 24 hours.

FILETTO IN CONZA

Serves 6

1 pound 2 ounces veal tenderloin

1 fresh rosemary sprig

8 fresh sage leaves, chopped

8 fresh basil leaves, chopped

1 onion, thinly sliced

thinly pared rind of 1 lemon, cut into strips

$1/2$–$2/3$ cup olive oil

juice of 2 lemons, strained

salt and pepper

MEAT MOLD

Preheat the oven to 350°F. Grease a soufflé dish or individual ramekins with butter and sprinkle with the bread crumbs, tipping out the excess. Melt the butter in a skillet, add the veal and cook, stirring occasionally, until browned. Transfer the veal to a bowl and add the ham. Season the béchamel sauce with salt and pepper and stir in the egg yolk, veal mixture and enough Parmesan, to achieve the desired consistency. Pour the mixture into the prepared dish or ramekins, sprinkle with a pinch of bread crumbs and bake for about 40 minutes until golden brown.

FLAN DI CARNE

Serves 4

2 tablespoons butter, plus extra for greasing

$3/4$ cup bread crumbs

$2\,1/4$ cups ground veal

2 ounces cooked, cured ham, chopped

1 quantity Béchamel Sauce (see page 50)

1 egg yolk

2–3 tablespoon Parmesan cheese, freshly grated

salt and pepper

VEAL BUNDLES WITH TRUFFLES

INVOLTINI AI TARTUFI

Serves 4

1 pound veal round steaks

1 white truffle, thinly shaved

1 ounce Parmesan cheese, thinly shaved

2 eggs

1¹/₂ cups bread crumbs • 3 tablespoons butter

salt

Pound the steaks with a meat mallet until thin and even, season with salt and sprinkle with a few shavings of truffle and Parmesan. Fold in half and press down well all around the edges. Beat the eggs with a pinch of salt in a shallow dish. Spread out the bread crumbs in another shallow dish. Dip each steak bundle into the beaten eggs and then into the bread crumbs. Melt the butter in a skillet, add the steak bundles and cook, turning frequently, for 10 minutes.

VEAL ROULADES WITH VEGETABLES

INVOLTINI ALLE VERDURE

Serves 4

1 pound veal slices • 2 carrots, cut into batons

1 celery stalk, cut into batons

3 tablespoons butter • 3 tablespoons olive oil

5 tablespoons dry white wine

4 tablespoons bottled strained tomatoes

salt and pepper

Pound the slices of veal with a meat mallet. Divide the carrots and celery among the slices of meat, then roll up and tie with kitchen string. Heat the butter and oil in a skillet, add the roulades and cook, turning frequently, until browned all over. Pour in the wine and cook until it has evaporated, then season with salt and pepper. Add the strained tomatoes, cover and simmer gently for 30 minutes.

SIMPLE POACHED VEAL

LESSO SEMPLICE

Serves 4

1 carrot • 1 celery stalk

1 onion • 2¹/₄-pound boned breast of veal

salt

Pour 4¹/₄ quarts water into a pan, add a pinch of salt, the carrot, celery and onion and bring to a boil. Add the veal, lower the heat, cover and simmer gently for about 2 hours. Drain the meat and serve while still hot with mustard or a choice of sauces.

VEAL ROULADES IN ASPIC

MESSICANI IN GELATINA

Serves 6

1 bread slice, crusts removed

1¹/₄ cups ground beef

¹/₃ cup prosciutto, chopped

²/₃ cup Parmesan cheese, freshly grated

1 egg

1 egg yolk

1 pound 2 ounces veal steaks

4 tablespoons olive oil

2 tablespoons butter

4–5 fresh sage leaves

³/₄ cup dry white wine

4 cups dissolved gelatin

salt and pepper

Tear the bread into pieces, place in a bowl, add water to cover and let soak for 10 minutes, then drain and squeeze out. Combine the beef, soaked bread, prosciutto and Parmesan in a bowl. Stir in the egg and egg yolk and season. Pound the veal steaks with a meat mallet until thin and divide the filling among them. Roll up and tie with kitchen string. Heat the oil and butter in a skillet, add the sage and roulades and cook, turning frequently, until browned. Pour in all but 1 tablespoon of the wine and cook until it has evaporated. Pour in ²/₃ cup water and cook for 15 minutes. Add 2–3 tablespoons water, increase the heat and cook for 1 minute. Remove the skillet from the heat and place the roulades on a serving dish. Prepare the gelatin according to the instructions, add the remaining wine and pour it over the roulades until completely covered. Chill in the refrigerator for a few hours until set.

VEAL NOISETTES IN BUTTER, SAGE AND ROSEMARY

Pound the noisettes lightly with a meat mallet and place in a pan with the butter. Sprinkle with the rosemary and sage and cook over medium heat for 4 minutes on each side. Season with salt and pepper, pour in the wine and cook until it has evaporated. Add the stock, lower the heat, cover and simmer for 30 minutes, adding more stock if necessary.

NODINI AL BURRO, SALVIA E ROSMARINO

Serves 4

4 veal noisettes

6 tablespoons butter, cut into pieces

2 fresh rosemary sprigs, chopped

8 fresh sage leaves, chopped

5 tablespoons white wine

1¼ cups Meat Stock (see page 208)

salt and pepper

VEAL NOISETTES À LA FINANCIÈRE

Melt half the butter in a skillet, add the mushrooms and cook over low heat, stirring occasionally, for 20 minutes. Add the peas, sweetbreads and bone marrow, pour in the Marsala and cook until it has evaporated. Season with salt and pepper and cook for a few minutes more. Melt the remaining butter in another skillet. Dust the veal noisettes with flour, add to the skillet and cook for 4 minutes on each side. Pour in the stock, cover and simmer until tender. Place the veal noisettes on a warm serving dish and spoon the sauce over them.

NODINI ALLA FINANZIERA

Serves 4

scant ½ cup butter

scant 1½ cups mushrooms, sliced

2 tablespoons frozen peas

5 ounces sweetbreads and

bone marrow, chopped

5 tablespoons dry Marsala

4 veal noisettes

all-purpose flour, for dusting

1¼ cups Meat Stock (see page 208)

salt and pepper

MILANESE OSSO BUCO

Melt the butter in a pan, add the onion and cook over low heat, stirring occasionally, for 5 minutes. Dust the veal with flour, add to the pan and cook over high heat, turning frequently, until browned all over. Season with salt and pepper and cook for a few minutes more, then pour in the wine and cook until it has evaporated. Add the stock, celery and carrot, lower the heat, cover and simmer for 30 minutes, adding more stock if necessary. Mix the tomato paste with 1 tablespoon hot water in a bowl and stir into the pan. Prepare the gremolata by combining the lemon rind and parsley in a bowl, add the mixture to the veal, turn carefully and cook for 5 minutes more.

OSSIBUCHI ALLA MILANESE

Serves 4

6 tablespoons butter • ½ onion, chopped

4 osso buco (2-inch thick rounds of

veal shank)

all-purpose flour, for dusting

5 tablespoons dry white wine

¾ cup Meat Stock (see page 208)

1 celery stalk, chopped

1 carrot, chopped

2 tablespoons tomato paste

salt and pepper

For the gremolata

thinly pared rind of ½ lemon, finely chopped

1 fresh flat-leaf parsley sprig, finely chopped

VEAL OSSO BUCO WITH PEAS

Lightly dust the veal with flour. Melt the butter in a skillet, add the onion, carrot and veal and cook over high heat, stirring and turning frequently, until the veal is browned all over. Pour in the wine and cook until it has evaporated. Put the tomatoes in a food processor, process to a purée and add to the pan with the peas and $2/3$ cup water. Season with salt and pepper, lower the heat, cover and simmer for about 1 hour.

OSSIBUCHI CON PISELLI

Serves 4

4 osso buco (2-inch thick rounds of veal shank)

all-purpose flour, for dusting

6 tablespoons butter

1 onion, finely chopped • 1 carrot, finely chopped

$3/4$ cup dry white wine

5 ounces canned tomatoes

$1 1/4$ cups fresh peas, shelled

salt and pepper

MEAT PIE

Pound the veal with a meat mallet until thin and even. Place one slice on the base of a deep heatproof dish (it should be just the right size to fit). Sprinkle with a little Parmesan and a pinch of salt and lay a slice of mortadella and a slice of ham on top. Spoon a little of the beaten eggs over the meat. Continue to make layers until all the ingredients are used, ending with beaten eggs. Stand the dish in pan and add water to come about halfway up the sides. Bring just to a boil, then lower the heat and simmer for 2 hours. Turn the pie out onto a dish — it should slide out easily. Put a weight on top and leave for about 1 hour. Drain off the jelly-like liquid which forms and use to garnish. Chill in the refrigerator, then serve cut into slices. This pie can even be served the next day.

PASTICCIO DI CARNE

Serves 6–8

4 thick lean veal slices

2 tablespoons Parmesan cheese, freshly grated

4 thick mortadella slices

4 cooked, cured ham slices

4 eggs, lightly beaten

salt

ROAST BREAST OF VEAL

Ask your butcher to pound the breast of veal into a fairly broad slice. Preheat the oven to 350°F. Grease a roasting pan with butter. Season the veal with salt and pepper, place the slices of prosciutto on top and sprinkle with the rosemary and sage. Roll up the meat and tie with kitchen string. Place the veal in the roasting pan, dot with the butter, drizzle with the oil and roast, basting and turning the meat occasionally, for about $1 1/2$ hours. Let stand for about 10 minutes before untying and carving into slices.

PETTO AL FORNO

Serves 6

$1/4$ cup butter, plus extra for greasing

$1 3/4$-pound boneless breast of veal

2 thick prosciutto slices

1 fresh rosemary sprig, chopped

4 fresh sage leaves, chopped

2 tablespoons olive oil

salt and pepper

BREAST OF VEAL
WITH MAYONNAISE

PETTO ALLA MAIONESE

Serves 4

1 pound 2-ounce boneless breast of veal

2 tablespoons butter

6 tablespoons Mayonnaise (see page 65)

3 dill pickles, drained and chopped

10 black olives, pitted and cut into fourths

salt and pepper

Season the veal on both sides with salt and pepper. Melt the butter in a skillet, add the veal and cook, turning frequently, until cooked through and golden brown all over. Remove from the skillet and let cool. Combine the mayonnaise, dill pickles and olives in a bowl and spread the mixture over the meat. Roll up and wrap securely in foil. Chill in the refrigerator for 3 hours before slicing and serving.

BREAST OF VEAL
WITH HERBS

PETTO ALLE ERBE

Serves 6

3 eggs

4 tablespoons Parmesan cheese, freshly grated

2¼-pound boneless breast of veal

11 ounce Swiss chard

1 fresh flat-leaf parsley sprig, chopped

1 fresh basil sprig, chopped

3 cooked, cured ham slices

1 garlic clove, chopped (optional)

2 tablespoons olive oil

3 tablespoons butter

2¼ cups Meat Stock (see page 208)

salt and pepper

Beat the eggs in a bowl, add the Parmesan, season with salt and make a small frittata (see page 382). Spread out the meat and place the frittata on top. Blanch the Swiss chard in salted, boiling water for a few minutes, then drain and chop. Combine the Swiss chard, parsley, basil, ham, and garlic if using. Sprinkle the mixture over the frittata and season with salt and pepper. Roll up the meat and tie with kitchen string. Heat the oil and butter in a skillet, add the veal and cook, turning frequently, until golden brown all over, then season with salt. Pour in the stock, cover and simmer over low heat, turning and basting occasionally, for 1½ hours. Remove the veal from the skillet and let stand for 10 minutes, then untie, slice and serve.

BREAST OF VEAL
WITH SAUSAGES

PETTO ALLE SALSICCE

Serves 6

6 small Italian sausages

4 tablespoons diced day-old bread

1 onion, chopped

1¼ cups Meat Stock (see page 208)

2¼-pound boneless breast of veal

4 tablespoons olive oil, plus extra for brushing

¼ cup butter

Cook the sausages without additional oil or fat in a skillet until browned and cooked through, then skin and crumble into a bowl. Add the bread and onion and mix well. If the mixture is too dry, stir in a little of the stock. Make a horizontal cut in the breast of veal along one of the long sides to create a 'pocket'. Spoon the mixture into the pocket and sew up the opening. Brush the veal with oil and put it into in a pan with the oil and butter. Cook over medium heat, turning occasionally, until browned all over. Cover and cook on low heat, turning the meat occasionally and gradually adding the stock as necessary, for 1½ hours. Carve into slices and spoon the cooking juices over them.

BRAISED BREAST OF VEAL

Open out the veal well and make several small incisions in the surface. Slip rosemary needles, a slice of garlic and a piece of pancetta dipped in pepper and a little salt into each incision. Roll up the meat and tie with kitchen string. Heat the butter and oil in a pan, add the veal and cook, turning frequently, until browned all over. Cover and cook over low heat, gradually adding the Marsala, for 1 hour or until cooked through and tender. Remove the meat from the pan and let stand. Add 1–2 tablespoons hot water to dilute the cooking juices, if necessary. Untie the veal, carve into slices, place on a warm serving dish and spoon the cooking juices over them. You could serve this with a side dish of spinach in butter.

PETTO ARROSTO

Serves 6

$2^1/_2$-pound boneless breast of veal

1 fresh rosemary sprig

1 garlic clove, sliced

$^1/_3$ cup pancetta, chopped

2 tablespoons butter

3 tablespoons olive oil

$^3/_4$ cup dry Marsala

salt and pepper

VEAL SCALLOPS IN LEMON

Pound the scallops lightly with a meat mallet and dust with a little flour. Melt 5 tablespoons of the butter in a skillet, add the scallops and cook over high heat for 5 minutes, turning several times, then season with salt. Combine the lemon juice with 4 tablespoons water, pour the mixture into the skillet and cook until slightly reduced. Sprinkle with the parsley, dot with the remaining butter, then remove from the heat when the butter has melted. Serve the veal scallops in the sauce.

PICCATA AL LIMONE

Serves 4

1 pound 2 ounces veal scallops

all-purpose flour for dusting

6 tablespoons butter

juice of 1 lemon, strained

1 fresh flat-leaf parsley sprig, chopped

salt

VEAL SCALLOPS WITH MARSALA

Dust the veal scallops with flour. Melt the butter in a large skillet, and when it turns hazel add the veal and cook over high heat for about 5 minutes on each side. Lower the heat, season with salt to taste and cook for a few more minutes more, then remove from the skillet and keep warm. Pour in the Marsala and cook over low heat, scraping up the sediment from the base of the pan with a wooden spoon. Place the scallops on a warm serving dish and spoon the sauce over them.

PICCATA AL MARSALA

Serves 4

1 pound 2 ounces veal scallops

all-purpose flour, for dusting

6 tablespoons butter

1 cup dry Marsala

salt

VEAL MEATLOAF

Combine the veal, ham, eggs and nutmeg in a bowl and season with salt and pepper. Shape the mixture into an ovoid and dust with flour. Heat the butter and oil in a pan, add the onion, carrot and celery and cook over low heat, stirring occasionally, for 10 minutes. Add the meatloaf and cook, turning carefully, until browned all over. Mix the tomato paste with 2 tablespoons warm water and stir into the pan. Cover and simmer gently for about 1 hour. Remove the meatloaf from the pan, cut into fairly thick slices, place them on a warm serving dish and spoon the cooking juices over them.

POLPETTONE CASALINGO

Serves 4

1 pound 2 ounces ground round of veal

generous $1/2$ cup cooked, cured ham, chopped

2 eggs, lightly beaten

pinch of freshly grated nutmeg

all-purpose flour, for dusting

$1/4$ cup butter

2 tablespoons olive oil

1 onion, chopped

1 carrot, chopped

1 celery stalk, chopped

2 teaspoons tomato paste

salt and pepper

ROMAN SALTIMBOCCA

This is the only main course in Italian cuisine whose recipe has been officially approved and laid down. This is the recipe that the panel of cooks agreed upon in Venice in 1962. Saltimbocca, incidentally, means jump into the mouth. Place a half-slice of prosciutto on each scallop, put a sage leaf on top and fasten with a toothpick. Melt the butter in a skillet and cook the veal over high heat on both sides until golden brown. Season with salt, pour in the wine and cook until it has evaporated, then remove the toothpicks and serve.

SALTIMBOCCA ALLA ROMANA

Serves 4

$3^{1}/2$ ounces prosciutto slices, halved

1 pound 2 ounces veal scallops

8–10 fresh sage leaves

$1/4$ cup butter

scant $1/2$ cup dry white wine

salt

VEAL SCALLOPS WITH MUSHROOMS

Heat half the oil and $1^{1}/2$ tablespoons of the butter in a skillet, add the mushrooms and garlic and cook over low heat, stirring occasionally, for 20 minutes. Remove the skillet from the heat, discard the garlic, season the mushrooms with salt and sprinkle with the parsley. Dust the veal scallops with flour. Heat the remaining oil and remaining butter in another skillet, add the veal and cook over high heat for 10 minutes on each side until golden brown. Season with salt and pepper, remove from the skillet and keep warm. Stir 2–3 tablespoons hot water into the cooking juices and add to the mushrooms. Place the veal scallops on a warm serving dish and pour the mushroom mixture over them.

SCALOPPINE AI FUNGHI

Serves 4

$1/2$ cup olive oil

$1/4$ cup butter

scant $4^{1}/2$ cups mushrooms, sliced

1 garlic clove

1 fresh flat-leaf parsley sprig, chopped

4 veal scallops

all-purpose flour, for dusting

salt and pepper

VEAL SCALLOPS PIZZAIOLA

Dust the veal scallops with flour. Heat the oil and butter in a skillet, add the onion and garlic and cook over low heat, stirring occasionally, for 5 minutes. Add the veal, increase the heat to high and cook for 5 minutes on each side. Add the tomatoes and cook for a few minutes more. Remove and discard the garlic, add the capers and the olives and season lightly with salt and pepper. Simmer for 5 minutes more, then transfer the veal scallops to a warm serving dish and spoon the cooking juices over them.

SCALOPPINE ALLA PIZZAIOLA

Serves 4

4 veal scallops

all-purpose flour, for dusting

3 tablespoons olive oil

3 tablespoons butter

$1/2$ onion, chopped

1 garlic clove

4 ripe tomatoes, peeled and chopped

2 tablespoons capers, drained and rinsed

10 green olives, pitted

salt and pepper

VEAL SCALLOPS WITH MUSTARD

Dust the veal scallops with flour. Heat the butter and oil in a large skillet, add the veal scallops and cook over medium heat for 8–10 minutes until golden brown on both sides. Season with salt, remove from the skillet and keep warm. Stir 1–2 tablespoons hot water into the cooking juices, add the mustard and mix well to dissolve. Chop the parsley, thyme and chives together, add to the skillet and cook for a few minutes. Pour the sauce over the veal scallops and serve.

SCALOPPINE ALLA SENAPE

Serves 4

4 veal scallops

all-purpose flour, for dusting

3 tablespoons butter

2 tablespoons olive oil

1 tablespoon Dijon mustard

1 fresh parsley sprig

1 fresh thyme sprig

4 fresh chives

salt

VEAL SCALLOPS WITH MILK

Lightly pound the veal scallops with a meat mallet and dust with flour. Beat the egg with a little salt and pepper in a shallow dish. Spread out the bread crumbs in another shallow dish. Dip the veal scallops first in the beaten egg, then in the bread crumbs and shake off the excess. Melt the butter in a skillet, add the veal and cook for 3 minutes on each side. Pour in the milk, cover the skillet and simmer for about 20 minutes until the veal is tender. Arrange the veal scallops on a warm serving dish. Stir the capers into the hot cooking juices and pour the mixture over the meat.

SCALOPPINE AL LATTE

Serves 4

4 veal scallops

all-purpose flour, for dusting

1 egg

1 cup bread crumbs

2 tablespoons butter

$2^{1}/4$ cups milk

1 tablespoon capers, drained,

rinsed and chopped

salt and pepper

VEAL SCALLOPS WITH HERBS

SCALOPPINE ALLE ERBE

Serves 4

¼ cup butter

1 tablespoon olive oil

¼ onion, in one piece

4 veal scallops

1 fresh rosemary sprig, chopped

1 fresh sage sprig, chopped

1 fresh thyme sprig, chopped

5 tablespoons dry white wine

salt and pepper

Heat the butter and oil in a skillet, add the onion and cook over low heat for 10 minutes, stirring occasionally to make sure the onion stays intact, then remove from the skillet. Add the veal scallops to the skillet and cook over high heat for 2 minutes on each side, then lower the heat and season with salt and pepper. Add the rosemary, sage and thyme and cook for a few minutes. Pour in the wine and cook over medium heat for about 10 minutes until the veal is tender. Remove the veal scallops from the skillet. Add 1–2 tablespoons hot water to the skillet and cook, scraping up the sediment from the base with a wooden spoon, then pour the sauce over the meat and serve.

VEAL SCALLOPS WITH GRAPEFRUIT

SCALOPPINE AL POMPELMO

Serves 4

3 tablespoons butter

1 fresh thyme sprig

4 veal scallops

all-purpose flour, for dusting

5 tablespoons dry white wine

juice of ½ grapefruit, strained

salt and pepper

grapefruit slices, to garnish

Heat the butter in a skillet and add the thyme. Lightly dust the veal scallops with flour, add to the skillet and cook over high heat until golden brown on both sides. Combine the wine and grapefruit juice and pour the mixture into the skillet. Cover and simmer over low heat for 15 minutes until the liquid has thickened. Season with salt and pepper. Transfer the veal scallops to a warm serving dish and spoon the cooking juices over them discarding the thyme. Garnish with slices of grapefruit.

VEAL FRITTERS

SGONFIOTTI DI CARNE

Serves 4

2 onions, chopped

1 garlic clove, chopped

1 chile, seeded and chopped

2¼ cups ground veal

¼ cup butter

2 eggs, hard-cooked and chopped

8 green olives, pitted and chopped

scant ½ cup golden raisins

pinch of dried oregano

9 ounces puff pastry dough, thawed if frozen

all-purpose flour, for dusting

1 egg, lightly beaten

vegetable oil, for deep-frying

salt and pepper

Combine the onions, garlic, chile and veal in a bowl. Melt the butter in a skillet, add the veal mixture and cook, stirring constantly, until evenly browned. Remove from the heat and let cool. Stir in the eggs, olives, golden raisins and oregano and season with salt and pepper. Roll out the dough on a lightly floured surface and stamp out 4-inch rounds. Put a little filling on each round, brush the edges with the beaten egg, fold in half and crimp to seal. Heat the oil in a large pan, add the fritters and cook until golden brown. Remove with a slotted spatula, drain and serve.

SIX–AROMA VEAL STEW

Season the veal with salt and pepper and place in a bowl with the garlic, parsley and basil. Add the lemon and orange juice, lime rind and cumin seeds and mix well. Let the veal marinate, stirring occasionally, for 2 hours. Heat the oil and butter in a pan. Drain the veal, reserving the marinade, add to the pan and cook, stirring frequently, for about 5 minutes. Strain the reserved marinade into the pan, cover and simmer for 45 minutes, adding a little warm water if necessary.

SPEZZATINO AI SEI PROFUMI

Serves 4

1³/₄ pounds boneless shoulder

of veal, cut into cubes

1 garlic clove, chopped

1 fresh flat-leaf parsley sprig, chopped

1 fresh basil sprig, chopped

juice of 1 lemon, strained

juice of 1 orange, strained

grated rind of 1 lime

1 tablespoon cumin seeds

3 tablespoons olive oil

3 tablespoons butter

salt and pepper

CURRIED VEAL

Heat the oil and butter in a pan, add the onions and cook over low heat, stirring occasionally, for 5 minutes. Lightly dust the veal with flour, add to the pan, increase the heat to high and cook, stirring frequently, for 5 minutes or until browned all over. Season with salt and pepper. Stir the curry powder into 2–3 tablespoons warm water in a bowl and pour the mixture over the meat. Mix well, cover and simmer over medium heat for 1 hour. Add the thyme and parsley, then transfer to a warm serving dish. This curry is delicious served with a pilaf or plain boiled rice.

SPEZZATINO AL CURRY

Serves 4

2 tablespoons olive oil

2 tablespoons butter

2 onions, chopped

1 pound 5 ounces boneless shoulder

of veal, cut into cubes

all-purpose flour, for dusting

2 tablespoons curry powder

leaves of 1 fresh thyme sprig

1 fresh flat-leaf parsley sprig, chopped

salt and pepper

VEAL AND VEGETABLE STEW

Heat the oil and butter in a pan, add the onion and celery and cook over low heat, stirring occasionally, for 5 minutes. Dust the veal with flour, add to the pan and cook over high heat, stirring frequently, until browned all over. Season with salt and pepper and cook for minutes more, then add the carrots and bottled strained tomatoes. Lower the heat, cover and simmer for about 45 minutes, occasionally adding 2–3 tablespoons warm water if the stew starts to dry out. Add the zucchini, re-cover the pan and cook for 15 minutes more.

SPEZZATINO CON VERDURE

Serves 4

2 tablespoons olive oil

2 tablespoons butter

1 onion, finely chopped

1 celery stalk, finely chopped

1 pound 5 ounces boned shoulder of veal, cut into cubes

all-purpose flour, for dusting

3 carrots, cut into thin batons

scant ¹/₂ cup bottled strained tomatoes

3 zucchini, cut into thin batons

salt and pepper

SPINACINO AI CARCIOFI

Serves 8

2¹/₂-pound boned breast of veal

11 ounces ground meat

²/₃ cup Parmesan cheese, freshly grated

1 egg, lightly beaten

3 very tender artichoke hearts

4 tablespoons olive oil

juice of ¹/₂ lemon, strained

2 tablespoons butter

salt

BREAST OF VEAL WITH ARTICHOKE HEARTS

Using a sharp knife, cut a deep 'pocket' in the veal. Combine the ground meat, Parmesan and egg in a bowl and season with salt. Place 2–3 tablespoons of the ground meat mixture in the veal 'pocket' and gently push it down towards the end. Insert an artichoke heart with the base towards the opening. Stuff the pocket with another 2–3 tablespoons of the ground meat mixture, pushing it down well, then insert another artichoke heart. Add another 2–3 tablespoons of the ground meat mixture, then the remaining artichoke heart and, finally, add the remaining ground meat mixture. Sew up the opening with trussing thread. Mix 1 tablespoon of the oil with the lemon juice in a small bowl and brush the mixture all over the veal. Heat the butter and the remaining oil in a large pan or flameproof casserole, add the veal, cover and cook over low heat for about 1 hour. After the first 30 minutes, start turning the veal occasionally. About 5 minutes before the end of the cooking time, remove the lid, increase the heat and cook the veal, turning frequently, until browned all over. Remove the pan from the heat and leave the veal to stand for 10 minutes before carving into slices. Arrange the slices on a serving dish and spoon some of the cooking juices over them.

STINCO AL SIDRO

Serves 6

²/₃ cup butter

4 shallots, thinly sliced

1 veal shank

1 tablespoon Calvados or applejack

4 cups hard cider

11 ounces pearl onions

4 red apples, cored and chopped

1 cup heavy cream

1 egg yolk

salt and pepper

SHANK OF VEAL IN HARD CIDER

Melt 4 tablespoons of the butter in a pan, add the shallots and cook over low heat, stirring occasionally, for 10 minutes. Increase the heat to high, add the veal shank and cook, turning frequently, for 10 minutes until browned all over. Season with salt and pepper, add the Calvados or applejock and cook until it has evaporated. Pour in the hard cider, add a little more salt, lower the heat, cover and simmer for about 1¹/₂ hours. Meanwhile, melt 4 tablespoons of the remaining butter in another pan, add the onions and cook over low heat, stirring occasionally, for 15 minutes. Melt the remaining butter in another pan, add the apples and cook over low heat, stirring occasionally, until just tender. Remove the meat from the pan and keep warm. Stir the cream into the cooking juices, then stir in the egg yolk and heat gently without letting the sauce boil. Carve the veal, place the slices on a warm serving dish, pour the sauce over them and surround with the apples and onions.

ROAST SHANK OF VEAL

STINCO ARROSTO

Serves 6

3 tablespoons olive oil

3 tablespoons butter

1 fresh myrtle sprig or 6 juniper berries

1 fresh rosemary sprig

2 shallots, finely chopped

1 veal shank

³/₄ cup red wine

salt and pepper

Preheat the oven to 375°F. Put the oil, butter, myrtle or juniper berries, rosemary and shallots in a roasting pan and cook over low heat, stirring occasionally, for 10 minutes. Add the veal and cook, turning frequently, until golden brown on all sides. Season with salt and pepper, transfer to the oven and roast for about 1 hour. Pour in the wine, return the pan to the oven and roast, basting occasionally, for 1 hour more. If necessary, add a ladleful of hot water. Remove the veal and carve it, then place the slices on a warm serving dish and spoon the cooking juices over them.

HOT VEAL IN TUNA SAUCE

VITELLO TONNATO CALDO

Serves 6

3 tablespoons butter • 3 tablespoons olive oil

1³/₄-pound veal round

³/₄ cup dry white wine

1 carrot • 1 celery stalk

2 salted anchovies, heads removed, cleaned and filleted (see page 596), soaked in cold water for 10 minutes, drained and rinsed

3¹/₂ ounces canned tuna in oil, drained and flaked

4 dill pickles, drained and chopped

juice of 1 lemon, strained

salt and pepper

Heat the butter and oil in a pan, add the veal and cook, turning frequently, until browned all over. Season with salt and pepper and cook for 5 minutes more, then pour in the wine and cook until it has evaporated. Add the carrot and celery and pour in ³/₄ cup water. Cover and simmer over low heat, turning the meat occasionally, for 1¹/₂ hours. Meanwhile, chop the anchovy fillets. Combine the anchovies, tuna, dill pickles and lemon juice in a bowl. When the meat is tender, remove it from the pan. Remove the carrot and celery, pour the tuna mixture into the pan and mix with the cooking juices. Carve the meat into fairly thin slices, place them on a warm serving dish and spoon the hot tuna sauce over them.

COLD VEAL IN TUNA SAUCE

VITELLO TONNATO FREDDO

Serves 6

1³/₄-pound veal round

1 carrot • 1 onion • 1 celery stalk

1 tablespoon white wine vinegar

1 tablespoon olive oil • salt

For the sauce

7 ounces canned tuna in oil, drained

3 canned anchovy fillets in oil, drained

2 tablespoons capers, drained and rinsed

2 hard-cooked egg yolks

3 tablespoons olive oil

juice of 1 lemon, strained

Tie the veal neatly with kitchen string. Bring a pan of salted water to a boil and add the veal, carrot, onion, celery, vinegar and olive oil. Cover and simmer over low heat for 2 hours until the meat is tender. Remove the pan from the heat and let the veal cool in the stock. For the sauce, put the tuna, anchovy fillets, capers and egg yolks through a grinder or process in a food processor. Stir in the olive oil, 2–3 tablespoons of the stock and the lemon juice. Untie the meat, carve into slices and place on a serving dish. Spoon the sauce over the slices and leave for a few hours for the flavors to mingle before serving.

SAUSAGES

Italian sausages include cotechino, cappello del prete, zampone and salame da sugo – or salamina, as this particular variety are more affectionately called by the inhabitants of Ferrara, who love it. Although the family of Italian sausages for cooking is not as big as the family of sausages eaten raw, the distinctiveness of their ingredients, their specific flavor and their aroma make them true delicacies which, particularly in the winter, provide comfort against the rigors of the climate and help create a cheerful mood. They are of very different shapes and sizes and include a wide variety of ingredients. For example, meat from the pig's snout predominates in cotechino. In boned feet, there is a mixture of a number of coarsely ground meats seasoned with spices. Lean meat predominates in sausages sold by length or in links, and the mixture must be fairly even. Prized cuts predominate in the salama da sugo – a sausage that seems to have no equivalent anywhere else in the world – such as tenderloin, lean meat and tongue. And every region of Italy, from Lombardy and Tuscany to Veneto, Emilia Romagna and Campania, boasts its special sausages. Lastly, the gastronomic symbol that marks the arrival of the new year in Italy is the zampone from Modena, which has rightly become part of Italian culinary tradition.

CAPPELLO DEL PRETE EN CROÛTE

Prick the sausage, wrap it in foil and boil for 1½ hours. Meanwhile, cook the beet greens in salted, boiling water for about 15 minutes until tender. Drain and squeeze out as much liquid as possible, then combine with the butter, garlic and Parmesan. Drain the cappello del prete and skin. Preheat the oven to 400°F. Roll out the pastry on a lightly floured counter to a triangle large enough to enclose the cappello del prete. Sprinkle half the beet greens on the dough, place the cappello del prete on top and cover with the remaining beet greens. Lift the dough corners up and over to the middle to enclose. Place on a cookie sheet, brush with egg yolk and bake for 40 minutes until golden brown.

CAPPELLO DEL PRETE IN CROSTA

Serves 4

1 cappello del prete sausage
 ('priest's-hat' pork sausage)
1 pound 2 ounces beet greens
2 tablespoons butter
1 garlic clove, finely chopped
2 tablespoons Parmesan cheese, freshly grated
11 ounces puff pastry dough, thawed if frozen
all-purpose flour, for dusting
1 egg yolk, lightly beaten
salt

COTECHINO

COTECHINO

Serves 4

1 pound 5-ounce cotechino sausage

Prick the cotechino all over and wrap in foil so that it does not burst. Place in a large pan, add water to cover, bring just to a boil, then lower the heat and simmer gently for about 2 hours. Leave in the water for 10 minutes before draining and slicing. It is worth noting that most cotechini sold outside Italy are pre-cooked, so this preliminary step is not required for cotechino recipes. You may, however, need to heat the cotechino before adding it to other ingredients or before serving.

WRAPPED COTECHINO

COTECHINO ARROTOLATO

Serves 6

9 ounces spinach

¼ cup butter

1 garlic clove, crushed

⅔ cup Parmesan cheese, freshly grated

1½-pound veal round steak

1 pound 5-ounce cooked cotechino, skinned

3 tablespoons olive oil

1 fresh rosemary sprig, chopped

6 fresh sage leaves, chopped

¾ cup dry white wine

salt and pepper

Preheat the oven to 375°F. Cook the spinach, in just the water clinging to the leaves after washing, for about 5 minutes, then drain, squeeze out as much liquid as possible and chop. Mix the spinach with half the butter and the garlic and season with salt and pepper. Put the spinach on the veal, sprinkle with the Parmesan and put the cotechino in the center. Roll up and tie with kitchen string. Heat the oil and the remaining butter in a flame-proof casserole, add the rosemary and sage and cook for a few minutes, then add the meat and cook, turning frequently, until browned all over. Pour in the wine and cook until it has evaporated, then season with salt and pepper. Transfer to the oven and roast for about 1 hour. Remove from the oven, let stand for 10 minutes, untie and carve into slices.

COTECHINO WITH LENTILS

COTECHINO CON LENTICCHIE

Serves 4

1¾ cups lentils

1 onion, halved

2 celery stalks

2 tablespoons olive oil

1½ tablespoons butter

1 pound 5-ounce cooked cotechino, skinned, sliced and heated through

salt and pepper

Put the lentils, one onion-half and one of the celery stalks in a large pan, add cold water to cover and bring to a boil, then lower the heat and simmer for 45–50 minutes until the lentils are tender. Meanwhile, chop the remaining onion-half and celery. Heat the oil and butter in a pan, add the chopped onion and celery and cook over low heat, stirring occasionally, for 5 minutes. Drain the lentils, discard the onion and celery and add to the pan. Cook over low heat, stirring constantly. Season with salt and pepper to taste, transfer to a warm serving dish and arrange the cotechino on top.

COTECHINO CON SALSA DI FUNGHI

Serves 6

2 tablespoons olive oil

1 shallot, chopped

9½ cups mushrooms, thinly sliced

scant 1 cup heavy cream

12 white bread slices

melted butter, for brushing

5 tablespoons milk

1 pound 5-ounce cooked cotechino, skinned, sliced and heated through

salt and pepper

COTECHINO WITH MUSHROOM SAUCE

Preheat the oven to 400°F. Heat the oil in a pan, add the shallot and cook over low heat, stirring occasionally, for 5 minutes. Add the mushrooms and cream, season with salt and pepper and cook for 10–20 minutes until tender. Meanwhile, stamp out 12 rounds from the slices of bread, brush with melted butter, place on a cookie sheet and cook in the oven until golden brown. Bring the milk to simmering point in a small pan. Transfer the mushroom mixture to a food processor, add the hot milk and process until smooth. Put a slice of cotechino on each round of bread and pour the mushroom sauce over the rounds.

COTECHINO VESTITO

Serves 4

1 cup dried mushrooms

11-ounce lean veal

14-ounce cooked cotechino, skinned

1½ tablespoons butter

¼ onion, finely chopped

1 celery stalk, finely chopped

1 carrot, finely chopped

⅓ cup pancetta, finely chopped

COTECHINO IN A JACKET

Put the mushrooms in a bowl, add warm water to cover and let soak for 15–30 minutes, then drain and squeeze out. Pound the veal with a meat mallet until thin and even, place the cotechino on top and roll up, then tie with kitchen string. Melt the butter in a pan, add the onion, celery, carrot and pancetta and cook over low heat, stirring occasionally, for about 5 minutes. Add the meat, increase the heat to medium and cook, turning frequently, until browned all over. Pour in enough water to half cover, add the mushrooms and simmer for about 1 hour. Remove the meat from the pan, untie, carve and serve with the cooking juices.

SALSICCE ALLE DIECI ERBE

Serves 4

8 Italian sausages

fresh rosemary needles, chopped

fresh sage leaves, chopped

fresh basil leaves, chopped

fresh thyme leaves, chopped

fresh flat-leaf parsley, chopped

fresh marjoram leaves, chopped

fresh mint leaves, chopped

fresh tarragon leaves, chopped

celery stalk(s), chopped

shallot(s), chopped

scant ½ cup dry white wine

TEN-HERB SAUSAGES

The quantities of the various herbs, celery and shallot to use depend on individual taste, but it is best to go easy with the stronger ones, such as rosemary. Prick the sausages, put them in a pan with 2 tablespoons water and cook, turning occasionally, for about 10 minutes until golden brown. Add the herbs, celery and shallot(s) and cook for a few minutes more. Pour in the wine and cook until it has evaporated, then serve.

SAUSAGES IN TOMATO

SALSICCE AL POMODORO

Serves 4

8 Italian sausages

scant $1/2$ cup dry white wine

1 cup bottled strained tomatoes

salt and pepper

Prick the sausages with a fork, put them in a pan, add 2 tablespoons water and cook over low heat, turning occasionally, for 10 minutes until golden brown. Pour in the wine and cook until it has evaporated. Add the strained tomatoes and season with salt and pepper to taste. Cover and simmer for a further 15 minutes, then serve the sausages in the sauce.

SAUSAGES WITH CARROTS

SALSICCE CON CAROTE

Serves 4

3 tablespoons butter

8 carrots, cut into thin batons

1 pound 2 ounces Italian sausages, cut into pieces

salt and pepper

Melt 2 tablespoons of the butter in a pan, add the carrots and cook over low heat, stirring occasionally, for 10 minutes. Put the sausages in a pan, add 2–3 tablespoons water and cook, stirring frequently, for about 10 minutes until browned. Add the carrots and remaining butter, season with salt and pepper to taste, cook for a few minutes and serve.

SAUSAGES WITH LEEKS AU GRATIN

SALSICCE CON PORRI AL GRATIN

Serves 4

3 leeks, trimmed and thinly sliced

1 quantity Meat Stock (see page 208)

butter, for greasing

8 small Italian sausages

$2/3$ cup heavy cream

Put the leeks in a small pan and pour in stock to cover. bring to a boil, then lower the heat and simmer for about 15 minutes until tender. Drain and let cool. Preheat the oven to 400°F. Grease an ovenproof dish with butter. Prick the sausages and cook in a pan, turning frequently, until browned all over. Put the leeks in the prepared dish and place the sausages on top. Spoon the cream over them and bake until hot and bubbling.

SAUSAGES WITH POTATO TART

SALSICCE CON TORTA DI PATATE

Serves 4

6 potatoes, unpeeled

11 ounces Italian sausages

3 tablespoons olive oil

2 onions, thinly sliced

salt and pepper

Cook the potatoes in a pan of lightly salted, boiling water for 25–30 minutes until tender. Drain, peel and mash with a fork. Prick the sausages, put them in a pan, add 2 tablespoons water and cook, turning frequently, for about 10 minutes until browned all over. Heat the oil in another pan, add the onions and cook over low heat, stirring occasionally, for about 5 minutes. Add the mashed potato, season with salt and pepper and stir well. Using a spatula, shape the mixture into a 1-inch thick round. Cook over high heat until brown and crisp on the underside, then turn over and brown the second side. Turn out the potato tart onto a warm serving dish and surround with the hot sausages.

SAUSAGES AND TURNIPS

Put the sausages, rosemary and garlic in a pan and cook, turning frequently, until browned all over. Remove the sausages from the pan, add the turnips and cook, stirring and turning frequently, for 5 minutes. Season lightly with salt and pepper, cover the pan and cook for about 30 minutes. If the turnips seem a little watery towards the end of the cooking time, remove the lid and reduce the liquid. Add the sausages and cook for a few minutes more. Place on a warm serving dish.

SALSICCE E RAPE

Serves 4

14 ounces Italian sausages, cut into pieces

1 fresh rosemary sprig

1 garlic clove, chopped

1 pound 5 ounces turnips, sliced

salt and pepper

FRIED SAUSAGES

Prick the sausages, place them in a pan and cook over medium-high heat, turning frequently, until browned all over. Pour in the wine and cook until it has evaporated. These sausages are good served with a side dish of Savoy cabbage cut into strips and seasoned with oil flavored with a clove of garlic.

SALSICCE IN TEGAME

Serves 4

8 Italian sausages

scant 1 cup dry white wine

FRANKFURTERS WITH SAVOY CABBAGE

Heat the oil in a pan, add the cabbage, season with salt and pepper and cook over medium heat, stirring frequently, for 5 minutes. Lower the heat, cover and cook for 1 hour. Drizzle the cabbage with vinegar and stir, then remove from the pan and place on a warm serving dish. Meanwhile, cook the frankfurters in simmering water for 10 minutes, then drain. Place on the bed of Savoy cabbage and serve.

WÜRSTEL CON VERZA

Serves 4

5 tablespoons olive oil

1 Savoy cabbage, shredded

white wine vinegar, for drizzling

8 frankfurter sausages

salt and pepper

ZAMPONE

Prick the skin of the zampone with a large needle. Wrap in cheesecloth, place in a pan, add water to cover and bring to a boil. Lower the heat, cover and simmer gently for 3 hours. (The cooking time increases by about 30 minutes for each additional 1 pound 2 ounces). Let stand in the water for 10 minutes, then drain and slice. Zampone goes well with mashed potatoes or stewed lentils.

ZAMPONE

Serves 4–6

2¹/₄-pound zampone (stuffed pig's foot), soaked overnight in cold water and drained

VARIETY MEATS

Pâté de foie gras is one of the gastronomic symbols of France, home of culinary elegance. Its sophisticated flavor has raised the prestige of liver to its highest level. It is, in fact, one of the most highly prized members of the vast family of variety meats, which also includes heart, lights, kidney ('red variety meats'), brains, sweetbreads, bone marrow ('white variety meats'), tripe and tongue, as well as the head, pig's feet and tail. Kidney is the basic ingredient of some very tasty recipes. Heart and liver have a lot of recipes in common. Lights and pluck, among the least popular and most inexpensive kinds of variety meats are, nevertheless, an essential ingredient for some authentic soups. Brains, sweetbreads and bone marrow are delicious and delicate. Fresh, pickled or smoked tongue is used in a variety of tasty and fairly popular recipes. Calf's head is also part of the same family. Pig's feet, which involve laborious preparation, are the key ingredient of the famous tasty nervetti. Variety meats may not suit every cook's sensibilities, but it forms an essential part of Italian meat cookery and can provide many of the richest and most delicious flavors of this cuisine.

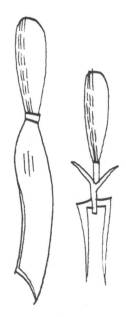

SWEETBREADS

Sweetbreads – almost always from calves, although lamb sweetbreads may also be available – are delicate and have a high nutritional value. The classic way to bring out their flavor is to fry them in butter. They are also delicious coated in bread crumbs and fried. They are highly recommended for thickening and softening stuffing and giving it a hint of sophistication.

QUANTITIES AND COOKING TIMES

→ Allow about 4 ounces per serving.

→ Soak the sweetbreads in plenty of cold water, changing it at least three or four times.

→ Parboil for 5–6 minutes in lightly salted, boiling water, drain and let cool.

→ Carefully remove all membrane, paying care not to damage the delicate texture.

ANIMELLE AL CRESCIONE

Serves 6

2 carrots

1 fresh flat-leaf parsley sprig

1 fresh thyme sprig

1³/₄ pounds sweetbreads, soaked and drained

5 tablespoons butter

1 onion, finely chopped

1 tablespoon all-purpose flour

scant ¹/₂ cup Madeira

1¹/₂ cups white wine

1 tablespoon heavy cream

1 bunch of watercress or young spinach

salt and pepper

SWEETBREADS WITH WATERCRESS

Put one of the carrots and the parsley and thyme into a pan, add about 4 cups water, bring to a boil and simmer for 30 minutes. Finely chop the remaining carrot. Remove the stock from the heat and let cool slightly, then add the sweetbreads and bring back to a boil. Lower the heat and simmer for 10 minutes, then drain and remove the membrane. Melt the butter in a pan, add the chopped carrot and the onion and cook over low heat, stirring occasionally, for 5 minutes. Add the sweetbreads and cook for a few minutes, then season with salt and pepper to taste. Stir in the flour, then stir in the Madeira and white wine and cook until evaporated. Add the cream and cook until thickened. Transfer the sweetbreads to a warm serving dish. Add the leaves and thinnest stems of the watercress to the pan and simmer for 10 minutes. Ladle the sauce into a food processor and process to a purée. Pour the sauce over the sweetbreads and serve.

SWEETBREADS AU GRATIN WITH PEAS

Parboil the sweetbreads in lightly salted, boiling water for 5–6 minutes, then drain, let cool slightly and remove the membrane. Melt 2 tablespoons of the butter in a pan, add the carrots and onions and cook over low heat, stirring occasionally, for 5 minutes. Add the thyme and season with salt and pepper. Add the sweetbreads to the pan, pour in the wine and $2/3$ cup water and cook for 5 minutes. Remove the sweetbreads from the pan, slice thinly and keep warm. Pass the cooking juices and vegetables through a food mill. Melt 4 tablespoons of the remaining butter in a skillet, stir in the flour and add the puréed cooking juices. Stir over low heat for about 10 minutes. Preheat the oven to 350°F. Grease an ovenproof dish with butter. Meanwhile, cook the peas in a pan with the remaining butter and 2 tablespoons warm water. In another pan combine the sauce made from the puréed cooking juices, the cream and the peas, season with salt and cook over medium heat until thickened. Place the sweetbreads in the prepared dish, spoon the pea sauce over them and sprinkle with the Parmesan. Bake for about 10 minutes until golden, then serve straight from the dish.

ANIMELLE AL GRATIN CON PISELLI

Serves 6

$1^1/2$ pounds sweetbreads, soaked and drained

$^1/2$ cup butter, plus extra for greasing

2 carrots, chopped

2 small onions, chopped

1 fresh thyme sprig

$^3/4$ cup dry white wine

$^1/3$ cup all-purpose flour

$2^1/4$ cups frozen peas

1 tablespoon heavy cream

$^1/3$ cup Parmesan cheese, freshly grated

salt and pepper

SWEETBREADS WITH CREAM AND MUSHROOMS

Lightly dust the sweetbreads with flour and gently shake off any excess. Melt 4 tablespoons of the butter in a pan, add the sweetbreads and cook, turning frequently, for about 10 minutes, then season with salt and pepper. Combine the cream and lemon juice in a bowl, pour the mixture over the sweetbreads, cover and cook over medium heat until thickened. Meanwhile, heat the remaining butter and the oil in another pan, add the mushrooms and cook over very low heat, stirring occasionally, for 20 minutes. Gently stir the mushrooms into the sweetbreads, season with salt and transfer to a warm serving dish.

ANIMELLE ALLA PANNA E FUNGHI

Serves 4

1 pound 2 ounces sweetbreads, soaked, drained and thinly sliced

all-purpose flour, for dusting

6 tablespoons butter

scant 1 cup heavy cream

juice of $^1/2$ lemon, strained

2 tablespoons olive oil

scant $4^1/2$ cups mushrooms, thinly sliced

salt and pepper

SWEETBREADS WITH MADEIRA

ANIMELLE AL MADERA

Serves 4

1 pound 5 ounces sweetbreads, soaked and drained

all-purpose flour, for dusting

3 tablespoons butter

³/₄ cup dry Madeira

salt and pepper

Parboil the sweetbreads in lightly salted water for 5–6 minutes, then drain and let cool slightly. Carefully remove the membrane with a small sharp knife, cut into even pieces and dust lightly with flour. Melt the butter in a pan, add the sweetbreads and cook over low heat, shaking the pan frequently, until golden brown. Season lightly with salt and pepper and cook for 10 minutes more. Pour in the Madeira, bring just to a boil and cook, stirring occasionally, until the cooking juices have thickened. Transfer to a warm serving dish.

SWEETBREADS IN WHITE WINE

ANIMELLE AL VINO BIANCO

Serves 4

1 pound 5 ounces sweetbreads, soaked and drained

all-purpose flour, for dusting

3 tablespoons butter

2 tablespoons olive oil

1 garlic clove

³/₄ cup dry white wine

1 fresh flat-leaf parsley sprig, chopped

salt

Parboil the sweetbreads in lightly salted water for 5–6 minutes, then drain and let cool slightly. Carefully remove the membrane and slice thinly. Dust lightly with flour. Heat the butter and oil in a pan, add the garlic and cook until browned, then remove and discard it. Add the sweetbreads and cook until browned on both sides. Pour in the wine, cook until it has evaporated, then lower the heat and cook for 10 minutes more. Season with salt to taste, sprinkle with the parsley and serve.

SWEETBREADS WITH GLOBE ARTICHOKES

ANIMELLE CON I CARCIOFI

Serves 4

juice of ¹/₂ lemon, strained

4 globe artichokes

¹/₄ cup butter

1 tablespoon olive oil

1 pound 2 ounces sweetbreads, soaked and drained

3¹/₂ ounces prosciutto, cut into strips

3¹/₄ cups dry white wine

salt and pepper

Half-fill a bowl with water and stir in the lemon juice. Break off the artichoke stems and remove the tough outer leaves and chokes. As each one is ready, place it in the acidulated water to prevent discoloration. Drain the artichokes, cut into wedges, then slice thinly. Heat 3 tablespoons of the butter and the olive oil in a pan, then add the artichokes and 5 tablespoons water and cook over low heat for about 30 minutes. Parboil the sweetbreads in lightly salted water for 5–6 minutes, then drain and let cool slightly. Carefully remove the membrane, then chop. Heat the remaining butter and the prosciutto in a skillet, add the sweetbreads, season lightly with salt and pepper and cook for 10 minutes. Add the cooked artichokes, sprinkle with the wine and cook until the liquid has evaporated. Transfer to a warm serving dish.

SWEETBREADS WITH JERUSALEM ARTICHOKES

Parboil the sweetbreads in lightly salted water for 5–6 minutes, then drain and let cool slightly. Carefully remove the membrane, then slice thinly. Melt the butter in a skillet, add the onion and cook over low heat, stirring occasionally, for about 10 minutes. Sprinkle with the Marsala and flour, season with salt and pepper and cook until the liquid has evaporated. Add the sweetbreads and cook for 10 minutes, adding the stock a ladleful at a time as it is absorbed. (You will not need it all.) Preheat the oven to 350°F. Generously grease an ovenproof dish with butter. Parboil the Jerusalem artichokes for 10 minutes, then drain and slice. Arrange them on the base of the prepared dish, sprinkle with the Parmesan, place the sweetbreads on top and spoon the cooking juices over them. Sprinkle with 5 tablespoons of the remaining stock and bake for 10 minutes. Serve straight from same dish.

ANIMELLE CON I TOPINAMBUR

Serves 4

1 pound 2 ounces sweetbreads, soaked and drained

¼ cup butter, plus extra for greasing

1 small onion, very finely chopped

scant ½ cup Marsala

1 tablespoon all-purpose flour

1 quantity Vegetable Stock (see page 209)

14 ounces Jerusalem artichokes

2 tablespoons Parmesan cheese, freshly grated

salt and pepper

SWEETBREADS IN BREAD CRUMBS

Parboil the sweetbreads in lightly salted water for 5–6 minutes, then drain and let cool slightly. Carefully remove the membrane, then slice thinly and dust with flour, shaking off any excess. Beat the egg with a pinch of salt in a shallow dish and spread out the bread crumbs in another shallow dish. Dip the sweetbreads first in the beaten egg, then in the bread crumbs. Melt the clarified butter in a skillet, add the sweetbreads and cook for 5–6 minutes until golden brown. Season with salt to taste, remove from the pan with a slotted spatula and drain on paper towels. Serve on a bed of Milanese risotto.

ANIMELLE IMPANATE

Serves 4

1 pound 5 ounces sweetbreads, soaked and drained

all-purpose flour, for dusting

1 egg

½ cup bread crumbs

¼ cup Clarified Butter (see page 88)

salt

Milanese Risotto (see page 330), to serve

BRAINS

Brains are delicate and have a high nutritional value. They should only be eaten when extremely fresh. They are mostly used in quick, simple dishes, for example cooked in butter or covered in bread crumbs and fried, or to soften and thicken meat and vegetable stuffings. Their flavor goes very well with the fragrance of truffles. In almost all recipes brains may be used interchangeably with sweetbreads. Outside Italy lamb's and sheep's brains are the most popular. Calf's and ox brains are also sometimes available. In some countries, brains can also be purchased frozen. Ox and calf's brains weigh 11–14 ounces, lamb's brains weigh about 4 ounces and sheep's brains about 5 ounces.

QUANTITIES AND COOKING TIMES

→ In general, allow about 5 ounces per serving.

→ Soak brains in warm water for 30 minutes. Remove the membrane and any traces of blood very gently with a small sharp knife.

→ Soak in cold water, which should be changed several times until the brains become white.

→ For recipes where the brains need pre-cooking, bring plenty of water to a boil with 1 tablespoon vinegar and the juice of half a lemon. Immerse ox brains and simmer for a few minutes. Calves' brains need a little less time. Drain and refresh under cold, running water.

→ To boil brains, first of all prepare a thick Vegetable Stock (see page 209), strain and let cool slightly. Immerse the brains in the stock, bring to a boil and cook over very low heat for about 10 minutes.

BRAINS WITH TOMATO SAUCE

Soak the brains in cold water for 10 minutes. Meanwhile, prepare the sauce. Combine the tomatoes, onion, garlic and basil in a bowl and blend for 2 minutes with a hand-held food processor. Stir in a dash of Tabasco, season with salt and pepper and set aside in a cool place. Drain the brains and cut into medium-sized cubes with a small sharp knife. Beat the egg with a pinch of salt in a shallow dish. Combine the cornstarch and lemon rind in another shallow dish and spread out the bread crumbs in a third. Dip the brains first in the egg, then in the cornstarch mixture and, finally, in the bread crumbs. Heat the oil and butter in a skillet, add the brains and cook over medium heat, turning once, for 4–5 minutes until golden brown. Season with salt, transfer to a warm serving dish and serve with the tomato sauce.

BOCCONCINI DI CERVELLA

Serves 4

1 pound 5 ounces lamb's brains, cleaned

1 egg • 3 tablespoons cornstarch

1 teaspoon grated lemon rind

2 tablespoons olive oil

1 cup bread crumbs • 2 tablespoons butter

salt

For the sauce

4 cherry tomatoes, peeled, seeded and chopped

1 onion, thinly sliced • 1 garlic clove

5–6 fresh basil leaves

dash of Tabasco sauce • salt and pepper

BRAINS WITH CAPERS

Preheat the oven to 350°F. Brush an ovenproof dish with olive oil. Put the brains in a pan, add water to cover, bring to a boil and cook for 1 minute. Drain, refresh under cold, running water and drain again. Cut in half and place in the prepared dish. Season with salt and pepper and sprinkle with the capers and olives. Sprinkle with the bread crumbs and drizzle the oil over them. Bake for about 20 minutes until golden brown and transfer to a warm serving dish.

CERVELLA AI CAPPERI

Serves 4

4 tablespoons olive oil, plus extra for brushing

1 pound 5 ounces brains, cleaned

1 tablespoon capers, drained and rinsed

10 black olives, pitted and sliced

$1/2$ cup fine bread crumbs

salt and pepper

BRAINS WITH BUTTER AND SAGE

Melt the butter in a skillet, add the sage and cook over low heat, stirring occasionally, for about 5 minutes. Add the brains and cook for about 10 minutes until golden brown on both sides. Season with salt and pepper to taste and arrange on a warm serving dish.

CERVELLA AL BURRO E SALVIA

Serves 4

3 tablespoons butter

8 fresh sage leaves

1 pound 5 ounces brains, cleaned and thinly sliced

salt and white pepper

BRAINS AU GRATIN

Preheat the oven to 350°F. Grease an ovenproof dish with butter and sprinkle with sea salt. Briefly blanch the brains in boiling water, then drain and slice. Place the brains in the prepared dish. Combine the bread crumbs and parsley and sprinkle the mixture over the brains. Dot with the butter and season with pepper. Bake for 15 minutes, then serve straight from the dish.

CERVELLA AL GRATIN

Serves 4

3 tablespoons butter, plus extra for greasing

1 pound 5 ounces brains, cleaned

4 tablespoons coarse bread crumbs

1 fresh flat-leaf parsley sprig, chopped

sea salt and white pepper

MILANESE-STYLE BRAINS

CERVELLA ALLA MILANESE

Serves 4

1 pound 5 ounces brains, cleaned and sliced

all-purpose flour, for dusting

2 eggs

1¹/₂ cups bread crumbs

7 tablespoons Clarified Butter (see page 88)

salt and pepper

lemon wedges, to garnish

Lightly dust the brains with flour. Beat the eggs with a pinch of salt in a shallow dish and spread out the bread crumbs in another shallow dish. Dip the brains first in the eggs and then in the bread crumbs to coat. Melt the clarified butter in a skillet over low heat, add the brains and cook until browned on both sides. Season with salt and pepper to taste. Remove with a slotted spatula and drain on paper towels. Place on a warm serving dish and garnish with wedges of lemon.

BRAINS AND BONE MARROW IN CURRY SAUCE

CERVELLA CON FILONI AL CURRY

Serves 4

11 ounces lamb's brains, cleaned

7 ounces calf's brains, cleaned

7 ounces bone marrow

1 onion, halved

1 carrot

1 celery stalk

¹/₄ cup butter, plus extra for greasing

3 tablespoons all-purpose flour

1 tablespoon curry powder

salt

Put the brains and bone marrow in a pan, add cold water to cover, one of the onion halves, the carrot and celery and season with salt. Bring to a boil, lower the heat and simmer for 20 minutes. Finely chop the remaining onion half. Melt the butter over low heat, add the chopped onion and cook for about 5 minutes. Sprinkle with the flour and stir in. Pour a ladleful of the brain cooking juices into a bowl, stir in the curry powder and pour the mixture into the pan with sauce. Cook over low heat, stirring frequently, for about 30 minutes. Preheat the oven to 350°F. Lightly grease an ovenproof dish. Drain and chop the meat, place in the prepared dish and pour the curry sauce over it. Bake for 10–15 minutes, then remove from the oven and let stand for 5 minutes. Serve straight from the dish.

BRAINS IN ANCHOVY SAUCE

CERVELLA IN SALSA DI ACCIUGHE

Serves 4

1 pound 5 ounces brains, cleaned • ¹/₂ onion

1 carrot • 1 celery stalk

1 fresh flat-leaf parsley sprig • salt

For the sauce

2 salted anchovies, heads removed, cleaned and filleted (see page 596), soaked in cold water for 10 minutes and drained • ¹/₄ cup butter

1 tablespoon capers, drained and rinsed

1 tablespoon fresh flat-leaf parsley, chopped

2 tablespoons white wine vinegar

salt and pepper

Put the brains in a pan, add cold water to cover, the onion, carrot, celery and parsley and season with salt. Bring to a boil, then lower the heat and simmer for 10–15 minutes. Drain, slice and place the brains on a warm serving dish. Set aside and keep warm. Make the sauce. Chop the anchovy fillets. Melt the butter in a skillet over low heat, add the parsley, capers and anchovies and mix well. Sprinkle with the vinegar and cook until it has evaporated, then season with salt and pepper to taste. Cook for 5 minutes more, then remove the pan from the heat, pour the sauce over the brains and serve.

BRAIN ROULADES WITH TRUFFLE

Blanch the brains briefly in boiling water, then drain and slice. Melt 2 tablespoons of the butter in a skillet, add the prosciutto, porcini and truffle and cook over low heat, stirring occasionally, for about 5 minutes. Season with salt and pepper and pour the mixture into the béchamel sauce. Cut the caul into eight or more squares and place two or more slices of brains and 1 tablespoon of the sauce mixture in the middle of each. Roll up and secure with toothpicks. Beat the egg with a pinch of salt in a shallow dish and spread out the bread crumbs in another shallow dish. Dip the roulades first in the egg and then in the bread crumbs. Melt the remaining butter in a skillet, add the roulades and cook, turning frequently, until browned all over. Remove with a slotted spatula and drain on paper towels. Place on a warm serving dish and garnish with lemon slices.

INVOLTINI DI CERVELLA AL TARTUFO

Serves 4

1 pound 5 ounces brains, cleaned

6 tablespoons butter

generous 1/2 cup prosciutto, diced

1 porcini, diced

1 small black truffle, diced

1 quantity Béchamel Sauce (see page 50)

1 pig's caul, soaked in warm water

for 3 minutes and drained

1 egg

1 1/2 cups fairly coarse bread crumbs

salt and pepper

lemon slices, to garnish

SMALL BRAIN MOLDS WITH HERBS

Heat the oil and butter in a pan, add the onion and cook over low heat, stirring occasionally, for 5 minutes. Stir in the herbs, add 2/3 cup water and simmer for 15 minutes. Add the brains, sprinkle with the lemon juice and season with salt and pepper. Simmer, uncovered, over low heat the until liquid has reduced Meanwhile, preheat the oven to 350°F. Grease four ramekins with butter. Remove the brains from the pan and chop. Beat the eggs with a pinch of salt, then stir them into the herb sauce. Divide the brains and sauce among the ramekins, place on a cookie sheet and bake for about 30 minutes or until a toothpick inserted into the molds comes out dry. Remove the molds from the oven, turn out in a ring on a warm serving dish and garnish with a few leaves of radicchio.

SFORMATINI ALLE ERBE

Serves 4

2 tablespoons olive oil

2 tablespoons butter, plus extra for greasing

1 onion, chopped

1 tablespoon chopped fresh chives

1 tablespoon chopped fresh tarragon

1 tablespoon fresh flat-leaf parsley, chopped

1 pound 5 ounces brains, cleaned

juice of 1/2 lemon, strained

5 eggs

salt and pepper

radicchio leaves, to garnish

OXTAIL

Oxtail is a very tasty, inexpensive cut of meat with lots of bone. It is particularly recommended for braising and stewing, and is an excellent ingredient in mixed boiled meat dishes. Calf's codino (literally: small tail) is something completely different. It is recommended for roasting and is a true cut of meat. It is called codino because it is the rump of the animal. Where fresh oxtail is difficult to obtain, frozen may be available.

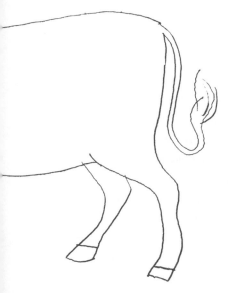

QUANTITIES AND COOKING TIMES

➜ Allow about 2¹/₄ pounds oxtail for four servings.

➜ Ask the butcher to cut the tail into fairly large pieces, then let soak in cold water for a few hours.

➜ To separate the meat from the bone more easily, it is useful to parboil the pieces for a few minutes in lightly salted water before following the recipe.

OXTAIL WITH PANCETTA

Soak the oxtail in three changes of cold water for a total of 2 hours, then drain and pat dry with paper towels. Heat the oil and butter in a pan, add the pancetta and cook, stirring occasionally, for 5 minutes. Add the oxtail and cook, turning frequently, until browned all over. Add the wine and cook until it has evaporated. Add the onion, carrots, celery and garlic and season with salt and pepper to taste. Stir and cook for a few minutes more, then add enough hot water to cover. Cover with a lid and simmer over medium heat for about 3 hours until the meat comes away from the bones and the cooking juices have thickened.

CODA DI MANZO ALLA PANCETTA

Serves 4

2¼ pounds oxtail, cut into pieces

2 tablespoons olive oil

2 tablespoons butter

scant ½ cup pancetta, chopped

¾ cup dry white wine

1 onion, finely chopped

2 carrots, finely chopped

1 celery stalk, finely chopped

1 garlic clove, finely chopped

salt and pepper

OXTAIL VACCINARA

Bring a large pan of salted water to a boil, add the oxtail, carrot, one of the onions and the bouquet garni and simmer for 1 hour. Chop the remaining onion. Heat the oil and pork fat in another pan, add the chopped onion and the garlic and cook until the garlic turns brown, then remove and discard it. Drain the oxtail, add it to the pan and cook, turning frequently, for a few minutes until browned all over. Pour in the wine and cook until it has evaporated. Season with salt and pepper, add the strained tomatoes, cover and simmer over medium heat for 1½ hours, adding a little stock if necessary. Stir in the celery and simmer gently for 10–15 minutes more until tender.

CODA DI MANZO ALLA VACCINARA

Serves 4

2¼ pounds oxtail, cut into pieces

1 carrot

2 onions

1 bouquet garni

4 tablespoons olive oil

2 ounces pork fat, pounded

1 garlic clove, lightly crushed

¾ cup dry white wine

3 cups bottled strained tomatoes

4 celery hearts, cut into batons

⅔–1¼ cups Meat Stock

(see page 208) (optional)

salt and pepper

ROASTING

COMMON
SQUARE PAN

PLUCK
AND LIGHTS

Lights refers only to the lungs, but the Italian expression coratella d'agnello and the somewhat archaic English term 'pluck' also include the heart, liver and other lamb variety meats. It is rarely, if ever, sold as pluck nowadays, outside Italy. This is a very tasty meat and suitable for a number of recipes.

QUANTITIES AND COOKING TIMES

→ Allow 5 ounces per serving.

→ The individual parts are normally used in this order: first the lungs, then the heart and other variety meats, and finally the liver, which cooks most rapidly.

TOMATO

Serves 4

¹/₄ cup butter

6 tablespoons olive oil

4 globe artichokes, cut into wedges

1 pound 2 ounces lights or pluck, chopped

salt and pepper

ROMAN LAMB'S LIGHTS

Heat half the butter and half the oil in a pan, add the artichokes and 2 tablespoons hot water and simmer for about 15 minutes until tender. Meanwhile, heat the remaining butter and oil in another pan, add the meat (in the order described above if using pluck) and cook until lightly browned all over and cooked through. Season with salt and pepper, add the meat to the artichokes and mix well. Cook for a few minutes more, then serve.

LIGHTS IN MARSALA

Lightly dust the meat with flour. Melt the clarified butter in a skillet, add the meat (in the order described opposite if using pluck) and cook over high heat until browned all over. Season with salt and pepper and remove the meat from the pan. Combine the flour and Marsala in a bowl, stir into the cooking juices and cook until reduced by half. Stir in the Worcestershire sauce and pour the mixture over the meat.

CORATELLA D'AGNELLO AL MARSALA

Serves 4

1 pound 5 ounces lights or pluck, sliced

1 tablespoon all-purpose flour, plus extra for dusting

5 tablespoons Clarified Butter (see page 88)

3/4 cup dry Marsala

dash of Worcestershire sauce

salt and pepper

GARDENER'S LIGHTS

Chop the lights. If using pluck, chop the lungs, heart, spleen and other variety meats and slice the liver. Combine the onion, carrot, garlic and parsley in a bowl. Heat the oil in a skillet, add the vegetable mixture and cook over low heat, stirring occasionally, for 5 minutes. Add the lights and cook for a few minutes, then, if using pluck, add all the other variety meats, except the liver, and cook for 3 minutes. Add the liver and cook for 2 minutes more. Season with salt and pepper to taste, stir in the lemon juice and serve.

CORATELLA D'AGNELLO DELL'ORTOLANO

Serves 4

1 pound 5 ounces lights or pluck

1 onion, finely chopped

1 carrot, finely chopped

1 garlic clove, finely chopped

1 fresh flat-leaf parsley sprig, chopped

3 tablespoons olive oil

juice of 1/2 lemon, strained

salt and pepper

FRIED LIGHTS

Dice the lights. If using pluck, dice the heart, spleen and other variety meats and slice the liver. Heat the oil and garlic in a skillet and cook until the garlic turns brown, then remove and discard it. Add the celery and carrots and cook for a few minutes. Add the lights, mix gently and cook for a few minutes, then add all the other variety meats except the liver and cook over medium heat for 3 minutes. Finally, add the liver, mix well and cook for 3–4 minutes more. Season with salt and pepper to taste, stir in the vinegar and cook until it has evaporated. Sprinkle with the thyme and serve.

CORATELLA D'AGNELLO IN TEGAME

Serves 4

1 pound 5 ounces lights or pluck

3 tablespoons olive oil

1 garlic clove

1 celery stalk, chopped

2 carrots, chopped

1/4 cup apple vinegar

2 fresh thyme sprigs, chopped

salt and pepper

859

HEART

Ox or calf's heart may be considered an excellent and economical alternative to other meat, as its nutritional value is equal to that of lean veal. However, owing to its tougher muscle fibres, it is more difficult to digest. A calf's heart weighs 1³/₄–2¹/₄ pounds. An ox heart may even reach 4¹/₂ pounds. When choosing, make sure the meat is elastic and the color bright. Heart is prepared by slicing, then removing any lumps together with the larger nodes with arteries and veins.

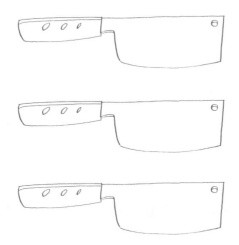

**QUANTITIES
AND COOKING TIMES**

→ Allow about 5–7 ounces per serving.

→ Broil ¹/₂-inch thick slices for 2 minutes on each side.

→ Allow no longer than 10 minutes in a skillet, turning halfway through the cooking time.

HEART KABOBS

Put the heart in a bowl. Combine the oil, lemon juice, wine, oregano and a pinch of pepper, pour the mixture over the meat and let marinate for 3 hours. Preheat the broiler. Drain the meat, reserving the marinade, and thread onto skewers, alternating with the bell pepper and onion slices. Brush with the reserved marinade and broil under medium-high heat, turning frequently, for 4 minutes. Season with salt and pepper and serve.

CUBETTI DI CUORE ALLO SPIEDO
Serves 4
1³/₄ pounds heart, cut into cubes
2 tablespoons olive oil • juice of 1 lemon, strained
³/₄ cup dry white wine
generous pinch of dried oregano
2 red bell peppers, halved, seeded and cut into thick slices
1 onion, sliced • salt and pepper

HEART WITH HERBS

Reserve 2 tablespoons of the olive oil and mix the remainder with the lemon juice in a dish. Add the heart and let marinate for 1 hour. Drain the heart and lard with the strips of pancetta. Heat the reserved oil and the butter in a skillet, add the onion and garlic and cook over low heat, stirring occasionally, for 5 minutes. Lightly dust the heart with flour, add to the skillet and cook for 2 minutes. Pour in the wine and cook until it has evaporated. Season with salt and pepper to taste and add the herbs. Add the stock or water, cover and simmer for 25 minutes. Slice the heart and serve in its gravy.

CUORE AGLI AROMI
Serves 4
³/₄ cup olive oil
juice of 1 lemon, strained
1³/₄ pounds heart, halved and cleaned
2 ounces pancetta, cut into strips • 2 tablespoons butter
1 onion, chopped • 1 garlic clove, crushed
all-purpose flour, for dusting
³/₄ cup dry white wine
1 fresh flat-leaf parsley sprig, chopped
4 fresh sage leaves, chopped
4 fresh basil leaves, chopped
²/₃ cup hot Meat Stock (see page 208) or water
salt and pepper

BROILED HEART

Preheat the broiler. Melt the butter with a little salt in a double boiler and brush on both sides of the slices of heart, then dip the slices in the bread crumbs. Place the bacon on the broiler rack and put a slice of heart on each. Broil for 2 minutes on each side. Transfer to a warm serving dish and serve with mashed potatoes.

CUORE ALLA GRIGLIA
Serves 4
¹/₄ cup butter
1³/₄ pounds heart, cut into ¹/₂-inch slices
1¹/₂ cups fine bread crumbs
3¹/₂ ounces bacon slices, halved
salt
mashed potatoes, to serve

HEART WITH ANCHOVIES

Heat the butter and olive oil in a skillet, add the heart and cook, turning frequently, for 5 minutes. Add the anchovies and cook until they have disintegrated. Sprinkle with the parsley and serve.

CUORE ALLE ACCIUGHE
Serves 4
2 tablespoons butter
2 tablespoons olive oil • 1³/₄ pounds heart, sliced
5 canned anchovy fillets in oil, drained and chopped
1 tablespoon fresh flat-leaf parsley, chopped

LIVER

Calf's liver is delicate and flavorsome, whereas ox liver is less tender. Both contain quite a bit of fat. The most valuable liver from the dietary point of view is pig's liver, followed by lamb's, ox, calf's and chicken's. Pâtés, terrines and numerous pies owe their distinctive flavor to liver.

QUANTITIES AND COOKING TIMES

→ Allow about 5 ounces per person.

→ Liver should be eaten extremely fresh and, like all variety meats, it needs careful rinsing in cold water.

→ Fresh liver is a brownish-red color. When it is not fresh it has tints of purple and a limp consistency.

→ Remove the membrane and any sinewy parts. Liver should be cooked for a few minutes over high heat and turned frequently.

→ Pig's liver takes longer to cook and is nearly always prepared by cutting it into small pieces and wrapping it in white caul fat.

→ Salt should be added after cooking, otherwise liver becomes tough.

FEGATELLI NELLA RETE

Serves 4

1 pig's caul

12–24 bay leaves

1 pound 5 ounces pig's liver, cut into large cubes

¼ cup lard or 4 tablespoons olive oil

salt and pepper

PIG'S LIVER IN A NET

Soak the caul in warm water for 3 minutes, then drain and cut into large squares. Place a bay leaf in the middle of each square with a cube of liver on top. Wrap the caul into a packet and secure with a toothpick. Melt the lard or heat the oil in a skillet, add the packets and cook, turning frequently, for a few minutes. Season with salt and pepper and stir. Transfer to a warm serving dish.

LIVER WITH SHALLOTS

Dust the liver with flour. Heat 2 tablespoons of the butter and the oil in a skillet, add the liver and cook for 2 minutes on each side. Season with salt and pepper. Transfer the liver to a serving dish and keep warm. Add the shallots to the skillet and cook over low heat, stirring occasionally, for about 10 minutes. Pour in the wine and cook until reduced by half. Add the remaining butter and remove the skillet from the heat. Pour the sauce over the liver and serve.

FEGATO AGLI SCALOGNI

Serves 4

1 pound 5 ounces liver, sliced

all-purpose flour for dusting

3 tablespoons butter

2 tablespoons olive oil

4 shallots, sliced

3/4 cup dry white wine

salt and pepper

LIVER WITH BUTTER AND SAGE

Beat the eggs with a pinch of salt in a shallow dish, add the liver and leave for a few minutes. Melt the butter over low heat with the garlic and sage in a skillet until they turn brown, then remove and discard. Drain the liver, add to the pan, increase the heat to medium and cook for 2 minutes on each side, then lower the heat cook for a few minutes more, turning frequently, until cooked through. Season with salt and pepper to taste and serve.

FEGATO AL BURRO E SALVIA

Serves 4

2 eggs

1 pound 5 ounces liver, sliced

1/4 cup butter

1 garlic clove

5—6 fresh sage leaves

salt and pepper

VENETO—STYLE LIVER

Heat the oil in a skillet, add the onions and cook over low heat, stirring occasionally, for about 10 minutes until lightly browned. Add the wine, increase the heat to high and cook until it has evaporated. Stir in the parsley and add the liver. Cook, turning frequently, for 4—5 minutes. Season with salt and pepper to taste and transfer to a warm serving dish.

FEGATO ALLA VENETA

Serves 4

4—5 tablespoons olive oil

9 ounces onions, thinly sliced

3/4 cup dry white wine

1 tablespoon fresh flat-leaf parsley, chopped

1 pound 2 ounces liver, sliced

salt and pepper

LIVER WITH LEMON

Lightly dust the liver with flour and shake off the excess. Heat the butter and oil in a skillet over low heat, add the liver, increase the heat to high and cook, turning frequently, for a few minutes until cooked through. Season lightly with salt and pepper and cook for a few minutes more. Transfer the liver to a serving dish and keep warm. Stir the lemon juice into the skillet and heat. Stir in the parsley, then pour the sauce over the liver and serve.

FEGATO AL LIMONE

Serves 4

1 pound 5 ounces liver, sliced

all-purpose flour, for dusting

2 tablespoons butter

2 tablespoons olive oil

juice of 1 lemon, strained

1 tablespoon fresh flat-leaf parsley, chopped

salt and pepper

LIVER UCCELLETTO

FEGATO ALL'UCCELLETTO

Serves 4

3 ounces prosciutto, sliced
1 pound 2 ounces liver, thinly sliced
8 fresh sage leaves • $^1/_3$ cup pancetta, diced
8 bread slices, crusts removed, cubed
2 tablespoons olive oil
2 tablespoons butter • salt and pepper

Put a small slice of prosciutto on each slice of liver and roll up. Thread the roulades onto long wooden or metal skewers, alternating with the sage leaves, pancetta and slices of bread. Heat the oil and butter in a skillet, add the kebobs and cook over high heat, turning frequently, for 5 minutes. Season lightly with salt and pepper and serve immediately.

LIVER IN MERLOT

FEGATO AL MERLOT

Serves 4

1 pound 5 ounces liver, thinly sliced
all-purpose flour, for dusting
$^1/_4$ cup butter
$^3/_4$ cup Merlot wine
salt and pepper

Lightly dust the liver with flour and shake off any excess. Melt the butter in a skillet over low heat, add the liver and cook for 2 minutes on each side. Add 1 tablespoon hot water and the wine, increase the heat to high and cook for 5 minutes or until the wine has evaporated. Season and transfer to a warm serving dish. This liver is traditionally served with fried polenta.

LIVER WITH GLOBE ARTICHOKES

FEGATO CON CARCIOFI

Serves 4

juice of 1 lemon, strained
4 globe artichokes stems,
outer leaves and chokes removed
7 tablespoons olive oil
1 pound 5 ounces liver, sliced
salt and pepper

Half-fill a bowl with water and stir in half the lemon juice. Cut the artichokes in half and add to the acidulated water as soon as each one is prepared to prevent discoloration. Drain and slice thinly. Heat 4 tablespoons of the oil in a pan, add the artichokes and cook over low heat for 20 minutes. Add 1 tablespoon hot water if necessary and season lightly with salt. Heat the remaining oil in a skillet, add the liver and cook for 2 minutes on each side, then sprinkle with the remaining lemon juice. Season with salt and pepper, stir well, then transfer to the pan of artichokes. Spoon the mixture onto a warm serving dish.

SWEET–AND–SOUR LIVER

FEGATO IN AGRODOLCE

Serves 4

scant 1 cup golden raisins, soaked in warm water
2 tablespoons butter
2 tablespoons olive oil
1 pound 5 ounces pig's liver, sliced
1 tablespoon all-purpose flour
1 tablespoon white wine vinegar
salt and pepper

Heat the butter and oil in a skillet, add the liver and cook, turning frequently, for a few minutes until tender. Season lightly with salt and pepper, then transfer to a serving dish and keep warm. Drain and squeeze out the golden raisins, dust with the flour and sprinkle into the skillet. Season lightly with salt and cook for 3 minutes, then stir well. Add the vinegar and 1 tablespoon cold water, season with pepper, increase the heat to high and cook until the liquid has evaporated. Simmer for a further 3 minutes, then pour the sauce over the liver and serve.

TONGUE

The most delicate tongue, as it is the smallest and most tender, is calf's tongue. Ox tongue is larger and heavier, and needs longer cooking which decreases its nutritional value. It also has a more powerful flavor. Tongue is delicious boiled, braised or pickled.

→ Allow about 2¼ pounds for 4 servings.

→ Both calf's and ox tongue are available whole or already cleaned.

→ Before cooking, soak the tongue in cold water for several hours, changing the water a number of times.

→ A calf's tongue weighs about 1 pound 2 ounces and cooks in 1–1½ hours. An ox tongue may weigh up to 4½ pounds and cooks in 3–3½ hours. A pig's tongue weighs 11–14 ounces and cooks in about 35 minutes.

→ To boil tongue, immerse it in cold, salted water with an onion, celery stalk, carrot and a few cloves. When cooked, drain and skin. Tongue should always be served with spicy sauces.

→ When the cooking liquid is to be used later as stock, parboil the tongue for 15 minutes, skin it and then return it to the pan and continue to cook it as normal.

→ Tongue should be sliced diagonally into very thin slices.

→ Preparing smoked tongue requires a lot of skill, so it is best to buy it ready smoked from a butcher or a delicatessen. It is delicious sliced and served with liver pâté and aspic.

QUANTITIES AND COOKING TIMES

BOILED SMOKED TONGUE

Fill a large pan with cold water, add the tongue, carrot, celery, onion and a pinch of salt and bring to a boil. Lower the heat and simmer for about 3 hours, depending on the thickness of the tongue. Drain the tongue, skin and slice. Serve with a selection of spicy sauces (see pages 64 to 76) or with mashed potatoes flavored with 2 tablespoons Parmesan cheese, freshly grated.

LINGUA AFFUMICATA E LESSATA

Serves 4

½ smoked tongue, soaked overnight
in cold water and drained

1 carrot

1 celery stalk

1 onion

salt

TONGUE WITH GREEN OLIVES

LINGUA ALLE OLIVE VERDI

Serves 4

1 tongue, soaked overnight in cold water and drained

2 tablespoons butter

1 tablespoon olive oil

1 onion, finely chopped

1 carrot, finely chopped

1 celery stalk, finely chopped

20 pitted green olives

salt and pepper

Cook the tongue in salted, boiling water for 20 minutes, then drain and skin without letting it cool. Heat the butter and oil in a skillet, add the onion, carrot and celery and cook over low heat, stirring occasionally, for 5 minutes. Meanwhile, coarsely chop 10 of the olives. Stir the chopped olives into the skillet, add the tongue, pour in $^2/_3$ cup warm water and simmer until the tongue is tender. Season with salt and pepper to taste, stir in the remaining olives, mix and cook for 3–4 minutes more. Slice the tongue, place on a warm serving dish and spoon the sauce over it.

BRAISED TONGUE

LINGUA BRASATA

Serves 4

1 tongue, soaked overnight in cold water and drained

3 tablespoons butter

3 tablespoons olive oil

2 onions, thinly sliced

3 carrots, sliced

$^3/_4$ cup dry white wine

9 ounces canned tomatoes

salt and pepper

Parboil the tongue in salted, boiling water for 20 minutes, then drain and skin. Meanwhile, heat the butter and oil in a pan, add the onions and carrots and cook over low heat, stirring occasionally, for 5 minutes. Add the tongue, cover and cook for 30 minutes. Pour in the wine and cook until it has evaporated, then season with salt and pepper to taste and cook for 2 minutes more. Mash the tomatoes with their can juices in a bowl, add to the pan, cover and simmer for about $1^1/_2$ hours until the tongue is tender. Remove the tongue from the pan. Ladle the cooking juices into a food processor and process to a purée. Reheat the purée for a few minutes. Slice the tongue, place on a warm serving dish and spoon the hot purée over it.

TONGUE IN TARTARE SAUCE

LINGUA IN SALSA TARTARA

Serves 4

1 pound 5 ounces tongue

$^3/_4$ cup white wine vinegar

1 garlic clove • salt and pepper

1 quantity Tartare Sauce (see page 73)

Prepare and boil the tongue as described on page 865. Drain, skin and cut into strips. Combine the vinegar and garlic in a dish, season with salt and pepper, add the tongue and let marinate for 4–5 hours. Just before serving, drain the tongue strips, place on a serving dish and spoon the tartare sauce over them.

SPICY TONGUE

LINGUA PICCANTE

Serves 4

3–4 tablespoons Dijon mustard

8 boiled tongue slices

$1^1/_2$ cups bread crumbs

3 tablespoons Clarified Butter (see page 88)

salt and pepper

Mix the mustard with a pinch of pepper in a bowl and spread the mixture on both sides of the tongue slices. Cover with the bread crumbs, pressing them in place with the palms of your hands. Melt the clarified butter in a skillet, add the slices of tongue and cook until golden brown on both sides. Season lightly with salt and pepper, remove with a slotted spatula and drain on paper towels.

KIDNEYS

Kidneys are highly regarded as ingredients in sophisticated European cuisine. They have a high nutritional value and contain some fat. It is advisable to buy lamb's or calf's kidneys as they have a more delicate and pleasant taste than ox or pig's kidneys, which are much tougher and have a decidedly stronger flavor.

→ Allow about 5 ounces per serving.

→ Kidneys should be eaten extremely fresh and must not be kept in the refrigerator for more than 24 hours.

→ If kidneys are not bought already cleaned, halve them vertically, wash carefully under cold, running water, skin with a small sharp knife and remove the inner white spongy core.

→ To reduce the strong flavor of ox kidneys, slice them and let soak in cold water with a little added lemon juice or vinegar.

→ To prevent kidneys from becoming tough during cooking, which in any case should take only a few minutes, chop or cut them into fairly thick slices.

→ Many chefs suggest pre-cooking before use. This consists of quickly sautéing sliced kidneys in a pan lightly brushed with oil, then leaving them to drain in a strainer for about 30 minutes.

→ Kidneys may be broiled, fried in butter and flambéed in brandy, or trifolato (sliced and fried with garlic and parsley).

QUANTITIES
AND COOKING TIMES

KIDNEYS WITH MUSTARD

ROGNONE ALLA SENAPE

Serves 4

¹/₄ cup butter

1 tablespoon olive oil

2 kidneys, cleaned and cored

³/₄ cup heavy cream

2 tablespoons Dijon mustard

salt and pepper

Heat the butter with the oil in a skillet, add the kidneys and cook over high heat for 4 minutes. Season with salt and pepper, remove from the skillet and keep warm. Combine the cream and mustard, stir into the cooking juices and cook until heated through. Thinly slice the kidneys, place on a warm serving dish and pour the sauce over them.

KIDNEYS IN MADEIRA

ROGNONE AL MADERA

Serves 4

¹/₄ cup butter

1¹/₂ teaspoons olive oil

2 kidneys, cleaned, cored and sliced

2 tablespoons all-purpose flour

2 tablespoons Madeira

salt and pepper

Melt 3 tablespoons of the butter with the oil in a skillet, add the kidneys and cook over high heat for 4 minutes. Season with salt and pepper, remove from the skillet, place on a warm serving dish and keep warm. Combine the remaining butter and the flour to make a paste — beurre manié. Stir 1 tablespoon hot water into the cooking juices, pour in the Madeira and heat gently. Gradually stir in the beurre manié (see page 88), small pieces at a time. As soon as the sauce has thickened, pour it over the kidneys.

KIDNEYS IN BORDEAUX

ROGNONE AL VINO DI BORDEAUX

Serves 6

3 kidneys, cleaned, cored and sliced

2 shallots, chopped

1¹/₂ teaspoons all-purpose flour

³/₄ cup red Bordeaux wine

³/₄ cup Meat Stock (see page 208)

2 ounces bone marrow, chopped

¹/₃ cup smoked pancetta, diced

scant 1 cup mushrooms, thinly sliced

salt and pepper

Heat a nonstick skillet, add the kidneys and cook for a few minutes. Remove from the skillet and keep warm. Add the shallots to the skillet and cook for about 5 minutes until soft. Sprinkle with the flour and mix well. Pour in the wine and stock and cook until the liquid has reduced. Season with salt and pepper, add the marrow and melt over low heat. Whisk the sauce gently. Cook the pancetta in another non-stick pan for about 5 minutes, then add the mushrooms and cook for 5 minutes more. Stir the mushroom mixture into the pan of shallots, add the kidneys, heat through for a few minutes and serve.

KIDNEYS WITH RAW SCALLIONS

Season the kidneys with salt and pepper. Heat the oil in a skillet, add the kidneys and stir gently with a wooden spoon, then add the shallot. When the kidneys are pink in color, add the cream and bring to a boil over low heat, stirring constantly. Remove the skillet from the heat, add the scallions and serve.

ROGNONE CON CIPOLLINE CRUDE

Serves 4

2 kidneys, cleaned, cored and thinly sliced diagonally

2 tablespoons olive oil

1 shallot, finely chopped

1 cup heavy cream

4 scallions, thinly sliced

salt and pepper

KIDNEYS, SAUSAGE AND MUSHROOMS

Put the mushrooms in a bowl, add warm water to cover and let soak for 2 hours. Cook the sausages in a pan with the wine for about 10 minutes until tender. Heat the oil in a skillet, add the garlic and cook over high heat until browned, then remove and discard it. Add the butter and when it has melted, add the kidneys and cook for 1 minute. Add the tomatoes, mash carefully and stir. Drain the mushrooms, reserving 1 tablespoon of the soaking liquid, and squeeze out. Add the mushrooms, reserved soaking liquid and stock to the skillet and simmer for 5 minutes. Drain the sausages, add to the skillet and cook for 15 minutes. Season with salt and pepper to taste and serve with mashed potatoes.

ROGNONE CON SALSICCIA E FUNGHI

Serves 4

1/3 cup dried mushrooms,

14 ounces Italian sausages, chopped

5 tablespoons dry white wine

2 tablespoons olive oil

1 garlic clove

1 1/2 tablespoons butter

2 kidneys, cleaned, cored and sliced

4 canned tomatoes

5 tablespoons Meat Stock (see page 208)

salt and pepper

mashed potato, to serve

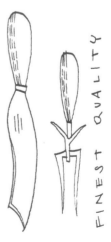

FINEST QUALITY

CALF'S HEAD

Although tasty, calf's head is not to everyone's taste. More than anything else, the thought of it is rejected both by those who have to cook it and those who are not 'brave enough' to eat it and therefore do not know what it tastes like. Nevertheless, calf's head is still an important ingredient in the Italian traditional dish of mixed boiled meats, albeit less frequently than in the past. It should not be used to make stock. Calf's head is normally bought from the butcher already boned and rolled. If bought whole, the following preparation, which takes some time, is necessary – singe, wash, soak in cold water for a few hours and parboil. A calf's head generally weighs around 11 pounds.

QUANTITIES AND COOKING TIMES

→ Allow about 5 ounces per serving.

→ A calf's head should be cooked on its own and not with other meat. It takes about 1½ hours if whole and 1¼ hours if boned. Add a pinch of salt to the water, and an onion, celery stalk and carrot or herbs, according to taste.

→ To keep the meat white, it is advisable to add a little lemon juice and 1–2 tablespoons all-purpose flour to the cooking water, and then stir quickly to prevent lumps from forming.

→ To check to see if the calf's head is cooked, prick with a fork. It is ready when it is no longer gelatinous.

→ Once drained, the calf's head should be left to cool, then chopped into small pieces. Discard the cooking liquid.

→ Calf's head may be eaten both hot and cold, together with spicy sauces – green sauce (see page 74) is particularly recommended.

BOILED CALF'S HEAD

Wash the calf's head, singe and let soak in cold water for a few hours. Pour 8³/₄ cups water into a large pan and bring to a boil. Stir the flour into a little water in a bowl and pour the mixture into the pan and stir well. Add the onion, carrot, celery, lemon juice, thyme, bay leaf, peppercorns and a generous pinch of salt. Simmer gently for 15 minutes, making sure the liquid does not boil over. Drain the calf's head, add to the pan, cover and simmer for about 2 hours. Check to see whether it is ready by pricking it with a fork. It should be tender but not jelly-like. Drain well, carve into thin slices and serve with two or three fairly spicy sauces.

TESTINA DI VITELLO BOLLITA

Serves 4

1 pound 5 ounces boned calf's head

2 tablespoons all-purpose flour

1 onion

1 carrot

1 celery stalk, chopped

juice of 1 lemon, strained

1 fresh thyme sprig

1 bay leaf

6 black peppercorns

salt and pepper

FRIED CALF'S HEAD

Bring a large pan of salted water to a boil with the onion, carrot and celery. Add the calf's head and simmer for 1¹/₂ hours. Drain, place a weight on top and let cool, then carve into slices. Beat 4 tablespoons of the oil with the lemon juice and a pinch each of salt and pepper in a dish, add the slices of calf's head and let marinate for 1 hour. Beat the eggs in a shallow dish and spread out the bread crumbs in another shallow dish. Drain the meat and dust lightly with flour. Dip in the beaten eggs and then in the bread crumbs. Heat the remaining oil in a skillet, add the meat and cook over medium heat, turning occasionally, until golden brown on both sides. Remove with a slotted spatula, drain on paper towels and serve.

TESTINA DI VITELLO FRITTA

Serves 4

1 onion

1 carrot

1 celery stalk

1 pound 5 ounces boned calf's head

¹/₂ cup olive oil

juice of 1 lemon, strained

2 eggs

1¹/₂ cups bread crumbs

all-purpose flour, for dusting

salt and pepper

CALF'S HEAD SALAD

Boil the calf's head as described above. Drain, let cool, then cut into strips. Line a salad bowl with lettuce leaves. Place the strips of calf's head in another bowl with the tuna, anchovy fillets and celery. Drizzle with olive oil, season with salt and pepper, transfer to the salad bowl and serve.

TESTINA DI VITELLO IN INSALATA

Serves 4

14 ounces boned calf's head

1 lettuce

5 ounces canned tuna, drained and flaked

10 canned anchovy fillets in oil, drained and chopped

1 celery heart, sliced

olive oil, for drizzling

salt and pepper

TRIPE

Tripe was always considered an excellent 'blue-collar' dish, but it is also enjoyed by those with sophisticated palates, although it has gone out of favor outside Italy and may be difficult to obtain. Italians serve tripe as a first course but it may be served as a main course, especially in the winter. Tripe may be ox or calf's, the latter being more tender and quicker to cook. It is divided into various types including plain and honeycomb, which is considered the best by connoisseurs.

QUANTITIES AND COOKING TIMES

→ Allow about 5 ounces per serving.

→ Rinse several times in cold water and then cut into thin strips.

→ If tripe is to be cooked the day after purchase, store it covered with water in the refrigerator.

→ Tripe does not have a particularly strong flavor, so choose a rich sauce and add vegetables and herbs when cooking.

→ The longer tripe cooks, the more flavor it has.

TRIPPA AI FUNGHI

Serves 4

¹/₄ cup dried mushrooms

6 tablespoons butter

2 tablespoons olive oil

1 onion, chopped

1 carrot, chopped

1 celery stalk, chopped

1¹/₂ pounds tripe, soaked, drained and cut into strips

1 pound 2 ounces tomatoes, peeled, seeded and diced

1 quantity Meat Stock (see page 208)

¹/₂ cup Parmesan cheese, freshly grated

salt and pepper

TRIPE WITH MUSHROOMS

Place the mushrooms in a bowl, add warm water to cover and let soak for 15–30 minutes, then drain and squeeze out. Heat half the butter and the oil in a pan, add the onion, carrot and celery and cook over medium heat, stirring occasionally, for 5 minutes. Add the mushrooms and cook for 5 minutes, then add the tripe and season with salt and pepper. Add the tomatoes and pour in just enough stock to cover. Bring to a boil, lower the heat, cover and simmer for 3 hours. Remove the pan from the heat, stir in the remaining butter and sprinkle with the Parmesan.

MILANESE–STYLE TRIPE

Heat 2 tablespoons of the butter and the oil in a pan, add the pancetta and cook over low heat, stirring occasionally, for 5 minutes. Add the onion and cook, stirring occasionally, for 5 minutes more, then add the tripe. Cook for about 15 minutes, then add the carrot, celery, tomatoes and eight of the sage leaves and season with salt and plenty of pepper. Cook for 10 minutes, then pour in the hot stock a little at a time. Bring to a boil and simmer for 3 hours or until the tripe is tender. Meanwhile, cook the beans separately in a large pan of boiling water with the remaining sage leaves and the garlic for about 3 hours until tender. Drain the beans, discarding the sage and garlic, and add to the tripe. Sprinkle with the Parmesan and serve.

TRIPPA ALLA MILANESE

Serves 6

6 tablespoons butter
2 tablespoons olive oil
scant 1 cup pancetta, chopped
1 onion, chopped
2¼ pounds tripe, soaked, drained and cut into strips
1 carrot, chopped
1 celery stalk, chopped
1 pound 2 ounces tomatoes,
peeled, seeded and diced
20 fresh sage leaves
4 cups hot Meat Stock (see page 208)
½ cup dried white beans,
soaked overnight and drained • 1 garlic clove
⅔ cup Parmesan cheese, freshly grated
salt and pepper

TRIPE WITH HERBS

Put the tripe in a large pan, add water to cover, the bouquet garni and one onion stuck with the cloves, and season with salt and pepper. Bring to a boil, then lower the heat and simmer for 1 hour. Meanwhile, thinly slice the remaining onions. Heat the olive oil in a pan, add the sliced onions, tomatoes and garlic and season with salt and pepper. Simmer gently, uncovered, for 15 minutes. Drain the tripe, cut into strips and stir it into the pan. Add the wine and simmer over low heat for 1 hour. Season with salt and pepper to taste, cover and simmer for 30 minutes more. Remove the pan from the heat, sprinkle with the parsley and serve.

TRIPPA AROMATICA

Serves 6

2¼ pounds tripe, soaked and drained
1 bouquet garni
3 onions
2 cloves
4 tablespoons olive oil
2¼ pounds tomatoes, peeled, seeded and diced
3 garlic cloves, unpeeled
¾ cup dry white wine
2 tablespoons fresh flat-leaf parsley, chopped
salt and pepper

SIMPLE TRIPE

Melt the butter in a pan, add the onion and cook over low heat, stirring occasionally, for 5 minutes. Add the tripe, cover and cook, occasionally adding a ladleful of the stock, for 3 hours or until tender. Season with salt and pepper, sprinkle with the Parmesan and serve.

TRIPPA IN BIANCO

Serves 4

scant ½ cup butter
1 onion, chopped
1½ pounds tripe, soaked, drained and cut into strips
1 quantity hot Meat Stock (see page 208)
generous 1 cup Parmesan cheese, freshly grated
salt and pepper

ROASTING

FORK

BEST WISHES

POULTRY →

POULTRY

The term poultry covers all domesticated birds bred and reared for eating. Even though some Italian breeders specify the birds are 'free-range', chickens, turkeys and geese are no longer free to scratch about in barnyards at will. Despite their often cramped conditions, Italian poultry farms are considered to offer birds a quality of life above average and the same is said for the flavor of the meat. That said, there is an increasing movement in some countries to raise free-range and organic birds, a trend that is widely supported by consumers. Poultry fit into two groups – white meat, such as chickens and turkeys, and red meat, such as ducks, guinea fowl and squab. Chicken is the most popular type of poultry as it is relatively inexpensive and can be prepared in an almost infinite number of ways. Guinea fowl, which have been domesticated since the sixteenth century, have a stronger flavor and firmer meat. Turkeys too have established a place in our eating habits – the breast is much sought after. Ducks and geese are almost exclusively eaten in Italy during the winter and are mainly part of the gastronomic traditions of a few regions, such as Lombardy and Veneto, where there are numerous farms. The same is true of squab, which are mainly eaten in Umbria. When buying frozen poultry, make sure the packaging is undamaged and thaw the meat completely before cooking.

DUCK

Ducks may be domesticated or wild, the latter being available in Italy during the hunting season. European domesticated ducks include large, fat fall birds, with strong-tasting meat, and spring ducks, which are smaller, more tender and with a more delicate flavor. Strictly speaking, a duckling does not become a duck until it is about two months old, at the stage of its second plumage. Most birds on sale are, in fact, ducklings and can weigh as much as 7 pounds oven-ready, although smaller specimens – 3¹/₄–3¹/₂ pounds – are also available. Ducklings are more tender than mature birds. Duck meat is tender and nutritious, but as it is very fatty it is not recommended for people on diets or with gastric problems. Ducks may be cooked in several ways – roasted, braised, in a casserole or as the now legendary à l'orange. Breast fillets are also available, as well as products such as the famous duck pâté de foie gras, terrines and pies. It is essential to follow a few rules when cooking a whole bird. Truss it with kitchen string so that it stays in shape while cooking. It must not be overcooked. Allow 30 minutes per 1 pound 2 ounces. Season the cavity with salt and pepper, then season the outside with a large pinch of salt. Pre-cooking is recommended although not essential. Season the cavity with salt and pepper, put the duck in a pan and pour in water to cover it by two-thirds. Add a large onion, bring to a boil and simmer for 20 minutes, then drain, pat dry and follow your chosen recipe.

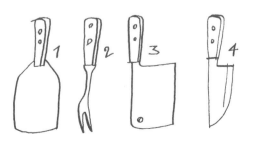

DUCK À L'ORANGE

ANATRA ALL'ARANCIA

Serves 4

3 tablespoons butter

3 fresh sage leaves

3¹/₄-pound duck

5 ounces lean pancetta, sliced

1 tablespoon olive oil

³/₄ cup white wine

¹/₂–²/₃ cup Chicken Stock
(see page 209)

5 oranges

salt and pepper

Put a pinch of salt, a pinch of pepper, 1 tablespoon of the butter and the sage in the cavity of the duck. Wrap it in the pancetta and truss with kitchen string. Heat the oil and remaining butter in a deep pan, add the duck and cook, turning frequently, for 15 minutes until browned all over. Pour in the wine and ²/₃ cup of the stock, cover and simmer, seasoning with salt and basting two or three times, for 1 hour until tender. If it seems to be drying out, add another ²/₃ cup hot stock. Meanwhile, pare the rind of two of the oranges and cut into thin strips. Blanch in boiling water for a few minutes, then drain. Squeeze the juice from two of the remaining oranges and cut the third into segments. Remove the duck from the pan and keep warm. Add the orange juice and strips of rind to the pan and heat gently without allowing the sauce to boil. Untie the duck and carve. Place the meat on a warm serving dish, spoon a little of the sauce on top and garnish with the orange segments. Serve with the remaining sauce.

DUCK COOKED IN BEER

ANATRA ALLA BIRRA

Serves 4

2 tablespoons butter

1 onion, thinly sliced

3¹/₄-pound duck

4 cups beer

1 fresh rosemary sprig

1 fresh thyme sprig

2 fresh sage leaves

1 tablespoon golden raisins

salt and pepper

Melt the butter in a deep pan, add the onion and cook over low heat, stirring occasionally, for 5 minutes. Add the duck and cook, turning frequently, for 15 minutes until browned all over. Pour in the beer, bring to a boil, then lower the heat to a simmer. Season with salt and pepper to taste, add the rosemary, thyme and sage and simmer, basting and turning occasionally, for 1 hour until tender. Meanwhile, place the golden raisins in a bowl, add lukewarm water to cover and let soak for 30 minutes, then drain and squeeze out. Remove the duck from the pan and keep warm. Remove and discard the herbs from the pan and increase the heat to thicken the cooking juices if necessary. Stir in the raisins and simmer for a few minutes. Cut the duck into pieces, place them on a warm serving dish and spoon the sauce over them.

DUCK IN ALMOND SAUCE

Set the liver aside and cut the bird into pieces. Season with salt and pepper and dust with flour. Heat 2 tablespoons of the oil in a pan over low heat, add the liver and cook for a few minutes until browned on the outside but still pink in the middle. Remove from the pan and set aside. Add the onion and garlic to the pan and cook over medium heat, turning frequently, for 8–10 minutes until browned all over. Remove from the pan and set aside with the liver. If necessary, add 1 tablespoon oil to the pan, then add the duck and cook, turning frequently, until browned all over. Add the tomatoes, lower the heat, cover and cook. Meanwhile, chop the almonds together with the liver, onion and garlic. Place in a bowl, stir in the wine and add the mixture to the duck. Add the parsley, season with salt, re-cover the pan and simmer gently for 1 hour more, adding a little warm water if necessary to prevent drying out. Place the pieces of duck in the middle of a warm serving dish, surround with two rings of potatoes mashed with cheese and serve.

ANATRA ALLA SALSA DI MANDORLE

Serves 6

$4^1/_2$-pound duck, with liver

all-purpose flour, for dusting

2–3 tablespoons olive oil

1 onion

1 garlic clove

3 tomatoes, chopped

12 blanched almonds, roasted

5 tablespoons dry white wine

1 fresh flat-leaf parsley sprig, chopped

salt and pepper

potatoes mashed

with Parmesan cheese, freshly grated to serve

DUCK WITH PEACHES

Place the duck in a pan with the sage and bay leaf and pour in water to cover. Season with salt and pepper and cook over low heat for $1^1/_2$ hours. Remove the duck from the pan. Remove and discard the skin, cut the breast fillets off the bones and return to the pan. Simmer over low heat until the liquid has evaporated completely. Cut the peach halves in half again. Melt the butter in a skillet, add the peaches and cook over low heat until lightly browned all over. Sprinkle with the cinnamon and cook for a few minutes more, then add to the duck. Season with salt and pepper to taste. Transfer the duck and peaches to a warm serving dish and serve with thickly sliced toast. This dish is also pleasant cold. The cold dish and peaches go well with white wines that have a peach-like aroma.

ANATRA ALLE PESCHE

Serves 4

$3^1/_4$-pound duck

3 fresh sage leaves

1 bay leaf

1 pound 2 ounces white peaches, peeled, halved and pitted

2 tablespoons butter

pinch of ground cinnamon

salt and pepper

thick toast slices, to serve

DUCK WITH GREEN PEPPERCORNS

ANATRA AL PEPE VERDE

Serves 6

3 tablespoons butter
1 onion, thinly sliced
1 carrot, sliced
1 celery stalk, sliced
1 fresh flat-leaf parsley sprig
1 fresh thyme, sprig
4¹/₂-pound duck
1 tablespoon green peppercorns
³/₄ cup dry white wine
1¹/₂ cups Chicken Stock (see page 209)
1 small red bell pepper, halved seeded and chopped
salt and pepper

Preheat the oven to 425°F. Heat 2 tablespoons of the butter in a roasting pan, add the onion and cook over low heat, stirring occasionally, for 5 minutes. Add the carrot, celery, parsley and thyme. Rub the skin of the duck with salt and pepper, put three of the peppercorns, the remaining butter and a pinch of salt inside the cavity and truss with kitchen string. Place in the roasting pan with the vegetables. Cover the pan with foil, transfer to the oven and cook for 15 minutes. Remove the duck from the oven and lower the temperature to 375°F. Pour the wine over the duck and cook over medium heat until it has evaporated. Add the stock and bring to a boil, then re-cover the roasting pan and return it to the oven for 45 minutes. If it seems to be drying out, add a little more stock. Do not switch off the oven, but remove the duck from the roasting pan and strain the cooking juices into a bowl. Stir in 5 tablespoons boiling water, pour back into the roasting pan and cook over medium heat until slightly reduced. Add the red bell pepper and remaining peppercorns. Return the duck to the roasting pan and roast in the oven for a further 15 minutes. Carve the duck, place on a warm serving dish and spoon the sauce over it.

STUFFED DUCK WITH HONEY

ANATRA FARCITA AL MIELE

Serves 6

4¹/₂-pound duck, with liver
2 tablespoons butter
3 tablespoons soy sauce
2 onions, chopped
¹/₂ garlic clove
5 tablespoons brandy
2 tablespoons honey
1 thick cooked, cured ham slice, chopped
salt

Preheat the oven to 350°F. Rub the inside and outside of the duck with salt. Melt the butter in a skillet, add the liver and cook over low heat, turning frequently, for a few minutes, then remove from the pan and chop. Combine the soy sauce, onions, garlic and brandy in a bowl. Transfer half the mixture to another bowl and stir in the honey. Rub the duck with the honey mixture making sure it penetrates well. Stir 1¹/₂ cups boiling water into the leftover mixture. Stir the liver and ham into the remaining soy, onion, garlic and brandy mixture and stuff the duck with it. Truss with kitchen string, place on a rack set over a roasting pan and pour a little water into the pan. Roast for about 1¹/₂ hours, basting occasionally with the diluted honey mixture. Remove the duck from the rack, untie, carve and place on a warm serving dish.

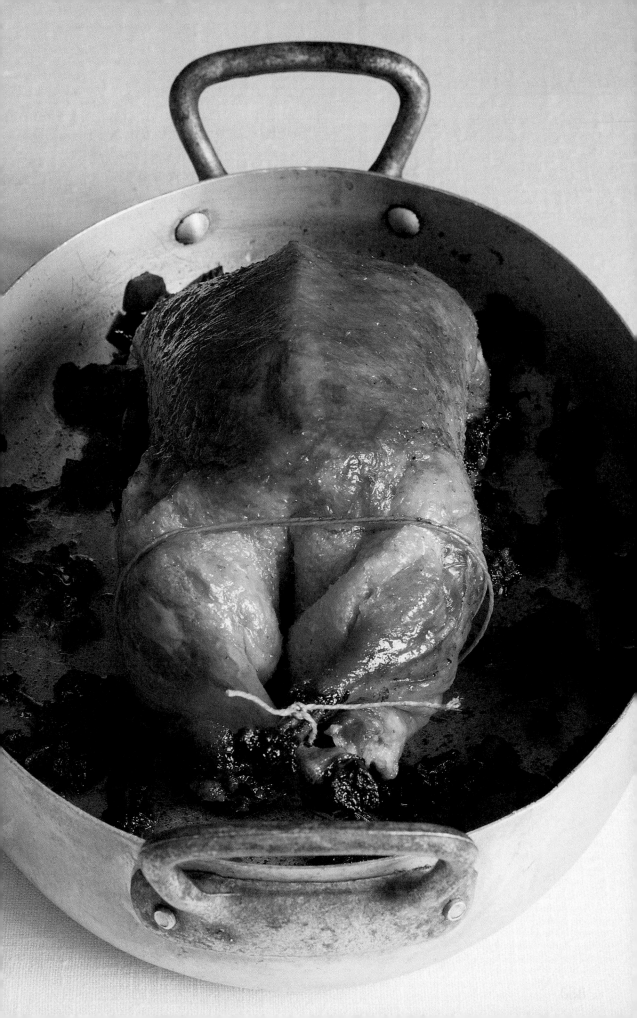

ANATRA IN AGRODOLCE

Serves 4

3¼-pound duck

3 tablespoons butter

2 onions, finely chopped

1 fresh sage leaf

1½ cups hot Chicken Stock (see page 209)

1 fresh mint sprig, chopped

2 tablespoons sugar

2 tablespoons white wine vinegar

salt and pepper

SWEET–AND–SOUR DUCK

Season the cavity of the duck with salt and pepper and truss with kitchen string. Melt the butter in a large pan or flameproof casserole, add the onions and cook over medium heat, stirring occasionally, for 5 minutes. Add the sage, then add the duck and cook, turning frequently, until browned all over. Pour in the hot stock, lower the heat, cover and simmer, turning the duck occasionally, for 1½ hours until tender. Remove the duck from the pan and keep warm. Add ⅔ cup boiling water to the cooking juices and sprinkle in the mint. Put the sugar and 1 tablespoon cold water in a pan, bring to a boil, stirring until the sugar has dissolved, then heat until caramelized and light golden in color. Pour the caramelized sugar onto the cooking juices, stir in the vinegar and season with salt to taste. Untie the duck and carve. Place on a warm serving dish and serve with the sauce.

ANATRA IN SALSA AROMATICA

Serves 6

2 tablespoons olive oil

1 small onion

2 fresh sage leaves

1 bay leaf

1 fresh rosemary sprig

1 fresh marjoram sprig

2 fresh thyme leaves

4½-pound duck

¼ cup butter

5 tablespoons balsamic vinegar

1 fresh chervil sprig

1 fresh tarragon sprig, chopped

6 fresh basil leaves, chopped

3 black peppercorns, lightly crushed

3 egg yolks

2 tablespoons tomato paste

2 tablespoons heavy cream

salt and pepper

DUCK IN HERB SAUCE

Preheat the oven to 350°F. Heat the oil in a small pan, then remove from the heat and set aside. Put the onion, sage, bay leaf, rosemary, marjoram and thyme in the cavity of the duck and season with salt and pepper. Truss with kitchen string, place in a roasting pan with half the butter and the hot oil, cover with foil and roast, basting and turning occasionally, for about 1½ hours. Meanwhile, pour the vinegar into a pan, add the chervil, tarragon, half of the basil and the peppercorns and cook over low heat until the liquid has reduced. Strain into a bowl and let cool slightly, then whisk the mixture into the egg yolks in a double boiler or heatproof bowl. Stir in the tomato paste and cream and season with salt and pepper. Heat over barely simmering water and gradually beat in the remaining butter in small pieces at a time. Carve the duck, place in the middle of a warm serving dish, spoon the herb sauce over it and sprinkle with the basil.

STUFFED DUCK IN TURNIP SAUCE

ANATRA RIPIENA IN SALSA DI RAPE

Serves 6

4¹/₂-pound duck, with giblets
¹/₃ cup smoked pancetta, diced
1 onion, chopped
1 garlic clove, chopped
4 leeks, white parts only thinly sliced
4 carrots, grated
1 tablespoon bread crumbs
1 egg white
¹/₄ cup ricotta cheese
pinch of freshly grated nutmeg
1³/₄ pounds turnips, sliced
2 tablespoons heavy cream
salt and pepper

Preheat the oven to 350°F. Chop the giblets. Cook the pancetta in a pan, without any additional oil or fat, over low heat, stirring frequently, for 5 minutes. Add the onion, garlic and giblets and cook over high heat for 5 minutes. Put the mixture into a bowl, add the leeks, carrots, bread crumbs, egg white, ricotta and nutmeg, season with salt and pepper and mix well. Stuff the duck with the mixture, sew up the opening and truss with kitchen string. Prick the skin all over with a fork, place in a roasting pan and roast for 1 hour. Meanwhile, steam the turnips for 30 minutes, then transfer to a food processor and process to a purée. Scrape the turnip purée into a bowl, stir in the cream, season with salt and pepper and keep warm. Remove the duck from the roasting pan, pull off the legs and wings and carve the breast. Place on a warm serving dish and spoon the turnip sauce over it.

JUGGED DUCK LEGS

COSCE IN SALMÌ

Serves 4

4 duck legs, boned
1¹/₂ cups red wine
2 garlic cloves
1 leek, sliced
1 bay leaf
2 carrots, thinly sliced
2 onions, thinly sliced
salt and pepper

Roll up the duck legs and tie with kitchen string. Combine 1 cup of the wine, the garlic, leek and bay leaf in a dish, season with salt, add the legs and let marinate, turning occasionally, for 6 hours. Preheat the oven to 400°F. Drain the legs, reserving the marinade, put in a roasting pan with the carrots and onions and roast for 20 minutes. Meanwhile, strain the marinade into a pan, season with salt and pepper according to taste and cook over low heat until the liquid has reduced. Remove the legs from the roasting pan and keep warm. Skim off the fat from the roasting pan and stir the remaining wine into the cooking juices, then pour into the pan. Heat gently until the sauce has reduced. Untie the legs and carve into slices. Arrange on a warm serving dish and spoon the sauce over them.

DUCK FILLETS WITH FIGS

FILETTI DI ANATRA AI FICHI

Serves 4

1 small duck, with liver
1 tablespoon olive oil
1/4 cup butter, plus extra for greasing
1 cup red wine
1 tablespoon lemon juice
5 1/2 pounds fresh figs
1/2 white loaf, sliced and crusts removed
1 lemon
salt and pepper

Preheat the oven to 450°F. Set the liver aside. Season the cavity of the duck with salt and pepper and truss with kitchen string. Place the duck in a roasting pan, add the oil and 1 1/2 teaspoons of the butter. Roast the duck for 1 hour, then remove from the oven and lower the temperature to 400°F. Cut off the wings, breast and legs and break up the carcass with a meat mallet. Stir the red wine into the roasting pan, add the carcass and cook in the oven for 10 minutes, then remove from the oven but do not switch it off. Pass the cooking juices through a food mill into a pan and stir in the lemon juice. Chop the liver and add to the sauce. Cut the figs almost in half and open out slightly. Grease another roasting pan with butter, add the figs and put a small piece of the remaining butter in each, then bake until lightly browned. Remove the figs from the oven and season with salt and pepper. Melt the remaining butter in a skillet, add the slices of bread and cook until golden brown on both sides. Carve the legs into slices and cut the breast into fillets. Place the fried bread and duck in the middle of a warm serving dish arrange the figs around them and spoon the sauce over the duck.

BREAST OF DUCK WITH GRAPEFRUIT

PETTO DI ANATRA AL POMPELMO

Serves 4

2 grapefruit
juice of 1 orange, strained
2 tablespoons sugar
2 black peppercorns, lightly crushed
pinch of ground cinnamon (optional)
2 duck breasts
1 tablespoon olive oil
5 tablespoons white wine vinegar
2 tablespoons butter
salt and pepper

Preheat the oven to 400°F. Holding the grapefruit over a bowl to catch the juice, peel and cut off the pith. Dice the flesh, add to the bowl and pour in the orange juice. Stir in the sugar, peppercorns, 1 tablespoon water and the cinnamon, if using. Pour into a pan and cook over medium heat for 15 minutes. Meanwhile, slash the thickest parts of the duck breasts. Heat the oil in a skillet, add the duck breasts and cook over high heat until lightly browned. Transfer to the oven and cook for 10 minutes. (If your skillet does not have an ovenproof handle, cover it with foil first.) Remove the duck from the skillet and keep warm. Stir the vinegar into the skillet, add 2 tablespoons of the juice mixture, season with salt and pepper and cook over low heat until reduced. Season with salt and pepper to taste and stir the butter into the mixture. Slice the duck diagonally, place on a warm serving dish and spoon the sweet-and-sour sauce over it.

CAPON

Capons are young roosters that have been castrated and fattened, producing birds with a weight range of 4¹/₂–5¹/₂ pounds. Despite their production having died out in many countries, capons are so popular in Italy that they are still commercially available there. Sometimes, large roasters outside Italy are described as 'capon-style' but this is not strictly accurate as they do not have the same tenderness or flavor as true capons, but they may be used as a substitute in the following recipes. In Italy, capon is synonymous with Christmas, when these delicious birds are much sought after for their flavorsome meat. They are generally cooked whole and served boiled with mixed pickles and mostarda, a preserve made with mustard, or with boiled rice and béchamel sauce flavored with curry powder. Skimmed capon stock is excellent for cooking cappelletti and raviolini. Capons may also be roasted.

CAPON ROAST IN A PACKET

CAPPONE AL CARTOCCIO

Serves 8

2¹/₂ cups dried mushrooms

2 tablespoons butter

1 tablespoon chopped fresh flat-leaf parsley

1 capon

3¹/₂ ounces pork fat or fatty bacon, sliced

2 carrots, sliced

2 onions, sliced

1 thick prosciutto slice, chopped

³/₄ cup Marsala

salt and pepper

Put the dried mushrooms in a bowl, add warm water to cover and let soak for 15–30 minutes, then drain, squeeze out and chop coarsely. Preheat the oven to 350°F. Combine the butter and parsley in a bowl and place the mixture in the cavity of the capon. Wrap the capon with the slices of pork fat or bacon and truss with kitchen string. Spread out a large sheet of foil, place the carrots and onions in the middle, sprinkle with the prosciutto and mushrooms and top with the capon. Fold over the sides of the foil and wrap the capon so that it is completely enclosed. Roast the capon for 1¹/₂–2 hours, depending on its size. Remove the capon from the oven, unwrap and untie, then cut into pieces and place on a warm serving dish. Tip the other ingredients in the packet into a food processor and process to a purée. Scrape the purée into a pan, stir in the Marsala and cook over low heat, stirring constantly, until hot. Season with salt and pepper to taste and serve the sauce with the capon.

CAPON IN CARDOON SAUCE

CAPPONE IN SALSA DI CARDI

Serves 4

¹/₂ capon, about 2¹/₄ pounds, with giblets

1³/₄ pounds cardoons (see page 423)

2 tablespoons all-purpose flour

1 lemon slice

2 tablespoons butter

4 tablespoons Parmesan cheese, freshly grated

salt

For the stock

1 veal shin

1 green celery stalk with leaves

1 carrot

1 onion

2 bay leaves

2 cloves

1 fresh flat-leaf parsley sprig

First, make the stock. Pour 8³/₄ cups water into a pan, add all the stock ingredients and the capon giblets and season with salt. Bring to a boil, lower the heat and simmer for 1¹/₂ hours. Strain the stock into a bowl and set aside. Wrap the capon in piece of cheesecloth, tie with kitchen string, place in a pan and add enough stock to cover. Cover the pan and simmer over low heat for 1¹/₂ hours. Meanwhile, trim, peel and chop the cardoons, place in a pan, add half the flour, the lemon, 1¹/₂ teaspoons of the butter and a pinch of salt and pour in water to cover. Bring to a boil, then lower the heat and simmer for 30–50 minutes until tender. Drain and pass through a food mill into a double boiler or heatproof bowl. Mix the remaining flour and remaining butter to a paste – beurre manié (see page 88). Heat the cardoon purée over barely simmering water and gradually stir in the beurre manié, a small piece at a time, and the Parmesan, then season with salt. Transfer the capon to a carving board, unwrap, remove the skin and carve the meat into thin slices. Place them on a warm serving dish and spoon the sauce over them.

POACHED CAPON

CAPPONE LESSATO

Serves 8

1 capon

1 onion • 1 carrot

1 celery stalk

salt and pepper

Green Sauce (see page 74)

or spicy fruit mostarda, to serve

Season the cavity of the capon with salt and pepper, place in a large pan and add plenty of water. Season with salt, add the onion, carrot and celery, bring just to a boil, then lower the heat and simmer gently for 2 hours until tender and cooked through. Remove from the heat and let cool slightly in the cooking liquid, then drain. Remove the skin, cut the capon into pieces and place on a serving dish. Serve with green sauce or spicy fruit mostarda.

STUFFED CAPON

CAPPONE RIPIENO

Serves 8

1 thick bread slice, crusts removed

generous ¹/₂ cup cooked, cured ham, chopped

generous ¹/₂ cup cooked tongue, chopped

generous ¹/₂ cup cooked spinach, chopped

1 carrot, chopped

1 fresh flat-leaf parsley sprig, chopped

2 eggs, lightly beaten

1 capon • 3 tablespoons olive oil

2 tablespoons butter • salt and pepper

new potatoes or mixed salad, to serve

Tear the bread into pieces, place in a bowl, add water to cover and let soak for 10 minutes, then drain and squeeze out. Combine the soaked bread, ham, tongue, spinach, carrot and parsley in a bowl, stir in the beaten eggs and season with salt and pepper. Stuff the capon with the mixture and truss with kitchen string. Heat the oil and butter in a large pan, add the capon and cook, basting occasionally with the cooking juices, for 1¹/₂–2 hours until tender and cooked through. If necessary, add 1–2 tablespoons warm water to prevent the bird from drying out. Serve the capon with new potatoes or a mixed salad.

TRUFFLED CAPON

Combine 1 tablespoon of the olive oil, the brandy and Marsala in a bowl, season with salt and pepper, add the truffles and let marinate for 1 hour. Preheat the oven to 350°F. Stir the pork fat or bacon into the truffle mixture and spoon it into the cavity of the capon. Sew up the opening. Put the remaining oil into a casserole, add the capon and roast for about 2 hours.

CAPPONE TARTUFATO

Serves 8

5 tablespoons olive oil

1 tablespoon brandy

1 tablespoon Marsala

$3^2/_3$ cups black truffles, chopped

$^1/_3$ cup pork fat or fatty bacon, chopped

1 capon

salt and pepper

SIMPLE CAPON GALANTINE

Bring a large pan of salted water to a boil, add the capon so that it is completely immersed and cook for 15 minutes. Remove the capon, let cool slightly, then peel off the skin, keeping the pieces as large as possible. Cut the meat off the bones and chop, then mix with the veal and ham in a bowl. Place the capon carcass, carrots and beef bone in a pan, add plenty of water and bring to a boil. Shape the chopped meat mixture into a meatloaf, then wrap first in the capon skin and then in cheese-cloth, tying both ends. Remove the carcass and beef bone from the stock, immerse the meatloaf and simmer for about 3 hours. Drain, cover and place a weight on top to flatten it evenly. (You can use a chopping board weighted down with several cans of tomatoes, beans, etc.) Let cool. Untie and discard the cheese-cloth, cut the capon into thin slices, place on a serving dish and garnish with diced gelatin.

GALANTINA SEMPLICE DI CAPPONE

Serves 8

1 capon

11 ounces lean veal, chopped

generous $^1/_2$ cup cooked, cured ham, chopped

2 carrots

1 beef bone

salt

diced gelatin, to garnish

TOMATO QUARTERS

GUINEA FOWL

Guinea fowl is a great choice for an elegant dinner party. It is much tastier than chicken with a flavor somewhat similar to that of pheasant. To guarantee success, choose a bird between eight and ten months old. If a guinea fowl is more than a year old its meat is rather tough and needs thorough hanging. It should be cooked over low heat for 40–60 minutes, depending on the size. When roasting guinea fowl, it is advisable to cover the breast with a few slices of pancetta or bacon so that the meat stays tender.

ARROSTO DI FARAONA

Serves 6

1 guinea fowl

1 fresh rosemary sprig

2 fresh sage leaves

2 ounces pancetta slices

3 tablespoons butter

3 tablespoons olive oil

³/₄ cup dry white wine

salt and pepper

POT ROAST GUINEA FOWL

Season the cavity of the guinea fowl with salt and pepper and place the rosemary, sage, one of the pancetta slices and 1 tablespoon of the butter in the cavity. Cover the breast of the bird with the remaining pancetta and tie with kitchen string. Season with salt and pepper. Heat the remaining butter and the oil in a pan, add the guinea fowl and cook, turning frequently, until browned all over. Add half the wine and cook until it has evaporated, then cover and cook over low heat for 50 minutes. Remove the pancetta slices, re-cover the pan and cook for a further 10 minutes. Remove the guinea fowl from the pan and keep warm. Stir the remaining wine into the pan and cook until reduced by half. Cut the guinea fowl into pieces, place on a warm serving dish and spoon the cooking juices over it.

GUINEA FOWL WITH ARTICHOKE HEARTS

Preheat the oven to 400°F. Season the cavity of the guinea fowl with salt and pepper. Heat 3 tablespoons of the oil with one of the garlic cloves in a pan, add the artichoke hearts and cook until tender, then sprinkle with the parsley and season lightly with salt and pepper. Let cool, then place in the cavity of the guinea fowl, sew up the opening and truss with kitchen string so that the bird keeps its shape. Place in a roasting pan with the remaining oil, the pancetta, butter, remaining garlic and rosemary. Roast until the upper surface is browned, then turn over to brown the other side. Add the wine, lower the oven temperature to 350°F and roast for about 1 hour until tender. Remove the guinea fowl from the roasting pan and untie. Carve the breast into fairly thick slices, pull off the wings and legs and cut the back into four pieces. Place the meat on a warm serving dish and spoon the hot cooking juices over it.

FARAONA AI CARCIOFI

Serves 6

1 guinea fowl, boned

5 tablespoons olive oil

2 garlic cloves

5 globe artichoke hearts

1 fresh parsley sprig, chopped

2 pancetta slices, chopped

2 tablespoons butter

1 fresh rosemary sprig

5 tablespoons dry white wine

salt and pepper

GUINEA FOWL WITH PINEAPPLE

Set two of the pineapple slices aside and chop the remainder. Heat the butter and oil in a pan, add the guinea fowl and cook, turning frequently, until browned all over. Season with salt and pepper, add the onion, carrot, celery, garlic and chopped pineapple and cook, stirring occasionally, for about 10 minutes. Pour in the stock, cover and simmer over low heat for 1 hour. Remove the pieces of guinea fowl and keep warm. Stir 2 tablespoons hot water into the pan, scraping up the sediment from the base, then pass the cooking juices through a food mill into a bowl and return to the pan. Stir in the cream and heat gently until slightly thickened. Place the pieces of guinea fowl on a warm serving dish, spoon the sauce over them and garnish with the reserved pineapple slices.

FARAONA ALL'ANANAS

Serves 6

$^1/_2$ pineapple, peeled, cored and sliced

2 tablespoons butter

3 tablespoons olive oil

1 guinea fowl, cut into pieces

1 onion, chopped

1 carrot, chopped

2 celery stalks, chopped

1 garlic clove, chopped

$1^1/_4$ cups Chicken Stock (see page 209)

1 cup heavy cream

salt and pepper

GUINEA FOWL WITH SAGE

FARAONA ALLA SALVIA

Serves 6

10 fresh sage leaves

3 tablespoons butter

1 guinea fowl

3¹/₂ ounces pancetta, sliced

2 tablespoons olive oil

salt and pepper

Preheat the oven to 350°F. Chop half the sage leaves and mix them with 1 tablespoon of the butter. Season the cavity of the guinea fowl with salt and pepper, place the sage and butter mixture inside the cavity and sew up the opening. Wrap the bird in the pancetta slices and truss with kitchen string. Place the guinea fowl in a roasting pan with the oil, half the remaining butter and the remaining sage leaves. Roast, turning occasionally, for about 1 hour until tender. Remove the guinea fowl from the roasting pan and place the pan over low heat. Stir 2 tablespoons hot water into the cooking juices, scraping up any sediment from the base of the pan, then stir in the remaining butter and pour into a sauceboat. Slice the breast of the bird, remove the wings and legs, cut the back into four pieces and serve with the sauce.

GUINEA FOWL ORTOLANA

FARAONA ALL'ORTOLANA

Serves 4

¹/₄ cup butter

6 tablespoons olive oil

4 fresh sage leaves

1 celery stalk, chopped

1 guinea fowl, cut into pieces

³/₄ cup white wine

8 pearl onions

3 potatoes, diced

scant 2¹/₂ cups diced pumpkin

salt and pepper

Heat half the butter and half the oil in a large pan with the sage, celery and a pinch each of salt and pepper, add the guinea fowl and cook, turning frequently and occasionally adding the wine, until browned all over. Heat the remaining butter and oil in another pan, add the onions, potatoes and pumpkin, season with salt and pepper and cook over low heat, stirring occasionally, for 40 minutes. Preheat the oven to 350°F. Transfer the vegetables and guinea fowl to a roasting pan and roast for about 30 minutes.

GUINEA FOWL WITH MASCARPONE

FARAONA AL MASCARPONE

Serves 6

²/₃ cup mascarpone cheese

¹/₂ cup brandy

1 guinea fowl

2 tablespoons butter

1 fresh rosemary sprig, chopped

salt and pepper

Combine the mascarpone and half the brandy in a bowl and spoon into the cavity of the guinea fowl. Sew up the opening and truss with kitchen string. Melt the butter in a pan, add the guinea fowl and cook, turning frequently, until browned all over. Season with salt and pepper, sprinkle with the rosemary, lower the heat and cover. Cook, turning occasionally, for 1 hour until tender. Transfer the guinea fowl to a warm serving dish, sprinkle with the remaining brandy and ignite. Carve when the flames have died down.

GUINEA FOWL WITH RED WINE

Dust the guinea fowl with flour. Heat the oil and 2 tablespoons of the butter in a pan, add the pancetta, onions and guinea fowl and cook over low heat, stirring and turning frequently, for 15 minutes. Season with salt and pepper, add the nutmeg and pour in the wine. Cover and simmer over low heat for 1 hour. Meanwhile, put the mushrooms in a bowl, add warm water to cover and let soak for 30 minutes, then drain and squeeze out. Remove the pieces of guinea fowl from the pan and keep warm. Stir 2 tablespoons hot water into the cooking juices, add the mushrooms, sausage and remaining butter and cook for 20 minutes. Place the guinea fowl on a warm serving dish and spoon the sauce over it.

FARAONA AL VINO ROSSO

Serves 6

1 guinea fowl, cut into pieces
all-purpose flour, for dusting
2 tablespoons olive oil
3 tablespoons butter
2 ounces pancetta
2 onions, chopped
pinch of freshly grated nutmeg
4 cups red wine
$^1/_3$ cup dried mushrooms
$3^1/_2$ ounces Italian sausages, chopped
salt and pepper

GUINEA FOWL WITH CREAM AND LEMON

Melt the butter in a pan, add the guinea fowl and cook over high heat, turning frequently, until browned all over. Season with salt and pepper, lower the heat, cover and cook for about 45 minutes. Stir in the cream, re-cover the pan and cook for a further 15 minutes. Transfer to a warm serving dish and sprinkle with the lemon juice.

FARAONA CON PANNA E LIMONE

Serves 6

$^1/_4$ cup butter
1 guinea fowl, cut into pieces
5 tablespoons heavy cream
juice of $^1/_2$ lemon, strained
salt and pepper

STUFFED GUINEA FOWL WITH MUSHROOMS

Chop the liver, place in a bowl, and add the sausages, mushrooms, onions, garlic, parsley and oregano and mix well. Season with salt and pepper and stir in the brandy. Heat 1 tablespoon of the oil in a skillet, add the mixture and cook over medium heat, stirring occasionally, for 5 minutes. Spoon the mixture into the cavity of the guinea fowl and sew up the opening. Cover the breast of the bird with the pancetta slices and truss with kitchen string. Heat the butter and the remaining oil in a pan, add the guinea fowl and cook over medium heat, turning frequently, until browned all over. Season with salt and pepper, lower the heat and cook for about 1 hour.

FARAONA FARCITA CON I FUNGHI

Serves 6

1 guinea fowl, with liver
5 ounces Italian sausages, chopped
$1^2/_3$ cups mushrooms, chopped
2 onions, chopped
1 garlic clove, chopped
1 fresh flat-leaf parsley sprig, chopped
1 fresh oregano sprig, chopped
$^1/_4$ cup brandy
3 tablespoons olive oil
2 ounces pancetta slices
2 tablespoons butter
salt and pepper

FARAONA RIPIENA CON UVETTA

Serves 6

1 ounce golden raisins

¼ cup brandy

1 thick bread slice, crusts removed

5 ounces Italian sausages, chopped

1 fresh thyme sprig, chopped

1 small fresh rosemary sprig, chopped

1 fresh flat-leaf parsley sprig, chopped

4 fresh sage leaves, chopped

pinch of freshly grated nutmeg

1 egg, lightly beaten

1 guinea fowl

2 tablespoons butter

2 tablespoons olive oil

salt and pepper

GUINEA FOWL STUFFED WITH GOLDEN RAISINS

Put the golden raisins in a bowl, add half the brandy, stir in 2 tablespoons water and let soak for 10 minutes, then drain. Tear the bread into pieces, place in another bowl, add water to cover and let soak for 10 minutes, then drain and squeeze out. Combine the sausages, soaked bread, half the golden raisins and the thyme, rosemary, parsley and sage in a bowl, stir in the nutmeg and egg and season with salt and pepper. Spoon the mixture into the cavity of the guinea fowl, sew up the opening and truss with kitchen string. Heat the butter and oil in a pan, add the guinea fowl and cook over medium heat, turning frequently, until browned all over. Season with salt and pepper, sprinkle with the remaining brandy, lower the heat and cook for about 30 minutes. Turn the bird over, sprinkle with the remaining golden raisins and cook for a further 30 minutes. To serve, thinly carve the stuffed part of bird and pull off the wings and legs.

FARAONA TARTUFATA AL CARTOCCIO

Serves 6

7 ounces lean veal, chopped

1 egg, lightly beaten

1 small white truffle, chopped

1¼ cups celery, chopped

1 carrot, chopped

1 fresh flat-leaf parsley sprig, chopped

2½ cups heavy cream

1 guinea fowl, boned

5 tablespoons olive oil

5 tablespoons white wine

1 fresh rosemary sprig, chopped

1 garlic clove, chopped

salt and pepper

mashed potatoes, to serve

GUINEA FOWL WITH TRUFFLES BAKED IN A PACKET

Preheat the oven to 400°F. Combine the veal, egg, truffle, celery, carrot and parsley in a large bowl, stir in the cream and season with salt and pepper. Spread out a sheet of baking parchment and place the guinea fowl on top. Stuff with the veal mixture, sew up the opening and fold over the baking parchment to enclose the bird completely. Pour 3 tablespoons of the oil into a roasting pan, add the packet and roast, occasionally sprinkling the packet with the wine, for about 1 hour. Remove the packet from the oven, open out slightly and let stand for 15 minutes, then remove the guinea fowl, thinly carve the stuffed part and pull off the wings and legs. Arrange on a serving dish and keep warm. Heat the remaining olive oil in a pan, add the rosemary and garlic and cook over low heat for a few minutes. Spoon the mixture over the meat and serve with mashed potatoes.

BOILING FOWL

It has long been known that mature birds – between 15 and 16 months old – make good stock. It is probably less well known that young hens, also known as pullets – between seven and eight months old – are excellent in stews and casseroles.

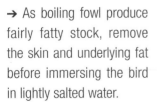

→ As boiling fowl produce fairly fatty stock, remove the skin and underlying fat before immersing the bird in lightly salted water.

→ Cooking takes 1 hour or more, depending on the size of the bird. If the hen is old, it takes at least 2 hours.

→ When the stock is ready, remove the fat by filtering it through a cheesecloth-lined strainer.

COOKING

897

GALLINA ALLA MELAGRANA

Serves 4

2 tablespoons olive oil

3 tablespoons butter

1 boiling fowl

2 pearl onions

$^1/_3$ cup dried mushrooms

4 pomegranates

1 cup heavy cream

4 fresh sage leaves, chopped

salt and pepper

CHICKEN WITH POMEGRANATE

Preheat the oven to 350°F. Heat half the oil and half the butter in a flameproof casserole, add the chicken and cook, turning frequently, until browned all over. Add one of the onions and sprinkle with hot water. Transfer to the oven and roast for about 1 hour. Meanwhile, place the mushrooms in a bowl, add warm water to cover and let soak for 15–30 minutes, then drain and squeeze out. Cut off and discard a slice from one end of a pomegranate, stand it upright and cut downwards through the skin at intervals. Bend back the segments and scrape the seeds into a bowl with your fingers. Repeat with the remaining pomegranates, then crush the seeds with a potato masher and pour the juice over the chicken. Return the casserole to the oven. Reserve the seeds. Chop the remaining onion. Heat the remaining oil and butter in a skillet, add the chopped onion and cook over low heat, stirring occasionally, for 5 minutes. Add the mushrooms and cook, stirring occasionally, for a further 15 minutes, then add to the casserole. When the bird is tender, remove it and the whole onion from the casserole. Transfer the cooking juices to a food processor and process to a purée. Scrape the purée into a pan, stir in the cream and sage, season and cook over low heat until thickened. Cut the bird into pieces and chop the onion. Serve the chicken with the sauce, reserved pomegranate seeds and chopped onion.

GALLINA CAMPAGNOLA

Serves 6

1 boiling fowl, with giblets

1 onion, thinly sliced

$^1/_2$ cup cooked, cured ham, chopped

2 tablespoons bread crumbs

1 fresh flat-leaf parsley sprig, chopped

1 egg yolk

3 tablespoons butter

1 ounce pancetta, sliced

12 pearl onions

$^3/_4$ cup dry white wine

3–4 potatoes, diced

salt and pepper

RUSTIC CHICKEN

Chop the giblets, place in a skillet with the onion and ham and cook over medium heat, stirring frequently, for a few minutes until browned. Remove the pan from the heat and stir in the bread crumbs, chopped parsley and egg yolk. Season with salt and pepper, return the skillet to the heat and cook for a few minutes more. Stuff the chicken with the mixture, sew up the opening and truss with kitchen string. Melt the butter in a flameproof casserole, add the chicken and cook over high heat, turning frequently, until browned all over. Add the pancetta and pearl onions, lower the heat to medium, cover and cook for about 10 minutes. Pour in the wine and cook, uncovered, until it has evaporated, then cover the casserole and simmer for 45 minutes. Add the potatoes and, if necessary, a little hot water to prevent drying out, and cook for a further 30 minutes. Remove the chicken from the casserole, untie and cut into pieces. Serve with the potatoes, pearl onions and cooking juices.

GALLINA CON CAROTE E CIPOLLE

Serves 4

2¹/₄-pound boiling fowl
2 tablespoons butter
11 ounces pearl onions
1 pound 2 ounces carrots, cut into thin batons
1¹/₂ cups dry white wine
salt and pepper

CHICKEN WITH CARROTS AND ONIONS

Season the cavity of the chicken with salt and pepper. Melt the butter in a pan, add the chicken and cook, turning frequently, until browned all over. Add the onions and carrots and cook, stirring frequently, for about 10 minutes until golden brown. Pour in the wine and cook until it has evaporated. Season with salt and pepper to taste, cover and cook over low heat for about 1 hour.

GALLINA IN SALSA ROSA

Serves 6

1 pound 2 ounces canned tomatoes
6 tablespoons butter
1 boiling fowl, cut into pieces
³/₄ cup white wine
³/₄ cup milk
salt and pepper
boiled or pilaf rice, to serve

CHICKEN IN PINK SAUCE

Pass the tomatoes through a food mill into a bowl. Melt the butter in a large pan, add the chicken pieces and cook, turning frequently, until browned all over. Add the wine, milk and tomatoes, season well with salt and pepper, cover and cook over medium heat for about 1¹/₂ hours. A thick, tasty pink sauce will have formed which, besides tasting exquisite, is also very attractive. Serve the chicken on a warm serving dish, completely covered with the sauce and accompanied with boiled or pilaf rice.

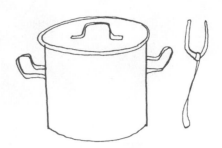

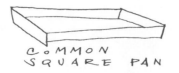

COMMON SQUARE PAN

GOOSE

Geese are beautiful, white, plump and appealing when alive, but not exactly easy to digest when cooked. By removing the excess fat, however, you can make goose meat much lighter and less of a strain on the digestive system. However, you should bear in mind that the youngest geese have the leanest meat. Generally, in Italy, geese are roasted with plenty of turnips and potatoes to help absorb the fat released during cooking. To make sure the skin is crisp, never baste a goose with its own cooking juices. It is best to place the bird on a rack so that the fat can drip into a roasting pan or tray beneath – pour about ³/₄ cup water into the pan before roasting. As far as cooking times are concerned, allow 1 hour for the first 2¹/₄ pounds and then 15 minutes for every additional 2¹/₄ pounds. If you are buying a whole goose, choose one aged between eight and nine months and weighing about 6¹/₂ pounds so that it can be roasted perfectly in an ordinary oven. When roasting a goose, parboiling is recommended to decrease its fattiness (see below).

COOKING

→ Season the cavity of the goose with salt, add a large pinch of rosemary needles and sew up the opening.

→ Fill a deep pan one-third full with water, add a large onion and the goose. Bring to a boil, cover and simmer for 30 minutes or more, depending on the size of the bird.

→ Drain the goose, discard the water and follow the recipe.

→ This method should also be used before roasting.

ROAST GOOSE WITH SWEET–AND–SOUR BELL PEPPERS

ARROSTO DI OCA CON PEPERONI
IN AGRODOLCE

Serves 8

6¹/₂-pound goose
12 ounces dried chestnuts
¹/₂ cup olive oil
1 onion, chopped
1 carrot, chopped
1 celery stalk, chopped
1 fresh rosemary sprig, chopped
³/₄ cup white wine
1 quantity hot Chicken Stock (see page 209)
2 yellow bell peppers, halved, seeded and cut into strips
2 red bell peppers, halved, seeded and cut into strips
2 green bell peppers, halved, seeded and cut into strips
2 tablespoons sugar
³/₄ cup white wine vinegar
salt and pepper

Season the cavity of the goose with salt and pepper, fill with the dried chestnuts and truss with kitchen string. Heat half the olive oil in a flameproof casserole, add the goose, onion, carrot, celery and rosemary and cook, turning the bird frequently, for about 20 minutes until well browned. Meanwhile, preheat the oven to 350°F. Pour the wine and 5 tablespoons of the hot stock into the casserole, then transfer to the oven and roast for 2 hours, adding a ladleful of hot stock every 15 minutes and turning the goose every 30 minutes. Heat the remaining oil in a pan, add all the bell peppers and cook over low heat, stirring occasionally, for 20 minutes. Stir in the sugar and vinegar and simmer gently for a further 10 minutes. Remove the goose from the oven and discard the chestnuts. Pass the cooking juices through a food mill. Carve the goose breast into slices, remove the legs and wings and place on a warm serving dish. Surround with the sweet-and-sour bell peppers and serve with the cooking juices.

SWEET–AND–SOUR GOOSE LEGS

COSCE DI OCA IN AGRODOLCE

Serves 4

1 cup balsamic vinegar
1 shallot
1 carrot
¹/₂ cup sugar
4 goose legs
¹/₄ cup butter
2 tablespoons cornmeal
salt

Pour the vinegar into a pan, add the shallot, carrot, 2 tablespoons of the sugar and the goose legs, season with salt and simmer until the goose is tender and cooked through. Drain the goose legs and let cool, then slice the meat off the bones. Strain the stock into a bowl and let cool, then remove and reserve the fat that solidifies on the surface. Melt the butter in a pan, add the goose meat and cook, turning frequently, until browned all over. Sprinkle with half the remaining sugar and a little of the reserved fat from the stock, then sprinkle with the remaining sugar and cook over low heat until caramelized. Remove the meat, place on a serving dish and keep warm. Stir the cornmeal into the pan and cook, stirring, for a few minutes, then gradually stir in ³/₄ cup of the stock and heat gently until thickened. Spoon the sauce over the slices of goose and serve.

GERMAN GOOSE WITH APPLES

Preheat the oven to 325°F. Chop half the apples and slice the remainder. Season the cavity of the goose with salt and stuff with the chopped apples, then sew up the opening and truss with kitchen string. Place on a rack set over a roasting pan or oven tray and pour a little water into the pan or tray. Roast until the goose has browned, then pat the skin dry with paper towels. Pour the wine over the goose, add $^2/_3$ cup warm water, return to the oven and roast for a further 2 hours. Meanwhile, blanch the apple slices in boiling water for 1 minute, then drain. Melt the butter in a skillet, add the sliced apples and cook over low heat, stirring frequently, until softened. Place the goose on a warm serving dish, surround with the apples and season with pepper.

OCA ALLA TEDESCA CON LE MELE

Serves 8

$2^1/_4$ pounds eating apples, peeled and cored

$6^1/_2$-pound goose

$^3/_4$ cup dry white wine

3 tablespoons butter

salt and pepper

BRAISED GOOSE

Preheat the oven to 300°F. Melt the butter in a flameproof casserole, add the goose and cook, turning frequently, until browned all over. Add the onions and garlic and cook over low heat, stirring occasionally, for 5 minutes. Pour in the wine, add the tomatoes and herbs and season with salt and pepper. Cover, transfer to the oven and cook for about 3 hours until the meat comes away from the bones. Remove the goose from the casserole, cut the meat off the bones, place on a serving dish and keep warm. Remove and discard the garlic and herbs and heat the cooking juices to reduce if necessary. Pour in the brandy and mix well, season with salt and pepper to taste and serve the goose with the sauce.

OCA BRASATA

Serves 8

$^1/_4$ cup butter

$6^1/_2$-pound goose, cut into pieces

2 onions, thinly sliced

2 garlic cloves

1 bottle (3 cups) dry white wine

6 large tomatoes, peeled, seeded and chopped

1 fresh rosemary sprig

2 fresh sage leaves

$^1/_4$ cup brandy

salt and pepper

GOOSE STUFFED WITH POTATOES

OCA RIPIENA DI PATATE

Serves 8

14 ounces potatoes, unpeeled
2 tablespoons butter
1 onion, chopped
1 fresh parsley sprig, chopped
pinch of chopped fresh rosemary
6¹/₂-pound goose
1¹/₄ cups hot Chicken Stock (see page 209)
salt and pepper

Cook the potatoes in salted, boiling water for 10 minutes, then drain, peel and dice. Preheat the oven to 400°F. Melt the butter in a pan, add the onion and parsley and cook over low heat, stirring occasionally, for 5 minutes. Add the potatoes, increase the heat to medium and cook, shaking the pan occasionally, until browned. Season with salt and pepper and stir in the rosemary. Stuff the goose with the vegetable mixture, sew up the opening and truss with kitchen string. Prick the skin all over with a fork. Place the goose, breast side down, on a rack set over a roasting pan or oven tray, cover with a sheet of foil and pour a little water into the pan or tray underneath. Roast for 1 hour, then lower the oven temperature to 350°F and roast for 1 hour more. Remove and discard the foil, turn the goose over, return to the oven and roast, basting occasionally with hot stock, for 1 more hour. Skim off the fat from the cooking juices and pour them into a sauceboat. Carve the goose and serve with the cooking juices.

BREAST OF GOOSE IN BALSAMIC VINEGAR

PETTO D'OCA ALL'ACETO BALSAMICO

Serves 4

2 tablespoons butter
2 tablespoons olive oil
2 garlic cloves
1 pound 2 ounces boneless breast of goose, sliced
6 tablespoons balsamic vinegar
salt and pepper

For the sauce
scant ¹/₂ cup olive oil
scant ¹/₂ cup balsamic vinegar
2 garlic cloves
¹/₂ fresh chile, seeded and chopped
salt

First, make the sauce. Whisk together the oil and vinegar in a bowl and add the garlic, chile and a pinch of salt, then set aside. Heat the butter and olive oil in a pan, add the garlic and cook over low heat until the cloves have turned brown, then remove and discard them. Add the goose slices to the pan, increase the heat to high and cook, turning frequently, for a few minutes until browned. Season with salt and pepper, sprinkle with the vinegar and cook for 15–20 minutes until reduced. Transfer to a warm serving dish and pour the sauce on top.

Serves 8

6^1/$_2$-pound goose

2 ounces pancetta, thinly sliced

2 tablespoons olive oil

1 bottle (3 cups) dry white wine

1^1/$_2$ cups white wine vinegar

1 quantity Chicken Stock (see page 209)

6 black peppercorns, lightly crushed

1 bay leaf

2 onions

pinch of chopped fresh marjoram

pinch of chopped fresh rosemary

For the sauce

2 salted anchovies, heads removed, cleaned and

filleted (see page 596), soaked in cold water for

10 minutes and drained

2 lemons

2 tablespoons butter

GOOSE STEW

Preheat the oven to 375°F. Wrap the goose in the slices of pancetta, place on a rack set over a roasting pan or oven tray and roast for 1^1/$_2$ hours. Take the goose out of the oven and remove the pancetta. Place the goose in a snug-fitting pan with the olive oil. Pour in the wine, vinegar and stock to cover. Add the peppercorns, bay leaf, onions, marjoram and rosemary and season with salt. Simmer over low heat for 1 hour, then remove the goose from the pan and keep warm. To make the sauce, first chop the anchovy fillets. Peel one of the lemons and cut off all traces of white pith. Dice the flesh and add to the goose cooking juices with the anchovies, heat through gently, then remove the pan from the heat and stir in the butter. Slice the remaining lemon. Carve the goose into slices and place on a warm serving dish. Spoon the sauce over it and garnish with the lemon slices.

SQUAB

Reared squab – young pigeons – have lean, white, tasty, easily digestible meat. In fact, experts say that only young birds should be cooked as they are sure to have tender, tasty flesh. Otherwise, you risk having tough, unpleasant meat on your plate. Squab are excellent roast, broiled or fried with peas. Wild squab have darker meat with a more gamy flavor. One squab is usually enough for two people.

ROAST SQUAB

ARROSTO DI PICCIONI

Serves 4

2 squab, with livers

4 thin pancetta slices

1 tablespoon olive oil

2 tablespoons butter

salt and pepper

Preheat the oven to 350°F. Chop the livers and set aside. Wrap each squab in two slices of pancetta and truss with kitchen string. Heat the oil and butter in a flameproof casserole, add the squab and cook, turning frequently, until browned all over. Season with salt and pepper to taste, transfer to the oven and roast for 40 minutes. Remove the pancetta, return the casserole to the oven and roast for a further 10 minutes. Remove the squab from the casserole and keep warm. Stir 1 tablespoon hot water into the cooking juices, add the chopped livers and cook over medium heat, stirring constantly, for a few minutes. Cut the squab in half, place on a warm serving dish and spoon the sauce over them.

BROILED SQUAB

PICCIONI ALLA GRIGLIA

Serves 4

5 tablespoons olive oil

1 fresh flat-leaf parsley sprig, chopped

juice of 2 lemons, strained

4 black peppercorns, lightly crushed

2 squab, halved • salt

potatoes baked in foil, to serve

Combine the oil, parsley, lemon juice and peppercorns in a dish, season with salt, add the squab and let marinate for 4–6 hours. Preheat the broiler. Drain the squab, reserving the marinade, and place under the broiler. Cook for 45 minutes, turning frequently and brushing with the reserved marinade. Serve with potatoes baked in foil.

PIQUANT SQUAB

PICCIONI ALL'AGRO

Serves 4

2 fresh rosemary sprigs, chopped

2 bay leaves

2 fresh sage leaves

2 pancetta slices

2 squab

juice of 2 lemons, strained

salt and pepper

boiled rice, to serve

Put a pinch of salt, a pinch of pepper, half the rosemary, a bay leaf, a sage leaf and a slice of pancetta in the cavity of each squab. Place in a pan, season with salt and pour in the lemon juice. Cover and cook over low heat for 45 minutes. Serve with boiled rice seasoned with a pat of butter.

SQUAB WITH OLIVES

PICCIONI ALLE OLIVE

Serves 4

2 ounces pancetta slices

2 squab

¹/₄ cup butter

1 onion, thinly sliced

1 teaspoon cornstarch

³/₄ cup white wine

1 cup hot Meat Stock (see page 208)

scant 1 cup pitted black olives

salt and pepper

Preheat the oven to 350°F. Put a pinch of salt and a slice of pancetta in the cavity of each squab. Place the remaining slices of pancetta over the breasts of the birds and truss with kitchen string. Season with salt and pepper. Place the squab in a casserole with 2 tablespoons of the butter and roast until well browned. Melt the remaining butter in a pan, add the onion and cook over low heat, stirring occasionally, for 5 minutes. Sprinkle in the cornstarch, then gradually stir in the wine and cook, stirring constantly, until it has evaporated. Pour in the stock, add the olives and cook until the sauce has thickened. Remove the squab from the casserole, untie and cut in half. Place on a warm serving dish and spoon the sauce over them.

STUFFED SQUAB

PICCIONI FARCITI

Serves 4

1 thick white bread slice, crusts removed

2 squab, with livers

¹/₃ cup cooked, cured ham, chopped

2 ounces prosciutto, chopped

1 fresh flat-leaf parsley sprig, chopped

¹/₄ cup butter

1 celery stalk, chopped

1 fresh sage leaf

³/₄ cup Meat Stock (see page 208)

³/₄ cup dry white wine

salt and pepper

Tear the bread into pieces, place in a bowl, add water to cover and let soak for 10 minutes, then drain and squeeze out. Chop the livers, place in a bowl, add the cooked ham, prosciutto, parsley and soaked bread and mix well. Season with salt and pepper and spoon the mixture into the cavities of the squab. Melt the butter in a pan, add the celery and sage and cook over low heat, stirring occasionally, for 5 minutes. Add the squab and cook, turning frequently, until browned all over. Pour in the stock and wine, cover and simmer over low heat for 1 hour.

CHICKEN

Chickens may be bought whole or in portions – breast, legs, wings, thighs and livers. Today most chickens in Italy and elsewhere are intensively reared and are sold plucked, gutted, without head, neck and feet and ready for cooking. There is increasing desire for free-range and organic birds and, although expensive, such chicken is growing in popularity. Chicken is tender and therefore cooks very quickly, but it is not always very tasty and the flavor sometimes needs enriching with marinades, sauces and herbs. The quality of chicken may be judged by its skin, which should have a velvety consistency and pale color with slight sky-blue glints.

JOINTING CHICKEN

→ A cooked or raw chicken may be easily cut along its joints with poultry shears or a short-bladed kitchen knife.

→ Always start from the legs. Cut into the point where they are attached to the body, then cut through the joint. Do the same with the wings. After removing the legs and wings, turn the chicken on its back, cut in along the central bone and remove the two breast fillets. Divide the body in half, first lengthwise, then crosswise.

COOKING

→ The chickens described here and used in the following recipes weigh about 2¹/₄ pound. To test whether the bird is cooked, pierce the thickest part with the point of a sharp knife. If the juices run clear, the chicken is ready, but if there are any traces of pink, it should be cooked for a little longer.

IN THE OVEN

It is best to cook chicken slowly at a moderate temperature, increasing the heat only towards the end of the cooking time, to brown the bird. That way the meat stays tender, especially if the bird is fairly large.

BROILING

The ideal method is over charcoal, but chicken can also be cooked successfully under a preheated conventional broiler. Open the bird out by cutting along its back and pounding to flatten it evenly. Cornish hens are excellent broiled as they cook in 45 minutes.

ROASTING

Always choose a young bird. To begin with, only season the cavity with salt. Near the end of the cooking time, season the outside too. It cooks in 40–45 minutes.

ON THE SPIT

Some modern ovens come with a spit. Season the cavity of the chicken with salt and occasionally brush the bird with oil or melted butter while it is cooking. It cooks in about 50 minutes.

STEWING

Cut the chicken into pieces. To provide extra flavor, add ingredients such as tomatoes, fresh or dried mushrooms, fragrant herbs, etc. It cooks in about 1 hour.

POACHING

Before immersing the chicken in water, rub the skin with half a lemon to keep the meat white. Always add a carrot, a celery stalk and an onion to the pan. When the chicken has finished cooking, drain it well, remove and discard the skin, carve the meat and serve, still warm, with a selection of sauces. It cooks in 1 hour.

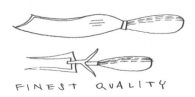

FINEST QUALITY

CHICKEN PIE

Preheat the oven to 350°F. Line the base and sides of a deep ovenproof pie dish with some of the bacon, place the chicken on top and cover with the slices of egg. Season very lightly with salt, bearing in mind that the bacon will be salty. Make a layer of the onion and parsley, top with a layer of the mushrooms and, finally, cover with the remaining bacon. Roll out the pastry dough on a lightly floured surface into a sheet large enough to cover the pie dish. Place the dough on top of the pie and tuck in the sides to seal. Brush with the egg yolk mixture and lightly prick all over the surface with a fork. Transfer to the oven and bake for 1¼ hours. Remove from the oven and let stand for about 10 minutes, then serve straight from the dish.

CHICKEN PIE

Serves 4

7 ounces smoked bacon rashers

3²/₃ cups boneless chicken, diced

2 eggs, hard-cooked, shelled and sliced

1 onion, chopped

2 tablespoons chopped fresh parsley

2 cups mushrooms, chopped

7 ounces puff pastry dough, thawed if frozen

all-purpose flour, for dusting

1 egg yolk beaten with 2 tablespoons water

salt

CHICKEN LEGS IN RED WINE

Put the mushrooms in a bowl, add hot water to cover and let soak for 15 minutes, then drain and squeeze out. Melt the butter in a pan, add the rosemary and bay leaf, then add the chicken legs and cook, turning frequently, until golden brown all over. Season with salt and pepper and add the mushrooms, then pour in the wine and cook until it has evaporated. Remove the chicken legs from the pan, wrap each in a slice of pancetta, secure with a toothpick and return to the pan. Cook, uncovered, over medium heat for 30 minutes until tender and cooked through. If necessary, thicken the cooking juices by adding a pinch of all-purpose flour stirred into 1 tablespoon water and cooking for a further 5 minutes.

GIAMBONETTI DI POLLO AL VINO ROSSO

Serves 4

¹/₂ cup dried mushrooms

2 tablespoons butter

1 fresh rosemary sprig

1 bay leaf

4 chicken legs

1¹/₂ cups red wine

4 pancetta slices

salt and pepper

AMERICAN CHICKEN SALAD

Put the chicken and celery in a bowl. Combine the mayonnaise and cream in another bowl, season with salt and pepper and stir gently into the chicken mixture. Transfer to a serving dish and sprinkle the capers and olives on top. Garnish the dish with the wedges of egg.

INSALATA DI POLLO ALL'AMERICANA

Serves 4

11 ounces cooked chicken, skinned and
cut into strips

1 bunch of white celery, cut into thin batons

1 cup Mayonnaise (see page 65)

2 tablespoons heavy cream

1 tablespoon capers, drained and rinsed

12 black olives

salt and pepper

2 eggs, hard-cooked, shelled and cut into wedges,
to garnish

CHICKEN AND CELERY ROOT SALAD

INSALATA DI POLLO CON SEDANO-RAPA

Serves 4

11 ounces cooked chicken, skinned and cut into strips

1 celery root, cut into thin batons

1 quantity Mayonnaise (see page 65)

3 tablespoons plain yogurt

1 teaspoon Dijon mustard

Put the chicken and celery root into a salad bowl. Combine the mayonnaise, yogurt and mustard in another bowl and season with salt. Gently stir the dressing into the salad and serve.

CHICKEN ROULADES WITH SAGE

INVOLTINI DI POLLO ALLA SALVIA

Serves 4

4 skinless, boneless chicken breast portions

8 fresh sage leaves

3½ ounces pancetta, thinly sliced

2 tablespoons olive oil

salt and pepper

radicchio salad, to serve

Lightly pound the chicken with a meat mallet. Place two of the sage leaves on each portion and season with salt and pepper. Roll up, wrap in the pancetta slices and secure with toothpicks. Heat the oil in a skillet, add the roulades and cook, turning frequently, until browned all over. Cover and cook over low heat for about 20 minutes, adding 1 tablespoon hot water if necessary. Serve with a radicchio salad.

CHICKEN, ANCHOVY AND CAPER ROULADES

INVOLTINI DI POLLO ALLE ACCIUGHE E CAPPERI

Serves 4

4 salted anchovies, soaked in water and drained

4 skinless, boneless chicken breast portions

3 tablespoons capers, drained and rinsed

2 tablespoons butter

1 tablespoon olive oil

1 onion, thinly sliced

¼ cup white wine

salt and pepper

Place the anchovies skin side up and press along the backbones with your thumb, then turn them over and remove the bones. Lightly pound the chicken with a meat mallet. Divide the boned anchovies and capers among the chicken portions, roll up and secure with toothpicks. Heat the butter and oil in a skillet, add the onion and cook over low heat, stirring occasionally, for 5 minutes. Add the roulades and cook, turning frequently, until browned all over. Season with salt and pepper, increase the heat to high, pour in the wine and cook until it has reduced slightly. Lower the heat, cover and simmer for 20 minutes. Transfer to a warm serving dish.

CHICKEN ROULADES WITH CHIVES

INVOLTINI DI POLLO
ALL'ERBA CIPOLLINA

Serves 4

4 skinless, boneless chicken breast portions

1/4 cup butter

2 tablespoons chopped fresh chives

all-purpose flour, for dusting

3 tablespoons olive oil

salt and pepper

peas in butter, to serve

Cut the chicken portions in half horizontally and pound to 1/4 inch thick with a meat mallet. Cut the butter in half and cut one of the halves into 4 slices. Put a slice of butter, a pinch of salt and a pinch of pepper on each chicken portion and divide the chives among them. Roll up the portions, dust with flour, shake off any excess and secure with toothpicks. Heat the olive oil and the remaining butter in a skillet, add the roulades and cook over high heat, turning frequently, until browned all over. Lower the heat to medium, cover and cook for 15 minutes. Serve the roulades with peas in butter.

POACHED STUFFED CHICKEN

LESSO RIPIENO

Serves 6

2 3/4 cups ground veal

1/3 cup Parmesan cheese, freshly grated

1 tablespoon bread crumbs

1 fresh flat-leaf parsley sprig, finely chopped

1 fresh rosemary sprig, finely chopped

1 garlic clove, finely chopped

1 egg, lightly beaten

1 chicken

1 carrot • 1 onion

1 celery stalk

salt and pepper

Combine the veal, Parmesan and bread crumbs in a bowl and add the parsley, rosemary and garlic. Stir in the beaten egg, season with salt and pepper and stuff the chicken with the mixture. Sew up the opening. Place the chicken in a pan, add the carrot, onion, celery and a pinch of salt and pour in water to cover. Bring just to a boil, then lower the heat and simmer for 25 minutes. Prick the chicken with a fork, return to the heat and simmer for a further 20 minutes until tender and cooked through. Remove the chicken from the pan, cut off the wings and legs and carve the central part filled with stuffing. Place on a warm serving dish. The stock may be used to cook cappelletti pasta.

CHICKEN IN VINEGAR

PETTI ALL'ACETO

Serves 4

4 skinless, boneless chicken breast portions

6 tablespoons butter

2 shallots, chopped

1 1/2 cups white wine vinegar

salt and pepper

Lightly pound the chicken portions with a meat mallet. Heat 4 tablespoons of the butter in a pan, add the chicken and cook over medium heat, turning occasionally, until browned on both sides. Season with salt and pepper, lower the heat, cover and cook for 20 minutes until tender and cooked through. Meanwhile, heat half the remaining butter in a small skillet, add the shallots and cook over low heat, stirring occasionally, for about 8 minutes until lightly golden. Pour in the vinegar and cook until reduced by half. Remove the skillet from the heat and stir in the remaining butter. Place the chicken on a warm serving dish, and pour the shallot sauce on top.

CHICKEN AND FENNEL AU GRATIN

PETTI CON FINOCCHI AL GRATIN

Serves 4

butter, for greasing

2 fennel bulbs, trimmed

4 skinless, boneless chicken breast portions, diced

1 quantity Béchamel Sauce (see page 50)

salt

Preheat the oven to 350°F. Grease a roasting pan with butter. If the fennel bulbs are young and tender, blanch in boiling water for 2–3 minutes, then drain. Otherwise cook the bulbs in boiling water for 5 minutes, then drain. Slice the fennel and spread out in the prepared roasting pan, then top with the chicken and season with salt. Spoon the béchamel sauce over the chicken and bake for 30 minutes or until golden brown.

CHICKEN STUFFED WITH MASCARPONE

PETTI FARCITI AL MASCARPONE

Serves 4

3 tablespoons butter, plus extra for greasing

9 ounces mushrooms

juice of 1 lemon, strained

1 garlic clove

1 tablespoon chopped fresh flat-leaf parsley

4 skinless, boneless chicken breast portions

2 cooked, cured ham slices, halved

scant ½ cup mascarpone cheese

1 tomato

salt and pepper

Preheat the oven to 400°F. Grease a roasting pan with butter. Chop the mushrooms and sprinkle with the lemon juice to prevent discoloration. Melt 2 tablespoons of the butter in a small skillet, add the garlic and cook until it turns brown, then remove and discard it. Add the parsley and mushrooms and cook over high heat, stirring occasionally, for 5 minutes. Season with salt and pepper and cook for a further 2 minutes, then remove the skillet from the heat. Slice horizontally through the chicken portions without cutting all the way through. Open out each portion like a book, pound with a meat mallet and season with salt and pepper. Place a piece of ham on one side of each piece of chicken, divide the mascarpone among the portions and top each one with 1 tablespoon of the mushrooms. Fold the portions together again and secure with toothpicks. Cut four slices out of the center of the tomato, put one on each chicken, season with salt and dot with the remaining butter. Place the chicken in the prepared roasting pan, cover with foil and roast for 15 minutes. Meanwhile, preheat the broiler. Discard the foil and brown the chicken under the broiler.

SOUSED CHICKEN

Pound the chicken with a meat mallet until evenly thin. Beat the eggs with a pinch of salt in a dish, add the chicken and let stand for 15 minutes. Spread out the bread crumbs in a shallow dish. Drain the chicken and dip in the bread crumbs to coat. Heat the butter and 2 tablespoons of the oil in a skillet, add the chicken and cook over medium heat, turning occasionally, for about 10 minutes until golden brown on both sides. Meanwhile, heat the remaining oil in another pan, add the onion, celery and carrot and cook over low heat, stirring occasionally, for 5 minutes. Season with salt and pepper to taste, add the vinegar and wine and bring to a boil, then immediately remove from the heat and add the sage and garlic. Place the chicken in a dish, pour the hot marinade over it, let cool, then chill in the refrigerator for at least 4 hours before serving. This dish can be prepared the day before.

PETTI IN CARPIONE

Serves 4

4 skinless, boneless chicken breast portions

2 eggs

1 1/2 cups bread crumbs

2 tablespoons butter

5 tablespoons olive oil

1 onion, thinly sliced

1 celery stalk, thinly sliced

1 carrot, thinly sliced

1 1/2 cups white wine vinegar

scant 1/2 cup dry white wine

4 fresh sage leaves

2 garlic cloves, sliced

salt and pepper

CHICKEN IN ALMOND SAUCE

Melt half the butter in a skillet, add the chicken and cook over low heat, turning occasionally, until lightly browned on both sides. Add the lemon juice, season with salt and pepper, cover and cook for 20 minutes. Remove the chicken from the pan and add half the remaining butter, the almonds, garlic and onion. Cook, stirring occasionally, until the almonds have browned, then add the remaining butter, pour in the wine and cook until it has evaporated. Return the chicken to the pan and heat through. Transfer the chicken to a warm serving dish, spoon the sauce over it and sprinkle with the parsley.

PETTI IN SALSA DI MANDORLE

Serves 4

3 tablespoons butter

4 skinless, boneless chicken breast portions

juice of 1/2 lemon, strained

1/3 cup almonds, chopped

1 garlic clove, crushed

1 onion, thinly sliced

1/4 cup dry white wine

2 tablespoons chopped fresh flat-leaf parsley

salt and pepper

CHICKEN WITH MUSHROOMS

Put the mushrooms in a bowl, add warm water to cover and let soak for 15 minutes, then drain and squeeze out. Lightly dust the chicken portions with the flour. Heat the butter and oil in a pan, add the chicken and cook, turning frequently, until browned all over. Add the mushrooms and onions and cook for a few minutes, then pour in the wine and cook until it has evaporated. Add the strained tomatoes and 3 tablespoons water and season with salt and pepper. Cover and cook over medium heat for about 1 hour until tender and cooked through. Place the chicken portions with their cooking juices on a warm serving dish and sprinkle with the parsley.

POLLO AI FUNGHI

Serves 4

2 1/2 cups dried mushrooms

1 chicken, cut into 4 portions

2 tablespoons all-purpose flour

2 tablespoons butter • 3 tablespoons olive oil

2 pearl onions, chopped

5 tablespoons dry white wine

2 tablespoons bottled strained tomatoes

2 tablespoons chopped fresh flat-leaf parsley

salt and pepper

POLLO AL CARTOCCIO

Serves 4

1 chicken

4 black peppercorns

4 fresh flat-leaf parsley sprigs

12 pearl onions

2 cloves

2 tablespoons butter, melted

sea salt

CHICKEN ROASTED IN A PACKET

Preheat the oven to 400°F. Sprinkle the cavity of the chicken with sea salt and add the peppercorns, two of the parsley sprigs and two of the onions studded with the cloves. Sew up the opening and fold the wings onto the back. Rub the outside of the bird with sea salt, brush with the melted butter and place in the middle of a fairly large sheet of foil. Surround with the remaining onions and parsley and wrap the foil over the chicken to enclose it completely. Roast for 30 minutes, then lower the oven temperature to 350°F and roast for a further 30 minutes until tender and cooked through. Serve in the packet and open at the table.

POLLO AL CURRY

Serves 4

2 tablespoons butter

1 chicken, cut into pieces

2 tablespoons curry powder

2 onions, chopped

2 apples, peeled, cored and chopped

2 tablespoons heavy cream

salt and pepper

boiled rice or pilaf (see page 314), to serve

CHICKEN CURRY

Melt the butter in a pan, add the chicken and cook, turning frequently, until very lightly browned, then season with salt and pepper. Stir the curry powder into $^2/_3$ cup hot water and add to the pan. Add the onions and apples, cover and cook over low heat for 35 minutes, adding a little hot water during cooking if necessary. Pour in the cream and cook for a further 10 minutes. Serve with boiled rice or pilaf.

POLLO ALLA BABI

Serves 4

1 chicken

5 tablespoons olive oil

1 garlic clove, crushed

1 fresh rosemary sprig

salt and pepper

CHICKEN BABI

In Piedmontese dialect, babi means toad. To make the chicken look like a toad, open it along the breast and pound several times with a meat mallet. Gently rub the inside of the bird with salt and pepper. Heat the oil in a heavy-based skillet, add the chicken and cook over high heat for about 15 minutes until browned on both sides. Add the garlic and rosemary, lower the heat and cook for a further 30 minutes until tender and cooked through. Drain the chicken carefully and serve.

CHICKEN IN LAGER

POLLO ALLA BIRRA

Serves 4

1 chicken

1 carrot, finely chopped • 1 onion, finely chopped

1 leek, trimmed and finely chopped

1 celery stalk, finely chopped

4 cups lager • salt and pepper

Season the chicken cavity with salt and pepper and place in a large pan. Add the carrot, onion, leek and celery and pour in the beer, which should almost completely cover the bird. Bring to a boil, then lower the heat and simmer, turning once, for about 1 hour until the beer has almost completely evaporated and the chicken is golden brown, tender and cooked through.

CHICKEN CACCIATORE

POLLO ALLA CACCIATORA

Serves 4

1 chicken, cut into pieces

2 tablespoons butter

3 tablespoons olive oil

1 onion

6 tomatoes, peeled, seeded and chopped

1 carrot, chopped

1 celery stalk, chopped

1 fresh flat-leaf parsley sprig, chopped

salt and pepper

Put the chicken in a flameproof casserole with the butter, oil and onion and cook over medium heat, stirring and turning frequently, for about 15 minutes until browned. Add the tomatoes, carrot and celery, pour in $^2/_3$ cup water, cover and simmer for 45 minutes until the chicken is tender and cooked through. Sprinkle in the parsley and season with salt and pepper. This is the simplest way to prepare chicken cacciatore – in some regions more celery and carrots are added, in others white wine is used instead of water or stock, and in still others sliced mushrooms are added.

DEVILED CHICKEN

POLLO ALLA DIAVOLA

Serves 4

1 chicken

3 tablespoons olive oil

generous pinch of chili powder

salt

Traditionally, deviled chicken is broiled, but this version is cooked on the stove. Open the chicken out lengthwise along the back and pound it well with a meat mallet. Heat the oil in a pan, add the chicken and cook, turning frequently, for 15 minutes until golden brown all over. Season with salt, sprinkle with the chili powder and cook over low heat for a further 45 minutes until tender and cooked through.

PHILIPPINES CHICKEN

POLLO ALLA FILIPPINA

Serves 4

2 tablespoons olive oil

1 chicken, cut into pieces

5 tablespoons white wine vinegar

3 tablespoons dark soy sauce

2 garlic cloves, chopped

1 bay leaf

4 black peppercorns

salt

Heat the oil in a pan, add the chicken and cook, stirring and turning frequently, until golden brown all over. Meanwhile, put the vinegar, soy sauce, garlic, bay leaf, peppercorns and a pinch of salt in a pan over low heat. When the chicken is evenly golden brown, pour the mixture over it, cover and simmer, basting occasionally, for 30 minutes until tender and cooked through. Remove the chicken from the pan and transfer to a warm serving dish. Stir 1 tablespoon hot water into the cooking juices, cook until heated through and pour into a sauceboat. Serve the chicken with the sauce.

CHICKEN WITH GARLIC

POLLO ALL'AGLIO

Serves 4

2 tablespoons butter

2 tablespoons olive oil

1 chicken, cut into pieces

1 garlic bulb, separated into unpeeled cloves

5 tablespoons dry white wine

salt and pepper

Heat the butter and oil in a pan, add the chicken and cook, stirring and turning frequently, for about 15 minutes until golden brown all over. Add the garlic cloves and cook until the papery skins have turned golden brown, then season well with salt and pepper. Pour in the wine and cook until it has evaporated, then cover the pan and simmer over low heat for 30 minutes until tender and cooked through. Remove the lid, increase the heat and cook until the sauce has thickened slightly. Remove the garlic and place the chicken on a warm serving dish.

GREEK CHICKEN

POLLO ALLA GRECA

Serves 4

1 chicken

5 tablespoons olive oil

juice of 1 lemon, strained

1 tablespoon chopped fresh oregano

salt and pepper

Gently rub the outside of the chicken with salt and pepper and put a pinch of each in the cavity. Whisk 4 tablespoons of the oil with the lemon juice and half the oregano in a bowl, season, add the chicken and let marinate for at least 2 hours. Preheat the oven to 350°F. Drain the chicken, reserving the marinade, and place in a roasting pan with the remaining oil. Roast, turning frequently and basting with the reserved marinade, for 1 1/2 hours until tender. Serve sprinkled with the remaining oregano.

CHICKEN WITH CREAM

POLLO ALLA PANNA

Serves 4

1 chicken, cut into pieces • all-purpose flour, for dusting

3 tablespoons butter • generous 1 cup heavy cream

juice of 1/2 lemon, strained

1/3 cup cooked, cured ham, chopped

salt and pepper

Season the chicken and dust with flour. Melt the butter in a pan, add the chicken and cook over low heat, turning occasionally, until lightly browned. Pour in the cream and simmer for about 30 minutes until tender and cooked through. Season to taste, pour in the lemon juice and mix thoroughly. Add the ham and cook for a further 2 minutes, then place on a warm serving dish.

CHICKEN RATATOUILLE

POLLO ALLA RATATOUILLE

Serves 4

1/4 cup butter • 6 tablespoons olive oil

2 onions, quartered • 3 zucchini, cut into cubes

2 eggplants, cut into cubes

3 red or yellow bell peppers, halved, seeded and thickly sliced

4 tomatoes, peeled, quartered and seeded

1 chicken, cut into pieces • 2 garlic cloves

salt and pepper

Heat half the butter and half the oil in a pan, add the onions, zucchini, eggplants and bell peppers, season with salt and pepper and cook over high heat for a few minutes. Lower the heat, add the tomatoes, cover and simmer gently for about 1 hour. Heat the remaining butter and oil in another pan, add the chicken and garlic and cook, stirring and turning frequently, until golden brown all over. Season with salt and pepper and cook for a further 30 minutes until tender and cooked through. Remove and discard the garlic and add the chicken to the vegetables. Mix well and serve.

CHICKEN WITH ONIONS

POLLO ALLE CIPOLLE

Serves 4

2 tablespoons butter

2 tablespoons olive oil

1 chicken, cut into pieces

1 large onion, thinly sliced

1 pound 2 ounces pearl onions

1 fresh thyme sprig

1 bay leaf

1 garlic clove

salt and pepper

Heat the butter and olive oil in a pan, add the chicken, sliced onion and pearl onions and cook over low heat, stirring and turning occasionally, until golden brown all over. Season with salt and pepper, add the thyme, bay leaf and garlic, cover and cook gently for 40 minutes until tender and cooked through. Remove and discard the bay leaf and garlic. Place the chicken and onions on a warm serving dish.

CHICKEN WITH APPLES

POLLO ALLE MELE

Serves 4

1 chicken

2 red apples, peeled, cored and grated

4 pork fat slices or 4 fatty bacon rashers

salt and pepper

Preheat the oven to 475°F. Season the cavity of the chicken with salt and pepper and stuff with the grated apples. Sew up the opening, wrap the chicken in the pork fat or bacon and tie with kitchen string. Place in a roasting pan and roast until the pork or bacon fat melts and collects on the base of the pan. Lower the oven temperature to 375°F and roast for 1 hour, basting frequently during the last 30 minutes, until tender and cooked through. If the skin seems to go brown too quickly, lower the temperature and cover the pan with a sheet of foil. Remove the chicken from the oven and untie. Cut off the legs and wings and carve the central part filled with stuffing.

CHICKEN WITH OLIVES

POLLO ALLE OLIVE

Serves 4

3 tablespoons olive oil

1 chicken, cut into pieces

$3/4$ cup white wine

6 tomatoes, peeled, seeded and chopped

2 garlic cloves, chopped

1 fresh thyme sprig, chopped

4 fresh sage leaves, chopped

1 fresh marjoram sprig, chopped

$1/2$ cup pitted black olives

juice of $1/2$ lemon, strained

6 fresh basil leaves

salt and pepper

Heat the oil in a pan, add the chicken and cook, stirring and turning frequently, for 15 minutes until golden brown all over. Season with salt and pepper, then remove from the pan and keep warm. Stir the wine into the pan and cook until it has evaporated. Add the tomatoes, garlic, thyme, sage and marjoram. Return the chicken to the pan and cook, stirring occasionally, for 30 minutes until tender and cooked through. Add the olives, lemon juice and basil and cook for a few minutes more, then serve.

CHICKEN WITH LEMON (1)

POLLO AL LIMONE (1)

Serves 4

1 chicken
1 lemon, halved
2 tablespoons butter
1 garlic clove
2 tablespoons olive oil
juice of 1 lemon, strained
1 fresh flat-leaf parsley sprig, chopped
salt and pepper

Preheat the oven to 350°F. Gently rub the chicken cavity with one of the lemon halves, then slice the remaining half. Stuff the cavity with the lemon slices, half the butter and the garlic. Place the chicken in a roasting pan with the olive oil and remaining butter, season with salt and pepper and roast for 35 minutes. Sprinkle the lemon juice over the chicken, return to the oven and roast for a further 40 minutes until tender and cooked through. Cut the back and breast of the chicken into four pieces, pull off the wings and legs and place the meat on a warm serving dish. Sprinkle with the parsley and serve.

CHICKEN WITH LEMON (2)

POLLO AL LIMONE (2)

Serves 4

1 lemon
1 chicken
olive oil, for brushing
salt

Preheat the oven to 350°F. Put the lemon and a pinch of salt in the cavity of the chicken and sew up the opening. Brush a roasting pan with oil, place the chicken in it, cover with a sheet of foil and roast for 1½ hours until tender and cooked through. Remove the string from the opening and take the lemon out. Cut the chicken into portions and place on a warm serving dish.

CHICKEN ON THE SPIT

POLLO ALLO SPIEDO

Serves 4

1 chicken
3 tablespoons olive oil
salt and pepper
green salad or roast new potatoes with rosemary, to serve

Fold the wings against the back, season the chicken inside and out and brush well with the oil. Thread the chicken onto a spit, put in the oven and turn slowly, basting occasionally with the cooking juices, for 35–50 minutes until tender and cooked through. If you are using an infrared oven, it is not necessary to brush the chicken with oil as the bird will cook in its own fat. Remove the chicken from the spit and season again. Serve hot with a green salad or roast new potatoes with rosemary.

CHICKEN WITH SPARKLING WINE

Heat the oil and butter in a large pan, add the chicken and cook, turning frequently, until golden brown all over, then remove from the pan and keep warm. Add the shallots to the pan and cook over low heat, stirring occasionally, for about 5 minutes, then return the chicken to the pan. Pour in the wine and stock, season with salt and pepper and add the chili powder, parsley, thyme and rosemary. Cover and simmer for 50 minutes until tender and cooked through. Transfer the chicken to a warm serving dish. Reduce the cooking juices slightly, stir in the cream and simmer for 3 minutes. Strain the sauce over the chicken and serve.

POLLO ALLO SPUMANTE

Serves 4

3 tablespoons olive oil

2 tablespoons butter

1 chicken, cut into pieces

2 shallots, sliced

1 1/2 cups sparkling dry white wine

1 1/2 cups Chicken Stock (see page 209)

pinch of chili powder

1 fresh flat-leaf parsley sprig, chopped

1 fresh thyme sprig, chopped

1 fresh rosemary sprig, chopped

scant 1/2 cup heavy cream

salt and pepper

CHICKEN WITH TUNA

Preheat the oven to 350°F. Heat the olive oil in a flameproof casserole, add the chicken and cook, turning frequently, until lightly golden all over. Add the wine and cook until it has evaporated. Season with salt and pepper and add the bay leaf, garlic, onion, carrot and celery. Cover, transfer to the oven and roast for about 1 hour until tender and cooked through. Meanwhile, chop the anchovy fillets. Combine the mayonnaise, tuna and anchovies, then stir in the capers. Remove the chicken from the casserole and let cool. Strain the cooking juices into the mayonnaise mixture. When the chicken is cold, cut it into pieces and place on a serving dish. Spoon the mayonnaise mixture over it and chill in the refrigerator for 2 hours.

POLLO AL TONNO

Serves 4

3 tablespoons olive oil

1 chicken

3/4 cup dry white wine

1 bay leaf • 1 garlic clove

1 onion, chopped • 1 carrot, chopped

1 celery stalk, chopped

2 salted anchovies, heads removed, cleaned and filleted (see page 596), soaked in cold water for 10 minutes and drained

1 quantity Mayonnaise (see page 65)

9 ounces canned tuna in oil, drained and flaked

1 tablespoon capers, drained and rinsed

salt and pepper

CHICKEN IN WHITE WINE

Preheat the oven to 350°F. Heat the oil in a roasting pan, add the garlic and rosemary, then add the chicken and cook, turning frequently, until golden brown all over. Season with salt and pepper and pour in the wine so that the chicken is almost covered. Cover the pan with a double layer of foil and roast for 30 minutes. Remove the foil, return the roasting pan to the oven and roast until the wine has evaporated and the chicken is tender and cooked through.

POLLO AL VINO BIANCO

Serves 4

2 tablespoons olive oil

1 garlic clove

1 fresh rosemary sprig

1 chicken, cut into pieces

1 bottle (3 cups) dry white wine

salt and pepper

CHICKEN IN RED WINE

POLLO AL VINO ROSSO

Serves 4

$^1/_4$ cup butter

generous $^1/_2$ cup pancetta, diced

$3^1/_2$ ounces pearl onions

1 garlic clove

$3^1/_2$ ounces mushrooms

1 fresh thyme sprig

1 tablespoon all-purpose flour

1 chicken, cut into pieces

$2^1/_4$ cups red wine

salt

Melt the butter in a pan, add the pancetta, onions, garlic, mushrooms and thyme and cook over low heat, stirring occasionally, for 5 minutes, then sprinkle with the flour. Remove and discard the garlic and add the chicken pieces. Cover and cook for 10 minutes, then pour in the wine and season with salt. Cover and simmer over low heat for about 30 minutes until tender and cooked through.

POT ROAST CHICKEN

POLLO ARROSTO

Serves 4

1 chicken

4 tablespoons olive oil

1 onion, chopped

1 carrot, chopped

1 celery stalk, chopped

1 fresh rosemary sprig

salt and pepper

carrots in butter, to serve

Lightly season the cavity of the chicken and tie with kitchen string. Heat the oil in a pan, add the onion, carrot, celery and rosemary and cook over low heat, stirring occasionally, for about 10 minutes. Place the chicken on top, increase the heat to high and cook, turning occasionally, for 15 minutes. Season with salt, lower the heat, cover and cook for 40–50 minutes until tender and cooked through. If necessary, add a little hot water to prevent the meat from drying out. Remove the chicken from the pan, untie, carve and serve with carrots in butter.

STUFFED CHICKEN

POLLO ARROSTO RIPIENO

Serves 4

4 bread slices, crusts removed

1 chicken, with giblets

2 chicken livers, thawed if frozen and chopped

generous $^1/_2$ cup prosciutto, chopped

$^1/_2$ cup Parmesan cheese, freshly grated

1 egg, lightly beaten

1 fresh rosemary sprig

4 fresh sage leaves

2 tablespoons butter

3 tablespoons olive oil

salt and pepper

Preheat the oven to 350°F. Tear the bread into pieces, place in a bowl, add water to cover and let soak for 10 minutes, then drain and squeeze out. Season the cavity of the chicken with salt and pepper. Chop the giblets and combine with the chicken livers, prosciutto, soaked bread and Parmesan in a bowl. Season with salt and pepper and stir in the beaten egg. Stuff the chicken with the mixture and sew up the opening. Fold the wings against the back and tuck the rosemary and sage underneath them. Put the chicken in a roasting pan with the butter and olive oil and roast, basting frequently, for about 1 hour until tender and cooked through. Season with salt to taste, cut the chicken into quarters, take out and slice the stuffing. Place the chicken and stuffing on a warm serving dish.

CHICKEN WITH YELLOW BELL PEPPERS

Preheat the broiler. Place the bell peppers on a cookie sheet and broil, turning frequently, until the skins are blistered and charred. Remove with tongs, place in a plastic bag and seal the top. When the bell peppers are cool enough to handle, rub off the skins, then halve, seed and cut into strips. Heat the oil and garlic in a pan until the garlic has turned brown, then remove and discard it. Add the chicken and cook, turning frequently, until browned all over. Season with salt and pepper, pour in the wine and cook until it has evaporated. Stir in the tomatoes and strips of bell pepper and simmer over medium heat, stirring occasionally, for about 20 minutes until the chicken is tender and cooked through.

POLLO CON PEPERONI GIALLI

Serves 4

3 large yellow bell peppers

2 tablespoons olive oil

1 garlic clove, lightly crushed

1 chicken, cut into pieces

3/4 cup dry white wine

1 pound 5 ounces tomatoes,

peeled, seeded and diced

salt and pepper

CHICKEN WITH GREEN BELL PEPPERS

Heat the butter and 4 tablespoons of the oil in a pan, add the chicken and cook, turning frequently, for 15 minutes until golden brown all over. Season with salt and pepper, cover and cook over low heat for about 20 minutes. Add the bell peppers, garlic and the remaining oil if necessary. Simmer over low heat for about 30 minutes until the chicken is tender and cooked through. If necessary, add 1–2 tablespoons hot water to prevent the pan from drying out.

POLLO CON PEPERONI VERDI

Serves 4

3 tablespoons butter

4–5 tablespoons olive oil

1 chicken, cut into pieces

11 ounces small, thin green bell peppers

1 garlic clove, chopped

salt and pepper

FRIED MARINATED CHICKEN

Season the chicken with salt and pepper. Combine 3/4 cup of the oil, the lemon juice, garlic, parsley, onion and bay leaf in a dish, add the chicken and let marinate for at least 2 hours. Drain the chicken, pat dry with paper towels and dust with flour. Beat the egg with a pinch of salt and dip the chicken in the mixture to coat. Heat the remaining oil in a skillet, add the chicken and cook over medium heat, turning frequently, for about 10 minutes until golden brown all over and cooked through. Remove the chicken from the skillet, drain well on paper towels, and garnish with slices of lemon.

POLLO FRITTO MARINATO

Serves 4

1 chicken, cut into pieces

1 cup olive oil

juice of 1 lemon, strained

1 garlic clove, chopped

1 fresh flat-leaf parsley sprig, chopped

1 onion, thinly sliced

1 bay leaf, crumbled

all-purpose flour, for dusting

1 egg

salt and pepper

lemon slices, to garnish

POLLO IMPANATO E FRITTO

Serves 4

³/₄ cup olive oil

juice of 1 lemon, strained

1 chicken, cut into pieces

2 eggs

1¹/₂ cups fresh bread crumbs

¹/₄ cup Clarified Butter (see page 88)

all-purpose flour, for dusting

salt and pepper

FRIED CHICKEN IN BREAD CRUMBS

Combine the olive oil and lemon juice in a dish and season with salt and pepper. Add the chicken and let marinate for 1 hour. Beat the eggs with a pinch of salt in a shallow dish and spread out the bread crumbs in another shallow dish. Drain the chicken, dust lightly with flour and dip first in the beaten eggs and then in the bread crumbs. Melt the clarified butter in a skillet, add the chicken and cook over medium-high heat, turning frequently, for 15–20 minutes until crisp on the outside and tender and cooked through on the inside. Remove the chicken from the skillet, drain on paper towels and serve.

POLLO IN CROSTA DI SALE

Serves 4

9 cups all-purpose flour

6³/₄ cups sea salt

1 egg white

1 chicken

1 fresh rosemary sprig

1 bay leaf

salt and pepper

CHICKEN IN A SALT CRUST

Preheat the oven to 325°F. Combine the flour, sea salt and egg white in a bowl until thoroughly mixed. Season the inside of the chicken with salt and pepper and put the rosemary and bay leaf in the cavity. Place the chicken in an oven-proof dish and cover completely with the salt mixture. Cover the dish tightly and bake for 1¹/₂ hours. Break the salt crust and cut the chicken into pieces.

POLLO IN TERRACOTTA

Serves 4

1 fresh rosemary sprig, chopped

1 fresh thyme sprig, chopped

1 fresh summer savory sprig, chopped

2 teaspoons dried oregano

4 fresh sage leaves, chopped

2 fresh flat-leaf parsley sprigs, chopped

1 chicken

salt and pepper

CHICKEN IN A BRICK

Preheat the oven to 425°F. Soak a chicken brick in warm water for 5 minutes, then tip out any excess water but do not dry. Combine all the herbs in a bowl and put half of them in the base of the chicken brick. Season the chicken with salt and pepper and tie neatly with kitchen string. Place the chicken in the brick and sprinkle with the remaining herbs. Roast for 1¹/₄ hours until tender and cooked through.

SPICY INDIAN MEATBALLS

POLPETTE PICCANTI ALL'INDIANA

Serves 4

2 onions

2 cloves

3¹/₂ cups ground chicken

1 garlic clove, finely chopped

1 small fresh red chile, seeded and chopped

¹/₄ cup butter

juice of 1 lemon, strained

salt

Finely chop one of the onions and stud the other with the cloves. Combine the chicken, chopped onion, garlic and chile in a bowl, season with salt and mix well. Shape the mixture into balls. Melt the butter in a skillet, add the remaining onion and cook over medium heat, turning frequently, until browned, then discard. Add the meatballs and cook, stirring frequently, for 10 minutes. Lower the heat and cook for 20 minutes, basting with 1 tablespoon hot water if necessary. Pour the lemon juice over the meatballs, stir and serve.

CHOPPED CHICKEN WITH LEMON BALM

SPEZZATINO ALLA MELISSA

Serves 4

10 fresh lemon balm leaves

2 tablespoons vegetable oil

2 tablespoons butter

1 chicken, cut into pieces

4 tablespoons sugar

2 tablespoons soy sauce

Put the lemon balm leaves in a heatproof bowl, pour in 5 tablespoons boiling water and let steep for 2 hours. Heat the oil and butter in a pan, add the chicken pieces and cook over medium heat, turning frequently, for 5 minutes. Meanwhile, put the sugar in a large pan, add 1 tablespoon water and cook, stirring until the sugar has dissolved, then boil without stirring until it has caramelized. Strain the lemon balm liquid into the caramelized sugar, stir in the soy sauce and add the chicken. Cook over low heat for 30 minutes. Mix well and serve.

CHICKEN STEW WITH OLIVES

SPEZZATINO ALLE OLIVE

Serves 4

2 tablespoons olive oil • 2 tablespoons butter

1 garlic clove • 1 chicken, cut into pieces

4 tomatoes, peeled and coarsely chopped

1¹/₄ cups pitted black olives

1 fresh flat-leaf parsley sprig, chopped

4 fresh basil leaves, chopped • salt and pepper

Heat the oil and butter in a pan with the garlic. Add the chicken and cook over medium-high heat, turning frequently, until browned all over. Season with salt and pepper, add the tomatoes and olives, lower the heat, cover and simmer for about 30 minutes. Transfer the mixture to a warm serving dish and sprinkle with the parsley and basil.

CHOPPED CHICKEN WITH ALMONDS

SPEZZATINO CON LE MANDORLE

Serves 4

4 skinless, boneless chicken breast portions, cut into strips

2 tablespoons vegetable oil

scant 1 cup blanched almonds

2 tablespoons soy sauce • salt

Cut the chicken strips into smaller pieces. Heat the oil in a skillet, add the chicken and almonds and stir-fry over high heat for a few minutes until golden brown all over. Pour in the soy sauce, season lightly with salt and stir in 1–2 tablespoons water. Lower the heat to medium, cover and simmer for 20 minutes.

OSTRICH

Ostrich could become the meat of the third millennium, so it is worth trying it straight away. It is already familiar in the United States and ostrich farms have also been established in several European countries as well as further afield, including Australia and New Zealand. Ostrich farms are multiplying in Italy – at the moment there are about 400. Some Italian supermarkets offer a variety of ostrich cuts and several restaurants have dishes devoted to this exotic bird on their menus. From a nutritional point of view its red, lean and tender meat deserves respect mainly because of its iron content and high levels of protein. In addition, its low fat content, compared with other more common red meats, makes it particularly digestible. It has minimal cholesterol and sodium levels too. As regards flavor, it is similar to beef but slightly stronger. Ostrich meat is lean and 3^1/$_2$ ounces provides 105 kcal. A 220–pound ostrich provides about 55–66 pounds of prime meat – fillets, steaks, etc. – and 11 pounds of other cuts – slices, ground meat, etc. Ostrich sausages and cold cuts, such as ham, salami and dried salted meat are also available. As ostrich is a suitable alternative to beef, and more or less the same preparation and cooking techniques apply, from carpaccio onwards. This has been proved conclusively since 1995 by chef Fabio Beretta at the Conte Rosso restaurant, the first in Milan – maybe in the whole of Italy – to offer this new meat on its menu. The recipes in this section are his.

OSTRICH EGGS

UOVA DI STRUZZO

Ostrich eggs weigh about 3^1/$_4$ pounds – the shell alone weighs 7 ounces The shell should be kept intact because of its commercial value. Drill a hole in the bottom with a ^{3}/$_4$-inch conical bit, insert a thin stick and whisk the yolk and white inside the egg. Pour the egg out through the hole and store in a screw-top jar in the refrigerator. Weigh out the required amount.

CONTE ROSSO OSTRICH FILLET

FILETTO DI STRUZZO ALLA CONTE ROSSO

Serves 4

2 porcini, cut into thin strips

1 teaspoon bread crumbs

1 garlic clove, chopped

3 fresh basil leaves, chopped

1 teaspoon chopped fresh rosemary needles

1 pound 9-ounce ostrich fillet

all-purpose flour, for dusting

4 tablespoons olive oil

1½ cups heavy cream

3 tablespoons butter

1 tablespoon Worcestershire sauce

dash of brandy

8 white bread slices, toasted and cut into triangles

salt

Combine the porcini, bread crumbs, garlic, basil and rosemary in a bowl. Cut the ostrich fillet into quarters, make a slit in each to create a 'pocket' and stuff with the porcini mixture. Secure with toothpicks and dust with flour. Heat the olive oil in a pan, add the ostrich fillets and cook for 5 minutes on each side. Pour off the oil, then add the cream, butter, Worcestershire sauce, brandy and a pinch of salt. Cook over low heat until the sauce is creamy. Place the fillets on a warm serving dish, spoon the sauce over them and arrange the toast triangles around them.

OSTRICH STEW

STRACOTTO DI STRUZZO

Serves 4

2 carrots, finely chopped

1 celery stalk, finely chopped

1 onion, finely chopped

7 tablespoons olive oil

1 pound 2 ounces ostrich slices, cut into large cubes

all-purpose flour, for dusting

2¼ cups white wine

2¼ cups Vegetable Stock (see page 209)

¾ cup tomato paste

1 bouquet garni, (1 bay leaf, 2 cloves, 1 fresh sage sprig,1 fresh rosemary sprig, 6 juniper berries, 1 small cinnamon stick and a pinch of freshly grated nutmeg in a cheesecloth square)

salt and pepper

Put the carrots, celery and onion in a deep pan, add 4 tablespoons of the olive oil and cook over medium heat, stirring occasionally, for 5 minutes. Dust the meat with flour. Heat the remaining oil in another pan, add the meat and cook, stirring and turning frequently, until browned. Transfer the meat to the pan of vegetables, add the wine, stock, tomato paste and bouquet garni and season with salt and pepper. Cover and cook over medium heat for 40 minutes.

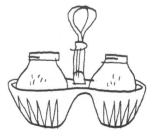

TURKEY

For nearly four centuries, turkey has been the honoured guest at the decorative Thanksgiving Day dinner table. The United States celebrates this festival every year on the fourth Thursday of November in remembrance of the landing of the Mayflower, the English vessel which brought the first group of European settlers to North America in 1620. The turkey is, in fact, native to America. Christopher Columbus wrote about it in his journals. However, the bird has been farmed for a long time and, through selective breeding, it has developed from a lean wild bird to a fat domesticated one. It is so large today that some turkeys are more than twice the size of their ancestors. They put on weight very quickly – with current breeding techniques, males reach 31–33 pounds and females 15–18 pounds in five months. Among the females, the most delicious are the three-month-olds. Turkey is often stuffed. Classic stuffings include chestnuts, prunes and sausage, celery and carrot, and sausage and bread crumbs.

COOKING

→ Before putting a turkey in the oven, brush it with oil or grease it with butter. Protect the breast with slices of pancetta or bacon.

→ Place the turkey on one side for the first 45 minutes, then on the other, so that the breast does not come into contact with the roasting pan. Finally, place it on its back.

→ Baste frequently while it is cooking. If there are not enough cooking juices, sprinkle with a little hot water.

→ As soon as the skin goes golden brown, cover with foil.

→ Cooking takes about 40 minutes per 2¼ pound, at a temperature of 425°F for the first hour, and 350°F after that.

POT ROAST TURKEY

ARROSTO DI TACCHINELLA

Serves 8

6¹/₂-pound turkey
2 fresh rosemary sprigs
4 fresh sage leaves
2 prosciutto slices, cut into strips
3¹/₂ ounces pancetta, sliced
3 tablespoons olive oil
2 tablespoons butter
2 tablespoons grappa
salt and pepper

Season the cavity of the turkey with salt and pepper and put one of the rosemary sprigs, the sage and prosciutto in the cavity. Sew up the opening, wrap the turkey breast with pancetta and truss with kitchen string. Put the oil, butter and remaining rosemary in a large shallow pan, add the turkey and cook over low heat, turning and basting occasionally, for 1³/₄–2 hours until tender and cooked through. Season lightly with salt once or twice during cooking. About 10 minutes before the end of the cooking time, remove the pancetta to allow the turkey to brown completely. Sprinkle with the grappa and ignite. Serve when the flames have died down.

TURKEY À L'ORANGE

ARROSTO DI TACCHINO ALL'ARANCIA

Serves 4

1³/₄-pound turkey breast
2 tablespoons butter
2 tablespoons olive oil
1 onion, chopped
1 celery stalk, chopped
1 carrot, chopped
2 oranges
5 tablespoons dry white wine
pinch of all-purpose flour (optional)
¹/₄ cup heavy cream
salt and pepper

Tie the turkey breast neatly with kitchen string. Heat the butter and oil in a pan, add the onion, celery and carrot and cook over low heat, stirring occasionally, for 10 minutes. Add the turkey, increase the heat to medium and cook, turning several times, until browned all over. Meanwhile, peel the oranges and blanch three or four pieces of rind, making sure that they are free of pith, in boiling water for a few minutes, then drain. Squeeze the juice from one of the oranges and strain. Separate the other orange into segments. As soon as the turkey is golden brown, pour in the wine and orange juice, add the blanched orange rind and season with salt and pepper. Lower the heat, cover and simmer for 1 hour until cooked through and tender. Remove the turkey from the pan, carve into slices and place on a warm serving dish. Stir 2 tablespoons hot water into the cooking juices, scraping up any sediment on the base of the pan. If the sauce seems a little thin, stir in a pinch of flour to thicken. Stir in the cream and season with a little pepper. Spoon the sauce over the slices of turkey and garnish with the orange segments.

TURKEY LEG WITH SPINACH

Open out the turkey leg like a book and pound with a meat mallet to flatten slightly. Tear the bread into pieces, place in a bowl, add all but 1 tablespoon of the wine and let soak for 10 minutes, then drain and squeeze out. Preheat the oven to 350°F. Cook the spinach, in just the water clinging to the leaves after washing, for about 5 minutes, then drain, squeeze out and chop. Melt half the butter in a skillet, add the onion, garlic and soaked bread and stir well, then add the spinach and marjoram and season with salt and pepper. Cook for a few minutes, then remove the skillet from the heat. Combine the spinach mixture with the beaten egg in a bowl, then spread it over the turkey and roll up. Tie with kitchen string, put in a roasting pan with the remaining butter and roast for about 50 minutes. Remove the turkey from the roasting pan and let stand for 10 minutes. Meanwhile, stir the remaining wine and 1 tablespoon warm water into the cooking juices, scraping up any sediment on the base of the pan, over low heat. Pour into a sauceboat and serve with the turkey carved into even slices.

COSCIA AGLI SPINACI
Serves 4
2-pound turkey leg, skinned and boned
1 thick bread slice, crusts removed
³/₄ cup dry white wine
9 ounces spinach
¹/₄ cup butter
1 onion, chopped
1 garlic clove, chopped
pinch of dried marjoram
1 egg, lightly beaten
salt and pepper

TURKEY LEG WITH HERBS

Finely chop the herbs in quantities according to taste, mix with 4 tablespoons of the butter and the lemon juice in a bowl and season with salt and pepper. Remove the skin from the turkey leg in one piece. Spread the herb butter over the leg, wrap it up in its skin and tie with kitchen string. Heat the olive oil and the remaining butter in a pan, add the turkey leg and cook, turning frequently, until browned all over. Cover and cook over low heat, adding a little hot water if necessary to prevent drying out, for 1 hour until tender and cooked through. Carve the meat into slices, place on a warm serving dish and spoon the cooking juices over. Serve with potatoes.

COSCIA ALLE ERBE AROMATICHE
Serves 4
fresh flat-leaf parsley
fresh tarragon
fresh thyme
fresh rosemary
fresh marjoram
fresh basil
fresh mint
fresh sage
6 tablespoons butter, softened
juice of ¹/₂ lemon, strained
2-pound turkey leg
4 tablespoons olive oil
salt and pepper
potatoes, to serve

TURKEY BREAST WITH CHEESE

FESA AL FORMAGGIO

Serves 4

1 pound 5 ounces turkey breast steaks

all-purpose flour, for dusting

2 tablespoons butter

¾ cup white wine

2 ounces Parmesan cheese, shaved

black truffle, thinly shaved (optional)

salt and pepper

Pound the turkey steaks with a meat mallet and dust with flour. Melt the butter in a pan, add the turkey steaks and cook, turning occasionally, until browned on both sides. Pour in the wine and cook until it has evaporated, then season with salt and pepper. Cook over low heat for about 10 minutes, then sprinkle each steak with Parmesan, cover and cook until the cheese has melted. Transfer to a warm serving dish. To enrich the dish, sprinkle with a few thin shavings of black truffle.

TURKEY BREAST WITH ALMONDS

FESA ALLE MANDORLE

Serves 4

3 tablespoons butter

1 onion, chopped

1 carrot, chopped

1 celery stalk, chopped

1 pound 5 ounces turkey breast steaks

5 tablespoons white wine

½ cup blanched almonds

¾ cup milk

1 tablespoon brandy

salt and pepper

Melt the butter in a pan, add the onion, carrot and celery and cook over low heat, stirring occasionally, for 5 minutes. Place the turkey steaks on top and cook until browned on both sides, then season with salt and pepper. Increase the heat to medium, pour in the wine and cook until it has evaporated, then cover and cook over low heat for about 10 minutes. Meanwhile, put the almonds in a pan, add the milk and brandy and simmer for 15 minutes. Transfer to a food processor and process to a purée. Pour the purée over the meat, simmer for a few more minutes and serve.

TURKEY FRICASSÉE WITH PORCINI

FRICASSEA AI PORCINI

Serves 4

3 tablespoons butter

3 tablespoons olive oil

1 pound 5 ounces skinless, boneless turkey breast, cut into medium cubes

1 small onion, chopped

2 garlic cloves

¾ cup dry white wine

14 ounces porcini, sliced

1 fresh flat-leaf parsley sprig, chopped

5 tablespoons hot chicken or turkey stock made with a stock cube

2 egg yolks

juice of ½ lemon, strained

salt and pepper

Heat the butter and 2 tablespoons of the olive oil in a pan, add the turkey and cook over high heat, stirring frequently, until golden brown. Remove with a slotted spatula and set aside. Lower the heat, add the onion and one of the garlic cloves to the pan and cook, stirring occasionally, for 5 minutes, then remove and discard the garlic. Return the turkey to the pan, add the wine, cover and simmer for 30 minutes. Brush the porcini with the remaining olive oil and stir into the pan. Chop the remaining garlic and add to the pan with the parsley, pour in the hot stock and simmer for about 30 minutes more. Beat the egg yolks with 1 tablespoon water, the lemon juice, a pinch of salt and a pinch of pepper in a bowl. Move the pan to the edge of the stove, pour in the egg mixture and mix quickly so that it does not curdle, but remains soft and creamy and coats the meat lightly. Transfer to a warm serving dish.

TASTY TURKEY ROULADES

Preheat the oven to 400°F. Place the yellow bell pepper on a cookie sheet and roast until the skin blackens and blisters, then remove from the oven, wrap in foil and set aside for 20 minutes. Meanwhile, chop the anchovy fillets. Tear the roll into pieces, place in a bowl, add water to cover and let soak for 10 minutes, then drain and squeeze out. Unwrap the bell pepper, peel, seed and cut into strips. Place the bell pepper, anchovies, soaked roll, parsley and a pinch of salt in a food processor and process to a purée. Place a slice of pancetta on each slice of turkey and spread with the purée, then roll up, tie with kitchen string and dust with the flour. Heat the oil and butter in a pan, add the onion and cook over low heat, stirring occasionally, for 5 minutes. Add the roulades and cook, turning frequently, until browned all over, then season with salt and pepper and cook for a few minutes more. Add the tomatoes and basil leaves and simmer for 10 minutes. Taste and add more salt if necessary. Transfer the roulades to a warm serving dish and spoon the cooking juices over them.

INVOLTINI SAPORITI
Serves 4

1 yellow bell pepper
4 salted anchovies, heads removed, cleaned and filleted (see page 596), soaked in cold water for 10 minutes and drained
1 bread roll, crust removed
1 fresh flat-leaf parsley sprig, coarsely chopped
3$\frac{1}{2}$ ounces pancetta, sliced
1 pound 5 ounces sliced turkey breast
$\frac{1}{4}$ cup all-purpose flour
2 tablespoons olive oil
2 tablespoons butter
$\frac{1}{2}$ onion, chopped
14 ounces canned chopped tomatoes
5 fresh basil leaves
salt and pepper

TURKEY ROLL WITH OLIVES

Spread out the turkey breast and pound well with a meat mallet. Place the ham and olives on top, season with salt and pepper, roll up and tie with kitchen string. Heat the butter and olive oil in a pan, add the sage, rosemary and rolled turkey and cook, turning frequently, for 10 minutes until browned all over. Pour in the wine and cook until it has evaporated. Season with salt and pepper, cover and cook over low heat for 1 hour. This dish is excellent both hot and cold.

ROTOLO ALLE OLIVE
Serves 4

1$\frac{3}{4}$-pound turkey breast, boned
3 ounces cooked, cured ham, sliced
$\frac{1}{2}$ cup green olives
2 tablespoons butter
2 tablespoons olive oil
4 fresh sage leaves
1 fresh rosemary sprig
5 tablespoons dry white wine
salt and pepper

TURKEY STEW WITH MUSTARD

SPEZZATINO ALLA SENAPE

Serves 4

2 tablespoons olive oil
2 tablespoons butter
1 onion, chopped
1 garlic clove, chopped
1 pound 5 ounces skinless, boneless turkey breast, cut into cubes
3/4 cup dry white wine
1 cup hot Chicken Stock (see page 209)
2 tablespoons Dijon mustard
1 fresh flat-leaf parsley sprig, chopped
salt and pepper

Heat the oil and butter in a skillet, add the onion and garlic and cook over low heat, stirring occasionally, for 5 minutes. Increase the heat to medium, add the turkey and cook, stirring frequently, for 10 minutes until golden brown. Season with salt and pepper, pour in the wine and cook until it has evaporated. Pour in 3/4 cup of the hot stock, cover and simmer for about 30 minutes. Combine the remaining stock and the mustard in a bowl and stir into the skillet. Sprinkle with the parsley and simmer for a further 15 minutes.

GLAZED TURKEY

TACCHINELLA GLASSATA

Serves 8–10

3 1/4-pound turkey
bunch of fresh mixed herbs
thinly pared rind of 1 orange, cut into thin strips
3 tablespoons olive oil
5 tablespoons dry white wine
3/4 cup hot Chicken Stock (see page 209)
1/3 cup dried mushrooms
1 carrot, chopped
1 celery stalk, chopped
1 onion, chopped
3 tablespoons butter
1 pound 2 ounces shelled chestnuts, boiled for about 45 minutes
5 tablespoons dry Marsala
salt and pepper

Preheat the oven to 400°F. Season the turkey inside and out with salt and pepper and place the herbs and orange rind in the cavity. Put the bird in a fairly large roasting pan, sprinkle with the olive oil and roast until the skin is golden brown. Lower the temperature to 350°F, sprinkle with the wine, return to the oven and roast, basting occasionally with the hot stock, for a further 1 1/2 hours. Meanwhile, place the mushrooms in a bowl, add hot water to cover and let soak for 30 minutes, then drain and squeeze out. Add the carrot, celery and onion to the roasting pan, cover the turkey with a sheet of foil, return to the oven and roast for a further 30 minutes. Melt the butter in a pan, add the chestnuts and mushrooms and cook over low heat, stirring occasionally, for about 10 minutes. Add the Marsala and 1 tablespoon of the turkey cooking juices, season with salt and pepper and simmer until thickened. Transfer the turkey to a warm serving dish and surround with the glazed chestnuts. Pour the sauce that remains into a sauceboat and serve with the turkey.

CHRISTMAS TURKEY

Preheat the oven to 425°F. First make the stuffing. Tear the bread into pieces, place in a bowl, add water to cover and let soak for 10 minutes, then drain and squeeze out. Chop the turkey giblets, pancetta and sausages together, place in a bowl, add the soaked bread, apples, prunes and chestnuts and mix well. Spoon the mixture into the cavity of the turkey, dip the butter into a pinch each of salt and pepper, add to the cavity and sew up the opening. Cover the turkey breast with the pancetta slices and put in a roasting pan with the butter. Roast for 1 hour, then lower the temperature to 350°F and roast, basting occasionally, for about a further 1¼ hours. Remove the pancetta, return the turkey to the oven and roast for 15 minutes more until golden brown, tender and cooked through.

TACCHINO DI NATALE

Serves 8

6½-pound turkey, with giblets
3½ ounces pancetta, sliced
¼ cup butter

For the stuffing
1 thick slice bread, crusts removed
1½ ounces pancetta
3½ ounces Italian sausages
2 apples, peeled, cored and sliced
scant ½ cup no-soak prunes
9 ounces shelled chestnuts, boiled
for about 45 minutes
2 tablespoons butter
salt and pepper

TURKEY STUFFED WITH CHESTNUTS

Peel off the skins and mash the chestnuts. Preheat the oven to 350°F. Add the sausages and olives to the chestnuts, season with salt and pepper and mix well. Spoon the mixture into the cavity of the turkey and sew up the opening. Cover the turkey breast with the pancetta slices, tie with kitchen string and season with salt and pepper. Generously brush a roasting pan with oil, put the turkey in it and roast, basting occasionally, for 1½ hours. Remove the pancetta slices, return the turkey to the oven and roast for a further 30 minutes until browned, cooked through and tender. Place the turkey on a warm serving dish and surround with large lettuce leaves as a garnish.

TACCHINO RIPIENO DI CASTAGNE

Serves 6–8

9 ounces shelled chestnuts, boiled for
about 45 minutes
11 ounces Italian sausages, skinned and crumbled
1¼ cups pitted green olives, chopped
6½-pound turkey
3½ ounces pancetta, sliced
olive oil, for brushing
salt and pepper
lettuce leaves, to garnish

TURKEY STUFFED
WITH BRUSSELS SPROUTS

Preheat the oven to 350°F. Cook the Brussels sprouts in a large pan of salted, boiling water, uncovered, for about 15 minutes, then drain and halve. Put them in a bowl, add the ham, season with salt and pepper and mix well. Spoon the mixture into the cavity of the turkey and sew up the opening. Cover the turkey breast with the pork fat or bacon, tie with kitchen string and season with salt and pepper. Generously brush a roasting pan with oil, put the turkey in it and roast, basting occasionally, for 1½ hours. Remove the slices of pork fat or bacon, return the turkey to the oven and roast for a further 30 minutes until browned, cooked through and tender. Remove the turkey from the roasting pan and let stand for about 10 minutes, then place on a warm serving dish.

TACCHINO RIPIENO
DI CAVOLINI DI BRUXELLES

Serves 6–8

11 ounces Brussels sprouts, trimmed

9 ounces cooked, cured ham, chopped

6½-pound turkey

3½ ounces pork fat, thinly sliced,

or fatty bacon slices

olive oil, for brushing

salt and pepper

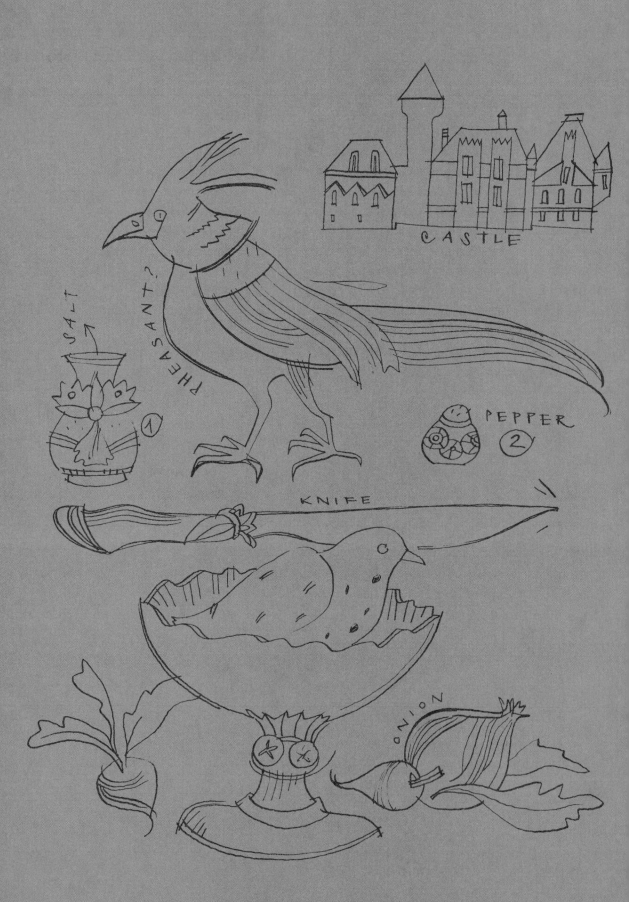

CASTLE

THEASANT?

SALT

①

PEPPER

②

KNIFE

ONION

GAME →

GAME

This chapter on game has been written in the hope that the reader will, whenever possible, buy farmed animals. Many game species, such as rabbit, deer and 'wild' boar, are reared nowadays in very much the same way as cattle and pigs. This helps to conserve wildlife in its natural habitat. Each individual section of this chapter provides specific details about the particular animal. However, in general, young game is more suitable for roasting, frying and broiling, whereas adult game is better stewed, braised and jugged. Jugged game is one of the most classic, traditional recipes. The flavor of game often goes well with some fruits, such as cherries, grapes, blueberries and apples, which may be added to the pan during cooking or served separately as sauces.

PHEASANT?

WOODCOCK AND SNIPE

Woodcock and snipe are similar-looking, migratory birds with characteristically long beaks. They are known as beccacce throughout Italy, but in the north they are also called gallinazze, pizzacre or pole and in the south, pizzarde or arcere. They are not farmed and are only found in Italy at certain times of year – in October and November and in February and March. Different countries specify various hunting seasons. Both woodcock and snipe are pleasantly tasty and need hanging for between three and five days. One woodcock or snipe is sufficient for two people.

FEATHERED GAME

CURRIED WOODCOCK

Season the birds with salt and pepper and dust with flour. Melt half the butter in a skillet, add the birds and cook over medium heat, turning frequently, for 15 minutes. Melt the remaining butter in another pan, add the onion and cook over low heat, stirring occasionally, for 5 minutes. Add the curry powder and hot stock and simmer for 20 minutes. Just before serving, transfer the birds to the curry sauce, heat through and add the lemon juice.

BECCACCIA AL CURRY

Serves 4

2 woodcock or snipe, drawn and plucked

all-purpose flour, for dusting

¹/₄ cup butter

1 onion, sliced

2 teaspoons curry powder

1¹/₄ cups Meat Stock (see page 208)

juice of ¹/₂ lemon, strained

salt and pepper

WOODCOCK WITH JUNIPER

BECCACCIA AL GINEPRO

Serves 4

12 juniper berries

7 tablespoons butter

4 fresh thyme sprigs

2 woodcock or snipe, drawn and plucked

3/4 cup gin

salt and pepper

Crush the juniper berries in a mortar with a pestle until mashed. Blend one-third of the berries with 3 tablespoons of the butter and shape the mixture into four balls. Put one butter ball and a sprig of thyme in the cavity of each bird. Heat the remaining butter in a pan, add the birds and cook over high heat, turning frequently, until browned. Season with salt and pepper, sprinkle with the remaining juniper berries, lower the heat to medium and cook until the birds are tender and cooked through. Gently heat the gin in a small pan, pour it over the birds and ignite, then serve.

WOODCOCK WITH TRUFFLE

BECCACCIA AL TARTUFO

Serves 4

2 woodcock or snipe, drawn and plucked with livers and hearts

3 ounces pancetta slices

2 tablespoons butter

2 tablespoons olive oil

1 carrot, chopped

1 celery stalk, chopped

1/2 onion, chopped

1 bay leaf

1 1/2 cups red wine

2 small black truffles, shaved

8 polenta slices

salt and pepper

Chop the livers and hearts and set aside. Tie the beaks of the birds between their legs, season the cavities with a pinch each of salt and pepper and wrap them with the pancetta. Heat the butter and olive oil in a pan, add the carrot, celery, onion and bay leaf and cook over low heat, stirring occasionally, for 10 minutes. Add the birds to the pan and cook, turning frequently, until browned all over. Season with salt and pepper, pour in 1 cup of the wine and simmer over low heat for about 20 minutes. Remove the birds from the pan, cut them in half and keep warm. Add the livers and hearts to the pan and mix well. Pour in the remaining wine, add half the truffle shavings and cook until the sauce is slightly reduced. Place the polenta on a warm serving dish and put the birds on top. Spoon the sauce over them and sprinkle with the remaining truffle.

WOODCOCK WITH GREEN APPLES

BECCACCIA CON MELE VERDI

Serves 4

2 woodcock or snipe, drawn and plucked

olive oil, for brushing

2 tablespoons butter

4 bread slices

2 green apples, peeled, cored and cut into 1/4-inch thick slices

salt and pepper

Preheat the oven to 425°F. Put the birds in a roasting pan, brush with olive oil and season with salt. Roast for 10 minutes or until golden brown and tender. Melt half the butter in a skillet, add the slices of bread and cook until golden brown on both sides, then remove from the skillet and set aside. Heat the remaining butter, add the apples and cook until lightly browned, then season with pepper. Serve the birds on the slices of fried bread surrounded by the hot apples.

PHEASANT

Pheasants are highly valued birds originating in Asia. The most obvious difference between the male and the female is that the former has colored feathers. The hen has duller plumage which merges into the vegetation. In Italy, farm-reared pheasants, which need hanging for about a day in the refrigerator, are the most widespread, but this is not usually necessary for pheasants bought commercially outside Italy. If the bird comes from a shoot, it needs to be hung for three days. A large cock pheasant is more or less enough for four people.

PHEASANT WITH FRUIT

Squeeze the juice from 3²/₃ cups of the grapes. Truss the pheasant with kitchen string. Melt half the butter in a pan, add the pheasant and cook, turning frequently, until browned all over. Pour the grape juice, orange juice, wine and brandy over the bird, season with salt and pepper, cover and simmer over low heat for 30 minutes. Meanwhile, blanch the remaining grapes in boiling water for 1 minute, then drain, refresh under cold water and peel. Add the grapes and walnuts to the pheasant and simmer for a further 10 minutes. Transfer the pheasant to a serving dish, remove the string and keep warm. Add the remaining butter to the cooking juices, sprinkle with the flour and stir well. Bring to a boil, add the orange rind and remove from the heat. Surround the pheasant with slices of orange and the peeled grapes and serve with the sauce.

FAGIANO ALLA FRUTTA

Serves 4

5¹/₄ cups mixed white and black grapes

1 pheasant, drawn and plucked

¹/₄ cup butter

juice of 2 oranges, strained

³/₄ cup dry white wine

¹/₄ cup brandy

20 shelled walnuts, coarsely chopped

1 tablespoon all-purpose flour

grated rind of ¹/₂ orange

salt and pepper

orange slices, to garnish

PHEASANT IN CREAM SAUCE

Season the cavity of the pheasant with salt and pepper, then wrap the breast in the pancetta slices and truss with kitchen string. Heat the olive oil and butter in a pan, add the pheasant and cook, turning frequently, until browned all over, then season lightly with salt. Lower the heat, cover and cook gently for about 30 minutes. Sprinkle the pheasant with the cream and cook, basting frequently, for a further 15 minutes. Finally, add the lemon juice to the sauce and serve.

FAGIANO ALLA PANNA

Serves 4

1 pheasant, drawn and plucked

4$\frac{1}{2}$ ounces pancetta, thinly sliced

2 tablespoons olive oil

2 tablespoons butter

4 tablespoons heavy cream

1 tablespoon lemon juice

salt and pepper

PHEASANT WITH OLIVES

Preheat the oven to 350°F. Season the cavity of the pheasant with salt and pepper and put the rosemary and 2 tablespoons of the butter in it. Wrap the bird in the pancetta and truss with kitchen string. Place in a flameproof casserole dish, dot with remaining the butter and roast, basting frequently with the Marsala and cooking juices, for about 1 hour. Remove the dish from the oven, sprinkle the olives over the pheasant and cook over low heat for a further 40 minutes.

FAGIANO ALLE OLIVE

Serves 4

1 pheasant, drawn and plucked

1 fresh rosemary sprig

6 tablespoons butter

6 pancetta slices

5 tablespoons dry Marsala

1$\frac{3}{4}$ cups pitted black olives

salt and pepper

STUFFED POT ROAST PHEASANT

If possible, choose a hen pheasant rather than a cock as the meat is more tender. Chop the liver, mix with the pork fat or bacon, parsley, and truffle if using, in a bowl and season with salt and pepper. Spoon the mixture into the cavity of the pheasant and sew up the opening. Cover the breast of the bird with the pancetta slices, tie with kitchen string and season with salt and pepper. Heat the butter in a pan, add the pheasant and cook for 20 minutes. Remove the pancetta to allow the meat to brown and cook for a further 10 minutes. Add the cream and cook for 15 minutes more, then serve.

FAGIANO ARROSTO RIPIENO

Serves 4

1 pheasant, drawn and plucked, with liver

$\frac{1}{3}$ cup smoked pork fat or fatty bacon, chopped

1 fresh flat-leaf parsley sprig, chopped

1 small black truffle, chopped (optional)

2 ounces pancetta, sliced

2 tablespoons butter

2 tablespoons heavy cream

salt and pepper

FAGIANO CON I FUNGHI

Serves 4

1 pheasant, drawn and plucked

1 tablespoon olive oil

$^1/_4$ cup butter

1 onion, chopped

1 shallot, chopped

1 carrot, chopped

generous $^1/_2$ cup cooked, cured ham, diced

1 fresh rosemary sprig

4 fresh sage leaves, chopped

1 bay leaf

4 cups Chicken Stock (see page 209)

7 ounces white mushrooms

7 ounces chanterelle mushrooms

1 garlic clove

1$^3/_4$ cups pitted green olives

salt and pepper

PHEASANT WITH MUSHROOMS

Season the cavity of the pheasant with salt and pepper and truss with kitchen string. Heat the olive oil and half the butter in a pan, add the pheasant and cook, turning frequently, until browned all over, then remove from the pan. Add the onion, shallot, carrot, ham and herbs to the pan, season with salt and pepper and pour in the stock. Cover and simmer over low heat for about 15 minutes. Return the pheasant to the pan, re-cover and simmer for a further 40 minutes. Melt the remaining butter in another pan, add the mushrooms and garlic and cook, stirring occasionally, for about 10 minutes. Remove the mushrooms from the pan, add the olives and cook gently for 5 minutes. Add the olives and mushrooms to the pheasant and cook for a few minutes more. Transfer the bird and vegetables to a warm serving dish, discarding the rosemary, bay leaf and garlic.

FILETTI DI FAGIANO ALL'ARANCIA

Serves 4

1 pheasant, drawn and plucked boned and carcass reserved

$^1/_4$ cup butter

5 juniper berries, lightly crushed

$^3/_4$ cup dry white wine

scant 1 cup Meat Stock (see page 208)

4 black peppercorns, lightly crushed

juice of 1 orange, strained

salt

PHEASANT WITH ORANGE

Slice the pheasant meat. Melt the butter in a skillet with the juniper berries, add the slices of pheasant and cook over medium heat, stirring and turning occasionally, for about 20 minutes. Meanwhile, put the wine, stock, peppercorns and a pinch of salt in another pan, add the carcass and bring to a boil, then cook until the liquid has reduced by half. Strain and skim off the fat if necessary. Bring the pheasant stock to a simmer, add the orange juice and slices of pheasant and simmer for a further 2 minutes. Transfer to a warm serving dish.

FINEST QUALITY

PARTRIDGE

Red-legged partridges, commonly eaten in Italy, are related to American partridges, which have now been introduced to Europe, particularly to France. Farmed partridges do not require hanging, but hunted birds should be hung for two to four days. Partridge meat is red and flavorsome and is excellent roasted in the oven or on a spit. Allow one small partridge or half a large one per serving. To cook, allow 20 minutes per 9 ounces.

PARTRIDGE WITH MUSTARD

PERNICE ALLA SENAPE

Serves 4

2 partridges, drawn and plucked with livers

pinch of chili powder

2 slices pork fat or fatty bacon

3 tablespoons olive oil

¹/₄ cup butter

²/₃ cup Meat Stock

(see page 208), plus extra for the sauce

¹/₄ cup all-purpose flour

¹/₂ teaspoon English mustard

3–4 tablespoons heavy cream

salt

Season the cavities of the partridges with the chili powder and a pinch of salt and wrap the birds in the pork fat or bacon. Heat the olive oil and 2 tablespoons of the butter in a pan, add the partridges and cook over a medium-high heat, turning frequently, until browned all over. Pour in the stock and simmer, basting occasionally, for 20–25 minutes. Meanwhile, finely chop the livers. Combine the flour and remaining butter in a bowl and stir in the mustard. Remove the partridges from the pan, place on a serving dish and keep warm. Add the mustard mixture and the partridge livers to the pan and pour in a little extra stock if necessary. Lower the heat and cook, stirring constantly, until the sauce has the desired consistency. Add the cream and cook over medium heat for a few minutes. Spoon the sauce over the partridges and serve.

STUFFED PARTRIDGE

PERNICE FARCITA

Serves 4

2 tablespoons butter, plus extra for greasing

1 thick bread slice, crusts removed

5 tablespoons milk

1 pound 2 ounces mushrooms

2 partridges, drawn and plucked
with livers and hearts

generous ¹/₂ cup smoked pancetta, diced

salt and pepper

Preheat the oven to 350°F. Generously grease an ovenproof dish with butter. Tear the bread into pieces, place in a bowl, add the milk and let soak for 10 minutes, then drain and squeeze out. Separate the caps of half the mushroom from their stems and chop the stems with the livers and hearts. Place in a bowl, stir in the soaked bread and season with salt and pepper to taste. Divide the mixture between the cavities of the partridges and sew up the openings. Chop the remaining mushrooms. Place the partridges in the prepared dish, surround them with the chopped mushrooms and pancetta and dot with the butter. Cover and roast for about 20 minutes. Remove the lid, stir in the cooking juices and roast until the partridges are cooked through and tender. Serve straight from the dish.

MARINATED PARTRIDGE

PERNICE MARINATA

Serves 4

4 partridges, drawn and plucked

4 tablespoons olive oil

1 onion, chopped

1 garlic clove, chopped

1 red bell pepper, halved, seeded and diced

¹/₂ celery root, diced

2 bay leaves

4 black peppercorns, lightly crushed

1¹/₄ cups dry white wine

1¹/₄ cups white wine vinegar

5 tablespoons Meat Stock (see page 208), optional

salt and pepper

Season the partridges inside and out with salt. Heat the olive oil in a skillet, add the partridges and cook, turning frequently, for 10 minutes until browned all over, then season with pepper. Transfer the birds to a flameproof dish and add the onion, garlic, red bell pepper, celery root, bay leaves, peppercorns, wine and vinegar. Cover and cook over low heat for about 1 hour, adding the stock if necessary to prevent drying out. Let the partridges cool slightly, then serve in their vegetable sauce, discarding the bay leaves.

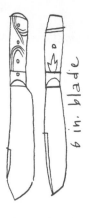

QUAIL

Quail are widespread and naturally live in fields and on grazing land. Most quail available in supermarkets are farmed and with no wild flavor. They are sold oven-ready, and have lean, easily digestible flesh. Frozen quail are also available.

QUAIL WITH YOGURT

Combine the lemon rind, onion, garlic and paprika in a bowl, strain in 2 tablespoons of the lemon juice and season with salt and pepper. Spread some of the mixture on the quail to cover. Place the birds in a skillet with the olive oil and cook for 10 minutes on each side. Add the remaining lemon mixture, pour in the hot stock, cover and cook for about 15 minutes. Transfer the quail to a warm serving dish. Stir the yogurt into the cooking juices and strain in the remaining lemon juice to taste. Cook until thickened, then serve the quail with the sauce.

QUAGLIE ALLO YOGURT

Serves 4

grated rind and juice of 1 lemon

1 onion, chopped

1 garlic clove, chopped

1 teaspoon paprika

8 quail

2 tablespoons olive oil

scant 1 cup hot Meat Stock (see page 208)

1³/₄ cups natural yogurt

salt and pepper

QUAIL IN WHITE WINE

Put half a garlic clove, 1 teaspoon of the rosemary needles and a sage leaf in the cavity of each bird and season with salt and pepper. Put the quail in a pan with the olive oil and cook, turning frequently, until browned all over. Season with salt, pour in the wine, cover and simmer over low heat for 20 minutes.

QUAGLIE AL VINO BIANCO

Serves 4

4 garlic cloves, halved

8 teaspoons fresh rosemary needles

8 fresh sage leaves

8 quail

2 tablespoons olive oil

³/₄ cup white wine

salt and pepper

QUAIL WITH RISOTTO

QUAGLIE CON RISOTTO

Serves 4

4 quail

6 tablespoons butter

2 tablespoons olive oil

2 tablespoons all-purpose flour

about 6¼ cups hot Chicken Stock

(see page 209)

1 fresh thyme sprig

1 bay leaf

¾ cup dry white wine

1 onion, chopped

scant 2 cups risotto rice

½ cup Parmesan cheese, freshly grated

salt and pepper

Truss the quail with kitchen string and season with salt and pepper. Heat 2 tablespoons of the butter and the oil in a pan, add the quail and cook over high heat, turning frequently, for about 10 minutes until golden brown. Sprinkle the quail with half the flour and mix well. Combine the remaining flour and ⅔ cup of the stock in a bowl. Add the thyme and bay leaf to the quail, pour in the wine and the flour mixture and cook for a further 10 minutes. Meanwhile, prepare a risotto (see page 328) with the remaining butter, the onion, rice and stock and sprinkle with the Parmesan. Spoon the risotto onto a warm serving dish, flatten slightly and top with the quail and the cooking juices, discarding the herbs.

QUAIL ON THE SPIT

SPIEDO DI QUAGLIE

Serves 4

2 tablespoons butter, softened

2 teaspoons fresh rosemary needles

1 small onion, finely chopped

8 quail

16 pancetta slices

8 country-style bread slices

olive oil, for brushing

salt and pepper

plain risotto, to serve

Preheat the oven to 350°F. Combine the butter, rosemary and onion in a bowl and season with salt and pepper. Divide the herb butter among the quails' cavities, then wrap each bird in two pancetta slices and truss with kitchen string. Thread the quail onto a spit, alternating with the slices of bread, brush with oil and roast for about 25 minutes. Brush occasionally with the cooking juices. Serve with a plain risotto.

GARLIC

CHAMOIS

FURRED GAME

Chamois, a wild mammal found in the Alps, is not widely available in other parts of the world. Even in Italy, chamois have become rare on the table and even rarer in the wild. The chamois meat found in shops is often frozen and is mainly imported. It tends to be less tasty, but more tender and is best jugged – the universal recipe for furred game. Other cooking methods are similar to those shown for venison (see pages 964 to 966), which may used as a substitute in this section. Mocetta is a speciality of Valle d'Aosta. It is cured meat made from a chamois leg that has been dried after soaking in a special marinade.

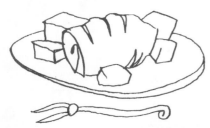

CAMOSCIO ALSAZIANO

Serves 8

4¹/₂ pounds chamois or venison, cut into large pieces

³/₄ cup olive oil

generous ¹/₂ cup pancetta, diced

¹/₄ cup butter

¹/₂ cup all-purpose flour

4 tablespoons heavy cream

salt and pepper

For the marinade

1 bottle (3 cups) white wine

5 tablespoons white wine vinegar

1 carrot

1 onion

1 garlic clove

2 celery stalks

1 fresh flat-leaf parsley sprig

4 juniper berries

4 black peppercorns

salt

ALSACE CHAMOIS

To make the marinade, pour the wine and vinegar into a pan, add the carrot, onion, garlic, celery, parsley, juniper berries, peppercorns and a pinch of salt, bring to a boil and simmer for 15 minutes. Pour the marinade into a bowl, add the meat and leave in a cool place, turning occasionally, for 12 hours. Drain the meat, reserving the marinade, and pat dry with paper towels. Heat the olive oil in a pan, add the pancetta and meat and cook over medium heat, stirring and turning frequently, until browned all over. Season with salt and pepper, lower the heat and cook, basting occasionally with the marinade until half has been used. Strain the remaining marinade into a bowl. Melt the butter in a pan, stir in the flour and cook, stirring constantly, until golden brown. Gradually stir in the remaining marinade and continue to cook, stirring constantly, until the sauce begins to thicken. Turn the heat to its lowest setting and simmer for 20 minutes. Just before serving, stir the cream into the sauce, season with salt and heat through. Serve the meat with the sauce.

CHAMOIS IN RED WINE

CAMOSCIO AL VINO ROSSO

Serves 6

1 bottle (3 cups) Barolo or Nebbiolo wine

2 cloves

4 juniper berries

2 bay leaves

1 celery stalk, sliced

1 carrot, sliced

1 onion, sliced

1 chamois or venison leg, cut into small pieces

2 tablespoons butter

3 tablespoons olive oil

1 apple, peeled, cored and chopped

salt and pepper

Pour the wine into a dish, add the cloves, juniper berries, bay leaves, celery, carrot and onion and season with salt and pepper. Add the meat and let marinate in a cool place, but not in the refrigerator, for at least 12 hours. Drain the meat, reserving the marinade, put it in a pan with the butter and olive oil and cook over medium heat, turning and stirring frequently, until browned all over. Pour in the reserved marinade, add the apple, lower the heat and simmer gently for about 2 hours. Remove the pan from the heat and, using a slotted spoon, transfer the meat to a warm serving dish. Strain the cooking juices, stir in a little warm water if they are too thick and reheat. Spoon the cooking juices over the meat and serve.

CHAMOIS CHOPS WITH MUSHROOMS AND DRIED FRUIT

COSTOLETTE DI CAMOSCIO AI FUNGHI E FRUTTA SECCA

Serves 4

$^3/_4$ cup dried porcini

16 prunes

16 dried apricots

$1^1/_4$ cups freshly brewed tea

2 tablespoons olive oil

$^1/_4$ cup butter

8 chamois or venison chops

2 tablespoons sugar

scant $^1/_2$ cup red wine vinegar

scant $^1/_2$ cup hot Meat Stock (see page 208)

3 juniper berries

salt

Put the porcini in a bowl, add hot water to cover and let soak for 30 minutes, then drain and slice thinly. Put the prunes and apricots in another bowl, add the tea and let soak for 30 minutes, then drain. Heat the olive oil and half the butter in a skillet, add the chops and cook for about 10 minutes on each side, then season with salt to taste. Transfer the chops to a serving dish. Put the sugar in the pan and cook over high heat for a few minutes but do not allow it to caramelize. Stir in the vinegar and cook over high heat until the liquid has reduced by about half. Add the dried fruit, hot stock and juniper berries, bring to a boil and simmer for 5 minutes. Remove the fruit with a slotted spoon and arrange it around the chops. Stir the remaining butter into the cooking juices, in small pieces at a time, add the porcini, cover and cook, occasionally adding a tablespoonful of hot water if necessary. Season with salt to taste, spoon the sauce over the chops and serve.

VENISON

Roe deer, which live in the mountains, especially the Alps, as well as on the plains, are the main source of venison in Italy. However, they are increasingly rare in the wild and rightly protected, but their numbers are increasing on farms. Farmed venison has a less gamy flavor and their meat needs hanging for only eight days. Besides deer meat, that of other animals, including elk and moose, are also classed as venison in the United States. Venison may be prepared in numerous ways – frozen meat may be used for stews and braising, the saddle of a young deer is ideal for roasting and the haunch and ribs are tasty broiled or fried.

ROAST VENISON

CAPRIOLO ARROSTO

Serves 6

1 leg or haunch of venison

3¹/₂ ounces pancetta, cut into thin strips

³/₄ cup olive oil, plus extra for brushing

2¹/₄ cups dry white wine

1 fresh thyme sprig, chopped

1 fresh summer savory sprig, chopped

1 fresh oregano sprig, chopped

salt and pepper

Make small incisions in the meat and insert the strips of pancetta. Combine the olive oil, wine and herbs in a dish, season with salt and pepper and add the meat. Cover and let marinate in a cool place overnight. Preheat the oven to 425°F. Generously brush a roasting pan with oil. Drain the leg of venison, reserving the marinade, place it in the roasting pan and roast for 10 minutes. Pour the reserved marinade into the pan, lower the temperature to 350°F and roast, basting frequently, for about 30 minutes. This will result in slightly rare venison. If you prefer it well done, roast for a further 10 minutes, but do not overcook or it will become tough. Remove the venison from the roasting pan and carve, then place the slices on a warm serving dish and spoon the cooking juices over them.

Serves 8

1 bottle (3 cups) red wine

2 pinches of freshly grated nutmeg

2 pinches of ground cinnamon

4 cloves

1 celery stalk, chopped

2 carrots, sliced

1 onion, chopped

1 garlic clove, chopped

4 fresh sage leaves

2 bay leaves

4¹/₂ pounds stewing venison, cut into cubes

3 tablespoons olive oil

¹/₄ cup butter

1 pancetta slice, diced

salt and pepper

VENISON STEW

Combine the wine, half the spices, the celery, carrots, onion, garlic, sage and bay leaves in a dish, season with salt and pepper and add the meat. Let marinate, stirring and turning occasionally, for 12 hours. Remove the venison from the marinade and pat dry with paper towels. Strain the marinade into a bowl and reserve the liquid and the vegetables separately, but discard the cloves and bay leaves. Heat the olive oil and butter in a pan, add the pancetta and cook, stirring occasionally, until crisp. Add the venison and cook, stirring frequently, until browned all over. Add the remaining spices, season with salt to taste and stir in the reserved vegetables. Cook, stirring occasionally, for 10 minutes, then pour in the reserved marinade and bring to a boil. Lower the heat, cover and simmer for 2 hours. Transfer the meat to a warm serving dish. Remove and discard the cloves and transfer the cooking juices to a blender. Process to a purée, pour into a sauceboat and serve with the venison.

Serves 6–8

1 saddle of venison

4 tablespoons olive oil

¹/₄ cup butter

2 carrots, chopped

1 onion, chopped

1 celery stalk, chopped

1 garlic clove

scant 1 cup hot Meat Stock (see page 208)

scant ¹/₂ cup red wine

3 tablespoons sugar

3¹/₂ cups cranberries, thawed if frozen

2 tablespoons heavy cream

salt and pepper

ROAST SADDLE OF VENISON WITH CRANBERRIES

Preheat the oven to 350°F. Gently rub the meat with salt and pepper. Heat the olive oil and half the butter in a large skillet, add the venison and cook, turning frequently, until browned all over. Transfer to a roasting pan, surround with the vegetables and garlic and roast, basting frequently with the cooking juices and stock, for 1¹/₂ hours. Remove the venison from the roasting pan, carve into thin slices, place on a serving dish and keep warm. Remove and discard the garlic from the cooking juices, pour in the wine and cook over high heat until reduced. Cut the remaining butter into small pieces, add to the roasting pan and stir until the sauce is thick and velvety, then spoon it over the venison. Stir the sugar into ³/₄ cup water to dissolve, then pour into a pan, bring to a boil and boil for a few minutes. Add the cranberries and simmer over low heat for 5 minutes. Stir in the cream and cook until thickened. Serve the venison with the warm cranberry sauce.

WILD BOAR

Italian wild boar are large and robust, sometimes reaching a weight of 397 pounds, and live in a few restricted areas of Tuscany and Lazio. Apart from a few places in Europe, most wild boar is, in fact, farmed. The cuts of meat and the most suitable cooking techniques correspond to those of pork. The loin, ribs and legs of young boar are popular for broiling and roasting. The loin is best for roasting and the ribs are recommended for cooking on the barbecue. Other cuts of young boar are best stewed. Adult wild boar are best fried or stewed after marinating. As with all other game, frozen wild boar is tastiest when stewed.

WILD BOAR WITH APPLES

Preheat the oven to 400°F. Melt half the butter in a flameproof casserole, add the meat and cook, stirring frequently, until browned. Stir in the onion and carrot, sprinkle in the flour and cook, stirring constantly, for 2–3 minutes, then gradually stir in the wine. Add the garlic and bay leaf, season with salt and pepper and bring to a boil. Transfer the casserole to the oven and cook for 1 hour, then stir in the brandy. Meanwhile, melt the remaining butter in a pan, add the apples and cook, stirring occasionally, for 10 minutes until golden. Discard the garlic and bay leaf, serve the meat in the cooking juices and hand the apples separately.

CINGHIALE ALLE MELE

Serves 4

1/4 cup butter

2 1/4 pounds lean wild boar, diced

1 onion, finely chopped

1 carrot, finely chopped

1 tablespoon all-purpose flour

1 2/3 cups red wine

1 garlic clove

1 bay leaf

1/4 cup brandy

3 apples, peeled, cored and sliced

salt and pepper

WILD BOAR WITH OLIVES

Pour the wine and vinegar into a large pan and add the carrot, garlic, onion, thyme, sage, bay leaves, parsley, peppercorns and a generous pinch of salt. Bring to a boil, then lower the heat and simmer for 15 minutes. Remove the pan from the heat, let cool and pour into a bowl. Add the meat, cover and let marinate in a cool place, stirring occasionally, for up to 2 days. Heat the olive oil and butter in a pan. Drain the meat, reserving the marinade, add to the pan and cook, stirring frequently, until browned all over. Season with salt and pepper, pour in about half the reserved marinade, bring to a boil, then lower the heat and simmer for $1\frac{1}{2}$ hours. Add the olives and simmer for a further 30 minutes. Discard the garlic and herbs and serve with mashed potatoes.

CINGHIALE ALLE OLIVE

Serves 6

1 bottle (3 cups) white wine

5 tablespoons white wine vinegar

1 carrot

1 garlic clove

1 onion

1 fresh thyme sprig

2 fresh sage leaves

2 bay leaves

1 fresh flat-leaf parsley sprig

6 black peppercorns

$2\frac{1}{2}$ pounds lean wild boar, diced

$\frac{3}{4}$ cup olive oil

2 tablespoons butter

$1\frac{1}{4}$ cups pitted green olives

salt and pepper

mashed potatoes, to serve

WILD BOAR IN SAUCE

First make the marinade. Put the carrots, onions, garlic, parsley, thyme, bay leaf, cloves, wine, vinegar and olive oil in a pan, season with salt and pepper and bring to a boil, then lower the heat and simmer for 15 minutes. Remove the pan from the heat and let cool, then pour into a dish. Gently rub the leg of boar with salt, place in the cooled marinade, cover and let marinate in a cool place for 24 hours. Preheat the oven to 400°F. Drain the meat, reserving the marinade, and pat dry with paper towels. Strain the marinade into a bowl. Place the meat in a roasting pan with the strips of pancetta and cook over medium heat, turning frequently, until browned all over. Add enough of the reserved marinade to half-cover the meat and transfer to the oven. Roast, turning occasionally, for $1\frac{3}{4}$ hours, covering the roasting pan with foil halfway through the cooking time. Remove the meat from the roasting pan and keep warm. Add the remaining marinade and cook over high heat until reduced by half, then purée the mixture with a hand-held blender. Season with pepper, remove from the heat and stir in the butter in small pieces at a time. Serve the wild boar with the sauce.

CINGHIALE IN SALSA

Serves 12

$5\frac{1}{2}$ pounds leg of wild boar

5 ounces pancetta, sliced into strips

2 tablespoons butter

salt and pepper

For the marinade

2 carrots, chopped

2 onions, chopped

1 garlic clove, chopped

1 fresh flat-leaf parsley sprig, chopped

1 fresh thyme sprig, chopped

1 bay leaf

2 cloves

$8\frac{3}{4}$ cups red wine

$\frac{3}{4}$ cup red wine vinegar

3 tablespoons olive oil

salt and pepper

RABBIT

Rabbit meat is white, lean, tender, tasty and eaten mainly in the winter. Both wild rabbits and farmed rabbits are widely available. The former have more flavorsome, aromatic meat as they are free to feed on the herbs found in the wooded areas where they live. The best rabbits for eating are between three months and a year old and at this age they have short necks and feet. Rabbit meat does not need hanging and may be bought whole or in pieces. Keep to the following few basic rules when cooking rabbit. Before starting to cook, soak the rabbit in a mixture of 6^1/$_4$ cups water and ^{3}/$_4$ cup white wine vinegar for 30 minutes. The best herbs for flavoring rabbit are rosemary, sage, bay leaf, thyme, fennel and basil. Do not forget to add one or more garlic cloves to the pan. Rabbit meat is a little watery, so heat it in a skillet for a few minutes until dry. It takes 45–60 minutes to cook, depending on its age.

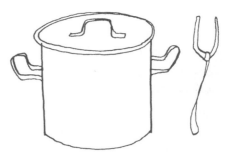

ROAST RABBIT

CONIGLIO AL FORNO

Serves 6

5 tablespoons olive oil
1 fresh rosemary sprig
2 garlic cloves
1 rabbit, cut into pieces
salt and pepper

Preheat the oven to 350°F. Heat the olive oil in a flameproof casserole with the rosemary and garlic, add the rabbit and cook, turning frequently, until browned all over. Season with salt and pepper, transfer the casserole to the oven and cook, stirring and turning occasionally, for 1 hour or until tender. Transfer to a warm serving dish.

RABBIT CACCIATORE

Melt the butter in a pan, add the onion and prosciutto and cook over low heat, stirring occasionally, for 5 minutes. Add the rabbit, increase the heat to medium and cook, turning frequently, until browned all over. Season with salt and pepper to taste, stir in the wine and add the thyme, then cover and cook for 20 minutes. Add the tomatoes, lower the heat and simmer for about 1 hour. If the cooking juices are too runny, thicken them by stirring in a pinch of flour. Transfer the stew to a warm serving dish, discarding the thyme, and serve with a soft polenta.

CONIGLIO ALLA CACCIATORA

Serves 6

2 tablespoons butter

1 onion, chopped

$^1/_3$ cup prosciutto, chopped

1 rabbit, cut into pieces

$^3/_4$ cup dry white wine

1 fresh thyme sprig

1 pound 2 ounces tomatoes, peeled, seeded and coarsely chopped

pinch of all-purpose flour (optional)

salt and pepper

soft polenta (see page 305), to serve

RABBIT IN VINEGAR

Heat the butter and olive oil in a pan, add the sage, rosemary and garlic, season with pepper and stir-fry for a few minutes. Add the rabbit and cook over medium heat, turning frequently, until browned all over. Mix the vinegar with 3 tablespoons water and add to the pan. Season with salt to taste, cover and simmer for about 50 minutes. Stir in the olives and capers and simmer for a further 10 minutes, then serve.

CONIGLIO ALL'ACETO

Serves 6

2 tablespoons butter

3 tablespoons olive oil

1 fresh sage sprig, chopped

1 fresh rosemary sprig, chopped

1 garlic clove, crushed

1 rabbit, cut into pieces

$^3/_4$ cup white wine vinegar

generous $^3/_4$ cup pitted green olives

$^1/_3$ cup capers, drained and rinsed

salt and pepper

RABBIT IN OLIVE OIL AND LEMON

Heat the olive oil in a pan, add the rosemary, sage, parsley, garlic and bay leaf and cook over medium heat, stirring occasionally, for 3 minutes. Add the rabbit and cook, turning frequently, until browned all over. Season with salt and pepper, pour in the wine and cook until it has evaporated. Lower the heat, cover and simmer for 45 minutes. Remove the lid and simmer for a further 15 minutes until tender. Remove and discard the garlic and bay leaf, stir in the lemon juice, increase the heat to high and cook for 5 minutes more.

CONIGLIO ALL'AGRO

Serves 6

5 tablespoons olive oil

1 fresh rosemary sprig, chopped

1 fresh sage leaf, chopped

1 fresh flat-leaf parsley sprig, chopped

1 garlic clove

1 bay leaf

1 rabbit, cut into pieces

$^3/_4$ cup dry white wine

juice of 2 lemons, strained

salt and pepper

RABBIT WITH BAY LEAVES

Heat the olive oil in a pan, add the rabbit and bay leaves and cook over medium heat for a few minutes. Lower the heat, cover and cook, turning the meat occasionally, for 1 hour. Season with salt and pepper, cook for 1 minute more and serve.

CONIGLIO ALL'ALLORO

Serves 6

5 tablespoons olive oil

1 rabbit, cut into pieces

6 bay leaves

salt and pepper

RABBIT WITH MUSTARD

Brush the rabbit with some of the olive oil and season generously with salt and pepper. Heat the remaining oil in a pan, add the rabbit and cook over medium heat, turning frequently, until browned all over. Pour in the wine and lemon juice, season lightly with salt and pepper and add the rosemary, marjoram, parsley, garlic, scallion and bay leaf. Lower the heat, cover and simmer for about 50 minutes. Mix the mustard with 1 tablespoon hot water, pour into the pan and simmer, uncovered, for a further 10 minutes until the sauce has thickened. Discard the bay leaf and serve with mashed potatoes.

CONIGLIO ALLA SENAPE

Serves 6

1 rabbit, cut into pieces

4 tablespoons olive oil

$^3/_4$ cup dry white wine

juice of 1 lemon, strained

1 fresh rosemary sprig, chopped

2 fresh marjoram leaves, chopped

1 fresh flat-leaf parsley sprig, chopped

1 garlic clove, crushed

1 scallion, white part only, sliced

1 bay leaf

2 tablespoons strong mustard

salt and pepper

mashed potatoes, to serve

RABBIT IN MILK

Melt the butter in a pan, add the onion and rosemary and cook over low heat, stirring occasionally, for 5 minutes. Dust the rabbit with flour, add to the pan, increase the heat to medium and cook, turning frequently, until browned all over. Season with salt and pepper, pour in the milk and bring to a boil, then lower the heat, cover and simmer for about 30 minutes. Add the fennel seeds, re-cover the pan and simmer for a further 30 minutes. Mix the cornstarch to a paste with 1 tablespoon water, add to the pan and cook, stirring constantly, until the sauce has thickened. Transfer the meat to a warm serving dish and spoon the sauce over it.

CONIGLIO AL LATTE

Serves 6

$^1/_4$ cup butter

1 onion, chopped

1 fresh rosemary sprig, chopped

1 rabbit, cut into pieces

all-purpose flour, for dusting

$2^1/_4$ cups milk

1 tablespoon fennel seeds

1 teaspoon cornstarch

salt and pepper

RABBIT WITH HONEY AND VEGETABLES

CONIGLIO AL MIELE CON VERDURE

Serves 4

6 tablespoons butter
1 tablespoon clear honey
1 rabbit, cut into pieces
5 tablespoons white wine vinegar
4 carrots, sliced
4 turnips, sliced
scant 1/2 cup peas
2/3 cup green beans
1 fresh tarragon sprig, chopped
salt and pepper

Preheat the oven to 400°F. Heat the butter and honey in a flame-proof casserole, add the rabbit and cook over medium heat, turning frequently, until browned all over. Season with salt and pepper, remove from the casserole and keep warm. Pour the vinegar into the casserole and cook, scraping up any sediment from the base with a wooden spoon, then simmer over low heat until the liquid has evaporated. Meanwhile, cook the vegetables in separate pans of salted, boiling water for 5 minutes, then drain. Return the rabbit to the casserole, add the vegetables and tarragon, cover, transfer to the oven and cook for about 45 minutes until tender.

RABBIT IN HARD CIDER

CONIGLIO AL SIDRO

Serves 6

2 tablespoons butter • 2 tablespoons olive oil
1 rabbit, cut into pieces
1 onion, sliced
generous 1/2 cup pancetta, diced
1 tablespoon all-purpose flour • 2 1/2 cups hard cider
3/4 cup Meat Stock (see page 208)
scant 1 1/2 cups mushrooms, sliced
1 fresh thyme sprig
strip of thinly pared lemon rind
salt and pepper

Heat the butter and oil in a pan, add the rabbit and cook over medium heat, turning frequently, until browned all over. Remove the rabbit from the pan and keep warm. Add the onion and pancetta to the pan and cook over low heat, stirring occasionally, for about 10 minutes. Sprinkle with the flour and stir well, then gradually stir in the cider and stock. When all the liquid has been incorporated, bring to a boil, stirring constantly. Return the rabbit to the pan, add the mushrooms, thyme and lemon rind and season with salt and pepper. Cover and cook over low heat for 1 hour until tender. Remove and discard the thyme and lemon rind, season with salt and pepper to taste and serve.

RABBIT IN RED WINE

CONIGLIO AL VINO ROSSO

Serves 6

1 rabbit, with liver
1 onion • 2 cloves
1 fresh thyme sprig, chopped
1 fresh rosemary sprig, chopped
1 fresh sage sprig, chopped
pinch of ground cinnamon
1 garlic clove
1 carrot, chopped • 1 celery stalk, chopped
1 bottle (3 cups) red wine
3 tablespoons butter • 2 tablespoons olive oil
salt and pepper

Chop the liver and set aside. Cut the rabbit into pieces. Put them in a dish, add the onion stuck with the cloves, the thyme, rosemary, sage, cinnamon, garlic, carrot and celery and pour in the wine. Let marinate, turning occasionally, for 12 hours. Drain the meat, reserving the marinade. Heat the butter and olive oil in a pan, add the rabbit and cook over medium heat, turning frequently, until browned all over. Season with salt and pepper, pour in the reserved marinade, lower the heat, cover and simmer for 30 minutes. Add the liver, re-cover and simmer for a further 30 minutes. Transfer the rabbit to a warm serving dish. Ladle the cooking juices into a blender and process to a purée. Spoon the sauce over the rabbit and serve

CONIGLIO ARROSTO AL ROSMARINO

Serves 6

4 fresh rosemary sprigs

1 rabbit

3 tablespoons olive oil

2 tablespoons butter

1 garlic clove

salt and pepper

roast potatoes, to serve

BRAISED RABBIT WITH ROSEMARY

Chop the needles of one of the rosemary sprigs and set aside. Brush the rabbit with some of the olive oil and stuff with the whole rosemary sprigs, half the butter and the garlic and season the cavity with a pinch of salt. Place in a pan with the remaining oil and butter, sprinkle with the chopped rosemary and season with salt and pepper to taste. Cover and cook over low heat, turning occasionally and adding a few tablespoons of hot water if necessary, for 1½ hours. Remove the rabbit from the pan, cut into pieces and place on a warm serving dish. Serve with roast potatoes.

CONIGLIO CON PEPERONATA

Serves 6

6 tablespoons olive oil

2 tablespoons butter

1 carrot, chopped

1 fresh sage sprig, chopped

1 fresh rosemary sprig, chopped

1 rabbit, cut into pieces

5 tablespoons white wine vinegar

1 red bell pepper, halved, seeded and thickly sliced

1 green bell pepper, halved, seeded and thickly sliced

1 yellow bell pepper, halved, seeded and thickly sliced

1 onion, thinly sliced

3 tomatoes, peeled, seeded and diced

salt and pepper

RABBIT WITH PEPERONATA

Heat half the olive oil and the butter in a pan, add the carrot, sage and rosemary and cook over low heat, stirring occasionally, for 5 minutes. Add the rabbit, increase the heat to medium and cook, turning frequently, for 10 minutes until browned all over, then season with salt and pepper to taste. Mix the vinegar with 5 tablespoons water, add to the pan, lower the heat, cover and simmer for 1 hour or until the rabbit is tender. Meanwhile, heat the remaining olive oil in a skillet, add the bell peppers and onion and cook over medium heat, stirring occasionally, for about 15 minutes. Add the tomatoes, lower the heat, cover and simmer until all the vegetables are softened and cooked through. Season with salt and pepper, transfer the bell pepper mixture to the pan of rabbit and cook for a few minutes more, then serve.

CONIGLIO FRITTO

Serves 6

2 eggs

1½ cups bread crumbs

1 rabbit, cut into pieces

⅔ cup olive oil

salt

lemon wedges, to garnish

FRIED RABBIT

Beat the eggs with a pinch of salt in a shallow dish and spread out the bread crumbs in another shallow dish. Dip the pieces of rabbit first into the beaten eggs and then in the bread crumbs to coat. Heat the oil in a skillet, add the pieces of rabbit and cook, turning frequently, for about 10 minutes until crisp and golden brown on the outside and tender and cooked through on the inside. Remove from the skillet and drain on paper towels. Serve immediately, garnished with wedges of lemon.

STEWED RABBIT

Heat the olive oil in a pan, add the rabbit and cook over medium heat, turning frequently, for 15 minutes until browned all over. Add the garlic, thyme and parsley, mix well and season with salt and pepper. Pour in the wine and cook until it has evaporated. Add the tomatoes, lower the heat, cover and simmer, stirring occasionally, for about 1¼ hours.

CONIGLIO IN UMIDO

Serves 6

3 tablespoons olive oil

1 rabbit, cut into pieces

1 garlic clove, chopped

1 fresh thyme sprig, chopped

1 fresh flat-leaf parsley sprig, chopped

³/₄ cup dry white wine

2 tomatoes, peeled, seeded and coarsely chopped

salt and pepper

MARINATED RABBIT

Stud the onion with the cloves and place in a dish with the wine, vinegar, celery, carrot and peppercorns. Add the rabbit and let marinate, turning occasionally, for at least 6 hours. Drain the meat, reserving the marinade, and pat dry with paper towels. Strain the marinade. Heat the butter and olive oil in a pan, add the pieces of rabbit and cook over medium heat, turning frequently, until browned all over. Season with salt and pepper, add 1¼ cups of the reserved marinade and cook until it has evaporated slightly. Lower the heat, cover and simmer for about 1¼ hours, adding 2–3 tablespoons of the remaining marinade if necessary.

CONIGLIO MARINATO

Serves 6

1 onion • 2 cloves

2¼ cups dry white wine

2 tablespoons white wine vinegar

1 celery stalk

1 carrot

6 black peppercorns

1 rabbit, cut into pieces

2 tablespoons butter

3 tablespoons olive oil

salt and pepper

STUFFED RABBIT

Preheat the oven to 400°F. Tear the bread into pieces, place in a bowl, add water to cover and let soak for 10 minutes, then drain and squeeze out. Chop the liver. Combine the ham and sausages in a bowl. Heat half the butter and the olive oil in a pan, add the liver and onion and cook over low heat, stirring occasionally, for 5 minutes. Remove the pan from the heat and stir in the soaked bread, then add the mixture to the bowl of ham and sausages, stir in the parsley, thyme and egg and season with salt and pepper. Spoon the mixture into the cavity of the rabbit and sew up the opening. Place the rabbit in a roasting pan, brush with olive oil, dot with the remaining butter and sprinkle with the garlic and carrot. Roast until golden brown, then pour in the wine, cover with foil and roast for a further 1½ hours.

CONIGLIO RIPIENO

Serves 6

1 thick bread slice, crusts removed

1 rabbit, with liver

generous ¹/₂ cup cooked, cured ham, chopped

7 ounces Italian sausages, skinned and crumbled

¹/₄ cup butter

1 tablespoon olive oil, plus extra for brushing

1 onion, chopped

1 fresh flat-leaf parsley sprig, chopped

1 fresh thyme sprig, chopped

1 egg, lightly beaten

1 garlic clove, finely chopped

1 carrot, chopped

1¹/₂ cups dry white wine

salt and pepper

RABBIT AND TUNA ROLL

ROTOLO DI CONIGLIO CON IL TONNO

Serves 6

generous 2 cups boneless rabbit, diced

all-purpose flour, for dusting

pinch of curry powder

2 tablespoons olive oil

6¹/₂ ounces canned tuna in oil, drained

1 canned anchovy fillet in oil, drained

¹/₂ cup heavy cream

3 egg yolks

¹/₂ cup pistachios

5 tablespoons white wine

1 shallot, chopped

2 tablespoons butter

2¹/₄ cups Meat Stock (see page 208)

1 tablespoon white truffle pâté

juice of ¹/₂ lemon, strained

scant 1 cup sunflower oil

2 tablespoons white wine vinegar

²/₃ cup arugula

salt and pepper

radicchio salad, to serve

Dredge one-third of the diced rabbit with flour and sprinkle with the curry powder. Heat the olive oil in a skillet, add the coated meat and cook over low heat, stirring occasionally, for 30 minutes. Put the remaining rabbit and the tuna and anchovy in a food processor and process. Add the cream and one of the egg yolks, season with salt and pepper and process again. Scrape into a bowl and stir in the pistachios, cooked rabbit, wine, shallot and butter. Knead the mixture and shape into a sausage. Wrap in cheesecloth and tie both ends. Bring the stock to a boil in a large pan, add the cheesecloth-wrapped roll and simmer for 20 minutes. Remove the pan from the heat and let the roll cool in the cooking liquid, then drain and chill in the refrigerator for at least 2 hours. Meanwhile, beat the remaining egg yolks with the truffle pâté and lemon juice in a bowl and season with salt. Gradually whisk in the sunflower oil until fully incorporated, then stir in the vinegar. Remove the rabbit roll from the refrigerator, unwrap and slice. Make a bed of arugula on a serving dish, place the slices of rabbit roll on top and spoon the sauce over them. Serve with a radicchio salad.

RABBIT STEW WITH ANCHOVIES

SPEZZATINO ALLE ACCIUGHE

Serves 6

5 tablespoons olive oil

1 fresh rosemary sprig

2 fresh sage leaves

1 garlic clove, chopped

1 rabbit, cut into pieces

4 salted anchovies, heads removed, cleaned and filleted (see page 596), soaked in cold water for 10 minutes and drained

5 tablespoons white wine vinegar

salt and pepper

Heat the olive oil in a large pan with the rosemary, sage and garlic. Add the rabbit and cook over high heat, turning frequently, until browned all over. Season, lower the heat, cover and cook, stirring occasionally, for 1¹/₄ hours until tender. Meanwhile, chop the anchovy fillets. Combine the anchovies, vinegar and 1 tablespoon water in a bowl. Remove the rabbit from the pan and drain well. Discard the herbs. Pour the vinegar and anchovy mixture into the pan, increase the heat and cook until reduced. Return the meat to the pan, lower the heat and cook for a further 10 minutes. Transfer to a warm serving dish.

RABBIT STEW
WITH WALNUTS

Put the garlic, thyme, rosemary and juniper berries in a dish, season with salt and pepper and pour in the wine and vinegar. Add the rabbit and let marinate, turning occasionally, for 12 hours. Drain the meat, reserving the marinade, and pat dry with paper towels. Melt the butter in a pan, add the rabbit and cook, turning frequently, until browned all over. Add about half the marinade and cook over high heat for 30 minutes or until the liquid has almost completely evaporated. Chop $1/2$ cup of the walnuts and stir into the cream, then pour into the pan and cook until thickened. Transfer the rabbit to a warm serving dish. Stir the remaining walnuts into the sauce, spoon it over the rabbit and serve.

SPEZZATINO ALLE NOCI

Serves 6

1 garlic clove, chopped

1 fresh thyme sprig, chopped

1 fresh rosemary sprig, chopped

3 juniper berries, lightly crushed

$1^2/_3$ cups dry white wine

1 tablespoon white wine vinegar

1 rabbit, cut into pieces

2 tablespoons butter

scant 1 cup shelled walnuts, halved

5 tablespoons heavy cream

salt and pepper

RABBIT STEW
WITH TOMATOES
AND BASIL

Heat the olive oil in a pan, add the rabbit and cook, turning frequently, until browned all over. Transfer to a plate, cover and keep warm. Add the tomatoes and onion to the pan and cook, stirring occasionally, for 20 minutes. Return the rabbit to the pan, add the garlic and season with salt and pepper. Cover and cook over low heat for 1 hour. Sprinkle with the basil and serve.

SPEZZATINO AL POMODORO
E BASILICO

Serves 6

3 tablespoons olive oil

1 rabbit, cut into pieces

$2^1/_4$ pounds tomatoes, peeled, seeded and diced

1 onion, thinly sliced

1 garlic clove, crushed

10 fresh basil leaves, chopped

salt and pepper

RABBIT 'TUNA'

Cook the rabbit in a large pan of simmering water with the onion, carrot, celery, bay leaf and a pinch of salt for $1^1/_2$ hours. Drain the rabbit, cut the meat off the bones and chop while still warm, then season with salt and pepper. Make a layer of meat in a glass or ceramic dish and sprinkle with some of the sage and garlic. Continue making layers until the dish is three-fourths full. Gently pour the olive oil over the surface, cover and let stand in a cool place for a few days.

'TONNO' DI CONIGLIO

Serves 6

1 rabbit

1 onion

1 carrot

1 celery stalk

1 bay leaf

6 fresh sage leaves, chopped

2 garlic cloves, finely chopped

$3/_4$ cup olive oil

salt and pepper

HARE AND JACK RABBIT

The European hare is often mistaken for a wild rabbit, but differs in that their ears and feet are longer. It is, in fact, the equivalent of the American jack rabbit. For the best results when cooking, the age of the animal should be considered as it will affect the choice of recipe. Young animals from two to four months old, weighing about 3¹/₄ pounds, can be roasted. One-year olds, weighing 5¹/₂–6¹/₂ pounds, are best jugged. Older animals, weighing 8³/₄–13 pounds, are best used in terrines. Young female jack rabbits are preferable for their tender meat. Hares should be hung for about two days. The Italian recipe titles still refer to hare.

JACK RABBIT CACCIATORE

LEPRE ALLA CACCIATORA

Serves 6–8

1 jack rabbit, cut into pieces
white wine vinegar, for rinsing
2 fresh thyme sprigs
2 fresh marjoram, sprigs
4 fresh sage leaves
2 bay leaves
1 bottle (3 cups) full-bodied red wine
4 tablespoons olive oil
1 garlic clove
2 tablespoons tomato paste
salt and pepper

Wash the pieces of rabbit in plenty of vinegar, then put the pieces in a bowl with a thyme sprig, a marjoram sprig, two sage leaves and a bay leaf and pour in the wine. Cover and let marinate in a cool place, turning occasionally, for at least 12 hours. Drain the meat, reserving the marinade, put in a pan and cook over high heat, turning frequently, for 10 minutes, then season. Add the olive oil, garlic and remaining herbs and cook, turning frequently, until the pieces of rabbit are browned all over. Strain the reserved marinade into the pan and bring to a boil, then lower the heat, cover and simmer for about 2 hours. If the meat seems to be drying out during cooking, add a little warm water. Mix the tomato paste with 2 tablespoons water, add to the pan, re-cover and simmer for a further 30 minutes. Transfer to a warm serving dish.

JACK RABBIT WITH WINE

Stud the onion with the cloves and place in a dish with the wine, carrot, shallot, thyme, bay leaf, sage leaf, juniper berries and vinegar. Set the liver and blood aside. Cut the rabbit into small pieces, season with pepper, add to the marinade and season with salt. Let marinate, turning occasionally, for at least 12 hours. Heat the butter and oil in a pan. Drain the meat, reserving the marinade, add to the pan and cook over medium heat, turning frequently, until lightly browned all over. Remove and discard the herbs from the marinade, pour it into a blender and process to a purée. Sprinkle the pieces of rabbit with the flour and mix well, then pour in the puréed marinade. If necessary, add a little warm water so that the liquid covers the meat. Lower the heat and simmer for 2 hours until tender. Meanwhile, finely chop the liver. Stir the blood, liver and cream into the pan and simmer for 3 minutes, then serve.

LEPRE AL VINO

Serves 6–8

1 onion

2 cloves

1 bottle (3 cups) full-bodied red wine

1 carrot, sliced

1 shallot, sliced

1 fresh thyme sprig

1 bay leaf

1 fresh sage leaf

6 juniper berries

1 tablespoon white wine vinegar

1 jack rabbit, with liver and blood

2 tablespoons butter

2 tablespoons olive oil

1 tablespoon all-purpose flour

5 tablespoons heavy cream

salt and pepper

JACK RABBIT WITH JUNIPER BERRIES

Combine the wine, juniper berries, bay leaf, shallot, garlic, onion, peppercorns and a pinch of salt in a dish. Add the pieces of rabbit, cover and let marinate in a cool place, turning occasionally, for at least 12 hours. Preheat the oven to 350°F. Generously brush a roasting pan with olive oil. Drain the meat, reserving the marinade, and pat dry with paper towels. Wrap the slices of pancetta around the pieces of rabbit, place in the prepared roasting pan and cook for 45–50 minutes or until the rabbit is medium rare. If you prefer well-done meat, cook for an extra 15 minutes. Strain the marinade into a pan, bring to a boil over high heat and cook until reduced by half. Remove the roasting pan from the oven and unwrap the pieces of rabbit. Gently heat the brandy in a small pan, pour it over the meat and ignite. When the flames have died down, transfer the rabbit to a warm serving dish. Strain the reduced marinade into the cooking juices and bring to a boil over high heat, scraping up any sediment from the base of the roasting pan with a wooden spoon. Remove the pan from the heat, stir in the butter and pour into a sauceboat. Serve the rabbit with the sauce.

LEPRE CON IL GINEPRO

Serves 6–8

2¼ cups dry white wine

10 juniper berries

1 bay leaf, torn into pieces

1 shallot, very finely chopped

1 garlic clove, crushed

1 onion, sliced

4 black peppercorns

1 jack rabbit, cut into fairly large pieces

olive oil, for brushing

3½ ounces pancetta, sliced

3 tablespoons brandy

2 tablespoons butter

salt

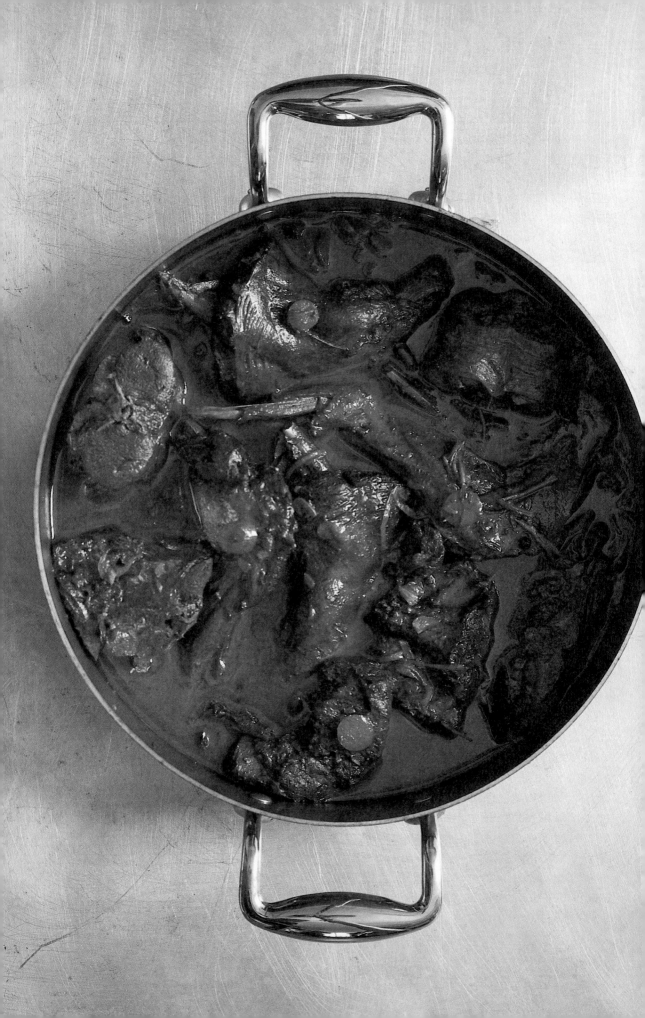

SWEET AND STRONG
JACK RABBIT

Heat the olive oil and butter in a pan, add the pancetta and rabbit and cook over medium heat, turning and stirring frequently, until the pieces of rabbit are browned all over. Season with salt and pepper, sprinkle with half the flour, mix well and cook for about 10 minutes. Pour in the wine and stock, add the bay leaf, lower the heat and simmer for about 1¹/₂ hours. Meanwhile, put the golden raisins in a bowl, add warm water to cover and let soak for 15 minutes, then drain and squeeze out. Stir the raisins and pine nuts into the pan and simmer for a further 30 minutes. Combine the chocolate, the remaining flour, the vinegar, sugar and a pinch of salt in a bowl, then stir in 3–4 tablespoons water. Pour the mixture into the pan and bring just to a boil. Taste and add more salt if necessary. Serve the rabbit covered in this ancient chocolate sauce.

LEPRE DOLCE FORTE

Serves 6–8

2 tablespoons olive oil

2 tablespoons butter

¹/₄ cup pancetta, diced

1 jack rabbit, cut into pieces

2 tablespoons all-purpose flour

³/₄ cup red wine

³/₄ cup Meat Stock (see page 208)

1 bay leaf

scant ¹/₂ cup golden raisins

¹/₄ cup pine nuts

2 tablespoons semi-sweet chocolate, grated

1 teaspoon white wine vinegar

2 teaspoons sugar

salt and pepper

ROASTING

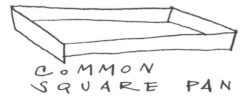

COMMON
SQUARE PAN

WILD GAME DISHES

Today it is unusual to buy game that is not farmed, but some animals are still hunted in the wild to be served at the table, and there may be occasions when you need to cook wild rabbit, snipe or venison, for example. Generally, the recipes are not particularly difficult, but they are often quite time consuming and complicated.

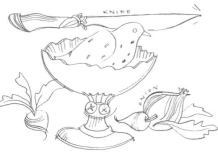

ANATRA SELVATICA CON I FICHI

Serves 4

1 wild duck, drawn and plucked, liver reserved

white wine vinegar, for rinsing

2 tablespoons olive oil

1 bottle (3 cups) red wine

2 teaspoons brandy

juice of 1 lemon, strained

14 ounces figs

2 tablespoons butter

salt and pepper

WILD DUCK WITH FIGS

Preheat the oven to 400°F. Rinse the duck well with plenty of vinegar and season the cavity with salt and pepper. Rinse and trim the liver and place in the cavity, then put the duck in a roasting pan with the olive oil and wine and roast for 1 hour until cooked through and tender. Remove the duck from the roasting pan, cut into slices and keep warm. Finely dice the liver. Reduce the oven temperature to 350°F. Stir the brandy and lemon juice into the cooking juices and cook over low heat, scraping up any sediment from the base of the pan with a wooden spoon. Stir in the liver. Meanwhile, cut the figs in half, leaving them attached at the stem. Place in an ovenproof dish, season with salt and pepper and dot with the butter. Transfer to the oven and cook for about 10 minutes. Place the slices of duck on a warm serving dish, spoon the sauce over them and surround with the figs.

VENISON WITH CREAM

First make the marinade. Stud the onion with the cloves. Pour the wine into a large pan, add the studded onion, carrot, celery, parsley, bay leaf, thyme, nutmeg and juniper berries and season with salt and pepper. Bring to a boil, then lower the heat and simmer for 15 minutes. Remove the pan from the heat and pour the marinade into a dish. Pound the venison with a meat mallet, add to the marinade, cover and let marinate in a cool place, stirring occasionally, for 3 days. Preheat the oven to 400°F. Generously brush a roasting pan with olive oil. Drain the venison, place in the roasting pan, add the carrot, onion and celery, pour in the wine, sprinkle with the bread crumbs and season lightly with pepper. Roast for 15 minutes, add the cream and season with salt to taste, then return to the oven and roast for a further 15 minutes. Carve the venison into slices and place on a warm serving dish. Add 2 tablespoons hot water to the cooking juices and heat gently, scraping up the sediment from the base of the pan with a wooden spoon. Strain the cooking juices over the slices of venison. Serve with sliced polenta.

CERVO ALLA PANNA

Serves 6

3¼ pounds loin or haunch of venison

olive oil, for brushing

1 carrot, chopped • 1 onion, chopped

1 celery stalk, chopped

4 cups dry white wine

1 tablespoon bread crumbs

⅔ cup heavy cream

salt and pepper

sliced polenta (see page 305), to serve

For the marinade:

1 onion • 2 cloves

4 cups dry white wine

1 carrot, thinly sliced • 1 celery stalk

1 tablespoon chopped fresh flat-leaf parsley

1 bay leaf • 1 fresh thyme sprig

pinch of freshly grated nutmeg

5 juniper berries

salt and pepper

MUSHROOM AND GAME PIE

Place the venison and partridge in a dish, add the carrot, shallot, celery, sage, bay leaf and juniper berries and season with salt and pepper. Pour in the wine and let marinate in a cool place, stirring occasionally, for 12 hours. Drain the meat, reserving the marinade. Heat the butter and olive oil in a pan, add the meat and cook over medium heat, stirring frequently, until browned all over. Remove the meat from the pan and set aside. Add the onion and ham to the pan and cook over low heat, stirring occasionally, for 10 minutes, then add the porcini. Cover and simmer gently for 20 minutes. Return the meat to the pan, pour in the reserved marinade, cover and cook over low heat for 1½ hours. Preheat the oven to 425°F. Divide the pastry into two pieces and roll out on a lightly floured surface. Line the base of a pie dish with one piece of pastry and spoon in the meat and porcini mixture. Cover with the remaining pastry, prick all over with a fork and brush with the beaten egg. Bake for 20 minutes, then lower the oven temperature to 375°F and bake for a further 15 minutes. Serve warm.

TORTA DI FUNGHI E SELVAGGINA

Serves 12

1 pound 2 ounces lean venison, diced

1 pound 2 ounces skinless, boneless partridge, diced

1 carrot, chopped • 1 shallot, chopped

1 celery stalk, chopped

1 fresh sage sprig

1 bay leaf

5 juniper berries

2¼ cups red wine

2 tablespoons butter

3 tablespoons olive oil

1 onion, chopped

⅓ cup cooked, cured ham, diced

1 pound 2 ounces fresh porcini

9 ounces puff pastry dough, thawed if frozen

all-purpose flour, for dusting

1 egg, lightly beaten

salt and pepper

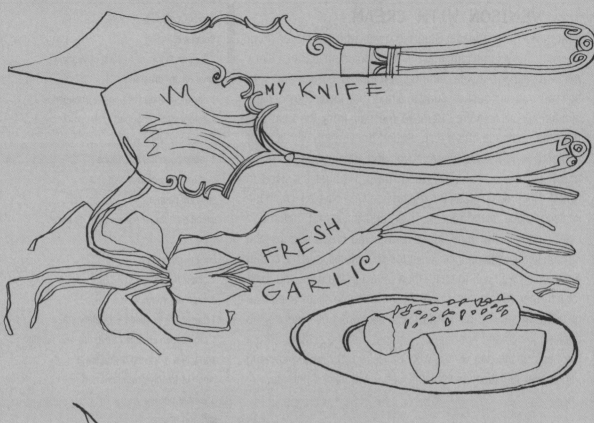

MY KNIFE

FRESH GARLIC

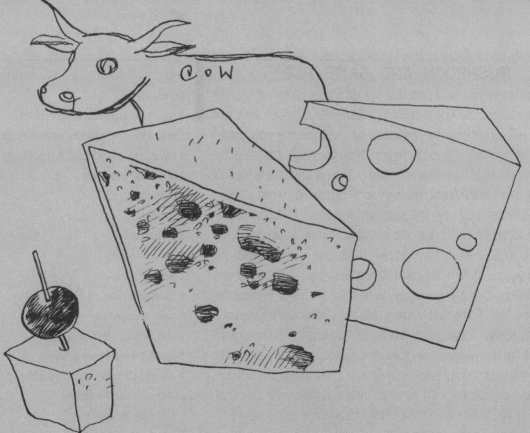

COW

CHEESE →

CHEESE

Parmesan and grana padano on pasta and risottos, mozzarella on pizzas, fontina in dishes from Valle d'Aosta, mascarpone in Tiramisu, Gorgonzola with polenta, macaroni with four cheeses – we could go on, as hundreds of antipasti, first courses, main dishes, lunches and snacks depend upon on at least 451 different kinds of cheese. That is the number of cheeses produced in Italy. Their quality is overseen by the various national consortia for each type. There are also Italian controlling bodies that assign cheeses the Denominazione di Origine Controllata, and European controlling bodies that assign them the coveted Protected Designation of Origin (PDO). As cheese is simultaneously both a food and a flavoring, it is important to follow some rules about how it is cooked and the quantity used. This is to avoid altering the flavor of the dish and of the cheese itself. Remember that cooking makes cheese taste stronger, so pay attention to the quantity specified in the recipe, the stage at which it is added and the way it is mixed.

ADVICE

→ Grated cheese should always be sprinkled on pasta before the sauce, which then softens and melts it. In the specific case of bucatini amatriciana, professional cooks advise serving the romano cheese separately so that guests can help themselves, thus preserving its fragrance.

→ As a general rule with risottos, the cheese or cheeses should not be added during cooking, but at the end after removing the pan from the heat. At most, the cheese may be added 3 minutes before the end of the cooking time for a stronger flavor, in which case, you should continue stirring to prevent it from sticking to the base of the pan.

→ In the case of soups and purées, freshly grated cheese should be handed separately at the table.

→ Grated cheese should be brought to the table in a cheese dish with lid, complete with a bone or other nonmetallic teaspoon. Metal teaspoons oxidize easily in contact with cheeses.

→ When using savory cheeses – whether grated, thinly sliced, melted or shaved – together with other ingredients (for example in soufflés, savory pies, fried mozzarella sandwiches, etc.) season the dish itself only lightly.

Store cheeses on the bottom shelf of the refrigerator in sealed plastic or glass containers. As they are in the least cold part of the refrigerator, they remain softer and, being sealed, do not transfer smells to other dishes and ingredients or absorb them.

→ Put one or two sugar cubes in the containers to absorb any moisture.

→ Place each kind of cheese in its own container or wrap it in foil.

→ Store mozzarella in its original packaging, complete with its original liquid, or transfer it to one of the upper shelves in a bowl full of a mixture of water and milk.

→ It is advisable to take cheeses out of the refrigerator 1 hour before serving and open the containers to allow them to breathe. When cold, they tend to be less flavorsome and more difficult to digest, especially fattier cheeses.

→ Avoid putting grana padano, provolone and romano cheese in the refrigerator. Simply store in a cool place instead.

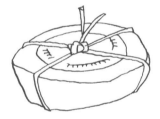

→ Remove cheeses from their wrappings and place on a wooden board or glass plate garnished with lettuce leaves.

→ Adjust quantities according to the number of guests. Offer at least three different types of cheese – soft, semi-hard and hard – ranging from mild to strong in flavor. Alternatively, serve an Italian mild or strong cheese, a French soft cheese and an English hard or medium cheese.

→ It is probably wise to avoid serving very strong-smelling cheeses, which are not to everyone's taste.

→ Provide one or two cheese knives or slicer.

→ For authentic Italian presentation, serve cheese before dessert and fruit, offering them once only.

→ The wines served at the table should come from the same regions as the cheeses.

ETIQUETTE

→ Hard cheeses: Cut one piece at a time with a knife, remove any rind, put on a bite-sized piece of bread or a biscuit and lift to the mouth.

→ Soft cheeses: Use only a fork.

TASTY COMBINATIONS

→ Blue cheeses and soft cheeses may be served with mixed broiled vegetables, or steamed vegetables dressed with olive oil.

→ Mascarpone and other cream cheeses go very well with mostarda (a preserve made with mustard).

→ Caciotta goes with both black and green olives.

→ Caprino loves radishes.

→ Gorgonzola and fontina go perfectly with polenta.

→ Almost all semi-hard and hard cheeses are good with walnuts, pears and grapes.

→ Blue, cream and ricotta-type cheeses mixed with icing sugar turn into delicate creams for decorating biscuits, fruit salads or sour black cherries in syrup.

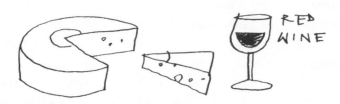

RED WINE

CAPRINO BAVAROIS

Serves 4

2 ounces gelatin sheets

scant ¹/₂ cup heavy cream

4 ounces caprino or other high-fat goats' cheese

olive oil, for drizzling and brushing

1 teaspoon white wine vinegar, plus extra for drizzling

2 egg whites

10 radishes, sliced

1 bunch of arugula, shredded

2 tomatoes, peeled, seeded and sliced

2 celery stalks, chopped

salt and pepper

Soak the sheets of gelatin in cold water for 10 minutes, then squeeze out. Heat a little water in a double boiler or in a heatproof bowl set over a pan of barely simmering water. Add the gelatin and dissolve, following the packet instructions. Stir into the cream in a bowl. Mash the cheese in another bowl with a fork, drizzle with olive oil and add the vinegar. Beat the mixture with a whisk until light and frothy. Pour in the cream mixture. Whisk the egg whites in a grease-free bowl and fold them into the cheese mixture, a little at a time. Season with salt and pepper to taste. Brush four molds with olive oil, then divide the mixture among them. Cover and leave in a cool place for a few hours to set. When set, turn out the molds and arrange the creams in the middle of a serving dish. Cover with the radish slices and a little shredded arugula and place the tomatoes around one side and the celery around the other. Drizzle with olive oil and a little vinegar and season with salt and pepper to taste.

BUFFALO MILK MOZZARELLA CAPRESE SALAD

Serves 4

11 ounces buffalo milk mozzarella cheese

3–4 tomatoes, peeled, seeded and sliced

8 fresh basil leaves

olive oil, for drizzling

salt

Drain the mozzarella and cut into ¹/₈-inch thick slices. Arrange the mozzarella and tomato slices alternately in concentric rings on a serving dish. Sprinkle with the basil leaves, drizzle with olive oil and season with salt. Keep in a cool place until ready to serve.

SCAMORZA CARPACCIO

Serves 4

14 ounces scamorza

or provolone cheese, peeled and thinly sliced

1 cucumber, thinly sliced

3 tablespoons olive oil

juice of ¹/₂ lemon, strained

salt and pepper

6 fresh mint leaves, to garnish

Place the cheese in the middle of a serving dish and arrange the cucumber slices around it. Whisk together the oil and lemon juice in a bowl and season with salt and pepper to taste. Pour the dressing over the cheese and garnish with the mint leaves.

CHEESE RINGS

CIAMBELLINE DI FORMAGGIO

Serves 4–6

7 tablespoons butter, softened

generous 1 cup Parmesan cheese, freshly grated

scant 1 cup all-purpose flour

1 egg yolk

1 tablespoon milk

salt

Preheat the oven to 300°F. Line a cookie sheet with baking parchment. Beat the butter with the Parmesan, flour and a pinch of salt in a bowl until smooth and combined. Roll into thin cylinders and shape into rings. Lightly beat the egg yolk with the milk and brush the rings with the mixture. Place on the prepared cookie sheet and bake for about 12 minutes. Remove the rings from the oven while they are still pale because overcooking makes the cheese taste unpleasantly strong and the rings become hard. These cheese rings go well with pre-dinner drinks.

MASCARPONE AND ANCHOVY CREAM

CREMA DI MASCARPONE E PASTA D'ACCIUGHE

Serves 4

scant 1 cup mascarpone cheese

scant 1/4 cup anchovy paste

lightly toasted croûtons, to serve

Gently beat the mascarpone and anchovy paste in a bowl until smooth and even. Put the cream into individual small bowls and serve with very hot, lightly toasted croûtons.

CREAM OF RICOTTA AND VEGETABLE SOUP

CREMA DI RICOTTA E VERDURE

Serves 4

2 small potatoes, diced

2 lettuces, finely chopped

generous 1 cup red sorrel or spinach, finely chopped

2 leeks, white parts only, finely chopped

scant 1 cup ricotta cheese

2 tablespoons olive oil

1 fresh flat-leaf parsley sprig, chopped

salt and pepper

Put the potatoes, lettuces, sorrel or spinach and leeks into a pan, pour in 4 cups water, bring to a boil and season with salt and pepper. Lower the heat to medium, cover and simmer for about 30 minutes. Remove the pan from the heat, transfer the mixture to a food processor and process until smooth, then pour back into the pan. Press the ricotta through a strainer, stir into the pan and set over medium-low heat. When the soup is heated through, pour it into a tureen and add the olive oil. Sprinkle with the parsley and serve.

POPPY SEED CROQUETTES

Serves 4

7 ounces potatoes, unpeeled

7 ounces Emmenthal cheese, shaved

1 tablespoon finely chopped mixed fresh herbs,

such as fresh basil, flat-leaf parsley,

thyme and marjoram

2 eggs

generous 1 cup bread crumbs

2 tablespoons poppy seeds

5 tablespoons olive oil

salt and pepper

Cook the potatoes in salted, boiling water for 20–25 minutes until tender, then drain, peel, place in a bowl and mash with a potato masher. Stir in the Emmenthal, and a pinch each of salt and pepper. Shape the mixture into round croquettes. Beat the eggs in a shallow dish and combine the bread crumbs and poppy seeds in another shallow dish. Dip the croquettes first in the beaten eggs and then in the bread crumb mixture. Heat the oil in a skillet, add the croquettes and cook until golden brown on both sides. Remove with a slotted spatula, drain on paper towels and serve.

TALEGGIO TOASTS

Serves 4

1 eggplant, cut lengthwise into 1/8-inch slices

1 zucchini, cut lengthwise into 1/8-inch slices

olive oil, for drizzling

8 bread slices, crusts removed

9 ounces taleggio cheese, sliced

salt and pepper

Preheat the oven to 350°F and the broiler. Place the eggplant and zucchini slices on the rack in the broiler pan and broil briefly on both sides. Drizzle with a little olive oil, season with salt and pepper and set aside. Broil the slices of bread on both sides, drizzle with oil and season lightly with salt. Divide the vegetables among the toasts, cover with two slices of Taleggio and season lightly with pepper. Place on a cookie sheet and bake for a few minutes without allowing the cheese to melt. Serve warm.

EGGPLANT AND MOZZARELLA ROUNDS

Serves 4

2 eggplants, cut into 1/2-inch thick slices

3 tablespoons olive oil

5 ounces mozzarella cheese, thinly sliced

3 tablespoons bottled strained tomatoes

salt

Put the eggplant slices in a colander, sprinkling each layer with salt, and let drain for 30 minutes, then rinse and pat dry. Preheat the oven to 350°F. Heat the oil in a skillet, add the eggplant slices, in batches if necessary, and cook until light golden brown on both sides. Remove from the pan with a slotted spatula and drain on paper towels. Place the eggplant slices in a single layer on a cookie sheet and top each with a slice of mozzarella. Put 1 teaspoon of the strained tomatoes on each slice of cheese and bake for a few minutes until the mozzarella has melted. Serve hot or cold.

SPICY BUNDLES

FAGOTTINI PICCANTI

Serves 4

scant ¹/₂ cup ricotta cheese

3¹/₂ ounces strong provolone cheese, shaved

pinch of paprika

8 prosciutto slices

¹/₂ melon, seeded

pepper

Combine the ricotta, provolone and paprika in a bowl. Spread out the prosciutto and place 1 tablespoon of the cheese mixture on each slice, then roll each up and secure with toothpicks. Scoop out balls from the melon using a melon baller. Place the roulades on a serving dish and surround with the melon balls. Just before serving, season with pepper.

PUFF PASTRY FLOWERS WITH TOMA

FIORE DI SFOGLIA CON TOMA

Serves 4

butter, for greasing

1 pound 2 ounces puff pastry dough, thawed if frozen

all-purpose flour, for dusting

2 egg yolks

7 ounces toma paglierina cheese

salt

Preheat the oven to 350°F. Grease a cookie sheet with butter. Roll out the pastry dough on a lightly floured surface and cut out four or five 6-inch rounds. Place one dough round on the base of the prepared cookie sheet and arrange the others, slightly over-lapping, all around it. Beat the egg yolks with 1 tablespoon water and brush the mixture over the dough rounds. Place the toma on the central round and season lightly with salt. Fold over the other rounds to form a flower shape. Bake for 15 minutes or until the cheese has completely melted. Serve hot.

SAVOYARD FONDUE

FONDUTA ALLA SAVOIARDA

Serves 4

1 garlic clove

1 pound 5 ounces Swiss cheese or Emmenthal cheese, diced

1 bottle (3 cups) dry white wine

1 teaspoon potato flour

¹/₄ cup kirsch

salt and pepper

triangles of lightly toasted bread, to serve

Rub the inside of a terracotta dish or ceramic fondue pot with the garlic. Put the cheese in the pot, pour in the wine and let stand for 3 hours. Combine the potato flour and kirsch in a small bowl. Place the fondue pot over medium heat and melt the cheese, stirring constantly, then gradually add the kirsch mixture, stirring constantly, until thickened and smooth. Season lightly with salt and pepper. Serve immediately in small warm dishes with triangles of lightly toasted bread.

PIEDMONTESE FONDUE

FONDUTA PIEMONTESE

Serves 4

14 ounces fontina cheese, diced

1 cup milk

2 tablespoons butter

4 egg yolks

1 white truffle, sliced

salt

triangles of lightly toasted bread, to serve

Put the fontina in a bowl and add the milk to cover. Let soften for at least 2 hours. Melt the butter in a double boiler or in a heatproof bowl set over a pan of barely simmering water. Stir in the fontina mixture and egg yolks and cook, stirring constantly, until the cheese has completely melted. Season lightly with salt and cook for a further 5 minutes but do not allow the mixture to boil. Pour into soup plates, sprinkle with slices of white truffle and serve with small triangles of lightly toasted bread.

SWISS CHEESE GOURGÈRE

GOURGÈRE ALLA GROVIERA

Serves 6

$^2/_3$ cup butter, plus extra for greasing

9 ounces Swiss cheese

$2^1/_4$ cups all-purpose flour, sifted

5 eggs

salt

For the garnish

6 tablespoons butter

2 eggplants, diced

2 zucchini, diced

3 tomatoes, peeled, seeded and diced

salt and pepper

Preheat the oven to 350°F. Grease a cookie sheet with butter. Grate 7 ounces of the Swiss cheese and dice the remainder. Bring $1^1/_4$ cups water to the boil in a pan and add the butter and a pinch of salt. When the butter has melted, remove the pan from the heat and tip in the flour all at once, stirring constantly. Return the pan to the heat and cook, stirring constantly, for 10 minutes. Let cool slightly, then beat in the eggs, one at a time. Stir the grated cheese into the mixture. Place tablespoons of the mixture in a ring on the prepared cookie sheet and sprinkle them with the diced cheese. Bake for about 30 minutes. Meanwhile, prepare the garnish. Melt the butter in a skillet, add the eggplants and zucchini and cook, stirring constantly, for 5 minutes, then add the tomatoes and cook until all the vegetables are tender and light golden brown. Season with salt and pepper. Transfer the gougère to a warm serving dish and spoon the vegetables into the center. If you prefer a stronger flavor, substitute mature provolone for the Swiss cheese.

BELGIAN ENDIVE, CHEESE AND WALNUTS

INDIVIA BELGA, FORMAGGIO E NOCI

Serves 4

16 walnuts

2 celery stalks, chopped

2 heads of Belgian endive, sliced

7 ounces Emmenthal cheese, diced

olive oil, for drizzling

salt and pepper

Blanch the walnuts, then drain, refresh under cold water, peel and chop coarsely. Put the walnuts, celery, Belgian endive and cheese in a salad bowl, drizzle with olive oil and season. Toss gently and leave in a cool place for a few minutes to allow the flavors to mingle.

BRESAOLA ROLLS WITH RICOTTA

INVOLTINI DI BRESAOLA ALLA RICOTTA

Serves 4

scant 1 cup ricotta cheese

7 ounces bresaola, thinly sliced

bunch of arugula, chopped

olive oil, for drizzling

salt

lightly toasted bread, to serve

Beat the ricotta in a bowl until smooth, then place a tablespoon of the cheese on each slice of bresaola. Sprinkle with the arugula, drizzle with a little olive oil and season with a pinch of salt. Roll up and put in a cool place. Serve with lightly toasted bread.

MIXED GREENS WITH CAPRINO

MISTO VERDE AL CAPRINO

Serves 4

4 potatoes

2^2/$_3$ cups snowpeas

3 green bell peppers

olive oil, for drizzling

11 ounces caprino

or other high-fat goats' cheese, sliced

salt and pepper

Preheat the broiler. Cook the potatoes in lightly salted, boiling water for 20–25 minutes until tender. Drain, peel and cut into wedges. Cook the snowpeas in lightly salted, boiling water for 8–10 minutes until tender, then drain. Meanwhile, place the green bell peppers on a cookie sheet and broil, turning frequently, until blackened and charred. Transfer to a plastic bag, seal the top and let cool, then peel, seed and cut into large slices. Place the potatoes, snowpeas and bell pepper slices in a salad bowl, drizzle with olive oil, season with salt and add the cheese. Season with pepper, toss gently and serve.

TOASTED MOZZARELLA

Beat the eggs in a shallow dish and mix together the bread crumbs, thyme and a pinch of salt in another shallow dish. Dust the mozzarella slices with flour, dip in the beaten eggs, then in the bread crumb mixture. Chill in the refrigerator for 2 hours. Place a cookie sheet under the broiler and preheat the broiler and the cookie sheet. Remove the mozzarella slices from the refrigerator and place on the hot cookie sheet. Brown under the broiler without melting the cheese. Place on a serving dish, drizzle with oil and sprinkle with the chopped parsley, capers and anchovies.

MOZZARELLA ALLA PIASTRA

Serves 4

2 eggs

1¼ cups bread crumbs

1 tablespoon fresh thyme leaves

8 mozzarella cheese slices

all-purpose flour, for dusting

olive oil, for drizzling

1 tablespoon chopped fresh flat-leaf parsley

1 tablespoon capers, rinsed

4 canned anchovy fillets, drained and chopped

salt

FRIED MOZZARELLA SANDWICHES

Place the slices of mozzarella on half the bread and top with the remaining bread to make sandwiches. Beat the eggs in a shallow dish with the milk and season with salt. Dust the sandwiches with flour and place in the beaten eggs, pressing down gently with a slotted spatula until they have absorbed some of the mixture. Heat the olive oil and butter in a skillet, add the sandwiches and cook for about 2 minutes on each side until crisp and golden brown. Remove with a slotted spatula and drain on paper towels. Serve hot.

MOZZARELLA IN CARROZZA

Serves 4

8 bread slices, halved

5 ounces mozzarella cheese, sliced

2 eggs

¾ cup milk

all-purpose flour, for dusting

scant ½ cup olive oil

2 tablespoons

salt

CHEESE AND HAM PÂTÉ

Beat the ricotta in a bowl until smooth, then stir in the ham, pine nuts, cream and brandy and season with salt and pepper. Line a rectangular mold with plastic wrap and pour in the mixture. Smooth the surface with a palette knife and chill in the refrigerator for 3—4 hours. Turn out on to a serving dish and serve with small, warm, brown bread croûtons.

PÂTÉ DI FORMAGGIO
E PROSCIUTTO COTTO

Serves 6

scant 1 cup ricotta cheese

scant 1½ cups cooked, cured ham, finely chopped

2 tablespoons pine nuts

5 tablespoons heavy cream

¼ cup brandy

salt and pepper

warm brown bread croûtons, to serve

997

ROTOLO DI FONTINA E PROSCIUTTO

Serves 4

2³/₄ cups all-purpose flour, plus extra for dusting

3 eggs

3¹/₂ ounces cooked, cured ham, sliced

7 ounces fontina cheese, sliced

3 tablespoons butter

6 fresh sage leaves

salt and pepper

FONTINA AND HAM ROLL

Sift the flour into a mond on the work surface and make a well in the center. Break the eggs into the well and add a pinch each of salt and pepper. Knead the mixture for 10 minutes, then gather into a ball, wrap in plastic wrap and let rest for 15 minutes. Roll out the dough on a lightly floured surface to a thin sheet. Place the dough on a linen cloth and sprinkle with the ham and fontina. Using the cloth to help you, roll up into a sausage shape and tie the ends with kitchen string. Bring a large pan of salted water to a boil, add the wrapped roll and simmer for 20 minutes. Meanwhile, melt the butter with the sage leaves. Drain the roll and unwrap. Slice, place on a serving dish and spoon the sage butter over the slices.

ROTOLO DI PATATE E FORMAGGIO

Serves 6

2¹/₄ pounds potatoes,

3 cups all-purpose flour

2 eggs, lightly beaten

3 ounces fontina cheese, sliced

3 ounces Taleggio cheese, sliced

7 tablespoons butter, melted

6 fresh sage leaves

²/₃ cup Parmesan cheese, freshly grated

salt

POTATO AND CHEESE ROLL

Cook the potatoes in lightly salted, boiling water for 20–25 minutes, then drain, peel, place in a bowl and mash with a potato masher. Stir in the flour and eggs and season with salt. Knead to an elastic dough, then roll out to a ¹/₂-inch thick round with a rolling pin and place on a dish towel. Place the cheese slices on the potato dough and roll up, using the dish towel to help you. Tie the ends of the roll with kitchen string. Bring a pan of salted water to a boil, add the wrapped roll and simmer for 20 minutes. Meanwhile, melt the butter with the sage leaves. Drain the roll and let cool slightly, then unwrap and place on a wooden chopping board. Cut into ¹/₂-inch thick slices and place on a serving dish. Sprinkle with the Parmesan and sage butter.

CHEESE PIE

Preheat the oven to 350°F. Line a pie pan with baking parchment and grease lightly with butter. Cut the pastry dough in half. Roll out one piece on a lightly floured surface and place in the prepared pan. Beat the ricotta in a bowl with a wooden spoon, stir in the mozzarella, Emmenthal, beaten eggs and Parmesan and season with salt and pepper to taste. Sprinkle the mixture over the pie shell. Roll out the remaining pastry dough, place it over the pie and press along the edges to seal. Lightly beat the egg yolk and brush it over the pie. Bake for about 35 minutes, then remove the pie from oven and let stand for 10 minutes before serving.

TORTA DI FORMAGGIO

Serves 6

butter, for greasing

9 ounces puff pastry dough, thawed if frozen

all-purpose flour, for dusting

generous 1 cup ricotta cheese

5 ounces mozzarella cheese, diced

5 ounces Emmenthal cheese, diced

2 eggs, lightly beaten

1 tablespoon Parmesan cheese, freshly grated

1 egg yolk

salt and pepper

ROBIOLA TRIANGLES

Preheat the oven to 350°F. Grease a cookie sheet with butter. Cut each slice of bread into two triangles, drizzle each with olive oil and season with a pinch of salt. Mash the robiola in a bowl and stir in the Parmesan, egg and cream until fully mixed. Spread the mixture on the bread triangles, place on the prepared cookie sheet and bake for about 10 minutes. Serve hot.

TRIANGOLINI ALLA ROBIOLA

Serves 4

butter, for greasing

8 bread slices, crusts removed

olive oil, for drizzling

7 ounces robiola cheese

1 tablespoon Parmesan cheese, freshly grated

1 egg, lightly beaten

2 tablespoon heavy cream

salt

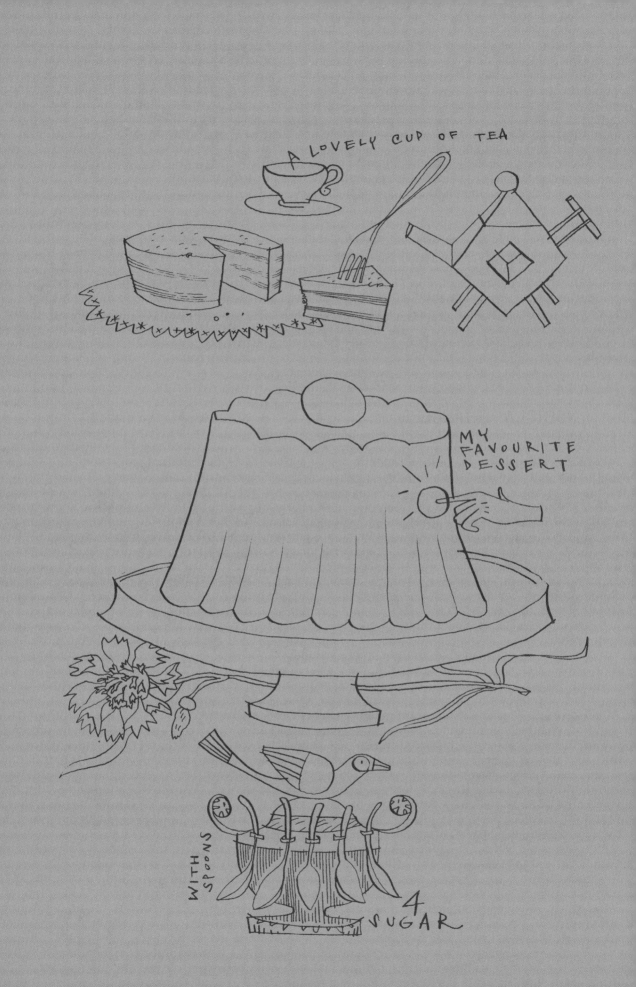

DESSERTS →

BAKING →

DESSERTS AND SWEET TREATS

Ready-made and instant puddings and commercial ice creams have not destroyed the sheer pleasure of homemade desserts, prepared by hand from recipes we have dreamed up ourselves or taken from books and magazines. It would, of course, be foolish, when time is often so short, to reject the benefits of ready-made dough and puff pastry dough, which halve the time and effort and are usually of excellent quality. However, the joy of savoring the aroma of a freshly baked tart, decorating a meringue with cream or frosting a cake never goes out of fashion. That is why desserts are talked about, invented and reinvented and why old recipes are revised, lightened and still made at home. The following is a survey of the various techniques.

PASTRY AND DOUGH

Flour, eggs, butter, sugar, milk or water and yeast are ingredients that appear time and again in numerous desserts and form the basis of pastries and cakes. The following pages provide recipes for them, and in some cases more than one recipe, as small variations on a theme mean greater choice and variety. The recipes may be divided into ones for pastries (firm) and doughs (soft). Pastries, such as pie, dough, puff and pâte brisée, are baked in pie or cake tins or on cookie sheets, and are eaten as they are or used as the base for creams, fillings, etc. Doughs, such as the mixtures for puffs, brioches and savarins, are kneaded with yeast or lightened with whisked egg white and cooked in special molds. They are eaten as they come or finished with creams, fillings and liqueurs, depending on the recipe.

FLOUR

Flour should be absolutely fresh, extremely fine, white and dry. When adding it to eggs, it is always a good idea to sift it first so that there will be no lumps. When rolling out pastry and dough, dust it and the counter lightly with flour to prevent it from sticking. The rolling pin may also be dusted with flour.

BUTTER

Like flour, butter must be extremely fresh, top quality and stored correctly. It should usually be removed from the refrigerator some time before use to soften it slightly. Sometimes it is added to flour in small pieces. When the recipe calls for melted butter, it is always best to heat it in a double boiler or a heatproof bowl set over a pan of barely simmering water. Sweet butter is invariably used in Italian recipes and is, in any case, the best choice for sweet dishes.

SUGAR

Always use the type of sugar specified in the recipe – superfine, confectioner's, granulated (simply described as sugar with no further qualification) or brown. You can grind coarse sugar in a food processor to make it finer if necessary. You can buy vanilla sugar, which usually has a very strong aroma, but it is better and more economical to make your own. Put a vanilla bean in a glass jar, fill the jar with sugar, seal and store in a cool place. In this way the sugar takes on a natural, delicate vanilla fragrance.

MILK

Of course milk should be fresh. Although long-life milk can give excellent results, fresh whole milk is preferable.

LEAVENING AGENTS

Fresh and dried yeast should always be activated in lukewarm water or milk before adding it to the other ingredients. Rapid-rise yeast can be added with the flour. The average amount of fresh yeast needed in summer is $1/4$–$3/8$ ounce for every 1 pound 2 ounces flour. In winter, use $1/2$–$3/4$ ounce for every 1 pound 2 ounces flour. Dried yeast is stronger, so use half these quantities, the equivalent of 2 teaspoons. With rapid-rise yeast, 1 envelope is the equivalent, but do check the packet instructions. After adding yeast to the mixture, let rise in a warm place and, when the dough has doubled in volume, put the dessert straight into the oven. In the case of baking powder, follow the packet instructions and remember that the leavening action begins immediately the baking powder becomes wet, so do not leave the mixture to stand unless instructed to do so in the recipe.

OCTAGON

DOUGH

It is always best to leave dough covered with a dish towel or wrapped in plastic wrap before use so that the surface does not become hard on contact with the air. To prevent dough from puffing up during baking, prick it all over with a fork after placing it in the pan, or cover with a sheet of baking parchment and sprinkle with baking beans, also known as pie weights. These may be metal or ceramic or simply dried beans, such as kidney beans, kept specifically for the purpose.

Most modern ovens are fitted with thermostats that will regulate the internal temperature and let dishes be cooked with as much accuracy as possible. The table below gives you the correspondence between the temperature shown on the thermostat and the general indications given in the recipes. Use one or the other system throughout.

LOW HEAT
225–275°F
MEDIUM
275–350°F
HOT
350–400°F
VERY HOT
400–475°F

Bear in mind, however, that dessert cooking times vary depending on the size, the material the pan or dish is made from and the quantity of ingredients. Individual ovens also vary and you should check the manufacturer's instructions if using a fan oven. As a general rule, it is advisable not to put desserts in a very hot oven and a medium temperature is usually preferable for even cooking. If desserts brown quickly on the surface, they are often not equally well cooked inside. To make sure, use the old trick of inserting a toothpick – if it comes out clean and dry, the dessert is ready.

Puddings, soufflés and custards may be cooked in a bain-marie, or water bath, in the oven and on the stovetop. This technique keeps the mixture softer. It consists of standing the cake pan or dish in another container half full of water that is kept constantly at simmering point. If the water starts to boil away too quickly, add more boiling water.

TURNING OUT CAKES

Cakes, including those served hot, should not be turned out immediately after they have been removed from the oven, but left to stand for a few minutes first. If you're not using a spring-form pan or a loose-based pan, put a plate on top and, holding the plate and pan firmly together, invert and tap the base of the pan so that the cake slides out onto the plate. Then gently lift off the pan. The cake will be upside down, so to serve it, cover with a serving dish and invert again immediately so that the surface is not damaged.

TURNING OUT MOLDS

After removing a mold from the refrigerator it is some-times necessary to wrap it in a dish towel wrung out in hot water to loosen its edges. To turn out the mold place a plate on top of it and, holding the plate and mold firmly together, invert, then tap the base of the mold. You can usually hear if the pudding slides onto the plate. If this doesn't work, wring out the dish towel in hot water again and repeat. You can also immerse the base of the mold in hot water and then invert onto a serving dish.

DECORATING

Whipped cream, candied fruit, walnuts, hazelnuts, candied violets, chopped almonds, silver balls and hundreds and thousands are among the most popular decorations. However, do not over-decorate your dessert as you may alter its flavor.

PASTRY AND DOUGH

This section provides basic recipes that are essential when tackling the vast subject of preparing pastry- or dough-based dishes, and they range from pie crust dough and pâte brisée to marzipan and Genoese pastry. These recipes are, of course, essential when preparing desserts but the section also contains recipes for cookie dough and two specialist pastries that are used for savory dishes – Savory Choux Paste and Easy Pâte Brisée. Desserts themselves are usually finished with custards, fruit, ricotta or other ingredients. Ready-made pastry dough may also be an invaluable aid – all you have to do is carefully follow the packet's instructions.

PÂTE BRISÉE

Sift the flour into a mound, make a well in the center, add the butter and a pinch of salt and rub in with your fingertips. Add just enough ice water to form a springy dough. Wrap in plastic wrap and chill in the refrigerator for about 1 hour. Preheat the oven to 350°F. Briefly knead the dough, then roll out on a lightly floured surface to a ¹/₈-inch thick sheet. If making a tart, place the dough in a tart pan greased with butter and bake for 40 minutes. If you are preparing barquettes or tartlet cases, bake for 15–20 minutes.

PASTA BRISÉE

Serves 6

2³/₄ cups all-purpose flour, plus extra for dusting

²/₃ cup sweet butter, cut into pieces

2–3 tablespoons ice water

salt

ALMOND PASTE (1)

Preheat the oven to 350°F. Grease a cookie sheet with butter. Combine the almonds and sugar in a bowl, crushing them to a coarse paste. Stiffly whisk the egg whites in another, grease-free bowl and fold into the almond mixture, then stir in the flour. Spoon the mixture into a pastry bag and squeeze out small balls onto the prepared cookie sheet, spacing them well apart. Bake for 15–20 minutes, then remove from the oven and let from one another cool.

PASTA DI MANDORLE (1)

Makes 30–35 petits fours

sweet butter, for greasing

scant ¹/₂ cup blanched almonds

¹/₂ cup superfine sugar

3 egg whites

¹/₄ cup all-purpose flour, sifted

ALMOND PASTE (2)

PASTA DI MANDORLE (2)

Sufficient to stuff 40 dates or make 20 bonbons

scant $1/2$ cup blanched almonds, finely chopped

scant 1 cup confectioner's sugar

2 egg whites

pink or green food dye (for dates)

1 tablespoon white rum (for dates) or strong coffee

or maraschino liqueur (for bonbons)

40 dates, pitted

1 quantity caramel (see page 1019), optional

superfine sugar, for decorating (for bonbons)

Combine the almonds and sugar in a bowl. Stiffly whisk the egg whites in another, grease-free bowl and fold into the almond mixture. If stuffing dates, stir a drop of your chosen food dye into the rum and then stir the rum into the almond paste until the color is even. Cut the dates in half and stuff with a little of the mixture. If you like, you can pour caramel over the dates. To make bonbons, add the coffee or liqueur to the almond mixture. Shape into 20 balls, roll in superfine sugar and arrange in fluted paper cases.

PIE CRUST DOUGH (1)

PASTA FROLLA (1)

Serves 6

$1^3/4$ cups all-purpose flour, plus extra for dusting

$1/2$ cup superfine sugar

scant $1/2$ cup sweet butter, softened and cut into pieces

2 egg yolks

2 teaspoons lemon rind, grated

salt

Sift the flour and sugar together into a mound, make a well in the center and add the butter, egg yolks, lemon rind and a pinch of salt. Mix thoroughly and knead briefly. Wrap the dough in plastic wrap and chill in the refrigerator for 1 hour. Roll out the dough on a lightly floured counter and use to line a pie pan. Trim the edges and follow the recipe instructions for your chosen pie.

PIE CRUST DOUGH (2)

PASTA FROLLA (2)

Serves 6

$1^3/4$ cups all-purpose flour, plus extra for dusting

$1/2$ cup superfine sugar

6 tablespoons sweet butter, softened and cut into pieces, plus extra for greasing

1 egg

1 egg yolk

preserve

salt

This recipe is used for extra-light tarts. Sift together the flour and sugar into a mound, make a well in the center and add the butter, egg, egg yolk and a pinch of salt. Knead together, then wrap the pastry in plastic wrap and chill in the refrigerator for at least 1 hour. Preheat the oven to 350°F. Grease a tart pan with butter. Take the dough out of the refrigerator and set a small piece aside, then roll out the remainder on a lightly floured counter to $1/8$ inch thick. To make a jam tart, place the dough in the prepared tart pan and spread with your chosen preserve. Roll out the reserved dough, cut into thin strips and place in a lattice pattern over the tart, securing at the rim with a little water. Alternatively, use a lattice cutter. Bake for about 20 minutes.

EGGLESS PIE CRUST DOUGH

PASTA FROLLA SENZA UOVA

Serves 6

²/₃ cup sweet butter, softened

¹/₂ cup superfine sugar

1 teaspoon grated lemon rind

1 cup all-purpose flour, plus extra for dusting

1 cup potato flour

Cream together the butter, sugar and lemon rind in a bowl. Sift together the all-purpose and potato flours into a mound, make a well in the center, add the creamed mixture and knead lightly. Wrap the dough in plastic wrap and chill in the refrigerator for 1 hour. Roll out the dough on a lightly floured counter and use according to the recipe. This dough has a more delicate flavor than the version with egg, but contains more butter.

GENOESE PASTRY

PASTA GENOVESE

Serves 6

¹/₄ cup sweet butter, softened, plus extra for greasing

1 cup all-purpose flour, plus extra for dusting

5 eggs

³/₄ cup superfine sugar

salt

Preheat the oven to 350°F. Grease a cake pan with butter and dust lightly with flour. Put the eggs and sugar in the top of a double boiler or in a heatproof bowl set over a pan of barely simmering water. Beat the mixture with a hand-held electric whisk or a balloon whisk until it doubles in volume, then remove from the heat and whisk until the mixture has cooled. Whisk in a pinch of salt, the butter and flour, a little at a time, and continue whisking until smooth. Pour the mixture into the prepared pan and bake for about 40 minutes.

MARGHERITA SPONGE

PASTA MARGHERITA

Serves 6

7 tablespoons sweet butter, melted, plus extra for greasing

1¹/₄ cups all-purpose flour, plus extra for dusting

6 eggs, separated

1 cup superfine sugar

¹/₂ cup potato flour

rind of 1 lemon, grated

salt

Preheat the oven to 350°F. Grease a cake pan with butter and dust lightly with flour. Beat the egg yolks with the sugar in a large bowl until pale and fluffy. Sift together the plain and potato flour onto a sheet of waxed paper, then add to the egg yolk mixture, a little at a time, followed by the melted butter, a pinch of salt and the lemon rind. Stiffly whisk the egg whites in another, grease-free bowl, then gently fold into the mixture. Pour into the prepared pan and bake for 30–35 minutes. This cake may be served sprinkled with confectioner's sugar and sliced and filled with preserve or cream.

CHOUX PASTE

Preheat the oven to 400°F. Grease a cookie sheet with butter and dust lightly with flour. Put 1 cup water, the butter, sugar and a pinch of salt in a pan, bring just to a boil and remove the pan from the heat. Tip in the flour, all in one go, and mix with a wooden spoon. Return the pan to the heat and cook, stirring constantly, for 7–8 minutes until the mixture comes away from the side of the pan. Remove the pan from the heat, let cool, then beat in the eggs, one at a time, making sure each egg has been fully absorbed before adding the next. Spoon the dough into a pastry bag and pipe walnut-size heaps onto the prepared cookie sheet, spacing them well apart. Alternatively, use two dessert spoons. Bake for about 20 minutes until the puffs have doubled in size. Transfer the puffs to a wire rack, making a slit in the side of each to allow the steam to escape and let cool, then fill with custard, chocolate or whipped cream.

PASTA PER BIGNÈ

Serves 6

7 tablespoons sweet butter, plus extra for greasing

1¼ cups all-purpose flour, sifted, plus extra for dusting

1 tablespoon superfine sugar

4 eggs

salt

SAVORY CHOUX PASTE

Preheat the oven to 350°F. Grease a cookie sheet with butter and dust lightly with flour. Pour 1 cup water into a pan, add the butter and a little salt and pepper and bring to a boil. Remove the pan from the heat, tip in the flour, all in one go, then cook, stirring constantly, until the mixture comes away from the sides of the pan. Remove the pan from the heat and let cool. Beat the eggs into the mixture, one at a time, making sure each egg has been fully absorbed before adding the next. Stir in the Parmesan. Scoop out a tablespoon of the mixture at a time, shape it into a walnut-size ball and place on the prepared cookie sheet. Bake for about 20 minutes until the puffs have doubled in size. Transfer the puffs to a wire rack, making a slit in the side of each to allow the steam to escape and let cool. Fill with melted cheese, béchamel sauce or other creamy, savory mixture. You can substitute generous 1 cup diced cooked ham or finely chopped Hungarian salami for the Parmesan. You can also use half Emmenthal and half Parmesan cheese.

PASTA PER BIGNÈ SALATA

Serves 6

7 tablespoons sweet butter, plus extra for greasing

1¼ cups all-purpose flour, sifted, plus extra for dusting

4 eggs

2⅓ cups Parmesan cheese, freshly grated

salt and white pepper

BRIOCHE

PASTA PER BRIOCHE

Serves 6–8

1/4 ounce fresh yeast

2 1/4 cups all-purpose flour, plus extra for dusting

4 eggs

1 tablespoon superfine sugar

scant 1 cup sweet butter,
softened and cut into pieces,
plus extra for greasing

salt

Pour a little lukewarm water into a bowl, add the yeast and mash with a fork to a smooth paste. Sift 1/2 cup of the flour into a mound, make a well in the center and add the dissolved yeast. Knead well and shape into a ball. Cut a cross in the surface, cover with a dish towel and let rise in a warm place for 2–3 hours. Sift the remaining flour into a mound, make a well in the center, break one of the eggs into it and add the sugar and a pinch of salt. Mix well, gradually incorporating the butter, then knead in two of the remaining eggs, one at a time. Once the first batch of dough has doubled in size, combine the two mixtures, knead into a large ball, cover with a dish towel and let rise in a warm place for 2–3 hours until doubled in size. Grease a brioche mold with butter. Lightly dust your hands with flour and lightly knead the dough again. Cut off one-third of the dough and set aside. Shape the larger piece of dough into a ball, place in the prepared mold and cut a cross in the top. Shape the smaller piece of dough into a pear shape and place, pointed end down, on top of the first piece, then let rise in a warm place for a further 30 minutes. Preheat the oven to 400°F. Lightly beat the remaining egg and brush it over the surface of the dough. Bake for about 50 minutes or until a toothpick inserted into the brioche comes out dry. You can use individual fluted molds to make small brioches. Shape as before, brush with beaten egg and prick with a fork. Bake for 15–20 minutes.

YEAST CAKE

PASTA PER DOLCI LIEVITATA

Serves 4–6

scant 1/2 cup lukewarm milk

2 tablespoons superfine sugar

3/4 teaspoon dried yeast

1 egg

3 tablespoons sweet butter, softened,
plus extra for greasing

2 cups all-purpose flour

Pour the milk into a bowl and stir in 1 teaspoon of the sugar. Sprinkle the yeast on the surface and let stand for 10–15 minutes until frothy, then stir to a smooth paste. Tip the yeast mixture into a mixing bowl and add the remaining sugar, the egg and butter. Sift the flour over the mixture, stirring constantly, then knead to a smooth dough. Cover and let rise in a warm place for 1 1/2 hours. Preheat the oven to 350°F. Grease two cake pans with butter. Divide the dough in half and roll out, leaving the edges fairly thick. Place in the prepared pans and bake for 30 minutes. Sandwich the cakes together with your chosen filling.

TART SHELL

Cream the butter with the sugar and a pinch of salt in a bowl, then stir in the egg and all the flour in one go. Turn out onto the counter and knead until the flour has been completely absorbed. Divide the dough into four pieces, put one on top of the other and press down. Repeat this process twice more, then wrap in plastic wrap and let stand for about 1 hour. Preheat the oven to 350°F. Grease a tart pan or cake pan with butter. Roll out the dough to a round $1/4$ inch thick and line the prepared pan with it. Cover the tart shell with a sheet of foil or waxed paper and fill with baking beans. Bake for about 25 minutes. Remove from the oven and remove the foil or paper and beans. Let cool before filling with fresh fruit or a filling of your choice.

PASTA PER FONDO TORTA

Serves 6

generous $1/4$ cup sweet butter,
plus extra for greasing
scant $1/2$ cup superfine sugar
1 egg, lightly beaten
$2^1/4$ cups all-purpose flour
salt

SPONGE CAKE

Preheat the oven to 350°F. Grease a cake pan with butter and dust lightly with flour. Beat the egg yolks with the sugar in a bowl until pale and fluffy. Stiffly whisk the egg whites in another, grease-free bowl, then gently fold into the egg yolk mixture. Sift in the potato flour and all-purpose flour, adding a little at a time. Spoon the mixture into the prepared pan and smooth the surface. Bake for about 40 minutes. Remove from the oven and let cool in the pan, then turn out. Slice horizontally and spread with the filling of your choice before sandwiching together again.

PASTA PER PAN DI SPAGNA

Serves 6

sweet butter, for greasing
$2/3$ cup all-purpose flour, sifted,
plus extra for dusting
6 eggs, separated
$3/4$ cup superfine sugar
$2/3$ cup potato flour, sifted

SABLÉ DOUGH

Chop the almonds together with half the sugar. Sift the flour into a mound, make a well in the center and add the butter, remaining sugar, egg yolks, almond mixture and a pinch of salt. Knead lightly and shape into a ball, then wrap in plastic wrap and let rest for 1 hour. Preheat the oven to 350°F. Roll out the dough into a fairly thick sheet on a lightly floured counter and stamp out rounds or other shapes with a cutter. Place on a dampened cookie sheet and bake for 15 minutes. Leave the cookies on the cookie sheet to cool.

PASTA PER SABLÉ

Serves 6

generous $1/2$ cup blanched almonds
$1/2$ cup superfine sugar
$1^3/4$ cups all-purpose flour, plus extra for dusting
$1/2$ cup sweet butter, softened
3 egg yolks
salt

SPEEDY PUFF PASTRY

PASTA SFOGLIA RAPIDA

Serves 6

scant ¹/₂ cup sweet butter

1¹/₄ cups all-purpose flour, plus extra for dusting

salt

Making puff pastry is so time-consuming that it is almost always best to buy it ready-made. However, if you want to make it at least once, it is worth trying this simplified version. Combine the butter and ¹/₄ cup of the flour using a metal spatula. (This helps to prevent the heat of your hands making the mixture too soft. In fact, the secret of successful puff pastry is the right balance of temperature between the different ingredients.) When the butter has absorbed all the flour, shape the dough into a ¹/₄-inch thick square on a lightly floured counter. Knead the remaining flour with a little water and a pinch of salt until soft. Shape into a round and place it in the middle of the dough square. Gently lift the four corners of the square and bring them together in the middle covering the round. Using a rolling pin, roll out into a rectangle with the short side toward you. Turn the dough a quarter turn. Lift up the right-hand short side and fold it in towards the middle of the rectangle. Do the same with the left-hand side. Fold the pastry in half again so that it looks like a sort of square book. This is the first 'pastry fold'. Roll out the square into a long rectangle, always rolling in the same direction, and repeat the pastry fold. Do this four times. Between each fold, chill the dough in the refrigerator for 10 minutes. Puff pastry should be baked in an oven preheated to 400–425°F for about 20 minutes for small dishes and slightly longer for petits fours and cakes.

EASY PÂTE BRISÉE

PASTA TIPO BRISÉE

Serves 6

2³/₄ cups all-purpose flour, plus extra for dusting

scant ¹/₂ cup sweet butter, softened and cut into pieces

1 egg

3–4 tablespoons milk

salt

Sift the flour into a mound, make a well in the center and add the butter, egg and a pinch of salt. Mix together with your fingertips until the mixture resembles bread crumbs. Add the milk, a little at a time, and knead briefly into a smooth dough. Wrap in plastic wrap and chill in the refrigerator for 1 hour. Remove the dough from the refrigerator, knead lightly, then roll out on a lightly floured counter to a sheet about ¹/₂ inch thick. This dough is used for savory pies.

SWEET SAUCES AND DECORATIONS

Sauces and decorations may be used to transform an ordinary ice-cream cake or plain homemade pudding into an elegant dessert. Just pour on melted chocolate, decorate with smooth liqueur-flavored frosting or liven up with colorful fruit sauces and wrap in a cloud of whipped cream. This section reveals the secrets, big and small, of how to present simple dishes with style.

MELTED CHOCOLATE

Pour generous 1 cup water into a pan, add the sugar and heat gently, stirring constantly, until the sugar has dissolved. Bring to a boil, then simmer, without stirring, until the syrup has reduced by half. Add the chocolate and melt over low heat, stirring constantly with a wooden spatula. Stir in the butter and when it has melted remove the pan from the heat. This chocolate sauce may be served with ice creams or used to decorate or fill cakes and puffs.

CIOCCOLATA FUSA

¹/₄ cup superfine sugar

5 ounces semisweet chocolate, broken into pieces

1¹/₂ teaspoons sweet butter

COLD FROSTING

This simple frosting is used to decorate cakes and petits fours. Put the sugar in a bowl and stir in 2–3 tablespoons water to make a fairly thick mixture. Stir in the liqueur, or the vanilla or orange rind. Stir the mixture with a wooden spatula until smooth and of a spreading consistency. To give the frosting a shine after it has been spread on a cake, put the cake in an oven preheated to 350°F for a few seconds.

GLASSA A FREDDO

1¹/₄ cups confectioner's sugar

2 tablespoons liqueur of your choice

or ¹/₂ teaspoon vanilla extract or orange rind, grated

BUTTER FROSTING

GLASSA AL BURRO

5 tablespoons sweet butter

3 cups confectioner's sugar, sifted

1–2 drops vanilla extract

2 tablespoons heavy cream

Cream the butter in a bowl with a wooden spoon, then beat in the sugar and vanilla. Add the cream, a little at a time, until the frosting has a spreading consistency. To make sure the frosting adheres well, spread the surface of the cake or the petits fours with a light film of gelatin first.

COFFEE FROSTING

GLASSA AL CAFFÈ

1¼ cups freshly brewed strong coffee

2¼ cups confectioner's sugar

Pour the hot coffee into a bowl and sift in the sugar, a little at a time, stirring until the mixture is fairly thick. Let cool. Spread the frosting evenly over the surface of the cake with a metal spatula. Place in an oven preheated to 350°F for a few seconds so that it becomes shiny.

CHOCOLATE FROSTING

GLASSA AL CIOCCOLATO

2 tablespoons confectioner's sugar

5 ounces semisweet chocolate, broken into pieces

Put the sugar in a pan, add ½ cup water and heat, stirring constantly, for a few minutes until thickened. Meanwhile, melt the chocolate in a heatproof bowl set over a pan of barely simmering water. Add the syrup to the melted chocolate, a drop at a time, stirring constantly. Spread the frosting over the cake while it is still hot.

DECORATIVE FROSTING

GLASSA PER DECORARE

1 egg white

1¼ cups vanilla confectioner's sugar (see page 1003)

Whisk the egg white in a grease-free bowl, then gradually sift in the sugar, whisking constantly. Add 2 tablespoons warm water, a drop at a time, and stir gently for 20 minutes with a regular movement from the bottom upwards to avoid knocking out the air. Use a pastry bag to decorate the cake.

MERINGUES

MERINGA

Makes 20

sweet butter, for greasing

all-purpose flour, for dusting

5 egg whites

1¾ cups confectioner's sugar, sifted

Preheat the oven to 300°F. Grease a cookie sheet with butter and dust lightly with flour. Stiffly whisk the egg whites in a grease-free bowl, then gently stir in the sugar. Spoon a little of the meringue into a pastry bag and squeeze out ½-inch thick rounds onto the prepared cookie sheet. Lower the oven temperature to its minimum setting and cook the meringues for 30–40 minutes without allowing them to brown. Meringues should not cook, but simply dry out.

WHIPPED CREAM

Chill a bowl in the freezer for 15–30 minutes, then remove and pour the cream into it. Whip with an electric mixer until thickened. If you want a sweetened cream, add the sugar to the cream before whipping.

PANNA MONTATA

1¼ cups heavy cream, chilled

1–2 tablespoons vanilla confectioner's sugar (optional, see page 1003)

BATTER FOR FRYING

Put the flour, wine and grappa into a large bowl, add a pinch of salt and mix well. Stir in the egg yolk to make a fairly thick, but still runny mixture. Let stand for 30 minutes. Whisk the egg white in a grease-free bowl, then fold it into the mixture. Quickly dip the ingredients to be fried in the batter and cook in hot oil – 350–375°F or until a cube of day-old bread browns in 30 seconds. Remove with a slotted spoon or slotted spatula and drain on paper towels.

PASTELLA PER FRIGGERE

1¼ cups all-purpose flour

5 tablespoons white wine

2 tablespoons grappa

1 egg, separated

salt

HOT CHOCOLATE SAUCE

Melt the chocolate in a heatproof bowl set over a pan of barely simmering water. Stir with a wooden spoon, then add the cream, a little at a time, stirring until the sauce has the required consistency. Remove the bowl from the heat just as the sauce reaches simmering point. This chocolate sauce may be poured onto molds and mousses, as well as various flavors of ice cream, such as hazelnut, banana or even chocolate ice cream itself.

SALSA AL CIOCCOLATO

9 ounces semisweet chocolate, broken into pieces

scant 1 cup heavy cream

COLD CHOCOLATE SAUCE

Whip the cream until thickened. Melt the chocolate in a heatproof bowl set over a pan of barely simmering water, then remove from the heat and let cool slightly. Stir in the custard and let cool completely, then fold in the whipped cream. This chocolate sauce may be used to fill sponge cakes.

SALSA AL CIOCCOLATO FREDDA

3 tablespoons heavy cream

2 ounces semisweet chocolate, broken into pieces

1 quantity Custard (see page 1039)

ORANGE SAUCE

SALSA ALL'ARANCIA

rind of 1 orange, finely pared
7 ounces orange jelly
7 ounces apricot jam
2 tablespoons orange liqueur

Slice the orange rind into fine strips and blanch in boiling water for 5 minutes, then drain and dry with paper towels. Press the orange jelly and apricot jam through a fine strainer into a pan and stir in the orange liqueur. Add the orange rind and heat gently, stirring constantly. This sauce may be poured, hot or cold, onto ice creams and creamy desserts.

APRICOT SAUCE

SALSA DI ALBICOCCHE

¾ cup superfine sugar
9 ounces apricots, pitted

Put the sugar and scant 1 cup water in a pan and bring to a boil over medium heat, stirring until the syrup thickens. Pass the apricots through a food mill, add to the syrup and heat until the sauce is thick enough to coat the back of a tablespoon. Pour the sauce through a cheesecloth-lined strainer into a bowl. This sauce is used for filling or covering desserts and cakes, especially those made with chocolate. It may be used hot or cold.

CHERRY SAUCE

SALSA DI CILIEGE

scant 2 cups cherries, pitted
generous ½ cup superfine sugar
¾ cup kirsch

Place the cherries and sugar in a small pan, pour in scant ½ cup water, cover and cook over medium heat until softened. Remove the cherries with a slotted spoon and pass through a food mill into a bowl. Reduce the cooking liquid over low heat, then remove from the heat and let cool. Stir the cooled liquid into the cherry purée, then add the kirsch. Serve this sauce with plain ice cream or panna cotta. It may also be used to fill cakes.

STRAWBERRY SAUCE

SALSA DI FRAGOLE

¼ cup superfine sugar
scant 3 cups strawberries
¼ cup kirsch or maraschino liqueur

Pour scant ½ cup water into a pan, add the sugar and cook over medium heat, stirring constantly, for 8–10 minutes. Pass the strawberries through a food mill, stir the purée into the syrup and add the liqueur. This sauce may be served with all types of ice cream, particularly pistachio.

HAZELNUT SAUCE

Preheat the oven to 400°F. Spread out the hazelnuts on a cookie sheet and place in the oven for about 10 minutes but do not let them brown. Tip the nuts onto a clean dish towel and rub to remove the skins, then crush finely and stir into the custard. Finally, stir in the brandy. This sauce goes particularly well with zabaglione ice cream or plain zabaglione.

SALSA DI NOCCIOLE

scant 1 cup hazelnuts, shelled

2 cups Confectioner's Custard

(see page 1039)

¼ cup brandy

THICK SYRUP

Pour 4 tablespoons water into a pan, add the sugar and heat gently, stirring constantly, until the sugar has dissolved. Bring to a boil, then simmer, without stirring, until the syrup has thickened. The quantities of sugar and water vary depending on the consistency required. For example, halve the amount of sugar for a runny syrup. When making syrup, it is best to use a stainless steel or heavy-based double boiler.

SCIROPPO DI ZUCCHERO DENSO

1 tablespoon superfine sugar

CARAMEL

Rinse out a small stainless steel pan with cold water, add the sugar and pour in ½ cup warm water. Cook over very low heat, stirring until the sugar has dissolved completely and turned golden brown and stringy. This may take as long as 30 minutes. Caramel is used for lining dessert molds and, in particular, when making classic Crème Caramel (see page 1028). It may also be poured over ice cream and is one of the main ingredients of mulled milk.

ZUCCHERO CARAMELLATO

½ cup superfine sugar

BAVARIAN CREAMS

All you need is a little practice and your Bavarian cream or Bavarois – a delicious dessert for all seasons of the year – is sure to make a great impression. This may be partly thanks to the tall, often fluted or decorated molds that give them an elegant shape or to their color – yellow, green, red or brown from fruit, coffee or chocolate. They may be two-color – cream and chocolate or strawberry and lemon – or even three-color – coffee, zabaglione and hazelnut. They are based on egg custard, whipped cream and flavored sugars. The bavarois is left to cool and set in the refrigerator and then turned out by inverting the mold. The dessert is completed to perfection with fresh fruit, fruit in syrup or a sauce handed separately.

ORANGE BAVARIAN CREAM

BAVARESE ALL'ARANCIA

Serves 6

3 gelatin leaves

3 oranges

$^{1}/_{2}$ cup superfine sugar

$1^{3}/_{4}$ cups evaporated milk

6–8 candied orange slices

Fill a small bowl with water, add the gelatin and let soak. Grate the rind of two of the oranges and squeeze the juice from all three. Strain the orange juice into a pan, add the sugar and orange rind, bring to a boil and cook until reduced by half. Drain the gelatin, squeeze out and stir into the warm orange syrup, one sheet at a time. Whisk the evaporated milk in a bowl until foamy, then whisk in the orange mixture. Arrange the slices of candied orange on the base of a cake pan and pour the mixture on top. Chill in the refrigerator for at least 4 hours until set, then turn out.

VANILLA BAVARIAN CREAM

Bring the milk just to a boil in a small pan, remove from the heat, add the vanilla bean and leave for about 1 hour, then remove the vanilla bean. Fill a small bowl with water, add the gelatin and let soak. Beat the egg yolks with the sugar until pale and fluffy, then fold in the flavored milk a little at a time. Drain the gelatin, squeeze out and stir into the mixture. Pour into a pan and cook over medium heat, stirring constantly, until thick enough to coat the back of the spoon. Do not let the mixture boil. Remove the pan from the heat, pour the resulting custard into a bowl and let cool, stirring occasionally to prevent a skin forming on the surface. Stiffly whip the cream, then gently fold into the cooled custard. Rinse out a cake pan with cold water and spoon the mixture into it. Cover and chill in the refrigerator for about 4 hours until set. To serve, dip the base of the cake pan in hot water for a few seconds, then invert onto a serving plate. This Bavarian cream, which is excellent on its own, is also used as the base for fruit, coffee, chocolate and other flavored Bavarian creams.

BAVARESE ALLA VANIGLIA

Serves 6

1 cup milk

1 vanilla bean, slit

1 gelatin leaf

4 egg yolks

³/₄ cup superfine sugar

2¹/₄ cups heavy cream

PLUM BAVARIAN CREAM

Place the plums in a dish, pour in the red wine and let soak for about 20 minutes. Line a loose-based cake pan with the Genoese pastry. Drain the plums and place five or six of them in a bowl with the brandy. Arrange some of remaining plums on the base of the lined pan and the remainder upright around the side. Fill a small bowl with water, add the gelatin and let soak for 3 minutes, then drain and squeeze out. Stir the gelatin into the custard in a bowl and let cool. Stiffly whip the cream and gently fold it into the custard. Pour the mixture into the cake pan, being careful not to disturb the plums. Chill in the refrigerator for at least 2 hours until set. Drain the remaining plums. Transfer the Bavarian cream to a serving dish and decorate with the drained plums.

BAVARESE ALLE PRUGNE

Serves 6

14 ounces plums, pitted

4 cups red wine

1 quantity Genoese Pastry (see page 1010)

³/₄ cup brandy

2 gelatin leaves

1 quantity Custard (see page 1039)

1³/₄ cups heavy cream

Serves 6

2 gelatin leaves

5 tablespoons sweet white wine

juice of ¹/₂ lemon, strained

4 eggs yolks

³/₄ cup superfine sugar

2¹/₄ cups heavy cream

sweet butter, for greasing

1 quantity Genoese Pastry (see page 1010)

all-purpose flour, for dusting

For the syrup

5 tablespoons sweet white wine

1¹/₂ cups black grapes

¹/₂ cup superfine sugar

WINE BAVARIAN CREAM

Fill a small bowl with water, add the gelatin and let soak. Gently heat the wine and lemon juice in a pan. Beat the egg yolks with the sugar in another pan until pale and fluffy. Whisk in the hot wine mixture and heat gently, stirring constantly, until thick enough to coat the back of the spoon. Remove from the heat and let cool slightly. Drain the gelatin and squeeze out, then stir into the custard and let cool completely. Stiffly whip the cream and gently fold it into the cold custard. Chill in the refrigerator. Preheat the oven to 350°F. Grease two shallow cake pans with butter. Make the syrup. Heat the wine, ¹/₃ cup of the grapes and the sugar in a pan, stirring until the sugar has dissolved. Drain and reserve the grapes and reserve the syrup. Place the remaining grapes in a food processor and process to a purée. Strain the purée into the hot syrup, mix well and let cool slightly. Divide the dough in half, place in the prepared pans to a depth of ³/₄ inch and bake for about 40 minutes. Remove from the oven and let cool. Place a pastry round on a serving dish, sprinkle with some of the syrup, spread a layer of Bavarian cream on top, then a layer of the reserved grapes, then another layer of Bavarian cream. Top with the second pastry round and sprinkle with syrup. Spread the remaining Bavarian cream over the whole cake. Keep cool until ready to serve, then decorate with the remaining grapes.

MOLDS
AND PUDDINGS

This group of desserts encompasses a large number of techniques and recipes. To Italians, molds bring back happy childhood memories and are often served as tempting snacks for children. They are made from milk, eggs and flour – and sometimes potato flour, semolina, rice and bread – and are flavored with vanilla or other ingredients, depending on what you like best. Molds are served cold with fruit sauces or cookies.

LITTLE SPOON

PIEDMONT PUDDING

Heat the milk to simmering point in a small pan, then remove from the heat. Beat the eggs with 4 heaping tablespoons of the sugar in a bowl until pale and fluffy. Gradually stir in the warm milk, then add the amaretti, chocolate, and rum if using. Mix well. Put the remaining sugar in a small pan, add 2 tablespoons water and heat until caramelized. When the sugar has begun to turn brown, remove it from the heat and pour into a warm rectangular mold, tipping and turning so that the caramel coats the base and sides evenly. Let cool. Preheat the oven to 350°F. Pour the chocolate mixture into the mold. Stand the mold in a roasting pan, add boiling water to come halfway up the sides and bake for 1 hour or until a toothpick inserted into the center comes out clean. Alternatively, simmer over low heat for 1 hour. Remove from the water bath and let cool, then turn out.

BONET

Serves 6

2¹/₄ cups milk

4 eggs

generous ³/₄ cup superfine sugar

1 cup amaretti, crumbled

3 tablespoons bittersweet chocolate, grated

¹/₄ cup rum (optional)

CHOCOLATE MOLD

BUDINO AL CIOCCOLATO

Serves 6

scant ¹/₂ cup sweet butter, softened,
plus extra for greasing
3 eggs, separated
¹/₂ cup superfine sugar
3¹/₂ ounces semisweet chocolate,
broken into pieces
2¹/₄ cups milk
¹/₂ cup all-purpose flour
Zabaglione (see page 1039) or whipped cream,
to serve (optional)

Preheat the oven to 350°F. Grease a mold with plenty of butter. Cream the butter in a bowl, then beat in the egg yolks, one at a time, followed by the sugar. Melt the chocolate in a heatproof bowl set over a pan of barely simmering water. Meanwhile, bring the milk just to a boil. Gradually add the milk to the chocolate, a little at a time, then pour onto the creamed mixture, mixing well. Pour into a pan, sift in the flour and simmer, stirring constantly, for 5 minutes. Remove from the heat and let cool, stirring occasionally. Stiffly whisk the egg whites in a grease-free bowl and fold into the mixture. Pour the chocolate mixture into the prepared mold. Stand the mold in a roasting pan, add boiling water to come halfway up the sides and bake for 30 minutes. Alternatively, set the roasting pan over low heat, add boiling water and simmer for 30 minutes. Remove the mold from the water bath and let cool, then turn out gently onto a serving dish. Serve with zabaglione or whipped cream, if you like.

LIME MOLD

BUDINO AL LIME

Serves 4–6

1 quantity Caramel (see page 1019)
5 eggs
1 cup superfine sugar
scant ¹/₂ cup lime juice, strained
lemon rind, thinly pared, to decorate

Prepare the caramel and pour into a mold, tipping and turning so that it covers the base and sides evenly. Beat the eggs with the sugar in a pan over low heat until pale and fluffy. Stir in the lime juice and pour the mixture into the prepared mold. Stand the mold in a roasting pan, add boiling water to come halfway up the sides and simmer for 1 hour or until a toothpick inserted into the dessert comes out dry. Remove the mold from the water bath and let cool. Turn out onto a serving dish and decorate with lemon rind.

HONEY PUDDING

BUDINO AL MIELE

Serves 4

2¹/₄ cups sweet white wine
²/₃ cup clear honey
pinch of ground cinnamon
1 teaspoon lemon rind, grated
6 eggs
²/₃ cup superfine sugar

Pour the wine into a pan and bring to a boil. Stir in the honey, cinnamon and lemon rind, then remove from the heat and let cool. Beat the eggs in a bowl and beat in the wine mixture. Prepare the caramel (see page 1019) with the quantity of sugar specified. Pour into a round mold, tipping and turning so that it coats the base and sides evenly, and let cool. Preheat the oven to 350°F. Pour the egg and wine mixture into the mold, place in a roasting pan and add boiling water to come halfway up the sides. Bake for 30 minutes, then remove from the water bath and let cool. Turn out just before serving.

CHESTNUT MOLD

Cook the chestnuts in a pan of boiling water for about 20 minutes, then drain and peel off the skins. Put them in a pan, add the milk and vanilla and season with a pinch of salt. Cover and cook over medium heat for about 35 minutes until tender. Press the chestnuts and their cooking liquid through a strainer into another pan. Toast the almonds in the oven or under the broiler, then chop. Gently heat the chestnut purée and stir in the sugar and almonds, then remove from the heat and stir in the cream. Pour the mixture into a mold, let cool and then chill in the refrigerator for 3 hours. Just before serving, turn out onto a dish and garnish with almonds.

BUDINO DI CASTAGNE

Serves 6

1 pound 2 ounces chestnuts, shelled

2¼ cups milk

a few drops of vanilla extract

scant 1 cup blanched almonds,

plus extra to garnish

¼ cup superfine sugar

⅔ cup light cream

salt

FRUIT JELLY

Pour the orange and lemon juices into a pan, add the sugar and cook over low heat, stirring constantly, until the sugar has dissolved. Add the jelly, prepared according to the packet instructions, bring just to a boil, then remove from the heat and strain. Place the strawberries in a food processor and process to a purée. Stir the purée into the fruit juice mixture, let cool slightly, then pour into a ring mold. Chill in the refrigerator for several hours or overnight until set. Using a melon baller, scoop out balls of melon flesh. Turn out the mold onto a serving dish, fill the center with the melon balls and serve.

BUDINO DI FRUTTA IN GELATINA

Serves 6

2¼ pounds oranges, strained

juice of 2 lemons, strained

scant 1 cup superfine sugar

1 tablespoon instant jelly

4½ cups strawberries

1 small melon, halved and seeded

ALMOND PUDDING

Preheat the oven to 350°F. Brush a marble slab or metal cookie sheet with oil. Grease a mold with butter. Spread out the almonds on another cookie sheet and bake for a few minutes, until dry. Melt the sugar in a pan, stir in the almonds and cook, stirring constantly, until they are golden brown. Pour the mixture onto the prepared slab or cookie sheet and let cool, then crush extremely finely. Stiffly whisk the egg whites in a grease-free bowl, then fold in the crushed almond mixture. Pour into the prepared mold, place in a roasting pan, pour in boiling water to come halfway up the sides and bake for 30 minutes or until a toothpick inserted in the center comes out clean. Turn out and serve cold.

BUDINO DI MANDORLE

Serves 4–6

sunflower or olive oil, for brushing

sweet butter, for greasing

1½ cups blanched almonds

scant 1 cup superfine sugar

8 egg whites

ENGLISH BREAD AND BUTTER PUDDING

Put both types of raisins in a bowl, add warm water to cover and let soak for 1 hour, then drain and squeeze out. Grease a large ovenproof dish with butter. Spread both sides of the slices of bread with the butter and make a layer of half the slices on the base of the prepared dish, cutting them into two or more pieces to fit well. Sprinkle with half the raisins and place the remaining bread on top. Beat the eggs with the sugar in a bowl, then stir in the milk, cream and remaining raisins, a little at a time. Pour the mixture over the bread and let stand for 30 minutes or until the bread has absorbed the liquid. Meanwhile, preheat the oven to 350°F. Cover the dish with foil and bake for 45 minutes. Remove and discard the foil, return the dish to the oven and bake for 15 minutes more. Serve warm with apricot sauce.

BUDINO DI PANE ALL'INGLESE

Serves 6

generous 1/2 cup golden raisins

generous 1/2 cup raisins

scant 1/2 cup sweet butter, softened, plus extra for greasing

8–10 white bread slices, crusts removed

4 eggs

2/3 cup superfine sugar

2 1/4 cups milk

scant 1 cup heavy cream

Apricot Sauce (see page 1018), to serve

SEMOLINA PUDDING

Put the golden raisins in a bowl, add warm water to cover and let soak for 15 minutes, then drain and squeeze out. Preheat the oven to 350°F. Grease a mold with butter and sprinkle with bread crumbs to coat. Pour the milk into a pan, add 1/2 cup water and the sugar and bring to a boil. Sprinkle in the semolina, add a pinch of salt and simmer, stirring constantly, for 10 minutes. Remove the pan from the heat and stir in the butter, golden raisins, lemon rind and eggs. Pour the mixture into the prepared mold and bake for 40 minutes. This pudding may be made more flavorsome by adding a little candied citron peel.

BUDINO DI SEMOLINO

Serves 6

scant 1/2 cup golden raisins

2 tablespoons sweet butter, plus extra for greasing

bread crumbs, for sprinkling

3 cups milk

1/2 cup superfine sugar

generous 3/4 cup fine semolina

grated rind of 1 lemon

4 eggs, lightly beaten

salt

SEMOLINA PUDDING WITH BLACK CHERRIES

Pour the milk into a pan, add the sugar, lemon rind and a pinch of salt and bring to a boil. Sprinkle in the semolina, stir quickly and immediately remove from the heat. Stir in the butter and cherries and let cool. Meanwhile, preheat the oven to 350°F. Grease an ovenproof dish with butter. Stir the egg yolks into the cooled semolina mixture, one at a time. Stiffly whisk the egg whites in a grease-free bowl and fold into the mixture. Pour into the prepared dish and bake for 40 minutes.

BUDINO DI SEMOLINO ALLE AMARENE

Serves 4

4 cups milk

1/2 cup superfine sugar

grated rind of 1 lemon

generous 1 cup semolina

1/4 cup sweet butter, plus extra for greasing

scant 2 cups black cherries, pitted

3 eggs, separated

salt

CRÈME CARAMEL

CRÈME CARAMEL

Serves 6

2¼ cups milk

1 vanilla bean, slit

2 eggs

3 egg yolks

¾ cup superfine sugar

Pour the milk into a pan, add the vanilla bean and bring to simmering point, then remove from the heat and let steep for 15 minutes. Remove the vanilla bean. Beat the eggs and egg yolks with a generous ½ cup of the sugar in a bowl until pale and fluffy. Gradually stir in the flavored milk, then strain the mixture into another bowl. Preheat the oven to 350°F. Put the remaining sugar and 1 tablespoon water into a nonstick pan and heat gently until caramelized. Remove from the heat and pour into individual molds, tipping and turning so that the base and sides are covered. Pour the custard into the molds, place them in a roasting pan, add boiling water to come halfway up the sides and bake for 20 minutes. Remove from the water bath and let cool, then turn out.

CHOCOLATE DELIGHT

DELIZIA AL CIOCCOLATO

Serves 4–6

sweet butter, for greasing

¼ cup all-purpose flour, plus extra for dusting

3½ ounces semisweet chocolate, broken into pieces

5 eggs, separated

1¾ cups confectioner's sugar

2 tablespoons vanilla sugar (see page 1003)

¼ cup sweet butter, melted

3 tablespoons cornstarch

Preheat the oven to 300°F. Grease a cake pan with butter and lightly dust with flour. Melt the chocolate in a heatproof bowl set over a pan of barely simmering water, then remove from the heat. Beat the egg yolks with half the confectioner's sugar and the vanilla sugar in a bowl. Beat in the melted butter and chocolate, sift in the flour and cornstarch and mix well. Stiffly whisk the egg whites in a grease-free bowl, then whisk in the remaining confectioner's sugar. Gently fold into the chocolate mixture and pour into the prepared pan. Bake for about 40 minutes, then remove from the oven and let cool. Chill in the refrigerator before turning out and serving.

RICE PUDDING

DELIZIA AL RISO

Serves 4

⅔ cup short-grain rice

1 cup milk

¾ cup superfine sugar

⅔ cup heavy cream

⅓ cup candied citron peel, chopped

Cook the rice in a pan of boiling water for 10 minutes, then drain immediately. Bring the milk to simmering point in another pan, add the rice and cook until all the milk has been absorbed. Stir in the sugar, then remove the pan from the heat and let cool. Stiffly whip the cream. Fold the citron peel and the whipped cream into the rice. Rinse out a ring mold with water, pour in the rice mixture and place in the freezer until the mixture becomes firm. Turn out and serve.

LATTE BRÛLÉE

Serves 6

4 cups milk

scant 1 cup superfine sugar

8 egg yolks

2 egg whites

whipped cream, to serve

MILK BRÛLÉE

Pour the milk into a pan, add $\frac{1}{2}$ cup of the sugar and cook over medium heat, stirring until the sugar has dissolved. Lower the heat and simmer for about 1 hour, then remove from the heat and let cool. Heat the remaining sugar in a small pan until it melts and turns golden brown, then pour into a mold, tipping and turning so that the base and sides are evenly covered. Return the excess caramelized sugar to the heat and cook until it turns dark brown. Add $\frac{2}{3}$ cup water to prevent the sugar from burning and cook, stirring constantly, until a thick, dark syrup forms. Remove the pan from the heat and let cool. Preheat the oven to 350°F. Beat together the egg yolks and egg whites in a pan with a fork, stir in the milk mixture and dark syrup and strain into the caramel-lined mold. Stand in a roasting pan, add boiling water to come halfway up the sides and bake for 20 minutes or until a toothpick inserted into the center comes out clean. Turn out and serve with whipped cream. This dessert has a sophisticated bitter-sweet flavor that finishes off a meal perfectly.

PANNA COTTA

Serves 6

2 gelatin leaves

scant $\frac{1}{2}$ cup milk

$2\frac{1}{4}$ cups heavy cream

$\frac{1}{2}$ cup superfine sugar

1 vanilla bean, slit

Hazelnut Sauce (see page 1019), to serve (optional)

PANNA COTTA

Fill a small bowl with water, add the gelatin and let soak. Pour the milk into a pan and bring to just below simmering point, then remove the pan from the heat. Do not let it boil. Drain and squeeze out the gelatin and add to the milk. Pour the cream into another pan, add the sugar and vanilla bean and bring to a boil over low heat, stirring constantly. Immediately remove the pan from the heat, remove the vanilla bean and stir in the milk mixture. Rinse out a rectangular cake pan with ice-cold water, shaking out any excess, and fill with the mixture. Chill in the refrigerator for several hours until set. Turn out onto a serving dish and serve by itself or with hazelnut sauce.

CHARLOTTES

A charlotte is a dessert based on fruit and custard, which may be covered or encircled in sliced bread, ladyfingers or sponge cake softened with fresh fruit juice, liqueur, tea or coffee.

AMARETTI CHARLOTTE

Beat the butter with ¹/₂ cup of the sugar in a bowl until pale and fluffy. Melt the chocolate with 2 tablespoons water in a heatproof bowl set over a pan of barely simmering water. Beat the egg yolk with the milk in a small bowl, then stir into the melted chocolate. Stir in the butter mixture. Mix the rum with 5 tablespoons water and the remaining sugar in another bowl. Make a layer of amaretti in a dish and sprinkle with some of the rum mixture. Make another layer of amaretti on top and sprinkle with the rum mixture again. Continue making layers in this way until all the amaretti have been used. Line the base and sides of a charlotte mold with some of the softened amaretti. Pour in a little of the chocolate mixture and make alternating layers of amaretti and chocolate mixture, ending with a layer of amaretti. Press down gently, cover and chill in the refrigerator for 4–5 hours. To make the frosting, put the chocolate, sugar, butter and 1 tablespoon water in a heatproof bowl set over a pan of barely simmering water and stir until melted and combined, then remove from the heat. Turn out the charlotte and spread with the frosting. If you want to make the frosting shiny, put the charlotte in a hot oven for a minute.

CHARLOTTE AGLI AMARETTI

Serves 6

¹/₂ cup sweet butter, softened

generous ¹/₂ cup superfine sugar

9 ounces semisweet chocolate,
broken into pieces

1 egg yolk

scant 1 cup milk

5 tablespoons rum

14 ounces small amaretti

For the frosting

2¹/₂ ounces semisweet chocolate,
broken into pieces

¹/₂ cup confectioner's sugar

2 tablespoons sweet butter

CHARLOTTE AI FRUTTI DI BOSCO

Serves 6

4 gelatin leaves

2¼ cups milk

a few drops of vanilla extract

6 egg yolks

¾ cup superfine sugar

24 sponge cake slices

scant ½ cup heavy cream

generous 1 cup raspberries

1¾ cups mixed red currants and
black currants, stripped

scant 1 cup blueberries

scant 1 cup strawberries

FRUITS OF THE FOREST CHARLOTTE

Fill a small bowl with water, add the gelatin and let soak. Pour the milk into a pan, add the vanilla and bring to simmering point, then remove from the heat. Beat the egg yolks with the sugar in a pan until pale and fluffy, then gradually stir in the hot milk. Drain the gelatin, squeeze out and add to the custard, then cook over low heat, stirring constantly, until thick enough to coat the back of the spoon. Remove from the heat and let cool. Preheat the broiler and lightly toast the slices of sponge cake, then line the base and sides of a charlotte mold with them, reserving enough to cover the top. Stiffly whip the cream and stir it into the cooled custard with the fruit. Pour the mixture into the mold and cover with the remaining slices of sponge cake. Cover the mold with foil and chill in the refrigerator for 24 hours.

*CHARLOTTE ALLE PRUGNE
E ALLE PERE*

Serves 6

1 pound 2 ounces pears, peeled,
cored and chopped

juice of ½ lemon, strained

¾ cup superfine sugar

7 ounces plums, pitted

4 cups red wine

3 tablespoons red currant jelly

1¼ cups heavy cream

sweet butter, for greasing

24 ladyfingers

PLUM AND PEAR CHARLOTTE

Place the pears and lemon juice in a food processor and process to purée, then scrape into a pan and stir in the sugar. Put the plums and wine into another pan, bring to a boil, then lower the heat and simmer for 15 minutes, then drain. Set aside a few plums for decoration and place the remainder in a food processor and process to purée. Add the plum purée to the pear purée and heat gently but do not let boil. Add the red currant jelly and stir until it has melted completely, then remove from the heat and let cool. Stiffly whip the cream and fold it into the fruit mixture. Grease a charlotte mold with butter and line the base and sides with ladyfingers. Reserve enough ladyfingers to cover the top of the mold and crumble the remainder. Make a layer of the fruit mixture in the mold and cover with a layer of crumbled ladyfingers. Continuing making layers, ending with the reserved whole ladyfingers. Chill in the refrigerator for 3 hours, then turn out and decorate with the reserved plums.

BLACK CURRANT CHARLOTTE

CHARLOTTE AL RIBES

Serves 6–8

1 quantity Custard (see page 1039)

2 gelatin leaves

2 tablespoons brandy

1³/₄ cups black currants

2¹/₂ tablespoons Chestnut Preserve (see page 1116)

4 egg whites

²/₃ cup heavy cream

ladyfingers

Let the custard cool slightly. Fill a small bowl with water, add the gelatin and let soak for 3 minutes, then drain and squeeze out. Stir the gelatin into the custard and let cool completely. Stir the brandy, black currants and chestnut jam into the custard. Stiffly whisk the egg whites in a grease-free bowl and fold into the custard. Line a mold with baking parchment, pour the mixture into it and chill in the refrigerator for 6 hours. Stiffly whip the cream. Turn out the charlotte onto a serving dish, spread the whipped cream over it and arrange upright ladyfingers all around it, leaving the top uncovered.

CHARLOTTE DELIGHT

CHARLOTTE DELIZIA

Serves 6

¹/₄ cup sweet butter

4 ounces semisweet chocolate, broken into pieces

5 eggs

scant ¹/₂ cup ricotta cheese

¹/₂ cup superfine sugar

3 tablespoons heavy cream

1 teaspoon instant coffee powder

5 ounces langues-de-chat

whipped cream, to serve

Put half the butter, the chocolate and 3 tablespoons water into a pan and cook over low heat, stirring constantly, until melted and combined, then remove the pan from the heat. Separate two of the eggs, stir the yolks into the chocolate mixture and let cool. Stiffly whisk the two egg whites in a grease-free bowl and fold into the cooled chocolate mixture, then chill in the refrigerator. Separate the remaining eggs and stir the yolks into the ricotta, one at a time. Stir in the sugar, cream and coffee powder. Stiffly whisk the egg whites in a grease-free bowl and fold into the ricotta mixture, then let stand in a cool place until ready to use. Grease a shallow round mold with the remaining butter, place a layer of langues-de-chat on the base and top with the chocolate mixture. Make another layer of langues-de-chat and top with the coffee mixture. Cover with a final layer of langues-de-chat. Cover the mold with foil and chill in the refrigerator for 24 hours. To serve, dip the base of the mold in warm water for a few seconds, then turn out. Serve with whipped cream.

BLACK GRAPE CHARLOTTE

Heat the wine in a pan, add the grapes and parboil for a few minutes, then drain, reserving the wine. Peel, halve and seed the grapes, then put them in a bowl. Return the wine to the pan, add ²/₃ cup of the sugar and heat gently, stirring constantly, until the sugar has dissolved, then remove from the heat and let cool slightly. Add half the grapes to the wine mixture and let steep for about 2 hours. Drain the grapes, reserving the wine mixture, and pat dry with paper towels. Stiffly whip the cream, fold in the remaining sugar and chill in the refrigerator until required. Dip the ladyfingers, one at a time, into the reserved wine and use some to line the base and sides of a charlotte mold. Spread a layer of whipped cream on the base and arrange a layer of wine-infused grapes on top. Continue making alternating layers until all the ingredients have been used, ending with a layer of ladyfingers. Chill in the refrigerator for 2 hours, then turn out onto a serving dish and decorate with the remaining grapes.

CHARLOTTE DI UVA NERA

Serves 6

1¹/₂ cups red wine

6 cups black grapes

³/₄ cup superfine sugar

³/₄ cup heavy cream

24 ladyfingers

CUSTARDS AND CREAMS

Custards and creams are an enormous family, a mainstay in dessert preparation, and have a truly wide and versatile range of uses. They are used to fill cakes, tartlets, puff pastry spirals and choux puffs, to enrich traditional cakes such as pandoro and panettone – Christmas cakes from Verona and Milan respectively – and to decorate charlottes, and can be served alone as mouthwatering desserts in their own right. Following a few basic rules and being a little patient when cooking will result in a delicious homemade cream that can even be prepared a few days in advance.

CREMA AI MARRONI

Serves 6

2¼ pounds chestnuts, shelled

1 cup superfine sugar

¼ cup vanilla sugar (see page 1003)

scant 1 cup heavy cream

salt

CHESTNUT CREAM

Blanch the chestnuts in boiling water for 5 minutes, then drain and peel. Bring a pan of lightly salted water to a boil, add the chestnuts and simmer for 30 minutes. Meanwhile, put the superfine sugar, vanilla sugar and 1 cup water into a pan and cook over low heat, stirring until the sugar has dissolved, then simmer for about 10 minutes. Drain the chestnuts, remove the syrup from the heat and add the chestnuts. Return the pan to the heat and boil for 10 minutes, then remove the chestnuts with a slotted spoon and pass through a food mill into a bowl. Stir the syrup into the chestnuts and let cool. Stiffly whip the cream and fold it into the cooled chestnut mixture, then divide among individual dishes and keep cool until ready to serve.

BLUEBERRY CREAM

CREMA AI MIRTILLI

Serves 4

1 tablespoon superfine sugar

1³/₄ cups blueberries

1 quantity Custard (see page 1039), cooled

Put the sugar and 2 tablespoons water in a pan and cook over low heat, stirring constantly, until the sugar has dissolved. Add the blueberries, reserving a few, increase the heat to medium and cook for 15 minutes, then remove from the heat and let cool, then drain. Divide the custard among individual dishes and decorate with the reserved fruit.

APRICOT CREAM

CREMA DI ALBICOCCHE

Serves 6

1 pound 5 ounces apricots, peeled, pitted and chopped

scant 1 cup superfine sugar

2 gelatin leaves

1¹/₄ cups light cream

1–2 ice cubes, crushed

1 egg white

Put the apricots and ²/₃ cup of the sugar in a pan and cook over low heat until tender. Meanwhile, fill a small bowl with water, add the gelatin and let soak. Transfer the apricots to a food processor and process to a purée, then scrape into a bowl. Drain and squeeze out the gelatin, stir it into the purée and chill in the refrigerator. Combine the cream and ice cubes and beat well. Stiffly whisk the egg white with the remaining sugar in a heatproof bowl over a pan of barely simmering water until firm and foamy. Remove from the heat and let cool. Combine the three mixtures and divide among individual dishes.

BANANA CREAM

CREMA DI BANANE

Serves 4

2 bananas

1³/₄ cups farmer's cheese

¹/₄ cup non-fat dry milk

2 tablespoons honey

generous pinch of ground cinnamon

Peel and slice the bananas, then place in a bowl with the cheese, dry milk, honey and cinnamon. Mash together thoroughly until evenly combined. Pour into a dish and chill in the refrigerator for at least 1 hour before serving.

MASCARPONE CREAM

CREMA DI MASCARPONE

Serves 6

3 eggs, separated

3 tablespoons superfine sugar

1¹/₃ cups mascarpone cheese

3 tablespoons rum

cookies, to serve

Beat the egg yolks with the sugar in a bowl until pale and fluffy. Stiffly whisk the egg whites in a grease-free bowl and fold into the egg yolk mixture, then fold in the mascarpone, a little at a time. Gently mix in the rum, pour into individual dishes and chill in the refrigerator until required. Serve with cookies.

CUSTARD

Pour the milk into a pan, stir in the vanilla sugar and bring just to a boil, then remove from the heat. Beat the egg yolks with the superfine sugar in another pan until pale and fluffy, then gradually pour in the hot milk. Cook over very low heat, stirring constantly, until the mixture is thick enough to coat the back of the spoon. Do not let it boil. Remove from the heat and let cool slightly. Custard may be served cold with light cookies as a simple dessert, or it may be used hot or cold as a sauce or filling for cakes or other desserts.

CREMA INGLESE

Serves 6

2¹/₄ cups milk

1 tablespoon vanilla sugar (see page 1003)

4 egg yolks

²/₃ cup superfine sugar

CONFECTIONER'S CUSTARD

Beat the egg yolks with the sugar in a pan until pale and fluffy. Gradually stir in the flour until evenly mixed. Bring the milk just to boiling point in another pan and add the vanilla or lemon rind, then remove from the heat. Gradually add the hot milk to the egg yolk mixture then cook over low heat, stirring constantly, for 3−4 minutes until thickened. Pour the custard into a bowl and let cool, stirring occasionally to prevent a skin from forming. This custard is used for filling a wide variety of pastries and cakes. The flour makes it thicker but a little less delicate than plain custard.

CREMA PASTICCERA

Serves 4

4 egg yolks

¹/₂ cup superfine sugar

¹/₄ cup all-purpose flour

2¹/₄ cups milk

a few drops of vanilla extract

or 1 teaspoon grated lemon rind

OLD−FASHIONED CREME BRÛLÉE

Pour the milk and cream into a small pan and bring to a boil. Beat the egg yolks with the sugar in another pan until pale and fluffy and pour in the hot milk mixture. Cook over low heat, stirring constantly, until thick enough to coat the back of the spoon. Pour the custard into a large flameproof dish and chill in the refrigerator for 5−6 hours. Preheat the broiler to high. Sprinkle the surface of the custard with sugar. Place the dish on a cookie sheet and surround with ice cubes, then cook under the broiler for a few minutes to caramelize the sugar. Return to the refrigerator until ready to serve.

CRÈME BRÛLÉE D'ALTRI TEMPI

Serves 6

2¹/₄ cups milk

scant ¹/₂ cup heavy cream

4 egg yolks

scant ¹/₂ cup superfine sugar

sugar, for sprinkling

ZABAGLIONE

Beat the egg yolks with the sugar in a heatproof bowl until pale and fluffy, then stir in the Marsala or wine, a little at a time. Place the bowl over a pan of barely simmering water and cook over low heat, stirring constantly, until the mixture starts to rise. Remove from the heat and serve hot or cold in glasses. Alternatively, zabaglione may be used as a sauce on coffee or hazelnut ice cream.

ZABAIONE

Serves 4

4 egg yolks

4 tablespoons superfine sugar

¹/₂ cup Marsala, dry white wine

or sparkling wine

SOUFFLÉS

Soufflés are classic dishes and both savory and sweet soufflés are seen as a test of culinary skill. However, following a few basic rules will help to insure success. The milk, flour and eggs – the basic ingredients – should be extremely fresh. The whisked egg whites should be folded into the mixture at the last minute and the spatula or spoon used should be turned very gently from the bottom to the top of the mixture to avoid knocking out the air. Other essential instructions are to never open the oven during cooking, as the soufflé will go flat, and to calculate the timing carefully so that the desert may be brought immediately to the table and served as soon as it is ready. The spongy airy structure of these desserts gives them a soft delicate taste.

CHOCOLATE SOUFFLÉ

SOUFFLÉ AL CIOCCOLATO

Serves 6

1 tablespoon sweet butter, plus extra for greasing

vanilla sugar (see page 1003), for dusting

3 ounces semisweet chocolate, broken into pieces

1¼ cups milk

scant ⅓ cup all-purpose flour

¼ cup superfine sugar

3 egg yolks

1 egg white

Preheat the oven to 400°F. Grease a soufflé dish with butter and dust with vanilla sugar. Put the chocolate and ¾ cups of the milk in a heatproof bowl set over a pan of barely simmering water and stir constantly until the chocolate has melted and the mixture is smooth. Put the flour in another pan, pour in the remaining milk and mix well. Stir in the sugar and chocolate mixture, bring to a boil and cook, stirring constantly, for 2–3 minutes. Remove from the heat and let cool slightly, then stir in the butter, then the egg yolks one at a time. Stiffly whisk the egg white in a grease-free bowl and gently fold it into the mixture. Spoon the mixture into the prepared dish so that it is two-thirds full and bake for about 30 minutes until risen and set. Serve immediately.

VANILLA SOUFFLÉ (BASIC RECIPE)

SOUFFLÉ ALLA VANIGLIA

Serves 6

1 tablespoon sweet butter,
plus extra for greasing

¼ cup superfine sugar, plus extra for sprinkling

scant 1 cup milk

1 vanilla bean, slit

scant ⅓ cup all-purpose flour

3 eggs, separated

1 egg white

salt

Vanilla soufflé is a basic recipe which can be adapted for other flavors. Preheat the oven to 400°F. Grease a soufflé dish with butter and sprinkle with sugar. Pour ½ cup of the milk into a small pan, add the sugar and a pinch of salt and bring to a boil. Remove the pan from the heat, add the vanilla bean and let steep for 15 minutes, then remove the vanilla bean. Put the flour in a small pan, stir in the remaining cold milk and gradually add the hot milk. Bring to a boil and cook, stirring constantly, for 2–3 minutes. Remove from the heat and let cool slightly. Stir in the egg yolks, one at a time, then stir in the butter. Stiffly whisk all the egg whites in a grease-free bowl, then gently fold into the mixture. Spoon the mixture into the prepared dish so that it is two-thirds full and bake for 30 minutes. Serve immediately.

RHUBARB SOUFFLÉ

SOUFFLÉ AL RABARBARO

Serves 6

7 ounces rhubarb, cut into thin batons

scant 1 cup confectioner's sugar

sweet butter, for greasing

3 tablespoons superfine sugar,
plus extra for sprinkling

4 egg whites

Custard (see page 1039), to serve

Place the rhubarb in a dish, sprinkle the confectioner's sugar over it and let soften for 2 hours. Preheat the oven to 325°F. Grease an ovenproof dish or mold with butter and sprinkle with superfine sugar. Stiffly whisk the egg whites in a grease-free bowl. Put the superfine sugar and 2 tablespoons water in a small pan and bring to a boil, then add the rhubarb and cook for 2 minutes. Pour the rhubarb mixture onto the egg whites and whisk with an electric mixer for 1 minute. Spoon the mixture into the prepared dish or mold and bake for 25 minutes. Serve with immediately with custard.

RUM SOUFFLÉ

SOUFFLÉ AL RUM

Serves 4

sweet butter, for greasing

¼ cup all-purpose flour

generous ½ cup superfine sugar

scant 1 cup milk

3 eggs, separated

¼ cup rum

1 egg white

Preheat the oven to 350°F. Grease a cake pan with butter. Combine the flour, sugar and milk in a pan and bring to just below boiling point, stirring constantly. Remove the pan from the heat as soon as the mixture thickens. Stir in the egg yolks, one at a time, then add the rum and let cool. Stiffly whisk the egg whites in a grease-free bowl and fold into the mixture. Spoon the mixture into the prepared cake pan and bake for 35–40 minutes. Serve immediately.

TORRONE SOUFFLÉ

Preheat the oven to 400°F. Grease a soufflé dish with butter and sprinkle with sugar. Bring 1 cup of the milk to a boil in a small pan, then remove from the heat and add the sugar, a pinch of salt and the vanilla bean. Cover and let steep for 15 minutes, then remove the vanilla bean. Combine the flour and remaining cold milk in a small pan, and bring to a boil over medium heat, stirring constantly. Stir in the vanilla milk, then as soon as the mixture thickens, remove from the heat and let cool slightly. Stir in the egg yolks, one at a time, then stir in the butter and torrone. Stiffly whisk the egg whites in a grease-free bowl and fold into the mixture. Spoon the mixture into the prepared dish and bake for 30 minutes. Serve immediately.

SOUFFLÉ AL TORRONE

Serves 6

2 tablespoons sweet butter, plus extra for greasing

¼ cup superfine sugar, plus extra for sprinkling

1¼ cups milk

1 vanilla bean, slit

scant ⅓ cup all-purpose flour

4 egg yolks

1½ ounces torrone (Italian nougat), finely chopped

5 egg whites

salt

ZABAGLIONE SOUFFLÉ

Preheat the oven to 400°F. Sprinkle the ladyfingers with the Marsala and use to line a soufflé dish. Cook the peaches in a pan with 1 tablespoon water for a few minutes, then drain and sprinkle them into the soufflé dish. Bring ½ cup of the milk to the boil with the sugar and a pinch of salt. Combine the flour and remaining milk, pour the mixture into the boiling milk and cook, stirring constantly, for 2–3 minutes. Remove from the heat and let cool, then stir into the zabaglione. Stiffly whisk the egg whites in a grease-free bowl, fold gently into the zabaglione mixture and pour the mixture over the peaches. Bake for 30 minutes. Serve immediately.

SOUFFLÉ CON ZABAIONE

Serves 6

3½ ounces ladyfingers

4 tablespoons Marsala

9 ounces peaches, peeled, pitted and diced

¾ cup milk

¼ cup superfine sugar

scant ⅓ cup all-purpose flour

1 quantity Zabaglione (see page 1039)

4 egg whites

salt

BAKING

Cakes, pastries, and other confectionery provide an opportunity to cook creatively. At first, the different doughs were shaped by hand, then molds were created that have ended up characterizing many desserts over time. Just think of the dozens of cookie shapes, from the shell-shaped madeleines, made famous by Marcel Proust, to the finger-shaped langues-de-chat (literally cats' tongues) not to mention the animals, stars, hearts, diamonds, houses and little figures so often seen in petits fours and cookies. Consider the numerous lovely cake pans, from babà, charlotte, plum cake and ciambella pans to other fluted or tower-shaped ones, with protrusions and indentations that produce amazing sculptures that are often small masterpieces of design in themselves. Then there is cake decoration – the search for the right combination of colors that turns a plate of assorted sweet pastries into a mosaic of jewels. Petits fours fall into this section, together with family cakes and other cakes from the simplest to the most elaborate. As a general rule, cakes should be brought to the table whole and guests should serve themselves by cutting their own portions with a serving knife. Remember also that soft cakes should be eaten with a special dough fork, whereas a knife may be required for firmer cakes and tarts. Cookies that accompany ice cream, for example, should be served directly from the tray or dish. The same goes for sweet pastries, which should be transferred from the tray or dish to the plate without removing the fluted paper cases.

FAMILY CAKES

This section includes some of the most popular, classic Italian recipes from ciambella – ring cake – to plum-cake – actually a dried fruit cake – as well as some treats from other corners of the world such as American-style muffins and British-style biscuits.

A LOVELY CUP OF TEA

CARROT RING CAKE

Preheat the oven to 350°F. Grease a ring mold with butter. Sift together the flour, sugar, baking powder, ginger, nutmeg and a pinch of salt into a bowl. Add the milk, oil, butter and eggs and mix well. Stir in the raisins and walnuts, followed by the carrots. Pour the mixture into the prepared mold and bake for about 1 hour. Remove from the oven and leave to cool in the mold, then turn out, sprinkle with plenty of confectioner's sugar and serve.

CIAMBELLA ALLE CAROTE

Serves 4–6

2 tablespoons sweet butter, melted,

plus extra for greasing

1 1/4 cups all-purpose flour

2/3 cup soft brown sugar

2 teaspoons baking powder

pinch of ground ginger

pinch of freshly grated nutmeg

2 tablespoons milk

5 tablespoons olive or sunflower oil

2 eggs, lightly beaten

generous 1/3 cup raisins

3 tablespoons shelled walnuts, chopped

2 carrots, finely chopped

confectioner's sugar, for sprinkling

salt

EASY RING CAKE

CIAMBELLA FACILE

Serves 4

scant ¹/₂ cup sweet butter, softened,
plus extra for greasing

all-purpose flour, for dusting

1 cup superfine sugar

3 eggs, separated

2¹/₄ cups potato flour

2 teaspoons baking powder

2 tablespoons vanilla sugar (see page 1003)

3 tablespoons milk

salt

Preheat the oven to 350°F. Grease a ring mold with butter and lightly dust with flour. Cream the butter with the superfine sugar until pale and fluffy, then beat in a pinch of salt and the egg yolks. Sift together the potato flour, baking powder and vanilla sugar into the butter mixture, mix gently and stir in the milk. Stiffly whisk the egg whites in a grease-free bowl and fold into the mixture. Half-fill the prepared mold with the mixture and bake for about 40 minutes. Let cool in the mold before turning out.

MARBLED RING CAKE

CIAMBELLA MARMORIZZATA

Serves 6–8

6 tablespoons sweet butter, melted,
plus extra for greasing

3¹/₂ cups all-purpose flour, plus extra for dusting

2 teaspoons baking powder

scant ¹/₂ cup superfine sugar

2 eggs

³/₄ cup milk

¹/₄ cup unsweetened cocoa powder

confectioner's sugar, for sprinkling

salt

Preheat the oven to 350°F. Grease a ring mold with butter and lightly dust with flour. Sift together the flour, baking powder, sugar and a pinch of salt into a bowl, add the eggs, melted butter and milk and mix until smooth and even. Pour one-third of the mixture into another bowl and stir in the cocoa powder. Pour the plain mixture into the prepared mold, then pour the cocoa mixture on top and bake for 35–40 minutes. Remove from the oven and let stand for 15 minutes, then turn out. Sprinkle with confectioner's sugar and serve.

VELVETY RING CAKE

CIAMBELLA VELLUTATA

Serves 4

5 tablespoons lukewarm milk

¹/₄ cup superfine sugar

1 teaspoon dried yeast

1³/₄ cups all-purpose flour

scant ¹/₂ cup sweet butter,
softened and cut into pieces,
plus extra for greasing

2 eggs

2 tablespoons rum

salt

Pour the milk into a bowl and stir in the sugar until it has dissolved. Sprinkle the yeast over the surface and let stand for 10–15 minutes until frothy, then stir into a paste. Sift the flour and a pinch of salt into a mound in a bowl, make a well in the center and add the yeast mixture. Mix well with a wooden spoon, then knead in the butter. Add the eggs, one at a time, and the rum, kneading after each addition. Cover with a dish towel and let rise for 8 hours. Preheat the oven to 350°F. Grease a ring mold with butter. Spoon the dough evenly into the ring mold and bake for 40 minutes. Remove from the oven and let stand for 15 minutes, then turn out.

KUGELHUPF

Serves 6

¾ cup muscatel raisins

¾ cup milk

1 ounce fresh yeast

2¾ cups all-purpose flour, plus extra for dusting

6 tablespoons sweet butter, plus extra for greasing

4 eggs

scant ½ cup superfine sugar, plus extra for sprinkling

grated rind of 1 lemon

5 tablespoons heavy cream

KUGELHOPF

Put the raisins in a bowl, add warm water to cover and let soak for 15 minutes, then drain and squeeze out. Heat 3 tablespoons of the milk until lukewarm, pour into a bowl and add the yeast. Mash with a fork to a smooth paste, then add 3 tablespoons of the flour and let rise. Preheat the oven to 350°F. Grease a kugelhopf mold with butter and lightly dust with flour. Cream the butter in a bowl, then beat in the eggs, sugar and lemon rind. When the yeast mixture has doubled in volume, add it to the butter mixture with the remaining flour, the raisins and cream and mix well. Gently heat the remaining milk and add just enough to make a soft dough. Place the dough in the mold and let rise until it reaches about 2 inches below the rim of the mold. Bake for 1¼ hours. Serve cold, sprinkled with sugar.

MUFFINS

Serves 6

¼ cup sweet butter, softened, plus extra for greasing

¼ cup superfine sugar

1 egg

5 tablespoons milk

1¾ cups all-purpose flour

2 teaspoons baking powder

salt

butter and preserves, to serve

MUFFINS

Preheat the oven to 350°F. Grease a six-cup muffin pan with butter or line the pans with paper cases. Cream the butter with the sugar in a bowl until pale and fluffy, then beat in the egg and milk. Sift together the flour, baking powder and a pinch of salt into the mixture and mix gently. Turn out and knead for about 15 minutes. Divide the dough among the prepared cups in the muffin pan, but do not fill them completely. Bake for 15 minutes until golden brown. Remove the muffins from the oven and serve hot with butter and preserves.

FRUIT CAKE

Preheat the oven to 350°F. Grease a rectangular cake pan with butter. Cream the butter in a bowl, then gradually beat in the sugar, a little at a time, until pale and fluffy. Beat in the eggs and egg yolks, one at a time, followed by the flour and a pinch of salt. Add the rum, raisins, currants, golden raisins and chopped peel. Pour the mixture into the prepared cake pan and bake for 30 minutes or until cooked through. Remove from the oven and let cool, then turn out.

PLUM–CAKE

Serves 8

generous 1 cup sweet butter, softened,
plus extra for greasing

1¼ cups superfine sugar

3 eggs

2 egg yolks

2¼ cups all-purpose flour

2 tablespoons rum

¾ cup muscatel raisins

¼ cup currants

generous ⅓ cup golden raisins

generous ½ cup candied peel, chopped

salt

ENGLISH BISCUITS

Cream the butter in a bowl and beat in the sugar and eggs. Sift together the flour, baking powder and a pinch of salt and stir into the mixture. Add just enough milk to make a soft dough, then shape into a ball, cover and let stand for 1 hour. Preheat the oven to 350°F. Grease a cookie sheet with butter. Roll out the dough to a ¾-inch thick sheet on a lightly floured counter. Stamp out rounds with a cookie cutter or the rim of an upturned glass and cut a cross in the surface of each. Place on the prepared cookie sheet and bake for 15 minutes until well risen. Remove and serve immediately while still very hot. Traditionally, English biscuits are served halved and spread with butter and preserves.

SCONES

Serves 4

¼ cup sweet butter, softened,
plus extra for greasing

2 tablespoons superfine sugar

2 eggs, lightly beaten

1¾ cups all-purpose flour, plus extra for dusting

2 teaspoons baking powder

2–3 tablespoons milk

salt

4 AFTERNOON

PETITS FOURS AND COOKIES

Making petits fours, cookies, pralines and meringues at home requires a little practice, but their flavor and aroma certainly reward the work involved.

BISCOTTI ALLA CANNELLA

Serves 6

2¼ cups all-purpose flour, plus extra for dusting

5 tablespoons olive oil

²/₃ cup superfine sugar

rind of 1 lemon, grated

sweet butter, for greasing

ground cinnamon, for dusting

CINNAMON COOKIES

Sift the flour into a mound, make a well in the center, pour in the oil and add the sugar and lemon rind. Mix until well combined, then let stand for about 20 minutes at room temperature. Preheat the oven to 400°F. Grease a cookie sheet with butter and dust lightly with flour. Shape the mixture into balls, flatten slightly and place on the prepared cookie sheet. Dust with cinnamon and bake for about 20 minutes. Remove the cookie sheet from the oven, let the cookies cool slightly, then transfer to a wire rack to cool completely.

BISCOTTI ALLO YOGURT

Serves 6

sweet butter, for greasing

1½ cups all-purpose flour, plus extra for dusting

4 eggs

1 cup superfine sugar

½ cup whole plain yogurt

YOGURT COOKIES

Preheat the oven to 425°F. Grease a cookie sheet with butter and dust lightly with flour. Beat the eggs with the sugar in a bowl until light and fluffy. Beat in the yogurt, then sift in the flour, stirring constantly until evenly combined and smooth. Spoon small heaps of the mixture onto the prepared cookie sheet and bake for 15 minutes. Remove from the oven and cool on a wire rack.

UGLY-BUT-GOOD COOKIES

Stiffly whisk the egg whites in a grease-free bowl, then gradually fold in the hazelnuts, sugar and vanilla. Pour the mixture into a nonstick pan and cook over low heat, stirring constantly with a wooden spoon, for about 30 minutes. Preheat the oven to 350°F. Grease a cookie sheet with butter and dust lightly with flour. Remove the pan from the heat and place tablespoons of the mixture on the prepared cookie sheet, spaced well apart. Bake for about 40 minutes without opening the oven door. Remove from the oven and let cool on the cookie sheet, then remove with a spatula.

BISCOTTI BRUTTI MA BUONI

Makes 20

6 egg whites

3$\frac{1}{2}$ cups toasted hazelnuts, finely chopped

1$\frac{2}{3}$ cups superfine sugar

a few drops of vanilla extract

sweet butter, for greasing

all-purpose flour, for dusting

ENGLISH COOKIES

Preheat the oven to 350°F. Cream the butter with both types of sugar in a bowl, then beat in the egg and vanilla. Combine the flour, baking powder and a pinch of salt in another bowl, then sift into the creamed mixture, beating constantly with a wooden spoon. If necessary, soften the mixture with a little milk. Stir in the hazelnuts and chocolate. Place about 15 tablespoons of the mixture, spaced well apart, on an ungreased cookie sheet and bake for about 7–8 minutes. Remove the cookie sheet from the oven and let cool slightly, then remove the cookies with a spatula and let cool on a wire rack. Cook the remaining mixture in the same way.

BISCOTTI INGLESI

Makes 30

scant $\frac{1}{2}$ cup sweet butter

$\frac{1}{4}$ cup soft brown sugar

$\frac{1}{4}$ cup superfine sugar

1 egg, lightly beaten

a few drops of vanilla extract

1$\frac{1}{2}$ cups all-purpose flour

2 teaspoons baking powder

2 tablespoons milk (optional)

$\frac{1}{2}$ cup shelled hazelnuts, coarsely chopped

2 ounces semisweet chocolate, coarsely chopped

salt

SABLÉS

Preheat the oven to 400°F. Grease a cookie sheet with butter. Sift the flour into a bowl, add the butter and 4 tablespoons of the sugar and mix until combined. Shape the mixture into three or four rolls, then cut into slices and flatten to about $\frac{1}{2}$ inch thick. Sprinkle with the remaining sugar and place on the prepared cookie sheet. Switch off the oven, put the cookie sheet inside and leave until the oven has cooled completely, by which the time the cookies will be ready.

BISCOTTI SABLÉ

Makes 20

6 tablespoons sweet butter, softened, plus extra for greasing

1 cup all-purpose flour

$\frac{1}{3}$ cup superfine sugar

BONBON DI DATTERI E NOCI

Serves 10–12

2¹/₂ cups superfine sugar

4¹/₂ cups ground almonds

scant ¹/₂ cup maraschino liqueur

a few drops of pink food coloring

a few drops of green food coloring

20 shelled walnuts, halved

20 dates, pitted

DATE AND WALNUT BONBONS

Put the sugar in a pan, add 4 tablespoons water and bring to a simmer over low heat. Simmer for 2 minutes, then remove the pan from the heat and stir in the almonds. Color half the maraschino liqueur with a drop of pink food coloring and half with a drop of green food coloring. Divide the almond mixture in half and knead the pink liqueur into one half and the green into the other until evenly colored. Shape the mixture into small balls. Sandwich each green ball between two walnut halves and press each pink ball into the center of a date. Place in fluted paper petits fours cases and arrange in alternate concentric rings.

CIALDE ARROTOLATE

Serves 6

scant ¹/₂ cup sweet butter, softened, plus extra for greasing

¹/₃ cup superfine sugar

²/₃ cup all-purpose flour, plus extra for dusting

2–3 egg whites

ROLLED WAFERS

Preheat the oven to 400°F. Grease a cookie sheet with butter. Cream the butter in a bowl until soft and fluffy, then beat in the sugar and flour. Stiffly whisk two of the egg whites in another, grease-free bowl and fold in gently. If the mixture seems too stiff, add another whisked egg white. Roll out the mixture on a lightly floured counter into a thin sheet, then stamp out rounds and place on the prepared cookie sheet. Bake for 7–8 minutes until golden brown, then remove from the oven. Lift the cookies off the cookie sheet with a spatula, roll up and let cool on a wire rack.

CROCCANTINI

Serves 6

olive oil, for brushing

²/₃ cup superfine sugar

¹/₄ cup blanched almonds, chopped

1 tablespoon sweet butter

¹/₂ teaspoon lemon juice

fresh bay leaves, to serve

PRALINE

Brush a marble slab or a cookie sheet with oil. Melt the sugar with 1¹/₂ teaspoons water in a heavy pan over medium-low heat. Stir in the almonds, then add the butter and lemon juice. Lower the heat and cook until the mixture is golden brown. Remove the pan from the heat and pour the mixture onto the oiled surface and spread out to ¹/₂ inch thick. Cut into diamond shapes with a knife and let cool and set. Break up the praline into diamonds and place each piece on a bay leaf.

MERINGUES WITH WHIPPED CREAM

MERINGHE ALLA PANNA MONTATA

Makes 24

sweet butter, for greasing

all-purpose flour, for dusting

3 egg whites

1¼ cups confectioner's sugar, plus extra for sprinkling

2¼ cups heavy cream

ground cinamon, grated chocolate, tamarind or black cherry syrup (optional)

Preheat the oven to 225°F. Grease a cookie sheet with a little butter and dust lightly with flour. Stiffly whisk the egg whites in a grease-free bowl, then gradually whisk in the sugar. Spoon the mixture into a pastry bag fitted with a round tip and pipe half-shell shapes onto the prepared cookie sheet. Sprinkle with sugar and place in the oven for 30–35 minutes. Meringues must not cook, but simply dry without browning. Remove from the oven and let cool. Whip the cream until thickened and quite stiff. Hollow out part of the flat side of each meringue with a teaspoon and fill with the cream. Leave the cream plain or sprinkle with ground cinnamon, grated chocolate, tamarind syrup or black cherry syrup. Put the meringues together in pairs and serve.

CARAMEL TARTLETS

TARTELETTE AL CARAMELLO

Makes 10

⅔ cup sweet butter, plus extra for greasing

scant 1 cup confectioner's sugar

1 egg, lightly beaten

2¼ cups all-purpose flour, plus extra for dusting

For the walnut paste

30 shelled walnuts, chopped

¼ cup confectioner's sugar

1 egg yolk

2 egg whites

For the walnut caramel

scant 1 cup heavy cream

1¼ cups superfine sugar

1 tablespoon honey

scant 1 cup shelled walnuts

Prepare the pastry dough the day before serving. Cream the butter and confectioner's sugar together in a bowl, then beat in the egg and stir in the flour. Knead the dough lightly, then shape into a ball, cover and let stand in a cool place until the next day. Preheat the oven to 400°F. Grease 10 cups in one or two muffin pans with butter. Roll out the dough on a lightly floured surface to ¼ inch thick. Stamp out rounds and place in the prepared muffin pans. Make the walnut paste. Combine the walnuts, confectioner's sugar and about 1 tablespoon water in a bowl, then stir in the egg yolk. Stiffly whisk the egg whites in another, grease-free bowl, then fold into the walnut paste, a little at a time. Spread the walnut paste in the dough shells. Bake for 30 minutes. Let cool, then remove from the pans. Meanwhile, prepare the walnut caramel. Pour the cream into a small pan and heat gently. Put the superfine sugar in another pan, add the honey and cook, without stirring, until golden brown. Remove the pan from the heat and stir in the hot cream and the walnuts. Pour the caramel over the tartlets and let cool, but do not chill.

DESSERT CAKES

The wide range of recipes here includes cakes from a number of countries and of various levels of difficulty, from the famous Viennese Sachertorte and babà to simpler strudels and light sponge cakes. The choice of dessert depends on the other dishes on the menu, although it is usually best to choose something light for the end of an evening meal or lunch. More elaborate layer cakes and substantial cakes may be offered at tea time.

CIAMBELLA

COFFEE BABÀ

Cream the yeast with the milk in a bowl, mashing it to a smooth paste with a fork. Sift the flour and a pinch of salt into a mound, make a well in the center and add the yeast and eggs. Mix well, then add the butter and sugar and mix again until thoroughly combined and smooth. Cover with a dish towel and let rise until almost doubled in volume. Grease a ring mold with butter. Shape the dough into a 'sausage' and place in the ring mold to half fill, then let rise until almost doubled in volume. Preheat the oven to 350°F, then bake the baba for about 40 minutes. Remove from the oven and let cool in the mold. Meanwhile, make the syrup. Pour the coffee and rum into a small pan, add the sugar and bring to a boil. Simmer gently until the sugar has dissolved. Turn out the cooled baba onto a serving dish and gradually pour the coffee syrup on top so that it is completely absorbed. Decorate with sweetened whipped cream.

BABÀ AL CAFFÈ

Serves 6

1/4 ounce fresh yeast

3/4 cup lukewarm milk

1 3/4 cups all-purpose flour

3 eggs

scant 1/2 cup sweet butter,

cut into pieces, plus extra for greasing

2 tablespoons superfine sugar

salt

sweetened whipped cream, to decorate

For the syrup

3/4 cup freshly brewed coffee

5 tablespoons rum

1/4 cup superfine sugar

CHESTNUT CAKE

CASTAGNACCIO

Serves 8

3 tablespoons sunflower or olive oil, plus extra for brushing and drizzling

3¹/₂ cups chestnut flour

1 cup milk

¹/₄ cup superfine sugar

3 tablespoons pine nuts

needles from 1 fresh rosemary sprig

salt

Preheat the oven to 350°F. Brush a ³/₄-inch deep layer pan with oil. Sift the flour into a bowl and gradually whisk in the milk and 1¹/₂ cups cold water until thoroughly combined but runny. Stir in the sugar, a pinch of salt and the oil, then spoon into the prepared pan. Sprinkle with the pine nuts and rosemary and drizzle with a little oil. Bake for 40 minutes, then let cool before serving.

APRICOT CLAFOUTIS

CLAFOUTIS ALLE ALBICOCCHE

Serves 6

1¹/₂ tablespoons sweet butter, melted, plus extra for greasing

1²/₃ cups superfine sugar

2 tablespoons vanilla sugar (see page 1003)

rind of 1 lemon, grated

1 pound 2 ounces apricots, halved and pitted

3 eggs, separated

¹/₂ cup all-purpose flour

²/₃ cup warm milk

Preheat the oven to 400°F. Grease a cake pan with butter. Pour 1 cup water into a pan, add 1¹/₄ cups of the superfine sugar, the vanilla sugar and the lemon rind and bring to a boil, stirring until the sugar has dissolved. Boil for 5 minutes, then add the apricots and simmer for a few minutes more. Drain and set aside. Beat the egg yolks with the remaining sugar in a bowl until pale and fluffy, then stir in the melted butter, flour and milk. Stiffly whisk the egg whites in a grease-free bowl and fold into the mixture. Pour into the prepared cake pan, arrange the apricot halves on top and then push them down into the mixture. Bake for 40 minutes and serve warm or cold.

CHERRY CLAFOUTIS

CLAFOUTIS ALLE CILIEGE

Serves 6

sweet butter, for greasing

scant 1 cup all-purpose flour

2 eggs, lightly beaten

¹/₂ cup superfine sugar

1 cup milk

scant 2 cup black cherries, pitted

vanilla sugar (see page 1003), for sprinkling

Preheat the oven to 400°F. Grease a cake pan with butter. Sift the flour into a mound in a bowl, make a well in the center, add the eggs, sugar and milk and mix well until smooth. Pour the mixture into the prepared pan so that it is two-thirds full. Sprinkle the cherries on top and bake for 40 minutes. Sprinkle with vanilla sugar before serving.

PEAR CROWN

CORONA ALLE PERE

Serves 6

6 Bartlett pears

juice of 1 lemon, strained

1¼ cups superfine sugar

4 cups red wine

¼ cup sweet butter, melted, plus extra for greasing

3 eggs, separated

3 tablespoons warm milk

1 cup all-purpose flour

pinch of baking powder

Peel and core the pears, leaving them whole, then sprinkle with the lemon juice to prevent discoloration. Place in a pan, sprinkle with ½ cup of the sugar and pour in the red wine. Bring to a boil over low heat and simmer gently for about 10 minutes. Remove the pan from the heat and let the pears cool in their syrup. Preheat the oven to 350°F. Grease a ring mold with butter. Beat the egg yolks with the remaining sugar in a bowl until pale and fluffy. Stir in the milk, sift in the flour and add the melted butter. Mix gently until combined. Stiffly whisk the egg whites in a grease-free bowl, then gently fold into the mixture. Finally, add the baking powder. Pour the mixture into the prepared ring mold and bake for about 30 minutes. Remove from the oven and let cool completely. Meanwhile, remove the pears from the syrup with a slotted spoon. Turn out the cake onto a serving dish. Reheat the pear syrup, then sprinkle it onto the cake, a little at a time, so that it is completely absorbed. Place the pears in the middle of the crown and serve warm or cold.

RHUBARB TART

CROSTATA AL RABARBARO

Serves 6

sweet butter, for greasing

all-purpose flour, for dusting

11 ounces pie crust dough (see page 1008)

2 eggs

1 cup superfine sugar

14 ounces rhubarb, chopped

vanilla confectioner's sugar (see page 1003), to decorate (optional)

Preheat the oven to 350°F. Grease a medium-sized rectangular pie dish with butter, dust with flour and shake out any excess. Roll out the dough into a very thin sheet on a lightly floured counter, place in the prepared dish and prick the base with a fork. Let rest for 10 minutes. Meanwhile, whisk the eggs with the sugar in a bowl until pale and fluffy, then gently stir in the rhubarb. Spoon the mixture evenly over the base of the pie and bake for 45–50 minutes. Remove from the oven, let cool and transfer to a serving dish. Sprinkle with vanilla confectioner's sugar if you like.

FIG TART

Cut the figs into fourths, without peeling, and place in a bowl. Sprinkle with the sugar and half the rum and set aside for about 1 hour. Preheat the oven to 350°F. Grease a tart pan with butter. Roll out two-thirds of the dough into a round on a lightly floured counter and place in the prepared tart pan. Prick the base with a fork, cover with foil and fill with baking beans. Bake for about 20 minutes, then remove from the oven but do not switch it off. Remove the foil and beans and let cool. Drain the figs and arrange them on the base of the tart shell. Combine the jam and remaining rum in a small pan and heat gently, stirring frequently, until smooth. Gently pour the mixture over the figs. Shape the remaining dough into very thin rolls and arrange in a lattice over the tart and as piping around the edge, pressing gently to seal. Bake for about 10 minutes, then remove from the oven and let cool.

CROSTATA DI FICHI

Serves 6

14 ounces ripe green figs

$^1/_4$ cup superfine sugar

1$^1/_2$ cups rum

sweet butter, for greasing

11 ounces Pie Crust Dough (see page 1008)

all-purpose flour, for dusting

3 tablespoons plum jam

BLACKBERRY TART

Preheat the oven to 350°F. Grease a tart pan with butter. Roll out the dough to a round on a lightly floured counter, place in the prepared pan and prick the base with a fork. Make sure the confectioner's custard has cooled well, then pour it into the tart shell and bake for 35–40 minutes. Meanwhile, set aside about 3–4 cups of the blackberries to use for decoration later and place the remainder in a food processor. Process them to a purée, scrape the blackberry purée into a bowl and stir in the raspberry jam, diluting the mixture with a little water, if necessary (the mixture should be thick). Remove the tart from the oven and let cool. Spread the purée evenly over the tart, then cover it with the reserved blackberries.

CROSTATA DI MORE

Serves 6

sweet butter, for greasing

11 ounces Pie Crust Dough (see page 1008)

all-purpose flour, for dusting

1 quantity Confectioner's Custard (see page 1039)

9 cups blackberries

$^3/_4$ cup raspberry jam

TUTTI FRUTTI TART

CROSTATA TUTTI FRUTTI

Serves 6

2 tablespoons sweet butter, plus extra for greasing

11 ounces Pâte Brisée (see page 1007)

all-purpose flour, for dusting

1 vanilla bean, slit

2¼ cups milk

4 egg yolks

½ cup superfine sugar

2 tablespoons all-purpose flour, sifted

2¼ cups black currants

scant 1 cup blueberries

1½ cups raspberries

8 apricots, peeled, pitted and sliced

1 kiwi fruit, peeled and sliced

Preheat the oven to 400°F. Grease a tart pan with butter. Roll out the dough into a round on a lightly floured counter and place in the prepared pan. Prick the base with a fork, cover with baking parchment and fill with baking beans, then bake for about 30 minutes. Remove from the oven, discard the parchment and beans and let cool. Meanwhile, place the vanilla bean in a pan with the milk and heat to simmering point. Beat the egg yolks with the sugar in another pan until pale and fluffy and add the flour. Remove the vanilla bean and gradually stir the flavored milk into the egg yolk mixture, then heat gently, stirring constantly, until thickened. Remove the pan from the heat, stir in the butter and let cool. Pour the cooled custard into the tart shell. Arrange all the fruit in a decorative pattern on top of the tart. Keep in a cool place until ready to serve.

WALNUT AND COFFEE CAKE

DOLCE ALLE NOCI E AL CAFFÈ

Serves 8–10

¼ cup sweet butter, softened, plus extra for greasing

5 eggs, separated

scant 2 cups superfine sugar

2¾ cups shelled walnuts, finely chopped

scant 1 cup all-purpose flour, sifted

½ cup freshly brewed espresso or strong black coffee

1 tablespoon rum

1 cup confectioner's sugar

walnut halves and coffee beans, to decorate

Preheat the oven to 400°F. Grease two shallow square cake pans with butter. Beat four of the egg yolks with 1¼ cups of the superfine sugar in a bowl until pale and fluffy. Stir in 2¼ cups of the walnuts, then stir in the flour, a little at a time. Stiffly whisk the egg whites in a grease-free bowl and gently fold into the mixture. Divide the mixture between the prepared pans and bake for 25 minutes, then remove from the oven and let cool. Cream the butter in a bowl, then beat in the remaining egg yolk and superfine sugar, half the coffee, the rum and the remaining walnuts. Spread this mixture on one cake, then place the other on top, aligning the sides. Sift the confectioner's sugar into a shallow bowl, stir in the remaining coffee and gradually add water until the mixture is spreadable. Pour the frosting over the cake and spread using a warm spatula. Let dry, then decorate with walnut halves and coffee beans.

CHERRY TART

To make the dough, beat together the sugar, egg, one of the egg yolks, the lemon rind and a pinch of salt in a bowl until pale and fluffy. Beat in the butter, a little at a time, then stir in the flour. Tip out onto a counter and knead gently, then shape into a ball and let rest in a cool place for 30 minutes. Lightly beat the remaining egg yolk. To make the filling, put the milk and vanilla bean in a pan and bring just to a boil, then remove from the heat. Beat together the egg yolks with $1/4$ cup of the sugar and stir in the flour. Remove the vanilla bean from the milk and add the milk to the mixture in a thin continuous trickle, stirring constantly. Pour the mixture into a pan and bring to a boil over low heat, stirring constantly. Remove the pan from the heat and place the butter on top, then spread it gently with a knife blade to prevent a skin from forming. Let cool. Put the cherries into a pan, sprinkle with the remaining sugar, add the brandy and bring to a boil over low heat, then simmer for 10 minutes. Meanwhile, preheat the oven to 400°F. Grease a tart pan with butter. Roll out two-thirds of the dough on a lightly floured counter and line the prepared pan. Pour in the cooled custard and spread the cherries evenly on top. Roll out the remaining dough into a round and place over the filling. Crimp the edges well to seal, brush with the beaten egg yolk, score with a fork and pierce with the point of a knife. Bake for 45 minutes, then let cool in the pan before serving.

DOLCE DI CILIEGE

Serves 6–8

$3/4$ cup superfine sugar

1 egg

2 egg yolks

rind of $1/2$ lemon, grated

$2/3$ cup sweet butter, softened
and diced, plus extra for greasing

$1 3/4$ cup all-purpose flour, sifted,
plus extra for dusting

salt

For the filling

1 cup milk

$1/2$ vanilla bean, slit

2 egg yolks

$1/2$ cup superfine sugar

$1/4$ cup all-purpose flour, sifted

$1 1/2$ tablespoons sweet butter

$1 1/2$ cups black cherries, pitted

2 tablespoons brandy

STRAWBERRY DESSERT

Melt the jelly over low heat with 3 tablespoons water until the mixture is syrupy. Sprinkle the sugar and lemon rind over the strawberries in a separate dish and spread them evenly in the tart shell. Spoon the raspberry syrup over them.

DOLCE DI FRAGOLE

Serves 6

scant 1 cup raspberry jelly

$1/4$ cup superfine sugar

rind of 1 lemon, grated

$3 1/2$ cups strawberries

1 Tart Shell (see page 1013), cooled

MASCARPONE DESSERT

DOLCE DI MASCARPONE

Serves 6

1/4 cup sweet butter, softened, plus extra for greasing

2 1/4 cups mascarpone cheese

3 3/4 cups superfine sugar

a few drops of vanilla extract

2 1/4 cups cornstarch

4 eggs

scant 1 cup heavy cream

2 teaspoons lemon juice

Preheat the oven to 300°F. Grease a round mold with butter. Beat together the butter and mascarpone in a bowl until evenly combined, then beat in the sugar, vanilla and cornstarch. Stir in the eggs, one at a time, then add the cream and lemon juice. The resulting mixture should be fairly thick. Pour into the prepared mold and bake for about 30 minutes until golden brown, then increase the oven temperature to 475°F and bake for 10 minutes more. Remove the mold from the oven and let cool, then turn out and store in the refrigerator until ready to serve.

THREE–CHOCOLATE MILLEFEUILLE

MILLEFOGLIE AI TRE CIOCCOLATI

Serves 6

1 pound 5 ounces puff pastry dough, thawed if frozen

all-purpose flour, for dusting

1 egg yolk, lightly beaten

3 1/2 ounces semisweet chocolate, broken into pieces

2/3 cup light cream

3 1/2 ounces milk chocolate, broken into pieces

3 1/2 ounces white chocolate, broken into pieces

Preheat the oven to 350°F. Line a cookie sheet with baking parchment. Roll out the dough on a lightly floured counter and cut out four 10-inch rounds. Place a round on the prepared cookie sheet, brush with the egg yolk and bake for 20 minutes. Transfer to a wire rack to cool and let the cookie sheet cool. Bake the remaining dough rounds in the same way, but without brushing with egg yolk. Meanwhile, melt the semisweet chocolate in a heatproof bowl over a pan of barely simmering water. Stir in 3 tablespoons of the cream, then remove from the heat and whisk until fairly thick. Repeat with the milk chocolate and 3 tablespoons of the cream and, finally, with the white chocolate and remaining cream. Place a plain dough round on a serving dish and spread with the semisweet chocolate cream. Top with a second plain round and spread with the white chocolate cream. Place the remaining plain dough round on top and spread with the milk chocolate cream. Cover with the glazed dough round, let stand for a few minutes, then serve.

MOCHA CAKE

Preheat the oven to 350°F. Grease a cake pan with butter and lightly dust with flour. To make the cake, beat the egg yolks with the superfine sugar and lemon rind in a bowl until the mixture has trebled in volume. Stiffly whisk the egg whites in a grease-free bowl and fold into the mixture. Sift in the flour, stirring gently. Pour the mixture into the prepared pan and bake for 30 minutes. Let stand in the pan for a few minutes, then turn out onto a wire rack to cool. To make the syrup, put the superfine sugar in a small pan, add 4 tablespoons water and bring to a boil, stirring until the sugar has dissolved. Remove the pan from the heat, add the brandy and let cool. To make the coffee cream, cream the butter in a bowl until light and smooth, then beat in the egg yolks, one at a time. Beat in the coffee and confectioner's sugar. Set 1 tablespoon of the cream aside. Slice the cake in half horizontally. Sprinkle the lower half with one-third of the syrup and spread with one-third of the cream. Top with the other half of the cake, spoon the remaining syrup over the top and sides and spread all except the reserved tablespoon of cream over the top and sides. Decorate the sides with the almonds and arrange the candied cherries and curls of the reserved coffee cream alternately on top.

MOKA

Serves 6

For the cake

sweet butter, for greasing

scant 1 cup all-purpose flour,

plus extra for dusting

4 eggs, separated

$^1/_2$ cup superfine sugar

grated rind of 1 lemon

For the syrup

$^1/_4$ cup superfine sugar

$^1/_2$ cup brandy

For the coffee cream

scant 1 cup sweet butter, softened

3 egg yolks

1 cup freshly brewed strong coffee

$1^1/_4$ cups confectioner's sugar

To decorate

$^1/_2$ cup blanched almonds, roasted

$^1/_4$ cup candied cherries

ITALIAN BREAD AND BUTTER PUDDING

Preheat the oven to 300°F. Grease an ovenproof dish with butter. Put the raisins in a bowl, add warm water to cover and let soak. Cut the slices of bread in half, spread them out on a cookie sheet and dry them in the oven. Remove the cookie sheet from the oven and increase the temperature to 350°F. Beat the eggs with the sugar in a bowl and stir in the milk. Drain the raisins and squeeze out. Spread the bread with the butter and place a layer on the base of the prepared dish, then sprinkle with the raisins and the egg mixture. Continue making layers, ending with a layer of moistened bread. Bake the pudding for about 40 minutes. Serve warm or cold in the same dish.

PAN DOLCE

Serves 4

$^3/_4$ cup sweet butter, plus extra for greasing

generous $^3/_4$ cup raisins

20 white bread slices, crusts removed

4 eggs

generous $^1/_2$ cup superfine sugar

4 cups milk

FRUITS OF THE FOREST CRUMBLE

SBRICIOLATA AI FRUTTI DI BOSCO

Serves 6

1³/₄ cups all-purpose flour

1 cup soft brown sugar

¹/₂ cup sweet butter

4¹/₂ cups mixed berries,
such as blackberries, blueberries and raspberries

Sift the flour into a large bowl, stir in half the sugar and add the butter. Cut the butter into the dry ingredients, then rub in with your fingertips. Let stand in a cool place, but not in the refrigerator, for about 30 minutes. Preheat the oven to 350°F. Meanwhile, put all the fruit in a deep ovenproof dish, sprinkle with the remaining sugar and mix well. Spoon the crumble mixture over the fruit to cover and bake for 30 minutes until golden brown. Serve warm.

SPLENDID MARIA—CAKE

SPLENDIDA TORTA MARIA

Serves 6–8

1¹/₄ cups blanched almonds

1 cup superfine sugar

9 ounces semisweet chocolate, broken into pieces

1 egg

4 egg yolks

generous 1 cup sweet butter,
softened and cut into pieces

6 egg whites

a few drops of vanilla extract

1 teaspoon potato flour

confectioner's sugar, for sprinkling

Preheat the oven to 300°F. Line a loose-based 10-inch round cake pan with baking parchment. Lightly toast the almonds in a heavy skillet over low heat until golden, then remove from the heat and let cool. Chop the almonds with 1 tablespoon of the sugar. Melt the chocolate in a heatproof bowl set over a pan of barely simmering water, then remove from the heat, stir gently and let cool. Beat the egg, egg yolks and remaining sugar in a large bowl until pale and fluffy, then stir in the butter, one piece at a time, until thoroughly combined. Stir in the cooled chocolate. Stiffly whisk the egg whites in a grease-free bowl and fold in the almond mixture, vanilla and potato flour, then fold the egg white mixture into the chocolate mixture. Pour into the prepared pan and bake for 1¹/₄ hours. If necessary, lower the oven temperature for the last 15 minutes of the cooking time. Remove the cake from the oven and let cool in the pan. Turn out onto a serving dish and sprinkle with confectioner's sugar.

APRICOT STRUDEL

STRUDEL DI ALBICOCCHE

Serves 4

2¹/₄ cups all-purpose flour, plus extra for dusting

1 egg

¹/₂ cup superfine sugar

scant ¹/₂ cup sweet butter, melted,
plus extra for greasing

2¹/₄ pounds apricots, peeled, pitted and sliced

salt

Sift the flour into a mound, make a well in the center and add the egg, ¹/₄ cup of the sugar, 6 tablespoons of the butter, a pinch of salt and 1–2 tablespoons water. Knead to a smooth, elastic dough, then let rest for 30 minutes. Preheat the oven to 425°F. Grease a cookie sheet with butter. Roll out the dough into a very thin rectangle on a lightly floured counter. Place the apricots along one side, sprinkle with the remaining sugar and roll into a sausage shape. Seal the ends and brush the surface with the remaining melted butter. Place the strudel on the prepared cookie sheet and bake for about 1 hour.

RICOTTA STRUDEL

Place the raisins in a bowl, add warm water to cover and let soak for 15 minutes, then drain and squeeze out. Preheat the oven to 425°F. Grease a cookie sheet with butter. Roll out the dough into a very thin rectangle on a lightly floured counter. Beat the ricotta in a bowl until smooth, then stir in the raisins, sugar, butter, egg, egg yolk and lemon rind. Spoon the mixture onto one half of the dough, roll up and seal the ends. Brush with the melted butter, place on the prepared cookie sheet and bake for about 1 hour.

STRUDEL DI RICOTTA

Serves 4

3 tablespoons raisins

¼ cup sweet butter, plus extra for greasing

9 ounces puff pastry dough, thawed if frozen,

or 1 quantity Speedy Puff Pastry (see page 1014)

all-purpose flour, for dusting

2¼ cups ricotta cheese

½ cup superfine sugar

1 egg

1 egg yolk

rind of 1 lemon, grated

1 tablespoon melted butter

SIMPLE STRUDEL

Place the raisins for the filling in a bowl, add warm water to cover and let soak for 15 minutes, then drain and squeeze out. Meanwhile, sift the flour into a mound, make a well in the center and add 1½ tablespoons of the butter, the egg, 6 tablespoons water and a pinch of salt. Knead to a smooth and elastic dough and let rest for 30 minutes. For the filling, beat the butter with the egg yolks and sugar, then stir in the cream, bread crumbs, raisins, grapes and cinnamon. Whisk the egg whites in a grease-free bowl and fold into the filling mixture. Preheat the oven to 425°F. Grease a cookie sheet with butter. Roll out the dough into a very thin rectangle on a lightly floured counter and spread the filling on top. Roll up, brush the surface with the remaining butter, place on the prepared cookie sheet and bake for about 30 minutes. Brush with milk, return the strudel to the oven and bake for 30 minutes more. Transfer the strudel to a serving dish and sprinkle with plenty of confectioner's sugar.

STRUDEL SEMPLICE

Serves 4

2¼ cups all-purpose flour, plus extra for dusting

scant ¼ cup sweet butter, melted,

plus extra for greasing

1 egg

milk, for brushing

confectioner's sugar, for sprinkling

salt

For the filling

½ cup raisins

5 tablespoons sweet butter, softened

4 eggs, separated

½ cup superfine sugar

1 cup heavy cream

1 cup bread crumbs

1 cup seedless grapes

pinch of ground cinnamon

TARTE TATIN

TARTE TATIN

Serves 6

1¼ cups all-purpose flour, plus extra for dusting

5 tablespoons sweet butter, cut into pieces, plus extra for greasing

scant ½ cup superfine sugar

light cream, to serve

For the filling

5–6 apples

generous ½ cup superfine sugar

Sift the flour into a mound, make a well in the center and add the butter and 5 tablespoons water. Knead to a smooth dough and let rest for 1 hour. Preheat the oven to 475°F. Generously grease a round ovenproof dish with butter and sprinkle with the sugar. To make the filling, peel, core and thickly slice the apples. Place half the apple slices in the prepared dish and sprinkle with half the sugar. Arrange another layer of apple slices on top and sprinkle with the remaining sugar. Roll out the dough into a 1¼-inch thick round on a lightly floured counter, place it over the apples to cover completely and tuck in around the side. Bake for 30 minutes. Meanwhile, preheat the broiler. Turn out the tart onto a flameproof dish and place under the broiler for 10 minutes until the sugar has caramelized. Serve the tart warm with cream.

CHOCOLATE CAKE

TORTA AL CIOCCOLATO

Serves 6

¼ cup sweet butter, plus extra for greasing

3½ ounces semisweet chocolate, broken into pieces

3 eggs

¾ cup superfine sugar

scant 1 cup all-purpose flour, sifted

salt

whipped cream, to serve

Preheat the oven to 325°F. Grease a cake pan with butter. Melt the butter and chocolate in a heatproof bowl set over a pan of barely simmering water, whisking occasionally. Beat the eggs with the sugar in another bowl, then stir in the flour and a pinch of salt. Stir the egg mixture into the chocolate mixture and continue to stir for about 10 minutes. Pour the mixture into the prepared cake pan and bake for 20 minutes. Remove the pan from the oven and let cool, then turn out. Serve the cake with whipped cream.

CHOCOLATE CAKE WITH APRICOT PRESERVE

TORTA AL CIOCCOLATO CON MARMELLATA

Serves 6

Chocolate Cake (see above)

¾ cup apricot preserve

2 tablespoons pineapple syrup

5 tablespoons rum

Cut the chocolate cake in half horizontally. Stir the preserve well. Combine the pineapple syrup and the rum in a bowl and sprinkle generously on both cake halves. Spread one half with preserve and top with the other. Let stand for 1 hour before serving.

CHOCOLATE AND PEAR TART

Make a pâte brisée (see page 1007) with the flour, 7 tablespoons of the butter, 5 tablespoons ice water, a pinch of salt and 1 teaspoon of the sugar and let stand for 1 hour. Meanwhile, peel, core and halve the pears, place in a dish and sprinkle with the remaining sugar and the Grand Marnier. Preheat the oven to 350°F. Roll out the dough on a lightly floured counter into a round $1/4$ inch thick and place in a tart pan. Cover the base with foil, fill with baking beans and bake for 10 minutes. Remove the tart from the oven, remove the foil and beans and place the pear halves in the tart shell. Return the tart to the oven and bake until the crust is golden brown, then remove and let cool. Meanwhile, melt the chocolate with 1 tablespoon water in a small pan over low heat, then stir in the remaining butter. Remove the pan from the heat and let cool. Whip the cream and fold it into the chocolate mixture. Pour the chocolate topping over the tart, sprinkle with the almonds and serve.

TORTA AL CIOCCOLATO E ALLE PERE

Serves 8

$1^3/4$ cups all-purpose flour, plus extra for dusting

$2/3$ cup sweet butter

scant $1/2$ cup superfine sugar

4 pears

4 tablespoons Grand Marnier

$4^1/2$ ounces semisweet chocolate, broken into pieces

scant $1/2$ cup heavy cream

$1/4$ cup blanched almonds, chopped

salt

CAKE WITH ORANGE FROSTING

Preheat the oven to 350°F. Grease a cake pan with butter. Melt the butter in a heatproof bowl set over a pan of barely simmering water. Whisk together the eggs, superfine sugar and half the confectioner's sugar in a large bowl until light and fluffy. Stir in the melted butter. Sift the flour and baking powder into the mixture, mix well and gently stir in half the orange juice. Pour the mixture into the prepared cake pan and bake for 20–25 minutes. Meanwhile, combine the remaining orange juice and the remaining confectioner's sugar in a bowl. Remove the cake from the oven and let cool, then turn out onto a serving dish. Spread the orange frosting evenly over the cake and let set in a cool place.

TORTA ALLA GLASSA D'ARANCIA

Serves 6

scant $1/2$ cup sweet butter, cut into small pieces, plus extra for greasing

2 eggs

$1/2$ cup superfine sugar

$1^3/4$ cups confectioner's sugar

scant 1 cup all-purpose flour

$3/4$ teaspoon baking powder

juice of 2 oranges, strained

LEMON TART

Preheat the oven to 350°F. Grease a tart pan with butter. Beat the eggs with the superfine sugar in a large bowl, stir in the lemon rind and lemon juice, then stir in the butter. Roll out the dough into a round on a lightly floured counter and place in the prepared tart pan. Trim the edges, then pour the lemon mixture into the tart shell. Bake for 30 minutes, then remove from the oven and transfer to a wire rack to cool. Place a few lemon leaves or decorative paper shapes on the surface of the tart, sprinkle with confectioner's sugar, then carefully remove the leaves or shapes.

TORTA AL LIMONE

Serves 6

$^2/_3$ cup sweet butter, softened,
plus extra for greasing
3 eggs
$^3/_4$ cup superfine sugar
rind of 2 lemons, grated
juice of $^1/_2$ lemon, strained
11 ounces Pie Crust Dough (see page 1008)
all-purpose flour, for dusting
confectioner's sugar, sifted, for sprinkling

YOGURT CAKE

Preheat the oven to 350°F. Grease a cake pan with butter. Combine an equal quantity of sugar and flour and dust the cake pan with the resulting mixture, tipping out any excess. Beat the eggs in a bowl, add the flour, cornmeal, yogurt, sugar, oil and a pinch of salt and stir well. Pour the mixture into the prepared cake pan and bake for about 40 minutes. Make sure you do not open the oven door for at least the first 20 minutes. Remove the cake from the oven and let cool, then turn out.

TORTA ALLO YOGURT

Serves 6

sweet butter, for greasing
$^3/_4$ cup superfine sugar, plus extra for dusting
$1^1/_2$ cups self-rising flour, plus extra for dusting
2 eggs
$1^1/_2$ cups cornmeal
$^1/_2$ cup plain yogurt
5 tablespoons sunflower or olive oil
salt

YOGURT AND RICOTTA CAKE

Preheat the oven to 400°F. Grease a cake pan with butter. Separate two of the eggs and beat the third in a small bowl. Pour the yogurt into a pan, sift the cornstarch over it and stir well. Add the sugar and cook over low heat, stirring constantly, until thickened. Stir in the ricotta, then remove from the heat and let cool. Stiffly whisk the egg whites in a grease-free bowl. Stir the egg yolks into the ricotta mixture, then gently fold in the egg whites. Pour the mixture into the prepared cake pan, smooth the surface and brush with the beaten egg. Bake for about 30 minutes, then remove from the oven and let the cake cool in the pan.

TORTA ALLO YOGURT E RICOTTA

Serves 6

butter, for greasing
3 eggs
$^2/_3$ cup plain yogurt
scant 1 cup cornstarch
$^1/_2$ cup superfine sugar
$1^3/_4$ cups mild ricotta cheese, crumbled

ALSACE TART

TORTA ALSAZIANA

Serves 6

1¼ cups superfine sugar

4 eggs

½ cup sweet butter,
cut into pieces, plus extra for greasing

2¼ cups all-purpose flour, plus extra for dusting

5 tablespoons milk

2 tablespoons heavy cream

4 eating apples

juice of 1 lemon, strained

Beat together ½ cup of the sugar and one of the eggs in a bowl until light and fluffy, then beat in the butter. Sift the flour into a mound in a bowl, make a well in the center, pour in the butter mixture and mix with your fingertips, then knead until smooth. Shape into a ball, wrap and let rest in the refrigerator for 1 hour. Preheat the oven to 400°F. Grease a tart pan with butter. Roll out the dough into a round on a lightly floured counter, place on the base of the prepared pan and set aside in a cool place. Meanwhile, whisk together the remaining eggs and remaining sugar in a pan. Combine the milk and cream, pour into the pan and cook over low heat, stirring constantly, until thickened and smooth, then remove from the heat. Peel the apples, cut into fourths, core and arrange in the cake pan. Sprinkle with the lemon juice, pour the custard on top, letting it cover the base of the tart, and bake for 30 minutes. Remove from the oven and let stand for 15 minutes, then turn out.

APPLE CAKE

TORTA CON LE MELE

Serves 6

6 tablespoons sweet butter, softened,
plus extra for greasing

2¾ cups self-rising flour, plus extra for dusting

3 eggs

¾ cup superfine sugar

3 apples, peeled, cored and chopped

whipped cream, to serve (optional)

Preheat the oven to 350°F. Grease a cake pan or mold with butter and dust lightly with flour. Whisk together the eggs and sugar until pale and fluffy, then beat in the butter until thoroughly combined. Sift the flour into the mixture, then add the apples and mix gently. Pour the mixture into the prepared pan or mold and bake for 30–40 minutes. Remove from the oven and let cool, then turn out, or serve immediately while hot. Serve with whipped cream, if you like.

ALMOND CAKE

TORTA DI MANDORLE

Serves 6–8

¼ cup sweet butter, softened,
plus extra for greasing

1 cup blanched almonds, chopped

4 egg yolks

1¼ cups superfine sugar

½ cup all-purpose flour

½ cup potato flour

2 tablespoons orange liqueur

sifted confectioner's sugar, for dusting

Preheat the oven to 350°F. Grease a cake pan with butter and sprinkle with 2 tablespoons of the almonds to coat. Whisk together the egg yolks and sugar in a bowl until pale and fluffy. Fold in both flours, the remaining almonds, the orange liqueur and butter until thoroughly mixed. Pour the mixture into the prepared pan and bake for about 40 minutes. Transfer the cake to a wire rack and let cool. Dust the surface with plenty of confectioner's sugar.

APPLE AND PEAR TART

TORTA DI MELE E PERE

Serves 6

6 tablespoons sweet butter, softened, plus extra for greasing

all-purpose flour, for dusting

generous ½ cup superfine sugar

scant 1 cup blanched almonds, finely chopped

3 apples

3 pears

11 ounces Pâte Brisée (see page 1007)

1 egg yolk, lightly beaten

Preheat the oven to 400°F. Grease a tart pan with butter and dust lightly with flour. Cream the butter and sugar in a bowl until smooth, then stir in the almonds. Peel, core and dice the apples and pears and stir into the mixture. Roll out two-thirds of the dough into a round on a lightly floured counter and place in the prepared pan. Spread the fruit mixture over the base of the tart shell. Roll out the remaining dough to a round and place it on top of the tart. Crimp the edges to seal, make a hole in the center and brush with the egg yolk. Bake for about 45 minutes and serve warm.

HAZELNUT CAKE

TORTA DI NOCCIOLE

Serves 6

scant 1 cup sweet butter, melted, plus extra for greasing

1¾ cups self-rising flour, plus extra for dusting

2 eggs

1 cup superfine sugar

1¾ cups toasted hazelnuts, finely chopped

grated rind of 1 lemon

¼ cup milk

Preheat the oven to 350°F. Grease a shallow cake pan with butter and lightly dust with flour. Sift the flour into a mound, make a well in the center, add the eggs, sugar, hazelnuts, melted butter, lemon rind and milk and mix well. Pour the mixture into the prepared pan and bake for about 30 minutes. Remove the cake from the oven, let stand for 15 minutes, then turn out.

WALNUT CAKE

TORTA DI NOCI

Serves 6

⅔ cup sweet butter, softened, plus extra for greasing

4 eggs, separated

¾ cup superfine sugar

1¾ cups shelled walnuts, chopped

1¼ cups all-purpose flour

2 teaspoons baking powder

grated rind of 1 lemon

pinch of ground cinnamon

1 tablespoon rum (optional)

Custard (see page 1039) or whipped cream, to serve

Preheat the oven to 350°F. Grease a cake pan with butter. Cream the butter with a wooden spoon, then beat in the egg yolks, one at a time. Stir in the sugar and walnuts, sift in the flour and baking powder and mix well. Add the lemon rind, cinnamon, and rum if using. Stiffly whisk the egg whites in a grease-free bowl and fold into the mixture. Pour into the prepared pan and bake for about 1 hour. Remove the cake from the oven, let cool and then turn out. Serve with custard or whipped cream.

TORTA DI NOCI E MIELE

Serves 6

sweet butter, for greasing

all-purpose flour, for dusting

scant 1 cup superfine sugar

²/₃ cup heavy cream

1 tablespoon honey

generous 1¹/₂ cups shelled walnuts, chopped

11 ounces Pie Crust Dough (see page 1008)

1 egg yolk, lightly beaten

WALNUT AND HONEY TART

Grease a tart pan with butter and lightly dust with flour. Caramelize the sugar (see page 1019) in a pan over low heat. When it has turned golden brown, add the cream and stir in the honey and walnuts, then remove from the heat and let cool. Preheat the oven to 350°F. Halve the pastry dough. Roll out one half on a lightly floured counter and place the prepared pan. Spoon the walnut mixture evenly on top. Roll out the remaining dough and place on top of the tart. Crimp the edges to seal, brush with the egg yolk and bake for 25–30 minutes. Let cool before serving.

TORTA DI PESCHE

Serves 6

sweet butter, for greasing

³/₄ cup bread crumbs

2¹/₄ pounds peaches, peeled, pitted and sliced

³/₄ cup superfine sugar

¹/₄ cup unsweetened cocoa powder

4 eggs, lightly beaten

3¹/₂ cups amaretti, crushed

PEACH PIE

Preheat the oven to 350°F. Grease an ovenproof dish with butter and sprinkle with the bread crumbs, tipping out any excess. Put the peaches in a pan with the sugar and cook over low heat for about 10 minutes. Remove from the heat and mash with a fork. Stir in the cocoa, eggs and amaretti, then pour the mixture into the prepared dish. Bake for about 30 minutes, then remove from the oven, let stand for a few minutes and serve.

TORTA DI RICOTTA

Serves 6

sweet butter, for greasing

2¹/₄ cups all-purpose flour, plus extra for dusting

4 eggs

scant ¹/₂ cup soft brown sugar, plus extra for sprinkling

1³/₄ cups ricotta cheese

grated rind of ¹/₂ lemon

5 tablespoons sunflower or olive oil

³/₄ cup milk

1 tablespoon baking powder

RICOTTA CAKE

Preheat the oven to 350°F. Grease a tart pan with butter and lightly dust with flour. Whisk together the eggs and sugar in a bowl until pale and fluffy. Stir in the ricotta, lemon rind, oil and milk. Sift in the flour and baking powder, mix well and pour into the prepared pan. Sprinkle with extra sugar and bake for about 40 minutes. Remove from the oven and let cool, then turn out.

RICOTTA AND RAISIN TART

TORTA DI RICOTTA E UVETTA

Serves 6

scant ¹/₂ cup golden raisins

5 tablespoons Marsala

generous 1¹/₂ cups all-purpose flour,
plus extra for dusting

¹/₂ cup sweet butter, plus extra for greasing

scant ¹/₂ cup superfine sugar

2 egg yolks

grated rind of 1 lemon

1¹/₂ cups ricotta cheese

¹/₂ cup bread crumbs

Put the golden raisins in a bowl, pour in the Marsala and let soak. Sift the flour into a mound, make a well in the center, add the butter, ¹/₄ cup of the sugar, one of the egg yolks and half the lemon rind and mix well. Shape the dough into a ball, wrap and let rest for 1 hour. Preheat the oven to 350°F. Grease and dust a tart pan. Drain the golden raisins and squeeze out. Beat the remaining egg yolk with the remaining sugar in a bowl until pale and fluffy, then add the ricotta, bread crumbs, golden raisins and remaining lemon rind. Halve the dough and roll out one piece on a lightly floured counter to a ¹/₄-inch thick round. Place in the prepared pan and sprinkle the ricotta mixture on top. Roll out the remaining dough, cut into strips and make a lattice on top of the tart. Arrange the remaining dough strips around the side and press lightly to seal. Bake for 45 minutes, remove from the oven and let cool.

RICOTTA AND SOUR CHERRY TART

TORTA DI RICOTTA E VISCIOLE

Serves 6

generous 1¹/₂ cups all-purpose flour,
plus extra for dusting

¹/₂ cup sweet butter, cut into pieces,
plus extra for greasing

¹/₂ cup superfine sugar

1 egg yolk

grated rind of ¹/₂ lemon

scant 2 cups sour cherries, pitted

1¹/₂ cups ricotta cheese

Sift the flour into a mound, make a well in the center, add the butter, half the sugar, the egg yolk and the lemon rind and mix well. Shape the dough into a ball, wrap and let rest for 1 hour. Put the cherries in a pan with 4 tablespoons water and the remaining sugar and cook over low heat for 20 minutes. Meanwhile, preheat the oven to 350°F. Grease and dust a tart pan. Place the ricotta in a bowl. Drain the cherries and stir them into the ricotta. Halve the dough and roll out one piece on a lightly floured counter to a ¹/₄-inch thick round. Place in the prepared pan and sprinkle the ricotta mixture on top. Roll out the remaining dough, cut into strips and make a lattice on top of the tart. Arrange the remaining dough strips around the side and press lightly to seal. Bake for 45 minutes, then remove from the oven and let cool.

PUMPKIN CAKE

TORTA DI ZUCCA

Serves 6–8

scant ¹/₂ cup sweet butter, softened,
plus extra for greasing

scant 1 cup cooked pumpkin or canned pumpkin purée

1 cup superfine sugar • 2 eggs

2 cups self-rising flour

grated rind of 1 lemon • 8 amaretti, crushed

5 tablespoons milk

Preheat the oven to 350°F. Grease a cake pan with butter. If using cooked pumpkin, pass it through a food mill. Cream the butter and sugar in a bowl, then beat in the eggs until the mixture is light and fluffy. Add the pumpkin purée, flour, lemon rind, amaretti and milk. (The exact quantity of amaretti may need to be adjusted to produce a soft mixture.) Pour the mixture into the prepared pan and bake for 45 minutes. Remove the cake from the oven, let cool and then turn out.

SACHERTORTE

Preheat the oven to 350°F. Grease a springform cake pan with butter and lightly dust with flour. Melt the chocolate with 2 tablespoons water in a heatproof bowl set over a pan of barely simmering water. Remove from the heat and let cool. Stiffly whisk the egg whites in a grease-free bowl. Cream the butter with the superfine sugar in a bowl, then stir in the egg yolks, one at a time. Stir in the chocolate and fold in the egg whites. Sift in the flour and vanilla sugar, stirring gently. Pour the mixture into the prepared pan, smooth the surface with a spatula and bake for about 1 1/2 hours. Remove the cake from the oven and let cool in the pan, then turn out and slice in half horizontally. Heat the jelly in a small pan until melted, then spread it over the lower half of the cake and top with the other half. Spread the chocolate frosting over the whole cake with a spatula, then leave until set.

TORTA TIPO SACHER

Serves 6

scant 1/2 cup butter, softened,

plus extra for greasing

1 1/4 cups all-purpose flour, plus extra for dusting

3 ounces semisweet chocolate, broken into pieces

6 eggs, separated

1/2 cup superfine sugar

2 tablespoons vanilla sugar (see page 1003)

3 tablespoons apricot jelly

1 quantity Chocolate Frosting (see page 1016)

VIENNESE APPLE PIE

Sift the flour and a pinch of salt into a mound, make a well in the center and add the sugar, lemon rind and eggs. Mix with your fingertips to a fine, crumbly mixture, then gradually work in the butter. Shape into a ball and let rest in a cool place for 1 hour. Meanwhile, prepare the filling. Place the golden raisins in a bowl, add warm water to cover and let soak for 15 minutes, then drain and squeeze out. Peel, core and dice the apples, place in a large bowl, add the ladyfingers, golden raisins, walnuts, sugar, cinnamon and melted butter and mix well. Preheat the oven to 350°F. Grease a rectangular pie dish with butter. Roll out two-thirds of the dough on a lightly floured counter and line the prepared dish. Spoon the filling evenly on top. Roll out the remaining dough, place on top of the pie and crimp the edges to seal. Brush with the beaten egg yolk and bake for 45 minutes. Let cool before serving.

TORTA VIENNESE ALLE MELE

Serves 8

scant 3 cups all-purpose flour,

plus extra for dusting

scant 1/2 cup superfine sugar

grated rind of 1/2 lemon

2 eggs

generous 2/3 cup sweet butter,

softened and cut into pieces,

plus extra for greasing

1 egg yolk, lightly beaten

salt

For the filling

3/4 cup golden raisins

4 apples

4 ladyfingers, crumbled

scant 1/2 cup shelled walnuts, chopped

1/3 cup superfine sugar

pinch of ground cinnamon

1 tablespoon melted sweet butter

FRUIT DESSERTS

This section includes a collection of delicious recipes based on a wide range of fruits presented in a variety of fabulous ways – with liqueur, cream, wine or custard. Fruit can be served hot, cold or iced and is always a popular way to end a meal.

SUMMER PINEAPPLE

ANANAS D'ESTATE

Serves 6

1 pineapple

1 orange

1 banana, sliced

1 1/2 cups raspberries

2 1/4 cups strawberries, halved if large

1 pear, peeled, cored and diced or 1 peach, peeled, pitted and diced

4 tablespoons superfine sugar

3/4 cup champagne or sparkling white wine

scant 1/2 cup brandy

vanilla ice cream, to serve

Cut the pineapple in half horizontally and scoop out the flesh, leaving the 'shells' intact. Core and dice the pineapple flesh and place it in a bowl. Peel the orange, removing all traces of pith, and cut into segments, then dice the flesh. Add the orange, banana, raspberries, strawberries and pear or peach to the bowl and mix well. Sprinkle with the sugar, champagne or wine and brandy. Chill the fruit salad and pineapple shells in the refrigerator for 2–3 hours. To serve, fill the shells with the fruit salad and top with a dome of vanilla ice cream. Make a layer of crushed ice on a serving dish, place the filled pineapple shells on top and serve.

WATERMELON WITH RUM

Cut a slice off the top of the watermelon about a fourth of the way down and reserve. Scoop out the flesh from the large part of the watermelon and discard the seeds. Dice the flesh, place it in a bowl and stir in the sugar, rum and brandy. Spoon the mixture into the watermelon 'shell' and cover with the reserved 'lid'. Chill in the refrigerator for 2–3 hours before serving.

ANGURIA AL RUM

Serves 6

4$^1/_2$-pound watermelon

$^1/_2$ cup superfine sugar

2 tablespoons rum

2 tablespoons brandy

CARAMELIZED ORANGES

Thinly pare the rind from the oranges, avoiding the white pith, and cut it into strips. Put the sugar in a pan, add 1 table-spoon water and heat gently, without stirring, until melted and golden brown. Combine the wine with 1 tablespoon water and stir it into the caramel, then stir in the brandy. Add the strips of orange rind and cook over very low heat for 1$^1/_2$ hours. Blanch the oranges in boiling water for 2–3 minutes, then drain, and cut off any white pith with a small, sharp knife. Place them on a serving dish, sprinkle with the syrup and candied orange rind and decorate with mint leaves.

ARANCE CARAMELLATE

Serves 4

4 oranges

1 cup superfine sugar

5 tablespoons dry white wine

5 tablespoons brandy

fresh mint leaves, to decorate

CHERRIES IN ALCOHOL

Spread out the cherries on a dish towel and let dry for 24 hours. Cut off the first half of the stems and pack the cherries into one or two sterilized Mason jars. Add two of the cloves, a cinnamon stick and a heaping tablespoon of sugar to each jar. Fill the jar or jars with vodka or eau-de-vie so that the fruit is completely covered with the alcohol. Seal the jars and store them in a cool, dark, dry place for at least 2 months before using.

CILIEGE SOTTO SPIRITO

2 pounds large firm cherries

2–4 cloves

2 x 2-inch cinnamon sticks

$^1/_3$ cup superfine sugar

1 bottle (3 cups) vodka or eau-de-vie

STRAWBERRY AND RHUBARB COMPOTE

Put the strawberries in a dish, add the orange juice and let soak. Blanch the rhubarb in boiling water for 5 minutes, then drain. Mix the vanilla with $^1/_2$ teaspoon water, stir into the syrup and bring to a boil over low heat. Add the rhubarb and simmer gently for 10 minutes. Pour the mixture over the strawberries and let cool, then chill in the refrigerator until ready to serve.

COMPOSTA DI FRAGOLE AL RABARBARO

Serves 6

2$^3/_4$ cups strawberries

juice of 1 orange, strained

14 ounces rhubarb,

trimmed and cut into short lengths

1 teaspoon vanilla extract

1 cup Thick Syrup (see page 1019)

FICHI ALLE SPEZIE

Serves 6

$^1/_2$ teaspoon ground cinnamon

$^1/_2$ teaspoon ground coriander

2 cloves

$^1/_2$ teaspoon ground ginger

$^1/_2$ cup superfine sugar

rind of 1 orange, thinly pared and cut into strips

12 ripe figs

SPICED FIGS

Put the spices, sugar and orange rind in a pan, add $2^1/_4$ cups water and bring to a boil. Lower the heat and simmer for 10 minutes, then add the figs and simmer for 5 minutes more. Do not let the syrup boil. Remove the pan from the heat and let cool. Drain the figs, reserving the syrup, and put them in a dish. Bring the syrup back to a boil and cook over medium heat until reduced by half, then pour it over the figs. Let cool completely.

FRAGOLE ALL'ARANCIA

Serves 6

$6^1/_2$ cups strawberries

$^2/_3$ cup superfine sugar

$^3/_4$ cup orange juice, strained

STRAWBERRIES WITH ORANGE

Put $2^1/_4$ cups of the strawberries in a food processor and process to a purée. Add half the sugar and the orange juice and process briefly again until mixed. Pour the mixture into a dish, arrange the remaining whole strawberries on top and sprinkle with the remaining sugar. Cover and chill until ready to serve.

FRUTTA FRESCA IN GELATINA

Serves 6

3 gelatin leaves

1 bottle (3 cups) sweet white wine

$^1/_2$ cup superfine sugar

1 apple

1 pear

1 banana

2 kiwi fruit

2 mandarins

12 raspberries

2 fresh mint leaves, chopped

FRESH FRUIT JELLY

Fill a small bowl with water, add the gelatin and let soak for 3 minutes, then drain and squeeze out. Pour the wine into a pan, add the sugar and gelatin and heat gently until the sugar and gelatin have dissolved. Remove from the heat, let cool and then chill in the refrigerator overnight. Peel, core and chop the apple and pear. Peel and chop the banana, kiwi fruit and mandarins. Arrange all the fruit in a fairly large dish, alternating the colors to make an attractive design. Chill in the refrigerator for 3–4 hours. Just before serving, pour the wine jelly – which should be slightly runny – into the dish. Sprinkle with the mint and serve.

MACEDONIA

Serves 6

$2^1/_4$ pounds mixed fresh fruit

juice of 1 lemon, strained

$^1/_4$ cup maraschino liqueur

$^1/_2$ cup slivered almonds

$^3/_4$ cup superfine sugar

vanilla or lemon ice cream, to serve

FRUIT SALAD

There should be equal quantities of each type of fruit. Prepare the fruit, peeling and coring as necessary, and cut it into cubes. Put it into a large dish, sprinkle with the lemon juice, maraschino liqueur, almonds and sugar and stir well. Leave in a cool place for a few hours to soak up the flavor before serving. Serve with ice cream.

EXOTIC FRUIT SALAD

MACEDONIA DI FRUTTA ESOTICA

Serves 8

1 pound 10 ounces pineapple

9 ounces papaya, halved and seeded

2 mangoes

3 kiwi fruit, peeled and diced

2 star fruits, trimmed and sliced

9 ounces lychees, peeled and pitted

4 tablespoons superfine sugar

$^3/_4$ cup sweet white wine

2 tablespoons rum

1 pomegranate

Cut off the leafy top of the pineapple, then cut off the skin, removing the 'eyes' from the flesh with a small, pointed knife. Cut the flesh into slices, core and dice. Cut the papaya halves in half again, then peel and dice the flesh. Cut a thick lengthwise slice from a mango, keeping the knife as close to the pit as possible. Turn the mango round and cut a lengthwise slice from the other side of the pit. Score the flesh in each thick slice in criss-cross lines, spaced about $^1/_2$ inch apart. Turn the skin inside out and cut off the flesh. Trim any remaining flesh from the pit. Repeat with the other mango. Put the pineapple, papaya, mangoes, kiwis, star fruits and lychees in a dish and sprinkle with the sugar, wine and rum. Cut off a thin slice from one end of the pomegranate, then stand it upright and cut through the skin at intervals. Bend back the segments and push the seeds into a bowl with your fingers. Remove all traces of pith and membrane, then sprinkle the seeds over the fruit salad. Cover the dish with plastic wrap and chill in the refrigerator for 4 hours. To serve, stir the fruit salad gently and let stand at room temperature for 10 minutes.

MELON FRUIT SALAD

MACEDONIA DI MELONI

Serves 6–8

$^1/_2$ watermelon

1 white-fleshed melon, halved and seeded

1 yellow-fleshed melon, halved and seeded

juice of 1 orange, strained

$^3/_4$ cup port

3 tablespoons superfine sugar

Cut a slice off the top of the watermelon about one-third of the way down the fruit. Cut decorative notches around the edge of the larger portion with a knife. Scoop out balls of melon flesh with a melon baller, discarding the seeds. Chill the empty 'shell' in the refrigerator. Scoop out balls of flesh from the other two melons and place them, with the watermelon balls, in a bowl. Sprinkle with the orange juice, port and sugar, cover and let steep in the refrigerator for 3 hours. To serve, spoon the mixture into the watermelon shell.

APPLE DUMPLINGS

MELE IN CROSTA

Serves 4

sweet butter, for greasing

9 ounces puff pastry dough, thawed if frozen

all-purpose flour, for dusting

4 cooking apples

4 tablespoons vanilla sugar (see page 1003)

$^2/_3$ cup heavy cream

1–1$^1/_2$ teaspoons ground cinnamon

1 egg yolk, beaten with 1 tablespoon water

Preheat the oven to 350°F. Grease an ovenproof dish with butter. Roll out the dough to $^1/_8$ inch thick on a lightly floured counter and cut it into four squares, each large enough to enclose an apple. Peel and core the apples and place one in the middle of each dough square. Sprinkle with the vanilla sugar and fill each cavity with a fourth of the cream and a pinch of cinnamon. Bring the corners of the dough squares up to the top of each apple and pinch together, leaving a small opening to let steam escape. Brush the dumplings with the egg yolk mixture, place in the prepared dish and bake for 40 minutes.

APPLES IN THEIR NESTS

MELE NEL NIDO

Serves 6

¹/₄ cup sweet butter, cut into pieces,
plus extra for greasing

6 russet apples, peeled and cored

2 eggs, separated • ¹/₃ cup superfine sugar

generous 1 cup all-purpose flour

2 tablespoons milk

4–6 tablespoons raspberry preserve

salt

Preheat the oven to 400°F. Grease an ovenproof dish with butter. Place the apples in the prepared dish. Beat the egg yolks with the sugar in a bowl until pale and fluffy. Sift in the flour with a pinch of salt, a little at a time, and stir in the milk. Stiffly whisk the egg whites in a grease-free bowl and fold into the mixture. Pour the batter around the apples, but do not cover them completely. Fill the cavities in the apples with raspberry preserve and pieces of butter. Bake for about 45 minutes or until golden brown. Remove from the oven and let cool slightly, then serve.

SPICED APPLES WITH RAISINS

MELE SPEZIATE CON UVETTA

Serves 4

generous ¹/₄ cup golden raisins

2 tablespoons sweet butter, plus extra for greasing

1 teaspoon ground cinnamon

¹/₂ teaspoon ground ginger

pinch of ground cumin • 4 apples

5 tablespoons moscato
or other sparkling sweet dessert wine

Put the golden raisins in a bowl, add hot water to cover and let soak for 15 minutes. Meanwhile, preheat the oven to 325°F. Grease an ovenproof dish with butter. Drain the golden raisins, squeeze out and sprinkle with the cinnamon, ginger and cumin. Core the apples, fill the cavities with the raisin mixture and place in the prepared dish. Dot the tops of the apples with the butter and sprinkle with the wine. Bake for about 30 minutes, then remove from the oven and let cool slightly before serving.

MELON SURPRISE

MELONE SORPRESA

Serves 6

1 melon, halved and seeded

2 cups raspberries

2 cups seedless white grapes

3 peaches, peeled, pitted and diced

4 tablespoons superfine sugar

5 tablespoons sweet liqueur, such as maraschino

Scoop out balls of the melon flesh using a melon baller and place in a bowl. Reserve the 'shells'. Add the raspberries, grapes and peaches to the melon balls and sprinkle with the sugar and liqueur. Divide the fruit salad between the melon shells and chill in the refrigerator for at least 2 hours before serving.

BLUEBERRIES IN SYRUP

MIRTILLI SCIROPPATI

Serves 4

4¹/₂ cups blueberries

2¹/₂ cups superfine sugar

5 tablespoons grappa

Put the blueberries in a pan, add 5 tablespoons water and heat gently for 10 minutes. Add the sugar and cook, stirring constantly until it has dissolved completely, then simmer, stirring occasionally, for 15 minutes. Remove from the heat and let cool slightly. Sprinkle with the grappa and let cool completely. Spoon the berries and syrup into one or two sterilized jars and seal the tops. Use for decorating a variety of desserts and for serving with ice cream.

PEARS IN CHOCOLATE

Preheat the oven to 325°F. Sprinkle half the sugar evenly over the base of an ovenproof dish. Peel, halve and core the pears, place them in the dish and sprinkle with the remaining sugar. Bake for 15 minutes. Meanwhile, melt the chocolate and butter in a heatproof bowl set over a pan of barely simmering water. Add the pear brandy and stir until smooth and velvety. Pour the chocolate sauce over the pears and serve warm.

PERE AL CIOCCOLATO

Serves 4

2 tablespoons superfine sugar

4 pears

3¹/₂ ounces semisweet chocolate,

broken into pieces

1¹/₂ tablespoons butter

1–2 tablespoons pear brandy

CINNAMON PEARS

Peel and core the pears, then sprinkle with half the lemon juice to prevent discoloration. Put them in a pan, add the wine, ¹/₂ cup of the sugar and the cinnamon and bring to a boil. Lower the heat and simmer for about 10 minutes, then let cool. Remove the pears with a slotted spoon and put one pear in the center of each of six individual dishes. Slice the remaining pears and arrange the slices around the whole pears like flower petals. Add the remaining lemon juice and remaining sugar to the cooking juices, bring to a boil and simmer over medium heat until reduced by about half. Strain the liquid through a fine strainer and pour it over the pears. Chill in the refrigerator for at least 2 hours before serving.

PERE ALLA CANNELLA

Serves 6

12 pears

juice of 2 lemons, strained

1 bottle (3 cups) rosé wine

²/₃ cup superfine sugar

1¹/₂-inch cinnamon stick

PEARS WITH LEMON

Peel, halve and core the pears. Cut into fourths, then cut each fourth into two or three wedges. Place the pear wedges in a fairly large dish, pour in the lemon juice to cover and sprinkle with the sugar. Chill in the refrigerator for 2–3 hours.

PERE AL LIMONE

Serves 6

8 pears

juice of 8 lemons, strained

¹/₄ cup superfine sugar

SPICY CANDIED PEARS

Peel the pears and leave whole. Place them upright in a pan, pour in water to cover and add the cinnamon, sugar, cloves, butter and orange rind. Bring to a boil, then lower the heat and simmer for 20 minutes. Drain the pears, reserving the syrup. Bring the syrup to a boil and cook until reduced by one-third. Strain into a clean pan, stir in the cream and bring to a boil. Remove from the heat, let cool slightly and then bring back to the boil. Slice the pears and arrange like the rays of the sun on a serving dish. Spoon the spicy cream over them and sprinkle the surface with a pinch of cinnamon. Serve with cookies.

PERE PRALINATE ALLE SPEZIE

Serves 4

4 pears

1 teaspoon ground cinnamon,

plus extra to sprinkle

1¹/₂ tablespoons superfine sugar

2 cloves

1¹/₂ tablespoons sweet butter

rind of 1 orange, thinly pared

¹/₂ cup heavy cream

cookies, to serve

PEACHES WITH CHOCOLATE

Blanch the white peaches in boiling water for a few minutes, then drain and peel carefully without damaging the flesh. Set aside. Place the canned peaches and their syrup in a food processor and process to a purée. Transfer to a bowl and chill in the freezer for 1 hour. Place the chocolate, cream and sugar in a pan and heat gently until melted and smooth. Remove the pan from the heat and let cool, stirring constantly. Remove the peach purée from the freezer when it starts to take on a granular consistency and before it becomes completely frozen and place on a serving dish. Cut the white peaches in half, remove the pits and arrange on top of the purée. Chill in the refrigerator. Pour the cold sauce over the peaches and decorate with the hazelnuts.

PESCHE AL CIOCCOLATO

Serves 4

4 white peaches

14 ounces canned peaches in syrup

3¹/₂ ounces bittersweet chocolate

¹/₄ cup heavy cream

¹/₄ cup confectioner's sugar

scant 1 cup hazelnuts, chopped, to decorate

PEACHES WITH STRAWBERRIES

Blanch the peaches in boiling water for a few minutes, then drain and peel. Halve and pit them, then place on a serving dish. Sprinkle with the sugar and fill the cavities with the strawberries. Dilute the preserve with the wine and pour the mixture over the strawberries. Leave in a cool place for a few hours to absorb the flavor before serving.

PESCHE ALLE FRAGOLINE

Serves 4

6 yellow peaches

¹/₂ cup superfine sugar

2³/₄ cups strawberries

3 tablespoons strawberry preserve

2–3 tablespoons sweet white wine

PEACHES IN RED WINE

Blanch the peaches in a pan of boiling water for 5 minutes, then drain and peel. Halve and pit them. Pour the wine into a pan, add the superfine sugar, vanilla sugar, clove and nutmeg and simmer for 10 minutes. Add the peaches and simmer for 10 minutes more. Remove the peaches with a slotted spoon and place in a dish. Bring the syrup to a boil and cook until reduced and thickened. Pour it over the peaches and let steep for 12 hours.

PESCHE AL VINO ROSSO

Serves 4

1³/₄ pounds white peaches

4 cups red wine

scant 1 cup superfine sugar

2 tablespoons vanilla sugar (see page 1003)

1 clove

pinch of freshly grated nutmeg

Serves 4

2 tablespoons sweet butter, plus extra for greasing

5 yellow peaches

$^1/_4$ cup superfine sugar

4 amaretti, crushed

2 egg yolks

$^1/_4$ cup unsweetened cocoa powder

STUFFED PEACHES

Preheat the oven to 325°F. Grease an ovenproof dish with butter. Peel, halve, pit and chop one of the peaches and place in a bowl. Halve and pit the remaining peaches. Scoop out a little flesh from the cavity of each and add to the bowl. Stir in the sugar, amaretti, egg yolks and cocoa. Divide the mixture among the cavities of the peach halves, piling it up into a dome. Dot each dome with the butter, place the peaches in the prepared dish and bake for 1 hour. Serve hot or warm.

Serves 6

1 bottle (3 cups) sweet rosé wine

pinch of ground cinnamon

$^2/_3$ cup superfine sugar

thinly pared rind of 1 lemon

2$^1/_4$ pounds plums, halved and pitted

PLUMS IN WINE

Combine the wine, cinnamon and sugar in a pan, add the lemon rind and bring to a boil over low heat. Add the plums, bring back to a boil and cook for 10 minutes. Transfer to a dish and let cool, then chill in the refrigerator until ready to serve.

SWEET CRÊPES

Crêpes may be either sweet or savory and can be filled with béchamel sauce, vegetables, custard, fruit, preserve and many other things. In fact, they are equally successful as an antipasto or a dessert. Crêpes are very easy to make – simply prepare a batter with milk, flour, eggs and sugar and you're ready to cook them. The real secret of success lies in their thinness, and achieving this soon comes with practice. An ordinary skillet will do when making crêpes, but to guarantee success it's worth buying a crêpe pan. Once you get the hang of it, making crêpes is quick and easy. Crêpes can also be prepared in advance. If you fill them, heat them at the last minute and serve them flambéed at the table – with the aroma of brandy, they are guaranteed to delight your guests.

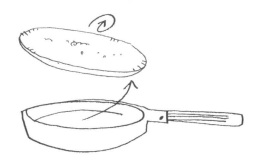

CHOCOLATE CRÊPES

Cook 12 crêpes, stack them, interleaved with waxed paper, on a plate and keep warm. Pour the milk into a pan, add the chocolate and melt over low heat, stirring constantly until smooth, then remove the pan from the heat. Gently stir in the butter and spread the filling over the crêpes while still hot. Fold each crêpe into a half-moon shape, arrange, slightly overlapping, on a serving dish and serve with whipped cream.

CRÊPES AL CIOCCOLATO

Serves 6

1 quantity Crêpe Batter (see page 155)

2 tablespoons milk

9 ounces semisweet chocolate, broken into pieces

2 tablespoons sweet butter

stiffly whipped heavy cream, to serve

CRÊPES WITH PRESERVE

CRÊPES ALLA MARMELLATA

Serves 6

1 quantity Crêpe Batter (see page 155)

2 tablespoons apricot preserve

2 teaspoons grated orange rind

2 tablespoons superfine sugar

¹/₄ cup brandy

vanilla sugar (see page 1003), for sprinkling

Cook 12 crêpes, stack them, interleaved with waxed paper, on a plate and keep warm. Put the apricot preserve, orange rind, sugar and 5 tablespoons water in a small pan and bring to a boil. Cook, stirring constantly, for a few minutes, then remove from the heat and add the brandy. Spread a little of the preserve mixture on each crêpe and fold into four. Place on a serving dish, sprinkle with vanilla sugar and serve warm.

APPLE CRÊPES

CRÊPES ALLE MELE

Serves 6

1 quantity Crêpe Batter (see page 155)

¹/₂ cup superfine sugar

¹/₂ teaspoon ground cinnamon

juice of 1 lemon, strained

strip of thinly pared lemon rind

1 pound 2 ounces apples, peeled, cored and diced

Cook 12 crêpes, stack them, interleaved with waxed paper, on a plate and keep warm. Pour ³/₄ cup water into a pan and add the sugar, cinnamon, lemon juice and strip of lemon rind. Bring to a boil, stirring until the sugar has dissolved, and cook for a few minutes over high heat until syrupy. Remove and discard the lemon rind, add the apples and cook, stirring frequently, until coated with caramel, then remove from the heat. Fill each crêpe with a little of the apple mixture and roll up loosely, then place on a serving dish. Serve warm.

SUGAR CRÊPES

CRÊPES ALLO ZUCCHERO

Serves 6

2 tablespoons sweet butter, cut into pieces

1 quantity Crêpe Batter (see page 155)

sugar, for sprinkling

Melt a piece of the butter in a small skillet over low heat. Pour in 1 tablespoon of the batter and tilt the skillet so that it covers the base evenly. Cook for a few seconds until the underside is set and golden brown, then flip over with a spatula and cook the second side for a few seconds more. Slide the crêpe out of the skillet onto a plate. Cook more crêpes in the same way, adding more butter as required. As the crêpes are cooked, stack them interleaved with waxed paper and keep warm. Sprinkle each crêpe with a little sugar, fold into four and place on a serving dish. Serve warm.

CRÊPES SUZETTE

CRÊPES SUZETTE

Serves 6

1 quantity Crêpe Batter (see page 155)

scant ¹/₂ cup sweet butter

¹/₂ cup superfine sugar

juice of 1 mandarin, strained • ¹/₄ cup curaçao

vanilla sugar (see page 1003), for sprinkling

Cointreau, or another sweet liquer (optional)

Cook 12 crêpes, stack them, interleaved with waxed paper, on a plate and keep warm. Cream the butter in a bowl, then beat in the sugar, mandarin juice and curaçao. Spread the crêpes with the mixture, fold into four and sprinkle with vanilla sugar. Place on a serving dish and serve warm. The crêpes may also be flambéed after sprinkling with Cointreau or another sweet liqueur.

PANCAKES

Sift together the flour, sugar and a pinch of salt into a bowl, make a well in the center, add the egg and beat well. Add the milk, oil and baking powder and mix well, then cover and let stand for 2 hours. Stir the batter. Melt a piece of the butter in a small skillet, pour in a ladleful of batter and tilt the skillet so that the batter covers the base evenly. Cook on both sides without letting the pancake brown too much. Continue making pancakes until all the batter is used, adding more butter as required. Serve the pancakes piping hot with a choice of syrups such as maple, apple or other fruits.

PANCAKES

Serves 4

scant 1 cup all-purpose flour

1 tablespoon superfine sugar

1 egg

$3/4$ cup milk

1 tablespoon sunflower or olive oil

1 teaspoon baking powder

2 tablespoons sweet butter, cut into pieces

salt

syrup of choice, to serve

BLUEBERRY PANCAKES

Sift together the flour, sugar, cinnamon and a pinch of salt into a bowl, make a well in the center, add the eggs and mix well. Add the milk, oil and baking powder and mix well, then cover and let stand for at least 2 hours. Stir the batter. Melt a piece of the butter in a small skillet, pour in a ladleful of batter, and cook on both sides. Continue making pancakes until all the batter is used, adding more butter as required. As the pancakes are ready, place on a serving dish and sprinkle with a little of the blueberries in syrup and some of the confectioner's sugar. Keep warm until ready to serve.

PANCAKES AI MIRTILLI

Serves 6

1 cup all-purpose flour

2 tablespoons superfine sugar

pinch of ground cinnamon

3 eggs

$1^1/4$ cups milk

1 tablespoon sunflower or olive oil

1 teaspoon baking powder

$1/4$ cup sweet butter, cut into pieces

$3/4$ cup Blueberries in Syrup

(see page 1084)

3 tablespoons confectioner's sugar

salt

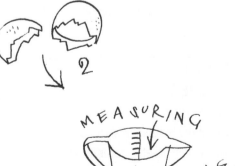

MEASURING SUGAR

SWEET OMELETS

Sweet omelets are made in the classic way, that is, cooked on one side only and usually folded. They are almost always filled with preserves or caramelized fruit, often enhanced with a few tablespoonfuls of liqueur. Omelets may round off a lunch or dinner menu consisting of fairly light dishes. They are also served as nourishing snacks for children. They may be decorated by sprinkling them with sugar and then caramelizing it with a hot skewer in a variety of patterns.

OMELETTE DOLCE (RICETTA BASE)

Serves 4

6 eggs

2 tablespoons superfine sugar

3 tablespoons sweet butter

SWEET OMELET (BASIC RECIPE)

Lightly beat the eggs with the sugar and 3 tablespoons water in a bowl. Melt 2 tablespoons of the butter in a skillet over low heat, pour in the egg mixture and tilt the skillet to cover the base evenly. Cook until the omelet is set underneath but still soft on top, then fold the left side over to the middle and the right side over on top of it. Slide the omelet onto a warm serving dish and 'glaze' by gently spreading the remaining butter over the surface. Alternatively, sprinkle with sugar and flash under the broiler.

APRICOT PRESERVE AND CREAM OMELET

Whip the cream, put it in a serving bowl and sprinkle with the almonds. Put the preserve and rum in a small pan and stir over medium heat until melted and smooth. Lightly beat the eggs with the sugar and 4 tablespoons water in a bowl. Melt the butter in a skillet over low heat, pour in the egg mixture and tilt the skillet to cover the base evenly. Cook until the omelet is set underneath but still soft on top. Spoon the preserve mixture over it, fold the left side in towards the middle and fold the right side over on top. Slide the omelet onto a warm serving dish. Serve the omelet immediately and hand the cream separately. This omelet can also be filled with canned fruit. In this case, drain and dice the fruit and place it in the middle of the omelet.

OMELETTE ALLA MARMELLATA DI ALBICOCCHE E PANNA

Serves 4

$2^1/_2$ tablespoons apricot preserve

2 tablespoons rum

6 eggs

2 tablespoons superfine sugar

2 tablespoons sweet butter

scant 1 cup heavy cream

2 tablespoons chopped blanched almonds

RASPBERRY OMELET

Put the preserve and kirsch in a small pan and stir over medium heat until melted and smooth. Lightly beat the eggs with the sugar and 4 tablespoons water in a bowl. Melt the butter in a skillet over low heat, pour in the egg mixture and tilt the skillet to cover the base evenly. Cook until the omelet is set underneath but still soft on top, then fold the left side over to the middle and the right side over on top of it. Slide the omelet onto a warm serving dish and pour the preserve mixture on top. Serve immediately.

OMELETTE DI LAMPONI

Serves 4

3 tablespoons raspberry preserve

2 tablespoons kirsch

6 eggs

$1^1/_2$ tablespoons superfine sugar

2 tablespoons sweet butter

OMELET WITH DRIED FRUIT AND ALMONDS

Put the raisins, prunes and apricots in a bowl, add warm water to cover and let soak. Lightly beat the eggs with the sugar, 4 tablespoons water and orange rind in another bowl. Melt the butter in a skillet over low heat, pour in the egg mixture and tilt the skillet to cover the base evenly with the egg mixture. Cook until the omelet is set underneath but still soft on top. Drain the fruit and squeeze out, then place it in the middle of the omelet. Fold the left side over the fruit and the right side over on top of it. Slide the omelet onto a warm serving dish, sprinkle with sugar almonds and the rum, ignite and serve.

OMELETTE CON FRUTTA SECCA ALLA FIAMMA

Serves 4

$^1/_3$ cup raisins

2 prunes, pitted

2 dried apricots, pitted and chopped

6 eggs

2 tablespoons superfine sugar,

plus extra for sprinkling

rind of 1 orange, grated

2 tablespoons sweet butter

2 tablespoons rum

chopped almonds, to serve

FRITTERS

Although they are sometimes a little heavy, these delicacies are almost irresistible. It is a good rule to fry only a few fritters at a time and to drain them on paper towels.

AMARETTI FRITTERS

AMARETTI FRITTI

Serves 4

generous 1 cup all-purpose flour

1 egg, separated

1 tablespoon brandy

1 tablespoon olive oil, plus extra for frying

7 ounces amaretti

2 tablespoons rum

confectioner's sugar, for dusting

Prepare a soft batter (see page 1017) with the flour, egg yolk, brandy, olive oil and as much water as required and let rest for 1 hour. Stiffly whisk the egg white in a grease-free bowl and fold into the batter. Soak the amaretti in the rum, then dip them in the batter. Heat the oil for frying in a skillet, add the amaretti and cook until golden brown. Drain on paper towels and dust with confectioner's sugar.

SWEET FRITTERS

CHIACCHIERE

Serves 6

2¼ cups all-purpose flour, plus extra for dusting

¼ cup superfine sugar

1 egg

1 egg yolk

2 tablespoons olive oil, plus extra for frying

¾ cup white wine

confectioner's sugar, for dusting

Sift the flour into a bowl, stir in the sugar and make a well in the center. Add the egg, egg yolk, olive oil and the wine, mix well and let rest for at least 30 minutes. Roll out the dough into a thin sheet on a lightly floured counter and, using a fluted pastry wheel, cut it into strips 4 inches long and 1¼ inches wide. Tie the strips together as if they were ribbons but do not pull too tightly. Heat the oil for frying in a skillet, add the fritters and cook until light golden brown. Remove with a slotted spoon and drain on paper towels. Dust with confectioner's sugar.

FRITTELLE DI FRUTTA
ALLO CHAMPAGNE

Serves 8

1 pineapple

4 apples

2 bananas

olive oil, for frying

$^1/_2$ cup confectioner's sugar

For the batter

1$^1/_4$ cups all-purpose flour

1 egg

scant $^1/_2$ cup sweet champagne

2 egg whites

For the sauce

3 cups raspberries

2–3 tablespoons confectioner's sugar

2 tablespoons kirsch

FRUIT AND CHAMPAGNE FRITTERS

To make the batter, sift the flour into a large bowl, make a well in the center and add the egg and half the champagne. Mix thoroughly with a whisk until smooth and even, then stir in the remaining champagne. Cover the bowl and let rest in a cool place for 1 hour. Stiffly whisk the egg whites in a grease-free bowl and gently fold them into the batter and set aside. Meanwhile, prepare the sauce. Mash the raspberries in a bowl and stir in sugar to taste and the kirsch. Press through a strainer into another bowl and keep in a cool place until required. Peel the pineapple and cut out the 'eyes' with a small, pointed knife. Cut the flesh into $^1/_2$-inch slices and stamp out the cores. Peel and core the apples, then cut into $^1/_2$-inch round slices. Peel the bananas and cut into $^3/_4$-inch diagonal slices. Heat plenty of oil in a large skillet. Dip the pieces of fruit in the batter and fry, a few at a time, until golden brown. Remove with a slotted spoon, drain on paper towels and keep warm. Dust with the confectioner's sugar and serve with the raspberry sauce.

FRITTELLE DI MELE

Serves 4

4 apples

scant $^1/_2$ cup rum

or juice of 1 lemon, strained

1 quantity Fruit

and Champagne Fritters batter (see above)

olive oil, for frying

confectioner's sugar, for dusting

APPLE FRITTERS

Peel and core the apples, then cut into fairly thick slices and sprinkle with the rum or lemon juice. Let stand for 15 minutes. Dip the apple slices in the batter, making sure they are evenly covered. Heat plenty of oil in a large skillet, add the apple slices, a few at a time, and fry until light golden brown. Remove with a slotted spoon, drain on paper towels and transfer to a warm serving dish. Dust with plenty of confectioner's sugar. Pineapple, peach, pear and other fruit fritters may be prepared in the same way.

DONUTS

Combine the yeast and superfine sugar in a bowl, add the milk and mash to a smooth paste. Stir in $^1/_2$ cup of the flour, knead well and shape into a miniature loaf, then let rise in a warm place for 20 minutes or until doubled in size. Sift the remaining flour onto a counter, place the miniature loaf in the center and add the butter, egg yolks and a pinch of salt. Knead thoroughly, then let rise in warm place for 1 hour. Roll out the dough on a lightly floured counter to about $^1/_4$ inch thick and stamp out 2-inch rounds with a plain cookie cutter or the rim of a glass. Put 1 tablespoon of preserve in the middle of half the rounds, brush the edges with a little milk and top with the remaining rounds, pressing down gently to seal. Let rise in a warm place for 30 minutes. Heat the oil in a deep pan, add the donuts, a few at a time, and cook until golden brown. Remove with a slotted spoon and drain on paper towels. Serve dusted with confectioner's sugar. You can also fill the donuts with Confectioner's Custard (see page 1039).

KRAPFEN

Makes 20

$^1/_2$ ounce fresh yeast

1 tablespoon superfine sugar

$^1/_2$ cup lukewarm milk, plus extra for brushing

$1^3/_4$ cups all-purpose flour, plus extra for dusting

$^1/_4$ cup sweet butter, melted

2 egg yolks

1 cup apricot preserve

sunflower or olive oil, for deep-frying

confectioner's sugar, for dusting

salt

FRITTERS

Sift the flour into a bowl, make a well in the center and add the superfine sugar, a pinch of salt, the butter and eggs. Knead lightly with your fingers to form a soft dough. Wrap in plastic wrap, flatten slightly with a rolling pin and let rest in the refrigerator for at least 12 hours. Roll out the dough on a lightly floured counter to a sheet about $1^1/_2$ inches thick. Stamp out shapes, such as stars, hearts or animals, with cookie cutters. Heat the oil in a deep pan. Add the fritters and cook for 5–6 minutes until puffed up and golden brown. Remove with a slotted spoon, drain on paper towels and dust with plenty of vanilla confectioner's sugar.

SGONFIOTTI

Serves 6

$2^1/_4$ cups all-purpose flour, plus extra for dusting

$^1/_2$ cup superfine sugar

$^1/_4$ cup sweet butter, softened

2 eggs, lightly beaten

sunflower or olive oil, for deep-frying

vanilla confectioner's sugar (see page 1003), for dusting

salt

ICE CREAMS AND SHERBETS

Homemade ice creams consist of a basic mixture of egg, milk, sugar and cream, combined with chocolate or other flavorings. Sherbets, on the other hand, are fat-free and based on syrup or fruit purée with additional sugar. As well as serving them as desserts, they make great palate cleansers between two savory courses. Both ice creams and sherbets are easy to make with an ice-cream maker, which allows the consistency of the mixture to be adjusted from firm and creamy to grainy. Ice creams and sherbets are wonderful with spirits such as whisky, vodka, rum and brandy, including fruit brandies. They also go with sweet liqueurs – coffee liqueur goes with creamy ice creams and orange liqueur with chocolate and vanilla ones.

FRUITS OF THE FOREST ICE CREAM

GELATO AI FRUTTI DI BOSCO

Serves 6

3½ cups berries, such as blackberries, loganberries and raspberries

juice of ½ lemon, strained

scant 1 cup superfine sugar

1 cup heavy cream

Put the berries into a food processor, add the lemon juice, sugar and cream and process until smooth. Pour the mixture into an ice-cream maker and freeze for about 20 minutes or according to the manufacturer's instructions.

MARRON GLACÉ ICE CREAM

GELATO AI MARRON GLACÉ

Serves 6

9 ounces marrons glacés

⅔ cup heavy cream

scant 1 cup milk

1 egg yolk

½ cup superfine sugar

liqueur of your choice

Put the marrons glacés, cream and milk in a food processor and process until combined. Beat the egg yolk with the sugar in a bowl until pale and fluffy, then stir in a dash of your choice of the liqueur and the marron glacé mixture. Pour into an ice-cream maker and freeze for about 20 minutes or according to the manufacturer's instructions.

COFFEE ICE CREAM

GELATO AL CAFFÈ

Serves 6

scant 1 cup milk

1 vanilla bean, halved

2 eggs

¾ cup superfine sugar

¾ cup extra strong coffee

scant 1 cup heavy cream

Pour the milk into a pan. Scrape the pulp from the vanilla bean into the milk and bring to a boil. Remove from the heat and let cool. Beat the eggs with the sugar in a bowl until pale and fluffy, then add the coffee, followed by the cream and vanilla milk. Mix well, then pour the mixture into an ice-cream maker and freeze for about 20 minutes or according to the manufacturer's instructions.

CARAMEL ICE CREAM

GELATO AL CARAMELLO

Serves 4

½ cup superfine sugar

3 egg yolks, lightly beaten

1½ cups heavy cream

Put the sugar in a pan with 1 tablespoon cold water and set over low heat until it has melted. Increase the heat to medium, skim and, when it goes golden red in color, pour in 5 tablespoons hot water and remove from the heat. Cover the pan and return to very low heat for about 20 minutes until a thick caramel has formed. Gradually whisk the caramel into the egg yolks in a bowl and continue whisking until the mixture is light, frothy and cool. Place the bowl in the freezer for 30 minutes. Stiffly whip the cream and fold it into the mixture. Pour into an ice-cream maker and freeze for about 20 minutes or according to the manufacturer's instructions.

CHOCOLATE ICE CREAM

GELATO AL CIOCCOLATO

Serves 6

3 cups milk

3½ ounces semisweet chocolate, broken into pieces

6 egg yolks

generous ½ cup superfine sugar

Bring the milk to a boil in a small pan, then remove from the heat. Place the chocolate and a few tablespoons of the milk in a heatproof bowl and melt the chocolate over a pan of barely simmering water. Pour the chocolate mixture into the hot milk. Beat the egg yolks with the sugar in a small pan until they are pale and fluffy, then gradually whisk in the chocolate mixture. Place the pan over low heat and cook, stirring constantly, until thickened. Make sure you do not let the mixture boil. Strain the mixture into a bowl and let cool, stirring occasionally. Pour into an ice-cream maker and freeze for about 20 minutes or according to the manufacturer's instructions.

VANILLA ICE CREAM

This is a basic recipe for several types of ice cream. Bring the milk to a boil in a small pan, remove from the heat and add the vanilla sugar. Beat the egg yolks with the superfine sugar in a pan until pale and fluffy. Set the pan over low heat and gradually beat in the hot milk. Do not let the mixture boil but continue beating until it is just thick enough to coat the back of the spoon. Remove from the heat, strain into a bowl and let cool, stirring occasionally. Pour into an ice-cream maker and freeze for about 20 minutes or according to the manufacturer's instructions.

GELATO DI CREMA ALLA VANIGLIA

Serves 6

3 cups milk

2 tablespoons vanilla sugar (see page 1003)

6 egg yolks

scant 1 cup superfine sugar

STRAWBERRY ICE CREAM

Set some whole strawberries aside for decoration and mash the remainder with a fork. Add the mashed strawberries to the ice cream, put the mixture in an ice-cream maker and freeze for about 20 minutes. Serve in individual dishes and decorate with the reserved whole strawberries. Peach, apricot and banana ice cream may be made in the same way.

GELATO DI FRAGOLE

Serves 6

$4^1/_2$ cups strawberries

1 quantity Vanilla Ice Cream (see above)

LEMON ICE CREAM

Beat together the lemon juice and sugar, using an electric mixer, then stir in the apple, milk and lemon syrup. Whip the cream in another bowl and very gently fold it into the mixture. Pour the mixture into an ice-cream maker and freeze for about 20 minutes or according to the manufacturer's instructions.

GELATO DI LIMONE

Serves 6

juice of 3 lemons, strained

$^3/_4$ cup superfine sugar

1 apple, peeled, cored and grated

$^1/_2$ cup milk • 2 tablespoons lemon syrup

scant 1 cup heavy cream

HAZELNUT ICE CREAM

Preheat the oven to 400°F. Spread out the hazelnuts on a cookie sheet and roast for 15–20 minutes. Tip the nuts onto a dish towel and rub off the skins, then chop finely and place in a bowl. Bring the milk to a boil and stir in the vanilla sugar. Mix a few tablespoons of the milk with the chopped hazelnuts, then stir in the remaining milk. Beat the egg yolks with the superfine sugar in a pan until pale and fluffy, then stir in the hazelnut mixture. Cook over medium heat, stirring constantly, until the mixture just comes to a boil. Remove from the heat and let cool, then pour the mixture into an ice-cream maker and freeze for about 20 minutes or according to the manu-facturer's instructions.

GELATO DI NOCCIOLE

Serves 6

scant 1 cup hazelnuts

3 cups milk

2 tablespoons vanilla sugar (see page 1003)

6 egg yolks

scant 1 cup superfine sugar

YOGURT ICE CREAM

GELATO DI YOGURT

Serves 4

2¼ cups natural yogurt • 2 tablespoons vanilla confectioner's sugar (see page 1003)

Pour the yogurt into an ice-cream maker and stir in the vanilla sugar. Freeze for about 20 minutes or according to the manufacturer's instructions.

RASPBERRY SEMIFREDDO

SEMIFREDDO AL LAMPONE

Serves 6–8

6 eggs

1¼ cups superfine sugar

1½ cups raspberries

3 cups heavy cream

Whisk the eggs with the sugar in a heatproof bowl set over a pan of barely simmering water until thickened, then remove from the heat and continue whisking the mixture until completely cool. Mash the raspberries in a shallow dish. Stiffly whip the cream and stir in the egg mixture and mashed raspberries. Line a rectangular loaf pan with plastic wrap, pour in the mixture and smooth the surface. Put in the freezer overnight or for at least 4 hours. To serve, turn out and remove the plastic wrap.

CREAM SEMIFREDDO

SEMIFREDDO ALLA PANNA

Serves 6

3 eggs, separated

2¼ cups heavy cream, chilled

¾ cup superfine sugar

7 ounces semisweet chocolate, chopped

Stiffly whisk the egg whites in a grease-free bowl. Stiffly whip the cream in another bowl. Beat the egg yolks with the sugar in a third bowl until pale and fluffy, then fold in the egg whites, followed by the whipped cream. Mix very gently. Line a mold with plastic wrap, sprinkle a layer of chocolate on the base and top with a layer of the cream mixture. Continue making alternate layers until all the ingredients are used. Chill in the freezer overnight. Turn out and remove the plastic wrap.

TORRONE SEMIFREDDO

SEMIFREDDO AL TORRONE

Serves 6

3 eggs, separated

¼ cup superfine sugar

11 ounces torrone (Italian nougat), chopped

2 tablespoons brandy

1½ cups heavy cream

Beat the egg yolks with the sugar until pale and fluffy, then stir in the torrone and brandy. Stiffly whisk the egg whites in a grease-free bowl. Stiffly whip the cream in another bowl. Gently fold the egg whites into the torrone mixture, followed by the cream. Line a mold with plastic wrap, pour in the mixture and place in the freezer overnight. Turn out the semifreddo 30 minutes before serving and remove the plastic wrap.

CREAM AND CHOCOLATE SEMIFREDDO

SEMIFREDDO DI CREMA DI CIOCCOLATO

Serves 6–8

3 eggs

1/2 cup superfine sugar

2 tablespoon all-purpose flour

1 cup milk

1/4 cup unsweetened cocoa powder

1 cup heavy cream

1 tablespoon vanilla sugar (see page 1003)

Make confectioner's custard (see page 1039) with the eggs, superfine sugar, flour and all but 3 tablespoons of the milk. Pour half the custard into a bowl and set aside. Stir the cocoa powder and remaining milk into the remaining custard and reheat for a few minutes, then pour into another bowl. When cold, chill both custards in the refrigerator. Stiffly whip the cream with the vanilla sugar and fold half into each custard. Line a mold with plastic wrap and pour in the first custard, followed by the second. Put in the freezer overnight. Turn out and remove the plastic wrap.

MARRON GLACÉ SEMIFREDDO

SEMIFREDDO DI MARRON GLACÉ

Serves 6–8

2 1/4 cups heavy cream

3 tablespoons superfine sugar

6 marrons glacés, chopped

5 ladyfingers, crumbled

1 teaspoon bitter cocoa powder

Hot Chocolate Sauce (see page 1017), to serve (optional)

Stiffly whip the cream with the sugar, then gently stir in the marrons glacés, lady fingers and cocoa. Line a mold with plastic wrap, pour in the mixture and smooth the surface. Put in the freezer overnight or for at least 4 hours. Turn out, remove the plastic wrap and serve with hot chocolate sauce, if you like.

KIWI SHERBET

SORBETTO AL KIWI

Serves 4

1 cup superfine sugar

4 kiwi fruits

juice of 1 lemon, strained

strawberries, to decorate

Pour 2 1/4 cups water into a pan, add the sugar and bring to a boil, stirring until the sugar has dissolved, then boil for about 15 minutes. Peel the kiwi fruits, place in a food processor and process to a purée. Combine the kiwi purée, syrup and lemon juice in a bowl, then pour the mixture into an ice-cream maker and freeze for about 20 minutes or according to the manufacturer's instructions. Serve decorated with strawberries.

SORBETTO ALLA BANANA

Serves 4

juice of 1 orange, strained

juice of 1 lemon, strained

³/₄ cup superfine sugar

2¹/₄ pounds bananas

BANANA SHERBET

Pour the orange and lemon juice into a pan, add the sugar and dissolve it over low heat, then remove the pan from the heat. Peel and coarsely chop the bananas, then place them in a food processor and process to a purée. Scrape the banana purée into the fruit juice and mix well. Pour the mixture into an ice-cream maker and freeze for about 20 minutes or according to the manufacturer's instructions.

SORBETTO AL LIMONE

Serves 6

3 lemons

1 cup superfine sugar

¹/₄ cup vodka

LEMON SHERBET

Thinly pare the rind of one of the lemons and squeeze the juice from all of them. Pour 2¹/₄ cups water into a pan, add the sugar and lemon rind and bring to a boil, stirring until the sugar has dissolved. Boil for 15 minutes, then remove from the heat. Remove and discard the lemon rind and let the syrup cool. Strain the lemon juice into the syrup and add the vodka. Pour into an ice-cream maker and freeze for about 20 minutes or according to the manufacturer's instructions.

OTHER
DESSERTS

Here are some desserts that do not fall neatly into any specific category. This section includes some very contemporary recipes together with other more traditional desserts.

BAKED CITRUS FRUIT WITH MINT

Preheat the oven to 400°F. Peel the oranges, grapefruit and lemons, removing all traces of pith, then cut each fruit into four, holding it over a bowl to catch the juice. Place the pieces of fruit in an ovenproof dish and reserve the juice. Beat the egg yolks with the sugar and vanilla in a pan, then beat in the reserved citrus juice. Cook over low heat, whisking constantly until thickened. Do not let the mixture boil. Remove the pan from the heat, stir in the chopped mint and pour the sauce over the fruit. Bake for 5–10 minutes until golden brown and heated through. Decorate with mint leaves and strips of lemon rind before serving.

GRATIN DI AGRUMI ALLA MENTA

Serves 4

4 oranges

4 grapefruit

4 lemons

3 egg yolks

1½ tablespoons superfine sugar

a few drops of vanilla extract

1 tablespoon chopped fresh mint

To decorate

fresh mint leaves

strips of lemon rind

GRATIN FRUITS OF THE FOREST WITH ZABAGLIONE

GRATIN DI FRUTTI DI BOSCO ALLO ZABAIONE

Serves 4

4¹/₂ cups mixed berries, such as strawberries, blackberries and blueberries

3 egg yolks

¹/₄ cup superfine sugar

2 tablespoons Grand Marnier

grated rind of ¹/₂ lemon

Preheat the broiler. Cut larger berries in half and place all the fruit in a flameproof dish or in individual ramekins. Beat together the egg yolks, sugar and Grand Marnier in a heatproof bowl. Set the bowl over a pan of barely simmering water and cook, whisking constantly, until the mixture has thickened. Do not let it boil. Remove from the heat and stir in the lemon rind. Pour the sauce over the fruit and cook under the broiler until golden brown. Serve hot, warm or cold.

CHOCOLATE MARQUISE

MARQUISE AL CIOCCOLATO

Serves 6

9 ounces semisweet chocolate, broken into pieces

2 tablespoons rum (optional)

scant 1 cup sweet butter, softened

5 eggs, separated

¹/₃ cup candied orange peel, chopped

scant ¹/₂ cup confectioner's sugar

Orange Sauce (see page 1018), to serve

Rinse out a mold with iced water and place in the refrigerator until required. Put the chocolate, and rum if using, in a heatproof bowl and melt over a pan of barely simmering water. Remove the bowl from the heat. Beat the butter with a wooden spoon until creamy, then add it to the melted chocolate. Beat well, then beat in the egg yolks, one at a time. Add the candied peel and sugar. Stiffly whisk the egg whites in a grease-free bowl, then gently fold into the chocolate mixture. Pour the mixture into the prepared mold and chill in the refrigerator for 24 hours. Turn out and serve with orange sauce.

PLUM MERINGUE

MERINGATA ALLE PRUGNE

Serves 6–8

11 ounces pitted plums

4 cups red wine

1 quantity Genoese Pastry, baked (see page 1010)

For the meringue

6 egg whites

2¹/₂ cups superfine sugar

juice of ¹/₂ lemon, strained

For the cream

1 cup milk

3 egg yolks

¹/₃ cup superfine sugar

generous ³/₄ cup sweet butter, softened

Preheat the oven to 225°F. Line a cookie sheet with baking parchment. First, make the meringue. Stiffly whisk the egg whites with the sugar and lemon juice in a grease-free bowl. Spoon or pipe the meringue into thin strips on the prepared cookie sheet and bake for 1¹/₂ hours. Remove from the oven. Meanwhile, place the plums in a pan, add the wine and bring to a boil, then lower the heat and simmer for about 20 minutes. Drain the plums, reserving the cooking liquid, and let cool, then chop. To prepare the cream, pour the milk into a small pan and bring to just below boiling point, then remove from the heat. Beat the egg yolks and sugar in another small pan until thick and frothy, then gradually add the hot milk. Cook over low heat, stirring constantly, until thick enough to coat the back of the spoon. Remove from the heat and let cool slightly, then stir in the butter. Let cool completely, then stir in the plums. Place the Genoese pastry on the base of a serving dish and sprinkle with the reserved cooking liquid. Pour half the cream on top and sprinkle with half the meringue strips. Top with the remaining cream. Crumble the remaining meringue and sprinkle them over the dessert.

GRAPE MERINGUE PIE

Crush half the grapes and strain the juice. Place the Genoese pastry on the base of a serving dish and sprinkle with the grape juice. Stiffly whip the cream and spread half of it over the dough base. Crumble the meringue. Reserve some of the meringue and a few grapes for decoration and sprinkle the remaining grapes and meringue over the cream. Cover with the remaining cream and decorate with the reserved meringue and grapes.

MERINGATA ALL'UVA

Serves 6

1 pound 5 ounces white grapes

1 quantity Genoese pastry, baked (see page 1010)

1³/₄ cups heavy cream

1 quantity Meringue (see Plum Meringue, opposite)

MONTEBIANCO

Tie the fennel seeds in a small square of cheesecloth. Bring a pan of lightly salted water to a boil, add the chestnuts and fennel seeds and simmer for about 40 minutes. Drain and peel the chestnuts, then place them in a pan, pour in the milk and simmer, mashing with a wooden spoon, for 15 minutes. If necessary, add a little more warm milk. As the mixture is just beginning to thicken, stir in the sugar and remove from the heat. Sprinkle in the rum and cocoa and mix well. Pass the mixture through a food mill onto a serving dish to create a cone of 'chestnut vermicelli'. Decorate with rosettes of whipped cream and candied violets.

MONTE BIANCO

Serves 6

pinch of fennel seeds

1³/₄ pounds chestnuts, shelled

³/₄ cup milk

¹/₄ cup superfine sugar • ¹/₄ cup rum

2 tablespoons unsweetened cocoa powder • salt

To decorate

1 quantity Whipped Cream

candied violets

CHOCOLATE PROFITEROLES

Preheat the oven to 375°F. Grease a cookie sheet with butter and dust with flour. Pour the milk and 5 tablespoons water into a small pan, add the butter and bring to a boil over low heat. Remove the pan from the heat, tip in the flour all at once and stir well. Return the pan to the heat and cook, stirring constantly until the mixture comes away from the base and sides. Remove from the heat and let cool, then beat in the eggs one at a time. Do not add the second egg until the first has been fully absorbed. Spoon the mixture into a pastry bag and pipe 16 mounds onto the prepared cookie sheet, spaced well apart. Bake for 15 minutes until the mounds are puffed up and golden brown. Transfer to a wire rack to cool. Meanwhile, prepare the topping. Melt the chocolate with 1 tablespoon water in a small pan over low heat. Stir in the butter and sugar and cook until thickened. Remove from the heat and let cool. Make a slit in the side of the puffs and fill them with the whipped cream. Arrange the puffs in a pyramid on a serving dish and pour the chocolate topping over them.

PROFITEROLES AL CIOCCOLATO

Serves 4–6

¹/₄ cup sweet butter, softened,

plus extra for greasing

scant ²/₃ cup all-purpose flour, plus extra for dusting

6 tablespoons milk

2 eggs

scant 1 cup heavy cream, whipped

For the topping

3¹/₂ ounces semisweet chocolate, broken into pieces

2 tablespoons sweet butter

¹/₄ cup superfine sugar

SEMOLINA WITH CHERRIES

SEMOLINO ALLE CILIEGE

Serves 6

sweet butter, for greasing
1 cup sweet white wine
²/₃ cup semolina
2 eggs
generous ¹/₂ cup superfine sugar
3 cups cherries, pitted
¹/₂ cup blanched almonds, chopped
1 egg white

Preheat the oven to 400°F. Grease a mold with butter. Pour the wine and 2¹/₄ cups water into a pan and bring to a boil. Sprinkle in the semolina and cook, stirring constantly, for 15 minutes. Remove the pan from the heat and let cool slightly. Stir in the eggs, one at a time, then stir in the sugar, cherries and almonds. Stiffly whisk the egg white in a grease-free bowl and fold into the semolina mixture. Pour the mixture into the prepared mold and place it in a roasting pan. Add boiling water to come about halfway up the sides and bake for 45 minutes. Remove from the oven and let cool to room temperature before turning out.

TIRAMISU

TIRAMI SU

Serves 6

2 egg whites • 4 egg yolks
1¹/₄ cups confectioner's sugar
1³/₄ cups mascarpone cheese
7 ounces ladyfingers
³/₄ cup freshly brewed extra strong coffee, cooled
7 ounces semisweet chocolate, grated
unsweetened cocoa powder, for dusting

Stiffly whisk the egg whites in a grease-free bowl. Beat the egg yolks with the sugar in another bowl until pale and fluffy. Gently fold in the mascarpone, then the egg whites. Make a layer of ladyfingers on the base of a deep, rectangular serving dish and brush them evenly with coffee. Cover with a layer of the mascarpone cream and sprinkle with a little grated chocolate. Continue making layers until all the ingredients are used, ending with a layer of mascarpone cream. Dust with cocoa and chill in the refrigerator for about 3 hours.

ZUCCOTTO

ZUCCOTTO

Serves 4–6

5 ounces ladyfingers
²/₃ cup Grand Marnier
1¹/₂ cups heavy cream
²/₃ cup unsweetened cocoa powder
2 tablespoons confectioner's sugar
3¹/₂ ounces semisweet chocolate, chopped
10 blanched almonds, chopped

You will need a hemispherical zuccotto mold for an authentic version of this dessert, but you can adapt the recipe for other shapes. Line the mold with some of the ladyfingers and sprinkle with a little Grand Marnier. Stiffly whip the cream and divide it between two bowls. Sift together the cocoa and sugar into one bowl of cream. Add the chocolate and almonds to the other bowl of cream. Spoon or pour the cocoa cream onto the base of the lined mold, then tap firmly on a counter to remove any pockets of air. Cover the cocoa cream with a layer of ladyfingers and sprinkle them evenly with Grand Marnier. Spoon or pour the almond cream on top and cover with the remaining ladyfingers. Sprinkle with the remaining Grand Marnier. Chill in the refrigerator for about 4 hours, then turn out onto a serving dish. If you prefer frozen zuccotto, put the mold in the freezer for 3–4 hours.

ZUPPA INGLESE

Serves 6

1 quantity Confectioner's Custard (see page 1039)

1 tablespoon cochineal

2 tablespoons rum

9 ounces sponge cake, sliced

To decorate

scant ¹/₂ cup heavy cream

mixed candied fruit

chocolate chips or fresh berries

ITALIAN TRIFLE

Reserve 1 cup of the confectioner's custard. Mix the cochineal with 1 tablespoon water in a shallow dish. Mix the rum with 1 tablespoon water in another shallow dish. Arrange a layer of sponge cake on the base of a broad glass dish, sprinkle with the cochineal mixture and pour on a layer of confectioner's custard. Make another layer of sponge cake, sprinkle with the rum and pour on another layer of confectioner's custard. Continue making alternating layers, ending with a layer of sponge cake. Chill in the refrigerator for 1 hour. Remove the bowl from the refrigerator and let stand for about 10 minutes. Meanwhile, stiffly whip the cream. Spread the reserved confectioner's custard on top of the last layer of sponge cake. Fill a pastry bag fitted with a star tip with the whipped cream and use to decorate the trifle, then add candied fruit and chocolate chips or fresh berries.

JELLIES
AND PRESERVES

Jellies and preserves are slightly different and made in slightly different ways. Raspberries, strawberries, apricots, apples and red currants are the best fruits for preparing delicate transparent jellies, while a wider variety of fruits may be used for preserves. Preparation is based on a few simple rules. The fruit should be ripe, in prime condition, well washed, and peeled and seeded. The quantity of sugar depends on the tartness of the fruit. As a general guide, the sharpest fruits require an equal weight in sugar, whereas sweeter ones need less. The fruit should not be cooked for too long as this may destroy the flavor or even leave a slightly burnt taste. It should not, however, be cooked too briefly either, or harmful fermentation may arise. To test for the setting point, remove the pan from the heat and put a teaspoon of jam on a cold saucer. Cool quickly, then push with your finger. If the surface wrinkles, the jam is ready.

---

strawberries

sugar

(See introduction for advice on quantities)

STRAWBERRY JELLY

Hull the strawberries, place them in a pan and cook over low heat, without adding any liquid and stirring constantly, for 8 minutes. Place a large strainer, or suspend a jelly bag, over a bowl, pour in the strawberries and let drain. If you want clear jelly, let drip without pressing or squeezing the fruit. When all the juice has collected, measure it and add the same quantity of sugar. Pour the juice into a pan and bring to a boil over medium heat, stirring constantly. When the juice comes to a boil, stop stirring, skim and cook for exactly 3 more minutes. Remove from the heat and let cool slightly, then ladle the warm jelly into warm, sterilized glass jars and let cool. Seal the jars and store in a cool, dry place.

QUINCE JELLY

Thinly slice the quinces, place them in a pan and add water to cover. Cook over medium heat until almost mushy. Place a large strainer, or suspend a jelly bag, over a bowl, pour in the quinces and let drain. If you want clear jelly, let drip without pressing or squeezing the fruit. When all the juice has collected, measure it and add the same quantity of sugar. Pour the juice into a pan and cook, stirring occasionally, until the jelly comes away from the spoon and falls in large drops. Add lemon juice to taste according to the quantity of jelly. Ladle into warm, sterilized glass jars while still hot, let cool and then seal. Store in a cool, dry place.

GELATINA DI MELE COTOGNE

quinces, unpeeled

sugar

freshly squeezed lemon juice, strained

(See introduction for advice on quantities)

RED CURRANT JELLY

Put the red currants in a pan and add water to cover. Cook over medium heat, stirring constantly, for about 8 minutes. Place a large strainer, or suspend a jelly bag, over a bowl, pour in the red currants and let drain. If you want clear jelly, let drip without pressing or squeezing the fruit. When all the juice has collected, measure it and add the same quantity of sugar. Pour the mixture into a pan and bring to a boil over low heat, stirring constantly. Do not stop stirring, skim carefully and cook for exactly 3 more minutes. Ladle the jelly into warm, sterilized glass jars and let cool. Seal and store in a cool, dry place.

GELATINA DI RIBES

red currants

sugar

(See introduction for advice on quantities)

GRAPE JELLY

Crush the grapes and strain the juice. Measure the juice and pour it into a pan. Add 1 1/3 cups sugar for every 4 cups juice. Bring the juice to a boil, stirring until the sugar has dissolved and skimming if necessary. Boil until reduced by about one-third. Remove from the heat and let cool slightly, then ladle into warm, sterilized glass jars. When cool, seal tightly and store in a cool, dry place.

GELATINA D'UVA

white grapes

sugar

(See introduction for advice on quantities)

MARMELLATA D'ALBICOCCHE

4 cups sugar

4½ pounds apricots, halved and pitted

APRICOT PRESERVE

Pour 2¼ cups water into a pan, add the sugar and bring to a boil over low heat, stirring constantly, then simmer for about 10 minutes. Add the apricots and cook, stirring and skimming occasionally, for about 2½ hours until the preserve reaches setting point. Ladle into warm, sterilized glass jars while still hot, let cool and seal tightly.

MARMELLATA D'ARANCE

4½ pounds oranges

sugar

(See introduction for advice on quantities)

ORANGE MARMALADE

Prick the oranges all over with a fork and place them in a large bowl. Add water to cover and let soak for 12 hours. Drain, dry and peel the oranges, reserving the rind from three of them. Using a small, sharp knife, remove all traces of white pith from the reserved rind and cut the rind into extremely thin strips. Bring a small pan of water to a boil, add the strips of orange rind and cook for 3–4 minutes, then drain. Weigh the peeled oranges, slice thinly and remove the seeds. Put the slices in a pan with an equal weight of sugar (2 cups sugar for each pound of oranges). Bring to a boil over medium heat and simmer gently, without adding any water, stirring frequently for about 1 hour or until the sugar starts to form threads. Add the strips of orange rind and cook, stirring constantly, for 2–3 minutes. Ladle the marmalade into warm, sterilized glass jars while still hot. Let cool and then seal tightly. Store in a cool, dry place.

MARMELLATA DI CASTAGNE

4½ pounds chestnuts, shelled

1 teaspoon sea salt

4½ cups sugar

scant 1 cup rum

CHESTNUT PRESERVE

Put the chestnuts in a pan and add the salt and enough water to cover. Cover and cook over medium heat for about 45 minutes. Drain, remove the skins and press through a strainer into a clean pan. Add the sugar and 1 cup water and cook over medium heat, stirring constantly, for about 40 minutes. About 10 minutes before removing the pan from the heat, add the rum and stir carefully. Ladle into warm, sterilized glass jars, let cool and seal tightly. This preserve should be thick and dry.

CHERRY PRESERVE

Place the cherries in a pan, add the sugar and let stand in a cool place for 3 hours. Sprinkle the cherries with the lemon juice and cook over medium heat, stirring occasionally, for about 1¹/₂ hours until the preserve is of an even consistency. Ladle into warm, sterilized glass jars while still hot and let cool, then seal tightly.

MARMELLATA DI CILIEGE

12 cups black cherries, pitted
4¹/₂ cups sugar
juice of 1 lemon, strained

FIG PRESERVE

Pour 2¹/₄ cups water into a pan, add the sugar and bring to a boil, stirring until the sugar has dissolved. Add the figs and cinnamon and cook the mixture over medium heat, stirring occasionally until the preserve thickens. Ladle into warm, sterilized glass jars while the preserve still hot, let cool then seal tightly.

MARMELLATA DI FICHI

2¹/₄ cups sugar
2¹/₄ pounds figs, peeled and chopped
pinch of ground cinnamon

STRAWBERRY PRESERVE

Hull the strawberries and place in a heavy pan. Add the sugar and bring to a boil over medium heat, stirring constantly. When the mixture starts to boil, gradually increase the heat and cook, stirring constantly, for 20–25 minutes. Ladle the preserve into warm, sterilized glass jars while still hot and let cool then seal and store in a cool, dry place.

MARMELLATA DI FRAGOLE

9 cups strawberries
4¹/₂ cups sugar

BERRY PRESERVE

Place the berries in a pan, add the sugar and cook over medium heat, without any additional liquid and stirring constantly, for 30 minutes. Remove the pan from the heat, let cool slightly, then ladle into warm, sterilized glass jars. When cool, seal the jars and store in a cool, dry place.

MARMELLATA DI FRUTTI DI BOSCO

9 cups mixed berries, such as raspberries, strawberries, blackberries, blueberries and red currants
2¹/₄ cups sugar

MARMELLATA DI KIWI

4¹/₂ pounds kiwi fruit, peeled and chopped

9 cups sugar

KIWI PRESERVE

Place the kiwis in a pan, add the sugar and cook over medium heat, stirring constantly, for 30 minutes. Ladle the preserve into warm, sterilized glass jars while still hot. When cool, seal the jars and store in a cool, dry place.

MARMELLATA DI MELE

4¹/₂ pounds apples, peeled and cored

juice of 2 lemons, strained

4¹/₂ cups sugar

APPLE PRESERVE

Brush the apples with the lemon juice to stop them from turning brown. Grate the apples into a pan, add the sugar and 4 tablespoons water and cook over low heat, stirring constantly, for 2¹/₂ hours. Ladle the preserve into warm, sterilized glass jars, let cool, then seal. Store in a cool, dry place. If you use russet apples, peel and thinly slice them, place them in a pan, add just enough water to cover and cook over very low heat. Pass through a food mill, then measure them and add an equal quantity of sugar. Return the mixture to the pan and cook until it reaches setting point.

MARMELLATA DI PERE

4¹/₂ pounds pears, peeled, cored and chopped

4¹/₂ cups sugar

juice of 1 lemon, strained

PEAR PRESERVE

Put the pears, sugar and lemon juice in a pan and cook over low heat, stirring constantly, for 1 hour. Ladle the preserve into warm, sterilized glass jars and let cool, then seal tightly. Store in a cool, dry place.

MARMELLATA DI PESCHE

4¹/₂ pounds peaches, peeled, halved and pitted

3¹/₂ cups sugar

PEACH PRESERVE

Slice the peach halves thinly and place in a pan. If the peaches are very ripe and juicy, it is not necessary to add water, otherwise add 5 tablespoons water. Cook over low heat until the peaches start to become mushy, then add the sugar and cook, stirring occasionally, for about 2¹/₂ hours. Ladle the preserve into warm, sterilized glass jars and let cool, then seal tightly. Store in a cool, dry place.

GREEN TOMATO PRESERVE

Put the tomatoes in a bowl and add the sugar, lemon juice and rind and a pinch of salt. Cover and let stand for a few hours. Pour the mixture into a pan and cook over medium heat until it reaches setting point. Ladle into warm, sterilized glass jars while still hot and let cool, then seal tightly. Store in a cool, dry place.

MARMELLATA DI POMODORI VERDI

2¼ pounds green tomatoes, chopped

1¾ cups sugar

juice and grated rind of ½ lemon

salt

PLUM PRESERVE

Put the plums in a pan, add the sugar and cook, stirring occasionally, for 35 minutes. Remove from the heat and let the preserve cool, then carefully ladle into warm, sterilized glass jars and seal. Store in a cool, dark place.

MARMELLATA DI PRUGNE

2¼ pounds plums, halved and pitted

2¼ cups sugar

RHUBARB PRESERVE

Put the rhubarb in a bowl, add the sugar, cover and let stand for 2 hours. Pour the mixture into a pan, bring to a boil and cook, stirring constantly, for about 30 minutes. To decide whether if it is done, pour a little of the mixture onto a small plate. If it slides slowly, when tilted the preserve is almost ready. Stir in the orange rind and cook for 5 minutes more. Ladle the preserve into warm, sterilized glass jars and let cool, then seal. Store in a cool, dry place.

MARMELLATA DI RABARBARO

4½ pounds rhubarb, trimmed and chopped

4½ cups sugar

grated rind of 1 orange

GRAPE PRESERVE

Any type of grapes may be used. Put the grapes in a pan and crush. Remove all the seeds but leave the skins. Add the sugar and cook over low heat, stirring occasionally, until the mixture reaches setting point. Ladle the preserve into warm, sterilized glass jars and seal tightly. Store in a cool, dry place.

MARMELLATA D'UVA

4½ pounds grapes

4½ cups sugar

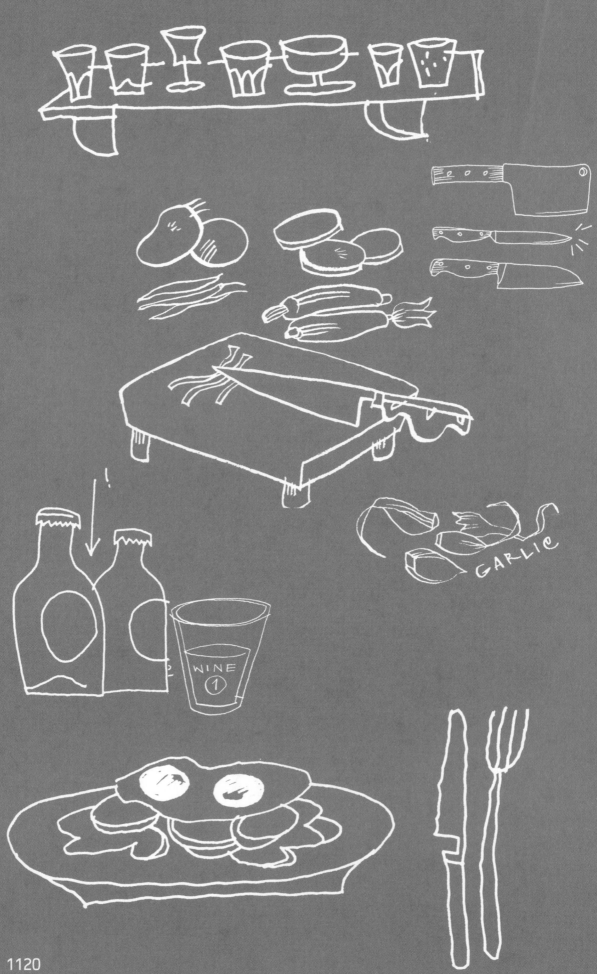

GARLIC

WINE
①

MENUS BY CELEBRATED CHEFS →

THE MENUS

Pulling together a menu requires equal amounts of skill and imagination. *The Silver Spoon* rounds off its presentation of over 2,000 recipes with a set of truly exquisite menus supplied by some of the best-known Italian chefs of the past fifty years.

Italian cuisine is revered throughout the world and, for this new English-language edition we have included a number of international chefs who are truly worldwide ambassadors of fine Italian cuisine. Though they may not be working in Italy (and, in fact, some of them were not even born there), each is playing their part in keeping the standard of Italian cuisine at the level of excellence now acknowledged throughout the world.

This section includes signature dishes from some of the most highly respected chefs in the world, be they Italian born or American, living in the center of Rome or the heart of Sydney. The list below illustrates not only the immense regard in which we hold Italian cuisine, but also its universal appeal.

The Silver Spoon Guest Chefs:

Aimo & Nadia	Italy
Lidia Bastianich	United States
Mario Batali	United States
Nino Bergese	Italy
Gianfranco Bolognesi	Italy
Carlo Brovelli	Italy
Arrigo Cipriani	Italy
Franco Colombani	Italy
Enzo Deprà	Italy
Maria Pia de Razza-Klein	New Zealand
Alfonso e Livia Jaccarino	Italy
Giorgio Locatelli	United Kingdom
Stefano Manfredi	Australia
Gualtiero Marchesi	Italy
Karen Martini	Australia
Gianluigi Morini	Italy
Fulvio Pierangelini	Italy
Stefano de Pieri	Australia
Ruth Rogers and Rose Gray	United Kingdom
Ezio Santin	Italy
Nadia Santini	Italy
Gianfranco Vissani	Italy
Aldo Zilli	United Kingdom

Aimo & Nadia

This is a perfect husband and wife partnership in the kitchen as well as in real life. Aimo knows the secrets of every type of meat, vegetable or other ingredient, while Nadia transforms Aimo's daily shopping trip into recipes. Having moved to Milan in 1946, Aimo started his long and splendid career as a kitchen help and quickly worked his way up, moving to manage his own restaurant in 1955. He has never forgotten the lessons learned from his mother (an excellent cook in private homes who spent seven years in France) and her recipes, which he has perfected with flair and skill. He is a keen researcher of raw ingredients, which are always strictly Italian and strictly seasonal, enhanced by the extra virgin olive oil that underlines the simplicity of all dishes by Aimo and Nadia. In their elegant Milan restaurant these two Tuscan nomads (they met when very young and have been married for over 40 years) test and test again, approve and change when change is needed. Chefs and custodians of Italian traditions, yet aware of modern ideas, Aimo and Nadia have strong principles – fast cooking, no cream, very little butter, a lot of olive oil as dressing and an abundance of vegetables and aromatic herbs. Typical dishes from their restaurant include cream of cannellini beans with black borlotti beans, fresh anchovies with a ricotta filling, spaghetti with scallions and red chile, warm Italian bacon with a purée of spinach, warm ricotta with radicchio, Norcia lamb with fresh ginger and frozen honey mousse.

Il Luogo di Aimo e Nadia
Via Montecuccoli 6
Milan
Italy

MENUS

ZUPPETTA DI MARE CON LENTICCHIE

SPAGHETTI AL CIPOLLOTTO E PEPERONCINO

CAPPELLO DI VITELLO SANATO ALL'UVA FRAGOLA

CROSTATA DI FARINA DI CASTAGNE FARCITA CON PERE

SEAFOOD STEW WITH LENTILS

ZUPPETTA DI MARE CON LENTICCHIE

Serves 4

3 tablespoons olive oil, plus extra for drizzling
1 celery stalk, chopped
1 carrot, chopped
1 onion, chopped
1/2 cup cooked lentils
9 ounces fish and seafood, such as sea bass fillets, prepared squid, peeled shrimp, peeled langoustines and scrubbed clams
1 1/4 cups Fish Stock (see page 208–9)
1 tomato, chopped
1 fresh flat-leaf parsley sprig, chopped
1 fresh basil sprig, chopped
salt and pepper

Heat 1 tablespoon of the olive oil in a skillet, add 1 tablespoon each of the celery, carrot and onion and cook over low heat, stirring occasionally, for 5 minutes. Stir in the lentils and cook for a few minutes more. Heat the remaining olive oil in a shallow pan, add the remaining celery, carrot and onion and cook over low heat, stirring occasionally, for 5 minutes. Add the sea bass and the squid, increase the heat to high and cook for 1 minute, then add the shrimp, langoustines, clams and lentil mixture. Pour in the stock, season with salt and pepper and cook until the fish is tender. Just before removing the pan from the heat, add the tomato, parsley and basil. Serve with a drizzle of olive oil.

SPAGHETTI WITH SCALLIONS AND RED CHILE

SPAGHETTI AL CIPOLLOTTO E PEPERONCINO

Serves 4

3 tablespoons olive oil, plus extra for drizzling
2 bay leaves
5 fresh thyme leaves
5 fresh oregano leaves
3 garlic cloves, chopped
6 cups scallions, white part only, cut into thin strips
3 1/2 ounces tomatoes, peeled, seeded and diced
1/2 tablespoon chopped fresh red chile
3/4 cup Vegetable Stock (see page 209)
11 ounces spaghetti
5 fresh basil leaves, shredded
salt

Heat the oil in a shallow pan with the bay leaves, thyme and oregano over low heat, add the garlic and scallions and cook for 15–20 minutes until the scallions are reduced in volume to about 60 per cent. Add the tomatoes and chile to the pan and cook for about 5 minutes, gradually adding the stock. Cook the pasta in a large pan of salted, boiling water for 8–10 minutes until al dente, then drain. Tip it into the sauce and toss over high heat for 1 minute. Garnish with the basil, drizzle with a little olive oil and serve.

SHOULDER OF VEAL WITH UVA FRAGOLA

Place the grapes in a pan, add ²/₃ cup of the stock and cook over medium heat for 15 minutes, then strain the liquid into a bowl. Put the celery, carrot, onion and shallot into a shallow pan. Season the veal with salt and pepper and add it to the pan with the pork fat or bacon, bouquet garni, cloves, garlic and olive oil. Cook over medium-high heat until the meat is browned all over, then lower the heat to medium and cook for 45 minutes, basting with the remaining stock. Pour in the grape juice and cook for a further 45 minutes, adding a little more stock if necessary. Lift the meat out of the pan and remove and discard the cloves, bouquet garni and pork fat or bacon. Strain the cooking juices into a pitcher and season with salt and pepper. Slice the meat, place it on a warm serving dish and pour the sauce over it. Serve with a purée of potatoes.

CAPPELLO DI VITELLO SANATO ALL'UVA FRAGOLA

Serves 4

7 ounces uva fragola

(strawberry-flavored grapes)

3 cups Meat Stock (see page 208)

¹/₂ celery stalk, chopped

¹/₂ carrot, chopped

¹/₂ onion, chopped

1 shallot, chopped

2¹/₄-pound shoulder of veal

1¹/₂ ounces pork fat or fatty bacon

1 bouquet garni

2 cloves

1 garlic clove

5 tablespoons olive oil

salt and pepper

puréed potatoes, to serve

CHESTNUT FLOUR PIE WITH PEARS

Sift together both types of flour into a mound and make a well in the center. Add the egg, 4 tablespoons of the sugar and the butter. Knead to make a smooth dough, then wrap and let rest in the refrigerator for 30 minutes. Chop 2 ounces of the pears, place in a pan with the remaining sugar and cook over medium heat for 30 minutes. Transfer the cooked pears to a food processor and process to a purée. Preheat the oven to 350°F. Cut off two-thirds of the dough and roll out on a lightly floured surface, then use to line a cake pan. Slice the remaining pears. Pour the confectioner's custard into the pastry case and top with the remaining pears. Spoon the melted chocolate over them. Roll out the remaining pastry and use to cover the pie, sealing and trimming the edges. Bake for 30 minutes.

CROSTATA DI FARINA DI CASTAGNE FARCITA CON PERE

Serves 4

¹/₂ cup all-purpose flour, plus extra for dusting

²/₃ cup chestnut flour

1 egg

¹/₃ cup superfine sugar

¹/₃ cup sweet butter

3¹/₂ ounces pears, peeled and cored

6 tablespoons Confectioner's Custard (see page 1039)

2 ounces semisweet or

bittersweet chocolate, melted

Lidia Bastianich

Felidia
243 East 58th Street
New York
United States of America

For Lidia Bastianich, every meal is a celebration. The genesis of this love for food, and the desire to share it, was her early childhood by the Adriatic Sea in the Istrian town of Pula. Her grandparents operated a trattoria, cultivating the produce that they ate and served. She has fond memories of distilling grappa and making wine, harvesting olives for olive oil, and curing meats such as prosciutto and pancetta. With her grandmother she would visit the communal mill to grind wheat for bread and pasta. In 1959 Lidia Bastianich and her family embarked on new lives in the United States of America. She mastered baking and cake decorating as a teenager working part time in a bakery, but soon opened her first restaurant where she refined further dishes. Other restaurant businesses followed. In 1981 her flagship, the award-winning Felidia, was launched, housed in an elegantly appointed brownstone building on the Upper East Side of Manhattan. Felidia clearly established Lidia Bastianich as a leader in the development of Italian cuisine: fine cooking with the freshest of ingredients; pure unaffected flavors; and provincial delicacies with an innovative touch. It is the culinary heritage and regional fare of her native soil, especially Friuli-Venezia-Giulia in northern Italy, that Lidia Bastianich interprets in her restaurants, on television and in print. She is renowned for the warmth and passion she brings to all her culinary endeavours and for encouraging families to cook and dine together. Lidia Bastianich's formative affinity with the yield of the land engendered her profound respect for seasonal ingredients and has delivered ongoing popular and critical acclaim.

MENUS

GAMBERI 'STILE SCAMPI'

ZITE CON SALSICCIA, CIPOLLE E FINOCCCHIO

POLLO E PATATE DI NONNA ERMINIA

CROSTATA DI CIOCCOLATO, NOCCIOLE E ARANCIA

SHRIMP IN THE SCAMPI STYLE

Heat the olive oil in a small skillet over medium heat. Add the garlic and cook for about 1 minute until pale golden. Stir in the shallots, season generously with salt and pepper and cook, shaking the skillet, for about 2 minutes until the shallots are wilted. Add half the wine, bring to a boil and cook until about half of the liquid has evaporated. Stir in 1 tablespoon of the lemon juice and cook until almost all the liquid has evaporated. Transfer the mixture to a small bowl and let cool completely. Add the butter, parsley and tarragon and beat until blended. Spoon the flavored butter onto a 12-inch length of plastic wrap and roll it into a log shape, wrapping it up completely. Chill in the refrigerator. (The flavored butter can be made several hours or up to a few days in advance.) Preheat the oven to 475°F. Peel the shrimp, leaving the tail and last shell segment intact, and devein them. Place the shrimp flat on a counter and, starting at the thick end, make a horizontal cut along the center of the shrimp extending about three-fourths of the way through. Pat the shrimp dry. Using some of the flavored butter, lightly grease a shallow baking pan, such as a jelly roll pan, or ovenproof sauté pan into which the shrimp will fit comfortably without touching. Place each shrimp on the counter with the underside of the tail facing away from you. With your fingers, roll each half of the slit part of the shrimp in towards and underneath the tail, forming a number 6-shape on each side of the shrimp and lifting the tail up. Arrange the shrimp, tails upwards, in the prepared pan as you work, leaving a space between them. Cut the remaining flavored butter into 1½-inch cubes and scatter them among the shrimp. Combine the remaining wine and lemon juice and add to the pan. Sprinkle the thyme sprigs over and around the shrimp, season with salt and pepper and roast for about 5 minutes until the shrimp are firm, crunchy and barely opaque in the center. Transfer the shrimp to a hot serving dish or divide among hot plates. Drain the cooking juices into a small pan. Bring to a boil over high heat and boil for 1–2 minutes until the sauce is slightly thickened. Spoon or strain the sauce over the shrimp and serve.

GAMBERI 'STILE SCAMPI'

Serves 6

2 tablespoons extra virgin olive oil

3 large garlic cloves, crushed

2 tablespoons finely chopped shallots

½ cup dry white wine

2 tablespoons freshly squeezed lemon juice, strained

½ cup sweet butter, at room temperature

2 teaspoons finely chopped fresh flat-leaf parsley

2 teaspoons finely chopped fresh tarragon

36 unpeeled raw jumbo shrimp (about 3½ pounds)

6–8 fresh thyme sprigs

salt and pepper

ZITE WITH SAUSAGE, ONIONS AND FENNEL

ZITE CON SALSICCIA, CIPOLLE E FINOCCHIO

Serves 6

1 tablespoon sea salt

1 pound sweet Italian sausage (without fennel seeds)

1 large fennel bulb with stem and fronds (about 1 pound), trimmed and halved lengthwise

5 tablespoons extra virgin olive oil

2 onions, halved and sliced

$1/2$ teaspoon salt

$1/2$ teaspoon chile flakes

$1/2$ cup tomato paste

1 pound zite (long tubes of dried pasta)

fennel fronds

1 cup romano, Parmesan or grana padano cheese, freshly grated

Bring a large pan of water with the salt to boiling point. Meanwhile, remove the sausage from its casing and break the meat up with your fingers. Slice the fennel halves lengthwise into $1/4$-inch thick slices. Separate the slivers of fennel if they are attached at the base and cut into 2-inch long batons. Heat the olive oil in a skillet over medium-high heat, add the sausage meat and cook, stirring and breaking it up with a wooden spoon, for about 1–$1^{1}/_{2}$ minutes until it is sizzling and beginning to brown. Push the sausage to one side, add the onion slices and cook, stirring constantly, for about 2 minutes until they are sizzling and wilting, then stir them in with the meat. Push the mixture to one side, add the fennel batons and cook for about 1 minute until wilted, then stir into the sausage and onion mixture. Sprinkle in half the salt and push to one side again. Add the chile flakes and toast for 30 seconds, then stir them in. Move the mixture to the sides of the pan, add the tomato paste and cook, stirring constantly, for 1–2 minutes until it is sizzling and caramelizing, then stir it into the sausage mixture. Ladle 3 cups of the salted, boiling water into the skillet, stir well and bring the liquid to a boil. Lower the heat and simmer for about 6 minutes until the fennel is soft but not mushy. Meanwhile, add the pasta to the pan of boiling water, stir and bring back to a boil, then cook for about 8 minutes until almost al dente. Check the sauce which should not become too thick – if necessary, stir in another 1 cup of the boiling pasta water. When the sauce is done, adjust the seasoning if necessary. When the pasta is al dente, lift it out of the pan with a spider (pasta spoon) or slotted spoon, drain briefly and add to the simmering sauce. Toss the pasta with the sauce, adding more pasta cooking water if the sauce seems too thick. Sprinkle with the fennel fronds and cook, tossing constantly, for 2 minutes until the pasta is perfectly al dente and coated with the sauce. Remove the skillet from the heat, sprinkle the grated cheese over the pasta and toss to combine. Transfer to warm pasta bowls and serve.

ERMINIA'S CHICKEN AND POTATOES

Trim off excess skin and all visible fat from the chicken and cut the drumsticks from the thighs. If using breast halves, cut into two small pieces. Halve the bacon slices crosswise, roll each strip into a neat, tight cylinder and secure with a toothpick, cutting off the end so only a small piece protrudes. Pour the canola oil into a skillet and set over high heat. Sprinkle the chicken with $1/4$ teaspoon salt on all sides. When the oil is very hot, add the chicken pieces skin side down, about 1 inch apart. Cook for several minutes to brown the underside, then turn and cook for 7–10 minutes until golden brown on all sides. If using breast pieces, cook for only about 5 minutes, removing them from the oil as soon as they are golden. Adjust the heat to maintain a steady sizzling and coloring. Remove the crisped chicken pieces with tongs to a bowl. Meanwhile, toss the potatoes with the olive oil and $1/4$ teaspoon salt in a bowl. When all the chicken has been cooked, pour off the frying oil from the pan. Return the pan to medium heat and, when hot, add all the potatoes, cut side down, in a single layer. Scrape all the olive oil out of the bowl into the skillet with a spatula; drizzle over a little more oil if the skillet seems dry. Cook the potatoes for about 4 minutes to form a crust, then move them around the skillet, still cut side down, for about 7 minutes more until brown and crisp. Turn them over and cook for a further 2 minutes. Add the onion wedges and rosemary to the skillet and toss with the potatoes. Return the chicken – but not breast pieces – to the skillet, together with any juices that have accumulated, and add the bacon rolls. Increase the heat slightly and carefully turn and tumble the chicken, potatoes and onion to coat with the pan juices. Spread everything out in the pan with as many potatoes on the base as possible to keep crisping up, and cover. Lower the heat to medium and cook, shaking the pan occasionally, for about 7 minutes, then uncover and tumble the chicken pieces and potatoes again. Cover and cook for a further 7–8 minutes, adding the breast pieces, if using, at this point. Tumble the mixture again, cover and cook for 10 minutes more. Remove the lid, turn the chicken pieces again and cook, uncovered, for about 10 minutes to evaporate the moisture and caramelize the mixture. Taste and adjust the seasoning if necessary. Turn the chicken pieces occasionally until they are golden and the potatoes are cooked through. Serve immediately.

POLLO E PATATE DI NONNA ERMINIA

Serves 4–6

$2^1/2$ pounds chicken legs or portions

4–6 ounces bacon slices

$1/2$ cup canola oil

$1/2$ teaspoon salt or more to taste

1 pound new potatoes, halved

2 tablespoons extra virgin olive oil,

plus extra if necessary

2 medium-small onions, cut into fourths lengthwise

2 fresh rosemary sprigs with plenty of needles

1–2 pickled cherry peppers, seeded

CROSTATA DI CIOCCOLATO,
NOCCIOLE E ARANCIA

Serves 6–8

1 quantity Shortcrust Pastry (1) (see page 1008), chilled

5 ounces semisweet chocolate, cut into pieces

whipped cream, to serve (optional)

For the filling

¹/₃ cup hazelnuts, toasted and skins rubbed off

1 orange

²/₃ cup sugar

6 tablespoons butter, softened

2 eggs

1 tablespoon all-purpose flour

3 ounces semisweet chocolate, chopped in very small pieces

2 tablespoons orange liqueur, such as Cointreau or Grand Marnier

CROSTATA WITH CHOCOLATE, HAZELNUTS AND ORANGE

Place a baking stone, if you have one, on the middle rack of the oven and preheat the oven to 350°F. Roll out the dough and use to line a 9-inch fluted, loose-based tart pan, then chill in the refrigerator. Melt the chocolate in a heat-proof bowl set over a pan of barely simmering water, stirring until it is completely smooth. Pour the chocolate into the tart shell and spread it evenly over the base. Put the hazelnuts in a food processor and pulse to chop finely but be careful not to overprocess. Tip the nuts into a bowl. Using a vegetable peeler, pare thin strips of orange rind about 2 inches long. Stack up a few strips at a time and slice them lengthwise into very thin slivers, then cut the slivers crosswise into tiny pieces like glitter or small confetti – you should have about 2 tablespoons. Put the sugar and butter in the food processor and process for about 30 seconds until smooth. With the motor running, add the eggs through the feeder tube and process for about 1 minute until smooth and slightly thickened. Scrape down the sides of the bowl. With the motor running, add the flour through the feeder tube and process until smooth. Scrape down the sides of the bowl again. Add the orange rind, chocolate and hazelnuts and pulse for 1–2 seconds to incorporate. Finally, add the orange liqueur and process for just 1 second. Scrape the filling from the sides and blade of the processor bowl, stir and pour it into the tart shell. Smooth the surface with a spatula. Bake for 35–40 minutes until the filling is puffed, firm in the center and a toothpick inserted in the center comes out clean. The crust should be nicely browned as well. Transfer the tart to a wire rack to cool and serve slightly warm or at room temperature, with whipped cream if you like.

Mario Batali

Across the West Village and theatre district of Manhattan, in an expanding empire of eateries, Mario Batali is reinventing and redefining Italian culinary traditions. His landmark restaurant is Babbo Ristorante e Enoteca where distinctive, innovative food with vibrant and complex flavors is served. After studying the Golden Age of Spanish theatre at university, Mario Batali briefly enrolled at Le Cordon Bleu in London, England. However, his real culinary adventure began in earnest with an apprenticeship to London's legendary chef Marco Pierre White. Several years of intense training followed in the small hillside village of Borgo Capanne in Northern Italy. Now, traditional and regionally inspired recipes and techniques steer his contemporary interpretations. Mario Batali's devotion to regional food extends outside Italy to the seasonal markets and artisan-made goods of New York's Greenwich Village. While Italian staples are imported, local farmers provide fresh produce including forgotten or heirloom varietals Mario Batali proudly makes his own salumi, such as pancetta and coppa. The overarching philosophy that guides him is to ask 'what are the best ingredients at hand today?' Accordingly, new, original dishes are constantly added to the menu at Babbo and full-bodied flavors abound. From marinated fresh anchovies with watermelon, radishes and lobster oil, to gooseliver ravioli with balsamic vinegar and brown butter, to yogurt cheesecake with lemon cream and black currant jam. In his cookbooks and on television he invites Americans to revel in spirited Italian cuisine. Combined with flattering reviews and prestigious awards this has made Mario Batali one of the most recognisable chefs in the United States.

Babbo Ristorante e Enoteca
110 Waverly Place
New York
United States of America

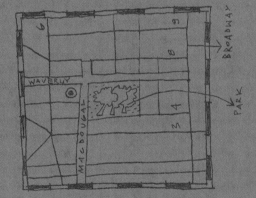

MENUS

SFORMATO DI PISELLI IN VINAIGRETTE DI CAROTA

RAVIOLI DI GUANCIA DI VITELLO CON FEGATINI E TARTUFO NERO

PICCIONE 'AL MATTONE' CON MOSTARDA DI PORCINI

BUDINO DI SEMOLINA CON RABARBARO E SCIROPPO DI MENTUCCIA

SFORMATO DI PISELLI

IN VINAIGRETTE DI CAROTA

Serves 6

cooking spray, for oiling

1 cup fresh mint leaves

3 cups fresh or frozen peas

3 eggs

³/₄ cup heavy cream

1 teaspoon freshly squeezed lemon juice

1¹/₄ cups carrot juice

1 teaspoon honey

1 tablespoon champagne vinegar

¹/₂ cup extra virgin olive oil

2 cups young pea vines

¹/₄ cup Parsley Oil (see below)

sea salt and pepper

Parmesan cheese shavings, to garnish

For the parsley oil

2 cups extra virgin olive oil

1 bunch of fresh flat-leaf parsley, chopped

1 teaspoon sea salt

SWEET PEA FLAN WITH CARROT VINAIGRETTE

Before preparing the parsley oil, chill the olive oil for 2 hours, then process all the ingredients in a food processor until nearly smooth and uniformly green. These quantities will make about 2 cups which may be stored in the refrigerator for 24 hours. Preheat the oven to 350°F. Oil six ramekins with cooking spray. Bring about 3 quarts water to a boil and add 1 tablespoon sea salt. Prepare an ice bath. Blanch the mint leaves and peas in the boiling water for 1 minute, then drain and immerse in the ice bath. Drain again, transfer to a food processor and process to a purée. Pass the mixture through a food mill into a bowl, stir in the eggs, cream and lemon juice and season with salt and pepper. Spoon the pea mixture into the ramekins so that they are about two-thirds full. Place the ramekins in a roasting pan, add boiling water to come about halfway up the sides and cover the pan with foil. Bake for 25–30 minutes until the mixture is just set in the centers. Remove from the oven and let cool. Meanwhile, bring 1 cup of the carrot juice to a boil in a heavy-based pan over high heat. Lower the heat to medium and cook until reduced to ¹/₄ cup. Pour the reduced juice into a bowl and whisk in the honey and vinegar. Gradually whisk in the olive oil and then stir in the remaining carrot juice. Season to taste with salt and pepper. To serve, carefully run a knife around the edge of each cooled flan and turn out onto the center of each of six chilled plates. Toss the pea vines with the carrot vinaigrette and season with salt and pepper if necessary. Divide the pea vines among the plates, partially covering the flans. Drizzle with any remaining vinaigrette and the parsley oil, garnish with the Parmesan and serve immediately.

BEEF CHEEK RAVIOLI

Preheat the oven to 400°F. Heat the olive oil in a large, ovenproof skillet with a lid. Add the onion and celery and cook over low heat, stirring occasionally, for about 10 minutes until very soft but not browned. Increase the heat to high, add the meat, in batches if necessary, and cook, turning frequently until browned all over. Add the wine and bring the mixture to a boil, stirring and scraping up the sediment from the base of the pan. Stir in the tomatoes and rosemary and bring back to a boil. Cover the pan, transfer to the oven and cook for 1 hour or until the meat is very tender. Remove from the oven and let cool, then skim off any excess fat. Transfer the mixture to a food processor and pulse until smooth. Roll out the pasta dough with a pasta machine on its thinnest setting, then cut the dough into 4-inch squares. Place 1 tablespoon of the beef filling in the center of each square, bring two opposite corners together to form a triangle and press the edges firmly together to seal. (You can freeze the ravioli on cookie sheets interleaved with waxed paper or baking parchment at this point.) Bring 6 quarts water to a boil and add 2 tablespoons salt. Meanwhile, heat the butter in a sauté pan over high heat until it begins to brown, then add the chicken canapés and cook for 1 minute. Add a few tablespoons of the salted, boiling water, then add the truffles and cook for 1 minute more. Cook the ravioli in the salted, boiling water for 2 minutes or until they rise to the surface, then remove with a slotted spoon and add to the sauté pan. Add half the chopped parsley and the romano and toss gently for 1 minute over medium heat. Place three ravioli on each of eight warmed plates, spoon the sauce over them, top with the remaining parsley and sprinkle with extra romano.

RAVIOLI DI GUANCIA DI VITELLO CON FEGATINI E TARTUFO NERO

Serves 8

3 tablespoons extra virgin olive oil

1 white onion, cut into ¼-inch dice

½ celery stalk, cut into ¼-inch dice

2 pounds beef cheeks, brisket

or chuck steak, trimmed

and cut into 1-inch cubes

2 cups red wine

1 cup fresh tomatoes, chopped

or drained canned chopped tomatoes

1 teaspoon fresh rosemary, chopped

1 quantity Fresh Pasta Dough (see page 268)

1 cup sweet butter

1 quantity Chicken Liver Canapés (see page 123)

2 tablespoons sliced black truffles

1 bunch of fresh flat-leaf parsley, chopped

4 tablespoons romano cheese, freshly grated, plus extra for serving

PICCIONE 'AL MATTONE' CON MOSTARDA DI PORCINI

Serves 4

2 tablespoons honey

¹/₄ cup balsamic vinegar

1 cup extra virgin olive oil

¹/₂ bunch of fresh thyme, leaves only

1 large red onion, thinly sliced

4 squab, cleaned and breast and backbones removed

salt and pepper

For the roasted beet farrotto

2 large red beets, trimmed

2 tablespoons extra virgin olive oil

2 tablespoons pomegranate molasses

1¹/₂ cups farro

¹/₂ cup Chicken Stock (see page 209)

sea salt and pepper

Parmesan cheese, freshly grated, to serve

For the porcini mustard

¹/₂ red onion, finely chopped

1 cup balsamic vinegar

1 cup dried porcini

¹/₄ cup Dijon mustard

¹/₄ cup extra virgin olive oil

¹/₄ cup black truffles, drained bottled or canned, finely chopped

BARBECUED SQUAB AL MATTONE WITH PORCINI MUSTARD

You will need four garden bricks, well wrapped in foil. Combine the honey, vinegar, olive oil, thyme leaves and onion in a nonmetallic dish large enough to hold the squab in one layer. Add the squab, turning to coat, cover and let marinate in the refrigerator, turning occasionally, for at least 4 hours. Meanwhile, make the porcini mustard. Combine the onion, vinegar, porcini and 1 cup water in a heavy-based pan and bring to a boil, then lower the heat and simmer until the liquid has reduced by half. Pour the mixture into a bowl and let cool, then transfer to a food processor, add the mustard and olive oil and process until thoroughly combined. Pass the mixture through a strainer into a bowl and stir in the truffles. This quantity makes 2 cups which may be stored in an airtight container in the refrigerator for up to 2 weeks. For the roasted beet farrotto, preheat the oven to 400°F and cut out two squares of foil each large enough to contain a beet. Place the beets on the foil squares, drizzle with the olive oil and season. Wrap and roast for about 40 minutes until tender. Remove from the oven and let cool enough to handle, then peel, halve and cut into half-moon slices about ¹/₄ inch thick. Place the slices in a bowl, toss gently with the molasses and season, then set aside. Bring 3 quarts water to a boil and add 1 tablespoon salt. Set up an ice bath. Cook the farro in the boiling water for about 20 minutes until tender but not quite cooked through, then drain and immerse in the ice bath. Drain again and transfer to a sauté pan. Add the stock and beets and toss over high heat for about 3 minutes until most of the stock has been absorbed and the farro is completely cooked through. Adjust the seasoning and sprinkle with the Parmesan. Preheat the barbecue. Place the bricks on the broiler and heat until very hot; use tongs to handle them from here on. Remove the squab from the marinade and pat dry with paper towels, then place them, breast side down, on the broiler. Carefully place a hot brick on top of each and cook for 6 minutes. Remove the bricks, turn the squab, replace the bricks and broil for a further 4–6 minutes until medium rare. To serve, divide the farrotto among four warm plates, placing it in the center of each. Place a squab on top of each mound and top each with 1 tablespoon porcini mustard.

SEMOLINA BUDINO WITH RHUBARB AND MINT MARMELLATA

Grease eight ramekins with butter, then sprinkle them with sugar, turning to coat evenly, and tip out the excess. Place the ramekins in a roasting pan large enough to hold them with at least 1 inch between them. Melt the remaining butter and let cool. Put the sliced rhubarb and $1/2$ cup of the sugar in a pan and scrape in the pulp from inside one vanilla bean using the point of a knife. Cook over medium heat, stirring frequently, for about 15 minutes until the rhubarb is soft. Remove from the heat and let cool completely. Meanwhile, preheat the oven to 400°F. Beat the egg yolks with $3/4$ cup of the remaining sugar with an electric mixer. Add the vanilla extract and melted butter, then beat in the milk. Combine the two types of flour in another bowl, then gradually beat them into the egg yolk mixture. Fold in the rhubarb with a rubber spatula. Whisk the egg whites with the salt until foamy, then gradually whisk in 2 tablespoons of the remaining sugar until soft peaks form. Fold the egg whites into the egg yolk mixture. Divide the mixture among the ramekins and add boiling water to the roasting pan to come about one-third of the way up their sides. Cover with foil and bake for 25–30 minutes until the budini begin to puff up. Remove the foil and bake for a further 10–15 minutes until the budini are pale golden in color and set. Transfer the ramekins to a rack to cool. To make the marmellata, put the rhubarb and sugar in a large pan and cook over low heat, stirring until the sugar has dissolved. Scrape the pulp from the inside of the vanilla bean into the pan, add the mint and cook, stirring, for about 10 minutes until the rhubarb is tender but not mushy. Transfer the mixture to a shallow dish and let cool, then discard the mint. Pour the cream into a bowl and scrape the pulp from the remaining vanilla bean into it. Whip with an electric mixer on medium speed until soft peaks form. Gradually add the remaining sugar and whip until the cream holds its shape. Turn out each budino onto individual plates, top with some of the marmellata and serve with a spoonful of the vanilla cream.

BUDINO DI SEMOLINA CON RABARBARO E SCIROPPO DI MENTUCCIA

Serves 8

$1/2$ cup sweet butter, plus extra for greasing

$1^1/2$ cups sugar, plus extra for sprinkling

3 rhubarb stalks, cut into $3/4$-inch slices

2 vanilla beans, split lengthwise

4 eggs, separated

$1/2$ teaspoon vanilla extract

$3/4$ cup milk

4 tablespoons semolina flour

$3/4$ cup cake flour

pinch of sea salt

1 cup heavy cream

For the rhubarb and mint marmellata

8 rhubarb stalks, finely chopped

$1^1/2$ cups sugar

1 vanilla bean, split lengthwise

3–4 large fresh mint sprigs

Nino Bergese

Nino Bergese was possibly the most authoritative Italian chef of the twentieth century. Even in retirement he still retained the unquestioned authority of a true master and every young chef would have loved to have worked within his great shadow. He was born in 1904 and died in 1977 and his career was meteoric. At the age of 16 he was already assistant chef in the distinguished kitchens of the Piedmont Count Costa Carrù della Trinità, at whose tables Italian and Egyptian royalty and the dukes of Aosta and Genoa were guests. He moved to work for Count Arborio Mella di Sant'Elia, master of ceremonies of the royal house of Savoy. The twenty-second birthday of Prince Umberto di Savoia was celebrated on September 15, 1926 at the royal family's summer residence at Villa Crocetta, between Intra and Pallanza. Bergese prepared his famous torta fiorentina for the heir to the Italian throne who went onto request it for a further three days. Later there were other great houses and other noble names, then all this was interrupted by war. With the return of peace, Bergese said goodbye to aristocratic homes and made his debut among the winding alleys of Genoa in Vico Indoratori. His tiny, yet chic restaurant La Santa became a landmark in the 1960s for all those intent on discovering culinary delights such as creamed risotto and spaghetti. 'Dishes should be created with the best ingredients and with a clear aim in mind,' explained Nino Bergese to those who, wanting to enter his profession, asked for his advice. His book Mangiare da Re (Eat Like a King) is a collection of 512 of his countless recipes – an expert's pantry from which we have taken three of his most famous dishes.

MENUS

RISO MANTECATO

SELLA DI VITELLO ALLA BERGESE

TORTA FIORENTINA

CREAMED RISOTTO

Heat the oil with ¼ cup of the butter in a deep pan, add the onion and cook over low heat, stirring occasionally, for about 20 minutes until golden brown. Pass the onion through a fine nylon strainer and return it to the pan. Add the wine and vegetable stock, bring to a boil, add the rice and cook for 15 minutes over medium heat. Remove the pan from the heat and stir in the remaining butter and the Parmesan. Serve the risotto in individual dishes, dressed with the meat stock.

RISO MANTECATO
Serves 8

4 tablespoons olive oil

1⅓ cups butter • 1 large onion, thinly sliced

1½ cups dry white wine

scant 2 cups Vegetable Stock (see page 209)

3 cups risotto rice

generous 1 cup Parmesan cheese, freshly grated

¾ cup hot Meat Stock (see page 208)

SADDLE OF VEAL ALLA BERGESE

Melt the butter in a large, flameproof pan, add the veal and cook, turning occasionally, until brown all over. Pour in the vodka and light it. When the flames have died, pour in the cream, bring to a boil and lower the heat. Add the pancetta and season with pepper. Cook, uncovered, over medium heat for about 40 minutes until tender. Season with salt if necessary and drain well. Using a sharp knife, detach the meat from the bones and place the bones on a warm serving dish. Slice the meat and arrange in tiers over the bones. Cover and keep warm. Strain the cooking liquid, reheat it if necessary and pour into a sauceboat. Serve the veal with the sauce and vegetables, such as finely diced, buttered carrots, potato browned in butter and pearl onions in a sweet and sour sauce.

SELLA DI VITELLO ALLA BERGESE
Serves 8

¼ cup butter

5½-pound saddle of veal

1½ cups vodka • 2¼ cups heavy cream

3 ounces smoked pancetta, sliced

salt and white pepper

FLORENTINE TART

Preheat the oven to 350°F. Grease one or two cookie sheets and dust lightly with flour. Prepare a shortcrust pastry dough (see page 1008). Roll out four sheets of dough on a floured counter to ¼ inch thick and 12 inches square. Place on the prepared cookie sheets and bake for 15 minutes, then remove from the oven and let cool. Meanwhile, make the confectioner's custard (see page 1039) and let cool, stirring occasionally. Spread the custard over three of the pastry squares, place them on top of each other and top with the fourth. Place the sugar and cocoa powder in a heatproof bowl set over barely simmering water and cook, stirring constantly, until melted and smooth. Remove from the heat, quickly cover the pastry with the mixture and let cool. To make the royal frosting, beat the egg white with 2 tablespoons of the confectioner's sugar in a bowl, beating in more sugar if necessary. Use a small pastry bag to decorate the tart with a lattice. Finally, place a dot of frosting in the center of each diamond.

TORTA FIORENTINA
Serves 8-10

For the dough

1⅓ cups sweet butter, plus extra for greasing

4½ cups all-purpose flour, plus extra for dusting

¾ cup superfine sugar

scant 1 cup unsweetened cocoa powder

For the confectioner's custard

scant 1 cup all-purpose flour • generous ½ cup sweet

butter • scant 1 cup unsweetened cocoa powder

4 cups milk • 1 cup superfine sugar

For the fondant

1¾ cups superfine sugar

¼ cup unsweetened cocoa powder

For the royal frosting

½ egg white • ⅓ cup confectioner's sugar

Gianfranco Bolognesi

La Frasca
Via Matteotti 38
Castrocaro Terme (FO)
Italy

Pellegrino Artusi's book La scienza in cucina o l'arte di mangiar bene (Science in the Kitchen or the Art of Eating Well), which was first published in 1891, is still a bestseller. However, the doctor from Forlimpopoli in the Romagna region was incapable of even cooking tagliatelle. It was simply a fondness for and an enjoyment of good cooking and a powerful cultural urge that led him to write this highly successful collection of recipes with wisdom and shrewdness. Today it remains an invaluable benchmark and guide. Gianfranco Bolognesi is an exponent and follower of the same philosophy. By adjusting the generous portions of recipes to modern dietary standards, he perpetuates Artusi's style and ideas. Although, like Artusi, he does not cook, unlike the famous master he can boast an expertise in wine that he puts into practice with great discernment when choosing specific wines to accompany the food. At La Frasca, his restaurant in Castrocaro, a team of chefs prepare typical local recipes to very high standards and, at the same time, develops ideas that have grown out of Bolognesi's research and creativity. Among the many dishes that regularly star on his menus, the rice savarin with goose salami and porcini, sole with rosemary, black truffle and crispy spinach and the Artusi vegetable mold with giblets must be mentioned. Such dishes have won him his much coveted Michelin stars and have been endorsed by diners, meal after meal, since 1971.

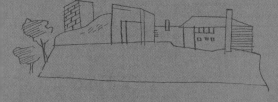

MENUS

TAGLIATELLE ALL'ANTICA CON TARTUFI

PERNICE CON VERZE, SALVIA FRITTA E VERDURE

PANNA COTTA, TORTA DI MANDORLE E ZABAIONE ARTUSIANO

TAGLIATELLE ALL'ANTICA WITH TRUFFLES

Make the pasta dough (see page 268) with the flour and eggs, forming a firm and elastic dough. Roll it out very thinly on a lightly floured counter and cut into $1/4$-inch ribbons. For the sauce, melt the butter in a skillet, add the prosciutto and cook over medium heat until softened, taking care that it does not color. Meanwhile, cook the tagliatelle in plenty of salted, boiling water until al dente, then drain and toss in the skillet with the prosciutto and butter. Add the Parmesan and mix carefully. Transfer the tagliatelle to a warm serving dish and garnish with the strips of truffle.

TAGLIATELLE ALL'ANTICA CON TARTUFI

Serves 4

For the pasta dough

$3^1/_2$ cups all-purpose flour, plus extra for dusting

4 eggs

For the sauce

scant $1/2$ cup butter

generous $1/2$ cup prosciutto, diced

$2/_3$ cup Parmesan cheese, freshly grated

$3^1/_2$ ounces black truffle, ideally from Dovadola (Forli), cut into thin strips

salt

PARTRIDGES WITH SAVOY CABBAGE, FRIED SAGE AND VEGETABLES

Steam or boil the diced vegetables until al dente. Heat 1 tablespoon of the olive oil in a skillet, add the cabbage, garlic and pancetta and cook over low heat, stirring occasionally, until crispy. Season to taste with salt and pepper. Separate the breasts and legs of the partridges. Heat 2 tablespoons of the remaining oil in a skillet, add the partridges and two of the sage leaves and cook, turning occasionally, until tender and golden brown. Remove from the skillet and keep warm. Drain off the oil and any fat from the pan, pour in the wine and heat until it has evaporated. Add the game stock and simmer over low heat for a few minutes, then stir in 2 tablespoons of the butter. Thinly slice the partridges. Toss the mixed vegetables with the remaining butter and spoon them onto one side of a warm serving dish. Spoon the crispy Savoy cabbage onto the other side, place the partridges on top and sprinkle with the slivers of truffle. Dust the remaining sage leaves with flour. Heat the remaining oil, add the sage leaves and fry until golden brown, then place in the center of the plate. Spoon the sauce over the partridges and serve. (Make game stock by simmering the discarded parts of the partridges, some vegetables, aromatic herbs and white wine for a few hours, occasionally adding a little Meat Stock [see page 208].)

PERNICE CON VERZE, SALVIA FRITTA E VERDURE

Serves 4

11 ounces mixed diced vegetables, such as carrots, fennel, pearl onions and new potatoes

$2/_3$ cup olive oil

2 cups Savoy cabbage, shredded

2 garlic cloves, chopped

generous $1/2$ cup lean pancetta, diced

4 partridges

18 fresh sage leaves

$3/_4$ cup dry white wine

$2/_3$ cup game stock

scant $1/2$ cup butter

2 ounces white truffle, cut into slivers

all-purpose flour, for dusting

salt and pepper

PANNA COTTA, TORTA DI MANDORLE

E ZABAIONE ARTUSIANO

Serves 4

For the panna cotta

3 eggs

2 egg yolks

generous $1/2$ cup superfine sugar

$2^1/4$ cups heavy cream

1 cup amaretti, lightly crushed

For the caramel

$3/4$ cup superfine sugar

$2/3$ cup water

For the tart

$3/4$ cup ground almonds

$3/4$ cup all-purpose flour

generous $1/2$ cup superfine sugar

$1/3$ cup sweet butter

pinch of salt

confectioner's sugar, for dusting

For the zabaglione

2 egg yolks

2 tablespoons superfine sugar

$3/4$ cup Marsala

To decorate

red fruits

fresh mint leaves

PANNA COTTA, ALMOND TART AND ZABAGLIONE

Preheat the oven to 350°F. To make the panna cotta, beat together the eggs, egg yolks and sugar until pale and fluffy, then beat in the cream. Strain the mixture into another bowl and stir in the amaretti crumbs. To make the caramel, stir the sugar and water in a pan over low heat until the sugar has dissolved, then cook until hazelnut in color. Pour the caramel into an ovenproof dish, tilting to coat the inside, then pour in the panna cotta mixture. Place the dish in a roasting pan, add boiling water to come about halfway up the side and bake for about 45 minutes. Remove from the oven, but do not switch it off, and let cool. Meanwhile, make the almond tart. Mix all the ingredients, except the confectioner's sugar, to a dough, then shape into a round about $1/2$ inch thick. Place on a cookie sheet and bake for about 10 minutes. To prepare the zabaglione, beat the egg yolks with the sugar in a heatproof bowl set over a pan of barely simmering water, gradually beating in the Marsala a little at a time. Cut the panna cotta into drop shapes and divide among four dishes, then pour the caramel over the shapes. Place a slice of almond tart, dusted with confectioner's sugar next to the panna cotta and pour the warm zabaglione on the other side. Decorate with red fruits and mint leaves.

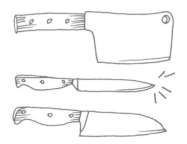

Carlo Brovelli

Ristorante Il Sole
Piazza Venezia 5
Ranco (VA)
Italy

In the 1950s, Il Sole in Ranco, on the Lombardy side of Lake Maggiore, was a traditional restaurant for day trippers and families. Fish from the lake, fried or cooked in a carpione (sweet and sour sauce), was excellent and finding a free table was no easy task. However, Carlo Brovelli, whose family had been restaurateur-chefs for four generations since 1872, decided that the time had come to change his style of cooking. He had learned all kinds of subtle ways of using local ingredients from his grandmother and uncle and had attended the excellent catering school at Stresa, yet he felt he needed more. As a result, he traveled the world for ten years, 'studying' in the greatest restaurants in Switzerland, France, Germany and Austria, where the excellence of the food is matched by the sophisticated presentation and service. Back in Ranco, assisted by his wife Itala, a wine expert, he revolutionized his old restaurant and, within a few years, had fulfilled his dream: the creation of haute cuisine with fish from his lake, such as red char al Barbaresco, shrimp pastries with foie gras and whitefish with jus, and masterpieces using game, such as mallard, duck and squab. His recipes are sophisticated yet never lose touch with local flavors. Carlo Brovelli should also be given credit for having taught a new generation of promising chefs, including his son Davide, who continues the family tradition.

MENUS

CAPPESANTE E SEDANO FRITTO

MARGHERITE ALLE UOVA E ASPARAGI

OSSOBUCO DI STORIONE IN GREMOLATA

SPUMONE D'ARANCIA E GRAND MARNIER

Serves 4

7 ounces shelled scallops,
skirts and corals reserved
1 cup milk
¹/₄ cup butter
¹/₄ cup dry white wine
1 tablespoon chopped fresh dill
1 tablespoon olive oil
1 celery stalk, cut into thin batons
salt and pepper

SCALLOPS AND FRIED CELERY

Rinse the scallops under cold running water for 15 minutes, then place in a bowl, add the milk and let soften. Melt the butter in a pan, add the scallop skirts and cook for about 4 minutes. Pour in the wine and 1 cup water, season with salt and pepper and bring to a boil. Add the dill, lower the heat and simmer for about 15 minutes, then remove from the heat and strain into a clean pan. Add the scallops and corals and cook for about 5 minutes until tender. Remove the scallops and corals with a slotted spoon, bring the cooking liquid to a boil and cook until slightly reduced. Meanwhile, heat the olive oil in a small pan, add the celery and cook, stirring, for a few minutes. Slice the scallops and arrange them like petals on four warm plates, alternating the white and the coral to create a colored flower shape. Drizzle with the reduced cooking liquid and garnish with the celery.

Serves 4

¹/₄ cup butter, melted
1 tablespoon chopped fresh basil

For the pasta dough
2¹/₄ cups all-purpose flour, plus extra for dusting
3 egg yolks
1 egg
scant 1 cup olive oil
salt

For the filling
1 bunch of wild asparagus
5 eggs
¹/₄ cup butter, melted
1 bunch of arugula, finely chopped
salt and pepper

RAVIOLI WITH EGGS AND ASPARAGUS

Prepare the pasta dough (see page 268). For the filling, cut off the asparagus spears and steam them until just al dente, then remove from the heat and dice. Beat the eggs with salt and pepper in a bowl. Combine the butter, eggs, asparagus spears and arugula. Roll out the pasta dough on a lightly floured counter. Spread the filling over one half of the dough. Fold over the other half of the dough and cut out the ravioli with a wheel into a flower shape. Cook in salted boiling water until al dente, then drain, toss gently with the melted butter and the basil.

STURGEON STEAKS IN GREMOLATA

Chop the parsley with the garlic, lemon rind, anchovies and sage. Pour the stock and wine into a pan, add the butter and cook over low heat until slightly reduced. Add the fish and simmer for 10 minutes. Shortly before the end of the cooking time, sprinkle the parsley mixture – gremolata – over the fish, cover and simmer for a further 2 minutes. Transfer the fish steaks to four warm plates and pour the sauce over them. Serve with mixed, boiled vegetables flavored with vanilla and cilantro.

OSSOBUCO DI STORIONE IN GREMOLATA
Serves 4

2 salted anchovies, heads removed, cleaned and filleted (see page 596) and soaked in cold water for 10 minutes and drained
2 fresh flat-leaf parsley sprigs
1 garlic clove
thinly pared rind of $1/2$ lemon
1 fresh sage sprig
1 cup Fish Stock (see page 208–9)
5 tablespoons dry white wine
$1/4$ cup butter
4 sturgeon steaks
mixed vegetables, to serve

ORANGE AND GRAND MARNIER MOUSSE

Grate the rind of two of the oranges and thinly pare the rind of the other two, avoiding all traces of bitter white pith. Separate the oranges into segments, carefully removing all traces of pith. Pour the milk into a pan, add the grated orange rind and $1/2$ cup of the sugar, stir well and bring to a boil. Beat the egg yolks in another pan, then pour in the milk in a steady stream, stirring constantly. Cook over low heat, stirring constantly, until thickened. Strain the mixture into a bowl and let cool completely. Stiffly whisk the egg whites in a grease-free bowl, then fold them into the egg yolk mixture, followed by the Grand Marnier. Pour the mousse into a mold or loaf pan and place in the freezer for 6 hours. Cut the remaining orange rind into thin strips. Pour 1 cup water into a pan, add the remaining sugar and the strips of orange rind and bring to a boil, stirring until the sugar has dissolved. Boil the mixture until a thick, translucent syrup forms. Turn out the mousse and cut it into $3/4$-inch slices. Place the slices on four plates, spoon the syrup and orange rind over them and decorate with the orange segments, arranged like flowers.

SPUMONE D'ARANCIA E GRAND MARNIER
Serves 4
4 oranges
1 cup milk
1 cup superfine sugar
4 eggs, separated
$1/4$ cup Grand Marnier

Arrigo Cipriani

Harry's Bar
Calle Vallaresso, 1323
Venice
Italy

Giuseppe Cipriani founded his legendary Harry's Bar in Venice in 1931 and was succeeded by his son Arrigo at the end of the 1950s. Nevertheless, he continued to eat at Harry's Bar at least twice a week, simply sitting at a table, perusing the menu, ordering and passing judgement on the dishes just like the other demanding customers. Indeed, Giuseppe Cipriani's school bears fruit: The Bellini, a cocktail made from white peach juice and sparkling white wine, was created in 1948, on the occasion of a great Venetian exhibition devoted to the painter Giovanni Bellini. His Carpaccio Cipriani consists of thin slices of meat covered with a special sauce, which was originally known as universal sauce. However, following the historic Carpaccio exhibition in Venice in 1950, it was renamed in honor of the painter. The colors of the dish – red and yellow – were his favourites. During those years Giuseppe Cipriani created other dishes – still on the menu today – with the aid of Berto Toffolo, his top-ranking chef. These include sole Casanova, langoustines armoricaine, croque monsieur and cream crêpes. Arrigo Cipriani has hired other talented chefs over the years and each one of them has contributed towards the fame of Harry's Bar, not just the original bar in Venice, but also his restaurant in New York, where the ambience and dishes match those which continue to attract swarms of illustrious guests to the Venetian lagoon each year.

MENUS

CARPACCIO CIPRIANI

RISOTTO ALLA PRIMAVERA

SCAMPI AL FORNO

CRESPELLE ALLA CREMA PASTICCIERA

CARPACCIO CIPRIANI

Trim all traces of fat, sinew and gristle from the beef, leaving a small, cylindrical piece, then chill in the refrigerator. When the meat is cold, cut it into extremely thin slices with a very sharp knife. Place the slices of meat on six plates to cover each one entirely. Season lightly with salt and chill in the refrigerator for at least 5 minutes. Stir the Worcestershire sauce and lemon juice into the mayonnaise and add just enough milk so that the sauce is thick enough to coat the back of a tablespoon. Add salt and pepper to taste and add more Worcestershire sauce or lemon juice if necessary. Chill in the refrigerator until required. Remove the meat and sauce from the refrigerator just before serving and drizzle the sauce over the beef.

CARPACCIO CIPRIANI

Serves 6

$1^1/_2$-pound lean sirloin

salt

For the Carpaccio sauce

1–2 teaspoons Worcestershire sauce

1 teaspoon lemon juice

scant 1 cup Mayonnaise (see page 65)

2–3 tablespoons milk

salt and white pepper

SPRING RISOTTO

To prepare the vegetables, heat the olive oil in a large skillet over medium heat, add the garlic and cook for about 30 seconds, then remove it from the pan. Add the mushroom caps and cook for 5–6 minutes until softened and the liquid has evaporated. Add the artichokes and cook for 8–10 minutes, then add the onion and cook for a further 2 minutes. Finally, add the zucchini, asparagus, red bell pepper and leek, increase the heat to high and cook for 10 minutes, stirring frequently. Season to taste with salt and pepper, remove the pan from the heat and set aside. To prepare the risotto, heat the olive oil in a large pan, add the onion and cook over medium heat, stirring occasionally, for 3–5 minutes. Stir in the rice, lower the heat, add about $1/_2$ cup of the stock and bring to a boil, stirring constantly. Gradually add more stock as each addition is absorbed. After about 10 minutes, when the risotto is half-cooked, add the vegetables and continue to cook for a further 10–15 minutes until the rice is tender and creamy. Remove the pan from the heat and stir in the butter and Parmesan. Season with salt and pepper to taste. For a softer risotto stir in a few more tablespoons of stock. Serve with extra grated Parmesan.

RISOTTO ALLA PRIMAVERA

Serves 6

For the spring vegetables

1 tablespoon olive oil

$1/_2$ garlic clove, crushed

$1^2/_3$ cups mushroom caps, thinly sliced

3 small artichokes, thinly sliced

1 teaspoon finely chopped onion

2 small zucchini, diced

6 asparagus spears, cut into short lengths

1 large red bell pepper slice, cut into pieces

1 small leek, white part only, cut into short lengths

salt and pepper

For the risotto

1 tablespoon olive oil

1 small onion, chopped

$1^1/_2$ cups risotto rice

$6^1/_4$ cups Chicken Stock (see page 209)

3 tablespoons butter

3 tablespoons freshly grated Parmesan cheese, plus extra for serving

salt and pepper

BAKED LANGOUSTINES

SCAMPI AL FORNO
Serves 6

2¹/₄ pounds peeled langoustines or jumbo shrimp
all-purpose flour, for dusting
scant ¹/₂ cup olive oil
¹/₄ cup butter
1 small fresh flat-leaf parsley sprig, chopped dash of Worcestershire sauce
juice of ¹/₂ lemon, strained
salt and pepper

Preheat the oven to 475°F. Season the langoustines or shrimp and dust with flour. Heat the oil in a skillet, add the langoustines or shrimp, a few at a time, and cook for 2–3 minutes until lightly colored. Remove with a slotted spoon, arrange in a single layer in an ovenproof dish and bake for 3–4 minutes. Drain off the oil from the skillet, add the butter and parsley and cook for about 30 seconds until the butter starts to darken. Remove from the oven, sprinkle with the Worcestershire sauce and lemon juice and pour the parsley butter on top.

ITALIAN CRÊPES WITH CUSTARD CREAM

CRESPELLE ALLA CREMA PASTICCIERA
Serves 6

1²/₃ cups milk
¹/₂ cup superfine sugar, plus extra for sprinkling
thinly pared rind of 2 lemons
3 large egg yolks
¹/₃ cup all-purpose flour
¹/₂ teaspoon vanilla extract
²/₃ cup Cointreau

For the Italian crêpes
3 eggs
¹/₄ cup all-purpose flour
1 tablespoon olive oil
¹/₂ cup milk
4–5 tablespoons sweet butter
salt

Pour the milk into a heavy pan, add half the sugar and the lemon rind and bring to a boil. Remove the pan from the heat and remove the lemon rind. Beat the egg yolks with the remaining sugar in a bowl, then beat in the flour. Gradually stir in the milk, then transfer the custard to a pan and cook over medium heat, stirring constantly, until thickened. Continue cooking for 3–4 minutes, then stir in the vanilla. Remove the pan from the heat and let cool, stirring frequently to prevent a skin from forming. When the custard is cold, chill in the refrigerator until required. To make the crêpes, beat the eggs in a bowl with the flour, oil and a pinch of salt. Stir in the milk and strain into a pitcher. Melt a little of the butter in a crêpe pan or small skillet (about 6 inches in diameter) over medium heat. Pour in enough batter to cover the base evenly and cook until golden brown on the underside, then flip over and lightly brown the other side. Slide out of the pan onto a dish towel. Continue making crêpes occasionally adding a little more butter to the pan as required. When the crêpes are served, the golden brown side of the crêpe – the one cooked first – should be on the outside, so fill the crêpes on the least cooked side. Sprinkle a tablespoon of the custard on one half, fold the other half over the top and fold again to form a triangle. Place on a cookie sheet and store in the refrigerator until ready to cook. Preheat the oven to 475°F. Sprinkle the crêpes with sugar and bake for 5–10 minutes until heated through and the sugar has melted. Bring the crêpes to the table on the cookie sheet, pour the Cointreau over and ignite carefully. Tip and turn the cookie sheet until the flames die down. Serve the crêpes in their hot juices.

Franco Colombani

'There is no nouvelle or traditional cuisine, just good or bad, and the client is the ultimate judge of a restaurateur's capabilities.' This is the pure and simple philosophy of Franco Colombani (1929–96), who spent a lifetime defending this firmly held view. A cultured and jealous guardian of Italian traditional cooking, Colombani was also the founder of Linea Italia in Cucina, an association for top-level restaurant owners committed to promoting local products and to using only produce in season. For over 60 years, his family owned the fifteenth-century inn Albergo del Sole in Maleo, near Lodi and this was where Colombani started to research traditional Italian recipes in 1958. (He was particularly interested in those of the areas around Cremona and Piacenza.) His mother and sister helped out initially, and then he was joined by his capable wife, Silvana. Today, she and the couple's sons, Francesco and Mario, continue the tradition and run the restaurant. The daily menu has always been restricted to a few dishes, but these are invariably rich in flavor – pesto minestrone, capon alla Stefani (named by a cook for the Gonzagas in the seventeenth century), braised beef with polenta in the Padania style and a fine pound cake with mascarpone cream. Finally, cured salami, one of the restaurant's specialities, should not be overlooked. This was always a feature of the celebrations in December each year.

Albergo del Sole
via Monsignor Trabattoni 22
Maleo (LO)
Italy

MENUS

INSALATA DI CAPPONE

STRACOTTO

SABBIOSA CON CREMA DI MASCARPONE

CAPON SALAD

INSALATA DI CAPPONE

Serves 4

1 tablespoon golden raisins
11 ounces poached capon or chicken
2 tablespoons candied citron peel, cut into thin strips
4 tablespoons extra virgin olive oil, plus extra for drizzling
1 1/2 teaspoons white wine vinegar, plus extra for drizzling
dash of balsamic vinegar
salad leaves
salt and pepper

Put the golden raisins in a bowl, add warm water to cover and let soak for 15 minutes, then drain and squeeze out. Carefully remove the skin and bones from the capon or chicken, then cut the meat into strips 1/2 inch thick and place them in a salad bowl. Add the raisins and candied peel, season and drizzle with the olive oil. Add the wine and balsamic vinegars and mix thoroughly. Make a bed of salad leaves on a serving dish and drizzle with olive oil and white wine vinegar. Spoon the meat mixture on top and serve.

BRAISED BEEF

STRACOTTO

Serves 4

2 1/4 pounds beef round
2 garlic cloves
1/4 cup butter • 3/4 cup olive oil
2 1/4 cups Barbera or other fruity red wine
2 onions, diced • scant 1/2 cup carrots, diced
1/2 cup celery, diced • 3 tablespoons bottled strained tomatoes
4 cups Meat Stock (see page 208)
3 cloves • pinch of freshly grated nutmeg
pinch of ground cinnamon
salt and pepper

Make two incisions in the meat and insert the garlic, then truss neatly with kitchen string. Heat the butter and oil in a pan, add the meat and cook, turning frequently, until browned all over. Pour in the wine and cook, turning the meat occasionally, until the liquid has reduced by half. Add the onions, carrots, celery and strained tomatoes and season with salt and a little pepper. Pour in the stock, add the spices, lower the heat, cover and simmer for about 2 hours until the meat is tender. Remove the meat from the pan and keep warm. Press the vegetables through a strainer and return to the pan. Reheat the sauce. Meanwhile, slice the beef and place it on a serving dish, then spoon the sauce over it.

POUND CAKE WITH MASCARPONE CREAM

SABBIOSA CON CREMA DI MASCARPONE

Serves 6

1 3/4 cups sweet butter, plus extra for greasing
bread crumbs, for sprinkling
1/4 cup brandy
1 sachet dried yeast
2 cups superfine sugar
3 1/2 cups potato flour
4 eggs

For the cream
5 eggs, separated
1/2 cup superfine sugar
2 1/4 cups mascarpone cheese
1/4 cup rum or brandy

Preheat the oven to 350°F. Grease a 12-inch round cake pan with butter and sprinkle with bread crumbs. To make the cake, pour the brandy into a small bowl, sprinkle the yeast on top and set aside for 10–15 minutes until frothy, then stir to a smooth paste. Beat the sugar with the butter, then add the potato flour and one egg at a time, beating well until thoroughly incorporated. Add the yeast mixture. Pour the mixture into the pan and bake until the cake has shrunk from the sides and a toothpick inserted in the center comes out clean. Do not open the oven door during baking. Leave the cake to cool. Meanwhile, prepare the cream. Beat the egg yolks with the sugar until pale and fluffy, then beat in the mascarpone a little at a time. Stiffly whisk the egg whites in a grease-free bowl and fold into the egg yolk mixture, followed by the rum or brandy.

Enzo Deprà

Enzo Deprà is the grandson and son of chefs. His Dolada restaurant in Pieve Dalpago in the province of Belluno is the same one that was opened by his grandfather in 1923. As a young man, like many others from the Veneto region, he emigrated to Switzerland, where he attended catering school and worked in his brother's restaurant. It was there that he learned the techniques of classic international cuisine and, also from his brother, (who had gained experience on cruise ships that sailed to the East), the secrets of Indonesian cooking. On his return to Italy in 1965 he was one of the first to take up nouvelle cuisine, a style in which he achieved wide acclaim. His skill led to his appointment as consultant to a large multinational company in the food industry, where he researched raw ingredients extensively. In 1982 he decided that the time had come to re-evaluate the produce from his locality and his restaurant succeeded in transforming traditional dishes into haute cuisine very quickly. He achieved yet another evolution in taste, replacing the sophisticated recipes of an aristocratic cuisine with traditional country dishes which he made lighter and tastier without altering their basic characteristics. His most celebrated creations include his patora soup of barley, corn and beans, exquisite chicken liver pâté with herbs and truffle and fillet of red deer served with small polenta gnocchi.

Dolada
località Plois
Pieve Dalpago (BL)
Italy

MENUS

TERRINA DI FEGATINI ALLE ERBE E TARTUFO

CASUNZJEI DI PATATE E RICOTTA FORTE

INTINGOLO DI CHIOCCIOLE AL SEDANO RAPA E DADOLATA DI POLENTA

DOLCE DI PANE CON SALSA ALLA VANIGLIA

TERRINA DI FEGATINI

ALLE ERBE E TARTUFO

Serves 4

1 tablespoon Madeira

1 tablespoon port

1¹/₃ cups butter

1 shallot, chopped

1 tablespoon white wine

14 ounces chicken livers,

thawed if frozen and trimmed

2 eggs • 4 teaspoons truffle juice

pinch of freshly grated nutmeg

1¹/₂ tablespoons chopped truffle

5 ounces unsalted pork fat

or fatty bacon, cut into thin strips

2 bay leaves

2 fresh thyme sprigs • 2 fresh marjoram sprigs

salt and pepper

CHICKEN LIVER PÂTÉ WITH HERBS AND TRUFFLE

Preheat the oven to 225°F or lower if possible. Pour the Madeira and port into a small pan and reduce by half over low heat, then let cool. Melt 1¹/₂ teaspoons of the butter in a shallow pan, add the shallot and cook over low heat for 3–4 minutes, then add the white wine and cook until reduced by half. Remove from the heat and let cool. Put the chicken livers, remaining butter, the eggs, truffle juice, Madeira mixture, wine mixture and nutmeg in a food processor, season with salt and pepper and process until smooth. Pass the mixture through a strainer into a bowl and gently stir in the truffle. Line a terrine or loaf pan with the pork fat or bacon and spoon the chicken liver mixture into it. Smooth the surface, place the bay leaves, thyme and marjoram on top and cover with the remaining slices of pork fat or bacon. Cover the terrine or loaf pan tightly with a lid or a double thickness of foil. Place in a roasting pan, add boiling water to come halfway up the sides and bake for 1 hour. Let cool completely before serving.

CASUNZJEI DI PATATE E RICOTTA FORTE

Serves 4

For the pasta

2³/₄ cups all-purpose flour, plus extra for dusting

2 eggs • 2 egg yolks • 1 tablespoon olive oil

For the filling

butter, for greasing

9 ounces potatoes, cut into thin batons

¹/₂ onion, finely chopped

¹/₄ cup mascarpone cheese

¹/₄ cup fresh ricotta cheese

1¹/₂ tablespoons Parmesan cheese, freshly grated

1 egg yolk • pinch of freshly grated nutmeg

1 tablespoon olive oil • salt and pepper

For the sauce

4 tablespoons olive oil • ¹/₂ onion, finely chopped

2 potatoes, diced

2 ounces fresh smoked ricotta cheese, very thinly sliced

salt and pepper

CASUNZJEI PASTA WITH POTATOES AND SEASONED RICOTTA

To make the filling, grease a skillet, make a layer of the potatoes and cook over low heat until browned on both sides. About 5 minutes before the end of cooking, add the onion and cook soften, then remove from the heat. When cooled, stir in the mascarpone, ricotta, Parmesan, egg yolk, nutmeg and olive oil and season. Make the pasta dough (see page 268) with the ingredients listed and roll out on a floured surface to a very thin sheet. Stamp out 3-inch rounds. Place a little filling in the center of each round, brush the edges with water and fold them in half, pressing firmly to seal. To prepare the sauce, heat 1 tablespoon of oil, add the onion and cook over low heat, stirring occasionally, for 5 minutes. Add the potatoes and 1¹/₄ cups water, increase the heat to medium and simmer for 30 minutes until tender. Pass the potato mixture through a food mill, add the remaining oil and season. Divide the sauce among four plates. Bring a large pan of salted water to a boil, add the casunzjei and cook for 3–4 minutes until al dente, then drain and arrange in a sunray pattern over the sauce. Top with the slices of ricotta.

RAGÙ OF SNAILS
WITH CELERY ROOT

Blanch the snails, shell them, and remove and discard the intestines (see page 730). Wash well and cut into small pieces. Heat the olive oil in a shallow pan, add the onion and celery and cook over low heat, stirring occasionally, for 5 minutes. Add the snails and cook for a few minutes, then pour in the wine, increase the heat to medium and cook until evaporated. Add the stock a little at a time and simmer for about 2 hours. Preheat the oven to 350°F. Season the snails with salt, if necessary, and plenty of pepper, add the celery root and cook for a further 5 minutes. Sprinkle with the bread crumbs, mix well and let stand for a few minutes. Meanwhile, heat the polenta in the oven, arrange it on a dish and drizzle with oil. Serve with the snail ragù.

INTINGOLO DI CHIOCCIOLE
AL SEDANO RAPA
E DADOLATA DI POLENTA
Serves 4
2¼ pounds snails
1 onion, finely chopped
2 green celery stalks, finely chopped
3 tablespoons olive oil, plus extra for drizzling
¾ cup aromatic white wine
4 cups Meat Stock (see page 208)
scant 1 cup celery root, diced
1 tablespoon bread crumbs
5 slices of polenta, cut into cubes
salt and pepper

BREAD PUDDING WITH
VANILLA SAUCE

Tear the bread into pieces and place it in a bowl. Bring the milk to a boil, remove from the heat and stir in the sugar until it has dissolved. Pour the mixture over the bread and leave until the liquid has been absorbed and the mixture has cooled. Place the golden raisins in another bowl, add warm water to cover and let soak for about 15 minutes, then drain and squeeze out. Dust with flour, gently shaking off any excess. Preheat the oven to 325°F. Grease individual molds with butter and dust them with sugar. Pass the soaked bread through a strainer into a bowl and add the raisins, liqueur, egg and egg yolk, mixing well. Spoon the mixture into the molds until they are three-fourths full. Dot the surface with the butter and bake for 20 minutes, then increase the oven temperature to 350°F and bake for a further 10 minutes. Remove from the oven, cool, then serve with the vanilla sauce. To make the vanilla sauce, bring the milk just to a boil, then remove from the heat. Meanwhile, put the egg yolks and sugar in a heatproof bowl and scrape in the contents of the vanilla bean. Beat vigorously until light and fluffy. Gradually beat in the hot milk. Set the bowl over a pan of barely simmering water and cook, stirring constantly with a wooden spoon until thickened, taking care that the eggs do not curdle. Strain and let the vanilla sauce cool before serving.

DOLCE DI PANE
CON SALSA ALLA VANIGLIA
Serves 8–10
3½ ounces day-old bread, crusts removed
1½ cups skimmed milk
1½ cups superfine sugar, plus extra for dusting
scant ½ cup golden raisins
all-purpose flour, for dusting
1 tablespoon sweet butter, plus extra for greasing
¼ cup fior d'agno or citrus liqueur
1 egg
1 egg yolk
Vanilla Sauce (see below), to serve

For the vanilla sauce
2¼ cups milk • 5 egg yolks
generous ½ cup superfine sugar
1 vanilla bean, halved lengthwise

Maria Pia de Razza-Klein

Maria Pia's Trattoria
55 Mulgrave Street
Thorndon, Wellington
New Zealand

Far from her adopted homeland of New Zealand, the town of Morciano di Leuca in Puglia is the setting for the early culinary education of Maria Pia de Razza-Klein. There, near the southeastern-most tip of the Italian Peninsula, she learnt to respect the products that were cultivated on her family's farm and made in their artisanal pasta shop. She produced handmade pasta such as orecchiette, pre-empting the rediscovery of regional cooking in Italy. From these lessons of the land emerged her adherence to a philosophy of holistic connections between food, well-being and the environment. She studied macrobiotics in Florence, and at the Steiner elementary school in Bologna she prepared meals for small, yet demanding, vegetarian children, which she found as satisfying as creating banquets for discerning gourmets. She now heads her local chapter of the worldwide Slow Food Movement. Concurrent with her quest for the integrity of ingredients is her observance of the traditions of the authentic Italian cuisine. Working in a restaurant in the Apennines of Emilia Romagna, Maria Pia de Razza-Klein was taught the secrets of Emilian cuisine by the women who were its custodians. She overheard and understood their declaration: 'But who invented tagliatelle? And tortellini? A statue, that's what they should dedicate to that person – a statue.' It is this philosophy of treasuring rustic dishes, along with her expertise in traditional and regional fare, that draws diners to Maria Pia's Trattoria in Wellington, New Zealand. Widely acclaimed for superb, truly homemade food, her restaurant's menu includes the freshly made pasta that began Maria Pia de Razza-Klein's gastronomic journey.

MENUS

INSALATA DI POLIPO SU LETTO DI FINOCCHIETTI E SCAGLIE DI PECORINO STAGIONATO

SPAGHETTI ALLA CHITARRA VERDI E BIANCHI CON SUGHETTO DI COZZE, POMODORINI ED OLIV

AGNELLO AL FORNO CON CONTORNO DI RADICCHIO TREVISANO ALLE MELE COTOGNE E PANCETT

RADICCHIO TREVISANO ALLE MELE COTOGNE E PANCETTA

FIOR DI LATTE ALLO ZAFFERANO CON SALSA ALLE ARANCE ROSSE E VINCOTTO

MARINATED OCTOPUS AND FENNEL SALAD WITH SHARP ROMANO CHEESE

Cut the tentacles from the head of the octopus. Remove and discard the eyes and innards, taking care not to break the ink sac. Remove the long strip of cartilage. Under running water remove the hard scales from the suckers on the tentacles, but do not remove the skin as it is the tastiest part and turns a lovely pink color when cooked. Beat the tentacles with a meat mallet for a few minutes until soft. Place the octopus in a large pan and add cold water to cover. Bring to a boil and skim off the foam from the surface for the first few minutes of cooking. Add the onion, bay leaves, celery, garlic, cloves and a cork, but do not add salt. Lower the heat and simmer for 1½ hours. Drain the octopus, reserving 1 cup of the cooking liquid. Discard the vegetables and flavorings, cut the octopus into 1½-inch long strips and transfer to a bowl. Add the lemon juice, reserved cooking liquid, olive oil and parsley, season, mix well and let marinate at room temperature for at least 1 hour before serving. Prepare the fennel by removing the feathery fronds and the base. Slice the bulb thinly and let soak in a bowl of very cold water. Just before serving, drain and pat dry. Arrange the fennel slices on the base of individual serving plates. Drain the strips of octopus and arrange them on top. Sprinkle with the romano. Add several spoonfuls of the marinade, drizzle with extra virgin olive oil and season with pepper. Serve with good bread such as pane pugliese, broiled and rubbed with garlic.

Serves 8

2¼-pound octopus (or 1 large or 2 small ones)
1 large onion
2 bay leaves
1 celery stalk
2 garlic cloves
2 cloves
juice of 3 lemons, strained
⅔ cup extra virgin olive oil, plus extra for drizzling
½ cup fresh flat-leaf parsley, finely chopped
3 large fennel bulbs
3½ ounces sharp romano cheese, shaved
salt and pepper
broiled garlic-flavored bread, to serve

In Puglia we are voracious eaters of seafood. We also know how to cook octopus and squid so that it is tender and not tough: we boil it together with a cork from a wine bottle. I learned this trick from my grandmother and my mother and can't tell you why it works but can assure that it does!

SPAGHETTI ALLA CHITARRA
VERDI E BIANCHI
CON SUGHETTO DI COZZE,
POMODORINI ED OLIVE

Serves 8

For the spinach pasta

7 ounces spinach

1³/₄ cups semolina flour plus extra for dusting

1³/₄ cups spelt flour

2 large eggs

1 egg yolk

1 tablespoon warm water (optional)

For the plain pasta

1³/₄ cups semolina flour

1³/₄ cups spelt flour

4 extra large eggs

For the sauce

2¹/₄ pounds New Zealand green lip mussels, scrubbed and beards removed

7 tablespoons extra virgin olive oil

3 garlic cloves, finely chopped

1 pound canned cherry tomatoes

scant 1 cup black olives, pitted

scant 1 cup green olives, pitted

1 tablespoon capers, drained

1 tablespoon rock salt

3 tablespoons finely chopped fresh flat-leaf parsley

salt and pepper

In Italy we use a tool called a chitarra to make the fresh spaghetti. It is a box strung with steel wire (it looks like a guitar) on to which the fresh pasta sheets are placed. They are then forced through the wires with a small rolling pin. If you don't have one, you can of course use the spaghetti form on your pasta machine. For this recipe I use our wonderful New Zealand green lip mussels which are so juicy and large. You can also use the black Mediterranean or other varieties.

FRESH 'GUITAR STRING' SPAGHETTI WITH MUSSELS, CHERRY TOMATOES AND OLIVES

For the spinach pasta, cook the spinach in a little boiling water until wilted. Drain and squeeze out well, then place in a food processor and process to a purée. Combine the two types of flour in a bowl, make a well in the center and add the eggs, egg yolk and puréed spinach in the well. Work with your hands to a soft and thoroughly mixed dough, adding the water if necessary. Knead for 15 minutes, cover with a clean dish towel and let rest for 20 minutes at room temperature. Halve the dough and roll out each piece on a lightly floured surface (preferably marble or stone) to ¹/₄-inch thick sheets. Sprinkle with flour and let dry for 30 minutes, turning once and sprinkling with more flour to prevent them from sticking. Make the pasta sheets into spaghetti and let rest until ready to cook. Follow the same process to make the plain pasta with the ingredients listed. Meanwhile, make the sauce. Discard any mussels with broken shells or that do not shut when sharply tapped. Pour water into a pan to a depth of about 4¹/₂ inches, add the mussels and cover with a tight-fitting lid. Bring to a boil and steam, shaking the pan occasionally, for 3–5 minutes until the shells have opened. Discard any mussels that are still closed. Remove the mussels with a slotted spoon, strain the cooking liquid through a fine strainer and reserve. Heat the olive oil in a pan, add the garlic and cook, stirring occasionally, until translucent. Add the tomatoes, olives, capers and reserved cooking liquid, bring to a boil and cook until reduced by half. Season with salt and pepper, then add the mussels and cook for 2–3 minutes. Meanwhile, bring 5¹/₄ quarts water to a boil, dissolve the rock salt and bring back to a boil. Add both pastas, stir gently with a wooden fork and cook for 3–5 minutes. Drain in a colander and toss with the sauce in a large bowl. Transfer to individual plates and arrange the mussels on the top and around the sides of each plate. Garnish with chopped parsley and season with freshly grated black pepper.

ROAST LAMB WITH RADICCHIO TREVISANO, QUINCE AND PANCETTA

Preheat the oven to 450°F. Season the lamb with the rosemary and garlic, then roll up and tie with kitchen string. Mix the paprika with 3 tablespoons of the olive oil and rub the mixture all over the lamb with your fingers. Place the lamb in a roasting pan and add the celery, onions, carrot and bay leaves. Pour over the remaining olive oil and roast uncovered for 20 minutes. Add the wine and stock, cover the pan with dampened baking parchment and foil, lower the oven temperature to 350°F and roast for 1 hour more until the meat is cooked but still tender and pink inside. Remove the lamb from the roasting pan and let rest. Strain the cooking liquid, reserving the vegetables but discarding the bay leaves, and skim off as much fat as possible. Pass the vegetables through a food mill or process in a food processor to reduce to a purée, adding half the strained cooking juices. Mix the other half of the cooking juices with the Vincotto in a pan, bring to a boil and cook until reduced by one-fourth. Season with salt and pepper. Slice the meat thickly and cover with the sauce. Serve with the radicchio Trevisano (see below).

AGNELLO AL FORNO CON CONTORNO DI
RADICCHIO TREVISANO
ALLE MELE COTOGNE E PANCETTA

Serves 8

4¹/₂-pound leg of lamb, boned and butterflied

2 tablespoons fresh rosemary, finely chopped

3 garlic cloves, crushed • 1 tablespoon sweet paprika

¹/₂ cup extra virgin olive oil

3 celery stalks, finely diced

3 onions, each cut into 6 wedges

1 carrot, coarsely chopped • 4 bay leaves,

2¹/₄ cups rosé wine

(preferably rosato del salento)

scant 1 cup Vegetable Stock (see page 209)

¹/₄ cup Vincotto

salt and pepper

Radicchio Trevisano

with Quince and Pancetta (see below), to serve

We Pugliese are not great carnivores but lamb is high on our list of preferred meats. Living in New Zealand, I naturally make great use of our delicious, grass-fed lamb and this recipe is one of my favorites.

RADICCHIO TREVISANO WITH QUINCE AND PANCETTA

Cook the quince in a small pan with 1¹/₂ cups of water for about 10 minutes until soft. Meanwhile, heat the butter and olive oil in a large skillet, add the pancetta and cook until crisp. Remove the pancetta from the pan and set aside. Add the onion and Jerusalem artichokes to the pan and cook over low heat for a few minutes, then add 2–3 tablespoons water and cook until the Jerusalem artichokes are soft. Add the radicchio leaves, the quince with its cooking liquid and the Vincotto and simmer for 10 minutes until most of the liquid has evaporated. Add the pancetta and cook for a further 5 minutes. Season with salt and pepper.

RADICCHIO TREVISANO ALLE MELE
COTOGNE E PANCETTA

Serves 8

1 quince, cut into fourths • 2 tablespoons butter

3 tablespoons extra virgin olive oil

scant 1 cup pancetta pepata

(pepper coated belly pork), diced

1 red onion, thinly sliced

3 Jerusalem artichokes, thinly sliced

3 heads of radicchio Trevisano,

leaves separated and kept whole

3 tablespoons Vincotto

salt and pepper

Radicchio Trevisano originates from the city of Treviso in the Veneto region. It has long red and white leaves and a slightly bitter taste that I absolutely adore.

FIOR DI LATTE ALLO ZAFFERANO
CON SALSA ALLE ARANCE ROSSE
E VINCOTTO

Serves 6

For the cooked milk puddings

sunflower or olive oil, for brushing

1 1/2 cups milk

1 cup heavy cream

generous 1/4 cup superfine sugar

1/4 teaspoon saffron threads, soaked
in 2 tablespoons boiling water

5 gelatin leaves

For the sauce

juice of 2 blood oranges, strained

juice of 1 lemon, strained

1/4 cup Vincotto

1 teaspoon honey, such as New Zealand Manuka
or other aromatic variety

2 tablespoons Grand Marnier or other orange liqueur

1 blood orange, to decorate

*I find fior di latte – literally 'flower of the milk' – to
be much lighter and more digestible than the
ubiquitous panna cotta. In this version I use saffron
to give it a gorgeous orange color. The sauce uses
Vincotto, a typical product of my region, Salento
(Puglia), made from the cooked must of
Negramaro and Malvasia grapes, which is
available from Italian speciality shops and
delicatessens.*

COOKED SAFFRON MILK PUDDINGS WITH BLOOD ORANGE AND VINCOTTO SAUCE

Lightly brush six individual molds with oil. Place the milk, cream and sugar in a pan and bring to a boil, stirring until the sugar has dissolved. Remove from the heat and stir in the saffron water. Soak the gelatin leaves in a small bowl of cold water for 5 minutes until softened, then drain and squeeze out. Stir the gelatin into the hot milk mixture and let cool to room temperature. Stir briefly, then pour into the prepared molds and chill in the refrigerator for at least 6 hours. To make the sauce, combine the orange juice, lemon juice and Vincotto in a small pan and bring to a boil. Stir in the honey until it dissolves, then remove from the heat. Stir in the Grand Marnier and let cool, then store in the refrigerator until ready to serve. To serve, loosen the edges the milk puddings with a knife and invert onto individual plates. Peel the orange, removing all traces of pith, cut into rounds and then divide each round into six triangular pieces. Spoon a small amount of the sauce on the fior di latte and spoon the remainder around the plates. Decorate with the orange triangles.

Alfonso e Livia Jaccarino

Four generations of Sorrento hoteliers have provided Alfonso Jaccarino with sufficient experience and skill to scale the heights of Italian and then European cuisine during the 1980s and 1990s. His talents as a chef are matched, at each stage, by those of his wife Livia, an authority on wine. Both travel a great deal, gathering wisdom in their visits to both vineyards and to fruit, meat and fish markets all over the world. This love of local producers and retailers led to their decision to study local food and wine in greater depth in order to discover how to preserve their characteristics and quality. This is how Le Peracciole farm came into being, a farm unique in the world and covering 7¹/₂ acres at Punta Campanella, looking out towards the island of Capri. Here, an ideal microclimate gives lettuce, tomatoes, potatoes, onions, aromatic herbs and olives those unique flavors and aromas that, when combined with the freshest of fish or most succulent meat, make the Jaccarino's cooking worthy of their coveted three Michelin stars — dishes such as vermicelli with clams and zucchini, swordfish with celery, lavender and wild spinach, and new potatoes with oysters, chives, shrimp and lentils. You also can't forget the desserts, with their delightful flavors and combinations, such as baked eggplant bound with a chocolate sauce.

Don Alfonso 1890
c.so Sant'Agata 11
Sant'Agata sui Due Golfi (NA)
Italy

MENUS

BACINI DI COZZE CON FIORI DI ZUCCA

RAVIOLI DI CACIOTTA AL POMODORINO E BASILICO

SCORFANO AL VINO BIANCO

PASTICCIO DI MELANZANE CON CIOCCOLATO

BACINI DI COZZE
CON FIORI DI ZUCCA

Serves 4

1 pound 5 ounces live mussels

zucchini, as required

1³/₄ cups bread crumbs

2 tablespoons chopped fresh flat-leaf parsley

¹/₄ cup olive oil

dry white wine, for drizzling

salt

MUSSEL PURSES WITH ZUCCHINI FLOWERS

Preheat the oven to 350°F. Open the mussels and remove the meat, reserving the shells. Carefully clean the zucchini flowers, remove and discard their pistils and steam briefly. Combine the bread crumbs, parsley and a pinch of salt in a bowl and add the mussels. Place the mussels, one by one, in each zucchini flower. Lay the flowers in the mussel shells, place in an ovenproof dish, drizzle with the olive oil and bake for 4 minutes. Remove the dish from the oven and drizzle the wine over the mussels. Transfer to a serving dish and serve.

RAVIOLI DI CACIOTTA
AL POMODORINO E BASILICO

Serves 4

3¹/₂ cups all-purpose flour, plus extra for dusting

scant ¹/₂ cup extra virgin olive oil

9 ounces fresh caciotta cheese, diced

1 fresh marjoram sprig, chopped

1 egg, separated

1 garlic clove, finely chopped

1 pound cherry tomatoes, cut into wedges

²/₃ cup bottled strained tomatoes

10 fresh basil leaves

salt

CACIOTTA RAVIOLI WITH TOMATO AND BASIL

Mix the flour with half the oil to a dough and let rest in a cool place. Meanwhile, prepare the filling. Combine the caciotta, marjoram, egg yolk and a pinch of salt. Lightly beat the egg white. Roll out the half the dough on a lightly floured counter and brush with beaten egg white to seal. Spoon the cheese mixture into a piping bag fitted with a ¹/₂-inch plain nozzle and pipe small mounds of filling at regular intervals on the dough. Roll out the remaining dough, brush with egg white and place on top of the first sheet. Press around the mounds of filling and cut out the ravioli using a small round cutter. Heat the remaining oil in a skillet, add the garlic and cook for 1–2 minutes, then add the tomatoes and strained tomatoes and season with salt if necessary. Add the basil, stir and turn off the heat. Cook the ravioli in a large pan of salted, boiling water for about 2 minutes, then drain well and tip into a serving dish. Pour the sauce over them and serve.

SCORPION FISH IN WHITE WINE

Preheat the oven to 350°F. Heat 3 tablespoons of the olive oil in a flameproof casserole, add the garlic cloves and cook for 2–3 minutes, then remove and discard them. Add the fish fillets and cook until lightly browned on both sides. Season lightly with salt, add the olives and capers, drizzle with the wine and cook until the liquid has evaporated. Sprinkle with the bread crumbs, transfer the casserole to the oven and bake for 20–30 minutes until tender. Meanwhile, roast the red bell pepper until charred and blackened, then remove from the oven. Peel, seed and dice the flesh. Heat the remaining oil in skillet, add the bread cubes and cook, turning frequently, until golden brown all over. Remove with a slotted spoon and drain on paper towels. Transfer the fish fillets to a warm serving dish and sprinkle with the croûtons, red bell pepper and parsley.

SCORFANO AL VINO BIANCO

Serves 4

4 tablespoons olive oil

2 garlic cloves

1 pound 5 ounces scorpion fish fillets

³/₄ cup pitted green olives

2 tablespoons capers, drained, rinsed and chopped

²/₃ cup dry white wine

1 cup fresh bread crumbs

1 red bell pepper

4 tomato bread slices, cut into cubes

2 tablespoons chopped fresh flat-leaf parsley

salt

EGGPLANT PIE WITH CHOCOLATE

Thoroughly combine the ricotta, sugar, candied fruit and 2 ounces of the chocolate in a bowl. Steam the eggplant slices until tender. Melt the remaining chocolate in a heatproof bowl set over a pan of barely simmering water, then remove from the heat and stir in the Marsala. Arrange the cubes of sponge cake on a serving dish and cover them with the ricotta mixture, mounding it up in the center. Place the eggplant slices on top and pour the melted chocolate over them.

PASTICCIO DI MELANZANE

CON CIOCCOLATO

Serves 4

²/₃ cup ricotta cheese

¹/₂ cup confectioner's sugar

scant ¹/₂ cup candied fruit, diced

9 ounces semisweet or bittersweet chocolate, broken into pieces

8 eggplant slices

2 tablespoons Marsala

1 sponge cake, cut into 1-inch cubes

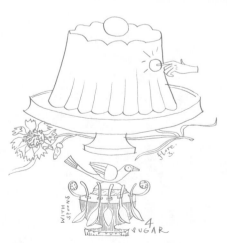

Giorgio Locatelli

Locanda Locatelli
8 Seymour Street
London
United Kingdom

Giorgio Locatelli is one of the finest Italian chefs in the United Kingdom, one who is celebrated for his use of the freshest and best quality produce. So vital is this to his cooking that he imports many of his ingredients directly from Italy. He was raised on the banks of Lake Maggiore in the village of Corgeno, where his family owned a Michelin-starred restaurant. This insured he enjoyed an intense appreciation and understanding of Northern Italian cuisine from an early age. Building on this solid foundation he honed his skills working in local restaurants in the north of Italy and in Switzerland. In 1986 he moved to England to join the kitchens of Anton Edelmann at The Savoy in London. Then he moved to Paris, cooking at Restaurant Laurent and La Tour D'Argent. On his subsequent return to London, Giorgio Locatelli became head chef at Olivio, Eccleston Street, and subsequently opened Zafferano in 1995. It was at Zafferano that his culinary talents received critical acclaim. He made his name in London and, at the same time, he earned international repute with a host of accolades including Best Italian Restaurant (Carlton London Restaurant Awards) and, in the best family tradition, his first Michelin star. Further restaurants in London followed but, in 2002, Giorgio Locatelli opened his first independent restaurant: the Michelin-starred Locanda Locatelli in Marylebone, London. The restaurant soon had a coveted Diploma di Cucina Eccellente, which was conferred on it by the Accademia Italiana della Cucina. Despite its prestigious status in the restaurant scene of London, Locanda Locatelli is renowned for its friendly service and relaxed atmosphere. Bambini are especially welcome. At Locanda Locatelli Giorgio Locatelli serves the traditional Italian dishes of his youth enhanced by his signature innovative interpretations: embracing the natural flavors of the freshest produce.

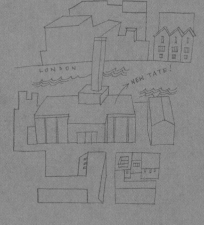

MENUS

CAPPESANTE ALL'ASPRETTO DI ZAFFERANO

RAVIOLI DI FAGIANO

CONIGLIO AL FORNO CON PROSCIUTTO CRUDO E POLENTA

DEGUSTAZIONE DI CIOCCOLATO AMEDEI

PAN-FRIED SCALLOPS WITH SAFFRON VINAIGRETTE

Put the vinegar into a pan with the saffron over low heat and let it reduce by half. Let it cool down. When cold, whisk in the oil and season with salt. If the scallops have been stored in the refrigerator, remove them and let them to come to room temperature before cooking. Preheat the oven to 350°F. To make the purée, put the celery root in an ovenproof dish with 5 tablespoons water, a pinch of salt and the olive oil, cover, seal completely with foil and bake for about 30 minutes until soft. Transfer the celery root mixture to a food processor and process, adding the cream as the motor is running, then pass through a fine strainer to produce a smooth purée. (It is important to process the celery root while it is still hot, as it makes the purée smoother and it will pass more easily through the strainer). Set the purée aside. Put the celery in a bowl with a handful of ice to crisp up. Combine the lemon juice and half the olive oil. Heat an ovenproof skillet – two if you have 12 scallops. When it is hot but not smoking, pour in the rest of the oil, then add the scallops (don't season at this stage as the salt will make them leach out their moisture and they will become dry). Cook the scallops for 1 minute (or 1½ minutes if large), until golden underneath, then turn them over and put into oven for 1 further minute. Season and transfer them to the bowl of saffron vinaigrette. Gently reheat the celery root purée in a small pan and season if necessary. Remove the pan from the heat and beat in the butter. Spoon the purée onto individual plates and arrange the scallops on top. Drain the celery from the ice, season with the lemon and oil mixture and arrange on top of the scallops. Drizzle the remaining saffron vinaigrette around.

CAPPESANTE ALL'ASPRETTO
DI ZAFFERANO

Serves 4

8 large scallops or 12 small ones, shelled and corals reserved

4–5 celery stalks, cut into thin batons

2 tablespoons lemon juice, strained

3 tablespoons extra virgin olive oil

4 tablespoons vinaigrette

salt and pepper

For the vinaigrette

scant 1 cup white wine vinegar

1 level tablespoon saffron threads

scant ½ cup extra virgin olive oil

freshly ground sea salt

For the purée

½ celery root, diced

1 tablespoon olive oil

3 tablespoons heavy cream

¼ cup butter

salt

PHEASANT RAVIOLI WITH ROSEMARY JUS

RAVIOLI DI FAGIANO

Serves 6

1 large drawn and plucked pheasant, boned

4 teaspoons vegetable oil

generous ¹/₂ cup pancetta, finely diced

3 shallots, finely chopped

³/₄ cup white wine

3 tablespoons Parmesan cheese, freshly grated

1 tablespoon fresh bread crumbs

1 egg, plus 1 egg, beaten, to brush the pasta

4 tablespoons heavy cream

¹/₂ quantity of Fresh Pasta Dough (see page 268)

¹/₄ cup sweet butter

1 fresh rosemary sprig

salt and pepper

Preheat the oven to 425°F. Cut the breasts of the pheasants in half crosswise, put them on a counter, skin side up, and season. Heat an ovenproof sauté pan (large enough to hold all the pheasant) until it smokes, then pour in the vegetable oil and add the pheasant, skin side down. Cook quickly until the skin turns golden, then add the pancetta and shallots, turn the pheasant over and cook for a further 2–3 minutes. Add the wine, cook for 1 minute to allow the alcohol to evaporate, then transfer to the oven for 2-3 minutes until the meat is cooked through, but not overcooked (it will continue to cook as it cools). Let the mixture cool then, while it is still warm, put it into a food processor and process to a coarse paste. Transfer the paste to a plate and then spoon a little at a time onto a chopping board. Pass the paste through a strainer or run over it with a spatula or table knife to feel whether any shot has been left in the meat. If so, remove it. Put the mixture into a bowl, add the Parmesan, bread crumbs and egg and season, if necessary. Gradually stir in the cream and then chill in the refrigerator. When the mixture is cold, scoop out small quantities, roll them into about 32 balls with your hands and place them ready to fill the pasta. Make the pasta dough and pass through a pasta machine to make strips. Mark a faint line along the center of the first pasta strip with the back of a knife. Brush one half with beaten egg, then place little mounds of the pheasant mixture, in pairs, on one side of the strip, leaving a space of about 1¹/₂ inches between each mound. Fold the other half of the pasta strip over the top, carefully matching the top edges and pressing them together. Then with your hand, gently press down over the rest (don't worry if you compress the filling a little), so that the two halves of pasta fit together. Press around each mound of filling, making sure the pasta is quite smooth. Using a fluted cutter about ¹/₂ inch bigger in circumference than the filling, cut out each raviolo. Discard the trimmings. Press out air trapped inside, by pinching with your thumbs around the outside of each raviolo until there are no air pockets left. (If you pierce the pasta, just pinch it together again.) Make more ravioli in the same way. Bring a large pan of salted water to a boil. Meanwhile, melt the butter with the rosemary in a large sauté pan and cook until the butter begins to foam. Cook the ravioli in the boiling water for 3-4 minutes, then drain with a slotted spoon and transfer to the pan of sauce. Toss gently for 1–2 minutes and serve.

RABBIT WITH PROSCIUTTO AND POLENTA

Preheat the oven to 250°F. Wrap each rabbit leg in two slices of prosciutto. Heat half the oil in a large, shallow, flameproof casserole, add the rabbit legs and cook over medium heat until they start to color, then add the butter. Turn the legs over and cook for a further 2 minutes. Cover the legs completely with the melted lard, then cover the casserole with foil and cook in the oven for 1 hour until very tender. Meanwhile, cook the polenta. Put it in a large pitcher so that it can be poured in a steady stream. Bring the milk to a boil in a large pan (it should half-fill the pan). Add 1 teaspoon salt and then gradually add the polenta in a continuous stream, stirring constantly with a long-handled whisk until completely blended. When the polenta starts to bubble vigorously, lower the heat to the lowest possible setting and cook, stirring occasionally, for 20 minutes. Cut each radicchio into three pieces and season with salt and pepper. Brush with the remaining oil and cook on a medium-hot griddle pan until wilted. Spoon the polenta onto individual serving plates and put the rabbit legs on top. Add the radicchio on the side and serve immediately.

CONIGLIO AL FORNO
CON PROSCIUTTO CRUDO E POLENTA

Serves 6

6 rabbit legs, boned

12 thin prosciutto slices

2 tablespoons peanut oil

$^1/_4$ cup butter

$2^1/_4$ cups lard, melted

scant 1 cup polenta

5 cups milk

2 heads of radicchio Trevisano

sea salt and pepper

DEGUSTAZIONE DI
CIOCCOLATO AMEDEI

Serves 4

For the dark chocolate mousse

$1/2$ gelatin leaf

5 tablespoons milk

3 ounces Amedei Chuao chocolate

$2^1/2$ ounces egg whites • 2 tablespoons dextrose

For the white chocolate mousse

$1/2$ gelatin leaf

$4^3/4$ ounces Amedei white chocolate

$2/3$ cup whipping cream

7 tablespoons milk • $1/2$ vanilla bean

For the nougatine

$1^1/2$ ounces fondant • $1^1/2$ tablespoons glucose

$1^1/2$ tablespoons honey

$1/2$ cup ground roasted pine nuts

For the chocolate crisps

scant 1 cup confectioner's sugar

1 tablespoon cocoa powder

$1/2$ cup all-purpose flour

pinch of ground cinnamon

$1/3$ cup sweet butter, melted

$3^1/2$ ounces egg whites • pine nuts, to decorate

For the crème anglaise

scant $1/2$ cup whipping cream

$1^3/4$ cups milk

thinly pared rind of $1/2$ orange

$1/2$ cup superfine sugar • $3^1/4$ ounces egg yolks

For the pine nut ice cream

scant $2^1/2$ cups milk

generous $2/3$ cup heavy cream • $2/3$ cup dextrose

$1/3$ cup non-fat dry milk

$1/4$ cup sacarose

$1/8$ ounce ice cream stabilizer

2 tablespoons inverted sugar

scant 1 cup pine nuts, roasted and chopped

AMEDEI CHOCOLATE TASTERS

To make the dark chocolate mousse, soak the gelatin for 5 minutes, then squeeze out. Bring the milk to a boil, then remove from the heat. Melt the chocolate over a pan of barely simmering water, then add the milk, making sure that the mixture doesn't split. Stir in the gelatin. Stiffly whisk the egg whites with the dextrose, then fold into the chocolate. To make the white chocolate mousse, soak the gelatin for 5 minutes, then squeeze out. Melt the chocolate over a pan of barely simmering water. Whip the cream. Pour the milk into a pan and scrape the seeds from the vanilla bean into the pan. Bring to a boil, then add to the chocolate, whisking constantly. Stir in the gelatin. Let the mixture cool to 95°F. Gently fold in the whipped cream. To make the nougatine, put the fondant, glucose and honey in a pan and heat the mixture to 325°F. Remove from the heat and stir in the pine nuts. Put the mixture between two sheets of baking parchment and roll as thinly as possible. Let cool. Preheat the oven to 330°F. Peel off the parchment, break into pieces, place on a cookie sheet and heat in the oven for 2 minutes until soft. Remove from the oven, flatten with the rolling pin and cut into $2^1/4$ x 4-inch rectangles, $1/24$ inch thick. Return to the oven for 20 seconds, then take out and roll around a metal cylinder or spoon, creating cylinder. To make the chocolate crisps, mix all dry ingredients together. Add the butter, mix well, then add the egg whites and mix again. Chill in the refrigerator for at least 2 hours. Preheat the oven to 350°F. With a palette knife, shape the mixture into $6^1/4$ x $1^1/4$-inch rectangles, place on a cookie sheet, sprinkle with pine nuts and bake for 5 minutes. Remove from the oven and place them on a rolling pin to cool. To make the crème anglaise, bring the cream, milk and orange rind to a boil, then let it cool for 30 minutes. Beat the egg yolks with the sugar. Remove the orange rind from the milk mixture and reheat to 140°F, then add the egg yolk mixture. Cook, stirring constantly, until 185°F, then remove from the heat and let cool. For the pine nut ice cream, put the milk, cream, dextrose and milk powder in a pan and heat, whisking with a hand-held blender, to 104°F. Add the sacarose, stabilizer and inverted sugar and bring to 185°F. Remove the pan from the heat and stand it in a bowl of iced water to cool the mixture, then chill in the refrigerator for 6–12 hours. Add the pine nuts to the mixture, then freeze in an ice cream machine. To serve, fill two of the cylinders with bittersweet chocolate mousse and one with white. Place on a plate, next to a bowl of ice cream with a crisp on top of it. Spoon some of the crème anglaise on the side.

Stefano Manfredi

Stefano Manfredi is a leading exponent of modern Italian cooking. Born in the Lombardy region of northern Italy, he settled on Australian shores with his family in 1961. His culinary journey was launched when his first restaurant opened in 1983. It transformed the way the cuisine of Italy was perceived and is the only Italian restaurant to have attained the coveted highest rating from The Sydney Morning Herald Good Food Guide. As one of Australia's leading chefs his success comes from paying tribute to his family's traditional fare in a revitalised contemporary context, in his eateries, cookbooks and food journalism. His latest venture after a distinguished line of restaurant projects is Manta Restaurant: Italian seafood dining located in an historic wharf building with spectacular views across the marina to the city skyline. Simplicity and freshness is the mantra at Manta Restaurant where exquisite dishes of unadulterated flavors are created. Stefano Manfredi believes that 'good cooking involves a lot of work even before one starts to cook'. At Manta Restaurant the selection and preparation of exceptional quality ingredients is fundamental and the menu is changed daily to honor seasonal availability. The fruits of the sea, in peak condition, are selected each morning at the fish market auction. Handpicked oysters are delivered directly from the grower. As each day's fish haul arrives in the kitchen, it is carefully dry-filleted, without using running water, to maintain the integrity of the texture and flavor. Dedicated to this freshest of produce, Stefano Manfredi has received critical and popular acclamation for his sophisticated reinvention of his proud Italian heritage.

Manta Restaurant
The Wharf,
Cowper Wharf Road
Woolloomooloo
Australia

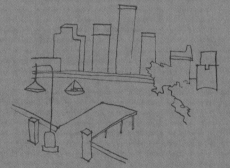

MENUS

CROSTINI CON PEPERONI E CIPOLLE AL AGRODOLCE

TAGLIATELLE CON GAMBERI DI FIUME, BURRO E SESAMO

FAGIANO ARROSTO CON VERZA, CASTAGNE E SALSA AL VINO ROSSO

TORTA SBRISOLONA CON MELA COTOGNA, CREMA DI MASCARPONE E VINCOTTO

CROSTINI WITH BELL PEPPERS AND ONIONS IN AGRODOLCE

CROSTINI CON PEPERONI E CIPOLLE AL AGRODOLCE

Serves 6

2 red bell peppers, seeded

2 yellow bell peppers, seeded

2 red onions

extra virgin olive oil, for drizzling and brushing

2 tablespoons balsamic vinegar

6 x 1/2-inch thick bread slices

salt and pepper

Preheat the oven to 350°F. Cut all the bell peppers into eight strips and cut both onions into eight wedges. Spread them out in a roasting pan, drizzle with olive oil, season with salt and pepper and toss well to coat. Bake for about 20 minutes until softened. Remove the pan from the oven, add the balsamic vinegar, mix well and let cool to room temperature. Preheat the broiler. Cut each slice of bread into three or four pieces, brush with olive oil and toast on both sides. Top the crostini with the vegetables and serve.

TAGLIATELLE WITH YABBIES, BUTTER AND SESAME SEEDS

TAGLIATELLE CON GAMBERI DI FIUME, BURRO E SESAMO

Serves 6

For the tagliatelle

5 1/4 cups all-purpose flour

6 eggs

For the topping

30 live yabbies or other freshwater crayfish

1/2 cup sesame seeds, toasted

1/2 cup butter, softened and thinly sliced

generous 1 cup grana padano, finely grated

salt and pepper

To make the tagliatelle, sift the flour into a mound on a counter and make a well in the center. Crack the eggs directly into the well and gradually bring the mixture together to form a dough. Add a little more flour if the mixture is too wet. Roll the dough through a pasta machine until it is very thin, then cut into 1/4 inch wide tagliatelle. For the topping, bring a large pan of salted water to a boil, add the yabbies or crayfish and bring to a boil, then immediately remove the seafood from the water, peel off the shells and cut each tail in half lengthwise. Cook the tagliatelle in a large pan of salted, boiling water for a few minutes until al dente, then drain and toss with the sesame seeds, butter, yabbies or crayfish, cheese and salt and pepper to taste. Serve immediately.

ROAST PHEASANT WITH SAVOY CABBAGE, CHESTNUTS AND RED WINE

For the red wine sauce, heat the olive oil in a pan, add the onion, celery and garlic and cook over low heat, stirring occasionally, for a few minutes until softened but not colored. Add the vinegar, increase the heat to medium and cook until the liquid has reduced by three-fourths. Pour in the wine and cook, skimming off any scum that rises to the surface, until the liquid has reduced by half. Strain the mixture through a cheesecloth-lined strainer into a clean pan, return to the heat and cook until reduced to 1 cup. To prepare the cabbage and chestnuts, heat the olive oil in a pan, add the onion and pancetta and cook over low heat, stirring occasionally, until softened and light golden brown. Add the cabbage, season with salt and cook, stirring constantly, until wilted. Add the chestnuts and simmer gently until the cabbage is tender but still retains a little texture. Season to taste. To prepare the pheasants, preheat the oven to 475°F. Rub each bird with a little olive oil, sprinkle with salt and place them in a roasting pan. Roast for 15–20 minutes until each pheasant is cooked through. Remove the roasting pan from the oven but do not switch off. Remove the pheasants from the roasting pan and let rest in a warm place for about 10 minutes. Meanwhile, add the red wine reduction to the roasting pan, mix thoroughly with the cooking juices and return the pan to the oven for 5–6 minutes. Strain the sauce through a cheesecloth-lined strainer and keep warm. To serve, cut the breast meat off the bones and remove the legs from each bird. Place half a bird on each of six plates and serve with the cabbage and chestnuts and red wine sauce.

FAGIANO ARROSTO CON VERZA, CASTAGNE E SALSA AL VINO ROSSO

Serves 6

3 x 1³/₄-pound pheasants, drawn and plucked
extra virgin olive oil, for rubbing
salt

For the red wine sauce
3 tablespoons extra virgin olive oil
1 onion, chopped
1 celery heart, chopped
10 garlic cloves, chopped
1 cup balsamic vinegar
6¹/₄ cups red wine

For the cabbage and chestnuts
3 tablespoons extra virgin olive oil
1 onion, finely diced
generous ¹/₂ cup pancetta, finely diced
¹/₂ Savoy cabbage, cored and shredded
30 chestnuts, cooked and peeled (see page 432)
salt and pepper

TORTA SBRISOLONA CON MELA COTOGNA,
CREMA DI MASCARPONE E VINCOTTO

Makes 20

For the torta sbrisolona

1 cup all-purpose flour

³/₄ cup fine polenta flour

scant 1 cup ground almonds

scant ¹/₂ cup superfine sugar

1 egg yolk

juice of ¹/₂ lemon

1 teaspoon vanilla extract

grated rind of 1 lemon

5 tablespoons butter

¹/₄ cup duck fat

For the quinces

6 quinces

4 cups dry white wine

1¹/₃ cups sugar

2 cinnamon sticks

8 black peppercorns

1–2 tablespoons vincotto

For the mascarpone cream

2 egg whites

generous ¹/₃ cup superfine sugar

1¹/₃ cups mascarpone cheese

1 teaspoon vanilla extract

TORTA SBRISOLONA WITH QUINCE, MASCARPONE CREAM AND VINCOTTO

Preheat the oven to 325°F. Line a cookie sheet with baking parchment. To make the torta sbrisolona, combine the flour, polenta, ground almonds, sugar, egg yolk, lemon juice, vanilla extract and lemon rind in a bowl. Add the butter and duck fat and gradually incorporate into the dry ingredients to form a dough. Roll out the dough to a thickness of ¹/₄ inch and stamp out rounds with an 3¹/₄-inch cookie cutter. Place the rounds on the prepared cookie sheet and bake for 30 minutes. Remove from the oven and let cool. Preheat the oven to 225°F. Peel the quinces, cut them into fourths, leaving the cores intact, place in an ovenproof dish and pour in the wine to cover. Sprinkle with the sugar and bake for 6–8 hours until tender. Remove from the oven and let cool, then core the fruit and thinly slice each fourth. To make the mascarpone cream, whisk the egg whites in a grease-free bowl until soft peaks form. Gradually whisk in the sugar until stiff peaks form. Fold in the mascarpone and vanilla extract. To serve, place a spoonful of mascarpone cream on each of the sbrisolona and top with the quince slices, then sprinkle with the vincotto.

CREAM

Gualtiero Marchesi

1977 witnessed the dawn of a new age in Italian food when Gualtiero Marchesi opened his restaurant in Via Bonvesin de la Riva in Milan. A single example of one of his dishes defines his nouvelle-cuisine style of conceptual cooking – 7 pasta penne, ³/₄ ounces sliced back Norcia truffle and 7 asparagus tips (bevel cut). However, this style of cooking was one with which the public grew weary. After fifteen years, Marchesi reconsidered his menu and at the Albereta, his new restaurant at Erbusco in Franciacorta, which opened in 1993, he reinvented the ancient recipe for lasagne. He opened out the pasta sheets instead of layering them, covered them with a light meat sauce and flour-free béchamel, using less stock and cream. Marchesi's fame travelled afar and for a few years he became for some 'the divine Marchesi', the first Italian to be awarded the prestigious three Michelin stars. On 22 October 2002, the International Academy of Gastronomy awarded Gualtiero Marchesi the Grand Prix Mémoire et Gratitude, the most prestigious prize that the Academy gives.

L'Albereta
Via Vittorio Emanuele 23
Erbusco (BS)
Italy

MENUS

INSALATA DI STORIONE CON LE SUE UOVA

RAVIOLO APERTO

FILETTO DI VITELLO ALLA ROSSINI

SFORMATO DI PANETTONE

INSALATA DI STORIONE
CON LE SUE UOVA

STURGEON SALAD WITH CAVIAR

INSALATA DI STORIONE CON LE SUE UOVA

Serves 4

4 tablespoons Vinaigrette
made with lemon juice (see page 76)
9-ounce sturgeon fillet
3¹/₂ ounces mixed salad greens
1 onion, finely chopped
3 tablespoons oscietra caviar
fresh chervil sprigs, to garnish

Pour 2 tablespoons of the vinaigrette into a dish. Thinly slice the sturgeon, pound the slices lightly and place carefully in the dish with the dressing. Toss the salad greens in 1 tablespoon of the remaining vinaigrette and divide them among four plates. Add the onion and caviar to the remaining vinaigrette. Place the slices of fish on the salad greens, sprinkle them with the caviar mixture and garnish them liberally with chervil.

OPEN RAVIOLO

RAVIOLO APERTO

Serves 6

For the parsley pasta dough
scant 1 cup all-purpose flour, plus extra for dusting
1 egg
1–2 tablespoons olive oil

For the green pasta dough
scant 1 cup all-purpose flour, plus extra for dusting
3 ounces spinach
1 egg
1–2 tablespoons olive oil
salt

For the filling
6 large parsley leaves
1 pound 5 ounces scallops, shelled
2-inch piece of fresh ginger root, grated
¹/₂ cup butter
scant ¹/₂ cup dry white wine
salt and white pepper

Make the parsley pasta dough (see page 268) with the flour, egg and oil and roll out on a lightly floured surface to ¹/₈ inch thick. Cut out twelve 2-inch squares. Place a parsley leaf in the center of half the squares, cover with the remaining squares and pass them through a pasta machine several times until the pasta is reduced to a thickness of about ¹/₂₅ inch. Make the green pasta dough (see page 268) and roll out on a lightly floured surface to ¹/₂₅ inch thick. Cut out six 4-inch squares. To prepare the filling, cut the scallops in half crosswise and season them with salt and pepper. Squeeze out the juice from the grated ginger and reserve 1 tablespoon. Melt 1¹/₂ tablespoons of the butter in a skillet, add the scallops and cook them for a few seconds, then pour in the wine and cook for a few minutes. Remove the scallops from the skillet. Heat the cooking liquid until it has reduced, add the ginger juice and whisk in the remaining butter to make the sauce. Return the scallops to the skillet and cook for a few minutes more. Cook the pasta squares in a large pan of salted, boiling water until al dente. Pour a tablespoon of sauce onto each of six warm plates, place a green pasta square on top, divide the scallops and remaining sauce among them and top with the parsley pasta.

FILLET OF VEAL ALLA ROSSINI

Preheat the oven to 350°F. Melt 1¹/₂ tablespoons of the butter in an ovenproof skillet, preferably a copper one. Season the veal with salt, add to the skillet and cook until lightly browned on both sides, then transfer to the oven and cook for 7 minutes. Remove the skillet from the oven, set the veal aside and keep warm. Set the skillet over low heat, pour in the Madeira and cook, stirring and scraping up the sediment from the base, until the liquid has evaporated. Add the truffle juice and cook until it has reduced, then add the stock and truffle and season with salt. Bring to a boil and whisk in 1¹/₂ teaspoons of the remaining butter. Briefly cook the four slices of foie gras in a nonstick pan and place them on the veal fillets. Put the golden raisins in a bowl, add warm water to cover and let soak for 5 minutes, then drain and squeeze out. Meanwhile, dry-fry the pine nuts until golden brown. Melt the remaining butter in another skillet, add the spinach and cook until just wilted, then add the pine nuts and raisins and season to taste. Arrange a bed of spinach on each of four warm plates, place the fillets on top and pour the sauce around them.

FILETTO DI VITELLO ALLA ROSSINI

Serves 4

¹/₄ cup butter

4 x 5-ounce veal fillets

¹/₄ cup Madeira

3 tablespoons truffle juice

scant ¹/₂ cup Meat Stock (see page 208)

³/₄ ounce black truffle, chopped

4 x 1¹/₂-ounce foie gras slices

2¹/₂ tablespoons golden raisins

3 tablespoons pine nuts

14 ounces spinach

salt and pepper

PANETTONE PUDDING

Cut the orange and lemon rinds into thin batons and place in a small pan with the orange juice, candied peel, golden raisins, candied orange, Grand Marnier and sugar syrup. Bring to a boil and cook until reduced by half. Meanwhile, soak the gelatin in cold water for 5 minutes, then squeeze out. Remove the pan from the heat and, while it is still warm, mix the resulting syrup with half the custard and the gelatin. Blend well and let cool, stirring occasionally. Meanwhile, stiffly whisk the egg whites and gently fold them into the mixture, then fold in the superfine sugar. Thickly whip the cream in another bowl and fold it into the mixture. Cut the panettone into cubes and add it to the mixture. Divide the mixture among four molds, and chill in the refrigerator for 3–4 hours. To serve, divide the remaining custard among four dishes, carefully turn the puddings out of their molds and place one in the center of each dish. To make the custard, pour the milk into a pan and bring to a boil, then remove from the heat. Beat the egg yolks with the sugar in another pan until pale and fluffy. Pour in the milk in a thin, continuous stream, whisking constantly. Cook the custard over medium heat, stirring constantly, until thickened. Do not allow it to boil.

SFORMATO DI PANETTONE

Serves 4

thinly pared rind of ¹/₂ orange

thinly pared rind of ¹/₂ lemon

2 tablespoons orange juice

2 tablespoons chopped candied citron peel

2¹/₂ tablespoons golden raisins, chopped

2¹/₂ tablespoons candied orange, chopped

2 tablespoons Grand Marnier

2 tablespoons Sugar Syrup (see page 1019)

2 gelatin leaves

1¹/₄ cups Custard (see below)

2 egg whites • 2 tablespoons superfine sugar

scant ¹/₂ cup heavy cream

3 ounces panettone, crusts removed

For the custard

1 cup milk

4 egg yolks

generous ¹/₂ cup superfine sugar

Karen Martini

Melbourne Wine Room
125 Fitzroy Street
St Kilda, Victoria
Australia

Definitively original, the cooking of Karen Martini is a Mediterranean affair of inventive flavor combinations. The celebrated Australian chef, restaurateur, writer and television presenter draws inspiration from her rich cultural heritage. Bistecca fiorentina, her signature dish, has its roots in Florence but thrives under her care. The aged rib-eye steak is charbroiled over charcoal or wood, encrusted in Sicilian sea salt and served with horseradish. Karen Martini determined when young that her sole aim was to cook. Her gastronomic direction was shaped by family influences, including those of her father's parents who hailed from Tuscany and Nice and had been pastry chefs in Tunisia. Karen Martini spent her youth learning Tuscan and other recipes from her province as well as the Italian-influenced cuisine of North Africa. Together with her grandparents, she prepared the classics that now comprise her style. At 15 years old her training commenced with apprenticeships followed by trade school. She went on to absorb the basics of French cuisine in the kitchens of Melbourne restaurant, Tansy's. Next, travelling in Europe, she consolidated her repertoire of regional Italian dishes. Returning to Australia she held several head-chef positions before becoming founding chef at The Melbourne Wine Room. The popular bustling wine bar with adjoining dining room has won numerous prestigious awards. Complemented by an impressive wine cellar, the menu is celebrated for its combinations of intense flavors and textures that excite without overwhelming the palate. The award-winning wine list, with over 800 listings, embraces outstanding wines from the world's boutique and smaller winemakers.

MENUS

CARPACCIO DI TONNO CON FINOCCHIO BOTTARGA

INSALATA DI GAMBERETTI E FAGIOLI BIANCHI, CONDITA CON OLIO DI TARTUFO

COSTOLETTINE DI AGNELLO CON PATATE E CONDITE CON FETA E ORIGANO

PASTA DI CHOUX CON CREMA PASTICCIERA DI MANDORLE E SALSA CIOCCOLATO
E MANDORLE CROCCANTI

YELLOW FIN TUNA CARPACCIO WITH SHAVED FENNEL AND LEMON AND BOTTARGA

Cut the tuna into four even-sized slices, place them between sheets of baking parchment and press out gently with the back of the knife to form four even rounds. Set aside. Stiffly whip the cream with the yogurt, then fold in salt and lemon juice to taste. Thinly shave the fennel into ribbons with a mandoline and sprinkle with the reserved fennel fronds. Place the tuna on four plates, season with salt and pepper and sprinkle with the diced shallot, fennel ribbons and lemon triangles. Add a spoonful of the cream mixture to each plate and thinly shave the bottarga over the plates using a sharp knife. Drizzle generously with the oil and place a grissini across each plate of carpaccio.

CARPACCIO DI TONNO CON FINOCCHIO E BOTTARGA

Serves 4

1 pound 2-ounce tuna mid-loin, sashimi grade

1/2 cup heavy cream

1 tablespoon natural yogurt

dash of lemon juice

1 fennel bulb, trimmed with fronds reserved

1 purple shallot, finely diced

1 lemon, peeled, segmented
and cut into little triangles

3 ounces bottarga • 4 grissini

scant 1 cup extra virgin olive oil

sea salt and pepper

SEARED SHRIMP WITH CANNELLINI BEAN SALAD AND TARTUFO DRESSING

Remove the shrimp heads, peel the bodies, but leave the tail shells intact, and devein. Combine the beans, half the lemon juice and the extra virgin olive oil in a bowl, season with salt and pepper and set aside in a warm place. Heat a large skillet, add a little oil for frying, then add the shrimp and stir-fry quickly without coloring. Season with salt and pepper, add the shallots and garlic to the skillet, then stir in the beans. Remove the skillet from the heat. Stir in the fennel, celery leaves and chives and transfer the mixture to a dish. To make the dressing, combine the truffle paste, lemon juice and olive oil and pour it over the shrimp and beans. Drizzle any extra dressing over the salad before serving. Finally, shave over the white truffle.

INSALATA DI GAMBERETTI E FAGIOLI BIANCHI, CONDITA CON OLIO DI TARTUFO

Serves 4

12 raw jumbo shrimp

generous 2 cups cooked cannellini beans,
drained and cooled to room temperature

scant 1/2 cup freshly
squeezed lemon juice, strained

2/3 cup extra virgin olive oil

olive oil, for frying • 3 shallots, finely diced

2 garlic cloves, finely diced

1 fennel heart, thinly shaved, with fronds reserved

fine yellow leaves of 1 celery heart, thinly sliced

1/2 bunch of chives, finely chopped

1 small fresh white truffle (optional)

salt and pepper

For the truffle dressing

1 tablespoon truffle paste

5 teaspoons lemon juice

scant 1/2 cup extra virgin olive oil

4 teaspoons truffle oil

1 tablespoon roasted garlic

filament scraped from 1 large,
broken-up field mushroom

COSTOLETTINE DI AGNELLO CON

PATATE E CONDITE CON FETA E

ORIGANO

Serves 6

2 racks of lamb, each with about 8 chops

6 garlic cloves, crushed with the flat of a knife

½ bunch of fresh oregano

scant ½ cup extra virgin olive oil,

plus extra for drizzling

juice of 1 lemon, strained

4 teaspoons sherry vinegar

12 potatoes, sliced lengthwise

7 ounces curly endive

2 bunches of baby leeks, trimmed

½ cup Vinaigrette (see page 76)

¾ cup Ligurian olives

7 ounces soft marinated feta cheese

salt and pepper

CHARBROILED LAMB CHOPS WITH OREGANO AND HOT FETA DRESSING

Trim the racks of lamb but leave a layer of fat, then score the fat in crisscross lines. Cut the racks into separate chops. Combine the garlic, half the oregano, the oil, lemon juice and vinegar in a large, nonmetallic dish, season with pepper, add the lamb and let marinate. Meanwhile, cook the potatoes in salted, boiling water until tender, then drain, drizzle with olive oil and season with salt and pepper. Add the curly endive while the potatoes are still hot, toss gently and set aside in a warm place. Preheat the broiler. Cook the leeks in another pan of boiling water for 2–3 minutes, then drain, drizzle with olive oil and season with salt and pepper. Drain the cutlets, season with salt and cook for 4–6 minutes until browned. Pour the vinaigrette into a shallow pan, add the olives, the remaining oregano leaves and the feta. Stir gently over low heat to warm through. Place the warm potatoes on a platter, top with the lamb cutlets, sprinkle with the leeks and spoon the hot dressing over the dish. Season with a little black pepper and serve.

CHOUX PASTRY CREST WITH ALMOND CREAM, PRALINE, CHOCOLATE SAUCE AND GOLD LEAF

Preheat the oven to 425°F. To make the choux paste, put the milk, butter, sugar and salt in a pan, add scant $^1/_2$ cup water and bring to a boil. Tip in the flour and beat well with a wooden spoon to combine. Cook over medium heat for 5 minutes. Remove the pan from the heat and beat the mixture with an electric mixer, then gradually beat in the eggs making sure that they are fully incorporated before the next addition. Spoon the mixture into a pastry bag fitted with a star tip and pipe donut-shaped rounds on a cookie sheet. Sprinkle the cookie sheet with a little water and bake for 5 minutes, then open the oven door and let the steam escape. Lower the oven temperature to 350°F and bake for a further 10–15 minutes until dried out. Remove from the oven and let cool. To make the almond cream, heat the milk, butter, half the sugar, the lemon rind and vanilla bean in a pan. Meanwhile, beat the egg yolks with the remaining sugar in a bowl, then whisk in the cornstarch in three batches. Remove the hot milk from the heat and stir it into the egg yolk mixture. Return the mixture to the pan and bring to simmering point, whisking constantly. Lower the heat and simmer gently for 5 minutes. Stir in the almond extract and discard the vanilla bean. Pour the cream into a tray and cover with plastic wrap. To make the chocolate sauce, place the chocolate, cream and honey in a pan over low heat. Whisk the unsweetened cocoa powder with 5 tablespoons water and the vanilla extract in a bowl and add to the chocolate mixture. Cook, stirring constantly, until melted and almost simmering. Remove from the heat and stir in the butter in small pieces at a time. Put the sugar in a pan, add about 2 tablespoons water and bring to a boil, then cook until the sugar caramelizes and turns golden brown. Stir in the almonds, remove the pan from the heat and pour the mixture onto an oiled cookie sheet. Let cool and set. Wrap a rolling pin in baking parchment and use to crush the praline, then store in an airtight container. Beat 1 cup of the almond cream with sufficient light cream to give a smooth consistency. Spoon into a pastry bag. Cut off a small 'lid' from each choux pastry and fill with the almond cream. Replace the lids. Place the pastries on a plate and pour the chocolate sauce over them. Sprinkle with the praline and confectioner's sugar or garnish with gold leaf filament.

PASTA DI CHOUX CON CREMA PASTICCIERA DI MANDORLE E SALSA CIOCCOLATO E MANDORLE CROCCANTI

Serves 6

1 quantity Choux Paste (see page 1011)

For the almond cream
2$^1/_4$ cups milk
2 tablespoons butter
$^1/_2$ cup superfine sugar
finely grated rind of $^1/_2$ lemon
$^1/_2$ vanilla bean
4 egg yolks
$^1/_2$ cup cornstarch
1 drop almond extract

For the chocolate sauce
7 ounces bittersweet chocolate, broken into pieces
scant $^1/_2$ cup heavy cream
$^1/_4$ cup unsweetened cocoa powder
scant $^1/_3$ cup honey
2 tablespoons butter, cut into small pieces
1 teaspoon vanilla extract

For the praline
olive oil, for brushing
2 tablespoons sugar
$^1/_2$ cup almonds, toasted

To serve
$^2/_3$ cup light cream
confectioner's sugar, for sprinkling (optional)
gold leaf filament (optional)

Gianluigi Morini

San Domenico
via Sacchi 1
Imola (BO)
Italy

Gianluigi Morini was born in Imola in 1935 in the very house where, on 7 March 1970, he opened the restaurant that was to become one of the most prestigious in Italy. A man with diverse interests, Morini had finally discovered his true vocation. But this was no passing whim – he sought out Nino Bergese, the legendary chef of kings, as his private tutor. It was not easy to persuade Bergese to leave his retirement in the peace and quiet of his home by the sea, but in the end Morini won him over. Bergese generously taught him the secrets of the trade, introduced him to the great dishes that had been created in the kitchens of the most prestigious Italian dynasties, drew up the menus at the San Domenico, organized service and guided the skills of the young chef Valentino Marcattilii. Today, Marcattilii is one of the most successful and internationally recognized Italian chefs, one who won his first Michelin star at the age of twenty and his second at twenty-two. Marcattilii's style became increasingly sophisticated, its success springing from the reintroduction of aristocratic dishes with a balanced blend of tradition and innovation. Morini meanwhile continued to perfect every detail of his restaurant, even providing a background of classical music each day that had been selected by Piero Buscaroli, a musicologist of world renown.

MENUS

TORTELLINI CON CREMA DI FEGATO D'OCA

QUAGLIE FARCITE CON VERDURE E PISELLI

CIOCCOCOCCO

TORTELLINI WITH GOOSE LIVER CREAM

Cook the goose liver in a nonstick pan with the bay leaves but without any additional fat for a few minutes. Remove the pan from the heat and let cool. Discard the bay leaves, put the liver in a food processor with the butter and process until smooth. Pass the mixture through a fine strainer into a bowl. Gently heat the cream in the same pan, add the liver mixture and nutmeg and season with salt and pepper if necessary. Cook the tortellini in a large pan of salted, boiling water until al dente, then drain and transfer to the pan of sauce. Cook, stirring constantly, for 2 minutes. Sprinkle with the Parmesan and serve with slivers of black truffle if you like.

TORTELLINI CON CREMA DI FEGATO D'OCA

Serves 4

7 ounces goose liver, sliced

3 bay leaves

scant ½ cup butter

scant ½ cup heavy cream

pinch of freshly grated nutmeg

14 ounces tortellini bolognesi

⅔ cup Parmesan cheese, freshly grated

salt and pepper

thinly shaved black truffle (optional), to serve

QUAIL STUFFED WITH GREEN VEGETABLES AND PEAS

Heat the half the oil and half the butter in a skillet, add the peas and spinach and cook over low heat, gradually adding the stock, until tender. Remove from the heat and let cool. Put the vegetable mixture in a food processor with the chicken and process until smooth. Combine the goose liver and eggs, season with salt and pepper if necessary and add the vegetable mixture. Stuff the quail with the mixture and let stand for about 3 hours. Preheat the oven to 350°F. Grease the reserved bones with the remaining oil and butter and place in an ovenproof dish with the quail. Season with salt and pepper, add the garlic and roast until the quail are browned all over and cooked through. (Test by piercing the thickest part with the point of a sharp knife. If the juices run clear, the quail are cooked.) Add the balsamic vinegar and return to the oven for a few minutes. Add the wine and cook until it has evaporated. Remove the quail, strain the cooking juices and season if necessary. Serve on warm plates with broiled or baked eggplant.

QUAGLIE FARCITE CON VERDURE E PISELLI

Serves 4

2 tablespoons olive oil

2 tablespoons butter

scant 1 cup shelled peas

5 ounces spinach

2 cups Chicken Stock (see page 209)

3½ ounces skinless, boneless chicken breast, coarsely chopped

5 ounces poached goose liver, cut into cubes

2 eggs

4 quail, boned with bones reserved

4 garlic cloves

5 tablespoons balsamic vinegar

¾ cup dry white wine

salt and pepper

broiled or baked eggplant, to serve

CHOCOCOCONUT

CIOCCOCOCCO

Serves 4

For the chocolate mousse
1 gelatin leaf
3 egg yolks
scant $^1/_2$ cup superfine sugar
3 tablespoons unsweetened cocoa powder
1$^1/_4$ cups milk
1 cup heavy cream

For the coconut mousse
1 gelatin leaf
3 egg yolks
scant $^1/_2$ cup superfine sugar
1$^1/_4$ cups milk
1$^2/_3$ cups dry unsweetened shredded coconut
1 cup heavy cream

For the caramel sauce
$^1/_2$ cup superfine sugar
1$^1/_4$ cups heavy cream

To decorate
4 fresh mint sprigs
1 ounces semisweet or bittersweet chocolate,
shaved

To make the chocolate mousse, soak the gelatin in a small bowl of cold water for 5 minutes, then squeeze out. Beat the egg yolks with the sugar and the cocoa powder until smooth and thoroughly combined. Bring the milk just to a boil and pour it into the egg mixture, stirring constantly, then add the gelatin and let cool, stirring occasionally. Stiffly whip the cream and fold it into the custard. Half-fill four large molds with the mixture and chill in the refrigerator until set. To make the coconut mousse, soak the gelatin in a small bowl of cold water for 5 minutes, then squeeze out. Beat the egg yolks with the sugar until thoroughly combined. Pour the milk into a pan, add the coconut and bring to a boil. Remove the pan from the heat and strain the milk into the egg yolk mixture, stirring constantly, then add the gelatin and let cool, stirring occasionally. Reserve the coconut and let dry. Stiffly whip the cream and fold it into the cooled custard. Remove the molds from the refrigerator, spoon in the coconut mixture and chill for several hours. To make the caramel sauce, put the sugar in a pan, add 5 tablespoons water and stir over low heat until the sugar has dissolved, then continue cooking until the mixture turns a golden color. Add the cream, bring to a boil, stirring constantly, and simmer for a few minutes. Remove the pan from the heat, strain the sauce and let cool. Pour the caramel sauce into four dishes. Turn out the chocococonut from the molds, place them on the sauce, dust with the reserved coconut and decorate with the mint and the chocolate shavings.

Fulvio Pierangelini

Fulvio Pierangelini's passion for cooking began at the age of fifteen. It was then he became convinved that he should study cooking techniques so that when he grew up he would be able to start work on solid foundations. He was pressured by his family to stay at school and then go to university to obtain a degree in political science, but he did not give up easily and spent his summer holidays working with high-calibre chefs to learn the techniques and culinary secrets that were later to create his distinctive style. His dishes show some affinity with nouvelle cuisine, but the ingredients are typically local, albeit being interpreted without being limited by tradition. In 1981 he opened Il Gambero Rosso, a restaurant on the San Vincenzo waterfront and, within a few years, became the most imitated chef in the whole of Tuscany. This imitation reached such a level that he felt compelled to put up a notice at the entrance to his restaurant controversially banning entry by fellow chefs. The cuisine of Fulvio Pierangelini, time after time sanctioned by Michelin stars, is part passion and part instinct, although he maintains that most of the results of his recipes are inspired by the quality of the raw ingredients which he checks and selects carefully and thoroughly each day. The most often discussed and applauded dishes on his menu include scallops à la coque with oil and lemon, ravioli with tomato and romano cheese with green garlic and squab casserole.

Il Gambero Rosso
piazza della Vittoria 13
S. Vincenzo (LI)
Italy

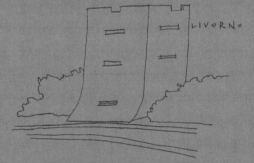

MENUS

PASSATINA DI CECI CON GAMBERI

RAVIOLI DI PESCE AI FRUTTI DI MARE

PICCIONI AL VINO ROSSO

SEMIFREDDO AI FRUTTI DI BOSCO

PASSATINA DI CECI CON GAMBERI

Serves 4

scant ½ cup garbanzo beans,
soaked overnight and drained

1 garlic clove

1 fresh rosemary sprig

1¾ pounds raw shrimp, peeled and deveined

extra virgin olive oil, for drizzling

salt and pepper

PURÉE OF GARBANZO BEANS WITH SHRIMP

Put the garbanzo beans, garlic and rosemary in a pan, add water to cover and bring to a boil, then lower the heat and simmer gently for about 2½ hours until the beans are tender. Drain well, discard the garlic and rosemary and pass the beans through a strainer into a bowl. Steam the shrimp for a few minutes until they change color. Spoon a pool of garbanzo bean purée onto each of four warm dishes and top with the shrimp. Drizzle with olive oil and season with salt and pepper to taste.

RAVIOLI DI PESCE AI FRUTTI DI MARE

Serves 4

For the pasta dough

1¾ cups all-purpose flour, plus extra for dusting

2 eggs

2 tablespoons chopped fresh flat-leaf parsley

For the filling

2¼-pound skate, cleaned and skinned

4 cups Fish Stock (see page 208–9)

For the sauce

5 tablespoons olive oil

2 garlic cloves

1 medium cuttlefish, skinned, cleaned
and cut into small pieces

1 small octopus, skinned, cleaned
and cut into small pieces

5 tablespoons dry white wine

7 ounces tomatoes, peeled and coarsely chopped

20 raw shrimp, peeled and deveined

10 mussels, shelled

salt and pepper

FISH RAVIOLI WITH SHELLFISH

To make the filling, place the skate in a pan, add the stock and bring just to a boil, then lower the heat and simmer for about 20 minutes. Remove the skate with a slotted spatula and let cool. Reserve the vegetables from the stock. When the fish is cold, remove the flesh from the cartilage and place in a food processor with the reserved vegetables. Process until thoroughly combined. Make the pasta dough (see page 268) with the flour and eggs and roll out on a lightly floured counter to a very thin sheet, then cut it into strips. Place cherry-size mounds of the filling on the long side of the strips at 1-inch intervals. Fold the pasta over them, pressing out the air, and seal the edges. Cut out the ravioli with a wheel and place on a lightly floured dish towel. To make the sauce, heat the oil in a shallow pan, add the garlic and cook for a few minutes, then remove and discard them. Add the cuttlefish and octopus and cook over medium-high heat, stirring frequently, until golden brown. Add the wine and cook until it has evaporated. Add the tomatoes, season with salt and pepper and cook for a few minutes, then add the shrimp and mussels and cook for a further 10 minutes. Cook the ravioli in a large pan of salted, boiling water, then drain well, dress with the shellfish sauce and sprinkle with the parsley.

SQUAB IN RED WINE

Heat half the olive oil in a skillet, add the garlic cloves and cook for a few minutes, then remove and discard, Add the squab and cook, turning occasionally, until golden brown all over and cooked through. Season with salt and pepper and remove them from the pan. Remove the breasts and legs from the squab, set aside and keep warm. Carefully bone the rest of the squab, reserving the carcasses. Heat the remaining oil in a skillet, add the shallots and carrots and cook over low heat, stirring occasionally, until softened. Place the squab carcasses in a shallow pan and heat gently. Add the wine and cook until it has reduced, then strain into a pitcher. Place the squab breasts on a warm serving dish, drizzle with the wine sauce and garnish with the shallots and carrots. Serve the legs separately.

PICCIONI AL VINO ROSSO

Serves 4

4 tablespoons olive oil

3 garlic cloves

4 x 14-ounce squab

2 shallots, chopped

2 carrots, chopped

1²/₃ cups full-bodied red wine

salt and pepper

FROZEN MOUSSE WITH FRUITS OF THE FOREST

Melt the butter in a nonstick pan, stir in the sugar and cook over medium heat until lightly caramelized. Add the berries to the pan and toss them in the caramel for a few minutes, then remove from the heat and let cool. To make the meringue, stiffly whisk the egg whites in a grease-free bowl, then gradually whisk in the sugar. Gently fold the berries into the meringue. Stiffly whip the cream in another bowl and fold into the meringue. Divide the mixture among four small molds and chill in the refrigerator for at least 6 hours until set. To make the custard, blanch the pistachios in boiling water for 1 minute, drain, rub off the skins and chop very finely. Pour the milk into a pan, add the pistachios and bring just to a boil, then remove the pan from the heat. Beat the egg yolks with the sugar in another pan until pale and fluffy. Gradually add the warm milk in a thin stream, stirring constantly. Cook the custard over low heat, stirring constantly, until thick enough to coat the back of the spoon. Do not allow the custard to boil. Remove the pan from the heat and place in a bowl of iced water. Meanwhile, melt the chocolate in a heatproof bowl set over a pan of barely simmering water. Divide the custard among four dishes, turn out the frozen mousses and place them in the center of each dish and decorate with wild strawberries and drizzled chocolate.

SEMIFREDDO AI FRUTTI DI BOSCO

Serves 4

¹/₄ cup sweet butter

2 tablespoons superfine sugar

3¹/₂ cups mixed berries, such as raspberries, strawberries, blueberries and blackberries

scant 1 cup heavy cream

For the meringue

2 egg whites

¹/₂ cup superfine sugar

For the custard

1 tablespoon pistachio nuts

1³/₄ cups milk

3 egg yolks

¹/₂ cup superfine sugar

To decorate

3¹/₂ ounces bittersweet or semisweet chocolate, broken into pieces

scant 1 cup wild strawberries

Stefano de Pieri

Stefano's
Mildura Grand Hotel
Seventh Street
Mildura, Victoria
Australia

The food of Stefano de Pieri comes straight from the heart. Raised on a tiny farm in Treviso near Venice, his family sold their produce at the local food market. Surrounded by superb regional cuisine, his palette received a fine education. As a young man, his sense of adventure turned him to Australia, and ultimately to the town of Mildura by the mighty Murray River in north-west Victoria, where he has settled. Here he has embraced wholeheartedly the local food and wine, establishing a series of renowned eateries that showcase the traditional cuisine of his native Veneto through the fabulous ingredients he finds in his new locality. Stefano de Pieri is largely self-taught, having undertaken only the briefest of formal culinary training. However, his real mentor was his mother, from whom he has inherited the unfailing instinct and expertise for which he is now recognised. Memories of the flavors of his childhood have inspired the hearty cuisine of Stefano's, his flagship restaurant, located in the atmospheric cantina cellar of the Mildura Grand Hotel. There, he serves five-course Northern Italian banquets using only the finest and freshest of local produce. As an enthusiastic proponent of the Slow Food movement, Stefano de Pieri's menu changes daily, presenting a parade of exciting seasonal dishes and buoyant combinations of tastes and aromas. Regular stars of his menus include Murray cod, silver perch, yabbies and scallops. Stefano de Pieri, and the food of his multi-award-winning restaurant, are enthusiastic ambassadors for his beloved region. He is an active campaigner for the care of the ecology of the Murray River, has founded a lively arts festival and, of course, has put his particular part of Australia firmly on the international culinary map.

MENUS

COZZE AL VAPORE CON ERBE AROMATICHE

ZUPPA DI PICCIONE

GUANCE DI MANZO BRASATE AL VINO

PANNA COTTA CARAMELLATA

MUSSELS WITH AROMATIC HERBS

Discard any mussels with broken shells or that do not shut immediately when sharply tapped. Chop the garlic, chile, ginger, cilantro and lime leaves, lemon rind or lemongrass. Heat the oil in a large pan and add all the herbs and flavorings. Add the mussels, cover and cook over high heat for 3–5 minutes until the mussels have opened. Discard any mussels that remain closed, tip the remainder into a bowl and serve.

COZZE AL VAPORE CON ERBE AROMATICHE

Serves 4

40 live mussels, scrubbed and beards removed

1 garlic clove, crushed with the back of a knife

$1/4$–$1/2$ fresh chile

6 thin slices of fresh root ginger

6 large fresh cilantro sprigs

3–4 kaffir lime leaves or thinly pared rind

of $1/4$ lemon or 2 lemongrass stalks

1 tablespoon olive oil

8 tablespoons coarsely chopped fresh flat-leaf parsley

SQUAB AND BREAD SOUP

Heat the oil in a pan, add the carrots, celery, onions and sage leaves and cook over low heat, stirring occasionally, for about 10 minutes or until lightly browned. Increase the heat to medium, add the squab and cook, turning frequently, until browned on all sides. Add the wine, season with salt and pepper, lower the heat and simmer for about 1 hour or until the squab are cooked through. If the mixture seems to be drying out during cooking, add a little hot water to the pan. Remove the squab from the pan and let cool. Pass the cooking juices and vegetables through a fine strainer into a bowl, let cool and then chill in the refrigerator until the fat has set on top. Remove and discard the fat. Using your fingers, pull the squab meat off the bones, including the legs, chop and set aside. Put the squab carcasses in a pan, add water to cover and cook over very low heat for about 2 hours. (Alternatively, use chicken stock instead of water for a stronger flavor.) Strain the squab stock into a bowl and discard the carcasses. Preheat the oven to 300°F. Make a layer of bread slices in the base of an ovenproof dish, ladle over enough stock to soak, sprinkle with a layer of the chopped squab meat, add spoonfuls of the de-fatted cooking juices and sprinkle generously with Parmesan. Continue making layers in this way until all the ingredients are used. Cover the dish with waxed paper and bake for 1 hour. Remove and discard the paper, increase the oven temperature to 350°F and bake until piping hot. Reheat the remaining stock. Divide the squab mixture among hot serving bowls with a little extra stock on the side, not the top, and serve.

ZUPPA DI PICCIONE

Serves 4

4 tablespoons olive oil

$2/3$ cup carrots, coarsely chopped

$2/3$ cup celery, coarsely chopped

$2/3$ cup onions, coarsely chopped

3–4 fresh sage leaves

4 squab, plucked and drawn

1 cup red wine

16–20 slices of day-old bread,

preferably sourdough, crusts removed

2 cups Parmesan cheese, freshly grated

salt and pepper

BRAISED BEEF CHEEKS

GUANCE DI MANZO BRASATE AL VINO

Serves 4

6 beef cheeks

6 ounces plum tomatoes, peeled

3 tablespoons olive oil

$1/3$ cup celery, coarsely chopped

$1/3$ cup carrots, coarsely chopped

$1/3$ cup onions, coarsely chopped

2 garlic cloves, chopped

2 bay leaves

$1^{1}/_{4}$ cups strong red wine

salt and pepper

polenta or mashed potatoes, to serve

Preheat the oven to 350°F. Line a baking tray, roasting pan or shallow ovenproof dish with waxed paper. Trim off the excess fat from the beef cheeks but do not cut off all the fat. Coarsely chop the tomatoes, reserving their juices. Place the tomato flesh and juices in a food processor and process to a purée. Heat the oil in a heavy pan, add the celery, carrots, onions and garlic and cook over low heat, stirring occasionally, for about 10 minutes until lightly browned. Increase the heat to medium, add the beef cheeks and cook, turning frequently, until browned all over. Season, add the bay leaves and wine and cook until the liquid has reduced. Add the puréed tomatoes and cook for a few minutes more, then transfer the mixture to the prepared tray, pan or dish, cover with waxed paper and foil and bake for $2^{1}/_{2}$ hours until the beef is very tender. Transfer the beef cheeks to another dish and pour the cooking juices into a pitcher or bowl. When cold, chill in the refrigerator. Remove the fat from the top of the cooking juices, pour the juices over the beef and reheat in a preheated oven at 350°F. Serve with polenta or mashed potatoes.

CARAMELIZED PANNA COTTA

PANNA COTTA CARAMELLATA

Serves 4

4 cups heavy cream

1 vanilla bean

1 cinnamon stick

pinch of coffee grains

thinly pared rind of 1 orange, 1 lemon or both

$1/2$ cup sugar, plus extra to taste

10 small egg whites or 8 medium egg whites

fruit, to serve

Pour the cream into a pan, add the vanilla, cinnamon, coffee and citrus rind and bring just to a boil. Stir in sugar to taste until it has dissolved, then remove from the heat and let cool. Meanwhile, put the sugar in a pan, add about 3 tablespoons water and bring to a boil, swirling the pan to dissolve the sugar, then cook for 4–5 minutes until caramelized and brown, but not burnt. Pour the caramel into four dariole molds to make a $1/8$–$1/4$-inch thick layer. When the cream is cold, remove and discard the flavorings. Preheat the oven to 275°F. Line a roasting pan with a dish towel. Whisk the egg whites until soft peaks form, then fold them into the cream. Divide the mixture among the molds, place them in the roasting pan and add boiling water to come halfway up the sides. Bake for 35–40 minutes until slightly risen. Remove from the oven and let cool. Do not worry if the creams fall slightly and appear unset. Chill in the refrigerator overnight, when they will acquire a soft creamy texture. To serve, place the molds in a bath of warm water to dissolve the caramel slightly or remove from the refrigerator well in advance. Serve with baked quinces, caramelized oranges or fruit of your choice.

Ruth Rogers and Rose Gray

In 1987, Ruth Rogers and Rose Gray opened The River Café in converted 19th-century warehouses on the banks of the Thames, at Hammersmith, London. Neither were following a traditional route: Ruth Rogers' mother-in-law had imbued her with a passion for good food; Rose Gray briefly cooked in the kitchen at Nell's Club in New York and had researched Italian recipes in Tuscany. From these unorthodox beginnings, The River Café has become one of the best known Italian restaurants, both in the United Kingdom and beyond. As firm exponents of seasonal and well sourced ingredients, both are at the forefront of the fresh-produce revolution. 'Good cooking is about fresh seasonal ingredients, used thoughtfully.' Rogers and Gray routinely journey to Italy, and have a flourishing vegetable and herb garden adjacent to the restaurant. Complimenting their respect for regional ingredients, they have introduced classic Italian cooking methods to diners at The River Café, and share their joy for rustic Italian cooking through their cookbooks and television projects. At The River Café, regional dishes, both robust and subtle, are served in a modern atmosphere, using sophisticated skill and materials in the kitchen, heralding Rose and Ruth's pleasure and excitement in cooking.

The River Café
Thames Wharf
Rainville Road
London
United Kingdom

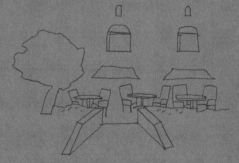

MENUS

PUNTARELLE ALLE ROMANA

TAGLIATELLE CON RUCOLA E CREMA DI LIMONE

TETRAONE CON BRUSCHETTA E CAVOLO NERO

NEMESIS

PUNTARELLE ALLA ROMANA

PUNTARELLE ALLA ROMANA

Serves 6

2 puntarelle heads

5 salted anchovies, heads removed, cleaned and filleted (see page 596)

2 tablespoons red wine vinegar

1 garlic clove, very finely chopped

1 teaspoon black pepper

2 dried chiles • 4 tablespoons extra virgin olive oil

1 lemon, cut into wedges

Fill a bowl with cold water and ice cubes. Pull the hollow buds from the puntarelle heads and thinly slice them lengthwise with a small knife. Put the sliced buds in the iced water for 1 hour or until crisped and curled up. Cut the anchovy fillets into 1/2-inch pieces. Place in a bowl, add the vinegar and stir until disintegrated. Add the garlic and pepper to the anchovies and crumble in the chiles. Let stand for 15 minutes, then stir in the olive oil. Drain the puntarelle and spin dry. Place in a bowl and spoon the sauce over it. Serve with the lemon wedges.

TAGLIATELLE WITH CRÈME FRAÎCHE AND ARUGULA

TAGLIATELLE CON RUCOLA E CREMA DI LIMONE

Serves 6

1 cup crème fraîche

finely grated rind and juice of 2 lemons

11 1/2 ounces egg tagliatelle

2 1/2 cups arugula leaves, coarsely chopped

1 2/3 cups Parmesan cheese, freshly grated

salt and pepper

Pour the crème fraîche into a bowl, stir in the lemon rind and juice and season with salt and pepper. Bring a large pan of salted water to a boil, add the tagliatelle and cook until al dente, then drain and return to the pan. Pour the lemon and cream sauce over the pasta, add the arugula and half the Parmesan and toss to combine. Serve with the remaining Parmesan.

GROUSE WITH BRUSCHETTA AND CAVOLO NERO

TETRAONE CON BRUSCHETTA E CAVOLO NERO

Serves 6

For the grouse with bruschetta

4 plucked and drawn grouse • 16 fresh thyme sprigs

scant 1 cup sweet butter

1 tablespoon extra virgin olive oil

1 1/2 cups red wine

1/4 sourdough loaf, thickly sliced

1 garlic clove, peeled

For the cavolo nero

4 heads cavolo nero (Tuscan cabbage), cored

3 tablespoons olive oil

2 garlic cloves, finely chopped

extra virgin olive oil, for drizzling

sea salt and pepper

For the grouse, preheat the oven to 425°F. Divide the thyme sprigs among the cavities and add a pat of butter to each. Season the birds and place on an oven tray, breast side down. Drizzle the olive oil over the birds and pour over 2/3 cup of the wine. Roast for 10 minutes, then turn them breast side up, pour 2/3 cup of the remaining wine over them and roast, basting occasionally, for a further 10 minutes. Add the rest of the wine and the remaining butter and roast for 5 minutes more. Remove from the oven. Toast the bread slices on both sides. Lightly rub one side of the toast with the garlic. Press the garlic side of each piece of toast into the grouse cooking juices and then invert onto warm plates. Place the grouse on top and pour the remaining cooking juices over the birds. Blanch the cavolo nero in salted, boiling water for 3 minutes, then drain. Heat the olive oil in a heavy pan, add the garlic and cook over low heat for a few minutes until it begins to color. Add the cavolo nero and season generously. Cook for about 5 minutes, then remove from the heat, drizzle with the olive oil and serve with the grouse.

NEMESIS

Preheat the oven to 250°F. Grease a 10-inch cake pan with butter and line with baking parchment. Put the chocolate and butter in a heatproof bowl and melt over a pan of barely simmering water, then remove from the heat. Using an electric mixer beat the eggs with ⅓ cup of the sugar until quadrupled in volume. Heat the remaining sugar with scant ½ cup water, stirring until the sugar has dissolved, then cook until a light syrup forms. Pour the hot syrup into the melted chocolate mixture and let cool slightly, then add the mixture to the egg mixture and beat slowly until combined. Pour the mixture into the prepared pan. Put a folded kitchen cloth on the base of a roasting pan, place the cake pan on top and pour in boiling water to come three-fourths of the way up the side. Bake for 50 minutes until set. Let the cake cool in the water bath before turning out.

NEMESIS

Serves 6

1 cup sweet butter, plus extra for greasing

11¾ ounces bittersweet chocolate, broken into pieces

5 eggs

generous 1 cup superfine sugar

Ezio Santin

Antica Osteria del Ponte
Cassinetta di Lugagnano (MI)
Italy

Colombina – or Bina – Santin, has a natural gift for cooking which her son Ezio has inherited. Sooner or later, these skills were bound to have been destined to find their rightful setting in the form of a restaurant. In 1976, a lovingly restored, charming and remote country house in Cassinetta di Lugagnano near Milan was reincarnated as the Antica Osteria del Ponte. Within a short time, it became a focus for gourmets, and won many coveted awards – a shower of Michelin stars from 1978 onward. These were the prize for Ezio Santin's true passion for cooking. Santin turned professional at the age of forty, having previously cooked only as a hobby. He loves Lombardy regional cooking and seeks out local produce, carefully judging the optimal cooking of Italian vegetables, 'in order not to eradicate their magnificent original flavor.' He also has a happy knack with fish, allowing him to explore such interesting ideas as red mullet in an orange sauce with candied onions and julienne rind. As far as desserts are concerned, Santin is very fond of chocolate, although he hands over this type of cooking to his son Maurizio who, after studying with the most celebrated maîtres pâtissiers in France, has become an excellent, creative maître pâtissier himself.

MENUS

INSALATA TIEPIDA DI GAMBERI, VERZE E LENTICCHIE

LASAGNETTE AI PORRI, CIPOLLOTTI E TARTUFI NERI

CREPINETTE DI CAPRETTO ALLE MANDORLE

TERRINA DI CIOCCOLATO E MANDORLE

SORBETTO CAFFE E CACAO

WARM SALAD OF SHRIMP, SAVOY CABBAGE AND LENTILS

Blanch the cabbage leaves in salted, boiling water until al dente, then drain and keep warm. Heat 1 tablespoon of the oil in a nonstick pan, add the shrimp and cook over medium-high heat for 2 minutes on each side, then season to taste with salt and pepper. Whisk together the remaining oil, the vinegar and the lentil cooking water in a small skillet, add the lentils and heat through. Cut the cabbage leaves in large pieces and place them in the center of four warm plates, arrange the shrimp on top of them and drizzle with the lentil vinaigrette.

INSALATA TIEPIDA DI GAMBERI, VERZE E LENTICCHIE

Serves 4

8 Savoy cabbage leaves

4 tablespoons olive oil

1 pound 5 ounces raw shrimp, peeled and deveined

1 tablespoon red wine vinegar

4 tablespoons cooked lentils,

plus 3 tablespoons of the cooking water

salt and pepper

LASAGNETTE WITH LEEKS, SCALLIONS AND BLACK TRUFFLES

Cook the lasagnette in salted, boiling water, then drain and refresh in iced water. Heat the butter and oil in a skillet, add the scallions and leeks and cook over low heat, stirring frequently, for 15 minutes. Season to taste with salt and pepper. Blanch the guanciale or pancetta in boiling water for 2 minutes, then drain and cook in a heated nonstick pan for a further 2 minutes until the fat runs. Remove from the pan, add to the scallion mixture with the truffles and cream and cook over medium heat, stirring constantly, for 6 minutes. Remove from the heat and let cool. Sandwich together the lasagnette in threes with the cooled filling, then steam for a few minutes to heat through. Meanwhile, make the dressing. Gently warm the oil, truffle juice and vinegar in a small pan. Serve the lasagnette with the warm dressing.

LASAGNETTE AI PORRI, CIPOLLOTTI E TARTUFI NERI

Serves 6

18 lasagnette (2$\frac{1}{2}$ x 4-inch pasta sheets)

$\frac{1}{4}$ cup butter

4 tablespoons olive oil

4$\frac{2}{3}$ cups scallions, thinly sliced

7 ounces leeks, white parts only, thinly sliced

2 ounces guanciale or pancetta, cut into strips

5 ounces black truffles, finely chopped

$\frac{3}{4}$ cup light cream

salt and pepper

For the dressing

6 tablespoons extra virgin olive oil

2 tablespoons black truffle juice

1 tablespoon balsamic vinegar

KID CRÉPINETTES WITH ALMONDS

CREPINETTE DI CAPRETTO ALLE MANDORLE

Serves 4

1 leg and fillet of a small kid
1 sheet caul fat, preferably from a kid
3 tablespoons blanched almonds, chopped
1/4 cup butter
2 tablespoons olive oil
3 tablespoons Chicken Stock (see page 209)
1/2 teaspoon Dijon mustard
salt and pepper
roasted new potatoes, to serve

Ask the butcher to fillet the kid leg completely. Soak the caul fat in warm water until it has softened, then drain. Cut the leg meat into medium pieces and cut the fillet into cubes. Put all of the meat into a bowl, add the almonds, season with salt and pepper and combine well. Divide the mixture into eight and roll each piece into a small ball. Cut the caul fat into eight pieces and use it to wrap the balls. Melt half the butter and the oil in a skillet, add the crépinettes and cook over medium-high heat for 6 minutes, then turn over and cook for a further 4 minutes. Meanwhile, bring the stock to a boil in a small pan, then remove from the heat. Stir in the mustard, whisk in the remaining butter and season to taste with salt and pepper. Place the crépinettes on a warm serving dish and spoon the sauce over them. Serve them with roasted new potatoes.

ALMOND AND CHOCOLATE LAYERS

TERRINA DI CIOCCOLATO E MANDORLE

Serves 6

sweet butter, for greasing
all-purpose flour, for dusting
6 egg whites
scant 1 cup superfine sugar
1 1/2 cups ground almonds
light chocolate sauce or coffee and cocoa sorbet (see below), to serve

For the chocolate ganache
1 cup heavy cream
11 ounces semisweet or bittersweet chocolate, broken into small pieces
2 tablespoons rum

Preheat the oven to 350°F. Lightly grease a jelly roll pan with butter and dust with flour. Stiffly whisk the egg whites in a grease-free bowl, then gradually whisk in the sugar, followed by the almonds. Spread out the mixture in the prepared pan to a depth of 3/4 inch and bake for 15–20 minutes until golden brown and just firm to the touch, then let cool. Meanwhile, prepare the ganache. Bring the cream to a boil in a small pan over medium heat. Put the chocolate in a heatproof bowl, pour the warm cream over it in a steady stream and let melt, then stir in the rum. Cut the almond cookie to fit a terrine or loaf pan in layers, then make alternating layers of cookie and chocolate ganache until all the ingredients are used, ending with a layer of chocolate. To serve, turn out onto a plate, cut into slices and serve with a light chocolate sauce on the side or with a coffee and cocoa sherbet.

COFFEE AND COCOA SHERBET

SORBETTO CAFFÉ E CACAO

Makes 1 pound 2 ounces sherbet
generous 1/2 cup still mineral water
scant 1 cup superfine sugar
2 tablespoons unsweetened cocoa powder
1 cup freshly brewed extra-strong coffee

Pour the mineral water into a small pan, add the sugar and bring to a boil, stirring constantly, then stir in the cocoa powder. Mix well and pour in the coffee. Strain the mixture into a bowl and let cool, then pour into an ice-cream maker and freeze for about 20 minutes or according to the manufacturer's instructions.

Nadia Santini

Nadia Santini is the first Italian female chef of renown and, currently, the only one to boast three Michelin stars. This is truly a record founded on the heritage of her culinary family. A small area of the countryside around Mantua, with its reeds and ponds, duck, geese and lush meadows – Canneto sull'Oglio – is the location for their Dal Pescatore restaurant, which opened in 1920. Antonio Santini comes from the third generation of a family of restaurant owners who have always applied the same management technique – husbands at the tables and wives in the kitchen. Antonio studied economics and business, Nadia political science, and they met at university in Milan. However, one day in 1974, they decided that their paths lay in another direction – that of haute cuisine. They sought advice from Franco Colombani, the great chef at Il Sole in Maleo and a valiant defender of regional cooking in the era of nouvelle cuisine. So, in the elegant rooms of their refurbished restaurant, they serve traditional dishes from the Padania region: pigs' feet with Savoy cabbage and pulses, duckling in balsamic vinegar and romano, ricotta and Parmesan tortelli. Nadia explains her work in the following simple terms, 'I feel drawn towards traditional, even lowly, cuisine, just for the pleasure of making it great.'

Dal Pescatore
Canneto sull'Oglio (MN)
Italy

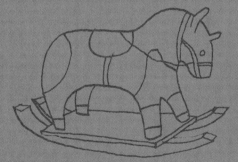

MENUS

TINCA IN CARPIONE

TORTELLI DI PECORINA, RICOTTA E PARMIGIANO AL TARTUFO BIANCO

ANATRA ALL'ACETO BALSAMICO

PIPASENER E ZABAIONE

TINCA IN CARPIONE

Serves 4

3 tablespoons olive oil, plus extra for drizzling

2 x 1 pound 5-ounce tench or catfish, cleaned and filleted

4 cups white wine vinegar

2¼ cups sweet white wine

½ cup sugar

2 onions, thinly sliced

pinch of ground cinnamon

2–3 cloves

pinch of freshly grated nutmeg

2 tablespoons chopped fresh flat-leaf parsley

balsamic vinegar, for drizzling

salt and pepper

SWEET–AND–SOUR TENCH

Heat the oil in a skillet, add the fish fillets and cook for about 10 minutes. Remove the fish from the skillet with a slotted spatula and drain on paper towels. Add the white wine vinegar, white wine, sugar, onions, cinnamon, cloves, nutmeg and a pinch each of salt and pepper to the skillet and cook, stirring occasionally, for about 15 minutes. Place the fish fillets in a heatproof dish, sprinkle with the parsley and pour the sauce over them. Cover the dish and let cool. Serve warm or cold, drizzled with olive oil and a few drops of balsamic vinegar.

TORTELLI DI PECORINA, RICOTTA E PARMIGIANO AL TARTUFO BIANCO

Serves 6

3 cups all-purpose flour, plus extra for dusting

2 eggs

salt

For the filling

⅓ cup ricotta cheese

2 eggs, lightly beaten

1 cup romano cheese, freshly grated

1 cup Parmesan cheese, freshly grated

For the sauce

¼ cup butter, melted

⅔ cup Parmesan cheese, freshly grated

2 ounces white truffle, thinly shaved

TUSCAN ROMANO, RICOTTA AND PARMESAN TORTELLI WITH WHITE TRUFFLE

First make the filling. Pass the ricotta through a strainer, then stir in the eggs, romano and Parmesan. Set aside and keep cool. Prepare the pasta dough with the flour, eggs and a pinch of salt (see page 268). Halve the dough and roll out one piece on a lightly floured counter into a thin sheet. Place small spoonfuls of the filling on it, spaced evenly apart. Roll out the second piece of dough and place it on top of the first, pressing down gently around the mounds of filling. Cut out tortelli with a small round, square or half-moon cutter, according to taste. Cook the tortelli in salted, boiling water for about 5 minutes, then drain and dress with the melted butter, grated Parmesan cheese and slivers of white truffle.

DUCKLING IN BALSAMIC VINEGAR

Preheat the oven to 300°F. Place the duckling in an ovenproof dish and spread the butter over it. Add the lemon juice, brandy, white wine, stock, 1 cup water, the rosemary and sage and season with salt and pepper to taste. Place the dish in the oven and cook for 1–1½ hours or until the duckling is golden brown. Remove the duckling from the dish and strain the cooking liquid into a pan. Pour in the red wine and reduce over low heat. Add the balsamic vinegar and cook until thickened. Cut the duck into fourths, place on individual dishes and pour the hot sauce over them.

ANATRA ALL'ACETO BALSAMICO

Serves 4

4½-pound duckling

⅔ cup butter

juice of ½ lemon, strained

5 tablespoons brandy

¾ cup white wine

1¼ cups Meat Stock (see page 208)

1 fresh rosemary sprig

1 fresh sage sprig

¾ cup full-bodied red wine

2 tablespoons balsamic vinegar

salt and pepper

PIPASENER PASTRY WITH ZABAGLIONE

Put the golden raisins in a bowl, add warm water to cover and let soak for 15 minutes, then drain and squeeze out. Pass the ricotta through a strainer. Combine the flour, sugar, eggs and ricotta in a bowl, then add the raisins, chocolate, rum and butter and knead lightly. Knead in the yeast. Grease a copper pan with butter and dust with flour, place the dough in the pan and cover with a copper lid. Cook over an open fire, placing the pan on the ashes and covering it with the embers and more ash. The dessert will be cooked after 1 hour. Prepare the zabaglione and serve it warm with the pastry.

PIPASENER E ZABAIONE

Serves 4

scant ½ cup golden raisins

scant 1 cup ricotta cheese

1¾ cups all-purpose flour, plus extra for dusting

1 cup superfine sugar

3 eggs

1½ ounces semisweet or bittersweet chocolate, broken into pieces

1 tablespoon rum

3 tablespoons sweet butter, plus extra for greasing

1 envelope rapid-rise yeast

Zabaglione made with 5 egg yolks (see page 1039)

Gianfranco Vissani

Gianfranco Vissani
Civitella del Lago
Baschi (TR)
Italy

When he was still only thirteen years old, Gianfranco Vissani's catering college already considered him to be promising, although it is unusual for chefs to display outstanding talent before their twentieth birthday. As an adult, the fact remains that Gianfranco Vissani has taken his rightful place in the history of cooking as one of the greatest chefs in Italy. Although penalized by the remote location of his restaurant, almost hidden in a corner of 'dolce Umbria', Vissani has succeeded in achieving world-wide fame. He never repeats his recipes – today the sea bass may be served with tomato, but tomorrow it will be accompanied by asparagus, and next month with artichokes and then with oranges. This is dictated by his creative sensitivity, a style that is capable of instantly grasping the potential of whatever ingredient he has before him. Vissani's was never nouvelle cuisine; his elegant and stylized dishes are solely the fruit of natural talent, one that tries out daring, yet always interesting flavors. Today, his cuisine is recognized as being typically Italian. Even if some recipes include foie gras or Belon oysters or basmati rice, Vissani always includes extra virgin olive oil and other typical local products, such as aromatic Norcia truffles or lentils from the hill area of Castelluccio.

MENUS

FILETTI DI SOGLIOLA CON SEDANO, SALSA AURORA E CAVIALE

ORZO PERLATO CON QUAGLIE E TIMO, SALSA DI PATATE E ARANCIA CON BRUNOISE D'OLIVE

SELLA DI DAINO CON TIMBALLO DI TARTUFI NERI

BABA CON SALSA D'ARANCIA

FILLETS OF SOLE WITH CELERY JULIENNE, AURORA SAUCE AND CAVIAR

Make a stock using the fish bones and herbs (see page 208–9). Heat 2 tablespoons of the oil in a skillet, add the celery and one garlic clove and cook over low heat for a few minutes. Remove the pan from the heat, drain the celery and discard the garlic. Divide the celery batons among the fish fillets, roll up and steam them until cooked through. Meanwhile, prepare the sauce. Coarsely chop the remaining garlic clove. Heat the remaining oil in a skillet, add the chopped garlic, tomatoes, shallot and chervil and cook over low heat, stirring occasionally, for about 10 minutes. Ladle the mixture into a food processor and process until smooth and thoroughly combined. Strain in enough stock to produce the desired consistency and season to taste with salt and white pepper. Pour a pool of sauce onto individual dishes, place the sole parcels on top and garnish with the caviar. Serve immediately.

FILETTI DI SOGLIOLA CON SEDANO, SALSA AURORA E CAVIALE

Serves 4

3 small sole, filleted with bones reserved

bunch of fresh mixed herbs

scant 1/2 cup extra virgin olive oil

4 tender celery stalks, cut into thin batons

2 garlic cloves

14 ounces cherry tomatoes, peeled and seeded

1 shallot, thinly sliced

2 fresh chervil sprigs, chopped

scant 1/2 cup caviar

salt and ground white pepper

PEARL BARLEY WITH QUAIL, THYME, POTATO AND ORANGE SAUCE WITH OLIVE BRUNOISE

Make a fairly light stock with the quail carcasses (see page 208), then strain. Dice the meat. Preheat the oven to 350°F. Heat 3 tablespoons of the oil in a pan, add three-fourths of the garlic, one bay leaf, one shallot, the quail meat, and cook over low heat, stirring occasionally, for about 5 minutes. Add the barley and cook briefly, then pour in a ladleful of the stock and cook, stirring constantly, until the liquid has been absorbed. Continue adding the stock, a ladleful at a time. When the mixture is cooked through and tender, remove from the heat and stir in the Parmesan and thyme. Remove and discard the bay leaf. Line four individual molds with the spinach, divide the barley mixture among them and bake for 10–15 minutes. Prepare the sauce. Heat 1 tablespoon of the remaining oil in a pan, add the remaining shallot and bay leaf, together with the pork rind, leek, potatoes and orange segments and cook over low heat, stirring occasionally, for 10 minutes or until the potatoes are tender. Transfer to a food processor and process until smooth, adding orange juice if necessary. Heat the remaining oil, add the olives and remaining garlic and cook over low heat for a few minutes. Pour a pool of the sauce onto individual dishes, turn out the barley cakes and place in the center and garnish with the black olives.

ORZO PERLATO CON QUAGLIE E TIMO, SALSA DI PATATE E ARANCIA CON BRUNOISE D'OLIVE

Serves 4

2 quail, boned and with carcasses reserved

4 tablespoons olive oil

3 garlic cloves, finely chopped

2 bay leaves

2 shallots, finely chopped

2 1/3 cups pearl barley

2/3 cup Parmesan cheese, freshly grated

1 fresh thyme sprig

2 ounces spinach

1 piece of pork rind, chopped

1 leek, white part only sliced

2 potatoes, par-boiled and sliced

2 oranges, cut into segments

juice of 1/2 orange, strained (optional)

scant 1 cup black olives, pitted and finely diced

SADDLE OF VENISON WITH BLACK TRUFFLE TIMBALE

SELLA DI DAINO CON TIMBALLO DI TARTUFI NERI

Serves 4

1 saddle of venison
3¹/₂ ounces pork fat or fatty bacon, cut into strips
4 tablespoons olive oil
1 garlic clove
1 fresh thyme sprig
1 bay leaf
1 quantity Béchamel Sauce (see page 50)
4 egg yolks
¹/₄ cup butter
5 ounces black truffle, thinly shaved
3 potatoes, boiled and sliced
salt and pepper

Place the strips of pork fat or bacon over the saddle of venison and tie in place with kitchen string. Heat the oil in a large pan, add the venison, garlic, thyme and bay leaf and season with salt and pepper. Cook, turning frequently to make sure that the meat stays moist, until tender and cooked through. Meanwhile, make the béchamel sauce and, while it is still warm, beat in the egg yolks one at a time. Make layers of the butter, truffle potatoes, alternating with the béchamel sauce in a timbale mold. Place the saddle of venison on a platter. Discard the garlic and herbs and drizzle the cooking liquid over it. Turn out the truffle timbale next to it.

BABÀ WITH ORANGE SAUCE

BABÀ CON SALSA D'ARANCIA

Serves 4

1 quantity Babà Dough (see page 1055)
1 quantity Confectioner's Custard (see page 1039), flavored with orange juice
thinly pared rind of ¹/₂ orange
¹/₃ cup orange marmalade
juice of 2 oranges, strained
scant ¹/₂ cup heavy cream

Prepare the babà and fill it with the orange-flavored confectioner's custard. Preheat the oven to 350°F. Meanwhile, prepare the orange sauce. Cut the orange rind into thin batons. Combine the marmalade, orange juice and orange rind in a pan, add the cream and simmer three times. Wrap the babà in foil and heat through in the oven for a few minutes. Remove the babà from the foil and pour the sauce over it.

Aldo Zilli

Signor Zilli
41 Dean Street
London
United Kingdom

Aldo Zilli grew up in the idyllic seaside township of Alba Adriatica, in the central Italian region of Abruzzo. The family's overflowing fruit and vegetable garden contained fifteen rosemary bushes. His father was a farmer and fishmonger. Surrounded by this fine harvest of the land and sea, and nurtured by his mother's magnificent cooking, Aldo Zilli's greatest ambition was to open a fish restaurant. Happily, his childhood dreams have been handsomely realised: Zilli is founder and chef patron of an award-winning group of London restaurants that bear his name. The Zilli establishments have become a magnet for people from the media and entertainment world seeking his modern Italian cuisine of traditional sauces, fresh pastas and superb seafood. After attending catering college in Pescara, Aldo Zilli set out to seek fame and fortune abroad. Settling in London, he initially ran Il Siciliano in Soho. Then in 1987 he opened his flagship restaurant, Signor Zilli, in the same neighbourhood. To suit English sensibilities he initially served fillets instead of the unfamiliar bones and heads of whole fish. The famous lobster spaghetti and the acclaimed skewered tiger shrimp with rosemary, garlic and chile are now his signature dishes. Zilli is fiercely proud of the provenance of his dishes and ingredients and divulges his culinary wisdom and skills at his cookery school, in cookbooks and in television appearances. His vision is to showcase the food of Abruzzo: whether by the mozzarella, olive oil and other produce he imports from his home region, or the new renditions of enduring recipes originally gleaned from his mother.

MENUS

FUNGHI DI BOSCO GRATINATI AL CAPRINO

LE CRESPELLE DI MIA COGNATA

SPIGOLA AL FINOCCHIO

SEMIFREDDO AI PINOLI

FUNGHI DI BOSCO GRATINATI
AL CAPRINO
Serves 4

8 portabello mushrooms

2 tablespoons extra virgin olive oil, plus extra for drizzling

8 x $\frac{1}{2}$-inch thick slices of goat cheese

$\frac{1}{2}$ cup Parmesan cheese, freshly grated

1 garlic clove, finely chopped (optional)

1 teaspoon ground black pepper

juice of 1 lemon, strained

balsamic vinegar, for drizzling

2 tablespoons chopped fresh flat-leaf parsley

PORTABELLO MUSHROOMS WITH GOAT CHEESE GRATIN

Preheat the broiler. Remove the stalks from the mushrooms, place the caps on a broiler rack, gill sides uppermost, brush with the oil and broil for 8 minutes. Place a slice of goat cheese over each mushroom, sprinkle with the Parmesan, garlic, pepper and lemon juice and broil for a further 5 minutes until golden and bubbling. Drizzle with balsamic vinegar and olive oil just before serving and garnish with the parsley.

LE CRESPELLE DI MIA COGNATA
Serves 4

For the stock

$3\frac{1}{4}$-pound chicken

1 celery stalk

2 carrots

4 bay leaves

1 onion, studded with 2 cloves

1 bunch of fresh flat-leaf parsley

4 garlic cloves

10–15 cups water

4 tablespoons Parmesan cheese, freshly grated

For the pancakes

4 eggs

$1\frac{1}{4}$ cups milk

$1\frac{3}{4}$ cups all-purpose flour

2 tablespoons chopped fresh flat-leaf parsley

1 large potato, halved

1 cup sunflower oil

salt and pepper

MARISA'S PANCAKE AND CHICKEN BROTH

To make the pancakes, whisk together the eggs, milk, flour and parsley to a lump-free batter and add salt and pepper to taste. Heat a nonstick pan or pancake pan until very hot, then insert a fork in the potato half and soak it in the sunflower oil. When the pan is hot, rub with the soaked potato and add a small ladleful of the batter. Cover the pan and leave until the pancake starts to move when you move the pan, turn the pancake with a spatula and cook the other side. Continue oiling the pan with the potato half and adding small ladlefuls of the batter until you have a stack of pancakes. To make the stock, put the chicken in a large pan with all the vegetables and herbs, pour in the water and bring to a boil. Lower the heat and simmer, occasionally skimming off the fat with a slotted spoon, for $1\frac{1}{2}$ hours. Remove the chicken, strain the stock into a soup tureen and place in the middle of the table with a ladle. Place the pancakes, cut into strips if you like, in individual soup bowls, ladle the stock over them and sprinkle the Parmesan. You can then serve the chicken with a good salad to complete the meal.

ROASTED SEA BASS & FENNEL

Preheat the oven to 375°F. Parboil the sliced potatoes for 2 minutes, then drain. Make several diagonal slashes across each side of the fish without cutting through to the bone. Place a small sprig of rosemary and a slice of garlic in each slash and put the remaining garlic, the lemon and the remaining rosemary inside the cavity. Rub the fish with 4 tablespoons of the olive oil and sprinkle with sea salt, half the fennel seeds and pepper. Slice the fennel lengthwise into 1/2-inch thick pieces and place on a cookie sheet with the potatoes. Sprinkle with the remaining fennel seeds and season. Place the fish on top, drizzle with the remaining olive oil, cover the cookie sheet with foil and bake for about 35 minutes until cooked through. Surround with the potatoes and fennel and garnish with rosemary.

SPIGOLA AL FINOCCHIO

Serves 6

2 baking potatoes, cut into 1/2-inch thick slices

3 1/4-pound sea bass, scaled and cleaned

2–4 fresh rosemary sprigs, plus extra to garnish

2 garlic cloves, lightly crushed

1/2 lemon, thinly sliced

6 tablespoons olive oil

1 1/2 tablespoons fennel seeds

2 fennel bulbs

sea salt and pepper

PINE NUT SEMIFREDDO

Preheat the oven to 350°F. Lightly brush a cookie sheet or tray with oil. Spread out the pine nuts on another cookie sheet and roast for 8 minutes until golden, but be very careful not to overcook them. Meanwhile, put the sugar and water into a heavy pan and set over medium-high heat. This mixture will first start bubbling and then turn to a clear syrup. When it starts to change color in parts, carefully shake the pan to mix. When it has become golden brown, tip the pan away from you and carefully pour in the pine nuts. Lower the heat to a simmer and stir gently to coat the nuts. When the caramel becomes a dark golden color, remove the pan from the heat and spread the mixture on the oiled cookie sheet or tray. Let it cool. Break up the cold praline and put half in a food processor, then pulse until quite fine. Set aside. Put the remaining praline in the food processor and pulse until crushed but not powdery, then set aside. To make the semifreddo, halve the vanilla bean lengthwise and scrape out the seeds with a teaspoon into a bowl. Add the egg yolks and sugar and whisk until the mixture turns pale. Whisk the cream in another bowl until soft peaks form. Whisk the egg whites with a pinch of salt in another, grease-free bowl until they form firm peaks. Fold the cream into the egg yolk mixture, then fold in the egg whites. Finally, fold in only the finely crushed praline. Pour the mixture into a freezerproof container and freeze for 3 hours until firm. Serve in scoops, decorated with the remaining praline.

SEMIFREDDO AI PINOLI

Serves 8

For the praline

sunflower oil, for brushing

1 1/4 cups pine nuts

1 cup superfine sugar

4 tablespoons water

For the semifreddo

1 vanilla bean

4 eggs, separated

4 tablespoons superfine sugar

1 1/4 cups heavy cream

salt

LIST OF RECIPES AND INDEX

LIST OF RECIPES

FISH, CRUSTACEANS AND SHELLFISH

HERRINGS
- **601** Smoked Herring with Grapefruit
- **601** Herring and Cauliflower Salad

SALT COD AND STOCKFISH
- **603** Salt Cod au Gratin
- **603** Salt Cod Livorno-style
- **603** Salt Cod with Olives and Capers
- **604** Salt Cod with Potatoes and Bell Peppers
- **604** Fried Salt Cod
- **604** Mediterranean Stockfish
- **605** Veneto-style Creamed Stockfish

WHITEBAIT
- **606** Whitebait in Egg Cream
- **606** Whitebait with Olive Oil and Lemon

SEA BASS
- **607** Sea Bass Baked in a Packet
- **609** Sea Bass with Fennel
- **609** Jellied Sea Bass
- **609** Baked Marinated Sea Bass

STRIPED GREY MULLET
- **610** Striped Grey Mullet in Vinegar
- **611** Striped Mullet with Parsley
- **611** Striped Mullet and Dill Parcels
- **611** Stuffed Striped Grey Mullet in Olive Sauce

GROUPER
- **612** Baked Grouper
- **614** Grouper with Avocado
- **614** Grouper with Olives

MONKFISH
- **615** Monkfish with Lemon
- **616** Monkfish in Red Wine
- **616** Monkfish with Cauliflower and Scallions
- **617** Monkfish with Anchovy Sauce
- **617** Monkfish and Shrimp Roulades
- **619** Monkfish Stew with Tumeric Rice

PORGY AND SEA BREAM
- **622** Porgy baked in a Salt Crust
- **622** Braised Porgy
- **622** Jellied Porgy
- **623** Broiled Porgy
- **623** Porgy with Fennel Bulbs
- **623** Baked Porgy
- **624** Porgy with Olives
- **624** Porgy with Zucchini
- **624** Aromatic Porgy
- **625** Roast Porgy
- **625** Porgy with Mushrooms
- **625** Fish Tartare with Kiwi Fruit
- **626** Marinated Porgy

COD
- **627** Cod with Leeks
- **627** Cod in Curry Sauce
- **628** Baked Cod with Vegetables
- **628** Provençal Cod
- **628** Sicilian Cod
- **629** Cod Stew with Olives and Capers
- **629** Cod and Walnut Terrine

HAKE
- **630** Hake with Potatoes
- **630** Hake in Green Sauce
- **632** Hake in Shallot Sauce
- **632** Fried Hake

TOPE
- **633** Tope with Vegetables
- **634** Tope with Celery
- **634** Tope with Potatoes au Gratin
- **634** Tope with Green Tomatoes

SWORDFISH
- **635** Fabulous Smoked Swordfish
- **635** Baked Swordfish
- **636** Swordfish Parcels
- **636** Braised Swordfish
- **638** Marinated Swordfish
- **638** Swordfish Steaks in Balsamic Vinegar

SKATE
- **639** Skate with Capers
- **639** Skate Niçoise

HALIBUT AND TURBOT
- **640** Halibut Fillets with Vegetables
- **641** Halibut Fillets with a Potato Topping
- **641** Baked Halibut with Lentil Sauce
- **642** Halibut in Orange
- **642** Halibut in Sparkling Wine
- **643** Halibut with Saffron in Clam Sauce
- **643** Halibut with Olive Sauce

SALMON
- **644** Salmon and Bacon Bites
- **644** Salmon and Belgian Endive Parcels
- **646** Salmon Patties
- **646** Salmon Tartare
- **646** Smoked Salmon Terrine

POMFRET AND JOHN DORY
- **647** John Dory Fillets in Sauce
- **648** John Dory Fillets in Béchamel Sauce
- **648** Baked John Dory Roulades
- **648** John Dory with Snow Peas

SARDINES
- **649** Sardine Rolls
- **649** Broiled Sardines
- **650** Sardines Marinara
- **650** Sardines with Shallots
- **650** Sardines in Bread Crumbs
- **652** Sardines Bellavista
- **652** Stuffed Sardines
- **652** Succulent Sardines

SCORPION FISH
- **654** Genoese Salad
- **655** Scorpion Fish with Mushrooms
- **655** Scorpion Fish with Thyme
- **655** Scorpion Fish in White Wine and Saffron

MACKEREL
- **656** Mackerel with Green Beans
- **656** Mackerel with Sage Butter
- **658** Greek Mackerel
- **658** Mackerel with Currants
- **658** Mackerel and White Wine Terrine

SOLE
- **659** Almond-coated Sole Fillets
- **661** Sole Salad
- **661** Sole and Shrimp Roulades
- **661** Sole with Mushrooms
- **662** Broiled Sole
- **662** Sole in Cider
- **662** Sole with Thyme
- **663** Sole in Melted Butter
- **663** Sole in Piquant Sauce

STURGEON
- **664** Sturgeon in Sweet-and-Sour Sauce
- **665** Sturgeon in Anchovy Sauce
- **665** Sturgeon in Balsamic Vinegar
- **665** Broiled Sturgeon
- **666** Sturgeon with Artichokes
- **666** Sturgeon with Red Bell Pepper Sauce

TUNA
- **667** Tuna in Vinegar
- **668** Tuna with Celery
- **668** Tuna and Bean Salad
- **668** Slow-cooked Tuna

RED SNAPPER AND RED MULLET
- **669** Red Snapper with Fennel
- **670** Red Snapper Livorno-style
- **670** Red Snapper with Herbs
- **670** Red Snapper with Beans

EEL
- **671** Breton Eel
- **672** Roast Eel
- **672** Eel with Savoy Cabbage
- **672** Eel in Green Sauce
- **673** Braised Eel
- **673** Eel Kabobs

CARP
- **674** Carp with Maître d'Hôtel Butter
- **675** Carp with Olives
- **675** Oriental Carp
- **675** Carp in Wine

WHITEFISH
- **676** Whitefish with Herbs
- **677** Fried Whitefish
- **677** Poached Whitefish with Horseradish Sauce
- **677** Whitefish and Potato Pie

LIVER

862 Pig's Liver in a Net
863 Liver with Shallots
863 Liver with Butter and Sage
863 Veneto-style Liver
863 Liver with Lemon
864 Liver Uccelletto
864 Liver in Merlot
864 Liver with Globe Artichokes
864 Sweet-and-Sour Liver

TONGUE

865 Boiled Smoked Tongue
866 Tongue with Green Olives
866 Braised Tongue
866 Tongue in Tartar Sauce
866 Spicy Tongue

KIDNEYS

868 Kidneys with Mustard
868 Kidneys in Madeira
868 Kidneys in Bordeaux
869 Kidneys with Raw Scallions
869 Kidneys, Sausage and
Mushrooms

CALF'S HEAD

871 Boiled Calf's Head
871 Fried Calf's Head
871 Calf's Head Salad

TRIPE

872 Tripe with Mushrooms
873 Milanese Tripe
873 Tripe with Herbs
873 Simple Tripe

POULTRY

DUCK

878 Duck à l'Orange
878 Duck Cooked in Beer
879 Duck in Almond Sauce
879 Duck with Peaches
880 Duck with Green Peppercorns
880 Stuffed Duck with Honey
882 Sweet-and-Sour Duck
882 Duck in Herb Sauce
884 Stuffed Duck in Turnip Sauce
884 Jugged Duck Legs
886 Duck Fillets with Figs
886 Breast of Duck with
Grapefruit

CAPON

887 Capon Roast in a Packet
888 Capon in Cardoon Sauce
888 Poached Capon
888 Stuffed Capon
889 Truffled Capon
889 Simple Capon Galantine

GUINEA FOWL

890 Pot-roast Guinea Fowl
891 Guinea Fowl with Artichoke Hearts
891 Guinea Fowl with Pineapple
892 Guinea Fowl with Sage
892 Guinea Fowl Ortolana
892 Guinea Fowl with Mascarpone
895 Guinea Fowl with Red Wine
895 Guinea Fowl with Cream and Lemon
895 Stuffed Guinea Fowl with Mushrooms
896 Guinea Fowl stuffed with
Goldens Raisins
896 Guinea Fowl with Truffles
Baked in a Packet

CHICKEN BOILING FOWL

898 Chicken with Pomegranate
898 Rustic Chicken
900 Chicken with Carrots and Onions
900 Chicken in Pink Sauce

GOOSE

902 Roast Goose with
Sweet-and-Sour Bell Peppers
902 Sweet-and-Sour Goose Legs
903 German Goose with Apples
903 Braised Goose
904 Goose stuffed with Potatoes
904 Breast of Goose in Balsamic Vinegar
906 Goose Stew

SQUAB

908 Roast Squab
908 Broiled Squab
910 Piquant Squab
910 Squab with Olives
910 Stuffed Squab

CHICKEN

913 Chicken Pie
913 Chicken Legs in Red Wine
913 American Chicken Salad
914 Chicken and Celery Root Salad
914 Chicken Roulades with Sage
914 Chicken, Anchovy and
Caper Roulades
916 Chicken Roulades with Chives
916 Poached Stuffed Chicken
916 Chicken Breasts in Vinegar
918 Chicken Breasts and
Fennel au Gratin
918 Chicken Breasts Stuffed with
Mascarpone
919 Soused Chicken Breasts
919 Chicken Breasts in Almond Sauce
919 Chicken with Mushrooms
920 Chicken Roasted in a Packet
920 Chicken Curry
920 Chicken Babi
922 Chicken Cacciatore
922 Deviled Chicken
922 Philippines Chicken
924 Chicken with Garlic

924 Greek Chicken
924 Chicken with Cream
924 Stuffed Chicken
924 Chicken Ratatouille
926 Chicken with Onions
926 Chicken with Apples
926 Chicken with Olives
928 Chicken with Lemon (1)
928 Chicken with Lemon (2)
928 Chicken on a Spit
929 Chicken with Sparkling Wine
929 Chicken with Tuna
929 Chicken in White Wine
930 Chicken in Red Wine
930 Pot Roast Chicken
930 Stuffed Chicken
931 Chicken with Yellow Bell Peppers
931 Chicken with Green Bell Peppers
931 Fried Marinated Chicken
932 Fried Chicken in Bread Crumbs
932 Chicken in Salt Crust
932 Chicken in a Brick
934 Spicy Indian Meatballs
934 Chopped Chicken with
Lemon Balm
934 Chicken Stew with Olives
934 Chopped Chicken with Almonds

OSTRICH

935 Ostrich Eggs
936 Conte Rosso Ostrich Fillet
936 Ostrich Stew

TURKEY

938 Pot Roast Turkey
938 Turkey à l'Orange
939 Turkey Leg with Spinach
939 Turkey Leg with Herbs
940 Turkey Breast with Cheese
940 Turkey Breast with Almonds
940 Turkey Fricassée with Porcini
941 Tasty Turkey Roulades
941 Turkey Roll with Olives
942 Turkey Stew with Mustard
942 Glazed Turkey
943 Christmas Turkey
943 Turkey stuffed with Chestnuts
945 Turkey stuffed with Brussels Sprouts

GAME

WOODCOCK

949 Curried Woodcock
950 Woodcock with Juniper
950 Woodcock with Truffle
950 Woodcock with Green Apples

PHEASANT

951 Pheasant with Fruit
953 Pheasant in Cream Sauce
953 Pheasant with Olives

1125 Shoulder of Veal with Uva Fragola
1125 Chestnut Flour Pie with Pears

LIDIA BASTIANICH
1127 Shrimp in the Scampi Style
1128 Zite with Sausage, Onions and Fennel
1129 Erminia's Chicken and Potatoes
1130 Crostata with Chocolate, Hazelnuts and Orange

MARIO BATALI
1132 Sweet Pea Flan with Carrot Vinaigrette
1133 Beef Cheek Ravioli
1134 Barbecued Squab Al Mattone with Porcini Mustard
1135 Semolina Budino with Rhubarb and Mint Marmellata

NINO BERGESE
1137 Creamed Risotto
1137 Saddle of Veal Alla Bergese
1137 Florentine Tart

GIANFRANCO BOLOGNESI
1139 Tagliatelle All'Antica with Truffles
1139 Partridges with Savoy Cabbage, Fried Sage and Vegetables
1140 Panna Cotta, Almond Tart and Zabaglione

CARLO BROVELLI
1142 Scallops and Fried Celery
1142 Ravioli with Eggs and Asparagus
1143 Sturgeon Steaks in Gremolata
1143 Orange and Grand Marnier Mousse

ARRIGO CIPRIANI
1145 Carpaccio Cipriani
1145 Spring Risotto
1146 Baked Langoustines
1146 Italian Crêpes with Custard Cream

FRANCO COLOMBANI
1148 Capon Salad
1148 Braised Beef
1148 Pound Cake with Mascarpone Cream

ENZO DEPRÀ
1150 Chicken Liver Pâté with Herbs and Truffle
1150 Casunzjei Pasta with Potatoes and Seasoned Ricotta
1151 Ragù of Snails with Celery Root
1151 Bread Pudding with Vanilla Sauce

MARIA PIA DE RAZZA–KLEIN
1153 Marinated Octopus and Fennel Salad with Mature Romano Cheese
1154 Fresh 'Guitar String' Spaghetti with Mussels, Cherry Tomatoes and Olives
1155 Roast Lamb with Radicchio

Trevisano, Quince and Pancetta
1155 Radicchio Trevisano with Quince and Pancetta
1156 Cooked Saffron Milk Puddings with Blood Orange and Vincotto Sauce

ALFONSO E LIVIA JACCARINO
1158 Mussel Purses with Zucchini Flowers
1158 Caciotta Ravioli with Tomato and Basil
1159 Scorpion Fish in White Wine
1159 Eggplant Pie with Chocolate

GIORGIO LOCATELLI
1161 Pan-Fried Scallops with Saffron Vinaigrette
1162 Pheasant Ravioli with Rosemary Jus
1163 Rabbit with Prosciutto and Polenta
1164 Amedei Chocolate Tasters

STEFANO MANFREDI
1166 Crostini with Bell Peppers and Onions in Agrodolce
1166 Tagliatelli with Yabbies, Butter and Sesame Seeds
1167 Roast Pheasant with Savoy Cabbage, Chestnuts and Red Wine
1168 Torta Sbrisolona with Quince, Mascarpone Cream and Vincotto

GUALTIERO MARCHESI
1170 Sturgeon Salad with Caviar
1170 Open Ravioli
1171 Fillet of Veal Alla Rossini
1171 Panettone Pudding

KAREN MARTINI
1173 Yellow Fin Tuna Carpaccio with Shaved Fennel and Lemon and Bottarga
1173 Seared Shrimp with Cannellini Bean Salad and Tartufo Dressing
1174 Charbroiled Lamb Chops with Oregano and Hot Feta Dressing
1175 Choux Pastry Crest with Almond Cream, Praline, Chocolate Sauce and Gold Leaf

GIANLUIGI MORINI
1177 Tortellini with Goose Liver Cream
1177 Quail Stuffed with Green Vegetables and Peas
1178 Chocococonut

FULVIO PIERANGELINI
1180 Purée of Chickpeas with Shrimp
1180 Fish Ravioli with Shellfish
1181 Squab in Red Wine
1181 Frozen Mousse with Fruits of the Forest

STEFANO DE PIERI
1183 Mussels with Aromatic Herbs
1183 Squab and Bread Soup
1184 Braised Beef Cheeks
1184 Caramelized Panna Cotta

RUTH ROGERS AND ROSE GRAY
1186 Puntarelle alla Romana
1186 Tagliatelle with Crème Fraîche and Arugula
1186 Grouse with Bruschetta and Cavolo Nero
1187 Nemesis

EZIO SANTIN
1189 Warm Salad of Shrimp, Savoy Cabbage and Lentils
1189 Lasagnette with Leeks, Scallions and Black Truffles
1190 Kid Crépinettes with Almonds
1190 Almond and Chocolate Layers
1190 Coffee and Cocoa Sorbet

NADIA SANTINI
1192 Sweet-and-Sour Tench
1192 Tuscan Romano, Ricotta and Parmesan Tortelli with White Truffle
1193 Duckling in Balsamic Vinegar
1193 Pipasener Pastry with Zabaglione

GIANFRANCO VISSANI
1195 Fillets of Sole with Celery Julienne, Aurora Sauce and Caviar
1195 Pearl Barley with Quail, Thyme, Potato and Orange Sauce with Olive Brunoise
1196 Saddle of Venison with Black Truffle Timbale
1196 Babà with Orange Sauce

ALDO ZILLI
1198 Portabello Mushrooms with Goats' Cheese Gratin
1198 Marisa's Pancake and Chicken Broth
1199 Roasted Sea Bass & Fennel
1199 Pine Nut Semifreddo

INDEX

Page numbers in *italic* refer to the illustrations

pirate's fish soup 728
potato and clam soup 255
seafood pie 182
seafood rice salad 324
swordfish packets 636, *637*
vermicelli with clams 304
clarified butter 88
clear stock 205
cockles
mixed shellfish soup 729
cocktail di scampi 105
cocktail sauce 72
cod 627–9
baked cod with vegetables 628
cod and mushroom pie 183
cod and walnut terrine 629
cod in curry sauce 627
cod stew with olives and capers 629
cod with leeks 627
mixed fish soup with orange 729
polenta with cod 307
Provençal cod 628
Sicilian cod 628
see also salt cod; stockfish
coda di manzo alla pancetta 857
coda di manzo alla vaccinara 857
coda di rospo al limone 615
coda di rospo al vino rosso 616
coda di rospo con cavolfiore e cipolle 616
coda di rospo con salsa d'acciughe 617
code di gamberi fritte in salsa rosa 694
codino arrosto 818
coffee
beef stew with coffee 800
coffee and cocoa sherbet 1190
coffee babá 1055
coffee frosting 1016
coffee ice cream 1100
mocha cake 1063
tiramisu 1110, *1111*
walnut and coffee cake 1060
cold chocolate sauce 1017
cold frosting 1015
composta di fragole al rabarbaro 1079
compote, strawberry and rhubarb 1079
concentrated stock 205
confectioner's custard 1039
blackberry tart 1059
hazelnut sauce 1019
Italian trifle 1112, *1113*
coniglio al forno 970
*coniglio al forno con prosciutto crudo e
polenta* 1163
coniglio al latte 973
coniglio al miele con verdure 974, *975*
coniglio al sidro 974
coniglio al vino rosso 974
coniglio alla cacciatora 971, *972*
coniglio alla senape 973
coniglio all'aceto 971
coniglio all'agro 971
coniglio all'alloro 973
coniglio arrosto al rosmarino 976

coniglio con peperonata 976
coniglio fritto 976
coniglio in umido 977
coniglio marinato 977
coniglio ripieno 977
consommé 205, 210
Conte Rosso ostrich fillet 936
cooked marinade 80
cookies and petits fours 1050–4
cinnamon cookies 1050
date and walnut bonbons 1052
English cookies 1051
rolled wafers 1052
sablés 1051
ugly-but-good cookies 1051
yogurt cookies 1050
coratella d'agnello al Marsala 859
coratella d'agnello alla Romana 859
coratella d'agnello dell'ortolano 859
coratella d'agnello in tegame 859
corn *see* sweetcorn
corn salad
bresaola with corn salad 496, *497*
truffle, chicken and corn salad 102
warm mushroom salad 483
corn soup 229
cornichons
cauliflower in green sauce 440
rice salad with pickled bell peppers 325
cornmeal
yogurt cake 1069
corona alle pere 1058
cosce di oca in agrodolce 902
cosce in salmì 884
coscia agli spinaci 939
coscia alle erbe aromatiche 939
cosciotto alla crema tartufata 753
cosciotto alla Perigordina 744
cosciotto alla Piemontese 754
cosciotto alla vodka 805
cosciotto arrosto 745
cosciotto con le rape 805, *806*
cosciotto in crosta d'erbe 745, *746*
cosciotto pasquale 754, *755*
costata alla Fiorentina 790
costata di bue al sale con salsa 790
costine con polenta 767
costolette al burro d'acciuga 745
costolette al burro e salvia 767
costolette al cavolo nero 768
costolette alla menta 747
costolette alla Milanese 819, *820*
costolette alla panna 754
costolette alla Valdostana 819
costolette alla Villeroy 819
costolette all'aceto 747
costolette all'Inglese 805
costolette con peperoni 768
*costolette di camoscio ai funghi e frutta
secca* 963
costolette a scottadito 747
*costolettine di agnello con patate e condito
con feta e origano* 1174

cotechino 840
cotechino in a jacket 842
cotechino with lentils 840, *841*
cotechino with mushroom sauce 842
cotechino arrotolato 840
cotechino con lenticchie 840, *841*
cotechino con salsa di funghi 842
cotechino vestito 842
cotolette al 'consumato di brodo' 821
cotolette alla Bolognese 821
country bonbons 150
country bouchées 150
court-bouillon 591
cozze al vapore con erbe aromatiche 1183
cozze alla crema 713
cozze alla marinara 714
cozze con peperoni verdi 714, *715*
cozze gratinate 714
crab 688, 700–2
cherry tomato and crab bites 104
cherry tomatoes stuffed with crab 700
crab and apple tartines 138
crab and langoustine cups 107
crab barquettes 143
crab meat omelet 392
crab rolls 702
crab salad *701,* 702
crab soufflé 177
crab soup 252, *253*
crab with avocado 702
rice and crab meat salad 325
see also spider crab
cranberries
roast saddle of venison with
cranberries 966
crauti con funghi e patate 443
crauti in umido 443
cream
apricot preserve and cream omelet 1093
baby carrots in cream 430
beef patties with cream and
mushrooms 785
black grape charlotte 1035
caprino Bavarian cream 991
chicken with cream 924
chocolate profiteroles 1109
cocktail sauce 72
cream and arugula risotto 336
cream and leek risotto 339
cucumbers with cream 452
curry and cream mayonnaise 67
eggplant with cream 510
grape meringue pie 1109
guinea fowl with cream and lemon 895
guinea fowl with truffles baked in a
packet 896
Italian trifle 1112, *1113*
Jerusalem artichokes in cream 574
kid chops with cream 754
leg of kid with truffle cream 753
meringues with whipped cream 1054
Montebianco 1109
mushrooms with cream 481